コスタス　カザジス

K.K.
1η Μαρτίου 2002

Merriam-Webster's Japanese–English Dictionary

*Published in collaboration with
Kenkyusha Limited*

Merriam-Webster, Incorporated
Springfield, Massachusetts

A GENUINE MERRIAM-WEBSTER

The name *Webster* alone is no guarantee of excellence. It is used by a number of publishers and may serve mainly to mislead an unwary buyer.

Merriam-Webster™ is the name you should look for when you consider the purchase of dictionaries or other fine reference books. It carries the reputation of a company that has been publishing since 1831 and is your assurance of quality and authority.

Merriam-Webster's Japanese-English Dictionary
Published in the United States by Merriam-Webster, Incorporated, by special arrangement with Kenkyusha Ltd., Tokyo, Japan
Copyright © 1993 by Kenkyusha Ltd.
Originally published by Kenkyusha Ltd., Tokyo, Japan, under the title: The Kenkyusha Japanese-English Learner's Pocket Dictionary

ISBN: 0-87779-918-0

56QP/B01

Contents

PREFACE

Merriam-Webster's Japanese-English Dictionary is designed to provide concise information about the words most widely used in written and spoken Japanese. It is a smaller, handier version of *Merriam-Webster's Japanese-English Learner's Dictionary*, published in 1993, and, as with that larger book, particular care has been taken to make the dictionary useful to beginners. Example sentences and phrases are regularly given at most entries so that users can gain a better understanding of typical uses of words and phrases. English translations follow each example in order to make the meaning and grammatical structure of each phrase or sentence as clear as possible. Tables of counters, tables of numbers, and other informative lists, including an Essential English-Japanese Vocabulary List, have been placed in appendixes for easy reference.

Another noteworthy feature of this dictionary is the marking of accent on each headword. This is a guide to accepted pronunciation and serves to distinguish those Japanese words that differ only in the ways that their syllables are accented.

The example phrases and sentences in this dictionary are shown in both romanized Japanese and in standard written Japanese. This makes it possible for students to familiarize themselves with the hiragana, katakana, and kanji characters used in Japanese writing.

Merriam-Webster's Japanese-English Dictionary was produced through a close collaboration between scholars of the Japanese and English languages and educators with long experience teaching Japanese as a foreign language. The editors of Merriam-Webster and Kenkyusha Limited are grateful to all of those who helped create this dictionary, and they join in the hope that this dictionary will prove helpful for travelers, students, businesspeople, or others who wish to learn to speak, read, and write Japanese.

Guide to the Use of the Dictionary

1. Romanization

The romanization used in this dictionary is based on the standard Hepburn system with the following modifications:

1.1 Long vowels are indicated by doubled vowel letters, '*aa*, *ii*, *uu*, *ee*, *oo*,' instead of the conventional transcription which, depending on the particular vowel, either uses macrons or doubles the vowel letter.

> to꜒oki とうき (earthenware)
> shu꜒uchuu しゅうちゅう (concentration)
> pa꜒atii パーティー (party)

1.2 When the vowel sequence '*ei*' is pronounced as a long '*e*,' it is written as '*ee*.'

> se꜒eto せいと (pupil)
> se꜒tsumee せつめい (explanation)

But a word like けいと (knitting wool) is written as *keito* in order to show that it is composed of two separate word elements, *ke* (wool) and *ito* (thread).

1.3 When there is a sequence of three or more identical vowel letters, a hyphen is used to clarify the word elements.

> ke꜒e-ee けいえい (management)
> so꜒o-oñ そうおん (noise)

1.4 '*ñ*' is used to transcribe the syllabic '*n*' (ん/ン).

> shi꜒ñbuñ しんぶん (newspaper)
> ke꜒ñkoo けんこう (health)

1.5 When the small 'っ/ッ' precedes a consonant, the sequence is transcribed as a double consonant, except in the case of '*ch*,' which is written '*tch*.'

> a꜒ppaku あっぱく (pressure)
> hi꜒tto ヒット (hit)
> shu꜒tchoo しゅっちょう (business trip)

1.6 The small 'っ / ッ' in interjections such as 'あっ' and 'え
っ' is transcribed with an apostrophe. This sign represents a glot-

tal stop (an abrupt tightening of the vocal cords) after the preceding vowel.

a′ あっ (Oh!)　　**e′** えっ (Eh!)

2.　Headwords

2. 1　Headwords are arranged in alphabetical order with accent marks. The accent of a prefix or suffix is not given unless the accent of the derived compound is invariant.

2. 2　Headwords are written in roman letters followed by the standard writing in *hiragana* or *katakana* (the two Japanese syllabaries), and, where appropriate, *kanji* (Chinese characters). This is followed by an abbreviation indicating the part of speech.

a⌐tama⌐ あたま (頭) *n*. head
bo⌐oeki ぼうえき (貿易) *n*. trade

2. 3　Numbered superscripts are used to distinguish different words with the same romanization.

ha⌐shi⌐[1] はし (橋) *n*. bridge
ha⌐shi[2] はし (箸) *n*. chopsticks

2. 4　Prefixes are followed, and suffixes preceded, by a hyphen, thus indicating position at either the beginning or end of a word.

da⌐i- だい (big; large) > *dai*-**toshi** (a *large* city)
-da⌐ñ だん (group) > **ooeñ**-*dañ* (a *group* of cheerleaders)

As a general principle, a word which can stand alone as a single unit is left as one word without a hyphen. However, in the case of examples which are listed under suffixes and prefixes which themselves constitute headwords, the hyphen is used to clarify the word elements.

oo-goe (大声) (under headword, **oo-**)
o⌐ogo⌐e (大声) (headword) a *loud* voice
jidoo-*sha* (自動車) (under headword, **-sha**)
ji⌐do⌐osha (自動車) (headword) a motor *vehicle*

2. 5　The swung dash, ～, is used to avoid repetition of the Japanese headword.

u⌐ndoo うんどう (exercise)
　uñdoo (o) suru (〜(を)する) (take exercise)

2.6　Set phrases are shown in boldfaced type.

atama ga kireru (〜が切れる) have a sharp mind
me ga mawaru (〜が回る) feel giddy

2.7　The raised dot in a headword distinguishes the stem of verbs and adjectives from the part to be inflected.

ka⌐k·u かく (書く), **a⌐buna·i** あぶない (危ない)

2.8　When a headword comprises more than one part of speech, each part is dealt with separately under a different subheading.

ma⌐nzoku まんぞく (満足) *n.* satisfaction; contentment.
——*a.n.* (〜 na, ni) satisfactory; contented.

The parts of speech of some words differ according to the context. In that case, they are given together.

3.　Meaning and usage

3.1　Different senses of a headword which are subsumed under one meaning are separated by semicolons.

na⌐yami⌐ なやみ (悩み) *n.* worry; trouble; sufferings; anguish.

3.2　When a headword has more than one meaning, each meaning is listed in a numbered sequence, with the most common and important meaning shown first.

ho⌐okoo ほうこう (方向) *n.*
　1　direction; way; course.
　2　aim; object; course.

3.3　Special notes on both the grammatical and social usage of words, and relevant cultural information are introduced by a ★.

4.　Illustrative examples

4.1　Example phrases and sentences are presented in the following order: romanized Japanese, normal Japanese orthography, the corresponding English translation.

Watashi wa maiasa hachi-ji ni ie o demasu. (私は毎朝8時に家を出ます) I *leave* the house at eight every morning.

4.2 Romanized Japanese is printed in italics with the headword of that particular entry set in upright style. In the illustrative phrase or sentence, the English translation of the headword is given in italics. The user should note that the parts of speech of the Japanese headword and its English translation equivalent will often be different, and also that it is sometimes difficult to define precisely the exact English word or words that correspond to the Japanese headword.

4.3 In example sentences featuring dialogue, Japanese style quotation marks, 「 」, are used in the Japanese text, and conventional English quotation marks in the romanization and translation.

> *"O-geñki desu ka?"* *"Okagesama de."* (「お元気ですか」「おかげさまで」) "How are you?" *"I'm fine, thank you."*

4.4 Many of the Japanese sentences are subject to several interpretations depending on context, which of course cannot be given in any detail in a dictionary such as this. It should be borne in mind that in Japanese the grammatical subject is often not expressed, and the distinction between singular and plural, or between definite (e.g. 'the pen') and indefinite (e.g. 'a pen'), is not as clearcut as in English.

5. Orthography

5.1 The orthography of headwords and entries reflects current educated usage, while at the same time taking into account the recommendations of the Government Committee on 'Chinese Characters for Daily Use' (1981). The general principles that have been followed are:

5.2 When there is a *kanji* listed after the *hiragana* immediately following the headword and all example phrases and sentences use that *kanji*, you may assume that the word is normally written in *kanji*, rather than *hiragana*.

> na⌈game⌉ru ながめる (眺める) *vt.* look at; watch; view: *mado kara soto o* nagameru (窓から外を眺める) *look* out of the window.

5.3 When there is a *kanji* listed after the *hiragana*, but no example phrases or sentences with that *kanji*, you may assume that whilst the *kanji* for that particular word does exist, it is common and perfectly acceptable not to use it in everyday written Japanese.

> **ma˥ku** まく（蒔く）*vt.* plant; sow:
> *hana no tane o* maku（花の種をまく）*plant* flower seeds.

5.4 You will also find illustrative examples in which example sentences using the headword is sometimes in *kana*, and sometimes in *kanji*. In such cases you may assume that both usages are perfectly acceptable, although some senses of the word may more commonly be written in *kana*, and other senses in *kanji*. (For example, see the entries under '**a˥taru**.')

6. Conjugations of verbs

6.1 Consonant-stem verbs

Consonant-stem verbs are marked Ⓒ in this dictionary and the two basic forms, to which '-*masu*' and '-*nai*' are attached, and the *te*-form are given in this order.

> **ka˥k·u** かく（書く）*vt.* (kak·i-; kak·a-; ka·i-te Ⓒ)
> **no˥m·u** のむ（飲む）*vt.* (nom·i-; nom·a-; noñ·de Ⓒ)

6.2 Vowel-stem verbs

Vowel-stem verbs are marked Ⓥ in this dictionary, and only the *te*-form is given, since the '-*masu*' and '-*nai*' are attached to the stem without any changes.

> **ta˥be˥·ru** たべる（食べる）*vt.* (tabe-te Ⓥ)

6.3 Irregular verbs

Irregular verbs are marked Ⓘ in this dictionary, and the two basic forms, to which '-*masu*' and '-*nai*' are attached, and the *te*-form are given.

> **s·u˥ru** する *vt.* (sh·i-; sh·i-; sh·i-te Ⓘ)
> **me˥ñs·u˥ru** めんする（面する）*vi.* (meñsh·i-; meñsh·i-; meñsh·i-te Ⓘ)
> **k·u˥ru** くる（来る）*vi.* (k·i-; k·o-; k·i-te Ⓘ)

6.4 With longer verbs, the conjugational information is given in abbreviated form in the interests of both clarity and economy of space.

> **chi˥rakas·u** ちらかす（散らかす）*vt.* (-kash·i-; -kas·a-; -kash·i-te Ⓒ) scatter; litter.

7. Conjugation of adjectives
7.1 Only the *ku*-form is given.

    ta⌈ka⌉·i たかい (高い) *a.* (-ku) high; tall; lofty.

7.2 Most adjectives are used attributively and predicatively. But in those cases in which adjectives are restricted in their usage, those that are used only attributively are marked '*attrib.*' (attributive), and those used only predicatively are marked '*pred.*' (predicative).

    shi⌈katana⌉·i しかたない (仕方ない) *a.* (-ku) (*pred.*) cannot help doing; be no use doing.

8. Adjectival nouns
The entry that follows an adjectival noun is as follows:

    shi⌉zuka しずか (静か) *a.n.* (~ na, ni) quiet

The word '*na*' is used to link the adjectival noun to a following noun or another adjectival noun which it modifies.

    shizuka *na ashioto* (*quiet* footsteps)

The '*ni*' indicates that the adjectival noun can be adverbialized.

    shizuka *ni aruku* (walk *quietly*)

9. Adverbs
Inflected forms of some verbs or adjectives are used as adverbs, and when such a form is common, it is listed as a headword.

    a⌈a-shite ああして *adv.* like that

When adverbs are commonly followed by '*to*,' or '*suru*,' this information is given in round brackets immediately following.

    do⌈shi⌉n どしん *adv.* (~ to) with a thud
    fu⌈rafura ふらふら *adv.* (~ suru) feel dizzy

When '*to*' is optional, an attempt is made to show this in the illustrative examples.

10. Levels of usage
Levels of usage or register are indicated as follows:

    formal = a word used in formal or official situations
    informal = a word used in relaxed and friendly situations

colloquial	=	an informal word used in conversation
polite	=	a polite word
honorific	=	a word indicating respect for others
humble	=	a word indicating humility
brusque	=	a potentially rough or abrupt word
rude	=	a potentially impolite or offensive word
literary	=	a word used in the written language

The above is to be taken only as a guide. There will be great variations in usage amongst native speakers of Japanese.

11. Cross-references
Reference to another word with a related meaning is indicated by ((→)).
Reference to a word with a contrasting meaning is indicated by ((↔)).

12. Brackets in illustrative examples
Round brackets ( ) indicate that omission is possible.
Square brackets [ ] indicate alternative possibilities.

13. Abbreviations

a.	adjective	*infl. end.*	inflected ending
a.n.	adjectival noun	*int.*	interjection
adv.	adverb	*n.*	noun
app.	appendix	*neg.*	negative
attrib.	attributive	*p.*	particle
colloq.	colloquial	*pred.*	predicative
conj.	conjunction	*pref.*	prefix
derog.	derogatory	*suf.*	suffix
fig.	figurative	*vi.*	intransitive verb
illus.	illustration	*vt.*	transitive verb

A Table of Japanese Sounds

Roomaji	Hiragana / Katakana

a	あ / ア	ka	か / カ	ga	が / ガ	sa	さ / サ	za	ざ / ザ	ta	た / タ	da	だ / ダ	na	な / ナ
i	い / イ	ki	き / キ	gi	ぎ / ギ	shi *si	し / シ	ji *zi	じ / ジ	chi *ti	ち / チ	ji *zi	ぢ / ヂ	ni	に / ニ
u	う / ウ	ku	く / ク	gu	ぐ / グ	su	す / ス	zu	ず / ズ	tsu *tu	つ / ツ	zu	づ / ヅ	nu	ぬ / ヌ
e	え / エ	ke	け / ケ	ge	げ / ゲ	se	せ / セ	ze	ぜ / ゼ	te	て / テ	de	で / デ	ne	ね / ネ
o	お / オ	ko	こ / コ	go	ご / ゴ	so	そ / ソ	zo	ぞ / ゾ	to	と / ト	do	ど / ド	no	の / ノ

kya	きゃ / キャ	gya	ぎゃ / ギャ	sha *sya	しゃ / シャ	ja *zya	じゃ / ジャ	cha *tya	ちゃ / チャ	ja *zya	ぢゃ / ヂャ	nya	にゃ / ニャ
kyu	きゅ / キュ	gyu	ぎゅ / ギュ	shu *syu	しゅ / シュ	ju *zyu	じゅ / ジュ	chu *tyu	ちゅ / チュ	ju *zyu	ぢゅ / ヂュ	nyu	にゅ / ニュ
kyo	きょ / キョ	gyo	ぎょ / ギョ	sho *syo	しょ / ショ	jo *zyo	じょ / ジョ	cho *tyo	ちょ / チョ	jo *zyo	ぢょ / ヂョ	nyo	にょ / ニョ

* Alternative romanization according to the Kunrei system.

Romanization

The romanization is based on the standard Hepburn system with the following modifications:

- Long vowels are indicated by double vowel letters. (paatii, shuuchuu)
- When the vowel sequence 'ei' is pronounced as a long vowel, it is indicated as 'ee.' (seeto, zeekiñ)
- The syllabic 'n' is transcribed as 'ñ.' (shiñbuñ)

ha	は ハ	ba	ば バ	pa	ぱ パ	ma	ま マ	ya	や ヤ	ra	ら ラ	wa	わ ワ	n̄	ん ン
hi	ひ ヒ	bi	び ビ	pi	ぴ ピ	mi	み ミ			rI	り リ	▲i	ゐ ヰ		
fu *hu	ふ フ	bu	ぶ ブ	pu	ぷ プ	mu	む ム	yu	ゆ ユ	ru	る ル				
he	へ ヘ	be	べ ベ	pe	ぺ ペ	me	め メ			re	れ レ	▲e	ゑ ヱ		
ho	ほ ホ	bo	ぼ ボ	po	ぽ ポ	mo	も モ	yo	よ ヨ	ro	ろ ロ	o	を ヲ		
hya	ひゃ ヒャ	bya	びゃ ビャ	pya	ぴゃ ピャ	mya	みゃ ミャ			rya	りゃ リャ				
hyu	ひゅ ヒュ	byu	びゅ ビュ	pyu	ぴゅ ピュ	myu	みゅ ミュ			ryu	りゅ リュ				
hyo	ひょ ヒョ	byo	びょ ビョ	pyo	ぴょ ピョ	myo	みょ ミョ			ryo	りょ リョ				

▲ Not used in modern Japanese

aa	ii	uu	ee	oo
ああ	いい	うう	ええ えい	おお おう
あー	いー	うー	えー	おー
アア	イイ	ウウ	エエ エイ	オオ オウ
アー	イー	ウー	エー	オー

Long vowels as described in this dictionary.

fa	fi	fo
ファ	フィ	フォ

Used for words of foreign origin.

A

aʹ¹ あっ *int.* oh; ah: ★ Used to express admiration, wonder, danger, etc. A', wakatta. (あっ、わかった) *Oh*, I see.

aʹaʹ¹ ああ *adv.* such; that; to such a degree; to such an extent: Niku ga takakute wa totemo kaemaseñ. (肉がああ高くてはとても買えません) If meat costs *that much*, I just cannot afford to buy it. (⇨ dooʹ; kooʹ; sooʹ)

aʹaʹ² ああ *int.* oh; ah; well; yes: ★ Used to express admiration, wonder, sorrow, etc. Aa, kiree da. (ああ、きれいだ) *Oh*, that's beautiful. (⇨ ooʹ)

aʹa-iu ああいう *attrib.* that; like that; that kind of; such: Watashi wa aa-iu zasshi ni wa kyoomi ga arimaseñ. (私はああいう雑誌には興味がありません) I am not interested in *that kind* of magazine. (⇨ doo-iu; koo-iu; soo-iu)

aʹa-shite ああして *adv.* like that; in that way: Kanojo wa aa-shite itsu-mo hito ni damasareru. (彼女はああしていつも人にだまされる) She is always deceived *like that* by people. (⇨ doo-shite; koo-shite; soo-shite)

aʹbaʹk·u あばく（暴く）*vt.* (aba-k·i-; abak·a-; aba·i-te Ⓒ) expose; disclose; reveal: himitsu o abaku (秘密を暴く) *expose* a confidence.

aʹbare-ru あばれる（暴れる）*vi.* (abare-te Ⓥ) act violently; rage; struggle: Kodomo wa chuusha o iyagatte abareta. (子どもは注射をいやがって暴れた) The child *struggled* to get away from the injection.

aʹbekobe あべこべ *n.* (*informal*) opposite; upside down; reverse.

aʹbi-ru あびる（浴びる）*vt.* (abi-te Ⓥ) 1 bathe: shawaa o abiru (シャワーを浴びる) *take* a shower.
2 get covered with: hokori o abiru (ほこりを浴びる) *get covered* with dust.
3 bask: nikkoo o abiru (日光を浴びる) *bask* in the sun.
4 be an object of praise [attack; criticism]: zessañ o abiru (絶賛を浴びる) *receive* great praise. (⇨ abi-seru)

aʹbise·ru あびせる（浴びせる）*vt.* (abise-te Ⓥ) 1 throw; pour (water): hito ni mizu o abiseru (人に水を浴びせる) *throw* water on a person.
2 (*fig.*) shower (with questions); heap (abuse on).

aʹbuna·i あぶない（危ない）*a.* (-ku) 1 dangerous; risky: Dooro de asobu no wa abunai. (道路で遊ぶのは危ない) It is *dangerous* to play in the road.
2 critical: Kaneko-sañ wa inochi ga abunai. (金子さんは命が危ない) Mr. Kaneko is in *critical* condition.

aʹburaʹ¹ あぶら（油）*n.* oil.

aʹburaʹ² あぶら（脂）*n.* fat; grease. (⇨ shibooʹ)

aʹburaʹe あぶらえ（油絵）*n.* an oil painting.

aʹchiʹ-kochi あちこち *n.* =achira-kochira.

aʹchira あちら *n.* 1 that place; that way; over there: ★ More polite than 'asoko' and 'atchi.' Achira ni irassharu no wa donata desu ka? (あちらにいらっしゃるのはどなたですか) Who is that person *over there*? (*polite*).
2 that thing; that person: ★ More polite than 'areʹ.' Achira ga yuumee na Nakamura señsee desu. (あちらが有名な中村先

生です) *That person over there* is
the famous Prof. Nakamura.
(⇨ dochira; kochira; sochira)

a￢chira-ko￢chira あちらこちら *n.*
here and there: ★ Abbreviated
to '*achi-kochi*.'
*Achira-kochira de sakura ga saki-
hajimeta.* (あちらこちらで桜が咲き始め
た) The cherry trees started to
bloom *here and there*.

a￢e￢g·u あえぐ (喘ぐ) *vi.* (aeg·i-;
aeg·a-; ae·i-de C) 1 pant;
gasp:
aegi aegi yama o noboru (あえぎあえ
ぎ山を登る) climb a mountain,
gasping for breath.
2 suffer:
fukyoo ni aegu (不況にあえぐ) *suffer*
an economic depression.

a￢fure￢·ru あふれる (溢れる) *vi.*
(afure-te V) 1 overflow; flood:
Ooame de kawa ga afureta. (大雨
で川があふれた) The river *overflowed*
because of the heavy rain.
2 be crowded with:
Shiñjuku wa hito de afurete iru.
(新宿は人であふれている) Shinjuku *is
crowded* with people.
3 be full of:
Kare wa kiboo ni afurete iru. (彼は
希望にあふれている) He *is full* of
hope.

a￢gar·u あがる (上がる) *vi.* (agar·i-;
agar·a-; agat-te C) 1 go up;
rise; come up:
*Kare wa go-kai made aruite agat-
ta.* (彼は5階まで歩いて上がった) He
walked up to the fifth floor.
2 (of degree, quantity, prices,
etc.) rise, be raised; be promoted:
oñdo ga agaru (温度が上がる) the
temperature *rises*. (⇨ ageru¹)
(↔ sagaru)
3 improve; make progress:
seeseki ga agaru (成績が上がる)
one's (school) grades *improve*.
(↔ ochiru; sagaru)
4 (of a child) enter (school):
*Kare no kodomo wa kotoshi shoo-
gakkoo ni agarimashita.* (彼の子ど

もは今年小学校に上がりました) His
child *started* elementary school
this year.
5 (of rain) stop; clear up:
Ame ga agarimashita. (雨が上がりま
した) The rain *has stopped*.
6 (of a person) get nervous; get
stage fright.
7 (*polite*) eat; drink:
Doozo o-agari kudasai. (どうぞお上
がりください) Please *help yourself*.
(⇨ nomu; taberu)

a￢ge·ru¹ あげる (上げる) *vt.* (age-te
V) 1 raise; lift:
*Shitsumoñ ga areba te o age
nasai.* (質問があれば手を上げなさい) If
you have any questions, please
raise your hands. (⇨ agaru)
2 give: ★ Not used toward
one's superiors.
Anata ni kono hoñ o agemasu. (あ
なたにこの本をあげます) I will *give* you
this book. (↔ kureru¹) (⇨ yaru²)
3 raise:
oñdo [nedañ] o ageru (温度[値段]を
上げる) *raise* the temperature
[price]. (↔ sageru) (⇨ agaru)
4 improve; increase:
nooritsu o ageru (能率を上げる)
improve the efficiency. (⇨ agaru)
-te ageru (て～) (used when
doing a favor for someone else):
*Watashi wa kare ni kasa o ka-
shite ageta.* (私は彼に傘を貸してあげ
た) I *lent* him an umbrella.

a￢ge·ru² あげる (揚げる) *vt.* (age-te
V) deep-fry: *sakana o ageru* (魚
を揚げる) *deep-fry* fish. (⇨ itameru)

a￢go¹ あご (顎) *n.* jaw; chin.

a￢go￢hige あごひげ (顎鬚) *n.*
beard. (⇨ hige)

a￢gura あぐら *n.* (way of sitting
with one's legs crossed).
agura o kaku (～をかく) sit cross-
legged.

a￢hiru あひる (家鴨) *n.* domestic
duck. (⇨ kamo)

a￢i あい (愛) *n.* love. (⇨ aisuru;
koi²)

a￢ida あいだ (間) *n.* 1 (of place)

between; among:

Gyoo to gyoo no aida *o sukoshi ake nasai*. (行と行の間を少しあけなさい) Leave a little space *between* the lines.

2 (of time) for; while; during:

Watashi wa nagai aida *matasareta*. (私は長い間待たされた) I was kept waiting *for* a long time.

3 (of relations) between; among:

Kanojo wa daigakusee no aida *de niñki ga aru*. (彼女は大学生の間で人気がある) She is popular *among* college students.

a⌈idagara あいだがら (間柄) *n*. relation; terms:

Takahashi to wa shitashii aidagara *desu*. (高橋とは親しい間がらです) I'm on friendly *terms* with Takahashi.

a⌈ijiñ あいじん (愛人) *n*. lover; love; mistress. (⇨ koibito)

a⌈ijoo あいじょう (愛情) *n*. love; affection; attachment.

a⌈ikagi あいかぎ (合鍵) *n*. duplicate key. (⇨ kagi)

a⌈ikawarazu あいかわらず (相変わらず) *adv*. still; as...as ever; as usual:

Kanojo wa aikawarazu *yoku hataraku*. (彼女は相変わらずよく働く) She works *as* hard *as ever*.

a⌈ikyo⌉o あいきょう (愛敬) *n*. charm; amiability. (⇨ aiso)

a⌈ima あいま (合間) *n*. interval; recess:

shigoto no aima *ni sukoshi uñdoo o suru* (仕事の合間に少し運動をする) do some exercise *during* one's work breaks.

a⌈imai あいまい (曖昧) *a.n.* (~ na, ni) vague; ambiguous:

aimai *na heñji o suru* (あいまいな返事をする) give a *vague* answer.

a⌈iniku あいにく (生憎) *adv*. unfortunately; unluckily:

Ainiku *kare wa fuzai datta*. (あいにく彼は不在だった) *Unfortunately*, he was not at home.

— *a.n.* (~ na/no) unfortunate;

unexpected:

Ainiku *no ame de eñsoku wa eñki sareta*. (あいにくの雨で遠足は延期された) The excursion was postponed on account of the *unexpected* rain.

a⌈isatsu あいさつ (挨拶) *n*.

1 greeting; salutation:

aisatsu *o kawasu* (あいさつを交わす) exchange *greetings*.

2 speech; address:

kaikai no aisatsu *o suru* (開会のあいさつをする) give an opening *address*.

3 call; visit:

shiññeñ no aisatsu *ni mawaru* (新年のあいさつに回る) make New Year's *calls*.

aisatsu (o) suru (~(を)する) *vi*. greet; salute.

a⌈iso⌉ あいそ (愛想) *n*. amiability; sociability; civility.

aiso ga ii (~がいい) get along well.

aiso ga tsukiru (~がつきる) be disgusted with.

aiso ga warui (~が悪い) be rather brusque.

... ni aiso o tsukasu (...に~をつかす) be out of patience with.... (↔ buaisoo) (⇨ aikyoo)

a⌈is·u⌉ru あいする (愛する) *vt*. (aish-i-; ais-a-; aish-i-te ⒸC) love:

Kare wa miñna ni aisarete iru. (彼はみんなに愛されている) He *is loved* by all. (⇨ ai; koi²)

a⌈ite⌉ あいて (相手) *n*. mate; partner; opponent; companion.

a⌈itsu あいつ *n*. that fellow [woman]; that one [thing]. (⇨ kanojo; kare)

a⌈izu あいず (合図) *n*. signal; sign; alarm.

... ni aizu (o) suru (...に~(を)する) *vi*. signal; make a sign: *Keekañ wa kuruma ni tomare to* aizu shita. (警官は車に止まれと合図した) The policeman *signaled* the car to stop.

a⌈ji¹ あじ (味) *n*. taste; savor; flavor. (⇨ ajiwau)

a⌈ji² あじ (鯵) *n*. horse mackerel.

a⌐jiwa¹·u あじわう（味わう）*vt.* (aji-wa·i-; ajiwaw·a-; ajiwat-te ⓒ)
1 taste; relish:
hoñba no Chuugoku-ryoori o aji-wau (本場の中国料理を味わう) *relish* real Chinese cooking.
2 enjoy; appreciate:
Tanoshii tabi o ajiwatta. (楽しい旅を味わった) I *enjoyed* a pleasant journey.
3 experience; go through:
kanashimi o ajiwau (悲しみを味わう) *experience* sorrow.

a⌐ka¹ あか（赤）*n.* red. (⇨ akai)

a⌐ka¹² あか（垢）*n.* dirt; grime.

a⌐kachañ あかちゃん（赤ちゃん）*n.* baby. ★ Usually refers to someone else's baby. (⇨ akañboo)

a⌐ka·i あかい（赤い）*a.* (-ku) red; crimson; scarlet. (⇨ aka¹)

a⌐kaji あかじ（赤字）*n.* the red; red figures; deficit. (↔ kuroji)

a⌐kañboo あかんぼう（赤ん坊）*n.* baby. (⇨ akachañ)

a⌐kari あかり（明り）*n.* light; lamp: *akari o tsukeru [kesu]* (明りをつける[消す]) turn on [off] the *light*.

a⌐karu·i あかるい（明るい）*a.* (-ku)
1 bright; light: *akarui iro* (明るい色) *bright* colors. (↔ kurai¹)
2 cheerful; happy: *akarui kibuñ* (明るい気分) a *happy* feeling. (↔ kurai¹)
3 (of prospects, etc.) bright: *akarui mirai* (明るい未来) a *bright* future. (↔ kurai¹)
4 be familiar with; be well informed:
Kare wa hooritsu ni akarui. (彼は法律に明るい) He *is well versed in* the law. (↔ kurai¹) (⇨ kuwashii)

a⌐kashi¹ñgoo あかしんごう（赤信号）*n.* red light; stoplight. (⇨ aoshiñgoo)

a⌐kas·u あかす（明かす）*vt.* (aka-sh·i-; akas·a-; akash·i-te ⓒ)
1 spend; pass (a night):
koya de ichi-ya o akasu (小屋で一夜を明かす) *spend* a night in a hut.
2 reveal; disclose (a secret, etc.):

shiñjitsu o akasu (真実を明かす) *tell* the truth.

a⌐kegata あけがた（明け方）*n.* dawn; daybreak.

a⌐ke·ru¹ あける（開ける）*vt.* (ake-te Ⓥ) open; unpack; unlock: *doa [hikidashi; kañzume] o akeru* (ドア[引き出し；缶詰]を開ける) *open* a door [drawer; can]. (↔ shimeru¹) (⇨ aku¹)

a⌐ke·ru² あける（明ける）*vi.* (ake-te Ⓥ) **1** (of day) break; dawn: *Moo sugu yo ga akeru.* (もうすぐ夜が明ける) The day will *break* soon.
2 (of a new year) begin: *toshi ga akeru* (年が明ける) a new year *begins*.
3 end; be over:
Yatto tsuyu ga aketa. (やっと梅雨が明けた) At last the rainy season *is over*. (⇨ owaru)

a⌐ke·ru³ あける（空ける）*vt.* (ake-te Ⓥ) **1** empty; vacate.
2 make room for.
3 make an opening:
kabe ni ana o akeru (壁に穴をあける) *make* a hole in the wall. (⇨ aku²)
4 make time:
Chotto o-jikañ o akete itadake-masu ka? (ちょっとお時間をあけていただけますか) Can you *spare* me a little time? (⇨ aki²; aku²)

a⌐ki¹ あき（秋）*n.* autumn; fall.

a⌐ki² あき（空き）*n.* **1** vacancy. (⇨ aku²)
2 space; room:
gyoo to gyoo no aida ni motto aki o toru (行と行の間にもっと空きをとる) leave more *space* between lines. (⇨ akeru³)
3 spare time. (⇨ akeru³)

a⌐kichi あきち（空き地）*n.* vacant land; empty lot. (⇨ tochi)

a⌐kikañ あきかん（空き缶）*n.* empty can.

a⌐ki¹raka あきらか（明らか）*a.n.* (~ na, ni) evident; obvious; clear:
Sono koto wa dare no me ni mo akiraka desu. (そのことはだれの目にも

明らかです) That is *evident* to everybody.

aˈkirame あきらめ (諦め) *n.* resignation; abandonment: Akirame *ga kañjiñ desu.* (あきらめが肝心です) We should know when to *give up.* (⇨ akirameru)

aˈkirameˌ·ru あきらめる (諦める) *vt.* (akirame-te Ⓥ) give up; abandon (a plan). (⇨ akirame; yameruˈ)

aˈkire·ru あきれる (呆れる) *vi.* (akire-te Ⓥ) be astonished; be dumbfounded: Kare no jooshiki no nasa ni wa akireta. (彼の常識のなさにはあきれた) I *was shocked* by his lack of common sense.

aˈkiˌ·ru あきる (飽きる) *vi.* (aki-te Ⓥ) get [be] tired of: Tokai no seekatsu ni wa akita. (都会の生活には飽きた) I *have become weary* of city life. (⇨ kikiakiru)

aˈkiya あきや (空き家) *n.* vacant [empty] house.

aˈkka あっか (悪化) *n.* worsening; deterioration; aggravation. **akka suru** (〜する) *vi.* become worse; deteriorate.

aˈkkenaˌ·i あっけない (呆気ない) *a.* (-ku) disappointingly short [brief; quick]: Is-shuukañ ga akkenaku sugita. (一週間があっけなく過ぎた) A week has passed *too quickly.*

aˈkogare あこがれ (憧れ) *n.* yearning; longing. (⇨ akogareru)

aˈkogare·ru あこがれる (憧れる) *vt.* (akogare-te Ⓥ) 1 long for; yearn for: Kanojo wa fasshoñ-moderu ni akogarete iru. (彼女はファッションモデルに憧れている) She *longs* to become a fashion model. (⇨ akogare) 2 admire: sutaa ni akogareru (スターに憧れる) *admire* a star. (⇨ akogare)

aˈkuˌ¹ あく (開く) *vi.* (ak·i·; ak·a·; a·i·te Ⓒ) open: Kono doa wa sayuu ni akimasu.

(このドアは左右にあきます) This door *opens* sideways. (↔ shimaruˈ) (⇨ akeruˈ; hiraku)

aˈk·uˌ² あく (空く) *vi.* (ak·i·; ak·a·; a·i·te Ⓒ) 1 get [be] empty [vacant]: Sumimaseñ ga, sono seki wa aite imasu ka? (すみませんが、その席はあいていますか) Excuse me, but *is* that seat *occupied?* (⇨ akeruˈ; akiˈ) 2 have a gap. (⇨ akeruˈ) 3 (of a hole) have an opening. (⇨ akeruˈ) 4 be free. (⇨ akeruˈ) 5 finish with something: Te ga aitara, kono shigoto o tetsudatte kudasai. (手があいたら、この仕事を手伝ってください) When you're *finished*, please help me with this job.

aˈkuˌ³ あく (悪) *n.* vice; evil. (↔ zeñˈ) (⇨ zeñaku)

aˈkubi あくび (欠伸) *n.* yawn: akubi *o suru* (あくびをする) give a *yawn.*

aˈkui あくい (悪意) *n.* ill will; malice; spite: akui *o idaku* (悪意を抱く) bear *ill will.*

aˈkuji あくじ (悪事) *n.* evil [wicked] deed; crime: akuji *o hataraku* (悪事を働く) do *evil.*

aˈkuma あくま (悪魔) *n.* devil; demon.

aˈkuˌmade (mo) あくまで (も) (飽く迄 (も)) *adv.* to the last; persistently.

aˈkuniñ あくにん (悪人) *n.* bad [wicked] person; villain.

aˈkuseñto アクセント *n.* 1 (pitch or stress) accent. ★ Not used in the sense of 'a (foreign) accent.' 2 emphasis; stress; accent: Ooki-na riboñ ga kanojo no fuku no akuseñto ni natte ita. (大きなリボンが彼女の服のアクセントになっていた) A large ribbon *set off* her dress.

aˈkushu あくしゅ (握手) *n.* handshake; handclasp. **akushu (o) suru** (〜(を)する) *vi.* shake hands.

aˈmaˌdo あまど (雨戸) *n.* sliding storm door made of thin boards; shutter.

aˈmae·ru あまえる (甘える) *vi.* (amae-te Ⅴ) **1** behave like a spoiled child; have a coquettish way:
Sono ko wa haha-oya ni amaeta. (その子は母親に甘えた) The child *behaved like a baby* with his mother.
2 depend on; take advantage of:
hito no kooi [shiñsetsu] ni amaeru (人の好意[親切]に甘える) *depend* on a person's goodwill [kindness].

aˈmaˌgu あまぐ (雨具) *n.* rainwear; umbrella; raincoat.

aˈma·i あまい (甘い) *a.* (-ku)
1 (of taste) sweet; sugary.
2 (of voice, melody, etc.) sweet; attractive.
3 not salty:
Kyoo no misoshiru wa chotto amai. (きょうのみそ汁はちょっと甘い) Today's miso soup is *not salty* enough. (↔ karai)
4 lenient; not severe in discipline:
Shujiñ wa kodomo ni amai. (主人は子どもに甘い) My husband is *too easy* on the children. (↔ karai)
5 optimistic; easygoing; underestimating the results.

aˈmaˌmizu あまみず (雨水) *n.* rainwater.

aˈmari¹ あまり (余り) *n.* the rest; the balance; remains. (⇨ amaru)

aˈmari² あまり (余り) *adv.* **1** too; very:
Kono ryoori wa amari karakute, taberarenai. (この料理はあまり辛くて、食べられない) This dish is *too peppery* for me to eat.
2 (with a negative) not...much; not very; seldom; rarely:
Yasai wa amari suki de wa arimaseñ. (野菜はあまり好きではありません) I don't like vegetables *very much*.

-aˈmari あまり (余り) *suf.* over...; more than...:

Nihoñ ni kite sañ-neñ-amari ni narimasu. (日本に来て3年あまりになります) I have been in Japan *over* three years now.

aˈma·ru あまる (余る) *vt.* (amar·i-; amar·a-; amat-te Ｃ)
1 be left (over):
Baageñ de yasuku kaeta no de, sañzeñ-eñ o-kane ga amatta. (バーゲンで安く買えたので、3,000円お金が余った) As I could buy it at a bargain, I *saved* 3,000 yen. (⇨ amari¹)
2 be in excess; be more than enough.

aˈmaˌs·u あます (余す) *vt.* (amash·i-; amas·a-; amash·i-te Ｃ)
1 leave:
Amasanai de, miñna tabe nasai. (余さないで、みんな食べなさい) *Don't leave* anything. Eat it all. (⇨ nokosu)
2 be left; remain. (⇨ nokosu)
amasu tokoro naku (～ところなく) completely; fully.

aˈmayaˌdori あまやどり (雨宿り) *n.* taking shelter from the rain.

aˈmayakaˌs·u あまやかす (甘やかす) *vt.* (-kash·i-; -kas·a-; -kash·i-te Ｃ) spoil; pamper.

aˈme¹ あめ (雨) *n.* rain. (⇨ amefuri; hare; kumori)

aˈme² あめ (飴) *n.* candy; sweet; lollipop:
ame o shaburu (あめをしゃぶる) suck a piece of *candy*.

aˈmeˌfuri あめふり (雨降り) *n.* rain; rainy weather. (⇨ ame¹)

aˈmi¹ あみ (網) *n.* net:
ami o haru (網を張る) lay a net / *ami o utsu* (網を打つ) cast a net.

aˈmiˌmono あみもの (編み物) *n.* knitting; crochet.

aˈm·u あむ (編む) *vt.* (am·i-; am·a-; añ-de Ｃ) knit; crochet; braid; weave:
keito no seetaa o amu (毛糸のセーターを編む) *knit* a woolen sweater.

aˈñ あん (案) *n.* plan; idea; proposal; draft.

a「na」 あな (穴) n. 1 hole; opening; perforation.

2 defect; deficit; loophole:
Kimi no keekaku ni wa ana ga aru. (君の計画には穴がある) There is a *defect* in your plan.

3 gap:
Sekiya-sañ no yasuñda ana o umenakereba naranai. (関谷さんの休んだ穴を埋めなければならない) We have to fill the *gap* left by Mr. Sekiya's absence.

a「nado」r・u あなどる (侮る) vt. (anador・i-; anador・a-; anadot-te ⓒ)
1 despise; look down on:
Wakai kara to itte kare o anadotte wa ikenai. (若いからといって彼を侮ってはいけない) You shouldn't *look down* on him just because he is young.

2 make light of.

a「na」ta あなた n. you: ★ Plural forms are 'anata-tachi', 'anata-gata' (polite) and 'anata-ra' (slightly derog.). Not used when addressing one's superiors.
Kore wa anata no desu ka? (これはあなたのですか) Is this *yours*? (⇒ kimi¹)

a「nau」ñsu アナウンス n. announcement.

a「ñba」rañsu アンバランス a.n. (~ na/ni) imbalance.

a「ñdo あんど (安堵) n. (formal) relief; reassurance. (⇒ añshiñ)
... ni añdo suru (...に~する) vi. be [feel] relieved.

a「ne あね (姉) n. one's older [elder; big] sister. (⇒ imooto)

a「ñgai あんがい (案外) adv. unexpectedly; against expectations.
— a.n. (~ na, ni) unexpected; surprising.

a「ñgoo あんごう (暗号) n. code; cipher; cryptogram.

a「ni あに (兄) n. one's older [elder; big] brother. (↔ otooto)

a「ñi あんい (安易) a.n. (~ na, ni) (formal) easy; easygoing; happy-go-lucky.

a「ñji あんじ (暗示) n. hint; suggestion; intimation.
añji suru (~する) vt. hint; suggest; imply.

a「ñji¹・ru あんじる (案じる) vt. (añji-te ⓥ) worry; be anxious:
Kare wa chichi-oya no keñkoo o añjite iru. (彼は父親の健康を案じている) He *is worried* about his father's health.

a「ñki あんき (暗記) n. memorization; memorizing.
añki suru (~する) vt. memorize; learn by heart.

a「ñma あんま (按摩) n. Japanese massage; masseur; masseuse.

a「ñmari あんまり a.n. (~ na/no, ni) beyond the ordinary degree; extreme:
Sore wa añmari da. (それはあんまりだ) That's going *too far*.
— adv. (colloq.) = amari².

a「ñmiñ あんみん (安眠) n. sound [good] sleep.

a「ñmoku あんもく (暗黙) n. implicitness; tacitness:
añmoku no ryookai (暗黙の了解) an *implicit* understanding.

a「ñna あんな attrib. such; like that:
Añna tokoro de asoñde wa abunai na. (あんな所で遊んでは危ないな) It is dangerous to play in *such* a place. (⇒ doñna; koñna; soñna)

a「ñna」i あんない (案内) n. 1 guidance; guide.
2 notice; invitation:
añnai-joo (案内状) an *invitation* letter [card].
añnai suru (~する) vt. guide; show.

a「ñna ni あんなに adv. such ; so:
Añna ni okoranakute mo yokkatta no ni. (あんなに怒らなくてもよかったのに) It was unnecessary for you to get so angry. (⇒ doñna ni; koñna ni; soñna ni)

a「no あの attrib. 1 that; the:
Asoko ni suwatte iru ano hito wa dare desu ka? (あそこに座っているあの

人はだれですか) Who is *that* person sitting over there?
2 that; the: ★ Refers to a person or thing that is, in time or space, distant from both the speaker and the listener.
"*Kinoo Akihabara e itte kimashita.*" "*Ano atari mo nigiyaka ni narimashita ne.*" (「きのう秋葉原へ行って来ました」「あの辺りもにぎやかになりましたね」) "I went to Akihabara yesterday." "*That* area has become a lively place, hasn't it?"
3 that: ★ Refers to a person or thing known to both the speaker and the listener.
"*Mada ano koto o ki ni shite iru ñ desu ka?*" "*Ano koto tte, nañ desu ka?*" (「まだあの事を気にしているんですか」「あの事って、何ですか」) "Are you still worried about *that* matter?" "What do you mean by *that* matter?" (⇨ dono; kono; sono)

a￢**noo** あのう *int.* excuse me; say; well:
Anoo, *Tookyoo-daigaku wa doo ittara ii deshoo ka?* (あのう、東京大学はどう行ったらいいでしょうか) *Excuse me*, but how can I get to Tokyo University?

a￢**ñpi** あんぴ (安否) *n.* safety:
Kare no añpi ga shiñpai desu. (彼の安否が心配です) I am worried about his *safety*.

a￢**ñsatsu** あんさつ (暗殺) *n.* assassination.

a￢**ñsee** あんせい (安静) *n.* rest; quiet; repose.
añsee ni suru (～にする) lie quietly in bed; take bed rest.

a￢**ñshiñ** あんしん (安心) *n.* peace of mind; relief.
añshiñ suru (～する) *vi.* feel relieved [assured].
— *a.n.* (～ na) safe; reassuring; secure.

a￢**ñshoo** あんしょう (暗礁) *n.*
1 reef.
2 (*fig.*) deadlock:

Kare-ra no hanashiai wa añshoo ni noriageta. (彼らの話し合いは暗礁に乗り上げた) Their talks came to a *deadlock*.

a￢**ñshoo-ba￢ñgoo** あんしょうばんごう (暗証番号) *n.* code number:
añshoo-bañgoo *o osu* (暗証番号を押す) enter one's *code number*.

a￢**ñta** あんた *n.* (*informal*) = anata.

a￢**ñtee** あんてい (安定) *n.* stability; balance; steadiness.
añtee suru (～する) *vi.* become stable; be stabilized.

a￢**ñzañ** あんざん (暗算) *n.* mental arithmetic [calculation].
añzañ suru (～する) *vt.* do sums in one's head.

a￢**ñzeñ** あんぜん (安全) *n.* safety; security.
— *a.n.* (～ na, ni) safe; secure.

a￢**ñzu** あんず (杏) *n.* apricot.

a￢**o** あお (青) *n.* **1** blue.
2 (of a traffic light, plants, vegetables, etc.) green:
ao-*yasai* (青野菜) *green* vegetables / ao-*riñgo* (青りんご) *a green apple*. (⇨ aoi; aojiroi; midori)

a￢**oa￢o to** あおあお (青々と) *adv.* (～ suru) (of trees, leaves, etc.) fresh and green; verdant.

a￢**o￢g·u**[1] あおぐ (仰ぐ) *vt.* (aog·i-; aog·a-; ao·i-de ⓒ) **1** look up at: *sora no hoshi o aogu* (空の星を仰ぐ) *look up* at the stars in the sky.
2 respect; look up to.

a￢**o￢g·u**[2] あおぐ (扇ぐ) *vt.* (aog·i-; aog·a-; ao·i-de ⓒ) fan:
uchiwa de jibuñ o aogu (うちわで自分をあおぐ) *fan* oneself with a round fan.

a￢**o￢·i** あおい (青い) *a.* (-ku) **1** blue.
2 green; unripe. (⇨ ao; midori)
3 (of a person's face, look) pale. (⇨ aojiroi)

a￢**ojiro￢·i** あおじろい (青白い) *a.* (-ku) **1** bluish white.
2 pale; pallid:
Kare wa aojiroi kao o shite iru. (彼は青白い顔をしている) He looks

pale. (⇨ aoi)

a⌐o¬r･u あおる (煽る) *vt.* (aor･i-; aor･a-; aot-te Ⓒ) **1** fan; flap: *Kaateñ ga kaze ni aorarete iru.* (カーテンが風にあおられている) The curtains *are flapping* in the wind. **2** stir up; incite: *kyoosooshiñ o aoru* (競争心をあおる) *arouse* a sense of rivalry.

a⌐oshi¬ñgoo あおしんごう (青信号) *n.* green light. (⇨ akashiñgoo)

a⌐ozame¬･ru あおざめる (青ざめる) *vi.* (aozame-te Ⓥ) turn pale. (⇨ aoi)

a⌐ozo¬ra あおぞら (青空) *n.* the blue (azure) sky.

a⌐pa¬ato アパート *n.* an apartment; an apartment house. (⇨ mañshoñ)

a⌐ppaku あっぱく (圧迫) *n.* pressure; oppression.

appaku suru (〜する) *vt.* oppress; suppress; strain.

a⌐ra あら *int.* my goodness; why. ★ Used by women to express wonder, surprise, etc. Men use '*are²*.' (⇨ maa²)

a⌐ra･i¹ あらい (荒い) *a.* (-ku) rough; rude; violent: *Kyoo wa nami ga arai.* (きょうは波が荒い) The sea is *rough* today. (↔ shizuka)

a⌐ra･i² あらい (粗い) *a.* (-ku) coarse; rough: *arai suna* (粗い砂) *coarse* sand. (↔ komakai)

a⌐rakajime あらかじめ *adv.* beforehand; in advance: *Kare wa jikeñ no naiyoo o arakajime shitte ita.* (彼は事件の内容をあらかじめ知っていた) He knew the details of the affair *in advance*.

a⌐rappo¬･i あらっぽい (荒っぽい) *a.* (-ku) rough; rude: *arappoi uñteñ* (荒っぽい運転) *unruly* driving.

a⌐rare あられ *n.* hail; hailstone.

a⌐rasa¬gashi あらさがし (粗探し) *n.* faultfinding; picking flaws: *hito no arasagashi o suru* (人のあらさがしをする) *find fault* with others.

a⌐rashi あらし (嵐) *n.* storm; tempest. (⇨ taifuu)

a⌐raso¬i あらそい (争い) *n.* dispute; quarrel; trouble. (⇨ arasou)

a⌐raso¬･u あらそう (争う) *vi.* (araso･i-; arasow･a-; arasot-te Ⓒ) **1** quarrel; dispute: *tochi no shoyuukeñ o arasou* (土地の所有権を争う) *dispute* the ownership of land. (⇨ arasoi) **2** compete: *Jookyaku wa saki o arasotte, deñsha ni noroo to shita.* (乗客は先を争って，電車に乗ろうとした) The passengers *pushed* in front of one another to get on the train.

a⌐ras･u あらす (荒らす) *vt.* (arash･i-; aras･a-; arash･i-te Ⓒ) **1** damage. (⇨ areru) **2** ransack; break in: *Doroboo ni heya o arasareta.* (泥棒に部屋を荒らされた) My room was *ransacked* by a thief.

a⌐rasuji あらすじ (粗筋) *n.* outline; synopsis; plot.

a⌐rata あらた (新た) *a.n.* (〜 na, ni) (*formal*) new; fresh. (⇨ atarashii)

a⌐ratama¬r･u あらたまる (改まる) *vi.* (-mar･i-; -mar･a-; -mat-te Ⓒ) **1** be improved. (⇨ aratameru) **2** (of a year, semester, etc.) begin; come around: *Toshi ga* aratamatta. (年が改まった) The new year *has come around*.

aratamatta (改まった) *attrib.* formal; ceremonious.

aratamatte (改まって) *adv.* in a formal way.

a⌐ratame¬･ru あらためる (改める) *vt.* (-me-te Ⓥ) **1** change; renew: *fukusoo o aratameru* (服装を改める) *change* one's clothes. (⇨ aratamaru) **2** correct; reform: *zeesee o aratameru* (税制を改める) *reform* the tax system. (⇨ aratamaru) **3** examine; check:

Keekañ wa kabañ no nakami o aratameta. (警官はかばんの中身を改めた) The policeman *checked* the contents of the bag.

a⌐rata⌐mete あらためて (改めて) *adv.* another time; again.

a⌐ra·u あらう (洗う) *vt.* (ara·i-; araw·a-; arat-te Ⓒ) 1 wash; clean: *sara o arau* (皿を洗う) *wash* the dishes.

2 wash; flow against [over]: *Nami ga kishi o aratte iru.* (波が岸を洗っている) Waves *are washing* the beach.

a⌐rau⌐mi あらうみ (荒海) *n.* rough [stormy] sea. (⇨ umi¹)

a⌐raware⌐·ru あらわれる (現れる) *vi.* (-ware-te Ⓥ) 1 appear; come out:
Kumo no aida kara tsuki ga ara-wareta. (雲の間から月が現れた) The moon *appeared* from behind the clouds. (⇨ arawasu³)

2 arrive; show up:
Sañjup-puñ matte, kare ga ara-warenakereba, saki ni ikimashoo. (30分待って、彼が現れなければ、先に行きましょう) We'll wait for thirty minutes and if he *doesn't show up,* let's go on ahead. (⇨ arawasu²)

3 (of hidden nature, facts, etc.) be discovered; be revealed.

a⌐rawa⌐s·u¹ あらわす (表す) *vt.* (-wash·i-; -was·a-; -wash·i-te Ⓒ) 1 show; reveal; express.

2 signify; stand for; symbolize:
Kono kigoo wa nani o arawashite imasu ka? (この記号は何を表していますか) What does this symbol *stand for?*

a⌐rawa⌐s·u² あらわす (現す) *vt.* (-wash·i-; -was·a-; -wash·i-te Ⓒ) 1 show up; appear; reveal:
Hisashiburi ni kare wa paatii ni sugata o arawashita. (久しぶりに彼はパーティーに姿を現した) He *showed up* at the party—the first time in quite a while. (⇨ arawareru)

2 take effect:
Kono kusuri wa sugu ni kooka o

arawashimasu. (この薬はすぐに効果を現します) This medicine will soon *take effect.*

a⌐rawa⌐s·u³ あらわす (著す) *vt.* (-wash·i-; -was·a-; -wash·i-te Ⓒ) (*formal*) write; publish:
hoñ o arawasu (本を著す) *write* a book.

a⌐rayu⌐ru あらゆる *attrib.* all; every:
arayuru kikai o riyoo suru (あらゆる機会を利用する) make use of *every* opportunity.

a⌐re¹ あれ *n.* 1 that over there: ★ Refers to something located at some distance from both the speaker and the listener.
Are wa Tookyoo-tawaa desu. (あれは東京タワーです) *That* is the Tokyo Tower. (⇨ dore¹; kore¹; sore¹)

2 that, it: ★ Refers to something, which is, in time or space, distant from both the speaker and the listener.
Are wa nañ-neñ-mae deshita kke. Izu ni jishiñ ga atta no wa? (あれは何年前でしたっけ、伊豆に地震があったのは) How many years ago was *it* when there was the earthquake in Izu? ˝

3 that, it: ★ Refers to something known to both the speaker and the listener.
"Nee, are kaita?" "Are tte geñgo-gaku no repooto no koto?" (「ねえ、あれ書いた」「あれって、言語学のレポートのこと」) "Say, have you written *that?*" "By 'that,' do you mean the linguistics paper?"

4 she; he: ★ Refers to one's wife or one's subordinate.
Kanai desu ka? Are wa ima jikka e itte imasu. (家内ですか。あれは今実家へ行っています) My wife? *She* is visiting her parents' house.

are irai (～以来) since then.

a⌐re² あれ *int.* oh; look; really. ★ Used by men to express surprise, doubt, etc. Women use 'ara.'

a⌈re de あれで *adv.* **1** with that:
Are de *kare wa jishiñ o torimodo-shita.* (あれで彼は自信を取り戻した) *With that*, he regained his self-confidence.
2 in one's own way:
Kare wa are de *nakanaka omoi-yari ga aru.* (彼はあれでなかなか思いやりがある) He is very considerate *in his own way.*

a⌈re-(k)kiri あれ(っ)きり *adv.* (with a negative) since then:
Are-(k)kiri *kare ni atte imaseñ.* (あれっきり彼に会っていません) I haven't met him *since then.* (⇨ kore-(k)kiri; sore-(k)kiri)

a⌈rel-kore あれこれ *adv.* this and that; one thing and another; in various ways:
Are-kore *yatte iru uchi ni, yoi hoo-hoo ga mitsukatta.* (あれこれやっているうちに, 良い方法が見つかった) While trying out *various ways*, I discovered a good method. (⇨ iroiro²)

a⌈re·ru あれる (荒れる) *vi.* (are-te ⓥ) **1** be stormy; be rough.
2 lie waste; be dilapidated. (⇨ arasu)
3 (of lips and skin) become rough:
Fuyu ni naru to te ga areru. (冬になると手が荒れる) In winter, my hands *become chapped.*
4 be in a bad mood.

a⌈rel·rugii アレルギー *n.* allergy.

a⌈ri あり (蟻) *n.* ant.

a⌈rifureta ありふれた (有り触れた) *attrib.* common; everyday; commonplace: arifureta *hanashi* (ありふれた話) just *another* story.

a⌈rigatal·i ありがたい (有り難い) *a.* (-ku) **1** thankful; grateful; pleasant:
Tetsudatte itadaketara, arigatai *desu.* (手伝っていただけたら, ありがたいです) I would be *grateful* if you helped me.
2 edifying and merciful:
Kyoo wa boosañ kara arigatai *hanashi o kiita.* (きょうは坊さんからありがたい話を聞いた) I listened to the *edifying* teachings of the Buddhist priest today.

a⌈ri⌉gatoo ありがとう (有り難う) thank you; thanks:
Arigatoo *gozaimasu.* (ありがとうございます) *Thank you* very much.

a⌈ri⌉sama ありさま (有様) *n.* state; circumstances; scenes.
★ Often refers to a bad state.

a⌈ru¹ ある (或る) *attrib.* a certain; some:
Aru *hi kare ga totsuzeñ tazunete kita.* (ある日彼が突然訪ねて来た) *One day* he suddenly called on me.

a⌈r·u² ある (有る・在る) *vi.* (ar-i-; at-te ⓒ) **1** be; exist; there is [are]:
Kagi wa tsukue no ue ni arimasu. (鍵は机の上にあります) The key *is* on the desk. (↔ nai) (⇨ da; desu; iru¹)
2 be located:
Sono shiro wa yama no naka ni arimasu. (その城は山の中にあります) The castle *is located* in the mountains. (↔ nai)
3 have:
Kanojo wa e no sainoo ga aru. (彼女は絵の才能がある) She *has* a talent for painting. (↔ nai)
4 (of quantity, height, width, etc.) be:
Taijuu wa dono kurai arimasu *ka?* (体重はどのくらいありますか) How much *do* you *weigh?*
5 be found:
Kono ki wa Nihoñ-juu doko ni mo arimasu. (この木は日本中どこにもあります) This tree *is found* throughout Japan. (↔ nai)
6 have the experience of:
Kare ni wa *atta koto ga* arimasu *ka?* (彼には会ったことがありますか) / *Have* you *ever* met him? (⇨ koto¹)
7 happen:
Yuube kiñjo de kaji ga arimashita. (ゆうべ近所で火事がありました) A fire *broke out* in the neighborhood

last night.

8 take place; be held:
Sakuneñ kono keñ de kokutai ga arimashita. (昨年この県で国体がありました) The National Athletic Meet *was held* in this prefecture last year.

a⌐ruba˥ito アルバイト *n.* part-time job; job on the side; part-timer.

a⌐ru˥iwa[1] あるいは (或は) *conj.* (*formal*) or; either...or:
Anata ka aruiwa watashi ga ikanakereba narimaseñ. (あなたあるいは私が行かなければなりません) Either you *or* I have to go. 《⇒ mata-wa》

a⌐ru˥iwa[2] あるいは (或は) *adv.* perhaps; probably: ★ Usually followed by '*ka mo shirenai.*'
Sono keekaku wa aruiwa chuushi ni naru ka mo shirenai. (その計画はあるいは中止になるかもしれない) The project will *probably* be halted.

a⌐rukari アルカリ *n.* alkali. 《↔ sañ[2]》

a⌐rukooru アルコール *n.* **1** alcohol. **2** alcoholic beverage.

a⌐ru˥k·u あるく (歩く) *vi.* (aruk·i-; aruk·a-; aru·i-te Ⓒ) walk:
Eki made aruite go-fuñ desu. (駅まで歩いて 5 分です) It takes five minutes to *walk* to the station.

a⌐rumi アルミ *n.* aluminum:
arumi sasshi (アルミサッシ) an *aluminum* window sash.

a⌐sa[1] あさ (朝) *n.* morning. 《↔ bañ[1]; yoru[1]》

a⌐sa[2] あさ (麻) *n.* hemp; hemp plant [cloth].

a⌐sabañ あさばん (朝晩) *n.* morning and evening. 《⇒ asayuu》
— *adv.* always; from morning till night.

a⌐sa˥gao あさがお (朝顔) *n.* morning glory plant.

a⌐sago˥hañ あさごはん (朝ご飯) *n.* breakfast. ★ More polite than '*asameshi.*' 《↔ bañgohañ》
《⇒ chooshoku; gohañ; hirugohañ》

a⌐sahi あさひ (朝日) *n.* morning [rising] sun. 《↔ yuuhi》

a⌐sa·i あさい (浅い) *a.* (-ku) **1** shallow:
asai nabe (浅い鍋) a *shallow* pan / *isu ni asaku koshikakeru* (いすに浅く腰掛ける) sit *on the edge* of a chair. 《↔ fukai》

2 (of time, etc.) short:
Kono kaisha wa dekite kara, hi ga asai. (この会社はできてから, 日が浅い) This company was established *not so long ago.*

3 (of experience, knowledge) lacking; green; superficial:
Kare wa mada keekeñ ga asai. (彼はまだ経験が浅い) He *doesn't have much* experience.

4 light; slight:
asai kizu (浅い傷) a *slight* cut. 《↔ fukai》

a⌐sameshi あさめし (朝飯) *n.* (*slightly rude*) breakfast. 《⇒ asagohañ; chooshoku》
asameshi mae (〜前) **1** before breakfast. **2** very easy.

a⌐sa˥ne あさね (朝寝) *n.* late rising.
asane (o) suru (〜を(を)する) *vi.* get up late. 《⇒ hirune》

a⌐sa-ne˥boo あさねぼう (朝寝坊) *n.* late riser. 《⇒ yofukashi》
asa-neboo (o) suru (〜を(を)する) *vi.* get up late in the morning.

a⌐sa˥tte あさって (明後日) *n.* the day after tomorrow. 《⇒ kyoo; myoogonichi》

a⌐sayake あさやけ (朝焼け) *n.* morning glow in the sky. 《↔ yuuyake》

a⌐sayuu あさゆう (朝夕) *n.* morning and evening. 《⇒ asabañ》

a⌐se あせ (汗) *n.* sweat; perspiration.

a⌐se˥r·u[1] あせる (焦る) *vi.* (aser·i-; aser·a-; aset-te Ⓒ) hurry; be impatient.

a⌐se˥r·u[2] あせる (褪せる) *vi.* (aser·i-; aser·a-; aset-te Ⓒ) fade; be discolored:
Kaateñ no iro ga asete kita. (カーテンの色があせてきた) The curtains

have faded.

a﹃shi﹄ あし（足・脚）*n*. **1** foot; leg; paw. ★ '脚' usually refers to some sort of support.
2 step; pace:
ashi *ga hayai* [*osoi*]（足が速い[遅い]）be quick [slow] of *foot*.
3 means of transport:
Kootsuu suto ga shimiñ no ashi o ubatta.（交通ストが市民の足を奪った）The transport strike deprived the citizens of *transportation*.
ashi ga deru（〜が出る）exceed the budget.
... kara ashi o arau（...から〜を洗う）wash one's hands of (crime).
... ni ashi o hakobu（...に〜を運ぶ）visit; make a call on.
... no ashi o hipparu（...の〜を引っ張る）get in a person's way; hold back (from success, etc.)

a﹃shia﹄to あしあと（足跡）*n*. footprint; track.

a﹃shibu﹄mi あしぶみ（足踏み）*n*.
1 stepping; stamping.
2 standstill:
ashibumi-*jootai ni aru*（足踏み状態にある）be at a *standstill*.
ashibumi (o) suru（〜を）する）*vi*. mark time.

a﹃shidori あしどり（足取り）*n*.
1 step; gate; pace:
Kare wa omoi [*karui*] ashidori *de ie e kaetta.*（彼は重い[軽い]足どりで家へ帰った）He returned home with heavy [light] *steps*.
2 trace; track:
Keesatsu wa hañniñ no ashidori o otta.（警察は犯人の足どりを追った）The police followed the *tracks* of the criminal.

a﹃shiga﹄kari あしがかり（足掛かり）*n*. footing; foothold.

a﹃shi﹄kubi あしくび（足首）*n*. ankle.

a﹃shimoto﹄ あしもと（足元）*n*. at (near) one's foot:
Ashimoto *ni ki o tsuke nasai.*（足元に気をつけなさい）Watch your *step*!

a﹃shinami あしなみ（足並み）*n*. (of two or more people) pace; step:
Kooshiñ-chuu ni miñna no ashinami ga midareta.（行進中にみんなの足並みが乱れた）They got out of *step* during the procession.

a﹃shioto﹄ あしおと（足音）*n*. sound of footsteps.

a﹃shita﹄ あした（明日）*n*. tomorrow. (⇨ kinoo¹; kyoo)

a﹃sobi あそび（遊び）*n*. play; game; fun; amusement.
asobi ni iku（〜に行く）visit; call on; make a trip for pleasure. (⇨ asobu)

a﹃sob·u あそぶ（遊ぶ）*vt*. (asob·i-; asob·a-; asoñ-de Ⓒ) **1** play; amuse oneself:
kooeñ de asobu（公園で遊ぶ）*play* in the park. (⇨ asobi)
2 be idle; idle away.
3 (of a place, a room, an instrument, etc.) be not in use:
asoñde iru *heya*（遊んでいる部屋）a room *not in use*.

a﹃soko あそこ *n*. **1** that place; over there: ★ Refers to a place which is some distance away from both the speaker and the listener.
Asoko *ni takai too ga mieru deshoo.*（あそこに高い塔が見えるでしょう）You should be able to see a tall tower *over there*.
2 that place: ★ Refers to a place which is removed from both the speaker and the listener, but is known to them.
Izu mo ii kedo, watashi wa asoko *yori Shiñshuu no hoo ga suki desu.*（伊豆もいいけど、私はあそこより信州の方が好きです）Izu is a nice place to visit, but I like Shinshu better. (⇨ soko¹)
3 that place: ★ Refers to a place which the speaker expects the listener to know about.
"*Koñbañ* asoko *e nomi ni ikanai?*" "*Ii ne. Ikimashoo.*" (「今晩あ

そこへ飲みに行かない」「いいね. 行きましょう」"How about going for a drink at *that place* this evening?" "Yes. Let's go."

2 that: ★ Used to emphasize a degree.

Kare ga asoko made gañbaru to wa omoimaseñ deshita. (彼があそこまでがんばるとは思いませんでした) I never thought that he would try *that* hard. (⇨ doko; koko[1]; soko[1])

a⌈ssa⌉ri あっさり *adv.* (~ to) easily; readily.

assari (to) suru (~(と)する) (of dish, appetite, desire, etc.) plain; simple; light: *Niku-ryoori no ato wa assari (to) shita mono ga tabetaku naru.* (肉料理の後はあっさり(と)したものが食べたくなる) After a meat dish, I feel like eating something *plain and simple*.

a⌈sseñ あっせん (斡旋) *n.* good offices; mediation; help.

asseñ suru (~する) *vt.* use one's good offices; mediate.

a⌈su⌉ あす (明日) *n.* = ashita.

a⌈tae·ru あたえる (与える) *vt.* (atae-te Ⅴ) **1** give; award.

2 give; cause (shock, damage, pain, etc.).

3 afford (pleasure, etc.).

4 assign; provide (a job, a question, etc.):

Hayashi-sañ wa ataerareta shigoto o isshoo-keñmee yatte imasu. (林さんは与えられた仕事を一生懸命やっています) Ms. Hayashi is putting her all into the work that *was assigned* to her.

a⌈takushi あたくし *n.* (*informal*) = watakushi. ★ Used mainly by women.

a⌈tama⌉ あたま (頭) *n.* **1** head: ★ Usually indicates the portion from the eyebrows up, or the top part covered with hair.

Atama ga itai. (頭が痛い) *I have a headache.*

2 brain: atama ga ii (頭がいい) *be smart* / atama o tsukau (頭を使う)

use one's *brains*. (⇨ chie)

3 hair: atama o arau (頭を洗う) shampoo one's *hair*. (⇨ kami-no-ke)

atama ga agaranai (~が上がらない) cannot compete with; be indebted to.

atama ga kireru (~が切れる) have a sharp mind.

atama ni kuru (~にくる) get angry.

atama o hineru (~をひねる) rack one's brains.

atama o itameru (~を痛める) be worried.

a⌈tamaka⌉zu あたまかず (頭数) *n.* the number of persons. (⇨ niñzuu)

a⌈tamakiñ あたまきん (頭金) *n.* down payment.

a⌈tarashi⌉·i あたらしい (新しい) *a.* (-ku) **1** new; latest. (↔ furui)

2 fresh. (↔ furui) (⇨ arata)

a⌈tari あたり (辺り) *n.* **1** neighborhood; vicinity. (⇨ heñ[2])

2 about; around: atari o mimawasu (辺りを見回す) look *around*.

a⌈tarimae あたりまえ (当たり前) *a.n.* (~ na/no, ni) **1** natural; reasonable. (⇨ toozeñ)

2 ordinary.

a⌈tar·u あたる (当たる) *vi.* (atar·i-; atar·a-; atat-te C) **1** hit; strike: *Booru ga kare no atama ni atatta.* (ボールが彼の頭に当たった) A ball *hit* him on the head. (⇨ ateru)

2 (of a prediction, a forecast) be right:

Kyoo no teñki-yohoo wa atatta. (きょうの天気予報は当たった) Today's weather forecast *was right*.

3 win:

Kono kuji ga it-too ni atarimashita. (このくじが一等に当たりました) This lottery ticket *won* first prize. (⇨ ateru)

4 make a hit; succeed:

Shiñ-seehiñ ga atatta. (新製品が当たった) The new product *was a hit*.

5 (of a date) fall on:
Kotoshi wa Kurisumasu ga nichi-yoo ni ataru. (ことしはクリスマスが日曜に当たる) This year Christmas *falls on* Sunday.

6 correspond; be equivalent to:
Ich-mairu wa it-teñ-rok-kiro ni ataru. (1 マイルは 1.6 キロに当たる) One mile *is equivalent* to 1.6 kilometers.

7 lie; be located:
Sono machi wa Tokyoo no kita ni ataru. (その町は東京の北に当たる) That town *lies* to the north of Tokyo.

8 be assigned; be allotted; be called on.
Koñdo no geki de kanojo wa ii yaku ni atatta. (今度の劇で彼女はいい役に当たった) In the recent play, she *was given* a good part. (⇨ ateru)

9 (of light, rays, etc.) shine; get sunshine. (⇨ ateru)

10 (of a person) be poisoned; get food poisoning:
fugu ni ataru (ふぐにあたる) *be poisoned* by globefish.

11 consult; look up; check (a source of information):
Jisho ni atatte, *kañji no imi o shirabeta.* (辞書にあたって、漢字の意味を調べた) I *looked* in the dictionary for the meaning of the Chinese character.

12 be hard on (a person):
Kimura-sañ wa itsu-mo watashi ni tsuraku ataru. (木村さんはいつも私につらく当たる) Mr. Kimura *is* always *hard* on me.

13 undertake; be in charge of. (⇨ ateru)

14 expose oneself to heat [wind, etc.]:
sutoobu ni ataru (ストーブにあたる) *warm oneself* at the heater.

*... (*suru*) ni wa ataranai* (...(する)にはあたらない) be not worth (doing).

... ni atari [atatte] (...するにあたり [あたって]) (*formal*) on the occasion

a⌈tashi あたし *n.* (*informal*)
= watakushi. ★ Used mainly by women.

a⌈tata⌉ka あたたか (暖か) *a.n.*
(~ na, ni) warm; mild. (⇨ atatakai)

a⌈tataka⌉·i あたたかい (暖かい・温かい) *a.* (-ku) (*informal* =attaka)
1 warm; mild:
Dañdañ atatakaku *natte kita.* (だんだん暖かくなってきた) It has become *warmer and warmer.* (↔ samui) (⇨ atataka)
2 warm-hearted; cordial:
Miñna wa kare o atatakaku *mukaeta.* (みんなは彼を温かく迎えた) They gave him a *cordial* welcome. (↔ tsumetai)

a⌈tatama⌉r·u あたたまる (暖まる・温まる) *vi.* (-mar·i-; -mar·a-; -matte C̄) get warm; warm up; be heated. (⇨ atatameru)

a⌈tatame⌉·ru あたためる (暖める・温める) *vt.* (-me-te V̄) **1** warm (up); heat. (⇨ atatamaru)
2 nurse (a thought); have (a plan) in mind.

a⌈tchi⌉ あっち *n.* (*colloq.*) =achira.

a⌈te あて (当て) *n.* **1** object; aim; goal. (⇨ mokuteki)
2 expectation; hope.
3 dependence; reliance:
Watashi-tachi wa anata o ate ni *shite imasu.* (私たちはあなたを当てにしています) We *depend* on you.

-ate あて (宛) *suf.* addressed to:
*Suzuki-sañ-*ate *no kozutsumi* (鈴木さんあての小包) a parcel *addressed to* Miss Suzuki.

a⌈tehama⌉r·u あてはまる (当てはまる) *vi.* (-hamar·i-; -hamar·a-; -hamat-te C̄) **1** hold true; fit:
Kono kotowaza wa geñdai ni mo atehamaru. (このことわざは現代にも当てはまる) This proverb *holds true* even in our time. (⇨ atehameru)
2 fulfill:
Koo-iu jookeñ ni atehamaru *hito wa nakanaka mitsukaranai.* (こうい

う条件に当てはまる人はなかなか見つから
ない) It is hard to find a person
who *fulfills* these conditions.
(⇨ atehameru)

a⌈tehame⌉・ru あてはめる（当てはめ
る) *vt.* (-hame-te Ⅴ) apply;
adapt:
*Gaikoku no shuukañ o subete
Nihoñ ni atehameru wake ni wa
ikanai.* (外国の習慣をすべて日本に当て
はめるわけにはいかない) You cannot
expect us to *adapt* all foreign customs to Japan. (⇨ atehamaru)

a⌈tena あてな（宛名) *n.* address.

a⌈te-ru あてる（当てる) *vt.* (ate-te
Ⅴ) 1 hit; strike:
Kare wa ya o mato ni ateta. (彼は
矢を的に当てた) He *shot* the arrow
into the target. (⇨ ataru)
2 put:
*Kanojo wa kodomo no hitai ni te o
ateta.* (彼女は子どもの額に手を当てた)
She *put* her hand to her child's
forehead.
3 guess; give a right answer:
Kare ga seekai o ateta. (彼が正解を
当てた) He *guessed* the right answer. (⇨ ataru)
4 expose:
*Nureta fuku o hi ni atete kawaka-
shita.* (ぬれた服を日に当てて乾かした) I
put the wet clothes out in the
sun to dry them. (⇨ ataru)
5 (of a lottery) win. (⇨ ataru)
6 use; spend (money, time, etc.):
*Kanojo wa ichi-nichi ichi-jikañ o
Nihoñgo no beñkyoo ni atete iru.*
(彼女は1日1時間を日本語の勉強に
当てている) She *devotes* an hour a
day to studying Japanese.
7 call on (somebody):
*Kyoo watashi wa señsee ni ate-
rareta.* (きょう私は先生に当てられた)
Today the teacher *called on* me
in class. (⇨ ataru)

a⌈tesaki あてさき（宛て先) *n.*
address; destination.

a⌈to¹ あと（後) *n.* 1 back; rear:
ato o ou (後を追う) *pursue* / *ato ni
tsuzuku* (後に続く) *follow*. (↔ mae)

2 after; later: ★ Usually in the
pattern '(...*no*/-*ta*) ato *de*.'
Ato de deñwa shimasu. (後で電話
します) I'll call you *later*. (↔ mae)
3 rest; remainder.

a⌈to² あと（跡) *n.* mark; trace;
track; ruins; remains:
kutsu no ato (靴の跡) the *marks* of
shoes.

a⌈to⌉ashi あとあし（後足) *n.* (of an
animal) hind leg. (↔ maeashi)

a⌈toka⌉tazuke あとかたづけ（後片
付け) *n.* clearing away; put back
in order:
shokuji no atokatazuke o suru (食
事の後片付けをする) *clear* the table
after a meal.

a⌈tosaki あとさき（後先) *n.* 1 before and behind; both ends.
2 consequences:
*Kare wa atosaki no kañgae mo
naku, keeyakusho ni saiñ shita.*
(彼は後先の考えもなく、契約書にサイン
した) He signed the contract
without any consideration of the
consequences.

a⌈toshi⌉matsu あとしまつ（後始末）
n. 1 putting things in order:
hi no atoshimatsu o suru (火の後始
末をする) *put* out a fire *completely*.
2 settlement:
*Chichi ga watashi no shakkiñ no
atoshimatsu o shite kureta.* (父が私
の借金の後始末をしてくれた) My
father *settled* my debts for me.

a⌈tsugami あつがみ（厚紙) *n.*
thick paper; cardboard; paste-
board.

a⌈tsugi あつぎ（厚着) *n.* heavy
[thick] clothes [clothing].
(↔ usugi)

a⌈tsu⌉・i¹ あつい（熱い) *a.* (-ku)
1 (of temperature) hot; heated.
(↔ tsumetai; nurui) (⇨ atsusa²)
2 emotionally excited.

a⌈tsu⌉・i² あつい（暑い) *a.* (-ku)
hot; very warm. (↔ samui)
(⇨ atsusa¹)

a⌈tsu・i³ あつい（厚い) *a.* (-ku)
1 thick; heavy:

Kono orenji wa kawa ga atsui.(こ のオレンジは皮が厚い) This orange has a *thick* skin. (↔ usui) (⇨ atsusa³; buatsui)

2 warm; hearty:
atsui *motenashi* (厚いもてなし) a *warm and friendly* welcome.

a¹tsukai あつかい (扱い) *n.* handling; dealing; treatment:
Gasoriñ no atsukai ni wa ki o tsukete kudasai.(ガソリンの扱いには気を つけてください) Please be careful when *handling* gasoline. (⇨ atsukau)

a¹tsukamashi¹·i あつかましい (厚か ましい) *a.* (-ku) impudent; shameless; presumptuous. (⇨ zuuzuushii)

a¹tsuka·u あつかう (扱う) *vt.* (-ka·i-; -kaw·a-; -kat-te C)
1 handle; operate.
2 treat; take care of; deal with:
Koko no teñiñ wa o-kyaku o taisetsu ni atsukaimasu.(ここの店員はお 客を大切に扱います) The clerks in this shop *treat* customers with courtesy.
3 accept; deal in.
4 write up in a newspaper or a magazine. (⇨ atsukai)

a¹tsukurushi¹·i あつくるしい (暑苦 しい) *a.* (-ku) sultry; humid and uncomfortable.

a¹tsumari¹ あつまり (集まり) *n.*
1 meeting; gathering.
2 attendance; collection:
Atsumari *ga yoi* [*warui*]. (集まりが よい[悪い]) There is a large [small] *attendance*.

a¹tsuma¹r·u あつまる (集まる) *vi.* (-mar·i-; -mar·a-; -mat-te C)
1 gather; assemble. (⇨ atsumari; atsumeru)
2 be collected. (⇨ atsumeru)
3 be concentrated; be centered:
Hitobito no doojoo ga kanojo ni atsumatta.(人々の同情が彼女に集ま った) Their sympathy *was centered* on her.

a¹tsume¹·ru あつめる (集める) *vt.*

(-me-te V) **1** gather; assemble:
gakusee o uñdoojoo ni atsumeru (学生を運動場に集める) *assemble* the students on the sports field. (⇨ atsumaru)
2 collect:
mezurashii kitte o takusañ atsumeru (珍しい切手をたくさん集める) *collect* many rare stamps. (⇨ atsumaru; shuushuu)
3 attract:
Sono nyuusu wa hitobito no kañshiñ o atsumeta.(そのニュースは人々 の関心を集めた) The news *attracted* people's interest.

a¹tsurae¹·ru あつらえる (誂える) *vt.* (-rae-te V) order (goods):
Yuumee na mise de suutsu o atsuraeta.(有名な店でスーツをあつらえ た) I *ordered* a suit at a famous store.

a¹tsu¹ryoku ありりょく (圧力) *n.* pressure; stress.

a¹tsusa¹ あつさ (暑さ) *n.* heat; hot weather; hotness. (↔ samusa) (⇨ atsui²)

a¹tsusa² あつさ (熱さ) *n.* hotness; heat; warmth:
furo no atsusa o miru (風呂の熱さを みる) check the *temperature* of a bath. (⇨ atsui¹)

a¹tsusa³ あつさ (厚さ) *n.* thickness. (⇨ atsui³)

a¹tta¹ka あったか (暖か) *a.n.* (*colloq.*) = atataka.

a¹ttoo あっとう (圧倒) *n.* being overwhelming.
attoo suru (～する) *vt.* overwhelm; overpower: *Wareware wa kazu no ue de teki o attoo shita.*(われわれは数の上で敵を圧倒した) We *overwhelmed* the enemy numerically.

a¹ttoo-teki あっとうてき (圧倒的) *a.n.* (～ na, ni) overwhelming:
attoo-teki *tasuu* (圧倒的多数) an *overwhelming* majority.

a¹·u¹ あう (会う・逢う・遇う) *vi.* (a·i-; aw·a-; at-te C) meet; see; come across: ★ Used with '*ni* [*to*].' A

more polite expression is '*o-me-ni-kakaru*.'
Watashi wa Ginza de kare ni battari atta. (私は銀座で彼にばったり会った) I *came across* him in Ginza.

a¹·u² あう (合う) *vi.* (a·i-; aw·a-; at-te Ⓒ) **1** fit; suit:
Kono fuku wa watashi ni pittari aimasu. (この服は私にぴったり合います) This dress *fits* me perfectly.
(⇨ awaseru)
2 agree with; correspond.
(⇨ awaseru)
3 (in the form of '*atte iru*') be correct; be right:
Kono tokee wa atte imasu. (この時計は合っています) This clock *has the right time*.
4 (with a negative) pay:
Kore ijoo yasuku shite wa (wari ni) awanai. (これ以上安くしては(割に)合わない) It *does not pay* if I sell at a lower price. (⇨ wari)

a¹·u³ あう (遭う) *vi* (a·i-; aw·a-; at-te Ⓒ) meet with; have an unfavorable experience:
jiko ni au (事故にあう) *meet with* an accident / *hidoi me ni au* (ひどい目にあう) *have a bad experience*.

a「wa¹ あわ (泡) *n.* bubble; foam; lather: *awa ga tatsu* (泡が立つ) *bubbles* form.
awa o kuu (～を食う) be confused. (⇨ awateru)

a「wa¹·i あわい (淡い) *a.* (-ku) (*literary*) **1** pale; light: *awai aoiro* (淡い青色) *pale* blue.
2 faint: *awai nozomi* (淡い望み) a *faint* hope.
3 transitory; fleeting: *awai koi* (淡い恋) a *fleeting* love.

a「ware あわれ (哀れ) *n.* pity: *aware o sasou* (哀れを誘う) arouse one's *pity*.
— *a.n.* (～ na, ni) pitiful; miserable; pathetic:
Hitori-gurashi no roojiñ o aware ni omou. (一人暮らしの老人を哀れに思う) I *pity* the old man living alone.

a「wase¹·ru あわせる (合わせる) *vt.* (awase-te Ⓥ) **1** put [join] together:
chikara o awaseru (力を合わせる) *unite* efforts. (⇨ au²)
2 add (up):
Zeñbu awasete ikura desu ka? (全部合わせていくらですか) How much does it come to *altogether*?
3 fit:
Karada ni awasete doresu o tsukutta. (体に合わせてドレスを作った) I had a dress made to *fit* me.
(⇨ au²)
4 adjust; set:
kamera no piñto o awaseru (カメラのピントを合わせる) *adjust* the focus of a camera. (⇨ au²)
5 accompany:
piano no bañsoo ni awasete utau (ピアノの伴奏に合わせて歌う) sing *to the accompaniment* of the piano.
6 adapt:
Watashi wa kare no yarikata ni awaseta. (私は彼のやり方に合わせた) I *adapted myself* to his way of working. (⇨ au²)
7 mix:
kechappu to mayoneezu o awaseru (ケチャップとマヨネーズを合わせる) *mix* ketchup and mayonnaise.

a「watadashi¹·i あわただしい (慌ただしい) *a.* (-ku) hasty; hurried; quick; busy.

a「watemono あわてもの (慌て者) *n.* rash person.

a「wate·ru あわてる (慌てる) *vi.* (awate-te Ⓥ) **1** hurry; panic.
2 get flustered; be confused.
(⇨ magotsuku)

a「yafuya あやふや *a.n.* (～ na, ni) vague; uncertain:
ayafuya na heñji (あやふやな返事) a *vague* answer.

a「yamachi¹ あやまち (過ち) *n.* mistake; error; fault; sin:
ayamachi o okasu (過ちを犯す) make a *mistake*.

a「yamari¹ あやまり (誤り) *n.* error; mistake; slip: ★ Interchangeable

with '*machigai*,' but more formal.
Ayamari *ga attara, naoshi nasai.*
(誤りがあったら, 直しなさい) Correct
errors, if any. (⇨ ayamaru²)

a⌐yama⌐r・u¹ あやまる (謝る) *vt.*
(-mar・i-; -mar・a-; -mat-te C̲)
apologize; beg a person's pardon.

a⌐yama⌐r・u² あやまる (誤る) *vi., vt.*
(-mar・i-; -mar・a-; -mat-te C̲)
make a mistake:
hoogaku o ayamaru (方角を誤る)
take the wrong direction.
(⇨ ayamari)

a⌐yame あやめ (菖蒲) *n.* sweet
flag; iris.

a⌐yashi⌐i あやしい (怪しい) *a.* (-ku)
1 suspicious; strange.
2 doubtful; dubious; uncertain.
3 clumsy; poor:
Kare wa ashimoto ga ayashikatta.
(彼は足元が怪しかった) He walked
unsteadily.

a⌐ya⌐s・u あやす *vi.* (ayash・i-; aya-
s・a-; ayash・i-te C̲) fondle; lull;
dandle; soothe:
akanboo o ayasu (赤ん坊をあやす)
cuddle a baby.

a⌐yatsu⌐r・u あやつる (操る) *vt.*
(ayatsur・i-; ayatsur・a-; ayatsut-
te C̲) manipulate; handle;
manage:
ningyoo o ayatsuru (人形を操る)
manipulate a puppet / *fune o* ayatsuru (船を操る) *steer* a boat.

a⌐za⌐yaka あざやか (鮮やか) *a.n.*
(~ na, ni) 1 bright; vivid;
fresh:
Ame no ato de, ki no midori ga
azayaka *datta.* (雨のあとで, 木の緑が
鮮やかだった) After the rain, the
green of the trees was *fresh.*

2 splendid, skillful:
azayaka *na engi* (鮮やかな演技) a
splendid performance.

a⌐zuka⌐r・u あずかる (預かる) *vt.*
(-kar・i-; -kar・a-; -kat-te C̲)
1 keep:
*Yamada-san ga anata no nimotsu
o* azukatte imasu. (山田さんがあなたの
荷物を預かっています) Mr. Yamada
has your baggage. (⇨ azukeru)
2 look after; take charge of:
Hoikuen wa kodomo o go-ji made
azukatte kureru. (保育園は子どもを 5
時まで預かってくれる) At the nursery,
they *look after* the children until
five o'clock. (⇨ azukeru)
3 withhold:
Kimi no jihyoo wa toriaezu azukatte okoo. (君の辞表はとりあえず預か
っておこう) I will *sit on* your resignation for the time being.
(⇨ azukeru)

a⌐zuke⌐ru あずける (預ける) *vt.*
(-ke-te V̲) 1 leave:
Kurooku ni mochimono o azuketa.
(クロークに持ち物を預けた) I *left* my
things in the cloakroom.
(⇨ azukaru)
2 deposit:
Ginkoo ni gomañ-en azuketa. (銀
行に 5 万円預けた) I *deposited*
50,000 yen in the bank.
(⇨ azukaru)
3 entrust:
Kodomo wa haha ni azukete, *shigoto ni ikimasu.* (子どもは母に預けて,
仕事に行きます) I *entrust* my child
to my mother's care and go to
work. (⇨ azukaru)

a⌐zuki あずき (小豆) *n.* adzuki
bean.

B

ba ば (場) *n.* **1** place; spot:
ba o hazusu (場を外す) leave the
room / ba o fusagu (場をふさぐ) take
up much *space*. (⇨ basho)
2 occasion; case:
sono ba *ni fusawashii fuku o kiru*
(その場にふさわしい服を着る) wear
clothes suitable for the *occasion*.
3 (of a drama) scene:
ni-maku sañ-ba (2 幕 3 場) Act 2,
Scene 3.

-ba[1] ば *infl. end.* [attached to the
conditional base of a verb, adjective or the copula] ★ The *ba*-
form of a verb is made by replacing the final '-*u*' with '*e*' and
adding '-*ba*,' and the *ba*-form of
an adjective by dropping the
final '-*i*' and adding '-*kereba*.'
The *ba*-form of the copula '*da*' is
'*naraba*.' (⇨ APP. 2)
1 if; provided; when:
a (the *ba*-form clause indicates a
condition and the following
clause the consequent result):
Ame ga fureba *eñsoku wa chuushi
desu.*(雨が降れば遠足は中止です) *If
it rains,* our outing will be can-
celed. (⇨ -tara)
b (the *ba*-form clause indicates
an assumed or possible situation
and the following clause the
speaker's intention, request,
advice, etc.):
Jikañ ga areba *Kyooto e mo ikitai.*
(時間があれば京都へも行きたい) *Pro-
vided there is time,* I would like
to go to Kyoto as well.
c (the *ba*-form clause indicates
an unfulfilled or unreal condition and the following clause the
speaker's judgment, wish, reaction, etc.):
Moo sukoshi gañbareba *dekita to
omoimasu.*(もう少しがんばればできたと

思います) I feel I could have succeeded *if I had tried a bit harder.*
(⇨ -tara)
2 when; whenever: ★ The *ba*-
form clause indicates a habitual
action in the past and the following clause the consequence of
that action.
Chichi wa nomeba *kanarazu
utatta mono da.*(父は飲めば必ず歌っ
たものだ) My father always used to
sing *when he drank.*
3 and; both...and; neither...nor:
★ Used to link similar items in a
parallel relationship.
Ano hito wa tabako mo sueba
sake mo nomu.(あの人はたばこも吸え
ば酒も飲む) He smokes *and* drinks.

-ba[2] ば (羽) *suf.* counter for birds
and rabbits. (⇨ APP. 4)

ba⌐**a** ばあ *int.* boo; bo. ★ Used
when playing with babies.

ba⌐**ai** ばあい (場合) *n.* **1** case; occasion; circumstance:
Sono kisoku wa kono baai *ate-
hamaranai.*(その規則はこの場合あては
まらない) That rule does not apply
in this *case.*
2 in case of; if; when:
Kaji no baai *wa beru ga narimasu.*
(火事の場合はベルが鳴ります) *In the
event of* fire, the bell will ring.
(⇨ toki)

ba⌐**asañ** ばあさん (婆さん) *n.* (*informal*) **1** one's grandmother.
2 old woman. (↔ jiisañ)
(⇨ o-baasañ)

ba⌐**chi**[1] ばち (罰) *n.* punishment
inflicted by gods or Buddha:
bachi ga ataru (罰が当たる) *be punished; get it.*

ba⌐**i** ばい (倍) *n.* double; twice:
Go-neñ de shuunyuu ga bai ni
natta.(5 年で収入が倍になった) My
income *doubled* in five years.

-bai[1] ばい (倍) *suf.* times; -fold: *Bukka ga sañ-bai ni natta.* (物価が 3 倍になった) Prices *tripled*.

-bai[2] ばい (杯) *suf.* =-hai. ((⇨ APP. 4))

ba˥ibai ばいばい (売買) *n.* buying and selling; trade.
baibai suru (〜する) *vt.* deal in; trade.

ba˥ieñ ばいえん (煤煙) *n.* soot; smoke.

ba˥ikai ばいかい (媒介) *n.* mediation; medium.
baikai suru (〜する) *vt.* mediate: *Mararia wa ka ni yotte* baikai *sareru.* (マラリアは蚊によって媒介され る) Malaria *is carried* by mosquitoes.

ba˥ikiñ ばいきん (ばい菌) *n.* germ; bacteria. ★ Informal equivalent for 'saikiñ,' emphasizing filthiness. ((⇨ saikiñ[2]))

ba˥imee ばいめい (売名) *n.* self-advertisement; publicity: *baimee o hakaru* (売名を図る) seek *publicity*.

ba˥ioriñ バイオリン *n.* violin. *baioriñ o hiku* (バイオリンを弾く) play the *violin*.

ba˥iritsu ばいりつ (倍率) *n.*
1 magnification; power.
2 competition: *Kono gakkoo wa* bairitsu *ga takai.* (この学校は倍率が高い) There is keen *competition* to enter this school.

ba˥ishoo ばいしょう (賠償) *n.* reparation; compensation: *baishoo o yookyuu suru* (賠償を要 求する) demand *reparations*.

ba˥ishuñ ばいしゅん (売春) *n.* prostitution: *baishuñ-fu* (売春婦) a *prostitute*.

ba˥ishuu ばいしゅう (買収) *n.*
1 buying up; purchase.
2 bribery; corruption.
baishuu (o) suru (〜(を)する) *vt.*
1 buy up; purchase (a building, land, etc.).
2 bribe; corrupt: *shooniñ o* bai-

shuu suru (証人を買収する) *corrupt* a witness.

ba˥iteñ ばいてん (売店) *n.* stand; stall; kiosk; store.

ba˥iu ばいう (梅雨) *n.* the rainy season. ((⇨ tsuyu[2]; uki[1]))

ba˥iyaku ばいやく (売約) *n.* sales contract.

ba˥jji バッジ *n.* badge; pin. ★ Usually refers to the badge that businessmen wear on their lapels to identify their companies.

ba˥ka ばか (馬鹿) *n.* fool; stupid [silly] person: *Soñna koto o suru to wa kare mo* baka *da.* (そんなことをするとは彼もばか だ) He is a *fool* to do such a thing.
baka ni naranai (〜にならない) be not negligible.
baka ni suru (〜にする) make a fool of.
baka o miru (〜を見る) feel like a fool.
— *a.n.* (〜 na) foolish; stupid; ridiculous; unreasonable.

ba˥ka- ばか (馬鹿) *pref.* too...; extremely; excessively: *baka-shoojiki* (ばか正直) *too* honest *for one's own good* / baka-teenee (ばかていねい) *excessive* politeness.

ba˥kabakashi˥-i ばかばかしい (馬 鹿馬鹿しい) *a.* (-ku) foolish; silly; absurd. ((⇨ bakarashii))

ba˥ka ni ばかに (馬鹿に) *adv.* awfully; terribly; very: *Kyoo wa* baka ni *isogashii.* (きょう はばかに忙しい) I'm *terribly* busy today.

ba˥kañsu バカンス *n.* vacation; holidays.

ba˥karashi˥-i ばからしい (馬鹿らし い) *a.* (-ku) foolish; silly; absurd; ridiculous. ((⇨ bakabakashii))

ba˥kari ばかり *p.* ★ Follows a noun, adjective or the dictionary form of a verb, or the *te*-form of a verb in the pattern '-te bakari iru.'
1 only; no other than...; nothing but:

Señsee wa watashi bakari *ni shitsumoñ suru.* (先生は私ばかりに質問する) The teacher asks questions to *no one but* me. (⇨ dake; nomi²)

2 just:

Nihoñ ni tsuita bakari *de mada nani mo mite imaseñ.* (日本に着いたばかりでまだ何も見ていません) I've *just* arrived in Japan, so I haven't yet seen anything.

3 about; approximately; thereabouts:

Juugo-fuñ bakari *matte kudasai.* (15分ばかり待ってください) Please wait for *about* fifteen minutes. (⇨ kurai²; hodo)

4 be about [ready] to do:

Itsu de mo shuppatsu dekiru bakari *ni yooi wa dekite imasu.* (いつでも出発できるばかりに用意はできています) We *are ready to* set off at any time.

5 just [simply] because:

Koñpyuutaa ga tsukaenai bakari *ni, ii shigoto no tsukaenakatta.* (コンピューターが使えないばかりに、いい仕事につけなかった) *Just because* I can't use a computer, I couldn't get a decent job.

6 (used for emphasis): ★ Emphatic form is '*bakkari.*'

Koñdo bakari *wa gamañ ga dekinai.* (今度ばかりはがまんができない) *This time* I am not going to put up with it.

ba￢ka￢s・u ばかす (化かす) *vt.* (bakash・i-; bakas・a-; bakash・i-te Ⓒ) bewitch; play a trick on:

Nihoñ de wa, kitsune ga hito o bakasu *to iwareru.* (日本では、狐が人を化かすといわれる) In Japan, it is said that foxes *play tricks* on people.

ba￢kemono￣ ばけもの (化け物) *n.* monster; ghost; specter.

ba￢ke￢・ru ばける (化ける) *vi.* (bake-te Ⓥ) **1** take the form of:

Mahootsukai ga raioñ ni baketa. (魔法使いがライオンに化けた) The witch *took the form of* a lion.

2 disguise oneself as:

Gootoo wa keekañ ni bakete ita. (強盗は警官に化けていた) The robber *disguised himself* as a policeman.

ba￢ketsu￣ バケツ *n.* bucket; pail.

ba￢kka￢ri ばっかり *p.* = bakari.

ba￢kkiñ￣ ばっきん (罰金) *n.* fine; penalty.

ba￢kku￣ バック *n.* back; background. (⇨ haikee²)

bakku suru (〜する) *vi.* reverse (a car).

ba￢kuchi￣ ばくち (博打) *n.* gambling; speculation. (⇨ kakegoto)

ba￢kudai￣ ばくだい (莫大) *a.n.* (〜 na) huge; enormous; vast:

bakudai *na kiñgaku* (莫大な金額) a *huge* sum of money.

ba￢kudañ￣ ばくだん (爆弾) *n.* bomb.

ba￢kufu￣ ばくふ (幕府) *n.* shogunate.

ba￢kugeki￣ ばくげき (爆撃) *n.* bombing.

bakugeki suru (〜する) *vt.* bomb.

ba￢kuhatsu￣ ばくはつ (爆発) *n.* explosion; eruption; burst.

bakuhatsu suru (〜する) *vi.* explode; blow up; burst.

ba￢kuro￣ ばくろ (暴露) *n.* exposure; disclosure.

bakuro suru (〜する) *vt.* expose; disclose: *himitsu o* bakuro suru (秘密を暴露する) *disclose* a secret.

ba￢kuzeñ￣ ばくぜん (漠然) *adv.* (〜 to) vaguely; aimlessly:

Kodomo no koro no koto wa bakuzeñ *to oboete imasu.* (子どものころのことは漠然と覚えています) I remember my childhood *vaguely*.

ba￢meñ￣ ばめん (場面) *n.* scene; sight; spectacle.

ba￢ñ¹ ばん (晩) *n.* evening; night. (↔ asa¹) (⇨ yoru¹; yuube¹; yuugata)

ba￢ñ² ばん (番) *n.* one's turn; order:

Saa kimi ga utau bañ *da.* (さあ君が歌う番だ) Now it's your *turn* to sing. (⇨ juñbañ)

ba⌐ñ³ ばん（番）n. watch; guard:
nimotsu no bañ o suru (荷物の番を
する) keep *watch* over the baggage.

ba⌐ñ⁴ ばん（盤）n. board; disk.

-bañ ばん（番）suf. **1** order in a
series:
Kare wa ni-bañ ni toochaku shita.
(彼は2番に到着した) He was the
second to arrive.
2 number:
Nañ-bañ ni o-kake desu ka? (何番
におかけですか) What *number* are
you phoning? (⇨ bañgoo)

ba⌐ñcha ばんちゃ（番茶）n. coarse
green tea. (⇨ o-cha; señcha)

ba⌐ñchi ばんち（番地）n. house
[street] number; address.

ba⌐ñdo バンド n. **1** strap; band:
tokee no bañdo (時計のバンド) a
watchband.
2 belt: *kawa no bañdo* (皮のバン
ド) a leather *belt*.
3 musical band: *burasu-bañdo*
(ブラスバンド) a brass *band*.

ba⌐ne ばね n. spring.

ba⌐ñgo⌐hañ ばんごはん（晩ご飯）n.
dinner; supper. ★ More polite
than '*bañmeshi*.'
(⇨ gohañ; hirugohañ; yuushoku)
(↔ asagohañ)

ba⌐ñgo⌐o ばんごう（番号）n. number. ★ When asking the number,
say '*nañ-bañ*,' not '*nañ bañgoo*.'
(⇨ -bañ)

ba⌐ñgumi ばんぐみ（番組）n.
program:
rajio [*terebi*] (*no*) *bañgumi* (ラジオ
[テレビ]（の）番組) a radio [television]
program.

ba⌐ñji ばんじ（万事）n. everything;
all:
Bañji umaku ikimashita. (万事うま
く行きました) *Everything* went well.

ba⌐ñkeñ ばんけん（番犬）n. watch-
dog. (⇨ inu)

ba⌐ñku⌐ruwase ばんくるわせ（番
狂わせ）n. unexpected result; surprise; upset.

-bañme¹ ばんめ（番目）suf. (des-

ignates the place in a sequence):
mae kara sañ-bañme (前から3番
目) *third* from the front.

ba⌐ñmeshi ばんめし（晩飯）n. (*informal*) supper. (⇨ bañgohañ;
yuushoku)

ba⌐ñneñ ばんねん（晩年）n. one's
later years.

ba⌐ñni⌐ñ ばんにん（番人）n. watch-
man; watch; guard.

ba⌐ñnoo ばんのう（万能）n. om-
nipotence:
bañnoo-*señshu* (万能選手) an *all-
around* player.

ba⌐ñsañ ばんさん（晩餐）n. (*formal*) dinner; banquet. (⇨ yuushoku)

-bañseñ ばんせん（番線）suf. platform; track:
Señdai-yuki no ressha wa go-
bañseñ *kara demasu.* (仙台行きの列
車は5番線から出ます) The train for
Sendai leaves from *track 5*.

ba⌐ñsoo ばんそう（伴奏）n. accompaniment.
bañsoo (o) **suru** (～（を）する) vi.
accompany (a song on the piano).

ba⌐ñsookoo ばんそうこう（絆創膏）
n. sticking plaster; adhesive tape.

ba⌐ñza⌐i ばんざい（万歳）n. cheers:
bañzai o sañshoo suru (万歳を三唱
する) give three *cheers*.

ba⌐ñzeñ ばんぜん（万全）n. abso-
lute sureness:
Taifuu ni taisuru sonae wa bañ-
zeñ *desu.* (台風に対する備えは万全で
す) We *are well prepared* against
typhoons.

ba⌐ra ばら（薔薇）n. rose.

ba⌐rabara¹ ばらばら a.n. (～ na/
no, ni) apart; in [to] pieces:
Kaze de shorui ga barabara *ni
natte shimatta.* (風で書類がばらばらに
なってしまった) The papers were *scattered* by the wind.

ba⌐rabara² ばらばら adv. (～ to)
(the sound of large drops of rain
or lots of small rocks pelting
down):
Barabara (*to*) *yuudachi ga futte*

kita. (ばらばら(と)夕立が降ってきた) The evening rain came *pelting down.*

baˈramaˈk·u ばらまく (ばら蒔く) *vt.* (-mak·i-; -mak·a-; -ma·i·te) Ⓒ
1 scatter; spread:
uwasa o baramaku (うわさをばらまく) *spread* the rumor.
2 hand out indiscriminately; throw around:
meeshi o baramaku (名刺をばらまく) *hand out* name cards indiscriminately.

baˈraňsu バランス *n.* balance:
baraňsu no toreta *shokuji* (バランスのとれた食事) a *well-balanced* diet. (↔ aňbaraňsu)

baˈree-boˈoru バレーボール *n.* volleyball. ★ Often abbreviated to simply 'baree.'

baˈsho ばしょ (場所) *n.* 1 place; spot; location. (⇨ ba; kasho)
2 space; room:
Piano wa basho *o toru.* (ピアノは場所をとる) The piano takes up a lot of *space.*
3 (of sumo wrestling) tournament:
*haru-*basho (春場所) the spring *sumo tournament.*

baˈssui ばっすい (抜粋) *n.* extract; excerpt.
bassui suru (〜する) *vt.* extract; excerpt.

baˈss·uru ばっする (罰する) *vt.* (bassh·i-; bassh·i-; bassh·i·te Ⓘ) punish; inflict punishment for (a crime). (⇨ batsu)

baˈsu バス *n.* bus; coach. (⇨ shibasu; tobasu²)

baˈsuketto-boˈoru バスケットボール *n.* basketball. ★ Often abbreviated to simply 'basuketto.'

baˈsutee バスてい (バス停) *n.* bus stop. (⇨ teeryuujo)

baˈtabata ばたばた *adv.* (〜 to)
1 (the sound of flapping, rattling or clattering):
Kaateň ga kaze de batabata (to) *oto o tatete iru.* (カーテンが風でばたば

た(と)音をたてている) The curtains are *flapping* in the wind.
2 in a flurry:
batabata (to) *beňkyoo o hajimeru* (ばたばた(と)勉強を始める) begin to study *in a fluster.*
3 one after another:
kaisha ga batabata (to) *toosaň suru* (会社がばたばた(と)倒産する) firms go bankrupt *one after another.*

baˈtsu ばつ (罰) *n.* punishment; penalty. (⇨ bassuru)

baˈtsuguň ばつぐん (抜群) *a.n.* (〜 no, ni) outstanding; unrivaled:
Kanojo wa uta ga batsuguň *ni umai.* (彼女は歌が抜群にうまい) Her singing *is unrivaled* in excellence.

baˈttaˈri ばったり *adv.* (〜 to)
1 with a thud:
battari (to) *taoreru.* (ばったり(と)倒れる) fall down *with a thud.*
2 unexpectedly; by chance:
Sakki Tanaka-saň to battari *aimashita.* (さっき田中さんとばったり会いました) I met Ms. Tanaka *by chance* a little while ago.
3 suddenly:
Kare kara no tegami ga battari *konaku natta.* (彼からの手紙がばったり来なくなった) His letters *suddenly* stopped coming.

baˈtterii バッテリー *n.* car battery. (⇨ deňchi)

-be べ (辺) *suf.* around; nearby; neighborhood:
kishi-be (岸辺) a *shore* / mado-be (窓辺) *by* the window.

Beˈekoku べいこく (米国) *n.* America; the United States (of America).

beˈesu ベース *n.* 1 base; basis:
*chiňgiň-*beesu (賃金ベース) the wage *base.*
2 (of baseball) base.

beˈesu-aˈppu ベースアップ *n.* pay raise [hike].

beˈki べき *n.* [follows the dictionary form of a verb, except that '*suru beki*' is usually '*su beki*.']

1 should; ought to:
Miñna ga kono teñ o kañgaeru beki desu.(みんながこの点を考えるべきです) Everyone *should* consider this point.
2 worthy of; deserve to be:
odoroku beki dekigoto (驚くべき出来事) a *remarkable* [*surprising*] incident / *kanashimu beki koto* (悲しむべきこと) a matter of *regret*.

be「kkyo べっきょ (別居) *n.* living apart; separation.
bekkyo suru (〜する) *vi.* live apart; separate. (⇨ rikoñ)

be「n べん (便) *n.* **1** convenience; facilities; service:
Kare no uchi wa kootsuu no beñ ga yoi. (彼の家は交通の便が良い) His house *is easy of access*.
2 feces; stool.

-beñ べん (遍) *suf.* (the number of) times. (⇨ APP. 4)

be「ñgo べんご (弁護) *n.* (legal) defense; justification.
beñgo (o) suru (〜(を)する) *vt.* defend; justify.

be「ñgoniñ べんごにん (弁護人) *n.* defense lawyer; counsel.

be「ñgo」shi べんごし (弁護士) *n.* lawyer; attorney.

be「ñjo」 べんじょ (便所) *n.* toilet; lavatory. ★ Avoid in polite conversation. Use '*tearai*' (*literally* 'hand-washing place') or '*o-te-arai*' (*polite*) instead.
(⇨ kooshuu-beñjo; toire)

be「ñkai べんかい (弁解) *n.* excuse; explanation.
beñkai suru (〜する) *vt.* make excuses; explain.

be「ñkyoo べんきょう (勉強) *n.*
1 study:
beñkyooo o namakeru (勉強を怠ける) neglect one's *studies*.
2 experience; lesson:
Shippai ga ii beñkyoo ni natta. (失敗がいい勉強になった) I *learned* much from my failure.

(⇨ taikeñ)
beñkyoo (o) suru (〜(を)する) *vi.*, *vt.* **1** study; work.
2 make a discount; reduce the price. (⇨ makeru)

be「ñpi べんぴ (便秘) *n.* constipation.
beñpi suru (〜する) *vi.* be constipated.

be「ñri べんり (便利) *a.n.* (〜 na, ni) convenient; useful; handy.
(↔ fubeñ) (⇨ choohoo)

be「ñshoo べんしょう (弁償) *n.* compensation; indemnification.
beñshoo (o) suru (〜(を)する) *vt.* compensate; indemnify; pay.

be「ñto」o べんとう (弁当) *n.* packed [box] lunch; lunch box.

be「rabera べらべら *adv.* (〜 to) glibly:
himitsu o berabera (to) hanasu (秘密をべらべら(と)話す) *babble out* a secret. (⇨ perapera')

be「rañda ベランダ *n.* veranda; porch.

be「sso」o べっそう (別荘) *n.* country [summer] house; villa; cottage.

be「suto ベスト *n.* best:
besuto o tsukusu (ベストをつくす) do one's *best*.

be「terañ ベテラン *n.* expert; experienced person:
beterañ no kañgofu (ベテランの看護婦) an *experienced* nurse.

be「tsu¹ べつ (別) *n.* distinction; exception.
betsu to shite (〜として) except:
Ookisa wa betsu to shite, iro ga ki ni iranakatta. (大きさは別として、色が気に入らなかった) *Regardless of* the size, I didn't like the color.

be「tsu² べつ (別) *a.n.* (〜 na/no, ni) another; different.

-betsu べつ (別) *suf.* classified by...; according to...:
shokugyoo-betsu deñwachoo (職業別電話帳) a *classified* telephone directory.

be「tsubetsu べつべつ (別々) *a.n.*

(~ na/no, ni) different(ly); separate(ly); respective(ly): *Futari wa betsubetsu no michi o itta.* (二人は別々の道を行った) The two of them went their *respective* ways.

be｢tsujoo べつじょう(別状) *n.* (with a negative) something wrong; something unusual: *Kare wa atama ni kega o shita ga, inochi ni wa* betsujoo *wa nakatta.* (彼は頭にけがをしたが, 命には別状なかった) He got hurt on the head, but his life *was not in danger*.

be｢tsu ni べつに(別に) *adv.* (with a negative) particularly; in particular: *Ima no tokoro* betsu ni *suru koto wa arimaseñ.* (今のところ別にすること はありません) I have nothing *particular* to do at the moment.

-bi び(日) *suf.* day: *kineñ*-bi (記念日) a memorial *day*. (⇨ APP. 5)

bi｢deo ビデオ *n.* video (tape); videocassette recorder.

bi｢jiñ びじん(美人) *n.* good-looking [beautiful] woman; beauty.

bi｢jutsu びじゅつ(美術) *n.* art; fine arts.

bi｢jutsu｢kañ びじゅつかん(美術館) *n.* art museum.

-biki びき(匹) *suf.* counter for small animals, fish and insects. (⇨ APP. 4)

bi｢kku｢ri s･uru びっくりする *vi.* (sh･i-; sh･i-; sh･i-te □) be surprised; be astonished; be amazed. (⇨ odoroku)

bi｢kubiku s･uru びくびくする *vi.* (sh･i-; sh･i-; sh･i-te □) be timid [nervous; afraid]: *machigai o* bikubiku suru (間違いを びくびくする) *be afraid* of mistakes. (⇨ osoreru)

bi｢myoo びみょう(微妙) *a.n.* (~ na, ni) delicate; subtle; nice; fine: bimyoo *na moñdai* (微妙な問題) a *delicate* matter.

bi｢ñ[1] びん(瓶) *n.* bottle; jar.

bi｢ñ[2] びん(便) *n.* flight; service: *Sono* biñ *wa shoogo ni demasu.* (その便は正午に出ます) The *flight* leaves at noon.

bi｢ñboo びんぼう(貧乏) *n.* poverty; destitution.
　biñboo suru (~する) *vi.* be poor; be badly off.
　— *a.n.* (~ na, ni) poor; needy. (⇨ mazushii)

bi｢ñboonin びんぼうにん(貧乏人) *n.* poor person. (↔ kanemochi)

bi｢ni｢iru ビニール *n.* plastic; vinyl. (⇨ purasuchikku)

bi｢ñjoo びんじょう(便乗) *n.* free ride in a car.
　biñjoo suru (~する) *vi.* 1 get a lift.
　2 take advantage of: *Kare-ra wa uñchiñ no neage ni* biñjoo shite, *nedañ o ageta.* (彼らは 運賃の値上げに便乗して, 値段を上げた) They *took advantage of* the rise in transport costs to increase their prices.

bi｢ñkañ びんかん(敏感) *a.n.* (~ na, ni) sensitive; susceptible: *Wakamono wa ryuukoo ni* biñkañ *da.* (若者は流行に敏感だ) Young people are *very aware* of changes in fashion. (↔ doñkañ)

bi｢ñseñ びんせん(便箋) *n.* letter paper; letterhead; writing pad.

bi｢ñshoo びんしょう(敏捷) *a.n.* (~ na, ni) agile; nimble; quick; prompt: biñshoo *ni koodoo suru* (敏しょうに行動する) act *promptly*. (⇨ subayai)

bi｢ñwañ びんわん(敏腕) *n.* (great) ability: biñwañ *o furuu* (敏腕をふ るう) show one's *ability*.
　— *a.n.* (~ na) able; capable: biñwañ *na keeji* (敏腕な刑事) a *shrewd* detective.

bi｢ñzume びんづめ(瓶詰) *n.* bottling; bottled food [beverage]. (⇨ kañzume)

bi｢ribiri びりびり *adv.* (~ to) (the sound of trembling or ripping):

Kare wa sono tegami o biribiri (to) yabuita. (彼はその手紙をびりびり(と)やぶいた) He *tore* the letter into pieces.

bi⌐roodo ビロード *n.* velvet.

bi⌐ru ビル *n.* building. ★ Shortened form of '*birudiñgu*' (building).

bi⌐rudiñgu ビルディング *n.* building. ★ Refers mainly to western-style structures three stories and over.

bi⌐shobisho びしょびしょ *a.n.* (～ na/no, ni) wet through; soaked:
bishobisho ni naru (びしょびしょになる) *get wet to the skin*.

bi⌐shoo びしょう (微笑) *n.* smile.
bishoo suru (～する) *vi.* make a smile. (⇨ hohoemu)

bi⌐suke⌐tto ビスケット *n.* cracker; cookie.

bi⌐yoo びよう (美容) *n.* personal beauty; beauty culture:
Earobikusu wa biyoo ni yoi. (エアロビクスは美容によい) Aerobics is good for *keeping your figure*.

bi⌐yo⌐oiñ びよういん (美容院) *n.* beauty shop [salon].

bo⌐chi ぼち (墓地) *n.* graveyard; cemetery.

bo⌐iñ ぼいん (母音) *n.* vowel:
tañ[choo]-boiñ (短[長]母音) a short [long] *vowel*. (⇨ APP. 1)

bo⌐ke⌐-ru ぼける (惚ける) *vi.* (bo-ke-te Ⓥ) grow senile:
Kare mo dañdañ bokete kita. (彼もだんだんぼけてきた) He too *became* increasingly *affected by senility*.

bo⌐ki ぼき (簿記) *n.* bookkeeping:
boki o tsukeru (簿記をつける) keep *books*.

bo⌐kiñ ぼきん (募金) *n.* fund-raising; collection of contributions.
bokiñ suru (～する) *vi.* raise funds; collect money.

bo⌐koku ぼこく (母国) *n.* one's mother country; one's homeland. (⇨ kuni)

bo⌐kokugo ぼこくご (母国語) *n.* one's mother tongue.

bo⌐koo ぼこう (母校) *n.* one's alma mater.

bo⌐ku ぼく (僕) *n.* I. ★ 'boku no' = my, 'boku ni/o' = me. Plural forms are '*boku-tachi*' or '*boku-ra*' (*humble*). (⇨ kimi¹; kare; kanojo)

bo⌐kuchiku ぼくちく (牧畜) *n.* stock farming; cattle breeding.

bo⌐kujoo ぼくじょう (牧場) *n.* stock farm; pasture; ranch.

bo⌐kushi ぼくし (牧師) *n.* clergyman; minister. (⇨ shiñpu)

bo⌐ñ¹ ぼん (盆) *n.* tray; server. ★ Usually with '*o*-'.

bo⌐ñ² ぼん (盆) *n.* Bon Festival. ★ '*Boñ*' is a Buddhist observance celebrated on July 15 or August 15, depending on the district.

-boñ ぼん (本) *suf.* counter for long cylindrical objects. (⇨ APP. 4)

bo⌐ñchi ぼんち (盆地) *n.* basin; valley: *Koofu Boñchi* (甲府盆地) the Kofu *Basin*.

bo⌐ñ-o⌐dori ぼんおどり (盆踊り) *n.* Bon dances. (⇨ boñ²)

bo⌐ñya⌐ri ぼんやり *adv.* (～ to; ～ suru) 1 absent-mindedly; vacantly; carelessly:
Boñyari shite ite, oriru eki o machigaete shimatta. (ぼんやりしていて, 降りる駅を間違えてしまった) I *carelessly* went and got off at the wrong station. (⇨ boyaboya suru)
2 idly:
Boñyari (to) tatte inai de, tetsudai nasai. (ぼんやり(と)立っていないで, 手伝いなさい) Don't stand there *doing nothing*. Give me a hand.
3 (of memory, sight, etc.) vaguely; unclearly; obscurely:
Kare no koto wa boñyari (to) shika oboete imaseñ. (彼のことはぼんやり(と)しか覚えていません) I only *vaguely* remember him. (⇨ bakuzeñ)
4 drowsy:

Nebusoku de atama ga boñyari *(to) shite iru.* (寝不足で頭がぼんやり (と)している) I feel *drowsy* because of lack of sleep.

boˈo ぼう(棒) *n.* stick; pole; rod.

boˈochoo ぼうちょう(膨張) *n.* expansion; swelling.

  boochoo suru (～する) *vi.* expand; swell.

boˈodoo ぼうどう(暴動) *n.* riot: boodoo *o okosu* [*shizumeru*] (暴動を起こす[しずめる]) start [suppress] a *riot.*

boˈoee ぼうえい(防衛) *n.* defense.

  booee suru (～する) *vt.* defend. (⇨ mamoru)

boˈoeki ぼうえき(貿易) *n.* trade; commerce.

  ... to booeki (o) suru (...と～(を)する) *vi.* carry on trade.

boˈoeñkyoo ぼうえんきょう(望遠鏡) *n.* telescope.

boˈofuˈu ぼうふう(暴風) *n.* storm; windstorm.

boˈogai ぼうがい(妨害) *n.* disturbance; obstruction; interference.

  boogai suru (～する) *vt.* disturb; obstruct; interfere.

boˈogyo ぼうぎょ(防御) *n.* defense; safeguard. (↔ koogeki)

  boogyo suru (～する) *vt.* defend. (⇨ mamoru)

boˈoi ボーイ *n.* waiter; bellboy; porter.

boˈoka ぼうか(防火) *n.* fire prevention.

boˈokeñ ぼうけん(冒険) *n.* adventure; venture; risk.

  bookeñ (o) suru (～(を)する) *vi.* make a venture; run a risk.

boˈokoo ぼうこう(暴行) *n.* violence; assault; rape.

  bookoo suru (～する) *vt.* use violence; make an assault; rape.

boˈomee ぼうめい(亡命) *n.* defection; asylum.

  boomee suru (～する) *vi.* defect; take [seek] asylum.

boˈonasu ボーナス *n.* bonus.

  ★ Japanese 'permanent' workers

usually receive extra remuneration, called '*boonasu*' twice a year in June and December.

boˈoneˈñkai ぼうねんかい(忘年会) *n.* year-end party.

boˈorubako ボールばこ(ボール箱) *n.* cardboard box; carton.

boˈorugami ボールがみ(ボール紙) *n.* cardboard.

boˈoru-peñ ボールペン *n.* ballpoint pen.

boˈoryoku ぼうりょく(暴力) *n.* violence; force.

boˈoryokuˈdañ ぼうりょくだん(暴力団) *n.* gang; crime syndicate: booryokudañ-*in* (暴力団員) a *gang* member.

boˈosañ ぼうさん(坊さん) *n.* Buddhist priest; bonze.

boˈoshi[1] ぼうし(帽子) *n.* hat; cap.

boˈoshi[2] ぼうし(防止) *n.* prevention; check.

  booshi suru (～する) *vt.* prevent; check. (⇨ fusegu)

boˈosui ぼうすい(防水) *n.* waterproofing.

boˈoto ボート *n.* rowboat: booto *o kogu* (ボートをこぐ) row a *boat.*

boˈribori ぼりぼり *adv.* (～ to) (the sound of scratching, crunching, etc.): *ka ni sasareta tokoro o* boribori *(to) kaku* (蚊に刺された所をぼりぼり(と)かく) *scratch away* at the place a mosquito has bitten one.

boˈroboro[1] ぼろぼろ *a.n.* (～ na/ no, ni) (the state of being worn or torn): *Watashi no kutsu wa moo* boroboro *desu.* (私の靴はもうぼろぼろです) My shoes are completely *worn out.*

boˈroboro[2] ぼろぼろ *adv.* (～ to) (the state of grains, drops, etc., falling down): *Furui kabe ga* boroboro *(to) kuzure-ochita.* (古い壁がぼろぼろ(と)くずれ落ちた) The old wall *fell down.*

boˈshuu ぼしゅう(募集) *n.* re-

cruitment; collection.
boshuu suru (～する) *vt.* recruit; collect.

bo˥sshuu ぼっしゅう (没収) *n.* confiscation; forfeit.
bosshuu suru (～する) *vt.* confiscate; impound. (⇨ **toriageru**)

bo˥tañ[1] ボタン *n.* button; push button.

bo˥tañ[2] ぼたん (牡丹) *n.* tree peony; *Paeonia suffruticosa.*

bo˥tchañ ぼっちゃん (坊ちゃん) *n.*
1 (*polite*) your son. (↔ **o-joosañ**)
2 (*derog.*) naive person:
Kare wa sekeñ shirazu no botchañ da. (彼は世間知らずの坊ちゃんだ) He is an *unsophisticated fellow* who knows nothing of the world.

bo˥ttoo ぼっとう (没頭) *n.* absorption; devotion.
bottoo suru (～する) *vi.* be absorbed; be devoted.

bo˥ya ぼや *n.* small fire.

bo˥yaboya s·uru ぼやぼやする *vi.* (sh·i-; sh·i-; sh·i-te □) be careless; be absent-minded:
Boyaboya shite iru to kuruma ni hikaremasu yo. (ぼやぼやしていると車にひかれますよ) If *you are not on your toes*, you will be hit by a car. (⇨ **boñyari**)

bu[1] ぶ (分) *n.* advantage.
bu ga aru (～がある) have an advantage.

bu[2] ぶ (分) *n.* (a unit of rate) one percent: ★ One tenth of '*wari*.' *hachi bu no rishi* (8 分の利子) eight *percent* interest. (⇨ **wari**)
...bu-doori (...～どおり) ten percent: *Geñkoo wa hachi-bu-doori kañsee shimashita.* (原稿は八分どおり完成しました) I have finished eighty *percent* of the manuscript.

bu[3] ぶ (部) *n.* 1 department: *hañbai-bu* (販売部) the sales *department.*
2 club; society:
tenisu-bu (テニス部) a tennis *club* / *eñgeki-bu* (演劇部) a theatrical *society.*

-**bu** ぶ (部) *suf.* 1 part:
Kono shoosetsu wa sañ-bu kara naru. (この小説は 3 部からなる) This novel consists of three *parts.*
2 (of a book) copy. (⇨ **-satsu**)

bu˥a˥isoo ぶあいそう (無愛想) *a.n.* (～ na, ni) unsociable; blunt:
Ano mise no teñiñ wa buaisoo da. (あの店の店員は無愛想だ) The clerks at that shop are *not courteous.* (↔ **aiso**)

bu˥atsu·i ぶあつい (分厚い) *a.* (-ku) thick: *buatsui hoñ* (分厚い本) a *thick* book. (⇨ **atsui**[2])

bu˥buñ ぶぶん (部分) *n.* part; portion.

bu˥buñ-teki ぶぶんてき (部分的) *a.n.* (～ na, ni) partial; partly:
Kanojo no iu koto wa bubuñ-teki ni wa tadashii. (彼女の言うことは部分的には正しい) What she says is *partly* right.

bu˥choo ぶちょう (部長) *n.* manager; the head [chief] of a department.

bu˥doo ぶどう (葡萄) *n.* grape; grapevine.

bu˥do˥oshu ぶどうしゅ (葡萄酒) *n.* wine.

bu˥e˥ñryo ぶえんりょ (無遠慮) *a.n.* (～ na, ni) rude; impolite; forwardness. (↔ **eñryo**)

bu˥hiñ ぶひん (部品) *n.* parts:
jidoosha no buhiñ (自動車の部品) automobile *parts.*

bu˥ji ぶじ (無事) *n.* safety; peace.
— *a.n.* (～ na, ni) safe; peaceful; all right:
Sono ko wa buji ni kyuushutsu sareta. (その子は無事に救出された) The child was rescued *safely.* (⇨ **añzeñ**)

bu˥joku ぶじょく (侮辱) *n.* insult; contempt; affront.
bujoku suru (～する) *vt.* insult.

bu˥ka ぶか (部下) *n.* subordinate (at a workplace).

bu˥ka˥kkoo ぶかっこう (不格好) *a.n.* (～ na, ni) unshapely; awkward; clumsy:

bukakko *na booshi* (不格好な帽子)
an *unshapely* hat. (⇨ kakkoo')

bu˺ki ぶき (武器) *n.* arms; weapon; ordnance.

bu˺kimi ぶきみ (無気味) *a.n.*
(~ na, ni) weird; uncanny:
bukimi *na oto* (無気味な音) a *weird*
noise.

bu˺ki˺yoo ぶきよう (不器用) *n.*
clumsiness; awkwardness.
— *a.n.* 1 (~ na, ni) clumsy; un-
skilled; awkward:
Watashi wa totemo bukiyoo *da.*
(私はとても不器用だ) I'm *all thumbs.*
(↔ kiyoo)
2 unable to deal with a situation
with finesse:
Watashi wa doomo bukiyoo *de
oseji mo ienai.* (私はどうも不器用でお
世辞も言えない) I am a *poor hand* at
paying compliments.

bu˺kka ぶっか (物価) *n.* (commodity) prices. ★ Means general
prices of commodities. The price
of a specific article is '*nedañ.*'
(⇨ kakaku)

Bu˺kkyoo ぶっきょう (仏教) *n.*
Buddhism.

bu˺kubuku ぶくぶく *adv.* 1 (~
to, ni) (the state of being fat or
baggy):
Kare wa saikiñ bukubuku *(to [ni])
futotte kita.* (彼は最近ぶくぶく(と
[に])太ってきた) He is getting *fatter*
these days.
2 (~ to) (the state of bubbling):
Fune wa bukubuku *(to) shizuñde
shimatta.* (船はぶくぶく(と)沈んでしま
った) The ship sank, *leaving a
trail of bubbles.*

bu˺ñ[1] ぶん (文) *n.* sentence; composition.

bu˺ñ[2] ぶん (分) *n.* 1 share; part;
portion:
Kore wa kimi no buñ *da.* (これは君
の分だ) This is your *share.*
2 place; station:
jibuñ no buñ *o shiru* (自分の分を知
る) know one's *place.*
3 condition:

Kono buñ *nara, bañji umaku iku
daroo.* (この分なら、万事うまく行くだろ
う) Under the present *conditions*,
everything should go well.
(⇨ chooshi)

-buñ ぶん (分) *suf.* (the amount
or percentage contained in materials): *too-buñ* (糖分) the *amount
[percentage]* of sugar / *eñ-buñ* (塩
分) salt *content.*

bu˺nañ ぶなん (無難) *n.* safety;
security.
— *a.n.* (~ na, ni) safe; passable:
*Sono koto ni tsuite wa damatte
iru hoo ga* bunañ *da.* (そのことについ
てはだまっているほうが無難だ) Regard-
ing that matter, it would be *safer*
to keep silent.

bu˺ñbo ぶんぼ (分母) *n.* denominator. (⇨ buñsuu)

bu˺ñbo˺ogu ぶんぼうぐ (文房具) *n.*
stationery; writing materials.

bu˺ñboogu˺teñ ぶんぼうぐてん (文
房具店) *n.* stationer's; stationery
store.

bu˺ñbuñ ぶんぶん *adv.* (~ to)
(the buzzing noise made when
bees or flies are flying; the dron-
ing noise made by the rotation of
motors):
katana [boo] o buñbuñ *(to) furima-
wasu* (刀[棒]をぶんぶん(と)振り回す)
wave a sword [club] about
vigorously.

bu˺ñgaku ぶんがく (文学) *n.* literature.

bu˺ñga˺kusha ぶんがくしゃ (文学
者) *n.* literary man; man of letters; writer.

bu˺ñgo ぶんご (文語) *n.* written
[literary] language. (↔ koogo)

bu˺ñjoo-ju˺utaku ぶんじょうじゅう
たく (分譲住宅) *n.* condominium;
house in a development project.
(⇨ chiñtai-juutaku)

bu˺ñka[1] ぶんか (文化) *n.* culture:
buñka *no kooryuu* (文化の交流) *cultural* exchange.

bu˺ñka[2] ぶんか (文科) *n.* the department of liberal arts; the

humanities. (⇨ rika)

bu￢ŋkai ぶんかい（分解）*n.* resolution; taking to pieces.

buŋkai suru（～する）*vi., vt.* resolve; take to pieces.

bu￢ŋka¹jiŋ ぶんかじん（文化人）*n.* person following an academic or artistic career; cultured person.

Bu￢ŋka-ku¹ŋshoo ぶんかくんしょう（文化勲章）*n.* Order of Culture.

bu￢ŋka-teki ぶんかてき（文化的）*a.n.* (～ na, ni) cultural; civilized:
buŋka-teki *na* seekatsu *o* suru [*okuru*]（文化的な生活をする［送る］）lead a *civilized* life.

bu￢ŋka¹zai ぶんかさい（文化財）*n.* cultural property [assets]:
juuyoo-buŋkazai（重要文化財）an Important *Cultural Property*.

bu￢ŋkeŋ ぶんけん（文献）*n.* books or documents on a particular subject; literature.

bu￢ŋmee ぶんめい（文明）*n.* civilization.

bu￢ŋmyaku ぶんみゃく（文脈）*n.* context.

bu￢ŋpai ぶんぱい（分配）*n.* distribution; division.

buŋpai suru（～する）*vt.* distribute; divide. (⇨ yamawake)

bu￢ŋpoo ぶんぽう（文法）*n.* grammar.

bu￢ŋpu ぶんぷ（分布）*n.* distribution; spread.

buŋpu suru（～する）*vi.* be distributed; range.

bu¹ŋraku ぶんらく（文楽）*n.* traditional Japanese puppet theater.

bu￢ŋretsu ぶんれつ（分裂）*n.* split; division.

buŋretsu suru（～する）*vi.* split; divide. (⇨ wakareru¹)

bu￢ŋri ぶんり（分離）*n.* separation; disunion.

buŋri suru（～する）*vi., vt.* separate: gyuunyuu kara kuriimu o buŋri suru（牛乳からクリームを分離する）*separate* cream from milk.

bu￢ŋrui ぶんるい（分類）*n.* classification; grouping.

buŋrui suru（～する）*vt.* classify; group.

bu￢ŋryo¹o ぶんりょう（分量）*n.* quantity or amount that can be measured. (⇨ ryoo¹)

bu￢ŋsaŋ ぶんさん（分散）*n.* dispersion; decentralization.

buŋsaŋ suru（～する）*vi., vt.* disperse; decentralize. (↔ shuuchuu)

bu￢ŋseki ぶんせき（分析）*n.* analysis.

buŋseki suru（～する）*vt.* make an analysis; analyze.

bu¹ŋshi ぶんし（分子）*n.* **1** numerator. (⇨ buŋsuu)
2 molecule; element.

bu¹ŋsho ぶんしょ（文書）*n.* document; writing.

bu¹ŋshoo ぶんしょう（文章）*n.* sentences; writing.

bu¹ŋsu¹u ぶんすう（分数）*n.* fraction. ★ The numerator is called '*buŋshi*'（分子）, and the denominator '*buŋbo*'（分母）. Y/X is read as '*X buŋ no Y*.'

bu￢ŋtai ぶんたい（文体）*n.* style of writing.

bu￢ŋtaŋ ぶんたん（分担）*n.* partial charge; allotment; share.

buŋtaŋ suru（～する）*vt.* share. (⇨ wakeru)

bu￢ŋtsuu ぶんつう（文通）*n.* correspondence.

buŋtsuu suru（～する）*vi.* correspond with; exchange letters. (⇨ tegami)

bu￢ŋya ぶんや（分野）*n.* field; sphere; branch:
Kare wa kono buŋya de yuumee desu.（彼はこの分野で有名です）He is famous in this *field*.

bu¹rabura ぶらぶら *adv.* (～ to; ～ suru) **1** (the state of legs or arms hanging loosely, or of a pendulum swinging):
burabura yureru（ぶらぶら揺れる）sway *back and forth*.
2 (the state of moving aimlessly about):

Kooen o bura-bura *sanpo shita.*(公園をぶらぶら散歩した) I went out for a *stroll* around the park.
3 (the state of idling about): *Sotsugyoo shite kara, ano hito wa mainichi* burabura *shite iru.*(卒業してから、あの人は毎日ぶらぶらしている) Since he graduated from school, he has been *lazing about* every day.

bu⌐ranko ぶらんこ *n.* swing.

bu⌐rasagar·u ぶらさがる(ぶら下がる) *vi.* (-sagar·i·; -sagar·a·; -sagat-te Ⓒ) hang:
tetsuboo ni burasagaru (鉄棒にぶら下がる) *hang* from a horizontal bar. (⇨ burasageru)

bu⌐rasage·ru ぶらさげる(ぶら下げる) *vt.* (-sage-te Ⓥ) hang:
kata kata baggu o burasageru (肩からバッグをぶら下げる) *sling* a bag on one's shoulder. (⇨ burasagaru)

bu⌐rashi ブラシ *n.* brush. (⇨ fude; hake)

bu⌐ree ぶれい(無礼) *n.* impolite behavior; rudeness: buree o hataraku(無礼をはたらく) *be rude.*
— *a.n.* (~ na) rude; impolite. (⇨ shitsuree)

-buri ぶり(振り) *suf.* **1** [with a noun or the continuative base of a verb] manner; way:
hanashi-buri (話しぶり) someone's *way* of talking.
2 after: ★ Used after words denoting duration and indicates that something occurred again after the interval of time stated. Gonen-buri *ni furusato e kaetta.*(五年ぶりにふるさとへ帰った) I went back to my hometown *for the first time in five years.*
(⇨ hisashiburi)

-bu⌐r·u ぶる *suf.* (vi.) (-bur·i·; -bur·a·; -but-te Ⓒ) pose as...; behave like...: ★ Used to form a verb from a noun, adjective, or adjectival noun. It conveys a derogatory meaning.
1 [after a noun] *Kare wa geeju*-tsuka-butte iru.(彼は芸術家ぶっている) He *poses as* an artist.
2 [after the stem of an adjective] era-buru (偉ぶる) *act* big.
3 [after an adjectival noun] *joo*-hin-buru (上品ぶる) *put on* airs; *pretend* to be refined.

bu⌐ruburu ぶるぶる *adv.* (~ to) (the state of the body or limbs shaking or quivering from cold, fear, etc.):
Watashi wa osoroshikute, buruburu (to) *furueta.*(私は恐ろしくて、ぶるぶる(と)震えた) I *trembled* with fear.

bu⌐sa¬hoo ぶさほう(無作法) *n.* bad manners; breach of etiquette.
— *a.n.* (~ na, ni) ill-mannered; impolite. (⇨ shitsuree)

bu⌐shi ぶし(武士) *n.* warrior; samurai. ★ A man of arms in the service of a feudal lord in Japan.

bu⌐sho¬o ぶしょう(不精・無精) *n.* laziness; indolence:
bushoo-*mono* (不精者) a *lazy* fellow / bushoo-hige (不精ひげ) a *stubbly beard.*
— *a.n.* (~ na, ni) lazy; indolent.
bushoo suru (~する) *vi.* be lazy; be remiss.

bu⌐shu ぶしゅ(部首) *n.* the radical of a Chinese character.
★ Used as a classificatory element in *kanji.* (⇨ hen³; tsukuri)

-bu⌐soku ぶそく(不足) *suf.* insufficient; short; lacking:
suimin-busoku(睡眠不足) *insufficient* sleep / *undoo*-busoku(運動不足) *lack* of exercise. (⇨ fusoku)

bu⌐soo ぶそう(武装) *n.* armaments; military equipment.
busoo suru (~する) *vi.* take up arms. (↔ hibusoo)

bu⌐sshi ぶっし(物資) *n.* goods; necessities; supplies:
kyuuen-busshi (救援物資) relief *supplies.*

bu⌐sshiki ぶっしき(仏式) *n.* Buddhist rites. (⇨ shinshiki)

bu⌐sshitsu ぶっしつ (物質) *n.*
matter; substance.

bu⌐sshitsu-teki ぶっしつてき (物
質的) *a.n.* (~ na, ni) material;
physical:
*Kanojo wa busshitsu-teki ni megu-
marete iru.* (彼女は物質的に恵まれて
いる) She *is well off*.

bu⌐sso⌐o ぶっそう (物騒) *n.* lack
of safety; danger.
— *a.n.* (~ na, ni) unsafe; dangerous. (⇨ kiken)

bu⌐ta ぶた (豚) *n.* pig; hog.

bu⌐tai ぶたい (舞台) *n.* 1 stage:
butai ni tatsu (舞台に立つ) appear
on the *stage*.
2 setting; scene.
butai-ura (~裏) backstage;
behind the scenes.

bu⌐taniku ぶたにく (豚肉) *n.* pork.

bu⌐too ぶとう (舞踏) *n.* (*formal*)
dance: *butoo-kai* (舞踏会) a *ball*.
(⇨ odori)

-butsu ぶつ (物) *suf.* thing;
object; matter:
iñsatsu-butsu (印刷物) printed
matter / *yuubiñ-butsu* (郵便物)
mail.

bu⌐tsubutsu¹ ぶつぶつ *adv.*
1 (the state of many small swell-
ings appearing):
kao ni nikibi ga butsubutsu dekiru
(顔ににきびがぶつぶつできる) have one's
face come out in *pimples*.
2 (the state of talking to oneself
in a low voice or mumbling complaints to someone):
*Kare wa ki ni iranai to sugu butsu-
butsu iu.* (彼は気に入らないとすぐぶつぶ
つ言う) When there is something
he doesn't like, he soon *grumbles*.
(⇨ fuhee)

bu⌐tsubutsu² ぶつぶつ *n.* rash;
pimple.

bu⌐tsudañ ぶつだん (仏壇) *n.* Buddhist altar for enshrining the
spirits of a family.

bu⌐tsukar·u ぶつかる *vt.* (-kar·i-;
-kar·a-; -kat-te Ⓒ) 1 bump into;
crash against; collide:

Kuruma ga kabe ni butsukatta.
(車が壁にぶつかった) A car *crashed
into* the wall. (⇨ butsukeru)
2 encounter; run into; meet
(difficulties, hardship, a problem,
etc.).
3 wrangle; have a run-in with:
*shigoto no koto de jooshi to butsu-
karu* (仕事のことで上司とぶつかる)
have a disagreement with one's
boss about the job. (⇨ shoototsu)

bu⌐tsuke·ru ぶつける *vt.* (-ke-te
Ⅴ) 1 bump; knock:
kuruma o deñchuu ni butsukeru
(車を電柱にぶつける) *drive* one's car
into a utility pole. (⇨ ataru; butsukaru)
2 throw:
*Neko ni ishi o butsukete wa ike-
maseñ.* (猫に石をぶつけてはいけません)
Don't *throw* stones at the cat.
3 give vent to:
fumañ o hito ni butsukeru (不満を
人にぶつける) *give vent* to one's discontent on somebody.

bu⌐tsuri ぶつり (物理) *n.* physics.
★ Shortened form of '*butsuri-
gaku*.'

bu⌐tsuri⌐gaku ぶつりがく (物理学)
n. physics.

bu⌐ttai ぶったい (物体) *n.* object;
thing; substance.

bu⌐yo⌐ojiñ ぶようじん (不用心) *a.n.*
(~ na, ni) unsafe; insecure; careless. (↔ yoojiñ)

byo⌐o¹ びょう (秒) *n.* second:
*Kono tokee wa go-byoo okurete
iru.* (この時計は5秒遅れている) This
watch is five *seconds* slow.
(⇨ fuñ¹; byooshiñ)

byo⌐o² びょう (鋲) *n.* tack; thumbtack; drawing pin. (⇨ gabyoo)

-byoo びょう (病) *suf.* disease:
shiñzoo-byoo (心臓病) heart
disease.

byo⌐obu びょうぶ (屏風) *n.* folding screen.

byo⌐odoo びょうどう (平等) *n.*
equality; impartiality.

— *a.n.* (~ na, ni) equal; impartial; even. (⇨ taitoo)

byoⁱoiñ びょういん (病院) *n.* hospital. (⇨ nyuuiñ; taiiñ)

byoⁱoki びょうき (病気) *n.* illness; sickness; disease:
byooki *ni naru* (病気になる) become *ill* / *Kare wa* byooki *da.* (彼は病気だ) He is *ill.* (⇨ hatsubyoo)

byoⁱoniñ びょうにん (病人) *n.* patient; sick person.

byoⁱosha びょうしゃ (描写) *n.* description; portrait.

byoosha suru (~する) *vt.* describe; portray.

byoⁱoshi びょうし (病死) *n.* death from a disease.

byooshi suru (~する) *vi.* die from an illness.

byoⁱoshiñ びょうしん (秒針) *n.* (of a clock) second hand. (⇨ byoo¹; fuñshiñ)

byoⁱoshitsu びょうしつ (病室) *n.* sickroom; ward.

byoⁱotoo びょうとう (病棟) *n.* ward (in a hospital).

C

cha ちゃ (茶) *n.* **1** tea; green tea. ★ When referring to the beverage, it is usually called 'o-cha.' **2** tea plant. **3** brown. (⇨ chairo)

chaⁱiro ちゃいろ (茶色) *n.* brown.

chaⁱkkaⁱri ちゃっかり *adv.* (~ to; ~ suru) shrewdly; smartly; cleverly:
Ano ko wa chakkari shite iru. (あの子はちゃっかりしている) That boy *is shrewd.*

-chaku¹ ちゃく (着) *suf.* (after a numeral) the order of arrival; place:
Marasoñ de it-chaku *ni natta.* (マラソンで1着になった) I came in *first* in the marathon. (⇨ -i¹)

-chaku² ちゃく (着) *suf.* [after a place name] arrival:
*gogo 2 ji Narita-*chaku *no biñ* (午後2時成田着の便) the plane *arriving* at Narita at two P.M.

-chaku³ ちゃく (着) *suf.* counter for dresses, suits, etc.

chaⁱkuchaku ちゃくちゃく (着々) *adv.* (~ to) steadily; according to plan; step by step:
Kooji wa chakuchaku *to susuñde imasu.* (工事は着々と進んでいます) The construction work is proceeding *according to plan.*

chaⁱkujitsu ちゃくじつ (着実) *a.n.* (~ na, ni) steady; sound; solid:
Keekaku wa chakujitsu *ni susuñde imasu.* (計画は着実に進んでいます) The plan is making *steady* progress.

chaⁱkuriku ちゃくりく (着陸) *n.* landing.
chakuriku suru (~する) *vi.* make a landing; land. (↔ ririku)

chaⁱkuseki ちゃくせき (着席) *n.* taking a seat; sitting.
chakuseki suru (~する) *vi.* sit down; have a seat.

chaⁱkushoku ちゃくしょく (着色) *n.* coloration; coloring.
chakushoku suru (~する) *vt.* color; paint.

chaⁱkushu ちゃくしゅ (着手) *n.* start; commencement.
chakushu suru (~する) *vi.* start; begin; set about. (⇨ hajimeru)

chaⁱkusoo ちゃくそう (着想) *n.* idea; conception.

-chañ ちゃん *suf.* **1** (used after a given name to address children affectionately): ★ The first name is often shortened. *Sachiko* >*Sat-*chañ, *Hiroshi* >*Hiro-*chañ. **2** (used after a kinship word by a small child):
o-nee-chañ (おねえちゃん) one's

older sister / o-jii-chañ (おじいちゃん) one's *grandfather*.

cha-「no-ma ちゃのま (茶の間) *n.* living [sitting] room. (⇨ ima²)

cha-「no-yu ちゃのゆ (茶の湯) *n.* tea ceremony. (⇨ sadoo)

cha「ñsu チャンス *n.* good chance; opportunity. ★ Used only with reference to a favorable occasion.

cha「nto ちゃんと *adv.* (~ suru) (of an action) properly done; without fail; exactly: *Kaze ga hairanai yoo ni doa o chañto shime nasai.* (風が入らないようにドアをちゃんと閉めなさい) Please shut the door *properly* to keep the wind out. (⇨ kichiñto)

cha「wañ ちゃわん (茶碗) *n.* teacup; rice bowl. (⇨ yunomi)

chi¹ ち (血) *n.* **1** blood: *chi o tomeru* (血を止める) stop the *bleeding*.
2 family relation: *Kare-ra wa chi no tsunagari ga aru.* (彼らは血のつながりがある) They are related by *blood*.

chi¹² ち (地) *n.* the earth; the ground; district.

chi「chi¹ ちち (父) *n.* **1** father. (↔ haha) (⇨ chichi-oya; o-too-sañ)
2 originator: *Kare wa Nihoñ no kiñdai-kagaku no chichi desu.* (彼は日本の近代科学の父です) He is the *father* of modern science in Japan.

chi「chi¹² ちち (乳) *n.* **1** milk: *akañboo ni chichi o nomaseru* (赤ん坊に乳を飲ませる) *breast-feed* a baby.
2 (mother's) breast.

chi「chi-oya ちちおや (父親) *n.* male parent; father. (↔ haha-oya) (⇨ chichi¹)

chi「e ちえ (知恵) *n.* wisdom; sense; brains.
chie o shiboru (~をしぼる) think hard: *Watashi-tachi wa miñna de chie o shibotta.* (私たちはみんなで知恵をしぼった) We all *racked our*

brains. (⇨ atama)

chi「gai ちがい (違い) *n.* difference; distinction; disparity. (⇨ sa¹)

-chigai ちがい (違い) *suf.* **1** mis-; error; mistake: ★ Attached to a noun or the continuative base of a verb.
kañ-chigai (勘違い) a *mistaken* idea / *kiki*-chigai (聞き違い) a *mis-* hearing. (⇨ hitochigai)
2 (with a numeral) difference: ★ Often the difference in age between siblings.
*Watashi to ani wa mittsu-*chigai *desu.* (私と兄は三つ違いです) My brother is three years *older* than me.

chi「gaina「i ちがいない (違いない) must; be certain; be sure: ★ Polite equivalent is '*chigai arimaseñ.*'
Kare ga itte iru koto wa hoñtoo ni chigainai. (彼が言っていることは本当に違いない) What he says *must be* true. (⇨ tashika)

chi「ga·u ちがう (違う) *vi.* (chigai-; chigaw·a-; chigat-te C)
1 be different; differ: *Kuni ni yotte kotoba ya shuukañ ga chigaimasu.* (国によって言葉や習慣が違います) Language and customs *differ* from country to country. (⇨ sooi¹)
2 wrong; incorrect: *Kotae ga chigatte iru.* (答えが違っている) The answer to the question *is wrong*.

chi「gi「r·u¹ ちぎる (千切る) *vt.* (chi-gir·i-; chigir·a-; chigit·te C)
tear off; tear to pieces: *Pañ o komakaku chigitte, tori ni yatta.* (パンを細かくちぎって、鳥にやった) I *broke* the bread *into pieces* and gave it to the birds.

chi「gi「r·u² ちぎる (契る) *vt.* (chi-gir·i-; chigir·a-; chigit·te C)
1 pledge; vow; promise: *Futari wa ee-eñ no ai o chigitta.* (二人は永遠の愛を契った) The two

pledged their eternal love.
2 share a bed.

chi「heeseñ ちへいせん (地平線) *n.*
horizon. ★ The line where the
sky and the land seem to meet.
(⇨ suiheeseñ)

chi「ho」o ちほう (地方) *n.* **1** district; region; area: ★ Refers to a
particular region of a country.
Kañtoo-chihoo (関東地方) the
Kanto *district*. (⇨ chiiki)
2 the country; the provinces.
(⇨ inaka)

chi「i ちい (地位) *n.* position; status; standing.

chi「iki ちいき (地域) *n.* area;
region; zone: ★ 'Chiiki' implies
a more limited area than 'chihoo.'
*Hiroi chiiki ni watatte sakumotsu
ga higai o uketa.* (広い地域にわたって
作物が被害を受けた) The crops
were badly damaged over a large
area. (⇨ chiku; chitai)

chi「isa」・i ちいさい (小さい) *a.* (-ku)
1 small; little:
chiisai kuruma (小さい車) a *small*
car. (↔ ookii)
2 trivial; petty:
*Chiisai koto ni kuyokuyo suru no
wa yame nasai.* (小さいことにくよくよ
するのはやめなさい) Don't worry
about *trivial* matters. (↔ ookii)
(⇨ komakai)

chi「isa-na ちいさな (小さな) *attrib.*
small; little; trivial:
*Kare wa chiisa-na moñdai ni wa
kodawaranai.* (彼は小さな問題にはこ
だわらない) He does not care about
trivial matters. (↔ ooki-na)
(⇨ chiisai)

chi「ji ちじ (知事) *n.* (prefectural)
governor:
keñ[fu]-chiji (県[府]知事) the *governor* of a prefecture.

chi「jimar・u ちぢまる (縮まる) *vi.*
(-mar・i-; -mar・a-; -mat・te C)
get shorter or smaller:
*Koñdo no taikai de kiroku ga ni-
byoo chijimatta.* (今度の大会で記録
が２秒縮まった) In this meet, two

seconds *were clipped off* the record. (⇨ chijimeru)

chi「jime・ru ちぢめる (縮める) *vt.*
(-me-te V) shorten; reduce:
sukaato no take o chijimeru (スカー
トの丈を縮める) *shorten* the length
of a skirt. (⇨ chijimaru)

chi「jim・u ちぢむ (縮む) *vi.* (chijim-
m・i-; chijim・a-; chijiñ-de C)
shrink; contract:
*Kono shatsu wa aratte mo chiji-
manai.* (このシャツは洗っても縮まない)
This shirt *doesn't shrink* in the
wash. (⇨ chijimeru)

chi「jiñ ちじん (知人) *n.* acquaintance; friend.

chi「jire-ru ちぢれる (縮れる) *vi.*
(chijire-te V) (of hair) wave;
curl; frizz.

chi「joo ちじょう (地上) *n.* the
ground; the land surface:
chijoo juuni-kai no biru (地上 12
階のビル) a building with twelve
stories above *the ground*.
(↔ chika)

chi「ka」 ちか (地下) *n.* underground:
Chuushajoo wa chika ni arimasu.
(駐車場は地下にあります) The park-
ing space is down in the *base-
ment*. (↔ chijoo)

chi「ka」doo ちかどう (地下道) *n.*
underground passage.

chi「ka」goro ちかごろ (近頃) *adv.*
(～ no) lately; recently; nowa-
days:
*Chikagoro no wakai hito wa yoku
kaigai e iku.* (近ごろの若い人はよく海
外へ行く) *Today's* youngsters frequently go abroad. (⇨ kono-goro)

chi「ka」・i」 ちかい (近い) *a.* (-ku)
1 near; close:
Tookyoo-eki wa koko kara chikai.
(東京駅はここから近い) Tokyo Sta-
tion is *near* here. (↔ tooi)
2 almost; nearly:
Natsu mo owari ni chikai. (夏も終
わりに近い) Summer is *almost* over.

chi「kai² ちかい (誓い) *n.* oath;
vow; pledge:

chikai *o tateru* (誓いをたてる) swear an *oath*. (⇨ chikau)

chiˈkaˈku ちかく (近く) *n.* neighborhood:
Kono chikaku ni wa suupaa ga takusañ arimasu. (この近くにはスーパーがたくさんあります) There are a lot of supermarkets *around here.*
(↔ tooku) (⇨ chikai¹)
— *adv.* 1 almost; nearly:
★ Often with a numeral.
Kare wa moo ik-kagetsu chikaku yasuñde iru. (彼はもう1か月近く休んでいる) He has been absent *nearly* a month now.
2 (of time) soon; before long:
Ano futari wa chikaku kekkoñ suru soo desu. (あの二人は近く結婚するそうです) I hear that those two are going to get married *soon.*

chiˈkaˈmichi ちかみち (近道) *n.* shortcut; the shortest way.
(↔ toomawari)

chiˈkaraˈ ちから (力) *n.* 1 power; ability:
Watashi no chikara de dekiru koto wa nañ de mo yarimasu. (私の力でできることは何でもやります) I will do everything in my *power.*
2 strength; force; might.
chikara-ippai (〜いっぱい) with all one's might.
chikara o ireru (〜を入れる) make efforts.

chiˈkarazuyoˈˈi ちからづよい (力強い) *a.* (-ku) powerful; strong; reassuring:
Kare kara chikarazuyoi hagemashi o uketa. (彼から力強い励ましを受けた) I received *reassuring* encouragement from him.

chiˈkatetsu ちかてつ (地下鉄) *n.* subway; underground railway.

chiˈkaˈˈu ちかう (誓う) *vt.* (chikai-; chikaw·a-; chikat-te C) swear; pledge; vow:
Shooniñ wa shiñjitsu o noberu to chikatta. (証人は真実を述べると誓った) The witness *swore* to tell the truth. (⇨ chikai²)

chiˈkayoˈˈr·u ちかよる (近寄る) *vi.* (-yor·i-; -yor·a-; -yot-te C) approach; get near:
Abunai tokoro ni wa chikayoranai hoo ga ii. (危ないところには近寄らないほうがいい) You'd better *keep away* from dangerous places.

chiˈkazukeˈˈl·ru ちかづける (近付ける) *vt.* (-zuke-te V) bring close; move nearer. (⇨ chikazuku)

chiˈkazuˈk·u ちかづく (近付く) *vi.* (-zuk·i-; -zuk·a-; -zu·i-te C) 1 approach; come [draw] near:
Taifuu ga Nihoñ ni chikazuite iru. (台風が日本に近づいている) A typhoon *is approaching* Japan.
2 become acquainted; approach:
Añna otoko ni wa chikazukanai hoo ga ii. (あんな男には近づかないほうがいい) You had better *keep away from* such a fellow. (⇨ chikazukeru)

chiˈkee ちけい (地形) *n.* the lay of the land; geographical features.

chiˈkoku ちこく (遅刻) *n.* late coming; being late.
chikoku suru (〜する) *vi.* be [come] late. (⇨ okureru)

chiˈku ちく (地区) *n.* district; zone; area: ★ Refers to a section or an area with some distinctive feature.
Kare wa kono chiku no daihyoo desu. (彼はこの地区の代表です) He is the representative of this *district.* (⇨ chiiki)

chiˈkuˈbi ちくび (乳首) *n.* nipple; teat.

chiˈkuseki ちくせき (蓄積) *n.* accumulation.
chikuseki suru (〜する) *vt.* accumulate; store up: *tomi o chikuseki suru* (富を蓄積する) *accumulate* a fortune.

chiˈkyuu ちきゅう (地球) *n.* the earth; the globe.

chiˈmamire ちまみれ (血塗れ) *n.* being bloody:
chimamire no taoru (血まみれのタオル) a *bloodstained* towel.

chi⌐mee ちめい（地名）*n*. place-name.

chi⌐me⌐eshoo ちめいしょう（致命傷）*n*. fatal wound [injury]; deathblow.

-chiñ ちん（賃）*suf*. pay; fare; rate; charge:
deñsha-chiñ（電車賃）a train *fare* / kari-chiñ（借り賃）a *rent*; *hire*.
((⇨ -ryoo; -dai²))

chi⌐ñbotsu ちんぼつ（沈没）*n*. sinking (of a ship).
chiñbotsu suru（～する）*vi*. sink; go down. ((⇨ shizumu))

chi⌐ñchiñ ちんちん *adv*. (the sound of whistling):
Yakañ ga chiñchiñ *natte iru.*（やかんがちんちんなっている）The kettle is *singing*.

chi⌐ñgiñ ちんぎん（賃金）*n*. wages; pay. ((⇨ gekkyuu; kyuuryoo))

chi⌐ñmoku ちんもく（沈黙）*n*. silence; reticence.
chiñmoku suru（～する）*vi*. hold one's tongue; be silent. ((⇨ damaru))

chi⌐noo ちのう（知能）*n*. intelligence; mental ability:
chinoo-*shisuu*（知能指数）an *intelligence* quotient. ((⇨ chisee))

chi⌐ñretsu ちんれつ（陳列）*n*. exhibition; display.
chiñretsu suru（～する）*vt*. exhibit; display.

chi⌐ñtai-ju⌐utaku ちんたいじゅうたく（賃貸住宅）*n*. rental house [apartment]. ((⇨ buñjoo-juutaku))

chi⌐rabar·u ちらばる（散らばる）*vi*. (-bar·i-; -bar·a-; -bat-te C̄) scatter; be strewn:
Akikañ ga hiroba ni takusañ chirabatte iru.（空き缶が広場にたくさん散らばっている）Many empty cans *are strewn* over the square. ((⇨ chiru))

chi⌐rachira ちらちら *adv*. (～ to; ～ suru) 1 (the state of something small and light falling slowly):
Yuki ga chirachira (to) *furi-haji-meta.*（雪がちらちら（と）降り始めた）

Snow has started to fall *lightly*.
2 (the state of small lights twinkling):
Terebi no gameñ ga chirachira *shite iru.*（テレビの画面がちらちらしている）There is a *flutter* on the TV screen.
3 (the state of seeing or hearing on and off):
Kare wa chirachira (to) *kochira o mita.*（彼はちらちら（と）こちらを見た）He kept *glancing* in my direction.

chi⌐rakar·u ちらかる（散らかる）*vi*. (-kar·i-; -kar·a-; -kat-te C̄) be scattered; be littered; be untidy:
Kare no heya wa chirakatte ita.（彼の部屋は散らかっていた）His room *was a mess*. ((⇨ chirakasu))

chi⌐rakas·u ちらかす（散らかす）*vt*. (-kash·i-; -kas·a-; -kash·i-te C̄) scatter; litter:
Gomi o chirakasanai de *kudasai.*（ごみを散らかさないでください）Don't litter, please. ((⇨ chirakaru))

chi⌐ras·u ちらす（散らす）*vt*. (chirash·i-; chiras·a-; chirash·i-te C̄) (*literary*) scatter:
Kaze ga niwa ichimeñ ni ko no ha o chirashita.（風が庭一面に木の葉を散らした）The wind *scattered* leaves all over the garden. ((⇨ chiru))

chi⌐ri¹ ちり（塵）*n*. dust; dirt. ((⇨ gomi; hokori²))

chi⌐ri² ちり（地理）*n*. geography; geography of a neighborhood.

chi⌐rigami ちりがみ（ちり紙）*n*. tissue; toilet paper (in separate sheets).

chi⌐rigami-ko⌐okañ ちりがみこうかん（ちり紙交換）*n*. an exchange of old newspapers and magazines for tissue or toilet rolls.

chi⌐r·u ちる（散る）*vi*. (chir·i-; chir·a-; chit-te C̄) 1 fall:
Ame de sakura no hana ga sukka-ri chitte shimatta.（雨で桜の花がすっかり散ってしまった）The cherry blossoms have all *fallen* in the rain. ((⇨ chirasu))

2 scatter; disperse:
Kooen ni kamikuzu ga chitte iru.
(公園に紙くずが散っている) *There is*
paper *all over* the park.
(⇨ chirasu)

chi⌐ryoo ちりょう(治療) *n.* medical treatment.
　chiryoo suru (～する) *vt.* treat; cure: *Watashi wa me o chiryoo shite moratta.* (私は眼を治療してもらった) I *had* my eyes *treated*.

chi⌐see ちせい(知性) *n.* intellect; intelligence. (⇨ chiteki)

chi⌐shiki ちしき(知識) *n.* knowledge; information; learning.

chi⌐sso ちっそ(窒素) *n.* nitrogen: *chisso-sankabutsu* (窒素酸化物) *nitrogen* oxide.

chi⌐ssoku ちっそく(窒息) *n.* suffocation; choking.
　chissoku suru (～する) *vi.* be suffocated; be choked.

chi⌐tai ちたい(地帯) *n.* zone; area; region; belt: *anzen-chitai* (安全地帯) a safety *zone*. (⇨ chiiki; chiku)

chi⌐teki ちてき(知的) *a.n.* (～ na, ni) intellectual; intelligent. (⇨ chisee; chinoo)

chi⌐tsu⌐jo ちつじょ(秩序) *n.* order; system: *shakai no chitsujo o tamotsu [midasu]* (社会の秩序を保つ[乱す]) maintain [disturb] social *order*.

chi⌐tto⌐-mo ちっとも *adv.* (with a negative) (not) a bit; (not) at all: *Kono bangumi wa chitto-mo omoshirokunai.* (この番組はちっともおもしろくない) This program is *not at all* interesting. (⇨ sukoshi mo)

chi⌐zu ちず(地図) *n.* map; atlas; chart.

-cho ちょ(著) *suf.* written by: *Kawabata Yasunari-cho "Yukiguni"* (川端康成著『雪国』) "*Snow Country*" *written by* Yasunari Kawabata.

cho⌐chiku ちょちく(貯蓄) *n.* savings.

chochiku suru (～する) *vi.* save up: *roogo ni sonaete chochiku suru* (老後に備えて貯蓄する) *save up* for one's old age. (⇨ chokin; yokin)

cho⌐kin ちょきん(貯金) *n.* savings; deposit.
　chokin suru (～する) *vi.*, *vt.* save; deposit: *Watashi wa maitsuki sanman-en chokin shite imasu.* (私は毎月3万円貯金しています) I *save* 30,000 yen every month. (⇨ yokin; chochiku)

cho⌐kkaku ちょっかく(直角) *n.* right angle.

cho⌐kkee ちょっけい(直径) *n.* diameter.

cho⌐kki チョッキ *n.* vest; waistcoat.

cho⌐kkoo ちょっこう(直行) *n.* going straight [direct].
　chokkoo suru (～する) *vi.* go straight [direct].

cho⌐kumen ちょくめん(直面) *n.* confrontation; facing.
　chokumen suru (～する) *vi.* be faced; be confronted. (⇨ butsukaru)

cho⌐kusen ちょくせん(直線) *n.* straight line. (↔ kyokusen)

cho⌐kusetsu ちょくせつ(直接) *adv.* (～ no) directly; immediately: *Kare to chokusetsu kooshoo shite mimasu.* (彼と直接交渉してみます) I will try to negotiate *directly* with him. (↔ kansetsu) (⇨ jika ni)

cho⌐kusetsu-teki ちょくせつてき(直接的) *a.n.* (～ na, ni) direct; immediate: (↔ kansetsu-teki) *chokusetsu-teki na genin* (直接的な原因) the *immediate* cause.

cho⌐o ちょう(腸) *n.* intestines; bowels.

cho⌐o ちょう(兆) *n.* one trillion (U.S.); one billion (Brit.). (⇨ APP. 3)

cho⌐o ちょう(蝶) *n.* butterfly.

cho⌐o ちょう(庁) *n.* agency; government office. (⇨ APP. 7)

cho⌐o- ちょう(超) *pref.* super-;
ultra-: choo-*tokkyuu* (超特急)
*super*express / choo-koosoobiru
(超高層ビル) a *skyscraper*.

-choo¹ ちょう(町) *suf.* town;
block; street. ★ An administrative division of a city or metropolitan area. (⇨ -machi; juusho)

-choo² ちょう(長) *suf.* head;
boss; chief; leader:
bu-choo (部長) the *head* of a division / *eki*-choo (駅長) a *stationmaster* / *iiñ*-choo (委員長) a *chairman*.

cho⌐obo ちょうぼ(帳簿) *n.* account book:
choobo o tsukeru [*shimeru*] (帳簿
をつける[締める]) keep [close] the
accounts. (⇨ choomeñ)

cho⌐ochi⌐ñ ちょうちん(提灯) *n.*
(paper) lantern.

cho⌐ocho(o) ちょうちょ(う)(蝶々)
n. = choo³.

cho⌐oda⌐i ちょうだい(頂戴) please;
please do [give] ...: ★ Used at
the end of a sentence and follows
a noun or the *te*-form of a verb.
Informal equivalent of '*kudasai*.'
Used mainly by children and
women, and by men to their
inferiors.
Kore o choodai. (これをちょうだい)
Please give this to me. / *Kono tegami o kare ni* watashite choodai.
(この手紙を彼に渡してちょうだい) *Please
hand over* this letter to him.

cho⌐odai s·uru ちょうだいする(頂
戴する) *vt.* (sh·i-; sh·i-; sh·i-te □)
1 (*humble*) receive; get:
Koko ni iñkañ o choodai shitai *no
desu ga.* (ここに印鑑をちょうだいしたい
のですが) May I *have* your seal
impression here?
2 (*humble*) eat; drink:
Moo juubuñ choodai shimashita.
(もう十分ちょうだいしました) I *have
had* enough, thank you. (⇨ itadaku)

cho⌐odo ちょうど(丁度) *adv.*
just; exactly:
Ima choodo *shichi-ji desu.* (今ちょ

うど 7 時です) It is *exactly* seven
o'clock.

cho⌐ofuku ちょうふく(重複) *n.*
overlap; duplication: repetition.
choofuku suru (〜する) *vi.* repeat; overlap.

cho⌐ohoo ちょうほう(重宝) *a.n.*
(〜 na) useful; handy; helpful.
(⇨ beñri)
choohoo suru (〜する) *vt.* find
something handy [useful].

cho⌐ohookee ちょうほうけい(長方
形) *n.* rectangle.

cho⌐oiñ ちょういん(調印) *n.* sign-
ing; signature.
... ni chooiñ suru (...に〜する) *vi.*
sign (a treaty, contract, etc.).
(⇨ saiñ)

cho⌐ojo ちょうじょ(長女) *n.* eldest
[oldest] daughter. (↔ choonañ)

cho⌐ojo⌐o ちょうじょう(頂上) *n.*
top; summit; peak.

cho⌐oka ちょうか(超過) *n.* excess;
surplus.
chooka suru (〜する) *vt.* exceed;
be more than. (⇨ koeru²)

cho⌐okañ¹ ちょうかん(朝刊) *n.*
morning paper; the morning edition of a paper. (↔ yuukañ²)
(⇨ shiñbuñ)

cho⌐okañ² ちょうかん(長官) *n.*
the director [head] of a (government) office.

cho⌐oki ちょうき(長期) *n.* a long
(period of) time. (↔ tañki¹)

cho⌐okoku ちょうこく(彫刻) *n.*
sculpture; carving.
chookoku suru (〜する) *vt.*
sculpt; carve.

cho⌐ome ちょうめ(丁目) *n.*
chome: ★ A section of a city,
larger than '*bañchi*.'
Giñza yoñ-choome (銀座 4 丁目)
Ginza 4-chome. (⇨ bañchi; juusho)

cho⌐ome⌐ñ ちょうめん(帳面) *n.*
notebook; account book:
choomeñ o tsukeru (帳面をつける)
keep an *account book*. (⇨ choobo;
nooto)

cho⌐omi⌐ryoo ちょうみりょう（調味料） *n.* seasoning; flavoring.

cho⌐onaⁿ ちょうなん（長男） *n.* eldest [oldest] son. (↔ choojo)

cho⌐ori⌐shi ちょうりし（調理師） *n.* qualified cook.

cho⌐osa ちょうさ（調査） *n.* investigation; survey; research.
  choosa suru (～する) *vt.* investigate; make a survey.

cho⌐osa⌐daⁿ ちょうさだん（調査団） *n.* survey group; investigating commission.

cho⌐osee ちょうせい（調整） *n.* adjustment; regulation.
  choosee suru (～する) *vt.* adjust; regulate.

cho⌐oseⁿ ちょうせん（挑戦） *n.* challenge; attempt.
  chooseⁿ suru (～する) *vi.* challenge; attempt; try. (⇨ idomu)

cho⌐osetsu ちょうせつ（調節） *n.* control; adjustment; regulation.
  choosetsu suru (～する) *vt.* control; adjust; regulate.

cho⌐oshi ちょうし（調子） *n.*
  1 condition:
  Kono kuruma wa chooshi *ga yoi.* （この車は調子が良い） This car is in good *condition.*
  2 way; manner:
  Sono chooshi *de yari nasai.* （その調子でやりなさい） Keep trying in that *way.*
  3 tune; tone:
  Kono gitaa wa chooshi *ga atte [hazurete] iru.* （このギターは調子が合って[はずれて]いる） This guitar is in [out of] *tune.*
  chooshi o awaseru (～を合わせる) adapt oneself; humor.

cho⌐osho ちょうしょ（長所） *n.* strong [good] point; merit; advantage. (↔ taⁿsho; ketteⁿ)

cho⌐oshoku ちょうしょく（朝食） *n.* breakfast. (⇨ asagohaⁿ; asameshi) (↔ baⁿgohaⁿ)

cho⌐oshuu ちょうしゅう（聴衆） *n.* audience; attendance.

cho⌐oteⁿ ちょうてん（頂点） *n.* peak; top; climax:
  chooteⁿ *ni tassuru* （頂点に達する） reach the *peak.*

cho⌐owa ちょうわ（調和） *n.* harmony.
  choowa suru (～する) *vi.* harmonize; match.

cho⌐sha ちょしゃ（著者） *n.* writer of a book; author.

cho⌐sho ちょしょ（著書） *n.* book written by the author; work.

cho⌐su⌐ichi ちょすいち（貯水池） *n.* reservoir.

cho⌐tto ちょっと *adv.* **1** (of degree, quality, quantity, etc.) just a little; slightly:
  Satoo o moo chotto *irete kudasai.* （砂糖をもうちょっと入れてください） Please add *a little more* sugar.
  2 (of time) just a minute; for a moment:
  Chotto o-machi kudasai. （ちょっとお待ちください） Please wait *a moment.*
  3 rather; pretty:
  Sore wa chotto *omoshiro-soo desu ne.* （それはちょっとおもしろそうですね） That sounds *rather* interesting.
  4 (with a negative) just; easily:
  Kare ni doko de atta ka chotto *omoidasenai.* （彼にどこで会ったかちょっと思い出せない） I *just* cannot remember where I met him.

cho⌐zoo ちょぞう（貯蔵） *n.* storage; preservation; stock.
  chozoo suru (～する) *vt.* store; preserve.

chu⌐u¹ ちゅう（中） *n.* middle; medium; average:
  Kare no seeseki wa chuu *no joo desu.* （彼の成績は中の上です） His school record is slightly above *average.*

chu⌐u² ちゅう（注） *n.* note; annotation:
  chuu *o tsukeru* （注をつける） *annotate.*

-chuu ちゅう（中） *suf.* **1** (used to express time) in; during; within; through; throughout:
  *Koⁿshuu-*chuu *ni reⁿraku itashimasu.* （今週中に連絡いたします） I

will get in touch with you *during* the week. (⇨ -juu')

2 (used to express a continuing state, condition or situation) under; in; during:
Sono dooro wa ima kooji-chuu desu.(その道路は今工事中です) The road is now *under* construction.

3 out of (the stated number):
Juuniñ-chuu hachi-niñ ga sono añ ni sañsee shita.(10人中8人がその案に賛成した) Eight *out of* ten were in favor of the proposal.

chu⌈uburu ちゅうぶる (中古) *n.* used [secondhand] article. (⇨ chuuko)

chu⌈ucho ちゅうちょ (躊躇) *n.* hesitation; indecision.
chuucho suru (～する) *vi.* hesitate; waver. (⇨ tamerau)

chu⌈udañ ちゅうだん (中断) *n.* discontinuance; interruption.
chuudañ suru (～する) *vi., vt.* stop; discontinue; interrupt.

chu⌈udoku ちゅうどく (中毒) *n.* poisoning:
shoku[gasu]-chuudoku(食[ガス]中毒) food [gas] *poisoning*.
chuudoku suru (～する) *vi.* be poisoned.

chu⌈uga⌉eri ちゅうがえり (宙返り) *n.* somersault; looping.

chu⌈uga⌉kkoo ちゅうがっこう (中学校) *n.* junior high school; lower secondary school. (⇨ gakkoo)

chu⌈ugaku ちゅうがく (中学) *n.* Shortened form of '*chuugakkoo*' (junior high school).

chu⌈uga⌉kusee ちゅうがくせい (中学生) *n.* junior high school pupil.

chu⌈ugata ちゅうがた (中型) *n.* medium size:
chuugata no kuruma(中型の車) a *medium-sized* car. (⇨ oogata; kogata)

chu⌈ugeñ ちゅうげん (中元) *n.* midyear gift. ★ Usually used with an honorific '*o-.*' In appreciation of special favors received, it is sent between July and August. (⇨ (o)seebo)

chu⌈ui ちゅうい (注意) *n.* **1** attention:
Dare mo kare no itta koto ni chuui *o harawanakatta.*(だれも彼の言ったことに注意を払わなかった) Nobody paid *attention* to what he said.

2 care; caution:
Kono shigoto wa tokubetsu no chuui *ga iru.*(この仕事は特別の注意がいる) This work needs special *care*.

3 warning:
Kanojo wa watashi no chuui *o mushi shita.*(彼女は私の注意を無視した) She disregarded my *warning*.
chuui suru (～する) *vi.* take care; caution; advise; warn: *Korobanai yoo ni chuui shi nasai.*(転ばないように注意しなさい) *Take care* that you don't fall.

chu⌈uibuka⌉i ちゅういぶかい (注意深い) *a.* (-ku) careful; cautious; watchful. (⇨ shiñchoo²; yoojiñbukai)

chu⌈ujitsu ちゅうじつ (忠実) *a.n.* (～ na, ni) **1** loyal; faithful:
Kare ni wa geñbuñ ni chuujitsu *na buka ga oozee iru.*(彼には忠実な部下がおおぜいいる) He has many *loyal* people working under him.

2 true to fact:
Kore wa geñbuñ ni chuujitsu *na yaku da.*(これは原文に忠実な訳だ) This is a translation *true* to the original.

chu⌈ujuñ ちゅうじゅん (中旬) *n.* the middle ten days of a month. (⇨ joojuñ; gejuñ)

chu⌈ukai ちゅうかい (仲介) *n.* intermediation; mediation:
ryoosha no chuukai o suru(両者の仲介をする) *mediate* between two parties.

chu⌈ukañ ちゅうかん (中間) *n.* interim; middle:
Eki wa sono futatsu no machi no chuukañ *ni dekimasu.*(駅はその二つの町の中間にできます) The train station will be built *in between* the

two towns.

chu⌐uka-ryo⌐ori ちゅうかりょうり (中華料理) *n.* Chinese dishes [food]; Chinese cooking [cuisine].

chu⌐uka-so⌐ba ちゅうかそば (中華そば) *n.* Chinese noodles. (⇨ raameñ)

chu⌐ukee ちゅうけい (中継) *n.* relay; hookup; transmission.
chuukee suru (～する) *vt.* relay.

chu⌐uko ちゅうこ (中古) *n.* used [secondhand] article:
chuuko-*sha* (中古車) a *secondhand* car. (⇨ chuuburu)

chu⌐ukoku ちゅうこく (忠告) *n.* advice; counsel
chuukoku suru (～する) *vt.* advise; counsel.

chu⌐uko⌐oneñ ちゅうこうねん (中高年) *n.* (people of) middle and advanced age; senior citizen. (⇨ chuuneñ)

chu⌐ukyuu ちゅうきゅう (中級) *n.* medium level. (⇨ shokyuu; jookyuu)

chu⌐umoku ちゅうもく (注目) *n.* attention; notice.
chuumoku suru (～する) *vi., vt.* pay attention; watch.

chu⌐umoñ ちゅうもん (注文) *n.*
1 order (of goods):
Chuumoñ *o sabaku no ni isogashii.* (注文をさばくのに忙しい) We are busy filling *orders.*
2 request; demand:
Soñna chuumoñ *ni wa oojirarenai.* (そんな注文には応じられない) I cannot comply with such a *demand.*
chuumoñ suru (～する) *vt.* give an order; order.

chu⌐uneñ ちゅうねん (中年) *n.* middle age:
chuuneñ *no fuufu* (中年の夫婦) a *middle-aged* couple.

chu⌐uo⌐o ちゅうおう (中央) *n.* center; middle. (⇨ mañnaka)

chu⌐uritsu ちゅうりつ (中立) *n.* neutrality:
chuuritsu *o mamoru* (中立を守る) observe *neutrality.*

chu⌐uryuu ちゅうりゅう (中流) *n.*
1 middle class:
chuuryuu *no katee* (中流の家庭) a *middle-class* family. (⇨ jooryuu; kasoo)
2 the middle of a river.

chu⌐usai ちゅうさい (仲裁) *n.* arbitration; mediation.
chuusai (o) suru (～(を)する) *vt.* arbitrate; mediate.

chu⌐usee ちゅうせい (中世) *n.* the Middle Ages; medieval times.
★ The Japanese Middle Ages comprise the Kamakura period (12th century) to the Azuchi-Momoyama period (late 16th–early 17th centuries). (⇨ APP. 9)

chu⌐useñ ちゅうせん (抽選) *n.* drawing; lot: chuuseñ *de kimeru* (抽選で決める) decide by *lot.*

chu⌐usha¹ ちゅうしゃ (駐車) *n.* parking:
Koko wa chuusha-*kiñshi desu.* (ここは駐車禁止です) *Parking* is prohibited here.
chuusha suru (～する) *vi.* park. (⇨ chuushajoo)

chu⌐usha² ちゅうしゃ (注射) *n.* injection; shot.
chuusha suru (～する) *vt.* inject.

chu⌐ushajoo ちゅうしゃじょう (駐車場) *n.* parking lot; car park. (⇨ chuusha¹)

chu⌐ushi ちゅうし (中止) *n.* stoppage; discontinuance; suspension.
chuushi suru (～する) *vt.* stop; call off; discontinue; suspend.

chu⌐ushiñ ちゅうしん (中心) *n.*
1 center:
Sono biru wa shi no chuushiñ *ni aru.* (そのビルは市の中心にある) That building is in the *center* of the city.
2 focus; core:
Kuruma no yushutsu ga wadai no chuushiñ *datta.* (車の輸出が話題の中心だった) Car exports were the *focus* of our discussions.

chu⌐ushoku ちゅうしょく (昼食) *n.*

(*formal*) lunch. 《⇨ hirumeshi; hirugohañ》

chu⌐ushoo ちゅうしょう（中傷）*n.* slander.

　chuushoo suru (～する) *vt.* slander; speak ill of.

chu⌐ushoo-ki˥gyoo ちゅうしょうきぎょう（中小企業）*n.* small and medium-sized enterprises.

chu⌐ushoo-teki ちゅうしょうてき（抽象的）*a.n.* (～ na, ni) abstract: chuushoo-teki *na giroñ* (抽象的な議論) *abstract* discussion. 《↔ gutai-teki》

chu⌐utai ちゅうたい（中退）*n.* leaving school in mid-course.

　chuutai suru (～する) *vi.* drop out; quit (school, university, etc.). 《⇨ taigaku》

chu⌐uto ちゅうと（中途）*n.* middle; the midway point: *Teñki ga warui no de* chuuto *de hikikaeshita.* (天気が悪いので中途で引き返した) We turned back *halfway* because the weather was bad. 《⇨ tochuu》

D

da だ *copula.* (*informal*) ★ The corresponding formal equivalent in the written language is '*de aru*,' and the polite colloquial equivalent is '*desu*.' 《⇨ APP. 2》
1 be [am/is/are]. ★ Indicates that the subject equals the complement.
Kare wa haisha da. (彼は歯医者だ) He *is* a dentist.
2 be located in a certain place: *Boku no kuruma wa doko* da? (僕の車はどこだ) Where *is* my car?
3 (indicates a situation or condition):
Kyoo wa ichi-nichi ame datta. (きょうは一日雨だった) It *rained* all day today.
4 (used as a verb substitute): *"Nomimono wa nani ni shimasu ka?" "Boku wa koohii* da." (「飲物は何にしますか」「僕はコーヒーだ」) "What would you like to drink?" "I'll *drink* coffee."

da⌐asu ダース *n.* dozen.

da⌐budabu だぶだぶ *a.n.* (～ na, ni) too large; baggy; loose.

da˥ ga だが *conj.* but; however: *Kare wa byooiñ e katsugi-komareta. Da ga osokatta.* (彼は病院へかつぎ込まれた. だが遅かった) He was carried into the hospital. *But* it was too late.

da⌐geki だげき（打撃）*n.* **1** hard hit; blow.
2 damage:
kañbatsu de hidoi dageki *o ukeru* (かんばつでひどい打撃を受ける) suffer serious *damage* because of the drought.
3 emotional disturbance; shock.
4 (of baseball) batting.

da˥i¹ だい（大）*n.* bigness; large size:
Dai *wa shoo o kaneru.* (*saying*) (大は小をかねる) '*Big*' always includes 'small.'

da˥i² だい（代）*n.* generation; time:
Sono mise wa kare no dai *ni sakaeta.* (その店は彼の代に栄えた) The shop flourished in his *time*.

da˥i³ だい（題）*n.* subject; theme.

da˥i-¹ だい（大）*pref.* **1** big; large: dai-*toshi* (大都市) a *large* city. 《↔ shoo-》
2 great: dai-*seekoo* (大成功) a *great* success.
3 serious; grave: dai-*moñdai* (大問題) a *serious* issue.

da˥i-² だい（第）*pref.* (indicates an ordinal number):
dai-niji *sekai-taiseñ* (第二次世界大戦) *the Second* World War.

-dai¹ だい (台) *suf*. **1** (counter for relatively large vehicles or machines):
Uchi ni wa terebi ga ni-dai *aru*. (うちにはテレビが 2 台ある) We have *two* TVs at home.
2 mark:
Kabuka ga niseñ-eñ-dai *ni tasshita*. (株価が 2,000 円台に達した) The price of the stock reached the 2,000-yen *mark*.
3 between...and...:
asa shichi-ji-dai *no deñsha* (朝 7 時台の電車) the trains *between seven and eight* in the morning.

-dai² だい (代) *suf*. fare; rate; charge:
takushii-dai (タクシー代) a taxi *fare* / *heya*-dai (部屋代) room *rent*. (⇨ -chiñ; -ryoo)

-dai³ だい (代) *suf*. age; period:
Kare wa mada sañjuu-dai *desu*. (彼はまだ 30 代です) He is still in his *thirties*.

da¹ibeñ だいべん (大便) *n*. feces; stool; excrement. (⇨ fuñ²; kuso)

da¹ibu だいぶ (大分) *adv*. considerably; quite; very:
Daibu *suzushiku natte kita*. (だいぶ涼しくなってきた) It has become *considerably* cool. (⇨ kanari)

da¹ibu¹buñ だいぶぶん (大部分) *n*. the greater part; most:
Daibuñ *no hito wa sono hooañ ni hañtai desu*. (大部分の人はその法案に反対です) *Most* of the people are against the bill.
— *adv*. mostly. (⇨ hotoñdo)

da¹ibutsu だいぶつ (大仏) *n*. huge statue of Buddha.

da¹ichoo だいちょう (大腸) *n*. the large intestine.

da¹idai だいだい (代々) *n*. from generation to generation; generation after generation.

da¹idoko(ro) だいどこ(ろ) (台所) *n*. kitchen. (⇨ katte¹)

da¹igaku だいがく (大学) *n*. university; college.

da¹igaku¹iñ だいがくいん (大学院) *n*. graduate school.

da¹iga¹kusee だいがくせい (大学生) *n*. university [college] student; undergraduate.

da¹igi¹shi だいぎし (代議士) *n*. Diet member. ★ Usually refers to a member of the House of Representatives (*Shuugiiñ*).

da¹ihyoo だいひょう (代表) *n*. representative; delegate.
daihyoo suru (〜する) *vt*. represent.

da¹ihyoo-teki だいひょうてき (代表的) *a.n*. (〜 na) typical; representative.

da¹i-ichi だいいち (第一) *n*. the first; the most important thing:
Keñkoo ga dai-ichi *da*. (健康が第一だ) Health is *everything*.
— *adv*. first; to begin with:
Dai-ichi *sore wa taka-sugimasu*. (第一それは高すぎます) *To begin with*, it is too expensive.

da¹iji¹ だいじ (大事) *a.n*. (〜 na, ni) important; valuable; precious. (⇨ o-daiji ni; juuyoo; taisetsu)

da¹iji² だいじ (大事) *n*. serious matter; crisis; emergency:
Kaji wa daiji *ni itaranakatta*. (火事は大事に至らなかった) The fire did not get *serious*. (⇨ ichidaiji)

da¹ijiñ だいじん (大臣) *n*. minister; secretary; cabinet member.

da¹ijo¹obu だいじょうぶ (大丈夫) *a.n*. (〜 na) all right; sure:
Watashi wa hitori de daijoobu *desu*. (私は一人でだいじょうぶです) I can *manage* it by myself.

da¹iki¹bo だいきぼ (大規模) *a.n*. (〜 na, ni) large-scale. (⇨ oogakari)

da¹ikiñ だいきん (代金) *n*. price; charge; bill. (⇨ ryookiñ)

da¹ikirai だいきらい (大嫌い) *a.n*. (〜 na) have a strong dislike; hate. (⇨ kirai) (↔ daisuki)

da¹ikoñ だいこん (大根) *n*. Japanese white radish. (⇨ hatsukadaikoñ)

da¹iku だいく (大工) *n*. carpenter.

((⇨ nichiyoo daiku))

-daime だいめ (代目) *suf.* the order of generations: go-daime no shachoo (5 代目の社長) the *fifth* president of the company.

da⌐imee だいめい (題名) *n.* title.

da⌐ime⌐eshi だいめいし (代名詞) *n.* pronoun; synonym; epithet.

da⌐imyo⌐o だいみょう (大名) *n.* daimyo. ★ Japanese feudal lord.

da⌐inashi だいなし (台無し) *a.n.* (~ ni) ruining; spoiling: Ame de ryokoo ga dainashi ni natta. (雨で旅行が台無しになった) Our trip *was spoiled* by the rain.

da⌐iri だいり (代理) *n.* representative; proxy: kachoo no dairi o tsutomeru (課長の代理を務める) *act* for the section chief.

da⌐ishoo だいしょう (大小) *n.* size; measure. ((⇨ ookisa))

da⌐isuki だいすき (大好き) *a.n.* (~ na) favorite: daisuki na tabemono (大好きな食べ物) one's *favorite* food. ((⇨ suki¹))

da⌐itai だいたい (大体) *n.* outline; summary; sketch.
— *adv.* about; almost; generally: Kare no toshi wa daitai watashi to onaji-gurai desu. (彼の年は大体私と同じくらいです) He is *almost* as old as I am.

da⌐ita⌐n だいたん (大胆) *a.n.* (~ na, ni) daring; bold; audacious.

da⌐ito⌐oryoo だいとうりょう (大統領) *n.* president (of a country).

da⌐iya¹ ダイヤ *n.* train [bus] schedule; timetable. ((⇨ jikokuhyoo))

da⌐iya² ダイヤ *n.* diamond.

da⌐iyaru ダイヤル *n.* dial. daiyaru suru (~する) *vi.* call on the phone; dial.

da⌐iyoo だいよう (代用) *n.* substitution. ((⇨ kawari))

da⌐izu だいず (大豆) *n.* soybean.

da⌐kara だから *conj.* so; therefore; because: Kinoo wa netsu ga atta. Da kara gakkoo o yasuñda. (きのうは熱があった。だから学校を休んだ) I had a temperature yesterday. *That's why* I took the day off from school.

da⌐ke だけ *p.* [follows a noun, the dictionary form and ta-form of a verb or adjective, an adjectival noun with 'na' or particles]
1 only; just; no more: ★ Used to indicate a limit.
Sore o shitte iru no wa watashi dake desu. (それを知っているのは私だけです) I am the *only* person who knows that.
2 as...as; enough to do: ★ Used for emphasis or to indicate a limit.
Doozo suki na dake meshiagatte kudasai. (どうぞ好きなだけ召し上がってください) Please go ahead and eat as much as you wish. ((⇨ nomi²; shika³))

da⌐kedo だけど *conj.* (*informal*) = da keredo (mo).

da⌐keredo (mo) だけれど(も) *conj.* but; however; yet: Ano hito wa uñdoo wa nañ de mo tokui desu. Da keredo (mo) oyogemaseñ. (あの人は運動は何でも得意です。だけれど(も)泳げません) He excels at all sorts of sports. *However*, he cannot swim.

da⌐ketsu だけつ (妥結) *n.* agreement; compromise settlement. daketsu suru (~する) *vi.* come to an agreement [a settlement].

da⌐kia⌐u だきあう (抱き合う) *vi.* (-a·i-; -a·wa-; -at-te Ⓒ) embrace [hug] each other.

da⌐kko だっこ *n.* carrying [holding] (a baby) in one's arms. dakko suru (~する) *vt.* carry [hold] (a baby) in one's arms. ((⇨ daku))

da⌐k·u だく (抱く) *vt.* (dak·i-; dak·a-; da·i-te Ⓒ) **1** hold (a thing; a person) in one's arms; hug; embrace. ((⇨ dakko))

2 (of a bird) sit on (an egg).

da｢kuoñ だくおん (濁音) *n.* syllables in Japanese that have a voiced consonant. ★ Indicated in writing with '゛' on the upper right-hand side of the *kana* letters. ガ (*ga*), ザ (*za*), ダ (*da*), バ (*ba*). (⇨ hañ-dakuoñ; seeoñ; APP. 1)

da｢kyoo だきょう (妥協) *n.* compromise; agreement.
dakyoo suru (～する) *vi.* compromise.

da｢ma｢r·u だまる (黙る) *vi.* (damar·i-; damar·a-; damat-te C) stop talking [crying]; keep silent.

da｢ma｢s·u だます (騙す) *vt.* (damash·i-; damas·a-; damash·i-te C) 1 cheat; trick; deceive.
2 coax (a child); use every trick to coax. (⇨ gomakasu; sagi¹)

da｢ma｢tte だまって (黙って) *adv.* without telling a person; without permission [notice]; without complaints.

da｢me¹ だめ (駄目) *a.n.* (～ na, ni)
1 no good; useless:
Kono kamisori wa zeñzeñ dame da. (このかみそりは全然だめだ) This razor is completely *useless.*
2 vain; of no use:
Doryoku shita ga dame datta. (努力したがだめだった) I made every effort, but *in vain.* (⇨ muda)
3 fail:
Shikeñ wa dame datta. (試験はだめだった) I *failed* in the examination.
4 cannot do; be poor at:
Ryoori wa dame na ñ desu. (料理はだめなんです) I am *not good* at cooking.
5 must not do; should not do:
O-sake o noñde wa dame desu. (お酒を飲んではだめです) You *shouldn't* drink. (⇨ ikemaseñ; ikenai)
dame ni naru (～になる) *vi.* be spoiled; be ruined; go bad.
dame ni suru (～にする) *vt.* spoil; ruin.

da｢ñ¹ だん (段) *n.* 1 step; stair; rung (of a ladder).

2 column:
*shiñbuñ no go-*dan *kookoku* (新聞の5段広告) a five-*column* newspaper advertisement.
3 (in judo, kendo, karate, go, shogi, etc.) a degree of proficiency. (⇨ kyuu²)
4 the holder of *dan.*

da｢ñ² だん (壇) *n.* platform; podium.

-dañ だん (団) *suf.* group; troupe; party: *ooeñ-*dañ (応援団) a *group* of cheerleaders.

da｢ñatsu だんあつ (弾圧) *n.* oppression; suppression; pressure.
dañatsu suru (～する) *vt.* oppress; suppress.

da｢ñboo だんぼう (暖房) *n.* heating of a room, building, etc.
dañboo suru (～する) *vt.* heat. (↔ reeboo)

da｢ñbo｢oru だんボール (段ボール) *n.* corrugated cardboard.

da｢ñchi だんち (団地) *n.* public apartment [housing] complex.

da｢ñdañ だんだん (段々) *adv.* (～ to, ni) gradually; little by little; one after another. (⇨ sukoshi-zutsu)

da｢ñjo だんじょ (男女) *n.* man and woman; both sexes.

da｢ñjo kyo｢ogaku だんじょきょうがく (男女共学) *n.* coeducation.
★ Sometimes abbreviated to '*kyoogaku.*'

da｢ñkai だんかい (段階) *n.* 1 step; stage; phase:
Ima no dañkai de wa happyoo dekimaseñ. (今の段階では発表できません) We cannot make an announcement at this *stage.*
2 grade; rank; level.

da｢ñketsu だんけつ (団結) *n.* union; solidarity.
dañketsu suru (～する) *vi.* unite; join together.

da｢no だの *p.* and; or; and the like; and so forth; and what not:
Watashi wa jisho dano sañkoosho dano o tsukatte shirabemashita.

(私は辞書だの参考書だのを使って調べました) I checked it using dictionaries, reference books *and so forth*. (⇨ ya¹; to ka)

da￢ñsee だんせい (男性) *n.* adult man; male. (↔ josee) (⇨ dañshi; otoko)

da￢ñsee-teki だんせいてき (男性的) *a.n.* (~ na, ni) (of men, women and things) manly; masculine; mannish. (⇨ josee-teki; otokorashii)

da￢ñshi だんし (男子) *n.* **1** boy. **2** man; male:
dañshi-*yoo toire* (男子用トイレ) the *men's* toilet. (↔ joshi') (⇨ dañsee)

da￢ñtai だんたい (団体) *n.* party; group; body.

da￢ñtee だんてい (断定) *n.* conclusion; decision.
dañtee suru (~する) *vt.* conclude; decide.

da￢ñtoo だんとう (暖冬) *n.* mild winter.

-dara だら *infl. end.* ⇨ -tara.

-da￢rake だらけ *suf. (n.)* [attached to a noun] be full of; be covered with: ★ Used in an unfavorable situation.
machigai-*darake* (間違いだらけ) *be full of* mistakes.

da￢rashina￢·i だらしない *a.* (-ku) **1** slovenly; sloppy; untidy. **2** weak-willed; spineless.

da￢re だれ (誰) *n.* who; whose; whom:
Kore wa dare *no kutsu desu ka?* (これはだれの靴ですか) *Whose* shoes are these? (⇨ donata)

da￢re-ka だれか (誰か) *n.* someone; anyone:
Dare-ka *kanojo no juusho o shirimaseñ ka?* (だれか彼女の住所を知りませんか) Doesn't *anyone* know her address? (⇨ donata-ka)

da￢re￢·ru だれる *vi.* (dare-te Ⓥ) become dull; become tedious; become listless.

-dari だり *infl. end.* ⇨ -tari.

da￢ro￢o だろう [follows a verb,

noun, adjectival noun, or adjective] (*polite*=deshoo) I think; I suppose; I wonder:
Ame wa furanai daroo. (雨は降らないだろう) I don't *think* it will rain. (⇨ da; deshoo)

da￢ru￢·i だるい *a.* (-ku) listless; feel languid [tired].

da￢sseñ だっせん (脱線) *n.* derailment; digression.
dasseñ suru (~する) *vi.* be derailed; digress.

da￢s·u だす (出す) *vt.* (dash·i-; das·a-; dash·i-te Ⓒ) **1** hold out; stick out:
mado kara kubi o dasu (窓から首を出す) *lean* out of the window.
2 take out:
kimerareta basho ni gomi o dasu (決められた場所にごみを出す) *take* the garbage *out* to the designated place.
3 issue; publish:
hoñ o dasu (本を出す) *publish* a book. (⇨ hakkoo; shuppañ')
4 give; hand in:
jihyoo o dasu (辞表を出す) *hand in* one's resignation.
5 send:
tegami o sokutatsu de dasu (手紙を速達で出す) *send* a letter by special delivery. (⇨ okuru')
6 serve (a dish); pay (expenses):
o-kyaku ni koohii o dasu (お客にコーヒーを出す) *serve* coffee to a visitor.
7 give out; break out:
Kaze o hiite, netsu o dashita. (かぜを引いて、熱を出した) I caught a cold and *ran* a fever.
8 show; display:
paatii ni kao o dasu (パーティーに顔を出す) *make an appearance* at a party.
9 put forth; stir (power, energy, etc.):
supiido o dasu (スピードを出す) *gather* speed / *Geñki o dashi nasai.* (元気を出しなさい) *Cheer up!*
10 start; result in; cause (a fire,

casualties, etc.):

Koñkai no jiko wa ooku no shi-shoosha o dashita. (今回の事故は多くの死傷者を出した) The accident *resulted in* many dead and injured.

11 draw; work out (a conclusion, an answer, etc.):
ketsuroñ o dasu (結論を出す) *draw* a conclusion.

12 open (a shop):
Amerika ni shiteñ o dasu (アメリカに支店を出す) *open* a branch office in America.

-da¹s·u だす (出す) (-dash·i·; -da-s·a·; -dash·i·te Ⓒ) ★ Occurs as the second element of compound verbs. Added to the continuative base of a verb.

1 [with a transitive verb] take out; put out; bring out:
mochi-dasu (持ち出す) carry *out* / *oi-dasu* (追い出す) drive *away*.

2 [with an intransitive verb] go out; come out:
nige-dasu (逃げ出す) run *away* / *nuke-dasu* (抜け出す) sneak *out*.

3 [with a transitive or intransitive verb] start; begin:
aruki-dasu (歩き出す) *start* walking / *furi-dasu* (降り出す) *begin* to rain [snow]. (⇨ **-hajimeru**)

da¹too だとう (妥当) *a.n.* (~ na) appropriate; proper; reasonable.

da¹ttai だったい (脱退) *n.* withdrawal; secession.
  dattai suru (~する) *vt.* withdraw; secede. (↔ **kanyuu**) (⇨ **nukeru (5)**)

da¹tte¹ だって *p.* [an informal variant of '*de mo*' and follows a noun] **1** even:
a (used to give an extreme example):
Koñna kañtañ na koto, kodomo datte shitte iru yo. (こんな簡単なこと, 子どもだって知っているよ) *Even* a child knows something as simple as this. (⇨ **de mo¹**)
b (with a number or quantity

expression, indicates an emphatic negative):
Ano hito ni wa ichi-eñ datte kashi-taku arimaseñ. (あの人には1円だって貸したくありません) I wouldn't lend him *even* one *single* yen.

2 always; everyone; everywhere: ★ Used with interrogatives such as '*itsu*,' '*dare*,' and '*doko*.'
Ano hito wa itsu datte hima-soo da. (あの人はいつだって暇そうだ) She *always* seems to have time on her hands. (⇨ **de mo¹**)

da¹tte² だって *conj.* (*informal*) because; but: ★ Used at the beginning of a sentence.
"Doo-shite okureta no?" "Datte basu ga okureta ñ da mono." (「どうして遅れたの」「だってバスが遅れたんだもの」) "Why are you late?" "Well, *because* the bus was late." (⇨ **de mo²**)

de¹ で *p.* [follows a noun]
1 (indicates the location of an action) at; in; on:
dooro de asobu (道路で遊ぶ) play *on* the street.

2 (indicates a means or method) by; with; in:
takushii de iku (タクシーで行く) go *by* taxi.

3 (indicates a substance or material) of; with:
Kono niñgyoo wa kami de dekite imasu. (この人形は紙でできています) This doll is made *of* paper.

4 (sets the limits of a time or space) in:
Nihoñ de ichi-bañ takai yama (日本で一番高い山) the highest mountain *in* Japan.

5 (indicates cause or reason) because of; by; owing to:
Byooki de kaisha o yasumima-shita. (病気で会社を休みました) I was absent from the company *due to* illness.

6 (delimits the time in which an action or event occurs) in:

Is-shuukañ de *sañ-satsu hoñ o yomimashita.* (一週間で 3 冊本を読みました) I read three books *in* a week.

7 (sets the limits of a price or quantity) for; by:

Riñgo wa sañ-ko de *hyaku-eñ desu.* (りんごは 3 個で 100 円です) Apples are 100 yen *for* three.

de[2] で *copula* [the *te*-form of '*da*'] be:

Chichi wa isha de, *ani wa kyooshi desu.* (父は医者で, 兄は教師です) My father *is* a doctor and my older brother is a teacher.

-de で *infl. end.* ⇨ -te.

de⌈a·u であう (出会う) *vi.* (dea·i-; deaw·a-; deat-te Ⓒ) **1** come across; run into; meet.

2 encounter (difficulties, hardship, etc.).

de⌈fure デフレ *n.* deflation. 《↔ iñfure》

de⌉guchi でぐち (出口) *n.* exit; way out. 《↔ iriguchi》

de⌈iri でいり (出入り) *n.* going in and out.

deiri suru (〜する) *vi.* go in and out; come and go.

de⌈iri⌉guchi でいりぐち (出入り口) *n.* entrance; doorway; gateway.

de⌈kake·ru でかける (出掛ける) *vi.* (dekake-te Ⓥ) go out; leave the house. 《⇨ gaishutsu》

de⌈ki でき (出来) *n.* **1** workmanship; craftsmanship; make.

2 crop; harvest.

3 result:

Shikeñ no deki *wa maamaa datta.* (試験の出来はまあまあだった) The *result* of the examination was not so bad.

de⌈kiagari できあがり (出来上がり) *n.* completion; workmanship. 《⇨ deki》

de⌈kiagar·u できあがる (出来上がる) *vi.* (-agar·i-; -agar·a-; -agat-te Ⓒ) be completed; be finished.

de⌈ki⌉goto できごと (出来事) *n.* occurrence; happening; event; accident.

de⌈kimo⌉no できもの (出来物) *n.* boil; tumor; eruption.

de⌈ki⌉·ru できる (出来る) *vi.* (deki-te Ⓥ) **1** be able to do; can do:

Watashi wa kuruma no uñteñ ga dekimasu. (私は車の運転ができます) I *can* drive a car.

2 be competent; be capable:

Kanojo wa suugaku ga dekiru. (彼女は数学ができる) She *is good* at mathematics.

3 be completed; be organized:

Sono biru wa ku-gatsu ni dekimasu. (そのビルは 9 月にできます) The building will *be completed* in September.

4 be ready:

Yuushoku no yooi ga dekimashita. (夕食の用意ができました) Dinner *is ready.*

5 be made:

Kono kutsu wa gañjoo ni dekite iru. (この靴はがんじょうにできている) These shoes *are made* strong.

6 form:

Kao ni nikibi ga dekita. (顔ににきびができた) Pimples have *come out* on my face.

7 grow; yield:

Kono chihoo de wa riñgo ga dekimasu. (この地方ではりんごができます) Apples *are grown* in this district.

de⌈kiru dake できるだけ (出来る丈) *adv.* as...as possible; to the best of one's ability:

Dekiru dake *hayaku kite kudasai.* (できるだけ早く来てください) Please come *as* early *as possible.*

de⌈koboko でこぼこ (凸凹) *a.n.* (〜 na, ni) uneven; rough.

de⌉ mo[1] でも *p.* [the *te*-form of '*da*' plus the particle '*mo*']

1 even:

a (used to give an extreme example):

Ame de mo *uñdookai wa okonaimasu.* (雨でも運動会は行います) *Even* if it rains, we will hold sports day. 《⇨ datte[1]》

b (used to emphasize the preceding noun):
Ichi-eṅ de mo yasuku kaitai mono desu. (1円でも安く買いたいものです) It is natural that we want to buy things *even* one yen more cheaply. (⇨ datte¹)
2 any: ★ Used with interrogatives such as '*itsu*,' '*dare*,' and '*doko*.'
Sono shina wa doko de mo te ni hairimasu. (その品はどこでも手に入ります) The goods are available *anywhere*. (⇨ datte¹)
3 or something:
Sono heṅ de koohii de mo ikaga desu ka? (その辺でコーヒーでもいかがですか) What about having a coffee *or something* over there?

de⌈mo² でも *conj.* (informal) but; and yet: ★ Used only at the beginning of a sentence.
De mo watashi wa haṅtai desu. (でも私は反対です) *But* I am against it. (⇨ datte²)

de⌈mukae でむかえ (出迎え) *n.* meeting; reception:
Eki made demukae ni kite kudasai. (駅まで出迎えに来てください) Please come to the station to *meet* me. (↔ miokuri) (⇨ demukaeru)

de⌈mukae-ru でむかえる (出迎える) *vt.* (-kae-te Ⓥ) meet; greet; receive:
kuukoo de kare o demukaeru (空港で彼を出迎える) *meet* him at the airport. (↔ miokuru) (⇨ demukae)

de⌈ṅatsu でんあつ (電圧) *n.* voltage.

de⌈ṅchi でんち (電池) *n.* battery; (electric) cell. (⇨ batterii)

de⌈ṅchuu でんちゅう (電柱) *n.* utility pole; electric light [telephone] pole.

de⌈ṅeṅ でんえん (田園) *n.* the country; rural districts.

de⌈ṅgeṅ でんげん (電源) *n.* power supply; switch; outlet:
deṅgeṅ o ireru [kiru] (電源を入れる*

[切る]) *turn the switch on [off].*

de⌈ṅki でんき (電気) *n.* **1** electricity:
deṅki-ryookiṅ (電気料金) *electric charges* / *deṅki-kigu* (電気器具) *electric appliances.*
2 electric light:
deṅki o tsukeru [kesu] (電気をつける [消す]) turn on [off] the *light.*

de⌈ṅki-go⌉tatsu でんきごたつ (電気炬燵) *n.* electric foot warmer. (⇨ kotatsu)

de⌈ṅki-sooji⌉ki でんきそうじき (電気掃除機) *n.* vacuum cleaner.

de⌈ṅki-suta⌉ṅdo でんきスタンド (電気スタンド) *n.* desk lamp; floor lamp.

de⌈ṅkyuu でんきゅう (電球) *n.* electric light bulb. (⇨ tama¹)

de⌈ṅpa でんぱ (電波) *n.* electric wave; radio wave.

de⌈ṅpoo でんぽう (電報) *n.* telegram; wire; telegraph.

de⌈ṅryoku でんりょく (電力) *n.* electric power; electricity.

de⌈ṅryuu でんりゅう (電流) *n.* electric current.

de⌈ṅseṅ¹ でんせん (電線) *n.* electric wire; telephone line.

de⌈ṅseṅ² でんせん (伝染) *n.* contagion; infection:
deṅseṅ-byoo (伝染病) an infectious *disease.*
deṅseṅ suru (～する) *vi.* be contagious; be infectious.

de⌈ṅsetsu でんせつ (伝説) *n.* legend; tradition.

de⌈ṅsha でんしゃ (電車) *n.* (electric) train; streetcar; tram (car). (⇨ ressha; kisha²)

de⌈ṅshi-re⌉ṅji でんしレンジ (電子レンジ) *n.* microwave oven.

de⌈ṅtaku でんたく (電卓) *n.* desk [pocket] calculator.

de⌈ṅtoo¹ でんとう (電灯) *n.* electric light.

de⌈ṅtoo² でんとう (伝統) *n.* tradition; heritage.

de⌈ṅtoo-teki でんとうてき (伝統的) *a.n.* (～ na, ni) traditional.

de˥ñwa でんわ（電話）*n.* telephone; (tele)phone call:
deñwa o kakeru [kiru]（電話をかける[切る]）*dial* [*hang up*].
　deñwa (o) suru（～を）する）*vt.* call up; telephone. （⇨ kooshuu-deñwa）

de˥ñwa-ba˥ñgoo でんわばんごう（電話番号）*n.* telephone number.

de˥ñwachoo でんわちょう（電話帳）*n.* telephone book [directory].

de˥pa˥ato デパート *n.* department store.

de˥·ru でる（出る）*vi.* (de-te Ⅴ)
1 go out; leave; depart:
Watashi wa maiasa hachi-ji ni ie o demasu.（私は毎朝 8 時に家を出ます）I *leave* the house at eight every morning. （⇨ shuppatsu）
2 go to; get to:
Kono michi o massugu ni iku to eki ni demasu.（この道をまっすぐに行くと駅に出ます）Go straight along this road, and you'll *get to* the station.
3 attend; take part in:
jugyoo [kaigi] ni deru（授業[会議]に出る）*attend* class [a meeting]. （⇨ shusseki）
4 appear; come out:
Nishi no sora ni tsuki ga deta.（西の空に月が出た）The moon *appeared* in the western sky.
5 graduate:
Daigaku o deta no wa go-neñ mae desu.（大学を出たのは 5 年前です）It is five years since I *graduated* from university. （⇨ sotsugyoo）
6 produce; yield:
Kono chihoo de wa oñseñ ga deru.（この地方では温泉が出る）There *are* hot springs in this area.
7 (of physiological phenomena) have:
Yoñjuu-do chikai netsu ga deta.（40度近い熱が出た）I *had* a fever of almost forty degrees.
8 (of liquid) run; flow; come out:
Kemuri ga shimite, namida ga deta.（煙がしみて、涙が出た）The smoke stung and made my eyes *water*.
9 (of emotions and spirits) show; raise:
Kore o nomeba geñki ga demasu.（これを飲めば元気が出ます）Drinking this will *raise* your spirits.
10 stick out:
Koñna tokoro ni kugi ga dete iru.（こんなところにくぎが出ている）There's a nail *sticking out* here.
11 be published; be printed:
Kono hoñ wa deta bakari desu.（この本は出たばかりです）This book *has* just *been published*. （⇨ shuppañ'）
12 be given:
Señsee kara shukudai ga deta.（先生から宿題が出た）Our teacher *gave* us homework.
13 be reached; come up with:
Yatto ketsuroñ ga deta.（やっと結論が出た）At last a conclusion *was reached*.
14 be found; turn up:
Ikura sagashite mo ano tegami ga dete konai.（いくら探してもあの手紙が出てこない）Although I've looked everywhere, the letter *has not been found*.
15 exceed; be over:
Kanojo wa sañjuu o sukoshi dete iru.（彼女は 30 を少し出ている）She *is* a little *over* thirty.
16 sell:
Kono hoñ wa saikiñ yoku demasu.（この本は最近良く出ます）This book *has been selling* very well recently. （⇨ ureru'）
17 take an attitude:
Aite ga doo deru ka ga moñdai desu.（相手がどう出るかが問題です）It is a question of what move the other party *makes*.

-de˥·ru でる（出る）(-de-te Ⅴ)
★ Occurs as the second element of compound verbs. Added to the continuative base of a verb.
1 [with an intransitive verb] appear; come out:

tsuki-deru (突き出る) stick *out* / *shimi*-deru (しみ出る) ooze *out.*

2 [with a transitive verb] apply; announce:
mooshi-deru (申し出る) *offer* / todo-ke-deru (届け出る) *report.*

deˈshi¹ でし (弟子) *n.* pupil; apprentice; disciple.

deshoo でしょう I suppose [wonder]: ★ Polite equivalent of '*daroo.*'
Chichi wa osoraku uchi ni iru deshoo. (父はおそらく家にいるでしょう) *I think* my father will probably be at home. (⇨ da; daroo)

desu です *copula.* (*polite*) (*informal*= da) **1** be [am/is/are]: ★ Indicates that the subject equals the complement.
"*Anata wa gakusee* desu *ka?*" "*Hai, soo* desu. [*Iie, soo* de wa arimaseñ.]" (「あなたは学生ですか」「はい、そうです[いいえ、そうではありません]」) "*Are* you a student?" "Yes, I *am.* [No, I *am not.*]" (⇨ APP. 2)

2 be located in a certain place:
Omocha-uriba wa sañ-gai desu. (おもちゃ売り場は3階です) The toy section *is* on the third floor. (⇨ aru²)

3 (indicates a situation or condition):
Kanojo wa byooki desu. (彼女は病気です) She *is* sick.

4 (used as a verb substitute):
"*Anata wa nani o chuumoñ shimashita ka?*" "*Watashi wa o-sushi* desu." (「あなたは何を注文しましたか」「私はおすしです」) "What did you order?" "I *ordered* sushi."

5 (after an adjective, makes the expression polite):
Kono riñgo wa totemo oishii desu. (このりんごはとてもおいしいです) This apple *is* very *delicious.*

deˈtarame でたらめ (出鱈目) *n.* nonsense; irresponsible remark; lie. (⇨ uso)
—— *a.n.* (~ na, ni) random; haphazard; irresponsible.

deˈ wa¹ では [used in conditional sentences] with: ★ The '*de wa*' clause indicates the condition and the second clause the natural or obvious result.
Kono chooshi de wa *kotoshi no keeki wa kitai dekimaseñ.* (この調子ではことしの景気は期待できません) *If* things are like this, we cannot expect good business this year.

deˈ wa² では *conj.* then; well; if so: ★ '*De wa*' becomes '*jaa*' in informal speech. (⇨ sore ja(a))
De wa *kore kara kaigi o hajimemasu.* (ではこれから会議を始めます) *Well then*, we will now start the meeting / De wa mata *ashita.* (ではまたあした) *So long*, see you again tomorrow.

-de wa では [*te*-form of '*da*' plus the paticle '*wa*'] ⇨ -te wa.

do ど (度) *n.* **1** (of myopia, glasses) degree:
do no tsuyoi [yowai] *megane* (度の強い[弱い]眼鏡) *strong* [*weak*] glasses.

2 extent; amount; limit.
do ga sugiru (~が過ぎる) carry things too far.

-do ど (度) *suf.* **1** (a unit of measure) degree: *sesshi nijuu-do* (摂氏20度) twenty *degrees* centigrade.

2 time: ichi-do (一度) *once* / ni-do (二度) *twice* / sañ-do (三度) three *times* (⇨ -kai¹)

doˈbuˈñ どぶん *adv.* (~ to) with a plop; with a splash: ★The sound of an object falling into water.
puuru e dobuñ *to tobikomu* (プールへどぶんと飛び込む) dive into a pool *with a splash.*

doˈchira どちら *n.* **1** where: ★ More polite than '*doko.*'
Deguchi wa dochira *desu ka?* (出口はどちらですか) *Where* is the exit?

2 which: ★ More polite than '*dotchi.*'
Koohii to koocha to dochira *ga suki desu ka?* (コーヒーと紅茶とどちら

が好きですか) *Which* do you like better, coffee or tea?
3 who:
Dochira-*sama deshoo ka?* (どちら様でしょうか) May I have your name? (*literally*, *Who* would you be?) 《⇨ achira; kochira; sochira》

do｢chira mo どちらも both; either:
Ryooshiñ wa dochira mo *señsee desu.*(両親はどちらも先生です) *Both* of my parents are teachers.

do｢ke･ru どける (退ける) *vt.* (doke-te Ⓥ) remove; take away. 《⇨ doku｣》

do｢kidoki どきどき *adv.* (~ to; ~ suru) (the state of one's heart beating faster):
Mune ga dokidoki *shita.* (胸がどきどきした) *There was a pounding* in my chest.

do｢ko どこ (何処) *n.* where; wherever:
Koobañ wa doko *desu ka?* (交番はどこですか) *Where* is the police box? / Doko *de mo suki na tokoro e iki nasai.*(どこでも好きな所へ行きなさい) You may go *wherever* you like. 《⇨ asoko; dochira; koko｣; soko｣》

do｢ko-ka どこか (何処か) somewhere; someplace:
Doko-ka *shizuka na tokoro e ryokoo shite mitai.*(どこか静かな所へ旅行してみたい) I want to take a trip to *someplace* quiet.
— *adv.* somewhat; something.

do｢ko made mo どこまでも (何処迄も) *adv.* to the last; endlessly:
Kare wa doko made mo *jibuñ no ikeñ o shuchoo shita.*(彼はどこまでも自分の意見を主張した) He *persistently* held to his opinion.

do｢ko mo どこも (何処も) *adv.* everywhere; (*neg.*) nowhere:
Natsu-yasumi ni naru to kaisui-yokujoo wa doko mo hito de ippai ni naru. (夏休みになると海水浴場はどこも人でいっぱいになる) With summer break starting, beaches every-

where become crowded.

do｢koro ka どころか *p.* [precedes a contradictory or qualifying statement]
1 far from; on the contrary:
Kare wa byooki dokoro ka, *totemo geñki desu.*(彼は病気どころか、とても元気です) *Far from* being ill, he is in excellent health.
2 not to mention; to say nothing of:
Uchi de wa jidoosha dokoro ka, *jiteñsha mo arimaseñ.*(うちでは自動車どころか、自転車もありません) We do not have a bicycle, *not to mention* a car.

do｢k･u¹ どく (退く) *vi.* (dok･i-; dok･a-; do･i-te Ⓒ) move; make room; step aside. 《⇨ dokeru》

do｢ku｣² どく (毒) *n.* poison; harm:
Tabako wa karada ni doku *da.*(たばこは体に毒だ) Smoking is *bad* for your health.

do｢kuji どくじ (独自) *a.n.* (~ na/no, ni) one's own; unique; original; personal.

do｢kuritsu どくりつ (独立) *n.* independence.
dokuritsu suru (~する) *vi.* become independent. 《⇨ hitoridachi》

do｢kusai どくさい (独裁) *n.* dictatorship; despotism.

do｢kuseñ どくせん (独占) *n.* monopoly; exclusive possession.
dokuseñ suru (~する) *vt.* monopolize.

do｢kusha どくしゃ (読者) *n.* subscriber; reader.

do｢kushiñ どくしん (独身) *n.* bachelorhood; spinsterhood.

do｢kusho どくしょ (読書) *n.* reading (a book).
dokusho (o) suru (~(を)する) *vi.* read (a book).

do｢kutoku どくとく (独特) *a.n.* (~ na/no, ni) characteristic; peculiar; unique. 《⇨ tokuyuu》

do｢kuyaku どくやく (毒薬) *n.* poison. (⇨ gekiyaku)

-do˦mo ども (共) *suf.* (used to form the plural of a noun).
1 (expresses humility): ★ Attached to a noun indicating the speaker. (⇨ -tachi)
Watashi-domo ni o-makase kudasai. (私どもにおまかせください) Please leave it to *us*.
2 (implies a contemptuous or belittling attitude): ★ Attached to a noun indicating others.
Wakamono-domo wa mattaku reegi o shiranai. (若者どもはまったく礼儀を知らない) *Young people* have no manners at all.

do˦na˦r·u どなる (怒鳴る) *vi.* (do-nár·i-; donar·a-; donat-te ⓒ) shout; cry; yell:
tasukete kure to donaru (助けてくれとどなる) *cry* for help. (⇨ sakebu)

do˦nata どなた (何方) *n.* (*polite*) = dare. who; whose; whom:
Kore wa donata no kasa desu ka? (これはどなたの傘ですか) *Whose* umbrella is this?

do˦nata-ka どなたか (何方か) *n.* (*polite*) =dare-ka. anyone:
Donata-ka tetsudatte kureru hito wa imaseñ ka? (どなたか手伝ってくれる人はいませんか) Isn't there *anyone* who can help me?

do˦ñbu˦ri どんぶり (丼) *n.* porcelain bowl; large rice bowl:
oyako-doñburi (親子どんぶり) a *bowl* of rice topped with chicken and eggs.

do˦ñdoñ¹ どんどん *adv.* (~ to) rapidly; steadily:
Yama-kaji ga doñdoñ (to) moe-hirogatta. (山火事がどんどん(と)燃え広がった) The forest fire spread *rapidly*.

do˦ñdoñ² どんどん *adv.* (~ to) (the sound made when knocking strongly on a door or beating a drum):
to o doñdoñ (to) tataku (戸をどんどん(と)たたく) *bang* at a door.

do˦ñkañ どんかん (鈍感) *a.n.*

(~ na, ni) insensible; insensitive; dull. (↔ biñkañ)

do˦ñkoo どんこう (鈍行) *n.* (*informal*) local [slow] train. (⇨ futsuu²)

do˦ñna どんな *attrib.* 1 what; what kind of:
Saikiñ doñna mono o yomimashita ka? (最近どんなものを読みましたか) *What* have you read recently?
2 however; no matter how:
Doñna chiisa-na koto de mo kiroku shite kudasai. (どんな小さなことでも記録してください) *However* minor it is, please make a record of it.
3 any; every:
Soñna koto wa doñna hito de mo shitte iru. (そんなことはどんな人でも知っている) *Everyone* is aware of such a thing. (⇨ añna; koñna; soñna)

do˦ñna ni どんなに *adv.* 1 how; how much; to what extent:
Sore ga doñna ni jyuuyoo ka wakatte imasu. (それがどんなに重要かわかっています) I know *how* important it is. (⇨ ika ni)
2 (with a negative) no matter how; whatever; however:
Doñna ni ooki-na jishiñ de mo kono biru wa taoremaseñ. (どんなに大きな地震でもこのビルは倒れません) *However* great the earthquake may be, this building will not collapse.
(⇨ añna ni; koñna ni; soñna ni)

do˦no どの *attrib.* 1 which; what; who:
Dono kisetsu ga ichibañ suki desu ka? (どの季節が一番好きですか) *Which* season do you like best?
2 any; every:
Koñshuu wa dono hi mo isogashii. (今週はどの日も忙しい) I am busy *every* day this week. (⇨ ano; kono; sono)

-do˦no どの (殿) *suf.* (one of the titles used after the addressee's name in a formal letter):
★ Used by public offices while '*-sama*' is used by private individuals.

Yamada Taroo-dono (山田太郎殿)
Mr. Taro Yamada.

do⌐no-kurai どのくらい（どの位）
adv. (~ no) how much [many;
long; far, etc.]. ★ Also '*dono-
gurai*.'
*Kono suutsukeesu no omosa wa
dono-kurai desu ka?* (このスーツケー
スの重さはどのくらいですか) *How much*
does this suitcase weigh?

do⌐o[1] どう *adv.* 1 how:
Kibuñ wa doo desu ka? (気分はどう
ですか) *How* are you feeling?
2 what:
*Moshi shippai shitara, doo shi-
masu ka?* (もし失敗したら、どうします
か) *What* if you should fail?
((⇨ aa[1]; koo; soo[1]))

do⌐o[2] どう（胴）*n.* the trunk of the
body. ★ The body not includ-
ing the head and limbs. ((⇨ dootai))

do⌐o[3] どう（銅）*n.* copper; bronze.

doo- どう（同）*pref.* 1 the same:
doo-sedai *no wakamono* (同世代の
若者) the youth of *one's generation*.
2 (used in documents, newspaper articles, etc. to avoid repetition of the same word):
*Higaisha wa chikaku no byooiñ ni
hakobare, doo-byooiñ de teate o
uketa.* (被害者は近くの病院に運ばれ、
同病院で手当を受けた) The injured
were taken to a nearby hospital
and treated in *that* hospital.

do⌐obutsu どうぶつ（動物）*n.*
1 animal. ★ Any living thing
that is not a plant.
2 any animal other than man:
doobutsu *o hogo [gyakutai] suru*
(動物を保護[虐待]する) protect [be
cruel to] *animals*.

do⌐obutsu[eñ どうぶつえん（動物
園）*n.* zoo. ((⇨ shokubutsueñ))

do⌐odoo どうどう（堂々）*adv.*
(~ to) 1 in a dignified manner;
magnificently.
2 (of competition, play, etc.)
fairly: doodoo to *tatakau* (堂々と

戦う) play *fair*.

do⌐ofuu どうふう（同封）*n.* enclos-
ing.
doofuu suru (~する) *vt.* enclose.

do⌐ogu[どうぐ（道具）*n.* tool;
utensil; instrument.

do⌐ohañ どうはん（同伴）*n.* company; accompanying.
doohañ suru (~する) *vt.* go with;
accompany; escort.

do⌐oi どうい（同意）*n.* agreement;
consent; assent.
... ni dooi suru (...に~する) *vt.*
agree with; consent to.

do⌐oigo どうご（同意語）*n.* synonym. ((↔ hañigo))

do⌐o i⌐tashima⌐shite どういたし
まして（どう致しまして）you're wel-
come; don't mention it; not at
all; it's my pleasure.

do⌐oitsu どういつ（同一）*a.n.*
(~ na/no, ni) identical; the
same. ((⇨ onaji))

do⌐o-iu どういう（どう言う）*attrib.*
how; why; what:
Sore wa doo-iu koto desu ka? (それ
はどういうことですか) *What* do you
mean by that? ((⇨ aa-iu; koo-iu;
soo-iu))

do⌐oji どうじ（同時）*n.* simulta-
neity; occurrence at the same
time. ((⇨ dooji ni))

do⌐oji ni どうじに（同時に）*adv.*
1 at the same time; simultaneously.
2 soon; immediately:
Yo ga akeru to dooji ni *ame ga
furi-dashita.* (夜が明けると同時に雨が
降りだした) *At* the break of day, it
started to rain.
3 as well as; while:
*Watashi-tachi wa kare-ra ni tabe-
ru mono to* dooji ni *kiru mono mo
ataeta.* (私たちは彼らに食べる物と同時
に着る物も与えた) We gave them
clothes *as well as* food.

do⌐oji-tsu⌐uyaku どうじつうやく
（同時通訳）*n.* simultaneous interpretation; simultaneous interpreter. ((⇨ tsuuyaku))

do⌐ojoo どうじょう（同情）*n*. sympathy; compassion.
... **ni doojoo suru**（...に～する）*vt*. sympathize.

do⌐o ka どうか *adv*. 1 please:
Doo ka *o-kane o kashite kudasai.*（どうかお金を貸してください）*Please* lend me some money.
2 if; whether:
Sore ga hoñtoo ka doo ka *shirimaseñ.*（それが本当かどうか知りません）I don't know *whether* that is true or not.
doo ka shite iru（～している）be strange; be wrong.

do⌐okañ どうかん（同感）*n*. agreement; feeling the same way.
... **ni dookañ suru**（...に～する）*vi*. agree; sympathize; feel the same way.

do⌐oki どうき（動機）*n*. motive; motivation; reason.

do⌐omee¹ どうめい（同盟）*n*. alliance; league; union.
... **to doomee suru**（...と～する）*vi*. make an alliance with; ally.

do⌐omee² どうめい（同名）*n*. the same name.

do⌐omo どうも *adv*. 1 very:
Doomo *arigatoo gozaimasu.*（どうもありがとうございます）Thank you *very* much. ★ '*Doomo*' is often used as an abbreviation of either '*doomo arigatoo*' or '*doomo sumimaseñ*' In that sense, '*doomo*' is more like 'thank you' or 'I'm sorry.' (⇨ señjitsu)
2 it seems...: ★ Used when making unfavorable judgments or predictions. In this usage '*yoo da*' or '*rashii*' often come at the end of the sentence.
Doomo *ano hanashi wa uso no yoo da.*（どうもあの話はうそのようだ）The story *seems* like a lie.
3 (with a negative) just cannot; there is no way:
Urusai oñgaku wa doomo *suki ni naremaseñ.*（うるさい音楽はどうも好きになれません）I *just don't seem* able

to enjoy loud music.
4 somehow:
Doomo *watashi-tachi wa itsu-mo keñka ni natte shimau.*（どうも私たちはいつもけんかになってしまう）*Somehow* we always end up arguing.

do⌐o ni ka どうにか *adv*.
= nañ to ka.

-do⌐ori どおり *suf*. = -toori.

do⌐oro どうろ（道路）*n*. road; way; street. (⇨ koosoku-dooro)

do⌐osa どうさ（動作）*n*. movement; manners; action.

do⌐ose どうせ *adv*. 1 after all:
★ Used when past experience suggests an unfavorable result.
Soñna hanashi wa doose *uso ni kimatte iru.*（そんな話はどうせうそに決まっている）*After all*, such a story must be a lie.
2 as a matter of course; anyhow: ★ Used when a certain limit is known and the speaker is pessimistic.
Doose *watashi no inochi wa nagaku nai no da.*（どうせ私の命は長くないのだ）*Anyhow*, I know that I cannot live long.

do⌐osee¹ どうせい（同性）*n*. 1 the same sex: doosee-*ai*（同性愛）*homosexual* love.
2 person of the same sex.

do⌐osee² どうせい（同姓）*n*. the same family name:
doosee doomee（同姓同名）*the same family* and given *names.*

do⌐osee³ どうせい（同棲）*n*. cohabitation; living together.
doosee suru（同せいする）cohabit; live together.

do⌐oshi どうし（動詞）*n*. verb. (⇨ APP. 2)

-do⌐oshi¹ どうし（同士）*suf*.
1 persons who belong to the same group or class:
*Kodomo-*dooshi *de keñka o hajimeta.*（子どもどうしでけんかを始めた）The children began to quarrel *among themselves.*
2 persons who stand in the same

relationship to each other:
Futari wa koibito-dooshi da. (二人
は恋人どうしだ) They *are lovers.*

-dooshi[2] どおし (通し) *suf.* keep
doing: ★ Added to the continuative base of a verb.
*Asa kara tachi-dooshi de tsuka-
reta.* (朝から立ち通しで疲れた) As I
have been standing since morning,
I am tired.

do͞o-shite どうして *adv.* 1 why:
Doo-shite *koñna koto ni natta no
ka, setsumee shite kudasai.* (どう
てこんなことになったのか、説明してくださ
い) Please explain *why* this happened.
2 how:
Kono moñdai wa doo-shite *toku ñ
desu ka?* (この問題はどうして解くんで
すか) *In what way* can we solve
this problem?
(⇨ aa-shite; koo-shite; soo-shite)

do͞o-shite mo どうしても *adv.*
1 by all means; at any cost.
2 (with a negative) just cannot:
Kare no iu koto wa doo-shite mo
shiñjirarenai. (彼の言うことはどうして
も信じられない) I *just cannot* believe
what he says.

do͞oso͞okai どうそうかい (同窓会)
n. alumni association [reunion].

do͞otai どうたい (胴体) *n.* trunk;
body; torso. (⇨ doo[2])

do͞otoku どうとく (道徳) *n.* mo-
rality; morals.

do͞otoku-teki どうとくてき (道徳
的) *a.n.* (~ na, ni) moral; mor-
ally.

do͞owa どうわ (童話) *n.* fairy
[nursery] tale; children's story.

do͞o-yara どうやら *adv.* 1 probably; apparently: ★ Usually
occurs with 'rashii,' 'yoo da,' etc.
Ashita wa doo-yara *ame no yoo
desu.* (あしたはどうやら雨のようです) It
certainly looks like rain tomorrow.
2 somehow:
Doo-yara *shujutsu wa seekoo
shita.* (どうやら手術が成功した) The

operation was *somehow* a success.

do͞oyoo[1] どうよう (同様) *a.n.*
(~ na, ni) the same; similar:
Dooyoo *na ikeñ wa hoka kara mo
deta.* (同様な意見はほかからも出た)
Similar opinions were given by
other people. (⇨ onaji)
— *adv.* in the same way; likewise.

do͞oyoo[2] どうよう (動揺) *n.* shaki-
ness; disturbance; agitation.
... ni dooyoo *suru vi.*
be shaken by; be disturbed by.

do͞oyoo[3] どうよう (童謡) *n.* children's song; nursery rhyme.

do͞ozo どうぞ (何卒) *adv.*
1 please:
Doozo *o-kake kudasai.* (どうぞお掛け
ください) *Please* have a seat.
2 certainly; sure; of course:
*"Deñwa o o-kari dekimasu ka?"
"Ee,* doozo.*" (「電話をお借りできます
か」「ええ、どうぞ」) "May I use your
telephone?" *"Certainly."*

do͞re[1] どれ (何れ) *n.* 1. which:
Dore *ga anata no nimotsu desu
ka?* (どれがあなたの荷物ですか) *Which*
one is your baggage?
2 whichever:
Dore *de mo ichibañ suki na mono
o tori nasai.* (どれでも一番好きなものを
とりなさい) Take *whichever* one
you like best.
3 all:
Karita hoñ wa dore *mo omoshiroku nakatta.* (借りた本はどれもおもしろ
くなかった) *All* the books I borrowed were boring.
(⇨ are[1]; kore; sore[1])

do͞re[2] どれ *int.* now; well; let me
see. (⇨ saa)

do͞ro どろ (泥) *n.* mud.

do͞roboo どろぼう (泥棒) *n.* thief;
robber; burglar.

do͞ru ドル (弗) *n.* dollar. (⇨ dorudaka; doruyasu)

do͞rubako ドルばこ (弗箱) *n.*
money-maker; gold mine.

do͞rudaka ドルだか (弗高) *n.*
strong dollar; appreciation of the

do゛**ruyasu** ドルやす (弗安) *n.* weak dollar; depreciation of the dollar. (↔ dorudaka)

do゛**ryoku** どりょく (努力) *n.* effort; endeavor.

doryoku suru (〜する) *vi.* make efforts; endeavor.

do゛**shi¹ñ** どしん *adv.* (〜 to) with a thud [thump]; plump:
Kuruma ga hee ni doshiñ to butsukatta. (車が塀にどしんとぶつかった) The car *thudded* into the wall.

do゛**soku** どそく (土足) *n.* with one's shoes on:
Kare wa dosoku no mama uchi ni agatta. (彼は土足のまま家にあがった) He entered the house *without removing his shoes.*

do゛**tchi** どっち *n.* (*colloq.*) = dochira. 1 which:
Waiñ wa aka to shiro, dotchi ni shimasu ka? (ワインは赤と白, どっちにしますか) *Which* will you have, red or white wine?
2 both; either:
Watashi-tachi wa dotchi mo sara-

riimañ desu. (私たちはどっちもサラリーマンです) We are *both* office workers. (⇒ atchi; kotchi; sotchi)

do゛**tchimichi** どっちみち *adv.* anyway; in either case; sooner or later.

do゛**te** どて (土手) *n.* bank; embankment.

do゛**tto** どっと *adv.* 1 (the state of giving a roar of laughter):
Kañkyaku wa dotto waratta. (観客はどっと笑った) The audience *burst* into laughter.
2 in a rush; all of a sudden:
Deñsha kara hito ga dotto orita. (電車から人がどっと降りた) People *rushed* off the train.

do゛**yadoya** どやどや *adv.* (〜 to) (the state of many people moving together in a crowd):
Siñbuñ-kisha ga kaijoo ni doya-doya (to) haitte kita. (新聞記者が会場にどやどや(と)入って来た) The reporters rushed *noisily* into the meeting room.

do゛**yo¹o(bi)** どよう(び) (土曜(日)) *n.* Saturday. (⇒ APP. 5)

E

e¹¹ え (絵) *n.* picture; drawing; painting. (⇒ egaku; kaiga)

e² え (柄) *n.* handle (of a tool, etc.).

e³ へ *p.* [follows a noun and indicates a direction or goal]
1 to; for:
Giñza e itte, eega o mimashoo. (銀座へ行って, 映画を見ましょう) Let's go *to* Ginza and see a film.
2 on; onto:
Kono hako o tana no ue e oite kudasai. (この箱を棚の上へ置いてください) Please put this box *on* the shelf.
3 in; into:
Shorui wa hikidashi e iremashita. (書類は引き出しへ入れました) I put the papers *in* the drawer.
★ In the above examples '*ni*' can

be used instead of '*e.*' (⇒ ni²)

e' えっ *int.* oh; hah; eh: ★ Used when one fails to hear what is said, or to indicate surprise.
E', nañ desu ka? (えっ, 何ですか) *What?* What did you say?

e゛**akoñ** エアコン *n.* air conditioner; air conditioning. (⇒ kuuraa)

e゛**bi** えび (海老) *n.* lobster; prawn; shrimp.

e゛**da** えだ (枝) *n.* branch; bough; twig; sprig.

e゛**e** ええ *int.* yes; no: ★ '*Ee*' literally means 'That's right' and is used to confirm a statement, whether affirmative or negative.
"Anata wa Nihoñjiñ desu ka?"

"*Ee, soo desu.*" (「あなたは日本人です
か」「ええ、そうです」) "Are you Japanese?" " *Yes*, I am." / "*Kore wa
anata no kasa de wa arimaseň
ne?*" "*Ee, chigaimasu.*" (「これはあな
たの傘ではありませんね」「ええ、違います」)
"Isn't this your umbrella?" "*No*,
it isn't." (⇨ hai¹; iie)

e⌐ebuň えいぶん (英文) *n*. En-
glish; English sentence.

e⌐ebu⌐ňgaku えいぶんがく (英文学)
n. English literature.

e⌐e-eň えいえん (永遠) *a.n*. (~ ni /
no) eternity; permanence.
(⇨ eekyuu)

e⌐ega えいが (映画) *n*. movie; the
movies; film.

e⌐ega⌐kaň えいがかん (映画館) *n*.
movie theater; cinema.

E⌐ego えいご (英語) *n*. English;
the English language.

e⌐egyoo えいぎょう (営業) *n*.
sales; business; trade:
Eegyoo-chuu. (*sign*) (営業中) *Open*
(for business).
　　eegyoo suru (~する) *vi*. do business.

E⌐ekoku えいこく (英国) *n*. Great
Britain; England; the United
Kingdom.

e⌐ekyoo えいきょう (影響) *n*. influence; effect; impact.
　　... ni eekyoo suru (...に~する) *vi*.
influence; affect.

e⌐ekyuu えいきゅう (永久) *a.n*. (~
ni / no) permanence; eternity:
eekyuu no heewa o negau (永久の
平和を願う) wish for *eternal* peace.
(⇨ ee-eň)

e⌐enichi-ji⌐teň えいにちじてん (英
日辞典) *n*. English-Japanese dictionary for English speaking people. (⇨ eewa-jiteň; nichiee-jiteň;
waee-jiteň)

e⌐esee¹ えいせい (衛生) *n*. hygiene; sanitation; health.

e⌐esee² えいせい (衛星) *n*. satellite: (⇨ jiňkoo-eesee)
eesee-*hoosoo* (衛星放送) *satellite*
broadcasting.

e⌐esee-teki えいせいてき (衛生的)
a.n. (~ na, ni) sanitary:
Shokudoo no eesee-teki *na kaňri
ga hitsuyoo desu.* (食堂の衛生的な
管理が必要です) Conditions in res-
taurants must be kept *sanitary*.

e⌐ewa-ji⌐teň えいわじてん (英和辞
典) *n*. English-Japanese dictionary for Japanese people. (⇨ ee-
nichi-jiteň; nichiee-jiteň; waee-
jiteň)

e⌐eyoo えいよう (栄養) *n*. nutrition; nourishment. (⇨ jiyoo)

e⌐eyuu えいゆう (英雄) *n*. hero.

e⌐ga⌐k·u えがく (描く) *vt*. (egak·i-;
egak·a-; ega·i-te ⓒ) 1 paint;
draw:
e o egaku (絵を描く) *draw* a picture. (⇨ kaku²)
2 take form; describe:
Booru wa aozora ni ko o egaite
toňde itta. (ボールは青空に弧を描いて
飛んで行った) The ball went flying,
describing an arc against the sky.
3 form a picture in the mind;
imagine.

e⌐gao えがお (笑顔) *n*. smile; smiling [beaming] face.

e-⌐ha⌐gaki えはがき (絵葉書) *n*.
picture postcard. (⇨ hagaki)

e⌐ho⌐ň えほん (絵本) *n*. picture
[illustrated] book.

e⌐ki えき (駅) *n*. (railroad) station.

e⌐kibeň えきべん (駅弁) *n*. box
lunch sold at a railroad station.

e⌐kichoo えきちょう (駅長) *n*.
stationmaster.

e⌐ki⌐iň えきいん (駅員) *n*. station
employee; station staff.

e⌐kimae えきまえ (駅前) *n*. the
place [street] in front of [near] a
(railroad) station.

e⌐kitai えきたい (液体) *n*. liquid;
fluid. (⇨ kitai²; kotai)

e⌐mono えもの (獲物) *n*. game;
catch; take:
Emono *ga wana ni kakatta.* (獲物が
わなにかかった) There was an *animal* caught in the trap.

e⌐ň¹ えん (円) *n*. yen. ★ The

monetary unit of Japan. (⇨ eñdaka; eñyasu; kooka³; shihee)

e¹ñ² えん (円) *n.* circle.

e¹ñ³ えん (縁) *n.* relation; connection; affinity:
Ano hito to wa eñ o kirimashita. (あの人とは縁を切りました) I broke off *relations* with him.

e¹ñchoo えんちょう (延長) *n.* extension; prolongation.
eñchoo suru (〜する) *vt.* extend; lengthen; prolong. (↔ tañshuku)

e¹ñdaka えんだか (円高) *n.* strong yen; appreciation of the yen. (↔ eñyasu)

e¹ñdañ えんだん (縁談) *n.* an offer of marriage; marriage arrangements.

e¹ñdoo えんどう (沿道) *n.* route; roadside:
Eñdoo wa keñbutsuniñ de ippai datta. (沿道は見物人でいっぱいだった) *Both sides of the street* were crowded with spectators.

e¹ñgañ えんがん (沿岸) *n.* coast; shore.

e¹ñgawa えんがわ (縁側) *n.* corridor-like veranda. ★ A long, narrow wooden floor laid outside the rooms of a Japanese house.

e¹ñgee えんげい (園芸) *n.* gardening; horticulture.

e¹ñgeki えんげき (演劇) *n.* play; theatrical performance. ★ Usually refers to dramatic performances as a branch of art.

e¹ñgi¹ えんぎ (演技) *n.* performance; acting.

e¹ñgi² えんぎ (縁起) *n.* omen; luck; portent:
Kore wa eñgi ga yoi [warui]. (これは縁起がよい[悪い]) This is a sign of good [bad] *luck*.
eñgi o katsugu (〜をかつぐ) be superstitious.

e¹ñji·ru えんじる (演じる) *vt.* (eñjite Ⅴ) perform; play; act:
Kooshoo ni atari, kare wa juuyoo na yakuwari o eñjita. (交渉にあたり, 彼は重要な役割を演じた) He *played* an important role in the negotiation.

e¹ñjo えんじょ (援助) *n.* help; aid; assistance; support.
eñjo suru (〜する) *vt.* help; aid; assist; support.

e¹ñka えんか (演歌) *n.* traditional Japanese popular songs. ★ Typically with sad lyrics and melancholy melodies.

e¹ñkai えんかい (宴会) *n.* party; dinner (party); banquet.

e¹ñkatsu えんかつ (円滑) *a.n.* (〜 na, ni) smooth; without a hitch:
Hanashiai wa eñkatsu ni susuñda. (話し合いは円滑に進んだ) The talks went off *smoothly*.

e¹ñki えんき (延期) *n.* postponement; adjournment.
eñki suru (〜する) *vt.* postpone; put off; adjourn. (⇨ nobasu²)

e¹ñogu えのぐ (絵の具) *n.* paints; colors.

e¹ñpitsu えんぴつ (鉛筆) *n.* pencil.

e¹ñryo えんりょ (遠慮) *n.* reserve; restraint; modesty.
eñryo suru (〜する) *vi.*, *vt.* 1 reserve: Watashi no hihañ wa eñryo shite okimasu. (私の批判は遠慮しておきます) I will *reserve* my criticism.
2 refrain: Tabako wa eñryo shite kudasai. (たばこは遠慮してください) Please *refrain* from smoking.

e¹ñshi えんし (遠視) *n.* farsightedness; longsightedness. (↔ kiñshi²)

e¹ñshutsu えんしゅつ (演出) *n.* production; direction.
eñshutsu suru (〜する) *vt.* produce; direct (a play).

e¹ñshuu えんしゅう (演習) *n.* 1 maneuvers.
2 seminar:
Nihoñ-buñgaku no eñshuu (日本文学の演習) a *seminar* in Japanese literature.

e¹ñsoku えんそく (遠足) *n.* outing; excursion; hike.

e￢ñsoo えんそう (演奏) n. (musical) performance; recital.
eñsoo suru (〜する) vt. play; perform.

e￢ñtotsu えんとつ (煙突) n. chimney; stovepipe; funnel.

e￢ñyasu えんやす (円安) n. weak yen; depreciation of the yen. (↔ eñdaka)

e￢ñzetsu えんぜつ (演説) n. address; speech; oration:
Kare wa mijikai enzetsu o shita. (彼は短い演説をした) He made a short speech. (⇨ kooeñ²)

e￢ra えら (鰓) n. gills.

e￢raￒb·u えらぶ (選ぶ) vt. (erab·i-; erab·a-; erañ-de C) 1 choose; select: okurimono o erabu (贈り物を選ぶ) choose a present.
2 elect (a chairman).

e￢raￒ·i¹ えらい (偉い) a. (-ku) 1 distinguished; high:
erai hito to au (偉い人) meet a distinguished person.
2 great; admirable:
Jibuñ de hataraite, daigaku o deta nañte erai desu ne. (自分で働いて、大学を出たなんて偉いですね) It is admirable that you worked your way through college. (⇨ rippa)

e￢raￒ·i² えらい a. (-ku) serious; awful:
Erai koto ni natta zo. (えらいことになったぞ) Now we are in a fix. (⇨ taiheñ)

e￢ri えり (襟) n. collar; neck; neckband; lapel.

e￢·ru える (得る) vt. (e-te V) gain; obtain; get:
Kanojo wa señsee no shikaku o eru tame ni beñkyoo shite imasu. (彼女は先生の資格を得るために勉強しています) She is studying to obtain a teaching certificate. (⇨ toru¹)
-zaru o enai (ざるを得ない) can do nothing but...: ★ Attached to the negative base of a verb; 'suru' is irregular: 'sezaru o enai.'
Sono keekaku wa akiramezaru o enai. (その計画はあきらめざるを得ない) We can do nothing but give up the plan.

e￢sa¹ えさ (餌) n. bait; food; feed.

F

fa￢·ito ファイト n. fight; fighting spirit:
faito o moyasu (ファイトを燃やす) be full of fight.
— int. a shout given when encouraging other people:
Faito! (ファイト) Stick to it [Come on]!

fa￢sunaa ファスナー n. zipper; zip fastener.

fu ふ (府) n. prefecture: ★ An administrative division of Japan, but only used with reference to Osaka (大阪) and Kyoto (京都).
Oosaka-fu (大阪府) Osaka Prefecture. (⇨ keñ¹)

fu- ふ (不) pref. not; un-; in-:
★ Gives a negative or contrary meaning to a word.
fu-goori na (不合理な) irrational / fu-hitsuyoo na (不必要な) unnecessary / fu-jiyuu (不自由) inconvenience.

fu￢añ ふあん (不安) n. worry; uneasiness; anxiety:
fuañ o kañjiru (不安を感じる) feel anxiety.
— a.n. (〜 na, ni) afraid; uneasy; anxious; worried. (⇨ shiñpai)

fu￢beñ ふべん (不便) n. inconvenience; unhandiness:
Teedeñ de zuibuñ fubeñ o shita. (停電でずいぶん不便をした) We were put to great inconvenience because of the power failure.

— *a.n.* (~ na, ni) inconvenient; not handy. (↔ beñri) (⇨ fujiyuu)

fu˺beˈñkyoo ふべんきょう (不勉強) *n.* laziness (in one's studies).
— *a.n.* (~ na) idle; lazy.
★ Not trying hard enough to acquire knowledge.

fu˺bo ふぼ (父母) *n.* parents; one's father and mother. (⇨ fukee)

fu˺buki ふぶき (吹雪) *n.* snowstorm; blizzard. (⇨ kamifubuki)

fu˺chi¹ ふち (縁) *n.* brim; rim; edge; brink.

fu˺choo ふちょう (不調) *n.* failure; bad condition:
fuchoo ni owaru (不調に終わる) end in *failure* / fuchoo de aru (不調である) be in *bad condition*. (↔ koochoo¹)

fu˺chuui ふちゅうい (不注意) *n.* carelessness; negligence.
— *a.n.* (~ na) careless; thoughtless; negligent:
fuchuui na ayamari (不注意な誤り) *careless* mistakes.

fu˺da ふだ (札) *n.* check; tag; card.

fu˺dañ ふだん (普段) *n., adv.* usual(ly); ordinary; ordinarily; always:
fudañ to kawaranai fukusoo o suru (普段と変わらない服装をする) wear the same clothes as *always*.

fu˺dañgi ふだんぎ (普段着) *n.* everyday clothes; casual wear.

fu˺de ふで (筆) *n.* writing brush (for Japanese calligraphy); brush for painting a picture.

fu˺doosañ ふどうさん (不動産) *n.* real estate [property]; immovables: fudoosañ-ya (不動産屋) a *real estate* agent.

fu˺e ふえ (笛) *n.* flute; whistle.

fu˺e˺-ru ふえる (増える・殖える) *vi.* (fue-te Ⅴ) 1 increase:
Taijuu ga ichi-kiro fueta. (体重が1キロ増えた) I *have gained* a kilo in weight. (↔ heru)
2 breed; propagate:

Neko ga fuete, komatte iru. (猫が殖えて、困っている) We don't know what to do about the cats *breeding*.

fu˺goo ふごう (符号) *n.* sign; mark; symbol. (⇨ kigoo)

fu˺hee ふへい (不平) *n.* dissatisfaction; discontent; complaint.

fu˺hitsu˺yoo ふひつよう (不必要) *a.n.* (~ na, ni) unnecessary; needless. (↔ hitsuyoo)

fu˺i ふい (不意) *n.* unexpectedness; suddenness; surprise.
fui o tsuku (~をつく) catch a person off guard.
— *a.n.* (~ na/no, ni) unexpected, sudden; all of a sudden:
Mukashi no tomodachi ga fui ni yatte kita. (昔の友だちが不意にやって来た) An old friend *unexpectedly* dropped by.

fu˺jiñ¹ ふじん (夫人) *n.* 1 wife:
Saitoo-sañ wa fujiñ doohañ de ryokoo shita. (斎藤さんは夫人同伴で旅行した) Mr. Saito went on a trip with his *wife*.
2 Mrs.:
Hiroma de Satoo fujiñ ni shookai sareta. (広間で佐藤夫人に紹介された) I was introduced to *Mrs*. Sato in the hall.

fu˺jiñ² ふじん (婦人) *n.* lady; female; adult woman. (⇨ josee; joshi¹; oñna)

fu˺jiñka ふじんか (婦人科) *n.* gynecology. (⇨ sañfujiñka)

fu˺jiñka˺-i ふじんかい (婦人科医) *n.* gynecologist.

fu˺jiñke˺ekañ ふじんけいかん (婦人警官) *n.* policewoman. (⇨ omawari-sañ)

fu˺jiyuu ふじゆう (不自由) *a.n.* (~ na) 1 (of one's lifestyle) inconvenient; needy:
Deñwa ga nai to nani-ka to fujiyuu desu. (電話がないと何かと不自由です) It is somewhat *inconvenient* to be without a telephone. (↔ beñri) (⇨ fubeñ)
2 physically handicapped; dis-

abled:

me no fujiyuu *na hito* (目の不自由な人) a person with *weak* eyes; a *blind* person.

fujiyuu suru (～する) *vi.* be inconvenient; be needy; be short of.

fuˈjuˈubuñ ふじゅうぶん (不十分) *a.n.* (～ na) not enough; unsatisfactory; imperfect:

Setsumee ga fujuubuñ *da.* (説明が不十分だ) The explanation is *insufficient.* (↔ juubuñ)

fuˈka ふか (不可) *n.* (of a grade rating) failure; F in schoolwork. (↔ ka[2])

fuˈkaˈ·i ふかい (深い) *a.* (-ku)

1 deep:

fukai *kawa* (深い川) a *deep* river / fukai *kizu* (深い傷) a *deep* wound. (↔ asai) (⇒ fukasa)

2 profound; deep:

fukai *kanashimi* (深い悲しみ) *deep* sorrow.

3 dense; thick:

fukai *kiri* (深い霧) a *dense* fog.

fuˈkamaˈr·u ふかまる (深まる) *vi.* (-mar·i-; -mar·a-; -mat-te [C])

deepen; become deeper:

Nihoñgo e no kyoomi ga fukamatta. (日本語への興味が深まった) My interest in the Japanese language *has deepened.* (⇒ fukameru)

fuˈkameˈ·ru ふかめる (深める) *vt.* (-me-te [V]) deepen; enrich:

chishiki o fukameru (知識を深める) *deepen* one's knowledge. (⇒ fukamaru)

fuˈkaˈnoo ふかのう (不可能) *n.* impossibility; impracticability.

— *a.n.* (～ na, ni) impossible; impracticable. (↔ kanoo)

fuˈkaˈñzeñ ふかんぜん (不完全) *a.n.* (～ na) incomplete; imperfect. (↔ kañzeñ)

fuˈkaˈsa ふかさ (深さ) *n.* depth:

Kono kawa wa fukasa *ga go-meetoru aru.* (この川は深さが5メートルある) This river is five meters *deep.* (⇒ fukai)

fuˈkaˈs·u[1] ふかす (吹かす) *vt.* (fukash·i-; fukas·a-; fukash·i-te [C])

1 puff:

tabako o fukasu (たばこを吹かす) *puff* on a cigarette.

2 race (an engine).

fuˈkaˈs·u[2] ふかす (蒸かす) *vt.* (fukash·i-; fukas·a-; fukash·i-te [C]) steam:

jagaimo [gohañ] o fukasu (じゃがいも[ご飯]をふかす) *steam* potatoes [rice]. (⇒ musu)

fuˈkeˈe ふけい (父兄) *n.* parents of schoolchildren. (⇒ fubo)

fuˈkeˈeki ふけいき (不景気) *n.* economic depression; hard times; recession; slump. (↔ keeki[2])

— *a.n.* (～ na) **1** dull; slack; depressed:

Doko mo fukeeki *da.* (どこも不景気だ) Business is *slack* everywhere. (⇒ fukyoo)

2 (*informal*) cheerless; gloomy:

Kare wa fukeeki *na kao o shite ita.* (彼は不景気な顔をしていた) He looked *gloomy.*

fuˈkeˈ·ru[1] ふける (老ける) *vi.* (fuke-te [V]) grow old; look old for one's age.

fuˈkeˈ·ru[2] ふける (更ける) *vi.* (fuke-te [V]) grow late:

Yoru mo daibu fukete kimashita *kara sorosoro o-itoma itashimasu.* (夜もだいぶ更けてきましたからそろそろおいとま致します) As *it is getting* quite late, I must be leaving now.

fuˈketsu ふけつ (不潔) *a.n.* (～ na) unclean; dirty; filthy; unsanitary. (↔ seeketsu)

fuˈkiˈñ[1] ふきん (付近) *n.* neighborhood; vicinity.

fuˈkiˈñ[2] ふきん (布巾) *n.* dish [tea] towel; dishcloth.

fuˈkiˈsoku ふきそく (不規則) *a.n.* (～ na, ni) irregular:

fukisoku *na seekatsu o suru* (不規則な生活をする) lead an *irregular* life.

fuˈkitobaˈs·u ふきとばす (吹き飛ばす) *vt.* (-tobash·i-; -tobas·a-;

-tobash·i·te C) blow off:
Kaze de booshi o fukitobasareta.
(風で帽子を吹き飛ばされた) My hat
was blown off by the wind.
(⇨ fukitobu)

fuˈkitobˌu ふきとぶ(吹き飛ぶ) *vi.*
(-tob·i-; -tob·a-; -toñ·de C)
blow off:
Shorui ga kaze de fukitoñda. (書類
が風で吹き飛んだ) The papers *flew
away* in the wind. (⇨ fukitobasu;
tobu¹)

fuˈkitsu ふきつ(不吉) *a.n.* (~ na)
ominous; unlucky:
Fukitsu na yokañ ga suru. (不吉な
予感がする) I have an *ominous* pre-
sentiment.

fuˈkitsukeˌ·ru ふきつける(吹き付け
る) (-tsuke-te Ⅴ) **1** *vi.* blow
against:
*Kaze ga shoomeñ kara hageshiku
fukitsuketa.* (風が正面から激しく吹き
付けた) The wind *blew* violently
from in front.
2 *vt.* spray:
kabe ni peñki o fukitsukeru (壁にペ
ンキを吹き付ける) *spray* paint on the
wall.

fuˈkkatsu ふっかつ(復活) *n.* re-
vival; restoration; resurgence.
fukkatsu suru [saseru] (~する[さ
せる]) *vi., vt.* come [bring] back;
revive; restore.

Fuˈkkatsuˌsai ふっかつさい(復活
祭) *n.* Easter; Easter Day [Sun-
day].

fuˈkoˌo ふこう(不幸) *n.* **1** unhappiness; misfortune.
2 death:
*Kanojo no uchi de fukoo ga atta
rashii.* (彼女の家で不幸があったらしい)
She seems to have had a *death* in
the family.
— *a.n.* (~ na, ni) unhappy; unlucky; unfortunate. (⇨ fushiawase)
fukoo chuu no saiwai (~中の幸
い) a stroke of good luck in the
midst of ill fortune.

fuˈkoˌohee ふこうへい(不公平) *n.*

unfairness; partiality; injustice.
— *a.n.* (~ na, ni) unfair; partial; unjust. (↔ koohee)

fuˈk·u¹ ふく(吹く) (fuk·i-; fuk·a-;
fu·i·te C) *vi.* blow:
Kaze ga fuite iru. (風が吹いている)
The wind *is blowing.*
— *vt.* **1** play a musical instrument:
fue [torañpetto] o fuku (笛[トランペッ
ト]を吹く) *play* the flute [trumpet].
2 send forth air; blow:
*Kare wa roosoku no hi o fuite,
keshita.* (彼はろうそくの火を吹いて, 消
した) He *blew* out the candle.
3 put forth a bud:
Sakura no ki ga me o fuita. (桜の木
が芽をふいた) The cherry trees *have
put forth* buds.

fuˈkuˌ² ふく(服) *n.* clothes; dress;
suit. (⇨ ifuku; yoofuku; wafuku)

fuˈk·uˌ³ ふく(拭く) *vt.* (fuk·i-; fu-
k·a-; fu·i·te C) **1** wipe (off);
clean:
mado o fuite, kiree ni suru (窓をふ
いて, きれいにする) *wipe* the windows
clean.
2 dry:
hañkachi de namida [ase] o fuku
(ハンカチで涙[汗]をふく) *dry* one's
tears [perspiration] with one's
handkerchief.

fuˈkuˌ⁴ ふく(福) *n.* good luck [for-
tune]; happiness.

fuˈkuˌ- ふく(副) *pref.* vice; deputy; assistant:
fuku-chiji (副知事) a *deputy* governor / *fuku-gichoo* (副議長) a *vice-*
chairman.

fuˈkumeˌ·ru ふくめる(含める) *vt.*
(fukume-te Ⅴ) include:
*Riñgo wa sooryoo o fukumete,
rokuseñ-eñ desu.* (りんごは送料を含め
て, 6千円です) The apples will be
6,000 yen, *including* delivery
charges. (⇨ fukumu)

fuˈkuˌm·u ふくむ(含む) *vt.*
(fukum·i-; fukum·a-; fukuñ·de
C) **1** contain; include:
Hooreñsoo wa bitamiñ o takusañ

fukuṇde iru. (ほうれん草はビタミンをたくさん含んでいる) Spinach *contains* plenty of vitamins.
2 hold a thing in one's mouth: *mizu o kuchi ni* fukuṇde, *ugai suru* (水を口に含んで、うがいする) *hold* water in one's mouth and gargle. (⇨ fukumeru)
3 imply: *Kare no kotoba wa hiniku o* fukuṇde ita. (彼の言葉は皮肉を含んでいた) *There was* sarcasm in his words.
4 bear in mind: *Doo ka kono teṇ o o-*fukumi *oki kudasai.* (どうかこの点をお含みおきください) Please *bear* this point *in mind.*

fuˈkurahagi ふくらはぎ (脹ら脛) *n.* calf of the leg.

fuˈkuramasˑu ふくらます (膨らます) *vt.* (-mashˑi-; -masˑa-; -mashˑiˑte Ⓒ) **1** inflate; swell; blow up: *kuchi de fuusen o* fukuramasu (口で風船をふくらます) *blow up* a balloon. (⇨ fukuramu)
2 puff out; expand: *Kare wa fumaṇ-soo ni hoo o* fukuramashita. (彼は不満そうにほおをふくらました) He *puffed out* his cheeks with apparent dissatisfaction. (⇨ fukureru)

fuˈkuramˑu ふくらむ (膨らむ) *vi.* (-ramˑi-; -ramˑaˑ; -raṇ-de Ⓒ) **1** swell; expand: *Hana no tsubomi ga* fukurami-*hajimeta.* (花のつぼみがふくらみ始めた) The flower buds *have begun to swell.* (⇨ fukureru)
2 bulge: *Kabaṇ wa nimotsu de* fukuraṇde ita. (かばんは荷物でふくらんでいた) The bag *was bulgy* with its contents.

fuˈkureˑru ふくれる (膨れる) *vi.* (fukure-te Ⓥ) **1** swell: *Mochi wa yaku to* fukureru. (もちは焼くとふくれる) Rice cakes *swell* when grilled.
2 sulk; become sulky: *Kare wa shikarareru to sugu ni* fukureru. (彼はしかられるとすぐにふくれ

る) He soon *sulks* when he is scolded.

fuˈkuro ふくろ (袋) *n.* bag; sack; pouch.

fuˈkusaˈyoo ふくさよう (副作用) *n.* side effect.

fuˈkuseṇ ふくせん (複線) *n.* two-track line; double track. (↔ taṇseṇ)

fuˈku-shaˈchoo ふくしゃちょう (副社長) *n.* executive vice president.

fuˈkuˈshi[1] ふくし (福祉) *n.* welfare; well-being: *shakai-*fukushi (社会福祉) social *welfare.*

fuˈkushi[2] ふくし (副詞) *n.* adverb. (⇨ APP. 1)

fuˈkushuu ふくしゅう (復習) *n.* review; revision. **fukushuu suru** (〜する) *vt.* review [go over] one's lessons. (↔ yoshuu)

fuˈkusoo ふくそう (服装) *n.* dress; costume; clothes: *Uchi no musuko wa* fukusoo *o amari kamawanai.* (うちの息子は服装をあまり構わない) My son doesn't care much about his *clothes.* (⇨ minari)

fuˈkuzatsu ふくざつ (複雑) *a.n.* (〜 na, ni) complicated; complex; intricate: fukuzatsu *na koozoo* (複雑な構造) a *complex* structure. (↔ kaṇtaṇ)

fuˈkyoo ふきょう (不況) *n.* recession; depression; slump. (↔ kookyoo[2]) (⇨ fukeeki)

fuˈkyuu ふきゅう (普及) *n.* popularization; spread; diffusion. **fukyuu suru** (〜する) *vi.* spread; diffuse; popularize. (⇨ hiromaru)

fuˈmaˈjime ふまじめ (不真面目) *a.n.* (〜 na, ni) not serious; frivolous; insincere. (↔ majime)

fuˈmaṇ ふまん (不満) *n.* dissatisfaction; discontent.
— *a.n.* (〜 na, ni) unsatisfactory; unsatisfied; dissatisfied: *Ima no kyuuryoo ni wa* fumaṇ

desu. (今の給料には不満です) I am *dissatisfied* with my present salary. (↔ mañzoku)

fu「mee ふめい (不明) *a.n.* (~ na/no) unclear; obscure; unknown: *kokuseki fumee no hikooki* (国籍不明の飛行機) an aircraft of *unidentified* nationality.

fu「me¹eyo ふめいよ (不名誉) *a.n.* (~ na) disgraceful; shameful; discreditable: *Booryoku o furuu no wa fumeeyo na koto da.* (暴力をふるうのは不名誉なことだ) It is a *disgraceful* act to use violence. (↔ meeyo)

fu「mikiri ふみきり (踏切) *n.* railroad crossing; level crossing.

ʈu「mitsuke¹·ru ふみつける (踏み付ける) *vt.* (-tsuke-te Ⅴ) trample; stamp: *Dare-ka ga kadañ o fumitsuketa.* (だれかが花壇を踏みつけた) Someone *trampled down* the flower bed.

fu「moto¹ ふもと (麓) *n.* lowest part of a mountain; foot of a hill.

fu「m-u ふむ (踏む) *vt.* (fum·i-; fu-m·a-; fuñ-de Ⓒ) 1 trample; step: *bureeki o fumu* (ブレーキを踏む) *step* on the brakes.
2 set foot on: *hajimete Amerika no chi o fumu* (初めてアメリカの地を踏む) *set foot* on American soil for the first time.
3 go through; follow (a procedure): *seeki no tetsuzuki o fumu* (正規の手続きを踏む) *go through* the due formalities.

fu「ñ¹ ふん (分) *n.* minute: *Sañ-ji go-fuñ mae [sugi] desu.* (3時5分前[過ぎ]です) It is five *minutes* to [past] three. (⇨ APP. 4)

fu「ñ¹ ふん (糞) *n.* excrement; feces; dung. (⇨ daibeñ; kuso)

fu「nabiñ ふなびん (船便) *n.* sea [surface] mail.

fu「ñba¹r·u ふんばる (踏ん張る) *vi.* (-bar·i-; -bar·a-; -bat-te Ⓒ)

1 stand firm; brace one's legs.
2 hold out: *Akirameru na. Ima koso fuñbaru toki da.* (あきらめるな. 今こそ踏ん張るときだ) Don't give up. Now is the time to *hang on.* (⇨ gañbaru)

fu「ne ふね (舟・船) *n.* boat; ship; vessel. ★ '舟' usually refers to a small vessel like a rowboat, and '船' to a large vessel like a steamship. (⇨ watashibune)

fu「neñ ふねん (不燃) *n.* nonflammability; incombustibility: *funeñ-butsu* (不燃物) *incombustibles.*

fu「ñeñ ふんえん (噴煙) *n.* smoke of a volcano.

fu「ñgai ふんがい (憤慨) *n.* indignation; resentment.
fuñgai suru (~する) *vi.* resent; be indignant.

fu「ñi¹ki ふんいき (雰囲気) *n.* mood; atmosphere; ambience.

fu「ñka ふんか (噴火) *n.* eruption; volcanic activity.
fuñka suru (~する) *vi.* erupt.

fu「ñka¹koo ふんかこう (噴火口) *n.* volcanic crater.

fu「ñshiñ ふんしん (分針) *n.* (of a clock) minute hand. (⇨ byooshiñ)

fu「ñshitsu ふんしつ (紛失) *n.* loss.
fuñshitsu suru (~する) *vt.* (*formal*) lose; miss. (⇨ nakusu¹)

fu「ñwa¹ri ふんわり *adv.* (~ to) softly; lightly; gently: *Akañboo ni moofu o fuñwari (to) kaketa.* (赤ん坊に毛布をふんわり(と)掛けた) I put a blanket *gently* over the baby. (⇨ fuwari)

fu「ñzuke¹·ru ふんづける (踏ん付ける) *vt.* (-zuke-te Ⅴ) (*informal*) = fumitsukeru.

fu「rafura¹ ふらふら *a.n.* (~ na, ni) unsteady; staggering; groggy: *Kare wa furafura to tachiagatta.* (彼はふらふらと立ち上がった) He *unsteadily* got to his feet.

fu「rafura² ふらふら *adv.* (~ to; ~ suru) 1 impulsively; uncon-

sciously:
Kanojo wa furafura to kare no sasoi ni notte shimatta. (彼女はふらふらと彼の誘いに乗ってしまった) She yielded to his temptation *in spite of herself.*
2 feel dizzy; be faint; waver:
Onaka ga suite furafura suru. (おなかがすいてふらふらする) I am *faint* with hunger.

fuˈrai フライ *n.* fried food.

fuˈraipañ フライパン *n.* frying pan; skillet.

fuˈre・ru ふれる (触れる) *vi.* (fure-te Ⓥ) **1** touch; feel:
E ni te o furenai de kudasai. (絵に手を触れないでください) *Don't touch* the paintings.
2 mention; refer to:
Kare wa jibuñ no misu ni tsuite hitokoto mo furenakatta. (彼は自分のミスについて一言も触れなかった) He *did not mention* even one word about his blunder.
3 affect the emotions or feelings of (a person):
Shachoo no ikari ni furete, kare wa kubi ni natta. (社長の怒りに触れて, 彼は首になった) Having *incurred* the president's anger, he was fired.
4 perceive; experience:
Me ni fureru mono subete ga watashi ni wa mezurashii. (目に触れるものすべてが私には珍しい) Everything that I *see* is new to me.
5 infringe (a law, a regulation, a rule, etc.).

fuˈri¹ ふり (不利) *n.* disadvantage; handicap.
— *a.n.* (~ na, ni) disadvantageous; unfavorable:
Kare ni totte furi na shooko ga mitsukatta. (彼にとって不利な証拠が見つかった) A piece of evidence *against* him has been found. (↔ yuuri)

fuˈri¹² ふり (振り) *n.* personal appearance.
... furi o suru (~をする) pretend; affect; feign: *neta furi o suru* (寝たふりをする) *pretend* to be asleep.

fuˈrigana ふりがな (振り仮名) *n.* 'kana' written next to or above Chinese characters to show the pronunciation. (⇨ kana)

fuˈrikaˈer・u ふりかえる (振り返る) *vi.* (-kaer-i-; -kaet-a-; -kaet-te Ⓒ) **1** turn around; look back.
2 recollect; look back:
kako [gakusee jidai] o furikaeru (過去[学生時代]を振り返る) *look back* on the past [one's college days].

fuˈrimuˈk・u ふりむく (振り向く) *vi.* (-muk-i-; -muk-a-; -mu-i-te Ⓒ) **1** turn one's face; turn around. (⇨ muku¹)
2 (with a negative) pay attention to; care for:
Kanojo wa kanemochi igai no otoko ni wa furimuki mo shinai. (彼女は金持ち以外の男には振り向きもしない) She *doesn't care for* men unless they are rich.

fuˈro¹ ふろ (風呂) *n.* **1** bath; bathtub: ★ Often with 'o-.'
furo ni hairu (ふろに入る) take a *bath.* (⇨ nyuuyoku)
2 public bath:
furo ni iku (ふろに行く) go to the *public bath.* ★ The public bath is called '*furoya*' or '*señtoo.*'

fuˈroba¹ ふろば (風呂場) *n.* a room with a bathtub; bathroom.

fuˈroku ふろく (付録) *n.* supplement; appendix.

fuˈroñto フロント *n.* (of a hotel) front desk; reception desk.

fuˈroñto-gaˈrasu フロントガラス *n.* windshield; windscreen.

fuˈroshiki ふろしき (風呂敷) *n.* wrapping cloth. ★ A square scarf-like cloth used for wrapping and carrying things.

fuˈroˈya ふろや (風呂屋) *n.* public bath. (⇨ señtoo¹)

fuˈr・u¹ ふる (降る) *vi.* (fur-i-; fur-a-; fut-te Ⓒ) **1** (of rain, snow, hail) fall:
Ame ga hageshiku futte iru. (雨が激しく降っている) *It is raining* hard.

2 (of ash, dust, etc.) fall; come down.

fuᒥru·ru² ふる（振る） *vt.* (fur·i-; fur·a-; fut-te C) **1** shake; move:
Keekañ wa te o futte, tomare to aizu shita.（警官は手を振って、止まれと合図した）The policeman *waved* his hand to signal me to halt.
2 sprinkle:
niku ni shio to koshoo o furu（肉に塩とこしょうを振る）*sprinkle* the meat with salt and pepper.
3 assign; add (a letter, a number, etc.):
kañji ni furigana o furu（漢字にふりがなを振る）*put* the corresponding 'furigana' next to the Chinese characters.
4 (often in the passive) refuse; abandon:
Kare wa koibito ni furareta.（彼は恋人に振られた）He *was jilted* by his girlfriend.

fuᒥrue·ru ふるえる（震える）*vi.* (furue-te V) tremble; shake; shiver; shudder. (⇨ furuwaseru)

fuᒥru¹·i ふるい（古い）*a.* (-ku) old; stale; old-fashioned; out-of-date. (↔ atarashii)

fuᒥruma¹·u ふるまう（振る舞う）*vi.* (-ma·i-; -maw·a-; -mat-te C)
1 behave; act:
Kare wa shachoo rashiku furumatta.（彼は社長らしく振る舞った）He *behaved* just as the president of a company should.
2 treat; entertain.

fuᒥru¹sato ふるさと（故郷）*n.* one's home; one's hometown.

fuᒥrushi¹ñbuñ ふるしんぶん（古新聞）*n.* old newspaper. (⇨ chiri-gami-kookañ)

fuᒥruwase·ru ふるわせる（震わせる）*vt.* (furuwase-te V) cause to tremble:
Shoojo wa samu-soo ni karada o furuwasete ita.（少女は寒そうに体を震わせていた）The girl *was shaking* all over as if she were cold. (⇨ furueru)

fuᒥryoo ふりょう（不良）*a.n.* (~ na/no) bad; poor; defective:
Kotoshi wa ine no sakugara ga furyoo da.（今年は稲の作柄が不良だ）We had a *poor* rice crop this year. (⇨ yoi¹)

fuᒥsa¹ ふさ（房）*n.* tuft; fringe; tassel; bunch.

fuᒥsagar·u ふさがる（塞がる）*vi.* (fusagar·i-; fusagar·a-; fusagat-te C) **1** close; be closed:
Kizuguchi ga yatto fusagatta.（傷口がやっとふさがった）The wound has *closed up* at last. (⇨ fusagu)
2 be blocked; be packed:
Jiko de dooro ga fusagatte, ugo-kenakatta.（事故で道路がふさがって、動けなかった）The road *was blocked* by the accident and we were stuck. (⇨ fusagu)
3 be occupied; be used:
Zaseki wa miñna fusagatte imasu.（座席はみんなふさがっています）The seats *are* all *occupied*.

fuᒥsag·u ふさぐ（塞ぐ）*vt.* (fusag·i-; fusag·a-; fusa·i-de C)
1 stop; cover:
Ana o ishi de fusaida.（穴を石でふさいだ）I *stopped up* the hole with a stone. (⇨ fusagaru)
2 block; occupy:
Ooki-na torakku ga michi o fusa-ide ita.（大きなトラックが道をふさいでいた）A large truck *was blocking* the road. (⇨ fusagaru)

fuᒥsa¹i ふさい（夫妻）*n.* husband and wife.

fuᒥsawashi¹·i ふさわしい *a.* (-ku) suitable; proper; appropriate:
sono ba ni fusawashii fuku（その場にふさわしい服）clothes *suitable* for the occasion. (⇨ tekisetsu)

fuᒥse¹ekaku ふせいかく（不正確）*n., a.n.* (~ na, ni) incorrect; inaccurate; inexact; uncertain. (↔ seekaku²)

fuᒥse¹g·u ふせぐ（防ぐ）*vt.* (fuse-g·i-; fuseg·a-; fuse·i-de C)
1 protect; defend:
Samusa o fusegu tame ni, jañpaa

o kita. (寒さを防ぐために, ジャンパーを着た) I wore a windbreaker to *protect* myself from the cold.
2 guard; prevent:
jiko o fusegu (事故を防ぐ) *prevent* an accident. (⇒ booshi²)

fuˈseˈru ふせる (伏せる) *vt.* (fusete Ⅴ) **1** put a thing upside down; put a thing face down.
2 look downward; lower one's eyes:
Kanojo wa hazukashi-soo ni me o fuseta. (彼女は恥ずかしそうに目を伏せた) She *lowered* her eyes bashfully.
3 keep a thing secret.

fuˈshiˈ¹ ふし (節) *n.* **1** knot:
Kono ita wa fushi ga ooi. (この板は節が多い) This plank is full of *knots*.
2 joint:
take no fushi (竹の節) a *joint* in a piece of bamboo.

fuˈshiˈ² ふし (節) *n.* melody; tune; strain.

fuˈshiaˈwase ふしあわせ (不幸せ) *n.* unhappiness; misfortune.
— *a.n.* (~ na, ni) unhappy; unfortunate. (↔ shiawase)
(⇒ fukoo)

fuˈshiˈgi ふしぎ (不思議) *n.* wonder; mystery; miracle.
— *a.n.* (~ na, ni) difficult to explain the reason or cause; mysterious; strange.

fuˈshiˈmatsu ふしまつ (不始末) *n.* carelessness; misconduct:
Kaji no geñiñ wa tabako no hi no fushimatsu *datta.* (火事の原因はたばこの火の不始末だった) The cause of the fire was *careless handling* of cigarette butts.

fuˈshiˈñsetsu ふしんせつ (不親切) *a.n.* (~ na, ni) unkind; insufficient inconsiderate. (↔ shiñsetsu)

fuˈshiˈzeñ ふしぜん (不自然) *a.n.* (~ na, ni) unnatural; artificial; forced. (↔ shizeñ)

fuˈshoo ふしょう (負傷) *n.* injury;

wound; cut; bruise. (⇒ kega)
fushoo suru (~する) *vi.* be injured; be wounded.

fuˈsoku ふそく (不足) *n.* shortage; lack; want; insufficiency.
fusoku suru (~する) *vi.* be short; be lacking. (⇒ -busoku)

fuˈsuma ふすま (襖) *n.* Japanese sliding door. ★ Both sides are covered with thick paper.

fuˈta ふた (蓋) *n.* lid; cap; cover:
nabe ni futa *o suru* (なべにふたをする) put the *lid* on a pot.

fuˈta- ふた (二) *pref.* double; two:
futa-keta (二桁) *double* digits / *futa-kumi* (二組) *two* pairs.

fuˈtañ ふたん (負担) *n.* burden; load; charge; obligation.
futañ suru (~する) *vt.* bear; share; cover: *Sooryoo wa kochira de* futañ *shimasu.* (送料はこちらで負担します) We *will cover* the postage.

fuˈtari¹ ふたり (二人) *n.* two persons; couple.

fuˈtaˈshika ふたしか (不確か) *a.n.* (~ na, ni) uncertain; unreliable. (↔ tashika)

fuˈtatabi ふたたび (再び) *adv.* again; once more; for the second time: ★ Similar in meaning to '*mata*' but slightly formal.
Kooshoo ga futatabi *hajimatta.* (交渉が再び始まった) The negotiations have started *once more*.

fuˈtatsu¹ ふたつ (二つ) *n.* couple; two. ★ Used when counting.
(⇒ ni¹; APP. 3)

fuˈteˈkitoo ふてきとう (不適当) *a.n.* (~ na, ni) unsuitable; unfit. (↔ tekitoo)

fuˈto ふと *adv.* suddenly; by chance; unexpectedly:
Futo ii aidea ga ukañda. (ふといいアイデアが浮かんだ) *Suddenly* a good idea came to me.

fuˈtoˈ·i ふとい (太い) *a.* (-ku)
1 (of round objects such as sticks or string) thick; bold:

futoi *keito* (太い毛糸) *thick* wool /
futoi *señ* (太い線) a *bold* line.
(↔ hosoi)
  2 (of a voice) deep. (↔ hosoi)

fu｢tokoro ふところ (懐) *n.* breast;
bosom; breast pocket.

fu｢tomomo ふともも (太股) *n.*
thigh. (⇨ momo¹)

fu｢toñ ふとん (布団) *n.* padded
floor mattress used as a bed; bedding; quilt.

fu｢too ふとう (不当) *a.n.* (~ na,
ni) unfair; unjust; unreasonable.
(↔ seetoo¹)

fu｢to｢r･u ふとる (太る) *vi.* (futor·i-;
futor·a-; futot-te Ⓒ) **1** grow fat;
gain weight.
  2 be fat; be plump: ★ '*Futotte
iru* ' is the pattern used in this
sense.
Futotte iru hito wa tsukare-yasui.
(太っている人は疲れやすい) *Fat* people
get tired easily.

fu｢tsuka ふつか (二日) *n.* two
days; the second day. (⇨ APP. 5)

fu｢tsukayoi ふつかよい (二日酔い)
n. hangover (from alcohol).

fu｢tsuu¹ ふつう (普通) *a.n.* (~ na/
no, ni) common; ordinary; normal; usual; average:
*Nihoñ de wa busshiki no sooshiki
ga* futsuu *desu*. (日本では仏式の葬式
が普通です) In Japan Buddhist
funerals are the *norm*.
  — *adv.* usually; commonly;
ordinarily; normally. (⇨ heejoo;
nami¹)

fu｢tsuu² ふつう (普通) *n.* local
train; one that stops at every station along the line. (⇨ doñkoo)

fu｢tsuu³ ふつう (不通) *n.* interruption; suspension:
Yamanote-señ wa ima futsuu *desu*.
(山の手線はいま不通です) The Yama-
note Line *is not in service* now.

fu｢ttoo ふっとう (沸騰) *n.* boiling;
seething.
  futtoo suru (~する) *vi.* **1** boil;
come to the boil.
  2 be heated:

Giroñ ga futtoo shita. (議論がふっと
うした) The discussion *became
heated*.

fu｢u¹ ふう (風) *n.* **1** look; appearance; air:
Kare wa nanigenai fuu *o shite ita*.
(彼は何気ない風をしていた) He *pre-
tended* nonchalance.
  2 way; manner:
Sore wa koñna fuu *ni yatte goran
nasai*. (それはこんな風にやってごらんなさ
い) Try to do it *in this manner*.
(⇨ guai)

fu｢u² ふう (封) *n.* seal:
tegami no fuu *o suru* [*kiru*] (手紙の
封をする[切る]) *seal* [*open*] a letter,

-fuu ふう (風) *suf.* style; type:
Nihoñ-fuu no furo (日本風のふろ) a
Japanese *style* bath.

fu｢ufu ふうふ (夫婦) *n.* man [hus-
band] and wife; married couple.

fu｢ufuu ふうふう *adv.* (~ to)
(used when blowing on something hot to cool it):
Miñna fuufuu *ii-nagara sukiyaki o
tabeta*. (みんなふうふう言いながらすき焼
きを食べた) Everyone was *blowing*
on the sukiyaki as they ate it.
  fuufuu iu (~言う) pant; breathe
hard. (⇨ aegu)

fu｢ukee ふうけい (風景) *n.* landscape; scene; scenery.

fu｢uki ふうき (風紀) *n.* social mo-
rality; discipline:
fuuki o midasu (風紀を乱す) corrupt *public morals*.

fu｢uñ¹ ふうん *int.* hum; oh.
★ Used to express a half-hearted
reply. It is rude to use this
expression in reply to one's
superiors.

fu｢uñ² ふうん (不運) *n.* bad luck;
misfortune.
  — *a.n.* (~ na, ni) unlucky; unfortunate:
fuuñ na jiko (不運な事故) an *unfortunate* accident. (↔ koouñ)

fu｢useñ ふうせん (風船) *n.* balloon.

fu｢ushuu ふうしゅう (風習) *n.* custom; manners; practices.

fu￼utoo ふうとう (封筒) *n.* envelope.

fu￼u-u ふうう (風雨) *n.* wind and rain; storm.

fu￼uzoku ふうぞく (風俗) *n.* manners; public morals.

fu￼uzoku-e￼egyoo ふうぞくえいぎょう (風俗営業) *n.* entertainment and amusement trades. ★ Usually used as a euphemism for prostitution.

fu￼wafuwa[1] ふわふわ *a.n.* (~ no, ni) gentle; soft: ★ Used for objects which are light and fluffy. *fuwafuwa no kusshoñ* (ふわふわのクッション) a *soft* cushion.

fu￼wafuwa[2] ふわふわ *adv.* (~ to, ~ suru) 1 lightly; buoyantly: *Sono fuuseñ wa doko-ka e fuwafuwa (to) toñde itta.* (その風船はどこかへふわふわ(と)飛んで行った) The balloon *gently* floated away somewhere.
2 restless; unsettled. ★ Used about people who cannot settle down or pay attention to what they should be doing.

fu￼wa￼ri ふわり *adv.* (~ to) gently; softly; lightly. ★ Used for objects moving slowly in the air. '*Fuñwari*' is also used when referring to something softer or lighter. (⇨ funwari)

fu￼ya￼s·u ふやす (増やす) *vt.* (fuyash·i-; fuyas·a-; fuyash·i-te Ⓒ) increase; add to: *hito o fuyasu* (人を増やす) *increase* the staff / *zaisañ o fuyasu* (財産を増やす) *add to* one's fortune.

fu￼yu[1] ふゆ (冬) *n.* winter.

fu￼yu￼kai ふゆかい (不愉快) *a.n.* (~ na, ni) unpleasant; disagreeable. (↔ yukai)

fu￼yu-ya￼sumi ふゆやすみ (冬休み) *n.* winter vacation.

fu￼zai ふざい (不在) *n.* absence: *Anata no fuzai-chuu ni raikyaku ga arimashita.* (あなたの不在中に来客がありました) A visitor came to see you during your *absence*.

fu￼zake￼-ru ふざける *vi.* (fuzakete Ⓥ) 1 joke; jest; talk nonsense: *Kare ga fuzakete itta koto nado, ki ni suru na.* (彼がふざけて言ったことなど、気にするな) Don't worry about something he said *in jest*.
2 frisk; frolic.

fu￼zoku ふぞく (付属) *n.* attachment; accessory. **fuzoku suru** (~する) *vi.* be attached; be affiliated.

G

ga[1] が *p.* 1 (used to mark the topic of a sentence): *Kyooto ni wa furui tatemono ga takusañ arimasu.* (京都には古い建物がたくさんあります) There are a lot of old *buildings* in Kyoto. ★ Generally speaking, '*ga*' is used to stress the subject and '*wa*' is used to emphasize the predicate. When a noun is first mentioned, it is usually followed by '*ga*,' but on later mentions, by '*wa*.' (⇨ wa[3])
2 [follows a nominalized verb which is the subject of its clause]: *Oñgaku o kiku no ga nani yori no tanoshimi desu.* (音楽を聞くのがなによりの楽しみです) Nothing is more enjoyable than *listening to music*.
3 (used with certain expressions indicating likes, dislikes, desires and wishes): *Watashi wa yasai ga kirai desu.* (私は野菜がきらいです) I dislike *vegetables*.
4 (used with certain expressions indicating ability or skill):

Yamada-sañ wa sukii *ga joozu desu.* (山田さんはスキーがじょうずです) Mrs. Yamada is good at *skiing.*

ga[2] が *p.* **1** but; although:

a (used to link two clauses, the second of which is an unexpected outcome or result of the first):

Yuujiñ ni ai ni ikimashita ga, ainiku rusu deshita. (友人に会いに行きましたが、あいにく留守でした) I went to see my friend, *but* unfortunately she was not at home. (⇨ kakawarazu; keredo (mo); no ni)

b (used to link two clauses that are in direct contrast):

Peñ wa arimasu ga, kami ga arimaseñ. (ペンはありますが、紙がありません) I have a pen, *but* no paper. (⇨ kakawarazu; keredo (mo); no ni)

2 (used in a non-contrastive way to link two clauses, the first of which is a preliminary to the second):

Sumimaseñ ga, eki e wa doo ikeba ii ñ deshoo ka? (すみませんが、駅へはどう行けばいいんでしょうか) *Excuse me, but* what would be the best way of going to the station?

3 and also: ★ Used to link two clauses, the second of which supplements the first.

Kanojo wa kiryoo mo ii ga, atama mo ii. (彼女は器量もいいが、頭もいい) She is good-looking, *and* what is more, clever.

4 (used at the end of an unfinished sentence to politely express modesty or reserve, or to avoid making an overly direct statement):

Anoo, sore watashi no na ñ desu ga ... (あのう、それ私のなんですが...) Excuse me, but *I think* that is mine.

ga⌐bugabu がぶがぶ *adv.* (~ to) (the sound of noisily drinking a liquid):

Kare wa mizu o nañbai mo gabu-gabu (to) noñda. (彼は水を何杯もがぶがぶ(と)飲んだ) He *noisily* drank several cups of water. (⇨ gatsugatsu)

ga⌐byoo がびょう(画鋲) *n.* thumbtack; drawing pin. (⇨ byoo²)

-gachi がち(勝ち) *suf.* tend to do; be apt [liable] to do: ★ Added to a noun or the continuative base of a verb. Often used when the tendency is unfavorable.

Kare wa karada ga yowai no de gakkoo o yasumi-*gachi desu.* (彼は体が弱いので学校を休みがちです) Since he is physically delicate, he *is often absent* from school.

ga⌐i がい(害) *n.* harm; damage:

Tabako wa keñkoo ni gai ga aru. (たばこは健康に害がある) Smoking *is harmful* to your health.

-gai がい(外) *suf.* outside:

*moñdai-*gai (問題外) *out of* the question / jikañ-gai roodoo (時間外労働) *overtime* work.

ga⌐iatsu がいあつ(外圧) *n.* external pressure:

gaiatsu *ni makeru* (外圧に負ける) yield to *external pressure.*

ga⌐ibu がいぶ(外部) *n.* **1** outside; exterior:

tatemono no gaibu (建物の外部) the *exterior* of a building. (↔ naibu)

2 outside (one's circle); external (to one's interests):

Himitsu ga gaibu *ni moreta.* (秘密が外部に漏れた) The secret leaked to *outsiders.* (↔ naibu)

ga⌐ido-bu⌐kku ガイドブック *n.*

1 guidebook for travelers or tourists.

2 manual; handbook.

ga⌐ijiñ がいじん(外人) *n.* foreigner. ★ Abbreviation of '*gaikokujiñ.*'

ga⌐ika がいか(外貨) *n.* foreign currency [money].

ga⌐ikañ がいかん(外観) *n.* appearance; exterior view.

ga⌐ikoku がいこく (外国) n. foreign country [land].

ga⌐ikokugo がいこくご (外国語) n. foreign language.

ga⌐ikoku¬jiñ がいこくじん (外国人) n. foreigner; alien.

ga⌐ikoo がいこう (外交) n. 1 diplomacy; foreign affairs.
2 door-to-door sales:
Kanojo wa hokeñ no gaikoo o shite iru. (彼女は保険の外交をしている) She *goes from house to house* selling insurance.

ga⌐iko¬oiñ がいこういん (外交員) n. salesman; saleswoman.

ga⌐iko¬okañ がいこうかん (外交官) n. diplomat.

ga⌐ineñ がいねん (概念) n. notion; general idea; concept.

ga⌐iraigo がいらいご (外来語) n. loanword; Japanized foreign word. ★ Usually written in 'katakana.'

ga⌐ishite がいして (概して) adv. (*formal*) generally; in general; on the whole:
Nihoñ no dooro wa gaishite semai. (日本の道路は概して狭い) Roads in Japan are *generally* narrow.

ga⌐ishoku がいしょく (外食) n. eating out.

ga⌐ishutsu がいしゅつ (外出) n. going out.
  gaishutsu suru (～する) vi. go out. (⇨ dekakeru)

ga⌐isoo がいそう (外装) n. the exterior (of a building, car, etc.); external ornament. (↔ naisoo)

ga⌐is·u がいす (害す) vt. (gaish·i-te Ⓥ) injure; hurt:
Kare wa kañjoo o gaishita rashii. (彼は感情を害したらしい) He seems to *be offended*.

ga⌐itoo¹ がいとう (該当) n. application; correspondence.
  gaitoo suru (～する) vi. come [fall] under; apply; correspond. (⇨ atehamaru)

ga⌐itoo² がいとう (街頭) n. street.

ga⌐itoo³ がいとう (街灯) n. street lamp.

ga⌐ito¬osha がいとうしゃ (該当者) n. applicable person:
Sono shoo no gaitoosha wa inakatta. (その賞の該当者はいなかった) There was nobody *deserving* of the prize.

ga⌐iyoo がいよう (概要) n. outline; summary. (↔ shoosai)

ga⌐ka がか (画家) n. painter; artist.

-ga¬kari¹ がかり (係) suf. 1 clerk:
añnai-gakari (案内係) a *receptionist*; an *usher*.
2 section (of a company, organization, etc.). (⇨ kakari)

-ga¬kari² がかり (掛かり) suf. take; require:
Sañ-niñ-gakari de piano o ugokashita. (三人がかりでピアノを動かした) It *took* three people to move the piano.

ga⌐ke がけ (崖) n. cliff; precipice; bluff.

ga⌐keku¬zure がけくずれ (崖崩れ) n. landslide.

ga⌐kka がっか (学科) n. 1 department (of a university).
2 subject; a course of study.

ga⌐kkai がっかい (学会) n. learned society; academic conference.

ga⌐kka¬ri がっかり adv. (～ suru) be disappointed; lose heart:
Shiai ga ame de chuushi ni nari, gakkari shita. (試合が雨で中止になり、がっかりした) I *was* very *disappointed*, because the game was rained out. (⇨ shitsuboo)

ga¬kki¹ がっき (学期) n. term; semester. ★ Japanese elementary schools and junior and senior high schools have three terms. Universites and colleges have two terms. (⇨ shiñgakki)

ga¬kki² がっき (楽器) n. (musical) instrument.

ga⌐kkoo がっこう (学校) n. school.

ga¬ku¹ がく (額) n. sum; amount.

ga¬ku² がく (額) n. framed picture; frame.

ga┐ku³ がく（学）*n.* learning; knowledge; education: *Ano hito wa gaku ga aru.*（あの人は学がある）He *is well-educated.*

-gaku がく（学）*suf.* science; study: butsuri-gaku（物理学）*physics* / geñgo-gaku（言語学）*linguistics.*

ga┐kubu がくぶ（学部）*n.* college; faculty; department; school: *koo-gakubu*（工学部）the *college* of engineering / *hoo-gakubu*（法学部）the *faculty* of law. 《⇒ bu³》

ga┐kuchoo がくちょう（学長）*n.* the president of a university; chancellor.

ga┐kufu がくふ（楽譜）*n.* (sheet) music; score.

ga┐kuhi がくひ（学費）*n.* school expenses; tuition.

ga┐ku┐moñ がくもん（学問）*n.* learning; study; education.

ga┐kuneñ がくねん（学年）*n.* school [academic] year; grade.

ga┐kureki がくれき（学歴）*n.* educational background; schooling.

ga┐kuryoku がくりょく（学力）*n.* academic ability; scholarship.

ga┐kusee がくせい（学生）*n.* student. ★ Refers to older students, especially college students. 《⇒ seeto》

ga┐kusetsu がくせつ（学説）*n.* theory.

ga┐kusha がくしゃ（学者）*n.* scholar; learned man.

ga┐kushuu がくしゅう（学習）*n.* learning; study. ★ Usually refers to the process of studying. **gakushuu suru**（～する）*vt.* learn; study.

ga┐kushu┐usha がくしゅうしゃ（学習者）*n.* learner.

ga┐mañ がまん（我慢）*n.* endurance; patience; perseverance. **gamañ ga naranai**（～ならない）cannot stand. **gamañ suru**（～する）*vt.* 1 endure; stand; put up with. 《⇒ shiñboo》

2 manage; make do with: *Kono fuyu wa furui oobaa de gamañ shita.*（この冬は古いオーバーで我慢した）I *made do with* my old overcoat this winter. **gamañ-zuyoi**（～強い）be very patient.

-gamashi┐i がましい *suf.* (*a.*) (-ku) sound like; smack of: *Kare no setsumee wa iiwake-ga-mashikatta.*（彼の説明は言い訳がましかった）His explanation *sounded like* an excuse.

ga┐migami がみがみ *adv.* (～ to) (the manner of insisting or needlessly saying something): *Uchi no kachoo wa itsu-mo gami-gami (to) urusai.*（うちの課長はいつもがみがみ（と）うるさい）Our section chief *is always nagging* us.

ga┐ñ がん（癌）*n.* cancer.

ga┐ñba┐r·u がんばる（頑張る）*vi.* (-bar·i-; -bar·a-; -bat-te C) 1 work hard; persevere: *Atarashii shokuba de gañbari-masu.*（新しい職場で頑張ります）I will *do my utmost* in my new place of work. 2 insist: *Kare wa jibuñ ga tadashii to gañ-batta.*（彼は自分が正しいと頑張った）He *insisted* that he was right. **Gañbatte (ne).**（頑張って（ね））Good luck. ★ Used in giving encouragement.

ga┐ñjoo がんじょう（頑丈）*a.n.* (～ na, ni) strong; firm; sturdy: *Kono hoñbako wa gañjoo ni dekite iru.*（この本箱はがんじょうにできている）This bookcase is *well put together.*

ga┐ñka がんか（眼科）*n.* ophthalmology: gañka-i（眼科医）an *eye doctor.* 《⇒ meisha》

ga┐ñkiñ がんきん（元金）*n.* monetary principal. 《↔ rishi》

ga┐ñko がんこ（頑固）*a.n.* (～ na, ni) 1 (of a person) stubborn; obstinate. 2 (of a disease, stains, etc.)

incurable; stubborn.

ga⌐ñpeki がんぺき (岸壁) *n.* quay; wharf.

ga⌐ñrai がんらい (元来) *adv.* originally; by nature. 《⇨ hoñrai (wa)》

ga⌐ñsho がんしょ (願書) *n.* (written) application; written request.

ga⌐ppee がっぺい (合併) *n.* merger; combination; amalgamation.
gappee suru (〜する) *vi., vt.* merge; combine.

ga⌐ra がら (柄) *n.* 1 pattern; design.
2 build:
Kare wa gara ga ookii. (彼は柄が大きい) He *has a large build.*

-gara がら (柄) *suf.* 1 pattern:
hana-gara no sukaato (花柄のスカート) a skirt with a flower *pattern.*
2 pertinent to the situation:
Shigoto-gara sake o nomu kikai ga ooi. (仕事柄酒を飲む機会が多い) *My job being what it is*, I often have occasion to drink.

ga⌐ragara¹ がらがら *a.n.* (〜 na/no, ni) empty. 《⇨ kara¹》

ga⌐ragara² ガラガラ *adv* (the sound of things crashing or collapsing):
Jishiñ de tatemono ga garagara (to) kuzureta. (地震で建物がガラガラ(と)崩れた) The earthquake caused the building to *come crashing down.*

ga⌐rakuta がらくた *n.* useless articles; junk; rubbish. 《⇨ kuzu》

ga⌐ra⌐ri to ガラリと *adv.* 1 with a clatter [noise]:
to o garari to akeru (戸をガラリと開ける) slide open a door *with a noise.* ★ Used only for sliding doors.
2 (of attitude, situation, etc.) completely; suddenly:
Machi no yoosu ga garari to kawatta. (町のようすがガラリと変わった) The look of the town has changed *completely.*

ga⌐rasu ガラス *n.* glass; pane

ga⌐reeji ガレージ *n.* garage.

★ '*Gareeji*' does not refer to a place where cars are repaired and gasoline sold. 《⇨ shako》

-gari がり *suf.* (*n.*) (refers to a person sensitive to the quality suggested by the adjective): ★ Attached to the stem of an adjective to form a noun. It is often followed by '*-ya (-sañ)*,' which implies familiarity.
samu-gari no hito (寒がりの人) a person *sensitive to the cold* / sabishi-gari-ya (寂しがり屋) a person *who always feels lonely and longs for company.*

ga⌐roo がろう (画廊) *n.* gallery.
★ Refers to a store that sells art work, usually Western art.

-ga⌐r·u がる *suf.* (*vi.*) (-gar·i-; -gar·a-; -gat-te ⓒ) [attached to the stem of an adjective or adjectival noun] ★ Not used when asking others about their feelings, emotions, etc.
1 (expresses the feelings or emotions of someone other than the speaker):
Kodomo-tachi wa miñna samu-gatte iru. (子どもたちはみんな寒がっている) The children are all *complaining that they are cold.*
2 pretend:
Kare wa tsuyo-gatte iru dake da. (彼は強がっているだけだ) He is only *pretending to be strong.*

ga⌐soriñ ガソリン *n.* gasoline; petrol.

ga⌐soriñ-suta⌐ñdo ガソリンスタンド *n.* gas [filling] station.

ga⌐sshoo がっしょう (合唱) *n.* chorus; concerted singing.

ga⌐sshuku がっしゅく (合宿) *n.* lodging together for training.

ga⌐su ガス *n.* gas; dense fog.

-gata がた (方) *suf.* toward:
ake-gata (明け方) daybreak / *yuu-gata* (夕方) evening.

ga⌐tagata¹ がたがた *adv.* (〜 to; suru) 1 rattle; clatter:
Tsuyoi kaze de mado ga gatagata

(to) natta.(強い風で窓ががたがた(と)鳴った) The windows *rattled* in the strong wind.
2 shiver; tremble:
Samukute, karada ga gatagata (to) furueta.(寒くて、体ががたがた(と)震えた) My body *trembled* with cold.

ga｢tagata² がたがた *a.n.* (~ na/ no, ni) shaky; rickety:
gatagata *no teeburu* (がたがたのテーブル) a *rickety* table.

-gata｢i がたい(難い) *suf.* (*a.*) (-ku) (*formal*) difficult; impossible:
★ Added to the continuative base of a verb.
Kare no koudou wa rikai shi-gatai. (彼の行動は理解しがたい) His behavior *is difficult* to understand. (↔ -yasui) (⇨ -nikui; -zurai)

-ga｢tera (ni) がてら(に) *suf.* while; at the same time; by way of: ★ Attached to the continuative base of volitional verbs or nouns that denote action. Note that the last verb phrase indicates the main action.
Sañpo-gatera (ni), *chotto yotte mita dake desu.*(散歩がてら(に)、ちょっと寄ってみただけです) I just dropped by *while taking a walk.*

ga｢tsugatsu がつがつ *adv.* (~ to; ~ suru) hungrily; greedily:
gatsugatsu (to) *taberu* (がつがつ(と)食べる) eat *greedily.* (⇨ gabugabu)

ga｢wa がわ(側) *n.* side:
migi [*hidari*]-gawa (右[左]側) the right [left] *side* / *ryoo*-gawa (両側) both *sides.*

ga｢yagaya がやがや *adv.* (~ to) (the noise made by many people talking and laughing):
gayagaya (to) *sawagu* (がやがや(と)騒ぐ) make *a lot of noise.* (⇨ zawazawa)

ge｢ げ(下) *n.* lowest grade [class]; inferiority. (⇨ chuu¹; joo²)

-ge げ(気) *suf.* (*a.n.*) (~ na, ni) (indicates the feeling or appearance of others): ★ Attached to the stem of an adjective.
tanoshi-ge *na waraigoe* (楽しげな笑い声) *happy* laughter.

ge｢e げい(芸) *n.* **1** art; skill.
2 trick:
Inu ni gee o shikoñda.(犬に芸を仕込んだ) I taught my dog *tricks.*

ge｢ejutsu げいじゅつ(芸術) *n.* art; fine arts.

ge｢ejutsuka げいじゅつか(芸術家) *n.* artist.

ge｢enoo げいのう(芸能) *n.* public entertainment; performing arts:
geenoo-jiñ (芸能人) *public entertainer; show business personality.*

ge｢eto-booru ゲートボール *n.* 'gate ball.' ★ A variant of croquet created in Japan.

ge｢hiñ げひん(下品) *a.n.* (~ na, ni) vulgar; coarse; unrefined:
gehiñ *na kotoba o tsukau* (下品な言葉を使う) use *coarse* language. (↔ joohiñ)

ge｢juñ げじゅん(下旬) *n.* the last ten days of a month. (⇨ chuujuñ; joojuñ)

ge｢ka げか(外科) *n.* surgery:
geka-i (外科医) a *surgeon.* (⇨ naika)

ge｢ki げき(劇) *n.* drama; play.

ge｢kijoo げきじょう(劇場) *n.* theater; playhouse.

ge｢kiree げきれい(激励) *n.* encouragement; urging.
gekiree suru (~する) *vt.* encourage; cheer up.

ge｢kiyaku げきやく(劇薬) *n.* powerful drug; poison. (⇨ dokuyaku)

ge｢kkañ げっかん(月間) *n.* by the month; monthly:
gekkañ *no uriage* (月間の売り上げ) *monthly* sales. (⇨ neñkañ)

ge｢kkyuu げっきゅう(月給) *n.* monthly pay [salary]. (⇨ chiñgiñ)

ge｢koo げこう(下校) *n.* leaving school.
gekoo suru (~する) *vi.* leave school. (↔ tookoo)

ge｢ñba げんば(現場) *n.* the scene;

the spot:
Koko ga jiko-geñba desu.(ここが事
故現場です) This is the *spot* where
the accident occurred.

ge「ñbaku げんばく (原爆) *n.* =
geñshi-bakudañ.

ge「ñchi げんち (現地) *n.* the spot;
the place:
*Geñchi kara no hookoku wa mada
kite imaseñ.*(現地からの報告はまだ来
ていません) Reports from *the scene*
have not yet come in.

ge「ñdai げんだい (現代) *n.* the
present age [day]; today. (⇨ kin-
dai)

ge「ñdai-teki げんだいてき (現代的)
a.n. (~ na, ni) modern:
geñdai-teki *na keñchiku* (現代的な
建築) *modern* architecture.

ge「ñdo げんど (限度) *n.* limit;
limitations; bounds.

ge「ñgo げんご (言語) *n.* language;
speech; words. (⇨ kokugo)

ge「ñgo」gaku げんごがく (言語学)
n. linguistics.

ge「ñgo」o げんごう (元号) *n.* an era
name. 《⇨ APP. 9》

ge「ñiñ げんいん (原因) *n.* cause;
factor; origin:
kaji no geñiñ *o shiraberu* (火事の原
因を調べる) try to find the *cause* of
the fire. (↔ kekka)

ge「ñjitsu げんじつ (現実) *n.* actu-
ality; reality:
Yume ga geñjitsu *to natta.* (夢が現
実となった) The dream came *true*.

ge「ñjitsu-teki げんじつてき (現実
的) *a.n.* (~ na, ni) realistic;
down-to-earth.

ge「ñjoo げんじょう (現状) *n.* the
present condition.

ge「ñjuu げんじゅう (厳重) *a.n.*
(~ na, ni) strict; severe; strong:
Kyootee-ihañ ni taishite, geñjuu *ni
koogi shita.*(協定違反に対して、厳重
に抗議した) We made a *strong* protest against their breach of the
agreement.

ge「ñju」usho げんじゅうしょ (現住
所) *n.* one's present address.

(⇨ juusho; sumai)

ge「ñkai げんかい (限界) *n.*
boundary; limit; limitations.

ge「ñkañ げんかん (玄関) *n.* front
door; entrance; porch.

ge「ñki げんき (元気) *n.* spirits;
vigor; energy.
geñki-zukeru (~づける) *vt.* encourage.
— *a.n.* (~ na, ni) 1 well; fine;
healthy: ★ The honorific 'o' ('o-
geñki') is often used when en-
quiring about someone's health,
but never used when referring to
oneself, one's family members,
etc.
*"O-*geñki *desu ka?" "Hai,* geñki
desu."(「お元気ですか」「はい、元気で
す」) "How are you?" "*Fine*,
thank you."
2 lively; high-spirited; energetic; vigorous; active.

ge「ñki」ñ[1] げんきん (現金) *n.* cash:
geñkiñ *de harau* (現金で払う) pay
in *cash*.

ge「ñki」ñ[2] げんきん (現金) *a.n.*
(~ na, ni) calculating; merce-
nary:
Kare wa geñkiñ *na otoko da.*(彼は
現金な男だ) He is a *calculating* fellow.

ge「ñki」ñ[3] げんきん (厳禁) *n.* strict
prohibition:
Chuusha geñkiñ. (*sign*) (駐車厳禁)
No Parking.
geñkiñ suru (~する) *vt.* strictly
prohibit [forbid].

ge「ñkoo げんこう (原稿) *n.* manuscript; copy.

ge「ñkoo-yo」oshi げんこうようし
(原稿用紙) *n.* manuscript [writ-
ing] paper:
yoñhyaku-ji-zume geñkoo-yooshi
(四百字詰め原稿用紙) *manuscript
paper* with four hundred squares
for characters.

ge「ñ ni げんに (現に) *adv.* actually; really:
Watashi wa geñ ni *sore o kono
me de mimashita.*(私は現にそれをこ

の目で見ました) I *actually* saw it with my own eyes.

ge`npatsu げんぱつ (原発) *n.* nuclear power plant. ★ Abbreviation of '*genshiryoku hatsuden-sho*.' (⇨ **genshiryoku**)

ge`nri げんり (原理) *n.* principle; theory.

ge`nron げんろん (言論) *n.* speech; writing:
genron no jiyuu (言論の自由) freedom of *speech*.

ge`nryo`o げんりょう (原料) *n.* raw materials; ingredient.

ge`nsaku げんさく (原作) *n.* the original (work).

ge`nshi げんし (原子) *n.* atom.

ge`nshi-ba`kudan げんしばくだん (原子爆弾) *n.* atomic bomb. (⇨ **genbaku**)

ge`nshi`kaku げんしかく (原子核) *n.* atomic nucleus.

ge`nshi`ro げんしろ (原子炉) *n.* nuclear reactor.

ge`nshi`ryoku げんしりょく (原子力) *n.* atomic energy; nuclear power. (⇨ **genpatsu**)

ge`nsho げんしょ (原書) *n.* the original (book) written in a foreign language.

ge`nshoo[1] げんしょう (減少) *n.* decrease; diminution.
genshoo suru (〜する) *vi.* decrease; diminish; lessen. (↔ zoo-dai; zooka)

ge`nshoo[2] げんしょう (現象) *n.* phenomenon.

ge`nshu げんしゅ (厳守) *n.* strict observance; rigid adherence.
genshu suru (〜する) *vt.* observe strictly.

ge`nshuu げんしゅう (減収) *n.* decrease in income [revenue]. (↔ zooshuu)

ge`nso げんそ (元素) *n.* chemical element.

ge`nsoku げんそく (原則) *n.* principle; general rule.
gensoku to shite (〜として) in principle.

ge`nzai げんざい (現在) *n.* the present time; now. (⇨ ima')
... genzai (...〜) as of...: Hachi-gatsu tooka genzai, oobosha wa gojuu-niñ desu. (8月10日現在, 応募者は50人です) The number of applicants is fifty *as of* August 10.

ge`nzoo げんぞう (現像) *n.* (of photography) development.
genzoo suru (〜する) *vt.* develop (a film).

ge`ppu げっぷ (月賦) *n.* monthly installment [payment].

ge`ragera げらげら *adv.* (〜 to) (the act of laughing loudly): geragera (to) warau (げらげら(と)笑う) *guffaw*.

ge`ri げり (下痢) *n.* diarrhea. (⇨ kudaru)

ge`sha げしゃ (下車) *n.* getting off (a train). (↔ joosha)
gesha suru (〜する) *vi.* get off (a train). (⇨ tochuu-gesha; oriru)

ge`shi げし (夏至) *n.* summer solstice (about June 21). (⇨ tooji')

ge`shuku げしゅく (下宿) *n.*
1 boardinghouse; rooming house.
2 boarding; lodging.
geshuku suru (〜する) *vi.* board; live in a rooming house.

ge`ssha げっしゃ (月謝) *n.* monthly tuition; tuition fee.

ge`sshoku げっしょく (月食) *n.* lunar eclipse. (⇨ nisshoku)

ge`ta げた (下駄) *n.* Japanese wooden sandals.

ge`tsumatsu げつまつ (月末) *n.* the end of the month. (⇨ shuu-matsu; nenmatsu)

ge`tsuyo`o(bi) げつよう(び) (月曜(日)) *n.* Monday. (⇨ APP. 5)

gi`choo ぎちょう (議長) *n.* chairperson; the speaker.

gi`dai ぎだい (議題) *n.* topic [subject] for discussion; agenda.

gi`iñ ぎいん (議員) *n.* Diet member; member of an assembly. (⇨ Shuugiiñ; Sangiiñ)

gi`jutsu ぎじゅつ (技術) *n.* technique; technology; art; skill.

gi⌐kai ぎかい (議会) *n.* assembly; the Diet; Congress; Parliament. (⇨ kokkai)

gi⌐kyoku ぎきょく (戯曲) *n.* play; drama.

-gimi ぎみ (気味) *suf.* touch; shade:
Watashi wa kaze-gimi *desu.* (私はかぜぎみです) I have a *bit* of a cold.

gi⌐moñ ぎもん (疑問) *n.* question; doubt; problem. (⇨ utagai)

gi⌐mu ぎむ (義務) *n.* duty; obligation:
gimu *o hatasu [okotaru]* (義務を果たす[怠る]) perform [neglect] one's *duty.* (↔ keñri)

gi⌐ñ ぎん (銀) *n.* silver.

gi⌐ñkoo ぎんこう (銀行) *n.* bank:
giñkoo *ni yokiñ suru* (銀行に預金する) deposit money in a *bank.*

gi⌐ñkoⁱoiñ ぎんこういん (銀行員) *n.* bank clerk.

gi⌐ragira ぎらぎら *adv.* (~ to) (the state of shining with unpleasant brightness):
Taiyoo ga giragira *(to) teritsukete ita.* (太陽がぎらぎら(と)照りつけていた) The sun *was glaring down.* (⇨ kirakira)

gi⌐ri¹ ぎり (義理) *n.* duty; obligation; debt of gratitude:
Watashi wa kare ni giri *ga aru.* (私は彼に義理がある) I am under an *obligation* to him.
giri no ... (~の...) ...-in-law: giri *no chichi [imooto]* (義理の父[妹]) a father[sister]-*in-law.*

gi⌐roñ ぎろん (議論) *n.* argument; discussion; dispute.
giroñ *(o) suru* (~(を)する) *vt.* argue; discuss; dispute.

gi⌐see ぎせい (犠牲) *n.* 1 sacrifice: gisee *o harau* (犠牲を払う) make *sacrifices.*
2 victim:
Chichi wa señsoo no gisee *to natte shiñda.* (父は戦争の犠牲となって死んだ) My father died, a *victim* of war.

gi⌐shi ぎし (技師) *n.* engineer.

gi⌐sshi⌐ri ぎっしり *adv.* (~ to) closely; tightly; to the full:
Hoñbako ni hoñ ga gisshiri *(to) tsumatte iru.* (本箱に本がぎっしり(と)詰まっている) The bookcase is *tightly* packed with books. (⇨ ippai²; mañiñ)

go¹ ご (語) *n.* 1 language:
gaikoku-go (外国語) a foreign *language.*
2 word:
Kono go *no imi wa nañ desu ka?* (この語の意味は何ですか) What does this *word* mean?
3 term: señmoñ-go (専門語) a technical *term.*

go¹² ご (碁) *n.* (the game of) go.

go¹³ ご (五) *n.* five. (⇨ itsutsu; APP. 3)

go- ご (御) *pref.* [added to a noun, usually of Chinese origin]
1 (indicates respect toward the listener):
Go-kekkoñ *wa itsu desu ka?* (ご結婚はいつですか) When is *your marriage?*
2 (indicates humility on the part of the speaker):
Watashi ga go-añnai *itashimasu.* (私がご案内いたします) I'll *show* you *around.*

-go ご (後) *suf.* after; in:
*Kare no shujutsu-*go *no keeka wa ryookoo desu.* (彼の手術後の経過は良好です) He is doing well *after* the operation. (⇨ -mae¹)

go-⌐busata ごぶさた (御無沙汰) *n.* long silence (not having been in touch). ★ Humble form of 'busata.' This word is only used with reference to oneself.
go-busata suru *(~する)* *vi.* do not see [write] for a long time:
Go-busata *shite imasu [shimashita].* (ご無沙汰しています[しました]) I *haven't seen [written to]* you *for a long time.*

go⌐chisoo ごちそう (御馳走) *n.* treat; feast; entertainment:

Kare wa watashi ni teñpura o gochisoo shite kureta. (彼は私にてんぷらをごちそうしてくれた) He *treated* me to tempura.

go⌐chisoosama ごちそうさま (御馳走さま) 1 (used to express thanks after a meal):
Gochisoosama (deshita). (ごちそうさま(でした)) *Thank you. I really enjoyed the meal.* (⇨ itadakimasu)
2 (used to express thanks for hospitality):
Kyoo wa hoñtoo ni gochisoosama deshita. (きょうは本当にごちそうさまでした) *Thank you very much for your hospitality* today.

go⌐gaku ごがく (語学) n. language study; linguistics.

go⌐-gatsu ごがつ (五月) n. May. (⇨ APP. 5)

go⌐geñ ごげん (語源) n. origin of a word; etymology.

go⌐go ごご (午後) n. afternoon; P.M. (↔ gozeñ)

go⌐hañ ごはん (ご飯) n.
1 (cooked [boiled]) rice:
Gohañ o ni-hai tabeta. (ご飯を2杯食べた) I ate two bowls of *rice*.
2 meal; food:
Ohiru da kara gohañ ni shiyoo. (お昼だからご飯にしよう) Since it is noon, let's have *lunch*. (⇨ asa-gohañ; bañgohañ; hirugohañ)

go⌐i ごい (語彙) n. vocabulary.

go⌐ju⌐u ごじゅう (五十) n. fifty.

go⌐juu-no⌐-too ごじゅうのとう (五重の塔) n. five-storied pagoda.

go⌐ju⌐uoñ ごじゅうおん (五十音) n. the Japanese syllabary. (⇨ inside front cover)

go⌐kai ごかい (誤解) n. misunderstanding; misapprehension.
gokai (o) suru (〜(を)する) vt. misunderstand; mistake.

go⌐ka⌐ku-kee ごかくけい (五角形) n. pentagon.

go⌐kiburi ごきぶり n. cockroach.

-go⌐kko ごっこ suf. play...:
o-isha-sañ-gokko o suru (お医者さんごっこをする) play *doctor*.

-gokochi ごこち (心地) suf. feeling:
sumi-gokochi ga ii (住み心地がいい) be comfortable to *live in*.

go⌐ku ごく (極) adv. very; extremely: (⇨ kiwamete)
Sore wa goku saikiñ no dekigoto desu. (それはごく最近のでき事です) That is a *very* recent occurrence.

go⌐ku⌐roo ごくろう (ご苦労) n. trouble:
Gokuroo o kakete, mooshiwake arimaseñ. (ご苦労をかけて、申し訳ありません) I am very sorry for causing so much *trouble*.
— a.n. (〜 na/no) painful; hard:
★ Sometimes used sarcastically.
Kono samui no ni suiee to wa gokuroo na koto da. (この寒いのに水泳とはご苦労なことだ) It is an *ordeal* to go swimming when it is cold like this. (⇨ gokuroosama)

go⌐ku⌐roosama ごくろうさま (御苦労様) thank you for your trouble; thank you very much. ★ Used to express thanks for a task well done or trouble expended. Not used to superiors.

go⌐maka⌐s·u ごまかす (誤魔化す) vt. (-kash·i-; -kas·a-; -kash·i-te Ⓒ) 1 cheat; deceive; take in. (⇨ damasu)
2 tell a lie:
neñree o gomakasu (年齢をごまかす) *lie* about one's age.
3 gloss over:
Kare wa shippai o waratte gomakashita. (彼は失敗を笑ってごまかした) He *laughed off* his blunder.
4 embezzle; (of accounts) cook.

go⌐meñ[1] ごめん (御免) excuse me; pardon me; I'm sorry. ★ '*Gomeñ nasai*' is more polite. (⇨ gomeñ kudasai)

go⌐meñ[2] ごめん (御免) n. (used to express refusal):
Soñna shigoto wa gomeñ da. (そんな仕事はごめんだ) That kind of job *is not for me.*

go⌐meñ kudasa⌐i ごめんください

(御免下さい) **1** excuse me:
★ Used when arriving or taking one's leave.
Kore de shitsuree shimasu.
Gomeñ kudasai. (これで失礼します. ごめんください) I will now say good-bye here. *Please excuse me.*
2 I am sorry; pardon [forgive] me. (⇨ gomeñ¹)

go⌐meñ nasa¹i ごめんなさい (御免なさい) I am sorry; excuse me; forgive me:
Okurete gomeñ nasai. (遅れてごめんなさい) *I'm sorry* to be late.

go⌐mi¹ ごみ (塵・芥) *n.* trash; rubbish; litter; garbage. (⇨ chiri¹)

go⌐mi¹bako ごみばこ (ごみ箱) *n.* trash [garbage] can; dustbin.

go⌐mu ゴム *n.* rubber.

-goo ごう (号) *suf.* **1** number:
taifuu juusañ-goo (台風 13 号) Typhoon *No.* 13.
2 issue (of a magazine).
3 building number. (⇨ juusho)

go⌐oiñ ごういん (強引) *a.n.* (~ na, ni) forcible; high-handed:
gooiñ *na seerusumañ* (強引なセールスマン) a *high-handed* salesman.

go⌐oka ごうか (豪華) *a.n.* (~ na, ni) luxurious; magnificent:
gooka *na kekkoñ-shiki* (豪華な結婚式) a *splendid* wedding ceremony.

go⌐okaku ごうかく (合格) *n.* passing (an examination); success.
gookaku suru (~ する) *vi.* pass; succeed: *keñsa ni* gookaku suru (検査に合格する) *pass* an inspection.

go⌐okee ごうけい (合計) *n.* total; sum; the sum total.
gookee suru (~ する) *vt.* sum up; total. (⇨ sashihiki)

go⌐orika ごうりか (合理化) *n.* rationalization.
goorika suru (~ する) *vt.* rationalize.

go⌐ori-teki ごうりてき (合理的) *a.n.* (~ na, ni) rational; reasonable; practical:
kaji o goori-teki ni suru (家事を合

理的にする) *streamline* housework.

go⌐orudeñ-ui¹iku ゴールデンウイーク *n.* 'Golden Week.' ★ Refers to the period from April 29 to May 5, which is full of national holidays. (⇨ APP. 6)

go⌐oru¹-iñ ゴールイン *n.* finish; breasting the tape.
gooru-iñ suru (~ する) **1** reach the finish line.
2 get married: *Futari wa yatto* gooru-iñ shita. (二人はやっとゴールインした) The two of them finally *got married.*

go⌐osee ごうせい (合成) *n.* synthesis; composition:
goosee-*señi* (合成繊維) *synthetic* fiber.

go⌐otoo ごうとう (強盗) *n.* **1** burglar; robber. (⇨ dorobo)
2 robbery:
gootoo *o hataraku* (強盗をはたらく) commit a *robbery.*

go⌐raku ごらく (娯楽) *n.* amusement; recreation; entertainment.

go⌐rañ ごらん (ご覧) *n.* (*honorific*) **1** see; look at:
Kore o gorañ *kudasai.* (これをご覧ください) Please *look at* this.
2 try:
Moo ichi-do yatte gorañ nasai (もう一度やってご覧なさい) *Try* it again.

-go⌐ro ごろ (頃) *suf.* about; around:
Juuji-goro *uchi ni kite kudasai.* (10 時ごろうちに来てください) I would like you to come to my house at *about* ten o'clock. (⇨ koro)

go⌐rogoro ごろごろ *adv.* (~ to) **1** (the sound of rolling, rumbling and purring):
Kaminari ga gorogoro (to) *natte iru.* (雷がゴロゴロ(と)鳴っている) The thunder *is rolling.*
2 (the state of something rolling):
Ooki-na iwa ga yama no shameñ o gorogoro (to) *ochite itta.* (大きな岩が山の斜面をゴロゴロ(と)落ちて行った) A large rock *rolled down* the

mountainside.

3 (the state of being plentiful):
Suisu de wa ni-ka-koku-go o hana-seru hito ga gorogoro *iru.* (スイスでは2か国語を話せる人がごろごろいる) In Switzerland *there are many* who can speak two languages.

4 (the state of being lazy):
Kare wa yasumi-juu ie de goro-goro (to) shite ita. (彼は休み中家でごろごろ(と)していた) He *lolled around* the house all through the holidays.

go'ro'ri ごろり *adv.* (~ to) (used to express the action of lying down):
Kare wa gorori *to tatami no ue ni yoko ni natta.* (彼はごろりと畳の上に横になった) He *plopped himself down* full length on the tatami.

-goshi ごし(越し) *suf.* **1** through; over:
*Kare wa megane-*goshi *ni watashi o niramitsuketa.* (彼は眼鏡越しに私をにらみつけた) He glared at me *over* his glasses.

2 [after a noun denoting a long period of time] for; over:
*Go-neñ-*goshi *no koi ga minotte, futari wa kekkoñ shita.* (五年越しの恋が実って、二人は結婚した) Their love of *five years* matured and they got married.

-goto ごと *suf.* and all; together with:
*riñgo o kawa-*goto *taberu* (りんごを皮ごと食べる) eat an apple, peel *and all*.

-go'to ni ごとに *suf.* **1** every; each:
*Sooji tooban wa ik-kagetsu-*goto *ni kawarimasu.* (掃除当番は1か月ごとに替わります) Cleaning duty changes *every* month.

2 every time; whenever; whoever:
*Kare wa au hito-*goto *ni sono hanashi o shite iru.* (彼は会う人ごとにその話をしている) He tells that story to *whoever* he meets.

go'zaima'su ございます(御座居ます) be; have; there is [are]:
★ Polite equivalent of '*arimasu.*' The polite equivalent of '*desu*' is '*de gozaimasu.*'
Nani-ka go-yoo ga gozaimashi-tara, o-shirase kudasai. (何かご用がございましたら、お知らせください) If *there is* anything I can do for you, please let me know.
Arigatoo gozaimasu. (ありがとうございます) Thank you very much.
Ohayoo gozaimasu. (お早うございます) Good morning.

go'zeñ ごぜん(午前) *n.* forenoon; morning; A.M. (↔ gogo) (⇨ asa)

go'zeñ-chuu ごぜんちゅう(午前中) *n., adv.* in the morning; any time from sunrise to noon.

go'zo'ñji ごぞんじ(ご存じ) (*honorific*) know; be aware:
*Kare no atarashii juusho o go-*zoñji *desu ka?* (彼の新しい住所をご存じですか) Do you *know* his new address? (⇨ zoñjiru)

gu'ai ぐあい(具合) *n.* **1** condition:
Onaka no guai *ga okashii.* (おなかのぐあいがおかしい) I *am sick* to my stomach.

2 convenience:
Kare wa guai *no warui toki ni yatte kita.* (彼はぐあいの悪いときにやって来た) He showed up at an *inconvenient* time.

3 manner; way:
Koñna guai *ni yareba, umaku iki-masu.* (こんなぐあいにやれば、うまく行きます) If you do it *this way*, you will succeed.

gu'ñ¹ ぐん(群) *n.* group; crowd.
guñ o nuku (~を抜く) excel [surpass] all.

gu'ñ² ぐん(軍) *n.* force; army; troops. (⇨ Jieitai)

gu'ñ³ ぐん(郡) *n.* county; district.

gu'ñbi ぐんび(軍備) *n.* armaments; military preparations.

gu'ñguñ ぐんぐん *adv.* (~ to) quickly; rapidly; steadily;

shiñchoo ga gunguñ (to) *nobiru* (身長がぐんぐん(と)伸びる) *shoot up* in height.

guʳñji-eˈñjo くんじえんじょ (軍事援助) *n.* military aid.

guˈñjiñ くんじん (軍人) *n.* military man; soldier; sailor; airman.

guˈñkañ くんかん (軍艦) *n.* warship; man-of-war.

guˈñshuu くんしゅう (群衆・群集) *n.* crowd; throng; mob.

guˈñtai くんたい (軍隊) *n.* armed forces; troops.

guˈñtoo くんとう (群島) *n.* a group of islands; archipelago. (⇨ rettoo¹)

guˈragura くらくら *adv.* (~ to)
1 (unstable shaking or moving): *Jishiñ de ie ga* guragura *(to) yureta.* (地震で家がぐらぐら(と)揺れた) The house shook *unsteadily* in the earthquake.
2 (the state of water boiling): *Yakañ no yu ga* guragura *(to) nitatte iru.* (やかんの湯がぐらぐら(と)煮立っている) The water in the kettle is boiling *vigorously*.

guˈrai くらい (位) *p.* = kurai².

guˈramu グラム *n.* gram.

guˈrañdo グランド *n.* playground; sports ground; stadium.

guˈriiñsha グリーンしゃ (グリーン車) *n.* 'green car'; first-class railway carriage.

guˈroˈobu グローブ *n.* glove.

guˈruguru ぐるぐる *adv.* (~ to) (the state of something moving around or rotating continuously): *Kare wa te o* guruguru *(to) mawashite aizu shita.* (彼は手をぐるぐる(と)回して合図した) He signaled by *waving* his hand *around*.

guˈruˈri ぐるり *adv.* = gurutto.

guˈruˈtto ぐるっと *adv.* (the action of looking around or the feeling of being completely surrounded): *koosoo-biru ni* gurutto *torikakomareta kooeñ* (高層ビルにぐるっと取り囲まれた公園) a park *completely* surrounded by high-rise buildings.

guˈssuˈri ぐっすり *adv.* (~ to) (the state of sleeping soundly): *Yuube wa* gussuri *(to) nemureta.* (ゆうべはぐっすり(と)眠れた) I was able to sleep *soundly* last night.

guˈtai-teki くたいてき (具体的) *a.n.* (~ na, ni) concrete; definite; physical: gutai-teki *na ree o ageru* (具体的な例をあげる) give *concrete* examples. (↔ chuushoo-teki)

guˈtto くっと *adv.* 1 suddenly; firmly; fast; hard: gutto *tsukamu* (くっとつかむ) grasp *firmly* / gutto *hipparu* (くっと引っ張る) pull *with a jerk*.
2 much; by far: *Kotchi no hoo ga* gutto *hikitatsu.* (こっちのほうがくっと引き立つ) This one looks *much* better.

guˈuguu くうくう *adv.* (~ to) (the sound of snoring or of an empty stomach): *Kare wa* guuguu *(to) ooki-na ibiki o kaite ita.* (彼はグウグウ(と)大きないびきをかいていた) He was snoring *loudly*.

guˈusuˈu くうすう (偶数) *n.* even number(s). (↔ kisuu)

guˈuzeñ くうぜん (偶然) *a.n.* (~ na/no, ni) chance; accident: guuzeñ *no dekigoto* (偶然の出来事) a *chance* occurrence.
— *adv.* by chance: *Watashi wa* guuzeñ*, sono jiko geñba ni ita.* (私は偶然、その事故現場にいた) I just *happened to be* at the scene of the accident. (⇨ tamatama)

guˈzuguzu くずくず *adv.* (~ to; ~ suru) slowly; lazily: *Guzuguzu shite iru to, okuremasu yo.* (ぐずぐずしていると、遅れますよ) If you *dawdle along*, you will be late.
guzuguzu *iu* (〜言う) grumble; complain. (⇨ fuhee)

gyaˈku ぎゃく (逆) *n.* reverse; contrary; opposite.

— *a.n.* (~ na/no, ni) reverse; contrary; opposite:
gyaku no hookoo (逆の方向) the *opposite* direction.

gyo¹gyoo ぎょぎょう (漁業) *n.* fishery; fishing industry. (⇨ noogyoo)

gyo¹kuro ぎょくろ (玉露) *n.* green tea of the highest quality. (⇨ bañcha; señcha)

gyo¹o ぎょう (行) *n.* **1** row of words; line:
ichi gyoo oki ni kaku (一行おきに書く) write on every other *line*.
2 (of the Japanese syllabary) series;
gojuuoñ-zu no ka gyoo (五十音図のカ行) the 'k' *series* in the list of the Japanese syllabary. (⇨ inside front cover)

gyo¹ogi ぎょうぎ (行儀) *n.* manners; behavior.

gyo¹oji ぎょうじ (行事) *n.* event; function.

gyo¹oretsu ぎょうれつ (行列) *n.*
1 line; queue.
2 procession; parade:
soogi no gyooretsu (葬儀の行列) a funeral *procession*.
gyooretsu suru (~する) *vi.* stand in line; queue up.

gyo¹osee ぎょうせい (行政) *n.* administration:

gyoosee-kaikaku (行政改革) *administrative* reform. (⇨ sañkeñbuñritsu)

gyo¹oseki ぎょうせき (業績) *n.* achievements; results; work:
Kaisha no gyooseki wa amari yoku arimaseñ. (会社の業績はあまり良くありません) Company *business* is not so good.

gyo¹osha ぎょうしゃ (業者) *n.* dealer; trader; manufacturer.

gyo¹oza ぎょうざ *n.* Chinese dumplings.

gyo¹señ ぎょせん (漁船) *n.* fishing boat [vessel].

gyo¹soñ ぎょそん (漁村) *n.* fishing village.

gyo¹tto s·uru ぎょっとする *vi.* (sh·i-; sh·i-; sh·i-te ▢) be startled; be frightened.

gyu¹ugyuu ぎゅうぎゅう *adv.* (~ to, ni) (the state of squeezing something, or of it being tightly packed):
Watashi wa kabañ ni irui o gyuugyuu (to [ni]) tsumeta. (私はかばんに衣類をぎゅうぎゅう(と[に])詰めた) I *squeezed* my clothes into the bag.

gyu¹uniku ぎゅうにく (牛肉) *n.* beef. (⇨ niku)

gyu¹unyuu ぎゅうにゅう (牛乳) *n.* cow's milk.

H

ha¹¹ は (歯) *n.* tooth:
ha o migaku (歯を磨く) brush one's *teeth*.
ha ga tatanai (~がたたない) be beyond one's power.

ha¹² は (刃) *n.* edge; blade.

ha³ は (葉) *n.* leaf; foliage.

ha¹a¹ はあ *int.* yes; indeed; well:
"Issho ni ikimasu ka?" "Haa, ikimasu." (「一緒に行きますか」「はあ、行きます」) "Are you coming with me?" "*Yes*, I am." (⇨ hai¹)

ha¹a² はあ *int.* what: ★ With a rising tone.
"Raishuu Chuugoku e ikimasu." "Haa?" (「来週中国へ行きます」「はあ」) "I am going to China next week." "*What did you say?*"

ha¹aku はあく (把握) *n.* grasp; hold; grip. ★ Usually used figuratively.
haaku suru (~する) *vt.* grasp; hold; seize: jitai o haaku suru (事態を把握する) *grasp* the situation.

(⇨ rikai; tsukamu)

ha⌈ba はば (幅) *n.* width; range; breadth. (⇨ nagasa; takasa)

ha⌈ba⌉m·u はばむ (阻む) *vt.* (habam·i·; habam·a·; habañ·de C) prevent; block; check. (⇨ jama)

ha⌈bu⌉k·u はぶく (省く) *vt.* (habuk·i·; habuk·a·; habu·i·te C) cut down; save; omit:
tema o habuku (手間を省く) *save a* labor.

ha⌈bu⌉rashi はブラシ (歯ブラシ) *n.* toothbrush.

ha⌈chi⌉[1] はち (八) *n.* eight. (⇨ yattsu; APP. 3)

ha⌈chi⌉[2] はち (鉢) *n.* flower pot; container; bowl; basin. (⇨ chawañ; doñburi)

ha⌈chi⌉[3] はち (蜂) *n.* bee; wasp.

ha⌈chi-gatsu はちがつ (八月) *n.* August. (⇨ APP. 5)

ha⌈chi⌉maki はちまき (鉢巻き) *n.* headband.

ha⌈da はだ (肌) *n.* **1** skin:
Kanojo wa hada ga shiroi. (彼女は肌が白い) She has fair *skin.*
2 temperament:
Kare wa geejutsuka-hada da. (彼は芸術家肌だ) He has an artistic *temperament.*

ha⌈dagi⌉[1] はだぎ (肌着) *n.* underwear; underclothes.

ha⌈daka はだか (裸) *n.* naked body; nakedness; nudity.

ha⌈dashi はだし (裸足) *n.* bare foot.

ha⌈de⌉[1] はで (派手) *a.n.* (~ na, ni)
1 showy; bright; gaudy:
Kono fuku wa sukoshi hade-sugiru. (この服は少し派手すぎる) This garment is a bit too *gaudy.* (↔ jimi)
2 spectacular; conspicuous:
Futari wa hade na keñka o shita. (二人は派手なけんかをした) The two of them had a *spectacular* fight.
3 lavish:
hade ni kane o tsukau (派手に金を使う) spend money *lavishly.*

ha⌈e はえ (蝿) *n.* fly.

ha⌈e⌉·ru[1] はえる (生える) *vi.* (hae·te V) **1** (of a plant) come out; grow:
Kono ki wa nettai dake ni haete iru. (この木は熱帯だけに生えている) This tree *grows* only in tropical regions.
2 (of tooth, hair, etc.) grow:
Akañboo ni ha ga haeta. (赤ん坊に歯が生えた) The baby *cut* a tooth. (⇨ hayasu)

ha⌈e⌉·ru[2] はえる (映える) *vi.* (hae·te V) **1** shine:
Fuji-sañ ga asahi ni haete, utsukushii. (富士山が朝日に映えて、美しい) Mt. Fuji is beautiful—*shining* in the morning sun.
2 look beautiful:
Kanojo ni wa shiroi doresu ga yoku haeru. (彼女には白いドレスがよく映える) White dresses *look very nice* on her.

ha⌈gaki はがき (葉書) *n.* postcard. (⇨ e-hagaki; oofuku-hagaki)

ha⌈gare⌉·ru はがれる (剥がれる) *vi.* (hagare·te V) peel [come] off:
Posutaa ga kaze de hagarete shimatta. (ポスターが風ではがれてしまった) The poster *came off* in the wind. (⇨ hagasu)

ha⌈ga⌉s·u はがす (剥がす) *vt.* (hagash·i·; hagas·a·; hagash·i·te C) peel off:
Fuutoo kara kitte o hagashita. (封筒から切手をはがした) I *peeled* the stamp off the envelope. (⇨ hagu; hagareru)

ha⌈gema⌉s·u はげます (励ます) *vt.* (-mash·i·; -mas·a·; -mash·i·te C) encourage; cheer up.

ha⌈ge⌉m·u はげむ (励む) *vi.* (hagem·i·; hagem·a·; hageñ·de C) work hard; apply oneself to.

ha⌈ge⌉·ru[1] はげる (剥げる) *vi.* (hage·te V) **1** come off; wear off:
Tokorodokoro peñki ga hagete iru. (ところどころペンキがはげている) The paint *has come off* in places. (⇨ hagasu)
2 (of color) fade. (⇨ aseru[2])

haˈge·ˌruˀ² はげる (禿る) *vi.* (hage-te Ⅴ) become bald: *Kare wa sukoshi* hagete iru. (彼は少しはげている) He *is* slightly *bald*.

haˈgeshiˌi·i はげしい (激しい) *a.* (-ku) intense; violent; severe: hageshii *atsusa* (激しい暑さ) *intense* heat / hageshii *itami* (激しい痛み) an *acute* pain.

haˈg·u はぐ (剥ぐ) *vt.* (hag·i-; hag·a-; ha·i-de Ⅽ) tear off; strip off; remove the skin. (⇨ hagasu)

haˈguˌruma はぐるま (歯車) *n.* cogwheel; gear.

haˈha はは (母) *n.* mother. (↔ chichiˌ) (⇨ haha-oya)

haˈhaa ははあ *int.* well; I see; oh; now: Hahaa, *sore de wakarimashita.* (はは あ、それでわかりました) *I see.* I understand now.

haˈha-oya ははおや (母親) *n.* female parent; mother. (↔ chichi-oya) (⇨ haha)

haˈiˀ¹ はい *int.* 1 yes; no: ★ '*Hai*' literally means 'That's right' and is used to confirm a statement, whether affirmative or negative. "*Kore wa kawa desu ka?*" "Hai, *soo desu.*" (「これは革ですか」「はい、そうです」) "Is this leather?" "*Yes*, it is." / "*Anata wa Nihoñ no kata de wa arimaseñ ne?*" "Hai, *Chuugokujiñ desu.*" (「あなたは日本の方ではありませんね」「はい、中国人です」) "You aren't Japanese, are you?" "*No*, I'm Chinese." (↔ iie)
2 (when the roll is called) yes; here; present: "*Suzuki(-kuñ).*" "Hai." (「鈴木(君)」「はい」) "Suzuki." "*Here.*"
3 certainly; of course: "*Deñwa o o-kari shite yoroshii desu ka?*" "Hai, *doozo.*" (「電話をお借りしてよろしいですか」「はい、どうぞ」) "May I use your phone?" "*Certainly.* Please go ahead."

haˈiˀ² はい (灰) *n.* ash.

haˈiˀ³ はい (肺) *n.* lungs.

-hai はい (杯) *suf.* cup; glass; bowl. ★ Liquid measure counter used to count glassfuls or cupfuls. (⇨ APP. 4)

haˈiagaˌru はいあがる (這い上がる) *vt.* (-agar·i-; -agar·a-; -agat-te Ⅽ) creep up; crawl up: *Kono gake o* haiagaru *no wa muzukashii.* (このがけをはい上がるのは難しい) It is difficult to *climb up* this cliff.

haˈiboku はいぼく (敗北) *n.* defeat. haiboku suru (～する) *vi.* be defeated be beaten. (↔ shoori) (⇨ makeru)

haˈiboˌoru ハイボール *n.* highball. ★ In Japan, refers to whisky and soda. (⇨ mizuwari)

haˈichi はいち (配置) *n.* arrangement; stationing. haichi suru (～する) *vt.* arrange; station; post.

haˈigañ はいがん (肺癌) *n.* lung cancer. (⇨ gañ)

haˈiguˌusha はいぐうしゃ (配偶者) *n.* (*legal*) spouse; one's husband; one's wife.

haˈi-iro はいいろ (灰色) *n.* gray.

haˈikeeˀ¹ はいけい (拝啓) *n.* Dear...; Gentlemen; Dear Sir or Madam. ★ Used in the salutation of a formal letter. (⇨ keegu; zeñryaku)

haˈikeeˀ² はいけい (背景) *n.* 1 background.
2 scenery; setting; scene: *Sono monogatari no* haikee *wa Yokohama desu.* (その物語の背景は横浜です) The *setting* of the story is Yokohama.

haˈikeñ はいけん (拝見) *n.* (humble equivalent of 'see' or 'read'): "*Doozo.*" "*De wa chotto* haikeñ." (「どうぞ」「ではちょっと拝見」) "Please go ahead." "Then let me *have a look* at it."
haikeñ suru (～する) *vt.* (*humble*) see; look at; watch; read: *O-tegami o* haikeñ shimashita. (お手紙を拝見しました) I *have read* your letter.

ha⌐ikiñgu ハイキング *n.* hike; hiking.

ha⌐iku はいく (俳句) *n.* haiku.
★ A poem with lines of five, seven, and five syllables.

ha⌐iretsu はいれつ (配列) *n.* arrangement; placement in order.
hairetsu suru (～する) *vt.* arrange; place in order.

ha⌐ir·u はいる (入る) *vi.* (hair·i-; hair·a-; hait-te C) ★ '*haitte iru*' =be in [inside]. 1 enter; come [go] in:
Deñsha ga hoomu ni haitte kita. (電車がホームに入ってきた) The train *pulled in* to the platform.
2 be admitted; enter; join:
daigaku ni hairu (大学に入る) *matriculate* at a university.
3 contain; include:
Kono biiru ni wa amari arukooru ga haitte imaseñ. (このビールにはあまりアルコールが入っていません) This beer *does not contain* much alcohol.
4 hold; seat:
Kono gekijoo wa gohyaku-niñ hairu. (この劇場は500人入る) This theater *accommodates* 500 people.
5 (of a season, a vacation, etc.) begin; set in:
Moo tsuyu ni hairimashita. (もう梅雨に入りました) We have already *entered* the rainy season.
6 get; obtain; have:
Dai-nyuusu ga haitta. (大ニュースが入った) We *have had* some big news.
7 be installed:
Kaku heya ni deñwa ga haitta. (各部屋に電話が入った) Telephones *have been installed* in each room. (⇨ setchi)

ha⌐iseki はいせき (排斥) *n.* exclusion; boycott; shut-out.
haiseki suru (～する) *vt.* expel; boycott; shut out.

ha⌐iseñ はいせん (敗戦) *n.* loss of a battle [game]; defeat.

ha⌐isha¹ はいしゃ (歯医者) *n.* dentist. (⇨ isha)

ha⌐isha² はいしゃ (敗者) *n.* loser; defeated peson. (↔ shoosha²)

ha⌐ishi はいし (廃止) *n.* abolition; discontinuance; repeal.
haishi suru (～する) *vt.* abolish; discontinue; repeal.

ha⌐isui はいすい (排水) *n.* draining; drainage.
haisui suru (～する) *vt.* drain; pump water out.

ha⌐itatsu はいたつ (配達) *n.* delivery.
haitatsu suru (～する) *vt.* deliver (newspapers, letters, etc.).

ha⌐iyaa ハイヤー *n.* chauffeur-driven limousine. ★ From 'hire.' (⇨ takushii)

ha⌐iyuu はいゆう (俳優) *n.* actor; actress. (⇨ yakusha)

ha⌐izara はいざら (灰皿) *n.* ashtray.

ha⌐ji¹ はじ (恥) *n.* shame; disgrace; humiliation:
Watashi wa miñna no mae de haji o kaita. (私はみんなの前で恥をかいた) I was put to *shame* in public.

ha⌐jike¹·ru はじける (弾ける) *vi.* (hajike-te V) burst [crack] open; pop:
Kuri ga hi no naka de hajiketa. (栗が火の中ではじけた) The chestnut *burst open* in the fire. (⇨ hajiku)

ha⌐ji¹k·u はじく (弾く) *vt.* (hajik·i-; hajik·a-; haji·i-te C) flip; fillip; repel:
Kono reeñkooto wa ame o yoku hajikimasu. (このレインコートは雨をよくはじきます) This raincoat *repels* rain well. (⇨ hajikeru)

ha⌐jimar·u はじまる (始まる) *vi.* (hajimar·i-; hajimar·a-; hajimat-te C) begin; start. (⇨ hajimeru)

ha⌐jime はじめ (初め) *n.* beginning; start:
Watashi wa kotoshi no hajime ni Nihoñ e kimashita. (私は今年の初めに日本へ来ました) I came to Japan at the *beginning* of this year.

ha⌐jimema¹shite はじめまして (始

めまして) How do you do?; I'm glad to meet you.

ha┌jime‧ru はじめる (始める) vt. (hajime-te V) begin; start: *Sore de wa jugyoo o* hajimemasu. (それでは授業を始めます) Now we'll *begin* the lesson. (⇨ hajimaru)

-hajime‧ru はじめる (始める) (-hajime-te V) start (doing): ★ Occurs as the second element of compound verbs. Added to the continuative base of a verb. *yomi*-hajimeru (読み始める) *start* reading / *tabe*-hajimeru (食べ始める) *begin* eating. (⇨ -dasu (3))

ha┌ji┌mete はじめて (初めて) adv. first; for the first time: *Fuji-sañ o mita no wa kore ga* haji-mete *desu.* (富士山を見たのはこれが初めてです) This is *the first time* that I have seen Mt. Fuji.

ha┌ji‧ru はじる (恥じる) vi. (haji-te V) feel ashamed: *Watashi wa jibuñ no chikara-busoku o* hajite iru. (私は自分の力不足を恥じている) I *am ashamed* of my lack of ability.

ha┌ka はか (墓) n. grave; tomb.

ha┌kai はかい (破壊) n. destruction; demolition.
   hakai suru (〜する) vt. destroy; demolish.

ha┌kai-teki はかいてき (破壊的) a.n. (〜 na, ni) destructive.

ha┌kama はかま (袴) n. Long pleated trousers chiefly worn by men over a kimono.

ha┌kama┌iri はかまいり (墓参り) n. visit to a grave. (⇨ higañ)

ha┌kari はかり (秤) n. balance; scales.

ha┌ka┌r‧u はかる (計る) vt. (hakar-i-; hakar‧a-; hakat-te C)
   1 record the time; time: *kuruma no sokudo o* hakaru (車の速度を計る) *time* the speed of a car.
   2 measure (blood pressure or temperature); take.

ha┌ka┌r‧u はかる (量る) vt. (hakar-i-; hakar‧a-; hakat-te C)

weigh; measure: *taijuukee de taijuu o* hakaru (体重計で体重を量る) *weigh* oneself on scales / *komugiko no ryoo o kappu de* hakaru (小麦粉の量をカップで量る) *measure* the amount of flour with a measuring cup.

ha┌ka┌r‧u はかる (測る) vt. (hakar-i-; hakar‧a-; hakat-te C)
   1 take the measurement; fathom: *kawa no fukasa o* hakaru (川の深さを測る) *measure* the depth of a river.
   2 = hakaru[2].

ha┌ka┌r‧u はかる (図る) vt. (hakar-i-; hakar‧a-; hakat-te C)
   1 strive; make an effort: *imeeji-appu o* hakaru (イメージアップを図る) *strive* to improve one's image.
   2 plan; attempt: *jisatsu o* hakaru (自殺を図る) *attempt* suicide.

ha┌ka┌r‧u はかる (謀る) vt. (hakar-i-; hakar‧a-; hakat-te C)
plot; attempt: *shushoo no añsatsu o* hakaru (首相の暗殺を謀る) *plot* the assassination of the prime minister.

ha┌kase はかせ (博士) n. doctor. (⇨ hakushi[1])

ha┌ke はけ (刷毛) n. flat brush. (⇨ burashi)

ha┌keñ はけん (派遣) n. dispatch.
   hakeñ suru (〜する) vt. dispatch; send.

ha┌kihaki はきはき adv. (〜 to) crisply; briskly; smartly: *Kanojo wa shitsumoñ ni* hakihaki (to) *kotaeta.* (彼女は質問にはきはき(と)答えた) She *briskly* replied to the questions.

ha┌kimono はきもの (履物) n. footwear; shoes.

ha┌kkeñ はっけん (発見) n. discovery; detection.
   hakkeñ suru (〜する) vt. discover; find; detect. (⇨ mitsukeru)

ha┌kki はっき (発揮) n. demonstration; display.

hakki suru (～する) *vt.* demonstrate; display; show: *jitsuryoku o hakki suru* (実力を発揮する) *show* one's ability.

ha⌐kki¬ri はっきり *adv.* (～ to; ～ suru) clearly; distinctly; definitely:
Sono koto wa asu ni nareba, hakkiri *shimasu.* (そのことは明日になれば、はっきりします) The matter will become *clear* tomorrow.
(⇨ akiraka)

ha⌐kkoo はっこう (発行) *n.* publication; issue.
hakkoo suru (～する) *vt.* publish; issue (a magazine). (⇨ dasu (3))

ha⌐kkutsu はっくつ (発掘) *n.* digging; excavation.
hakkutsu suru (～する) *vt.* dig out; unearth; excavate.

ha⌐ko はこ (箱) *n.* box; case.

ha⌐kob·u はこぶ (運ぶ) (hakob·i-; hakob·a-; hakoñ-de [C])
1 *vt.* carry; transport:
Keganiñ wa kyuukyuusha de byooiñ ni hakobareta. (けが人は救急車で病院に運ばれた) The injured *were taken* to the hospital by ambulance.
2 *vt.* move forward; carry out:
umaku koto o hakobu (うまくことを運ぶ) *carry out* a plan smoothly.
3 *vi.* make progress; go:
Shigoto wa umaku hakoñde imasu. (仕事はうまく運んでいます) The work *is going* forward nicely.

ha⌐k·u¬¹ はく (履く) *vt.* (hak·i-; hak·a-; ha·i-te [C]) put on (footwear, trousers, skirts, etc.):
★ 'haite iru' = wear.
Kono jiiñzu o haite mite mo ii desu ka? (このジーンズをはいてみてもいいですか) May I *try* on these jeans?

ha⌐k·u¬² はく (掃く) *vt.* (hak·i-; hak·a-; ha·i-te [C]) sweep:
niwa o haku (庭を掃く) *sweep* the garden.

ha⌐k·u¬³ はく (吐く) *vt.* (hak·i-; hak·a-; ha·i-te [C]) 1 vomit; spit:
Michi ni tsuba o haite wa ikema-

señ. (道につばを吐いてはいけません)
You must not *spit* on the street.
2 send out; emit; belch:
Yukkuri iki o haite kudasai. (ゆっくり息を吐いてください) Please *breathe out* slowly.

-haku はく (泊) *suf.* counter for overnight stays.
(⇨ tomaru²; APP. 4)

ha⌐kubutsu¬kañ はくぶつかん (博物館) *n.* museum.

ha⌐kusa¬i はくさい (白菜) *n.* Chinese cabbage.

ha⌐kuseñ はくせん (白線) *n.* white line:
Hakuseñ no uchigawa ni o-sagari kudasai. (station announcement) (白線の内側にお下がりください) Please keep behind the *warning line.*

ha⌐kushi¬¹ はくし (博士) *n.* doctor:
buñgaku-hakushi (文学博士) a *Doctor* of Literature. (⇨ hakase)

ha⌐kushi¬² はくし (白紙) *n.* white paper; blank paper.
hakushi ni modosu (～に戻す) make a fresh start.

ha⌐kushu はくしゅ (拍手) *n.* applause; hand clapping.
hakushu suru (～する) *vi.* clap one's hands.

ha⌐me·ru はめる (嵌める) *vt.* (hame-te [V]) 1 put on (gloves, rings, etc.): ★ 'hamete iru' = have on; wear.
Kare wa kawa no tebukuro o hamete ita. (彼は革の手袋をはめていた) He *was wearing* leather gloves.
2 fit; put:
Watashi wa sono e o gaku ni hameta. (私はその絵を額にはめた) I *set* the picture into the frame.
3 take in; entrap:
hito o wana ni hameru (人をわなにはめる) *entrap* a person.

ha⌐mi¬gaki はみがき (歯磨き) *n.* toothpaste; dental cream.

ha⌐ñ¬¹ はん (班) *n.* group; squad.

ha⌐ñ¬² はん (判) *n.* seal; stamp.
★ A seal is used in Japan instead

of a signature. (⇒ iñkañ)

ha「ñ³ はん (版) *n*. edition; printing:

*Kono jisho wa go-*hañ *o kasaneta.*
(この辞書は 5 版を重ねた) This dictionary has gone through five *printings*.

hañ- はん (反) *pref*. **1** anti-:
hañ-*kaku uñdoo* (反核運動) an *anti*-nuclear campaign.

2 re-:
hañ-*sayoo* (反作用) a *reaction*.

-ha「ñ はん (半) *suf*. half:
*Kesa wa go-ji-*hañ *ni okimashita.*
(今朝は 5 時半に起きました) I got up *at five thirty this morning*.

ha「na¹ はな (鼻) *n*. **1** (of a human being) nose.

2 (of an animal) muzzle; snout; trunk.

3 nasal mucus:
Hana o kami nasai. (はなをかみなさい)
Blow your *nose*.

4 the sense of smell:
Kare wa hana ga kiku. (彼は鼻がきく) He has a good *nose*.

ha「na¹² はな (花) *n*. flower; blossom. (⇒ o-hana)

ha「nabanashi¹·**i** はなばなしい (華々しい) *a*. (-ku) brilliant; splendid; active:
hanabanashii *katsuyaku o suru* (はなばなしい活躍をする) lead an *active* career.

ha「nabi はなび (花火) *n*. fireworks; sparkler.

ha「nabi¹**ra** はなびら (花びら) *n*. petal.

ha「nahada はなはだ (甚だ) *adv*. (*formal*) very; greatly; extremely:
Sono soo-oñ wa hanahada *mee-waku da.* (その騒音ははなはだ迷惑だ)
The noise is *terribly* annoying.

ha「nahadashi¹·**i** はなはだしい (甚だしい) *a*. (-ku) serious; gross; excessive:
Mattaku gokai mo hanahadashii.
(全く誤解もはなはだしい) It is a *gross* misunderstanding.

ha「nami¹ はなみ (花見) *n*. cherry blossom viewing. ★ Often with '*o-*.'

ha「namu¹**ko** はなむこ (花婿) *n*. bridegroom. (↔ hanayome)

ha「nare-ba¹**nare** はなればなれ (離れ離れ) *n*. being separated; being split up:
hanare-banare *ni kurasu* (離ればなれに暮らす) live *separately*.

ha「nare¹·**ru**¹ はなれる (離れる) *vi*. (hanare-te Ⓥ) **1** separate; be separated:
Kare wa kazoku to hanarete, *kurashite iru.* (彼は家族と離れて、暮らしている) He is living *apart* from his family. (⇒ hanasu²)

2 leave:
kokyoo o hanareru (故郷を離れる)
leave one's hometown.

3 be away from; be apart from:
Watashi no ie wa eki kara ni-kiro hanarete imasu. (私の家は駅から 2 キロ離れています) My house *is* two-kilometers *away* from the station.

ha「nare¹·**ru**² はなれる (放れる) *vi*. (hanare-te Ⓥ) get free:
Tora ga ori o hanarete *nigeta.* (虎がおりを放れて逃げた) The tiger *got free* from its cage and escaped.

ha「nase¹·**ru** はなせる (話せる) *vi*. (hanase-te Ⓥ) ★ Potential form of '*hanasu*¹.'

1 be able to speak:
Kono tori wa kotoba ga hanaseru.
(この鳥は言葉が話せる) This bird *can talk*.

2 talk sense; be understanding:
Kare wa hanaseru *otoko da.* (彼は話せる男だ) He is an *understanding* person.

ha「nashi¹ はなし (話) *n*. **1** talk; chat; conversation:
Kare to hanashi *o shita.* (彼と話をした) I had a *talk* with him.

2 speech; address.

3 topic; subject:
Hanashi *o kaemashoo.* (話をかえましょう) Let's change the *subject*.

4 story; tale:

Kodomo ga neru mae ni hanashi o *shite yatta.* (子どもが寝る前に話をしてやった) I told my child a *story* before he went to sleep.

5 rumor:
Kare wa byooki da to iu hanashi *desu.* (彼は病気だという話です) There is a *rumor* that he is ill.

haˈnashiai はなしあい (話し合い) *n.* talks; consultation; negotiations.

haˈnashiaˈ・u はなしあう (話し合う) *vi.* (-a・i-; -aw・a-; -at-te Ⓒ) talk with; consult with; discuss:
Keekaku wa miñna to hanashiatte *kara kimemasu.* (計画はみんなと話し合ってから決めます) I will decide on a plan after *discussing* it with the others.

haˈnashigoˈe はなしごえ (話し声) *n.* voice; the sound of voices.

haˈnashikakeˈ-ru はなしかける (話し掛ける) *vt.* (-kake-te Ⓥ) speak to; address; begin to speak [talk]:
Watashi wa kare ni Nihoñgo de hanashikaketa. (私は彼に日本語で話しかけた) I *spoke* to him in Japanese.

haˈnashi-koˈtoba はなしことば (話し言葉) *n.* spoken language; speech. (↔ kaki-kotoba)

haˈnashite はなして (話し手) *n.* speaker; the person (in a conversation) who is talking. (↔ kikite)

haˈnaˈs・u¹ はなす (話す) *vi.* (hanash・i-; hanas・a-; hanash・i-te Ⓒ) talk; speak; tell:
Motto yukkuri hanashite *kudasai.* (もっとゆっくり話してください) Will you please *speak* a little more slowly? (⇨ hanaseru; kataru)

haˈnaˈs・u² はなす (離す) *vt.* (hanash・i-; hanas・a-; hanash・i-te Ⓒ) **1** separate; part; keep apart; isolate. (⇨ hikihanasu)

2 (with a negative) do without:
Kono jiteñ wa hanasu *koto ga dekinai.* (この辞典は離すことができない) I *cannot do without* this dictionary.

haˈnaˈs・u³ はなす (放す) *vt.* (hanash・i-; hanas・a-; hanash・i-te Ⓒ) **1** let go; take one's hand off:
Kare wa roopu kara te o hanashita. (彼はロープから手を放した) He *let go* of the rope.

2 let loose; set free (an animal):
Sakana o kawa e hanashite yatta. (魚を川へ放してやった) I *put* the fish *back* into the river.

haˈnawa はなわ (花輪) *n.* floral wreath.

haˈnaˈyaka はなやか (華やか) *a.n.* (~ na, ni) bright; flowery; gorgeous; luxurious:
hanayaka *na doresu* (華やかなドレス) a *gorgeous* dress.

haˈnaˈyome はなよめ (花嫁) *n.* bride. (↔ hanamuko)

haˈñbai はんばい (販売) *n.* sale; selling; marketing.
hañbai suru (~する) *vt.* sell; deal. (⇨ uruˈ)

haˈñ-Bee はんべい (反米) *n.* anti-American. (↔ shiñ-Bee)

haˈñbuˈñ はんぶん (半分) *n.* half.
— *adv.* half:
Shigoto wa hañbuñ *owarimashita.* (仕事は半分終わりました) The work is now *half* finished. (⇨ nakaba)

haˈñ-daˈkuoñ はんだくおん (半濁音) *n. kana* letters with ' ° ' attached. These change the original consonant pronunciation to '*p*': パ (*pa*), ピ (*pi*), プ (*pu*), ペ (*pe*) and ポ (*po*). (⇨ dakuoñ; seeoñ; APP. 1)

haˈñdañ はんだん (判断) *n.* judgment; decision:
Dochira ga hoñmono ka hañdañ *ga tsukanai.* (どちらが本物か判断がつかない) I *cannot tell* which is genuine.
hañdañ suru (~する) *vt.* judge; decide.

haˈñdo-baˈggu ハンドバッグ *n.* handbag; purse.

haˈñdoru ハンドル *n.* **1** steering wheel.

2 (of a bicycle) handlebars.

ha⌐ne はね（羽）*n.* feather; wing; plume.

ha⌐ñee[1] はんえい（繁栄）*n.* prosperity.

hañee suru（〜する）*vi.* prosper; thrive; flourish.

ha⌐ñee[2] はんえい（反映）*n.* reflection.

hañee suru（〜する）*vt.* reflect.

ha⌐nekaes·u はねかえす（跳ね返す）*vt.* (-kaesh·i·; -kaes·a-; -kaesh·i·te Ⓒ) repel; reject: *Teki no koogeki o* hanekaeshita. （敵の攻撃を跳ね返した）We *repelled* the attack of the enemy.

ha⌐ne⌐·ru はねる（跳ねる）*vi.* (hane-te Ⓥ) **1** jump; leap; spring; bound: *Koi ga ike de* haneta. （こいが池で跳ねた）A carp *jumped* in the pond. **2** (of mud, water, etc.) splash. **3** (of a performance) close; be over.

ha⌐ñga はんが（版画）*n.* woodblock print; woodcut.

ha⌐ñgaku はんがく（半額）*n.* half the price.

ha⌐ñgeki はんげき（反撃）*n.* counterattack.

hañgeki suru（〜する）*vi.* counterattack; fight back.

ha⌐ñhañ はんはん（半々）*n.* half-and-half; fifty-fifty: *rieki o* hañhañ *ni wakeru* （利益を半々にわける）divide the profit *equally*.

ha⌐ñi はんい（範囲）*n.* scope; sphere; range: *Kare no kyoomi wa hiroi* hañi *ni wataru.* （彼の興味は広い範囲にわたる）His interests are wide *ranging*.

ha⌐ñi⌐go はんいご（反意語）*n.* antonym. (↔ dooigo)

ha⌐ñji はんじ（判事）*n.* judge.

ha⌐ñjoo はんじょう（繁盛）*n.* (of business) prosperity.

hañjoo suru（〜する）*vi.* (of business) prosper; thrive; flourish.

ha⌐ñjuku はんじゅく（半熟）*n.* half-

boiled egg. (⇨ tamago)

ha⌐ñkachi ハンカチ *n.* handkerchief.

ha⌐ñkan はんかん（反感）*n.* antipathy; ill feeling.

ha⌐ñkee はんけい（半径）*n.* radius.

ha⌐ñko[1] はんこ（判子）*n.* seal; stamp. (⇨ hañ[2])

ha⌐ñkyoo はんきょう（反響）*n.* echo; sensation; repercussion: *Sono eega wa ooki-na* hañkyoo *o yoñda.* （その映画は大きな反響を呼んだ）The movie created a great *sensation*.

hañkyoo suru（〜する）*vi.* echo; reverberate.

ha⌐ñnichi はんにち（半日）*n.* half a day; a half day.

ha⌐ñniñ はんにん（犯人）*n.* criminal; culprit; offender.

ha⌐ñnoo はんのう（反応）*n.* reaction; response; effect.

hañnoo suru（〜する）*vi.* react: respond. (⇨ eekyoo)

ha⌐ñrañ はんらん（反乱）*n.* rebellion; revolt; insurrection: *hañrañ o okosu* （反乱を起こす）rise in *rebellion*.

ha⌐ñsee はんせい（反省）*n.* reflection; reconsideration; introspection.

hañsee suru（〜する）*vt.* reflect; feel sorry.

ha⌐ñsha はんしゃ（反射）*n.* reflection; reflex.

hañsha suru（〜する）*vt.* reflect.

ha⌐ñshite はんして（反して）be contrary to: ★ Used in the pattern '... ni hañshite.' *Kare wa oya no kiboo ni* hañshite, *isha ni naranakatta.* （彼は親の希望に反して、医者にならなかった）*Contrary to* his parents' wishes, he did not become a doctor. (⇨ hañsuru)

ha⌐ñshoku はんしょく（繁殖）*n.* breeding; propagation.

hañshoku suru（〜する）*vi.* breed; propagate.

ha⌐ñs·u⌐ru はんする（反する）*vi.* (hañsh·i-; hañsh·i·; hañsh·i·te

[1]) be against; breach (a regulation, rule, contract, etc.):
Sore wa keeyaku ni hañsuru.(それ は契約に反する) That *breaches* the contract. (⇨ hañshite; ihañ)

ha￢ñtai はんたい (反対) *n.* 1 opposite; contrary:
Kono e wa jooge hañtai *da.*(この絵 は上下反対だ) This picture is *upside-down*.
2 opposition; objection:
Watashi wa sono ikeñ ni hañtai *desu.*(私はその意見に反対です) I am *against* that opinion. (↔ sañsee￢)
hañtai suru (～する) *vi.* oppose.

ha￢ñ-ta￢isee はんたいせい (反体制) *n.* anti-establishment. (↔ taisee)

ha￢ñtee はんてい (判定) *n.* judgment; decision.
hañtee suru (～する) *vt.* judge; decide.

ha￢ñtoo はんとう (半島) *n.* peninsula.

ha￢ñtoshi はんとし (半年) *n.* six months; half a year.

ha￢ñtsuki[1] はんつき (半月) *n.* fortnight; two weeks; half a month.

ha￢ñzai はんざい (犯罪) *n.* crime; offense; delinquency.

ha￢ori はおり (羽織) *n.* short overgarment. ★ Usually worn over a kimono.

ha￢ppi はっぴ (法被) *n.* happi coat.

ha￢ppyoo はっぴょう (発表) *n.* announcement; publication; release.
happyoo suru (～する) *vt.* announce; publish; release. (⇨ dasu (3))

ha￢ra[1] はら (腹) *n.* 1 belly; bowels; stomach: ★ Informal expression used by men. '*Onaka*' is more polite.
Hara ga itai.(腹が痛い) I *have a stomachache*.
2 mind; heart:
Hara *no naka de kanojo wa kare o keebetsu shite ita.*(腹の中で彼女は 彼を軽蔑していた) She despised him in her *heart*.

hara ga tatsu (～が立つ) be [get] angry.
hara o kimeru (～を決める) make up one's mind.
hara o tateru (～を立てる) lose one's temper.

ha￢ra[2] はら (原) *n.* field; plain. (⇨ nohara)

ha￢ra￢gee はらげい (腹芸) *n.* implicit mutual understanding.

ha￢rahara はらはら *adv.* (～ suru) (the state of being nervous or uneasy):
Kare ga nani o ii-dasu ka wakaranai no de harahara *shita.*(彼が何を 言い出すかわからないのではらはらした) I didn't know what he was going to say, so I felt *uneasy*. (⇨ fuañ; shiñpai)

ha￢rappa はらっぱ (原っぱ) *n.* field; plain. (⇨ nohara)

ha￢ra￢·u はらう (払う) *vt.* (hara·i-: haraw·a-: harat-te [C]) 1 pay; pay back: *Kuruma ni ni-hyaku-mañ-eñ* haratta.(車に 200 万円払っ た) I *paid* two million yen for the car.
2 dust; brush; clear:
hoñ no hokori o harau (本のほこりを 払う) *dust* the books.
3 pay; show (attention):
hokoosha no añzeñ ni chuui o harau (歩行者の安全に注意を払う) *pay* attention to the safety of pedestrians.

ha￢re[1] はれ (晴れ) *n.* fine [clear] weather:
Asu wa hare *deshoo.*(あすは晴れでし ょう) It is likely to be *fine* tomorrow. (⇨ hareru￢; ame￢; kumori)
hare no (～の) 1 fine; fair:
hare no *hi* (晴れの日) a *clear* day.
2 auspicious; grand: hare no *butai* (晴れの舞台) a *grand* occasion.

ha￢re￢·ru[1] はれる (晴れる) *vi.* (hare-te [V]) 1 (of weather, sky) clear up; become clear. (⇨ hare)
2 be cheered up; be refreshed:
Sañpo de mo sureba ki ga hare-

masu *yo*. (散歩でもすれば気が晴れます
よ) If you were to, say, go for a
stroll, you'd *feel much better*.
3 be cleared; be dispelled:
Kare ni taisuru utagai ga hareta.
(彼に対する疑いが晴れた) The suspi-
cion against him *has been dispelled*.

haˈreˈru² はれる (腫れる) *vi*. (hare-
te Ⓥ) swell up; become swollen.

haˈri¹ はり (針) *n*. **1** needle.
2 the hands of a clock.
3 fishhook. (⇨ tsuriˈ)

haˈri² はり (鍼) *n*. acupuncture.

haˈrigane はりがね (針金) *n*. wire.

haˈrikiˈrˈu はりきる (張り切る) *vi*.
(ˌkiruˌ, ˌkiraˈ; ˌkitˈto Ⓒ) be in
high spirits; be full of vitality;
be fired up:
Kanojo wa atarashii shigoto ni
harikitte imasu. (彼女は新しい仕事に
張り切っています) She *is very enthusiastic* about her new job.

haˈru¹ はる (春) *n*. spring:
Moo sugu haru ga kuru. (もうすぐ春
が来る) *Spring* will come soon.

haˈru² はる (貼る) *vt*. (har·i·; har-
r·a-; hat-te Ⓒ) put; stick:
kabe ni posutaa o haru (壁にポスター
をはる) *stick* a poster on the wall.

haˈrˈu³ はる (張る) *vi*., *vt*. (har·i·;
har·a-; hat-te Ⓒ) **1** set up; put
up; spread:
teñto o haru (テントを張る) *pitch* a
tent / *ho o haru* (帆を張る) *set* a sail.
2 stretch; strain:
Geñba ni wa tsuna ga hatte atte,
dare mo hairemaseñ. (現場には綱が
張ってあって、だれも入れません) A rope
is stretched around the spot and
no one can get in.
3 cover; freeze; tile:
Ike ni koori ga hatta. (池に氷が張っ
た) Ice *covered* the pond.

haˈrubaˈru はるばる (遥々) *adv*.
(~ to) all the way; from afar:
Kinoo haha ga kyoori kara haru-
baru (*to*) *dete kimashita*. (きのう母が
郷里からはるばる(と)出てきました) Yes-
terday my mother came up *all*

the way from our hometown.

haˈruka はるか (遥か) *adv*. **1** (of
distance) far away:
*Haruka mukoo ni Fuji-sañ ga mi-
eta*. (はるか向こうに富士山が見えた) I
could see Mt. Fuji *far away* over
there.
2 (of time) far back:
Haruka mukashi no koto na no de
yoku oboete imaseñ. (はるか昔のこと
なのでよく覚えていません) It is some-
thing that happened *a very long
time ago*, so I don't remember
clearly.

haˈruka ni はるかに (遥かに) *adv*.
much; by far:
Kono kuruma no hoo ga haruka ni
seenoo ga ii. (この車のほうがはるかに性
能がいい) This car's performance
is *far* better. (⇨ zutto)

haˈru-yaˈsumi はるやすみ (春休み)
n. spring vacation. ★ Schools
are on vacation from the middle
of March until the beginning of
April. (⇨ yasumi)

haˈsami¹ はさみ (鋏) *n*. scissors;
shears.

haˈsaˈm·u はさむ (挟む) *vt*. (ha-
sam·i·; hasam·a-; hasañ-de Ⓒ)
put in; insert; catch in:
doa ni yubi o hasamu (ドアに指を挟
む) *get* one's fingers *caught* in the
door.

haˈsañ はさん (破産) *n*. bankruptcy; insolvency.
hasañ suru (~する) *vi*. go bankrupt.

haˈshi¹ はし (橋) *n*. bridge.

haˈshi² はし (箸) *n*. chopsticks.

haˈshi³ はし (端) *n*. end; edge.

haˈshigo はしご (梯子) *n*. ladder;
stairs.

haˈshira はしら (柱) *n*. pillar;
post; column.

haˈshiˈr·u はしる (走る) *vi*. (ha-
shir·i·; hashir·a-; hashit-te Ⓒ)
1 (of people and animals) run;
dash; rush; jog. (⇨ kakeruˈ)
2 (of vehicles) run; travel:
Kono dooro wa basu ga hashitte

imasu. (この道路はバスが走っています)
Buses *run* along this street.
3 (of a railroad, a road, etc.)
run:
Kono michi wa toozai ni hashitte
imasu. (この道は東西に走っています)
This road *runs* east-west.

ha'soñ はそん (破損) *n.* damage;
breakage.
hasoñ suru (～する) *vi.* be damaged; be broken.

ha'ssee はっせい (発生) *n.* occurrence; outbreak.
hassee suru (～する) *vi.* occur;
break out: *Jiko ga* hassee shita.
(事故が発生した) An accident has
occurred.

ha'ssha はっしゃ (発車) *n.* (of a
train, bus, etc.) departure.
hassha suru (～する) *vi.* start;
leave; depart. (↔ teesha)

ha'sumu'kai はすむかい (斜向かい)
n. the diagonally opposite side:
hasumukai *no ie* (はす向かいの家) a
house standing *diagonally opposite*.

ha'ta' はた (族) *n.* flag; banner.

ha'tachi はたち (二十歳) *n.* twenty years of age.

ha'take はたけ (畑) *n.* field; farm.
hatake chigai (～違い) outside
one's field: *Kagaku wa* hatake
chigai *desu.* (化学は畑違いです)
Chemistry is *outside my field*.

ha'taki' はたき (叩き) *n.* duster.
★ Made of strips of cloth tied at
the end of a long stick.

ha'tame'k･u はためく *vi.* (-mek-
k･i-; -mek･a-; -me･i-te Ⓒ) (of a
flag) flutter; wave.

ha'tañ はたん (破綻) *n.* failure;
breakdown; rupture.
hatañ suru (～する) *vi.* fail; break
down; rupture.

ha'taraki はたらき (働き) *n.*
1 work; service:
hataraki *ni deru* (働きに出る) go to
work.
2 function; operation:
i no hataraki (胃の働き) the *func-*

tion of the stomach.
hataraki o suru (～をする) *vi.* do
work; make a contribution:
★ Preceded by a modifier.
Kare wa mezamashii hataraki o
shita. (彼は目覚ましい働きをした) He
has done remarkable *work*.

ha'tarak･u はたらく (働く) *vi., vt.*
(hatarak･i･; hatarak･a-; hatara･i-
te Ⓒ) **1** work; labor; serve:
giñkoo de hataraku (銀行で働く)
work at a bank.
2 function; work:
Kyoo wa atama ga hatarakanai.
(きょうは頭が働かない) My brain is
not working today.
3 commit (violence, a crime, etc.):
nusumi o hataraku (盗みを働く) *commit* theft.

ha'ta'shite はたして (果たして) *adv.*
(often in questions) really; as was
expected; sure enough:
Hatashite *hoñtoo daroo ka?* (はたし
て本当だろうか) Is it *really* true?

ha'to はと (鳩) *n.* pigeon; dove.

ha'tsu- はつ (初) *pref.* first:
hatsu-*koi* (初恋) one's *first* love /
hatsu-*yuki* (初雪) the *first* snow
of the winter.

-hatsu' はつ (発) *suf.* **1** (of a
train, bus, etc.) leaving:
Ueno-hatsu *no shiñdaisha* (上野発
の寝台車) the sleeper *leaving*
Ueno.
2 (of a news source) from; datelined:
Pekiñ-hatsu *no nyuusu* (北京発のニ
ュース) news *datelined* Beijing.

-hatsu' はつ (発) *suf.* counter for
bullets, shells and large fireworks.
(⇒ APP. 4)

ha'tsubai はつばい (発売) *n.* sale.
hatsubai suru (～する) *vt.* sell;
put on sale. (⇒ uru')

ha'tsubyoo はつびょう (発病) *n.*
onset of a disease; attack.
hatsubyoo suru (～する) *vi.* become sick; be taken ill.
(⇒ byooki)

ha'tsugeñ はつげん (発言) *n.*

speech; remark.

hatsugeñ suru (～する) *vi*. speak; utter; say a word.

haˈtsu-hiˈnode はつひので (初日の出) *n*. the sunrise on New Year's Day.

haˈtsuiku はついく (発育) *n*. development; growth.

hatsuiku suru (～する) *vi*. grow; develop.

haˈtsuka はつか (二十日) *n*. twenty days; the twentieth. (⇨ APP. 5)

haˈtsuka-daˈikoñ はつかだいこん (二十日大根) *n*. radish. (⇨ daikoñ)

haˈtoumee はつめい (発明) *n*. invention.

hatsumee suru (～する) *vt*. invent.

haˈtsumoˈode はつもうで (初詣) *n*. the first New Year's visit to a shrine or a temple.

haˈtsuoñ[1] はつおん (発音) *n*. pronunciation.

hatsuoñ suru (～する) *vt*. pronounce. (⇨ APP. 1)

haˈtsuˈoñ[2] はつおん (撥音) *n*. the Japanese syllabic nasal, written 'ñ' in this dictionary: hatsuoñ-*biñ* (はつ音便) the *nasal sound change*. (⇨ sokuoñ; yoo-oñ; APP. 1)

haˈttatsu はったつ (発達) *n*. development; growth.

hattatsu suru (～する) *vi*. grow; develop: *Taifuu ga minami no kaijoo de* hattatsu shite iru. (台風が南の海上で発達している) A typhoon *is developing* over the ocean in the south. (⇨ hatteñ)

haˈtteñ はってん (発展) *n*. expansion; development; progress.

hatteñ suru (～する) *vi*. develop; grow; expand. (⇨ hattatsu)

haˈtteñ-tojoˈo-koku はってんとじょうこく (発展途上国) *n*. developing country.

haˈtto はっと *adv*. (～ suru) (the state of being startled):

Watashi wa ushiro kara yobika-kerarete, hatto shita. (私は後ろから呼びかけられて、はっとした) I was *startled* when called to from behind.

haˈu はう (這う) *vi*. (ha·i-; ha-w·a-; hat-te Ⓒ) creep; crawl.

haˈusu ハウス *n*. hothouse; (plastic) greenhouse.

haˈyaˈi[1] はやい (早い) *a*. (-ku) (of time) early; soon: *Akirameru no wa mada* hayai. (あきらめるのはまだ早い) It is still too *early* to give up. (↔ osoi)

haˈyaˈi[2] はやい (速い) *a*. (-ku) (of motion) fast; quick; rapid; speedy: *Kono kawa wa nagare ga* hayai. (この川は流れが速い) The current in this river is very *fast*. (↔ osoi)

haˈyakuchi はやくち (早口) *n*. fast talking: *Kanojo wa* hayakuchi *da*. (彼女は早口だ) She *talks fast*.

haˈyamaˈr·u はやまる (早まる) *vi*. (-mar·i-; -mar·a-; -mat-te Ⓒ) (of time) be made earlier; be brought forward: *Dañtoo de sakura no kaika ga* ha-yamatta. (暖冬で桜の開花が早まった) Because of the warm winter, the opening of the cherry blossoms occurred early. (⇨ hayameru[1])

haˈyameˈr·u[1] はやめる (早める) *vt*. (-me-te Ⓥ) 1 hasten; speed up: *Karoo ga kare no shi o* hayameta. (過労が彼の死を早めた) Overwork *hastened* his death. (⇨ hayamaru) 2 advance; bring forward: *Kare-ra wa kekkoñ-shiki o ni-shuukañ* hayameta. (彼らは結婚式を2週間早めた) They *advanced* their wedding by two weeks. (⇨ hayamaru)

haˈyameˈr·u[2] はやめる (速める) *vt*. (-me-te Ⓥ) quicken; hasten: *Kuruma wa supiido o* hayameta. (車はスピードを速めた) The car *speeded up*.

haˈyaˈne はやね (早寝) *n*. going to bed early.

hayane (o) suru (~(を)する) *vi*. go to bed early.

ha⌐ya⌐oki はやおき (早起き) *n*. early rising.

hayaoki (o) suru (~(を)する) *vi*. get up early; rise early.

ha⌐ya⌐r·u はやる (流行る) *vi*. (hayar·i-; hayar·a-; hayat-te ⓒ)
1 be popular; be in fashion:
Ima sono uta ga hayatte imasu. (今その歌がはやっています) That song *is* now *popular*. (⇨ ryuukoo)
2 (of a shop, an enterprise, etc.) prosper; do good business:
Ano mise wa hayatte iru. (あの店ははやっている) That shop *is doing well*.
3 (of disease) be raging; be prevalent:
Ryuukañ ga Nihoñ-juu de hayatte imasu. (流感が日本中ではやっています) Influenza *is prevalent* throughout Japan.

ha⌐yasa はやさ (速さ) *n*. speed; quickness; rapidity. (⇨ sokudo; supiido)

ha⌐yashi はやし (林) *n*. grove; woods. ★ A large area of land more thickly covered with trees than 'hayashi' is called 'mori' (森).

ha⌐ya⌐s·u はやす (生やす) *vt*. (hayash·i-; hayas·a-; hayash·i-te ⓒ) grow (a beard, etc.): ★ '*hayashite iru*'=wear.
Kare wa hige o hayashite iru. (彼はひげを生やしている) He *wears* a beard. (⇨ haeru')

ha⌐zu はず (筈) *n*. supposed; expected:
Tanaka-sañ wa jimusho ni iru hazu desu. (田中さんは事務所にいるずです) Miss Tanaka *is supposed* to be in the office. (⇨ hazu wa nai)

ha⌐zukashi¹·i はずかしい (恥ずかしい) *a*. (-ku) ashamed; shameful:
Koñna kañtañ na koto ga dekinakute, hazukashii. (こんな簡単なことができなくて、恥ずかしい) I feel *ashamed* that I cannot do such a simple

thing. (⇨ kimari ga warui)

ha⌐zumi はずみ (弾み) *n*. momentum; impulse:
hazumi *ga tsuku* (はずみがつく) gain *momentum*. (⇨ hazumu)

ha⌐zum·u はずむ (弾む) *vi*. (hazum·i-; hazum·a-; hazuñ-de ⓒ)
1 bounce; bound:
Kono booru wa yoku hazumu. (このボールはよく弾む) This ball *bounces* well. (⇨ hazumi)
2 become lively; bound:
Watashi-tachi no hanashi wa hazuñda. (私たちの話は弾んだ) Our conversation *became lively*.

ha⌐zure·ru はずれる (外れる) *vi*. (hazure-te Ⓥ) 1 come off; be undone; be out of joint:
Juwaki ga hazurete imasu. (受話器が外れています) The receiver *is off the hook*. (⇨ hazusu)
2 miss (a target); fail; (of a prediction, a forecast, a guess, etc.) prove wrong.
3 be out of the way; be contrary:
chuushiñ kara hazureru (中心からはずれる) *be off* center.

ha⌐zus·u はずす (外す) *vt*. (hazush·i-; hazus·a-; hazush·i-te ⓒ)
1 take off; remove:
megane [tokee] o hazusu (眼鏡[時計]を外す) *take off* one's glasses [watch] / *botañ o* hazusu (ボタンをはずす) *undo* a button. (⇨ hazureru)
2 leave (one's seat); slip away from:
Kare wa kaigi-chuu, seki o hazushita. (彼は会議中、席をはずした) He *left* his seat in the middle of the meeting.

ha⌐zu wa na¹i はずはない (筈は無い) (*formal*='hazu wa arimaseñ') be hardly possible; cannot expect:
Soñna hazu wa nai. (そんなはずはない) That's *impossible*.
★ Note the use of a double negative, 'nai hazu wa nai': *Kimi ga sore o* shiranai hazu wa nai. (君が

それを知らないはずはない) *There is no reason* for you *not to know* that.

he˻bi へび (蛇) *n.* snake; serpent.

he˻e へい (塀) *n.* wall; fence.

he˻eboñ へいぼん (平凡) *a.n.*
(~ na, ni) ordinary; common; uneventful:
Heeboñ *da keredo, shiawase na mainichi o okutte imasu.* (平凡だけれど、幸せな毎日を送っています) I lead an *uneventful*, but happy life.
((⇨ futsuu˻))

he˻ehoo へいほう (平方) *n.* square:
ni-meetoru heehoo (2 メートル平方) 2 meters *square* / *ni*-heehoo *meetoru* (2 平方メートル) two *square* meters.
heehoo suru (~する) *vt.* square.
((↔ rippoo˻))

he˻ejitsu へいじつ (平日) *n.* weekday; workday. ((⇨ kyuujitsu; shukujitsu; shuumatsu))

he˻ejoo へいじょう (平常) *n.* normal; usual:
Shiñkañseñ no daiya wa heejoo *ni modotta.* (新幹線のダイヤは平常に戻った) The schedule of the Shinkansen has returned to *normal*.
((⇨ futsuu˻))

he˻ekai へいかい (閉会) *n.* closing of a meeting [session].
heekai suru (~する) *vi.* close [adjourn] a meeting. ((↔ kaikai))

he˻eki˻ へいき (平気) *n.* indifference; calmness:
Kanojo wa heeki *o yosootta.* (彼女は平気を装った) She assumed an air of *indifference*.
— *a.n.* (~ na, ni) calm; cool; indifferent; unconcerned:
Nani o iwarete mo watashi wa heeki *desu.* (何を言われても私は平気です) I *do not care* what is said to me.

he˻eki˻² へいき (兵器) *n.* weapon; arms.

he˻ekiñ˻ へいきん (平均) *n.* average; mean: heekiñ *o dasu* (平均を出す) find the *average*.
heekiñ suru (~する) *vi.* calculate

the average: Heekiñ shite, *futari ni hitori ga megane o kakete imasu.* (平均して、二人に一人が眼鏡をかけています) *On the average*, every second person wears glasses.

he˻ekiñ² へいきん (平均) *n.* balance:
heekiñ *o tamotsu* [ushinau] (平均を保つ[失う]) keep [lose] one's *balance*.

he˻ekoo˻ へいこう (平行) *n.* parallel.

he˻ekoo² へいこう (並行) *n.* going side by side.

he˻ekoo³ へいこう (閉口) *n.* being annoyed; being bothered.
heekoo suru (~する) *vi.* be annoyed; be bothered: *Shichoo no nagai eñzetsu ni wa* heekoo shita. (市長の長い演説には閉口した) We *got fed up* with the mayor's long speech.

he˻emeñ へいめん (平面) *n.* level; plane.

he˻eme˻ñzu へいめんず (平面図) *n.* floor [ground] plan.

he˻etai へいたい (兵隊) *n.*
1 a group of soldiers; troops.
2 soldier; sailor. ★ Especially those lower in rank. Often figuratively refers to a common company employee. ((⇨ guñjiñ))

he˻ewa へいわ (平和) *n.* peace.
— *a.n.* (~ na, ni) peaceful: heewa *ni kurasu* (平和に暮らす) live in *peace*. ((↔ señsoo))

he˻eya へいや (平野) *n.* plain; open field.

he˻ñ˻ へん (変) *a.n.* (~ na, ni) strange; odd; queer; peculiar:
Kono kuruma wa tokidoki heñ *na oto ga suru.* (この車はときどき変な音がする) This car sometimes makes a *strange* noise.

he˻ñ² へん (辺) *n.* **1** part; region; neighborhood:
Kare no ie wa kono heñ *ni aru hazu desu.* (彼の家はこの辺にあるはずです) His house should be *around* here. ((⇨ atari))

2 degree; range; limit:
Kyoo wa kono heñ de owari ni shiyoo. (きょうはこの辺で終わりにしよう) Let's finish up *here* today.

heˈñ³ へん (偏) *n.* the left-hand radical of a Chinese character. (⇨ bushu; tsukuri)

-heñ へん (遍) *suf.* counter for the number of times. (⇨ -kai¹; APP. 4)

heˈñi へんい (変異) *n.* variation: *totsuzeñ-heñi* (突然変異) *mutation.*

heˈñji¹ へんじ (返事) *n.* answer; reply:
Yobaretara, sugu heñji o shi nasai. (呼ばれたら, すぐ返事をしなさい) *Answer* immediately when your name is called. (⇨ kotaeru)

heˈñka へんか (変化) *n.*
1 change; variation; alteration:
Kono atari no keshiki wa heñka ni toñde iru. (この辺りの景色は変化に富んでいる) The landscapes around here are full of *variety.*
2 inflection; conjugation:
dooshi no heñka (動詞の変化) *conjugation* of verbs.
heñka suru (〜する) *vi.* **1** change; vary; alter.
2 inflect; conjugate.

heˈñkeñ へんけん (偏見) *n.* prejudice; bias.

heˈñkoo へんこう (変更) *n.* change; alteration; modification.
heñkoo suru (〜する) *vt.* change; alter; modify: *yotee o heñkoo suru* (予定を変更する) *change* one's schedule.

heˈñsai へんさい (返済) *n.* repayment; refund.
heñsai suru (〜する) *vt.* pay back; repay; refund.

heˈñshuu へんしゅう (編集) *n.* editing; compilation.
heñshuu suru (〜する) *vi.* edit; compile: *bideo o heñshuu suru* (ビデオを編集する) *edit* video tapes.

heˈñshuˈuchoo へんしゅうちょう (編集長) *n.* editor-in-chief; chief editor.

heˈrasˈu へらす (減らす) *vt.* (herash·i-; heras·a-; herash·i·te Ⓒ) reduce; decrease; cut down; diminish:
Anata wa taijuu o herashita hoo ga yoi. (あなたは体重を減らしたほうがよい) You should *lose* weight. (⇨ heru)

heˈrˑu へる (減る) *vi.* (her·i-; her·a-; het-te Ⓒ) **1** become less [fewer]; decrease:
Kuruma no gasoriñ ga hette kita. (車のガソリンが減ってきた) The car *has run low* on gas. (↔ fueru)
2 (of shoes, tires) wear out.
3 get hungry:
Onaka ga hette kita. (おなかが減ってきた) I've gotten *hungry.* ★ '*Onaka ga suite kimashita.*' is more polite. (⇨ suku¹)

heˈso へそ (臍) *n.* navel. ★ Often '*o-heso.*'

heˈtaˈ へた (下手) *a.n.* (〜 na, ni) poor; bad:
Watashi wa uñteñ ga heta desu. (私は運転がへたです) I am *not* very *good* at driving. (↔ joozu)
heta o suru to (〜をすると) if one is not careful; if not properly handled.

heˈte へて (経て) via; by way of:
Kare wa Hawai o hete Tookyoo ni tsukimashita. (彼はハワイを経て東京に着きました) He arrived in Tokyo *via* Hawaii. (⇨ keeyu¹)

heˈyaˈ へや (部屋) *n.* room; chamber; apartment.

hi¹ ひ (日) *n.* **1** day (24 hours); time:
Doñdoñ hi ga tatte yuku. (どんどん日がたってゆく) The *days* go by so quickly.
2 date:
Shuppatsu no hi wa mitee desu. (出発の日は未定です) The *date* of departure is not fixed yet.

hi² ひ (日) *n.* **1** the sun.
2 sun (=sunbeam):
Kono heya ni wa hi ga sasanai. (こ

の部屋には日がささない) The *sun* does not shine into this room.
3 period of light; day (as opposed to night):
Hi *ga nagaku [mijikaku] natta.* (日が長く[短く]なった) The *days* are getting longer [shorter].

hi[13] ひ (火) *n.* fire:
tabako ni hi *o tsukeru* (たばこに火をつける) *light* a cigarette.

hi[14] ひ (灯) *n.* light:
hi *o tomosu [kesu]* (灯をともす[消す]) turn on [off] a *light*.

hi[15] ひ (比) *n.* ratio. (⇨ hiritsu)

hi[6] ひ (碑) *n.* monument.

hi[1]- ひ (非) *pref.* un-; non-:
hi-*kyooryoku-teki na taido* (非協力的な態度) an *un*cooperative attitude.

-hi ひ (費) *suf.* expenses:
kootsuu-hi (交通費) traveling *expenses* / *seekatsu*-hi (生活費) living *expenses*.

hi「**atari** ひあたり (日当たり) *n.* exposure to the sun; sunshine:
hiatari *no yoi heya* (日当たりのよい部屋) a *sunny* room. (⇨ hikage; hinata)

hi「**bachi** ひばち (火鉢) *n.* brazier.
★ The hibachi has no grill. It is used basically for heating, not cooking.

hi「**bana** ひばな (火花) *n.* sparks.

hi「**bari** ひばり (雲雀) *n.* skylark; lark.

hi「**bashi** ひばし (火箸) *n.* chopsticks made of metal. ★ Used like tongs and fire irons to tend heated charcoal, etc.

hi「**bi** ひび *n.* **1** crack:
Kono koppu ni wa hibi *ga haitte iru.* (このコップにはひびが入っている) There is a *crack* in this glass.
2 split:
Sono koto de futari no kañkee ni hibi *ga haitta.* (そのことで二人の関係にひびが入った) The incident caused a *split* in their relationship.

hi「**biki**[1] ひびき (響き) *n.* sound; peal; echo. (⇨ hibiku)

hi「**bik·u** ひびく (響く) *vi.* (hibik·i-; hibik·a-; hibi·i-te [C]) **1** sound; ring; resound; echo:
Tera no kane ga mura-juu ni hibiita. (寺の鐘が村中に響いた) The bell of a temple *resounded* throughout the village. (⇨ hibiki)
2 affect; have an unfavorable influence on:
Naga-ame ga sakumotsu no shuukaku ni hibiita. (長雨が作物の収穫に響いた) The long rains *had an adverse effect* on the harvest.

hi「**bu**「**soo** ひぶそう (非武装) *n.* demilitarization. (↔ busoo)

hi「**dari** ひだり (左) *n.* left. (↔ migi)

hi「**darigawa** ひだりがわ (左側) *n.* left side. (↔ migigawa)

hi「**darikiki** ひだりきき (左利き) *n.* left-handed person. (↔ migikiki)

hi「**darite** ひだりて (左手) *n.*
1 left hand. (↔ migite)
2 left direction:
Hidarite *ni kawa ga mieru.* (左手に川が見える) I can see a river on the *left*. (↔ migite)

hi「**do**「**i** ひどい (酷い) *a.* (-ku) **1** serious; hard; violent:
Ame ga hidoku *natte kita.* (雨がひどくなってきた) It has started to rain *hard*.
2 cruel; terrible:
Ano otoko wa hidoi *yatsu da.* (あの男はひどいやつだ) He is a *cruel* man.

hi「**e**「**·ru** ひえる (冷える) *vi.* (hie-te [V]) get cold [chilly; cool]:
Yoru ni natte, dañdañ hiete kita. (夜になって、だんだん冷えてきた) It *is* gradually *getting cold* as night comes on. (⇨ hiyasu)

hi「**fu** ひふ (皮膚) *n.* skin. (⇨ hada)

hi「**fuka** ひふか (皮膚科) *n.* dermatology.

hi「**gaeri**[1] ひがえり (日帰り) *n.* day-trip; one day trip.

hi「**gai** ひがい (被害) *n.* **1** damage.
2 loss:
Sono kaisha no uketa higai *wa wazuka datta.* (その会社の受けた被害

はわずかだった）The *loss* the company sustained was slight.

hi⌈ga⌉isha ひがいしゃ（被害者）*n.* victim; sufferer.

hi⌈ga⌉ñ ひがん（彼岸）*n.* the equinoctial week. ★ Politely 'o-higañ.' It is a Japanese custom to visit one's family grave during the spring and autumn equinoctial weeks. (⇨ hakamairi)

hi⌈gashi⌉ ひがし（東）*n.* east; (～ ni/e) eastward. (↔ nishi)

hi⌈ge ひげ（髭）*n.* general term for facial hair:
hige *o* hayasu（ひげを生やす）grow a *beard*. (⇨ kuchihige)

hi⌈geki ひげき（悲劇）*n.* tragedy. (↔ kigeki)

hi⌈goro ひごろ（日頃）*n.* everyday; always; usually:
Higoro *no doryoku ga taisetsu desu.*（日ごろの努力が大切です）One's *daily* efforts are important.

hi⌈hañ ひはん（批判）*n.* criticism. hihañ suru（～する）*vt.* criticize.

hi⌈hyoo ひひょう（批評）*n.* comment; criticism; review.
hihyoo suru（～する）*vt.* criticize; review; comment.

hi⌈ji⌉ ひじ（肘）*n.* elbow.

hi⌈joo ひじょう（非常）*n.* emergency; contingency:
Hijoo *no baai wa koko kara deraremasu.*（非常の場合はここから出られます）You can go out this way in an *emergency*.
— *a.n.* (～ na, ni) great; extreme; very:
Kare wa hijoo ni *yorokoñde imashita.*（彼は非常に喜んでいました）He was *absolutely* delighted. (⇨ taiheñ; taisoo²)

hi⌈jo⌉oguchi ひじょうぐち（非常口）*n.* emergency exit.

hi⌈joo ni ひじょうに（非常に）*adv.* ⇨ hijoo.

hi⌈jooseñ ひじょうせん（非常線）*n.* police cordon.

hi⌈jo⌉oshiki ひじょうしき（非常識）*a.n.* (～ na, ni) lacking in common sense; unreasonable.

hi⌈kae⌉shitsu ひかえしつ（控室）*n.* anteroom; waiting room.

hi⌈kage ひかげ（日陰）*n.* shade. (↔ hinata)

hi⌈kaku ひかく（比較）*n.* comparison; parallel. (⇨ kuraberu)
hikaku suru（～する）*vt.* compare.

hi⌈kaku-teki ひかくてき（比較的）*adv.* comparatively; relatively:
★ Note that this word is an adverb, not an adjectival noun.
Moñdai wa hikaku-teki *yasashikatta.*（問題は比較的やさしかった）I found the problems *comparatively* easy.

hi⌈kari⌉ ひかり（光）*n.* light; ray.

hi⌈ka⌉r·u ひかる（光る）*vi.* (hikar·i-; hikar·a-; hikat-te C)
1 shine; twinkle; gleam; glitter:
Tooku de nani-ka ga hikatta.（遠くで何かが光った）Something *glinted* in the distance.
2 stand out; be prominent:
Kono zasshi de wa kare no shoosetsu ga hikatte iru.（この雑誌では彼の小説が光っている）His novel *figures prominently* in this magazine.

-hiki ひき（匹）*suf.* counter for small animals, fish and insects. (⇨ APP. 4)

hi⌈kiage⌉·ru ひきあげる（引き上げる・引き揚げる）*vt.* (-age-te V)
1 pull up; salvage:
Chiñbotsu shita fune o hikiageta.（沈没した船を引き揚げた）We *salvaged* the sunken ship.
2 raise:
chiñgin o hikiageru（賃金を引き上げる）*raise* wages. (↔ hikisageru)
3 withdraw (an army):
guñtai o hikiageru（軍隊を引き揚げる）*withdraw* troops.

hi⌈kidashi ひきだし（引き出し）*n.* drawer.

hi⌈kida⌉s·u ひきだす（引き出す）*vt.* (-dash·i-; -das·a-; -dash·i-te C)
1 draw (a conclusion, etc.).
2 draw (money from a deposit):
giñkoo kara hyakumañ-eñ hiki-

dasu (銀行から100万円引き出す) *withdraw* one million yen from the bank.

hiˈkihanaˌs·u ひきはなす (引き離す) *vt.* (-hanash·i·-; -hanas·a·-; -hanash·i·te |C|) 1 outdistance; outrun:
aite o hikihanasu (相手を引き離す) *run ahad of* one's competitors.
2 separate:
hahaoya kara kodomo o hikihanasu (母親から子どもを引き離す) *separate* a mother from her child. ((⇨ hanasu²)

hiˈkikaˌes·u ひきかえす (引き返す) *vi.* (-kaesh·i·-; -kaes·a·-; -kaesn·i·te |C|) come [go] back; return:
Hikooki wa enjin no koshoo de tochuu kara hikikaeshita. (飛行機はエンジンの故障で途中から引き返した) The plane *turned back* half way because of engine trouble.

hiˈkiniku ひきにく (挽き肉) *n.* ground meat; minced meat.

hiˈkinobashi¹ ひきのばし (引き延ばし) *n.* delaying; postponement. ((⇨ hikinobasu²)

hiˈkinobashi² ひきのばし (引き伸ばし) *n.* enlargement. ((⇨ hikinobasu²)

hiˈkinobaˌs·u¹ ひきのばす (引き延ばす) *vt.* (-nobash·i·-; -nobas·a·-; -nobash·i·te |C|) extend; prolong; put off:
Shiharai kigeñ o hikinobashite moratta. (支払い期限を引き延ばしてもらった) The payment deadline *was extended* for me. ((⇨ hikinobashi¹)

hiˈkinobaˌs·u² ひきのばす (引き伸ばす) *vt.* (-nobash·i·-; -nobas·a·-; -nobash·i·te |C|) enlarge:
Shashiñ o hikinobashite moratta. (写真を引き伸ばしてもらった) I had the photograph *enlarged*. ((⇨ hikinobashi²)

hiˈkinuˌk·u ひきぬく (引き抜く) *vt.* (-nuk·i·-; -nuk·a·-; -nu·i·te |C|) 1 pull out; draw; extract:
kugi o hikinuku (くぎを引き抜く)

pull out a nail. ((⇨ nuku)
2 hire away; transfer:
Uchi no kaisha de wa shaiñ o sañniñ hikinukareta. (うちの会社では社員を3人引き抜かれた) Three people *were hired away* from our company.

hiˈkisagaˌr·u ひきさがる (引き下がる) *vi.* (-sagar·i·-; -sagar·a·-; -sagat·te |C|) withdraw; leave:
Kumiaiiñ-tachi wa sunao ni hikisagaranakatta. (組合員たちは素直に引き下がらなかった) The union members *did not withdraw* obediently. ((⇨ hiku¹)

hiˈkisageˌ·ru ひきさげる (引き下げる) *vt.* (-sage·te |V|) lower; reduce; cut [bring] down:
nedañ o hikisageru (値段を引き下げる) *lower* the price. ((⇨ hikiageru)

hiˈkitateˌ·ru ひきたてる (引き立てる) *vt.* (-tate·te |V|) 1 favor; patronize; support:
Kachoo wa itsu-mo kare o hikitatete iru. (課長はいつも彼を引き立てている) Our boss *is* always *favoring* him.
2 set off:
Bakku no aozora ga kanojo no fukusoo o hikitatete iru. (バックの青空が彼女の服装を引き立てている) The blue sky in the background *sets off* her clothes.

hiˈkitaˌts·u ひきたつ (引き立つ) *vi.* (-tach·i·-; -tat·a·-; -tat·te |C|) look nice; be set off:
Soko ni hana o ikeru to issoo hikitachimasu. (そこに花を生けるといっそう引き立ちます) If you put a flower arrangement there, the place will *look much better*. ((⇨ hikitateru)

hiˈkitomeˌ·ru ひきとめる (引き止める・引き留める) *vt.* (-tome·te |V|) keep; prevent:
Kare o hikitomeru koto wa dekinakatta. (彼を引き止めることはできなかった) We could not *prevent* him *from leaving*.

hiˈkitoˌr·u ひきとる (引き取る) *vt.* (-tor·i·-; -tor·a·-; -tot·te |C|)

1 take [buy] back:
Urenokotta shinamono wa hikitori-masu.(売れ残った品物は引き取ります)
We will *take back* unsold goods.
2 take care of; take in (a child, an old person, etc.).

hi⌐kitsuke¹·ru ひきつける（引き付ける） *vt.* (-tsuke-te Ⓥ) **1** attract; charm; magnetize:
Kare no eñzetsu wa chooshuu o hikitsuketa.(彼の演説は聴衆を引きつけた) His speech *charmed* the audience.
2 (of a magnet) attract.

hi⌐kiuke¹·ru ひきうける（引き受ける） *vt.* (-uke-te Ⓥ) take; undertake:
Sono yakume wa watashi ga hiki-ukemasu.(その役目は私が引き受けます) I will *undertake* that duty.

hi⌐kiwake ひきわけ（引き分け） *n.* drawn game; draw; tie. (⇨ hiki-wakeru)

hi⌐kiwake¹·ru ひきわける（引き分ける） *vi.*, *vt.* (-wake-te Ⓥ) draw; tie:
Jaiañtsu wa Taigaasu to no shiai o hikiwaketa.(ジャイアンツはタイガースとの試合を引き分けた) The Giants *drew* in the game with the Tigers. (⇨ hikiwake)

hi⌐kiwata¹s·u ひきわたす（引き渡す） *vt.* (-watash·i-; -watas·a-; -wa-tash·i-te Ⓒ) hand over; deliver:
Kare-ra wa doroboo o keesatsu ni hikiwatashita.(彼らは泥棒を警察に引き渡した) They *handed* the thief *over* to the police. (⇨ watasu)

hi⌐ki¹zañ ひきざん（引き算） *n.* (of arithmetic) subtraction. (↔ tashizañ)

hi⌐kizur·u ひきずる（引きずる） *vt.* (-zur·i-; -zur·a-; -zut-te Ⓒ) drag; trail: *ashi o hikizuru*（足を引きずる） *drag* one's feet / *kimono no suso o hikizuru*（着物の裾を引きずる） *trail* the hem of one's kimono.

hi⌐kkaka¹r·u ひっかかる（引っ掛かる） *vi.* (-kakar·i-; -kakar·a-; -kakat-te Ⓒ) **1** get caught:
Zuboñ ga kugi ni hikkakatta.(ズボ

ンがくぎに引っ掛かった) My trousers *got caught* on a nail. (⇨ hikka-keru)
2 fall for; be deceived:
Kanojo wa sagi ni hikkakatta.(彼女は詐欺に引っ掛かった) She *fell for* a confidence trick. (⇨ hikkakeru)

hi⌐kkake¹·ru ひっかける（引っ掛ける） *vt.* (-kake-te Ⓥ) **1** catch:
Kare wa shatsu o kugi ni hikka-keta.(彼はシャツをくぎに引っ掛けた) He *caught* his shirt on a nail. (⇨ hikkakaru)
2 (of clothes) throw on:
Kare wa uwagi o hikkakete, soto ni deta.(彼は上着を引っ掛けて、外に出た) He *threw on* his jacket and went out.
3 splash:
Kodomo-tachi wa otagai ni mizu o hikkakete, asoñda.(子どもたちはお互いに水を引っ掛けて、遊んだ) The children played, *splashing* water at each other. (⇨ hikkakaru)
4 deceive; trap; seduce:
Kare o hikkakeyoo to shite mo, muda desu.(彼を引っ掛けようとしても、無駄です) It is no use trying to *deceive* him. (⇨ hikkakaru)

hi⌐kki ひっき（筆記） *n.* note-taking; writing.
hikki suru (～する) *vt.* take notes.

hi⌐kko¹m·u ひっこむ（引っ込む） *vi.* (-kom·i-; -kom·a-; -koñ-de Ⓒ) **1** retire; withdraw:
Kare wa kokyoo ni hikkoñda.(彼は故郷に引っ込んだ) He *retired* to his hometown.
2 stand back:
Kare no ie wa dooro kara yaku gojuu-meetoru hikkoñde iru.(彼の家は道路から約 50 メートル引っ込んでいる) His house *stands back* about fifty meters from the road.

hi⌐kkoshi ひっこし（引っ越し） *n.* move; removal. (⇨ hikkosu)

hi⌐kko¹s·u ひっこす（引っ越す） *vi.* (-kosh·i-; -kos·a-; -kosh·i-te Ⓒ) move:
Ikka wa Nagoya kara Oosaka e

hikkoshita. (一家は名古屋から大阪へ引っ越した) The family *moved* from Nagoya to Osaka. 《⇨ hikkoshi》

hi「kkurika」er・u ひっくりかえる (ひっくり返る) *vi.* (-kaer・a-; -kaer・i-; -kaet-te C̲) overturn; upset:
Tsuri-bune ga hikkurikaetta. (釣り舟がひっくり返った) The fishing boat *overturned.* 《⇨ hikkurikaesu》

hi「kkurika」es・u ひっくりかえす (ひっくり返す) *vt.* (-kaesh・i-; -kaes・a-; -kaesh・i-te C̲) turn over; upset:
Kare wa koppu o hikkurikaeshita. (彼はコップをひっくり返した) He *upset* the glass. 《⇨ hikkurikaeru》

hi「koo ひこう (飛行) *n.* flight; flying.
 hikoo suru (～する) *vi.* fly; make a flight.

hi「koojoo ひこうじょう (飛行場) *n.* airfield; airport. 《⇨ kuukoo》

hi「ko」oki ひこうき (飛行機) *n.* airplane; plane.

hi「kooseñ ひこうせん (飛行船) *n.* airship; dirigible; blimp.

hi「k・u」¹ ひく (引く) *vt.* (hik・i-; hik・a-; hi・i-te C̲) **1** pull; draw; tow; tug:
Himo o hiite, deñki o tsuketa. (ひもを引いて, 電気をつけた) I switched on the light by *pulling* the cord.
2 lead by the hand:
Kanojo wa kodomo no te o hiite, aruita. (彼女は子どもの手を引いて, 歩いた) She walked along, *leading* her child *by the hand*.
3 catch; attract:
chuui o hiku (注意を引く) *attract* someone's attention.
4 consult (a dictionary); look up:
Jisho o hiite, sono imi o shirabeta. (辞書を引いて, その意味を調べた) I *consulted* a dictionary and checked the meaning.
5 lay; install:
suidoo o hiku (水道を引く) *lay* a water pipe / *deñwa o hiku* (電話を引く) *install* a telephone.

6 draw (a line):
señ o hiku (線を引く) *draw* a line.
7 subtract; take:
Juu kara sañ o hiku to nana noko-ru. (10 から 3 を引くと 7 残る) *Take* 3 from 10 and it leaves 7. 《↔ tasu》
8 catch (a cold).
9 *vi.* go down; subside:
Netsu wa hikimashita ka? (熱は引きましたか) *Has* the fever *subsided?*
10 *vi.* yield; pull out:
Kare wa ip-po mo ato e hikana-katta. (彼は一歩も後へ引かなかった) He *did not yield* a single step.
11 (of the tide) ebb. 《↔ michiru》

hi「k・u」² ひく (弾く) *vt.* (hik・i-; hik・a-; hi・i-te C̲) play (a musical instrument):
Kanojo wa joozu ni piano o hiku. (彼女は上手にピアノを弾く) She *plays* the piano well.

hi「k・u」³ ひく (轢く) *vt.* (hik・i-; hik・a-; hi・i-te C̲) hit; run over [down]:
Kare no kuruma wa neko o hiita. (彼の車は猫をひいた) His car *ran over* a cat.

hi「ku」・i ひくい (低い) *a.* (-ku)
1 (of height) low; short:
Chichi wa watashi yori se ga hi-kui. (父は私より背が低い) My father is *shorter* than me. 《↔ takai》
2 (of a position, degree, level) low:
Kyoo wa kinoo yori oñdo ga hikui. (きょうはきのうより温度が低い) Today the temperature is *lower* than yesterday. 《↔ takai》
3 (of sound, voice) not loud; low:
hikui koe de hanasu (低い声で話す) speak in a *low* voice. 《↔ takai》

hi「kyo」o ひきょう (卑怯) *a.n.* (～ na, ni) foul; unfair; cowardly; mean:
Imasara te o hiku nañte hikyoo da. (いまさら手を引くなんてひきょうだ) It is *cowardly* of you to back out now.

hi「ma ひま (暇) *n.* time; free time; leisure.

— *a.n.* (~ na) free; not busy:
*Kyoo wa kyaku ga sukunakute,
hima desu.* (きょうは客が少なくて、暇で
す) There are only a few customers today, so we are *not busy.*
(↔ isogashii)

hima o dasu (~を出す) dismiss;
fire. (⇨ kubi)

hiˈmee ひめい (悲鳴) *n.* shriek;
scream: himee *o ageru* (悲鳴を上
げる) give a *scream.*

hiˈmitsu ひみつ (秘密) *n.* secret.

hiˈmo ひも (紐) *n.* string; cord;
band.

hiˈñ ひん (品) *n.* elegance; grace;
refinement: hiñ no yoi *fujiñ* (品
の良い婦人) an *elegant* lady.
(⇨ hiñi)

hiˈna ひな (雛) *n.* chick; young
bird.

hiˈnamaˈtsuri ひなまつり (雛祭り)
n. the Doll Festival celebrated
on March 3. ★ Also known as
the Girls' Festival.

hiˈnañ[1] ひなん (非難) *n.* blame;
criticism; attack.
hinañ suru (~する) *vt.* criticize;
blame; attack.

hiˈnañ[2] ひなん (避難) *n.* shelter;
refuge; evacuation.
hinañ suru (~する) *vi.* take shelter [refuge]; evacuate.

hiˈnaniˈñgyoo ひなにんぎょう (雛人
形) *n.* a doll made of paper or
clay, usually colorfully clad.
(⇨ hinamatsuri)

hiˈnata ひなた (日向) *n.* sunny
place. (↔ hikage) (⇨ hiatari)
hinata-bokko (~ぼっこ) sunbath:
hinata-bokko o suru (日なたぼっこを
する) *bask in the sun.*

hiˈneˈrˑu ひねる (捻る) *vt.* (hiner-
ri; hinerˑa; hinet-te Ⓒ)
turn (a faucet, tap, knob); twist:
Kare wa sukeeto de ashi o hinetta.
(彼はスケートで足をひねった) He *twist-
ed* his foot ice-skating.

hiˈñi ひんい (品位) *n.* dignity;
grace; elegance. (⇨ hiñ)

hiˈniku ひにく (皮肉) *n.* irony; sar-

casm; cynicism.
— *a.n.* (~ na, ni) ironic:
*Gyaku no kekka ni naru to wa hi-
niku da.* (逆の結果になるとは皮肉だ)
It's *ironic* that things turned out
exactly opposite.

hiˈñjaku ひんじゃく (貧弱) *a.n.*
(~ na, ni) poor; feeble:
hiñjaku *na karadatsuki* (貧弱な体つ
き) a *feeble* body.

hiˈnode ひので (日の出) *n.* sunrise.

hiˈnoiri ひのいり (日の入り) *n.* sunset. (↔ hinode)

hiˈñshi ひんし (品詞) *n.* part of
speech. (⇨ APP. 2)

hiˈñshitsu ひんしつ (品質) *n.*
quality:
hiñshitsu *ga yoi [warui]* (品質が良
い[悪い]) be good [bad] in *quality.*

hiˈñyookika ひにょうきか (泌尿器
科) *n.* urology department.

hiˈppaˈrˑu ひっぱる (引っ張る) *vt.*
(-par·i-; -par·a-; -pat-te Ⓒ)
1 pull; tug; jerk:
*Dare-ka ga watashi no sode o hip-
patta.* (だれかが私のそでを引っ張った)
Someone *tugged* at my sleeve.
2 bring; take (a person):
Kare wa keesatsu e hipparareta.
(彼は警察へ引っ張られた) He *was
taken along* to the police.
3 lead:
*Kare wa chiimu no hoka no mono
o yoku hippatte iru.* (彼はチームの他
の者をよく引っ張っている) He *leads*
the others in the team well.

hiˈragaˈna ひらがな (平仮名) *n.*
the Japanese cursive syllabary.
(⇨ inside front cover)

hiˈrahira ひらひら *adv.* (~ to)
(the motion of light, thin or soft
things, fluttering, swaying, or
falling):
*Choochoo ga hirahira (to) toñde
iru.* (蝶々がひらひら(と)飛んでいる) The
butterflies are *fluttering* around.

hiˈrakeˈˑru ひらける (開ける) *vi.*
(hirake-te Ⓥ) **1** (of a place)
become modernized [civilized];
develop:

Kono machi wa saikiñ hirakema-shita.（この町は最近開けました）This town *has* recently *developed*.
2 (of scenery) open; spread out:
Me no mae ni utsukushii keshiki ga hiraketa.（目の前に美しい景色が開けた）A beautiful view *opened* in front of our eyes.

hi⌐raki¹ ひらき（開き）n.
1 opening:
Kono tobira wa hiraki ga warui.（このとびらは開きが悪い）This door *won't open* easily.（⇨ hiraku）
2 difference:
Futari no ikeñ ni wa ooki-na hiraki ga aru.（二人の意見には大きな開きがある）There is a great *difference* of opinion between them.
3 fish cut open, flattened and dried:
aji no hiraki（あじの開き）a horse mackerel *cut open and dried*.

hi⌐ra⌐k·u ひらく（開く）(hirak·i-; hirak·a-; hira·i-te Ⓒ)
1 *vt.* open; undo; unpack; unseal:
Kare wa doa o hiraite, heya ni haitta.（彼はドアを開いて、部屋に入った）He *opened* the door and went into the room.（⇨ akeru¹）
2 *vi.* (of an office, etc.) start; begin; establish; found:
Yuubiñkyoku wa ku-ji ni hiraki-masu.（郵便局は9時に開きます）The post office *opens* at nine.（⇨ aku¹）
3 *vt.* hold (a meeting); give (a party).
4 *vi.* (of flowers) come out:
Sakura ga hiraki-hajimemashita.（桜が開き始めました）The cherry blossoms have started to *open*.

hi⌐rata·i ひらたい（平たい）a. (-ku) flat; even:
hiratai sara（平たい皿）a *flat* plate / *hyoomeñ o hirataku suru*（表面を平たくする）make a surface *even*.（⇨ taira）

hi⌐ritsu ひりつ（比率）n. ratio; percentage.（⇨ hi⌐）

hi⌐roba ひろば（広場）n. open space; square; plaza.

hi⌐rogar·u ひろがる（広がる）vi. (hirogar·i-; hirogar·a-; hirogat-te Ⓒ) **1** extend; expand; widen:
Eki no mae no michi ga hirogatta.（駅の前の道が広がった）The road in front of the station *widened*.（⇨ hirogeru）
2 (of a rumor) spread.（⇨ hiromaru）

hi⌐roge·ru ひろげる（広げる）vt. (hiroge-te Ⓥ) **1** spread; unfold; unroll:
Sono tori wa tsubasa o hirogeta.（その鳥は翼を広げた）The bird *spread its wings*.（⇨ hirogaru）
2 widen (a field of activity); enlarge; extend:
shoobai o hirogeru（商売を広げる）*expand* one's business.（⇨ hirogaru）

hi⌐ro·i ひろい（広い）a. (-ku) large; big; wide; broad:
hiroi ie（広い家）a *roomy* house / *hiroi chishiki*（広い知識）*broad* knowledge.（↔ semai）

hi⌐romar·u ひろまる（広まる）vi. (hiromar·i-; hiromar·a-; hiromat-te Ⓒ) spread; come into fashion; be circulated:
Sono uwasa wa machi-juu ni hiromatta.（そのうわさは町中に広まった）The rumor *spread* throughout the town.（⇨ hiromeru）

hi⌐rome·ru ひろめる（広める）vt. (hirome-te Ⓥ) spread; popularize:
kañkyoo-hakai ni kañsuru chishiki o hiromeru（環境破壊に関する知識を広める）*spread* knowledge about environmental destruction.（⇨ hiromaru）

hi⌐roo¹ ひろう（疲労）n. fatigue; tiredness; exhaustion.
hiroo suru（〜する）vi. be tired; be fatigued; be exhausted.（⇨ kutabireru; tsukareru）

hi⌐roo² ひろう（披露）n. introduction; announcement.
hiroo suru（〜する）vt. introduce;

announce; show: *Kare wa watashi-tachi ni atarashii sakuhiñ o hiroo shita.*(彼は私たちに新しい作品を披露した) He *showed* us his new work.

hiˈrosa ひろさ (広さ) *n.* area; extent; size; width:
Sono heya no hirosa wa dono kurai desu ka?(その部屋の広さはどのくらいですか) What is the *size* of that room?

hiˈro·u ひろう (拾う) *vt.* (hiro·i-; hirow·a-; hirot-te Ⓒ) 1 pick up; find:
Saifu o hirotte, keesatsu ni todoketa.(財布を拾って、警察に届けた) I *picked up* a wallet and turned it in to the police.
2 get; pick up (a taxi).

hiˈru ひる (昼) *n.* noon; day; daytime. (⇨ asa¹)

hiˈrugoˈhañ ひるごはん (昼ご飯) *n.* lunch. ★ More polite than '*hirumeshi*.' (⇨ asagohañ; bañgohañ; chuushoku; gohañ)

hiˈrumaˈ ひるま (昼間) *n.* daytime.

hiˈrumeshi ひるめし (昼飯) *n.* (*informal*) lunch. (⇨ hirugohañ; chuushoku)

hiˈru¹m·u ひるむ (怯む) *vi.* (hirum·i-; hirum·a-; hiruñ-de Ⓒ) flinch (from); shrink (from):
Kare wa kikeñ ni mo hirumanakatta.(彼は危険にもひるまなかった) He *did not shrink* from danger.

hiˈrune ひるね (昼寝) *n.* nap.

hiˈruyaˈsumi ひるやすみ (昼休み) *n.* lunch break; noon recess.

hiˈryoo ひりょう (肥料) *n.* manure; fertilizer.

hiˈsaˈisha ひさいしゃ (被災者) *n.* victim (of a disaster); sufferer.

hiˈsañ ひさん (悲惨) *a.n.* (~ na, ni) wretched; miserable; terrible; tragic:
hisañ na jiko(悲惨な事故) a *tragic* accident.

hiˈsashi ひさし (庇) *n.* 1 eaves.
2 visor (to a cap).

hiˈsashiburi ひさしぶり (久し振り)

a.n. (~ na/no, ni) after a long time [silence; separation]:
Hisashiburi desu ne.(久しぶりですね) It's *a long time* since I saw you last. ★ In greetings, '*o-hisashiburi desu ne*' is more polite.

hiˈsaˈshiku ひさしく (久しく) *adv.* (*formal*) for a long time:
Suzuki-sañ to wa hisashiku atte imaseñ.(鈴木さんとは久しく会っていません) I haven't met Mrs. Suzuki *for a long time*.

hiˈsho¹¹ ひしょ (秘書) *n.* secretary.

hiˈsho¹² ひしょ (避暑) *n.* summering; going somewhere cool during the hot months.

hiˈsoˈka ひそか (密か) *a.n.* (~ na, ni) in secret; in private:
Kagekiha wa hisoka ni bakudañ o tsukutte ita.(過激派はひそかに爆弾を作っていた) The radicals were *secretly* making bombs.

hiˈssha ひっしゃ (筆者) *n.* writer; author.

hiˈsshi ひっし (必死) *a.n.* (~ na/no, ni) desperate; frantic:
Kare wa hisshi ni nigeta.(彼は必死に逃げた) He ran away *desperately*.

hiˈssoˈri ひっそり *adv.* (~ to; ~ suru) (the state of being quiet, still or deserted):
Mori no naka wa hissori (to) shite ita.(森の中はひっそり(と)していた) All was *hushed* in the forest.

hiˈtai ひたい (額) *n.* forehead; brow.

hiˈtar·u ひたる (浸る) *vi.* (hitar·i-; hitar·a-; hitat-te Ⓒ) 1 be flooded; be under water:
Koozui de hatake ga mizu ni hitatta.(洪水で畑が水に浸った) The fields *were inundated* because of flooding. (⇨ hitasu)
2 be immersed in; be given to:
Kare wa sono ba no tanoshii fuñiki ni hitatta.(彼はその場の楽しい雰囲気に浸った) He *steeped himself* in the merry atmosphere of the place.

hiˈtas·u ひたす (浸す) *vt.* (hita-

sh·i-; hitas·a-; hitash·i-te C)
dip; soak:
mame o mizu ni hitasu (豆を水に浸
す) *soak* beans in water.
(⇨ hitaru)

hi「tee ひてい (否定) *n.* denial;
negation.
hitee suru (〜する) *vt.* deny;
make a denial. (↔ kootee')

hi「to ひと (人) *n.* **1** person; man;
woman: ★ In polite speech, '*kata*' is used.
Ano hito wa dare desu ka? (あの人
はだれですか) Who is that *man
[woman]*? (⇨ kata')
2 (other) people:
Wakai hito ga urayamashii. (若い
人がうらやましい) I envy young *people.*
3 human being; man:
Hito *wa dare de mo shinu.* (人はだ
れでも死ぬ) *Man* is mortal.
4 worker; hand:
Hito *ga tarinai.* (人が足りない) We
are short of *workers.* (⇨ hitode)

hi「to-[1] ひと (一) *pref.* one:
Watashi wa ichi-nichi ni tabako o
hito-*hako suimasu.* (私は一日にたば
こを一箱吸います) I smoke *a* pack of
cigarettes a day.

hi「to-[2] ひと (一) *pref.* a [an]:
★ Precedes a noun and indicates
one (short) action.
hito-*shigoto suru* (一仕事する) do *a*
job of work / hito-*nemuri suru* (一
眠りする) have *a* nap.

hi「to「bito ひとびと (人々) *n.*
(many) people.

hi「tochi「gai ひとちがい (人違い) *n.*
mistaking a person for somebody
else:
Gomeñ nasai. Hitochigai deshita.
(ごめんなさい. 人違いでした) I'm sorry.
I *took you for someone I know.*
(⇨ -chigai)

hi「tode ひとで (人手) *n.*
1 worker; hand:
Hitode *ga tarinai.* (人手が足りない)
We are short of *hands.* (⇨ hito)
2 another's help:

Kono shigoto wa hitode *o karizu
ni, yarimashita.* (この仕事は人手を借
りずに, やりました) I have done this
work without *anyone else's help.*
3 another's possession:
Sono uchi wa tsui-ni hitode *ni
watatta.* (その家はついに人手に渡った)
The house finally passed into
another's possession.

hi「todoori ひとどおり (人通り) *n.*
pedestrian traffic.

hi「togara ひとがら (人柄) *n.* personality; personal character.

hi「togomi ひとごみ (人込み) *n.*
crowd:
Depaato wa taiheñ na hitogomi
datta. (デパートは大変な人込みだった)
The department store was very
crowded.

hi「togoto ひとごと (人事) *n.*
other people's affairs: ★ Often
used with a negative.
Sono jiko wa hitogoto de wa nai.
(その事故はひと事ではない) *Everyone
has the possibility* of encoun-
tering such an accident.

hi「tokage ひとかげ (人影) *n.*
shadow of a person; human
figure.

hi「to「koto ひとこと (一言) *n.* single word:
Kare wa kaigi-chuu, hitokoto mo
shaberanakatta. (彼は会議中, ひと言
もしゃべらなかった) He *remained
silent* during the meeting.

hi「toma「kase ひとまかせ (人任せ)
n. leaving a matter to others:
Kare wa nañ de mo hitomakase
da. (彼は何でも人まかせだ) He *leaves
everything to others.*

hi「tomane ひとまね (人真似) *n.*
(of people) mimicry; imitation:
Oomu wa hitomane *ga umai.* (おう
むは人まねがうまい) Parrots are good
at *copying what people say.*

hi「to「mazu ひとまず *adv.* first (of
all); for a while; for the time
being:
Hitomazu, *yasumi o torimashoo.*
(ひとまず, 休みをとりましょう) Let's

take a break *for a while*.

hiˈtoˈme[1] ひとめ (一目) *n.* look; sight; glance:
Kare wa hitome *de kanojo ga suki ni natta.*（彼はひと目で彼女が好きになった）With *one glance*, he took a fancy to her.

hiˈtome[2] ひとめ (人目) *n.* public attention; notice:
Sono atarashii biru wa hitome *o hiita.*（その新しいビルは人目を引いた）The new building attracted *public attention*.

hiˈtoˈmi ひとみ (瞳) *n.* pupil of the eye.

hiˈtoˈri ひとり (一人・独り) *n.* one (person); each; by oneself:
Kanojo wa hitori *de kurashite imasu.*（彼女は一人で暮らしています）She lives *by herself*.

hiˈtoridachi ひとりだち (独り立ち) *n.* independence.
hitoridachi suru（～する）*vi.* become independent; stand on one's own feet. (⇨ dokuritsu)

hiˈtoride ni ひとりでに (独りでに) *adv.* by itself; automatically:
Kono deñtoo wa kuraku naru to hitoride ni *tsukimasu.*（この電灯は暗くなるとひとりでにつきます）When it gets dark, this light comes on *automatically*. (⇨ shizeñ ni)

hiˈtorigoto ひとりごと (独り言) *n.* soliloquy; talking to oneself.

hiˈtori-hitoˈri ひとりひとり (一人一人) *n.* every one; one by one; one after another.

hiˈtosashiˈyubi ひとさしゆび (人差し指) *n.* forefinger; index finger. (⇨ yubi)

hiˈtoshiˈi ひとしい (等しい) *a.* (-ku)
1 equal; the same:
Kono futatsu no kozutsumi wa mekata ga hitoshii.（この二つの小包は目方が等しい）These two parcels are *equal* in weight.
2 almost; practically:
Rieki ga tatta señ-eñ de wa nai ni hitoshii.（利益がたった千円ではないに等しい）The profit was only one

thousand yen, which is *almost nothing*.

hiˈtoˈtobi ひととび (一飛び) *n.* jump; hop:
Hikooki nara, Tookyoo to Fukuoka wa hitotobi *desu.*（飛行機なら、東京と福岡はひととびです）It is just a *hop* between Tokyo and Fukuoka if you go by airplane.

hiˈtotoori ひととおり (一通り) *n.* all; generality; ordinariness:
hitotoori *no setsumee* (一通りの説明) a *general* explanation.
—— *adv.* briefly; hurriedly; roughly:
maiasa hitotoori *shiñbuñ ni me o toosu* (毎朝一通り新聞に目を通す) glance *through* newspapers every morning. (⇨ zatto)

hiˈtoˈtsu[1] ひとつ (一つ) *n.* 1 one; single: ★ Used when counting.
Kore o hitotsu *kudasai.* (*at a store*) （これを一つ下さい）Give me *one* of these, please. (⇨ APP. 3)
2 one-year old:
Kono ko wa hitotsu *hañ desu.* （この子は一つ半です）This child is *one* and a half years old.

hiˈtoˈtsu[2] ひとつ *adv.* just; anyway; at any rate:
Mono wa tameshi da. Hitotsu *yatte miyoo.*（ものは試しだ。ひとつやってみよう）You will never know if you don't try. Let's have *a go*.

hiˈtoˈtsuki ひとつき (一月) *n.* one month.

hiˈtoˈyasumi ひとやすみ (一休み) *n.* a short rest; break.
hitoyasumi suru（～する）*vi.* take a short rest. (⇨ kyuukee)

hiˈtsuji ひつじ (羊) *n.* sheep.

hiˈtsuyoo ひつよう (必要) *n.* necessity; need.
—— *a.n.*（～ na, ni）necessary; essential; indispensable:
Hitsuyoo ga mono ga attara, osshatte kudasai.（必要なものがあったら、おっしゃってください）If there is anything you *need*, please let me know. (↔ fuhitsuyoo)

hi⸢tsuzeñ-teki ひつぜんてき（必然的）*a.n.* (~ na, ni) necessary; natural; inevitable:
hitsuzeñ-teki na kekka（必然的な結果）an *inevitable* result.

hi⸢tto ヒット *n.* 1 (of baseball) hit; single.
2 great success; hit.
hitto suru (~する) *vi.* make a hit.

hi⸢ya-a⸣se ひやあせ（冷や汗）*n.* cold sweat:
hiya-ase o kaku（冷や汗をかく）break into a *cold sweat*.

hi⸢yaka⸣s･u ひやかす（冷やかす）*vt.* (hiyakash･i-; hiyakas･a-; hiyakash･i-te [C]) 1 make fun of; tease:
Futari ga aruite iru no o mite, hiyakashite yatta.（二人が歩いているのを見て、冷やかしてやった）We saw the couple strolling and *made fun of* them.
2 window-shop:
Mise o hiyakashite jikañ o tsubushita.（店を冷やかして時間をつぶした）I idled away the time *window-shopping*.

hi⸢yake ひやけ（日焼け）*n.* sunburn; suntan.
hiyake suru (~する) *vi.* get sunburned; get a suntan.

hi⸢ya⸣s･u ひやす（冷やす）*vt.* (hiyash･i-; hiyas･a-; hiyash･i-te [C]) cool; ice; refrigerate:
reezooko de biiru o hiyasu（冷蔵庫でビールを冷やす）*cool* beer in the fridge. (⇨ hieru)

hi⸢ya⸣yaka ひややか（冷ややか）*a.n.* (~ na, ni) cold; coldhearted; cool; icy:
Kare wa hiyayaka na me de watashi o mita.（彼は冷ややかな目で私を見た）He gave me a *cold* look.

hi⸢yoko ひよこ *n.* chick; chicken.

hi⸢yoo ひよう（費用）*n.* expense; expenditure; cost.

hi⸢za ひざ（膝）*n.* knee; lap.

hi⸢zashi ひざし（日差し）*n.* sunlight; sun.

hi⸢zuke ひづけ（日付）*n.* date.

hi⸢zumi ひずみ（歪み）*n.* warp; distortion:
keezai no hizumi（経済のひずみ）*distortions* in the economy.

ho[1] ほ（穂）*n.* (of a plant) ear.

ho[2] ほ（帆）*n.* sail:
ho o ageru [orosu]（帆を揚げる[下ろす]）hoist [lower] a *sail*.

-ho ほ（歩）*suf.* counter for steps. (⇨ APP. 4)

ho⸢bo ほぼ *adv.* almost; nearly; about:
Biru wa hobo dekiagarimashita.（ビルはほぼでき上がりました）The building is *almost* completed.

hodo ほど（程）*p.* 1 about; some:
Ato juugo-fuñ hodo de Narita ni tsukimasu.（あと15分ほどで成田に着きます）We will be arriving at Narita in *about* fifteen minutes. (⇨ kurai)
2 not as [so]...as: ★ Follows a noun and used with a negative.
Kotoshi no natsu wa kyoneñ hodo atsuku nai.（今年の夏は去年ほど暑くない）This summer is *not as hot as* last year's.
3 the more...the more:
Reñshuu sureba suru hodo umaku narimasu.（練習すればするほどうまくなります）*The more* you practice, *the better* you become.
4 so...that:
Tsukarete, moo ip-po mo arukenai hodo datta.（疲れて、もう一歩も歩けないほどだった）I was *so* exhausted *that* I was unable to take even one step more.
5 almost:
Sono shirase o kiite tobiagaru hodo bikkuri shita.（その知らせを聞いて飛び上がるほどびっくりした）On hearing the news, I *almost* jumped up in surprise.

ho⸢do⸣k･u ほどく（解く）*vt.* (hodok･i-; hodok･a-; hodok･i-te [C]) undo; untie; unpack; unfasten:
kutsu no himo o hodoku（靴のひもをほどく）*untie* one's shoelaces / seetaa o hodoku（セーターをほどく）*un-*

ravel a sweater.

ho⌐doo ほどう (歩道) *n.* sidewalk; pavement. (↔ shadoo)

ho⌐dookyoo ほどうきょう (歩道橋) *n.* pedestrian overpass.

ho⌐e⌐l·ru ほえる (吠える) *vi.* (hoe-te Ⓥ) bark; howl; roar: *Sono inu wa watashi ni mukatte hoeta.* (その犬は私に向かってほえた) The dog *barked* at me.

ho⌐ga⌐raka ほがらか (朗らか) *a.n.* (~ na, ni) cheerful; bright: *hogaraka na seekaku* (朗らかな性格) a *cheerful* disposition.

ho⌐go ほご (保護) *n.* protection; guardianship; preservation. **hogo suru** (~する) *vt.* **1** protect; take care of; preserve. **2** take into protective custody; shelter.

ho⌐ho ほほ (頬) *n.* cheek. (⇒ hoo⌐)

ho⌐hoe⌐m·u ほほえむ (微笑む) *vi.* (-em·i-; -em·a-; -eñ-de Ⓒ) smile. (⇒ bishoo)

ho⌐ka ほか (外・他) *n.* other; another; else: *Kono kutsu wa sukoshi ooki-sugimasu. Hoka no o misete kudasai.* (この靴は少し大き過ぎます。ほかのを見せてください) These shoes are a bit too big. Can you show me some *others*? (⇒ sono-hoka; ta no)

ho⌐kahoka ほかほか *a.n.* (~ no) nice and warm; steaming hot: *hokahoka no satsumaimo* (ほかほかのさつまいも) *steaming* hot sweet potatoes.
— *adv.* (~ suru) warm: *Furo ni hairu to karada ga hokahoka suru.* (ふろに入ると体がほかほかする) You will feel *warm* after taking a bath.

ho⌐kañ ほかん (保管) *n.* safekeeping; custody; storage. **hokañ suru** (~する) *vt.* keep; have a thing in one's custody.

ho⌐ka ni ほかに (他に) *adv.* **1** besides; else; as well as: *Hoka ni nani-ka suru koto wa arimasu ka?* (ほかに何かすることはありますか) Is there anything *else* left to do? (⇒ sono-hoka)
2 except (for): *Kare no hoka ni sore ga dekiru mono wa imaseñ.* (彼のほかにそれができる者はいません) *Except for* him, there is no one who can do that.

ho⌐keñ[1] ほけん (保険) *n.* insurance; assurance: *Kuruma ni hokeñ o kaketa.* (車に保険をかけた) I've taken out *insurance* on my car.

ho⌐keñ[2] ほけん (保健) *n.* preservation of health; health.

ho⌐keñjo ほけんじょ (保健所) *n.* health center.

ho⌐ke⌐ñshoo ほけんしょう (保険証) *n.* = keñkoo-hokeñshoo.

ho⌐keñ-ta⌐iiku ほけんたいいく (保健体育) *n.* health and physical education.

Ho⌐kkyoku ほっきょく (北極) *n.* North Pole. (↔ Nañkyoku)

ho⌐kori[1] ほこり (誇り) *n.* pride: *Kare wa musuko o hokori ni omotte iru.* (彼は息子を誇りに思っている) He takes *pride* in his son. (⇒ hokoru)

ho⌐kori[2] ほこり (埃) *n.* dust. (⇒ chiri[1]; gomi)

ho⌐korobi⌐ru ほころびる (綻びる) *vi.* (hokorobi-te Ⓥ) **1** be torn; come apart: *nuime ga hokorobiru* (縫い目がほころびる) *come apart* at the seams. **2** (of a flower bud) begin to bloom.

ho⌐kor·u ほこる (誇る) *vt.* (hokor·i-; hokor·a-; hokot-te Ⓒ) be proud; boast; brag: *Kare wa umare no yoi no o hokotte iru.* (彼は生まれの良いのを誇っている) He *is proud* of being well-born. (⇒ hokori[1])

ho⌐me⌐l·ru ほめる (褒める) *vt.* (home-te Ⓥ) praise; speak well of; compliment: *Señsee wa kare no Nihoñgo no hatsuoñ o hometa.* (先生は彼の日本語の発音をほめた) The teacher *praised* his Japanese pronunciation. (↔ kenasu)

hoñ ほん (本) *n.* book; volume.

hoñ- ほん (本) *pref.* **1** real; genuine; regular:
hoñ-*shiñju* (本真珠) a *genuine* pearl / hoñ-*shikeñ* (本試験) the *final* examination.
2 (*formal*) this; current:
hoñ-*añ* (本案) *this* plan.

-hoñ ほん (本) *suf.* counter for long objects. (⇨ APP. 4)

hoñba ほんば (本場) *n.* center of production; home:
Riñgo no hoñba wa Aomori desu. (りんごの本場は青森です) The *home* of Japanese apple *production* is Aomori.

hoñbako ほんばこ (本箱) *n.* bookcase. (⇨ hoñdana)

hoñbuñ ほんぶん (本文) *n.* text; body:
keeyakusho no hoñbuñ (契約書の本文) the *text* of a contract.

hoñdana ほんだな (本棚) *n.* bookshelf. (⇨ hoñbako)

hone ほね (骨) *n.* **1** bone:
Kono sakana wa hone ga ooi. (この魚は骨が多い) This fish has a lot of *bones*.
2 rib; frame:
Kasa no hone ga ip-poñ orete shimatta. (傘の骨が一本折れてしまった) A *rib* of my umbrella broke.
3 hardness; difficulty:
Sono yama ni noboru no wa hone da. (その山に登るのは骨だ) It *is* hard to climb that mountain.
4 backbone; pluck:
Kare wa hone no aru otoko da. (彼は骨のある男だ) He is a man with *backbone*.
hone o oru (〜を折る) take great pains.

hoñgoku ほんごく (本国) *n.* one's own country; one's home country. (⇨ bokoku)

hoñjitsu ほんじつ (本日) *n.* today; this day. ★ Formal equivalent of 'kyoo.'

hoñkaku-teki ほんかくてき (本格的) *a.n.* (〜 na, ni) full; full-scale; real:
hoñkaku-teki na Furañsu ryoori (本格的なフランス料理) *real* French cooking.

hoñkañ ほんかん (本館) *n.* the main building; this building.

hoñki ほんき (本気) *n.* earnestness; seriousness:
Tanaka-sañ wa joodañ o hoñki ni shita. (田中さんは冗談を本気にした) Ms. Tanaka *took* the joke *seriously*. (⇨ majime)
— *a.n.* (〜 na, ni) earnest; serious:
Kare-ra wa hoñki ni natte, choosa o hajimeta. (彼らは本気になって、調査を始めた) They have become *serious* and started the investigation.

hoñmono ほんもの (本物) *n.* genuine article; the real thing.

hoñmyoo ほんみょう (本名) *n.* one's real name. (⇨ namae)

hoñne ほんね (本音) *n.* real intention [feeling]:
Ano hito wa nakanaka hoñne o iwanai. (あの人はなかなか本音を言わない) He doesn't readily disclose his *real intentions [feelings]*. (⇨ tatemae)

hoñneñ ほんねん (本年) *n.* the current year; this year. ★ More formal than 'kotoshi.'

hoñniñ ほんにん (本人) *n.* the person in question:
Hoñniñ wa sono jijitsu o hitee shite imasu. (本人はその事実を否定しています) *The man himself* denies the fact. (⇨ tooniñ)

hoñno ほんの (本の) *attrib.* only; mere; just: (⇨ wazuka)
Shio o hoñno sukoshi irete kudasai. (塩をほんの少し入れてください) Please add *just* a little salt.

hoñnoo ほんのう (本能) *n.* instinct.

hoñnoo-teki ほんのうてき (本能的) *a.n.* (〜 na, ni) instinctive:
Doobutsu wa hoñnoo-teki ni ki-

keñ o kañjiru. (動物は本能的に危険を感じる) Animals sense danger *instinctively.*

hoˈnoo ほのお (炎) *n.* flame; blaze.

hoˈñrai (wa) ほんらい(は)(本来(は)) *adv.* 1 originally; by nature: *Sushi wa hoñrai (wa) hozoñshoku de atta.* (すしは本来(は)保存食であった) Sushi was *originally* a preserved food.
2 essentially: *Kore to sore wa hoñrai (wa) betsu no mono da.* (これとそれは本来(は)別のものだ) This and that are *essentially* different matters. (⇨ gañrai; motomoto)

hoˈñryoo ほんりょう (本領) *n.* one's real ability; one's specialty: *Kare wa hañbaibu de hoñryoo o hakki shita.* (彼は販売部で本領を発揮した) He showed *what he could do* in the sales department.

hoˈñshitsu ほんしつ (本質) *n.* essence; substance; real nature: *Kare-ra no ikeñ wa hoñshitsu ni oite onaji desu.* (彼らの意見は本質において同じです) Their opinions are the same in *essence.*

hoˈñshitsu-teki ほんしつてき (本質的) *a.n.* (~ na, ni) essential; intrinsic: *Ryoosha no aida ni hoñshitsu-teki na chigai wa nai.* (両者の間に本質的な違いはない) There is not an *essential* difference between the two of them.

hoˈñteñ ほんてん (本店) *n.* head office; main store.

hoˈñto ほんと *n., a.n.* (*informal*) = hoñtoo.

hoˈñtoo ほんとう (本当) *n.* truth; fact; reality: *Hoñtoo no koto o itte kudasai.* (本当のことを言ってください) Please tell me the *truth.*
— *a.n.* (~ na, ni) true; actual; real: *Sono hanashi wa hoñtoo desu.* (その話は本当です) The story is *true.*

hoˈñya ほんや (本屋) *n.* book-store; bookshop.

hoˈñyaku ほんやく (翻訳) *n.* translation.
hoñyaku suru (~する) *vt.* translate. (⇨ yaku')

hoˈo¹ ほう (法) *n.* 1 law: *Kimi no kooi wa hoo ni hañsuru.* (君の行為は法に反する) Your conduct is against the *law.*
2 method; way: *Watashi wa ii keñkoo-hoo o shitte imasu.* (私はいい健康法を知っています) I know a very effective *way* of keeping one's health. (⇨ hoohoo)

hoˈo² ほう (方) *n.* 1 direction: *Kare wa dotchi no hoo e ikimashita ka?* (彼はどっちの方へ行きましたか) In which *direction* did he go?
2 (as far as) something [someone] (is concerned): ★ Used in comparison or contrast. *Boku no hoo ga kare yori mo se ga takai.* (ぼくのほうが彼よりも背が高い) *I* am taller than him.

hoˈo³ ほお (頬) *n.* cheek. (⇨ hoho)

hoˈoañ ほうあん (法案) *n.* bill: *Sono hooañ wa gikai o tsuuka shita.* (その法案は議会を通過した) The *bill* passed the Diet.

hoˈobi ほうび (褒美) *n.* reward; prize: *Watashi wa hoobi ni mañneñhitsu o moratta.* (私はほうびに万年筆をもらった) I got a fountain pen as a *prize.*

hoˈoboo ほうぼう (方々) *n.* every direction; everywhere; here and there: *Kagi o hooboo sagashita ga, mitsukaranakatta.* (鍵をほうぼう捜したが、見つからなかった) I searched for the key *high and low*, but it did not turn up.

hoˈochi ほうち (放置) *n.* leaving (a thing).
hoochi suru (~する) *vt.* leave; let alone: *Jiteñsha o koko ni hoochi shinai de kudasai.* (自転車をここに放置しないでください) Please *don't leave* your bicycle here.

ho⌐ochoo ほうちょう (包丁) *n.* kitchen knife.

ho⌐odoo ほうどう (報道) *n.* news; report; information.
hoodoo suru (〜する) *vt.* report; inform.

ho⌐odo⌐ojiñ ほうどうじん (報道陣) *n.* a group of reporters; the press.

ho⌐ofu ほうふ (豊富) *a.n.* (〜 na, ni) plentiful; ample; rich:
Ano kañgofu-sañ wa keekeñ ga hoofu desu.(あの看護婦さんは経験が豊富です) That nurse has *a lot of* experience.

ho⌐o ga ⌐i⌐i ほうがいい (方が良い)
★ Used in the patterns, '*n.*+*no hoo ga ii*; *a.n.*+*na hoo ga ii*; *v.* [*a.; attrib.*]+*hoo ga ii*.'
1 be better:
Chiisai no yori ookii hoo ga ii. (小さいのより大きいほうがいい) The big one *is better* than the small one.
2 I suggest...; be better; had better (do); should (do): ★ Used in making recommendations.
Hokkaidoo nara, hikooki de itta hoo ga ii ka mo shiremaseñ.(北海道なら, 飛行機で行ったほうがいいかもしれません) If you are going to Hokkaido, *it might be better* to go by plane.

ho⌐ogaku ほうがく (方角) *n.* direction; bearings.

ho⌐oge⌐ñ ほうげん (方言) *n.* dialect.

ho⌐ohige ほおひげ (頬髭) *n.* whiskers. (⇒ hige)

ho⌐ohoo ほうほう (方法) *n.* method; way; measure. (⇒ hoo¹)

ho⌐oji·ru ほうじる (報じる) *vt.* (hooji-te Ⅴ) report; inform; broadcast; televise:
Dono shiñbuñ mo sono kuni no jishiñ no koto o hoojita. (どの新聞もその国の地震のことを報じた) All the newspapers *reported* the earthquake in that country.

ho⌐okai ほうかい (崩壊) *n.* (*formal*) collapse; breakdown; disintegration.

hookai suru (〜する) *vi.* collapse; disintegrate; decay. ((⇒ kowareru; kuzureru))

ho⌐okeñ-shu⌐gi ほうけんしゅぎ (封建主義) *n.* feudalism.

ho⌐okeñ-teki ほうけんてき (封建的) *a.n.* (〜 na, ni) feudal; feudalistic:
hookeñ-teki na kañgaekata (封建的な考え方) a *feudalistic* way of thinking.

ho⌐oki¹ ほうき (放棄) *n.* abandonment; renunciation.
hooki suru (〜する) *vt.* give up; abandon; renounce.

ho⌐oki² ほうき (箒) *n.* broom.

ho⌐okoku ほうこく (報告) *n.* report.
hookoku suru (〜する) *vt.* report; inform; give an account.

ho⌐okoo ほうこう (方向) *n.*
1 direction; way; course.
2 aim; object; course:
jibuñ no shoorai no hookoo o kimeru (自分の将来の方向を決める) make a decision about the future *course* of one's life.

ho⌐ome⌐ñ ほうめん (方面) *n.*
1 district:
Taifuu wa Shikoku hoomeñ o osotta. (台風は四国方面を襲った) The typhoon hit the Shikoku *district*.
2 direction:
Kare wa Ueno hoomeñ e ikimashita. (彼は上野方面へ行きました) He went in the *direction* of Ueno.
3 field:
Yamada-hakase wa kono hoomeñ no keñi desu. (山田博士はこの方面の権威です) Dr. Yamada is an authority in this *field*.

ho⌐omoñ ほうもん (訪問) *n.* visit; call.
hoomoñ suru (〜する) *vt.* call at [on]; visit.

ho⌐omu¹ ホーム *n.* platform.

ho⌐omu² ホーム *n.* home; asylum: *roojiñ-hoomu* (老人ホーム) an old people's *home*.

ho￢omu³ ホーム *n.* (of baseball) home plate.

ho￢omu￢r·u ほうむる (葬る) *vt.* (hoomur·i-; hoomur·a-; hoomutte C) 1 bury (a dead body): *Kare wa kono bochi ni hoomurarete imasu.* (彼はこの墓地に葬られています) He *is buried* in this graveyard.
2 shelve (a plan); hush up (an incident): *Sono oshoku-jikeñ wa yami ni hoomurareta.* (その汚職事件は闇に葬られた) The corruption case *was swept under the carpet.*

ho￢oreñsoo ほうれんそう (菠薐草) *n.* spinach.

ho￢oritsu ほうりつ (法律) *n.* law.

ho￢or·u¹ ほうる (放る) *vt.* (hoor·i-; hoor·a-; hoot-te C) throw; toss; pitch: *Sono booru o hootte kudasai.* (そのボールを放ってください) Please *throw* the ball to me. (⇨ nageru)

ho￢oru² ホール *n.* hall. ★ Used for public events.

ho￢osaku¹ ほうさく (豊作) *n.* good crop; rich harvest.

ho￢osaku² ほうさく (方策) *n.* measures; plan; means: *hoosaku ga tsukiru* (方策が尽きる) *be at one's wits' end.* (⇨ shudañ)

ho￢oseki ほうせき (宝石) *n.* jewel; gem; jewelry.

ho￢oshi ほうし (奉仕) *n.* service. *... ni hooshi suru* (...に～する) *vt.* serve: *shakai ni hooshi suru* (社会に奉仕する) *serve* the community. (⇨ tsukusu)

ho￢oshiñ ほうしん (方針) *n.* policy; course; principle: *atarashii hooshiñ o tateru* (新しい方針を立てる) make a new *policy.*

ho￢oshuu ほうしゅう (報酬) *n.* remuneration; reward; fee.

ho￢osoku ほうそく (法則) *n.* law; rule: *juyoo to kyookyuu no hoosoku* (需要と供給の法則) the *law* of supply and demand.

ho￢osoo¹ ほうそう (放送) *n.* broadcasting; broadcast.
hoosoo suru (～する) *vt.* broadcast; televise; put on the air.

ho￢osoo² ほうそう (包装) *n.* packing; wrapping.
hoosoo suru (～する) *vt.* pack; wrap. (⇨ tsutsumu)

ho￢oso￢ogeki ほうそうげき (放送劇) *n.* radio [TV] drama.

ho￢oso￢okyoku ほうそうきょく (放送局) *n.* broadcasting station; radio [TV] station.

ho￢otai ほうたい (包帯) *n.* bandage; dressing: *kizuguchi ni hootai o suru* (傷口に包帯をする) put a *bandage* on the wound.

ho￢ra ほら *int.* look; look here; listen: *Hora, mukoo ni shima ga mieru yo.* (ほら, 向こうに島が見えるよ) *Look!* You can see an island over there.

ho￢ra-ana ほらあな (洞穴) *n.* cave; cavern.

ho￢ri¹ ほり (堀) *n.* moat; canal.

ho￢robi·ru ほろびる (滅びる) *vi.* (horobi-te V) fall; die out; be ruined; perish: *Sono kuni wa sañzeñ-neñ mae ni horobimashita.* (その国は3千年前に滅びました) That country *perished* 3,000 years ago. (⇨ horobosu)

ho￢robo￢s·u ほろぼす (滅ぼす) *vt.* (horobosh·i-; horobos·a-; horobosh·i-te C) destroy; ruin: *Kaku-señsoo wa jiñrui o horoboshimasu.* (核戦争は人類を滅ぼします) Nuclear war will *destroy* humanity. (⇨ horobiru)

ho￢r·u¹ ほる (掘る) *vt.* (hor·i-; hor·a-; hot-te C) dig; excavate: *ana o horu* (穴を掘る) *dig* a hole.

ho￢r·u² ほる (彫る) *vt.* (hor·i-; hor·a-; hot-te C) carve; engrave; chisel; inscribe: *Kare wa ki o hotte niñgyoo o tsukutta.* (彼は木を彫って人形を作った) He made a doll by *carving* the wood.

ho⌐ryo ほりょ (捕虜) *n.* prisoner (of war); captive.

ho⌐shi ほし (星) *n.* star.

ho⌐shi⌐.i ほしい (欲しい) *a.* (-ku) want; would like; wish; hope: *Motto jikan ga hoshii.* (もっと時間が欲しい) I *want* more time.

ho⌐shi⌐mono ほしもの (干し物) *n.* washing; clothes for drying. (⇨ señtaku¹; señtakumono)

ho⌐shoo¹ ほしょう (保証) *n.* guarantee; warranty; assurance.
hoshoo suru (〜する) *vt.* guarantee; warrant; assure.

ho⌐shoo² ほしょう (保障) *n.* security: *shakai-hoshoo* (社会保障) social *security*.
hoshoo suru (〜する) *vt.* secure; guarantee.

ho⌐shoo³ ほしょう (補償) *n.* compensation; indemnity.
hoshoo suru (〜する) *vt.* compensate; indemnify.

ho⌐shoonin ほしょうにん (保証人) *n.* guarantor.

ho⌐shu ほしゅ (保守) *n.* conservatism:
hoshu-too (保守党) a conservative party. (↔ kakushin²)

ho⌐shu-teki ほしゅてき (保守的) *a.n.* (〜 na, ni) conservative. (↔ shiñpo-teki)

ho⌐so⌐.i ほそい (細い) *a.* (-ku)
1 (of round objects such as sticks or string) thin; small; fine: *hosoi hari* (細い針) a *thin* needle / *hosoi señ* (細い線) a *fine* line. (↔ futoi)
2 (of a voice) thin. (↔ futoi)

ho⌐sonaga⌐.i ほそながい (細長い) *a.* (-ku) long and narrow; slender: *Kono heya wa hosonagakute tsukainikui.* (この部屋は細長くて使いにくい) This room is *long and narrow*, and awkward to use. (⇨ hosoi; nagai)

ho⌐ssoku ほっそく (発足) *n.* start; inauguration.
hossoku suru (〜する) *vi.* make a start; be inaugurated.

ho⌐s.u ほす (干す) *vt.* (hosh·i-; hos·a-; hosh·i-te C) **1** dry: *Kanojo wa nureta taoru o hinata ni hoshita.* (彼女はぬれたタオルを日なたに干した) She *dried* the wet towel in the sun.
2 drink up; empty: *Kare wa koppu no biiru o hoshita.* (彼はコップのビールを干した) He *drained* the beer in the glass.

ho⌐taru ほたる (蛍) *n.* firefly.

ho⌐tchikisu ホッチキス *n.* stapler.

ho⌐toke¹ ほとけ (仏) *n.* **1** the Buddha.
2 the deceased: *hotoke ni hana o sonaeru* (仏に花を供える) offer flowers before *the deceased.*

ho⌐to⌐ndo ほとんど (殆ど) *n., adv.*
1 almost; nearly: *Sono ie wa hotoñdo dekiagarimashita.* (その家はほとんどでき上がりました) The house is *nearly* completed.
2 (with a negative) hardly; few; little: *Watashi wa sore ni tsuite wa hotoñdo shirimaseñ.* (私はそれについてはほとんど知りません) I *hardly* know anything about that.

ho⌐tto ほっと *adv.* (〜 suru) (the state of being relieved): *Shikeñ ga owatte, hotto shita.* (試験が終わって、ほっとした) I *was relieved* when the exam was over.

ho⌐yahoya ほやほや *n.* (the state of being new or fresh): *Kare-ra wa shiñkoñ hoyahoya desu.* (彼らは新婚ほやほやです) They have *just* married.

ho⌐zoñ ほぞん (保存) *n.* preservation; conservation.
hozoñ suru (〜する) *vt.* preserve; keep.

ho⌐zo⌐ñshoku ほぞんしょく (保存食) *n.* preserved food; emergency provisions.

hya⌐kkaji⌐teñ ひゃっかじてん (百科事典) *n.* encyclopedia.

hya⌐ku¹ ひゃく (百) *n.* one hundred. (⇨ APP. 3)

hyo⌈ito ひょいと *adv.* unexpectedly; suddenly; casually; lightly:
Michi no kado kara hyoito jiteñsha ga dete kite, bikkuri shita. (道の角からひょいと自転車が出て来て, びっくりした) I was surprised when a bicycle *suddenly* came around the corner.

hyo⌈o ひょう(表) *n.* table; list.

hyo⌈obañ ひょうばん(評判) *n.* reputation; popularity; rumor.

hyo⌈ogeⁿ ひょうげん(表現) *n.* verbal expression; representation.
hyoogeñ suru (～する) *vt.* express; represent.

hyo⌈ojo⌈o ひょうじょう(表情) *n.* facial expression; look.

hyo⌈ojuñ ひょうじゅん(標準) *n.* standard; normal; average.

hyo⌈ojuñgo ひょうじゅんご(標準語) *n.* the standard language. ★ Often called '*kyootsuugo.*'

hyo⌈ojuñ-teki ひょうじゅんてき(標準的) *a.n.* (～ na, ni) standard; average; typical.

hyo⌈oka ひょうか(評価) *n.* valuation; appraisal; rating; assessment.
hyooka suru (～する) *vt.* value; appraise; estimate.

hyo⌈omeⁿ ひょうめん(表面) *n.*
1 surface:
Teeburu no hyoomen wa pika-pika shite ita. (テーブルの表面はぴかぴかしていた) The *surface* of the table was shiny.
2 outside:
Tatemono no hyoomeñ wa rippa datta. (建物の表面はりっぱだった) The *outside* of the building was gorgeous.
3 appearance:
Kare wa hyoomeñ wa otonashi-soo ni mieru. (彼は表面はおとなしそうに見える) In *appearance*, he seems easy to deal with.

hyo⌈oroñ ひょうろん(評論) *n.* criticism; review; critical essay.

hyo⌈oryuu ひょうりゅう(漂流) *n.* drifting.
hyooryuu suru (～する) *vt.* drift; go adrift.

hyo⌈oshi ひょうし(表紙) *n.* the cover of a book or a magazine. ★ Often refers to the jacket of a book. (⇨ kabaa)

hyo⌈rohyoro¹ ひょろひょろ *adv.* (～ to; ～ suru) 1 tall and thin: hyorohyoro (to) nobita kusa (ひょろひょろ(と)伸びた草) grass which has grown *tall and thin.*
2 staggeringly; totteringly:
Kare wa sake ni yotte hyoro-hyoro (to) aruita. (彼は酒に酔ってひょろひょろ(と)歩いた) He *staggered* along drunk. (⇨ yoroyoro)

hyo⌈rohyoro² ひょろひょろ *a.n.* (～ na, ni) lanky; slender; frail; feeble:
Kare wa karada ga hyorohyoro de tayorinai. (彼は体がひょろひょろで頼りない) He is *tall and slim* and looks unreliable.

I

i い(胃) *n.* stomach.

-i¹ い *suf.* place; rank:
hyaku-meetoru kyoosoo de ni-i ni naru (百メートル競走で2位になる) come in *second* in the 100-meter race.

-i² い(医) *suf.* medical doctor; general practitioner:
gañka-i (眼科医) an eye *doctor* / *geka-i* (外科医) a *surgeon* / *naika-i* (内科医) a *physician.* (⇨ isha)

i⌈ba⌈r·u いばる(威張る) *vi.* (ibar·i-; ibar·a-; ibat-te Ⓒ) put on airs; boast; be haughty. (⇨ karaibari)

i⌈basho いばしょ(居場所) *n.* whereabouts.

i｢biki¹ いびき (鼾) *n.* snore.

i｢chi¹¹ いち (一・壱) *n.* one; the first; No. 1:
Nihoñ-ichi (日本一) *No. 1* in Japan. (⇨ hitotsu¹; APP. 3)

i｢chi² いち (位置) *n.* position; location; situation.
ichi suru (～する) *vi.* lie; be located.

i｢chiba いちば (市場) *n.* market.
★ Never used to mean 'supermarket' or 'store.'

i｢chi｢bañ¹ いちばん (一番) *n.* first.

i｢chibañ² いちばん (一番) *adv.*
most; best:
Dono kisetsu ga ichibañ suki desu ka? (どの季節がいちばん好きですか)
Which season do you like *best*?

i｢chi｢bu いちぶ (一部) *n.* (a) part; portion; section.
— *adv.* partially; in part:
sekkee o ichibu shuusee suru (設計を一部修正する) correct the design *in part*.

i｢chibu｢buñ いちぶぶん (一部分) *n.* (a) part; section. (⇨ ichibu)

i｢chida｢iji いちだいじ (一大事) *n.* serious [grave] matter. (⇨ daiji²)

i｢chidañ いちだん (一団) *n.* group; party; body:
Kare-ra wa ichidañ to natte heya kara dete itta. (彼らは一団となって部屋から出て行った) They walked out of the room *in a body*. (⇨ -dañ)

i｢chido いちど (一度) *n.* once; one time.

i｢chido¹ ni いちどに (一度に) *adv.*
all at once; at a time; at the same time.

i｢chido¹o いちどう (一同) *n.* everyone; all present:
ichidoo o daihyoo shite, aisatsu suru (一同を代表して、挨拶する)
make an address as the representative of *all those present*.

i｢chi¹gai ni いちがいに (一概に) *adv.*
(～ wa) (with a negative) generally; necessarily; indiscriminately:
Kare ga machigatte iru to wa ichi-

gai ni (wa) kimeraremaseñ. (彼が間違っているとは一概に(は)決められません) We cannot *necessarily* conclude that he is wrong.

i｢chi-gatsu¹ いちがつ (一月) *n.* January. (⇨ APP. 5)

i｢chigo いちご (苺) *n.* strawberry.

i｢chiguñ いちぐん (一軍) *n.* (of baseball) the first team; major league. (⇨ niguñ)

i｢chiha¹yaku いちはやく (逸早く) *adv.* quickly; without delay.

i｢chi¹ichi いちいち (一々) *adv.* in detail; one by one:
Chichi wa watashi no suru koto ni ichiichi kuchi o dasu. (父は私のすることにいちいち口を出す) My father meddles in *everything* I do.

i｢chi¹ji いちじ (一時) *adv.* 1 once; at one time:
Sono uta wa ichiji hayatta koto ga arimasu. (その歌は一時はやったことがあります) That song was *at one time* popular.
2 for a while; for the time being:
Watashi wa sañ-neñ hodo mae ni ichiji koko ni suñde ita koto ga arimasu. (私は三年ほど前に一時ここに住んでいたことがあります) Three years ago I used to live here *for a while*.

i｢chijirushi¹·i いちじるしい (著しい) *a.* (-ku) remarkable; marked; noticeable.

i｢chimeñ いちめん (一面) *n.* 1 one side; one aspect:
Anata wa yo-no-naka no ichimeñ shika mite inai. (あなたは世の中の一面しか見ていない) You have only seen *one side* of life.
2 the front page of a newspaper.
— *adv.* 1 on the other hand:
Kanojo wa yasashii ga ichimeñ kibishii tokoro mo aru. (彼女は優しいが一面厳しい所もある) She is tenderhearted, but *on the other hand* she has a strict side.
2 all over; the whole place:
Mizuumi wa ichimeñ koori de oowarete ita. (湖は一面氷でおおわれて

いた) *The whole surface* of the lake was covered with ice.

i￢**chinichi-juu** いちにちじゅう (一日中) *adv.* all day (long).

i￢**chioo** いちおう (一応) *adv.* anyway; just in case; for the time being:
Kare ga iru ka doo ka wakaranai ga, ichioo *reñraku shite mimashoo.* (彼がいるかどうかわからないが、一応連絡してみましょう) I don't know if he is there or not, but *anyway* let's try to get in touch with him. (⇨ toriaezu)

i￢**chiritsu** いちりつ (市立) *n.* = shiritsu².

i￢**chiryuu** いちりゅう (一流) *n.* first-class; first-rate:
ichiryuu *no hoteru* (一流のホテル) a *first-rate* hotel. (⇨ ikkyuu; sañryuu)

i￢**chi￢ya** いちや (一夜) *n.* a [one] night:
Watashi wa sono koya de ichiya *o sugoshita.* (私はその小屋で一夜を過ごした) I spent *a night* in the hut.

i￢**dai** いだい (偉大) *a.n.* (～ na, ni) great; grand: idai *na sakka* (偉大な作家) a *great* novelist.

i￢**do** いど (井戸) *n.* well.

i￢**do￢m･u** いどむ (挑む) *vt.* (idom･i･; idom･a･; idoñ-de C) try; challenge; defy: *shiñ-kiroku ni* idomu (新記録に挑む) *try to set a* new record. (⇨ chooseñ)

i￢**doo¹** いどう (移動) *n.* **1** movement; transfer.
2 removal; migration:
miñzoku no idoo (民族の移動) a racial *migration*.
idoo suru (～する) *vi., vt.* move; travel; migrate.

i￢**doo²** いどう (異動) *n.* personnel change; reshuffle.

i￢**e¹¹** いえ (家) *n.* home; house. ★A little more formal than '*uchi*¹.'

i￢**e¹²** いえ *int.* no. ★Less formal than '*iie*.'

i￢**ede** いえで (家出) *n.* running away from home.

i￢**emoto¹** いえもと (家元) *n.* master [leader] of a school (of flower arrangement, tea ceremony, etc.).

i￢**fuku** いふく (衣服) *n.* clothes; clothing. (⇨ fuku²)

i￢**gai** いがい (意外) *a.n.* (～ na, ni) unexpected; surprising:
igai *na dekigoto* (意外な出来事) an *unexpected* occurrence.

-i￢**gai** いがい (以外) *suf.* **1** except; but; other than:
*Mokuyoo-*igai *nara, itsu de mo kekkoo desu.* (木曜以外なら、いつでもけっこうです) As long as it is a day *other than* Thursday, anytime is fine.
2 in addition to; besides:
*Kare wa hyooroñ-*igai *ni shoosetsu mo kakimasu.* (彼は評論以外に小説も書きます) *In addition to* reviews, he also writes novels.

i￢**gaku** いがく (医学) *n.* medical science; medicine.

i￢**gañ** いがん (胃癌) *n.* stomach [gastric] cancer. (⇨ gañ)

i￢**geñ** いげん (威厳) *n.* dignity; majesty: igeñ *o tamotsu [sokonau]* (威厳を保つ[損なう]) maintain [impair] one's *dignity*.

i￢**gi¹** いぎ (意義) *n.* meaning; significance:
Oriñpikku wa sañka suru koto ni igi *ga aru.* (オリンピックは参加することに意義がある) In the Olympics, the *importance* lies in participating.

i￢**gi²** いぎ (異議) *n.* objection; dissent; protest: igi *o tonaeru* (異議を唱える) raise an *objection*.

i￢**go¹** いご (以後) *n.* after this; from that time on; ever since:
Sono kaisha wa sekiyu shokku igo, *sugu ni tachinaotta.* (その会社は石油ショック以後、すぐに立ち直った) The company recovered soon *after* the oil crisis. (↔ izeñ¹)

i￢**go²** いご (囲碁) *n.* the game of go.

i￢**hañ** いはん (違反) *n.* violation; breach.
... ni ihañ suru (...に～する) *vt.* vio-

late; break. (⇨ hañsuru)

i'i いい (良い) a. good; nice; fine:
★ Used only in this form. More
informal than 'yoi[1]' and often
used ironically.
Kanojo wa fukusoo no señsu ga ii.
(彼女は服装のセンスがいい) She has
good taste in clothes.

i'iarawa'su いいあらわす (言い表す)
vt. (-arawash·i·; -arawas·a·;
-arawash·i·te C) say; express;
describe.

i'ia'u いいあう (言い合う) vt. (-a·i·;
-aw·a·; -at·te C) quarrel; dispute. (⇨ arasou)

i'ida'su いいだす (言い出す) vt.
(-dash·i·; -das·a·; -dash·i·te C)
start speaking; propose; suggest.

i'ie[1] いいえ int. no; yes: ★ '*Iie*'
literally means 'That's wrong',
and is used to confirm a statement, whether affirmative or
negative.
"Ima isogashii desu ka?" "Iie, iso-
gashiku arimaseñ." (「今忙しいです
か」「いいえ、忙しくありません」) "Are
you busy now?" "*No,* I am not."
/ *"Moo sukoshi o-nomi ni narima-*
señ ka?" "Iie, moo kekkoo desu."
(「もう少しお飲みになりませんか」「いいえ、
もう結構です」) "Won't you have a
bit more to drink?" "*No,* thank
you. (↔ hai[1]) (⇨ iya[2])

i'ika'es·u いいかえす (言い返す) vi.
(-kaesh·i·; -kaes·a·; -kaesh·i·te
C) talk back; retort.

i'ikageñ いいかげん (いい加減) a.n.
(~ na, ni) irresponsible; non-
committal; vague:
Kare wa suru koto ga iikageñ da.
(彼はすることがいいかげんだ) He *never*
takes responsibility for what he
does.
— adv. rather; pretty:
Tañjuñ na shigoto na no de iika-
geñ iya ni natta. (単純な仕事なのでい
いかげんいやになった) Since it is a
monotonous job, I am *rather*
bored with it.
Iikageñ ni shinai ka. (~にしない

か) That's enough! Come off it!

i'ikata いいかた (言い方) n. expression; way of speaking:
Kanojo wa mono no iikata ga tee-
nee da. (彼女は物の言い方が丁寧だ)
Her *manner of speaking* is polite.

i'ikase'·ru いいきかせる (言い聞か
せる) vi. (-kikase-te V) tell a person to (do); persuade; admonish.

i'iñ いいん (委員) n. member of a
committee.

i'i'ñchoo いいんちょう (委員長) n.
chairman; chairperson.

i'i'ñkai いいんかい (委員会) n. committee; committee meeting.

i'itsuke'·ru いいつける (言い付ける)
vi., vt. (-tsuke-te V) 1 tell a person to (do):
Kare wa musuko ni shigoto o to-
tsudau yoo iitsuketa. (彼は息子に仕
事を手伝うよう言いつけた) He *told* his
son to help him with his work.
2 tell on:
Soñna koto o shitara, señsee ni ii-
tsukemasu yo. (そんなことをしたら、先
生に言いつけますよ) If you do such a
thing, I will *tell* the teacher *on*
you.

i'itsutae いいつたえ (言い伝え) n.
tradition; legend.

i'iwake いいわけ (言い訳) n. excuse; explanation; justification:
kurushii iiwake o suru (苦しい言い
訳をする) *make* a poor *excuse*.

i'iji[1] いじ (意地) n. 1 pride:
Watashi ni mo iji ga aru. (私にも意
地がある) I, too, have my *pride*.
2 nature; disposition:
Ano hito wa iji ga warui. (あの人は
意地が悪い) She is *ill-natured*.
iji o haru (~を張る) do not give
in.

i'iji[2] いじ (維持) n. maintenance;
upkeep.
iji suru (~する) vt. maintain;
keep up: *keñkoo o iji suru* (健康を
維持する) *keep* oneself in good
health.

i'ijime·ru いじめる (苛める) vt. (iji-
me-te V) tease; annoy; bully.

i'jiwa'ru いじわる（意地悪）n. nastiness; maliciousness.
— a.n. (~ na, ni) nasty; ill-natured; malicious.

i'joo¹ いじょう（以上）n. 1 the above; the foregoing:
Ijoo ga watashi no kiita koto no subete desu.（以上が私の聞いたことのすべてです）The foregoing is everything I heard. (↔ ika¹)
2 that's all; concluded:
Ijoo, watashi no kañgae o nobesasete itadakimashita.（以上、私の考えを述べさせていただきました）That is what I wanted to say.

i'joo² いじょう（以上）conj. since; once; as long as:
Yakusoku shita ijoo, watashi wa kanarazu jikkoo shimasu.（約束した以上、私は必ず実行します）Once I have made a promise, I will certainly carry it out.

i'joo³ いじょう（異常）a.n. (~ na, ni) abnormal; unusual; extraordinary. (↔ seejoo)

-i'joo いじょう（以上）suf. 1 above; over; not less than:
Juuhas-sai-ijoo nara dare de mo meñkyo ga toremasu.（18歳以上ならだれでも免許が取れます）Anybody who is eighteen and over can get a driver's license. (↔ -ika)
★ '-ijoo' includes the preceding number, so, strictly speaking, '18-ijoo' means 'more than 17.'
2 more than:
Kono mae kanojo ni atte kara ichi-neñ-ijoo ni narimasu.（この前彼女に会ってから一年以上になります）It is now more than a year since I last met her.

i'juu いじゅう（移住）n. migration; emigration; immigration.
ijuu suru (~する) vi. migrate; emigrate; immigrate.

i'ka¹ いか（以下）n. the following; as follows:
Kare kara kiita hanashi wa ika no toori desu.（彼から聞いた話は以下の通りです）What I heard from him is as follows: (↔ ijoo¹)

i'ka² いか（烏賊）n. cuttlefish; squid. (⇨ surume)

-i'ka いか（以下）suf. 1 less than:
Kono kuruma wa juumañ-eñ ika no kachi shika nai.（この車は10万円以下の価値しかない）This car only has a value of less than 100,000 yen. ★ '-ika' includes the preceding number, so, strictly speaking, '19 ika' means 'less than 20.' (↔ -ijoo) (⇨ -mimañ)
2 below; under:
Koñdo no watashi no seeseki wa heekiñ-ika datta.（今度の私の成績は平均以下だった）My grades this time were below average.

i'kada いかだ（筏）n. raft.

i'ka'ga いかが（如何）adv.
1 how:
O-karada wa ikaga desu ka?（お体はいかがですか）How is your health?
2 Would you like...?: ★ Used when offering food, drink, etc.
Biiru wa ikaga desu ka?（ビールはいかがですか）Would you like some beer?
3 How [What] about...?:
Kare o sasottara ikaga desu ka?（彼を誘ったらいかがですか）What about inviting him?
4 what:
Anata no go-ikeñ wa ikaga desu ka?（あなたのご意見はいかがですか）What is your opinion?

i'ka'iyoo いかいよう（胃潰瘍）n. an ulcer of the stomach.

i'ka'ni いかに（如何に）adv. 1 (of degree) how:
Itte minai to sono taki ga ika ni ookii ka wakarimaseñ.（行って見ないとその滝がいかに大きいかわかりません）You will not appreciate how large the waterfall is unless you go and see for yourself.
2 (of manner) how:
Ika ni shite uriage o nobasu ka ga moñdai desu.（いかにして売上を伸ばすかが問題です）The question is how to increase sales.

3 (*formal*) however:
Ika ni kurushikute mo kono shi-goto o tsuzukeru tsumori desu. (いかに苦しくてもこの仕事を続けるつもりです) *However* painful it is, I intend to continue this work.

i˺ka˺ ni mo いかにも（如何にも）*adv.*
really; truly; typically:
Sono hanashi wa ika ni mo hoñtoo ni kikoeru. (その話はいかにも本当に聞こえる) That story sounds as if it were *really* true.

i˺kari いかり（怒り）*n.* anger; rage; wrath. (⇨ okoru²)

i˺ka˺s·u いかす（生かす）*vt.* (ika-shi˺ː; ikas·a˺ː; ikaɕ·iɹ·te Ⓒ)
make the most of:
jibuñ no chishiki [sainoo; keekeñ] o ikasu (自分の知識[才能; 経験]を生かす) *make good use of* one's knowledge [talent; experience].

i˺ke˺ いけ（池）*n.* pond. (⇨ numa)

i˺ke˺bana いけばな（生け花）*n.*
flower arrangement. (⇨ ikeru)

i˺kemase˺ñ いけません ★Polite equivalent of '*ikenai*.'
1 must not (do); will not (do); be no good:
Uchi no inu o ijimete wa ikemase-ñ. (うちの犬をいじめてはいけません) You *must not* tease our dog. (⇨ dame)
2 (with a negative verb) must (do); have to (do):
Anata wa kanojo ni ayamaranaku-te wa ikemaseñ. (あなたは彼女に謝らなくてはいけません) You *must* apologize to her. (⇨ beki; dame)

i˺keñ いけん（意見）*n.* **1** opinion; view; idea:
jibuñ no ikeñ o noberu (自分の意見を述べる) express one's *opinion*.
2 advice:
isha no ikeñ ni shitagau (医者の意見に従う) follow one's doctor's *advice*.

i˺kena·i いけない *a.* (-ku) bad; wrong:
Doko-ka ikenai tokoro ga arimasu ka? (どこかいけないところがありますか) Is

there anything *wrong* with it?
-te wa ikenai (ては〜) **1** must not (do); should not (do): *Soñna koto o shite wa ikenai.* (そんなことをしてはいけない) You *should not do* such a thing. (⇨ dame)
2 (with a negative verb) must (do); should (do): *Sugu ikana-kereba ikenai.* (すぐ行かなければいけない) I *must* go at once.
... to ikenai kara [no de] (...と〜から[ので]) in case: *Ame ga furu to ikenai kara, kasa o motte iki nasai.* (雨が降るといけないから、傘を持って行きなさい) Take an umbrella with you in case it rains.
★ Polite forms are '*ikenai desu, ikemaseñ.*'

i˺ke˺·ru いける（生ける）*vt.* (ike-te Ⓥ) arrange (flowers). (⇨ ike-bana)

i˺ki¹ いき（息）*n.* breath; breathing.
iki ga kireru (〜が切れる) be out of breath.
iki o hikitoru (〜を引き取る) breathe one's last.
iki o korosu (〜を殺す) hold one's breath.
iki o tsuku (〜をつく) take a rest.

i˺ki² いき（行き）*n.* (=yuki²) going (to the destination):
Iki wa takushii, kaeri wa basu deshita. (行きはタクシー、帰りはバスでした) The *trip there* was by taxi, and the return by bus. (↔ kaeri)

i˺ki³ いき（粋）*a.n.* (〜 na, ni) chic; stylish; smart.

i˺kichigai いきちがい（行き違い）*n.*
crossing each other. (⇨ yukichi-gai)

i˺kidomari いきどまり（行き止まり）*n.* dead end. (⇨ yukidomari)

i˺kigire いきぎれ（息切れ）*n.* being short of breath. (⇨ iki¹)

i˺ki-i˺ki いきいき（生き生き）*adv.*
(〜 to) vividly:
Mizu o yattara, nae ga iki-iki to shite kita. (水をやったら、苗が生き生きとしてきた) When I watered the young plants, they *freshened up*.

i˥kikaer·u いきかえる（生き返る）*vi.*
(-kaer·i-; -kaer·a-; -kaet-te ©)
1 revive; come to life.
2 feel refreshed:
Tsumetai shawaa o abitara, iki-
kaetta *yoo na kokochi ga shita*.
(冷たいシャワーを浴びたら、生き返ったよ
うな心地がした) I *felt refreshed* after
taking a cold shower.

i˥ki˥mono いきもの（生き物）*n.*
living thing; creature; animal.
(⇨ seebutsu)

i˥kinari いきなり *adv.* all of a sudden; abruptly; without notice.

i˥kinoko˥r·u いきのこる（生き残る）
vi. (-nokor·i-; -nokor·a-; -nokot-
te ©) survive.

i˥kio˥i¹ いきおい（勢い）*n.* force;
might; vigor; energy; influence:
Miñna de booto o ikioi yoku *koida*.
(みんなでボートを勢いよくこいだ) We all
rowed the boat *powerfully*.

i˥kio˥i² いきおい（勢い）*adv.* in the
course of; consequently; naturally; necessarily:
Ikioi, *sono yaku o hikiukeru koto
ni natte shimatta*.(勢い、その役を引
き受けることになってしまった) *By force
of circumstances*, I ended up accepting the role.

i˥ki˥·ru いきる（生きる）*vi.* (iki-te
Ⓥ) **1** live: ★ '*ikite iru*'=be
alive. (↔ shinu)
Sono inu wa mada ikite imasu.(そ
の犬はまだ生きています) The dog *is
still alive*.
2 (of a rule, convention, etc.) be
valid; be good; live. ★ Usually
used in '*ikite iru*.'

i˥kisatsu いきさつ（経緯）*n.* circumstances; story; reason:
Kanojo to shiriatta ikisatsu *o kare
ni hànashita*.(彼女と知り合ったいきさ
つを彼に話した) I told him the *story*
of how I had come to know her.

i˥kka いっか（一家）*n.* family:
Yamada-sañ ikka *wa Yokohama e
hikkoshimashita*.(山田さん一家は横
浜へ引っ越しました) *The Yamadas*
moved to Yokohama.

i˥kkoo¹ いっこう（一行）*n.* party;
group; company.

i˥kkoo² いっこう（一向）*adv.* (～ ni)
(with a negative) at all; in the
least:
Kare no gorufu wa ikkoo ni *joota-
tsu shinai*.(彼のゴルフは一向に上達し
ない) His golf does not improve *at
all*. (⇨ sappari²)

i˥kkyuu いっきゅう（一級）*n.* first
class [rate]; top grade. (⇨ ichiryuu; saikoo)

-i˥koo いこう（以降）*suf.* after; on
or after:
*Yoru hachi-ji-*ikoo *ni o-deñwa o
kudasai*.(夜8時以降にお電話を下さ
い) Please phone me *after* eight in
the evening. ★ '*-ikoo*' includes
the preceding number, so, strictly speaking, '*sañ-ji-ikoo*' means '
at and after three o'clock.'

i˥k·u いく（行く）*vi.* (ik·i-; ik·a-; itte ©) ★ Also pronounced
'*yuku*,' an alternate form of '*iku*,'
which is somewhat formal and
old-fashioned but is used in
forming compounds.
1 go away; leave:
Kare wa moo ikimashita.(彼はもう
行きました) He *has* already *left*.
(↔ kuru)
2 go; come:
Kanojo wa kotoshi Oosutoraria ni
ikimasu.(彼女は今年オーストラリアに
行きます) She *is going* to Australia
this year. (↔ kaeru¹)
3 go doing: ★ Used with a
noun in '... *ni iku*.'
Kanojo wa suupaa e kaimono ni
ikimashita.(彼女はスーパーへ買い物に
行きました) She *has gone* shopping
at the supermarket.
4 go in order to do: ★ Used
with a verb in '... *ni iku*.'
Kinoo wa eega o mi ni ikimashita.
(きのうは映画を見に行きました) I *went*
to see a movie yesterday.
5 proceed; go:
Subete ga umaku ikimashita.(すべ
てがうまくいきました) Everything

went smoothly. ★ Note that '*iku*' is equivalent to 'come' in the following kind of situation.

"*Hayaku, kochira ni kite kudasai.*"
"*Hai, ima* ikimasu." (「早く、こちらに来てください」「はい、いま行きます」)
"Please come here quickly."
"All right, I'm coming (literally '*going*') now."

i˺ku- いく (幾) *pref.* (*formal*)
1 how many:
Fune de iku-nichi kakarimashita ka?(船で幾日かかりましたか) *How many* days did it take by ship? (⇨ **nañ**)
2 some; several:
Sono jiko de iku-niñ mo keganiñ ga deta.(その事故で幾人もけが人が出た) *Several* people were injured in that accident. (⇨ **nañ**)

i˺kubuñ いくぶん (幾分) *adv.*
(~ ka) a little; somewhat; more or less. (⇨ **ikura ka**)

i˺ku-do いくど (幾度) *adv.* how often. (⇨ **nañ-do**)
Iku-do ittara wakaru ñ da. (いくど言ったらわかるんだ) *How many times* do I have to tell you before you understand?
iku-do mo (~も) very often; again and again.

i˺kuji ga nai いくじがない (意気地がない) *Kare wa* ikuji ga nai. (彼は意気地がない) He *has no guts*.

i˺kura いくら (幾ら) *adv.* (of a price) how much.
ikura mo (~も) (with a negative) not many [much]: *Kono biñ ni wa uisukii ga ikura mo nokotte inai.* (このびんにはウイスキーがいくらも残っていない) There is *not much* whisky left in this bottle.
ikura ... -te [-de] mo (~...て[で]も) (with a negative) no matter how; however:
Ikura hayaku aruite mo, kare ni oitsukenakatta. (いくら速く歩いても、彼に追いつけなかった) *No matter how* fast I *walked*, I could not catch

up with him.

i˺kura ka いくらか (幾らか) *adv.* a little; somewhat; more or less: *Kanojo wa* ikura ka *Nihoñ-go ga hanasemasu.* (彼女はいくらか日本語が話せます) She *can* speak Japanese *after a fashion*. (⇨ **ikubuñ**)

i˺kusaki いくさき (行く先) *n.* destination. (⇨ **yukusaki**)

i˺kutsu いくつ (幾つ) *adv.* (of a number, age) how many; how old. (⇨ **APP. 3**)
ikutsu ka (~か) some; several: *Kono hoñyaku ni wa* ikutsu ka *machigai ga aru.* (この翻訳にはいくつか間違いがある) There are *some* mistakes in this translation.
ikutsu mo (~も) many; a large number of; a lot of. (⇨ **takusañ**)

i˺ma[1] いま (今) *n.* now; at present; at the moment.
— *adv.* **1** at once; right [just] now: Ima (*sugu*) ikimasu. (今(すぐ)行きます) I am coming (right) *now*.
2 more: Ima *shibaraku matte kudasai.* (今しばらく待ってください) Please wait a little *longer*.

i˺ma[2] いま (居間) *n.* living room; sitting room. (⇨ **cha-no-ma**)

i˺magoro いまごろ (今頃) *n.* now; (about) this time:
Kanojo wa imagoro *ni natte, ikanai to ii-dashita.* (彼女は今ごろになって、行かないと言い出した) *At this stage* she has announced that she is not going.

i˺ma ma˺de いままで (今迄) *adv.* (~ no) until now; so far: Ima made, *doko e itte ita ñ desu ka?* (今まで、どこへ行っていたんですか) Where have you been *until now*?

i˺ma ni いまに (今に) *adv.* soon; before long: Ima ni *anata mo Nihoñgo ga hanaseru yoo ni narimasu yo.* (今にあなたも日本語が話せるようになりますよ) *Before long* you too will be able to speak Japanese.

i˺ma ni mo いまにも (今にも) *adv.*

at any moment; be ready to:
Ima ni mo *ame ga furi-soo da.* (今
にも雨が降りそうだ) It looks as if it
will rain *at any moment.*

i｢**masara** いまさら (今更) *adv.*
1 (with a negative) now; after so
long; at this late stage:
Imasara, *iya to wa ienai.* (いまさら、
いやとは言えない) I can't say no *at
this stage.*
2 (with a negative) again:
Imasara *iu made mo nai ga, ashita
wa chikoku shinai yoo ni.* (いまさら
言うまでもないが、あしたは遅刻しないよう
に) It is hardly necessary to tell
you *again,* but make sure that
tomorrow you are not late.

i｢**meeji** イメージ *n.* image; picture; impression.

i｢**meeji-a｢ppu** イメージアップ *n.*
improving one's image.
(↔ meeji-dauñ)

i｢**meeji-che｢ñji** イメージチェンジ *n.*
changing one's image.

i｢**meeji-da｢uñ** イメージダウン *n.*
damaging one's image.
(⇨ imeeji-appu)

i｢**mi** いみ (意味) *n.* **1** meaning;
sense; implication:
Kono go ni warui imi *wa arimaseñ.* (この語に悪い意味はありません)
This word has no bad *implica-
tions.*
3 significance:
Kare no shite iru koto wa imi *ga
arimasu.* (彼のしていることは意味があり
ます) What he is doing has *significance.*

i｢**miñ** いみん (移民) *n.* **1** emigration; immigration.
2 emigrant; immigrant.
imiñ suru (〜する) *vi.* emigrate;
immigrate.

i｢**mo**[1] いも (芋) *n.* potato; sweet
potato; taro.

i｢**mooto** いもうと (妹) *n.* one's
younger sister. ★ When referring to someone else's sister,
'*imooto-sañ*' is usually used.
(↔ ane)

-**iñ** いん (員) *suf.* person in
charge; member: *eki*-iñ (駅員) a
station *employee* / *kaisha*-iñ (会社
員) a company *worker.*

i｢**na** いな (否) *n.* (*formal*) no; nay.
(↔ ka?)
... **ya ina ya** (...やいなや) as soon
as; hardly...when: *Kodomo-tachi
wa watashi o miru* ya ina ya *nige-
dashita.* (子どもたちは私を見るやいなや
逃げ出した) *The moment* the children saw me, they ran away.

-**i｢nai** いない (以内) *suf.* within;
in:
Hoñ wa ni-shuukañ-inai *ni kaeshite kudasai.* (本は2週間以内に返
してください) Please return the book
in two weeks. ★ '-*inai*' includes
the preceding number, so, strictly speaking, '*hyaku-eñ-inai*'
means '100 yen or less than 100
yen.'

i｢**naka** いなか (田舎) *n.* **1** the
country; the countryside.
2 one's home; one's hometown.

i｢**nazuma** いなずま (稲妻) *n.* lightning.

i｢**ñboo** いんぼう (陰謀) *n.* plot;
intrigue; conspiracy.

i｢**ñchiki** いんちき *n.* (*colloq.*) fake;
fraud; forgery:
Iñchiki o suru *na yo.* (いんちきをする
な よ) Don't *cheat.*
— *a.n.* (〜 na, ni) (*colloq.*) fake;
fraudulent; bogus:
Kono shorui wa iñchiki *da.* (この書
類はいんちきだ) These documents
are *forgeries.*

i｢**ne** いね (稲) *n.* rice plant.
(⇨ kome)

i｢**ñfure** インフレ *n.* inflation.
(↔ defure)

i｢**ñkañ** いんかん (印鑑) *n.* personal
seal; stamp. (⇨ hañ?)

i｢**ñmetsu** いんめつ (隠滅) *n.* destruction; disappearance.
iñmetsu suru (〜する) *vt.* destroy: *shooko o* iñmetsu suru (証
拠を隠滅する) *destroy* evidence.

i｢**nochi** いのち (命) *n.* life:

Sono jiko de shichi-niñ ga inochi *o ushinatta.* (その事故で7人が命を失った) Seven people lost their *lives* in that accident.

inochi-gake de (〜がけで) at the risk of one's life.

i**「noko」r・u** いのこる (居残る) *vi.* (inokor・i-; inokor・a-; inokot-te C) stay; remain; work overtime. (⇨ nokoru)

i**「nori」** いのり (祈り) *n.* prayer; grace. (⇨ inoru)

i**「no」r・u** いのる (祈る) *vi., vt.* (inor・i-; inor・a-; inot-te C) pray; wish:
Koouñ [Seekoo] o inorimasu. (幸運 [成功]を祈ります) I wish you good luck [success]. (⇨ inori)

i**「ñryoku** いんりょく (引力) *n.* gravitation.

i**「ñryo」osui** いんりょうすい (飲料水) *n.* drinking water.

i**「ñsatsu** いんさつ (印刷) *n.* printing; print; press.
iñsatsu suru (〜する) *vt.* print; put into print.

i**「ñsatsu」butsu** いんさつぶつ (印刷物) *n.* printed matter.

i**「ñshi** いんし (印紙) *n.* = shuu-nyuu-iñshi.

i**「ñshoo** いんしょう (印象) *n.* impression:
Kare wa miñna ni yoi iñshoo o ataeta. (彼はみんなに良い印象を与えた) He made a good *impression* on everybody.

i**「ñshoo-teki** いんしょうてき (印象的) *a.n.* (〜 na, ni) impressive.

in**「sutañto ra」ameñ** インスタントラーメン *n.* instant Chinese noodles. (⇨ raameñ)

i**「ñteri** インテリ *n.* intellectual; the intelligentsia.

i**「nu」** いぬ (犬) *n.* dog. (⇨ bañkeñ)

i**「nugoya** いぬごや (犬小屋) *n.* doghouse; kennel.

i**「ñyoo** いんよう (引用) *n.* quotation; citation.
iñyoo suru (〜する) *vt.* quote; cite.

i**「ppai」** いっぱい (一杯) *n.* 1 a cup [glass; bowl]:
koohii ippai (コーヒー一杯) *a cup* of coffee. (⇨ -hai; APP. 4)
2 (having) a drink:
Kaeri ni ippai yarimaseñ ka? (帰りに一杯やりませんか) Won't you have *a drink* on the way back?
ippai kuwasu (〜食わす) deceive; cheat. (⇨ damasu)

i**「ppai²** いっぱい (一杯) *a.n.* (〜 na/no, ni) be full; be filled; be crowded:
Depaato wa hito de ippai datta. (デパートは人でいっぱいだった) The department store was *crowded* with people.

i**「ppai」** いっぱい *adv.* until (the end of):
Kono shigoto wa koñgetsu ippai kakarimasu. (この仕事は今月いっぱいかかります) This job will take *until the end of* this month.

i**「ppañ ni** いっぱんに (一般に) *adv.* generally; in general.

i**「ppo」o¹** いっぽう (一方) *n.* 1 one end [side]; the other end [side].
2 one-way: ippoo-*tsuukoo* (一方通行) *one-way* traffic.
3 continuation:
Tochi no nedañ wa agaru ippoo desu. (土地の値段は上がる一方です) Land prices *continue* to rise.

i**「ppo」o²** いっぽう (一方) *conj.* on the other hand; while:
Shuunyuu wa fueta ga, ippoo, iso-gashiku natta. (収入は増えたが、一方、忙しくなった) My income has gone up, but, *on the other hand*, I have become busier.

i**「rai** いらい (依頼) *n.* 1 request:
hito no irai o kotowaru (人の依頼を断る) decline a person's *request*.
2 dependence; reliance:
Kanojo wa irai-shiñ ga tsuyoi. (彼女は依頼心が強い) She *relies too much* on other people.
irai suru (〜する) *vt.* ask; request.

-i**「rai** いらい (以来) *suf.* since; after:
Sotsugyoo-irai kare to wa atte

imaseñ. (卒業以来彼とは会っていませ
ん) I have not seen him *since*
graduation.

i⌐rainiñ いらいにん (依頼人) *n.*
client. (⇨ kyaku)

i⌐raira いらいら *adv.* (~ suru) (the
state of being impatient [ner-
vous]):
Kare o matte mo konai no de ira-
ira *shite kita.* (彼を待っても来ないので
いらいらしてきた) I waited for him
but he did not come, so I got
impatient.

i⌐rassha⌐i いらっしゃい = irasshaimase.

i⌐rasshaima⌐se いらっしゃいませ
1 (to a visitor) welcome:
Irasshaimase. *Doozo o-hairi kudasai.* (いらっしゃいませ。どうぞお入りくださ
い) *Welcome.* Please come in.
2 (to a customer at a store) welcome.

i⌐rassha⌐r·u いらっしゃる *vi.* (iras-
sha·i-; irasshar·a-; irasshat-te
C) ★ Honorific form of 'kuru,
iku, iru.' The te-form is often
pronounced 'irashite.'
1 come:
Yoku irasshaimashita. (よくいらっし
ゃいました) I am glad you *have
come.*
2 go:
Kyooto e wa itsu irasshaimasu
ka? (京都へはいついらっしゃいますか)
When *are* you *going* to Kyoto?
3 be; be present:
Señsee wa ima irasshaimasu ka?
(先生は今いらっしゃいますか) *Is* the
teacher *in* now?

i⌐rechigai ni いれちがいに (入れ違い
に) *adv.* passing [crossing] each
other:
Anata to irechigai ni Tanaka-sañ
ga miemashita. (あなたと入れ違いに田
中さんが見えました) *Just as you went
out,* Miss Tanaka came to see
you.

i⌐re⌐esai いれいさい (慰霊祭) *n.* memorial service.

i⌐rekae⌐l·ru いれかえる (入れ替える)

vt. (-kae-te V) replace; substitute; change.
2 refresh:
kuuki o irekaeru (空気を入れ替える)
change the air (of a room).
(⇨ irekawaru)

i⌐rekawa⌐r·u いれかわる (入れ代わ
る) *vi.* (-kawar·i-; -kawar·a-;
-kawat-te C) be replaced;
change:
Kaichoo ga irekawatta. (会長が入
れ代わった) The company chair-
man *was replaced.* (⇨ irekaeru)

i⌐remono いれもの (入れ物) *n.*
container; vessel.

i⌐re·ru いれる (入れる) *vt.* (ire-te
V) 1 put in [into]; pour; fill:
koohii ni satoo o ireru (コーヒーに砂
糖を入れる) *put* sugar into coffee.
2 insert; enclose:
Tegami ni shashiñ o ireta. (手紙に
写真を入れた) I *enclosed* some pho-
tos with the letter.
3 let in:
Mado o akete shiñseñ na kuuki o
ireta. (窓を開けて新鮮な空気を入れた)
I opened the windows and *let in*
some fresh air.
4 send (a person to school, an
organization, etc.):
*Kare wa musuko o gaikoku no dai-
gaku ni* ireta. (彼は息子を外国の大
学に入れた) He *sent* his son to a
university overseas.
5 include:
Tesuuryoo o irete, *goseñ-eñ ni narimasu.* (手数料を入れて、5千円になり
ます) It comes to 5,000 yen, *including* commission.
6 admit:
Sono kai no meñbaa ni irete
moratta. (その会のメンバーに入れてもら
った) I *was admitted* as a member
of the society.
7 accept (a demand, request, etc.):
*Kaisha-gawa wa kumiai no yoo-
kyuu o* ireta. (会社側は組合の要求を
入れた) The management *accepted*
the union's demands.
8 switch on:

terebi no suitchi o ireru(テレビのスイッチを入れる) *switch on* the television.

i￼**riguchi** いりぐち (入り口) *n*. entrance; way in; doorway. (↔ deguchi)

i￼**rita**￼**mago** いりたまご (煎り卵) *n*. scrambled eggs.

i￼**ro**[1] いろ (色) *n*. color; tint; complexion.

Kanojo wa iro ga shiroi.(彼女は色が白い) She has a fair *complexion*.

iro o tsukeru (～をつける) add a little something extra.

i￼**roiro**[1] いろいろ (色々) *n*. variety: *choo wa* iroiro (蝶のいろいろ) a *variety of* butterflies.

— *a.n.* (～ na, ni) various; all kinds of. (⇨ samazama)

i￼**roiro**[2] いろいろ (色々) *adv*. (～ to) variously; differently; all kinds of:

iroiro *yatte miru* (いろいろやってみる) try *all sorts of things*.

i￼**rojiro** いろじろ (色白) *a.n.* (～ na/ no) fair-complexioned:

irojiro *no bijiñ* (色白の美人) a *fair-skinned* beauty.

i￼**roñna** いろんな *attrib*. (*informal*) various; all kinds of. (⇨ iroiro[1])

i・￼**ru**[1] いる (居る) *vi*. (i-te Ⓥ)

1 (of a person, animal) be; there is [are]; exist: ★ When the subject is animate (a person or animal), '*iru*' is used, while '*aru*' is used to indicate the existence of something inanimate (a thing or plant).

Kare wa niwa ni imasu.(彼は庭にいます) He *is* in the garden.

2 have:

Watashi ni wa ani ga hitori imasu.(私には兄が一人います) I *have* one older brother.

3 live:

Ryooshiñ wa Hokkaidoo ni imasu.(両親は北海道にいます) My parents *live* in Hokkaido.

4 be present:

Anata ga ite kuretara, tasukarima-su.(あなたがいてくれたら、助かります) If you *are present*, it will be of great help to us.

-te [-de] iru (て[で]～) ★ Attached to the *te*-form of a verb, it indicates a continuing action, the state of being engaged in something, or a resulting state.

Kanojo wa gakkoo de Nihoñgo o oshiete imasu.(彼女は学校で日本語を教えています) She *teaches* Japanese at a school.

i・￼**ru**[2] いる (要る) *vi*. (ir·i-; ir·a-; it-te Ⓒ) need; want; be necessary: *Kono hoñ wa moo* irimaseñ.(この本はもう要りません) I *no longer need* this book.

i・￼**ru**[3] いる (煎る) *vt*. (ir·i-; ir·a-; it-te Ⓒ) roast (beans); parch.

i・￼**ru**[4] いる (射る) *vt*. (i-te Ⓥ) shoot (an arrow); hit.

i￼**rui** いるい (衣類) *n*. clothing; clothes; garments.

i￼**ryoo**[1] いりょう (医療) *n*. medical treatment.

i￼**ryoo**[2] いりょう (衣料) *n*. clothing; clothes.

i￼**ryoohiñ** いりょうひん (衣料品) *n*. articles of clothing.

i￼**samashi**￼**·i** いさましい (勇ましい) *a*. (-ku) brave; courageous: isamashiku *tatakau* (勇ましく戦う) fight *bravely*.

i￼**see**[1] いせい (異性) *n*. the opposite [other] sex.

i￼**see**[2] いせい (威勢) *n*. spirits: *Kare-ra wa* isee yoku, *shuppatsu shita*.(彼らは威勢よく、出発した) They set out *in high spirits*.

i￼**sha** いしゃ (医者) *n*. doctor; physician:

isha *ni mite morau* (医者に診てもらう) consult a *doctor*. (⇨ -i[2])

i￼**shi**[1] いし (石) *n*. stone; rock; pebble.

i￼**shi**[2] いし (意志) *n*. will: *Kare wa* ishi *ga tsuyoi* [*yowai*].(彼は意志が強い[弱い]) He is a man of strong [weak] *will*.

i￼**shi**[3] いし (意思) *n*. intention.

i'**shi'** いし（医師）n. doctor.
(⇨ isha)

i'**shiki** いしき（意識）n. consciousness; one's senses.
ishiki suru (〜する) vt. be conscious [aware] of.

i'**shoku** いしょく（移植）n. transplantation; grafting.
ishoku suru (〜する) vt. transplant; graft.

i-'**shoku'-juu** いしょくじゅう（衣食住）n. food, clothing and shelter.

i'**shoo** いしょう（衣装）n. clothes; dress; costume.

i'**sogashi'-i** いそがしい（忙しい）a. (-ku) busy:
shigoto de isogashii（仕事で忙しい）*be busy* with one's work.
(↔ hima) (⇨ taboo)

i'**soga's-u** いそがす（急がす）vt. (isogash-i-; isogas-a-; isogash-i-te Ⓒ) hurry; hasten.
(⇨ isogu)

i'**so'g-u** いそぐ（急ぐ）vi. (isog-i-; isog-a-; iso-i-de Ⓒ) hurry; make haste; hasten. (⇨ isogasu)

i'**ssai** いっさい（一切）n. all; everything.
— adv. (with a negative) not at all:
Watashi wa sono mondai to issai *kankee arimasen.*（私はその問題と一切関係ありません）I am *not in any way* connected with that matter.

i'**ssaku'jitsu** いっさくじつ（一昨日）n. (*formal*) =ototoi.

i'**ssakunen** いっさくねん（一昨年）n. (*formal*) =ototoshi.

i'**ssee¹** いっせい（一斉）adv. (〜 ni) at the same time; all together; simultaneously.

i'**ssee²** いっせい（一世）n. Issei; Japanese immigrant, usually to North and South American countries. (⇨ nisee; sansee²)

i'**sshi'n ni** いっしんに（一心に）adv. earnestly; fervently:
kami ni isshin ni *inoru*（神に一心に祈る）pray to God *intently*.

i'**ssho** いっしょ（一緒）n. the same:
Watashi wa Yamada to kurasu ga issho *datta.*（私は山田とクラスがいっしょだった）I was in *the same* class as Yamada. (⇨ onaji)

i'**ssho ni** いっしょに（一緒に）adv. (all) together; at the same time.
issho ni naru (〜なる) meet; get married.
issho ni suru (〜する) put together; mix up.

i'**sshoo** いっしょう（一生）n. lifetime; life:
Kare wa isshoo *dokushin de sugoshita.*（彼は一生独身で過ごした）He was a bachelor *all his life*.

i'**sshoo-kenmee** いっしょうけんめい（一生懸命）a.n. (〜 na, ni) very hard; with all one's might:
isshoo-kenmee *(ni) hataraku*（一生懸命(に)働く）work *as hard as one could.* (⇨ kenmee²)

i'**sshu** いっしゅ（一種）n. kind; sort; variety:
Kono ki wa sakura no isshu *desu.*（この木は桜の一種です）This tree is *a variety* of cherry.

i'**sshun** いっしゅん（一瞬）n. an instant; a moment.
— adv. for a moment:
Kare wa isshun *ishiki o ushinatta.*（彼は一瞬意識を失った）He lost consciousness *for just a moment*.

i'**sshuu** いっしゅう（一周）n. one round.
isshuu suru (〜する) vi. go around: *sekai o* isshuu suru（世界を一周する）*travel around* the world.

i'**sso** いっそ adv. rather; preferably; once and for all.
isso no koto (〜の事) rather; preferably: Isso no koto saisho kara yarinaoshita hoo ga ii.（いっその事最初からやり直したほうがいい）We *had better* do it all over again from the beginning.

i'**ssoo** いっそう（一層）adv. (〜 no) all the more; further; still:
issoo *doryoku suru*（いっそう努力す

る) make *even* greater efforts.

i˥**su** いす (椅子) *n.* **1** chair; stool. **2** post; position: *shachoo no isu o nerau* (社長のいすをねらう) aim for the *post* of president.

i˥**ta** いた (板) *n.* board; plank.

i˥**taba˥sami** いたばさみ (板挟み) *n.* dilemma; fix: *giri to niñjoo no itabasami ni naru* (義理と人情の板挟みになる) *be torn between* duty and sentiment. (⇨ nayamu)

i˥**tadakima˥su** いただきます (頂きます・戴きます) ★ This is what the Japanese say before they start eating. Literally it means, "We are going to eat [partake]." (⇨ Itadaku; gochisousama)

i˥**tadak·u** いただく (頂く・戴く) *vt.* (itadak·i-; itadak·a-; itada·i-te C̄) **1** (*humble*) have; get; take; receive: *Kinoo, o-tayori o itadakimashita.* (きのう, お便りをいただきました) I *received* your letter yesterday. (⇨ morau) **2** (*humble*) eat; drink: *Moo juubuñ itadakimashita.* (もう十分いただきました) I *have had* plenty, thanks. (⇨ choodai suru; itadakimasu; taberu; nomu) **3** (*literary*) be capped: *yuki o itadaita yama* (雪をいただいた山) a mountain *capped* with snow. (⇨ oou)

-te itadaku [itadakeru] (ていただく[いただける]) (*humble*) have something done for one; be allowed to do something. ★ Used when asking a favor of a person, who is higher in status. When the person is equal or lower in status, '-te morau' is used. *Eki e iku michi o oshiete itadakemasu ka?* (駅へ行く道を教えていただけますか) *Would you be kind enough to tell me* the way to the station?

i˥**ta˥·i** いたい (痛い) *a.* (-ku) painful; sore:

Ha ga itai. (歯が痛い) I *have a toothache.*

i˥**tame˥·ru** いためる (炒める) *vt.* (itame-te V̄) fry; panfry; sauté: *niku o abura de itameru* (肉を油でいためる) *fry* meat in oil. (⇨ ageru²)

i˥**tami˥** いたみ (痛み) *n.* pain; ache: *Senaka ni itami o kañjiru.* (背中に痛みを感じる) I can feel a *pain* in my back. (⇨ itamu; itai)

i˥**ta˥m·u** いたむ (痛む) *vi.* (itam·i-; itam·a-; itañ-de C̄) **1** hurt; ache; have a pain: *Ha ga mada itamu.* (歯がまだ痛む) My tooth still *hurts.* (⇨ itami) **2** (of one's heart) ache: *Sono ko no koto o omou to kanojo wa kokoro ga itañda.* (その子のことと思うと彼女は心が痛んだ) When she thought of the child, her heart *ached.* (⇨ itami)

i˥**tashima˥su** いたします (致します) *vt.* = itasu.

i˥**tas·u** いたす (致す) *vt.* (itash·i-; itas·a-; itash·i-te C̄) do: ★ The humble form of 'suru.' Usually used in the *masu*-form. *Asu o-ukagai itashimasu.* (あすお伺いいたします) I *will* call on you tomorrow.

i˥**tawa˥r·u** いたわる (労る) *vt.* (itawar·i-; itawar·a-; itawat-te C̄) treat kindly; be kind; take care of: *roojiñ o itawaru* (老人をいたわる) *be kind* to old people.

i˥**tazura** いたずら (悪戯) *n.* mischief; prank: *itazura o suru* (いたずらをする) play a *trick.* — *a.n.* (~ na) naughty; mischievous.

i˥**tchi** いっち (一致) *n.* agreement; accord; coincidence. **itchi suru** (~する) *vi.* match; agree; accord; coincide.

i˥**to**¹ いと (糸) *n.* thread; yarn; string.

i˥**to**² いと (意図) *n.* intention; purpose.

ito suru (～する) *vt.* intend; aim at. (⇨ mokuromu)

i˻to˺guchi いとくち (糸口) *n.*
1 the end of a thread.
2 beginning; clue; lead:
hanashi no itoguchi o mitsukeru (話の糸口を見つける) try to *break the ice in a conversation.*

i˻to˺ko いとこ (従兄弟・従姉妹) *n.* cousin. ★ '従兄弟' is used to refer to male cousins or a mixed group of male and female cousins. '従姉妹' refers to female cousins.

i˻toma いとま (暇) *n.* (*formal*)
1 spare time. (⇨ hima)
2 taking one's leave: ★ Often with 'o-.'
Moo o-itoma shinakereba narimaseñ. (もうおいとましなければなりません) I must *be leaving* now.

i˻tona˺m·u いとなむ (営む) *vt.* (itonam·i-; itonam·a-; itonañ-de Ⓒ) run; be engaged in; lead: Kare wa ryokañ o itonañde iru. (彼は旅館を営んでいる) He *runs* a Japanese inn. (⇨ kee-ee)

i˻tsu いつ (何時) *adv.* when; what time:
Kono koinu wa itsu umaremashita? (この小犬はいつ生まれました) *When* was this puppy born? / Anata wa itsu made Hokkaidoo ni iru yotee desu ka? (あなたはいつまで北海道にいる予定ですか) *How long* do you plan to stay in Hokkaido?

i˻tsu de mo いつでも (何時でも) *adv.* 1 always; all the time.
2 at any time; whenever:
Kaesu no wa itsu de mo kekkoo desu. (返すのはいつでもけっこうです) You can return it *anytime.*

i˻tsuka いつか (五日) *n.* five days; the fifth day of the month. (⇨ APP. 5)

i˻tsu-ka いつか (何時か) *adv.*
1 (of future) someday; sometime:
Sono shiñsoo wa itsu-ka wakaru deshoo. (その真相はいつかわかるでしょ

う) The truth will come out *someday.*
2 (of the past) once; before:
Kanojo ni wa itsu-ka doko-ka de atta oboe ga arimasu. (彼女にはいつかどこかで会った覚えがあります) I have a recollection of meeting her somewhere *sometime before.*

i˻tsu made mo いつまでも (何時迄も) *adv.* forever; endlessly; as long as (one likes).

i˻tsu-mo いつも (何時も) *adv.* (～ no) always; usually:
Itsu-mo neru mae ni shawaa o abimasu. (いつも寝る前にシャワーを浴びます) I *usually* take a shower before going to bed. (⇨ maido; shotchuu)

i˻tsu-no-ma-ni˺-ka いつのまにか (何時の間にか) *adv.* before one knows it; too soon.

i˻tsu˺tsu いつつ (五つ) *n.* five. ★ Used when counting. (⇨ go³; APP. 3)

i˻ttai¹ いったい (一体) *n.* one; one body:
Futatsu no kaisha ga gappee shite, ittai to natta. (二つの会社が合併して、一体となった) The two companies merged and became *one.*

i˻ttai² いったい (一体) *adv.* (with an interrogative) on earth; in the world; even:
Ittai nani ga okotta no desu ka? (いったい何が起こったのですか) What *on earth* has happened?

i˻ttañ いったん (一旦) *adv.* 1 once:
Ittañ hajimeta koto wa saigo made yari nasai. (いったん始めたことは最後までやりなさい) *Once* you have started something, continue until you have finished it.
2 temporarily; for a while:
Watashi wa raishuu ittañ kuni ni kaerimasu. (私は来週いったん国に帰ります) I am going home *for just a short while* next week.

i˻tte いって (一手) *n.* 1 monopoly; exclusiveness:
Kono shina wa kare no kaisha ga

itte *ni hañbai shite iru.* (この品は彼の会社が一手に販売している) This article is sold *exclusively* by his company.

2 (of chess, shoogi, go, etc.) move.

i˻ttee いってい (一定) *n.* fixed (condition); definite (condition); uniform (circumstances).

ittee no (〜の) fixed; regular: *Watashi wa ittee no sokudo de uñteñ shita.* (私は一定の速度で運転した) I drove at a *steady* speed.

ittee suru (〜する) *vi.* fix; set; standardize: *Okiru jikañ wa ittee chito imaseñ* (起きる時間は一定していません) The time I get up *is irregular.*

i˻tte-kimasu いってきます (行って来ます) I'll go and come back. ★ A set expression used when leaving home. A more polite form is '*itte-mairimasu.*' (⇨ itte-(i)rasshai)

i˻tte-(i)rasshai いって(い)らっしゃい (行って(い)らっしゃい) Please go and come back. ★ A set expression used when someone is going out. (⇨ itte-kimasu)

i˻ttoo いっとう (一等) *n.* first class; first prize; first place. (⇨ nitoo)

i˻u いう (言う) *vt.* (i·i·; iw·a·; it-te ⒞) ★ '言う' (*iu*) is often pronounced '*yuu.*' In the *te*-form and the past '*yutte*' and '*yutta*' are common, but slightly more informal than the equivalent standard form, '*itte*' and '*itta.*'

1 say; tell; talk; speak: *Kare wa watashi ni「Isoge」to itta.* (彼は私に「急げ」と言った) He *said* "Hurry up" to me.

2 mention; refer to: *Shachoo wa atarashii keekaku ni tsuite nani mo iwanakatta.* (社長は新しい計画について何も言わなかった) The president *did not refer* to the new project.

3 express; call: *Anata no kañgae o itte kudasai.*

(あなたの考えを言ってください) Please *express* your thoughts.

4 tell; order: *Kare-ra ni sugu dete iku yoo ni itta.* (彼らにすぐ出て行くように言った) I *told* them to get out at once.

... to iu (…と〜) **1** people say: *Kare wa kaisha o yameru to iu uwasa ga aru.* (彼は会社を辞めるといううわさがある) Rumor has it *that* he will quit his company.

2 (used for emphasis or explanation): *Watashi wa mada tako to iu mono o tabeta koto ga nai.* (私はまだたこというものを食べたことがない) I have not yet eaten *octopus.*

i˻wa いわ (岩) *n.* rock; crag. (⇨ ishi)

i˻waba いわば (言わば) *adv.* so to speak; as it were, in a sense; practically.

i˻wa˺i いわい (祝い) *n.* **1** celebration; congratulation. ★ Usually with '*o-.*' (⇨ iwau)

2 present: *kekkoñ no o-iwai* (結婚のお祝い) a wedding *present.*

i˻washi いわし (鰯) *n.* sardine.

i˻wa˺·u いわう (祝う) *vt.* (iwa·i-; iwaw·a-; iwat-te ⒞) celebrate; congratulate: *tañjoobi o iwau* (誕生日を祝う) *cele-brate* a birthday. (⇨ iwai; shukusu)

i˻wa˺yuru いわゆる (所謂) *attrib.* what is called; so-called.

i˻ya[1] いや (嫌) *a.n.* (〜 na, ni) disagreeable; disgusting; horrible: *Beñkyoo ga iya ni natta.* (勉強がいやになった) I *am fed up* with my studies.

i˻ya[2] いや *int.* no; yes: ★ '*Iya*' literally means 'That's wrong,' and is used to confirm a statement, whether affirmative or negative. *"Kare wa kimasu ka?" "Iya, konai to omoimasu."* (「彼は来ますか」「いや、来ないと思います」) "Is he

coming?" "*No*, I do not think
so." / "*Mada ame wa yamimaseñ
ka?*" "*Iya, yamimashita.*" (「まだ雨
はやみませんか」「いや、やみました」)
"Hasn't the rain stopped yet?"
"*Yes*, it has." (⇨ iie)
iya to iu (〜と言う) say no.

iˈyagarase いやがらせ (嫌がらせ) *n.*
harassment:
iyagarase *no deñwa* (嫌がらせの電
話) a *harassing* phone call.
(⇨ sekuhara)

iˈyagaˈr・u いやがる (嫌がる) *vt.* (iya-
gar・i-; iyagat・a-; iyagat-te Ⓒ)
dislike; hate; be unwilling; be
reluctant.

iˈyaiya いやいや *adv.* unwillingly;
reluctantly; against one's will.

iˈyarashiˈ・i いやらしい *a.* (-ku) disgusting; offensive; nasty:
iyarashii *yatsu* (いやらしいやつ) a
nasty fellow.

iˈyashi・i いやしい (卑しい) *a.* (-ku)
1 vulgar; coarse.
2 greedy; gluttonous:
Kare wa kane ni iyashii. (彼は金に
卑しい) He is *mean* with money.

iˈyoˈiyo いよいよ *adv.* **1** more
and more; all the more. (⇨ masumasu)
2 at last; finally:
Iyoiyo *ashita wa nyuugaku-shikeñ
da.* (いよいよあしたは入学試験だ) To-
morrow is the entrance exam *at
long last.*

iˈyoku いよく (意欲) *n.* will; eager-

ness; desire; volition:
Kanojo ni wa beñkyoo shitai to iu
iyoku ga aru. (彼女には勉強したいとい
う意欲がある) She *is eager* to study.

iˈyoku-teki いよくてき (意欲的)
a.n. (〜 na, ni) eager; active;
positive enthusiastic.

iˈzeñ¹ いぜん (以前) *n.* **1** before a
certain time:
Kyoo wa shichi-ji izeñ *ni kaerimasu.* (きょうは7時以前に帰ります)
Today I'll return *before* seven.
(↔ igo¹)
2 ago; once; formerly:
Kare ni atta no wa zutto izeñ *desu.*
(彼に会ったのはずっと以前です) It was
a long time *ago* that I met him.

iˈzeñ² いぜん (依然) *adv.* (〜 to
shite) still; as ever; as before:
Eñ wa izeñ (*to shite*) *agari tsuzukete iru.* (円は依然(として)上がり続け
ている) The Japanese yen *still*
shows a tendency to go up.

iˈzumi いずみ (泉) *n.* spring; fountain.

iˈzure いずれ (何れ) *adv.* (〜 no)
some day; one day; before long.
izure ni shite mo [seyo] (〜にし
ても[せよ]) in any event; at any rate.

iˈzure mo いずれも (何れも) *adv.*
both; either; any; all:
Sono ni-satsu no shoosetsu wa
izure mo *yomimashita.* (その2冊の
小説はいずれも読みました) I have read
both those novels.

J

ja じゃ *conj.* = jaa.

jaˈa じゃあ *conj.* (*formal* = de wa)
well; then:
Jaa, *mata ashita.* (じゃあ、またあした)
Well, I'll see you tomorrow.

jaˈbujabu じゃぶじゃぶ *adv.* (〜 to)
(the sound or action of water
splashing around):
kawa o jabujabu (*to*) *wataru* (川をじ

ゃぶじゃぶ(と)渡る) *splash* one's way
across a river.

jaˈgaimo じゃがいも (じゃが芋) *n.*
potato.

jaˈguchi じゃぐち (蛇口) *n.* tap;
faucet.

jaˈma じゃま (邪魔) *n.* disturbance; hindrance; interference.
jama (o) suru (〜(を)する) *vt.*

1 disturb; hinder; interfere.
2 visit: ★ Usually with '*o-*.'
Asu o-jama shimasu.(あすおじゃまします) I'll *visit* you tomorrow.
— *a.n.* (~ na, ni) obstructive; hampering; burdensome:
Soko ni iru to jama desu.(そこにいるとじゃまです) You are *in the way*.

ja˥ñkeñ じゃんけん *n.* the game of 'paper, scissors, stone.'

ja˥re˩ru じゃれる *vi.* (jare-te Ⅴ) play with:
Neko ga mari to jarete iru.(猫がまりとじゃれている) The cat *is playing* with a ball.

-jau じゃう *suf.* ⇨ shimau².

je˥tto˩ki ジェットき(ジェット機) *n.* jet (plane).

ji˥ じ(字) *n.* **1** letter; character. (⇨ moji)
2 handwriting:
Kare no ji wa yomi-nikui.(彼の字は読みにくい) His *handwriting* is hard to read.

-ji¹ じ(時) *suf.* o'clock:
gozeñ roku-ji (午前6時) *six* in the morning. (⇨ jikañ)

-ji² じ(寺) *suf.* temple:
Hooryuu-ji (法隆寺) Horyuji *Temple.* (⇨ tera)

-ji³ じ(次) *suf.* the number in a series; order:
ichi-ji (一次) the *first* / *ni-ji* (二次) the *second* / *seki*-ji (席次) seating *order.*

ji˩bi-iñ˥kooka じびいんこうか(耳鼻咽喉科) *n.* otolaryngology; ear, nose and throat department.

ji˩bika じびか(耳鼻科) *n.* = jibi-iñkooka.

ji˩biki じびき(字引) *n.* dictionary. ★ Not as common as '*jisho*' anymore. (⇨ jisho²; jiteñ)

ji˩buñ じぶん(自分) *n.* oneself:
Jibuñ no koto wa jibuñ de shi nasai.(自分のことは自分でしなさい) *You yourself* do *your own* business.

ji˥chi˩ じち(自治) *n.* self-government; autonomy.

ji˥choo じちょう(次長) *n.* deputy chief; vice-director.

ji˥dai じだい(時代) *n.* **1** era; period; age. (⇨ APP. 9)
2 days: *gakusee jidai* (学生時代) one's student *days.*
3 times:
Kimi no kañgae wa jidai-okure da. (君の考えは時代遅れだ) You ideas are behind the *times.*

ji˩dai-sa˥kugo じだいさくご(時代錯誤) *n.* anachronism.

ji˩doo¹ じどう(自動) *n.* automatic: *jidoo-shooteñ no kamera* (自動焦点のカメラ) an *automatic* focusing camera

ji˩doo² じどう(児童) *n.* child; juvenile. (⇨ kodomo)

ji˩do˥osha じどうしゃ(自動車) *n.* car; automobile; motor vehicle. (⇨ kuruma)

ji˩do˥oshi じどうし(自動詞) *n.* intransitive verb. (↔ tadooshi) (⇨ APP. 2)

ji˥ee じえい(自衛) *n.* self-defense.
jiee suru (~する) *vi.* defend oneself.

Ji˩eetai じえいたい(自衛隊) *n.* the Self-Defense Forces:
Rikujoo [Kaijoo; Kookuu] Jieetai (陸上[海上; 航空]自衛隊) the Ground [Maritime; Air] *Self-Defense Force.* (⇨ guñ²)

ji˥goku˩ じごく(地獄) *n.* hell.

ji˥gyoo じぎょう(事業) *n.* business; enterprise:
jigyoo ni seekoo [shippai] suru (事業に成功[失敗]する) succeed [fail] in *business.*

ji˩hi˥biki じひびき(地響き) *n.* rumbling of the ground:
Sono ki wa jihibiki o tatete, taoreta.(その木は地響きを立てて、倒れた) The tree fell *with a thud.*

ji˥hyoo じひょう(辞表) *n.* resignation:
jihyoo o dasu (辞表を出す) hand in one's *resignation.*

ji˩isañ じいさん(爺さん) *n.* (*informal*) **1** one's grandfather.

2 old man. (↔ baasañ) (⇨ o-jiisañ)

ji꜀jitsu[1] じじつ(事実) *n*. fact; truth; reality:
Kono shoosetsu wa jijitsu *ni moto-zuite imasu.* (この小説は事実に基づいています) This novel is based on *fact.*
jijitsu joo (no) (〜上(の)) actual:
Kare wa jijitsu joo (no) *shachoo no yoo ni furumatte iru.* (彼は事実上(の)社長のように振る舞っている) He carries on as if he were the *actual* president.

ji꜀jitsu[2] じじつ(事実) *adv*. as a matter of fact; actually:
Jijitsu kare wa soo iimashita. (事実彼はそう言いました) *As a matter of fact,* he said so.

ji꜀jo じじょ(次女・二女) *n*. one's second daughter.

ji꜀joo じじょう(事情) *n*. **1** circumstances; conditions:
Jijoo ga yuruseba sono kai ni shusseki shimasu. (事情が許せばその会に出席します) I'll attend the party if *circumstances* permit.
2 reasons:
Kanojo wa katee no jijoo *de kai-sha o yamemashita.* (彼女は家庭の事情で会社を辞めました) She left the company for family *reasons.*
3 affairs:
Kare wa Nihoñ no jijoo *o yoku shitte iru.* (彼は日本の事情をよく知っている) He is familiar with Japanese *affairs.*

ji꜀kai じかい(次回) *n*. next; next time:
jikai no kaigi (次回の会議) the *next* meeting. (⇨ tsugi)

ji꜀kaku じかく(自覚) *n*. consciousness; awareness.
jikaku suru (〜する) *vt*. realize; awaken; be aware of: *Watashi wa chiimu no kyaputeñ to shite jikaku shite imasu.* (私はチームのキャプテンとして自覚しています) I *am well aware* that I am captain of this team.

ji꜀kañ じかん(時間) *n*. **1** time; period:
Jikañ wa juubuñ ni arimasu. (時間は十分にあります) We have plenty of *time.*
2 time; hour:
Shuppatsu no jikañ ga heñkoo ni natta. (出発の時間が変更になった) The *hour* of departure has been changed.
3 lesson; class:
Tsugi no jikañ wa suugaku desu. (次の時間は数学です) The next *lesson* is mathematics.

-ji꜀kañ じかん(時間) *suf*. hour:
Hakone made kuruma de sañ-jikañ kakatta. (箱根まで車で3時間かかった) It took three *hours* to Hakone by car.

ji꜀ka ni じかに(直に) *adv*. directly; at first hand; in person:
Sono hanashi wa kare kara jika ni *kikimashita.* (その話は彼からじかに聞きました) I heard the news *directly* from him. (⇨ chokusetsu)

ji꜀kañwari じかんわり(時間割) *n*. class schedule.

ji꜀keñ じけん(事件) *n*. **1** event; affair:
Kare wa sono jikeñ *ni makikoma-reta.* (彼はその事件に巻き込まれた) He was involved in that *affair.*
2 incident; case.

ji꜀ki[1] じき(時期) *n*. **1** time:
Ima ga ichineñ-juu de ichibañ iso-gashii jiki desu. (今が一年中で一番忙しい時期です) This is the busiest *time* of the whole year. (⇨ toki)
2 season:
Aki wa ryokoo o suru no ni ichi-bañ ii jiki desu. (秋は旅行をするのに一番いい時期です) Autumn is the best *season* for traveling.

ji꜀ki[2] じき(時機) *n*. opportunity; chance.

ji꜀ki[3] じき(磁器) *n*. porcelain; china. (⇨ tooki[1])

ji꜀ki ni じきに(直に) *adv*. **1** soon; in a moment:
Shujiñ wa jiki ni modotte kimasu.

（主人はじきに戻ってきます）My husband will *soon* be back.
2 easily; readily:
Yasui shinamono wa jiki ni *kowareru.*（安い品物はじきに壊れる）Cheap goods *easily* break.

ji⌐kkan じっかん（実感）*n.* actual feeling; realization.
jikkañ suru（～する）*vt.* fully realize.

ji⌐kkeñ じっけん（実験）*n.* experiment; test.
jikkeñ (o) suru（～(を)する）*vt.* make an experiment.

ji⌐kkeñdai じっけんだい（実験台）*n.*
1 laboratory table.
2 the subject of an experiment: jikkeñdai *ni sareru*（実験台にされる）be used as a *guinea pig.*

ji⌐kke⌐ñshitsu じっけんしつ（実験室）*n.* laboratory.

ji⌐kkoo じっこう（実行）*n.* practice; action; execution.
jikkoo suru（～する）*vt.* carry out; execute: *yakusoku o* jikkoo suru（約束を実行する）*fulfill* a promise.

ji⌐kku⌐ri じっくり *adv.*（～ to）closely; carefully; thoroughly: *Watashi wa kanojo to sono koto ni tsuite* jikkuri (to) *hanashiatta.*（私は彼女とそのことについてじっくり(と)話し合った）I discussed the matter *thoroughly* with her.

ji⌐ko¹ じこ（事故）*n.* accident: jiko *o okosu*（事故を起こす）cause an *accident.*

ji⌐ko² じこ（自己）*n.* self; oneself: jiko-*mañzoku*（自己満足）*self-satisfaction.*

ji⌐koku じこく（時刻）*n.* time: *Tokee o tadashii* jikoku *ni awaseta.*（時計を正しい時刻に合わせた）I set my watch to the right *time.*

ji⌐kokuhyoo じこくひょう（時刻表）*n.* (train) schedule; timetable. （⇨ daiya）

ji⌐ko-sho⌐okai じこしょうかい（自己紹介）*n.* self-introduction.
jiko-shookai (o) suru（～(を)する）*vi.* introduce oneself.

ji⌐ku¹ じく（軸）*n.* axis; axle; shaft.

ji⌐mañ じまん（自慢）*n.* pride; boast:
Kare wa haha-oya no jimañ no *tane da.*（彼は母親の自慢の種だ）He is his mother's *pride.*
jimañ (o) suru（～(を)する）*vt.* be proud of; boast; brag.

ji⌐meñ じめん（地面）*n.* surface of the earth; ground.

ji⌐mi じみ（地味）*a.n.*（～ na, ni）plain; quiet; modest:
jimi *na nekutai*（地味なネクタイ）a *quiet* tie. (↔ hade)

Ji⌐miñtoo じみんとう（自民党）*n.* =Jiyuu Miñshutoo. （⇨ APP, 8）

ji⌐mu じむ（事務）*n.* office [clerical] work; business.

ji⌐mu⌐iñ じむいん（事務員）*n.* office worker; clerk; secretary.

ji⌐mu⌐shitsu じむしつ（事務室）*n.* office room.

ji⌐mu⌐sho じむしょ（事務所）*n.* office.

-jiñ じん（人）*suf.* person: *geenoo-*jiñ（芸能人）a show business [TV] *personality.*

ji⌐nañ じなん（次男・二男）*n.* one's second son.

ji⌐ñbuñka⌐gaku じんぶんかがく（人文科学）*n.* the humanities.

ji⌐ñbutsu じんぶつ（人物）*n.*
1 character:
Kare no jiñbutsu *wa hoshoo shimasu.*（彼の人物は保証します）I vouch for his *character.*
2 person; figure.

ji⌐ñja じんじゃ（神社）*n.* Shinto shrine. （⇨ tera）

ji⌐ñji じんじ（人事）*n.* personnel affairs:
Atarashii jiñji *ga happyoo ni natta.*（新しい人事が発表になった）The new *personnel appointments* were announced.

ji⌐ñkaku じんかく（人格）*n.* character; personality.

ji⌐ñkoo じんこう（人口）*n.* population.

ji⌐ñkoo-e⌐esee じんこうえいせい

（人工衛星）n. artificial satellite.
(⇨ eesee²)

ji「ňkoo-ko「kyuu じんこうこきゅう
（人工呼吸）n. artificial respiration.

ji「ňkoo-teki じんこうてき（人工的）
a.n. (~ na, ni) artificial:
jiňkoo-teki ni ame o furaseru (人
工的に雨を降らせる) make rain fall
artificially.

ji「ňmee じんめい（人命）n. human
life.

ji「ňmi「ň じんみん（人民）n. the people; the members of a nation-
state.

ji「ňrui じんるい（人類）n. human-
kind; the human race.
(⇨ niňgeň)

ji「ňsee じんせい（人生）n. human
life; life:
Kanojo wa shiawase na jiňsee o
okutta. (彼女は幸せな人生を送った)
She lived a happy *life*.

ji「ňshu じんしゅ（人種）n. race;
ethnic group:
jiňshu-sabetsu (人種差別) *racial*
discrimination.

ji「ňtai じんたい（人体）n. human
body. (⇨ karada)

ji「ňushi じぬし（地主）n. land-
owner; landlord. (⇨ ooya)

ji「ňzoo じんぞう（腎臓）n. kidney.

ji「rojiro じろじろ adv. (~ to)
jirojiro (to) miru (~（と）見る)
stare at.

ji「satsu じさつ（自殺）n. suicide.
jisatsu suru (~する) vi. commit
suicide; kill oneself.

ji「shiň¹ じしん（自信）n. confidence; assurance:
Watashi wa shikeň ni ukaru jishiň
ga aru. (私は試験に受かる自信がある)
I *am confident* of passing the examination.

ji「shiň² じしん（地震）n. earthquake; earth tremor.

ji「shiň³ じしん（自身）n. oneself;
itself:
Kare jishiň ga soo iimashita. (彼自
身がそう言いました) He told me so
himself.

ji「sho¹ じしょ（地所）n. land;
ground; lot.

ji「sho² じしょ（辞書）n. dictionary.
★ More formal than '*jibiki*.'
(⇨ jibiki; jiteň)

ji「shuu じしゅう（自習・自修）n.
studying for [by] oneself.
jishuu suru (~する) vi. study for
[by] oneself.

ji「ssai じっさい（実際）n. fact;
truth; practice:
Sono hanashi wa jissai to chigaimasu. (その話は実際と違います) Your
story differs from the *facts*.
jissai wa (~は) as a matter of
fact: Kare wa reetaň ni mieru ga
jissai wa shiňsetsu na hito desu.
(彼は冷淡に見えるが実際は親切な人で
す) He appears coldhearted, but
he is *really* a kind man.
— adv. (~ no, ni) actually;
really.

ji「ssai-teki じっさいてき（実際的）
a.n. (~ na, ni) practical; matter-
of-fact:
jissai-teki na chishiki (実際的な知
識) *practical* knowledge.

ji「sseki じっせき（実績）n. actual
results; one's achievements.

ji「sseň じっせん（実践）n. practice.
jisseň suru (~する) vt., vi. practice: Jibuň ga shiňjiru yoo ni jisseň shi nasai. (自分が信じるように実
践しなさい) *Act* in accordance with
your beliefs.

ji「sshi じっし（実施）n. enforce-
ment; operation.
jisshi suru (~する) vt. enforce;
carry out; put into force.

ji「sshitsu-teki じっしつてき（実質
的）a.n. (~ na, ni) substantial;
essential; material.

ji「sshuu じっしゅう（実習）n. practice; practical training:
ryoori no jisshuu o suru (料理の実
習をする) *practice* cooking.

ji「tai じたい（事態）n. situation:
Saiaku no jitai wa sakerareta. (最
悪の事態は避けられた) We were able
to avert *the worst*.

ji⌐taku じたく（自宅）*n.* one's own house; one's home.

ji⌐teñ じてん（辞典）*n.* dictionary. ★ More formal than '*jisho*.' Usually used in the title of a dictionary. (⇨ jisho²; jibiki)

ji⌐teñsha じてんしゃ（自転車）*n.* bicycle: jiteñsha *ni noru* (自転車に乗る) ride a *bicycle*.

ji⌐tsubutsu じつぶつ（実物）*n.* real thing; original: *Kono e wa* jitsubutsu *sokkuri da.* (この絵は実物そっくりだ) This picture looks just like the *real thing*.

ji⌐tsugeñ じつげん（実現）*n.* realization; materialization **jitsugeñ suru** (〜する) *vi., vt.* come true; realize.

ji⌐tsujoo じつじょう（実情）*n.* actual circumstances; the real state of affairs.

ji⌐tsu¹ ni じつに（実に）*adv.* very; terribly; really; extremely: *Koko kara miru Fuji-sañ wa* jitsu ni *utsukushii.* (ここから見る富士山は実に美しい) Mt. Fuji seen from here is *very* beautiful.

ji⌐tsuree じつれい（実例）*n.* example; instance: *Kare wa* jitsuree *o agete, setsumee shita.* (彼は実例をあげて、説明した) He explained by giving *examples*.

ji⌐tsuryoku じつりょく（実力）*n.* **1** real ability; merit: jitsuryoku *o hakki suru* (実力を発揮する) demonstrate one's *ability*. **2** force: jitsuryoku *o kooshi suru* (実力を行使する) use *force*.

ji⌐tsu¹-wa じつは（実は）*adv.* to tell the truth; actually; as a matter of fact.

ji⌐tsuyoo じつよう（実用）*n.* practical use; utility: *Kono doogu wa* jitsuyoo *ni wa yakudatanai.* (この道具は実用には役立たない) This tool is of little *practical use*.

ji⌐tsuyooka じつようか（実用化）*n.*

practical use. **jitsuyooka suru** (〜する) *vt., vi.* put [turn] (a thing) to practical use.

ji⌐tsuyoo-teki じつようてき（実用的）*a.n.* (〜 na, ni) practical.

ji⌐ttai じったい（実態）*n.* actual condition: *Roodoosha no* jittai *o shirabeta.* (労働者の実態を調べた) We researched the *actual conditions* of the workers.

ji⌐tto じっと *adv.* **1** still; quietly; motionlessly: *Shashiñ o torimasu kara* jitto *shite ite kudasai* (写真を撮りますからじっとしていてください) I am going to take a photo, so please keep *still*. **2** fixedly; steadily; intently; attentively: jitto *mitsumeru* (じっと見つめる) stare *intently*. **3** patiently: *Watashi wa sono itami o* jitto *gamañ shita.* (私はその痛みをじっと我慢した) I *patiently* endured the pain.

ji⌐yoo じよう（滋養）*n.* nourishment; nutrition. (⇨ eeyoo)

ji⌐yu¹u じゆう（自由）*n.* freedom; liberty: *Iku ikanai wa kimi no* jiyuu *da.* (行く行かないは君の自由だ) It is *up to* you whether you go or not. — *a.n.* (〜 na, ni) free; easy.

ji⌐yuushu¹gi じゆうしゅぎ（自由主義）*n.* liberalism.

ji⌐zeñ じぜん（慈善）*n.* charity.

ji⌐zoo じぞう（地蔵）*n.* guardian deity of children and travelers.

-jo じょ（所）*suf.* office; institute; works: *iñsatsu*-jo (印刷所) printing *plant* / *keñkyuu*-jo (研究所) a research *institute* / *seesaku*-jo (製作所) a *factory*. (⇨ -sho¹)

jo⌐do¹oshi じょどうし（助動詞）*n.* auxiliary verb.

jo⌐gai じょがい（除外）*n.* exclusion; exception.

jogai suru (〜する) *vt.* exclude; except.

jo「koo じょこう (徐行) *n.* going slow.

jokoo suru (〜する) *vi.* go slow; slow down.

jo「kyo「oju じょきょうじゅ (助教授) *n.* assistant professor.

jo「o¹ じょう (情) *n.* **1** affection; love:
oyako no joo (親子の情) the *affection* between parent and child.
2 feeling; sentiment:
Kare wa joo ni moroi. (彼は情にもろい) He *is easily moved emotionally*.
joo ga utsuru (〜が移る) become attached.

jo「o² じょう (上) *n.* the best; the top:
Kono shina wa joo no bu desu. (この品は上の部です) This article is one of the *best*.

-joo¹ じょう (場) *suf.* ground; links; track:
uñdoo-joo (運動場) a *playground* / *yakyuu-joo* (野球場) a baseball *ground* / *gorufu-joo* (ゴルフ場) golf *links* / *keeba-joo* (競馬場) a race *track*.

-joo² じょう (状) *suf.* letter:
shootai-joo (招待状) an *invitation* / *suiseñ-joo* (推薦状) a *letter* of recommendation. 《⇒ tegami》

-joo³ じょう (状) *suf.* -like; -shaped; form:
kyuu-joo no (球状の) *globular* / *kuriimu-joo no* (クリーム状の) *creamy*. 《⇒ jootai》

-joo⁴ じょう (上) *suf.* concerning; from the viewpoint of:
kyooiku-joo konomashiku nai (教育上好ましくない) be unsuitable *from the educational point of view*.

-joo⁵ じょう (畳) *suf.* counter for tatami mats:
roku-joo ma (6 畳間) a six-*mat* room / *hachi-joo no heya* (8 畳の部屋) a room with eight *mats*. 《⇒ tatami》

jo「obu じょうぶ (丈夫) *a.n.* (〜 na, ni) **1** (of a person) healthy.
2 (of substance) strong; durable; firm; tough.

jo「ocho じょうちょ (情緒) *n.* **1** atmosphere: *ikoku-joocho* (異国情緒) an exotic *atmosphere*.
2 emotion:
Kare wa joocho ga fuañtee da. (彼は情緒が不安定だ) He is *emotionally* unstable.

jo「oda「ñ じょうだん (冗談) *n.* joke; humor; fun:
Joodañ hañbuñ ni itta dake desu. (冗談半分に言っただけです) I just said it in *fun*.
joodañ deshoo (〜でしょう) you're kidding.
joodañ ja nai (〜じゃない) you can't be serious.
joodañ wa sate oki (〜はさておき) joking apart.

jo「oee じょうえい (上映) *n.* showing of a movie.
jooee suru (〜する) *vt.* show; present.

jo「oeñ じょうえん (上演) *n.* (of a play) presentation; performance.
jooeñ suru (〜する) *vt.* present; perform; put on the stage.

jo「oge じょうげ (上下) *n.* **1** upper and lower parts:
sebiro no jooge (背広の上下) the *jacket and trousers* of a suit.
2 social standing:
jooge kañkee (上下関係) the *pecking order*.
3 up and down:
hata o jooge ni furu (旗を上下に振る) wave a flag *up and down*.
jooge suru (〜する) *vi.* rise and fall; fluctuate. 《↔ sayuu》《⇒ ue-shita》

jo「ohatsu じょうはつ (蒸発) *n.* **1** evaporation; vaporization.
2 (of a person) disappearance.
joohatsu suru (〜する) *vi.* **1** evaporate; vaporize.
2 (of a person) disappear; run away.

jo⌐ohi¹ñ じょうひん（上品）a.n.
(～ na, ni) graceful; elegant;
refined. (↔ gehiñ)

jo⌐ohoo じょうほう（情報）n. information; intelligence.

jo⌐ojuñ じょうじゅん（上旬）n. the
first ten days of a month.
(⇨ chuujuñ; gejuñ)

jo⌐oke¹ñ じょうけん（条件）n. condition; terms:
jookeñ o tsukeru（条件をつける）
impose conditions.

jo⌐oki じょうき（蒸気）n. steam;
vapor.

jo⌐oki¹geñ じょうきげん（上機嫌）n.
good humor; high spirits.

jo⌐oko⌐okyaku じょうこうきゃく（乗
降客）n. passengers getting on
and off.

jo⌐okuu じょうくう（上空）n. the
sky:
Hikooki wa Tookyoo-wañ jookuu
o señkai shita.（飛行機は東京湾上空
を旋回した）The airplane circled
over Tokyo Bay.

jo⌐okyaku じょうきゃく（乗客）n.
passenger.

jo⌐okyoo¹ じょうきょう（状況）n.
situation; circumstances; conditions.

jo⌐okyoo² じょうきょう（上京）n.
going [coming] up to Tokyo.
jookyoo suru（～する）vi. go
[come] up to Tokyo.

jo⌐okyuu じょうきゅう（上級）n.
advanced course. (⇨ chuukyuu;
shokyuu)

jo⌐omae じょうまえ（錠前）n. lock:
to ni joomae o kakeru（戸に錠前を
掛ける）lock a door. (⇨ kagi)

jo⌐omu (to⌐rishimari¹yaku)
じょうむ（とりしまりやく）（常務（取締役））
n. managing director.

jo⌐onetsu じょうねつ（情熱）n.
passion; enthusiasm:
Kare wa joonetsu o komete ka-
tatta.（彼は情熱を込めて語った）He
spoke with passion.

jo⌐onetsu-teki じょうねつてき（情
熱的）a.n. (～ na, ni) passionate;

enthusiastic; ardent:
joonetsu-teki na odori（情熱的な踊
り）a passionate dance.

jo-⌐o¹o じょおう（女王）n. queen.
(↔ oo¹)

jo⌐o-oñ じょうおん（常温）n. normal [room] temperature; fixed
temperature.

jo⌐oriku じょうりく（上陸）n. landing; disembarkation.
jooriku suru（～する）vi. land; dis-
embark: Taifuu ga Kyuushuu ni
jooriku shita.（台風が九州に上陸した）
The typhoon came ashore in Kyu-
shu.

jo⌐oruri じょうるり（浄瑠璃）n. narrative ballad sung for traditional
puppet theater.

jo⌐oryuu じょうりゅう（上流）n.
1 the upper course [reaches] of a
river. (↔ karyuu)
2 the upper class. (⇨ chuuryuu;
kasoo)

jo⌐osee じょうせい（情勢）n. the
state of affairs; situation; conditions.

jo⌐osha じょうしゃ（乗車）n. boarding a train [bus]; taking a taxi.
joosha suru（～する）vt. get on a
train [bus, etc.]. (↔ gesha)
(⇨ noru¹)

jo⌐osha¹keñ じょうしゃけん（乗車
券）n. train [bus] ticket.

jo⌐oshl じょうし（上司）n. one's
superior; boss.

jo⌐oshiki じょうしき（常識）n.
common knowledge; common
sense.
jooshiki hazure（～はずれ）eccen-
tric; absurd: jooshiki hazure no
furumai（常識はずれの振る舞い）sense-
less behavior.

jo⌐oshiki-teki じょうしきてき（常識
的）a.n. (～ na, ni) common-
sense; practical; ordinary; commonplace:
Sono nedañ wa jooshiki-teki da to
omou.（その値段は常識的だと思う）I
think that price is reasonable.

jo⌐oshoo じょうしょう（上昇）n.

rise; ascent.

jooshoo suru (〜する) *vi.* rise; go up. (↔ kakoo²; teeka¹)

jo⌐otai じょうたい (状態) *n.* state; condition:
Kono ie wa hidoi jootai *da.* (この家はひどい状態だ) This house is in a bad *state*.

jo⌐otoo じょうとう (上等) *a.n.* (〜 na, ni) of good quality; excellent.

jo⌐owan じょうわん (上腕) *n.* upper arm. (⇨ ude)

jo⌐oyaku じょうやく (条約) *n.* treaty:
jooyaku *ni chooiñ suru* (条約に調印する) sign a *treaty*.

jo⌐oyoo-ka⌐ñji じょうようかんじ (常用漢字) *n.* Chinese characters in common use. ★ The 1945 characters designated by the Cabinet in 1981 for everyday use. (⇨ kañji¹)

jo⌐ozu⌐ じょうず (上手) *a.n.* (〜 na, ni) good; well:
Nakanaka joozu *ni utaenai.* (なかなかじょうずに歌えない) I can't sing at all *well*. (↔ heta) (⇨ umai)

jo⌐see じょせい (女性) *n.* adult woman; lady; female. ★ A more refined word than 'oñna,' which often sounds rude. (↔ dañsee) (⇨ fujiñ²; joshi¹; oñna)

jo⌐see-teki じょせいてき (女性的) *a.n.* (〜 na, ni) (of women, men and things) womanly, feminine; womanish. (↔ dañsee-teki) (⇨ oñnarashii)

jo⌐shi¹ じょし (女子) *n.* 1 girl. 2 woman; lady; female. (↔ dañshi) (⇨ fujiñ²; josee; oñna)

jo⌐shi² じょし (助詞) *n.* (postpositional) particle. (⇨ APP. 2)

jo⌐shidai じょしだい (女子大) *n.* women's university. ★ Shortened form of 'joshi-daigaku.'

jo⌐shi-da⌐igaku じょしだいがく (女子大学) *n.* women's university. (⇨ daigaku; joshidai)

jo⌐shu じょしゅ (助手) *n.* assistant; helper; tutor.

jo⌐yuu じょゆう (女優) *n.* actress. (⇨ haiyuu)

ju⌐gyoo じゅぎょう (授業) *n.* lesson; class; school:
Señsee wa Nihoñgo de jugyoo (*o*) *shita.* (先生は日本語で授業(を)した) The teacher conducted her *class* in Japanese.

ju⌐keñ じゅけん (受験) *n.* taking an (entrance) examination.
jukeñ suru (〜する) *vt.* take an (entrance) examination.

ju⌐kugo じゅくご (熟語) *n.* 1 compound word consisting of two or more Chinese characters. *e.g.* 手荷物 (*tenimotsu*), 登山 (*tozañ*). 2 idiom; set phrase.

ju⌐ku⌐s・u じゅくす (熟す) *vi.* (jukush・i-; jukus・a-; jukush・i-te [C])
1 ripen:
Kono kaki wa jukushite iru. (この柿は熟している) This persimmon *is ripe*.
2 (of opportunity, etc.) be ripe:
Ki no jukusu *no o matoo.* (機の熟すのを待とう) Let's wait until the time *is ripe*.

ju⌐myoo じゅみょう (寿命) *n.* life span; life:
jumyoo *ga nagai [mijikai]* (寿命が長い[短い]) be *long-lived* [*short-lived*].
jumyoo ga chijimaru (〜が縮まる) one's life is shortened: *Sono jiko de* jumyoo ga chijimatta. (その事故で寿命が縮まった) The accident *took years off my life*.

ju⌐ñ¹ じゅん (順) *n.* order; turn:
Se no takai juñ *ni narabi nasai.* (背の高い順に並びなさい) Line up in *order* of height. (⇨ juñbañ; juñjo)
juñ o otte (〜を追って) in the proper order.

ju⌐ñ² じゅん (純) *a.n.* (〜 na) pure; innocent; simplehearted:
Juñ *na hito hodo damasare-yasui.* (純な人ほどだまされやすい) Those who are *unsophisticated* are apt to be taken in easily.

juñ-¹ じゅん (準) *pref.* quasi-;

semi-; associate:
juṅ-*kyuu* (*ressha*) (準急(列車)) a
semi-express train / juṅ-*kesshoo*
(準決勝) a *semi*-final match
[game].

juﾛ̄n-² じゅん (純) *pref.* pure; all:
juṅ-*kiṅ* (純金) *pure* gold / juṅ-*moo*
(純毛) *all* wool.

juﾛ̄nbaṅ じゅんばん (順番) *n.* one's
turn:
naraṅde, juṅbaṅ o matsu (並んで，
順番を待つ) line up and wait for
one's *turn*.

juﾛ̄nbi じゅんび (準備) *n.* preparation; arrangements.

juﾛ̄nchoo じゅんちょう (順調) *a.n.*
(~ *na, ni*) smooth; favorable; all
right:
*Shujutsu-go no keeka wa juṅchoo
desu.* (手術後の経過は順調です)
Post-operative progress has been
satisfactory.

juﾛ̄neṅ じゅんえん (順延) *n.* postponement of something scheduled.
juṅeṅ suru (~する) *vt.* postpone;
put off. (⇨ nobasu¹)

juﾛ̄njo じゅんじょ (順序) *n.* order:
Juṅjo ga gyaku desu. (順序が逆です)
The *order* is reversed. (⇨ juṅ¹)

juﾛ̄njoo じゅんじょう (純情) *a.n.*
(~ *na*) unsophisticated; naive;
pure.

juﾛ̄njuﾛ̄n ni じゅんじゅんに (順々に)
adv. one by one.

juﾛ̄nkaṅ じゅんかん (循環) *n.* circulation; rotation.
juṅkaṅ suru (~する) *vi.* circulate;
cycle. (⇨ mawaru)

juﾛ̄nkyuu じゅんきゅう (準急) *n.*
semi-express train. (⇨ kyuukoo¹)

juﾛ̄nsa じゅんさ (巡査) *n.* policeman (the lowest rank in the police).

juﾛ̄nsui じゅんすい (純粋) *a.n.*
(~ *na, ni*) pure; genuine:
juṅsui *na Akita-keṅ* (純粋な秋田犬)
a *pure-blooded* Akita dog.

juﾛtsugo じゅつご (術語) *n.* technical term.

juﾛu¹ じゅう (十) *n.* ten.
jut-chuu hakku (~中八九)
highly likely to occur.
(⇨ too¹; APP. 3)

juﾛu² じゅう (銃) *n.* gun; rifle.

-juu¹ じゅう (中) *suf.* **1** through;
throughout:
Ichinichi-juu ame ga futta. (一日中
雨が降った) It rained *all* day *long*.
(⇨ -chuu)
2 all over:
Kare wa sekai-juu o ryokoo shita.
(彼は世界中を旅行した) He has trav-
eled *all over* the world.

-juu² じゅう (重) *suf.* -fold:
ni-juu *no* (二重の) *twofold* / saṅ-juu
no (三重の) *threefold* / go-juu-*no-
too* (五重の塔) a *five-storied* pagoda.

juﾛubuﾛ̄n じゅうぶん (十分) *a.n.*
(~ *na, ni*) enough; sufficient;
ample:
Jikaṅ wa juubuṅ ni arimasu. (時間
は十分にあります) We have *plenty of*
time. (↔ fujubuṅ)
—— *adv.* enough; to the full;
thoroughly:
Aṅzeṅ ni juubuṅ go-chuui kudasai.
(安全に十分ご注意ください) Please
pay *close* attention to safety.

juﾛudai じゅうだい (重大) *a.n.*
(~ *na*) serious; important;
grave:
Kare no sekiniṅ wa juudai desu.
(彼の責任は重大です) His responsibility is *great*.

juﾛudeṅ じゅうでん (充電) *n.*
charge of electricity.
juudeṅ suru (~する) *vt.* charge.

juﾛudoo じゅうどう (柔道) *n.* judo.

juﾛufuku じゅうふく (重複) *n.*
= choofuku.

juﾛu-gatsu じゅうがつ (十月) *n.*
October. (⇨ APP. 5)

juﾛugoya じゅうごや (十五夜) *n.*
a full moon night.

juﾛugyoﾛoiṅ じゅうぎょういん (従業
員) *n.* employee; worker.
(⇨ shaiṅ)

juﾛuichi-gatsu じゅういちがつ (十

一月) *n*. November. (⇨ APP. 5)

ju⌐uji˥ro じゅうじろ (十字路) *n*. crossroads. (⇨ koosateñ)

ju⌐ujitsu じゅうじつ (充実) *n*. fullness; substantiality.

juujitsu suru (~する) *vi*. be rich in content: *Kono gakkoo wa uñdoo shisetsu ga* juujitsu *shite iru*. (この学校は運動施設が充実している) This school has a *full range* of sports facilities.

ju⌐ukyo じゅうきょ (住居) *n*. dwelling; residence. (⇨ sumai)

ju⌐umiñ じゅうみん (住民) *n*. inhabitant; dweller; resident.

ju⌐uni-gatsu˥ じゅうにがつ (十二月) *n*. December. (⇨ APP. 5)

ju⌐uni˥shi じゅうにし (十二支) *n*. the twelve Chinese year signs.

ju⌐usho じゅうしょ (住所) *n*. one's address; one's dwelling place.

ju⌐usu ジュース *n*. soft drink; juice. ★ Usually refers to sweetened and flavored carbonated drinks. Fruit and vegetable juice is called '*nama (no) juusu*' (fresh juice).

ju⌐utaku じゅうたく (住宅) *n*. house; housing.

ju⌐utañ じゅうたん (絨毯) *n.* carpet; rug.

ju⌐uteñ じゅうてん (重点) *n*. stress; importance; priority:
Kono gakkoo de wa supootsu ni juuteñ *o oite iru*. (この学校ではスポーツに重点を置いている) This school lays *stress* on sports.

ju⌐uteñ-teki じゅうてんてき (重点的) *a.n*. (~ na, ni) intensive; preponderant:
juuteñ-teki *ni soosaku suru* (重点的に捜索する) make an *intensive* search.

ju⌐uyaku じゅうやく (重役) *n*. corporate executive; company director.

ju⌐uyoo じゅうよう (重要) *a.n*. (~ na) important; major; essential.

ju⌐uyu じゅうゆ (重油) *n*. heavy oil. (↔ keeyu˥)

ju⌐wa˥ki じゅわき (受話器) *n*. (telephone) receiver.

ju⌐yoo じゅよう (需要) *n*. demand; request:
Kyookyuu ga juyoo *ni oitsukanai*. (供給が需要に追いつかない) The supply does not meet the *demand*. (↔ kyookyuu)

ju⌐yo˥osha じゅようしゃ (需要者) *n*. consumer; user; customer.

K

ka[1] か (蚊) *n*. mosquito.

ka[2] か (可) *n*. **1** (of a grade rating) being passable; C or D in schoolwork. (⇨ fuka; ryoo'; yuu²) **2** (*formal*) approval. (↔ ina)

ka[3] か *p*. **1** (used to make questions): ★ Changes an ordinary declarative sentence to an interrogative sentence.
Anata wa Tanaka-sañ desu ka? (あなたは田中さんですか) *Are you* Mrs. Tanaka?
2 won't you...; what about...; shall I [we]...: ★ Used in invitations, requests or proposals.

Koohii de mo nomimaseñ ka? (コーヒーでも飲みませんか) *Won't you have* a coffee, or something?
3 I wonder. ★ Used with the tentative of the copula.
Ashita wa teñki ni naru daroo ka? (あしたは天気になるだろうか) *I wonder* if it will be fine tomorrow.
4 (used rhetorically when confirming a fact to oneself):
Are, moo koñna jikañ ka. (あれ、もうこんな時間か) What! *Is it* already *so late*?
5 (used rhetorically when encouraging oneself to do some-

thing):
Sorosoro kaeru ka. (そろそろ帰るか) I *must be off on my way* now.
6 (used when questioning or refuting someone's opinion):
Soñna kodomo ni nani ga dekiru ka. (そんな子どもに何ができるか) *What can a child like that do?*

ka⁴ か *p.* **1** (used after interrogatives to form indefinites):
Nani-ka tsumetai mono o kudasai. (何か冷たいものを下さい) Please give me *something* cold to drink.
2 perhaps [probably] because: ★ Used to indicate a possible reason or cause.
Tsukarete iru see ka shokuyoku ga arimaseñ. (疲れているせいか食欲がありません) *Perhaps* it is *because* I am tired, but I have no appetite.
3 or: ★ Used when listing examples from among two or more alternatives.
Kyooto ka Nara e ikitai. (京都か奈良へ行きたい) I want to go to *either* Kyoto *or* Nara.
4 (used with embedded questions):
Tsugi no deñsha wa nañ-ji ni deru ka shitte imasu ka? (次の電車は何時に出るか知っていますか) Do you know *what time the next train leaves*?
5 whether or...; whether or not: ★ Used with embedded alternate questions.
Kare ni heñji o dashita ka, doo ka oboete imaseñ. (彼に返事を出したか、どうか覚えていません) I can't remember *whether* I sent him the answer *or not*. ★ Note that '*ka*' can be followed by other particles, particularly '*wa*', '*ga*' and '*o.*' *e.g.* Doko e iku ka wa, *mada kimete imaseñ.* (どこへ行くかは、まだ決めていません) I have not yet decided *where to go.* / Doo kaiketsu suru ka ga, *moñdai desu.* (どう解決するかが、問題です) The problem is *how we are going to solve it.*

-ka¹ か (日) *suf.* day:
futsu-ka (二日) the 2nd (*day*); two *days* / *too*-ka (十日) the 10th (*day*); ten *days*. (⇨ APP. 5)

-ka² か (下) *suf.* under; below:
... *no shihai*-ka (...の支配下) *under* the rule of... / *ree*-ka (零下) *below* zero (degrees).

-ka³ か (化) *suf.* -ization: ★ A change into the stated condition. *eega*-ka (映画化) *making* into a movie / *goori*-ka (合理化) *rationalization*.
-ka suru (〜する) *vt., vi.* -ize: *kikai*-ka suru (機械化する) *mechanize*.

-ka⁴ か (科) *suf.* course; department; studies:
Nihoñgo gak-ka (日本語学科) a Japanese language *course* / *nai*-ka (内科) the *department* of internal medicine.

-ka⁵ か (課) *suf.* **1** lesson; work: *dai ik*-ka (第一課) *Lesson* 1 / *nik*-ka (日課) daily *work*.
2 section (of a company): *jiñji*-ka (人事課) the personnel *section*.

-ka⁶ か (家) *suf.* **1** (signifies a possessor):
shihoñ-ka (資本家) a *capitalist*.
2 a person of the stated quality or tendency:
kuusoo-ka (空想家) a *dreamer*.
3 specialist:
oñgaku-ka (音楽家) a *musician*.

-ka⁷ か (箇) *suf.* counter used with numerals: ★ Sometimes 'ヶ' is used instead of 'か.'
ni-ka-*getsu* (二か月) *two* months / *go*-ka-*koku* (五か国) *five* countries.

ka¹asañ かあさん (母さん) *n.* (*informal*) momma; mother.
★ Usually with '*o*-.' (↔ toosañ)
(⇨ haha; haha-oya; o-kaasañ)

ka¹baa カバー *n.* **1** cover; covering:
sofaa ni kabaa o kakeru (ソファーにカバーをかける) put a *cover* on the sofa.
2 dust jacket; wrapper.

(⇨ hyooshi)

kabaa suru (〜する) *vt.* **1** cover; make up: *akaji o kabaa suru* (赤字をカバーする) *make up* the deficit. **2** (of baseball) cover; back up.

ka「bañ かばん (鞄) *n.* bag; satchel; briefcase.

ka「ba'‧u かばう (庇う) *vt.* (kaba‧i‧; kabaw‧a‧; kabat‧te ⓒ) protect; defend: *Dare mo kanojo o kabawanakatta.* (だれも彼女をかばわなかった) *Nobody pleaded* for her.

ka「bayaki かばやき (蒲焼き) *n.* broiled eels. ★ Eels are split and barbecued over a charcoal fire. (⇨ unagi)

ka「be かべ (壁) *n.* **1** wall. **2** obstacle; deadlock: *Jiñshu-moñdai ga kabe ni natte iru.* (人種問題が壁になっている) The racial problem constitutes an *obstacle.*

ka「bi かび (黴) *n.* mold.

ka「biñ かびん (花瓶) *n.* flower vase.

ka「bocha かぼちゃ *n.* pumpkin; squash.

ka「bu[1] かぶ (株) *n.* **1** stock; share. (⇨ kabukeñ; kabunushi) **2** roots; stump: *Pañjii no nae o sañ-kabu katta.* (パンジーの苗を3株買った) I bought three pansy *seedlings.*

ka「bu[2] かぶ (蕪) *n.* turnip.

ka「bukeñ かぶけん (株券) *n.* stock [share] certificate.

ka「buki かぶき (歌舞伎) *n.* Japanese traditional drama.

ka「bu'nushi かぶぬし (株主) *n.* stockholder; shareholder. (⇨ kabu)

ka「bu'r‧u かぶる (被る) *vt.* (kabur‧‧i‧; kabur‧a‧; kabut‧te ⓒ) **1** put on (headwear): ★ '*kabutte iru*'=wear. *Giñkoo-gootoo wa fukumeñ o kabutte ita.* (銀行強盗は覆面をかぶっていた) The bank robber *wore* a mask. (⇨ kabuseru)

2 be covered: *hokori o kaburu* (ほこりをかぶる) *be covered* with dust. (⇨ kabuseru) **3** take on (responsibility): *Kare wa hitori de sono jikeñ no sekiniñ o kabutta.* (彼は一人でその事件の責任をかぶった) He alone *took* responsibility for the affair.

ka「buse'‧ru かぶせる (被せる) *vt.* (kabuse‧te Ⓥ) put...on; cover... with: *kodomo ni booshi o kabuseru* (子どもに帽子をかぶせる) *put* a cap on a child's head. (⇨ kaburu)

ka「bushikiga'isha かぶしきがいしゃ (株式会社) *n.* incorporated company; joint-stock company. (⇨ kaisha)

ka「chi[1] かち (価値) *n.* worth; value; merit. (⇨ neuchi)

ka「chi[2] かち (勝ち) *n.* victory. (↔ make)

ka「chikachi[1] かちかち *a.n.* (〜 no, ni) **1** be frozen hard: *Ike (no mizu) ga kachikachi ni kootte iru.* (池(の水)がかちかちに凍っている) The (water in the) pond is frozen *hard.* **2** tense: *Sono oñna-no-ko wa kiñchoo shite, kachikachi ni natte ita.* (その女の子は緊張して、かちかちになっていた) The girl was *rigid* with tension.

ka「chikachi[2] カチカチ *adv.* (〜 to) (tick of a clock): *Kono tokee wa amari* kachikachi *(to) iwanai.* (この時計はあまりカチカチ(と)いわない) This clock hardly makes any *ticking sound.*

ka「chiku かちく (家畜) *n.* livestock; domestic animal.

ka「choo かちょう (課長) *n.* section chief; manager.

ka「dai かだい (課題) *n.* **1** problem; question. **2** assignment: *natsu-yasumi no* kadai (夏休みの課題) *assignments* for the summer vacation.

ka「do[1] かど (角) *n.* corner.

ka˺do² かど（過度）a.n. (~ no, ni) excessive; too much:
Kado *no kitai wa kiñmotsu desu.* (過度の期待は禁物です) You should not expect *too much.*

ka˹do˺matsu かどまつ（門松）n. New Year's pine decorations.

ka˹eri˺ かえり（帰り）n. return:
Koñya wa kaeri *ga osoku nari-masu.* (今夜は帰りが遅くなります) I will *be coming home* late this evening. (↔ iki²; yuki²)

ka˹erimi˺·ru かえりみる（顧みる）vt. (kaerimi-te Ⓥ) 1 look back on:
jibuñ no kako o kaerimiru（自分の過去を顧みる）*look back on* one's past.
2 think of; pay attention:
Isogashikute, kazoku o kaerimiru hima mo nakatta.（忙しくて、家族を顧みるひまもなかった）I was so busy that I did not even have time to *consider* my family.

ka˹er·u˺¹ かえる（帰る）vi. (kaer·i-; kaer·a-; kaet·te Ⓒ) (of a person) come back; return:
Moo kaeranakereba narimaseñ.（もう帰らなければなりません）I *must be going* now. (↔ iku) (⇨ modoru)

ka˹er·u˺² かえる（返る）vi. (kaer·i-; kaer·a-; kaet·te Ⓒ) (of an object) return; get back:
Nusumareta e wa buji ni mochinushi no tokoro e kaetta.（盗まれた絵は無事に持ち主の所へ返った）The stolen picture *was* safely *returned* to its owner. (⇨ modoru)

ka˹e·ru˺³ かえる（変える）vt. (kae-te Ⓥ) change; alter:
Taifuu wa shiñro o kaeta.（台風は進路を変えた）The typhoon *altered* its course. (⇨ kawaru²)

ka˹e·ru˺⁴ かえる（代える・替える・換える）vt. (kae-te Ⓥ) change:
ichimañ-eñ satsu o señ-eñ satsu ni kaeru（一万円札を千円札にかえる）*change* a 10,000-yen bill into 1,000-yen bills. (⇨ kawaru²)

ka˹er·u˺⁵ かえる（孵る）vi. (kaer·i-; kaer·a-; kaet·te Ⓒ) hatch; be hatched.

ka˹eru˺⁶ かえる（蛙）n. frog; toad.

ka˹es·u かえす（返す）vt. (kaesh·i-; kaes·a-; kaesh·i-te Ⓒ) return; give back. (⇨ modosu)

ka˹ette かえって（却って）adv. on the contrary; after all; rather:
Kuruma yori aruita hoo ga, kaette hayai koto ga arimasu.（車より歩いたほうが、かえって早いことがあります）Walking, *rather* than going by car, is sometimes quicker.

ka˹fuñshoo かふんしょう（花粉症）n. hay fever; pollen allergy.

ka˹gaku¹ かがく（科学）n. science.

ka˹gaku² かがく（化学）n. chemistry. ★ Sometimes called '*bake-gaku*' to distinguish it from '*ka-gaku¹*.'

ka˹ga˺kusha¹ かがくしゃ（科学者）n. scientist.

ka˹ga˺kusha² かがくしゃ（化学者）n. chemist.

ka˹gaku-teki かがくてき（科学的）a.n. (~ na, ni) scientific:
kagaku-teki *ni setsumee suru*（科学的に説明する）explain something *scientifically.*

ka˹game·ru かがめる（屈める）vt. (kagame-te Ⓥ) bend; stoop:
mi o kagameru（身をかがめる）*bend down.* (⇨ kagamu)

ka˹gami˺ かがみ（鏡）n. mirror; looking glass.

ka˹gami˺-mochi かがみもち（鏡餅）n. round rice cake offered to gods at New Year's time. (⇨ mochi)

ka˹gam·u かがむ（屈む）vi. (ka-gam·i-; kagam·a-; kagañ-de Ⓒ) bend; stoop; crouch:
kagañde kusa o toru（かがんで草を取る）*bend down* and pull up the weeds. (⇨ kagameru)

ka˹gayaki˺ かがやき（輝き）n. brightness; brilliance; radiance. (⇨ kagayaku)

ka˹gaya˺k·u かがやく（輝く）vi. (-yak·i-; -yak·a-; -ya·i-te Ⓒ) 1 shine; flash; glitter; twinkle.

2 be radiant; sparkle:
Shoojo no kao wa yorokobi de kagayaite ita.(少女の顔は喜びで輝いていた)The girl's face *was radiant* with joy.

ka⌐ge¹ かげ(影) *n.* **1** shadow.
2 silhouette:
Shooji ni hito no kage *ga utsutta.* (障子に人の影が映った)*The outline of a figure* was cast onto the paper sliding door.
3 reflection:
Mizuumi ni yama no kage *ga utsutte iru.*(湖に山の影が映っている)The *image* of the mountain is reflected in the lake.

ka⌐ge² かげ(陰) *n.* **1** shade.
2 back; rear:
Otoko wa kaateñ no kage *ni kakureta.*(男はカーテンの陰に隠れた)The man hid *behind* the curtain.
3 behind one's back; behind the scenes.

ka⌐geki かげき(過激) *a.n.* (~ na, ni) extreme; radical:
kageki *na shisoo*(過激な思想)*radical* ideology.

ka⌐geñ かげん(加減) *n.* **1** addition and subtraction.
2 state; condition:
Kyoo no kañja no kageñ *wa yosa* [waru]-soo da.(きょうの患者のかげんは良さ[悪]そうだ)The *condition* of the patient today seems to be good [bad].
kageñ suru (~する) *vt.* regulate; adjust (something physical):
heya no oñdo o kageñ *suru* (部屋の温度を加減する)*regulate* the temperature of the room.

ka⌐gi かぎ(鍵) *n.* key. ★ Can also refer to a lock. (⇨ aikagi)

ka⌐giri かぎり(限り) *n.* **1** limit:
Niñgeñ no yokuboo ni wa kagiri *ga nai.*(人間の欲望には限りがない)There are no *bounds* to human greed. (⇨ kagiru)
2 end:
Kono teñrañkai wa koñgetsu-kagiri de owari desu.(この展覧会は

今月限りで終わりです)This exhibition finishes at the *end* of this month.
... kagiri (...~) as long as; as far as: *Miwatasu* kagiri, *umi ga hirogatte ita.*(見渡す限り、海が広がっていた)The sea extended *as far as* the eye could see.

ka⌐gi⌐r.u かぎる(限る) *vt.* (kagir·i-; kagir·a-; kagit-te ⓒ)
1 limit; restrict:
Kono shoohiñ wa kazu ga kagirarete imasu.(この商品は数が限られています)These goods *are limited* in quantity. (⇨ kagiri)
2 be (the) best; be (the) most suitable:
Natsu wa biiru ni kagirimasu.(夏はビールに限ります)In summer *there is nothing like* beer.
... ni kagiri (...に限り) just: *Koñdo ni* kagiri, *muryoo to shimasu.*(今度に限り、無料とします)*Just this once*, we will make it free.
... ni kagitte (...に限って) be the last person: *Kare ni* kagitte, *soñna koto wa shimaseñ.*(彼に限って、そんなことはしません)*He is the last person* to do a thing like that.

ka⌐go かご(籠) *n.* basket; cage.

ka⌐goo かごう(化合) *n.* chemical combination.
kagoo suru (~する) *vi.* combine with.

ka⌐gu¹ かぐ(家具) *n.* furniture.

ka⌐g·u² かぐ(嗅ぐ) *vt.* (kag·i-; kag·a-; ka·i-de ⓒ) smell; scent; sniff:
Kanojo wa bara no hana no nioi o kaida.(彼女はばらの花のにおいをかいだ)She *smelled* the roses.

ka⌐ha⌐ñsuu かはんすう(過半数) *n.* majority; the greater number.

ka⌐hee かへい(貨幣) *n.* money; currency. (⇨ kane¹)

ka⌐i¹ かい(会) *n.* **1** meeting; party; assembly; gathering.
2 society; club:
Yamada-shi o ooeñ suru kai *o tsukutta.*(山田氏を応援する会をつくった)

We organized a *society* in support of Mr. Yamada.

ka⌐i² かい (貝) *n.* shellfish; shell.

-kai¹ かい (回) *n.* **1** time:
Watashi wa ik-kagetsu ni ni-kai Oosaka e ikimasu. (私は1か月に2回大阪へ行きます) I go to Osaka *twice* a month. ((⇨ -do))
2 (of baseball) inning.

-kai² かい (界) *suf.* community; world; circle; kingdom:
buñgaku-kai (文学界) the literary *world* / *keezai*-kai (経済界) financial *circles*.

-kai³ かい (階) *n.* **1** (used for counting floors):
ik-kai (1階) the first *floor* / *ni*-kai (2階) the second *floor*. ★ The floors of a house or a building are counted in the same way as in the U.S.A., the ground floor being the first floor.
2 (used for naming floors):
Omocha wa go-kai de utte imasu. (おもちゃは5階で売っています) Toys are sold on the fifth *floor*. ((⇨ APP. 4))

-kai⁴ かい (会) *suf.* party; gathering:
kañgee-kai (歓迎会) a welcome *party* / *soobetsu*-kai (送別会) a farewell *party*.

-kai⁵ かい (海) *suf.* sea:
Nihoñ-kai (日本海) the *Sea* of Japan / *Kasupi*-kai (カスピ海) the Caspian *Sea*.

ka⌐iage⌐·ru かいあげる (買い上げる) *vt.* (-age-te Ⓥ) (of a government) buy; purchase:
Seefu wa kome o nooka kara kaiagete iru. (政府は米を農家から買い上げている) The government *purchases* rice from farmers. ((⇨ kau¹))

ka⌐ichoo かいちょう (会長) *n.* the president (of a company); the chairman (of a corporation).

ka⌐ichuude⌐ñtoo かいちゅうでんとう (懐中電灯) *n.* flashlight; electric torch.

ka⌐ichuudo⌐kee かいちゅうどけい (懐中時計) *n.* pocket watch.

ka⌐idañ¹ かいだん (階段) *n.* stairs; steps; staircase.

ka⌐idañ² かいだん (会談) *n.* talks; conference.
... to kaidañ suru (...と～する) *vi.* talk together with; confer with.

ka⌐ifuku かいふく (回復) *n.* **1** recovery:
Kare no kaifuku wa hayakatta. (彼の回復は早かった) He made a quick *recovery*.
2 restoration:
shiñyoo no kaifuku o hakaru (信用の回復を図る) seek to *restore* one's reputation.
kaifuku suru (～する) *vt.*, *vi.* restore; improve; recover.

ka⌐iga かいが (絵画) *n.* picture; painting. ((⇨ e¹; egaku))

ka⌐igai かいがい (海外) *n.* lands beyond the sea; overseas countries:
kaigai-ryokoo (海外旅行) an *overseas* trip. ((↔ kokunai)) ((⇨ kokugai))

ka⌐igañ かいがん (海岸) *n.* seashore; coast; beach.

ka⌐igara かいがら (貝殻) *n.* seashell.

ka⌐igi かいぎ (会議) *n.* conference; meeting; council:
Kare wa kaigi-chuu desu. (彼は会議中です) He is in *conference*.

ka⌐igo かいご (介護) *n.* nursing; care.
kaigo suru (～する) *vt.* nurse; look after; care for.

ka⌐igoo かいごう (会合) *n.* meeting; gathering; assembly.

ka⌐iguñ かいぐん (海軍) *n.* navy; naval forces. ((⇨ Jieetai; kuuguñ; rikuguñ))

ka⌐ihatsu かいはつ (開発) *n.* development; exploitation.
kaihatsu suru (～する) *vt.* develop; exploit.

ka⌐ihoo¹ かいほう (解放) *n.* release; liberation.
kaihoo suru (～する) *vt.* release;

free; liberate: *hitojichi o* kaihoo
suru (人質を解放する) *free* hostages.

ka⌐ihoo² かいほう (開放) *n.* opening.

  kaihoo suru (～する) *vt.* be open
(to the public); leave open.

ka⌐ihyoo かいひょう (開票) *n.* ballot [vote] counting.

  kaihyoo suru (～する) *vi.* count
the ballots [votes].

ka⌐iiñ かいいん (会員) *n.* member;
membership.

ka⌐ijoo¹ かいじょう (会場) *n.* meeting place; site.

ka⌐ijoo² かいじょう (海上) *n.* the
sea:
Sono booto wa kaijoo *o hyooryuu
shita.* (そのボートは海上を漂流した)
The boat was adrift on *the sea.*
《⇒ kuuchuu; rikujoo》

ka⌐ikai かいかい (開会) *n.* the
opening of a meeting [session].

  kaikai suru (～する) *vi., vt.* open
a meeting. 《↔ heekai》

ka⌐ikaku かいかく (改革) *n.* reform; revision.

  kaikaku suru (～する) *vt.* reform;
revise: *zeesee o* kaikaku suru (税
制を改革する) *make reforms* in the
taxation system.

ka⌐ikee かいけい (会計) *n.* 1 accounts; accounting.
  2 payment; check; bill:
Kaikee *wa sumasemashita.* (会計は
済ませました) I paid the *bill.*
《⇒ shiharai》

ka⌐ikeñ かいけん (会見) *n.* interview.

  kaikeñ suru (～する) *vi.* have an
interview.

ka⌐iketsu かいけつ (解決) *n.* solution; settlement.

  kaiketsu suru (～する) *vi., vt.*
solve; settle; clear up.

ka⌐iko かいこ (解雇) *n.* dismissal;
discharge; layoff.

  kaiko suru (～する) *vt.* dismiss;
lay off. 《⇒ kubi》

ka⌐ikyoo かいきょう (海峡) *n.*
strait; channel:

*Tsugaru-*kaikyoo (津軽海峡) the
Tsugaru *Straits.*

Ka⌐ikyoo かいきょう (回教) *n.*
Islam.

ka⌐ikyuu かいきゅう (階級) *n.*
  1 class:
jooryuu [chuuryuu; kasoo] kaikyuu (上流[中流; 下層]階級) the
upper [middle; lower] *class.*
  2 rank.

ka⌐imono かいもの (買い物) *n.*
shopping; purchase:
yasui [takai] kaimono *o suru* (安い
[高い]買い物をする) make a good
[bad] *purchase.*

ka⌐inañ かいなん (海難) *n.* ship-
wreck; sea disaster; marine accident.

ka⌐iryoo かいりょう (改良) *n.* improvement; reform.

  kairyoo suru (～する) *vt.* improve; reform. 《⇒ kaizeñ》

ka⌐iryuu かいりゅう (海流) *n.*
ocean current:
*Nihoñ-*kairyuu (日本海流) the
Japan *Current.*

ka⌐isai かいさい (開催) *n.* holding
(of a conference, exhibition, etc.).

  kaisai suru (～する) *vt.* hold;
open. 《⇒ hiraku》

ka⌐isañ かいさん (解散) *n.* break-
up; dissolution.

  kaisañ suru (～する) *vi., vt.* break
up (a meeting); dissolve.

ka⌐isatsu かいさつ (改札) *n.* examination of tickets.

  kaisatsu suru (～する) *vt.* punch
[inspect] tickets.

ka⌐isee¹ かいせい (改正) *n.* revision; amendment.

  kaisee suru (～する) *vt.* revise;
amend: *keñpoo o* kaisee suru (憲
法を改正する) *amend* the constitution.

ka⌐isee² かいせい (快晴) *n.* fine
weather. 《⇒ teñki》

ka⌐isetsu¹ かいせつ (解説) *n.* explanation; commentary (by an
expert).

  kaisetsu suru (～する) *vt.* explain,

comment: *jiji-moñdai o* kaisetsu suru (時事問題を解説する) *comment* on current events.

ka˥isetsu² かいせつ (開設) *n.* establishment; foundation; inauguration.
kaisetsu suru (～する) *vt.* establish; set up: *jibuñ no jimusho o* kaisetsu suru (自分の事務所を開設する) *set up* one's own office.

ka˥isha かいしゃ (会社) *n.* 1 company; corporation; firm.
2 office:
Kaisha *o deru no wa roku-ji-goro desu.* (会社を出るのは 6 時ごろです) It is at about six o'clock that I leave the *office.*

ka˥isha˥iñ かいしゃいん (会社員) *n.* company employee; office worker. ★ Considered an occupational category.

ka˥ishaku かいしゃく (解釈) *n.* interpretation; explanation.
kaishaku suru (～する) *vt.* interpret; construe.

ka˥ishi かいし (開始) *n.* beginning; start; opening.
kaishi suru (～する) *vt.* begin; start; open. (↔ shuuryoo) (⇨ hajimeru)

ka˥ishoo かいしょう (解消) *n.* cancellation; annulment.
kaishoo suru (～する) *vt.* cancel (a contract); annul; break off.

ka˥isu˥iyoku かいすいよく (海水浴) *n.* sea bathing.

ka˥isu˥u かいすう (回数) *n.* the number of times; frequency:
Basu no deru kaisuu wa ichi-jikañ ni ni-hoñ desu. (バスの出る回数は 1 時間に 2 本です) The bus runs twice each hour.

ka˥isu˥ukeñ かいすうけん (回数券) *n.* coupon; ticket:
juu-mai tsuzuri no kaisuukeñ (十枚つづりの回数券) a book of 10 *bus* [*train*] *tickets.*

ka˥itaku かいたく (開拓) *n.* 1 reclamation; cultivation.
2 opening up.

kaitaku suru (～する) *vt.* 1 reclaim; cultivate: *arechi o* kaitaku suru (荒れ地を開拓する) *cultivate* waste land.
2 open up a new field [market, etc.]: *atarashii shijoo o* kaitaku suru (新しい市場を開拓する) *develop* a new market.

ka˥iteñ¹ かいてん (回転) *n.* 1 revolution; rotation; spin:
kaiteñ-*doa* (回転ドア) a *revolving* door.
2 turnover; circulation:
Ano mise wa kyaku no kaiteñ *ga ii.* (あの店は客の回転がいい) That store has a *constant flow* of customers.
kaiteñ suru (～する) *vi.* 1 revolve; rotate; spin.
2 circulate; turn over.

ka˥iteñ² かいてん (開店) *n.* opening of a store.
kaiteñ suru (～する) *vt., vi.* open [set up] a store.

ka˥itoo¹ かいとう (回答) *n.* reply; answer.
kaitoo suru (～する) *vt.* reply; answer: *buñsho de* kaitoo suru (文書で回答する) *reply* in writing.

ka˥itoo² かいとう (解答) *n.* solution; answer.
kaitoo (o) suru (～(を)する) *vt.* answer; solve. (⇨ toku¹).

ka˥itoo³ かいとう (解凍) *n.* thawing; defrosting.
kaitoo suru (～する) *vt.* thaw; defrost: *reetoo-shokuhiñ o* kaitoo suru (冷凍食品を解凍する) *thaw out* frozen food.

ka˥iwa かいわ (会話) *n.* conversation; talk; dialogue.

ka˥iyoo かいよう (潰瘍) *n.* ulcer. (⇨ ikaiyoo)

ka˥izeñ かいぜん (改善) *n.* improvement; betterment.
kaizeñ suru (～する) *vt.* improve; better: *roodoo-jookeñ o* kaizeñ suru (労働条件を改善する) *improve* labor conditions. (⇨ kairyoo)

ka˥ji¹ かじ (家事) *n.* housework;

household chores; housekeeping.
kaji no tsugoo (〜の都合) family reasons.

ka˺ji² かじ (火事) *n.* fire:
Sakuya kiñjo de kaji ga atta. (昨夜近所で火事があった) There was a *fire* in the neighborhood last night.

ka˺ji³ かじ (舵) *n.* tiller; rudder; helm.

ka˹jiritsu˺k·u かじりつく (齧り付く) *vt.* (-tsuk·i-; -tsuk·a-; -tsu·i-te C̄) 1 bite at [into]:
Kare wa ooki-na riñgo ni kajiritsuita. (彼は大きなりんごにかじりついた) He *bit* into a large apple.
2 hold on to; cling to:
Kanojo wa sutoobu ni kajiritsuite ita. (彼女はストーブにかじりついていた) She *stayed close up to* the heater.

ka˹ji˺r·u かじる (齧る) *vt.* (kajir·i-; kajir·a-; kajit-te C̄) 1 gnaw; bite:
Sono kaki o kajittara, shibukatta. (その柿をかじったら，渋かった) When I *took a bite* of the persimmon, it was bitter.
2 know a little of (learning):
Watashi wa Rateñgo o sukoshi kajirimashita. (私はラテン語を少しかじりました) I *have learned* a bit of Latin.

ka˹kae·ru かかえる (抱える) *vt.* (kakae-te Ⅴ) 1 have [hold] (a parcel, bag, baggage, etc.) in [under] one's arms.
2 have (a problem, difficulty, etc.):
Kare wa dai-kazoku o kakaete iru. (彼は大家族を抱えている) He *has* a large family to support.

ka˹kage·ru かかげる (掲げる) *vt.* (kakage-te Ⅴ) fly; put up; hang up (a flag, sign, etc.):
kañbañ o kakageru (看板を掲げる) *put up* a signboard.

ka˹kaku かかく (価格) *n.* price; cost; value:
kakaku o ageru [sageru] (価格を上げる[下げる]) raise [lower] the *price*.

ka˹kari かかり (係り) *n.* charge;

duty; a person in charge:
Kare wa eñkai no kakari desu. (彼は宴会の係りです) He is in *charge* of the banquet. ((⇨ -gakari¹))

ka˹kari˺choo かかりちょう (係長) *n.* group chief; chief clerk.

ka˹ka˺r·u かかる (掛かる) *vi.* (ka-kar·i-; kakar·a-; kakat-te C̄) 1 (of time) take:
Koko kara eki made aruite, dono kurai kakarimasu ka? (ここから駅まで歩いて，どのくらいかかりますか) How long does it *take* to walk from here to the station? ((⇨ kakeru²))
2 (of money) cost:
Terebi no shuuri ni goseñ-eñ kakatta. (テレビの修理に5千円かかった) The television repair *cost* me five thousand yen. ((⇨ kakeru²))
3 hang:
Kabe ni hana no e ga kakatte imasu. (壁に花の絵が掛かっています) There is a picture of flowers *hanging* on the wall. ((⇨ kakeru¹))
4 be locked; button:
Kono kuruma wa kagi ga kakatte inai. (この車は鍵がかかっていない) This car *is not locked*. ((⇨ kakeru¹))
5 be caught:
Kare wa wana ni kakatta. (彼はわなにかかった) He *was caught* in a trap.
6 splash:
Mizu ga zuboñ ni kakatta. (水がズボンにかかった) Water *splashed* on my trousers. ((⇨ kakeru¹))
7 (of suspicion) rest:
Kare ni utagai ga kakatta. (彼に疑いがかかった) Suspicion *has rested* on him.
8 (of tax) be imposed:
Gasoriñ ni wa zeekiñ ga kakatte imasu. (ガソリンには税金がかかっています) *There is* a tax on gasoline.
9 consult (a doctor):
Hayaku isha ni kakari nasai. (早く医者にかかりなさい) You should *consult* a doctor immediately.
10 be telephoned:
Kanojo kara deñwa ga kakatta. (彼女から電話がかかった) *There was a*

phone call from her. (⇨ kakeru[1])

11 work:
Kuruma no eñjiñ wa sugu ni ka-katta. (車のエンジンはすぐにかかった) The car engine soon *started*. (⇨ kakeru[1])

12 be covered:
Sora ni kumo ga kakatte kita. (空に雲がかかってきた) The sky *became cloudy*.

13 begin start; set about:
shigoto ni kakaru (仕事にかかる) *start* a job.

ka⌐ka⌐r·u² かかる (架かる) *vi.* (kakar·i-; kakar·a-; kakat-te Ⓒ) span:
Kono kawa ni chikai uchi ni hashi ga kakarimasu. (この川に近いうちに橋がかかります) A bridge will *span* this river in the near future. (⇨ kakeru[3])

ka⌐ka⌐r·u³ かかる (罹る) *vi.* (kakar·i-; kakar·a-; kakat-te Ⓒ) become [fall] sick [ill]; catch (a disease):
Kono ko wa kaze ni kakari-yasui. (この子はかぜにかかりやすい) This child *catches* colds *easily*.

ka⌐ka⌐r·u⁴ かかる (懸かる) *vi.* (kakar·i-; kakar·a-; kakat-te Ⓒ) appear; form:
Sora ni niji ga kakatta. (空に虹がかかった) A rainbow *formed* in the sky.

ka⌐kato かかと *n.* heel.

ka⌐kawa⌐razu かかわらず (拘らず) irrespective of; regardless of:
★ Used in the pattern, '… *ni kakawarazu.*'
Neñree ni kakawarazu, dare de mo sañka dekimasu. (年齢にかかわらず、だれでも参加できます) Anyone can take part, *irrespective of* age.

… ni mo kakawarazu (…にも～) although; in spite of: *Nañ-do mo chuui shita ni mo kakawarazu, kare wa aikawarazu kuru no ga osoi.* (何度も注意したにもかかわらず、彼は相変わらず来るのが遅い) *Although* I have repeatedly warned him, he

still continues to arrive late. (⇨ ga²; keredo (mo); no ni)

ka⌐kawa⌐r·u かかわる (関わる) *vi.* (kakawar·i-; kakawar·a-; kaka-wat-te Ⓒ) **1** have to do with; concern; affect:
hito no inochi ni kakawaru moñdai (人の命にかかわる問題) a problem *affecting* people's lives. (⇨ kañkee)

2 get involved; involve oneself with:
Yopparai ni wa kakawaranai hoo ga yoi. (酔っ払いにはかかわらないほうがよい) You had better *not get involved* with drunks.

ka⌐ke かけ (賭け) *n.* bet; stake; gamble: *kake o suru* (賭けをする) make a *bet*. (⇨ kakeru[4])

ka⌐ke⌐ashi かけあし (駆け足) *n.* run; gallop.

kakeashi de (～で) hurriedly:
Watashi wa Amerika o kakeashi de ryokoo shita. (私はアメリカを駆け足で旅行した) I made a *quick* tour of the United States.

ka⌐kebu⌐toñ かけぶとん (掛け布団) *n.* covers; quilt; eiderdown.

ka⌐kedas·u かけだす (駆け出す) *vi.* (-dash·i-; -das·a-; -dash·i-te Ⓒ) run out; start running.

ka⌐kedo⌐kee かけどけい (掛け時計) *n.* wall clock.

ka⌐kee かけい (家計) *n.* family budget; housekeeping expenses.

ka⌐kego⌐e かけごえ (掛け声) *n.* shout; cheer: *kakegoe o kakeru* (掛け声をかける) *call out*.

ka⌐ke⌐goto かけごと (賭事) *n.* gambling. (⇨ bakuchi; kake)

ka⌐ke⌐jiku かけじく (掛け軸) *n.* hanging scroll. ★ Traditionally hung in the '*tokonoma*.'

ka⌐kekomi かけこみ (駆け込み) *n.* running into:
Kakekomi-joosha wa kikeñ desu. (駆け込み乗車は危険です) It is dangerous to try to *dash onto a train* just before it leaves. (⇨ kakekomu)

ka「kekomu かけこむ(駆け込む) vi. (-kom·i-; -kom·a-; -koñ-de ⓒ) run into; seek refuge:
Kanojo wa tasuke o motomete koo-bañ ni kakekoñda.(彼女は助けを求めて交番に駆け込んだ) Seeking help, she took refuge in a police box. (⇨ kakekomi)

ka「kemawar·u かけまわる(駆け回る) vi. (-mawar·i-; -mawar·a-; -mawat-te ⓒ) 1 run about. (⇨ kakaru')
2 busy oneself (doing):
Kare-ra wa kifu-atsume ni kake-mawatte iru.(彼らは寄付集めに駆け回っている) They are busying themselves collecting contributions.

ka「kera かけら(欠片) n. fragment; broken piece. (⇨ kakaru⁶)

ka「ke」·ru¹ かける(掛ける・懸ける) vt. (kake-te Ⅴ) 1 hang:
kabe ni e o kakeru(壁に絵をかける) hang a picture on the wall. (⇨ kakaru')
2 set up:
yane ni hashigo o kakeru(屋根にはしごをかける) set up a ladder against the roof. (⇨ kakaru²)
3 place; put:
hi ni nabe o kakeru(火になべをかける) put a pot on the fire.
4 put on: ★'kakete iru' = wear.
Kanojo wa hoñ o yomu toki, itsumo megane o kakete iru.(彼女は本を読むとき、いつも眼鏡をかけている) She always wears glasses for reading.
5 cover; lay; put:
Samui no de hiza ni moofu o kaketa.(寒いのでひざに毛布をかけた) It was cold, so I covered my knees with a blanket.
6 lock:
mado ni kagi o kakeru(窓に鍵をかける) lock the window. (⇨ kakaru')
7 telephone; make a phone call:
Ato de deñwa o kakete kudasai. (あとで電話をかけてください) Please phone me later. (⇨ kakaru')
8 play; start; switch on:

rekoodo o kakeru(レコードをかける) put a record on / rajio o kakeru(ラジオをかける) turn on the radio. (⇨ kakaru')
9 sit down; take a seat:
beñchi ni koshi o kakeru(ベンチに腰をかける) sit down on a bench.
10 fasten; tie; bind:
furu-shiñbuñ no taba ni himo o kakeru(古新聞の束にひもをかける) bind up a sheaf of old newspapers with a cord.
11 pour; sprinkle; splash; water:
Sono kuruma wa watashi no fuku ni doromizu o kaketa.(その車は私の服に泥水をかけた) The car splashed muddy water on my clothes. (⇨ kakaru')

ka「ke」·ru² かける(掛ける) vt. (kake-te Ⅴ) spend; take:
Kare wa sono sakuhiñ no kañsee ni go-neñ kaketa.(彼はその作品の完成に5年かけた) He took five years to complete the work. (⇨ kakaru')

ka「ke」·ru³ かける(掛ける) vt. (kake-te Ⅴ) multiply:
Sañ kakeru ni wa roku desu.(3掛ける2は6です) Three times two is six. (↔ waru)

ka「ke」·ru⁴ かける(賭ける) vt. (kake-te Ⅴ) 1 bet; stake; gamble:
Kare wa sono reesu ni gomañ-eñ kaketa.(彼はそのレースに5万円賭けた) He bet 50,000 yen on the race. (⇨ kake)
2 risk: inochi o kakeru(命を賭ける) risk one's life.

ka「ke」·ru⁵ かける(架ける) vt. (kake-te Ⅴ) build; span:
kawa ni tsuribashi o kakeru(川につり橋をかける) build a suspension bridge across a river. (⇨ kakaru²)

ka「ke·ru⁶ かける(欠ける) vi. (kake-te Ⅴ) 1 chip; break:
Kono chawañ wa fuchi ga kakete iru.(この茶碗は縁が欠けている) The rim of this rice bowl is chipped.

2 lack; want; missing:
Kono hoñ wa ni-peeji kakete imasu.(この本は２ページ欠けています)
This book *is missing* two pages.

ka「ke¹•ru⁷ かける（駆ける）*vi.* (kake-te V) run. 《⇨ hashiru》

ka「ketsuke•ru かけつける（駆け付ける）*vi.* (-tsuke-te V) run [rush] to; come running:
Keekañ ga sugu sono genba ni kaketsuketa.（警官がすぐその現場に駆けつけた）A policeman *rushed to* the scene immediately. 《⇨ isogu》

ka「keyor•u かけよる（駆け寄る）*vi.* (-yor・i-; -yor・a-; -yot-te C) run up (to a child).

ka「ke¹zañ かけざん（掛け算）*n.* (of arithmetic) multiplication.
《⇨ kakeru³》《↔ warizañ》

ka「ki¹ かき（柿）*n.* persimmon.

ka「ki² かき（牡蠣）*n.* oyster.

ka「ki³ かき（夏期）*n.* summer; summertime:
kaki-*kyuuka*（夏期休暇）*summer* vacation [holidays]. 《⇨ tooki⁴; shuñki; shuuki²》

ka「kiarawa¹s•u かきあらわす（書き表す）*vt.* (-arawash・i-; -arawas・a-; -arawash・i-te C) describe in writing:
Sono kimochi wa kotoba de wa kakiarawasemaseñ.（その気持ちは言葉では書き表せません）I *cannot express* that feeling in writing.

ka「kidas•u かきだす（書き出す）*vt.* (-dash・i-; -das・a-; -dash・i-te C) make a list of:
kau mono o kakidasu（買う物を書き出す）*make a* shopping *list*.

ka「kiire•ru かきいれる（書き入れる）*vt.* (-ire-te V) write [put] in; enter. 《⇨ kakikomu》

ka「kikae•ru かきかえる（書き換える）*vt.* (-kae-te V) **1** rewrite; retell; paraphrase. 《⇨ kakinaosu》
2 renew (a license, certificate, etc.).

ka「kika¹ta かきかた（書き方）*n.* manner of writing; how to write; how to fill in [out].

ka「kikom•u かきこむ（書き込む）*vt.* (-kom・i-; -kom・a-; -koñ-de C) write; jot down; fill in [out]:
yooshi ni kakikomu（用紙に書き込む）*fill out* a form.

ka「ki-ko¹toba かきことば（書き言葉）*n.* written language; literary expression. 《↔ hanashi-kotoba》

ka「kimawas•u かきまわす（掻き回す）*vt.* (-mawash・i-; -mawas・a-; -mawash・i-te C) **1** stir; rummage:
Hikidashi o kakimawashite *hañko o sagashita*.（引き出しをかき回してはんこを捜した）I *rummaged around* in the drawer looking for my seal.
2 ruin; throw into confusion:
liñkai wa kare hitori ni kakimawasarete iru.（委員会は彼一人にかき回されている）The committee *has been thrown into confusion* just by him.

ka「kinaos•u かきなおす（書き直す）*vt.* (-naosh・i-; -naos・a-; -naosh・i-te C) rewrite; write again.
《⇨ kakikaeru》

ka「kine かきね（垣根）*n.* fence; hedge.

ka「kitate•ru かきたてる（書き立てる）*vt.* (-tate-te V) write up:
Shiñbuñ wa issee ni sono jikeñ o kakitateta.（新聞は一斉にその事件を書き立てた）All the newspapers *played up* that affair.

ka「kitome かきとめ（書留）*n.* registered mail.

ka「kitome•ru かきとめる（書き留める）*vt.* (-tome-te V) write [jot] down:
deñwa-bañgoo o kakitomeru（電話番号を書き留める）*write down* a telephone number.

ka「kitori かきとり（書き取り）*n.* dictation. 《⇨ kakitoru》

ka「kitor•u かきとる（書き取る）*vt.* (-tor・i-; -tor・a-; -tot-te C) write down; dictate; copy. 《⇨ kakitori》

ka「kitsuke•ru かきつける（書き付ける）*vt.* (-tsuke-te V) note [jot] down. (⇨ kakitomeru)

ka⌐kizome かきぞめ (書き初め) *n.* the New Year's writing.

ka⌐kko かっこ (括弧) *n.* parentheses; brackets; braces.

ka⌐kkoi·i かっこいい *a.* (kakkoyo-ku) (*informal*) good-looking; handsome; stylish: ★ Abbreviation of 'kakkoo ga ii.'
Kare wa kakkoii *kuruma o motte iru.* (彼はかっこいい車を持っている) He has a *stylish* car.

ka⌐kkoku かっこく (各国) *n.* every country; each nation; various countries.

ka⌐kkoo¹ かっこう (格好) *n.* appearance; shape; style:
kakkoo *ga onaji* (格好が同じ) be similar in *shape* / kakkoo ga ii (格好がいい) *look nice* / kakkoo no warui (格好の悪い) *unattractive.*
(↔ bukakko) (⇨ teesai)
— *a.n.* (~ na/no) suitable; fit; ideal: kakkoo *na nedañ* (格好な値段) a *reasonable* price.

ka⌐kkoo² かっこう (郭公) *n.* Japanese cuckoo.

ka⌐ko かこ (過去) *n.* the past:
Kako *no koto wa wasuremashoo.* (過去のことは忘れましょう) Let's forget *the past.*

ka⌐koi かこい (囲い) *n.* enclosure; fence; railing. (⇨ kakou)

ka⌐kom·u かこむ (囲む) *vt.* (ka-kom·i-; kakom·a-; kakoñ-de Ⓒ)
1 enclose; surround:
Sono mura wa yama ni kakoma-rete iru. (その村は山に囲まれている) The village *is surrounded* by mountains.
2 circle:
Tadashii kotae o maru de kakomi nasai. (正しい答えを丸で囲みなさい) *Circle* the correct answers.

ka⌐koo¹ かこう (加工) *n.* processing; manufacturing.
kakoo suru (~する) *vt.* process; manufacture; work: geñryoo o kakoo suru (原料を加工する) *process* raw materials.

ka⌐koo² かこう (下降) *n.* descent; fall; downturn.
kakoo suru (~する) *vi.* go down; descend; decline. (↔ jooshoo)

ka⌐ko·u かこう (囲う) *vt.* (kako·i-; kakow·a-; kakot-te Ⓒ) enclose; fence:
Shikichi o saku de kakotta. (敷地を柵で囲った) I *enclosed* the site with a fence. (⇨ kakoi)

ka⌐ku¹ かく (書く) *vt.* (kak·i-; ka-k·a-; ka·i-te Ⓒ) write:
tegami [shi] o kaku (手紙[詩]を書く) *write* a letter [poem].
kaite aru (書いてある) be written; say: Shiñbuñ ni wa nañ to kaite arimasu ka? (新聞には何と書いてありますか) What does it *say* in the paper?

ka⌐ku² かく (描く) *vt.* (kak·i-; ka-k·a-; ka·i-te Ⓒ) draw; paint:
kabe ni e o kaku (壁に絵をかく) *draw* a picture on the wall. (⇨ egaku)

ka⌐ku³ かく (掻く) *vt.* (kak·i-; ka-k·a-; ka·i-te Ⓒ) 1 scratch:
kayui tokoro o kaku (かゆい所をかく) *scratch* where it itches.
2 shovel: yuki o kaku (雪をかく) *shovel* snow away.

ka⌐ku⁴ かく (格) *n.* status; rank; class; grade.
kaku ga chigau (~が違う) be not comparable: Kare to watashi de wa kaku ga chigau. (彼と私では格が違う) I *am just not in his class.*

ka⌐ku⁵ かく (核) *n.* 1 nucleus:
kaku-*jikkeñ* (核実験) a *nuclear* test.
2 core; kernel.

ka⌐ku⁶ かく (角) *n.* angle. (⇨ kakudo; shikaku²)

ka⌐ku- かく (各) *pref.* each:
kaku-*katee* (各家庭) *each* family.

-ka⌐ku かく (画) *suf.* 1 (of rooms) partition:
ik-kaku (一画) a *partition.*
2 (of Chinese characters) stroke:
rok-kaku *no kañji* (6 画の漢字) a Chinese character of six *strokes.*

ka⌐kuchi かくち (各地) *n.* various parts of the country.

ka⌐kudai かくだい (拡大) *n.* expansion; magnification.
kakudai suru (～する) *vi., vt.* expand; magnify; enlarge: *kaigaieñjo no waku o* kakudai suru (海外援助の枠を拡大する) *increase* the range of overseas aid. (↔ shukushoo)

ka⌐kudo かくど (角度) *n.* 1 angle.
2 viewpoint:
Sono moñdai o chigau kakudo kara keñtoo shite mimashoo. (その問題を違う角度から検討してみましょう) Let's examine the problem from a different *viewpoint*.

ka⌐kugo かくご (覚悟) *n.* 1 preparedness; readiness:
Hinañ wa kakugo no ue desu. (非難は覚悟のうえです) I *am prepared* for criticism.
2 resolution; determination:
Watashi wa jihyoo o dasu kakugo desu. (私は辞表を出す覚悟です) I *am determined* to hand in my resignation.
kakugo suru (～する) *vt.* 1 be prepared; be ready.
2 be determined; be resigned:
shi o kakugo suru (死を覚悟する) *be resigned* to death.

ka⌐kuho かくほ (確保) *n.* securing; ensuring; guarantee.
kakuho suru (～する) *vt.* secure; ensure: *zaseki o kakuho suru* (座席を確保する) *secure* a seat.

ka⌐kuji かくじ (各自) *n.* (*formal*) each person. (⇨ meemee; onoono)

ka⌐kujitsu かくじつ (確実) *a.n.* (～ na, ni) certain; sure:
Tanaka-shi no tooseñ wa hobo kakujitsu desu. (田中氏の当選はほぼ確実です) Mr. Tanaka's victory in the election is almost *certain*.

ka⌐kumee かくめい (革命) *n.* revolution.

ka⌐kumee-teki かくめいてき (革命的) *a.n.* (～ na, ni) revolutionary.

ka⌐kuneñ かくねん (隔年) *n.* every other [second] year.

ka⌐kuniñ かくにん (確認) *n.* confirmation; verification.
kakuniñ suru (～する) *vt.* confirm; make sure: *hoteru no yoyaku o kakuniñ suru* (ホテルの予約を確認する) *confirm* the hotel reservation.

ka⌐kure⌐ñbo(o) かくれんぼ(う) (隠れん坊) *n.* hide-and-seek.

ka⌐kure⌐ru かくれる (隠れる) *vi.* (kakure-te Ⅴ) hide; hide oneself. (⇨ kakusu)

ka⌐kuritsu[1] かくりつ (確立) *n.* establishment.
kakuritsu suru (～する) *vi., vt.* establish; build up: *yuukookañkee o kakuritsu suru* (友好関係を確立する) *build up* friendly relations.

ka⌐kuritsu[2] かくりつ (確率) *n.* probability; likelihood:
Kare ga seekoo suru kakuritsu wa takai [hikui]. (彼が成功する確率は高い[低い]) There is a good [small] *chance* of his success.

ka⌐kushiñ[1] かくしん (確信) *n.* conviction; confidence.
kakushiñ suru (～する) *vt.* be convinced; strongly believe.

ka⌐kushiñ[2] かくしん (革新) *n.*
1 reform; innovation:
gijutsu no kakushiñ (技術の革新) technological *innovation*.
2 reformist; progressive; reformist [progressive] party. (↔ hoshu)
kakushiñ suru (～する) *vt.* reform; innovate. (⇨ kaikaku)

ka⌐kushu かくしゅ (各種) *n.* various kinds; all kinds:
kakushu *no mihoñ* (各種の見本) *all kinds* of samples.

ka⌐kushuu かくしゅう (隔週) *n.* every other [second] week.

ka⌐ku⌐s·u かくす (隠す) *vt.* (kakush·i-; kakus·a-; kakush·i-te Ⓒ)
1 hide; put out of sight. (⇨ kakureru)

2 keep secret from; conceal; cover up:
Nani mo kakusazu ni hanashi nasai. (何も隠さずに話しなさい) Speak out *without concealing* anything.

ka｢kutee かくてい (確定) *n.* decision; settlement.
kakutee suru (～する) *vi., vt.* decide; settle; fix: *Hikoku no yuuzai ga kakutee shita.* (被告の有罪が確定した) The defendant's guilt *was decided*.

ka｢kutoku かくとく (獲得) *n.* acquisition; acquirement.
kakutoku suru (～する) *vt.* acquire; win; obtain.

ka｢ma[1] かま (釜) *n.* iron pot; kettle.

ka｢ma[2] かま (鎌) *n.* sickle; scythe.

ka｢mae｣-ru かまえる (構える) *vt.* (kamae-te Ⓥ) **1** take a posture; prepare oneself:
pisutoru o kamaeru (ピストルを構える) *have* a pistol *ready*.
2 set up; build:
mise o kamaeru (店を構える) *set up* a shop.

ka｢ma｣-u かまう (構う) *vi., vt.* (kama-i-; kamaw-a-; kamat-te Ⓒ)
1 (in the negative) (not) mind:
"Tabako o sutte mo kamaimaseñ ka?" "Ee, kamaimaseñ." (「たばこを吸ってもかまいませんか」「ええ、かまいません」) "Do you *mind* if I smoke?" "No, I *don't*."
2 (in the negative) (not) meddle; (not) interfere:
Hito [Watashi] ni kamau na. (ひと [私]にかまうな) *Leave* me *alone*.
3 (in the negative) (not) look after; (not) care for; (not) pay attention to.

ka｢me かめ (亀) *n.* tortoise; turtle. (⇨ tsuru[3])

ka｢mera｣mañ カメラマン *n.* photographer; cameraman.

ka｢mi[1] かみ (紙) *n.* paper.

ka｢mi[2] かみ (髪) *n.* hair.

ka｢mi[3] かみ (神) *n.* deity; god; God. ★ Often called '*kamisama*.'

ka｢mi- かみ (上) *pref.* **1** upper:
kami-*te* (上手) the *upper* part; the right of the stage / kami-*za* (上座) the seat of *honor*. (↔ shimo-)
2 the first:
kami-*hañki* (上半期) the *first* half of the year. (↔ shimo-)

ka｢mia｣·u かみあう (噛み合う) *vi.* (-a·i-; -aw·a·; -at·te Ⓒ) **1** (of gears) mesh; engage.
2 (of an opinion, view, etc.) agree: ★ Used usually in the negative.
Futari no ikeñ wa kamiawanakatta. (二人の意見はかみ合わなかった) They *argued on different planes*.

ka｢mifu｣buki かみふぶき (紙吹雪) *n.* confetti. (⇨ fubuki)

ka｢mikuda｣k·u かみくだく (噛み砕く) *vt.* (-kudak·i·; -kudak·a·; -kuda·i·te Ⓒ) **1** crush with one's teeth. (⇨ kamu)
2 explain in easy words.

ka｢miku｣zu かみくず (紙屑) *n.* wastepaper.

ka｢mina｣ri かみなり (雷) *n.* thunder; lightning.

ka｢mi-no｣-ke かみのけ (髪の毛) *n.* hair of the head. (⇨ kami[2]; ke[1])

ka｢misama かみさま (神様) *n.* deity; god; God. (⇨ kami[3])

ka｢misori[1] かみそり (剃刀) *n.* razor.

ka｢mo かも (鴨) *n.* wild duck. (⇨ ahiru)

ka｢moku かもく (科目) *n.* subject; course of study.

ka｢mo shirenai かもしれない (かも知れない) (polite＝'ka mo shiremaseñ' or 'ka mo shirenai desu')
1 it may be; perhaps:
Sore wa hoñtoo ka mo shirenai. (それは本当かもしれない) It *might be* true.
2 there is no way to tell...:
Itsu ame ga furi-hajimeru ka mo shirenai. (いつ雨が降り始めるかもしれない) *There is no telling* when it might start raining.

ka｢motsu かもつ (貨物) *n.*

freight; goods; cargo.

ka¹m·u かむ (噛む) *vt.* (kam·i-; kam·a-; kañ-de ⒸC) bite; chew; gnaw:
Inu ni te o kamareta. (犬に手をかまれた) My hand *was bitten* by a dog.

ka¹ñ¹ かん (缶) *n.* can; tin:
kañ-*kiri* (缶切り) a *can* opener.

ka¹ñ² かん (管) *n.* pipe; tube.
(⇨ shikeñkañ; shiñkuukañ; sui-dookañ)

ka¹ñ³ かん (勘) *n.* intuition; perception:
Watashi wa kañ *de wakatta.* (私は勘でわかった) I felt it *intuitively*.

-kañ¹ かん (間) *suf.* **1** (of places, persons, etc.) between; among:
*Tookyoo Oosaka-*kañ (東京・大阪間) *between* Tokyo and Osaka.
2 (of time, period) in; for; during:
*Is-shuu-*kañ *Señdai ni taizai shita.* (一週間仙台に滞在した) I stayed in Sendai *for* a week.

-ka¹ñ² かん (巻) *suf.* volume; reel.
★ Counter for books, dictionaries, and reels of film.

ka¹na かな (仮名) *n.* Japanese syllabary. ★ There are two systems, 'hiragana' and 'katakana.' (⇨ furigana; inside front cover)

ka¹na かな *p.* **1** I wonder (if):
★ Usually used in addressing oneself. Most often used by men; women use 'ka shira.' 'Ka naa' is a variant.
Ashita wa teñki ka na? (あしたは天気かな) Will the weather be fine tomorrow, *I wonder*?
2 I don't know (whether or not):
Kimi ni kore wakaru ka na? (君にこれわかるかな) *I don't know whether or not* you can understand this.

ka¹naa かなあ *p.* = ka na.

ka¹nai かない (家内) *n.* one's own wife. (↔ otto; shujiñ) (⇨ tsuma)

ka¹namonoya かなものや (金物屋) *n.* hardware dealer; hardware

store; ironmonger.

ka¹narazu かならず (必ず) *adv.* certainly; surely; without fail; by all means.

ka¹narazu¹-shimo かならずしも (必ずしも) *adv.* (with a negative) always; necessarily:
Kanemochi ga kanarazu-shimo *shiawase to wa kagiranai.* (金持ちが必ずしも幸せとは限らない) The rich are not *always* happy.

ka¹nari かなり (可成) *adv.* pretty; fairly; considerably:
Yasuñdara, kanari *geñki ni nari-mashita.* (休んだら、かなり元気になりました) I took a day off, so I feel *pretty* good now. (⇨ daibu)

ka¹nashi·i かなしい (悲しい) *a.* (-ku) sad; sorrowful:
kanashii *monogatari* (悲しい物語) a *sad* tale. (↔ ureshii) (⇨ kanashi-mi; kanashimu)

ka¹nashimi かなしみ (悲しみ) *n.* sadness; sorrow; grief:
kanashimi *ni shizumu* (悲しみに沈む) be deep in *grief*. (↔ yorokobi) (⇨ kanashimu; kanashii)

ka¹nashi¹m·u かなしむ (悲しむ) *vt.* (kanashim·i-; kanashim·a-; kanashiñ-de ⒸC) feel sad; grieve; mourn; lament. (↔ yorokobu) (⇨ kanashimi; kanashii)

ka¹na¹·u かなう (適う) *vi.* (kana·i-; kanaw·a-; kanat-te ⒸC) suit; meet; serve:
Sore wa rikutsu ni kanatte·iru. (それは理屈にかなっている) That *is in conformity* with logic.

ka¹nawa¹nai かなわない (適わない) cannot bear [compete]: ★ The *nai*-form of the verb 'kanau.'
Mushiatsukute kanawanai. (蒸し暑くてかなわない) I *cannot stand* this sultry weather. ★ 'Kanaimseñ' and 'kanawanai desu' are polite forms.

ka¹nazu¹chi かなづち (金槌) *n.*
1 hammer:
kanazuchi *de kugi o utsu* (金づちで釘を打つ) drive a nail in with a

hammer.

2 (*colloq.*) a person who can not swim at all.

ka⌐nazu⌐kai かなづかい (仮名遣い) *n.* rules for the use of *kana*.

ka⌐ñbañ かんばん (看板) *n.* signboard; sign.

ka⌐ñbatsu かんばつ (干魃) *n.* drought; dry weather.

ka⌐ñbeñ かんべん (勘弁) *n.* pardon; excuse; tolerance.
kañbeñ suru (～する) *vt.* pardon; forgive; excuse. (⇨ yurusu)

ka⌐ñbu かんぶ (幹部) *n.* management; executives; leaders.

ka⌐ñbyoo かんびょう (看病) *n.* nursing; attendance.
kañbyoo (o) suru (～(を)する) *vt.* nurse; attend (a patient).

ka⌐ñchoo かんちょう (官庁) *n.* government office. (⇨ APP. 7)

ka⌐ñdañkee かんだんけい (寒暖計) *n.* thermometer. (⇨ oñdokee)

ka⌐ñdoo かんどう (感動) *n.* deep emotion; strong impression.
kañdoo suru (～する) *vi.* be impressed; be moved; be touched.

ka⌐ñdo⌐oshi かんどうし (感動詞) *n.* (of grammar) interjection. (⇨ APP. 2)

ka⌐ne¹ かね (金) *n.* money.
★ Often used with '*o*-.'
(⇨ kahee; kiñseñ; kooka³; shihee)

ka⌐ne² かね (鐘) *n.* bell; gong; chime.

ka⌐nemo⌐chi かねもち (金持ち) *n.* rich person; wealthy person; the rich. (↔ biñbooniñ)

ka⌐ne¹·ru かねる (兼ねる) *vt.* (kane-te Ⓥ) serve both as; double as:
Kono heya wa shosai to oosetsuma o kanete imasu. (この部屋は書斎と応接間を兼ねています) This room *serves both as* a study and a reception room.

-kane¹·ru かねる (-kane-te Ⓥ) cannot; be unable to; be not allowed to: ★ Occurs as the second element of compound verbs. Added to the continuative base of a verb.
Ano hito nara sore o yari-kanenai. (あの人ならそれをやりかねない) He *is likely* to do that.

ka⌐nete かねて (予て) *adv.* before; beforehand; previously:
kanete *yotee sarete ita yoo ni* (かねて予定されていたように) as *previously* scheduled.

ka⌐netsu¹ かねつ (加熱) *n.* heating.
kanetsu suru (～する) *vt.* heat; cook. (↔ reekyaku) (⇨ nessuru)

ka⌐netsu² かねつ (過熱) *n.* overheating.
kanetsu suru (～する) *vi.* overheat; (*fig.*) go to excess.

ka⌐ñga⌐e かんがえ (考え) *n.*
1 thought:
kañgae *o matomeru* (考えをまとめる) collect one's *thoughts*. (⇨ kañgaeru)
2 idea:
Sore wa yoi kañgae *da.* (それはよい考えだ) That is a good *idea*.
3 opinion; view:
Watashi no kañgae *de wa, anata no* kañgae *wa machigatte imasu.* (私の考えでは、あなたの考えは間違っています) In my *opinion*, your *view* is wrong.
4 intention:
Ima no shigoto wa yameru kañgae *desu.* (今の仕事はやめる考えです) I *intend* to quit my present job.

ka⌐ñgaeko⌐m·u かんがえこむ (考え込む) *vi.* (-kom·i-; -kom·a-; -koñ-de Ⓒ) think hard; brood over; be lost in thought.

ka⌐ñgaenao⌐s·u かんがえなおす (考え直す) *vt.* (-naosh·i-; -naos·a-; -naosh·i-te Ⓒ) reconsider; rethink; give up.

ka⌐ñgae¹·ru かんがえる (考える) *vt.* (kañgae-te Ⓥ) **1** think; consider:
Yoku kañgaete *kara kimetai to omoimasu.* (よく考えてから決めたいと思います) I would like to decide

after I *have considered* carefully.
((⇨ kañgae)

2 expect; imagine:
Sono shigoto wa kañgaete ita yori mo kañtañ datta. (その仕事は考えていたよりも簡単だった) The job was easier than I *had expected.*
((⇨ omou)

3 regard; take; believe:
Watashi wa ima made ano hito o shiñshi da to kañgaete imashita. (私は今まであの人を紳士だと考えていました) Up to now I *had believed* that he was a gentleman.

4 devise:
Kore wa watashi ga kañgaeta omocha desu. (これは私が考えたおもちゃです) This is a toy which I *thought up.*

ka「ñgaetsu¹k・u かんがえつく(考え付く) *vt.* (-tsuk・i-; -tsuk・a-; -tsui-te Ⓒ) think of; hit upon; call to mind; recollect.

ka「ñgai¹ かんがい(感慨) *n.* deep emotion; strong feelings:
kañgai ni fukeru (感慨にふける) be overcome by *deep emotion.*

ka「ñgai² かんがい(灌漑) *n.* irrigation.
kañgai suru (～する) *vt.* irrigate; water: *tochi o kañgai suru* (土地をかんがいする) *irrigate* land.

ka「ñgee かんげい(歓迎) *n.* welcome; reception.
kañgee suru (～する) *vt.* welcome.

ka「ñgeki かんげき(感激) *n.* deep emotion; strong impression.
kañgeki suru (～する) *vi.* be deeply moved; be impressed.

ka「ñgo かんご(看護) *n.* nursing.
kañgo suru (～する) *vt.* nurse; look after: *byooniñ o kañgo suru* (病人を看護する) *care for* a sick person.

ka「ñgo¹fu かんごふ(看護婦) *n.* female nurse.

ka「ni かに(蟹) *n.* crab.

ka「ñja かんじゃ(患者) *n.* patient; sufferer; case.

ka「ñji¹ かんじ(感じ) *n.* **1** impres-

sion; effect:
Kare wa kañji ga yoi [warui]. (彼は感じが良い[悪い]) He makes a good [bad] *impression.*

2 feeling; feel:
Watashi no kañji de wa kare wa konai to omou. (私の感じでは彼は来ないと思う) I have a *feeling* that he will not come.

ka「ñji² かんじ(漢字) *n.* Chinese character; 'kanji.' (⇨ jooyoo-kañji)

ka「ñji³ かんじ(幹事) *n.* secretary; manager; steward:
booneñ-kai no kañji (忘年会の幹事) the *organizer* of a year-end party.

ka「ñjiñ かんじん(肝心) *a.n.* (～ na, no) essential; important:
Nañ de mo hajime ga kañjiñ desu. (何でも初めが肝心です) In all things the first step is the most *important.* (⇨ juuyoo; taisetsu)

ka「ñji・ru かんじる(感じる) *vt.* (kañji-te Ⓥ) feel; sense; be impressed:
nani-ka kikeñ o kañjiru (何か危険を感じる) *sense* some danger.

ka「ñjo¹o¹ かんじょう(勘定) *n.*
1 calculation; count:
Gookee no kañjoo ga awanai. (合計の勘定が合わない) The *figures* for the total do not come out right.

2 account; payment; bill:
Kañjoo wa watashi ga haraimasu. (勘定は私が払います) I'll pay the *bill.*

3 consideration; account:
Kare no koto wa kañjoo ni irete nakatta. (彼のことは勘定に入れてなかった) I did not take him into *consideration.*
kañjoo suru (～する) *vt.* count; calculate. (⇨ kazoeru)

ka「ñjoo² かんじょう(感情) *n.* feeling(s); emotion; sentiment:
Kare no kotoba wa kanojo no kañjoo o gaishita. (彼の言葉は彼女の感情を害した) His words hurt her *feelings.*

ka「ñjoo-teki かんじょうてき(感情的) *a.n.* (～ na, ni) emotional;

sentimental:

Kare wa sugu kanjoo-teki *ni naru.*
(彼はすぐ感情的になる) He soon
gives way to his feelings.

ka⌐nkaku[1] かんかく (間隔) *n.*
interval; space:

juugo-fuñ kankaku *de* (15分間隔
で) at fifteen-minute *intervals* /
kankaku *o akeru* (間隔をあける)
leave a *space.*

ka⌐nkaku[2] かんかく (感覚) *n.*
sense; sensation:

*Kanojo wa shikisai-*kankaku *ga
sugurete iru.*(彼女は色彩感覚がすぐ
れている) She has an excellent *sense*
of color.

ka⌐nkaku-teki かんかくてき (感覚
的) *a.n.* (~ na, ni) sensuous;
related to the senses.

ka⌐nkañ[1] かんかん *adv.* (~ to)
1 (used to describe the heat and
brightness of the sun):

Hi ga kankañ (to) *tette iru.* (日がか
んかん(と)照っている) The sun *is
blazing hot.*

2 clang; loud ringing sound.

ka⌐nkañ[2] かんかん *a.n.* (~ ni)
furious:

Chichi wa kankañ *ni natte okotta.*
(父はかんかんになって怒った) My
father *flew into a rage.*

ka⌐nkee かんけい (関係) *n.*
1 connection:

Kare wa shigoto no kankee *de
Oosaka e ikimashita.*(彼は仕事の関
係で大阪へ行きました) He went to
Osaka *in connection with* his
business.

2 relation; relationship:

*Kanojo wa watashi no uchi to nañ
no* kankee *mo arimaseñ.*(彼女は私
の家と何の関係もありません) She is of
no *relation* to my family.

3 concern; involvement:

Anata ni wa kankee *no nai koto
desu.*(あなたには関係のないことです) It
is *none of your business.*

4 influence:

*Teñkoo wa shuukaku ni juuyoo
na* kankee *ga arimasu.*(天候は収穫

に重要な関係があります) The weath-
er has an important *influence* on
the harvest.

5 sexual relations.

kankee suru (~する) *vi.* be concerned; be involved; be related;
be affected. (↔ mukankee)

ka⌐nke⌐esha かんけいしゃ(関係者)
n. person concerned.

ka⌐nki[1] かんき (喚起) *n.* arousing;
stirring up.

kañki suru (~する) *vt.* arouse; stir
up: *hitobito no chuui o* kañki
suru (人々の注意を喚起する) *arouse*
the attention of people.

ka⌐nki[2] かんき (乾期) *n.* dry season.
(↔ uki[1])

ka⌐nkoo かんこう (観光) *n.* sightseeing; tourism.

kankoo suru (~する) *vt.* see the
sights.

ka⌐nkyaku かんきゃく (観客) *n.*
audience; spectator.
(⇒ keñbutsuniñ)

ka⌐nkyoo かんきょう (環境) *n.*
(natural) environment; surroundings.

ka⌐nkyoo-e⌐lesee かんきょうえいせ
い (環境衛生) *n.* environmental
hygiene [sanitation].

ka⌐nkyoo-ha⌐lkai かんきょうはかい
(環境破壊) *n.* environmental destruction.

ka⌐nmuri かんむり (冠) *n.* crown.

ka⌐nneñ かんねん (観念) *n.*
1 sense:

Kare wa jikañ no kanneñ *ga nai.*
(彼は時間の観念がない) He has no
sense of time.

2 idea: *kotee-*kanneñ (固定観念)
fixed *ideas.*

kanneñ suru (~する) *vi.* give up;
resign oneself to.

ka⌐nnushi かんぬし (神主) *n.*
Shinto priest.

ka⌐nojo かのじょ (彼女) *n.* 1 she.
★ 'kanojo no'=her; 'kanojo o'=
her. (↔ kare)

2 girlfriend.

ka⌐noo かのう (可能) *a.n.* (~ na,

ni) possible; practicable.
(↔ fukanoo)

ka⌐nsoku かのうせい (可能性) *n.*
possibility; potentiality.

ka⌐npa カンパ *n.* fund-raising
campaign; contribution.
kaṅpa suru (～する) *vt.* make a
contribution.

ka⌐npai かんぱい (乾杯) *n.* toast.
kaṅpai suru (～する) *vi.* drink a
toast.

ka⌐nreṅ かんれん (関連) *n.* relation; connection; association.
kaṅreṅ suru (～する) *vi.* be related; be connected.

ka⌐nri かんり (管理) *n.* administration; management; control:
kaṅri-niṅ (管理人) a *janitor*; a *con-
cierge*.
kaṅri suru (～する) *vt.* administer; manage; take care of.

ka⌐nroku かんろく (貫録) *n.*
presence; dignity:
Kare wa kaṅroku *ga aru.* (彼は貫録
がある) He is a man of *presence*.

ka⌐nryoo[1] かんりょう (完了) *n.*
completion.
kaṅryoo suru (～する) *vi., vt.*
complete; finish. (⇒ owaru)

ka⌐nryoo[2] かんりょう (官僚) *n.*
bureaucrat; bureaucracy.

ka⌐nryoo-teki かんりょうてき (官僚
的) *a.n.* (～ na, ni) bureaucratic.

ka⌐nsaṅ かんさん (換算) *n.* (of nu-
merical units) conversion;
change.
kaṅsaṅ suru (～する) *vt.* convert;
change: eṅ o doru ni kaṅsaṅ suru
(円をドルに換算する) *convert* yen
into dollars.

ka⌐nsatsu かんさつ (観察) *n.* observation.
kaṅsatsu suru (～する) *vt.* observe; watch: hoshi no ugoki o
kaṅsatsu suru (星の動きを観察する)
observe the movement of the
stars.

ka⌐nsee かんせい (完成) *n.* completion; perfection.
kaṅsee suru (～する) *vt., vi.* com-

plete; finish. (↔ mikaṅsee)

ka⌐nseṅ かんせん (感染) *n.* infection; contagion; transmission.
kaṅseṅ suru (～する) *vi.* catch;
contract. (⇒ utsuru[1])

ka⌐nsetsu[1] かんせつ (間接) *n.* in-
directness; being secondhand:
Sono koto wa kaṅsetsu *ni kikimashita.* (そのことは間接に聞きました) I
heard it *indirectly*. (↔ chokusetsu)

ka⌐nsetsu[2] かんせつ (関節) *n.* (of
a body) joint.

ka⌐nsetsu-teki かんせつてき (間接
的) *a.n.* (～ na, ni) indirect;
secondhand. (↔ chokusetsu teki)

ka⌐nsha かんしゃ (感謝) *n.*
thanks; gratitude.
kaṅsha suru (～する) *vt., vi.*
thank; be grateful; be thankful.

ka⌐nshi かんし (監視) *n.* watch;
surveillance.
kaṅshi suru (～する) *vt.* watch;
observe.

ka⌐nshiṅ[1] かんしん (感心) *n.*
admiration.
kaṅshiṅ suru (～する) *vi.* be impressed; admire.
— *a.n.* (～ na) admirable; good;
praiseworthy.

ka⌐nshiṅ[2] かんしん (関心) *n.* interest; concern:
seeji ni kaṅshiṅ ga aru (政治に関心
がある) be *interested* in politics.

ka⌐nshoo[1] かんしょう (鑑賞) *n.*
(usually of works of art, etc.)
appreciation.
kaṅshoo suru (～する) *vt.* appreciate; enjoy: oṅgaku o kaṅshoo
suru (音楽を鑑賞する) *listen to and
enjoy* music.

ka⌐nshoo[2] かんしょう (干渉) *n.* interference; intervention.
kaṅshoo suru (～する) *vi.* interfere; meddle.

ka⌐nshuu[1] かんしゅう (慣習) *n.* custom; convention.

ka⌐nshuu[2] かんしゅう (観衆) *n.*
audience; spectators.

ka⌐nsoku かんそく (観測) *n.* obser-

vation; survey:
kishoo no kansoku (気象の観測)
meteorological *observation*.
kansoku suru (～する) *vt.*
observe; survey.

ka⌐nsoo[1] かんそう (乾燥) *n.* dryness:
kansoo-zai (乾燥剤) a *desiccant*.
kansoo suru (～する) *vt., vi.* dry;
desiccate.

ka⌐nsoo[2] かんそう (感想) *n.* impression; thoughts; comment:
kansoo o noberu (感想を述べる)
give one's *impressions*.

ka⌐ns·u⌐ru かんする (関する) *vi.*
(kansh·i-; kansh·i-; kansh·i-te
①) concern.
... ni kanshite (…に関して) concerning; about: *Sono koto ni kanshite, shitte iru koto o o-hanashi shimasu.* (そのことに関して、知っていることをお話しします) I will tell you what I know *concerning* that matter.
... ni kansuru (…に～) concerning; about: *Nihon ni kansuru hon* (日本に関する本) a book *about* Japan.

ka⌐ntai かんたい (寒帯) *n.* frigid zone. 《↔ nettai; ontai》

ka⌐ntan かんたん (簡単) *a.n.* (～ na, ni) 1 easy; simple: *Sonna mondai wa kantan ni tokeru.* (そんな問題は簡単に解ける) I can *easily* solve a problem like that.
2 brief: kantan *ni ieba* (簡単に言えば) *briefly* speaking.

ka⌐ntoku かんとく (監督) *n.*
1 supervision:
Watashi-tachi wa kare no kantoku no moto ni hataraita. (私たちは彼の監督のもとに働いた) We worked under his *supervision*.
2 supervisor; foreman; manager; director.
kantoku suru (～する) *vt.* supervise.

ka⌐ntsuu かんつう (貫通) *n.* penetration.

kantsuu suru (～する) *vi.* penetrate; go through.

ka⌐nwa かんわ (緩和) *n.* relaxation; mitigation.
kanwa suru (～する) *vt., vi.* relax; ease: *seegen o* kanwa *suru* (制限を緩和する) *relax* restrictions. 《⇨ yurumeru》

ka⌐nwa-ji⌐ten かんわじてん (漢和辞典) *n.* dictionary of Chinese explained in Japanese.

ka⌐nyuu かにゅう (加入) *n.* joining; entry; admission.
... ni kanyuu suru (…に～する) *vi.* join; enter. 《↔ dattai》

ka⌐nyu⌐usha かにゅうしゃ (加入者) *n.* member; subscriber:
hoken kanyuusha (保険加入者) a *holder* of an insurance policy.

ka⌐nzee かんぜい (関税) *n.* customs; customs duties; tariff.

ka⌐nzen かんぜん (完全) *n.* perfection; completeness:
kanzen-*hanzai* (完全犯罪) a *perfect* crime.
— *a.n.* (～ na, ni) perfect; complete; fully. 《↔ fukanzen》

ka⌐nzoo かんぞう (肝臓) *n.* liver.

ka⌐nzume[1] かんづめ (缶詰) *n.* canned [tinned] food.

ka⌐o かお (顔) *n.* 1 face; features.
2 look; expression:
Kanojo wa kanashi-soo na kao o shite ita. (彼女は悲しそうな顔をしていた) She *looked* sad.
3 head: ★ The part of the head where hair grows is called 'atama.' *mado kara kao o dasu* (窓から顔を出す) put one's *head* out of the window.
4 honor; influence:
Kare wa oji no kao de kono kaisha ni haitta. (彼は叔父の顔でこの会社に入った) He got into this company through the *influence* of his uncle.
kao ga hiroi (～が広い) know a lot of people.
kao ga kiku (～がきく) have influence.

kao o dasu (〜を出す) make an appearance.

kao o tateru (〜を立てる) save a person's face.

ka⌐odachi かおだち (顔立ち) *n.* features; looks:

Kanojo no kaodachi wa haha-oya ni nite iru. (彼女の顔立ちは母親に似ている) Her *features* resemble her mother's.

ka⌐oiro かおいろ (顔色) *n.* complexion; look; expression.

kaoiro o kaeru (〜を変える) change color: *Kare wa* kaoiro o kaete *okotta.* (彼は顔色を変えて怒った) He *turned red* with anger.

ka⌐oku かおく (家屋) *n.* (*literary*) house; building. (⇨ ie¹; uchi¹)

ka⌐ori かおり (香り) *n.* smell; fragrance; aroma:

Kono bara wa yoi kaori *ga suru.* (このバラはよい香りがする) This rose *smells* sweet. (⇨ nioi)

ka⌐otsuki かおつき (顔付き) *n.* looks; countenance:

kiñchoo shita kaotsuki (緊張した顔つき) a strained *look.*

ka⌐ppa かっぱ (河童) *n.* imaginary Japanese river-sprite.

ka⌐ppatsu かっぱつ (活発) *a.n.* (〜 na, ni) lively; active:

Giroñ ga kappatsu *ni natte kita.* (議論が活発になってきた) The discussion has become *heated.*

ka⌐ra¹¹ から (空) *n.* emptiness:

Sono hako wa kara *desu.* (その箱は空です) The box is *empty.*

ka⌐ra¹² から (殻) *n.* shell; husk; hull.

kara³ から *p.* [follows a noun]

1 (indicates a point of origin in time or space) from:

Soko wa eki kara *aruite, dono kurai kakarimasu ka?* (そこは駅から歩いて、どのくらいかかりますか) How long does it take to go there on foot *from* the station? (↔ made)

2 (indicates a source) from:

Tomodachi kara *purezeñto o moraimashita.* (友達からプレゼントをもら

いました) I received a present *from* a friend.

3 (indicates origin or provenance) from:

Waiñ wa budoo kara *tsukuraremasu.* (ワインはぶどうから作られます) Wine is made *from* grapes.

4 (indicates movement or action from or through a place) from; through:

Watashi no ie kara *Fuji-sañ ga miemasu.* (私の家から富士山が見えます) Mt. Fuji is visible *from* my house.

5 (indicates the first item in a series) from; with:

Chiisai hito kara *juñ ni narañde kudasai.* (小さい人から順に並んでください) Please line up in order, starting *with* the smaller children.

6 (indicates cause or reason) from:

Chotto shita kooroñ kara *oogeñka ni natta.* (ちょっとした口論から大げんかになった) A big fight developed *from* a minor argument.

kara⁴ から *p.* so; therefore; because: ★ Follows a verb, adjective or the copula and indicates cause or reason.

Sukoshi samui kara *sutoobu o tsukemashoo ka?* (少し寒いからストーブをつけましょうか) *As* it's a bit chilly, shall I put on the heater? (⇨ da kara; no de)

... kara da (...〜だ) because: *Nihoñgo o narai-hajimeta no wa Nihoñ de beñkyoo shitakatta* kara desu. (日本語を習い始めたのは日本で勉強したかったからです) It is *because* I wanted to study in Japan that I started studying Japanese.

ka⌐rada からだ (体) *n.* **1** body; physique; build; constitution.

2 health:

Kare wa karoo de karada *o kowashita.* (彼は過労で体をこわした) He injured his *health* by overwork.

ka⌐radatsuki からだつき (体つき) *n.* one's figure; build.

ka「ra」l·i からい (辛い) *a.* (-ku)
1 salty; hot; peppery; spicy.
2 severe; strict:
Ano señsee wa saiteñ ga karai. (あ
の先生は採点が辛い) That teacher is
strict in grading. ((↔ amai))

ka「rai」bari からいばり (空威張り) *n.*
bravado; bluff.
karaibari suru (〜する) *vi.* blus-
ter; bluff. ((⇒ ibaru))

ka「rakara からから *a.n.* (〜 na/no,
ni) dry; thirsty:
karakara no teñki (からからの天気)
dry weather.

ka「raka」·u からかう *vt.* (karaka-
i-; karakaw·a-; karakat-te C)
tease; play a trick; make fun of.

ka「raoke カラオケ *n.* karaoke;
recorded musical backing for
vocal accompaniment.

ka「rappo からっぽ *a.n.* (〜 na/
no, ni) empty. ((⇒ kara』))

ka「rashi からし (芥子) *n.* mustard.

ka「rasu」¹ からす (烏) *n.* crow;
raven.

ka「ras·u」² からす (枯らす) *vt.* (kara-
sh·i-; karas·a-; karash·i-te C)
wither; kill (a plant). ((⇒ kareru))

ka「rasumu」gi からすむぎ (烏麦) *n.*
oats.

ka「rate」¹ からて (空手) *n.* state of
being empty-handed:
Kanojo wa karate de kaette kita.
(彼女は空手で帰って来た) She came
back *empty-handed*.

ka「rate」² からて (空手) *n.* karate.

ka「re かれ (彼) *n.* **1** he. ★ 'kare
no'=his, 'kare o'=him.
2 boyfriend. ((↔ kanojo))

ka「re·ru かれる (枯れる) *vi.* (kare-
te V) (of a plant) die; wither.
((⇒ karasu²))

ka「ri かり (借り) *n.* debt:
Kare ni wa ooki-na kari ga aru.
(彼には大きな借りがある) I am greatly
in *debt* to him. ((↔ kashi²))
((⇒ kariru))

ka「ri ni かりに (仮に) *adv.* **1** if;
even if; supposing:
Kari ni ame dattara doo shimasu

ka? (かりに雨だったらどうしますか) *Supposing* it rains, what shall we do?
((⇒ moshi (mo)))
2 for the time being; temporarily:
*Kono heya wa kari ni kyooshitsu
ni shiyoo shite imasu.* (この部屋はか
りに教室に使用しています) We are
using this room as a classroom
for the time being.

ka「ri·ru かりる (借りる) *vt.* (kari-te
V) **1** borrow; rent; lease.
((↔ kasu))
2 use (equipment, facilities, etc.):
Deñwa o o-kari dekimasu ka? (電
話をお借りできますか) Can I *use* your
phone? ((↔ kasu))
3 receive; need:
hito no chikara o kariru (人の力を借
りる) *receive* someone's help.

ka「roñji·ru かろんじる (軽んじる) *vt.*
(karoñji-te V) neglect; make little [light] of. ((⇒ omoñjiru))

ka「roo かろう (過労) *n.* overwork;
strain. ((⇒ karooshi))

ka「ro」ojite かろうじて (辛うじて)
adv. barely; narrowly:
karoojite shikeñ ni ukaru (かろうじ
て試験に受かる) *barely* pass the examination.

ka「ro」oshi かろうし (過労死) *n.*
death from overwork. ((⇒ karoo))

ka「r·u かる (刈る) *vt.* (kar·i-; ka-
r·a-; kat-te C) cut; reap; crop;
mow:
Kami o mijikame ni katte kudasai.
(髪を短めに刈ってください) Please *cut*
my hair a bit short.

ka「ru·i かるい (軽い) *a.* (-ku) **1** (of
weight) light. ((↔ omoi¹))
2 easy:
*Watashi wa karui kimochi de
demo ni sañka shita.* (私は軽い気持
ちでデモに参加した) I *casually* partici-
pated in the demonstration.
3 (of crime, disease, etc.) slight;
minor:
Karui kaze o hiita. (軽いかぜをひいた)
I have caught a *slight* cold.
((↔ omoi¹))

4 relieved; relaxed:
Ima wa kibuñ mo karui. (今は気分も軽い) I feel *relieved* now. (↔ omoi[1])

ka￢ruta カルタ *n.* traditional Japanese playing cards; card game.

ka￢ryoku かりょく (火力) *n.* heat; heating power:
karyoku-hatsudeñsho (火力発電所) a *thermal* power plant. (↔ suiryoku)

ka￢ryuu かりゅう (下流) *n.* lower course [reaches] of a river. (↔ jooryuu)

ka￢sa かさ (傘) *n.* umbrella; parasol. (⇨ amagu)

ka￢sai かさい (火災) *n.* fire:
★ More formal than '*kaji.*'
Shiñriñ ni kasai ga hassee shita. (森林に火災が発生した) A *fire* broke out in the forest.

ka￢sakasa[1] カサカサ *adv.* (~ to) (the sound of a thin, light object moving):
kasakasa to iu oto (カサカサという音) a *rustling* sound.

ka￢sakasa[2] かさかさ *a.n.* (~ no, ni) (the state of being dry):
Fuyu ni naru to te ga kasakasa ni naru. (冬になると手がかさかさになる) Whenever winter comes, my hands get *dry*.

ka￢sanar·u かさなる (重なる) *vi.* (kasanar·i-; kasanar·a-; kasanat-te C) **1** happen at the same time; occur one after another:
Kyuujitsu ga nichiyoo to kasanaru. (休日が日曜と重なる) The public holiday *falls* on Sunday.
2 pile up:
Tsukue no ue ni shorui ga kasanatte iru. (机の上に書類が重なっている) There *are* papers *piled up* on the desk. (⇨ kasaneru)

ka￢sane·ru かさねる (重ねる) *vt.* (kasane-te V) **1** pile up; put on top:
tsukue no ue ni hoñ o kasaneru (机の上に本を重ねる) *pile* books *up*

on the desk. (⇨ kasanaru; tsumu[1])
2 repeat:
Kare no kasaneta kuroo ga mi o musuñda. (彼の重ねた苦労が実を結んだ) His *repeated* toil produced favorable results.

ka￢segi かせぎ (稼ぎ) *n.* income; earnings:
Kare wa kasegi ga ii. (彼は稼ぎがいい) He *earns* a good income. (⇨ kasegu; shuunyuu)

ka￢se￢g·u かせぐ (稼ぐ) *vt.* (kaseg·i-; kaseg·a-; kase·i-de C) earn; make money; work. (⇨ kasegi)

ka￢seki かせき (化石) *n.* fossil.

ka￢shi[1] かし (菓子) *n.* confectionery; cake; candy; sweets.
★ Often '*o-kashi.*' (⇨ keeki[1])

ka￢shi[2] かし (貸し) *n.* loan:
★ Used both literally and figuratively.
Kare ni wa takusañ kashi ga aru. (彼にはたくさん貸しがある) He *owes* me a lot. (↔ kari)

ka￢shidashi かしだし (貸し出し) *n.* loan; lending service:
Sono hoñ wa kashidashi-chuu desu. (その本は貸し出し中です) That book is out on *loan*. (⇨ kashidasu)

ka￢shida￢s·u かしだす (貸し出す) *vt.* (-dash·i-; -das·a-; -dash·i-te C) lend [loan] out; rent. (⇨ kashidashi; kasu)

ka￢shiko かしこ *n.* Yours sincerely. ★ Used at the end of a woman's letter. (⇨ keegu; tegami)

ka￢shiko[1]·i かしこい (賢い) *a.* (-ku) wise; clever; smart:
kashikoi ko (賢い子) a *bright* child. (⇨ rikoo)

ka￢shikomarima￢shita かしこまりました (畏まりました) certainly:
★ Indicates that the speaker will carry out an order or request given by a superior. Often used by service personnel to customers.

"Kono hañkachi o kudasai." "Ka-shikomarimashita."（「このハンカチをください」「かしこまりました」）*"Please let me have this handkerchief." "Certainly."*

ka⌐shima かしま（貸間）*n.* = kashishitsu.

ka shira かしら *p. (informal)*
1 I wonder: ★ Used, often rhetorically, to indicate a question or express doubt. Used mainly by women. Men use '*ka na*.'
Ano hito wa ima-goro nani o shite iru ka shira.（あの人は今ごろ何をしているかしら）*I wonder* what he is doing at the moment.
2 (used to pose a question):
Anata wa ashita o-taku ni irassharu ka shira.（あなたはあしたお宅にいらっしゃるかしら）*Are* you *going to be* home tomorrow?
-nai ka shira（ない〜）I hope; I would like: *Hayaku yasumi ni naranai ka shira.*（早く休みにならないかしら）*I hope* the vacation begins soon.

ka⌐shishitsu かししつ（貸し室）*n.* room for rent; room to let.

ka⌐shiya¹ かしや（貸家）*n.* house for rent; house to let.

ka⌐shi⌐ya² かしや（菓子屋）*n.* confectioner; confectionery.

ka⌐sho かしょ（箇所）*n.* place; spot; point:
Kono shirushi wa kikeñ na kasho o shimeshimasu.（この印は危険な箇所を示します）These marks show the dangerous *places*. 《⇨ basho》

-ka⌐sho かしょ（箇所）*suf.* part; place; passage:
Shikeñ de ni-kasho machigaeta.（試験で 2 か所間違えた）I made *two* mistakes in the examination.

ka⌐shu かしゅ（歌手）*n.* singer; vocalist.

ka⌐soo かそう（下層）*n.* **1** lower layer [stratum].
2 the lower class. 《⇨ chuuryuu; jooryuu》

ka⌐s·u かす（貸す）*vt.* (kash·i·-; ka-

s·a-; kash·i·te C) **1** lend; loan; rent; lease:
tochi o kare ni kasu（土地を彼に貸す）*lease* the land to him.
《↔ kariru》《⇨ kashi²》
2 let use (equipment, facilities, etc.). 《↔ kariru》
3 give:
hito ni chikara o kasu（人に力を貸す）*give* a person assistance.
《↔ kariru》

ka⌐suka かすか（微か）*a.n.* (〜 na, ni) faint; vague; dim:
Tooku ni akari ga kasuka ni mieta.（遠くに明りがかすかに見えた）I could see a light shining *dimly* in the distance.

ka⌐sumi かすみ（霞）*n.* haze; mist.

ka⌐sum·u かすむ（霞む）*vi.* (kasum·i·-; kasum·a·-; kasuñ·de C)
1 (of a view, sky, etc.) be hazy.
2 (of vision) be blurred.

ka⌐ta¹¹ かた（肩）*n.* shoulder.
kata no ni ga oriru（〜の荷がおりる）a load off one's mind.
kata o motsu（〜をもつ）take sides.

ka⌐ta¹² かた（型）*n.* **1** pattern:
doresu no kata o toru（ドレスの型をとる）make a *pattern* of a dress.
2 type; style; model:
ichibañ atarashii kata（一番新しい型）the latest *model*.
3 mold:
zerii o kata ni nagashikomu（ゼリーを型に流し込む）pour jelly into a *mold*.

ka⌐ta¹³ かた（方）*n. (polite)* person; lady; gentleman:
Kono kata ga Suzuki-sañ desu.（この方が鈴木さんです）This *lady* is Miss Suzuki. 《⇨ hito》

-kata¹ かた（方）*suf.* care of:
Itoo-sama-kata Suzuki-sama（伊藤様方鈴木様）Mr. Suzuki *c/o* Mr. Ito.

-kata² かた（方）*suf.* way; manner: ★ Added to the continuative base of a verb.
Kono kudamono no tabe-kata ga wakarimaseñ.（この果物の食べ方がわ

かりません) I don't know *how to* eat this fruit.

ka⌐tachi かたち (形) *n.* shape; form; figure; appearance:
marui katachi *no tatemono* (丸い形の建物) a building with a round *shape* / Shiki *to itte mo,* katachi *dake no mono datta.* (式と言っても、形だけのものだった) Although it was a ceremony, it was only a matter of *form.*

ka⌐tagaki かたがき (肩書) *n.* title; degree:
Nihoñ de wa katagaki *ga mono o iu.* (日本では肩書がものをいう) In Japan *titles* have weight.

ka⌐ta⌐gata かたがた (方々) *n.* (*polite*) the people (concerned).

ka⌐tagawa かたがわ (片側) *n.* one side:
michi no katagawa *o tooru* (道の片側を通る) pass on *one side* of the road. (⇨ ryoogawa)

ka⌐tagu⌐ruma かたぐるま (肩車) *n.* riding on someone's shoulders.
kataguruma suru (〜する) *vt.* give someone a piggyback.

ka⌐tahashi かたはし (片端) *n.* one end; one side:
tsuna no katahashi *o hipparu* (綱の片端を引っ張る) pull *one end* of the rope. (↔ ryoohashi)

ka⌐ta⌐hoo かたほう (片方) *n.* one side; one of a pair; the other:
Tebukuro no katahoo *o nakushite shimatta.* (手袋の片方をなくしてしまった) I have lost *one of* my gloves. (⇨ ryoohoo)

ka⌐ta·i かたい (堅い・固い・硬い) *a.* (-ku) **1** hard; solid; stiff; firm; tough:
Daiyamoñdo wa katai. (ダイヤモンドは硬い) Diamonds are *hard.* (↔ yawaraka; yawarakai)
2 stiff:
Kare wa katai *buñshoo o kaku.* (彼は硬い文章を書く) He writes in a *stiff* style.
3 firm; tight:
Kono musubime wa katakute,

hodokenai. (この結び目は固くて、ほどけない) This knot is so *tight* I cannot undo it.
4 sure:
Ano señshu no nyuushoo wa katai. (あの選手の入賞は堅い) That player's winning the prize is a *sure* thing.
5 steady; sound; serious:
Katai *hanashi wa kore-gurai ni shimashoo.* (堅い話はこれぐらいにしましょう) Let's talk no more of *serious* matters.
6 obstinate; stubborn:
Uchi no kachoo wa atama ga katai. (うちの課長は頭が固い) Our section chief is *obstinate* in his way of thinking.

ka⌐taka⌐na かたかな (片仮名) *n.* one of the Japanese syllabaries. (⇨ inside front cover)

ka⌐taki かたき (敵) *n.* enemy; foe; rival:
*shoobai-*gataki (商売がたき) a *rival* in business. ★ The initial /k/ changes to /g/ in compounds.
kataki o utsu (〜を討つ) revenge oneself.

ka⌐tamari かたまり (塊) *n.* lump; mass; clod; chunk:
koori no katamari (氷の塊) a *lump* of ice.

ka⌐tamar·u かたまる (固まる) *vi.* (-mar·i-; -mar·a-; -mat-te C) become hard; harden; set:
Kono semeñto wa mada katamatte *imaseñ.* (このセメントはまだ固まっていません) This cement *has* not *set* yet. (⇨ katameru)

ka⌐tame·ru かためる (固める) *vt.* (-me-te V) **1** harden:
yuki o fuñde katameru (雪を踏んで固める) *tread down* the snow. (⇨ katamaru)
2 strengthen; tighten; fortify:
ketsui o katameru (決意を固める) *make a firm* resolution. (⇨ katamaru)

ka⌐tamichi かたみち (片道) *n.* one-way (ticket). (↔ oofuku)

ka⌐tamuke┐・ru かたむける（傾ける）
vt. (-muke-te Ⅴ) **1** incline;
lean; slant; tilt. (⇨ katamuku)
2 devote (one's energy).

ka⌐tamuki┐ かたむき（傾き）*n.*
1 slant; slope; tilt. (⇨ katamuku)
2 tendency; trend:
*Kare wa monogoto o karuku miru
katamuki ga aru.* (彼は物事を軽く見
る傾きがある) He has a *tendency* to
take things lightly. (⇨ keekoo)

ka⌐tamu┐k・u かたむく（傾く）*vi.*
(-muk・i-; -muk・a-; -mu・i-te Ⓒ)
1 lean; slope; slant; tilt:
Kono to wa sukoshi katamuite iru.
(この戸は少し傾いている) This door
leans slightly to one side.
(⇨ katamukeru; katamuki)
2 be inclined; lean:
Kare wa tasuu-ha ni katamuite iru.
(彼は多数派に傾いている) He *is in-
clining* toward the majority fac-
tion.
3 (of the sun or the moon) go
down; sink; set.

ka⌐tana┐ かたな（刀）*n.* sword:
katana o nuku (刀を抜く) draw a
sword.

ka⌐tar・u かたる（語る）*vt.* (katar・i-;
katar・a-; katat-te Ⓒ) (*slightly
formal*) talk; tell; relate.
shiñsoo o kataru (真相を語る) *tell*
the truth. (⇨ hanasu¹; shaberu)

ka⌐tasa かたさ（堅さ・固さ・硬さ）*n.*
1 hardness; solidity; firmness;
stiffness. (⇨ katai)
2 stubbornness. (⇨ katai)

ka⌐tate かたて（片手）*n.* one hand.
(⇨ ryoote)

ka⌐tayo┐r・u かたよる（偏る）*vi.*
(-yor・i-; -yor・a-; -yot-te Ⓒ) be
partial; be prejudiced; be slanted.

ka⌐tazuke┐・ru かたづける（片付ける）
vt. (-zuke-te Ⅴ) **1** put in order;
tidy up; put away.
2 settle (a dispute); solve (a problem); finish (a job).

ka⌐tee¹ かてい（家庭）*n.* home;
family; household.

ka⌐tee² かてい（仮定）*n.* assump-

tion; supposition; hypothesis.
katee suru (〜する) *vi.*, *vt.* assume; suppose; postulate.

ka⌐tee³ かてい（過程）*n.* process;
course:
seezoo-katee (製造過程) the *course*
of production.

ka⌐tee-teki かていてき（家庭的）
a.n. (〜 na, ni) homely; home-
like; domestic:
katee-teki *na josee* (家庭的な女性)
a *domestic* woman.

ka⌐ts・u¹ かつ（勝つ）*vi.* (kach・i-;
kat・a-; kat-te Ⓒ) **1** win; beat;
defeat:
tatakai ni katsu (戦いに勝つ) *win* a
battle. (↔ makeru)
2 overcome (temptation, difficulties, etc.). (↔ makeru)

ka⌐tsu² かつ（且つ）*conj.* (*formal*)
and; moreover; also:
hitsuyoo katsu juubuñ na jookeñ
(必要かつ十分な条件) a necessary
and sufficient condition.

ka⌐tsudoo かつどう（活動）*n.*
activity; action; operation.
katsudoo suru (〜する) *vi.* be
active; work.

ka⌐tsudoo-teki かつどうてき（活動
的）*a.n.* (〜 na, ni) active; energetic.

ka⌐tsu┐g・u かつぐ（担ぐ）*vt.* (ka-
tsug・i-; katsug・a-; katsu・i-de Ⓒ)
1 carry (a burden) on one's
shoulder.
2 play a trick on; make a fool
of; take in. (⇨ damasu)

ka⌐tsuji かつじ（活字）*n.* printing
type.

ka⌐tsute かつて（曽て）*adv.*
(〜 no) **1** once; at one time; formerly:
Katsute *kanojo wa niñki-kashu
datta.* (かつて彼女は人気歌手だった)
She was a popular singer *at one
time*.
2 ever; never:
Koñna keekeñ wa imada katsute
shita koto ga arimaseñ. (こんな経験
はいまだかつてしたことがありません) So

far I have *never* had this kind of experience.

ka⌐tsuyaku かつやく (活躍) *n.*
remarkable activity.
katsuyaku suru (〜する) *vi.* take an active part; participate actively: *terebi de* katsuyaku suru (テレビで活躍する) *be active* in TV.

ka⌐tsuyoo かつよう (活用) *n.*
1 practical use; utilization.
2 (of grammar) inflection; conjugation.
katsuyoo suru (〜する) 1 *vt.* make use of; utilize; make the most of.
2 *vi.* inflect; conjugate.

ka⌐tte[1] かって (勝手) *n.* 1 kitchen.
★ Usually with '*o-*.' (⇨ daidokoro)
2 way; convenience:
Kono apaato wa katte ga warui. (このアパートは勝手が悪い) This apartment *is inconvenient*.

ka⌐tte[2] かって (勝手) *n.* selfishness; willfulness:
Soñna katte wa yurusenai. (そんな勝手は許せない) I won't stand for that sort of *selfish behavior*.
— *a.n.* (〜 na, ni) selfish:
katte *na hito* (勝手な人) a *selfish* person. (⇨ wagamama)

ka·u[1] かう (買う) *vt.* (ka·i-; kaw·a-; kat-te [C]) 1 buy; purchase; get. (↔ uru[1]) (⇨ koonyuu)
2 incur; take up (an ill feeling, quarrel, etc.):
hito no urami o kau (人の恨みを買う) *incur* a person's ill will.
3 recognize; think much of (a person's ability).

ka·u[2] かう (飼う) *vt.* (ka·i-; kaw·a-; kat-te [C]) keep (an animal); have; raise; rear.

ka⌐wa[1] かわ (川) *n.* river; stream; brook.

ka⌐wa[2] かわ (皮) *n.* skin; hide; peel; rind; bark.

ka⌐wa[3] かわ (革) *n.* leather.

ka⌐wa[4] かわ (側) *n.* = gawa.

ka⌐waiga⌐r·u かわいがる (可愛がる)

vt. (-gar·i-; -gar·a-; -gat-te [C]) love; pet; caress.

ka⌐wai[1]·i かわいい (可愛い) *a.* (-ku)
1 cute; pretty; lovely.
2 dear:
Seeto wa miñna kawaii. (生徒はみんなかわいい) My pupils are all *dear* to me.
3 (of a vehicle, instrument, etc.) little; tiny.

ka⌐wairashi[1]·i かわいらしい (可愛らしい) *a.* (-ku) = kawaii.

ka⌐waiso⌐o かわいそう (可哀相) *a.n.* (〜 na, ni) poor; pitiful; miserable; sad:
Sono hanashi o kiite, roojiñ ga kawaisoo ni natta. (その話を聞いて, 老人がかわいそうになった) I felt *sorry* for the old man when I heard the story.

ka⌐waka⌐s·u かわかす (乾かす) *vt.* (-kash·i-; -kas·a-; -kash·i-te [C]) dry (wet things). (⇨ kawaku)

ka⌐wa⌐k·u かわく (乾く) *vi.* (kawak·i-; kawak·a-; kawa·i-te [C]) dry. (⇨ kawakasu)

ka⌐wara かわら (瓦) *n.* roof tile.

ka⌐wari かわり (代わり) *n.* substitute; replacement:
Dare ga kare no kawari o tsutomemashita ka? (だれが彼の代わりをつとめましたか) Who acted as his *substitute*?

ka⌐wari ni かわりに (代わりに) *adv.*
1 instead (of):
Kare ga ikenakereba, watashi ga kawari ni ikimasu. (彼が行けなければ, 私が代わりに行きます) If he cannot go, I will go *instead*.
2 in return; in exchange.

ka⌐war·u かわる (変わる) *vi.* (kawar·i-; kawar·a-; kawat-te [C])
1 change; turn:
Shiñgoo ga aka kara ao ni kawatta. (信号が赤から青に変わった) The traffic light *changed* from red to green. (⇨ kaeru[2])
2 differ; vary:
Kuni ni yotte fuuzoku shuukañ wa kawaru. (国によって風俗習慣は

変わる) Manners and customs *differ* from country to country. (⇨ kaeru³)

ka「war·u² かわる (代わる・替わる) *vi.* (kawar·i-; kawar·a-; kawat-te C̲) replace; displace; substitute: *Kaeri wa watashi ga kuruma no uñteñ o kare to* kawatta. (帰りは私が車の運転を彼と代わった) On the way back I did the driving *instead of* him. (⇨ kaeru¹)

ka「waru-ga「waru かわるがわる (代わる代わる) *adv.* (~ ni) by turns; in turn. (⇨ kootai)

ka「wase かわせ (為替) *n.*
1 money order.
2 monetary exchange:
kawase-*sooba* (為替相場) the *exchange* rate.

ka「yo「o(bi) かよう(び) (火曜(日)) *n.* Tuesday. (⇨ APP. 5)

ka「yo「okyoku かようきょく (歌謡曲) *n.* popular song.

ka「yo·u かよう (通う) *vi.* (kayo·i-; kayow·a-; kayot-te C̲) 1 go; commute:
Kare wa kuruma de kaisha e kayotte imasu. (彼は車で会社へ通っています) He *commutes* to his office by car.
2 (of a vehicle) run:
Sono machi made basu ga kayotte imasu. (その町までバスが通っています) There are buses *running* as far as that town.

ka「yowa「·i かよわい (か弱い) *a.* (-ku) weak; frail; helpless:
kayowai *josee* (か弱い女性) a *frail* woman.

ka「yu「·i かゆい (痒い) *a.* (-ku) itchy; itching:
Senaka ga kayui. (背中がかゆい) My back is *itching*.

ka「zañ かざん (火山) *n.* volcano.

ka「zari かざり (飾り) *n.* decoration; ornament. (⇨ kazaru)

ka「zar·u かざる (飾る) *vt.* (kazar·i-; kazar·a-; kazat-te C̲)
1 decorate; ornament:
heya o hana de kazaru (部屋を花で

飾る) *decorate* a room with flowers. (⇨ kazari)
2 display:
heya ni Nihoñ-niñgyoo o kazaru (部屋に日本人形を飾る) *display* a Japanese doll in a room.

ka「ze¹ かぜ (風) *n.* wind; draft; breeze:
Kaze *ga yañda.* (風がやんだ) The *wind* has died down.

ka「ze² かぜ (風邪) *n.* cold; influenza:
kaze o hiku (かぜをひく) catch a *cold*.

ka「zoe「doshi かぞえどし (数え年) *n.* a person's age counted on the basis of the calendar year. (⇨ toshi)

ka「zoe「·ru かぞえる (数える) *vt.* (kazoe-te V̲) count:
ichi kara juu made kazoeru (1 から 10 まで数える) *count* from one to ten. (⇨ kañjoo¹)

ka「zoku かぞく (家族) *n.* family:
Uchi wa roku-niñ kazoku *desu.* (うちは6人家族です) We have six *family members*.

ka「zu かず (数) *n.* number. (⇨ APP. 3)

ke¹ け (毛) *n.* 1 (body) hair:
Kare wa ke *ga koi [usui].* (彼は毛が濃い[薄い]) He has thick [thin] *hair*. (⇨ kami-no-ke)
2 fur; feather; wool: ke no *kooto* (毛のコート) a *woolen* coat.

ke² け (気) *n.* sign; touch; taste:
Doko ni mo hi no ke *wa nakatta.* (どこにも火の気はなかった) There was no *sign* of fire.

-ke け (家) *suf.* family:
*Yamada-*ke (山田家) the Yamada *family* / Maeda-ke (前田家) *the Maedas.*

ke「chi けち *n.* stinginess; stingy person; miser.
— *a.n.* (~ na, ni) 1 stingy; mean; miserly.
2 narrow-minded:
kechi *na kañgae* (けちな考え) a *narrow-minded* idea.

ke「damono けだもの (獣) *n.*

beast; brute. ★ More emphatic than '*kemono*' and often has a derogatory connotation. (⇨ kemono)

ke⌐e[1] けい (刑) *n.* punishment; penalty; sentence: kee *ni fuku-suru* (刑に服する) serve a *sentence*.

ke⌐e[2] けい (計) *n.* 1 total; sum: kee *o dasu* (計を出す) figure out a *sum*. (⇨ gookee)
2 plan; plot: *Ichi-neñ no* kee *wa gañtañ ni ari.* (一年の計は元旦にあり) New Year's Day is the day to make your *plans* for the year. (⇨ keekaku)

-kee けい (形) *suf. shape; form;* type: *kyuu* kee (球形) a round *shape* / *chi-*kee (地形) the *lay* of the land.

ke⌐eba けいば (競馬) *n.* horse racing.

ke⌐ebetsu けいべつ (軽蔑) *n.* contempt; scorn; disdain.
keebetsu suru (〜する) *vt.* look down on; despise; disdain.

ke⌐e-ee けいえい (経営) *n.* management; administration.
kee-ee suru (〜する) *vt.* manage; operate; run (a shop). (⇨ uñee; itonamu)

ke⌐e-e-esha けいえいしゃ (経営者) *n.* manager; the management; proprietor.

ke⌐ego けいご (敬語) *n.* honorific; polite expression. ★ Comprising the three categories of honorific, polite and humble expressions.

ke⌐egu けいぐ (敬具) *n.* Yours truly; Sincerely yours. ★ Used in the complimentary close of a letter. (⇨ haikee[1]; kashiko)

ke⌐ehi けいひ (経費) *n.* expense; cost; upkeep:
keehi *o kiritsumeru* (経費を切り詰める) cut down on *expenses*.

ke⌐eji けいじ (刑事) *n.* 1 (police) detective.
2 criminal affairs:
keeji-*jikeñ* (刑事事件) a *criminal* case. (⇨ miñji)

ke⌐eka けいか (経過) *n.* 1 progress; development; course: *jikeñ no* keeka (事件の経過) the *development* of an affair.
2 lapse; passage: *Ip-puñ* keeka. (1 分経過) One minute *has passed*.
keeka suru (〜する) *vi.* pass: ★ More formal than '*tatsu*'. *Sutaato shite kara sañjup-puñ* keeka shimashita. (スタートしてから 30 分経過しました) Thirty minutes *have passed* since they started.

ke⌐ekai[1] けいかい (警戒) *n.* caution; precaution; watch; guard.
keekai suru (〜する) *vt.* be cautious of; look [watch] out for; guard against

ke⌐ekai[2] けいかい (軽快) *a.n.* (〜 na, ni) light; nimble: keekai *na ashidori de aruku* (軽快 な足どりで歩く) walk with *light steps*.

ke⌐ekaku けいかく (計画) *n.* plan; design; project; scheme: keekaku *o tateru* (計画を立てる) work out a *plan*.
keekaku suru (〜する) *vt.* plan; project; scheme.

ke⌐ekañ けいかん (警官) *n.* policeman; police officer. ★ More formal than '*omawari-sañ*'. (⇨ fujiñkeekañ; keesatsu)

ke⌐ekeñ けいけん (経験) *n.* experience:
keekeñ *o tsumu* (経験を積む) gain *experience*. (⇨ taikeñ)
keekeñ suru (〜する) *vt.* experience; go through; undergo.

ke⌐eki[1] ケーキ *n.* cake. ★ Japanese confectionery is called '*kashi*.' (⇨ kashi)

ke⌐eki[2] けいき (景気) *n.* business; economy; economic conditions: Keeki *ga yoi* [*warui*]. (景気が良い [悪い]) *Business* is brisk [slow].

ke⌐eko けいこ (稽古) *n.* practice; exercise; lesson; rehearsal: *señsee ni tsuite ikebana no* keeko *o suru* (先生について生け花の稽古をす

る) take *lessons* in ikebana from a teacher.

ke￢ekoku けいこく(警告) *n.* warning; caution.
keekoku suru(〜する) *vt.* warn; caution. (⇨ chuui)

ke￢ekoo けいこう(傾向) *n.* tendency; trend; inclination:
Kare wa chikagoro monowasure o suru keekoo ga aru.(彼は近ごろ物忘れをする傾向がある) He *is inclined* to be forgetful these days.

ke￢ekootoo けいこうとう(蛍光灯) *n.* fluorescent lamp.

ke￢ekoo-to￢ryoo けいこうとりょう(蛍光塗料) *n.* fluorescent [luminous] paint.

ke￢ereki けいれき(経歴) *n.* career; background; one's personal history. (⇨ rireki)

ke￢esai けいさい(掲載) *n.* publication; insertion.
keesai suru(〜する) *vt.* publish; insert; print:
Sono kookoku wa shiñbuñ ni keesai sareta.(その広告は新聞に掲載された) That advertisement *appeared* in a newspaper. (⇨ noseru²)

ke￢esañ けいさん(計算) *n.* calculation; sums; figures.
keesañ ni ireru(〜に入れる) take account of.
keesañ suru(〜する) *vt.* calculate; count; reckon; figure.

ke￢esa￢ñki けいさんき(計算機) *n.* calculator.

ke￢esatsu けいさつ(警察) *n.* the police; police station. (⇨ keekañ)

ke￢esatsusho けいさつしょ(警察署) *n.* police station.

ke￢esee-ge￢ka けいせいげか(形成外科) *n.* plastic surgery.

ke￢esha けいしゃ(傾斜) *n.* slant; slope; inclination:
yane no keesha(屋根の傾斜) the *slope* of a roof.
keesha suru(〜する) *vi.* incline; slant; slope; descend. (⇨ katamuku)

Ke￢eshi￢-choo けいしちょう(警視庁) *n.* Metropolitan Police Department.

ke￢eshiki けいしき(形式) *n.* form; formality:
keeshiki ni kodawaru(形式にこだわる) stick to *formalities*. (↔ naiyoo)

ke￢eshiki-teki けいしきてき(形式的) *a.n.* (〜 na, ni) formal; perfunctory:
keeshiki-teki na aisatsu(形式的なあいさつ) a *perfunctory* greeting.

ke￢esotsu けいそつ(軽率) *a.n.* (〜 na, ni) careless; rash; hasty:
keesotsu na koto o suru(軽率なことをする) do something *rash*. (↔ shiñchoo²)

ke￢etai けいたい(携帯) *n.* carrying: keetai-hiñ(携帯品) one's *personal effects*.
keetai suru(〜する) *vt.* carry a thing with one.

ke￢eto けいと(毛糸) *n.* = keito.

ke￢etoo けいとう(系統) *n.*
1 system:
Meeree-keetoo ga barabara da.(命令系統がばらばらだ) The *system* of command is in disorder.
2 lineage; descent:
Ano hito wa Geñji no keetoo o hiite iru.(あの人は源氏の系統を引いている) He *is descended* from the Genji family.

ke￢etoo-teki けいとうてき(系統的) *a.n.* (〜 na, ni) systematic.

ke￢eyaku けいやく(契約) *n.* contract; agreement.
keeyaku suru(〜する) *vi.* make a contract.

ke￢eyakusho けいやくしょ(契約書) *n.* (written) contract:
keeyakusho o torikawasu(契約書を取り交わす) exchange *written contracts*.

ke￢eyoo けいよう(掲揚) *n.* (of a flag) hoist; fly.
keeyoo suru(〜する) *vt.* hoist; raise.

ke￢eyu¹ けいゆ(経由) *n.* by way of; via:

Roñdoñ keeyu *de Pari e iku* (ロンドン経由でパリへ行く) go to Paris *via* London. (⇨ hete)

ke⌐eyu² けいゆ (軽油) *n*. light oil. (↔ juuyu)

ke⌐ezai けいざい (経済) *n*. economy; finance: keezai *seechoo-ritsu* (経済成長率) *economic* growth rate.

ke⌐ezai-teki けいざいてき (経済的) *a.n.* (~ na, ni) **1** economic; financial: *Kare wa* keezai-teki *ni moñdai ga aru yoo da.* (彼は経済的に問題があるようだ) He seems to have *financial* problems. **2** economical: *Chiisai kuruma no hoo ga* keezai-teki *da.* (小さい車のほうが経済的だ) Small cars are more *economical*.

ke⌐ezoku けいぞく (継続) *n*. continuation; renewal. keezoku suru (~する) *vi., vt.* continue; go on. ★ More formal than 'tsuzuku.'

ke⌐ga¹ けが (怪我) *n*. injury; hurt; wound. kega (o) suru (~(を)する) *vt.* injure; wound; hurt: *te ni* kega *o suru* (手にけがをする) *hurt* one's hand.

ke⌐hai けはい (気配) *n*. sign; indication: *Heya ni wa hito no* kehai *wa nakatta.* (部屋には人の気配はなかった) There were no *signs* of life in the room.

ke⌐ito けいと (毛糸) *n*. woolen yarn; knitting wool.

ke⌐kka けっか (結果) *n*. result; effect; consequence; outcome: *geñiñ to* kekka (原因と結果) cause and *effect*. (↔ geñiñ)

ke⌐kkaku けっかく (結核) *n*. tuberculosis.

ke⌐kkañ¹ けっかん (欠陥) *n*. flaw; defect; shortcomings: kekkañ *shoohiñ* (欠陥商品) *defective* merchandise. (⇨ ketteñ)

ke⌐kkañ² けっかん (血管) *n*. blood

vessel; vein; artery.

ke⌐kkoñ けっこん (結婚) *n*. marriage; matrimony. kekkoñ suru (~する) *vi.* marry; get married.

ke⌐kko⌐ñshiki けっこんしき (結婚式) *n*. wedding ceremony: kekkoñshiki *o ageru* (結婚式を挙げる) hold a *wedding ceremony*.

ke⌐kkoo¹ けっこう (結構) *a.n.* (~ na, ni) good; nice; excellent; splendid: kekkoo *na okurimono* (結構な贈り物) a *nice* present. kekkoo desu (~です) **1** fine: *Nani-ka kakumono o kashite kudasai. Nañ de mo* kekkoo desu. (何か書くものを貸してください。何でも結構です) Please lend me something to write with. Anything is *fine*. **2** (refusal) no, thank you: "*Moo ip-pai biiru o ikaga desu ka?*" "*Moo* kekkoo *desu.*" (「もう一杯ビールをいかがですか」「もう結構です」) "What about another glass of beer?" "*No, thank you.*" (⇨ takusañ)

ke⌐kkoo² けっこう (結構) *adv*. fairly; quite; rather: *Sono gekijoo wa heejitsu de mo* kekkoo *koñde imasu.* (その劇場は平日でもけっこう込んでいます) The theater is *quite* crowded even on weekdays.

ke⌐kkoo³ けっこう (決行) *n*. carrying out as scheduled. kekkoo suru (~する) *vt.* carry out as scheduled.

ke⌐kkoo⁴ けっこう (欠航) *n*. cancellation (of a flight, voyage). kekkoo suru (~する) *vi.* do not fly [sail].

ke⌐kkyoku けっきょく (結局) *adv*. after all; in the end; in the long run.

ke⌐mono けもの (獣) *n*. beast; wild animal. (⇨ kedamono)

ke⌐mu·i けむい (煙い) *a*. (-ku) smoky: *Takibi ga* kemui. (たき火が煙い)

The bonfire is *smoky*. (⇨ kemu-tai)

ke「muri けむり (煙り) *n.* smoke; fumes. (⇨ kemuru)

ke「mur·u けむる (煙る) *vi.* (kemur·i-; kemur·a-; kemut-te ⒞)
1 smoke; smolder:
Kono dañro wa hidoku kemuru. (この暖炉はひどく煙る) This fireplace *smokes* badly. (⇨ kemuri)
2 look dim; be obscured:
Shima wa kiri ni kemutte ita. (島は霧に煙っていた) The island *was shrouded* in fog.

ke「muta·i けむたい (煙たい) *a.* (-ku)
1 smoky:
Heya ga kemutai. (部屋が煙たい) The room is *smoky*. (⇨ kemui)
2 unapproachable; uncomfortable:
Kono-goro chichi ga kemutaku natte kita. (このごろ父が煙たくなってきた) These days I have begun to feel *awkward* in my father's presence.

ke「ñ¹ けん (県) *n.* prefecture.
★ A basic administrative unit in Japan. (⇨ inside back cover)

ke「ñ² けん (券) *n.* ticket; coupon.

-keñ¹ けん (軒) *suf.* counter for a house [door]. (⇨ APP. 4)

-keñ² けん (権) *suf.* right:
señkyo-keñ (選挙権) the *right* to vote / *jiñ-keñ* (人権) human *rights*.

ke「nas·u けなす (貶す) *vt.* (kenash·i-; kenas·a-; kenash·i-te ⒞)
speak ill of; run down; criticize.

ke「ñbeñ けんべん (検便) *n.* stool test.
keñbeñ (o) suru (〜(を)する) *vi.* examine a person's stool.

ke「ñbutsu けんぶつ (見物) *n.* sightseeing; visit; sightseer; spectator.
keñbutsu suru (〜する) *vt.* see; see the sights of; watch.

ke「ñbutsuniñ けんぶつにん (見物人) *n.* spectator; onlooker.

ke「ñchi けんち (見地) *n.* viewpoint; standpoint:

kotonatta keñchi *kara ikeñ o noberu* (異なった見地から意見を述べる) express one's opinion from a different *viewpoint*.

ke「ñ-chi¹ji けんちじ (県知事) *n.* (prefectural) governor. (⇨ chiji)

ke「ñchiku けんちく (建築) *n.* building; construction; architecture. (⇨ tatemono)
keñchiku suru (〜する) *vt.* build; put up: ★ More formal than '*tateru²*.'

ke「ñchoo けんちょう (県庁) *n.* prefectural office.

ke「ñdoo けんどう (剣道) *n.* Japanese swordsmanship [fencing]; kendo.

ke「ñgaku けんがく (見学) *n.* study by observation; study visit.
keñgaku suru (〜する) *vt.* visit for study; inspect; observe:
Ashi o kega shita no de, taiiku wa keñgaku shita. (足をけがしたので、体育は見学した) As I had injured my leg, I only *observed* the physical education class.

ke「ñi けんい (権威) *n.* authority; expert.

ke「ñji けんじ (検事) *n.* public prosecutor.

ke「ñka けんか (喧嘩) *n.* quarrel; fight; brawl.
keñka (o) suru (〜(を)する) *vi.* quarrel; have a fight.
keñka o uru (〜を売る) pick a fight.

ke「ñkai けんかい (見解) *n.* opinion; view; outlook.

ke「ñketsu けんけつ (献血) *n.* blood donation.
keñketsu suru (〜する) *vi.* donate [give] blood.

ke「ñkoo けんこう (健康) *n.* health:
keñkoo-*shiñdañ* (健康診断) a *medical* checkup / keñkoo-*hokeñ* (健康保険) *health* insurance.
— *a.n.* (〜 na, ni) healthy; healthful.

ke「ñkoo-hoke「ñshoo けんこうほ

けんしょう（健康保険証）n. health insurance card.

ke┌ñkyuu けんきゅう（研究）n. study; research; investigation.
keñkyuu suru（～する）vt., vi. make a study; do research.

ke┌ñmee[1] けんめい（賢明）a.n.
(～ na, ni) wise; sensible; judicious.

ke┌ñmee[2] けんめい（懸命）a.n.
(～ na/no, ni) eager; hard; strenuous:
Keñmee na soosa ga tsuzukerareta.（懸命な捜査が続けられた）A diligent investigation was carried out.（⇨ isshoo-keñmee）

ke┌ñpoo けんぽう（憲法）n. constitution:
keñpoo-ihañ（憲法違反）a breach of the constitution.

ke┌ñri けんり（権利）n. right; claim; privilege:
keñri o yookyuu suru（権利を要求する）claim a right.（↔ gimu）

ke┌ñrikiñ けんりきん（権利金）n.
key money; premium. ★ Money additional to the rent requested when renting an apartment or house.（⇨ reekiñ; shikikiñ; yachiñ）

ke┌ñryoku けんりょく（権力）n.
power; authority:
Kare wa kono kaisha de keñryoku ga aru.（彼はこの会社で権力がある）He is an influential man in this company.

ke┌ñsa けんさ（検査）n. inspection; examination; test:
hiñshitsu no keñsa o suru（品質の検査をする）carry out quality inspections.

ke┌ñsaku けんさく（検索）n. reference; access; retrieval.
keñsaku suru（～する）vt. refer to; look up; search.

ke┌ñsatsu[1] けんさつ（検札）n. inspection of tickets.

ke┌ñsatsu[2] けんさつ（検察）n. prosecution.

ke┌ñsetsu けんせつ（建設）n. construction; establishment.
keñsetsu suru（～する）vt. build; construct; establish.

ke┌ñshoo けんしょう（懸賞）n. prize; prize contest; reward.

ke┌ñshu┌usee けんしゅうせい（研修生）n. trainee.

ke┌ñsoñ けんそん（謙遜）n. modesty; humility.
keñsoñ suru（～する）vi. be modest; be humble.

ke┌ñto┌o[1] けんとう（見当）n.
1 guess; estimate; idea:
keñtoo o tsukeru（見当をつける）make a guess.
2 direction:
Byooiñ wa daitai kono keñtoo ni arimasu.（病院は大体この見当にあります）The hospital is roughly in this direction.
keñtoo-chigai[-hazure]（～違い[はずれ]）be wrong; be off the point.

ke┌ñtoo[2] けんとう（検討）n. examination; study; investigation.
keñtoo suru（～する）vt. examine; study; investigate.

ke┌ñtoo[3] けんとう（健闘）n. good fight; strenuous efforts.
keñtoo suru（～する）vi. put up a good fight; make strenuous efforts.

ke┌ñyaku けんやく（倹約）n. thrift; economy.
keñyaku suru（～する）vt. save; economize: shokuhi o keñyaku suru（食費を倹約する）economize on food expenses.（↔ roohi）

ke┌ñzeñ けんぜん（健全）a.n.
(～ na, ni) healthy; wholesome; sound:
keñzeñ na yomimono（健全な読み物）wholesome reading.

ke┌ppaku けっぱく（潔白）n. innocence; guiltlessness:
mi no keppaku o shoomee suru（身の潔白を証明する）prove one's innocence.

ke┌redo (mo) けれど(も)conj.
but; however:

Kanojo wa kai ni shootai sareta. Keredo mo shusseki shinakatta. (彼女は会に招待された. けれども出席しなかった) *Though* she was invited, she did not attend the party. (⇨ ga²; kakawarazu; no ni)

ke⌐r·u ける(蹴る) *vt.* (ker·i-; ke-r·a-; ket-te Ⓒ) 1 kick.
2 reject; refuse (a request, demand, etc.):
Kare wa watashi-tachi no yookyuu o ketta. (彼は私たちの要求をけった) He *rejected* our demands.

ke⌐sa けさ(今朝) *n.* this morning. (↔ myoochoo; yokuasa)

ke⌐shigomu けしごむ(消しゴム) *n.* eraser; rubber.

ke⌐shiki けしき(景色) *n.* scenery; scene; landscape; view.

ke⌐sho⌐o けしょう(化粧) *n.* makeup: keshoo-shitsu(化粧室) a *toilet*; a *restroom*.
keshoo (o) suru (〜(を)する) *vi.* make oneself up; paint.

ke⌐ssaku けっさく(傑作) *n.* masterpiece.

ke⌐ssañ けっさん(決算) *n.* closing accounts; settlement of accounts.
kessañ (o) suru (〜(を)する) *vt.* settle [balance] accounts.

ke⌐ssee けっせい(結成) *n.* organization; formation.
kessee suru (〜する) *vt.* organize; form: *atarashii too o kessee suru*(新しい党を結成する) *form* a new political party.

ke⌐sseki けっせき(欠席) *n.* absence.
kesseki suru (〜する) *vt.* stay away; absent oneself: *gakkoo o kesseki suru*(学校を欠席する) *be absent* from school. (↔ shusseki)

ke⌐sshiñ けっしん(決心) *n.* decision; determination; resolution.
kesshiñ suru (〜する) *vi., vt.* make up one's mind; decide; determine; resolve.

ke⌐sshite けっして(決して) *adv.* (with a negative) never; by no means; not at all:
Kanojo wa kesshite *yakusoku o yaburanai.*(彼女は決して約束を破らない) She *never* breaks a promise.

ke⌐sshoo¹ けっしょう(決勝) *n.* final game [match]; finals.

ke⌐sshoo² けっしょう(結晶) *n.* 1 crystal; crystallization.
2 (*fig.*) result; fruit:
ase no kesshoo(汗の結晶) the *result* of much effort.

ke⌐ssoñ けっそん(欠損) *n.* deficit; loss:
hyakumañ-eñ no kessoñ o dasu (100万円の欠損を出す) have a *deficit* of a million yen. (↔ rieki)

ke⌐s·u けす(消す) *vt.* (kesh·i-; ke-s·a-; kesh·i-te Ⓒ) 1 extinguish; put out; blow out:
kaji o kesu(火事を消す) *extinguish* a fire / *akari o kesu*(明かりを消す) *put out* a light. (⇨ kieru)
2 switch off; turn off:
Rajio o keshite kudasai.(ラジオを消してください) Please *turn off* the radio.
3 erase; rub [wipe] off; cross out:
Kare wa kanojo no namae o meebo kara keshita.(彼は彼女の名前を名簿から消した) He *crossed* her name *off* the list. (⇨ kezuru)
4 remove; deaden; absorb:
iya na nioi o kesu(いやなにおいを消す) *get rid of* a bad smell. (⇨ kieru)

ke⌐tobas·u けとばす(蹴飛ばす) *vt.* (-tobash·i-; -tobas·a-; -tobas·i-te Ⓒ) kick (away). (⇨ keru)

ke⌐tsuatsu けつあつ(血圧) *n.* blood pressure:
ketsuatsu ga takai [hikui](血圧が高い[低い]) have a high [low] *blood pressure.*

ke⌐tsudañ けつだん(決断) *n.* decision; determination; resolution.
ketsudañ suru (〜する) *vi.* decide; determine; resolve.

ke⌐tsu⌐eki けつえき(血液) *n.* blood: ketsueki-*gata*(血液型) a

blood type.

ke⌐tsui けつい (決意) *n.* determination; resolution.

ketsui suru (〜する) *vt.* determine; resolve: *jiniñ o ketsui suru* (辞任を決意する) *decide* to resign one's post.

ke⌐tsuroñ けつろん (結論) *n.* conclusion:
ketsuroñ o dasu (結論を出す) form a *conclusion*.

ke⌐ttee けってい (決定) *n.* decision; determination; conclusion; settlement.
kettee suru (〜する) *vi., vt.* decide; determine; conclude; settle: *nani o suru ka o kettee suru* (何をするかを決定する) *decide* what to do. (⇨ kimeru; kimaru)

ke⌐tteñ けってん (欠点) *n.* fault; drawback; weak point:
jibuñ no ketteñ o naosu (自分の欠点を直す) correct one's *weak points.* (↔ choosho) (⇨ tañsho)

ke⌐washi¹·i けわしい (険しい) *a.* (-ku) **1** steep:
kewashii yama-michi (険しい山道) a *steep* mountain path.
2 grim; severe; critical:
Joosee ga kewashiku natte kita. (情勢が険しくなってきた) The situation has become *grave.*

ke⌐zur·u けずる (削る) *vt.* (kezur·i-; kezur·a-; kezut-te Ⓒ)
1 shave; plane; sharpen:
ita o taira ni kezuru (板を平らに削る) *plane* a board smooth / *eñpitsu o kezuru* (鉛筆を削る) *sharpen* a pencil.
2 delete; cross out. (⇨ kesu)
3 reduce; curtail; cut:
koosaihi o kezuru (交際費を削る) *cut down* on entertainment expenses.

ki¹¹ き (木) *n.* **1** tree; shrub.
2 wood; lumber; timber.

ki² き (気) *n.* **1** mind; mood; feeling:
Kare wa shippai suru yoo na ki ga suru. (彼は失敗するような気がする) I

have a *feeling* that he will fail.
2 nature; disposition; temper:
Kare no musume wa ki ga tsuyoi ga, musuko wa ki ga yowai. (彼の娘は気が強いが, 息子は気が弱い) His daughter is *unyielding*, but his son is *timid.*
3 intention; will:
Ano hito to kekkoñ suru ki wa arimaseñ. (あの人と結婚する気はありません) I have no *intention* of marrying him.
ki ga au (〜が合う) get along well.
ki ga chiisai (〜が小さい) be timid.
ki ga chiru (〜が散る) be distracted.
ki ga kiku (〜が利く) be considerate; be attentive; be thoughtful.
ki ga omoi (〜が重い) be heavy-hearted.
ki ga sumu (〜が済む) be satisfied.
ki ga tsuku (〜がつく) notice; come to one's senses.
ki ni iru (〜に入る) like; be pleased.
ki ni kuwanai (〜に食わない) be disagreeable.
ki ni naru (〜になる) bother; get on one's nerves.
ki ni suru (〜にする) worry; mind; care.
ki o kubaru (〜を配る) be attentive to.
ki o tsukeru (〜をつける) be careful; take care.

-ki¹ き (器) *suf.* **1** -ware; utensil; apparatus:
too-ki (陶器) ceramic *ware* / *gak-ki* (楽器) a musical *instrument* / *juwa*-ki (受話器) a telephone *receiver.*
2 organ: *shooka*-ki (消化器) the digestive *organs.*

-ki² き (機) *suf.* **1** plane:
hikoo-ki (飛行機) an *airplane* / *jetto*-ki (ジェット機) a jet *plane.*
2 machine:
señtaku-ki [*sentak*-ki] (洗濯機) a washing *machine* / *señpuu*-ki (扇風機) an electric *fan.*

ki⌐atsu きあつ (気圧) *n.* atmospheric pressure.

ki'bishi'·i きびしい (厳しい) *a.* (-ku) severe; stern; strict: *Kanojo wa kodomo ni* kibishii. (彼女は子どもに厳しい) She is *strict* with her children.

ki'bo きぼ (規模) *n.* scale; size: *Sono taikai wa kokusai-teki na* kibo *de hirakareta.* (その大会は国際的な規模で開かれた) The convention was held on an international *scale*.

ki'boo きぼう (希望) *n.* hope; wish; request; expectation: kiboo *o idaku* (希望を抱く) cherish a *hope* / kiboo *o ushinau* (希望を失う) lose *hope*.
kiboo suru (〜する) *vt.* hope; wish. (⇨ nozomu')

ki'buñ きぶん (気分) *n.* feeling; mood; sentiment: *Kyoo wa* kibuñ *ga yoi [warui].* (きょうは気分が良い[悪い]) I feel [*don't feel*] *well* today.

ki'chi きち (基地) *n.* base: *guñji-kichi* (軍事基地) a military *base*.

ki'chi'ñto きちんと *adv.* neatly; exactly; properly; in good order: *hikidashi o* kichiñto *seeri shite oku* (引き出しをきちんと整理しておく) keep the drawers *tidy*. (⇨ chañto)

ki'choo きちょう (貴重) *a.n.* (〜 na) precious; valuable: *kichoo na taikeñ* (貴重な体験) a *precious* experience.

ki'choohiñ きちょうひん (貴重品) *n.* (one's) valuables.

ki'dootai きどうたい (機動隊) *n.* riot police [squad].

ki'dor·u きどる (気取る) *vi., vt.* (kidor·i-; kidor·a-; kidot-te Ⓒ)
1 put on airs; give oneself airs.
2 pose as: *Kare wa gakusha o* kidotte iru. (彼は学者を気取っている) He *affects* to be a scholar.

ki'e·ru きえる (消える) *vi.* (kie-te Ⓥ) 1 (of a fire, light, etc.) go out; die out. (⇨ kesu)
2 disappear; vanish; go out of sight. (⇨ kesu)
3 (of snow) melt away.
4 go away; die out: *Itami ga* kieta. (痛みが消えた) The pain *has gone away*.

ki'fu きふ (寄付) *n.* contribution; donation: kifu *o atsumeru* (寄付を集める) collect *contributions*.
kifu suru (〜する) *vt.* contribute; donate.

ki'gae きがえ (着替え) *n.* change of clothes: kigae *o suru* (着替えをする) *change one's clothes.* (⇨ kigaeru)

ki'gae'·ru きがえる (着替える) *vt.* (kigae-te Ⓥ) change one's clothes. (⇨ kigae)

ki'gai きがい (機外) *n.* outside an airplane. (↔ kinai)

ki'ga'kari きがかり (気掛り) *a.n.* (〜 na, ni) worry; anxiety; concern: *Musuko no shoorai ga* kigakari *desu.* (息子の将来が気がかりです) We *are worried* about our son's future. (⇨ shiñpai)

ki'gane きがね (気兼ね) *n.* constraint.
kigane suru (〜する) *vi.* feel constrained; worry about giving trouble: *Shuuto ni wa* kigane *shite imasu.* (しゅうとには気兼ねしています) I *feel ill at ease* with my mother-in-law.

ki'garu きがる (気軽) *a.n.* (〜 na, ni) lighthearted; cheerful; buoyant: *Kigaru ni asobi ni kite kudasai.* (気軽に遊びに来てください) Please feel *free* to come and visit us. (⇨ kiraku)

ki'geki きげき (喜劇) *n.* comedy. (↔ higeki)

ki'geñ' きげん (期限) *n.* time limit; deadline: *Koñgetsu de keeyaku no* kigeñ *ga kireru.* (今月で契約の期限が切れる) The agreement *expires* this month.

ki⌐geñ[2] きげん（機嫌）*n.* humor; temper; mood: kigeñ *ga ii [warui]*（きげんがいい[悪い]）be in good [bad] *humor* today.
kigeñ o toru（～を取る）play up to: *Kare wa uwayaku no go-kigeñ o totta.*（彼は上役のごきげんを取った）He *got on the right side of* his boss.

ki⌐geñ[3] きげん（起源）*n.* origin; beginning: *seemee no* kigeñ（生命の起源）the *origin* of life.

ki⌐goo きごう（記号）*n.* mark; sign; symbol.（⇨ fugoo）

ki⌐gu きぐ（器具）*n.* appliance; utensil; instrument.

ki⌐gyoo きぎょう（企業）*n.* company; business; enterprise.

ki⌐hoñ きほん（基本）*n.* fundamentals; basics; basis; standard: Kihoñ *o wasureru na.*（基本を忘れるな）Never forget *basics.*（⇨ kiso）

ki⌐hoñ-teki きほんてき（基本的）*a.n.*（～ na, ni）fundamental; basic.

ki⌐iro きいろ（黄色）*n.* yellow.（⇨ kiiroi）

ki⌐iro·i きいろい（黄色い）*a.* (-ku) yellow.（⇨ kiiro）

ki⌐ji[1] きじ（記事）*n.* news; article: *Sono* kiji *wa kesa no shiñbuñ de yomimashita.*（その記事は今朝の新聞で読みました）I read the *news* in this morning's paper.

ki⌐ji[2] きじ（生地）*n.* cloth; material; texture.

ki⌐ji[3] きじ（雉）*n.* pheasant.

ki⌐jitsu きじつ（期日）*n.* fixed date; deadline; appointed day: *Kare wa itsu-mo* kijitsu *o mamoranai.*（彼はいつも期日を守らない）He always fails to meet the *deadline.*

ki⌐juñ[1] きじゅん（基準）*n.* standard; criterion; basis: *Yosañ wa sakuneñ-do no jisseki o* kijuñ *ni shite iru.*（予算は昨年度の実績を基準にしている）The budget was made on the *basis* of last year's actual results.

ki⌐juñ[2] きじゅん（規準）*n.* norm; standard.

ki⌐kai[1] きかい（機械）*n.* machine; machinery.

ki⌐kai[2] きかい（機会）*n.* opportunity; chance; occasion: *ii* kikai *o nogasu*（いい機会を逃す）miss a good *opportunity.*

ki⌐kaika きかいか（機械化）*n.* mechanization. **kikaika suru**（～する）*vt.* mechanize: *noogyoo o* kikaika suru（農業を機械化する）*mechanize* farming.

ki⌐kaku[1] きかく（企画）*n.* plan; project; planning: kikaku *o tateru*（企画を立てる）make a *plan.* **kikaku suru**（～する）*vt.* plan; arrange.

ki⌐kaku[2] きかく（規格）*n.* standard; requirements.

ki⌐kañ きかん（期間）*n.* term; period: *Keeyaku no* kikañ *wa go-neñ desu.*（契約の期間は 5 年です）The *term* of the contract is five years.

-ki⌐kañ きかん（機関）*suf.* **1** engine: *jooki*-kikañ（蒸気機関）a steam *engine.* **2** institution; system; means: *kyooiku*-kikañ（教育機関）an educational *institution* / *kootsuu*-kikañ（交通機関）a *means* of transport.

ki⌐kañsha きかんしゃ（機関車）*n.* locomotive.

ki⌐kas·u きかす（聞かす）*vt.* (kikash·i·; kikas·a·; kikash·i·te Ⓒ) tell; let hear: *Sono hanashi wa nañ-do mo* kikasareta.（その話は何度も聞かされた）I *was told* the story many times.（⇨ kiku[1]）

ki⌐keñ[1] きけん（危険）*n.* danger; peril; risk; hazard: kikeñ *o kañjiru*（危険を感じる）sense *danger.*
— *a.n.*（～ na）dangerous; perilous; risky; hazardous; unsafe.

ki⌐keñ[2] きけん（棄権）*n.* abstention; withdrawal.

kikeñ suru (～する) *vt.* abstain; withdraw; default: *toohyoo o kikeñ suru* (投票を棄権する) *abstain* from voting.

ki┌**ki** きき (危機) *n.* crisis; emergency.
kiki-ippatsu (～一髪) a hair's breadth: *Kare wa kiki-ippatsu de shi o manugareta.* (彼は危機一髪で死を免れた) He escaped death *by the skin of his teeth.*

ki┌**kiaki**┐**·ru** ききあきる (聞き飽きる) *vi.* (-aki-te Ⅴ) be tired of hearing. (⇨ akiru)

ki┌**kichigae**┐**·ru** ききちがえる (聞き違える) *vt.* (-chigae-te Ⅴ) mishear; hear a thing wrong. (⇨ kikichigai)

ki┌**kichigai** ききちがい (聞き違い) *n.* hearing wrongly: *Sore wa anata no kikichigai desu.* (それはあなたの聞き違いです) You *didn't hear* me *correctly.* (⇨ kikichigaeru)

ki┌**kida**┐**s·u** ききだす (聞き出す) *vt.* (-dash·i-; -das·a-; -dash·i-te Ⓒ) get (information); find out: *Kare kara nani mo kikidasu koto ga dekinakatta.* (彼から何も聞き出すことができなかった) We could not *find out* anything from him.

ki┌**kigurushi**┐**·i** ききぐるしい (聞き苦しい) *a.* (-ku) disagreeable to hear; harsh to the ear: *Kare no iiwake wa kikigurushikatta.* (彼の言い訳は聞き苦しかった) I *could not bear* to listen to his excuses.

ki┌**kika**┐**es·u** ききかえす (聞き返す) *vt.* (-kaesh·i-; -kaes·a-; -kaesh·i-te Ⓒ) repeat a question; ask again. (⇨ kikinaosu)

ki┌**kime** ききめ (効き目) *n.* effect; efficacy; virtue: *Kare ni chuukoku shite mo, kikime wa nakatta.* (彼に忠告しても、効き目はなかった) Although I warned him, it had no *effect.* (⇨ kiku²; kooka¹)

ki┌**kinao**┐**s·u** ききなおす (聞き直す)

vt. (-naosh·i-; -naos·a-; -naosh·i-te Ⓒ) ask again. (⇨ kikikaesu)

ki┌**kinoga**┐**s·u** ききのがす (聞き逃す) *vt.* (-nogash·i-; -nogas·a-; -nogash·i-te Ⓒ) fail to hear: *Sono nyuusu wa kikinogashimashita.* (そのニュースは聞き逃しました) I *failed to hear* the news.

ki┌**kisokona**┐**·u** ききそこなう (聞き損なう) *vt.* (-sokona·i-; -sokonaw·a-; -sokonat·te Ⓒ) hear amiss; fail to catch: *Kare ga itta koto o kikisokonaimashita.* (彼が言ったことを聞き損ないました) I *could not catch* what he said. (⇨ -sokonau)

ki┌**kite** ききて (聞き手) *n.* hearer; listener; interviewer; audience. (↔ hanashite)

ki┌**kito**┐**r·u** ききとる (聞き取る) *vt.* (-tor·i-; -tor·a-; -tot·te Ⓒ) hear; catch: *Watashi no iu koto ga kikitoremasu ka?* (私の言うことが聞き取れますか) *Can* you *hear* what I am saying?

ki┌**koe**┐**·ru** きこえる (聞こえる) *vi.* (kikoe-te Ⅴ) **1** hear; be audible: *Deñwa ga tookute, yoku kikoemaseñ.* (電話が遠くて、よく聞こえません) I *cannot hear* you properly because of the bad phone connection.
2 sound (like...): *Anata no kotoba wa iiwake ni kikoeru.* (あなたの言葉は言い訳に聞こえる) What you say *sounds* like an excuse.

ki┌**koku** きこく (帰国) *n.* return to one's country [homeland].

ki┌**koku-shi**┐**jo** きこくしじょ (帰国子女) *n.* Japanese children [students] who have recently returned home from living abroad.

ki┌**koo** きこう (気候) *n.* climate; weather.

ki┌**k·u**¹ きく (聞く・聴く・訊く) *vt.* (ki-k·i-; kik·a-; ki·i-te Ⓒ) **1** listen to:

Maiasa shichi-ji no nyuusu o kiki-masu. (毎朝 7 時のニュースをききます) Every morning I *listen to* the seven o'clock news.

2 hear of [about]:
Soñna koto wa kiita *koto ga arima-señ.* (そんなことは聞いたことがありません) I *have* never *heard of* such a thing.

3 ask; inquire:
Keesatsukañ ni eki e iku michi o kiita. (警察官に駅へ行く道を聞いた) I *asked* a policeman the way to the station.

4 obey; follow:
Sono ko wa oya no iu koto o yoku kiku. (その子は親の言うことをよく聞く) That boy faithfully *obeys* what his parents tell him. (⇨ shitagau)

ki「k·u² きく（効く・利く）*vi.* (kik·i-; kik·a-; ki·i-te [C]) **1** (of medicine, remedy, etc.) have an effect; work.

2 (of apparatus) act; work:
Kono jiteñsha wa bureeki ga kikanai. (この自転車はブレーキが利かない) The brakes on this bicycle *do not work.*

... ga kiku (…が～) can be done:
señtaku ga kiku (洗濯がきく) *be washable* / shuuri ga kiku (修理がきく) *be repairable.* (⇨ dekiru)

ki「ku¹³ きく（菊）*n.* chrysanthemum.

ki「ku¹bari きくばり（気配り）*n.* attention; care; consideration.

ki「kyoo ききょう（帰郷）*n.* homecoming.

kikyoo suru (～する) *vi.* return to one's hometown.

ki「mae ga i¹i きまえがいい（気前がいい）generous; liberal; open-handed:
Ano hito wa itsu-mo kimae ga ii. (あの人はいつも気前がいい) He *is* always *generous* with his money.

ki「magure きまぐれ（気紛れ）*n.* caprice; whim; fancy.
— *a.n.* (～ na, ni) capricious;

whimsical:
Kimagure ni itta koto ga hoñtoo ni natta. (気まぐれに言ったことが本当になった) What I had said *frivolously* came true.

ki「mama きまま（気まま）*a.n.* (～ na, ni) easy; carefree:
kimama ni kurasu (気ままに暮らす) live an *easy* life.

ki「mari きまり（決まり）*n.* **1** rule; regulation:
kimari o mamoru [yaburu] (決まりを守る[破る]) obey [break] a *rule.*

2 settlement; conclusion:
Hayaku kono shigoto ni kimari o tsuketai. (早くこの仕事に決まりをつけたい) I *want to finish up* this job as soon as possible.

3 habit; custom:
Yuuhañ mae ni biiru o nomu no ga kare no kimari desu. (夕飯前にビールを飲むのが彼の決まりです) It is his *custom* to have a beer before dinner.

ki「mari ga waru¹i きまりがわるい（きまりが悪い）feel embarrassed. (⇨ hazukashii)

ki「mar·u きまる（決まる）*vi.* (kimar·i-; kimar·a-; kimat-te [C]) be decided; be settled; be fixed:
Sono hanashi wa sugu ni kimatta. (その話はすぐに決まった) The negotiations *were* soon *concluded.* (⇨ kimeru)

kimatta (決まった) regular: *Kare ni wa* kimatta *shoku ga nai.* (彼には決まった職がない) He has no *regular* job. (⇨ kettee)

kimatte (決まって) always: *Kaigi ni kare wa* kimatte *okureru.* (会議に彼は決まって遅れる) He is *always* late for meetings.

ki「me·ru きめる（決める）*vt.* (kime-te [V]) **1** decide; determine:
Doko e iku ka mada kimete *ima-señ.* (どこへ行くかまだ決めていません) I have not yet *made up my mind* where to go. (⇨ kimaru)

2 arrange (a time, a place, etc.); fix; settle. (⇨ kimaru)

ki⌐mi[1] きみ (君) *n.* you. ★ The plural forms are '*kimi-tachi*' and '*kimi-ra*' (*slightly derog.*).
★ Used by men when talking to close friends, subordinates, or juniors. (⇒ anata)

ki⌐mi[2] きみ (気味) *n.* **1** feeling; sensation:
Ii kimi da. (いい気味だ) It serves you *right*.
2 tendency.
kimi ga ii (〜がいい) feel satisfied.
kimi ga warui (〜が悪い) weird; creepy; uncanny.

ki⌐mitsu きみつ (機密) *n.* secret [classified] information:
kimitsu-*buñsho* (機密文書) a *secret* [*confidential*] document.

ki⌐mochi きもち (気持ち) *n.* feeling; mood:
Kare no kimochi wa wakaru. (彼の気持ちはわかる) I know *how he feels*.
kimochi ga yoi [**warui**] (〜が良い [悪い]) feel good [sick].

ki⌐mono きもの (着物) *n.* **1** kimono; traditional Japanese costume.
2 clothes; clothing.

ki⌐muzukashi·i きむずかしい (気難しい) *n.* (-ku) hard to please; grouchy:
Kaneko-sañ wa kimuzukashii. (金子さんは気難しい) Mr. Kaneko is *hard to please*.

ki⌐myoo きみょう (奇妙) *a.n.* (〜 na, ni) strange; odd; queer:
Kimi ga sono koto o shiranai nañte kimyoo da. (きみがそのことを知らないなんて奇妙だ) It is rather *odd* that you know nothing about that.

ki⌐ñ[1] きん (金) *n.* gold.

ki⌐ñ[2] きん (菌) *n.* germ; bacterium; fungus.

ki⌐nai きない (機内) *n.* inside an airplane:
kinai ni ooki-na nimotsu o mochi-komu (機内に大きな荷物を持ち込む) take large items of luggage *onto the plane*. (↔ kigai)

ki⌐ñbeñ きんべん (勤勉) *n.* diligence; industry. (↔ namakeru)
— *a.n.* (〜 na, ni) hardworking; diligent:
Ano hito wa kiñbeñ da. (あの人は勤勉だ) He is *industrious*.

ki⌐ñchoo きんちょう (緊張) *n.* strain; tension.
kiñchoo suru (〜する) *vi.* feel nervous; tense up.

ki⌐ñdai きんだい (近代) *n.* modern ages [times]:
kiñdai-*kokka* (近代国家) a *modern* nation. (⇒ gendai)

ki⌐ñdaika きんだいか (近代化) *n.* modernization.
kiñdaika suru (〜する) *vt.* modernize: mura o kiñdaika suru (村を近代化する) *modernize* a village.

ki⌐neñ きねん (記念) *n.* souvenir; commemoration.
kineñ suru (〜する) *vt.* commemorate. (⇒ kineñbi)

ki⌐ñeñ きんえん (禁煙) *n.* prohibition of smoking: kiñeñ-*sha* (禁煙車) a *no-smoking* (railroad) car.
kiñeñ suru (〜する) *vi.* give up smoking.

ki⌐neñbi きねんび (記念日) *n.* memorial [commemoration] day; anniversary.

ki⌐ñgaku きんがく (金額) *n.* amount [sum] of money.

ki⌐ñgañ きんがん (近眼) *n.* nearsightedness; shortsightedness.

ki⌐ñgyo きんぎょ (金魚) *n.* goldfish.

ki⌐ñiro きんいろ (金色) *n.* color of gold; gold.

ki⌐ñji·ru きんじる (禁じる) *vt.* (kiñjite Ⅴ) forbid; prohibit; ban:
Koko de wa kitsueñ ga kiñjirarete imasu. (ここでは喫煙が禁じられています) Smoking *is prohibited* here.

ki⌐ñjo きんじょ (近所) *n.* neighborhood; vicinity.

ki⌐ñjo-me⌐ewaku きんじょめいわく (近所迷惑) *n.* a nuisance to the neighbors.

ki⌐ñko きんこ (金庫) *n.* safe:
o-kane o kiñko ni shimau (お金を金

庫にしまう) put money in a *safe*.

ki「ṅkoo きんこう (均衡) *n.* balance; equilibrium:
chikara no kiṅkoo o tamotsu [yaburu] (力の均衡を保つ[破る]) maintain [upset] the *balance* of power.

ki「ṅkyuu きんきゅう (緊急) *n.* emergency; urgency.
— *a.n.* (~ na, ni) urgent; pressing; immediate:
Kiṅkyuu na yooji ga dekimashita. (緊急な用事ができました) Some *pressing* business has come up.

ki「ṅmotsu きんもつ (禁物) *n.* prohibited thing; taboo:
Yudaṅ wa kiṅmotsu desu. (油断は禁物です) Carelessness is *not tolerated*.

ki「ṅmu きんむ (勤務) *n.* service; duty; work:
kiṅmu-jikaṅ (勤務時間) *office* hours / *kiṅmu-saki* (勤務先) one's place of *employment*.
kiṅmu suru (~する) *vi.* be on duty; be at work. (⇨ tsutomeru[1])

ki「ṅniku きんにく (筋肉) *n.* muscle; brawn:
Kare wa kiṅniku takumashii ude o shite iru. (彼は筋肉たくましい腕をしている) He has *brawny* arms.

ki「nodoku[1] きのどく (気の毒) *a.n.* (~ na, ni) pitiable; pitiful; unfortunate; regrettable; sorry:
Sore wa o-kinodoku desu. (それはお気の毒です) I'm *sorry* to hear that.

ki「noko きのこ *n.* mushroom.

ki「noo[1] きのう (昨日) *n.* yesterday. (⇨ ashita; kyoo; myoogonichi)

ki「noo[2] きのう (機能) *n.* function:
kinoo-shoogai (機能障害) a *functional* disorder (of the body).
kinoo suru (~する) *vi.* function; work. (⇨ ugoku)

ki「ṅpatsu きんぱつ (金髪) *n.* blond [golden] hair.

ki「ṅseṅ きんせん (金銭) *n.* money; cash. (⇨ kane[1])

ki「ṅshi[1] きんし (禁止) *n.* prohibition; ban:

Koko wa chuusha kiṅshi desu. (ここは駐車禁止です) Parking *is prohibited* here.
kiṅshi suru (~する) *vt.* prohibit; forbid; ban. (↔ kyoka)

ki「ṅshi[2] きんし (近視) *n.* nearsightedness; shortsightedness. (↔ eṅshi; kiṅgaṅ)

ki「nu きぬ (絹) *n.* silk.

ki「ṅyo「o(bi) きんよう(び) (金曜(日)) *n.* Friday. (⇨ APP. 5)

ki「ṅyuu さにゅう (記入) *n.* entry.
kinyuu (o) suru (~(を)する) *vt.* make an entry; write; fill out.

ki「ṅzoku きんぞく (金属) *n.* metal

ki「oku きおく (記憶) *n.* memory; recollection; remembrance:
kioku o ushinau (記憶を失う) lose one's *memory*.
kioku suru (~する) *vt.* remember; memorize. (⇨ mono-oboe; oboe)

ki「oṅ きおん (気温) *n.* (atmospheric) temperature.

ki「ppa「ri きっぱり *adv.* (~ to) flatly; definitely; for good:
kippari (to) sake o yameru (きっぱり(と)酒をやめる) give up drinking *for good*.

ki「ppu きっぷ (切符) *n.* ticket:
oofuku-kippu (往復切符) a round-trip *ticket*. (⇨ keṅ[2])

ki「rai きらい (嫌い) *a.n.* (~ na) dislike; hate:
Toku ni kirai na tabemono wa arimaseṅ. (特に嫌いな食べ物はありません) There isn't any food I *dislike* in particular. (↔ suki[1]) (⇨ kirau)

ki「rakira きらきら *adv.* (~ to) (the state of things that shine brightly):
kirakira (to) hikaru (きらきら(と)光る) *glitter*; *glisten*. (⇨ giragira)

ki「raku きらく (気楽) *a.n.* (~ na, ni) carefree; easy; comfortable:
Doozo, kiraku ni shite kudasai. (どうぞ, 気楽にしてください) Please make yourself *comfortable*. (⇨ noṅbiri; noṅki)

ki´ra`ri きらり *adv.* (~ **to**) shine or glitter briefly:
Kanojo no me ni namida ga kirari *to hikatta.* (彼女の目に涙がきらりと光った) The tears *glistened* in her eyes.

ki´ra·u きらう (嫌う) *vt.* (kira·i-; kiraw·a-; kirat-te Ⓒ) dislike; hate:
hito ni kirawareru (人に嫌われる) *be disliked* by everyone. (⇒ kirai)

ki´re[1] きれ (切れ) *n.* cloth; rag. (⇒ nuno)

-kire きれ (切れ) *suf.* piece; slice; strip:
niku go-kire (肉 5 切れ) five *pieces* of meat / *pañ hito-kire* (パン 1 切れ) a *slice* of bread.

ki´ree きれい (綺麗) *a.n.* (~ **na, ni**) 1 beautiful; pretty; lovely:
kiree *na josee* [keshiki] (きれいな女性[景色]) a *beautiful* woman [view] (⇒ utsukushii)
2 clean; clear; tidy; neat:
Heya o kiree *ni sooji shita.* (部屋をきれいに掃除した) I *cleaned* the room thoroughly. (↔ kitanai)
3 (~ **ni**) completely; wholly; entirely:
Sono koto wa kiree *ni wasurete ita.* (そのことはきれいに忘れていた) I had *completely* forgotten that. (⇒ sukkari)
4 (~ **na**) (of politics) fair; clean:
kiree *na señkyo* (きれいな選挙) a *clean and fair* election.

ki´re`·ru きれる (切れる) *vi.* (kire-te Ⓥ) 1 (of a blade, knife, sword, etc.) cut; be sharp:
Kono naifu wa (yoku) kireru. (このナイフは(よく)切れる) This knife *cuts* well.
2 (of a thread, rope, etc.) break; be broken; snap:
Ito [*Tsuna*] *ga* kireta. (糸[綱]が切れた) The thread [rope] *broke*. (⇒ kiru¹)
3 (of a telephone, communication, relations, etc.) cut off:
Deñwa ga tochuu de kireta. (電話

が途中で切れた) I *was cut off* in the middle of my phone call. (⇒ kiru¹)
4 (of a bank, dam) collapse; burst:
Totsuzeñ damu ga kireta. (突然ダムが切れた) The dam suddenly *burst*.
5 (of food, goods) run out; be out of stock:
Bataa ga kirete shimatta. (バターが切れてしまった) The butter *has run out*.
6 (of a contract, deadline, etc.) expire:
Kono keeyaku wa kotoshi de kire-masu. (この契約は今年で切れます) This contract *expires* this year.
7 (of a person) able; competent:
Kanojo wa kireru. (彼女は切れる) She is *very able*.

ki´ri[1] きり (霧) *n.* fog; mist.

ki´ri[2] きり (錐) *n.* drill; gimlet; awl.

-kiri きり (切り) *suf.* 1 only:
★ The emphatic form is '**-kkiri**.'
*Josee wa watashi hitori-*kiri *datta.* (女性は私一人きりだった) I was the *only* woman there.
2 since:
*Kare wa itta-*kiri *kaette konakatta.* (彼は行ったきり帰って来なかった) He has never returned *since* he left.

ki´riage·ru きりあげる (切り上げる) *vt.* (-age-te Ⓥ) 1 knock off; leave off; finish:
go-ji ni shigoto o kiriageru (5 時に仕事を切り上げる) *knock off* work at five.
2 raise; round up:
shoosuu-teñ ika o kiriageru (小数点以下を切り上げる) *raise* the decimals to the nearest whole number. (⇒ kirisuteru; shisha-gonyuu)
3 revalue:
tsuuka o juugo-paaseñto kiriageru (通貨を 15% 切り上げる) *revalue* the currency by fifteen percent.

ki´ridas·u きりだす (切り出す) *vi.*, *vt.* (-dash·i-; -das·a-; -dash·i-te

C) **1** begin to talk:
Kare wa yooyaku sono moñdai o kiridashita. (彼はようやくその問題を切り出した) He finally *broached* the matter.

2 cut down; log; quarry:
ki o kiridasu (木を切り出す) *cut down* a tree.

ki`rihana`s·u きりはなす (切り離す) *vt.* (-hanash·i·; -hanas·a·; -hanash·i-te C) cut off; separate.

ki`rikae·ru きりかえる (切り替える) *vt.* (-kae-te V) change; renew; switch:
chañneru o kirikaeru (チャンネルを切り替える) *change* the (TV) channel.

ki`rinuk·u きりぬく (切り抜く) *vt.* (-nuk·i·; -nuk·a·; -nu·i-te C) clip; cut out:
Sono kiji o shiñbuñ kara kirinuita. (その記事を新聞から切り抜いた) I *clipped* the article out of the newspaper.

ki`risage·ru きりさげる (切り下げる) *vt.* (-sage-te V) **1** cut; reduce:
nedañ o subete go-paaseñto kirisageru (値段をすべて5%切り下げる) *reduce* all prices by five percent.

2 devalue:
tsuuka o juugo-paaseñto kirisageru (通貨を15%切り下げる) *devalue* the currency by fifteen percent.

ki`risute·ru きりすてる (切り捨てる) *vt.* (-sute-te V) round down; cut off; omit:
hasuu o kirisuteru (端数を切り捨てる) *cut off* fractions. (⇨ kiriageru; shisha-gonyuu)

Ki`risuto キリスト *n.* Christ.

Ki`risuto-kyoo キリストきょう (基督教) *n.* Christianity:
Kirisuto-kyooto (キリスト教徒) a *Christian*.

ki`ritor·u きりとる (切り取る) *vt.* (-tor·i·; -tor·a·; -tot-te C) cut away [off]; clip:
ki no eda o kiritoru (木の枝を切り取る) *cut away* the branches of a tree.

ki`ritsu きりつ (規律) *n.* **1** rules; regulations:
kiritsu o mamoru [*yaburu*] (規律を守る[破る]) observe [break] the *rules*.

2 order; discipline.

ki`ritsume·ru きりつめる (切り詰める) *vt.* (-tsume-te V) cut down; reduce; shorten:
keehi o kiritsumeru (経費を切り詰める) *cut down* on expenses.

ki`ro キロ *n.* ★ Shortened form of '*kiromeetoru*' and '*kiroguramu*.'

ki`rogu`ramu キログラム *n.* kilogram. (⇨ kiro)

ki`roku きろく (記録) *n.* record; minutes.
kiroku suru (〜する) *vt.* record; write down: *kaigi no naiyoo o kiroku suru* (会議の内容を記録する) *record* the content of a meeting.

ki`rome`etoru キロメートル *n.* kilometer. (⇨ kiro)

ki`r·u[1] きる (切る) *vt.* (kir·i·; kir·a·; kit-te C) **1** cut; chop; slice; saw; shear:
Kanojo wa hoochoo de yubi o kitta. (彼女は包丁で指を切った) She *cut* her finger with a kitchen knife.

2 sever (relations):
Kare wa sono kai to eñ o kitta. (彼はその会と縁を切った) He *severed* his connection with the society. (⇨ kireru)

3 hang up (a telephone):
Deñwa o kiranai de kudasai. (電話を切らないでください) Please *do not hang up.* (⇨ kireru)

4 switch off:
deñki (*no suitchi*) *o kiru* (電気(のスイッチ)を切る) *switch off* the electricity.

5 punch (a ticket):
kippu o kitte morau (切符を切ってもらう) *get* one's ticket *punched.*

6 drain:
hooreñsoo no mizu o kiru (ほうれん草の水を切る) *drain* water from

spinach.

7 be less than...:
Kare wa hyaku-meetoru de juu-ichi-byoo o kitta. (彼は100メートルで11秒を切った) He *did* 100 meters *in less than* eleven seconds.

8 shuffle:
toranpu o kiru (トランプを切る) *shuffle* playing cards.

ki·ru² きる (着る) *vt.* (ki-te Ⅴ)
1 put on:
Kare wa oobaa o kinai de soto e deta. (彼はオーバーを着ないで外へ出た) He went out *without putting on* his overcoat. (⇨ kiseru)
2 wear; have on. ★ Used in 'kite iru.'
Yamada-san wa wafuku o kite ita. (山田さんは和服を着ていた) Miss Yamada *was wearing* Japanese clothes.

ki⸢seɴ きせん (汽船) *n.* steamer; steamship; steamboat.

ki⸢se·ru きせる (着せる) *vt.* (kise-te Ⅴ) dress; clothe:
kodomo ni wafuku o kiseru (子どもに和服を着せる) *dress* a child in Japanese style clothes. (⇨ kiru²)

ki⸢seꞮtsu きせつ (季節) *n.* season; time of the year.

ki⸢sha¹ きしゃ (記者) *n.* reporter; journalist.

ki⸢sha¹² きしゃ (汽車) *n.* train. (⇨ ressha; deɴsha)

ki⸢sha-kaꞮikeɴ きしゃかいけん (記者会見) *n.* press conference.

ki⸢shi¹ きし (岸) *n.* bank; shore; coast.

ki⸢shitsu きしつ (気質) *n.* disposition; temper; nature:
kimuzukashii [yasashii] kishitsu no otoko (気難しい[優しい]気質の男) a man of grumpy [affectionate] *disposition*.

ki⸢shoo¹ きしょう (気性) *n.* temper; disposition; nature:
Kare wa kishoo ga hageshii. (彼は気性が激しい) He has a fiery *temper*. (⇨ kishitsu)

ki⸢shoo² きしょう (気象) *n.* weath-er conditions.

ki⸢shoo³ きしょう (起床) *n.* getting up; rising.
kishoo suru (〜する) *vi.* rise from one's bed. (⇨ okiru)

ki⸢so¹ きそ (基礎) *n.* foundation; basis; base; basics. (⇨ kihoɴ)

ki⸢so¹ku きそく (規則) *n.* rule; regulations.

ki⸢soku-teki きそくてき (規則的) *a.n.* (〜 na, ni) regular; systematic:
kisoku-teki na seekatsu o suru (規則的な生活をする) lead a *well-regulated* life.

ki⸢so-teki きそてき (基礎的) *a.n.* (〜 na, ni) fundamental; basic; elementary:
kiso-teki na buɴpoo (基礎的な文法) *elementary* grammar.

ki⸢ssaꞮteɴ きっさてん (喫茶店) *n.* coffeehouse; coffee shop; tearoom.

ki⸢su¹u きすう (奇数) *n.* odd number(s). (↔ guusuu)

ki⸢ta きた (北) *n.* north; (〜 ni/e) northward. (↔ minami)

ki⸢tae¹·ru きたえる (鍛える) *vt.* (ki-tae-te Ⅴ) train; build up; strengthen:
wakai uchi ni karada o kitaeru (若いうちに体を鍛える) *harden* one's body while young.

ki⸢tai¹ きたい (期待) *n.* expectation; anticipation; hope:
kitai-hazure (期待外れ) a *disappointment*.
kitai suru (〜する) *vt.* count on; expect; anticipate; hope for.

ki⸢tai² きたい (気体) *n.* gas. (⇨ ekitai; kotai)

ki⸢taku きたく (帰宅) *n.* returning home.
kitaku suru (〜する) *vi.* return home. (⇨ kaeru¹)

ki⸢tana¹·i きたない (汚い) *a.* (-ku)
1 dirty; filthy; foul. (↔ kiree)
2 mean; low; dirty:
Ano hito wa o-kane ni kitanai. (あの人はお金に汚い) He is *mean* with

his money.
3 indecent; filthy; nasty:
kitanai *kotoba* (汚い言葉) *indecent*
language.

ki⌐tee きてい (規定) *n.* rule; regulation; stipulation.
kitee suru (〜する) *vt.* prescribe; provide. (⇨ sadameru)

ki⌐teñ きてん (起点) *n.* starting point. (⇨ shuuteñ)

ki⌐tsueñ きつえん (喫煙) *n.* smoking. (⇨ tabako)
kitsueñ suru (〜する) *vi.* have a smoke.

ki⌐tsu·i きつい *a.* (-ku) **1** tight:
Kono sukaato wa sukoshi kitsui.
(このスカートは少しきつい) This skirt
is a bit *tight.* (↔ yurui; yuruyaka)
2 hard; severe:
Kono-goro no samusa wa kitsui.
(この頃の寒さはきつい) The recent
cold weather has been *severe.*
3 stern; strong-minded:
kitsui *seekaku* (きつい性格) a *stern*
and *strong-minded* personality.

ki⌐tsune きつね (狐) *n.* fox.

ki⌐tte きって (切手) *n.* postage stamp.

ki⌐tto きっと *adv.* surely; without fail; undoubtedly:
Kare wa kitto *kimasu.* (彼はきっと来
ます) He will *certainly* come.
(⇨ kanarazu)

ki⌐wa⌐mete きわめて (極めて) *adv.*
(*formal*) extremely; exceedingly.

ki⌐yo⌐·i きよい (清い) *a.* (-ku) (*literary*) clean; pure:
kiyoku *suñda nagare* (清く澄んだ流
れ) a *crystal clear* stream.
(⇨ kiyoraka)

ki⌐yoo きよう (器用) *a.n.* (〜 na, ni) **1** skillful; handy; deft:
Kanojo wa tesaki ga kiyoo *da.* (彼
女は手先が器用だ) She is *good* with
her hands. (↔ bukiyoo)
2 clever: kiyoo *na hito* (器用な人)
a *clever* person.

ki⌐yo⌐raka きよらか (清らか) *a.n.*
(〜 na, ni) (*literary*) pure; clear;
noble:

kiyoraka *na hitomi* (清らかなひとみ)
bright, clear eyes. (⇨ kiyoi)

ki⌐zam·u きざむ (刻む) *vt.* (kizam·i·; kizam·a·; kizañ-de ⓒ)
1 mince; chop up:
tamanegi o kizamu (たまねぎを刻む)
chop up an onion.
2 carve; engrave.

ki⌐zetsu きぜつ (気絶) *n.* fainting; faint; swoon.
kizetsu suru (〜する) *vi.* faint:
Kanojo wa kizetsu *shite taoreta.*
(彼女は気絶して倒れた) She fell *in a
faint.*

ki⌐zoku きぞく (貴族) *n.* aristocracy; noble; nobleman; peer; peeress.

ki⌐zu¹ きず (傷) *n.* injury; wound; hurt; cut.

ki⌐zu² きず (疵) *n.* crack; flaw; bruise; defect.
kizu o tsukeru (〜をつける) damage; ruin; spoil.

ki⌐zu⌐kai きづかい (気遣い) *n.* worry; fear:
Kare ga shippai suru kizukai *wa
arimaseñ.* (彼が失敗する気遣いはあり
ません) There is no *fear* of his
failing. (⇨ kizukau)

ki⌐zuka⌐·u きづかう (気遣う) *vt.*
(kizuka·i·; kizukaw·a·; kizukat-
te ⓒ) be anxious about; worry
about:
hito no añpi o kizukau (人の安否を
気づかう) *be anxious* about a person's safety. (⇨ kizukai)

ki⌐zu⌐k·u¹ きづく (気付く) *vi.* (ki-
zuk·i·; kizuk·a·; kizu·i-te ⓒ)
become aware; notice; find out:
buñshoo no ayamari ni kizuku (文
章の誤りに気づく) *notice* a mistake
in a sentence.

ki⌐zu⌐k·u² きづく (築く) *vt.* (kizu-
k·i·; kizuk·a·; kizu·i-te ⓒ)
build; construct; erect:
ooki-na zaisañ o kizuku (大きな財産
を築く) *build up* a large fortune.

ki⌐zuna きずな (絆) *n.* bond; ties:
Futari wa tsuyoi yuujoo no kizuna
de musubarete ita. (二人は強い友情

のきずなで結ばれていた) The two of them were bound together by firm *ties* of friendship.

ki┌zutsuke┐·ru きずつける(傷付ける) *vt.* (-tsuke-te Ⅴ) wound; injure; hurt (physically or mentally). (⇨ kizutsuku)

ki┌zutsu┐k·u きずつく(傷付く) *vi.* (-tsuk·i-; -tsuk·a-; -tsu·i-te ⒸC) be [get] injured; be [get] hurt (usually mentally):
Sono uwasa de kanojo no kokoro wa kizutsuita. (そのうわさで彼女の心は傷ついた) She *was deeply hurt* by the rumor. (⇨ kizutsukeru)

ko こ(子) *n.* 1 child; son; daughter: ★ Usually used with a modifier.
otoko-no-ko (男の子) a *boy* / oñna-no-ko (女の子) a *girl*. (⇨ kodomo)
2 (of animals) the young:
inu no ko (犬の子) a *puppy* / neko no ko (猫の子) a *kitten*. (↔ oya)

ko-[1] こ(小) *pref.* small; little:
ko-*tori* (小鳥) a *little* bird / ko-*zeni* (小銭) *small* change / ko-*same* (小雨) *light* rain.

ko┐-[2] こ(故) *pref.* the late; the deceased:
ko-*Yamada-shi* (故山田氏) *the late* Mr. Yamada.

-ko[1] こ(個) *suf.* piece; item: ★ Counter for small objects.
tamago sañ-ko (卵3個) *three eggs* / sekkeñ go-ko (石けん5個) *five cakes* of soap.

-ko[2] こ(戸) *suf.* house: nijuk-ko no ie (20戸の家) twenty *houses*.

-ko[3] こ(粉) *suf.* powder; flour:
karee-ko (カレー粉) curry *powder* / komugi-ko (小麦粉) wheat *flour*.

-ko[4] こ(湖) *suf.* lake:
Kawaguchi-ko (河口湖) *Lake* Kawaguchi.

ko┌ba┐m·u こばむ(拒む) *vt.* (kobam·i-; kobam·a-; kobañ-de ⒸC) refuse (a demand, request); decline. (⇨ kotowaru)

ko┌bore┐·ru こぼれる(零れる) *vi.* (kobore-te Ⅴ) (of fluid, grains, etc.) fall; slop; spill:
Kanojo no me kara namida ga koboreta. (彼女の目から涙がこぼれた) Tears *fell* from her eyes. (⇨ kobosu)

ko┌bo┐s·u こぼす(零す) *vt.* (kobosh·i-; kobos·a-; kobosh·i-te ⒸC)
1 spill (fluid, grains, etc.); shed; drop. (⇨ koboreru)
2 complain; grumble:
Kanojo wa itsu-mo kodomo no koto o koboshite iru. (彼女はいつも子どものことをこぼしている) She *is* always *grumbling* about her children.

ko┌chira こちら *n.* 1 this place; this way; here: ★ Refers to a direction or a place close to the speaker. More polite than 'koko' and 'kotchi.'
Kochira ga o-tearai desu. (こちらがお手洗いです) *This* is the bathroom. (⇨ mukoo[1])
2 this thing; this person: ★ More polite than 'kore.'
Kochira wa hoñjitsu no tokubetsu ryoori desu. (こちらは本日の特別料理です) *This* is today's special dish.
3 I; we:
Ato de kochira kara moo ichido o-deñwa itashimasu. (あとでこちらからもう一度お電話いたします) *I* will call you back again later. (⇨ achira; dochira; sochira)

ko┌choo こちょう(誇張) *n.* exaggeration; overstatement.
kochoo suru (～する) *vt.* exaggerate; overstate.

ko┐dai こだい(古代) *n.* ancient times; remote ages.

ko┌doku こどく(孤独) *n.* loneliness; solitude.
— *a.n.* (～ na, ni) lonely; solitary:
kodoku na seekatsu o suru (孤独な生活をする) lead a *solitary* life.

ko┌domo こども(子供) *n.* child; boy; girl. (↔ otona) (⇨ ko)

ko┐e こえ(声) *n.* 1 human voice; cry:

koe o dashite, *hoñ o yomu* (声を出して、本を読む) read a book *aloud*.
2 sound; note; song:
mushi no koe o kiku (虫の声を聞く) listen to the *singing* of insects.
3 opinion; view:
kokumiñ no koe (国民の声) the *opinions* of the people.

ko⌐e¬ru[1] こえる (越える) *vi.* (koe-te ⊻) go beyond; go over:
yama o koeru (山を越える) *go over* a mountain / *kawa o koeru* (川を越える) *cross* a river.

ko⌐e¬ru[2] こえる (超える) *vi.* (koe-te ⊻) exceed; be more than:
Kanojo wa sañjuu o koete iru. (彼女は00を超えている) *She is more than* thirty. (⇨ kosu[2])

ko⌐e¬ru[3] こえる (肥える) *vi.* (koe-te ⊻) **1** be fertile:
Kono tochi wa koete iru. (この土地は肥えている) This soil *is fertile*.
2 grow fat; put on flesh.
... ga koete iru (…が肥えている) have a delicate…: *me ga koete iru* (目が肥えている) *have an eye for* (beauty).

ko⌐fuñ こふん (古墳) *n.* ancient tomb; old mound. (⇨ APP. 9)

ko⌐ga¬s·u こがす (焦がす) *vt.* (kogash-i-; kogas·a-; kogash·i-te ⊡) burn; singe; scorch:
airoñ de shatsu o kogasu (アイロンでシャツを焦がす) *scorch* one's shirt with an iron. (⇨ kogeru)

ko⌐gata こがた (小型) *n.* small size; pocket size:
kogata no kuruma (小型の車) a *small* car / *kogata no kamera* (小型のカメラ) a *pocket* camera. (⇨ oogata; chuugata)

ko⌐ge¬ru こげる (焦げる) *vi.* (koge-te ⊻) burn; scorch:
Mochi ga makkuro ni kogete shimatta. (餅が真っ黒に焦げてしまった) The rice cake *has been burned* black. (⇨ kogasu)

ko⌐gi¬tte こぎって (小切手) *n.* check; cheque: *kogitte de harau* (小切手で払う) pay by *check*.

ko⌐goe こごえ (小声) *n.* low voice; whisper. (↔ oogoe)

ko⌐goe·ru こごえる (凍える) *vi.* (kogoe-te ⊻) freeze; be frozen:
Samukute, te ga kogoeta. (寒くて、手が凍えた) My hands *were* numb with the cold.

ko⌐g·u こぐ (漕ぐ) *vt.* (kog-i-; kog·a-; ko·i-de ⊡) **1** row; paddle:
booto o kogu (ボートをこぐ) *row* a boat.
2 pedal; swing: *jiteñsha o kogu* (自転車をこぐ) *pedal* a bicycle.

ko⌐i[1] こい (濃い) *a.* (-ku) **1** (of color) dark; deep:
koi iro (濃い色) a *dark* color / *koi aka* (濃い赤) *deep* red. (↔ usui)
2 (of taste, density, etc.) thick; strong; dense:
Ani wa hige ga koi. (兄はひげが濃い) My brother has a *thick* beard. (↔ usui)
3 (of degree) strong:
Kare ga sore o shita utagai ga koi. (彼がそれをした疑いが濃い) The suspicion he did that is *strong*.

ko⌐i[2] こい (恋) *n.* love:
koi ni ochiru (恋に落ちる) fall in *love*. (⇨ ai; aisuru)

ko⌐i[3] こい (故意) *n.* intention; deliberation; purpose:
Watashi wa koi ni okureta wake de wa arimaseñ. (私は故意に遅れたわけではありません) I did not come late *intentionally*. (⇨ waza-to)

ko⌐i[4] こい (鯉) *n.* carp. (⇨ koi-nobori)

ko⌐ibito こいびと (恋人) *n.* boyfriend; girlfriend; love. ★ Refers to a steady male or female companion. (⇨ aijiñ)

ko⌐ino¬bori こいのぼり (鯉のぼり) *n.* carp streamer. ★ Carp-shaped streamers traditionally flown on Children's Day (May 5).

ko⌐ishi こいし (小石) *n.* small stone [rock]. (⇨ ishi[1])

ko⌐ishi¬·i こいしい (恋しい) *a.* (-ku) miss; long for; beloved:
Kokyoo ga koishiku natte kita. (故

郷が恋しくなってきた) I have come to *long for* my hometown.

ko⌐is·u⌐ru こいする (恋する) *vt.* (ko-ish·i-; koish·i-; koish·i-te ①) love; fall in love. (⇨ koi²)

ko⌐ji こじ (孤児) *n.* orphan.

ko⌐jin¹ こじん (個人) *n.* 1 individual:
kojiñ *no jiyuu* [*keñri*] (個人の自由 [権利]) the freedom [rights] of the *individual*.
2 each person:
Mochimono wa kojiñ kojiñ *de chuui shite kudasai.* (持ち物は個人個人で注意してください) *Each person* please take care of his or her possessions.

ko⌐jin² こじん (故人) *n.* the deceased. (⇨ ko²-)

ko⌐jin-teki こじんてき (個人的) *a.n.* (~ na, ni) personal; private:
Kare wa kojiñ-teki *na riyuu de tsutome o yamemashita.* (彼は個人的な理由で勤めをやめました) He quit his job for *private* reasons.

ko⌐ke¹ こけ (苔) *n.* moss.

ko⌐kka¹ こっか (国家) *n.* nation; state; country.

ko⌐kka² こっか (国歌) *n.* national anthem.

ko⌐kka³ こっか (国花) *n.* national flower.

ko⌐kkai こっかい (国会) *n.* national assembly; legislature of a nation; the Diet. ★ The Japanese Diet is made up of the House of Representatives (*Shuugiiñ*) and the House of Councilors (*Sañgiiñ*). (⇨ Shuugiiñ; Sañgiiñ)

ko⌐kkee こっけい (滑稽) *a.n.* (~ na, ni) funny; humorous; comical; ridiculous:
kokkee *na koto o iu* (滑稽なことを言う) say something *foolishly comical.*

ko⌐kki こっき (国旗) *n.* national flag.

ko⌐kkoo こっこう (国交) *n.* diplomatic relations; national friendship:

kokkoo *o musubu* (国交を結ぶ) establish *diplomatic relations.*

ko⌐kkyoo こっきょう (国境) *n.* national border; frontier of a country.

ko⌐ko¹ ここ (此処) *n.* 1 here; this place: ★ Refers to a place close to the speaker.
Koko *kara eki made dono kurai arimasu ka?* (ここから駅までどのくらいありますか) How far is it from *here* to the station?
2 here; this place: ★ Used when the speaker indicates a location by way of explanation, etc.
Kono chizu no koko *ga watashi-tachi no machi desu.* (この地図のここが私たちの町です) *This part* of the map is our town.
3 this: ★ Refers to something the speaker has just mentioned or intends to mention.
Kyoo no koogi wa koko *made desu.* (きょうの講義はここまでです) *This* concludes my lecture for today.
4 next; past: ★ Refers to a period of time.
Kare wa koko *shibaraku byooki deshita.* (彼はここしばらく病気でした) He had been sick for some time *past.*
5 so far: ★ Refers to a time in the present.
Koko *made wa subete umaku iki-mashita.* (ここまではすべてうまくいきました) *So far* everything has gone well. (⇨ asoko; doko; soko¹)

ko⌐ko² ここ (個々) *n.* (*formal*) individual; each:
Sore wa koko *no hito no sekiniñ desu.* (それは個々の人の責任です) *Each individual* person is responsible for it.

ko⌐kochi ここち (心地) *n.* feeling; sensation:
Kono isu wa kokochi *ga yoi.* (このいすは心地がよい) This chair *is comfortable.*

ko⌐koku ここく (故国) *n.* homeland [country].

ko⌈konoka⌉ ここのか（九日）*n.*
nine days; the ninth day of the
month. (⇨ APP. 5)

ko⌈ko⌉notsu ここのつ（九つ）*n.*
nine. ★ Used when counting.
((⇨ ku¹; kyuu¹; APP. 3))

ko⌈ko⌉ro こころ（心）*n.* heart;
mind; spirit:
kokoro o kimeru（心を決める）make
up one's *mind*. (⇨ shiñ²)

kokoro kara（～から）from the
bottom of one's heart.

kokoro o utsu（～を打つ）strike
home.

ko⌈koroa⌉tari こころあたり（心当た
り）*n.* idea; clue:
Kare ga doko ni iru ka kokoroa-
tari wa arimasu ka?（彼がどこにいる
か心当たりはありますか）Do you have
any *idea* where he is?

ko⌈koroboso⌉・i こころぼそい（心細
い）*a.* (-ku) lonely; helpless; uncertain:
kokorobosoku omou（心細く思う）
feel *helpless*.

ko⌈koro⌉e こころえ（心得）*n.*
knowledge; skill:
Kanojo wa ikebana no kokoroe ga
arimasu.（彼女は生け花の心得がありま
す）She has a good *knowledge* of
flower arrangement.

ko⌈koroe⌉・ru こころえる（心得る）
vt. (kokoroe-te Ⅴ) know; be
aware:
Sono heñ no jijoo wa yoku koko-
roete imasu.（その辺の事情はよく心得
ています）I *am well aware* of that
situation.

ko⌈korogake⌉ こころがけ（心掛け）*n.*
care; prudence; intention:
Kare wa itsu-mo kokorogake ga
yoi.（彼はいつも心がけがよい）He *is*
always *prudent*. (⇨ kokoroga-
keru)

ko⌈korogake⌉・ru こころがける（心
掛ける）*vt.* (-gake-te Ⅴ) try; keep
in mind; do one's best.
(⇨ kokorogake)

ko⌈korogurushi⌉・i こころくるしい

（心苦しい）*a.* (-ku) feel sorry; painful. (⇨ sumanai)

ko⌈koromi⌉ こころみ（試み）*n.* trial; attempt; test:
kokoromi ni sore o yatte miru（試
みにそれをやってみる）give it a *try*.
(⇨ kokoromiru)

ko⌈koromi⌉・ru こころみる（試みる）
vt. (-mi-te Ⅴ) try; attempt; experiment. (⇨ kokoromi; kuwadateru)

ko⌈koromochi⌉ こころもち（心持ち）
adv. a little; a bit; slightly:
Kyoo wa kokoromochi atatakai.
（きょうは心持ち暖かい）It is *a bit*
warm today.

ko⌈koroyo⌉・i こころよい（快い）*a.*
(-ku) pleasant; agreeable; de-
lightful.

ko⌈korozashi⌉ こころざし（志）*n.*
one's will; resolution; ambition:
kokorozashi o tateru（志を立てる）
make up one's *mind*.
(⇨ kokorozasu)

ko⌈koroza⌉s・u こころざす（志す）*vt.*
(-zash・i-; -zas・a-; -zash・i-te Ⅽ)
intend; aim; plan:
Kare wa sakka o kokorozashite
iru.（彼は作家を志している）He *has
set his heart* on becoming a writer. (⇨ kokorozashi)

ko⌈korozu⌉kai こころづかい（心遣
い）*n.* thoughtfulness; consideration.

ko⌈korozuyo⌉・i こころづよい（心強
い）*a.* (-ku) reassuring:
Anata ga ite kureru to kokorozu-
yoi.（あなたがいてくれると心強い）Your
presence *reassures* me.

ko⌈kubañ こくばん（黒板）*n.*
blackboard.

ko⌈kuboo こくぼう（国防）*n.* national defense.

ko⌈kudo こくど（国土）*n.* country; territory; land area.

ko⌈ku⌉gai こくがい（国外）*n.* outside the country; abroad; overseas. (↔ kunai) (⇨ kaigai)

ko⌈kugo こくご（国語）*n.* 1 Japanese language (as an academic

subject in Japan). (⇨ **Nihoñgo**)
2 language; one's mother tongue.
(⇨ **geñgo**)

ko⸢kuhaku こくはく (告白) *n.* confession; declaration.
kokuhaku suru (～する) *vt.* confess; declare.

ko⸢kuhoo こくほう (国宝) *n.* National Treasure.

ko⸢kumee こくめい (国名) *n.* name of a country.

ko⸢kumiñ こくみん (国民) *n.* nation; people; citizen:
kokumiñ *no shukujitsu* (国民の祝日) a *national* holiday. (⇨ **APP. 6**)

ko⸢kumu-da¹ijiñ こくむだいじん (国務大臣) *n.* minister of state.

ko⸢ku¹nai こくない (国内) *n.* inside the country; domestic; home:
Kare wa Nihoñ kokunai *o jiteñsha de ryokoo shita.* (彼は日本国内を自転車で旅行した) He has traveled *around Japan* by bicycle.
(↔ **kokugai**; **kaigai**)

ko⸢kuritsu こくりつ (国立) *n.* national; state:
kokuritsu-*daigaku* (国立大学) a *national* university / kokuritsu-*kooeñ* (国立公園) a *national* park.

ko⸢kusai- こくさい (国際) *pref.* international: kokusai-*kaigi* (国際会議) an *international* conference.

ko⸢kusaika こくさいか (国際化) *n.* internationalization.
kokusaika suru (～する) *vi.* internationalize: Kono moñdai wa kokusaika shi-soo da. (この問題は国際化しそうだ) This problem will *become a matter of international concern.*

ko⸢kusai-teki こくさいてき (国際的) *a.n.* (～ na, ni) international: kokusai-teki *ni katsuyaku shite iru pianisuto* (国際的に活躍しているピアニスト) a pianist who is active *on the world stage.*

ko⸢kusañ こくさん (国産) *n.* domestic production; home-pro-

duced:
kokusañ-*sha* (国産車) a *domestically produced* car.

ko⸢kuseki こくせき (国籍) *n.* (country of) nationality; citizenship:
Kare no kokuseki *wa Nihoñ desu.* (彼の国籍は日本です) His *country of nationality* is Japan.

ko⸢kuyuu こくゆう (国有) *n.* national; state:
kokuyuu-*chi* (国有地) *state-owned* land / kokuyuu-*riñ* (国有林) a *state* forest.

ko⸢kyoo こきょう (故郷) *n.* one's home; one's birthplace; hometown:
Watashi no kokyoo wa Hokkaidoo desu. (私の故郷は北海道です) I *come from* Hokkaido.

ko⸢kyuu こきゅう (呼吸) *n.*
1 breathing; respiration:
Byooniñ wa kokyuu *ga arakatta.* (病人は呼吸が荒かった) The patient was *breathing* hard. (⇨ **iki¹**)
2 knack; trick; craft:
Watashi wa yatto sono shigoto no kokyuu ga nomikometa. (私はやっとその仕事の呼吸が飲み込めた) Finally I got the *hang* of how to do the work.
3 harmony:
Shikisha to eñsoosha no kokyuu wa pittari atte ita. (指揮者と演奏者の呼吸はぴったり合っていた) The conductor and musicians were in perfect *harmony.*
kokyuu suru (～する) *vi., vt.* breathe; respire.

ko⸢ma¹ka こまか (細か) *a.n.* (～na, ni) fine; attentive; detailed:
komaka *na chuui* (細かな注意) *meticulous* care / komaka *ni shiraberu* (細かに調べる) examine *minutely.* (⇨ **komakai**)

ko⸢maka¹·i こまかい (細かい) *a.* (-ku) **1** (of grains, particles, etc.) very small; fine. (↔ **arai²**)
(⇨ **komaka**)
2 (of money) small:

señ-eñ satsu o komakaku suru (千円札を細かくする) *change* a 1000-yen bill.

3 detailed; careful:
Komakai koto wa ato de setsumee shimasu. (細かいことはあとで説明します) I will explain the *details* later.

4 minor; trifling:
komakai koto de kuyokuyo suru (細かいことでくよくよする) worry about *trifling* matters.

5 thrifty; stingy:
Kare wa kane ni komakai. (彼は金に細かい) He is *tight* with money.

ko⌐ma·r·u こまる (困る) *vi.* (komar·i-; komar·a-; komat-te C)
1 be in an awkward position, be in a fix; have a hard time.
2 be in financial difficulties; be hard up.

ko⌐me こめ (米) *n.* rice.
★ With '*o-*' in polite speech.

ko⌐me·ru こめる (込める) *vt.* (kome-te V) load:
juu ni tama o komeru (銃に弾を込める) *load* a gun.

ko⌐mori⌐uta こもりうた (子守歌) *n.* lullaby.

ko⌐m·u こむ (込む・混む) *vi., vt.* (kom·i-; kom·a-; koñ-de C) be crowded; be packed; be full; be jammed. (⇨ koñzatsu)

ko⌐mu⌐gi こむぎ (小麦) *n.* wheat.

ko⌐mugiko こむぎこ (小麦粉) *n.* wheat flour.

ko⌐ñ こん (紺) *n.* dark blue; navy blue.

ko⌐ñ- こん (今) *pref.* this; the present; the coming:
koñ-*nendo* (今年度) *this* year / koñ-*seeki* (今世紀) *the present* century.

ko⌐na こな (粉) *n.* powder; flour; meal.

ko⌐naida こないだ *n.* (*informal*) recently; the other day:
Sore wa tsui konaida *no dekigoto da.* (それはついこないだの出来事だ) That is a very *recent* event.
(⇨ kono-aida)

ko⌐ñbañ こんばん (今晩) *n.* this evening; tonight. (⇨ koñya)

ko⌐ñbañ wa こんばんは (今晩は)
Good evening.

ko⌐ñbu こんぶ (昆布) *n.* sea tangle; kelp. ★ Also called '*kobu.*'

ko⌐ñchuu こんちゅう (昆虫) *n.* insect; bug. (⇨ mushi)

ko⌐ñdate こんだて (献立) *n.* menu: *kyoo no* koñdate (きょうの献立) today's *menu*.

ko⌐ñdo こんど (今度) *n.* **1** this time; now:
Koñdo wa kimi no bañ desu. (今度は君の番です) *Now*, it's your turn.

2 next time:
Koñdo wa itsu kimasu ka? (今度はいつ来ますか) When are you coming *next time*?

3 recently:
Kare wa koñdo *hoñ o dashita.* (彼は今度本を出した) He has *recently* published a book.

ko⌐ñgetsu こんげつ (今月) *n.* this month. (⇨ señgetsu; raigetsu)

ko⌐ñgo こんご (今後) *n., adv.* after this; from now on; in the future.

koñgo tomo (〜とも) continually:
Koñgo tomo yoroshiku o-negai itashimasu. (今後ともよろしくお願いいたします) I'm looking forward to enjoying good relations with you.
★ Set phrase used upon meeting someone for the first time.

ko⌐ñgoo こんごう (混合) *n.* mixing; mixture.

koñgoo suru (〜する) *vi., vt.* mix; mingle; blend. (⇨ majiru, mazeru)

ko⌐ñjoo こんじょう (根性) *n.* spirit; guts: *koñjoo no aru otoko* (根性のある男) a man of *spirit*.

ko⌐ñkai こんかい (今回) *n.* this time:
Koñkai wa nyuushoo shita hito ga inakatta. (今回は入賞した人がいなかった) There was nobody who won the prize *this time*.

ko⌐ñku⌐uru コンクール *n.* contest; competition.

ko⌐nkyo こんきょ (根拠) n.
1 basis; foundation; ground:
Sono uwasa wa mattaku koñkyo *ga arimaseñ.* (そのうわさは全く根拠がありません) The rumor is completely without *foundation*.
2 reason:
Kare ga soo iu no ni wa koñkyo *ga aru.* (彼がそう言うのには根拠がある) He has his *reasons* for saying so.

ko⌐nmo⌐ri こんもり adv. (~ to; ~ suru) thick; dense:
koñmori to shita *mori* (こんもりとした森) *thick* woods.

ko⌐nna こんな attrib. this; like this: ★ Refers to something close to the speaker.
Koñna *sakana wa mita koto ga arimaseñ.* (こんな魚は見たことがありません) I have never seen a fish *like this.* (⇨ añna; doñna; soñna)

ko⌐nnañ こんなん (困難) n. difficulty; hardship; trouble:
koñnañ *ni taeru* (困難に耐える) endure *hardships*.
— a.n. (~ na, ni) difficult; hard; troublesome:
Kono moñdai wa kaiketsu ga koñnañ *desu.* (この問題は解決が困難です) It is *difficult* to solve this problem.

ko⌐nna ni こんなに adv. this; like this; so:
Koñna ni *osoku made doko ni ita no?* (こんなに遅くまでどこにいたの) Where have you been until *so* late? (⇨ añna ni; doñna ni; soñna ni)

ko⌐nnichi こんにち (今日) n. today; the present day:
koñnichi *no sekai* (今日の世界) the world of *today.* (⇨ hoñjitsu; kyoo)

ko⌐nnichi wa こんにちは (今日は) Good day; Good morning; Good afternoon; Hello.

ko⌐nnyaku こんにゃく n. devil's tongue. ★ Jelly-like food made from the starch of devil's tongue root.

ko⌐no この (此の) attrib. **1** this: ★ Refers to a person or thing that is close to the speaker.
Kono *fairu o tana ni modoshite kudasai.* (このファイルを棚に戻してください) Please put *this* file back on the shelf.
2 this: ★ Refers to a time in the immediate future.
Kono *natsu-yasumi wa doko-ka e ikimasu ka?* (この夏休みはどこかへ行きますか) Are you going anywhere *this* summer vacation?
3 this: ★ Introduces something as a subject of conversation.
Kono *koto wa dare ni mo iwanai de kudasai.* (このことはだれにも言わないでください) Please don't tell anybody about *this.* (⇨ ano; dono; sono)

ko⌐no-aida このあいだ (此の間) n. the other day; some time ago; recently: ★ *informal* = konaida.
Kono-aida *wa o-sewa ni narimashita.* (この間はお世話になりました) Thank you for the kindness I received *the other day.* (⇨ konomae)

ko⌐no-goro このごろ (此の頃) adv. (~ no) now; these days; recently. (⇨ chikagoro; saikiñ)

ko⌐no-ma⌐e このまえ (此の前) n. the other day; last; the last time:
Kono-mae *no kaigi ni wa demaseñ deshita.* (この前の会議には出ませんでした) I did not attend the *last* meeting. (⇨ kono-aida)

ko⌐no-mama このまま (此の儘) n. the present state; as it is; as they are:
Kono shorui wa kono-mama *koko ni oite oite kudasai.* (この書類はこのままここに置いておいてください) Please leave these papers here *just as they are.* (⇨ mama)

ko⌐nomashi⌐i このましい (好ましい) a. (-ku) good; desirable; favorable: (⇨ nozomashii)
Kitsueñ wa keñkoo-joo konomashiku *nai.* (喫煙は健康上好ましくない)

Smoking is not *good* for the health.

ko˞nomi¹ このみ (好み) *n*. liking; taste; fancy:
Kono nekutai wa watashi no konomi ni atte iru. (このネクタイは私の好みに合っている) This tie is to my *taste*. (⇨ konomu)

ko˞no˩m·u このむ (好む) *vt*. (konom·i-; konom·a-; konoñ-de C) like; prefer. ★ '*suki da* [*desu*]' is more common. (⇨ konomi)

ko˞no˩-tabi このたび (此の度) *n*. (*formal*) this (present; previous) time [occasion]:
Watashi wa kono-tabi Shiñgapooru ni teñkiñ ni narimashita. (私はこの度シンガポールに転勤となりました) I have been transferred to Singapore *this time*. (⇨ koñdo)

ko˞no-tsugi¹ このつぎ (此の次) *n*. next:
Kono-tsugi no deñsha ni noroo. (この次の電車に乗ろう) Let's take the *next* train.

ko˞no-ue このうえ (此の上) *n*. more; further; in addition to this.
kono-ue (mo) nai (~(も)ない) most; greatest: kono-ue mo nai *kooee* (この上もない光栄) the *greatest* honor.

ko˞ñpoñ こんぽん (根本) *n*. foundation; basis; root.

ko˞ñpoñ-teki こんぽんてき (根本的) *a.n.* (~ na, ni) fundamental; basic.

ko˞ñrañ こんらん (混乱) *n*. confusion; disorder; chaos.
koñrañ suru (~する) *vi*. be confused; be mixed up: *Jishiñ no tame ressha no daiya ga koñrañ shita.* (地震のため列車のダイヤが混乱した) The train schedule *was disrupted* because of the earthquake. (⇨ midareru)

ko˞ñseñto コンセント *n*. electrical outlet; wall socket.

ko˞ñshuu こんしゅう (今週) *n*. this week. (⇨ señshuu)

ko˞ñya こんや (今夜) *n*. this evening; tonight. (⇨ koñbañ)

ko˞ñyaku こんやく (婚約) *n*. marriage engagement.
koñyaku suru (~する) *vi*. get engaged.

ko˞ñzatsu こんざつ (混雑) *n*. congestion; jam.
koñzatsu suru (~する) *vi*. be crowded; be jammed. (⇨ komu)

ko˞o こう (斯う) *adv*. **1** this; like this: ★ Refers to something close to the speaker.
Koo atsukute wa gaishutsu shitaku nai. (こう暑くては外出したくない) I don't want to go out in *such* heat.
2 this: ★ Refers to something just mentioned or about to be mentioned.
Kono hoñ ni wa koo kaite arimasu. (この本にはこう書いてあります) This book says *as follows*: (⇨ aa¹; doo¹; soo¹)

-koo こう (港) *suf*. port; harbor:
Yokohama-koo (横浜港) Yokohama *Harbor* / *Niigata*-koo (新潟港) the *port* of Niigata.

ko˞oba こうば (工場) *n*. factory; workshop. ★ Refers to a small factory, often under private management. (⇨ koojoo¹)

ko˞obai こうばい (勾配) *n*. slope; grade; slant:
kyuu na koobai no yama-michi (急な勾配の山道) a mountain path with a steep *slope*.

ko˞obañ こうばん (交番) *n*. police box. (⇨ keesatsu)

ko˞obutsu¹ こうぶつ (好物) *n*. one's favorite food.

ko˞obutsu² こうぶつ (鉱物) *n*. mineral.

ko˞ocha こうちゃ (紅茶) *n*. black tea. (⇨ o-cha)

ko˞ochi¹ コーチ *n*. coach.
koochi suru (~する) *vt*. coach (a team).

ko˞ochi² こうち (耕地) *n*. cultivated land; arable land.

ko'ochi[3] こうち (高地) n. highlands; upland. (↔ teechi)

ko'ochoo[1] こうちょう (好調) a.n. (~ na, ni) in good shape [condition]; favorable; satisfactory. ((↔ fuchoo))

ko'ochoo[2] こうちょう (校長) n. principal; headmaster; headmistress.

ko'odai こうだい (広大) a.n. (~ na) extensive; vast:
koodai na sabaku (広大な砂漠) an extensive desert.

ko'odeñ こうでん (香典) n. monetary offering to a departed soul.

ko'odo[1] コード n. electrical cord; flex.

ko'odo[2] こうど (高度) n. height; altitude:
koodo goseñ-meetoru (高度5千メートル) a height of 5,000 meters.

ko'odo[3] こうど (高度) a.n. (~ na/no, ni) advanced; highly developed:
koodo ni hattatsu shita kagaku-gijutsu (高度に発達した科学技術) scientific technology which has developed to a high level.

ko'odo[4] こうど (硬度) n. hardness.

ko'odoo[1] こうどう (行動) n. act; action; behavior; conduct.
koodoo suru (~する) vi. act; behave; conduct oneself.

ko'odoo[2] こうどう (講堂) n. lecture hall; auditorium; assembly hall.

ko'oeñ[1] こうえん (公園) n. park; public playground.

ko'oeñ[2] こうえん (講演) n. lecture; speech; talk.
kooeñ (o) suru (~(を)する) vi. give a lecture; make a speech. ((⇒ eñzetsu))

ko'oeñ[3] こうえん (公演) n. public performance.
kooeñ suru (~する) vt. perform; present (a play). ((⇒ jooeñ))

ko'oeñ[4] こうえん (後援) n. support; sponsorship:
kooeñ-kai (後援会) a supporters'
association; a fan club.
kooeñ suru (~する) vt. support; sponsor.

ko'ofu こうふ (交付) n. issue; grant.
koofu suru (~する) vt. issue (a passport); grant.

ko'ofuku こうふく (幸福) n. happiness; fortune.
— a.n. (~ na, ni) happy; fortunate. ((⇒ shiawase))

ko'ofuñ こうふん (興奮) n. excitement; stimulation.
koofuñ suru (~する) vi. be [get] excited.

ko'ogai[1] こうがい (郊外) n. suburbs; outskirts:
Kare wa koogai no ie ni hikko-shita. (彼は郊外の家に引っ越した) He moved to a house on the outskirts of town. ((⇒ shigai)[2])

ko'ogai[2] こうがい (公害) n. pollution; public nuisance.

ko'ogaku こうがく (高額) n. large sum of money:
Kare wa koogaku no kifu o shita. (彼は高額の寄付をした) He made a large contribution. ((↔ teegaku)[2])

ko'ogeehiñ こうげいひん (工芸品) n. craftwork.

ko'ogeki こうげき (攻撃) n. attack; criticism; offensive.
koogeki suru (~する) vt. attack; criticize. ((↔ boogyo; shubi))

ko'ogeñ こうげん (高原) n. plateau; tableland; highlands.

ko'ogi[1] こうぎ (抗議) n. protest; objection.
koogi suru (~する) vi. protest; object.

ko'ogi[2] こうぎ (講義) n. lecture.
koogi (o) suru (~(を)する) vt. give a lecture; lecture.

ko'ogo こうご (口語) n. spoken [colloquial] language:
koogo-tai (口語体) colloquial style. ((↔ buñgo))

ko'ogo ni こうごに (交互に) adv. by [in] turns; alternately:
Futari wa koogo ni keebi ni tsuite

ita. (二人は交互に警備についていた) The two persons were on guard *in turns*.

ko⌐ogo⌐o こうごう (皇后) *n.* empress:

Koogoo *Heeka* (皇后陛下) Her Majesty the *Empress*. (⇨ teñnoo)

ko⌐ogu こうぐ (工具) *n.* tool; implement.

ko⌐ogyoo¹ こうぎょう (工業) *n.* industry: koogyoo-chitai (工業地帯) an *industrial* district.

ko⌐ogyoo² こうぎょう (鉱業) *n.* mining (industry).

ko⌐ohai こうはい (後輩) *n.* one's junior; underclassman: *Watashi wa kare no ichi-neñ* koohai *desu.* (私は彼の一年後輩です) I am his *junior* by a year. (↔ señpai)

ko⌐ohaku こうはく (紅白) *n.* red and white.

ko⌐ohañ こうはん (後半) *n.* second [latter] half. (↔ zeñhañ)

ko⌐ohee こうへい (公平) *n.* fairness; impartiality:

— *a.n.* (~ na, ni) fair, just; impartial: koohee *na saibañ* (公平な裁判) a *fair* trial. (↔ fukoohee)

ko⌐ohi⌐i コーヒー (咖啡) *n.* coffee: koohii *o ireru* [*nomu*] (コーヒーを入れる[飲む]) make [drink] *coffee*.

ko⌐oho こうほ (候補) *n.* **1** candidacy; candidature; candidate: kooho ni tatsu (候補に立つ) run [*stand*] *for election*.
2 favorite:
Kare no chiimu wa yuushoo kooho *da.* (彼のチームは優勝候補だ) His team is the top *favorite*.

ko⌐ohoo¹ こうほう (広報) *n.* public information; public relations.

ko⌐ohoo² こうほう (公報) *n.* official bulletin.

ko⌐oi¹ こうい (行為) *n.* act; action; deed; behavior; conduct.

ko⌐oi² こうい (好意) *n.* goodwill; kindness; favor:
Kanojo wa kimi ni kooi *o motte*

iru *yoo da.* (彼女は君に好意を持っているようだ) She seems to *be fond of* you. (↔ tekii)

ko⌐oiñ こういん (工員) *n.* factory worker.

ko⌐oi-teki こういてき (好意的) *a.n.* (~ na, ni) friendly; kind; favorable: kooi-teki *na heñji* (好意的な返事) a *favorable* reply.

ko⌐o-iu こういう (斯ういう) *attrib.* like this; thus: ★ Refers to something close to the speaker. koo-iu *koto* (こういうこと) *this sort of* thing. (⇨ aa-iu; doo-iu; soo-iu)

ko⌐oji こうじ (工事) *n.* construction work:
Kooji-*chuu.* (sign) (工事中) Under *Construction*. / kooji-*geñba* (工事現場) a *construction* site.

kooji suru (~する) *vi.* construct; work on.

ko⌐ojo⌐o¹ こうじょう (工場) *n.* factory; mill; plant; workshop. ★ Refers to a larger, well-equipped factory. More formal than '*kooba*.'

ko⌐ojoo² こうじょう (向上) *n.* rise; improvement; progress:
gijutsu no koojoo (技術の向上) an *improvement* in techniques.

koojoo suru (~する) *vi.* rise; improve; progress.

ko⌐oka¹ こうか (効果) *n.* effect; efficacy; efficiency:
Kono kusuri wa zutsuu ni kooka *ga arimasu.* (この薬は頭痛に効果があります) This medicine *is effective* for headaches.

ko⌐oka² こうか (高価) *a.n.* (~ na, ni) expensive; high-priced; costly:
kooka *na shinamono* (高価な品物) *high-priced* goods. (↔ yasui) (⇨ takai)

ko⌐oka³ こうか (硬貨) *n.* coin. (↔ satsu; shihee)

ko⌐okai¹ こうかい (公開) *n.* open to the public.

kookai suru (~する) *vt.* make public; exhibit; release.

ko⌐okai² こうかい（航海）*n.* voyage; navigation; cruise; sailing.
　kookai suru（〜する）*vi.* go by sea; sail; cruise.

ko⌐okai³ こうかい（後悔）*n.* regret; repentance.
　kookai suru（〜する）*vi.*, *vt.* regret; repent; feel remorse.

ko⌐okai⁴ こうかい（公海）*n.* the high seas.

ko⌐okañ こうかん（交換）*n.* exchange; replacement; barter.
　kookañ suru（〜する）*vt.* change; exchange; replace; barter. (⇨ torikaeru)

ko⌐oka-teki こうかてき（効果的）*a.n.* (〜 na, ni) effective; successful: kooka-teki *na taisaku* (効果的な対策) *effective* measures.

ko⌐okee こうけい（光景）*n.* scene; sight; view:
Sono tani no kookee *wa ima de mo oboete imasu.* (その谷の光景は今でも覚えています) I still remember the *view* of that valley.

ko⌐oki こうき（後期）*n.* latter half of the year; second term [semester]. (↔ zeñki)

ko⌐oki⌐shiñ こうきしん（好奇心）*n.* curiosity; inquisitiveness:
Kare wa kookishiñ *ga tsuyoi.* (彼は好奇心が強い) He *is very inquisitive.* (⇨ kyoomi; yajiuma)

ko⌐okoku こうこく（広告）*n.* advertisement:
shiñbuñ *ni* kookoku *o dasu [noseru]* (新聞に広告を出す[載せる]) put an *advertisement* in a newspaper.
　kookoku suru（〜する）*vt.* advertise. (⇨ señdeñ)

ko⌐okoo¹ こうこう（高校）*n.* (senior) high school. ★ Shortened form of 'kootoo-gakkoo.'

ko⌐okoo² こうこう（孝行）*n.* being obedient (to one's parents).
　— *a.n.* (〜 na) good; obedient; dutiful: kookoo *na musuko* (孝行な息子) a *dutiful* son.

ko⌐oko⌐osee こうこうせい（高校生）*n.* (senior) high school student.

ko⌐oku⌐ubiñ こうくうびん（航空便）*n.* airmail:
tegami *o* kookuubiñ *de okuru [dasu]* (手紙を航空便で送る[出す]) send a letter by *airmail.*

ko⌐oku⌐ukeñ こうくうけん（航空券）*n.* airline ticket.

ko⌐oku⌐uki こうくうき（航空機）*n.* airplane; aircraft.

Ko⌐okyo こうきょ（皇居）*n.* the Imperial Palace.

ko⌐okyoo¹ こうきょう（公共）*n.* the community; public:
kookyoo *no fukushi* (公共の福祉) *public* welfare.

ko⌐okyoo² こうきょう（好況）*n.* brisk market; prosperous conditions. (↔ fukyoo)

ko⌐okyuu こうきゅう（高級）*a.n.* (〜 na, ni) high-class; high-grade; exclusive:
kookyuu *(na) hoteru* (高級(な)ホテル) an *exclusive* hotel / kookyuu-*sha* (高級車) a *high-class* car.

ko⌐omi⌐ñkañ こうみんかん（公民館）*n.* public hall; community center.

ko⌐omiñ⌐keñ こうみんけん（公民権）*n.* civil rights.

ko⌐omoku こうもく（項目）*n.* item; heading; clause.

ko⌐omu⌐iñ こうむいん（公務員）*n.* public worker; government employee; civil servant.

ko⌐omu⌐r·u こうむる（被る）*vt.* (-mur·i-; -mur·a-; -mut-te ⓒ) receive; sustain; suffer:
taifuu *de ooki-na higai o* koomuru (台風で大きな被害を被る) *suffer* heavy damage from the typhoon. (⇨ ukeru)

ko⌐omyoo こうみょう（巧妙）*a.n.* (〜 na, ni) clever; cunning; smart; crafty:
koomyoo *na yarikata* (巧妙なやり方) a *clever* trick.

ko⌐onyuu こうにゅう（購入）*n.* purchase; buying.
　koonyuu suru（〜する）*vt.* buy; purchase. (⇨ kau¹)

ko￢o-oñ こうおん（高温）*n.* high temperature. (↔ teeoñ)

ko￢ori こおり（氷）*n.* ice.

ko￢oritsu[1] こうりつ（公立）*n.* public; prefectural; municipal: kooritsu no toshokañ（公立の図書館）a *public* library. (↔ shiritsu[1])

ko￢oritsu[2] こうりつ（効率）*n.* efficiency: kooritsu o takameru（効率を高める）increase the *efficiency*.

ko￢oritsu-teki こうりつてき（効率的）*a.n.* (～ na, ni) efficient: kooritsu-teki na kikai（効率的な機械）an *efficient* machine.

ko￢or-u こおる（凍る）*vi.* (koor·i-; koor·a-; koot-te |C|) freeze: Kesa niwa no ike ga kootta.（けさ庭の池が凍った）This morning the pond in the garden *was frozen*.

ko￢oryo こうりょ（考慮）*n.* (*formal*) consideration: Sono kikaku wa kooryo-chuu desu.（その企画は考慮中です）The project is now under *consideration*.
kooryo suru（～する）*vt.* consider; take into account.

ko￢oryoku こうりょく（効力）*n.* effect; force; validity: Sono hooritsu wa mada kooryoku ga arimasu.（その法律はまだ効力があります）That law is still in *force*.

ko￢osa こうさ（交差）*n.* crossing; intersection.
koosa suru（～する）*vi.* cross; intersect. (⇨ majiwaru)

ko￢osai こうさい（交際）*n.* company; association; friendship; acquaintance: koosai-hi（交際費）an *expense* account; *entertainment* [*social*] expenses.
koosai suru（～する）*vi.* keep company; associate.

ko￢osaku[1] こうさく（工作）*n.*
1 handicraft; woodwork: koosaku de take no fue o tsukuru（工作で竹の笛を作る）make a bamboo flute in *handicraft class*.

2 maneuvering; move: Kare wa kooshoo no ura de koosaku o shita.（彼は交渉の裏で工作をした）He *maneuvered* behind the scenes at the negotiations.

ko￢osaku[2] こうさく（耕作）*n.* cultivation: koosaku-chi（耕作地）*cultivated* land.
koosaku suru（～する）*vt.* cultivate. (⇨ tagayasu)

ko￢osa￢teñ こうさてん（交差点）*n.* crossing; intersection. (⇨ juujiro)

ko￢osee[1] こうせい（構成）*n.* make-up; organization; composition; structure.
koosee suru（～する）*vt.* make up; organize; compose: Iñkai wa shichi-niñ de koosee sarete imasu.（委員会は7人で構成されています）The committee *is made up* of seven members.

ko￢osee[2] こうせい（校正）*n.* proof-reading: zasshi o koosee suru（雑誌を校正する）*read proofs* of a magazine.

ko￢oseñ こうせん（光線）*n.* light; beam; ray: taiyoo no kooseñ（太陽の光線）the *rays* of the sun.

ko￢osha[1] こうしゃ（校舎）*n.* school building; schoolhouse. (⇨ gakkoo)

ko￢osha[2] こうしゃ（後者）*n.* (*formal*) the latter: Washitsu to yooshitsu de wa, koosha no hoo ga suki desu.（和室と洋室では、後者のほうが好きです）Between a Japanese-style room and a western-style room, I prefer *the latter*. (↔ zeñsha)

ko￢oshi[1] こうし（講師）*n.* lecturer; instructor.

ko￢oshi[2] こうし（公使）*n.* minister (in the diplomatic service): chuu-Nichi Furansu kooshi（駐日フランス公使）the French *minister* to Japan.

ko￢oshi￢kañ こうしかん（公使館）*n.* legation.

ko￢oshiki[1] こうしき（公式）*n.* official; formal: kooshiki *hoomoñ* (公式訪問) a *formal* visit. (⇨ seeshiki)

ko⌐oshiki[2] こうしき (公式) *n.* formula: *suugaku no kooshiki* (数学の公式) a mathematical *formula*.

ko⌐oshiñ こうしん (行進) *n.* march; parade: kooshiñ-*kyoku* (行進曲) a musical *march*. **kooshiñ suru** (～する) *vi.* march; parade.

ko⌐oshi¹see こうしせい (高姿勢) *n.* aggressive [high-handed] attitude. (↔ teeshisee)

ko⌐o-shite こうして *adv.* in this way: *Isogashikute,* koo-shite *jitto suwatte wa irarenai.* (忙しくて、こうしてじっとすわってはいられない) I am too busy to sit around *in this way* doing nothing. (⇨ aa-shite; soo-shite)

ko⌐oshoo こうしょう (交渉) *n.*
1 negotiations; talks: *Sono* kooshoo *wa matomarimashita.* (その交渉はまとまりました) The *negotiations* were concluded.
2 connection; relations: *Watashi wa seejika to wa nañ no* kooshoo *mo arimaseñ.* (私は政治家とは何の交渉もありません) I have no *connections* with politicians. **kooshoo suru** (～する) *vt.* negotiate.

ko⌐oshuu こうしゅう (公衆) *n.* the general public: Kooshuu *no meñzeñ de haji o kakasareta.* (公衆の面前で恥をかかされた) I was put to shame in *public*.

ko⌐oshuu-be¹ñjo こうしゅうべんじょ (公衆便所) *n.* public lavatory [toilet]. (⇨ beñjo)

ko⌐oshuu-de¹ñwa こうしゅうでんわ (公衆電話) *n.* public telephone; pay phone. (⇨ deñwa)

ko⌐oshuu-do¹otoku こうしゅうどうとく (公衆道徳) *n.* public morals. (⇨ dootoku)

ko⌐osoku-do¹oro こうそくどうろ (高速道路) *n.* expressway; free-

way; motorway. (⇨ dooro)

ko⌐osoo こうそう (構想) *n.* plan; idea; design; plot: koosoo *o tateru [neru]* (構想を立てる[練る]) map out [refine] a *plan*. **koosoo suru** (～する) *vt.* plan; design; plot.

ko⌐osu コース *n.* 1 (of lessons) course: *Nihoñgo no shokyuu* koosu (日本語の初級コース) the beginners' Japanese *course*.
2 (of a race) course; lane: *dai-sañ* koosu *o hashiru* (第3コースを走る) run in *Lane* No. 3.
3 (of a meal) course: *furu-*koosu *no shokuji* (フルコースの食事) a meal with all the *courses*.

ko⌐osui こうすい (香水) *n.* perfume; scent.

ko⌐otai こうたい (交替) *n.* shift; change: *Watashi-tachi wa* kootai *de uñteñ o shita.* (私たちは交替で運転をした) We took *turns* doing the driving. **kootai suru** (～する) *vi.* take turns; change.

ko⌐otee[1] こうてい (肯定) *n.* affirmation; affirmative. **kootee suru** (～する) *vt.* affirm; acknowledge; confirm. (↔ hitee)

ko⌐otee[2] こうてい (皇帝) *n.* emperor. ★ The Japanese emperor is known as '*teñnoo*.'

ko⌐oteñ-teki こうてんてき (後天的) *a.n.* (～ na, ni) acquired; a posteriori: kooteñ-teki *na seekaku* (後天的な性格) a personality *acquired because of one's upbringing and environment*. (↔ señteñ-teki)

ko⌐oto[1] コート *n.* coat; overcoat; raincoat; trenchcoat.

ko⌐oto[2] コート *n.* court: *tenisu* kooto (テニスコート) a tennis *court*.

ko⌐otoo こうとう (高等) *a.n.* (～ na) high; higher; advanced: kootoo-*kyooiku* (高等教育) *higher* education.

ko⌐otoo-ga¹kkoo こうとうがっこう

(高等学校) *n.* senior high school; upper secondary school. (⇨ koo-koo)

ko╹otsuu こうつう (交通) *n.* traffic; transportation; communication.

ko╹otsuu-do╹otoku こうつうどうとく (交通道徳) *n.* good driving manners; consideration for others when driving. (⇨ doo-toku)

ko╹otsu╹uhi こうつうひ (交通費) *n.* traveling expenses; carfare.

ko╹otsuu-ji╹ko こうつうじこ (交通事故) *n.* traffic accident.

ko╹ouñ こううん (幸運) *n.* good luck [fortune].
— *a.n.* (〜 na, ni) lucky; fortunate. (↔ fuuñ)

ko╹oyoo こうよう (紅葉) *n.* red leaves; autumn colors [tints].
kooyoo suru (〜する) *vi.* turn red [yellow]. (⇨ momiji)

ko╹ozañ[1] こうざん (鉱山) *n.* mine.

ko╹ozañ[2] こうざん (高山) *n.* high mountain.

ko╹ozeñ こうぜん (公然) *a.n.* (〜 no / to; 〜 taru) open; public: *Sore wa koozeñ no himitsu desu.* (それは公然の秘密です) It is an *open secret.*

ko╹ozoo こうぞう (構造) *n.* structure; construction: *buñ [shakai] no koozoo* (文[社会]の構造) the *structure* of a sentence [society].

ko╹ozui こうずい (洪水) *n.* flood; inundation.

ko╹pii コピー *n.* copy; photocopy.
kopii suru (〜する) *vt.* copy; photocopy.

ko╹ppu コップ *n.* glass; tumbler.

ko╹ra こら *int.* (*rude*) hey (you)!; hi!; there! ★ Used by men when reprimanding someone.

ko╹rae╹ru こらえる (堪える) *vt.* (korae-te Ⓥ) **1** bear; stand; endure: *itami o koraeru* (痛みをこらえる) *endure* pain. (⇨ gamañ)
2 control; subdue; suppress:

namida o koraeru (涙をこらえる) *keep back* one's tears.

ko╹re これ (此れ) *n.* **1** this: ★ Refers to something or someone that is close to the speaker. *Kore wa dare no hoñ desu ka?* (これはだれの本ですか) Whose book is *this?*
2 this: ★ Introduces or refers to one's own wife or child. *Kore ga uchi no kanai [musuko] desu.* (これがうちの家内[息子]です) *This* is my wife [son].
3 this; it: ★ Refers to something or someone that was previously mentioned or that is about to be mentioned. *Zairyoo o yoku maze, kore ni tamago o kuwaemasu.* (材料をよく混ぜ、これに卵を加えます) Mix the ingredients well, and then add the egg to *it.*
4 this; that: ★ Refers to a continuing state or action. *Kore de yoshi.* (これでよし) *This* will do.
5 this; that: ★ Used for emphasis. *Kore wa hidoi netsu da.* (これはひどい熱だ) What a fever *this* is! (⇨ are[1]; dore[1]; sore[1])

ko╹re de これで (此れで) *adv.* now; under the circumstances; with this: *Kore de añshiñ shita.* (これで安心した) I *now* feel relieved.

ko╹re kara[1] これから (此れから) **1** now: *Kore kara shusseki o torimasu.* (これから出席をとります) I am *now* going to take attendance.
2 from now on; after this; in the future. (⇨ are[1] irai; sore kara)

ko╹re-(k)kiri これっきり (此れっきり) *adv.* (with a negative) **1** (of future) never: *Kore-kkiri kanojo to wa aenai ka mo shirenai.* (これっきり彼女とは会えないかもしれない) I'm afraid I will *never* be able to see her again.

2 (of a thing) only:

O-kane wa kore-kkiri shika motte imaseñ. (お金はこれっきりしか持っていません) This is the *only* money I have. (⇨ are-(k)kiri; sore-(k)kiri)

koʳre maˡde これまで (此れ迄)

1 so far; until now:

Kare wa kore made gakkoo o yasuñda koto ga arimaseñ. (彼はこれまで学校を休んだことがありません) *So far* he has not missed a day from school.

2 here:

Kyoo wa kore made. (きょうはこれまで) Let us finish *here* today.

koʳriˡ·ru こりる (懲りる) *vi.* (kori-te Ⓥ)

1 learn a lesson:

Kare wa mada sono shippai ni korinai yoo da. (彼はまだその失敗に懲りないようだ) It seems he *has not learned a lesson* from his failure.

2 have enough (on); be soured:

Kekkoñ ni wa korite imasu. (結婚には懲りています) I've *had a bitter experience* with marriage.

koˡro ころ (頃) *n.* the time:

Sakura wa ima ga ichibañ ii koro desu. (桜は今がいちばんいいころです) Now is the best *time* for cherry blossoms. (⇨ -goro)

koʳrob·u ころぶ (転ぶ) *vi.* (korob·i-; korob·a-; koroñ-de Ⓒ) fall; tumble:

Kare wa ne ni tsumazuite koroñda. (彼は根につまずいて転んだ) He tripped on a root and *fell*. (⇨ taoreru)

koʳrogar·u ころがる (転がる) *vi.* (-gar·i-; -gar·a-; -gat-te Ⓒ)

1 roll; fall; tumble:

Booru ga saka o korogatte itta. (ボールが坂を転がっていった) The ball *rolled down* away the slope. (⇨ korogasu)

2 lie down:

shibafu ni korogaru (芝生に転がる) *lie down* on the lawn.

koʳrogasˡ·u ころがす (転がす) *vt.* (-gash·i-; -gas·a-; -gash·i-te Ⓒ)

roll; tumble over:

Sono ooki-na ishi o korogashite ugokashita. (その大きな石を転がして動かした) We moved that large stone by *rolling* it along. (⇨ korogaru)

koˡrokoro ころころ *adv.* (~ to) (the sound or manner of a small, round object rolling):

Booru ga korokoro (to) korogatte kita. (ボールがころころ(と)転がって来た) A ball came *rolling up* to me.

koʳroˡri ころり *adv.* (~ to) **1** easily; suddenly:

Kanojo wa kare ni korori to damasareta. (彼女は彼にころりとだまされた) She was *easily* taken in by him.

2 quite; entirely:

Sono yakusoku o korori to wasurete ita. (その約束をころりと忘れていた) I *quite* forgot the appointment.

koʳros·u ころす (殺す) *vt.* (korosh·i-; koros·a-; korosh·i-te Ⓒ)

1 kill; murder.

2 suppress (breathing, a yawn, etc.); restrain.

koˡr·uˡ こる (凝る) *vi.* (kor·i-; kor·a-; kot-te Ⓒ) be crazy; be devoted:

Kare wa gorufu ni kotte iru. (彼はゴルフに凝っている) He *is crazy* about golf.

koˡr·u² こる (凝る) *vi.* (kor·i-; kor·a-; kot-te Ⓒ) (of shoulders) be stiff.

koʳsame こさめ (小雨) *n.* light rain; drizzle. (↔ ooame)

koˡsee こせい (個性) *n.* individuality; personality:

kosee o nobasu (個性を伸ばす) develop one's *individuality*.

koʳsee-teki こせいてき (個性的) *a.n.* (~ na, ni) distinctive:

Ano haiyuu wa kosee-teki na kao o shite iru. (あの俳優は個性的な顔をしている) The actor has a *distinctive* face.

koʳseki こせき (戸籍) *n.* family register.

koˡshi こし (腰) *n.* waist; hip:

isu ni koshi o orosu (椅子に腰を下

ろす) *sit* on a chair. (⇨ shiri)

ko「shikake¹ こしかけ (腰掛け) n.
1 chair; stool:
koshikake ni suwaru (腰掛けに座る)
sit on a *chair*. (⇨ isu; koshikakeru)
2 temporary work; makeshift
job:
Kanojo no shigoto wa kekkoñ
made no koshikake da. (彼女の仕事
は結婚までの腰掛けだ) Her job is a
temporary one until marriage.
(⇨ riñji)

ko「shikake¹·ru こしかける (腰掛け
る) vi. (-kake-te Ⅴ) sit down;
take a seat. (⇨ koshikake)

ko「shirae·ru こしらえる (拵える) vt.
(-rae-te Ⅴ) make; build:
inugoya o koshiraeru (犬小屋をこし
らえる) *make* a doghouse. (⇨ tsukuru¹)

ko「shoo¹ こしょう (故障) n. breakdown; trouble.
koshoo suru (〜する) vi. go out
of order; break down; be in trouble. (⇨ kowareru)

ko「sho¹o² こしょう (胡椒) n. pepper.

koso こそ p. indeed; just:
★ Used to emphasize the preceding word.
Koñdo koso seekoo shite miseru.
(今度こそ成功して見せる) *This one
time* I will show you I can succeed.

ko「sso¹ri こっそり adv. (〜 to)
secretly; stealthily; in private:
Kare wa kanojo ni kossori (to)
atte ita. (彼は彼女にこっそり(と)会って
いた) He was meeting with her *secretly*.

ko「s·u¹ こす (越す) vt. (kosh·i-;
kos·a-; kosh·i-te Ⓒ) 1 go over;
cross:
Kare no utta booru wa feñsu o
koshita. (彼の打ったボールはフェンスを
越した) The ball he hit *went over*
the fence.
2 move (to a new house). (⇨ hikkoshi)

3 spend (time):
Kare wa Hokkaidoo de sukii o
shite, fuyu o koshita. (彼は北海道で
スキーをして, 冬を越した) He *spent*
winter skiing in Hokkaido.
(⇨ sugosu)

ko「s·u² こす (超す) vt. (kosh·i-;
kos·a-; kosh·i-te Ⓒ) be over;
be more than:
Shachoo wa nanajuu o koshite iru.
(社長は 70 を超している) Our president *is more than* seventy.
(⇨ koeru²)

ko「su¹r·u こする (擦る) vt. (kosu-
r·i-; kosur·a-; kosut-te Ⓒ) rub;
scrub: (⇨ masatsu)
Kare wa nemui me o kosutta. (彼
は眠い目をこすった) He *rubbed* his
sleepy eyes.

ko「ta¹e こたえ (答え) n. answer;
reply; response. (⇨ kotaeru)

ko「tae¹·ru こたえる (答える) vi.
(kotae-te Ⅴ) answer; reply:
Sono ko wa nani o kiite mo kota-
enakatta. (その子は何を聞いても答えな
かった) Whatever I asked the child,
he *did not reply*. (⇨ kotae)

ko「tai こたい (固体) n. solid.
(⇨ ekitai; kitai²)

ko「tatsu こたつ (炬燵) n. Japanese foot warmer. (⇨ deñki-
gotatsu)

ko「tchi¹ こっち n. (colloq.) =
kochira.
1 this; here:
Kare wa ma-mo-naku kotchi e
kimasu. (彼は間もなくこっちへ来ます)
He will be *here* very soon.
2 we; I:
Kotchi ni wa sekiniñ wa arimaseñ.
(こっちには責任はありません) *We* are
not to blame. (⇨ atchi; dotchi;
sotchi)

ko「tee こてい (固定) n. fixation.
kotee-shisañ zee (固定資産税) a
fixed property tax.
kotee suru (〜する) vt. fix; settle.

ko「teñ こてん (古典) n. classics.

ko「to¹ こと (事) n. 1 thing; matter; affair; fact: ★ The meaning

is defined by the preceding noun or modifier.

Kyoo wa suru koto ga takusañ aru. (きょうはすることがたくさんある) I have a lot of *things to do* today.

2 incident; problem; plan: *Koto wa juñchoo ni susuñde imasu.* (ことは順調に進んでいます) The *plan* is well under way.

3 (used in giving impersonal orders or instructions): *Shimee oyobi juusho o kinyuu no koto.* (氏名および住所を記入のこと) *Enter* both full name and address.

... koto ga aru (…～がある) have experienced: ★ Preceded by the past form of a verb and refers to experiences in the past. *Kare wa chuugaku de oshieta koto ga arimasu.* (彼は中学で教えたことがあります) He *has experience* of teaching at a junior high school.

... koto ga dekiru (…～ができる) be able to do: ★ Preceded by the dictionary form of a verb. *Sono ooki-na iwa wa ugokasu koto ga dekinakatta.* (その大きな岩は動かすことができなかった) We *were unable to* move that large rock.

... koto ni natte iru (…～になっている) be supposed [scheduled] to do: ★ Preceded by the dictionary form of a verb. *Kare to wa go-ji ni au koto ni natte imasu.* (彼とは5時に会うことになっています) I *am set to* meet him at five.

... koto ni shite iru (…～にしている) make it a rule to do: ★ Preceded by the dictionary form of a verb. *Asa wa hayaku okiru koto ni shite imasu.* (朝は早く起きることにしています) I *make it a rule to* get up early in the morning.

... koto ni suru (…～にする) decide to do: ★ Preceded by the dictionary form of a verb. *Kuuraa o kau koto ni shimashita.* (クーラーを買うことにしました) I *decided to* buy an air conditioner.

ko˥to² こと (琴) *n.* koto; traditional Japanese harp.

ko˥to³ こと (古都) *n.* ancient city [capital]. ★ Often refers to Kyoto or sometimes to Nara.

ko˥toba˩ ことば (言葉) *n.* language; word; speech.

ko˥tobazu˥kai ことばづかい (言葉遣い) *n.* wording; language; one's way of speaking.

ko˥togara˩ ことがら (事柄) *n.* thing; matter; subject: *Kore wa hijoo ni juuyoo na kotogara desu.* (これは非常に重要な事柄です) This is a very important *matter.* (⇨ koto!)

ko˥togo˥toku ことごとく (悉く) *adv.* (*formal*) entirely; utterly: *Yatoo wa yotoo no teeañ ni, kotogotoku hañtai shite iru.* (野党は与党の提案に, ことごとく反対している) The opposition is *utterly* against the ruling party's proposal.

ko˥tona˩r·u ことなる (異なる) *vi.* (-nar·i-; -nar·a-; -nat-te Ⓒ) differ; vary; be different: ★ More formal than '*chigau*'. *Watashi-tachi no kañgae-kata wa kotonatte iru.* (私たちの考え方は異なっている) Our ways of thinking *are different.*

ko˥to ni ことに (殊に) *adv.* (*formal*) especially; particularly. (⇨ toku ni)

ko˥to ni yoru to ことによると (事に依ると) *adv.* probably; possibly: *Koto ni yoru to gogo wa ame ga furu ka mo shirenai.* (ことによると午後は雨が降るかもしれない) There will *probably* be rain in the afternoon.

ko˥tori ことり (小鳥) *n.* little bird.

ko˥toshi ことし (今年) *n.* this year. (⇨ kyoneñ; raineñ)

ko˥towa˩r·u ことわる (断る) *vt.* (-war·i-; -war·a-; -wat-te Ⓒ)
1 refuse (a demand, request, admission, etc.); decline; reject; turn down. (⇨ o-kotowari)
2 get permission: *Kuruma o tsukau toki wa watashi*

ni kotowatte *kudasai*. (車を使うとき
は私に断ってください) When you are
going to use the car, please *get
permission* from me.
3 give notice:
Kare wa arakajime kotowaranai
de kaisha o yamete shimatta. (彼は
あらかじめ断らないで会社を辞めてしまっ
た) *Without giving notice* beforehand, he just went and quit the
company.

ko⌐towaza ことわざ (諺) *n.* proverb; saying.

ko⌐tozuke¬·ru ことづける (言付ける)
vt. (-zuke-te Ⅴ) leave a message;
ask a person to do. (⇨ tanomu)

ko⌐tsu こつ (骨) *n.* knack; secret:
Kare wa tsuri no kotsu *o shite iru*.
(彼は釣りのこつを知っている) He has
the *knack* of fishing.

ko⌐tsukotsu こつこつ *adv.*
(~ to) **1** (the sound of a step;
tap):
Kotsukotsu *to dare-ka no kutsu no
oto ga kikoeru*. (こつこつとだれかの靴
の音が聞こえる) I hear the *clicking*
sound of someone's heels.
2 steadily; patiently; little by
little:
kotsukotsu (*to*) *kane o tameru* (こつ
こつ(と)金をためる) save money *little
by little*.

ko⌐uri こうり (小売り) *n.* retail:
Kore wa kouri *de gohyaku-eñ
desu*. (これは小売りで 500 円です)
This is 500 yen *retail*. (⇨ oroshi)

ko⌐waga¬r·u こわがる (怖がる) *vi.*
(-gar·i-; -gar·a-; -gat·te Ⅽ) be
afraid; be frightened; be scared:
takai tokoro o kowagaru (高い所を
怖がる) *be afraid* of heights.
(⇨ kowai)

ko⌐wa¬·i こわい (怖い) *a.* (-ku)
1 dreadful; horrible; frightening:
kowai *omoi o suru* (怖い思いをする)
have a *frightening* experience.
(⇨ kowagaru; osoroshii)
2 strict:
Yamada señsee wa kowai. (山田先

生は怖い) Our teacher, Mr. Yamada, is very *strict*.

ko⌐ware¬·ru こわれる (壊れる) *vi.*
(koware-te Ⅴ) **1** break; be broken; be damaged:
Kabiñ ga yuka ni ochite kowareta.
(花びんが床に落ちてこわれた) The vase
fell on the floor and *broke*.
(⇨ kowasu)
2 get out of order:
Kono terebi wa kowarete imasu.
(このテレビはこわれています) This television *is out of order*. (⇨ koshoo¬)
3 (of a hope, dream, etc.) be destroyed; be broken off.
(⇨ kowasu)

ko⌐wa¬·su こわす (壊す) *vt.* (ko-
wash·i-; kowas·a-; kowash·i-te
Ⅽ) **1** break; pull down:
Dare-ka ga doa o kowashita. (だれ
かがドアをこわした) Someone *broke*
the door. (⇨ kowareru)
2 wreck; destroy; ruin; spoil (a
hope, dream, etc.):
shizeñ o kowasu (自然をこわす) *destroy* nature / *yume o* kowasu (夢
をこわす) *ruin* one's dreams.
(⇨ kowareru)
3 injure (health); upset:
Kare wa muri o shite karada o
kowashita. (彼は無理をして体をこわし
た) He *injured* his health by over-
working.

ko⌐ya こや (小屋) *n.* hut; shack;
shed.

ko⌐yomi¬ こよみ (暦) *n.* calendar;
almanac.

ko⌐yubi こゆび (小指) *n.* little
finger; little toe.

ko⌐yuki こゆき (小雪) *n.* light
snow. (⇨ ooyuki; yuki¬)

ko⌐yuu こゆう (固有) *a.n.* (~ na/
no, ni) peculiar; characteristic;
inherent:
Shiñtoo wa Nihoñ koyuu *no shuukyoo desu*. (神道は日本固有の宗教で
す) Shinto is a religion *peculiar* to
Japan.

ko⌐zukai こづかい (小遣い) *n.* allowance; pocket money.

ko⌐zu⌐tsumi こづつみ (小包) n.
parcel; package; parcel post.

ku[1] く (九) n. nine: ★「九」 is
sometimes pronounced 'kyuu.'
For counting days, the ninth day
is pronounced 'kokonoka.'
(⇨ kokonotsu; APP. 3)

ku[2] く (区) n. 1 ward. ★ The
basic administrative unit in
metropolitan areas. (⇨ kuyakusho)
2 district; zone:
Basu wa ik-ku hyakuhachijuu-eñ
desu. (バスは1区 180円です) The
bus fare is 180 yen per zone.

ku[3] く (句) n. phrase.

ku⌐ba⌐r・u くばる (配る) vt. (kuba-
r・i-; kubar・a-; kubat-te C) distribute; deliver; pass out:
bira o kubaru (ビラを配る) distribute
handbills / shiñbuñ o kubaru (新聞
を配る) deliver newspapers.
(⇨ haitatsu)

ku⌐betsu くべつ (区別) n. distinction; difference.
kubetsu suru (～する) vt. tell...
from; distinguish; discriminate.

ku⌐bi くび (首) n. neck; head:
Mado kara kubi o dasu to kikeñ
desu. (窓から首を出すと危険です) It is
dangerous to stick your head out
of the window. (⇨ atama)
kubi ni naru (～になる) be dis-
missed [fired]. (⇨ kaiko)
kubi o tsukkomu (～を突っ込む)
consciously involve oneself; stick
one's nose into.

ku⌐cha⌐kucha くちゃくちゃ adv.
(～ to) (the sound of chewing
things):
mono o taberu toki, kuchakucha
(to) oto o saseru (物を食べるとき、くち
ゃくちゃ(と)音をさせる) make a
smacking noise while eating food.

ku⌐chi[1] くち (口) n. 1 mouth.
2 (of a container) mouth:
biñ no kuchi (びんの口) the mouth
of a bottle.
kuchi ga karui (～が軽い) indis-
creet; talkative.

kuchi ga omoi (～が重い) be close-
mouthed. (⇨ mukuchi)
kuchi ga suberu (～が滑る) let
slip.
kuchi ga umai (～がうまい) be a
smooth talker.
kuchi ga warui (～が悪い) have a
sharp tongue.
kuchi ni au (～に合う) suit one's
taste.

ku⌐chi[2] くち (口) n. job; position;
opening:
taipisuto no kuchi (タイピストの口) a
job as a typist.

ku⌐chibeni くちべに (口紅) n.
rouge; lipstick.

ku⌐chibiru くちびる (唇) n. lip.

ku⌐chi⌐guchi ni くちぐちに (口々
に) adv. unanimously; in uni-
son; at once:
Miñna wa kuchiguchi ni kanojo no
e o hometa. (みんなは口々に彼女の絵
をほめた) They were all in agreement in praising her painting.

ku⌐chihige くちひげ (口髭) n.
mustache. (⇨ hige)

ku⌐da くだ (管) n. pipe; tube.

ku⌐dake⌐ru くだける (砕ける) vi.
(kudake-te V) break; go to
pieces:
Ishi ga atatte, kagami ga kudaketa. (石が当たって、鏡が砕けた) A
stone hit the mirror and it
smashed. (⇨ kudaku)

ku⌐da⌐keta くだけた 1 (of language) colloquial; informal:
kudaketa iikata (くだけた言いかた) a
colloquial expression.
2 (of a person) affable:
kudaketa hito (くだけた人) an affable person.

ku⌐da⌐k・u くだく (砕く) vt. (kuda-
k・i-; kudak・a-; kuda・i-te C)
1 break; smash; shatter; crush.
2 destroy; ruin (a hope, dream,
etc.). (⇨ kudakeru)

ku⌐da⌐mono くだもの (果物) n.
fruit.

ku⌐darana・i くだらない a. (-ku)
1 worthless; trivial:

ku「dari くだり（下り）n. **1** descent; downhill slope. (↔ nobori) (⇨ kudaru)
2 down train. ★ The train going away from Tokyo or a major city. (↔ nobori)

ku「dar・u くだる（下る）vi. (kudar・i-; kudar・a-; kudat-te C)
1 descend; go down; come down:
yama o kudaru (山を下る) *go down a mountain.* (↔ noboru)
2 (of an order) be passed; be issued:
Kare-ra ni shuppatsu no meeree ga kudatta. (彼らに出発の命令が下った) The order for departure *was issued* to them.
3 have loose bowels:
Watashi wa o-naka ga kudatte iru. (私はおなかが下っている) My bowels *are loose.* (⇨ geri)

ku「dasa「i ください（下さい）[the imperative of '*kudasaru*']
1 (*polite*) please give me; let me have: *O-cha o ip-pai kudasai.* (お茶を一杯下さい) *Please give me* a cup of tea.
2 (*polite*) please do (for me): ★ Preceded by the *te*-form of a verb. *Moo sukoshi yukkuri hanashite kudasai.* (もう少しゆっくり話して ください) *Speak* more slowly, *please.*
3 (*honorific*) please do: ★ Preceded by '*o-*'+the continuative base of a verb. *Doozo o-kake kudasai.* (どうぞお掛けください) *Please have a seat.*
-nai de kudasai (ないで〜) (*polite*) please do not: *Doo-ka ikanai de kudasai.* (どうか行かないでください) *Please don't go away.*

ku「dasa「r・u くださる（下さる）vt. (-sa・i-; -sar・a-; -sat-te C) give me [us] (something): ★ Honorific alternative of '*kureru*[1].'
Señsee wa watashi ni nooto o kudasatta. (先生は私にノートを下さった) The teacher *gave me* a notebook.
-te kudasaru (て〜) (used when a person's superior does something for that person): *Kore wa ano yuumee na gaka ga kaite kudasatta e desu.* (これはあの有名な画家が かいてくださった絵です) This is the picture which that famous painter *drew* for me.

ku「fuu くふう（工夫）n. idea; device; contrivance.
kufuu suru (〜する) vt. devise; contrive; think out.

ku「-gatsu くがつ（九月）n. September. (⇨ APP. 5)

ku「gi くぎ（釘）n. nail:
kugi o utsu [nuku] (釘を打つ[抜く]) drive [pull out] a *nail.*

ku「gi「r・u くぎる（区切る）vt. (kugir・i-; kugir・a-; kugit-te C) divide; partition; space; punctuate:
heya o futatsu ni kugiru (部屋を2つ に区切る) *divide* a room into two.

ku「i くい（杭）n. stake; pile; post:
kui o utsu (杭を打つ) drive in a *pile.*

ku「izu クイズ n. quiz: ★ Not used in the sense of a short exam.
kuizu bañgumi (クイズ番組) a *quiz* show.

ku「ji くじ（籤）n. lot; lottery. (⇨ takarakuji)

ku「ji「k・u くじく（挫く）vt. (kujik・i-; kujik・a-; kuji・i-te C) **1** sprain; wrench:
ashikubi o kujiku (足首をくじく) *sprain* one's ankle.
2 frustrate; baffle; crush:
yowaki o tasuke, tsuyoki o kujiku (弱きを助け、強きをくじく) help the weak and *crush* the strong.

ku「ki[1] くき（茎）n. stalk; stem.

ku「kyoo くきょう（苦境）n. difficult situation; adversity.

ku「ma[1] くま（熊）n. bear.

ku「mi[1] くみ (組) *n.* **1** class:
Watashi-tachi wa onaji kumi *desu.*
(私たちは同じ組です) We are in the
same *class.* (⇨ kurasu[2])

2 group; party; team:
*Go-niñ-zutsu, sañ-*kumi *ni wakareta.* (五人ずつ、3組に分かれた) We
were divided into three *groups* of
five.

3 set; pair:
*Kono sara wa go-ko de, hito-*kumi
desu. (この皿は5個で、ひと組です)
These plates come five to a *set.*

ku「miai くみあい (組合) *n.* union;
association. (⇨ roodoo-kumiai)

ku「miawase くみあわせ (組み合わ
せ) *n.* combination; pairing:
shiai no kumiawase (試合の組み合
わせ) the *pairings* for a tournament. (⇨ kumiawaseru)

ku「miawase・ru くみあわせる (組み
合わせる) *vt.* (-awase-te Ⅴ) put
together; combine; match.
(⇨ kumiawase)

ku「mitate くみたて (組み立て) *n.*
assembly; structure; construction; composition:
buhiñ no kumitate (部品の組み立て)
the *assembly* of parts. (⇨ kumitateru)

ku「mitate・ru くみたてる (組み立て
る) *vt.* (-tate-te Ⅴ) put together;
assemble; construct; compose:
mokee hikooki o kumitateru (模型
飛行機を組み立てる) *build* a model
airplane. (⇨ kumitate)

ku「mo[1] くも (雲) *n.* cloud.

ku「mo[2] くも (蜘蛛) *n.* spider.

ku「mori[1] くもり (曇り) *n.* cloudi-
ness; cloudy weather. (⇨ ame[1];
hare; kumoru)

ku「mori-ga「rasu くもりガラス (曇
りガラス) *n.* frosted glass; ground
glass. (⇨ garasu)

ku「mo「r・u くもる (曇る) *vi.* (ku-
mor・i-; kumor・a-; kumot-te Ⓒ)
1 become cloudy; cloud over;
become overcast. (↔ hareru[1])
(⇨ kumori)

2 fog up; collect moisture:

Yuge de megane ga kumotta. (湯
気で眼鏡が曇った) My glasses *mist-
ed up* with the steam.

3 (of a facial expression) grow
cloudy.

ku「m・u[1] くむ (組む) *vt.* (kum・i-;
kum・a-; kuñ-de Ⓒ) **1** cross;
fold:
ude o kuñde *aruku* (腕を組んで歩く)
walk *arm in arm.*

2 cooperate; pair with:
*Watashi wa tenisu de Yamada-
sañ to* kuñda. (私はテニスで山田さんと
組んだ) I *paired up* with Mr.
Yamada for tennis.

3 put together; assemble:
retsu o kumu (列を組む) *form* a line.

ku「m・u[2] くむ (汲む) *vt.* (kum・i-;
kum・a-; kuñ-de Ⓒ) **1** draw;
ladle; scoop up; pump:
baketsu ni mizu o kumu (バケツに水
をくむ) *ladle* water into a bucket.

2 understand (a person's feeling); take into consideration:
Kare wa watashi no kimochi o
kuñde kureta. (彼は私の気持ちをくん
でくれた) He *took* my feelings *into
consideration.*

ku「ñ くん (訓) *n.* the Japanese
reading of a Chinese character.
★ A single Chinese character
with different meanings may
have more than one '*kuñ*' reading. (⇨ oñ[2])

-kuñ くん (君) *suf.* Mr.:
★ Added to either the given or
family name of male friends or
someone of lower status.
(⇨ -sañ[1])
*Suzuki-*kuñ (鈴木君) (*Mr.*) Suzuki.

ku「ni くに (国) *n.* country;
nation; home; hometown.
(⇨ furusato; kokyoo)

ku「ñreñ くんれん (訓練) *n.* training; drill; practice.
kuñreñ (o) suru (〜を)する) *vt.*
train; drill.

ku「rabe・ru くらべる (比べる) *vt.*
(kurabe-te Ⅴ) compare:
hoñyaku to geñsho o kuraberu (翻

訳と原書を比べる) *compare* the translation with the original. ((⇒ hikaku; terashiawaseru))

ku「ra·i[1] くらい (暗い) *a.* (-ku)
1 dim; dark:
Soto ga kuraku natte kita. (外が暗くなってきた) It is getting *dark* outside. ((↔ akarui))
2 (of character, mood, etc.) gloomy; shadowy:
Suzuki-san wa itsu-mo kurai kao o shite iru. (鈴木さんはいつも暗い顔をしている) Miss Suzuki always *has a long face.* ((↔ akarui))
3 (of prospects, etc.) gloomy; dark:
Keezai no mitooshi wa kurai. (経済の見通しは暗い) The economic outlook is *gloomy.* ((↔ akarui))
4 (of knowledge) be unfamiliar with:
Watashi wa hooritsu ni kurai. (私は法律に暗い) I am *unfamiliar* with the law. ((↔ akarui))

ku「rai[2]/**gu「rai** くらい/ぐらい (位) *p.*
★ In the following examples, '*kurai*' can be replaced by '*gurai.*' ((⇒ bakari; hodo))
1 (of time and quantity) about; approximately:
Go-fun kurai de modorimasu. (5分くらいで戻ります) I will be back in *approximately* five minutes.
2 like; such that:
Konna koto kurai kodomo datte dekiru. (こんなことくらい子どもだってできる) Even a child can do something *like* this.
3 too...to:
Watashi wa ip-po mo arukenai kurai tsukareta. (私は一歩も歩けないくらい疲れた) I was *too* tired *to* take another step forward.
4 not as [so]...as: ★ Follows nouns and occurs with a negative.
Anata kurai isogashii hito wa hoka ni imasen. (あなたくらい忙しい人はほかにいません) There is *no one* who is *as* busy *as* you.
5 only; at least:

Sonna baka na koto o kangaeru no wa kimi kurai no mono da. (そんなばかなことを考えるのは君くらいのものだ) You are the *only* person that would think of something idiotic like that.

... kurai nara (...~なら) if:
Tochuu de nagedasu kurai nara, hajime kara yaranai hoo ga ii. (途中で投げ出すくらいなら、初めからやらないほうがいい) *If* you are going to give up halfway through, you had better not start at all.

ku「rashi くらし (暮らし) *n.* life; living; livelihood. ((⇒ kurasu[1]))

ku「rashi¹kku (o¹ngaku クラシックおんがく (クラシック音楽) *n.* classical music.

ku「ras·u[1] くらす (暮らす) *vi., vt.*
(kurash·i-; kuras·a-; kurash·i-te Ⓒ) live; make a living; get along; stay:
Sono sakka wa ik-ka-getsu hoteru de kurashita. (その作家は一か月ホテルで暮らした) The author *stayed* at a hotel for a month.

ku¹rasu[2] クラス *n.* class.

ku「re くれ (暮れ) *n.* end of the year. ((⇒ kureru[1]))

ku「regu¹re mo くれぐれも (呉々も) *adv.* please: ★ Used as an intensifier in expressions indicating one's sincere desire.
Kuregure mo kenkoo ni go-chuui kudasai. (くれぐれも健康にご注意ください) *Please* take good care of yourself.

ku「re·ru[1] くれる (呉れる) *vt.* (kure-te Ⓥ) give: ★ '*Kudasaru*' is the honorific alternative.
Kare wa watashi ni jisho o kureta. (彼は私に辞書をくれた) He *gave* me a dictionary.

-te kureru (て~) (used when a person's equal or subordinate does something for that person):
Yamada-san wa shinsetsu ni mo watashi o eki made okutte kureta. (山田さんは親切にも私を駅まで送ってくれた) Mr. Yamada was kind

enough to *take* me to the station.
(↔ ageru¹)

ku⌐re·ru² くれる (暮れる) *vi.* (kure-te ▽) **1** (of a day) get dark.
2 (of a year) draw to an end:
Kotoshi mo kurete kita. (今年も暮れてきた) The year *is drawing to an end*. (⇨ kure)
...ni kureru (...に暮れる) be lost (in thought): *Doo shite yoi ka tohoo ni kureta.* (どうしてよいか途方に暮れた) I *was at a loss* what to do.

ku⌐rii⌐niñgu クリーニング *n.* cleaning; laundry:
Zuboñ o kuriiniñgu ni dashita. (ズボンをクリーニングに出した) I sent my trousers to the *cleaner's*.

ku⌐rika⌐es·u くりかえす (繰り返す) *vt.* (-kaesh·i-; -kaes·a-; -kaesh·i-te ⓒ) repeat; do over again:
onaji machigai o kurikaesu (同じ間違いを繰り返す) *repeat* the same mistake.

Ku⌐risu⌐masu クリスマス *n.* Christmas.

ku⌐ro くろ (黒) *n.* **1** black; brown: kuro *no kutsu* (黒の靴) *black* shoes.
2 guilty:
Kare wa kuro *da to omou.* (彼は黒だと思う) I think he is *guilty*.
(↔ shiro¹)

ku⌐ro¹·i くろい (黒い) *a.* (-ku)
1 black; dark; tanned. (⇨ kuro)
2 (of rumors, etc.) dark:
Ano kaisha wa saikiñ kuroi *uwasa ga aru.* (あの会社は最近黒いうわさがある) Recently there have been *dark* rumors concerning that company.

ku⌐roji くろじ (黒字) *n.* black-ink balance; surplus:
Kaisha wa kuroji *desu.* (会社は黒字です) Our company is in the *black*.
(↔ akaji)

ku⌐roo くろう (苦労) *n.* trouble; difficulty; hardship; pains.
kuroo suru (〜する) *vi.* have trouble [difficulty]; have a hard time.
(⇨ gokuroosama)

ku⌐rooto くろうと (玄人) *n.* expert; professional; specialist.
(↔ shirooto)

k·u⌐ru くる (来る) *vi.* (k·i-; k·o-; k·i-te ①) **1** come; arrive:
Koko ni kite *kudasai.* (ここに来てください) Please *come* here. (↔ iku)
2 come from; be caused:
Kare no byooki wa karoo kara kita. (彼の病気は過労からきた) His illness *was caused* by overwork.
-te kuru (て〜) become [come to ...]: *Dañdañ samuku* natte kita. (だんだん寒くなってきた) It *has become* colder and colder.

ku⌐rukuru くるくる *adv.* (〜 to)
1 (used to express an object rotating):
Fuusha ga kurukuru *to mawatte ita.* (風車がくるくると回っていた) The sails of the windmill were turning *round and round*.
2 (used to express the state of being unstable):
Kare wa kañgae ga kurukuru *(to) kawaru.* (彼は考えがくるくる(と)変わる) His ideas are *always* changing.

ku⌐ruma くるま (車) *n.* **1** vehicle; car; automobile.
2 taxi:
Kuruma o yoñde kudasai. (車を呼んでください) Please call me a *taxi*.
3 wheel; caster.

ku⌐ru¹m·u くるむ *vt.* (kurum·i-; kurum·a-; kuruñ-de ⓒ) wrap:
Kanojo wa akañboo o moofu de kuruñda. (彼女は赤ん坊を毛布でくるんだ) She *wrapped* her baby in a blanket.

ku⌐ru⌐ri to くるりと *adv.* **1** (used to express the action of turning around):
Kare wa kururi *to ushiro o furi-muita.* (彼はくるりと後ろを振り向いた) He *spun around* and looked back.
2 suddenly; abruptly:
Kare wa kururi *o keekaku o kaeta.* (彼はくるりと計画を変えた) He *suddenly* changed his plan.

ku⌐rushi¹·i くるしい (苦しい) *a.*

(-ku) **1** painful; hard:
Sono tozañ wa kurushikatta. (その登山は苦しかった) The mountain climb was *very hard*. (⇨ kurushimu)

2 needy:
Koñgetsu wa kakee ga kurushii. (今月は家計が苦しい) This month we are in financially *straitened circumstances* at home.

3 awkward:
Watashi no tachiba ga kurushiku *natte kita*. (私の立場が苦しくなってきた) My position has become *awkward*.

kuˈrushimeˈ·ru くるしめる (苦しめる) *vt.* (-shime-te Ⅴ) distress; annoy; torment:
Shakkiñ ga kare o kurushimete iru. (借金が彼を苦しめている) The loan *is causing* him *distress*. (⇨ kurushimu)

kuˈrushimiˈ くるしみ (苦しみ) *n.* pain; hardship; agony:
kurushimi *ni taeru* (苦しみに耐える) bear *hardship*. (⇨ kurushimu)

kuˈrushiˈm·u くるしむ (苦しむ) *vi.* (-shim·i-; -shim·a-; -shiñ-de Ⅽ)
1 suffer from; feel pain; be afflicted:
ue ni kurushimu (飢えに苦しむ) *suffer* from hunger. (⇨ kurushimeru; kurushimi)

2 be troubled; be worried; be at a loss:
Kare wa iiwake ni kurushiñda. (彼は言い訳に苦しんだ) He *was at a loss* for an excuse.

3 have difficulty:
Kare no koodoo wa rikai ni kurushimu. (彼の行動は理解に苦しむ) I *have difficulty* in understanding his behavior.

kuˈsaˈ くさ (草) *n.* grass; weed. (⇨ zassoo; shiba; shibafu)

kuˈsaˈbana くさばな (草花) *n.* flowering plant.

kusaˈ·i くさい (臭い) *a.* (-ku)
1 smelly; stinking:
Kono kutsushita wa kusai. (この靴下は臭い) These socks are *smelly*.

2 suspicious; dubious; fishy:
Sono hanashi wa kusai. (その話は臭い) That story is *dubious*.

-kuˈsaˈi くさい (臭い) *suf.*
1 smelly; stinking:
*koge-*kusai (焦げ臭い) have a burnt smell / *sake-*kusai (酒臭い) *reek* of alcohol.

2 seem; look; sound:
*iñchiki-*kusai (インチキくさい) be phony *sounding* / *uso-*kusai (うそくさい) *seem like* a lie.

3 (used as an intensifier):
*baka-*kusai (ばかくさい) *completely foolish* / *meñdoo* kusai (面倒くさい) *very* troublesome.

kuˈsaˈki くさき (草木) *n.* grass and trees; plants.

kuˈsari くさり (鎖) *n.* chain.

kuˈsaˈr·u くさる (腐る) *vi.* (kusar·i-; kusar·a-; kusat-te Ⅽ) **1** go bad; decay; rot.

2 be discouraged:
Koto ga umaku ikanakute, kare wa kusatte iru. (ことがうまくいかなくて, 彼はくさっている) Things have gone wrong for him, so he *is discouraged*.

kuˈseˈ くせ (癖) *n.* **1** habit:
tsume o kamu kuse (つめをかむ癖) a *habit* of biting one's nails.

2 peculiarity:
Kare wa kuse *no aru ji o kaku*. (彼は癖のある字を書く) He writes in a *characteristic* way.

kuˈseˈ ni くせに (癖に) although; when; in spite of: ★ Usually belittling or disparaging.
Kare wa nani mo shiranai kuse ni, *nañ de mo shitte iru yoo ni hanasu*. (彼は何も知らないくせに, 何でも知っているように話す) *Although* he knows nothing, he talks as if he knew everything.

kuˈshakusha くしゃくしゃ *adv.* (~ no, ni) (used to express something that is wrinkled, creased or crumpled):
Kami no ke ga kushakusha *da*. (髪

の毛がくしゃくしゃだ) My hair is all *messed up*.

ku「sha¹mi くしゃみ *n.* sneeze: *Kare wa nañ-do mo* kushami (o) shita. (彼は何度もくしゃみ(を)した) He *sneezed* many times.

ku「shi¹ くし (櫛) *n.* comb.

ku「shi¹ñ くしん (苦心) *n.* pains; hard work; effort.
kushiñ suru (〜する) *vi.* take pains; work hard; make great efforts.

ku「so¹ くそ (糞) *n.* shit. ★ Often used as an exclamation of disgust, anger, etc. (⇨ daibeñ; fuñ²)

ku「sudama くすだま (薬玉) *n.*
1 decorative paper ball.
★ It is usually hung on festive occasions.
2 ornamental scent bag.

ku「sugur·u くすぐる (擽る) *vt.* (-gur·i·; -gur·a·; -gut-te Ⓒ) tickle (a person).

ku「sugutta¹·i くすぐったい *a.* (-ku) tickling; ticklish: *Senaka ga* kusuguttai. (背中がくすぐったい) My back is *ticklish*.

ku「su¹kusu くすくす *adv.* (〜 to) (used to express the manner of giggling [tittering; chuckling]): *hitori de* kusukusu (to) warau (ひとりでくすくす(と)笑う) *chuckle* to one-self.

ku「suri くすり (薬) *n.* medicine; drug: kusuri *o nomu* (薬を飲む) take *medicine*. (⇨ naifukuyaku)

ku「suriya くすりや (薬屋) *n.* pharmacy; drugstore. (⇨ yak-kyoku)

ku「suri¹yubi くすりゆび (薬指) *n.* ring finger.

ku「tabire¹·ru くたびれる *vi.* (-bi-re-te Ⓥ) 1 be tired; get tired; get exhausted: *Kanojo wa sugu ni* kutabireru. (彼女はすぐにくたびれる) She soon *gets tired out*.
2 (of clothes) be worn out: *Kare wa* kutabireta *kutsu o haite ita.* (彼はくたびれた靴をはいていた) He

was wearing *worn-out* shoes.

ku「takuta くたくた *adv.* (〜 ni) dead tired; exhausted: *Kare wa tsukarete* kutakuta *datta.* (彼は疲れてくたくただった) He was *utterly exhausted*.

ku「teñ くてん (句点) *n.* period. ★ The Japanese period is '。'. (⇨ tooteñ)

ku「to¹oteñ くとうてん (句読点) *n.* punctuation marks. (⇨ kuteñ; tooteñ)

ku「tsu¹ くつ (靴) *n.* shoes; boots.

ku「tsu¹shita くつした (靴下) *n.* socks; stockings: kutsushita *o haku* [*nugu*] (靴下をはく[脱ぐ]) put on [take off] one's *socks*. (⇨ tebukuro)

ku「tsuu くつう (苦痛) *n.* pain; pang; agony: kutsuu *o kañjiru* (苦痛を感じる) feel *pain*.

ku¹·u くう (食う) *vt.* (ku·i·; ku-w·a·; kut-te Ⓒ) 1 (*rude*) eat: ★ '*Taberu*' is more polite and usual.
Kyoo wa mada nani mo kutte inai. (きょうはまだ何も食っていない) I *have not eaten* anything yet today.
2 (*rude*) live; earn a living: ★ '*Taberu*' is more polite.
Kare wa arubaito o shite, kutte iru. (彼はアルバイトをして, 食っている) He *gets by* doing a part-time job.
3 (of an insect) eat; bite: *Kono moofu wa mushi ga* kutte iru. (この毛布は虫が食っている) The moths *have eaten* this blanket.
4 (of time, fuel, etc.) consume; waste: *Ookii kuruma wa gasoriñ o* kuu. (大きい車はガソリンを食う) Large cars *consume* lots of gasoline.
5 be taken in: *Sono te wa* kuwanai *zo.* (その手は食わないぞ) I *will not fall* for that trick.

ku「uchuu くうちゅう (空中) *n.* the air; the sky: kuuchuu *ni tadayou* (空中に漂う) float in *the air*. (⇨ kaijoo²; rikujoo)

ku⌐ufuku くうふく (空腹) *n.* hunger; empty stomach.

ku⌐uguň くうぐん (空軍) *n.* air force. (⇨ Jieetai; kaiguň; rikuguň)

ku⌐ukaň くうかん (空間) *n.* space; room: kuukaň *o akeru* (空間をあける) make *room*.

ku⌐uki くうき (空気) *n.* air: *heya no* kuuki *o irekaeru* (部屋の空気を入れ替える) *air* a room.

ku⌐ukoo くうこう (空港) *n.* airport. (⇨ hikoojoo)

ku⌐upoňˈkeň クーポンけん (クーポン券) *n.* coupon ticket.

ku⌐uraa クーラー *n.* air conditioner. (⇨ eakoň)

ku⌐uraň くうらん (空欄) *n.* blank column [space].

ku⌐usoo くうそう (空想) *n.* fancy; imagination; daydream.
kuusoo suru (〜する) *vt.* fancy; imagine; daydream.

ku⌐wadateˈru くわだてる (企てる) *vt.* (-date-te Ⅴ) **1** attempt; try: *jisatsu o* kuwadateru (自殺を企てる) *attempt* suicide.
2 plan: *Sono kaisha wa atarashii koojoo no keňsetsu o* kuwadatete iru. (その会社は新しい工場の建設を企てている) The company *is planning* the construction of a new factory.

ku⌐wae-ru くわえる (加える) *vt.* (-e-te Ⅴ) **1** add; sum up; include; join: (⇨ tsukekuwaeru) *Satoo o moo sukoshi* kuwaete *kudasai.* (砂糖をもう少し加えてください) Please *add* a little more sugar.
2 increase; gather; pick up: *Kuruma wa shidai ni sokudo o* kuwaeta. (車は次第に速度を加えた) The car gradually *picked up* speed. (⇨ kuwawaru)
3 give; put; deal: *hito ni atsuryoku o* kuwaeru (人に圧力を加える) *put* pressure on a person.

ku⌐washiˈ·i くわしい (詳しい) *a.* (-ku) **1** full; detailed; minute:

Kuwashii koto wa shirimaseň. (詳しいことは知りません) I do not know the *full details*.
2 (of knowledge) well versed; familiar.

ku⌐wawaˈr·u くわわる (加わる) *vi.* (-war·i-; -war·a-; -wat-te Ⅽ) **1** join; take part in: *Kanojo mo sono asobi ni* kuwawatta. (彼女もその遊びに加わった) She too *joined* in the game. (⇨ kuwaeru)
2 increase; gain: *Higoto ni samusa ga* kuwawatte *imasu.* (日ごとに寒さが加わっています) It *is getting* colder day by day.

ku⌐yaˈkusho くやくしょ (区役所) *n.* ward office. ★ The equivalent of city hall in metropolitan areas. (⇨ ku²; shiyakusho)

ku⌐yashiˈ·i くやしい (悔しい) *a.* (-ku) mortifying; regrettable: *Makete* kuyashii. (負けて悔しい) How *mortifying* it is to be defeated.

ku⌐zu くず (屑) *n.* **1** waste; rubbish; trash. (⇨ garakuta)
2 (*informal*) worthless [useless] person: *Aitsu wa niňgeň no* kuzu *da.* (あいつは人間のくずだ) He is a *good-for-nothing*.

ku⌐zureˈ·ru くずれる (崩れる) *vi.* (-re-te Ⅴ) **1** collapse; break; be destroyed; give way: *Toňneru ga* kuzureta. (トンネルがくずれた) The tunnel *caved in*. (⇨ kuzusu)
2 lose shape: *Sono fuku wa katachi ga* kuzurete *iru.* (その服は形がくずれている) Those clothes *have lost* their shape.
3 (of weather) change; deteriorate: *Teňki ga* kuzure-soo *da.* (天気がくずれそうだ) The weather is likely to *deteriorate*.
4 (of money) be changed: *Ichimaň-eň satsu* kuzuremasu ka? (一万円札くずれますか) Can you

change a ¥10,000 note?
((⇨ kuzusu))

ku⌐zu╵s·u くずす (崩す) *vt.* (-sh·i-; -s·a-; -sh·i-te C) **1** break down; pull down: *furui biru o kuzusu* (古いビルをくずす) *knock down* an old building. ((⇨ kuzureru))
2 change (money); break: *Ichimañ-eñ o kuzushite, señ-eñ satsu ni shita.* (一万円をくずして、千円札にした) I *have changed* ¥10,000 into thousand yen notes. ((⇨ kuzureru))
3 write (letters, characters) in a cursive style.

kya⌐betsu キャベツ *n.* cabbage.

kya⌐kkañ-teki きゃっかんてき (客観的) *a.n.* (~ na, ni) objective: *kyakkañ-teki na mikata* (客観的な見方) an *objective* point of view. ((↔ shukañ-teki))

kya╵ku きゃく (客) *n.* **1** caller; visitor; guest. ★ Polite form is 'o-kyaku(-sañ).'
2 customer; client; audience; spectator; passenger.

kya⌐kuhoñ きゃくほん (脚本) *n.* play; drama; scenario; screenplay.

kya⌐kuma きゃくま (客間) *n.* drawing room; guest room.

kya⌐kuseñ きゃくせん (客船) *n.* passenger boat [ship].

kya⌐kushoku きゃくしょく (脚色) *n.* dramatization; adaptation.
kyakushoku suru (~する) *vt.* dramatize; adapt.

kya⌐sshu-ka╵ado キャッシュカード *n.* debit card; bank card.

kyo⌐dai きょだい (巨大) *a.n.* (~ na, ni) huge; gigantic: *kyodai na tatemono* (巨大な建物) a *huge* building. ((⇨ ookii))

kyo╵hi きょひ (拒否) *n.* refusal; rejection; denial; veto.
kyohi suru (~する) *vt.* refuse; reject; deny; turn down; veto. ((⇨ kotowaru))

kyo╵ka きょか (許可) *n.* permis-

sion; license; approval; leave: *gaishutsu no kyoka o morau* (外出の許可をもらう) get *permission* to go out. ((⇨ shooniñ[1]; yurushi))
kyoka suru (~する) *vt.* permit; allow; license; approve. ((↔ kiñshi[1])) ((⇨ yurusu))

kyo╵ku きょく (曲) *n.* music; tune.

-kyoku きょく (局) *suf.* **1** bureau; department: *Seesoo-kyoku* (清掃局) Public Sanitation *Department*. ((⇨ -ka[5]))
2 office; station: *yuubiñ-kyoku* (郵便局) a post *office* / *heñshuu-kyoku* (編集局) an editorial *office* / *hoosoo-kyoku* (放送局) a broadcasting *station*.

kyo╵kuseñ きょくせん (曲線) *n.* curve; curved line. ((⇨ chokuseñ))

kyo⌐kuta╵ñ きょくたん (極端) *n.* extreme: *kyokutañ ni hashiru* (極端に走る) go to *extremes*.
— *a.n.* (~ na, ni) extreme; radical: *kyokutañ na ikeñ* (極端な意見) an *extreme* opinion.

kyo╵neñ きょねん (去年) *n.* last year. ((⇨ kotoshi; raineñ))

kyo╵o きょう (今日) *n.* today; this day. ((⇨ ashita; koñnichi; kinoo[1]))

-kyoo きょう (鏡) *suf.* -scope: *booeñ-kyoo* (望遠鏡) a *telescope* / *keñbi-kyoo* (顕微鏡) a *microscope*.

kyo⌐ochoo きょうちょう (強調) *n.* emphasis; stress.
kyoochoo suru (~する) *vt.* emphasize; stress.

kyo╵odai きょうだい (兄弟) *n.* sibling; brother; sister.

kyo⌐odoo きょうどう (共同) *n.* collaboration; partnership: *kyoodoo jigyoo* (共同事業) a *joint* venture / *kyoodoo seemee* (共同声明) a *joint* statement.
kyoodoo suru (~する) *vt.* share; combine one's efforts.

kyo⌐ofu きょうふ (恐怖) *n.* fear; terror; horror: *kyoofu ni osowareru* (恐怖に襲われる) be seized with *fear*.

kyo⌐oge╵ñ きょうげん (狂言) *n.*

1 traditional comic drama.
★ Performed as supplementary entertainment to fill the intervals between Noh plays.
2 sham; make-believe:
Kare no shita koto wa kyoogeñ datta. (彼のしたことは狂言だった) What he did was a *sham*.
((⇒ shibai))

kyo¯ogi¹ きょうぎ (競技) *n.* contest; competition; match; game; event:
kyoogi-joo (競技場) a *sports ground*; a *stadium*.
kyoogi suru (～する) *vt.* play a game; have a contest; compete.

kyo¯ogi² きょうぎ (協議) *n.* conference; discussion; deliberation.
kyoogi suru (～する) *vt.* discuss; talk; consult. ((⇒ soodañ))

kyo¯oguu きょうぐう (境遇) *n.* surroundings; circumstances:
Kanojo wa megumareta kyooguu ni sodatta. (彼女は恵まれた境遇に育った) She grew up in favorable *surroundings*.

kyo¯ohaku きょうはく (脅迫) *n.* threat; intimidation; menace:
kyoohaku-joo (脅迫状) a *threatening* [*blackmail*] letter.
kyoohaku suru (～する) *vt.* threaten; intimidate; menace.

kyo¯oiku きょういく (教育) *n.* education; teaching; training.
kyooiku suru (～する) *vt.* educate; train.

kyo¯oiñ きょういん (教員) *n.* teacher. ((⇒ señsee))

kyo¯oju きょうじゅ (教授) *n.* (full) professor. ((⇒ jokyooju; kooshi¹))

kyo¯oka きょうか (強化) *n.* strengthening; reinforcement; buildup: kyooka-garasu (強化ガラス) *reinforced* glass.
kyooka suru (～する) *vt.* strengthen; reinforce; build up: *keebi o kyooka suru* (警備を強化する) *strengthen* the guard.

kyo¯okai¹ きょうかい (境界) *n.* boundary; border. ((⇒ sakai))

kyo¯okai² きょうかい (教会) *n.* church.

kyo¯oka¯sho きょうかしょ (教科書) *n.* textbook; schoolbook.

kyo¯okuñ きょうくん (教訓) *n.* lesson; moral:
Sono shippai wa yoi kyookuñ ni natta. (その失敗は良い教訓になった) The failure was a good *lesson* to me.

kyo¯okyuu きょうきゅう (供給) *n.* supply; service:
deñryoku no kyookyuu (電力の供給) the *supply* of electric power.
((↔ juyoo))
kyookyuu suru (～する) *vt.* supply; provide.

kyo¯omi きょうみ (興味) *n.* interest:
Watashi wa seeji ni wa kyoomi ga nai. (私は政治には興味がない) I have no *interest* in politics.
((⇒ kañshiñ²))

kyo¯oretsu きょうれつ (強烈) *a.n.* (～ na, ni) strong; intense:
Sono jishiñ wa kyooretsu datta. (その地震は強烈だった) The earthquake was very *strong*.

kyo¯ori きょうり (郷里) *n.* one's hometown; one's home

kyo¯oryoku¹ きょうりょく (協力) *n.* cooperation; collaboration; working together.
kyooryoku suru (～する) *vi.* cooperate; collaborate; work together. ((⇒ kyoodoo))

kyo¯oryoku² きょうりょく (強力) *a.n.* (～ na, ni) strong; powerful. ((⇒ chikarazuyoi))

kyo¯osañshu¯gi きょうさんしゅぎ (共産主義) *n.* communism.

Kyo¯osañtoo きょうさんとう (共産党) *n.* = Nihoñ Kyoosañtoo. ((⇒ APP. 8))

kyo¯osee きょうせい (強制) *n.* compulsion; coercion.
kyoosee suru (～する) *vt.* force; compel; coerce.

kyo¯osee-teki きょうせいてき (強制的) *a.n.* (～ na, ni) compulsory;

obligatory:
Watashi-tachi wa kyoosee-teki ni sore o yarasareta. (私たちは強制的にそれをやらされた) We were made to do it *by force*.

kyoˈoshi きょうし (教師) *n.* teacher; instructor. (⇨ señsee)

kyoˈoshiˈñshoo きょうしんしょう (狭心症) *n.* angina (pectoris).

kyoˈoshitsu きょうしつ (教室) *n.* classroom; schoolroom.

kyoˈoshuku きょうしゅく (恐縮) *n.* being obliged; feeling sorry:
Wazawaza oide itadaite, kyooshuku *desu.* (わざわざお出ていただいて、恐縮です) I am much obliged to you for taking the trouble to come.
kyooshuku suru (～する) *vi.* be obliged; feel sorry.

kyoˈosoñ きょうそん (共存) *n.* co-existence.
kyoosoñ suru (～する) *vi.* coexist; live together.

kyoˈosoo きょうそう (競争) *n.* competition; contest:
kyoosoo *ni katsu [makeru]* (競争に勝つ[負ける]) win [lose] in a *competition*.
kyoosoo suru (～する) *vt.* compete; contest.

kyoˈotsuu きょうつう (共通) *a.n.* (～ na/no, ni) common; mutual:
wareware kyootsuu *no rieki* (われわれ共通の利益) our *mutual* advantage.
kyootsuu suru (～する) *vi.* have in common.

kyoˈotsuugo きょうつうご (共通語) *n.* common language. (⇨ kokugo)

kyoˈowaˈkoku きょうわこく (共和国) *n.* republic.

kyoˈoyoo きょうよう (教養) *n.* culture; education:
kyooyoo *o mi ni tsukeru* (教養を身につける) acquire *education and culture*.

kyoˈri きょり (距離) *n.* distance; interval:

kyori *o hakaru* (距離を測る) measure the *distance*.

kyoˈrokyoro きょろきょろ *adv.* (～ to; ～ suru) (used to express the action of looking around nervously or restlessly):
kyorokyoro *suru* (きょろきょろする) *look around restlessly*.

kyuˈu¹ きゅう (急) *n.* emergency; urgency:
Kono keñ wa kyuu o yoo shimasu. (この件は急を要します) This matter demands *immediate attention*.
— *a.n.* (～ na, ni) 1 urgent; pressing:
Kare wa kyuu na yooji de Oosaka e ikimashita. (彼は急な用事で大阪へ行きました) He went to Osaka on *urgent* business.
2 sudden; unexpected:
Kare no shi wa amari ni mo kyuu datta. (彼の死はあまりにも急だった) His death was very *sudden*.
3 steep; sharp:
Kono saka wa kyuu da. (この坂は急だ) This slope is *steep*.
4 swift; rapid:
Koko no nagare ga kyuu da. (ここは流れが急だ) The flow of the river is *swift* hereabouts.

kyuˈu² きゅう (級) *n.* 1 class; grade; rank:
daijiñ kyuu *no jiñbutsu* (大臣級の人物) a person of ministerial *rank*.
2 (in judo, kendo, karate, go, shogi, etc.) the name for the degree given to the less proficient:
*karate no ni-*kyuu (空手の2級) a second *grade* in karate.
3 the holder of *kyuu*. (⇨ dañ¹)

kyuˈu³ きゅう (旧) *n.* old; former:
kyuu *shoogatsu* (旧正月) New Year's Day according to the *old* [*lunar*] *calendar*.
— *pref.* ex-: kyuu-*shichoo* (旧市長) an *ex-*mayor. (⇨ moto²)

kyuˈu⁴ きゅう (球) *n.* globe; sphere; ball; bulb.

kyuˈu⁵ きゅう (九) *n.* nine.

★ Also pronounced '*ku.*'
(⇨ kokonotsu; APP. 3)

kyu⌈ubyoo きゅうびょう (急病) *n.*
sudden illness; acute disease.

kyu⌈ugaku きゅうがく (休学) *n.*
temporary absence from school.
kyuugaku suru (〜する) *vi.* withdraw from school temporarily.

kyu⌈ugeki きゅうげき (急激) *a.n.*
(〜 na, ni) sudden; abrupt;
rapid:
*Saikiñ no yo-no-naka wa heñka ga
kyuugeki desu.* (最近の世の中は変化
が急激です) The changes in recent
society are very *rapid*.

kyu⌈ugyoo きゅうぎょう (休業) *n.*
suspension of business; shutdown.
kyuugyoo suru (〜する) *vi.* suspend business; be closed; take a
holiday. (⇨ yasumu)

kyu⌈ujiñ きゅうじん (求人) *n.* offer
of a situation [job]:
kyuujiñ-*kookoku ni oobo suru* (求
人広告に応募する) apply for a job
in the *wanted* ads.

kyu⌈ujitsu きゅうじつ (休日) *n.*
holiday. (⇨ APP. 6)

kyu⌈uka きゅうか (休暇) *n.* vacation; holiday:
Isogashikute, kyuuka *ga torenai.*
(忙しくて、休暇がとれない) I am too
busy to *take time off.* (⇨ yasumi)

kyu⌈ukee きゅうけい (休憩) *n.*
break; rest; intermission:
kyuukee-*jikañ* (休憩時間) a *recess*;
an *intermission*. (⇨ kyuusoku;
yasumi)
kyuukee suru (〜する) *vt.* take
[have] a break [rest]. (⇨ hito-
yasumi)

kyu⌈ukoo[1] きゅうこう (急行) *n.*
express train. (⇨ futsuu[2]; tokkyuu)

kyu⌈ukoo[2] きゅうこう (休講) *n.* no
lecture.
kyuukoo suru (〜する) *vt.* cancel
a class [lecture].

kyu⌈ukutsu きゅうくつ (窮屈) *a.n.*

(〜 na, ni) **1** small; close; tight:
Kono kuruma wa roku-niñ noru to,
kyuukutsu *desu.* (この車は6人乗ると、
窮屈です) If six people get in this
car, it will *be cramped*.
2 (of regulations, etc.) strict;
rigid:
Kono gakkoo no kisoku wa kyuukutsu *da.* (この学校の規則は窮屈だ)
The rules at this school are *strict*.
3 stiff; formal; serious; uncomfortable:
Soñna ni kyuukutsu *ni kañgaenai
de kudasai.* (そんなに窮屈に考えないで
ください) Don't take it so *seriously*.

kyu⌈ukyuu きゅうきゅう (救急) *n.*
emergency:
kyuukyuu-*bako* (救急箱) a *first-aid*
kit / kyuukyuu-*byooiñ* (救急病院)
an *emergency* hospital / kyuukyuusha (救急車) an *ambulance*.

kyu⌈uri きゅうり (胡瓜) *n.* cucumber.

kyu⌈uryoo きゅうりょう (給料) *n.*
pay; wages; salary:
kyuuryoo *o morau* (給料をもらう)
get one's *salary*. (⇨ chiñgiñ)

kyu⌈ushoku[1] きゅうしょく (求職) *n.*
job hunting:
kyuushoku *no mooshikomi o suru*
(求職の申し込みをする) ask for *employment* [*a position*].

kyu⌈ushoku[2] きゅうしょく (給食) *n.*
provision of meals; school meal
[lunch].
kyuushoku suru (〜する) *vt.* provide lunches [meals] (for schoolchildren, employees, etc.).

kyu⌈ushuu きゅうしゅう (吸収) *n.*
absorption; suction.
kyuushuu suru (〜する) *vt.* absorb; suck in. (⇨ suu[1])

kyu⌈usoku きゅうそく (休息) *n.*
rest; repose.
kyuusoku suru (〜する) *vi.* take
[have] a rest. (⇨ kyuukee)

kyu⌈uyoo きゅうよう (急用) *n.* urgent business.

M

ma ま(間) *n.* **1** time; interval:
Isogashikute, yasumu ma mo nai.
(忙しくて、休む間もない) I am so busy
I do not even have *time* to rest.
2 interval; space:
*ie to dooro no aida ni ittee no ma
o toru* (家と道路の間に一定の間を取
る) leave a certain *space* between a
house and a road.
3 room. (⇨ heya; -ma)
ma ga [no] warui (～が[の]悪い)
unlucky; unfortunate; be embarrassed; feel awkward.
-ma ま(間) *suf.* room: ★ Also
used as counter for rooms.
Nihoñ-ma (日本間) a Japanese-
style *room* / *roku-joo-ma* (六畳間)
a six-tatami-mat *room.* (⇨ heya;
ma)
maa¹ まあ *adv.* (*informal*) **1** just:
Maa chotto yatte mimashoo. (まあち
ょっとやってみましょう) I will *just*
have a quick try.
2 well; say; probably; now:
★ Used to soften a statement or
opinion.
Maa kañgaete okimasu. (まあ考えて
おきます) *Well,* I will give it some
thought.
3 about; by and large:
*Kanojo wa maa sañ-juu gurai
desu.* (彼女はまあ30くらいです) She
would be, *about,* thirty.
maa² まあ *int.* oh; well; good
heavens; goodness: ★ Used by
women to express surprise, em-
barrassment or admiration.
Maa, odoroita. (まあ、驚いた) *Well!* I
am surprised! (⇨ ara)
maaku マーク *n.* mark; sign;
insignia; design.
maaku suru (～する) *vt.* **1** make
a mark.
2 keep an eye on: *Keesatsu de
wa kare o maaku shite iru.* (警察で

は彼をマークしている) The police *are
keeping a close eye* on him.
maamaa まあまあ *adv.* so-so;
not so bad; all right.
— *int.* come now; well:
*Maamaa, soñna ni koofuñ shinai
de.* (まあまあ、そんなに興奮しないで)
Come now, do not get so excited.
mabushi·i まぶしい(眩しい) *a.*
(-ku) glaring; dazzling.
mabuta まぶた(瞼) *n.* eyelid.
machi まち(町・街) *n.* town;
city; street. (⇨ mura)
-machi まち(町) *suf.* town;
block; street. ★ An administrative division of a town.
(⇨ -choo¹)
machiaishitsu まちあいしつ(待
合室) *n.* waiting room.
machiawase まちあわせ(待ち合わ
せ) *n.* meeting by appointment.
(⇨ machiawaseru)
machiawase·ru まちあわせる(待
ち合わせる) *vt.* (-awase-te Ⅴ)
meet a person by appointment.
(⇨ machiawase)
machidooshi·i まちどおしい(待
ち遠しい) *a.* (-ku) look forward to;
wait anxiously for; long for.
(⇨ machinozomu)
machigae·ru (間違え
る) *vt.* (-gae-te Ⅴ) make a mistake; make an error; confuse:
*Dare-ka ga machigaete, watashi
no kutsu o haite itta.* (だれかが間違え
て、私の靴をはいて行った) Someone
mistakenly put on my shoes and
went off. (⇨ machigai)
machigai まちがい(間違い) *n.*
1 mistake; error; blunder; fault:
machigai o suru (間違いをする)
make a *mistake.* (⇨ machigau)
2 accident; trouble:
machigai o okosu (間違いを起こす)
get into *trouble.* (⇨ jiko¹; misu¹)

ma⌐chiga⌐l·u まちがう（間違う）*vi.,
vt.* (-ga·i-; -gaw·a-; -gat·te C)
be wrong: ★ Usually in the
phrase '*machigatte iru*.'
Kono deñwa bañgoo wa machigatte iru.（この電話番号は間違ってい
る）This telephone number *is
wrong*. (⇨ machigaeru; machigai)

ma⌐chi⌐machi まちまち *a.n.*
(～ na/no, ni) different; various;
divided:
Ikeñ ga machimachi ni wakareta.
（意見がまちまちに分かれた）Opinion
was divided *in many ways*.

ma⌐chinozom·u まちのぞむ（待ち
望む）*vt,* (-nozom·i-; -nozom·a-;
-nozoñ-de C) wait for; look forward to. (⇨ machidooshii)

ma⌐da まだ（未だ）*adv.* 1 (with a
negative) yet:
Kanojo wa mada *kite imaseñ.*（彼
女はまだ来ていません）She has not
come *yet*.
2 still:
Kare wa mada *miseeneñ desu.*（彼
はまだ未成年です）He is *still* under
age.
3 more:
Taifuu wa mada *yatte kuru deshoo.*（台風はまだやって来るでしょう）
Some *more* typhoons will be
coming our way.
4 only:
Nihoñ ni kite, mada *hañtoshi desu.*
（日本に来て、まだ半年です）It is *only*
six months since I came to Japan.

ma⌐damada まだまだ（未だ未だ）
adv. still; (not) yet:
Kono shoobai wa madamada *kore
kara nobimasu.*（この商売はまだまだこ
れから伸びます）This business will
expand *still* more from now.

ma⌐de まで（迄）*p.* 1 to; till; as
far as: ★ Indicates the forward
limits of an action or state in
time or space. Often used with
'*kara*.'
Mainichi asa ku-ji kara gogo go-ji
made *hatarakimasu.*（毎日朝 9 時か
ら午後 5 時まで働きます）I work

from nine in the morning *till*
five in the afternoon every day.
(↔ kara³)
2 till: ★ Follows the dictionary
form of a verb and indicates the
time limit of an action or state.
Shiñbuñ o yomu made *sono jikeñ
no koto wa shiranakatta.*（新聞を読
むまでその事件のことは知らなかった）I
didn't know about the incident
till I read the paper. (⇨ made ni)
3 also; even: ★ Emphasizes an
extreme limit.
Kodomo ni made *baka ni sareta.*
（子どもにまではかにされた）I was made
a fool of *even* by the children

ma⌐de ni までに（迄に）1 by; before; not later than: ★ Follows
time expressions. (⇨ made)
Kono shigoto wa getsumatsu made ni *shiagete kudasai.*（この仕事は
月末までに仕上げてください）Please
finish up this work *by* the end of
this month.
2 by the time: ★ Follows the
dictionary form of a verb.
Kodomo-tachi ga kaette kuru made ni *yuuhañ no shitaku o shita.*
（子どもたちが帰って来るまでに夕飯の支
度をした）I had prepared dinner *by
the time* the children got back.

ma⌐do まど（窓）*n.* window:
mado *o akeru [shimeru]*（窓を開ける
[閉める]）open [shut] the *window*.

ma⌐do⌐guchi まどぐち（窓口）*n.*
window; wicket; clerk at the window.

ma⌐e まえ（前）*n.* 1 front:
★ '*Mae*' covers the meanings
'front' and 'in front (of).' *e.g.*
biru no mae＝the front of the
building; in front of the building. (↔ ura; ushiro) (⇨ shoomeñ)
2 the first part:
Sono monogatari no mae *no bubuñ wa taikutsu desu.*（その物語の
前の部分は退屈です）The *first part*
of the story is tedious. (↔ ato¹)
3 the previous [former] time;
ago; before:

Mae *wa koko ni eki ga arimashita.*
(前はここに駅がありました) In *former
times* there was a station here.
((⇒ izen¹))

-mae¹ まえ(前) *suf.* **1** in front
of:
*Kono basu wa shiyakusho-mae ni
tomarimasu.* (このバスは市役所前に止
まります) This bus stops *in front of*
the city hall.
2 ago; before:
*Kanojo wa hito-tsuki-mae ni
Nihoñ e kimashita.* (彼女は一月前に
日本へ来ました) She came to Japan
one month *ago.* (⇒ -go; -sugi)

-mae² まえ(前) *suf.* for (the
stated number of people):
shokuji o go-niñ-mae tanomu (食
事を5人前頼む) order food *for
five.*

ma⌐eashi まえあし(前足) *n.* (of
an animal) forefoot; foreleg.
(↔ atoashi)

ma⌐egaki まえがき(前書き) *n.*
preface; foreword.

ma⌐emuki まえむき(前向き) *n.*
1 facing front.
2 positive attitude:
*moñdai ni motto maemuki ni tori-
kumu* (問題にもっと前向きに取り組む)
take a more *positive attitude* to
the problem. (⇒ sekkyoku-teki)

ma⌐garikado まがりかど(曲がり角)
n. **1** street corner; bend; turn.
2 turning point:
*Gakkoo kyooiku wa magarikado
ni kite iru.* (学校教育は曲がり角に来
ている) School education is now at
a *turning point.*

ma⌐gar·u まがる(曲がる) *vi.* (ma-
gar·i·; magar·a·; magat-te C)
1 bend; curve:
koshi ga magaru (腰が曲がる) *be
bent over* at the waist.
((⇒ mageru))
2 turn; wind:
*Tsugi no shiñgoo o hidari ni ma-
gari nasai.* (次の信号を左に曲がりなさ
い) *Turn* left at the next traffic
light.

ma⌐ge·ru まげる(曲げる) *vt.* (ma-
ge-te V) **1** bend:
harigane o mageru (針金を曲げる)
bend a wire. (⇒ magaru)
2 depart from (one's principles);
deviate from:
*Watashi no kotoba o magete
toranai de kudasai.* (私の言葉を曲げ
て取らないでください) Please do not
wrongly interpret my words.

ma⌐gira¹s·u まぎらす(紛らす) *vt.*
(-rash·i·; -ras·a·; -rash·i·te C)
divert; beguile:
oñgaku o kiite ki o magirasu (音楽
を聞いて気を紛らす) *divert oneself* by
listening to music.
((⇒ magireru))

ma⌐gire¹·ru まぎれる(紛れる) *vi.*
(-re-te V) **1** get mixed up:
yami ni magirete nigeru (闇に紛れ
て逃げる) run away *under cover of*
darkness.
2 be diverted:
*Tabi ni dereba ki ga magireru de-
shoo.* (旅に出れば気が紛れるでしょう) If
you go on a trip, you will *be diverted from worry.* (⇒ magirasu)

ma⌐go¹ まご(孫) *n.* grandchild;
grandson; granddaughter.

ma⌐gomago まごまご *adv.*
(～ suru) **1** get confused; lose
one's presence of mind.
2 loiter; hang around:
*Magomago shite iru to deñsha ni
maniaimaseñ yo.* (まごまごしていると
電車に間に合いませんよ) If you *waste
time,* we will not be in time for
the train.

ma⌐gotsuk·u まごつく *vi.* (-tsu-
k·i·; -tsuk·a·; -tsu·i·te C) get
confused; be embarrassed; be at
a loss.

ma⌐guro まぐろ(鮪) *n.* tuna.

ma¹hi まひ(麻痺) *n.* paralysis;
numbness.
mahi suru (～する) *vi.* be paralyzed; be numbed.

ma⌐hoo まほう(魔法) *n.* magic;
witchcraft.

mai- まい(毎) *pref.* every; each:

mai-*nichi* (毎日) every day / mai-*shuu* (毎週) every week.

-mai[1] まい *infl. end.* [attached to the dictionary form of a consonant-stem verb or the continuative base of a vowel-stem verb]
1 think not; probably not:
Osoraku kare wa ikumai. (おそらく彼は行くまい) Probably he *will not go.* / *Koñna mono wa inu de mo tabemai.* (こんなものは、犬でも食べまい) Even a dog *wouldn't eat* stuff like this. (⇨ daroo)
2 do not want to: ★ Often in the pattern '*ni-do to ...-mai to omou.*'
Kare ni wa ni-do to aumai to omotte imasu. (彼には二度と会うまいと思っています) I am determined *never to meet* him again.

-mai[2] まい 《枚》 *suf.* sheet; piece; leaf; slice: ★ Counter for flat objects.
kami yoñ-mai (紙 4 枚) four *sheets* of paper / *garasu ni-mai* (ガラス 2 枚) two *panes* of glass.

ma͞iasa まいあさ (毎朝) *n.* every morning.

ma͞ibañ まいばん (毎晩) *n.* every evening; every night.

ma͞ido まいど (毎度) *n.* every [each] time; always:
Kare ga moñku o iu no wa maido no koto da. (彼が文句を言うのは毎度のことだ) His complaining is an *everyday affair.*
— *adv.* often; frequently. (⇨ itsu-mo)

maido arigatoo (〜ありがとう) thank you: *Maido arigatoo gozaimasu.* (毎度ありがとうございます) *Thank you* very much. ★ A set phrase used by service personnel.

ma͞igo まいご (迷子) *n.* lost [stray; missing] child:
maigo ni naru (迷子になる) *lose one's way.*

ma͞i-ho͞omu マイホーム *n.* one's own home.

ma͞i-ka͞ra マイカー *n.* one's own car; private [family] car.

ma͞ikai まいかい (毎回) *adv.* every [each] time; every inning [round].

ma͞iku マイク *n.* microphone.

ma͞inasu マイナス *n.* 1 minus:
mainasu go-do (マイナス 5 度) five degrees *below zero.*
2 disadvantage; handicap:
Sono koto wa wareware ni totte mainasu da. (そのことはわれわれにとってマイナスだ) That is a *disadvantage* to us. (↔ purasu)

mainasu suru (〜する) *vt.* subtract.

ma͞inichi まいにち (毎日) *n.* every day.

ma͞ir·u[1] まいる (参る) *vi.* (mair·i-; mair·a-; mait-te C) 1 (*humble*) go; come:
Sugu mairimasu. (すぐ参ります) I *am coming* right away. / *Itte mairimasu.* (行って参ります) I *am going out* (and will be back soon).
2 visit a shrine [temple]; go to worship. (⇨ omairi)

ma͞ir·u[2] まいる (参る) *vi.* (mair·i-; mair·a-; mait-te C) 1 cannot stand; give up:
Kono atsusa ni wa maitta. (この暑さには参った) I *cannot stand* this heat.
2 be defeated:
Kare wa maitta to itta. (彼は参ったと言った) He admitted his *defeat.*
3 be at a loss; be embarrassed:
Doo shite yoi ka wakarazu, maitta. (どうしてよいかわからず、参った) I *was at a loss* what to do.

ma͞ishuu まいしゅう (毎週) *n.* every week.

ma͞itoshi まいとし (毎年) *n.* every [each] year.

ma͞itsuki まいつき (毎月) *n.* every [each] month.

ma͞ijime まじめ (真面目) *a.n.* (〜 na, ni) serious; honest; sober; earnest. (↔ fumajime) (⇨ hoñki)

ma͞iji͞r·u まじる (混じる) *vi.* (majir·i-; majir·a-; majit-te C) be mixed; be mingled. (⇨ koñgoo; mazeru)

ma「jiwa」r·u まじわる (交わる) vi. (-war·i-; -war·a-; -wat-te C)
1 cross; intersect:
Sono futatsu no dooro wa yaku ichi-kiro saki de majiwatte imasu. (その二つの道路は約1キロ先で交わっています) The two roads *cross each other* about one kilometer ahead. (⇨ koosa)
2 associate (with a person); get along with.

ma「kase」·ru まかせる (任せる) vt. (makase-te V) leave; trust:
Sono shigoto wa watashi ni makase nasai. (その仕事は私に任せなさい) Please *leave* that job to me.

ma「kas·u まかす (負かす) vt. (makash·i-; makas·a-; makash·i-te C) beat; defeat. (⇨ makeru)

ma「ke まけ (負け) n. defeat; loss; lost game. (↔ kachi²) (⇨ makeru)

ma「keoshimi まけおしみ (負け惜しみ) n. sour grapes: Kare wa makeoshimi ga tsuyoi. (彼は負け惜しみが強い) He is a *bad loser*.

ma「ke·ru まける (負ける) vi. (make-te V) **1** be beaten [defeated]; lose. (↔ katsu¹) (⇨ makasu; make)
2 discount; reduce; cut:
Sukoshi makete kuremaseñ ka? (少しまけてくれませんか) Can't you *reduce* the price slightly?
3 give in (to temptation); yield. (↔ katsu¹)

ma「kiko」m·u まきこむ (巻き込む) vt. (-kom·i-; -kom·a-; -koñ de C) involve:
Watashi wa sono keñka ni makikomarete shimatta. (私はそのけんかに巻き込まれてしまった) I *got involved* in the fight.

ma「kka」 まっか (真っ赤) a.n. (~ na, ni) (deep) red; crimson; scarlet: makka ni natte okoru (まっかになって怒る) become *red* with anger. (↔ massao)

ma「kko」o kara まっこうから (真っ向から) adv. head-on; squarely:
Kare wa sono keekaku ni makkoo kara *hantai shita*. (彼はその計画にまっこうから反対した) He opposed that plan *head-on*.

ma「kku」ra まっくら (真っ暗) a.n. (~ na, ni) pitch-dark.

ma「kku」ro まっくろ (真っ黒) a.n. (~ na, ni) coal-black; tanned all over. (↔ masshiro)

ma「koto ni まことに (誠に) adv. (formal) very; very much; truly:
Makoto ni *mooshiwake arimaseñ*. (まことに申しわけありません) I am *sincerely* sorry.

ma「k·u¹ まく (巻く) vt. (mak·i-; mak·a-; ma·i-te C) **1** wind; wrap:
ude ni hootai o maku (腕に包帯を巻く) *wind* a bandage around one's arm.
2 roll up; coil up:
roopu o guruguru maku (ロープをぐるぐる巻く) *coil* a rope *up*.

ma「ku」² まく (幕) n. **1** curtain (in a theater).
2 act:
sañ-maku no kigeki (3幕の喜劇) a comedy in three *acts*.

ma「k·u³ まく (蒔く) vt. (mak·i-; mak·a-; ma·i-te C) plant; sow:
hana no tane o maku (花の種をまく) *plant* flower seeds.

ma「ku」⁴ まく (膜) n. membrane; film.

ma「ku-no」-uchi(-be」ñtoo) まくのうち(べんとう)(幕の内弁当) n. Japanese-style variety box lunch.

ma「kura まくら (枕) n. pillow.

ma「ma」¹ まま (儘) n. **1** remaining in the same state [condition]:
Deñsha wa mañiñ de, zutto tatta mama datta. (電車は満員で, ずっと立ったままだった) The train was full, and I *remained standing* all the way. (⇨ kono-mama; sono-mama)
2 with; having:
Kanojo wa booshi o kabutta ma-

ma, *heya ni haitta.* (彼女は帽子をかぶったまま，部屋に入った) She entered the room *with* her hat on.

3 as it is:
Watashi wa mita mama (no koto) o keesatsu ni hanashita. (私は見たまま(のこと)を警察に話した) I reported it to the police just *as I saw it happen.*

4 in accordance with; as:
Watashi wa iwareru (ga) mama ni soko e itta. (私は言われる(が)ままにそこへ行った) I went there *as I was told to.*

ma⌐ma² ママ *n.* mom; mum; mommy; mammy; mother. (→ papa)

ma⌐mahaha ままはは(継母) *n.* stepmother.

ma⌐me¹ まめ(豆) *n.* bean; pea.

ma⌐me¹² まめ *n.* blister; corn.

ma⌐me³ まめ *a.n.* (~ na, ni) faithful; hardworking:
mame ni hataraku (まめに働く) *work like a beaver.*

ma⌐metsu まめつ(摩滅) *n.* wear and tear.
mametsu suru (~する) *vi.* be worn down [out]. (⇨ heru)

-mamire まみれ(塗れ) *suf.* (*n.*)
[after a noun] be covered:
★ Used in an unfavorable situation.
ase-mamire (汗まみれ) *covered* in sweat / *chi-mamire* (血まみれ) *all bloody.*

ma⌐mire⌐ru まみれる(塗れる) *vi.* (mamire-te Ⅴ) be covered; be smeared:
Kare no zuboñ wa doro ni mamirete ita. (彼のズボンは泥にまみれていた) His trousers *were covered* in mud.

ma-⌐mo⌐-naku まもなく(間も無く) *adv.* soon; shortly; before long.

ma⌐mo⌐r-u まもる(守る) *vt.* (mamor-i-; mamor-a-; mamot-te C)
1 defend:
kuni o mamoru (国を守る) *defend* one's country. (↔ semeru¹)

2 protect; guard:

kodomo-tachi o kootsuu-jiko kara mamoru (子どもたちを交通事故から守る) *protect* children from traffic accidents.

3 keep (a promise); observe (a rule, etc.).

ma⌐ñ まん(万) *n.* ten thousand. (⇨ APP. 3)

ma⌐naa マナー *n.* manners:
manaa ga yoku nai (マナーがよくない) have no *manners.*

ma⌐nab·u まなぶ(学ぶ) *vt.* (manab·i-; manab·a-; manañ-de C) learn; study; take lessons. (⇨ narau)

ma⌐ne まね(真似) *n.* imitation; mimicry:
señsee no mane o suru (先生のまねをする) *mimic* a teacher. (⇨ maneru)

ma⌐neki まねき(招き) *n.* invitation. (⇨ maneku; shootai¹)

ma⌐ne⌐k·u まねく(招く) *vt.* (manek·i-; manek·a-; mane·i-te C)
1 invite; call:
Kanojo wa watashi o paatii ni maneite kureta. (彼女は私をパーティーに招いてくれた) She *invited* me to the party. (⇨ maneki)

2 beckon; gesture:
Watashi wa sono ko o te de maneita. (私はその子を手で招いた) I *beckoned* the child over.

3 cause (an accident, trouble, etc.); result in; bring about.

ma⌐ne·ru まねる(真似る) *vt.* (mane-te Ⅴ) imitate; copy; mimic:
dezaiñ o maneru (デザインをまねる) *copy* a design.

ma⌐ñga まんが(漫画) *n.* cartoon; comics; caricature.

ma⌐ñgetsu まんげつ(満月) *n.* full moon. (⇨ tsuki²)

ma⌐nia⌐l·u まにあう(間に合う) *vi.* (-a·i-; -aw·a-; -at-te C)
1 be in time:
shuudeñ ni maniau (終電に間に合う) *be in time* for the last train.

2 be useful; be enough; do:
Kono jisho de maniaimasu. (この辞書で間に合います) I can make *do*

with this dictionary.

ma⌐nichi まんいち (万一) *n.* emergency; the worst: ★ Literally 'one out of ten thousand.' Mañichi *no baai wa koko ni reñraku shite kudasai.* (万一の場合はここに連絡してください) In the event of an *unforseen occurrence*, please contact this place.
— *adv.* in case; by some chance.

ma⌐niñ まんいん (満員) *n.* being full; no vacancy; full house.

ma⌐ñjoo-itchi まんじょういっち (満場一致) *n.* unanimity:
Sono keekaku wa mañjoo-itchi *de kimatta.* (その計画は満場一致で決まった) The plan was *unanimously* adopted. (⇨ itchi)

ma⌐ñnaka まんなか (真ん中) *n.* the middle; center:
machi no mañnaka (町の真ん中) the *heart* of town. (⇨ chuuoo)

ma⌐ñne⌐ñhitsu まんねんひつ (万年筆) *n.* fountain pen.

ma⌐ñseki まんせき (満席) *n.* full house; the seats being filled.

ma⌐ñshoñ マンション *n.* 1 condominium; apartment complex.
2 individual unit of same.

ma⌐ñte⌐ñ まんてん (満点) *n.* full marks; perfect score:
mañteñ o toru (満点を取る) get *full marks*.

ma⌐ñza⌐i まんざい (漫才) *n.* comic dialogue on stage. ★ A vaudeville act performed by a pair of comedians.

ma⌐ñzoku まんぞく (満足) *n.* satisfaction; contentment.
mañzoku suru (～する) *vi.* be satisfied; be contented.
— *a.n.* (～ na, ni) 1 satisfactory; contented. (⇨ fumañ)
2 enough; complete; proper:
Isogashikute, kono mikka-kañ mañzoku *na shokuji o shite imaseñ.* (忙しくて、この3日間満足な食事をしていません) I have not had a *proper* meal these three days as I have been so busy.

ma⌐ppu⌐tatsu まっぷたつ (真っ二つ) *n.* right in half [two].

ma⌐re まれ (希) *a.n.* (～ na, ni) rare; uncommon; unusual. (⇨ mezurashii)

ma⌐ri¹ まり (鞠) *n.* ball.

ma⌐ru まる (丸) *n.* circle. (⇨ marui)

ma⌐ru- まる (丸) *pref.* full; whole:
Kañsee made ni wa maru-ik-ka-getsu kakarimasu. (完成までには丸1か月かかります) It will take a *whole* month before completion.

-maru まる (丸) *suf.* (attached to the name of a Japanese civilian vessel).

ma⌐rude まるで (丸で) *adv.*
1 (with a negative) absolutely; entirely; quite; altogether:
Watashi no Nihoñgo wa marude dame desu. (私の日本語はまるでだめです) My Japanese is *absolutely* useless.
2 just (like; as if): ★ Used with 'yoo da.'
Sono oñna-no-ko wa marude otona no yoo na kuchi o kiku. (その女の子はまるで大人のような口をきく) The girl talks *just as if* she were an adult.

ma⌐ru·i まるい (丸い) *a.* (-ku)
1 round; spherical; circular. (⇨ maru; shikakui)
2 plump; chubby:
akañboo no marui hoo (赤ん坊の丸いほお) the *chubby* cheeks of a baby.
3 bent; stooped:
Kare wa toshi o totte, senaka ga maruku natte kita. (彼は年をとって、背中が丸くなってきた) As he grew older, he became *stooped*.

ma⌐rume·ru まるめる (丸める) *vt.* (marume-te Ⅴ) form into a ball; roll (up): kami o marumeru (紙を丸める) *roll up* a piece of paper.

ma⌐saka まさか *adv.* surely (not); cannot be: ★ Used to express unlikelihood or unwillingness to believe.

Sore wa masaka hoñtoo no hana-shi ja nai deshoo ne? (それはまさか本当の話じゃないでしょうね) That is not *really* a true story, is it?

masaka no toki (〜のとき) (*formal*) in case of emergency [need].

ma˥sa ni まさに (正に) *adv.*
1 just; exactly; really; surely:
Masa ni *anata no ossharu toori desu.* (まさにあなたのおっしゃるとおりです) It is *just* as you say.
2 be about to (do); be just going to (do):
Eki ni tsuitara, deñsha ga masa ni deyoo to shite ita. (駅に着いたら、電車がまさに出ようとしていた) When I arrived at the station, the train was *just about to* pull out.

ma˥sa˥ru まさる (勝る) *vi.* (masar-i-; masar-a-; masat-te C̲) surpass; excel; exceed.

ma˥satsu まさつ (摩擦) *n.* rubbing; friction; discord:
booeki-masatsu o okosu (貿易摩擦を起こす) give rise to trade *friction*.
masatsu suru (〜する) *vt., vi.* rub. (⇒ kosuru)

ma˥shite まして *adv.* 1 (with a negative) much [still] less; let alone:
Chuugokugo wa hanasemaseñ shi, mashite kaku koto wa dekimaseñ. (中国語は話せませんし、まして 書くことはできません) I cannot speak Chinese, *much less* write it.
2 (with an affirmative) much [still] more; even more.

ma˥ssa˥ichuu まっさいちゅう (真っ最中) *n.* right in the middle (of); (at) the height (of). (⇒ saichuu)

ma˥ssa˥ki まっさき (真っ先) *n.* the very first; (at) the head (of).

ma˥ssa˥o まっさお (真っ青) *a.n.* (〜 na, ni) 1 (deep) blue; azure.
2 pale; white:
Kare wa kyoofu de massao ni natta. (彼は恐怖で真っ青になった) He grew *pale* with terror. (↔ makka)

ma˥sshi˥ro まっしろ (真っ白) *a.n.* (〜 na, ni) pure-white; white as

snow. (↔ makkuro)

ma˥sshiro˥·i まっしろい (真っ白い) *a.* (-ku) pure-white; white as snow.

ma˥ssu˥gu まっすぐ (真っ直ぐ) *a.n.* (〜 na, ni) 1 straight; direct.
massugu *na michi* (真っすぐな道) a *straight* road.
2 upright; honest:
Kare wa massugu na seekaku o shite iru. (彼は真っすぐな性格をしている) He has an *honest and upright* personality.

ma˥s·u˥ ます (増す) *vi.* (mash·i-; mas·a-; mash·i-te C̲) increase; gain; add. ★ Slightly more formal than '*fueru.*'

ma˥su˥² ます (鱒) *n.* trout.

ma˥su˥³ ます (升) *n.* small square measuring box.

-masu ます *infl. end.* [attached to the continuative base of a verb] ★ Used to make the style of speech polite without adding any concrete meaning. (⇒ APP. 2)
Watashi wa maiasa shiñbuñ o yomimasu. (私は毎朝新聞を読みます) I *read* the newspaper every morning. / *Watashi wa tabako o suimaseñ.* (私はたばこを吸いません) I *don't* smoke.

ma˥sukomi マスコミ *n.* mass media; journalism.

ma˥suku マスク *n.* (face) mask; features.

ma˥su˥masu ますます (益々) *adv.* more and more; less and less; increasingly. (⇒ iyoiyo)

ma˥sutaa˥¹ マスター *n.* mastery.
masutaa suru (〜する) *vt.* master: *Nihoñgo o masutaa suru* (日本語をマスターする) *master* the Japanese language.

ma˥sutaa˥² マスター *n.* owner (of a bar, club, etc.); proprietor. (⇒ shujiñ)

ma˥ta˥¹ また (股) *n.* crotch; thigh.

ma˥ta˥² また (又) *adv.* 1 again:
Mata, *kare wa chikoku da.* (また、彼は遅刻だ) He is late *again.*

2 also; too:
Kare wa isha de ari, mata sakka de mo aru.(彼は医者であり、また作家でもある) He is a doctor and *also* a writer.

ma⌐ta³ また (又) *conj.* moreover; besides; what is more. (⇨ sara ni)

ma⌐taga⌐r·u またがる (跨る) *vi.* (matagar·i-; matagar·a-; mata-gat-te ©) **1** straddle; sit astride (a horse).
2 extend; span:
Fuji-san wa futatsu no ken ni matagatte imasu.(富士山は2つの県にまたがっています) Mt. Fuji *sits on* two prefectures.

ma⌐ta⌐g·u またぐ (跨ぐ) *vt.* (matag·i-; matag·a-; mata·i-de ©) step over; cross:
Kare wa mizutamari o mataida.(彼は水たまりをまたいだ) He *stepped over* the puddle.

ma⌐ta⌐-wa または (又は) *conj.* or:
kuro mata-wa ao no boorupen (黒または青のボールペン) a black *or* a blue ballpoint pen. (⇨ aruiwa¹; moshikuwa)

ma⌐to まと (的) *n.* mark; target; object; focus:
chuumoku no mato (注目の的) the *focus* of public attention.
mato-hazure (〜外れ) off the point.

ma⌐tomari まとまり (纏り) *n.*
1 unity; organization; solidarity. (⇨ matomaru)
2 coherence; order:
Kare no hanashi wa matomari ga nai.(彼の話はまとまりがない) His talk lacks *coherence*.

ma⌐tomar·u まとまる (纏まる) *vi.* (matomar·i-; matomar·a-; matomat-te ©) **1** be collected; be brought together. (⇨ matomeru)
2 be united; be organized:
Kangae wa mada matomatte imasen.(考えはまだまとまっていません) My thoughts *are not organized* yet. (⇨ matomeru; matomari)

3 (of a negotiation, contract, etc.) be settled; be concluded; come to an agreement. (⇨ matomeru)

ma⌐tome まとめ (纏め) *n.* summary; conclusion. (⇨ matomeru)

ma⌐tome·ru まとめる (纏める) *vt.* (matome-te ▽) **1** collect; gather together:
Kamikuzu o matomete moyashita.(紙くずをまとめて燃やした) I *collected* the wastepaper and burned it.
2 arrange; put into shape:
Kare wa sono endan o matometa.(彼はその縁談をまとめた) He *arranged* the marriage. (⇨ matomaru)
3 settle (a negotiation, contract, etc.); mediate. (⇨ matomaru)

ma⌐ts·u¹ まつ (待つ) *vt.* (mach·i-; mat·a-; mat-te ©) wait; look forward to:
Dare o matte iru n desu ka? (だれを待っているんですか) Who *are* you *waiting* for?

ma⌐tsu² まつ (松) *n.* pine (tree):
matsu-*kazari* (松飾り) the New Year's pine decorations. (⇨ kado-matsu; shoo-chiku-bai)

-matsu まつ (末) *suf.* the end:
shuu-matsu (週末) the week-*end* / *getsu*-matsu (月末) the *end* of the month. (⇨ sue)

ma⌐tsuri まつり (祭り) *n.* festival; fete.

ma⌐tsur·u まつる (祭る) *vt.* (matsur·i-; matsur·a-; matsut-te ©) deify; enshrine.

ma⌐tsutake まつたけ (松茸) *n.* matsutake. ★ A large brown edible mushroom. (⇨ kinoko)

ma⌐ttaku まったく (全く) *adv.*
1 completely; utterly:
Sore wa mattaku bakageta hanashi da.(それはまったくばかげた話だ) That is an *utterly* ridiculous story.
2 (with a negative) (not) at all:
Watashi wa mattaku oyogemasen.(私はまったく泳げません) I cannot swim *at all*. (⇨ zenzen)
3 really; indeed:

"Kyoo wa ii teñki desu ne." "Mattaku *desu."* (「きょうはいい天気ですね」
「まったくです」) "It is nice weather
today." "It *certainly* is."

ma·ˈu まう (舞う) *vi.* (ma·i-; ma-
w·a-; mat-te C̄) dance; flutter;
whirl.

maˈwari まわり (回り・周り) *n.*
1 circumference; edge:
ike no mawari *o aruku* (池の周りを
歩く) walk around the *edge* of a
pond.
2 neighborhood; environment:
Watashi no ie no mawari *ni takusañ ie ga tachimashita.* (私の家の周
りにたくさん家が建ちました) Many
houses were built in my *neighborhood.*

maˈwariˈmichi まわりみち (回り
道) *n.* detour; roundabout
course: mawarimichi *o suru* (回
り道をする) make a *detour.*

maˈwar·u まわる (回る) *vi.* (ma-
war·i-; mawar·a-; mawat-te C̄)
1 turn; rotate; revolve; spin:
Kono koma wa yoku mawaru. (この
こまはよく回る) This top *spins* well.
(⇨ mawasu)
2 make the rounds; look
around:
Keekañ ga kono heñ o mawatte
iru no o mimashita. (警官がこの辺を
回っているのを見ました) I saw a policeman *making the rounds* in this
area.
3 come around; go around:
Uraguchi e mawatte *kudasai.* (裏
口へ回ってください) Please *come
around* to the back door.

-mawar·u まわる (回る) (-mawar-
r·i-; -mawar·a-; -mawat-te C̄)
★ Occurs as the second element
of compound verbs. Added to
the continuative base of a verb.
go about; move around:
aruki-mawaru (歩き回る) walk
about / *kake*-mawaru (駆け回る)
run *around.*

maˈwas·u まわす (回す) *vt.* (ma-
wash·i-; mawas·a-; mawash·i-

te C̄) 1 turn; rotate; spin:
daiyaru o mawasu (ダイヤルを回す)
dial a number / *totte o* mawasu
(取っ手を回す) *rotate* a handle.
(⇨ mawaru)
2 send around; pass; forward:
Sono shio o mawashite *kudasai.*
(その塩を回してください) *Pass* me the
salt, please.
3 (of a phone call) transfer.

maˈyoˈnaka まよなか (真夜中) *n.*
midnight; the middle of the
night.

maˈyoneˈezu マヨネーズ *n.* mayonnaise.

maˈyoˈ·u まよう (迷う) *vi.* (mayo-
i-; mayow·a-; mayot-te C̄)
1 get lost; lose one's way.
2 be puzzled; be at a loss:
Watashi wa nañ to itte yoi ka ma-
yotta. (私は何と言ってよいか迷った) I
was at a loss what to say.
3 hesitate; be undecided:
*Kare wa dare ni toohyoo suru ka
mada* mayotte iru. (彼はだれに投票す
るかまだ迷っている) He *is* still *undecided* who to vote for.

maˈyu まゆ (眉) *n.* eyebrow:
mayu *o hisomeru* (眉をひそめる) knit
one's *eyebrows.*

maˈyuge まゆげ (眉毛) *n.* eyebrow.

maˈzaˈr·u まざる (混ざる) *vi.* (ma-
zar·i-; mazar·a-; mazat-te C̄)
= majiru. (⇨ mazeru)

maˈzeˈ·ru まぜる (混ぜる) *vt.* (ma-
ze-te V̄) mix; combine; mingle;
blend. (⇨ majiru)

maˈzu まず (先ず) *adv.* 1 first of
all; to begin with.
2 probably; almost certainly:
Gogo wa mazu *ame deshoo.* (午後
はまず雨でしょう) It will *probably*
rain this afternoon.

maˈzuˈ·iˈ¹ まずい (不味い) *a.* (-ku)
1 (of taste) not good; bad.
(↔ oishii)
2 awkward; unfavorable:
Kanojo wa mazui *toki ni kita.* (彼
女はまずいときに来た) She showed up
at an *awkward* moment.

ma˥zu˩·i² まずい (拙い) *a.* (-ku) (of skill) clumsy; poor:
mazui *hoñyaku* (まずい翻訳) a *poor* translation. (⇨ heta)

ma˥zushi˩·i まずしい (貧しい) *a.* (-ku) poor; needy. (↔ yutaka) (⇨ biñboo)

me˥¹ め (目) *n.* **1** eye:
Haha wa hidari no me ga mienai. (母は左の目が見えない) My mother is blind in the left *eye*.
2 eyesight; sight:
Me ga waruku natte kita. (目が悪くなってきた) My *sight* began to fail.
3 viewpoint:
Oya no me kara mireba, dono ko mo kawaii. (親の目から見れば、どの子もかわいい) In the *eyes* of the parents, all children are sweet and dear.
4 bad experience:
Ikka wa hidoi me ni atta. (一家はひどい目にあった) The whole family had a very bad *experience*.
5 eye-like object:
hari no me (針の目) the *eye* of a needle / *taifuu no me* (台風の目) the *eye* of a typhoon.
me ga mawaru (～が回る) feel giddy.
me o hikaraseru (～を光らせる) keep a sharp eye out.
me o hiku (～を引く) attract a person's attention.
me o mawasu (～を回す) faint; be astonished.
me o toosu (～を通す) run one's eye over.
me o tsukeru (～をつける) have one's eye (on something). (⇨ ome-ni-kakaru)

me˥² め (芽) *n.* shoot; sprout; bud.

-me¹ め (目) *suf.* (the position of something in an ordered group or arrangement):
hidari kara ni-keñ-me *no uchi* (左から2軒目の家) the *second* house from the left.

-me² め *suf.* (degree or tendency): ★ Added to the stem of an adjective.
haya-me *ni shuppatsu suru* (早めに出発する) start *a bit early* / ooki-me *no kutsu* (大きめの靴) a pair of shoes *on the large side*.

me˥atarashi˩·i めあたらしい (目新しい) *a.* (-ku) new; fresh; novel; original. (⇨ atarashii)

me˥ate めあて (目当て) *n.* **1** aim; object:
o-kane meate *ni hataraku* (お金目当てに働く) work *for* money.
2 guide; landmark:
Ano takai biru o meate *ni aruite iki nasai.* (あの高いビルを目当てに歩いて行きなさい) Continue walking, *keeping an eye on* that tall building.

me˥chakucha めちゃくちゃ *a.n.* (～ na, ni) messy; unreasonable; reckless:
Kare no yookyuu wa mechakucha *da.* (彼の要求はめちゃくちゃだ) His demands are *unreasonable*.

me˥chamecha めちゃめちゃ *a.n.* (～ na, ni) (*informal*) smashed up; ruined; messed up.

me˥da˩ts·u めだつ (目立つ) *vi.* (medach·i-; medat·a-; medat-te ⓒ) stand out; be conspicuous; be prominent.

me˥deta˩·i めでたい (目出度い) *a.* (-ku) happy; joyful:
Musuko wa medetaku *daigaku ni gookaku shimashita.* (息子はめでたく大学に合格しました) *Happily* my son was able to pass the exam to university. (⇨ omedetai)

me˥e めい (姪) *n.* niece.
★ When another family's niece is referred to, '*meego-sañ*' is used. (↔ oi¹)

me˥e- めい (名) *pref.* famous; great; excellent:
mee-*bameñ* (名場面) a *famous* scene / mee-*señshu* (名選手) a *star* player.

-mee めい (名) *suf.* number of people:

nijuu-mee (20 名) twenty *people*.

me⌐eañ[1] めいあん (名案) *n.* good idea; splendid plan.

me⌐eañ[2] めいあん (明暗) *n.* light and shade; bright and dark sides.

　meeañ o wakeru (~を分ける) decide: *Sono dekigoto ga kare no jiñsee no meeañ o waketa.* (その出来事が彼の人生の明暗を分けた) The incident *decided* his fate.

me⌐ebo めいぼ (名簿) *n.* name list; directory; roll.

me⌐ebutsu めいぶつ (名物) *n.* special [noted] product; specialty.

me⌐echuu めいちゅう (命中) *n.* hit.

　meechuu suru (~する) *vt.* hit the target. (⇨ ataru)

me⌐ehaku めいはく (明白) *a.n.* (~ na, ni) clear; obvious; plain; evident. (⇨ meeryoo)

me⌐eji'ñ めいじん (名人) *n.* expert; master: *tsuri no meejiñ* (つりの名人) an *expert* at fishing.

me⌐eji·ru めいじる (命じる) *vt.* (meeji-te Ⅴ) 1 tell; order; command. (⇨ meeree)
2 appoint; place: *Kare wa koochoo ni meejirareta.* (彼は校長に命じられた) He *was appointed* school principal.

me⌐ekaku めいかく (明確) *a.n.* (~ na, ni) clear and accurate; distinct; definite.

me⌐eme'e めいめい (銘々) *n.* (~ ni) each; individually. (⇨ kakuji; ono-ono)

me⌐eree めいれい (命令) *n.* order; command; instructions.

　meeree suru (~する) *vt.* order; command; instruct.

me⌐eroo めいろう (明朗) *a.n.* (~ na, ni) 1 cheerful; open-hearted:
　meeroo na hito (明朗な人) an *open-hearted* person. (⇨ hogaraka)
2 (of accounts, bills, etc.) clean; aboveboard.

me⌐eryoo めいりょう (明瞭) *a.n.* (~ na, ni) clear; evident; articulate:

Sono jijitsu wa dare ni mo mee-ryoo desu. (その事実はだれにも明瞭です) That fact is *evident* to everyone. (⇨ meehaku)

me⌐esaku めいさく (名作) *n.* fine work; masterpiece.

me⌐eshi[1] めいし (名刺) *n.* calling [visiting] card; business card.

me⌐eshi[2] めいし (名詞) *n.* noun; substantive. (⇨ APP. 2)

me⌐eshiñ めいしん (迷信) *n.* superstition.

me⌐esho めいしょ (名所) *n.* noted place; place of interest; sights to see.

me⌐eshoo めいしょう (名称) *n.* name; title:
shiñ-seehiñ ni meeshoo o tsukeru (新製品に名称をつける) give a *name* to a new product.

me⌐etaa メーター *n.* meter:
gasu [suidoo; deñki] no meetaa (ガス [水道; 電気] のメーター) a gas [water; electricity] *meter*.

me⌐etoru メートル (米) *n.* meter.

me⌐ewaku めいわく (迷惑) *n.* trouble; annoyance; nuisance: *hito ni meewaku o kakeru* (人に迷惑をかける) cause a person *trouble*. (⇨ meñdoo)

　meewaku suru (~する) *vi.* be annoyed; be bothered.
　— *a.n.* (~ na) annoying; bothering; troublesome; inconvenient.

me⌐eyo めいよ (名誉) *n.* honor; glory:
Subarashii shoo o itadaite meeyo ni omoimasu. (素晴らしい賞をいただいて名誉に思います) I *am honored* to have received such a wonderful prize.
　— *a.n.* (~ na) honorable. (↔ fumeeyo)

me⌐eyoki'soñ めいよきそん (名誉棄損) *n.* defamation; libel; slander.

me¹gane めがね (眼鏡) *n.* glasses; spectacles:
megane o kakeru [hazusu] (眼鏡を

かける[はずす] put on [take off] one's *glasses*.

me「gumare・ru めぐまれる (恵まれる) *vi.* (megumare-te V) **1** be blessed; be gifted:
kenkoo ni megumareru (健康に恵まれる) be blessed with good health.
2 be rich:
Sono kuni wa tennen shigen ni megumarete iru. (その国は天然資源に恵まれている) That country *is rich* in natural resources.

me「gum・u めぐむ (恵む) *vt.* (megum-i-; megum-a-; megun-de C) give in charity; do a person a kindness.

me「gur・u めぐる (巡る) *vt.* (megur-i-; megur-a-; megut-te C)
1 come around; make a tour. (⇨ mawaru)
2 concern; relate:
Isan o megutte, *kyoodai ga ara-sotte iru.* (遺産を巡って兄弟が争っている) The brothers are fighting *over* the legacy.

me「gu「suri めぐすり (目薬) *n.* eye-wash; eye lotion.

me「isha めいしゃ (目医者) *n.* eye doctor; oculist. (⇨ ganka)

me「kata めかた (目方) *n.* weight:
tsutsumi no mekata o hakaru (包みの目方を計る) *weigh* a parcel. (⇨ omosa)

me「kki めっき (鍍金) *n.* plating; gilding.
mekki suru (〜する) *vt.* plate; gild.

me「kur・u めくる (捲る) *vt.* (mekur-i-; mekur-a-; mekut-te C) turn over [up]:
peeji o mekuru (ページをめくる) *turn over* a page.

me「ma「i めまい (眩暈) *n.* giddi-ness; dizziness: memai ga suru (めまいがする) *feel dizzy*.

me「mo メモ *n.* memo; note.
memo suru (〜する) *vt.* put down; make a note of.

me「mori「 めもり (目盛り) *n.* scale; graduation (on a thermometer).

me「n「[1] めん (面) *n.* **1** mask; face guard.
2 plane; surface: *suihee-*men (水平面) a horizontal *plane*.
3 aspect; side:
monogoto no akarui men *o miru* (物事の明るい面を見る) look on the bright *side* of things.
4 (of a newspaper) page:
*shinbun no dai ichi-*men (新聞の第一面) the front *page* of a news-paper.

me「n「[2] めん (綿) *n.* cotton:
men *no kutsushita* (綿の靴下) *cotton* socks. (⇨ momen; wata)

me「nboku めんぼく (面目) *n.* hon-or; face; prestige:
Anna machigai o shite, menboku nai. (あんな間違いをして, 面目ない) I *am ashamed* of having made such a mistake.

me「ndo「o めんどう (面倒) *n.*
1 trouble; inconvenience:
Hito ni mendoo *wa kaketaku ari-masen.* (人に面倒はかけたくありません) I don't want to cause any *trouble* to others. (⇨ meewaku)
2 care:
Ane ga byooki no haha no men-doo *o mite imasu.* (姉が病気の母の面倒を見ています) My sister takes *care* of our sick mother.
— *a.n.* (〜 na, ni) troublesome; difficult; complicated. (⇨ yakkai)

me「ndookusa「・i めんどうくさい (面倒臭い) *a.* (-ku) troublesome; wearisome; reluctant:
Ame ga futte iru no de gaishutsu suru no wa mendookusai. (雨が降っているので外出するのは面倒くさい) It is raining, so I am *reluctant* to go out.

me「nji・ru めんじる (免じる) *vt.* (menji-te V) (*formal*) exempt; excuse:
shiken o menjiru (試験を免じる) *ex-empt* a person from an examina-tion. (⇨ menjo)
... ni menjite (...に免じて) in con-sideration of: *Watashi* ni menjite

kare o yurushite yatte kudasai. (私に免じて彼を許してやってください)
Please forgive him *for my sake.*

me｢ñjo めんじょ (免除) *n.* exemption; remission.
meñjo suru (～する) *vt.* exempt; remit: *zeekiñ ga* meñjo *sareru* (税金が免除される) *be exempted* from taxation.

me｢ñkai めんかい (面会) *n.* interview; meeting.
meñkai suru (～する) *vt.* see; meet; visit; interview.

me｢ñkyo めんきょ (免許) *n.* license; certificate.

me｢ñkyo｣joo めんきょじょう (免許状) *n.* license; certificate.

me｢ñkyo｣shoo めんきょしょう (免許証) *n.* license; driver's license.

me｢ñmoku めんもく (面目) *n.* honor. ((⇨ meñboku))

me｢ñseki めんせき (面積) *n.* area; size; floor space. ((⇨ taiseki))

me｢ñs·u·ru めんする (面する) *vi.* (meñsh·i-; meñsh·i-; meñsh·i-te ⬜) face; look out: *Sono heya wa minami [umi] ni* meñshite iru. (その部屋は南[海]に面している) The room *faces* south [the sea].

me｢ñyuu メニュー *n.* menu; bill of fare.

me｢ñzee めんぜい (免税) *n.* tax exemption: meñzee-*hiñ* (免税品) a *duty-free* article.

me｢rodii メロディー *n.* melody; tune.

-me｣·ru める *suf.* (*v.*) (-me-te ⬜) make; -en: ★ Added to the stem of an adjective describing quality.
haya-meru (早める) *hasten; quicken* / usu-meru (薄める) *make* thinner.

me｢shi｣ めし (飯) *n.* ★ Used by men. **1** (*informal*) (cooked [boiled]) rice: meshi *o taku* (飯を炊く) cook [boil] *rice.* ((⇨ gohañ))
2 (*informal*) meal; food: *Saa* meshi *no jikañ da.* (さあ飯の時

間だ) Well, now it's time *to eat.* ((⇨ asameshi; bañmeshi; hirumeshi))
3 (*informal*) living; livelihood: *Kono kyuuryoo de wa* meshi *wa kuenai.* (この給料では飯は食えない) I *cannot make a living* on this salary.

me｢shiagar·u めしあがる (召し上がる) *vt.* (-agar·i-; -agar·a-; -agat-te ⬜) ★ Honorific equivalent of '*taberu*' and '*nomu*.'
eat; drink; have: *Nani o* meshiagarimasu *ka?* (何を召し上がりますか) What would you like to *have?*

me｢shita めした (目下) *n.* one's inferior; subordinate. ((↔ meue))

me｢su｣ めす (雌) *n.* female; she: mesu *no niwatori* (めすの鶏) a *hen* / mesu *inu* (めす犬) a *female* dog. ((↔ osu))

me｢tsuboo めつぼう (滅亡) *n.* fall; downfall.
metsuboo suru (～する) *vi.* fall; perish; collapse. ((⇨ horobiru))

me｢tsuki めつき (目付き) *n.* look; eyes: *surudoi* metsuki (鋭い目つき) a piercing *look.*

me｢tta めった (滅多) *a.n.* (～ na) rash; thoughtless; reckless: Metta *na koto wa iwanai hoo ga ii.* (めったなことは言わないほうがいい) You had better *be careful about what you say.*

me｢tta ni めったに (滅多に) *adv.* (with a negative) rarely; seldom; hardly ever: *Koñna ii chañsu wa* metta ni nai. (こんないいチャンスはめったにない) One *seldom has* a chance as good as this.

me｢ue めうえ (目上) *n.* one's superior. ((↔ meshita))

me｢zamashi｣·i めざましい (目覚ましい) *a.* (-ku) remarkable; startling; wonderful.

me｢za｣s·u めざす (目指す) *vt.* (mezash·i-; mezas·a-; mezash·i-te ⬜) aim:

Fune wa Ooshima o mezashite *shukkoo shita.* (船は大島を目指して出港した) The ship left port, *heading for* Oshima.

me｢zurashi¹·i めずらしい (珍しい) a. (-ku) rare; unusual; uncommon.

mi¹ み (身) n. 1 one's body; person; oneself:
doa no ushiro ni mi *o kakusu* (ドアの後ろに身を隠す) hide *oneself* behind the door.
2 position; place:
Watashi no mi *ni mo natte kudasai.* (私の身にもなってください) Please put yourself in my *place*.
mi ni shimiru (〜にしみる) touch one's heart.
mi ni tsukeru (〜につける) put on; acquire.

mi² み (実) n. fruit; nut; berry.
mi o musubu (〜を結ぶ) yield fruit; (*fig.*) bear fruit.

mi- み (未) pref. un-:
mi-*tee* (未定) *un*decided / mi-*kañ-see* (未完成) *un*finished.

-mi み (味) suf. taste:
ama-mi (甘味) *sweetness* / kara-mi (辛味) a hot *taste*.

mi｢age·ru みあげる (見上げる) vt. (-age-te Ⓥ) look up at; raise one's eyes toward. ((↔ miorosu))

mi｢ai みあい (見合い) n. an arranged meeting with a view to marriage. ★ Often with '*o-*.'
miai (o) suru (〜を(を)する) vi. see each other with a view to marriage. ((⇨ nakoodo))

mi｢awase·ru みあわせる (見合わせる) vt. (-awase-te Ⓥ) 1 look at each other.
2 put off; postpone.

mi｢buñ みぶん (身分) n. social status [standing]; position.

mi｢buñ-shoomeesho みぶんしょうめいしょ (身分証明書) n. identification card; ID (card).

mi¹buri みぶり (身振り) n. gesture; motion; way of acting.

mi｢chi¹ みち (道) n. 1 road; way; street; path.

2 course; means:
Kore ga nokosareta tada hitotsu no michi *desu.* (これが残されたただ一つの道です) This is the only *course* left open to us.
3 field:
Yamada-shi wa kono michi *no keñi desu.* (山田氏はこの道の権威です) Mr. Yamada is an authority in this *field*.
4 public morals; the path of righteousness.

mi¹chi² みち (未知) n. unknown:
michi *no sekai* (未知の世界) the *unknown* world.

mi｢chibi¹k·u みちびく (導く) vt. (-bik·i-; -bik·a-; -bi·i-te Ⓒ) guide; lead:
Kakegoto ga kare o hametsu e michibiita. (賭け事が彼を破滅へ導いた) Gambling *led* him to his ruin.

mi｢chigae·ru みちがえる (見違える) vt. (-gae-te Ⓥ) mistake for:
Kare to kare no niisañ o michigaete shimatta. (彼と彼の兄さんを見違えてしまった) I *mistook* his older brother for him.

mi｢chijuñ みちじゅん (道順) n. route; way; course:
Kare ni yuubiñkyoku made no michijuñ *o oshiete yatta.* (彼に郵便局までの道順を教えてやった) I told him the *way* to the post office. ((⇨ michi))

mi｢chi¹·ru みちる (満ちる) vi. (mi-chi-te Ⓥ) 1 be filled; be full:
Sono machi wa kakki ni michite *ita.* (その町は活気に満ちていた) The town *was full* of activity.
2 (of the tide) rise; come in. ((↔ hiku¹))

mi｢dare¹·ru みだれる (乱れる) vi. (midare-te Ⓥ) be in disorder; be in a mess; be confused; be disrupted. ((⇨ midasu))

mi｢da¹s·u みだす (乱す) vt. (midash·i-; midas·a-; midash·i-te Ⓒ) put into disorder; disturb; confuse; disrupt:
Retsu o midasanai de kudasai. (列

を乱さないでください) Please *do not fall out of* line. (⇨ midareru)

mi「dori みどり (緑) *n.* green; greenery; verdure. (⇨ ao; aoi; midori-iro)

mi「dori-iro みどりいろ (緑色) *n.* green color. (⇨ ao; midori)

mi「e¹・ru みえる (見える) *vi.* (mie-te Ⅴ) **1** be seen; be visible; be in sight:
Kiri de nani mo mienakatta. (霧で何も見えなかった) We *could see nothing* because of the fog. (⇨ miru)
2 look; seem:
Kanojo wa toshi yori mo wakaku mieru. (彼女は年よりも若く見える) She *looks* young for her age.
3 (*honorific*) come; appear:
Shachoo wa mada miemaseñ. (社長はまだ見えません) The president *has not appeared* yet.

mi「gak・u みがく (磨く) *vt.* (migak・i-; migak・a-; miga・i-te Ⅽ) **1** polish; shine; brush:
kutsu o migaku (靴を磨く) *shine* one's shoes.
2 improve (one's skill); cultivate (one's character).

mi「gi みぎ (右) *n.* right:
tsumami o migi *e mawasu* (つまみを右へ回す) turn a handle to the *right*. (↔ hidari)

mi「gigawa みぎがわ (右側) *n.* right side. (↔ hidarigawa)

mi「gikiki みぎきき (右利き) *n.* right-handed person. (↔ hidari-kiki)

mi「gite みぎて (右手) *n.* **1** right hand. (↔ hidarite)
2 right direction:
Migite ni Fuji-sañ ga mieta. (右手に富士山が見えた) We saw Mt. Fuji on our *right*. (↔ hidarite)

mi「goto みごと (見事) *a.n.* (~ na, ni) splendid; wonderful; excellent; beautiful. (⇨ subarashii)

mi「gurushi¹・i みぐるしい (見苦しい) *a.* (-ku) unsightly; indecent; disgraceful.

mi「harashi みはらし (見晴らし) *n.* view:
miharashi *no yoi heya* (見晴らしのよい部屋) a room with a good *view*.

mi「hari みはり (見張り) *n.* watch; guard. (⇨ miharu)

mi「har・u みはる (見張る) *vt.* (-har・i-; -har・a-; -hat-te Ⅽ) keep watch; keep a lookout:
teki o miharu (敵を見張る) *keep a lookout* for the enemy.

mi「hoñ みほん (見本) *n.* sample; specimen.

mi「idas・u みいだす (見い出す) *vt.* (-dash・i-; -das・a-; -dash・i-te Ⅽ) find; discover:
Watashi-tachi wa nañ to ka kaiketsu-saku o miidashita. (私達はなんとか解決策を見いだした) We managed somehow to *find* the solution.

mi「jika みぢか (身近) *a.n.* (~ na, ni) familiar; close; near oneself:
Watashi wa sono chosha o mijika *ni kañjita.* (私はその著者を身近に感じた) I felt myself *close* to the author.

mi「jika¹・i みじかい (短い) *a.* (-ku) **1** (of length, distance) short:
Kanojo wa kami o mijikaku *shite iru.* (彼女は髪を短くしている) She wears her hair *short*. (↔ nagai)
2 (of time) short; brief:
Kare no supiichi wa mijikakatta. (彼のスピーチは短かった) His speech *was short*. (↔ nagai)

mi「jime みじめ (惨め) *a.n.* (~ na, ni) miserable; wretched; pitiful:
mijime *na seekatsu o okuru* (惨めな生活を送る) lead a *miserable* life.

mi「ka¹iketsu みかいけつ (未解決) *n., a.n.* (~ na/no, ni) unsolved; unsettled. (↔ kaiketsu)

mi「kake みかけ (見掛け) *n.* appearance; look; show:
Hito wa mikake *ni yoranai.* (人は見かけによらない) People's *appearances* are deceptive.

mi「kake-ru みかける (見掛ける) *vt.* (-kake-te Ⅴ) happen to see; come across; catch sight of.

miˈkañ みかん (蜜柑) *n*. mandarin orange.

miˈkaˈñsee みかんせい (未完成) *a.n.* (~ na/no, ni) unfinished; incomplete. (↔ kañsee)

miˈkata[1] みかた (見方) *n*. point of view; standpoint; attitude.

miˈkata[2] みかた (味方) *n*. friend; side; ally; supporter:
Ano hito wa watashi-tachi no mikata desu. (あの人は私たちのみかたです) He is *on our side.* (↔ teki)

miˈkazuki みかづき (三日月) *n*. crescent; new moon. (⇒ tsuki[2])

miˈki みき (幹) *n*. main stem of a tree; trunk.

miˈkka みっか (三日) *n*. three days; the third day of the month. (⇒ APP. 5)

miˈkomi みこみ (見込み) *n*.
1 hope; chance; possibility:
Seekoo no mikomi wa gobu-gobu desu. (成功の見込みは五分五分です) There is a fifty-fifty *chance* of success. (⇒ chañsu)
2 expectation; prospect:
Watashi-tachi no mikomi wa atatta [hazureta]. (私たちの見込みは当たった[はずれた]) Our *expectations* proved right [wrong].
mikomi no aru (~のある) promising.

miˈkoñ みこん (未婚) *n*. unmarried; single:
mikoñ *no haha* (未婚の母) an *unmarried* mother.

miˈkudas·u みくだす (見下す) *vt.* (-kudash·i-; -kudas·a-; -kudash·i-te C) look down on; despise.

miˈkurabe·ru みくらべる (見比べる) *vt.* (-kurabe-te V) compare. (⇒ hikaku; kuraberu)

miˈmai みまい (見舞い) *n*. 1 visit (to a hospital or a sick person); call; inquiry. ★ Often with '*o-*.' (⇒ mimau)
2 expression of one's sympathy [concern]:
Shichoo wa higaisha ni mimai no kotoba *o nobeta.* (市長は被害者に見舞いの言葉を述べた) The mayor expressed his *sympathy* for the victims.

-miˈmañ みまん (未満) *suf.* under; below; less than:
Juuhas-sai-mimañ wa nyuujoo dekimaseñ. (18歳未満は入場できません) Those *under* eighteen years of age are not permitted to enter. ★ '*-mimañ*' does not include the preceding number, so, strictly speaking, '*jus-sai-mimañ*' is 'under nine years of age.' (⇒ -ika)

miˈma·u みまう (見舞う) *vt.* (mima·i-; mimaw·a-; mimat-te C)
1 visit; inquire after:
Kinoo nyuuiñ-chuu no itoko o mimatta. (きのう入院中のいとこを見舞った) Yesterday I *visited* my cousin who is in the hospital. (⇒ mimai)
2 (of disaster) hit; strike.

miˈmawari みまわり (見回り) *n*. patrol; inspection:
koojoo no mimawari *o suru* (工場の見回りをする) make an *inspection* visit to a factory. (⇒ mimawaru)

miˈmawar·u みまわる (見回る) *vt.* (-mawar·i-; -mawar·a-; -mawat-te C) patrol; make one's rounds; inspect. (⇒ mimawari)

miˈmawas·u みまわす (見回す) *vt.* (-mawash·i-; -mawas·a-; -mawash·i-te C) look around [about].

miˈmi みみ (耳) *n*. 1 ear.
2 hearing:
Kare wa mimi *ga tooi.* (彼は耳が遠い) He is hard of *hearing*.
mimi o sumasu (~を澄ます) strain one's ears; listen carefully.

miˈna みな (皆) *n., adv.* all; everyone; everything. (⇒ miñna)

miˈnami みなみ (南) *n*. south; (~ ni/e) southward. (↔ kita)

miˈnara·u みならう (見習う) *vt.* (-nara·i-; -naraw·a-; -narat-te C) follow a person's example;

imitate; learn:
shigoto o minarau (仕事を見習う) *learn* a job.

mi⌐nari みなり (身なり) *n.* appearance; dress; clothes:
Kare wa minari o kamawanai. (彼は身なりを構わない) He is indifferent about his *appearance*. (⇨ fukusoo)

mi⌐na¹-sama みなさま (皆様) *n.* (*honorific*) = mina-sañ.

mi⌐na¹-sañ みなさん (皆さん) *n.*
1 everybody; everyone; all:
Mina-sañ, *ohayoo gozaimasu.* (皆さん, お早うございます) Good morning, *everybody*.
2 ladies and gentlemen:
Mina-sañ, *kore o gorañ kudasai.* (皆さん, これをご覧ください) *Ladies and gentlemen*, please look at this.

mi⌐nas·u みなす (見なす) *vt.* (minash·i-; minas·a-; minash·i-te Ⓒ) regard; consider:
Sañjup-puñ ijoo tatte mo konai hito wa kesseki to minashimasu. (30 分以上たっても来ない人は欠席とみなします) Those who are over thirty minutes late will *be considered* absent.

mi⌐nato みなと (港) *n.* port; harbor.

mi⌐ne みね (峰) *n.* mountain peak; ridge.

mi⌐niku¹·i¹ みにくい (見難い) *a.* (-ku) hard [difficult] to see.

mi⌐niku¹·i² みにくい (醜い) *a.* (-ku)
1 ugly:
minikui *kizu* (醜いきず) an *ugly* scar.
2 (of conduct, trouble, etc.) scandalous; ignoble:
minikui *arasoi* (醜い争い) a *scandalous* dispute.

mi⌐ñji みんじ (民事) *n.* (of law) civil affairs: miñji-*soshoo* (民事訴訟) a *civil* action. (⇨ keeji)

mi⌐ñkañ みんかん (民間) *n.* private; civilian:
miñkañ-*kigyoo* (民間企業) a *private* enterprise.

mi⌐ña¹ みんな (皆) *n., adv.* all;

everyone; everything:
miñna *no ikeñ o kiku* (みんなの意見を聞く) listen to *everyone*'s opinion. (⇨ mina)

mi⌐no¹r·u みのる (実る) *vi.* (minor·i-; minor·a-; minot-te Ⓒ)
1 bear fruit.
2 (of an effort, etc.) have results:
Kare no doryoku wa amari mino-ranakatta. (彼の努力はあまり実らなかった) His efforts *hardly produced anything*.

mi⌐noshirokiñ みのしろきん (身代金) *n.* ransom.

mi⌐noue みのうえ (身の上) *n.* one's personal affairs; one's personal history.

mi⌐ñshuku みんしゅく (民宿) *n.* private home which takes in paying guests.

mi⌐ñshu-shu¹gi みんしゅしゅぎ (民主主義) *n.* democracy.

mi⌐¹k·u みぬく (見抜く) *vt.* (-nuk·i-; -nuk·a-; -nu·i-te Ⓒ) see through; figure out; perceive:
hito no kokoro o minuku (人の心を見抜く) *see into* a person's mind.

mi⌐ñyoo みんよう (民謡) *n.* folk song; popular ballad.

mi⌐¹ñzoku みんぞく (民族) *n.* race; people; nation:
miñzoku *no dai-idoo* (民族の大移動) a *racial* migration.

mi⌐oboe みおぼえ (見覚え) *n.* recognition; remembrance:
Ano otoko ni wa mioboe *ga aru.* (あの男には見覚えがある) I *remember* having seen that man.

mi⌐okuri みおくり (見送り) *n.* send-off; seeing a person off. (↔ demukae) (⇨ miokuru)

mi⌐okur·u みおくる (見送る) *vt.* (-okur·i-; -okur·a-; -okut-te Ⓒ)
1 see off:
Tookyoo-eki de kare o miokutta. (東京駅で彼を見送った) We *saw* him *off* at Tokyo Station. (↔ demukaeru) (⇨ miokuri)
2 pass up (one's turn, opportunity, etc.).

mi｢oros·u みおろす (見下ろす) *vt.*
(-orosh·i-; -oros·a-; -orosh·i-te
Ⓒ) look down; overlook; command. (↔ miageru)

mi｢otoshi みおとし (見落とし) *n.*
oversight; careless mistake.
(⇨ miotosu)

mi｢otos·u みおとす (見落とす) *vt.*
(-otosh·i-; -otos·a-; -otosh·i-te
Ⓒ) overlook; miss:
*Watashi wa sono machigai o mio-
toshite ita.* (私はその間違いを見落とし
ていた) I *missed* the mistake.
(⇨ miotoshi)

mi｢rai みらい (未来) *n.* future.

mi｢ri ミリ *n.* millimeter; milligram. ★ Shortened form of
'*miri-meetoru*' and '*miri-guramu*.'

mi｢ri-gu｢ramu ミリグラム (瓱) *n.*
milligram. ★ Shortened form,
'*miri*' is more common. (⇨ miri)

mi｢ri-me｢etoru ミリメートル (粍)
n. millimeter. ★ Shortened
form, '*miri*' is more common.
(⇨ miri)

mi｢ri-ri｢ttoru ミリリットル (竓) *n.*
milliliter.

mi｢ru みる (見る・診る) *vt.* (mi-te
Ⓥ) 1 see; look at; watch.
2 read; look through:
Kyoo no shinbun o mimashita ka?
(きょうの新聞を見ましたか) Have you
read today's paper?
3 inspect; check; consult:
Haisha de ha o mite moratta. (歯
医者で歯を診てもらった) I *had* my
teeth *looked at* by the dentist.
4 look after; help:
Kono kaban o mite ite kudasai. (こ
のかばんを見ていてください) Will you
please *keep an eye* on this bag?
-te miru (て〜) try doing:
*Atarashii waapuro wa tsukatte
mimashita ka?* (新しいワープロは使っ
てみましたか) Have you *tried using*
your new word processor?

mi｢ruku ミルク *n.* milk. ★ Often
refers to processed milk and
creamers. Cows' milk is called
'*gyuunyuu*.'

mi｢ryoku みりょく (魅力) *n.*
charm; attraction; appeal; fascination.

mi｢sage·ru みさげる (見下げる) *vt.*
(misage-te Ⓥ) = mikudasu.

mi｢saki みさき (岬) *n.* cape;
promontory.

mi｢se みせ (店) *n.* store; shop.

mi｢sebiraka｢s·u みせびらかす (見
せびらかす) *vt.* (-kash·i-; -kas·a-;
-kash·i-te Ⓒ) show off.

mi｢semono みせもの (見せ物) *n.*
show; exhibition.

mi｢se｢·ru みせる (見せる) *vt.* (mi-
se-te Ⓥ) 1 show; display; let a
person see.
2 show on purpose; pretend:
*Heya o hiroku miseru tame ni tee-
buru o ugokashita.* (部屋を広く見せ
るためにテーブルを動かした) I moved
the table so that the room *would
look* larger.
-te miseru (て〜) 1 show how to
do: *oyoide miseru* (泳いで見せる)
show someone *how* to swim.
2 (show a firm decision): *Kondo
koso kare o makashite miseru.* (今
度こそ彼を負かして見せる) You just
watch me *beat* him this time.

mi｢shin ミシン *n.* sewing machine.

mi｢so みそ (味噌) *n.* soybean
paste; miso.

mi｢soshi｢ru みそしる (味噌汁) *n.*
miso soup.

mi｢ssetsu みっせつ (密接) *a.n.*
(〜 na, ni) close; closely related:
missetsu na kankee ga aru (密接な
関係がある) have a *close* relation.

mi｢su¹ ミス *n.* mistake; error.
misu (o) suru (〜(を)する) *vi.*
make a mistake. (⇨ machigai)

mi｢su² ミス *n.* Miss; being single.

mi｢suborashi｢·i みすぼらしい *a.*
(-ku) humble; scruffy; shabby;
wretched.

mi｢sui みすい (未遂) *n.* attempt:
satsujin-misui (殺人未遂) an *at-
tempted* murder.

mi｢sumisu みすみす *adv.* before

one's eyes; helplessly:
Kare wa misumisu *sono kikai o
nogashite shimatta.* (彼はみすみすその
機会を逃してしまった) He *helplessly*
let the chance slip by.

mi「sute·ru みすてる (見捨てる) *vt.*
(-sute-te Ⅴ) forsake; desert;
leave.

mitai みたい *a.n.* (~ na, ni)
[immediately follows a preceding
noun or adjectival noun] 1 similar to; like:
yume mitai *na hanashi* (夢みたいな
話) a story *like* a dream.
2 such as; like: ★ Refers to
something by way of example.
Kare mitai *ni atama no yoi hito ni
wa atta koto ga nai.* (彼みたいに頭の
よい人には会ったことがない) I have
never met a smart person *like*
him.
3 seem; appear:
Kanojo wa kanemochi mitai *da.*
(彼女は金持ちみたいだ) She *appears*
to be rich. (⇨ rashii; soo²; yoo²)

mi「ta's·u みたす (満たす) *vt.* (mi-
tash·i·; mitas·a·; mitash·i·te Ⓒ)
1 fill up:
koppu ni biiru o mitasu (コップにビー
ルを満たす) *fill* a glass with beer.
2 satisfy (desire); meet (a condition, etc.).

mi「tee みてい (未定) *n.* undecided; uncertain.

mi「tome·ru みとめる (認める) *vt.*
(mitome-te Ⅴ) 1 recognize;
admit; concede:
Kare wa jibuñ no machigai o
mitometa. (彼は自分の間違いを認め
た) He *admitted* his mistake.
2 allow; approve:
Chichi wa watashi no gaihaku o
mitomete kuremaseñ. (父は私の外
泊を認めてくれません) My father *does
not allow* me to sleep out.
3 see; find; notice (an unusual
thing, change, etc.).

mi「tooshi みとおし (見通し) *n.*
1 visibility:
Kono atari wa mitooshi *ga ii*

[*warui*]. (このあたりは見通しがいい[悪
い]) *Visibility* is good [poor]
around here.
2 prospects; outlook:
Shoobai no mitooshi *wa akarui.*
(商売の見通しは明るい) Business
prospects are bright.

mi「tsu みつ (蜜) *n.* honey; molas-
ses; treacle.

mi「tsu」bachi みつばち (蜜蜂) *n.*
honeybee.

mi「tsudo みつど (密度) *n.* density:
jiñkoo mitsudo (人口密度) population *density*.

mi「tsukar·u みつかる (見付かる) *vi.*
(-kar·i·; -kar·a·; -kat-te Ⓒ) be
found; be discovered; be caught.
(⇨ mitsukeru)

mi「tsuke·ru みつける (見付ける) *vt.*
(-tsuke-te Ⅴ) find; discover;
catch:
Kinoo yasui mise o mitsuketa. (き
のう安い店を見つけた) Yesterday I
found a shop with good prices.
(⇨ mitsukaru; sagasu)

mi「tsume·ru みつめる (見詰める)
vt. (-tsume-te Ⅴ) gaze; stare;
study.

mi「tsumori みつもり (見積もり) *n.*
estimate; quotation:
shuuri no mitsumori *o dasu* [*suru*]
(修理の見積もりを出す[する]) make an
estimate for the repairs.
(⇨ mitsumoru)

mi「tsumor·u みつもる (見積もる)
vt. (-tsumor·i·; -tsumor·a·;
-tsumot-te Ⓒ) estimate; make
an estimate. (⇨ mitsumori)

mi「ttomona」·i みっともない *a.*
(-ku) shabby; clumsy-looking;
shameful; disgraceful.

mi「ttsu」 みっつ (三つ) *n.* three.
★ Used when counting. (⇨ sañ¹;
APP. 3)

mi「ushina·u みうしなう (見失う) *vt.*
(-ushina·i·; -ushinaw·a·; -ushi-
nat-te Ⓒ) lose sight [track] of.

mi「wake·ru みわける (見分ける) *vt.*
(-wake-te Ⅴ) distinguish; tell

from. (⇨ kubetsu)

mi「watas·u みわたす (見渡す) *vt.*
(-watash·i-; -watas·a-; -watash·i-te Ⓒ) look around; survey.

mi「yage みやげ (土産) *n.* present;
souvenir. ★ Something you buy
as a present when returning
from a trip or visiting someone.
(⇨ o-miyage; purezeñto)

mi「yako みやこ (都) *n.* capital;
metropolis; city.

mi「zo みぞ (溝) *n.* ditch; gutter;
groove.
2 gap; gulf:
Futari no aida ni mizo ga dekita.
(二人の間に溝ができた) A *gulf* has
developed between the couple.

mi「zu みず (水) *n.* water; cold
water.
mizu ni nagasu (～に流す) forgive
and forget.

mi「zugi みずぎ (水着) *n.* swim-
suit; bathing suit.

mi「zuiro みずいろ (水色) *n.* pale
[light] blue.

mi「zukara みずから (自ら) *adv.*
personally; in person:
*Shachoo mizukara sono kooshoo
ni atatta.* (社長自らその交渉にあたった)
The president *personally* carried
on the negotiations.

mi「zumushi みずむし (水虫) *n.*
athlete's foot.

mi「zusashi「 みずさし (水差し) *n.*
pitcher; water jug.

mi「zuu「mi みずうみ (湖) *n.* lake.
(⇨ ike)

mi「zuwari みずわり (水割り) *n.*
whisky and water. (⇨ haibooru)

mo[1] も (藻) *n.* waterweed; sea-
weed.

mo[2] も *p.* **1** also; too; besides:
Watashi mo ikitai. (私も行きたい) I
want to go, *too*.
2 both...and; either...or; neither...nor: ★ Usually occurs as a
pair.
*Kare wa sukii mo sukeeto mo
dekimasu.* (彼はスキーもスケートもでき
ます) He can *both* ski *and* skate.

*Watashi wa hima mo okane mo
arimaseñ.* (私は暇もお金もありません) I
have *neither* time *nor* money.
3 even: ★ Used to emphasize a
situation by giving one extreme
negative example.
*Isogashikute, deñwa mo kakera-
renai.* (忙しくて、電話もかけられない)
I'm so busy that I can't *even*
make a phone call. (⇨ sae; sura)
4 (used with interrogatives to
emphasize a negative):
Kinoo wa doko e mo ikanakatta.
(きのうはどこへも行かなかった) I did
not go *anywhere* yesterday.
5 as many as; as much as:
★ Used with a number or quantity expression to emphasize that
the number or quantity is unexpectedly either large or small.
*Kekkoñ-shiki ni hyaku-niñ mo
kite kureta.* (結婚式に100人も来てく
れた) A *full* hundred people came
to our wedding.
6 within, as little as: ★ Used
with number or quantity expressions to indicate a limit.
*Ichi-neñ mo sureba, shigoto ni na-
reru deshoo.* (一年もすれば、仕事に慣
れるでしょう) I am sure you will get
used to the job *in* a year.
7 not one; not any; not a single:
★ Follows counters and used
with a negative for emphasis.
*Gaikoku e wa ichi-do mo itta koto
ga arimaseñ.* (外国へは一度も行った
ことがありません) I have not been
abroad *even once*.
8 (used in sentences expressing
emotion, especially nostalgia):
Natsu-yasumi mo moo owari da.
(夏休みももう終わりだ) Ah! The sum-
mer vacation is now over.

mo「chi もち (餅) *n.* rice cake.
(⇨ mochitsuki; yakimochi)

mo「chiage·ru もちあげる (持ち上げ
る) *vt.* (-age-te Ⓥ) **1** lift; heave.
2 flatter; cajole:
*Kare wa mochiagerarete jookigeñ
datta.* (彼は持ち上げられて上機嫌だっ

た) He *was flattered* into good spirits.

mo⌐chidas·u もちだす (持ち出す) *vt.* (-dash·i·; -das·a·; -dash·i·te Ⓒ) **1** take out:
Kono hoñ wa damatte, mochidasanai de kudasai. (この本は黙って、持ち出さないでください) Please *do not take out* this book without asking.
2 bring up; propose (a plan, suggestion, etc.).

mo⌐chii¹·ru もちいる (用いる) *vt.* (mochii-te Ⓥ) use; make use of; employ. (⇨ tsukau)

mo⌐chikomi もちこみ (持ち込み) *n.* bringing in;
Kikeñbutsu no mochikomi kiñshi. (*sign*) (危険物の持ち込み禁止) Dangerous Articles *Prohibited*. (⇨ mochikomu)

mo⌐chikom·u もちこむ (持ち込む) *vt.* (-kom·i·; -kom·a·; -koñ-de Ⓒ) carry into; lodge:
kujoo o mochikomu (苦情を持ち込む) *lodge* a complaint. (⇨ mochikomi)

mo⌐chi¹mono もちもの (持ち物) *n.* one's belongings; one's property; one's personal effects.

mo⌐chi¹nushi もちぬし (持ち主) *n.* owner; possessor; proprietor.

mo⌐chi¹roñ もちろん (勿論) *adv.*
1 of course; certainly; sure.
2 (~ no koto) not to mention; to say nothing of:
Kanojo wa Nihoñ no geñdai-buñ wa mochiroñ (no koto), koteñ mo yomemasu. (彼女は日本の現代文はもちろん(のこと)、古典も読めます) She can read the Japanese classics, *to say nothing of* contemporary writing.

mo⌐chitsuki もちつき (餅つき) *n.* making of rice cake. (⇨ mochi)

mo⌐do¹r·u もどる (戻る) *vi.* (mo-dor·i·; modor·a·; modot-te Ⓒ)
1 go [come] back; return. (⇨ kaeru¹; kaeru²)
2 be restored; regain:
Shiñkañseñ no daiya wa heejoo ni

modorimashita. (新幹線のダイヤは平常に戻りました) The Shinkansen schedule *has been restored* to normal. (⇨ modosu)

mo⌐do¹s·u もどす (戻す) *vt.* (mo-dosh·i·; modos·a·; modosh·i·te Ⓒ) **1** put back; return; restore. (⇨ kaesu; modoru)
2 throw up; vomit.

mo⌐e·ru もえる (燃える) *vi.* (moe-te Ⓥ) **1** burn; blaze.
2 glow (with hope, ambition, etc.); burn:
Kanojo wa kiboo ni moete ita. (彼女は希望に燃えていた) She *was burning* with hope. (⇨ moyasu)

mo⌐ga¹k·u もがく *vi.* (mogak·i·; mogak·a·; moga·i·te Ⓒ) struggle; writhe:
Inu wa ana kara deyoo to mogaite ita. (犬は穴から出ようともがいていた) The dog *was struggling* to get out of the hole.

mo¹g·u もぐ *vt.* (mog·i·; mog·a·; mo·i-de Ⓒ) pick (fruit); pluck.

mo¹gumogu もぐもぐ *adv.* (~ to) mumblingly:
nani-ka mogumogu (to) iu (何かもぐもぐ(と)言う) *mumble* something.

mo¹gu¹r·u もぐる (潜る) *vi.* (mo-gur·i·; mogur·a·; mogut-te Ⓒ)
1 dive; go [stay] underwater.
2 get into (a hole, the ground, etc.); creep into; hide.

mo⌐hañ もはん (模範) *n.* model; example; pattern.

mo¹haya もはや (最早) *adv.* now; by now; already:
Mohaya ososugimasu. (もはや遅すぎます) It is too late *now*.

mo¹ji もじ (文字) *n.* letter; character. (⇨ ji)

mo¹jimoji もじもじ *adv.* (~ to; ~ suru) hesitatingly; timidly; reservedly:
Kanojo wa meñsetsu no toki moji-moji (to) shite ita. (彼女は面接のときもじもじ(と)していた) She acted *nervously* at the interview.

mo⌐¹kee もけい (模型) *n.* model;

miniature: mokee *hikooki* (模型飛行機) a *model* plane.

mo⌐kka もっか (目下) *n.*, *adv.* (*formal*) now; currently; at present. (⇨ geñzai)

mo⌐kuhi⌐keñ もくひけん (黙秘権) *n.* the right of silence.

mo⌐kuhyoo もくひょう (目標) *n.* goal; target; object; mark.

mo⌐kuji もくじ (目次) *n.* table of contents.

mo⌐kumoku もくもく (黙々) *adv.* (~ to) in silence; without saying anything:
mokumoku *to hataraku* (黙々と働く) work *without saying anything*.

mo⌐kuroku もくろく (目録) *n.* catalog; list.

mo⌐kuromi¹ もくろみ (目論見) *n.* plan; scheme; intention:
Watashi no mokuromi *wa hazureta.* (私のもくろみははずれた) My *plan* fell through. (⇨ mokuromu)

mo⌐kuro⌐m·u もくろむ (目論む) *vt.* (-rom·i-; -rom·a-; -roñ-de C̄) plan; scheme; intend:
Kare wa nani-ka mokuroñde *iru.* (彼は何かもくろんでいる) He *is up to* something. (⇨ mokuromi)

mo⌐kuteki もくてき (目的) *n.* purpose; aim; objective.

mo⌐kuteki⌐chi もくてきち (目的地) *n.* one's destination; one's; goal.

mo⌐kuyo⌐o(bi) もくよう(び) (木曜(日)) *n.* Thursday. (⇨ APP. 5)

mo⌐ku⌐zai もくざい (木材) *n.* wood; lumber; timber.

mo⌐kuzoo もくぞう (木造) *n.* made of wood; wooden:
Kono jiñja wa mokuzoo *desu.* (この神社は木造です) This shrine is *built of wood*.

mo⌐meñ もめん (木綿) *n.* cotton; cotton thread. (⇨ meñ²; wata)

mo⌐me·ru もめる (揉める) *vi.* (mo-me-te V̄) have trouble; have an argument.

mo⌐miji もみじ (紅葉) *n.* maple; autumn [red] leaves. (⇨ kooyoo)

mo⌐mo¹ もも (股) *n.* thigh.

mo⌐mo² もも (桃) *n.* peach; peach tree.

mo⌐moiro ももいろ (桃色) *n.* pink. ★ Has a pornographic implication like English 'blue.' (⇨ piñku)

mo⌐m·u もむ (揉む) *vt.* (mom·i-; mom·a-; moñ-de C̄) massage; rub.

mo⌐ñ もん (門) *n.* gate.

mo⌐naka もなか (最中) *n.* Japanese wafer cake. (⇨ wagashi)

mo⌐ñdai もんだい (問題) *n.*
1 question; issue; problem:
moñdai *o kaiketsu suru* (問題を解決する) settle a *question*.
2 problem (to be answered):
moñdai *o toku* (問題を解く) solve a *problem*. (↔ tooañ) (⇨ kotae)
3 matter:
Sore wa betsu moñdai *desu.* (それは別問題です) That is another *matter*.
4 trouble:
Kare wa mata moñdai *o okoshita.* (彼はまた問題を起こした) He has once more caused *trouble*.

mo⌐ñdo⌐o もんどう (問答) *n.* argument; questions and answers.
moñdoo *suru* (~する) *vi.* have an argument. (⇨ tooroñ)

mo⌐ñku もんく (文句) *n.* **1** words; phrase: *kimari-*moñku (決まり文句) a set *phrase*.
2 complaint; objection.

mo⌐no¹ もの (物) *n.* **1** thing; material; article:
Nani-ka taberu mono *wa arimasu ka?* (何か食べる物はありますか) Is there any*thing* to eat?
2 one's possessions:
Kore wa watashi no mono *da.* (これは私のものだ) This is *mine*.
3 quality:
Kono shina wa mono *ga ii.* (この品は物がいい) This article is of good *quality*.
4 word:
Tsukarete, mono *mo ienai.* (疲れて、物も言えない) I am too tired to

even say a *word*.

mono ni naru (〜になる) make good: *Sono keekaku wa* mono ni *naranakatta.* (その計画はものにならなかった) The plan *did not materialize*.

mono ni suru (〜にする) master.

mo⌐no⌐¹² もの(者) *n*. person; fellow; one: *Kare wa kono kaisha no* mono *de wa arimaseñ.* (彼はこの会社の者ではありません) He is not an *employee* of this company. (⇨ hito; kata³)

-mono もの(物) *suf*. thing; article; clothes: *uri*-mono (売り物) an *article* for sale / *fuyu*-mono (冬物) winter *clothes*.

mo⌐no⌐ da もの⌐ だ 1 be natural: ★ Polite form is '*mono desu*.' Denotes that a certain result or consequence is natural under given circumstances.

Ryokoo ni deru to hoñ ga yomi-taku naru mono da. (旅行に出ると本が読みたくなるものだ) When one goes on a trip, one *usually* feels like reading a book.

2 used to (do): ★ Refers to past habits and states.

Mukashi wa kono kono atari ni norainu ga takusañ ita mono desu. (昔はこのあたりに野良犬がたくさんいたものです) There *used to* be many stray dogs around this place a while back.

3 should (do): ★ Denotes obligation or duty.

Hito ni mono o morattara, oree o iu mono da. (人に物をもらったら、お礼をいうものだ) When you receive something from someone, you *should* say 'thank you.'

4 how...! ★ Denotes the speaker's sentiment.

Hito no isshoo wa mijikai mono da. (人の一生は短いものだ) *How* short life is!

5 how could...? ★ Denotes the speaker's criticism or judgment.

Baka na koto o shita mono da. (ばかなことをしたものだ) *It was* very

foolish of me.

mo⌐noga¹tari ものがたり(物語) *n*. story; tale; narrative.

mo⌐nogata¹r·u ものがたる(物語る) *vt*. (-gatar·i-; -gatar·a-; -gatat-te ⌐C⌐) tell of; show; describe.

mo⌐no⌐goto ものごと(物事) *n*. things; everything: *Anata wa* monogoto *o majime ni kangae-sugiru.* (あなたは物事をまじめに考え過ぎる) You take *things* too seriously.

mo⌐no¹ ka ものか (*informal*) never: ★ Placed at the end of a sentence to express strong negation. *Añna yatsu to moo kuchi o kiku* mono ka. (あんなやつともう口をきくものか) *Do you expect* me to talk to a fellow like him again?

mo⌐no-o¹boe ものおぼえ(物覚え) *n*. memory: *Kare wa* mono-oboe *ga ii.* (彼は物覚えがいい) He has a good *memory*. (⇨ kioku)

mo⌐nooki¹ ものおき(物置) *n*. storeroom; shed; closet.

mo⌐nooto¹ ものおと(物音) *n*. (strange) sound; noise: Monooto *hitotsu shinai.* (物音一つしない) There is no *sound*.

mo⌐nosa¹shi ものさし(物差し) *n*. ruler; measure.

mo⌐nosugo¹·i ものすごい(物凄い) *a*. (-ku) (*informal*) terrible; terrific: *Kare wa kimi no koto o* monosu-goku *okotte iru zo.* (彼は君のことをものすごく怒っているぞ) He is *hopping* mad at you.

mo⌐no¹zuki ものずき(物好き) *n*. strange [eccentric] person. —— *a.n*. (〜 na, ni) curious; weird; eccentric.

mo⌐o¹ もう *adv*. **1** already; yet; now: *Depaato wa* moo *hiraite imasu ka?* (デパートはもう開いていますか) Are the department stores open *yet*? **2** more; further; again:

Moo *ichi-do sono eega o mitai.* (もう一度その映画を見たい) I would like to see that film once *more*.

3 soon; before long:
Moo *sorosoro kanojo wa kuru to omoimasu.* (もうそろそろ彼女は来ると思います) I think she will be coming *soon*. (⇨ moo sugu)

mo⌐o- もう(猛) *pref.* hard; heavy; intensive:
moo-*beñkyoo* (猛勉強) *hard* study / moo-*reñshuu* (猛練習) *intensive* training.

mo⌐ochoo もうちょう(盲腸) *n.* appendix:
moochoo-*eñ* (盲腸炎) *appendicitis*. ★ '*Chuusuieñ*' (虫垂炎) is the technical term.

mo⌐ofu もうふ(毛布) *n.* blanket.

mo⌐o jiki もうじき *adv.* soon; shortly. (⇨ moo sugu)

mo⌐oka⌐r·u もうかる(儲かる) *vi.* (-kar-i-; -kar-a-; -kat-te C) make money; make a profit; be profitable. (⇨ mookeru¹; mooke)

mo⌐oke もうけ(儲け) *n.* profit; gains; earnings. (↔ soñ) (⇨ mookeru¹; mookaru; rieki)

mo⌐oke⌐·ru¹ もうける(儲ける) *vt.* (-ke-te V) make money; make a profit:
Kare wa kabu de ni-hyakumañ-eñ mooketa. (彼は株で200万円もうけた) He *made* two million yen on stocks. (⇨ mookaru; mooke)

mo⌐oke⌐·ru² もうける(設ける) *vt.* (-ke-te V) set up (an organization, rule, etc.); lay down:
shiteñ o mookeru (支店を設ける) *set up* a branch office.

mo⌐oretsu もうれつ(猛烈) *a.n.* (～ na, ni) violent; fierce; terrible:
mooretsu *na taifuu* (猛烈な台風) a *violent* typhoon.

mo⌐oshiage·ru もうしあげる(申し上げる) *vt.* (-age-te V) express; say: ★ Humble equivalent of '*iu*.' More humble than '*moosu*.'
Hoñ-neñ mo yoroshiku onegai

mooshiagemasu. (*on a New Year's card*) (本年もよろしくお願い申し上げます) I *would appreciate* your further kindness this year.

o[go]-... mooshiagemasu (お[ご]...申し上げます) (*humble*) will do:
O-seki e go-añnai mooshiagemasu. (お席へご案内申し上げます) I *will show* you to your seat.

mo⌐oshide·ru もうしでる(申し出る) *vt.* (-de-te V) propose; offer; request; apply for.

mo⌐oshikomi もうしこみ(申し込み) *n.* application; offer; proposal; request. (⇨ mooshikomu)

mo⌐oshikom·u もうしこむ(申し込む) *vt.* (-kom·i-; -kom-a-; -koñ-de C) apply for; propose:
Kare wa kanojo ni kekkoñ o moo-shikoñda. (彼は彼女に結婚を申し込んだ) He *proposed* marriage to her. (⇨ mooshikomi)

mo⌐oshiwake もうしわけ(申し訳) *n.* apology; excuse.

mooshiwake arimaseñ (～ありません) I am sorry; excuse me. (⇨ mooshiwake nai)

mo⌐oshiwake na⌐·i もうしわけない(申し訳ない) (-ku) be sorry:
Go-meewaku o o-kakeshite, moo-shiwake naku *omotte orimasu.* (ご迷惑をおかけして、申し訳なく思っております) I *feel very sorry* for causing you so much trouble.

mo⌐os·u もうす(申す) *vt.* (moo-sh·i-; moos-a-; moosh·i-te C) (*humble*) say; tell; call:
Chichi wa sugu ni mairu to moo-shite orimasu. (父はすぐに参ると申しております) My father *says* that he will soon come.

o-... mooshimasu (お...申します) (*humble*) will do: *Nochi-hodo* o-ukagai mooshimasu. (後ほどお伺い申します) I *will call on* you later. (⇨ mooshiageru)

mo⌐o su⌐gu もうすぐ *adv.* soon; shortly; before long.

mo⌐ppara もっぱら(専ら) *adv.* exclusively; wholly; mostly.

mo⌐ra⌐s·u もらす（漏らす）*vt.* (mo-rash·i-; moras·a-; morash·i-te C) 1 let leak (water, oil, etc.); let out (a secret, complaint, etc.). (⇨ moreru)

2 fail to do: ★ Attached to the continuative base of a verb. *kiki*-morasu（聞き漏らす）*fail to hear* / *kaki*-morasu（書き漏らす）*fail to* write down.

mo⌐ra·u もらう（貰う）*vt.* (mora·i-; moraw·a-; morat-te C) get; receive (a present).

-te morau（て～）★ Used when asking someone to do something, or when receiving benefit from someone.

Kanojo ni tegami o taipu shite moratta.（彼女に手紙をタイプしてもらった）I *had* her *type* the letter *for me.* (⇨ itadaku)

mo⌐re⌐·ru もれる（漏れる）*vi.* (more-te V) 1 (of water) leak; escape; (of a secret) leak out. (⇨ morasu; moru)

2 be left out (of a list, selection, etc.); be omitted.

mo⌐ri もり（森）*n.* woods; forest. (⇨ hayashi; shiñriñ)

mo⌐ribachi もりばち（盛り鉢）*n.* bowl. (⇨ wañ¹)

mo⌐ro⌐·i もろい（脆い）*a.* (-ku)

1 fragile; weak.

2 (of feeling, emotion, etc.) be moved easily: *Haha wa joo ni moroi.*（母は情にもろい）My mother *is easily moved* emotionally.

mo⌐r·u¹ もる（漏る）*vi.* (mor·i-; mor·a-; mot-te C) leak: *Kono heya wa ame ga moru.*（この部屋は雨が漏る）Rain *leaks* into this room. (⇨ moreru)

mo⌐r·u² もる（盛る）*vt.* (mor·i-; mor·a-; mot-te C) pile up; heap up. (⇨ tsumu¹)

mo⌐shi (mo) もし（も）（若し（も））*adv.* if; in case: *Moshi mo ashita yoi teñki nara, pikunikku ni ikimasu.*（もしもあした良い天気なら、ピクニックに行きます）We are going on a picnic *if* it is fine tomorrow. (⇨ kari ni)

mo⌐shi-ka shitara もしかしたら（若しかしたら）*adv.* perhaps; maybe; possibly.

mo⌐shi-ka suru to もしかすると（若しかすると）*adv.* = moshi-ka shitara.

mo⌐shikuwa もしくは（若しくは）*conj.* (formal) or: *hoñniñ moshikuwa dairiniñ*（本人もしくは代理人）*either* the person in question *or* his or her representative. (⇨ aruiwa; mata-wa)

mo⌐shimoshi もしもし *int.*

1 hello: ★ Used when answering a telephone call. *Moshimoshi, Yamada-sañ desu ka?*（もしもし、山田さんですか）*Hello.* Is that Mrs. Yamada?

2 excuse me: ★ Used when addressing a stranger. *Moshimoshi, kippu o otoshimashita yo.*（もしもし、切符を落としましたよ）*Excuse me.* You have dropped your ticket.

mo⌐tara⌐s·u もたらす *vt.* (-rash·i-; -ras·a-; -rash·i-te C) bring (about); lead to: *yoi kekka o motarasu*（良い結果をもたらす）*produce* good results. (⇨ shoojiru)

mo⌐tare⌐·ru もたれる（凭れる）*vi.* (-re-te V) 1 lean: *kabe ni motareru*（壁にもたれる）*lean* against a wall.

2 (of food) sit heavy on one's stomach; be hard to digest.

mo⌐tenas·u もてなす（持て成す）*vt.* (-nash·i-; -nas·a-; -nash·i-te C) entertain; treat: *kyaku o atsuku motenasu*（客を厚くもてなす）*give* a guest *warm welcome.*

mo⌐te⌐·ru もてる（持てる）*vi.* (mote-te V) be popular; be a favorite: *Kare wa oñna-no-ko ni yoku moteru.*（彼は女の子によくもてる）He *is* *very popular* with the girls.

mo「to¹ もと (元・基・本・素) *n.*

1 cause; beginning; origin:
keñka no moto (けんかの元) the *cause* of a quarrel.

2 basis; foundation:
Kono deeta wa nani o moto ni shite imasu ka? (このデータは何を基にしていますか) What is the *basis* for these data?

3 material; basic ingredient:
Miso no moto wa daizu desu. (みその素は大豆です) The *basic material* for miso is soybeans.

4 capital; funds. (⇨ motode)

mo「to² もと (元・旧) *n.* original [former] state:
teeburu o moto no toori naraberu (テーブルをもとの通り並べる) put the tables *as they were.* (⇨ kyuu³; zeñ-²)

mo「tode もとで (元手) *n.* capital; funds. (⇨ shihoñ; shikiñ)

mo「tome¹・ru もとめる (求める) *vt.* (-me-te Ⅴ) **1** request; demand.

2 seek; look for:
shoku o motomeru (職を求める) *look for* employment.

3 buy; purchase.

mo「tomoto もともと (元々) *adv.* from the first [beginning]; by nature.

motomoto da (〜だ) remain unchanged: *Soñ shite motomoto da.* (損してもともとだ) Even if I lose money, I will be *none the worse* for it.

mo「tozu¹k・u もとづく (基づく) *vi.* (-zuk・i-; -zuk・a-; -zu・i-te Ⓒ) be based on; be founded on.

mo「ts・u もつ (持つ) *vt.* (moch・i-; mot・a-; mot-te Ⓒ) **1** take; hold; carry:
Sono nimotsu wa watashi ga mochimashoo. (その荷物は私が持ちましょう) I'll *take* that luggage.

2 possess; own: ★ Usually used in the form '*motte iru.*'
Kare wa supootsukaa o motte iru. (彼はスポーツカーを持っている) He *has*

a sports car. (⇨ shoyuu)

3 cherish (a feeling); harbor (a desire):
Watashi wa Nihoñ no rekishi ni kyoomi o motte imasu. (私は日本の歴史に興味を持っています) I *have* an interest in Japanese history.

4 last; hold; keep; wear:
Kono fuku wa ato go-neñ mochimasu. (この服はあと5年もちます) These clothes *will last* five more years.

5 bear; cover; pay:
Kañjoo wa kare ga motta. (勘定は彼が持った) He *paid* the bill. (⇨ harau)

mo「ttaina¹・i もったいない (勿体無い) *a.* (-ku) **1** wasteful:
Jikañ ga mottainai. (時間がもったいない) It is a *waste* of time.

2 too good:
Watashi ni wa mottainai heya desu. (私にはもったいない部屋です) This is a room that is *too good* for me. (⇨ oshii)

mo「tte ik・u もっていく (持って行く) *vt.* (ik・i-; ik・a-; it-te Ⓒ) take (a thing with one); carry:
pikunikku ni iroiro na tabemono o motte iku (ピクニックにいろいろな食べ物を持って行く) *take* various foods to a picnic. (↔ motte kuru)

mo「tte k・u¹ru もってくる (持って来る) *vt.* (k・i-; k・o-; k・i-te Ⅰ) bring; get:
Kasa o motte kuru no o wasurete shimatta. (かさを持って来るのを忘れてしまった) I forgot to *bring* my umbrella. (↔ motte iku)

mo「tto もっと *adv.* more:
Motto motte kite kudasai. (もっと持って来てください) Please bring some *more.*

mo「tto¹mo¹ もっとも (最も) *adv.* most:
Nihoñ de mottomo takai yama (日本で最も高い山) the *highest* mountain in Japan. (⇨ ichibañ²)

mo「tto¹mo² もっとも (尤も) *a.n.* (〜 na, ni) reasonable; natural;

right. (⇒ toozeñ)

mo｢ttomo³ もっとも (尤も) *conj.* however; but; though: *Kanojo wa keesañ ga hayai. Mottomo tokidoki machigaeru.* (彼女は計算が速い. もっともときどき間違える) She is quick at figures. *But* she sometimes makes mistakes. (⇒ tadashi)

mo｢yas·u もやす (燃やす) *vt.* (mo-yash·i-; moyas·a-; moyash·i-te [C]) burn (wastepeper). (⇒ moeru)

mo｢yoo もよう (模様) *n.* **1** pattern; design: *hana no moyoo no kabegami* (花の模様の壁紙) wallpaper with a floral *pattern*. **2** look; appearance: *Kaigi wa eñki ni naru moyoo da.* (会議は延期になるもようだ) It *looks like* the meeting is going to be postponed. **3** development; circumstances: *Kare wa sono kuni no saikiñ no moyoo o hanashite kureta.* (彼はその国の最近のもようを話してくれた) He told us about the latest *developments* in the country. (⇒ yoosu)

mo｢yooshi もよおし (催し) *n.* meeting; party; function. (⇒ moyoosu)

mo｢yoos·u もよおす (催す) *vt.* (mo-yoosh·i-; moyoos·a-; moyoosh·i-te [C]) **1** hold; have; give (a party). (⇒ hiraku; moyooshi) **2** feel: *nemuke o moyoosu* (眠気を催す) *feel* sleepy / *samuke o moyoosu* (寒気を催す) *feel* a chill.

mu¹ む (無) *n.* nothing; naught; nil: *Watashi-tachi no doryoku wa subete mu ni natta.* (私たちの努力はすべて無になった) All our efforts have come to *nothing*.

mu- む (無) *pref.* un-; -less; free: *mu-yoku* (無欲) *unselfish* / *mu-zai* (無罪) *innocent*.

mu｢cha むちゃ (無茶) *n.* being unreasonable; being absurd: *mucha o suru* (無茶をする) do *reckless things*. — *a.n.* (~ na, ni) unreasonable; absurd; reckless.

mu｢chakucha むちゃくちゃ (無茶苦茶) *a.n.* (~ na, ni) (*informal*) absurd; reckless; awful. (⇒ mucha; mechamecha)

mu｢chi¹ むち (無知) *n.* ignorance; innocence. — *a.n.* (~ na) ignorant.

mu¹chi² むち (鞭) *n.* whip; lash.

mu｢chuu むちゅう (夢中) *a.n.* (~ na, ni) absorbed; crazy: *terebi-geemu ni muchuu ni naru* (テレビゲームに夢中になる) *be absorbed* in a video game. **muchuu de** (~ で) for one's life: *Watashi wa muchuu de nigeta.* (私は夢中で逃げた) I ran *for my life*.

mu｢da むだ (無駄) *n.* waste; uselessness: *muda o habuku* (無駄を省く) cut down on *waste*. — *a.n.* (~ na, ni) wasteful; useless. (⇒ dame)

mu｢dañ むだん (無断) *n.* without permission [leave; notice]: *mudañ de gakkoo o yasumu* (無断で学校を休む) be absent from school *without notice*.

mu｢dazu¹kai むだづかい (無駄遣い) *n.* waste; wasting: *zeekiñ no mudazukai* (税金のむだづかい) a *waste* of tax money. **mudazukai suru** (~する) *vt.* waste.

mu¹eki むえき (無益) *a.n.* (~ na, ni) useless; futile: *mueki na arasoi* (無益な争い) a *useless* controversy. (↔ yuueki)

mu¹gai むがい (無害) *a.n.* (~ na, ni) harmless; innocuous. (↔ yuugai)

mu｢geñ むげん (無限) *n.* boundless; limitless: *mugeñ no yorokobi* (無限の喜び) *boundless* joy.

— *a.n.* (~ na, ni) infinite;
boundless; limitless.

mu「gi むぎ (麦) *n.* wheat; barley;
oats.

mu「goǹ むごん (無言) *n.* silence;
muteness:
Kare wa mugoǹ de heya kara dete
itta. (彼は無言で部屋から出て行った)
He went out of the room *without a word*. (⇨ damatte)

mu「hoǹ むほん (謀反) *n.* rebellion:
muhoǹ o okosu (謀反を起こす) *rebel*.

mu「ika むいか (六日) *n.* six days;
the sixth day of the month.
(⇨ APP. 5)

mu「ii**mi** むいみ (無意味) *a.n.*
(~ na, ni) meaningless; sense-
less: muimi *na giroǹ* (無意味な議
論) *meaningless* arguments.

mui**jaki** むじゃき (無邪気) *a.n.*
(~ na, ni) innocent; childlike:
Kodomo wa mujaki da. (子どもは無
邪気だ) Children are *without
guile*.

mui**ji** むじ (無地) *n.* plain; having
no pattern or design.

mui**jiǹ** むじん (無人) *n.* vacant;
uninhabited:
mujiǹ-*fumikiri* (無人踏切) an *un-
attended* railroad crossing.

mu「juǹ むじゅん (矛盾) *n.* contradiction; inconsistency; incom-
patibility.

mujuǹ suru (~する) *vi.* contra-
dict; be inconsistent; be incom-
patible.

mu「kae・ru むかえる (迎える) *vt.*
(mukae-te Ⅴ) **1** meet; come to
meet; welcome; receive:
Watashi-tachi wa kare o eki de
mukaemashita. (私たちは彼を駅で迎
えました) We *met* him at the station.
2 invite:
kyaku o yuushoku ni mukaeru (客
を夕食に迎える) *invite* a guest to
dinner.
3 greet (a new year); see (one's
birthday); attain.

mu「kai むかい (向かい) *n.* opposite
side [place]:
Gakkoo no mukai ni hoǹya ga arimasu. (学校の向かいに本屋がありま
す) There is a bookstore *across*
from the school. (⇨ mukau)

mu「kai**ǹkee** むかんけい (無関係)
a.n. (~ na, ni) unrelated; irrele-
vant:
Watashi wa koǹdo no jikeǹ to wa
mukaǹkee desu. (私は今度の事件とは
無関係です) I *have nothing to do*
with this affair. (↔ kaǹkee)

mu「kashi むかし (昔) *n.* the past;
old days; ancient times.
(↔ ima¹)

mu「kashi-bai**nashi** むかしばなし
(昔話) *n.* old tale [story].

mu「kashi-mukashi むかしむかし
(昔々) *n.* once upon a time.

mu「ka・u むかう (向かう) *vi.* (muka-
i-; mukaw・a-; mukat-te Ⓒ)
1 face; front:
Mukatte *migi ni mieru no ga shiyakusho desu.* (向かって右に見えるの
が市役所です) The building *you
can see* on the right is the town
hall. (⇨ mukai)
2 head; leave for...:
Hikooki wa Tookyoo kara Oosaka
e mukatta. (飛行機は東京から大阪へ
向かった) The airplane *set course*
from Tokyo for Osaka.
3 against; to:
Seǹsee ni mukatte, *soǹna koto o
itte wa ikemaseǹ.* (先生に向かって、
そんなことを言ってはいけません) You
must not say that kind of thing
directly *to* your teacher.

-muke むけ (向け) *suf.* for:
kodomo-*muke no baǹgumi* (子ども
向けの番組) a program *for* children. (⇨ muki)

mu「ke・ru むける (向ける) *vt.* (mu-
ke-te Ⅴ) **1** turn; direct:
Kare wa kanojo no hoo ni me o
muketa. (彼は彼女のほうに目を向けた)
He *turned* his eyes toward her.
(⇨ muku¹)
2 aim; point:

Gootoo wa keekañ ni juu o muketa.(強盗は警官に銃を向けた) The robber *aimed* his pistol at the policeman.

mu¹ki むき(向き) *n.* **1** way; direction:
Kaze no muki *ga kawatta.*(風の向きが変わった) The *direction* of the wind has changed. 《⇨ muku¹》
2 suitable; suited:
Kono fuku wa wakai hito muki *desu.*(この服は若い人向きです) These clothes are *suitable* for young people. 《⇨ muku¹》

mu¹ko むこ(婿) *n.* **1** bridegroom.
2 son-in-law. 《↔ yome》

mu⌐koo¹ むこう(向こう) *n.* **1** the other [opposite] side; over there. 《↔ kochira》
2 (used to refer to the third person) the other party; he; she; they:
Warui no wa mukoo *da.*(悪いのは向こうだ) It is *they* who are in the wrong. 《↔ kochira》
3 destination:
Mukoo *ni tsuitara, o-shirase shimasu.*(向こうに着いたら, お知らせします) I will let you know when I reach my *destination.*
4 the near future; the coming period of time:
Mukoo *is-shuukañ kyuugyoo shimasu.*(向こう一週間休業します) We will be closed for business for the *next* week.

mu⌐koo² むこう(無効) *a.n.* (~ na) invalid; no good; void. 《↔ yuukoo²》

mu⌐koozune むこうずね(向こう脛) *n.* shin.

mu⌐k·u¹ むく(向く) *vi.* (muk·i·; muk·a·; mu·i·te [C]) **1** turn; look: *ushiro o* muku (後ろを向く) *look* back. 《⇨ mukeru》
2 face:
Watashi no heya wa nishi ni muite imasu.*(私の部屋は西に向いています) My room *faces* west. 《⇨ mukeru; muki》

3 be fit; be suitable; suit:
Kono shigoto wa kanojo ni muite iru.*(この仕事は彼女に向いている) This work *suits* her. 《⇨ fusawashii》

mu⌐k·u² むく(剝く) *vt.* (muk·i·; muk·a·; mu·i·te [C]) peel; pare.

mu¹kuchi むくち(無口) *a.n.* (~ na) taciturn; reticent:
Kare wa mukuchi *desu.*(彼は無口です) He *does not talk much.* 《⇨ kuchi¹》

mu⌐mee むめい(無名) *n.* nameless; unknown:
mumee *no sakka* (無名の作家) an obscure *writer.* 《⇨ yuumee》

mu⌐nashi¹·i むなしい(空しい) *a.* (-ku) fruitless; futile; empty:
munashii *doryoku* (むなしい努力) *fruitless* efforts. 《⇨ muda》

mu¹ne むね(胸) *n.* **1** chest; breast; bust.
2 heart:
Mada mune *ga dokidoki shite iru.* (まだ胸がどきどきしている) My *heart* is still pounding.
mune ga ippai ni naru (~ がいっぱいになる) one's heart is full of (emotion).
mune ga itamu (~ が痛む) pain one's heart.

mu¹noo むのう(無能) *a.n.* (~ na) incompetent; incapable. 《↔ yuunoo》

mu⌐ra むら(村) *n.* village:
mura-*yakuba* (村役場) a *village* office. 《⇨ machi》

-mura むら(村) *suf.* village:
Ogawa-mura (小川村) Ogawa *Village.*

mu⌐ra⌐saki むらさき(紫) *n.* purple; violet.

mu⌐re むれ(群れ) *n.* group; crowd:
hitsuji no mure (羊の群れ) a *flock* of sheep / *ushi no* mure (牛の群れ) a *herd* of cattle.

mu⌐ri むり(無理) *n.* unreasonable; unjust:
Amari muri *o iwanai de kudasai.*

(あまり無理を言わないでください) Do not be so *unreasonable*.

muri (o) suru (〜(を)する) *vi.* overwork; strain oneself.
— *a.n.* (〜 na, ni) impossible; unreasonable; unjust.

muˈriˈkai むりかい (無理解) *n., a.n.* (〜 na) lack of understanding [sympathy]; inconsiderate. (↔ rikai)

muˈri-shiˈnˌjuu むりしんじゅう (無理心中) *n.* forced double suicide. (⇨ shiñjuu)

muˈroñ むろん (無論) *adv.* = mochiroñ.

muˈryoku むりょく (無力) *a.n.* (〜 na/no) powerless; helpless; incompetent. (↔ yuuryoku)

muˈryoo むりょう (無料) *n.* no charge; free:
Sooryoo wa muryoo desu. (送料は無料です) The postage is *free*. (↔ yuuryoo)

muˈseñ むせん (無線) *n.* radio; wireless.

muˈshi[1] むし (虫) *n.* insect; bug; worm; vermin.
mushi ga [no] yoi (〜が[の]よい) be selfish. (⇨ wagamama)

muˈshi[2] むし (無視) *n.* disregard; neglect.
mushi suru (〜する) *vt.* ignore; disregard.

muˈshiatsu[1]ˈi むしあつい (蒸し暑い) *a.* (-ku) sultry; hot and humid. (⇨ musu)

muˈshiba むしば (虫歯) *n.* decayed [bad] tooth; cavity; caries.

muˈshiro むしろ (寧ろ) *adv.* rather (than):
Kare wa shoosetsuka to iu yori, mushiro shijiñ desu. (彼は小説家というより, むしろ詩人です) He is *more* of a poet than a novelist.

muˈshirˈu むしる *vt.* (mushir-i-; mushir-a-; mushit-te C) pull up (weeds); pluck (feathers).

muˈsˈu むす (蒸す) (mush-i-; mus-a-; mush-i-te C) 1 *vt.* steam:
jagaimo o musu (じゃがいもを蒸す)

steam potatoes. (⇨ fukasu[2])
2 *vi.* (of weather, place, etc.) be sultry; be stuffy.

muˈsubi むすび (結び) *n.* 1 end; finish; conclusion:
Kare ni musubi no kotoba o tanoñda. (彼に結びの言葉を頼んだ) We asked him to make some *closing* remarks. (⇨ musubu)
2 rice ball. (⇨ omusubi)

muˈsubitsukeˈ1ˈru むすびつける (結び付ける) *vt.* (-tsuke-te V)
1 tie; fasten:
inu no kusari o ki ni musubitsukeru (犬の鎖を木に結び付ける) fasten the dog's chain to a tree.
2 link; relate:
Sono futatsu no hañzai o musubitsukeru shooko wa nani mo nai. (その二つの犯罪を結び付ける証拠は何もない) There is no evidence at all that *links* the two crimes.

muˈsubˈu むすぶ (結ぶ) *vt.* (musub-i-; musub-a-; musuñ-de C)
1 tie (a ribbon); knot (a rope). (⇨ musubi)
2 link; connect:
Hoñshuu to Shikoku o musubu hashi ga kañsee shita. (本州と四国を結ぶ橋が完成した) The bridges which *link* Honshu and Shikoku have been completed. (⇨ musubitsukeru)
3 (*fig.*) bind:
Kare-ra wa yuujoo de musubarete ita. (彼らは友情で結ばれていた) They *were bound* together by their friendship.
4 conclude (a treaty, contract); form (an alliance).

muˈsuko むすこ (息子) *n.* son. ★ Another person's son is called '*musuko-sañ*.' (↔ musume)

muˈsume[1] むすめ (娘) *n.*
1 daughter. ★ Another person's daughter is called '*musume-sañ*.' (↔ musuko)
2 unmarried young woman; girl.

musuˈu むすう (無数) *a.n.* (〜 ni) countless; numberless.

mu｢ttsu¹ むっつ (六つ) *n.* six.
★ Used when counting.
(⇨ roku; APP. 3)

mu｜udo ムード *n.* atmosphere.

mu｢yami むやみ (無闇) *a.n.* (~ na,
ni) 1 reckless; excessive:
Muyami *ni uñdoo suru no wa
karada ni yoku nai.* (むやみに運動す
るのは体によくない) Exercising *excessively* is not good for you.
2 indiscriminate:
Muyami *ni kodomo o shikaranai
hoo ga yoi.* (むやみに子どもをしからない
ほうがよい) You should not *indiscriminately* scold children.

mu｢yoku むよく (無欲) *a.n.* (~ na,
ni) disinterested; unselfish.
(↔ yokubari)

mu｢yoo むよう (無用) *a.n.* (~ na,
ni) unnecessary; useless:
Shiñpai *wa muyoo desu.* (心配は無
用です) There is *no need* to worry.

mu｢zukashi·i むずかしい (難しい) *a.*
(-ku) 1 hard; difficult:
Kyoo no tesuto wa muzukashi-

katta. (きょうのテストは難しかった)
Today's test *was difficult.*
(↔ yasashii¹)
2 (of a procedure, a situation,
etc.) troublesome; complicated.
★ Often used as a euphemism
for the impossible.
3 (of character, personality, etc.)
difficult to please; particular.

mya｢ku¹ みゃく (脈) *n.* pulse.

myo｜o みょう (妙) *a.n.* (~ na, ni)
strange; queer; funny; odd.

myo｢obañ みょうばん (明晩) *n.*
(*formal*) tomorrow evening;
tomorrow night. (↔ koñbañ)

myo｢ochoo みょうちょう (明朝) *n.*
adv. (*formal*) tomorrow morning.
(↔ kesa)

myo｢ogo¹nichi みょうごにち (明後
日) *n.* the day after tomorrow.
★ Formal equivalent of 'asatte.'

myo｜oji みょうじ (名字) *n.* family
name; surname. (⇨ namae)

myo｜onichi みょうにち (明日) *n.*
(*formal*) tomorrow. (⇨ ashita)

N

ñ ん [the contracted form of
either the noun or particle 'no']
★ In speech, 'no da [desu]' is
often contracted to 'ñ da [desu].'
Kono kasa wa watashi ñ [no]
desu. (この傘は私ん[の]です) This
umbrella is *mine.* / Doo sureba ii
ñ [no] deshoo ka? (どうすればいいん
[の]でしょうか) What shall I do?
(⇨ no¹, no² (3))

na¹ な (名) *n.* 1 name; title.
(⇨ namae)
2 fame; reputation:
Kare wa Nihoñ de wa na ga shi-
rarete iru. (彼は日本では名が知られて
いる) He is *well-known* in Japan.
na mo nai (~もない) nameless;
obscure.

na² な *p.* (*rude*) do not (do):
★ Used to indicate prohibition

or to give a negative order. Used
usually by men.
Shibafu ni hairu na. (芝生に入るな)
Do not walk on the grass.

na³ な *p.* (*rude*) (used to give an
order): ★ An abbreviation of '
nasai.'
Motto hayaku aruki na. (もっと速く
歩きな) *Walk* faster.

na(a) な(あ) *p.* 1 (used to indicate emotion):
Ii teñki da na. (いい天気だな) What
nice weather it is!
2 (used when seeking agreement): ★ Used mainly by men.
Ashita wa atsui deshoo na. (あした
は暑いでしょうな) It will be hot tomorrow, *won't it?*

na｜be なべ (鍋) *n.* pan; pot.

na｢bi｜k·u なびく (靡く) *vi.* (nabi-

k·i-; nabik·a-; nabi·i-te Ⓒ)
(of a flag) flutter; wave; stream.

na「daka¹·i なだかい (名高い) *a.*
(-ku) famous; well-known;
noted. (⇨ yuumee)

na「dare¹ なだれ (雪崩) *n.* snow-
slide; avalanche.

na「de¹·ru なでる (撫でる) *vt.* (na-
de-te Ⓥ) stroke; pat; pet:
kodomo no atama o naderu (子ども
の頭をなでる) *stroke* a child's head.

na¹do など (等) *p.* 1 such as; and
the like: ★ Used to give examples. Follows nouns, usually in
the pattern 'ya … (ya) … nado.'
*Kono machi ni wa jiñja ya tera
nado furui tatemono ga takusañ
arimasu.* (この町には神社や寺など古い
建物がたくさんあります) In this town
there are lots of old buildings,
such as temples and shrines.
2 or whatever: ★ Used when
giving one representative example.
*Sono heñ de biiru nado ip-pai
ikaga desu ka?* (その辺でビールなど一
杯いかがですか) What about a beer,
or whatever, over there?
3 (used to express humility
when referring to oneself, one's
relatives, or one's possessions):
*Watashi no koto nado doozo o-
kamai naku.* (私のことなどどうぞおかま
いなく) Please don't worry yourself *about me*.
4 (used in expressions of negation, disavowal, or scorn):
*Koñna tsumaranai koto de keñka
nado yoshi nasai.* (こんなつまらないこ
とでけんかなどよしなさい) Don't argue
about *something* that is as unim-
portant as this. (⇨ nañte²)
5 (used to add emphasis):
*Kare wa uso nado tsuku yoo na
hito de wa arimaseñ.* (彼はうそなどつ
くような人ではありません) He is not
the kind of person that would do
something like tell a lie.

na¹e なえ (苗) *n.* seedling; young
plant.

na「fuda なふだ (名札) *n.* name
card; tag; nameplate.

na「ga- なが (長) *pref.* long:
naga-*ame* (長雨) a *long* rain / na-
ga-*banashi* (長話) a *long* talk.

na「gabi¹k·u ながびく (長引く) *vi.*
(-bik·i-; -bik·a-; -bi·i·te Ⓒ) be
prolonged; drag on.

na「gagutsu ながぐつ (長靴) *n.*
boots; rubber boots; Wellington
boots.

na「ga¹·i ながい (長い) *a.* (-ku)
1 (of length, distance) long:
Nihoñ de ichibañ nagai kawa (日
本で一番長い川) the *longest* river in
Japan. (↔ mijikai) (⇨ nagasa)
2 (of time) long:
*Koochoo señsee no hanashi wa
totemo nagakatta.* (校長先生の話は
とても長かった) The headmaster's
speech was very *long*.
(↔ mijikai)

na「gaiki¹ ながいき (長生き) *n.* long
life; longevity.
nagaiki (o) suru (~(を)する) *vi.*
live long; outlive.

na「game¹ ながめ (眺め) *n.* view;
scene; prospect. (⇨ nagameru)

na「game¹·ru ながめる (眺める) *vt.*
(nagame-te Ⓥ) look at; watch;
view:
mado kara soto o nagameru (窓から
外を眺める) *look* out of the window.
(⇨ nagame)

na「ganeñ ながねん (長年) *n.* many
years; a long time.

-nagara ながら (乍ら) *suf.* [at-
tached to the continuative base
of a verb, an adjectival noun or
the dictionary form of an adjec-
tive]
1 while; as: ★ Used to show
that two actions are simultaneous.
*Watashi wa sutereo o kiki-nagara,
beñkyoo shimasu.* (私はステレオを聞
きながら、勉強します) I study *while*
listening to the stereo.
2 though; yet: ★ Used to indicate a contrast or an unexpected

result or situation.
Karada ni warui to shiri-nagara, tabako wa yameraremaseñ. (体に悪いと知りながら、たばこはやめられません) *Though* I know cigarettes are bad for me, I cannot give them up.
3 (used in fixed, introductory expressions):
Zañneñ-nagara, kono jiko de ooku no kata ga nakunarimashita. (残念ながら、この事故で多くの方が亡くなりました) *To my deep regret,* a great many people died in this accident.

na┌gare┐ ながれ (流れ) n. **1** flow; stream:
Kono kawa wa nagare ga hayai. (この川は流れが速い) This river *flows fast.* (⇨ nagareru)
2 current; momentum:
Kare wa toki no nagare ni umaku notta. (彼は時の流れにうまくのった) He skillfully took advantage of the *current* of the times.

na┌gare┐·ru ながれる (流れる) vi. (nagare-te Ⅴ) **1** flow; run; stream. (⇨ nagare)
2 (of a bridge, building, etc.) be washed away. (⇨ nagasu)
3 pass:
Are kara juu-neñ no saigetsu ga nagareta. (あれから10年の歳月が流れた) Ten years *have passed* since then. (⇨ nagare)
4 (of a game, meeting, etc.) be rained out. (⇨ chuushi)

na┌gasa ながさ (長さ) n. length. (⇨ haba; nagai)

na┌gashi┐[1] ながし (流し) n. sink.

na┌gashi┐[2] ながし (流し) n. cruising (taxi): *nagashi no takushii* (流しのタクシー) a *cruising* taxi.

na┌ga┐s·u ながす (流す) vt. (nagash-i-; nagas-a-; nagash-i-te Ⅽ) **1** pour; let flow; shed:
furo no mizu o nagasu (ふろの水を流す) *let* the bath water *out.* (⇨ nagareru)
2 wash away (a bridge, etc.):

Taifuu de hashi ga nagasareta. (台風で橋が流された) A bridge *was washed away* in the typhoon. (⇨ nagareru)
3 wash down:
Señtoo de kare no senaka o nagashite yatta. (銭湯で彼の背中を流してやった) I *washed down* his back in the public bath.

na┌ge┐k·u なげく (嘆く) vi. (nagek·i-; nagek·a-; nage·i-te Ⅽ) grieve; deplore; regret. (⇨ kanashimu)

na┌ge┐·ru なげる (投げる) vt. (nage-te Ⅴ) **1** throw; hurl; fling; pitch; toss: *inu ni ishi o nageru* (犬に石を投げる) *throw* a stone at a dog. (⇨ hooru)
2 abandon (a plan, attempt, etc.); give up.

na┌gori┐ なごり (名残) n. **1** parting; farewell:
Futari wa nagori o oshiñda. (二人は名残を惜しんだ) The couple were *reluctant to part.*
2 trace; remains:
Sono mura ni wa mada señsoo no nagori ga atta. (その村にはまだ戦争の名残があった) There were still *traces* of the war in the village.

na┌go┐yaka なごやか (和やか) a.n. (～ na, ni) peaceful; friendly.

na┌gu┐r·u なぐる (殴る) vt. (nagur·i-; nagur·a-; nagut-te Ⅽ) strike; hit; knock; beat.

na┌gusame┐·ru なぐさめる (慰める) vt. (nagusame-te Ⅴ) comfort; console; cheer up.

na┌·i ない (無い) a. (-ku) ★ Not used attributively. Polite forms are 'arimaseñ' and 'nai desu.'
1 no; do not exist:
Kono buñ ni machigai wa nai. (この文に間違いはない) There are *no* mistakes in this sentence. (↔ aru[2])
2 no; do not have:
Hoñ o yomu hima ga nai. (本を読む暇がない) I *have no* time to read. (↔ aru[2])

3 be free (from):
Kare no seekatsu wa mattaku ku-roo ga nai. (彼の生活はまったく苦労がない) His life *is* quite *free* from care. (↔ aru²)
4 (of a thing, an article, etc.) be missing: (↔ aru²)
★ Follows the *ku*-form of other adjectives to make the negative form. *Kyoo wa isogashiku* nai. (きょうは忙しくない) I am *not* busy today.

-na·i¹ ない *infl. end.* (-ku) [attached to the negative base of a verb, and inflected like an adjective] do not; will not; cannot:
Kono mado wa dooshite mo aka-nai. (この窓はどうしても開かない) This window *won't* open.

-na¹·i² ない (無い) *suf.* (a.) (-ku) [added to a limited number of nouns to make a negative adjective]
nasake-nai (情けない) *shameful /* shikata-nai (仕方ない) *unavoidable.*

-nai³ ない (内) *suf.* in; inside; within:
Sha-nai no o-tabako wa go-eñryo kudasai. (車内のおたばこはご遠慮ください) Please refrain from smoking *in* the vehicle.

na¹ibu ないぶ (内部) *n.* **1** inside; interior:
kyookai no naibu (教会の内部) the *interior* of a church. (↔ gaibu)
2 internal affairs. (↔ gaibu)

na¹ifu ナイフ *n.* knife. ★ 'Kitchen knife' is called '*hoochoo.*'

na¹ifuku¹yaku ないふくやく (内服薬) *n.* medicine to be taken internally. (⇨ kusuri)

na¹ika ないか (内科) *n.* internal medicine: naika-i (内科医) a *physician.* (⇨ geka)

na¹ikaku ないかく (内閣) *n.* cabinet:
naikaku o soshiki [kaizoo] suru (内閣を組織[改造]する) form [re-shuffle] a *cabinet.*

Na¹ikaku-so¹orida¹ijiñ ないかく

そうりだいじん (内閣総理大臣) *n.* the Prime Minister.

na¹ishi ないし (乃至) *conj.* (*formal*)
1 from...to...; between...and...:
Kono shigoto wa kañsee made ni, tooka naishi *ni-shuukañ kakari-masu.* (この仕事は完成までに、10日ないし2週間かかります) It will take *be-tween* ten days *and* two weeks before this job is finished. (⇨ mata-wa)
2 or:
Dairiniñ wa haiguusha naishi *oyako ni kagirimasu.* (代理人は配偶者ないし親子に限ります) The proxy must be a spouse, *or* parent or child.

na¹ishiñ ないしん (内心) *n., adv.* one's inmost heart; at heart; inwardly:
Kare wa naishiñ *bikubiku shite ita.* (彼は内心びくびくしていた) He was *inwardly* nervous. (⇨ kokoro)

na¹isho¹ ないしょ (内緒・内証) *n.* secrecy; secret:
Kono keekaku wa kare ni wa nai-sho *ni shite kudasai.* (この計画は彼にはないしょにしてください) Please keep this plan a *secret* from him.

na¹isoo ないそう (内装) *n.* interior decoration [furnishings]; upholstery. (↔ gaisoo)

na¹iyoo ないよう (内容) *n.* contents; substance. (⇨ keeshiki)

na¹iyoo-mi¹hoñ ないようみほん (内容見本) *n.* sample pages; prospectus.

na¹izoo ないぞう (内臓) *n.* internal organs.

na¹ka¹ なか (中) *n.* **1** inside; interior:
Kono koppu wa naka *ga yogorete iru.* (このコップは中が汚れている) This glass is dirty on the *inside.*
(↔ soto) (⇨ uchi²)
2 in:
Uchi no naka *e hairi nasai.* (家の中へ入りなさい) Please come *into* the house. (↔ soto)
3 middle:

Kare-ra wa fubuki no naka *o deka-keta.*（彼らは吹雪の中を出かけた）
They went out in the *middle* of the blizzard.
4 of; among:
Sono shinamono no naka *ni wa furyoohiñ ga atta.*（その品物の中には不良品があった）There were some defective items *among* the goods.

na¹ka² なか（仲）*n*. relation; terms: naka *ga ii [warui]*（仲がい[悪い]）be on good [bad] *terms*.

na¹kaba¹ なかば（半ば）*n*. middle; halfway:
sañ-gatsu nakaba（三月半ば）*mid-March*.
— *adv*. half; partly:
Ima no wa nakaba *joodañ desu.*（今のは半ば冗談です）I was *half* joking.（⇨ hañbuñ）

na¹kama¹ なかま（仲間）*n*. friend; fellow; comrade:
Watashi wa sono nakama *ni haitta.*（私はその仲間に入った）I joined the *group*.

na¹ka¹mi なかみ（中身）*n*. contents; substance.（⇨ naiyoo）

na¹kanaka なかなか（中々）*adv*.
1 very; quite:
Kanojo no Nihoñgo wa nakanaka *umai.*（彼女の日本語はなかなかうまい）Her Japanese is *pretty* good.
2 (with a negative) easily; readily:
Kono futa wa nakanaka *torenai.*（このふたはなかなか取れない）This lid will not come off *easily*.

na¹kana¹ori なかなおり（仲直り）*n*. reconciliation.
nakanaori suru（〜する）*vi*. be reconciled; make up.

na¹kas·u なかす（泣かす）*vt*. (nakash·i-; nakas·a-; nakash·i-te Ⓒ) = nakaseru.

na¹kase·ru なかせる（泣かせる）*vt*. (nakase-te Ⓥ) **1** make a person cry; move a person to tears.（⇨ naku¹）
2 (*fig*.) cause trouble [a problem].

na¹kayoku s·uru なかよくする（仲良くする）*vi*. (sh·i-; sh·i-; sh·i-te Ⓘ) make friends with; get on well.

na¹ka¹yubi なかゆび（中指）*n*. middle finger.

-na¹kereba i¹kenai なければいけない (*polite*='-*nakereba ikemaseñ*') must do (something): ★ Literally 'Unless someone does..., it cannot go.'
Isha ni kono kusuri o nomana-kereba ikenai *to iwareta.*（医者にこの薬を飲まなければいけないと言われた）I was told by the doctor that I *had to take* this medicine.

-na¹kereba na¹ra¹nai なければならない (*polite*='-*nakereba narima-señ*') must do (something): ★ Literally, 'Unless someone does..., it will not do.'
Koñshuu-chuu ni kore o shina-kereba naranai.（今週中にこれをしなければならない）I *must finish* this within this week.

na¹kigo¹e¹ なきごえ（泣き声）*n*. cry; sob; whine.（↔ waraigoe）

na¹kigo¹e² なきごえ（鳴き声）*n*. song; note; bark:
kotori no nakigoe（小鳥の鳴き声）a little bird's *song*.（⇨ naku²）

na¹ko¹odo なこうど（仲人）*n*. matchmaker; go-between:
nakoodo *o suru*（仲人をする）act as *go-between*.（⇨ miai）

na¹k·u¹ なく（泣く）*vi*. (nak·i-; nak·a-; na·i-te Ⓒ) cry; weep; sob; shed tears.（⇨ nakaseru）

na¹k·u² なく（鳴く）*vi*. (nak·i-; nak·a-; na·i-te Ⓒ) **1** (of insects, birds) sing; cry.
2 (of animals) bark; roar; bleat.

na¹kunar·u¹ なくなる（無くなる）*vi*. (-nar·i-; -nar·a-; -nat-te Ⓒ)
1 run out:
Kozukai ga nakunatte shimatta.（小遣いがなくなってしまった）I *have used up* all my pocket money.（⇨ nakusu¹）
2 be missing:
Kono hoñ wa ni-peeji nakunatte

iru. (この本は 2 ページなくなっている)
This book *is missing* two pages.
3 be gone; disappear:
Ha no itami ga nakunatta. (歯の痛みがなくなった) The pain in my tooth *has gone.*

na⌐kunar·u² なくなる (亡くなる) *vi.*
(-nar·i-; -nar·a-; -nat-te ⦿) pass away; die. ★ Euphemistic equivalent of '*shinu.*' (⇨ nakusu²)

na⌐kus·u¹ なくす (無くす) *vt.* (nakush·i-; nakus·a-; nakush·i-te ⦿) 1 lose:
Watashi wa kurejitto kaado o nakushite shimatta. (私はクレジットカードをなくしてしまった) I *have lost* my credit card. (⇨ nakunaru¹)
2 get rid of; abolish:
Koñna warui shuukañ wa nakusu beki da. (こんな悪い習慣はなくすべきだ) This kind of evil custom should *be abolished.*

na⌐kus·u² なくす (亡くす) *vt.* (nakush·i-; nakus·a-; nakush·i-te ⦿) lose (a close relative); be bereft of:
Kare wa tsuma o gañ de nakushita. (彼は妻をがんで亡くした) He *lost* his wife to cancer. (⇨ nakunaru²)

na⌐ma なま (生) *n.* 1 raw; uncooked:
Kono sakana wa nama de taberaremasu. (この魚は生で食べられます) You can eat this fish *raw.*
2 live; direct: nama *no oñgaku* (生の音楽) *live* music.

na⌐ma- なま (生) *pref.* 1 raw; fresh: nama-*yasai* (生野菜) *raw* vegetables.
2 live: nama-*hoosoo* (生放送) a *live* broadcast.

na⌐ma-bi⌐iru なまビール (生ビール) draft beer. ★ Beer not sterilized by heating.

na⌐mae なまえ (名前) *n.* 1 name.
2 given name. (⇨ myooji; na¹)

na⌐magusa⌐i なまくさい (生臭い) *a.* (-ku) (of smell) fishy:
namagusai *nioi* (生臭いにおい) a

fishy smell.

na⌐maiki なまいき (生意気) *a.n.* (~ na, ni) cheeky; saucy; impudent; impertinent.

na⌐make⌐·ru なまける (怠ける) *vi.* (namake-te Ⓥ) be lazy; idle away; neglect. (↔ kiñbeñ)

na⌐manuru⌐·i なまぬるい (生温い) *adj.* (-ku) 1 (of liquid) lukewarm; tepid.
2 (of a method) mild; soft; wishy-washy.

na⌐mari¹ なまり (訛) *n.* dialect; accent.

na⌐mari¹² なまり (鉛) *n.* lead.

na⌐ma-ta⌐mago なまたまご (生卵) *n.* raw egg.

na⌐me⌐raka なめらか (滑らか) *a.n.* (~ na, ni) smooth.

na⌐me⌐·ru なめる (嘗める) *vt.* (name-te Ⓥ) 1 lick; lap.
2 suck (candy); eat:
ame o nameru (あめをなめる) *suck* a candy.
3 make light of:
aite o nameru (相手をなめる) *underestimate* one's rival.

na⌐mi¹ なみ (並) *n.* average; medium; ordinary; common. (⇨ futsuu¹)

na⌐mi¹² なみ (波) *n.* wave; surf.

-nami なみ (並み) *suf.* ordinary; the same level:
*Kare wa kazoku-*nami *ni atsukawareta.* (彼は家族並みに扱われた) He was treated *like* a member of the family.

na⌐mida なみだ (涙) *n.* tear:
namida *o nagasu* (涙を流す) shed *tears.*

na⌐miki なみき (並木) *n.* row of trees.

na⌐ñ なん (何) *n.* ★ Variant of '*nani.*' (⇨ nani)
1 what:
Are wa nañ *desu ka?* (あれは何ですか) *What* is that?
2 how:
Anata wa kono kaisha ni nañ-*neñ tsutomemashita ka?* (あなたはこの会

社に何年勤めましたか) *How* many years have you worked for this company? (⇨ iku-)

3 many:
Kono shigoto o oeru no ni nañ-neñ *mo kakarimashita.* (この仕事を終えるのに何年もかかりました) It took *many* years to finish this work.

na⎡na なな（七）*n.* seven. ★ Usually used in compounds. (⇨ nanatsu; shichi; APP. 3)

na⎡na⎤me ななめ（斜め）*a.n.* (~ no, ni) **1** oblique; slant:
michi o naname ni oodañ suru (道を斜めに横断する) cross a road *diagonally.*

2 in a bad humor:
Kanojo wa ima go-kigeñ naname *da.* (彼女は今ご機嫌斜めだ) She is now *in a bad mood.*

na⎡na⎤tsu ななつ（七つ）*n.* seven; the seventh. ★ Used when counting. (⇨ nana; shichi; APP. 3)

na⎡ñboku なんぼく（南北）*n.* north and south. (⇨ toozai)

na⎡ñ da ka なんだか（何だか）*adv.* somehow; somewhat:
Kyoo wa nañ da ka *kibuñ ga warui.* (きょうは何だか気分が悪い) Today I feel *somewhat* out of sorts.

na⎡ñ de なんで（何で）*adv.* why:
Kare wa nañ de *okotta ñ desu ka?* (彼は何で怒ったんですか) *Why* is it that he got angry? (⇨ naze)

na⎡ñ de mo なんでも（何でも）*adv.* **1** anything; everything; whatever:
Nañ de mo *hoshii mono ga attara, ii nasai.* (何でも欲しいものがあったら、言いなさい) If there is *anything* you want, please mention it.

2 I hear; they say: ★ Used to avoid direct agreement, judgment, or opinion.
Nañ de mo *kare no byooki wa omoi rashii.* (何でも彼の病気は重いらしい) *They say* that his illness seems grave.

3 (with a negative) nothing:

Koñna shigoto wa nañ de mo *nai.* (こんな仕事は何でもない) There is *nothing* to this kind of job.

na⎡ñ-do なんど（何度）*adv.* **1** how many times; how often:
Kyooto ni wa nañ-do *ikimashita ka?* (京都には何度行きましたか) *How often* have you been to Kyoto?

2 how many degrees:
Netsu wa nañ-do *arimasu ka?* (熱は何度ありますか) *How much* is your temperature?

nañ-do mo (~ も) many times.

na⎡ni なに（何）*n.* what:
Nani *ga atta ñ desu ka?* (何があったんですか) *What* happened? (⇨ nani-ka)
— *int.* what; why:
Nani, *kare ga jiko o okoshita tte.* (なに、彼が事故を起こしたって) *What!* You mean he has caused an accident!

na⎡ni-ka なにか（何か）*n., adv.* something; anything:
Nani-ka *nomimono o kudasai.* (何か飲み物を下さい) Please give me *something* to drink.

na⎡ni mo なにも（何も）*adv.* (with a negative) nothing:
Watashi wa kare to nani mo *kañkee arimaseñ.* (私は彼と何も関係ありません) I have *nothing* to do with him.

na⎡ni-shiro なにしろ（何しろ）*adv.* at any rate; anyway:
Nani-shiro *yatte miru koto desu.* (何しろやってみることです) *At any rate*, the important thing is to try.

na⎡ni-yara なにやら（何やら）*adv.* some; something:
Inaka kara nani-yara *okutte kita.* (田舎から何やら送ってきた) I have received *something* sent from the country.

na⎡ni-yori なにより（何より）*adv.* (~ no) better [more] than anything else:
Keñkoo ga nani-yori *desu.* (健康が何よりです) Health is the *most important* thing.

nañ-ka なんか（何か）*n., adv.*
(*informal*) = nani-ka.

nañkyoku なんきょく（難局）*n.*
difficult situation; difficulty.

Nañkyoku なんきょく（南極）*n.*
South Pole:
Nañkyoku-*tairiku*（南極大陸）the
Antarctic Continent. （↔ Hok-
kyoku）

nanoka[1] なのか（七日）*n.* seven
days; the seventh day of the
month. ★ Also pronounced
'*nanuka*.' （⇨ APP. 5）

nañra-ka なんらか（何らか）*adv.*
some; any:
Fukeeki ni taishite nañra-ka *no
taisaku o tateru hitsuyoo ga aru.*
（不景気に対してなんらかの対策を立てる
必要がある）We have to take *some*
measures against the business
depression.

nañte[1] なんて（何て）*adv.* how;
what:
Kesa wa nañte *samui ñ daroo.*（今
朝は何て寒いんだろう）*How* cold it is
this morning!

nañte[2] なんて *p.* such; like:
★ Follows a noun or the dictionary form of a verb and implies a
degree of criticism.
Ano hito ga nusumi o suru nañte
shiñjirarenai.（あの人が盗みをするなん
て信じられない）I cannot believe
that he would do *such* a thing *as*
steal.

nañ to なんと（何と）*adv.*
1 what: ★ Used in a question.
Kare wa ima nañ to iimashita ka?
（彼はいま何と言いましたか）*What* did
he say just now?
2 how; in what way:
Nañ to o-wabi shite yoi ka wakarimaseñ.（何とおわびしてよいかわかりませ
ん）I do not kow *how* I can apologize.
3 what; how; ★ Used in an exclamation of surprise.
Nañ to kare wa kyuujus-sai datta.
（何と彼は90歳だった）*To my sur-
prise*, he was ninety.

nañ to ka なんとか（何とか）*adv.*
one way or another; anyhow;
somehow:
Nañ to ka *shikeñ ni gookaku shimashita.*（何とか試験に合格しました）I
barely passed the exam.

nañ to ka suru （～する）manage
to do: Kono keñ *wa getsumatsu
made ni* nañ to ka shimasu.（この件
は月末までに何とかします）I will *man-
age to do* it by the end of this
month.

nañ-to-naku なんとなく（何と無
く）*adv.* somehow; vaguely; for
some reason or other:
Kyoo wa nañ-to-naku, sore o yaru
ki ga shinai.（きょうは何となく、それを
やる気がしない）*Somehow* I have no
mind to do it today.

nañnuka なんぬか（七日）*n.* = nanoka. （⇨ APP. 5）

nao[1] なお（尚）*adv.* still; even:
Daibu yoku natte kimashita ga
nao *chuui ga hitsuyoo desu.*（だいぶ
よくなってきましたがなお注意が必要です）
You have gotten much better,
but care is *still* necessary.

nao[2] なお（尚）*conj.* furthermore:
Nao, *shoosai wa nochi-hodo o-
shirase itashimasu.*（なお、詳細は後
ほどお知らせいたします）*Furthermore*,
we will inform you of the details
later.

naor·u[1] なおる（直る）*vi.* (naor·i-;
naor·a-; naot-te Ⓒ) 1 be fixed;
be mended; be repaired.
（⇨ naosu[1]）
2 (of a mistake) be corrected.
（⇨ naosu[1]）
3 (of a mood, temper) be restored:
Kanojo no kigeñ ga naotta.（彼女の
機嫌が直った）Her good mood *has
been restored.* （⇨ naosu[1]）

naor·u[2] なおる（治る）*vi.* (naor·i-;
naor·a-; naot-te Ⓒ) (of a person,
injury, illness, etc.) recover; get
well; be cured; be healed.
（⇨ naosu[2]）

nao-sara なおさら（尚更）*adv.* all

the more; still more.

na·o·s·u¹ なおす（直す）*vt.* (nao-sh·i·; naos·a·; naosh·i·te Ⓒ)
1 mend; repair; fix. (⇨ naoru¹)
2 correct (a mistake); remedy.
3 adjust:
tokee no hari o naosu（時計の針を直す）*adjust* a watch.
4 translate; convert; turn:
Nihoñgo o Eego ni naosu（日本語を英語に直す）*translate* Japanese into English. (⇨ yakusu)

na·o·s·u² なおす（治す）*vt.* (nao-sh·i·; naos·a·; naosh·i·te Ⓒ)
cure (a disease); heal. (⇨ naoru²)

nara なら [provisional form of '*da*'] ★ The more literary variant '*naraba*' can be used to emphasize the idea of condition.
1 when it comes to...; as far as... is concerned; if:
Deñsha nara, *nijip-puñ mo kakari-maseñ.*（電車なら、20分もかかりません）*If* you go by train, it won't even take twenty minutes.
2 provided that; if:
Tanaka-sañ ga ikanai no nara, *boku mo ikimaseñ.*（田中さんが行かないのなら、ぼくも行きません）*If* Miss Tanaka does not go, I will not go, either.
3 the more...the more:
Fukuzatsu nara *fukuzatsu na ho-do tsukai nikui.*（複雑なら複雑なほど使いにくい）*The more* complicated it is, *the harder* it is to use.
(⇨ -ba¹; to¹; -tara)

na·rabe·ru ならべる（並べる）*vt.* (narabe-te Ⓥ) 1 arrange; line up:
tsukue o ichi-retsu ni naraberu（机を一列に並べる）*arrange* the desks in one row. (⇨ narabu)
2 display; spread (dishes). (⇨ narabu)

na·rabi ni ならびに（並びに）*conj.* (*formal*) and; as well as:
Nihoñ narabi ni *Kañkoku*（日本ならびに韓国）Japan *and* Korea. (⇨ soshite; to²)

na·rab·u ならぶ（並ぶ）*vi.* (narab·i·; narab·a·; narañ-de Ⓒ)
1 stand in a row; form a line [queue]. (⇨ naraberu)
2 rank; be equal:
Watashi-tachi no aida de wa go-rufu de kare ni narabu *mono wa imaseñ.*（私たちの間ではゴルフで彼に並ぶものはいません）In our group, there is no one *equal* to him in golf.

na·ra·nai ならない (polite = nari-maseñ) 1 must not; should not:
★ Used in the pattern '-*te wa* naranai' to indicate prohibition.
Kono koto o kare ni itte wa naranai.（このことを彼に言ってはならない）You *should not* tell him about this matter.
2 must; have to; need to:
★ Used in the pattern '-*nakereba* [-*nakute wa*] naranai' to indicate necessity.
Moo ikanakereba naranai.（もう行かなければならない）I *must* be going now.
3 cannot help: ★ Used with a *te*-form of a verb, adjective or the copula to indicate that one cannot prevent oneself from doing something.
Kare wa uso o tsuite iru yoo ni omoete naranai.（彼はうそをついているように思えてならない）I *cannot help* thinking that he is telling a lie.
4 cannot:
Moo gamañ ga naranai.（もうがまんがならない）I *cannot* stand any more.

na·ras·u¹ ならす（鳴らす）*vt.* (na-rash·i·; naras·a·; narash·i·te Ⓒ)
1 ring (a bell); sound (a siren); blow (a horn). (⇨ naru²)
2 (of a person) be popular.

na·ra·s·u² ならす（慣らす）*vt.* (na-rash·i·; naras·a·; narash·i·te Ⓒ)
accustom; train:
Nihoñgo no hatsuoñ ni mimi o narasu（日本語の発音に耳を慣らす）*accustom* one's ears to the pronunciation of Japanese.
(⇨ nareru)

na⌐ra¹·u ならう (習う) *vt.* (nara·i-; naraw·a-; narat-te C) learn; study; practice; take lessons: *piano o* narau (ピアノを習う) *take* piano lessons. (⇨ manabu)

na⌐renareshi¹·i なれなれしい (馴れ馴れしい) *a.* (-ku) overfamiliar; too friendly.

na⌐re¹·ru なれる (慣れる) *vi.* (nare-te V) become accustomed: *Nihoñ no seekatsu ni* nareru (日本の生活に慣れる) *become accustomed* to life in Japan. (⇨ narasu²)

nari¹ なり *p.* or: ★ Follows a noun or the dictionary form of a verb and implies a choice among two or more alternatives. *Wakaranai toki wa señsee ni kiku* nari *jisho de shiraberu* nari *shi nasai.* (わからないときは先生に聞くなり辞書で調べるなりしなさい) When you do not understand, ask the teacher, look it up in your dictionary, *or* do something. (⇨ aruiwa¹; mata-wa)

nari² なり *p.* as soon as: ★ Follows the dictionary form of a verb. *Kare wa kaette kuru* nari, *nete shimatta.* (彼は帰ってくるなり、寝てしまった) He went straight to sleep *as soon as* he returned.

na⌐ritats·u なりたつ (成り立つ) *vi.* (-tach·i-; -tat·a-; -tat-te C) **1** be made up; consist. **2** materialize; be realized: *Shikiñ ga areba kono kikaku wa* naritachimasu. (資金があればこの企画は成り立ちます) Provided we have the funds, this project will *be realized.* (⇨ seeritsu)

na⌐r·u¹ なる (成る) *vi.* (nar·i-; nar·a-; nat-te C) **1** (of a person) become; grow: *Kare wa isha ni* natta. (彼は医者になった) He *became* a doctor. **2** (of time, season, etc.) come; grow; set in: *Yatto haru ni* natta. (やっと春になった) At last spring *has come.*

3 come to do; begin to do: *Watashi wa kare ga suki ni* natta. (私は彼が好きになった) I *have come* to like him.

4 change; turn: *Shiñgoo ga ao ni* natta. (信号が青になった) The traffic light *turned* green.

5 become of: *Sono go kare ga doo* natta *ka shirimaseñ.* (その後彼がどうなったか知りません) I do not know what *became of* him after that.

6 (of a number, quantity, etc.) amount; total: *Zeñbu de ikura ni* narimasu *ka?* (全部でいくらになりますか) How much does it *come* to altogether?

7 (of age) reach: *Kanojo wa raineñ hatachi ni* narimasu. (彼女は来年二十歳になります) She will *be* twenty next year.

8 (*formal*) (of time) pass: *Nihoñ ni kite, ni-neñ ni* narimasu. (日本に来て、2年になります) Two years *have passed* since I came to Japan.

9 act; serve: *Kare wa sono kaigi de gichoo to* natta. (彼はその会議で議長となった) He *was elected* chairman at the meeting.

10 be made up; consist: *Kono kurasu wa yoñjuugo-niñ kara* natte imasu. (このクラスは45人からなっています) This class *is made up* of forty-five people. ★ Honorific expressions are formed with '*o-*' plus the continuative base of a verb plus '*ni naru.*' e.g. *Kono hoñ o* o-yomi ni narimasu *ka?* (この本をお読みになりますか) Would you like to *read* this book?

na⌐r·u² なる (鳴る) *vi.* (nar·i-; nar·a-; nat-te C) ring; sound; chime; toll. (⇨ narasu¹)

na⌐r·u³ なる (生る) *vi.* (nar·i-; nar·a-; nat-te C) (of a plant) bear fruit; (of fruit) grow.

na⌐rubeku なるべく（成る可く）*adv.*
1 as...as possible; to the best of
one's ability:
*Narubeku ooki-na koe de hana-
shite kudasai.* (なるべく大きな声で話
してください) Please speak *as* loudly
as possible.
2 if possible:
*Narubeku (nara) ashita made ni
kono shigoto o shiagete kudasai.*
(なるべく(なら)あしたまでにこの仕事を仕
上げてください) I want you to finish
this work by tomorrow, *if possible.*

na⌐ruhodo なるほど（成る程）*adv.*
1 I see; I admit:
*Naruhodo, watashi no machigai
deshita.* (なるほど、私の間違いでした) *I
admit* it was my mistake.
2 indeed; to be sure.

na⌐sai なさい (used to express an
imperative): ★ The imperative
form of '*nasaru*.' Follows the continuative base of a verb.
Tsugi no mondai o toki nasai. (次
の問題を解きなさい) *Solve* the following problems.

na⌐sake なさけ（情け）*n.* sympathy; mercy; charity; kindness:
hito ni nasake o kakeru (人に情けを
かける) show *sympathy* to a person.

na⌐sakebuka⌐i なさけぶかい（情け
深い）*a.* (-ku) kindhearted; warm-
hearted; merciful.

na⌐sakena⌐i なさけない（情けない）
a. (-ku) shameful; deplorable;
miserable.

na⌐sa⌐r・u なさる（為さる）*vt.* (nasa-
i-; nasar・a-; nasat-te C) do:
★ Honorific equivalent of '*suru*.'
Ashita wa doo nasaimasu ka? (あ
したはどうなさいますか) What are you
going to *do* tomorrow?
《⇨ nasai》

na⌐shi¹ なし（無し）*n.* nothing:
Ijoo nashi. (異常なし) There is
nothing abnormal. 《⇨ nai》

na⌐shi¹² なし（梨）*n.* pear; pear
tree.

na⌐su¹ なす（茄子）*n.* eggplant.

na⌐s・u² なす（為す）*vt.* (nash・i-; na-
s・a-; nash・i-te C) (*formal*) do:
*Kare ni wa kare no nasu beki koto
ga aru.* (彼には彼のなすべきことがある)
He has to do what he has to *do.*

na⌐tsu¹ なつ（夏）*n.* summer.
《⇨ shiki¹》

na⌐tsukashi⌐i なつかしい（懐かしい）
a. (-ku) dear; good old; longed-
for:
Furusato ga natsukashii. (ふるさとが
懐かしい) I *long for* my hometown.

na⌐tsumi⌐kañ なつみかん（夏蜜柑）
n. Chinese citron.

na⌐tsu-ya⌐sumi なつやすみ（夏休
み）*n.* summer vacation. 《⇨ yasu-
mi》

na⌐ttoku なっとく（納得）*n.* understanding; satisfaction.
nattoku saseru (～させる) *vt.* con-
vince; persuade.
nattoku suru (～する) *vi.* understand; be satisfied.

na⌐tto⌐o なっとう（納豆）*n.* fer-
mented soybeans.

na⌐wa¹ なわ（縄）*n.* rope; cord.

na⌐yamashi⌐i なやましい（悩ましい）
a. (-ku) sexy; amorous; volup-
tuous.

na⌐yami¹ なやみ（悩み）*n.* worry;
trouble; sufferings; anguish.
《⇨ nayamu》

na⌐ya⌐m・u なやむ（悩む）*vi.* (na-
yam・i-; nayam・a-; nayañ-de C)
worry; suffer:
*Kare wa doo shitara yoi ka naya-
ñde imasu.* (彼はどうしたらよいか悩んで
います) He *is worrying* about what
to do. 《⇨ nayami》

na⌐ze なぜ（何故）*adv.* why; what
for:
*Naze paatii ni konakatta ñ desu
ka?* (なぜパーティーに来なかったんですか)
Why didn't you come to our
party? 《⇨ nañde》

na⌐ze nara(ba) なぜなら(ば)（何故
なら(ば)）*conj.* the reason is; that
is so because. ★ Used at the beginning of a sentence.

na⌐zo なぞ（謎）*n.* mystery; enig-

ma; riddle; puzzle:
nazo *o toku* (謎を解く) solve a *mystery* [*riddle*].

na⌈zonazo なぞなぞ (謎々) *n.* riddle. (⇨ nazo)

na⌈zuke¹·ru なづける (名付ける) *vt.* (nazuke-te ⓥ) name; call:
Ryooshiñ wa kodomo o Akemi to nazuketa. (両親は子どもを明美と名づけた) The parents *named* their child Akemi. (⇨ namae)

ne¹¹ ね (根) *n.* 1 root:
Sono ki wa sugu ni ne ga tsuita. (その木はすぐに根がついた) The tree soon took *root*.
2 (*fig.*) root:
aku no ne o tatsu (悪の根を断つ) eradicate the *root* of evil.

ne² ね (値) *n.* price; cost. (⇨ nedañ)

ne³ ね *p.* 1 (used when seeking agreement from someone):
Ashita kimasu ne. (あした来ますね) You are coming tomorrow, *aren't you?*
2 (used after a phrase to obtain confirmation from the listener):
★ Overuse sounds too familiar.
Ano ne, kinoo ne, Giñza de ne, shokuji shite ne ... (あのね、きのうね、銀座でね、食事してね...) *Look...*yesterday, *okay?* In Ginza, *understand?* We had a meal, *right?*
3 (used as an exclamation, or to indicate surprise):
Zuibuñ muzukashii desu ne. (ずいぶん難しいですね) Well, it is very difficult, *isn't it?*
4 (used to slightly emphasize one's opinion):
Hayaku kaetta hoo ga ii to omoimasu ne. (早く帰ったほうがいいと思いますね) *I think* you had better go back soon.

ne¹⁴ ね *int.* look; listen; say:
★ Used to get attention.
Ne, kore kiree deshoo. (ね、これきれいでしょう) *Look*, isn't this lovely?

ne⌈agari ねあがり (値上がり) *n.* increase in price; appreciation.

neagari suru (〜する) *vi.* (of a price) rise; go up. (↔ nesagari)

ne⌈age ねあげ (値上げ) *n.* price rise; increase; raise.

neage suru (〜する) *vt.* raise the price. (↔ nesage)

ne⌈bari¹ ねばり (粘り) *n.* 1 stickiness; adhesiveness. (⇨ nebaru)
2 tenacity; perseverance:
Kimi wa nebari *ga tarinai.* (きみは粘りが足りない) You lack *tenacity*. (⇨ nebaru)

ne⌈ba¹r·u ねばる (粘る) *vi.* (nebar·i-; nebar·a-; nebat-te ⓒ)
1 be sticky; be glutinous. (⇨ nebari)
2 (of a person) stick; persist. (⇨ nebari)

ne⌈biki ねびき (値引き) *n.* discount; reduction in price. (⇨ waribiki)

nebiki suru (〜する) *vt.* discount; reduce a price.

ne⌈boke¹·ru ねぼける (寝惚ける) *vi.* (-boke-te ⓥ) be half asleep; be not fully awake.

ne⌈boo ねぼう (寝坊) *n.* late riser; sleepyhead; oversleeping.

neboo suru (〜する) *vi.* oversleep; get up late.

ne⌈dañ ねだん (値段) *n.* price; cost. (⇨ ne²)

ne⌈da¹r·u ねだる *vt.* (nedar·i-; nedar·a-; nedat-te ⓒ) ask; beg; press; plead.

ne⌈doko ねどこ (寝床) *n.* bed:
nedoko *ni hairu* (寝床に入る) go to *bed*. (⇨ neru¹)

ne⌈esañ ねえさん (姉さん) *n.* one's own older sister. (⇨ ane; niisañ)

ne⌈fuda ねふだ (値札) *n.* price tag [label].

ne⌈ga¹i ねがい (願い) *n.* wish; desire; request: *heewa e no* negai (平和への願い) *desire* for peace. (⇨ o-negai; negau)

ne⌈ga¹·u ねがう (願う) *vt.* (nega·i-; negaw·a-; negat-te ⓒ) wish; desire; hope:
Mata o-me ni kakareru koto o

negatte imasu.(またお目にかかれること を願っています) I *hope* to see you again. (⇨ negai)

ne¹gi ねぎ (葱) *n.* Welsh onion; scallion. (⇨ tamanegi)

ne¹ji ねじ *n.* **1** screw:
neji o shimeru [yurumeru] (ねじを締 める[ゆるめる]) turn [loosen] a *screw*.
2 the spring of a watch.

ne¹jire·ru ねじれる (捩れる) *vi.* (ne-jire-te V) be twisted. (⇨ nejiru)

ne¹ji·ru ねじる (捩る) *vt.* (nejir·i-; nejir·a-; nejitte C) twist; screw; wring:
futa o nejitte shimeru [akeru] (ふた をねじって閉める[開ける]) screw a cap on [off]. (⇨ nejireru)

ne¹kase·ru ねかせる (寝かせる) *vt.* (nekase-te V) put to bed; let sleep. (⇨ nekasu)

ne¹kas·u ねかす (寝かす) *vt.* (ne-kash·i-; nekas·a-; nekash·i-te C) put to bed; let sleep. (⇨ neru¹)

ne¹ko ねこ (猫) *n.* cat.

ne¹koro¹b·u ねころぶ (寝転ぶ) *vi.* (-korob·i-; -korob·a-; -koroñ-de C) lie down; throw oneself down. (⇨ neru¹)

ne¹maki ねまき (寝巻) *n.* night-clothes; nightgown; pajamas.

ne¹mu·i ねむい (眠い) *a.* (-ku) sleepy; drowsy:
Kaigi no toki, totemo nemukatta. (会議のとき、とても眠かった) I *felt* very *drowsy* during the meeting.

ne¹mure·ru ねむれる (眠れる) *vi.* (nemure-te V) be able to sleep. (⇨ nemuru)

ne¹mur·u ねむる (眠る) *vi.* (ne-mur·i-; nemur·a-; nemut-te C) sleep; fall asleep:
Akañboo wa gussuri nemutte imasu. (赤ん坊はぐっすり眠っています) The baby *is sleeping* soundly. (⇨ nemureru; neru¹)

ne¹muta·i ねむたい (眠たい) *a.* (-ku) = nemui.

ne¹ñ¹ ねん (年) *n.* **1** year:
Kare wa neñ ni ichi-do gaikoku e

iku.(彼は年に一度外国へ行く) He goes abroad once a *year*.
2 grade:
Musuko wa kookoo ichi-neñ desu. (息子は高校1年です) My son is in the first *year* of high school. (⇨ gakuneñ)

ne¹ñ² ねん (念) *n.* sense; feeling:
Kimi wa kañsha no neñ ga tarinai. (きみは感謝の念が足りない) You lack a *sense* of gratitude.
neñ no tame (〜のため) just in case.
neñ o ireru (〜を入れる) do with great care.

ne¹ñbutsu ねんぶつ (念仏) *n.* Buddhist invocation.

ne¹ñchoo ねんちょう (年長) *n.* seniority:
Kare wa watashi yori mittsu neñ-choo desu.(彼は私より3つ年長です) He is *older* than me by three years. (⇨ toshi-ue)

ne¹ñdai ねんだい (年代) *n.* gen-eration; date; age; period. (⇨ jidai; APP. 9)

ne¹ñdo¹ ねんど (年度) *n.* year; fiscal [financial] year:
rai-neñdo no yosañ (来年度の予算) the budget for the next *year*.

ne¹ñdo² ねんど (粘土) *n.* clay.

ne¹ñga ねんが (年賀) *n.* New Year's greetings.

ne¹ñga-ha¹gaki ねんがはがき (年賀 葉書) *n.* New Year's greeting postcard. (⇨ neñgajoo)

ne¹ñgajoo ねんがじょう (年賀状) *n.* New Year's card. (⇨ neñga-hagaki)

ne¹ñga¹ppi ねんがっぴ (年月日) *n.* date. ★ A particular day, month and year.

ne¹ñgetsu ねんげつ (年月) *n.* time; years:
Sono toñneru o kañsee suru no ni nagai neñgetsu ga kakatta.(そのト ンネルを完成するのに長い年月がかかった) It took many *years* to build the tunnel. (⇨ toshitsuki; tsukihi)

ne¹ñgo¹o ねんごう (年号) *n.* the

name of an era; the posthumous name of a Japanese emperor and of his reign. (⇨ APP. 9)

ne⌐ñjuu ねんじゅう (年中) *n.*, *adv.* all the year round; throughout the year; always.

ne⌐ñkañ ねんかん (年間) *n.* year: *Watashi wa juugo-neñkañ mujiko desu.* (私は15年間無事故です) I've had a clean driving record *for fifteen years*. (⇨ gekkañ)

ne⌐ñmatsu ねんまつ (年末) *n.* the end of the year. (↔ neñtoo)

ne⌐ñree ねんれい (年齢) *n.* age. (⇨ toshi¹)

ne⌐ñryo⌐o ねんりょう (燃料) *n.* fuel.

-ne⌐ñsee ねんせい (年生) *suf.* a student of the stated academic year: *shoogaku roku-neñsee* (小学6年生) a sixth *year* elementary school pupil.

ne⌐ñtoo ねんとう (年頭) *n.* the beginning of a year. (↔ neñmatsu)

ne⌐rai ねらい (狙い) *n.* aim; mark; target; purpose: *mato ni nerai o sadameru* (的にねらいを定める) take *aim* at a target. (⇨ nerau)

ne⌐ra·u ねらう (狙う) *vt.* (nera·i-; neraw·a-; nerat-te C) 1 take aim; set one's sights. (⇨ nerai) 2 aim (a goal, victory, success, etc.). (⇨ nerai)

ne⌐ru¹ ねる (寝る) *vi.* (ne-te V) 1 go to bed; sleep. (⇨ nekasu) 2 be sick in bed: (⇨ yasumu) *Kinoo wa kaze de nete imashita.* (きのうはかぜで寝ていました) I *was sick in bed* with a cold yesterday. 3 lie down. (⇨ nesoberu)

ne⌐r·u² ねる (練る) *vi.* (ner·i-; ner·a-; net-te C) 1 knead: *komugi-ko no kiji o neru* (小麦粉の生地を練る) *knead* dough. 2 work out (a plan, etc.) carefully; elaborate.

ne⌐sagari ねさがり (値下がり) *n.* fall in price; depreciation.

(↔ neagari)

nesagari suru (〜する) *vi.* fall; go down; become cheaper.

ne⌐sage ねさげ (値下げ) *n.* reduction in price; price cut. (↔ neage)

nesage suru (〜する) *vt.* reduce; cut the price; mark down.

ne⌐sobe⌐r·u ねそべる (寝そべる) *vi.* (nesober·i-; nesober·a-; nesobet-te C) lie down; sprawl; stretch.

ne⌐sshiñ ねっしん (熱心) *a.n.* (〜 na, ni) eager; hardworking; devoted.

ne⌐ss·u⌐ru ねっする (熱する) *vi.*, *vt.* (nessh·i-; nessh·i-; nessh·i-te I) heat; become hot. (⇨ kanetsu¹; netsu)

ne⌐takiri ねたきり (寝たきり) *n.* bedridden: *Chichi wa netakiri desu.* (父は寝たきりです) My father is *bedridden*.

ne⌐tsu⌐ ねつ (熱) *n.* 1 heat: *taiyoo no netsu* (太陽の熱) the *heat* of the sun. 2 fever; temperature: *Kono ko wa netsu ga aru.* (この子は熱がある) This child has a *fever*. 3 enthusiasm; craze.

ne⌐ttai ねったい (熱帯) *n.* torrid zone; tropics. (↔ kañtai; oñtai)

ne⌐ttoo ねっとう (熱湯) *n.* boiling water. (⇨ o-yu)

ne⌐uchi ねうち (値打ち) *n.* value; worth; price. (⇨ kachi¹)

ne⌐zumi ねずみ (鼠) *n.* mouse; rat.

ni¹ に (二) *n.* two. (⇨ APP. 3)

ni² に *p.* 1 (indicates a place): **a** at; in: ★ Indicates existence at a location. *Ashita wa watashi wa uchi ni imasu.* (あしたは私は家にいます) I will be *at* home tomorrow. **b** on; onto: ★ Indicates the final location of an object that is moved. *Hoñ wa tsukue no ue ni oite kudasai.* (本は机の上に置いてください) Put the book *on* the desk, please.

c to; toward: ★ Indicates direction or final destination. Used with verbs of movement.
Watashi wa mainichi gakkoo ni *ikimasu.* (私は毎日学校に行きます) I go *to* school every day. ★ Direction can also be indicated by '*e*.' (⇨ *e³*)

2 to; from; by: ★ Indicates the direction of giving or receiving.
Nokorimono o inu ni *yatta.* (残り物を犬にやった) I gave the leftovers *to* the dog. (⇨ kara³)

3 at; in: ★ Indicates the time of an action or event.
Watashi wa maiasa rokuji ni *okimasu.* (私は毎朝6時に起きます) I get up *at* six every morning.

4 in; to: ★ Used in expressions of frequency or proportion.
Kare wa ichi-nichi ni *tabako o futa-hako suimasu.* (彼は1日にたばこを2箱吸います) He smokes two packs of cigarettes *in* a day.

5 to; into: ★ Indicates a change or resulting condition.
Shiñgoo ga aka kara ao ni *kawatta.* (信号が赤から青にかわった) The traffic lights changed from red *to* green.

6 (used with verbs of decision):
Kaisha o yameru koto ni *kimeta.* (会社をやめることに決めた) I have decided *to* quit the company.

7 to: ★ Indicates a recipient.
Gaikoku no tomodachi ni *tegami o kaita.* (外国の友だちに手紙を書いた) I wrote a letter *to* a friend abroad.

8 by: ★ Indicates the agent of a passive sentence.
Kyoo wa señsee ni *homerareta.* (きょうは先生にほめられた) I was praised *by* my teacher today. ★ '*Kara*' can also be used. (⇨ kara³)

9 (indicates the person who is made or allowed to do an action): ★ Used with a causative verb.
Sono shigoto o watashi ni *sasete kudasai.* (その仕事を私にさせてくださ

い) I beg you to let *me* do the job.

10 for: ★ Used when comparing, differentiating, estimating, etc.
Kono doresu wa watashi ni *choodo ii.* (このドレスは私にちょうどいい) This dress is just right *for* me.

11 in order to; for the purpose of: ★ Indicates purpose or reason. Used with verbs of movement, especially '*iku*' and '*kuru*.'
Sañpo ni *ikimashoo.* (散歩に行きましょう) Let's go *for* a walk.

12 for; as: ★ Indicates purpose or means.
Kono sakana wa shokuyoo ni *naranai.* (この魚は食用にならない) This fish is not fit *for* food.

13 from; by: ★ Indicates the cause or reason for a state or situation.
Shigoto ni *tsukaremashita.* (仕事に疲れました) I am tired *from* work.

14 at; in: ★ Used in expressions indicating ability, skill or knowledge.
Kare wa suugaku ni *tsuyoi.* (彼は数学に強い) He is good *at* math.

15 in (a stated way): ★ Used in expressions indicating manner.
Kare wa sono buñshoo ni *machigawazu ni yoñda.* (彼はその文章を間違わずに読んだ) He read the sentence *faultlessly*.

ni³ に *p.* and: ★ Used in listing, recalling or restating things.
Kyoo kau mono wa tamago ni *miruku desu.* (きょう買うものは卵にミルクです) Today I have to buy eggs *and* milk. (⇨ to²; ya¹; yara)

ni⁴ に (荷) *n.* load; freight; cargo: *kuruma* ni *o tsumu* (車に荷を積む) *load up* a car. (⇨ kamotsu; nimotsu)

ni「a」·u にあう (似合う) *vi.* (nia·i-; niaw·a-; niat-te 〔C〕) suit; become. (⇨ au²)

ni「bu」·i にぶい (鈍い) *a.* (-ku) dull; blunt; slow:
Mada ki ga tsukanai nañte kare

mo nibui *desu ne.*(まだ気がつかないな
んて彼も鈍いですね) He still does not
understand. He is a bit *slow*,
isn't he? (↔ surudoi)

-nichi にち(日) *suf.* day:
*Ni, sañ-nichi koko ni taizai shi-
masu.* (2, 3 日ここに滞在します) I will
stay here for a few *days*.

ni⌈chiee-ji⌉teñ にちえいじてん(日
英辞典) *n.* a Japanese-English
dictionary for English-speaking
people. ★ A Japanese-English
dictionary for Japanese is called '
waee-jiteñ'(和英辞典). (⇨ jiteñ)

ni⌈chiji にちじ(日時) *n.* time and
date.

ni⌈chijoo-ka⌉iwa にちじょうかいわ
(日常会話) *n.* everyday conversation.

ni⌈chijoo-se⌉ekatsu にちじょう
せいかつ(日常生活) *n.* daily life.

ni⌈chiyoo da⌉iku にちようだいく
(日曜大工) *n.* Sunday [weekend]
carpenter. (⇨ daiku)

ni⌈chiyo⌉o(bi) にちよう(び)(日曜
(日)) *n.* Sunday. (⇨ APP. 5)

ni⌈chiyoohiñ にちようひん(日用品)
n. daily necessities.

ni⌈e-ru にえる(煮える) *vi.* (nie-te
Ⓥ) cook; be cooked. (⇨ niru¹)

ni⌈ga⌉·u にがい(苦い) *a.* (-ku)
1 (of taste) bitter. (↔ amai)
2 (of experience) hard; bitter:
nigai *keekeñ o suru* (苦い経験をす
る) have a *bitter* experience.
3 (of a countenance) sour; unpleasant: nigai *kao o suru* (苦い顔
をする) make a *wry* face.

ni⌈ga⌉s·u にがす(逃がす) *vt.* (niga-
sh·i-; nigas·a-; nigash·i-te Ⓒ)
set free; let go; let escape.
(⇨ nigeru; torinigasu)

ni⌈gate¹ にがて(苦手) *a.n.* (~ na)
1 one's weak point. (↔ tokui)
2 person who is hard to deal
with; tough customer.

ni-⌈gatsu¹ にがつ(二月) *n.* February. (⇨ APP. 5)

ni⌈gedas·u にげだす(逃げ出す) *vi.*
(-dash·i-; -das·a-; -dash·i·te Ⓒ)

run away; take to one's heels.

ni⌈ge⌉·ru にげる(逃げる) *vi.* (nige-
te Ⓥ) run away; escape; flee.
(⇨ nigasu; nogareru)

ni⌈giri にぎり(握り) *n.* 1 grip;
handle. (⇨ nigiru)
2 = nigirizushi.

ni⌈giri⌉zushi にぎりずし(握り鮨) *n.*
hard-rolled sushi. (⇨ sushi)

ni⌈gir·u にぎる(握る) *vt.* (nigir·i-;
nigir·a-; nigit-te Ⓒ) 1 grasp;
grip; hold.
2 dominate (an organization);
rule; control:
Kare ga kaisha no subete o nigitte
iru.(彼が会社のすべてを握っている) He
controls everything in the company.

ni⌈giwa⌉·u にぎわう(賑わう) *vi.*
(-wa·i-; -waw·a-; -wat-te Ⓒ)
be crowded; be alive; be prosperous. (⇨ nigiyaka)

ni⌈gi⌉yaka にぎやか(賑やか) *a.n.*
(~ na, ni) 1 (of place) busy;
crowded. (⇨ nigiwau)
2 (of people, crowds, etc.)
merry; lively; cheerful; noisy.
(↔ sabishii)

ni⌈gori にごり(濁り) *n.* 1 mud-
diness; unclearness:
Kono mizu wa nigori *ga aru.* (この
水は濁りがある) This water is *not
clear.* (⇨ nigoru)
2 voiced consonant. (⇨ dakuoñ;
nigoru)

ni⌈go⌉r·u にごる(濁る) *vi.* (nigo-
r·i-; nigor·a-; nigot-te Ⓒ)
1 become muddy; become
cloudy. (⇨ nigori)
2 (of some *kana* letters) be
voiced:
'Ta' ga nigoru *to 'da' ni narimasu.*(「た」が濁ると「だ」になります)
'Da' is the *voiced* equivalent of
'ta.' (⇨ nigori)

ni⌈guñ にぐん(二軍) *n.* (of baseball) farm team [club]; the
minors. (⇨ ichiguñ)

Ni⌈ho⌉ñ にほん(日本) *n.* Japan.
★ Also '*Nippoñ*.' (⇨ Nippoñ)

Ni‖hoñgo にほんご (日本語) n.
Japanese language; Japanese.
(⇨ kokugo)

Ni‖hoñji‖ñ にほんじん (日本人) n.
Japanese people; Japanese.

ni‖isañ にいさん (兄さん) n. one's
own older brother. (⇨ ani; nee-
sañ)

ni‖ji にじ (虹) n. rainbow.

ni‖ji‖m·u にじむ (滲む) vi. (nijim·i-;
nijim·a-; nijiñ-de Ⓒ) (of ink)
run; blot; get blurred.

ni‖kai にかい (二階) n. the second
(American) floor; the first (British) floor.

ni‖kka にっか (日課) n. one's daily
work [task]:
*Maiasa jogiñgu o suru no ga
nikka desu.* (毎朝ジョギングをするのが
日課です) I make a *practice* of jog-
ging every morning.

ni‖kki にっき (日記) n. diary.

ni‖kkoo にっこう (日光) n. sunlight; sunshine; sun.

ni‖kko‖ri にっこり adv. (~ to;
~ suru) with a smile:
*Sono oñna-no-ko wa watashi ni
mukatte nikkori (to) waratta.* (その
女の子は私に向かってにっこり(と)笑った)
The girl gave me a *smile*.

ni‖koniko にこにこ adv. (~ to;
~ suru) with a smile:
*Kanojo wa itsu-mo nikoniko shite
iru.* (彼女はいつもにこにこしている) She
is always *smiling cheerfully.*

ni‖ku‖ にく (肉) n. meat; flesh.

ni‖ku‖·i にくい (憎い) a. (-ku)
1 hateful. (⇨ nikumu)
2 (*ironic*) smart; clever:
*Kimi mo nakanaka nikui koto o iu
ne.* (君もなかなか憎いことを言うね)
Well said.

-niku‖·i にくい (難い) suf. (a.) (-ku)
hard; difficult: ★ Added to the
stem of a volitional verb.
Kono doogu wa tsukai-nikui. (この
道具は使いにくい) This tool is *difficult* to handle. (↔ -yasui)
(⇨ -gatai)

ni‖ku‖m·u にくむ (憎む) vt. (ni-
kum·i-; nikum·a-; nikuñ-de Ⓒ)
hate; abhor; despise. (⇨ niku-
shimi)

ni‖kurashi‖·i にくらしい (憎らしい)
a. (-ku) hateful; spiteful:
*Dañdañ kare ga nikurashiku natte
kita.* (だんだん彼が憎らしくなってきた)
He has gradually become *detest-
able* to me.

ni‖kushimi にくしみ (憎しみ) n.
hatred; hate; enmity.
(⇨ nikumu; nikui)

ni‖kutai にくたい (肉体) n. body;
the flesh. (⇨ karada)

ni‖ku‖ya にくや (肉屋) n. butcher;
meat shop.

ni‖kyuu にきゅう (二級) n. second
class; second rate. (⇨ ikkyuu)

ni‖motsu にもつ (荷物) n. load;
baggage; luggage.

-niñ にん (人) suf. counter for people: *Kodomo wa sañ-niñ desu.*
(子どもは3人です) I have *three* children. ★ Exceptions are '*hitori*'
(one person) and '*futari*' (two
persons).

ni‖na‖·u になう (担う) vt. (nina·i-;
ninaw·a-; ninat-te Ⓒ) (*formal*)
bear (a burden); take (responsibility).

ni‖ñgeñ にんげん (人間) n. human
being; man. (⇨ hito; jiñrui)

ni‖ñgyoo にんぎょう (人形) n.
doll; puppet.

ni‖ñjiñ にんじん (人参) n. carrot.

ni‖ñjoo にんじょう (人情) n. human nature; humanity; kindness:
niñjoo no atsui [usui] hito (人情の
厚い[薄い]人) a *warmhearted* [*coldhearted*] man.

ni‖ñki にんき (人気) n. popularity;
public interest.

ni‖ñmu にんむ (任務) n. duty;
task; office:
niñmu o hatasu [okotaru] (任務を果
たす[怠る]) fulfill [neglect] one's
duty.

ni‖ñshiki にんしき (認識) n. understanding; recognition:

niñshiki *ga tarinai* (認識が足りない) have little *understanding*.

niñshiki suru (～する) *vt.* understand; recognize; be aware of. (⇨ rikai)

ni⌐ñshiñ にんしん (妊娠) *n.* pregnancy.

niñshiñ suru (～する) *vi.* become pregnant.

ni⌐ñzuu にんずう (人数) *n.* the number of people. (⇨ atamakazu)

ni⌐o⌐i におい (匂い・臭い) *n.* smell; odor; fragrance. (⇨ kaori; niou)

ni⌐o⌐·u におう (匂う・臭う) *vi.* (nioi-; niow·a-; niot-te C) smell; be fragrant; stink. (⇨ nioi)

Ni⌐ppo⌐ñ にっぽん (日本) *n.* Japan. ★ Both '*Nippoñ*' and '*Nihoñ*' are often used in isolation interchangeably. Generally, however, '*Nihoñ*' is preferred when forming compounds. (⇨ Nihoñ)

ni⌐ra⌐m·u にらむ (睨む) *vt.* (niram·i-; niram·a-; nirañ-de C)
1 glare; stare.
2 (in the passive) be in disfavor: *Kare wa buchoo ni* niramarete iru. (彼は部長ににらまれている) He *is in disfavor* with the general manager.
3 suspect; spot.

ni·⌐ru¹ にる (煮る) *vt.* (ni-te Ⅴ) boil; simmer; cook. (⇨ nieru)

ni·⌐ru² にる (似る) *vi.* (ni-te Ⅴ) resemble; be like; be similar.

ni⌐ryuu にりゅう (二流) *n.* second-class; second-rate. (⇨ ichiryuu; sañryuu)

ni⌐se にせ (偽) *n.* sham; counterfeit; imitation: nise *no daiya* (偽のダイヤ) a *fake* diamond.

ni⌐see にせい (二世) *n.* Nisei; the second-generation of Japanese immigrants; a member of this generation. (⇨ issee²; sañsee²)

ni⌐semono にせもの (偽物) *n.* forgery; counterfeit; imitation.

ni⌐shi にし (西) *n.* west; (～ ni/e)

westward. (↔ higashi)

ni shiro にしろ ★ The particle '*ni*' plus the imperative of '*suru*.'
1 even if: ★ Used to form a weak conditional.
Oseji ni shiro, *homerarereba dare de mo warui ki wa shinai.* (お世辞にしろ, ほめられればだれでも悪い気はしない) *Even if* it is flattery, no one feels displeased when he is praised.
2 and; or: ★ Used to give illustrative examples or possibilities.
Beñkyoo ni shiro *uñdoo* ni shiro, *mainichi no doryoku ga taisetsu desu.* (勉強にしろ運動にしろ, 毎日の努力が大切です) In *both* studies *and* physical training, continued daily effort is important.

ni shi⌐te⌐ mo にしても even if: *Joodañ* ni shite mo, *do ga sugiru.* (冗談にしても, 度が過ぎる) *Even if* you did it in jest, you've carried things too far. (⇨ ni shiro)

ni shi⌐te⌐ wa にしては 1 even if; for: ★ Used when the speaker accepts the situation or explanation in the first clause, but finds that the consequent result, as specified in the second clause, is contrary to normal expectation. *Kare wa daigaku o deta* ni shite wa, *jooshiki ni kakete iru.* (彼は大学を出たにしては, 常識に欠けている) *For* someone who graduated from college, he lacks common sense.
2 considering; for: ★ Follows a noun and indicates that, considering the characteristics normally associated with that noun, the judgment the speaker makes is contrary to expectation. *Ano hito wa gaikoku-jiñ* ni shite wa, *Nihoñgo ga umai.* (あの人は外国人にしては, 日本語がうまい) *For* a foreigner, his Japanese is good.

ni⌐sshoku にっしょく (日食) *n.* solar eclipse. (⇨ gesshoku)

ni⌐ssu⌐u にっすう (日数) *n.* the

ni「ta「ts·u にたつ（煮立つ）*vi.*
(-tach·i-; -tat·a-; -tat·te C)
(of water, vessel) boil; come to a
boil.

ni「tchuu にっちゅう（日中）*n.* the
daytime. (↔ yakañ¹)

ni「too にとう（二等）*n.* second
class; second prize; second place.
(⇨ Ittoo)

ni「ttee にってい（日程）*n.* one's
day's schedule; itinerary.

ni「wa にわ（庭）*n.* garden; yard;
court.

ni¹ wa には *p.* for; to; in:
*Kore wa watashi ni wa taisetsu
na shashiñ desu.* (これは私には大切な
写真です) This is a photo which is
important *for* me. (⇨ ni²; wa³)

ni「waka にわか（俄か）*a.n.* (~ na,
ni) sudden; immediate; unexpected:
Niwaka ni ame ga furi-dashita. (に
わかに雨が降りだした) It *suddenly*
started raining.

ni「waka-a「me にわかあめ（俄か雨）
n. rain shower.

ni「watori にわとり（鶏）*n.* chick-
en; rooster; hen. (⇨ hiyoko)

ni「yaniya にやにや *adv.* (~ to;
~ suru) (the manner of grinning
[smirking]):
niyaniya (to) warau (にやにや（と）笑
う) *grin broadly.*

ni「zu「kuri にづくり（荷造り）*n.*
packing:
hikkoshi no nizukuri o suru (引っ越
しの荷造りをする) do the *packing* for
moving.

no¹ の *p.* 1 of; at; in; on:
★ Used to link two nouns. The
first noun describes the latter in
some way.
kinu no hañkachi (絹のハンカチ) a
silk handkerchief / *watashi* no
hoñ (私の本) a book *of* mine /
machi no *yuubiñkyoku* (町の郵便
局) a post office *in* town.
★ Also note the pattern: noun +
particle +'*no*'+ noun. *e.g.* tomo-

dachi kara no *deñwa* (友だちからの
電話) a phone call *from* a friend /
haha e no *tegami* (母への手紙) a letter *to* my mother.
2 (used as the subject marker in
a clause modifying a noun):
*Watashi no yomitai hoñ wa kore
desu.* (私の読みたい本はこれです) The
book *I* want to read is this one.
3 (used to link two nouns,
which are in apposition):
beñgoshi no *Tanaka-sañ* (弁護士の
田中さん) Mr. Tanaka, *who is* a
lawyer.
★ Note the ambiguity: '*isha* no
tomodachi' (医者の友だち) has two
meanings, 'the doctor's friend'
(as in 1) and 'my friend, who is a
doctor' (as in 3).
4 (used to link quantity expressions to a following noun):
sañ-biki no *kobuta* (三匹のこぶた)
three little pigs.

no² の *n.* 1 one: ★ Used to substitute for another noun and
often modified by a verb or adjective.
Motto yasui no wa arimaseñ ka?
(もっと安いのはありませんか) Isn't there
a cheaper *one*?
2 the fact; that: ★ Used to nom-
inalize the previous clause.
*Kanojo ga nyuuiñ shita no o shitte
imasu ka?* (彼女が入院したのを知って
いますか) Do you know *that* she
was hospitalized?
3 (used in giving explanations,
or in eliciting or confirming information): ★ Added to the end of
a clause as '*no da*' or '*no desu*.'
In speech, usually '*ñ da*' or '*ñ
desu*.'
Nani-ka atta ñ desu ka? (何かあった
んですか) *Has* something *happened*?

no³ の *p.* (*colloq.*) [added to the
end of a sentence]
1 (signifies a question): ★ With
rising intonation. Equivalent to
'*no desu ka*.'

Doko e iku no? (どこへ行くの)
Where *are* you *off* to?
2 (suggests an explanation):
★ With falling intonation. Used mainly by women and children. Equivalent to '*no desu*.'
"Doo shita?" "Atama ga itai no."
(「どうした」「頭が痛いの」) "What's the matter? " " I have a headache. "

no⁴ の (野) *n.* field. (⇨ nohara)

no⌈ba⌉s·u¹ のばす (伸ばす) *vt.* (no-bash·i-; nobas·a-; nobash·i-te Ⓒ) **1** lengthen; make longer.
2 straighten; stretch; reach:
Kanojo wa te o nobashite posutaa o hagashita. (彼女は手を伸ばしてポスターをはがした) She *reached out* and pulled down the poster.
3 smooth out (a wrinkle, surface, etc.); iron out. (⇨ nobiru¹)
4 let grow (a beard, hair). (⇨ nobiru¹)
5 develop; improve; better:
Kare wa mata kiroku o nobashita. (彼はまた記録を伸ばした) He *bettered* his record once more. (⇨ nobiru¹)

no⌈ba⌉s·u² のばす (延ばす) *vt.* (no-bash·i-; nobas·a-; nobash·i-te Ⓒ) **1** extend; prolong:
taizai kikañ o nobasu (滞在期間を延ばす) *extend* one's length of stay. (⇨ nobiru²)
2 postpone; put off:
shuppatsu o nobasu (出発を延ばす) *postpone* one's departure. (⇨ eñki)

no⌈be- のべ (延べ) *pref.* aggregate; total number:
Nyuujoosha wa nobe-hasseñ-niñ ni tasshita. (入場者は延べ 8,000 人に達した) *The total number* of visitors reached 8,000.

no⌈be⌉·ru のべる (述べる) *vt.* (no-be-te Ⓥ) state (an opinion); express (one's ideas); mention.

no⌈bi⌉·ru¹ のびる (伸びる) *vi.* (nobi-te Ⓥ) **1** (of a plant, hair, etc.) grow. (⇨ nobasu¹)
2 lengthen, extend:

Kare wa saikiñ shiñchoo ga kyuu ni nobita. (彼は最近身長が急に伸びた) He *has* recently *shot up* in height.
3 improve; develop; increase:
Yushutsu wa nobiru keekoo ni arimasu. (輸出は伸びる傾向にあります) Exports show a tendency to *increase*. (⇨ nobasu¹)
4 (*colloq.*) be tired out; pass out.

no⌈bi⌉·ru² のびる (延びる) *vi.* (nobi-te Ⓥ) **1** lengthen; be extended:
Hi ga nobimashita ne. (日が延びましたね) The days *have gotten longer*, haven't they?
2 be postponed; be delayed. (⇨ nobasu²)

no⌈bori のぼり (上り) *n.* **1** ascent. (↔ kudari)
2 up train. ★ '*Nobori*' is a train going in the direction of a major city, especially Tokyo, and '*kudari*' is a train going out of a major city. (↔ kudari)

no⌈bor·u¹ のぼる (上る) *vi.* (nobo-r·i-; nobor·a-; nobot-te Ⓒ)
1 go up; ascend:
kaidañ [saka] o noboru (階段[坂]を上る) *go up* stairs [a slope]. (↔ oriru)
2 amount to; reach:
Sono jiko ni yoru shishoosha wa gojuu-niñ ijoo ni nobotta. (その事故による死傷者は 50 人以上に上った) The dead and injured in the accident *reached* more than fifty.
3 rise:
shachoo no chii ni noboru (社長の地位に上る) *rise* to the position of president.

no⌈bor·u² のぼる (昇る) *vi.* (nobo-r·i-; nobor·a-; nobot-te Ⓒ) go up; rise. (⇨ agaru)

no⌈bor·u³ のぼる (登る) *vi.* (nobo-r·i-; nobor·a-; nobot-te Ⓒ) climb (a mountain).

no⌈chi⌉ のち (後) *n.* later; after. (⇨ ato¹)

no⌈chi-hodo のちほど (後程) *adv.* later (on):

Nochi-hodo *go-reñraku itashimasu.* (後ほどご連絡いたします) I will get in touch with you *later on*.

no de のて because; so; owing to; therefore:
Sakuya wa osoku made shigoto o shita no de, nemui. (昨夜は遅くまで仕事をしたので、眠い) I worked late last night and I am *therefore* sleepy. (⇒ kara⁴)

no¹do のど (喉) *n.* throat:
Nodo ga kawaita. (のどが渇いた) I *am* thirsty.

no¹doka のどか (長閑) *a.n.* (~ na, ni) calm; peaceful:
nodoka na haru no hi (のどかな春の日) a *calm* spring day.

no¹gare¹-ru のがれる (逃れる) *vi.* (nogare-te Ⅴ) escape; run away; avoid. (⇒ nigeru; nogasu)

no¹ga¹s-u のがす (逃す) *vt.* (nogash-i-; nogas-a-; nogash-i-te Ⓒ) miss (a chance, an opportunity, etc.); lose; let slip. (⇒ nigasu; nogareru)

no¹hara のはら (野原) *n.* field; plain. (⇒ hara²; harappa; no⁴)

no¹iro¹oze ノイローゼ *n.* neurosis; nervous breakdown.

no¹ki のき (軒) *n.* eaves.

no¹kku ノック *n.* 1 knock.
2 (of baseball) hitting grounders and flies for practice.
nokku suru (~する) *vt.* rap on a door; knock.

no¹kogiri¹ のこぎり (鋸) *n.* saw.

no¹ko¹razu のこらず (残らず) *adv.* all; entirely; without exception. (⇒ subete; zeñbu)

no¹kori¹ のこり (残り) *n.* the remainder; the rest; leftovers.

no¹ko¹r-u のこる (残る) *vi.* (nokor-i-; nokor-a-; nokot-te Ⓒ) remain; be left:
Watashi wa shibaraku sono ba ni nokotta. (私はしばらくその場に残った) I *remained* there for a short while. (⇒ inokoru; nokosu)

no¹ko¹s-u のこす (残す) *vt.* (nokosh-i-; nokos-a-; nokosh-i-te Ⓒ) leave (behind); set aside; reserve. (⇒ amasu; nokoru)

no¹mi¹ のみ (鑿) *n.* chisel.

no¹mi² のみ *p.* (formal) only; alone: ★ Used after a noun or verb to express a limit.
Watashi wa jibuñ ga shitte iru koto nomi hanashita. (私は自分が知っていることのみ話した) I told *only* what I knew. (⇒ bakari; dake; shika³)

... nomi narazu ... mo (...~ならず...も) not only...but also: *Kono hoñ wa kodomo nomi narazu otona ni mo omoshiroi.* (この本は子どものみならず大人にもおもしろい) This book is interesting, *not only* for children, *but also* for adults.

no¹mikom-u のみこむ (飲み込む) *vt.* (-kom-i-; -kom-a-; -koñ-de Ⓒ)
1 swallow; gulp; choke down.
2 understand; learn; grasp:
Kanojo wa watashi no setsumee o sugu nomikoñda. (彼女は私の説明をすぐ飲み込んだ) She *grasped* my explanation right away.

no¹mi¹mizu のみみず (飲み水) *n.* drinking water.

no¹mi¹mono のみもの (飲み物) *n.* drink; beverage.

no¹m-u のむ (飲む) *vt.* (nom-i-; nom-a-; noñ-de Ⓒ) 1 drink (coffee, milk, etc.); take alcohol; take (medicine).
2 accept (a demand, request, etc.); agree.

no¹ñbi¹ri のんびり *adv.* (~ to; ~ suru) leisurely; quietly; peacefully.

no ni のに although; but; in spite of:
Isshoo-keñmee hataraite iru no ni seekatsu wa raku ni naranai. (一生懸命働いているのに生活は楽にならない) *In spite of* my working hard, life has not become any easier. (⇒ ga²; kakawarazu; keredo (mo))

no¹ñki のんき (呑気) *a.n.* (~ na, ni) easygoing; happy-go-lucky; carefree; optimistic.

no̱¹o¹ のう(脳) n. brain; brains.

no̱¹o² のう(能) n. Noh play.

no̱¹ochi のうち(農地) n. farm-land; agricultural land.

no̱¹oeñ のうえん(農園) n. farm; plantation. (⇨ noojoo)

no̱¹ogyoo のうぎょう(農業) n. agriculture; farming.

no̱¹oi¹kketsu のういっけつ(脳溢血) n. cerebral hemorrhage.

no̱¹ojoo のうじょう(農場) n. farm; ranch.

no̱¹oka のうか(農家) n. farm-house; farmer.

no̱¹oke¹sseñ のうけっせん(脳血栓) n. cerebral thrombosis.

no̱¹oko¹osoku のうこうそく(脳梗塞) n. cerebral infarction.

no̱¹omiñ のうみん(農民) n. landed farmer; peasant.

no̱¹oritsu のうりつ(能率) n. effi-ciency:
shigoto no nooritsu o ageru (仕事の能率を上げる) improve the *effi-ciency* of the work.

no̱¹oritsu-teki のうりつてき(能率的) a.n. (~ na, ni) efficient.

no̱¹oryoku のうりょく(能力) n. ability; capacity; faculty.

no̱¹oshi のうし(脳死) n. brain death.

no̱¹osoñ のうそん(農村) n. farm village; farming district.

no̱¹oto ノート n. notebook. (⇨ choomeñ)
nooto suru (~ する) vt. write down; take notes.

no̱¹oyaku のうやく(農薬) n. arti-ficially synthesized fertilizers and pesticides.

no̱¹rainu のらいぬ(野良犬) n. homeless dog; stray dog.

no̱¹reñ のれん(暖簾) n. short split curtain. ★ Hung outside the entrance of a Japanese-style shop, restaurant, bar, etc.

no̱¹ri¹ のり(糊) n. glue; paste; starch. (⇨ norizuke)

no̱¹ri¹² のり(海苔) n. laver; sea-weed. (⇨ norimaki)

no̱¹riage¹·ru のりあげる(乗り上げる) vi. (-age-te Ⅴ) run onto; run aground.

no̱¹riba のりば(乗り場) n. stop; stand; platform:
Chikatetsu no noriba wa doko desu ka? (地下鉄の乗り場はどこですか) *Where* can I take the subway?

no̱¹rida¹s·u のりだす(乗り出す) vi. (-dash·i·; -das·a·; -dash·i·te Ⓒ)
1 sail out:
araumi ni noridasu (荒海に乗り出す) *sail out* on the rough sea.
2 set about; embark; start (an enterprise):
atarashii jigyoo ni noridasu (新しい事業に乗り出す) *embark* on a new business.
3 lean forward:
mado kara noridasu (窓から乗り出す) *lean* out of a window.

no̱¹riire のりいれ(乗り入れ) n.
1 driving (a car) into:
Kuruma no noriire kiñshi. (*sign*) (車の乗り入れ禁止) No *Entry* for Motor Vehicles. (⇨ noriireru)
2 the extension of (a railroad line) into (another line). (⇨ noriireru)

no̱¹riire¹·ru のりいれる(乗り入れる) vi. (-ire-te Ⅴ) **1** drive [ride] into (a place). (⇨ noriire)
2 extend into:
Raineñ wa chikatetsu ga kono eki made noriiremasu. (来年は地下鉄がこの駅まで乗り入れます) The subway will *be extended* to this station next year. (⇨ noriire)

no̱¹rikae のりかえ(乗り換え) n. change; transfer. (⇨ norikaeru)

no̱¹rikae¹·ru のりかえる(乗り換える) vi. (-kae-te Ⅴ) change; transfer:
Ueno de Giñza-señ ni norikaeru (上野で銀座線に乗り換える) *change* at Ueno for the Ginza Line. (⇨ norikae)

no̱¹rikoe¹·ru のりこえる(乗り越える) vi. (-koe-te Ⅴ) get over; climb over; overcome.

no̱¹riko¹m·u のりこむ(乗り込む) vi.

(-kom·i-; -kom·a-; -koñ-de Ⓒ)
1 get on [in] (a vehicle); board:
takushii ni norikomu (タクシーに乗り
込む) *get in* a taxi.
2 march [ride] into (a place).

no'rikoshi のりこし (乗り越し) *n.*
riding beyond one's station.
(⇨ norikosu)

no'riko'su のりこす (乗り越す) *vt.*
(-kosh·i-; -kos·a-; -kosh·i-te Ⓒ)
ride past one's station.
(⇨ norikoshi)

no'ri'maki のりまき (海苔巻き) *n.*
vinegared rice rolled in dried
laver. (⇨ nori²)

no'rimono のりもの (乗り物) *n.*
vehicle; (a means of) transport.

no'riokure'·ru のりおくれる (乗り
遅れる) *vi.* (-okure-te Ⓥ) fail to
catch (a train, bus, etc.); miss.

no'ri'ori のりおり (乗り降り) *n.* getting on and off trains.
noriori suru (〜する) *vi.* get on
and off.

no'risokona'·u のりそこなう (乗り
損なう) *vt.* (-sokona·i-; -soko-
naw·a-; -sokonat-te Ⓒ) fail to
catch (a train, bus, etc.); miss.

no'rizuke のりづけ (糊付け) *n.*
pasting; gluing. (⇨ nori¹)

no'ro'·i のろい (鈍い) *a.* (-ku)
(*colloq.*) (of motion, work, etc.)
slow; dull.

no'ronoro のろのろ *adv.* (〜 to;
〜 suru) slowly; sluggishly.

no'r·u¹ のる (乗る) *vi.* (nor·i-;
nor·a-; not-te Ⓒ) **1** take (a bus,
train, etc.); ride (a horse);
get on. (↔ oriru) (⇨ noseru¹)
2 step on; get on:
*Kanojo wa isu ni notte, sono hoñ
o totta.* (彼女はいすに乗って、その本を
取った) She *got on* a chair and got
the book.
3 give advice; take an interest:
Kare wa watashi no soodañ ni
notte kureta. (彼は私の相談に乗って
くれた) He was kind enough to
give me *advice*.

no'r·u² のる (載る) *vi.* (nor·i-; no-

r·a-; not-te Ⓒ) **1** lie on; rest:
*Shiryoo wa anata no tsukue no ue
ni notte imasu.* (資料はあなたの机の
上にのっています) The data *are on*
your desk.
2 (of an article, advertisement,
etc.) appear (in a magazine, newspaper, etc.); (of a name, etc.) be
listed. (⇨ noseru²)

no'se·ru¹ のせる (乗せる) *vt.* (nosete Ⓥ) give a ride; load; pick up.
(↔ orosu¹) (⇨ noru¹)

no'se·ru² のせる (載せる) *vt.* (nosete Ⓥ) **1** put on; load:
*Watashi wa sono tsutsumi o tana
no ue ni noseta.* (私はその包みを棚の
上に載せた) I *put* the parcel on the
shelf.
2 publish:
Kono kiji wa san-gatsu-goo ni
nosemasu. (この記事は 3 月号に載せ
ます) We are going to *publish* this
article in the March issue.
(⇨ noru²)

no'shi¹ のし (熨斗) *n.* decoration
for gifts. ★ Thin strip of dried
abalone wrapped in red and
white paper. These days the abalone is usually omitted.

no'zok·u¹ のぞく (除く) *vt.* (nozok-
k·i-; nozok·a-; nozo·i-te Ⓒ)
remove; exclude; get rid of.
(⇨ torinozoku)

no'zok·u² のぞく (覗く) *vt.* (nozo-
k·i-; nozok·a-; nozo·i-te Ⓒ)
peep; look in.

no'zomashi¹·i のぞましい (望ましい)
a. (-ku) desirable; preferable.
(⇨ konomashii)

no'zomi のぞみ (望み) *n.* **1** wish;
desire; hope. (⇨ nozomu¹)
2 chance; prospect; likelihood:
*Shoori no nozomi wa mada juu-
buñ ni arimasu.* (勝利の望みはまだ十
分にあります) We still have a good
chance of victory.

no'zom·u¹ のぞむ (望む) *vt.* (nozo-
m·i-; nozom·a-; nozoñ-de Ⓒ)
1 want; wish; hope for.
(↔ nozomi)

2 like; prefer:
Inaka no seekatsu o nozomu hito ga ooi.(田舎の生活を望む人が多い) There are many people who *prefer* life in the country. (⇨ nozomi)

no˹zom·u² のぞむ (臨む) *vi.* (nozom·i-; nozom·a-; nozoń-de C)
1 face (a place); overlook.
2 attend (a ceremony).
3 face (danger, crisis, etc.).

nu˹g·u ぬぐ (脱ぐ) *vt.* (nug·i-; nu-g·a-; nu·i-de C) take off; get undressed. (↔ haku¹; kiru²)

nu˹karumi ぬかるみ (泥濘) *n.* mud; muddy place.

nu˹keda˺s·u ぬけだす (抜け出す) *vi.* (-dash·i-; -das·a-; -dash·i-te C) get away; slip away; get out of: *heya kara nukedasu* (部屋から抜け出す) *slip* out of a room.

nu˹ke·ru ぬける (抜ける) *vi.* (nuke-te V) **1** come out; fall (out): *Kugi ga nakanaka nukenai.*(くぎがなかなか抜けない) The nail *won't come out* easily. (⇨ nuku)
2 come off; go off; wear off: *Baketsu no soko ga nukete shimatta.*(バケツの底が抜けてしまった) The bottom of the bucket *came out.* (⇨ nuku)
3 be missing; be left out: *Kono geñkoo wa sañ-mai nukete imasu.*(この原稿は3枚抜けています) This manuscript *is missing* three pages. (⇨ nuku)
4 go through: *Deñsha wa toñneru o nuketa.*(電車はトンネルを抜けた) The train *went* through the tunnel.
5 leave (a group, organization, etc.); quit. (⇨ dattai; nuku)

nu˹kito˹r·u ぬきとる (抜き取る) *vt.* (-tor·i-; -tor·a-; -tot-te C) pull out; extract; take out. (⇨ nuku)

nu˹k·u ぬく (抜く) *vi., vt.* (nuk·i-; nuk·a-; nu·i-te C) **1** pull out; extract: *biiru no señ o nuku* (ビールの栓を抜く) *open* the bottle of beer.

(⇨ hikinuku; nukeru)
2 take out; remove (a stain). (⇨ nukeru)
3 beat; outrun; outstrip: *mae o hashitte iru kuruma o nuku* (前を走っている車を抜く) *overtake* the car traveling in front.

nu˹ma˺ ぬま (沼) *n.* swamp; marsh. (⇨ ike)

nu˹no ぬの (布) *n.* cloth. (⇨ kire)

nu˹ras·u ぬらす (濡らす) *vt.* (nurash·i-; nuras·a-; nurash·i-te C) wet; moisten; dampen. (⇨ nureru)

nu˹re·ru ぬれる (濡れる) *vi.* (nure-te V) get wet; be moistened. (⇨ nurasu)

nu˹r·u ぬる (塗る) *vt.* (nur·i-; nur·a-; nut-te C) paint; spread; plaster; apply.

nu˹ru˺·i ぬるい (温い) *a.* (-ku) lukewarm; tepid. (⇨ atsui¹)

nu˹shi ぬし (主) *n.* the person: *Ano hito ga uwasa no nushi desu.* (あの人がうわさの主です) He is *the person* we have been talking about. (⇨ hoññiñ)

nu˹sumi˺ ぬすみ (盗み) *n.* theft; pilferage; stealing: *nusumi o hataraku* (盗みを働く) commit *theft.* (⇨ nusumu)

nu˹su˺m·u ぬすむ (盗む) *vt.* (nusum·i-; nusum·a-; nusuñ-de C) steal; rob; pilfer. (⇨ nusumi; toru¹)

nu˺·u ぬう (縫う) *vt.* (nu·i-; nu-w·a-; nut-te C) sew; stitch:

nyo˹o にょう (尿) *n.* urine.

nyu˹u- にゅう (入) *pref.* entry; entrance: *nyuu-koku* (入国) *entry* into a country / *nyuu-koo* (入港) *arrival* of a ship in port.

nyu˹ugaku にゅうがく (入学) *n.* entrance into a school; admission to a school.
nyuugaku suru (〜する) *vi.* start to go to school; be admitted to a school. (↔ sotsugyoo)

nyu˹uga ́ñ にゅうがん (乳癌) *n.*

breast cancer. ((⇨ gañ))

nyu⌐uiñ にゅういん (入院) *n.* admission to a hospital; hospitalization.
nyuuiñ suru (〜する) *vi.* be hospitalized; enter the hospital.
((↔ taiiñ)) ((⇨ byooiñ))

nyu⌐ujoo にゅうじょう (入場) *n.* entrance; admission:
Kodomo wa nyuujoo *o-kotowari.*
(*sign*) (子どもは入場お断わり) No *Admission* to Children.
nyuujoo suru (〜する) *vi.* enter; be admitted. ((↔ taijoo)) ((⇨ hairu))

nyu⌐ujo⌐okeñ にゅうじょうけん (入場券) *n.* admission ticket.

nyu⌐ukoku にゅうこく (入国) *n.* entry into a country:
nyuukoku-*tetsuzuki* (入国手続き) *immigration* formalities.

nyuukoku suru (〜する) *vi.* enter a country. ((↔ shukkoku))

nyu⌐usha にゅうしゃ (入社) *n.* joining a company.
nyuusha suru (〜する) *vi.* join a company. ((↔ taisha))

nyu⌐ushoo にゅうしょう (入賞) *n.* winning a prize.
nyuushoo suru (〜する) *vi.* win a prize.

nyu⌐usu ニュース *n.* news:
Nani ka ii nyuusu *wa arimasu ka?*
(何かいいニュースはありますか) Do you have any good *news?*

nyu⌐uyoku にゅうよく (入浴) *n.* bath; bathing ((⇨ furo))
nyuuyoku suru (〜する) *vi.* take a bath.

O

o¹ お (尾) *n.* **1** tail. ((⇨ shippo))
2 (of a comet) trail.

o² を *p.* [follows a noun]
1 (indicates the direct object):
Maiasa shiñbuñ o *yomimasu.* (毎朝新聞を読みます) I read the *newspaper* every morning.
2 (indicates location or movement):
Tsugi no kado o *hidari e magari nasai.* (次の角を左へ曲がりなさい) Turn left *at* the next corner.
3 (indicates movement away from a place, institution, etc.):
Kyoneñ koko no daigaku o *demashita.* (去年ここの大学を出ました) I graduated *from* a university here last year.

o- お *pref.* [added to a noun, verb or adjective to indicate respect, humility or politeness]
1 (respect toward the listener):
O-tegami *arigatoo gozaimashita.* (お手紙ありがとうございました) Thank you for *your letter.* ★ Verbs are used in the following pattern: '*o-*

+*v.* (continuative base)+*ni naru.*'
((⇨ naru¹))
2 (humility on the part of the speaker):
Ato de o-deñwa *itashimasu.* (あとでお電話いたします) I'll give you a *call* later. ★ Verbs are used in the following pattern: '*o-+v.* (continutative base)+*suru* [*itasu*].'
((⇨ suru¹))
3 (politeness):
o-kashi (お菓子) *sweets* / o-kane (お金) *money* / o-kome (お米) *rice.*

o⌐ba おば (伯母・叔母) *n.* one's aunt. ★ Older sisters of one's father or mother are '伯母,' and younger sisters are '叔母.' ((⇨ obasañ))

o-⌐ba⌐asañ おばあさん (お祖母さん・お婆さん) *n.* ★ '祖母' is used for 1, while '婆' is used for 2.
1 one's grandmother. ((⇨ sobo))
2 old woman. ((⇨ baasañ))

o⌐basañ おばさん (伯母さん・叔母さん・小母さん) *n.* ★ '伯母, 叔母' are used for 1, while '小母' is used for 2. ((⇨ oba))

1 one's aunt.

2 middle-aged woman.

o**bi** おび (帯) *n.* obi; belt for a kimono; broad sash.

o**biyaka·s·u** おびやかす (脅かす) *vt.* (-kash·i·-; -kas·a·-; -kash·i·te C) threaten; menace; frighten.

o**bo·e** おぼえ (覚え) *n.* memory; remembrance; recollection: *Kanojo ni wa mae ni doko-ka de atta oboe ga aru.* (彼女には前にどこかで会った覚えがある) I *remember* seeing her somewhere before. (⇨ kioku)

o**boe·ru** おぼえる (覚える) *vt.* (oboe-te V) 1 remember; memorize. (⇨ omoidasu)
2 learn:
Suiee wa doko de oboemashita ka? (水泳はどこで覚えましたか) Where *did* you *learn* swimming?

o**bore·ru** おぼれる (溺れる) *vi.* (o-bore-te V) 1 (almost) drown; be (almost) drowned.
2 indulge in (excessibly):
sake ni oboreru (酒におぼれる) *abandon oneself* to drink.

o**busa·r·u** おぶさる (負ぶさる) *vi.* (obusar·i·-; obusar·a·-; obusat-te C) ride on a person's back; rely on. (⇨ onbu)

o-**cha** おちゃ (お茶) *n.* 1 tea; green tea:
O-cha o nomimaseñ ka? (お茶を飲みませんか) How about a cup of *tea*? ★ This expression often implies "Let's have a chat." (⇨ cha)
2 tea break:
O-cha ni shimashoo. (お茶にしましょう) Let's have a *tea break*.
3 tea ceremony:
o-cha o narau (お茶を習う) learn the *tea ceremony*.

o**chiba** おちば (落ち葉) *n.* fallen leaves.

o**chi·ru** おちる (落ちる) *vi.* (ochi-te V) 1 come [go] down; fall; drop. (⇨ otosu)
2 fall [drop] off:
Koñgetsu wa uriage ga ochita. (今

月は売上が落ちた) This month's sales *have fallen off*. (↔ agaru)
3 fail an examination. (⇨ otosu)
4 (of stains) come out [off]. (⇨ otosu)
5 (of a name, item, etc.) be missing. (⇨ otosu)

o**chitsuk·u** おちつく (落ち着く) *vi.* (-tsuk·i·-; -tsuk·a·-; -tsu·i·te C) 1 calm down; cool down.
2 (of trouble, a quarrel, etc.) subside; die down.
3 settle down (in an apartment).

o-**chuugeñ** おちゅうげん (お中元) *n.* = chuugeñ.

o-**dai** おだい (お代) *n.* price; rate; charge; fare. (⇨ -dai)

o-**daiji ni** おだいじに (お大事に) take care of yourself. ★ An idiomatic expression of sympathy to a sick person.

o**date·ru** おだてる (煽てる) *vt.* (odate-te V) flatter; incite.

o**da·yaka** おだやか (穏やか) *a.n.* (~ na, ni) 1 calm; quiet; peaceful. (⇨ shizuka)
2 (of personality, atmosphere, etc.) mild; gentle; amicable.

o**de·ki** おでき *n.* = dekimono.

o**de·ñ** おでん *n.* Japanese hotchpotch.

o**dokas·u** おどかす (脅かす) *vt.* (odokash·i·-; odokas·a·-; odokash·i·te C) threaten; frighten; startle. (⇨ odosu)

o**do-odo** おどおど *adv.* (~ to) timidly; shyly.
odo-odo suru (~する) *vi.* be timid. (⇨ bikubiku suru)

o**dori** おどり (踊り) *n.* dance; dancing. (⇨ butoo; odoru)

o**doriba** おどりば (踊り場) *n.* landing (of stairs).

o**doroka·s·u** おどろかす (驚かす) *vt.* (-kash·i·-; -kas·a·-; -kash·i·te C) surprise; astonish; startle. (⇨ odoroku)

o**doroki** おどろき (驚き) *n.* surprise; astonishment; shock. (⇨ odoroku) o⌐**doro**⌐**k·u** おどろく (驚く) *vi.* (o-dorok·i-; odorok·a-; odoro·i-te C) 1 be surprised; be astonished; be shocked. ((⇨ odorokasu))

2 wonder; marvel:
Sono sakuhiñ no amari no dekibae ni odorokimashita. (その作品のあまりのできばえに驚きました) I *marveled* at that wonderful work. ((⇨ odoroki))

o⌐**dor·u** おどる (踊る) *vi.* (odor·i-; odor·a-; odot-te C) dance:
warutsu o odoru (ワルツを踊る) *dance* a waltz. ((⇨ odori))

o⌐**doshi** おどし (脅し) *n.* threat; menace; bluff. ((⇨ odosu))

o⌐**dos·u** おどす (脅す) *vt.* (odosh·i-; odos·a-; odosh·i-te C) threaten; menace. ((⇨ odoshi))

o⌐**e·ru** おえる (終える) *vt.* (oe-te V) finish; end; complete. ((⇨ owaru))

o⌐**ga**⌐**m·u** おがむ (拝む) *vt.* (ogam·i-; ogam·a-; ogañ-de C) pray; worship:
hotoke-sama o ogamu (仏様を拝む) *worship* the Buddha.

o⌐**gawa** おがわ (小川) *n.* brook; small stream.

o⌐**gina**⌐**·u** おぎなう (補う) *vt.* (ogina·i-; oginaw·a-; oginat-te C) make up for; compensate; fill:
akaji o oginau (赤字を補う) *make up* the deficit.

o⌐**gor·u**¹ おごる (奢る) *vt.* (ogor·i-; ogor·a-; ogot-te C) treat:
Kyoo no o-hiru wa watashi ga ogorimasu. (きょうのお昼は私がおごります) I'll *treat* you to lunch today.

o⌐**gor·u**² おごる (驕る) *vi.* (ogor·i-; ogor·a-; ogot-te C) be proud; be haughty:
Saikiñ yuumee ni natte, kare wa sukoshi ogotte iru. (最近有名になって, 彼は少しおごっている) Recently he has become famous and *is* a little *proud and arrogant*.

o⌐**go**⌐**soka** おごそか (厳か) *a.n.* (~ na, ni) solemn; grave; dignified.

o⌐**ha**⌐**gi** おはぎ (お萩) *n.* glutinous rice ball coated with sweet red-bean paste or soybean powder.

o-⌐**hana** おはな (お花) *n.* flower arrangement; ikebana. ((⇨ hana; ikebana))

o⌐**hayoo** おはよう (お早よう) good morning. ★ Expression used when people first see each other in the early morning. 'Ohayoo.' is used between close friends or when addressing a person lower in status. The more polite expression is 'Ohayoo gozaimasu.'

o-⌐**hi**⌐**ru** おひる (お昼) *n.* noon; lunch:
O-hiru wa doko de tabemashita ka? (お昼はどこで食べましたか) Where did you have *lunch*? ((⇨ shoogo))

o⌐**i**¹ おい (甥) *n.* nephew. ★ When another family's nephew is referred to, 'oigo-sañ' is used. ((↔ mee))

o⌐**i**² おい *int.* (*rude*) hey; hi; say; hello; look: ★ Used by men.
Oi. *Doko e iku ñ da.* (おい。どこへ行くんだ) *Hey!* Where are you going?

o⌐**ida**⌐**s·u** おいだす (追い出す) *vi.* (-dash·i-; -das·a-; -dash·i-te C) drive out; expel; oust.

o⌐**ide** おいで (お出で) *n.* ★ Both 'oide desu' and 'oide ni naru' are honorific equivalents of 'iru,' 'kuru' and 'iku.'

1 presence:
O-kaasañ wa oide *desu ka?* (お母さんはおいでですか) *Is* your mother *in*? ((⇨ iru))

2 coming:
Doozo oide *kudasai.* (どうぞおいでください) Please *come and visit* us. ((⇨ kuru))

3 going:
Dochira e oide *desu ka?* (どちらへおいでですか) Where *are* you *going*? ((⇨ iku))

4 be present; go; come: ★ Shortened form of 'oide nasai,' which implies an order or request.
Koko ni shibaraku oide. (ここにしばら

くおいで） *Stay* here for a while.

o「hara.u おいはらう (追い払う)
vt. (-hara.i.; -haraw.a.-; -harat-te
C) (*informal*=opparau) drive [turn]
away; disperse.

o「ikake」.ru おいかける (追い掛ける)
vt. (-kake-te V) run after; chase;
pursue.

o「iko」s.u おいこす (追い越す) vt.
(-kosh.i.; -kos.a.; -kosh.i.te C)
pass; overtake; outstrip. (⇨ oi-
tsuku)

o「inu」k.u おいぬく (追い抜く) vt.
(-nuk.i.; -nuk.a.; -nu.i.te C)
overtake. (⇨ oikosu)

o「ishi.i おいしい (美味しい) a. (-ku)
delicious; tasty; good. (↔ mazui「)
(⇨ umai「)

o「ite おいて (於いて) ★ Used in the
pattern '... *ni oite*.' Compared to '
de,' it is a written form. Before a
noun '... *ni okeru*' or '... *ni oite no*.'
1 in: ★ Indicates location in
place or time.
Shikeñ wa kaigishitsu ni oite *oko-
nawareta.* (試験は会議室において行われ
た) The examination was given *in*
the conference room.
2 as for; in the matter of:
Kono teñ ni oite *watashi wa kare
to ikeñ ga kuichigatte imasu.* (この
点において私は彼と意見が食い違ってい
ます) *As for* this point, my opinion
differs from his.

o「itsu」k.u おいつく (追い付く) vt.
(-tsuk.i.; -tsuk.a.; -tsu.i.te C)
catch up with; overtake.
(⇨ oikosu)

o「ji おじ (伯父・叔父) n. one's uncle.
★ Older brothers of one's father
or mother are '伯父,' and younger
brothers are '叔父.' (⇨ ojisañ)

o「jigi おじぎ (お辞儀) n. bow:
*Sono ko wa watashi ni teenee ni
ojigi o shita.* (その子は私にていねいにお
じぎをした) The child *bowed* politely
to me.

o-「ji」isañ おじいさん (お祖父さん・お爺
さん) n. ★ '祖父' is used for 1,
while '爺' is used for 2.

1 one's grandfather. (⇨ sofu)
2 old man. (⇨ jiisañ)

o「jisañ おじさん (伯父さん・叔父さん・
小父さん) n. ★ '伯父, 叔父' is used
for 1, while '小父' is used for 2.
1 one's uncle. (⇨ oji)
2 middle-aged man.

o-「jo」osañ おじょうさん (お嬢さん) n.
1 your [his; her] daughter.
2 young lady; girl. (↔ botchañ)

o「ka おか (丘) n. hill; heights.
(⇨ yama)

o-「ka」achañ おかあちゃん (お母ちゃん)
n. mother; mom. ★ Used chiefly
by small children. (↔ o-toochañ)

o-「ka」asañ おかあさん (お母さん) n.
mother; mom. (↔ o-toosañ)
(⇨ haha)

o「kaeri nasa」i おかえりなさい (お帰り
なさい) welcome home; I'm glad
you're home again. ★ Literally
'You've come home.' A set phrase
used in response to '*Tadaima*.'
(I'm home.) (⇨ tadaima[2])

o「kage おかげ (お陰) n. thanks to;
owing to:
Anata ga tetsudatte kureta okage
de, mikka de shigoto ga owarimashita.* (あなたが手伝ってくれたおかげで、3
日で仕事が終わりました) *Thanks to*
your help, I was able to finish the
work in three days. (⇨ see[5])

o「kagesama de おかげさまで (お
陰さまで) ★ An idiomatic expression used in response to a greeting.
*"O-geñki desu ka?" "Okagesama
de."* (「お元気ですか」「おかげさまで」)
"How are you?" "*I'm fine, thank
you.*"

o-「kane おかね (お金) n. = kane[1].

o-「ka」shi おかし (お菓子) n. confectionery; cake; sweets; candy.
(⇨ kashi[1])

o「kashi」.i おかしい (可笑しい) a.
(-ku) 1 amusing; funny; ridiculous. (⇨ okashi-na; omoshiroi)
2 strange; odd:
Kare ga mada konai no wa okashii.
(彼がまだ来ないのはおかしい) His not

arriving yet is *strange*.

3 queer; unusual:

I no guai ga chotto okashii. (胃の具合がちょっとおかしい) My stomach feels a bit *queer*.

o｢ka¹shi-na おかしな (可笑しな) *attrib.* **1** amusing; funny; ridiculous. (⇨ okashii)

2 strange; queer; odd. (⇨ okashii)

o｢ka¹s·u¹ おかす (犯す) *vt.* (okash·i-; okas·a-; okash·i-te Ⓒ) commit (a crime); violate (a law); break.

o｢ka¹s·u² おかす (侵す) *vt.* (okash·i-; okas·a-; okash·i-te Ⓒ) invade; infringe; violate:

hoka no hito no puraibashii o okasu (ほかの人のプライバシーを侵す) *invade* another person's privacy.

o｢kazu おかず (お数) *n.* side dish.

o｢ke おけ (桶) *n.* tub; pail; wooden bucket.

o｢ke¹ru おける (於ける) at; in: ★ Used in the pattern '… *ni okeru.*'

Igaku ni okeru shinpo wa subarashii. (医学における進歩はすばらしい) The progress *in* medical science is remarkable. (⇨ oite)

o｢ki おき (沖) *n.* offing; open sea.

-o｢ki おき (置き) *suf.* every; at intervals of:

ichi-meetoru-oki ni kui o utsu (1 メートルおきにくいを打つ) drive in the stakes *at intervals of* one meter.

o｢kiba おきば (置き場) *n.* place (for leaving something); space; room.

o｢kido¹kee おきどけい (置き時計) *n.* table [desk; mantel] clock. (⇨ tokee)

o｢kimono おきもの (置物) *n.* ornament. ★ China, carving, figurines, etc., that are displayed in one's home.

o｢ki¹·ru おきる (起きる) *vi.* (oki-te Ⓥ) **1** get up; rise. (⇨ okosu)

2 wake up; stay awake. (⇨ okosu)

3 happen; occur. (⇨ okosu)

o｢kiwasure¹·ru おきわすれる (置き忘れる) *vt.* (-wasure-te Ⓥ) leave;

forget; put down and forget:

deñsha ni kasa o okiwasureru (電車に傘を置き忘れる) *leave* one's umbrella in a train. (⇨ wasureru; wasuremono)

o｢kona·u おこなう (行う) *vt.* (okona·i-; okonaw·a-; okonat-te Ⓒ) hold; give; practice:

shikeñ o okonau (試験を行なう) *give* an examination.

o｢kori¹ おこり (起こり) *n.* **1** cause:

Koto no okori wa nañ desu ka? (事の起こりは何ですか) What is the *cause* of this?

2 origin; source:

buñmee no okori (文明の起こり) the *origin* of civilization.

o｢ko¹r·u¹ おこる (起こる) *vi.* (okor·i-; okor·a-; okot-te Ⓒ) **1** happen; occur; take place.

2 be caused; stem from:

Sono jiko wa fuchuui kara okotta. (その事故は不注意から起こった) The accident *stemmed* from carelessness. (⇨ okiru; okosu)

o｢ko¹r·u² おこる (怒る) (okor·i-; okor·a-; okot-te Ⓒ) **1** *vi.* get angry; lose one's temper.

2 *vt.* scold. (⇨ shikaru)

o｢ko¹r·u³ おこる (興る) *vi.* (okor·i-; okor·a-; okot-te Ⓒ) spring up; come into existence.

o-｢kosañ おこさん (お子さん) *n.* (*polite*) someone else's child.

o｢ko¹s·u おこす (起こす) *vt.* (okosh·i-; okos·a-; okosh·i-te Ⓒ) **1** wake up; awake:

Asu no asa roku-ji ni okoshite kudasai. (あすの朝6時に起こしてください) Please *wake* me *up* at six tomorrow morning. (⇨ okiru)

2 raise; set up:

Kare wa taoreta saku o okoshita. (彼は倒れたさくを起こした) He *raised* the fallen fence.

3 cause (an accident, trouble); bring about:

jiko [moñdai] o okosu (事故[問題]を起こす) *cause* an accident [trouble]. (⇨ okiru)

4 start (a movement):
shoohisha-uñdoo o okosu (消費者運動を起こす) *start* a consumer movement. (⇨ okiru)

5 produce:
deñki o okosu (電気を起こす) *produce* electricity. (⇨ okiru)

o-'kotowari おことわり (お断り) *n.*
refusal; rejection; prohibition:
★ Used as a warning.
Meñkai wa o-kotowari desu. (面会はお断りです) We *cannot accept* visitors. (⇨ kotowaru)

o'ku-u¹ おく (置く) *vt.* (ok·i-; ok·a-; o·i-te C) **1** put; keep; place:
Kasa wa doko ni oitara yoi deshoo ka? (傘はどこに置いたらよいでしょうか) Where should I *put* my umbrella?

2 leave:
Kagi o doko e oita ka wasurete shimatta. (鍵をどこへ置いたか忘れてしまった) I have forgotten where I *left* the keys.

3 have for sale; deal in:
Kono mise wa iroiro na buñboogu o oite imasu. (この店はいろいろな文房具を置いています) At this shop they *handle* a variety of stationery goods.

4 take in; have:
Kare wa shiyooniñ o oite imasu. (彼は使用人を置いています) He *has* a servant.

-te[-de] oku (て[で]〜) leave a thing as it is; do something in advance: *Tomodachi ga sugu kuru kara doa o akete oite kudasai.* (友だちがすぐ来るからドアを開けておいてください) A friend is coming soon, so please *leave* the door *open*.

o'ku² おく (奥) *n.* inner part; interior; back.

o'ku³ おく (億) *n.* one hundred million. (⇨ APP. 3)

o'kubyo'o おくびょう (臆病) *a.n.* (〜 na, ni) cowardly; timid.

o'kujoo おくじょう (屋上) *n.* roof; rooftop. (↔ chika)

o'kurase·ru おくらせる (遅らせる) *vt.* (okurase-te V) delay; put off;

turn back. (⇨ okureru)

o'kure おくれ (遅れ) *n.* delay:
Kootsuu juutai ga okure no geñiñ datta. (交通渋滞が遅れの原因だった) The traffic jam was the cause of the *delay*. (⇨ okureru)

o'kure·ru おくれる (遅れる) *vi.* (okure-te V) **1** be late; be behind time:
Yakusoku no jikañ ni okurete shimatta. (約束の時間に遅れてしまった) I *was later* than the time agreed on. (⇨ chikoku; okure)

2 (of a clock, watch) be slow; lose. (↔ susumu)

3 fall behind; behind.

o'kurigana おくりがな (送り仮名) *n.* (inflectional) 'kana' ending.
★ The 'kana' added to a Chinese character to help show its Japanese grammatical ending.

o'kurimono おくりもの (贈り物) *n.* present; gift. (⇨ miyage; pureze-ñto)

o'kur·u¹ おくる (送る) *vt.* (okur·i-; okur·a-; okut-te C) **1** send:
Kare ni kookuubiñ de hoñ o okutta. (彼に航空便で本を送った) I *sent* him a book by airmail. (⇨ dasu (5))

2 see off; see home; take:
Kanojo o uchi made okutte yari nasai. (彼女を家まで送ってやりなさい) Please *see* her home.

3 pass; spend; lead:
Kare wa megumareta seekatsu o okutte imasu. (彼は恵まれた生活を送っています) He *leads* a privileged life.

o'kur·u² おくる (贈る) *vt.* (okur·i-; okur·a-; okut-te C) give; present:
Kanojo no kekkoñ iwai ni kabiñ o okutta. (彼女の結婚祝いに花瓶を贈った) I *gave* her a vase for a wedding present.

o'kusama おくさま (奥様) *n.* (*polite*) someone else's wife; married woman. (⇨ okusañ)

o'kusañ おくさん (奥さん) *n.* someone else's wife; married woman.
★ Used when addressing some-

one else's wife or referring to her.
A more polite word is '*okusama*.'
The speaker's wife is referred to
as '*kanai*.'

o-「**kyaku-sañ** おきゃくさん (お客さん)
n. 1 (*polite*) caller; visitor; guest.
2 customer; client; audience;
spectator; passenger. (⇨ kyaku)

o「**machidoosama** まちどうさま
(お待ちどうさま) (*informal*) = omatase shimashita.

o「**mae** おまえ (お前) *n*. (*rude*) you:
★ Used by men in addressing
inferiors, particularly children.
The plural forms are '*omae-tachi*'
and (*derog.*) '*omae-ra*.'
Omae *mo kuru ka?* (おまえも来るか)
You coming with me? (⇨ ore)

o「**mairi** おまいり (お参り) *n*. visit to
a temple [shrine]; going to worship at a temple [shrine].
omairi suru (〜する) *vi*. visit [go
to] a temple [shrine]. (⇨ sañpai)

o「**mamori** おまもり (お守り) *n*. good
luck talisman [charm].

o「**matase shima¬shita** おまたせ
しました (お待たせしました) (*humble* = '
omatase itashimashita') I am
sorry to have kept you waiting.

o「**ma¬wari-sañ** おまわりさん (お巡り
さん) *n*. policeman; cop. (⇨ keekañ)

o「**medeta** おめでた (御目出度) *n*.
happy event. ★ Often used with
reference to a forthcoming birth.

o「**medeta·i** おめでたい (御目出度い)
a. (-ku) 1 = medetai.
2 (*derog.*) simple-minded.

o「**medetoo** おめでとう (御目出度う)
congratulations: ★ '*Omedetoo
gozaimasu*' is more polite.
Tañjoobi omedetoo. (誕生日おめでと
う) *Many happy returns of the day.*

o「**medetoo gozaima¬su** おめで
とうございます (御目出度う御座います)
= omedetoo.

o「**me-ni-kaka¬r·u** おめにかかる (お
目に掛かる) *vt*. (-kakar·i·-, -kaka-
r·a-; -kakat-te C) meet; see:
★ Humble equivalent of '*au*.'

Mata ome-ni-kakarete *ureshii desu*.
(またお目にかかれてうれしいです) I'm
glad to *see* you again.

o「**mikuji** おみくじ (御神籤) *n*. sacred lot from a shrine; written ora-
cle. ★ The fortune is written on
a slip of paper.

o-「**miyage** おみやげ *n*. present;
gift; souvenir. (⇨ miyage; okurimono)

o「**mo¬cha** おもちゃ *n*. toy; play-
thing.
omocha ni suru (〜にする) toy
[play] with.

o「**mo·i**[1] おもい (重い) *a*. (-ku)
1 heavy. (↔ karui) (↔ omoo)
2 important; grave:
Watashi wa sono omoi *sekiniñ o
hikiukeru koto ni shita.* (私はその重い
責任を引き受けることにした) I've decid-
ed to assume that *grave* responsibility. (↔ karui)
3 (of crime, disease, etc.) serious.
(↔ karui)

o「**mo¬i**[2] おもい (思い) *n*.
1 thought; idea:
omoi *ni fukeru* (思いにふける) be lost
in *thought*.
2 wish; expectation:
Subete wa omoi-doori *umaku ikimashita.* (すべては思い通りうまくいきまし
た) Everything went off well, *as we
had wished.*
3 attachment; affection:
Kare wa kanojo ni omoi *o yosete
ita.* (彼は彼女に思いを寄せていた) He
had an *attachment* for her.
4 feeling:
Kodomo ni wa kanashii omoi *o
sasetaku nai.* (子どもには悲しい思いをさ
せたくない) I do not want to make
my children *feel sad.*

o「**moichigai** おもいちがい (思い違い)
n. misunderstanding; mistake.

o「**moida¬s·u** おもいだす (思い出す)
vt. (-dash·i·-, -das·a-; -dash·i·te
C) remember; recall; remind:
mukashi *o* omoidasu (昔を思い出す)
think of the good old days.
(⇨ oboeru)

o'**moide** おもいで (思い出) *n.* recollections; memory; reminiscence.

o'**moigakena**̧l·**i** おもいがけない (思いがけない) *a.* (-ku) unexpected: Omoigakenaku, *tomodachi ga tazunete kita.* (思いがけなく、友だちが訪ねて来た) A friend *unexpectedly* visited me.

o'**moikiri**[1] おもいきり (思い切り) *n.* decisiveness; decision: *Kare wa* omoikiri *ga yoi [warui].* (彼は思い切りがよい[悪い]) He *is decisive [indecisive].* (⇨ omoikiru)

o'**moikiri**[2] おもいきり (思い切り) *adv.* thoroughly; to one's heart's content. (⇨ omou-zoñbuñ)

o'**moiki**̧l**r·u** おもいきる (思い切る) *vt.* (-kir·i-; -kir·a-; -kit-te ⓒ) give up; abandon; decide. (⇨ omoikiri[1]; omoikitte)

o'**mo**̧l**ikitte** おもいきって (思い切って) *adv.* decisively; resolutely: *Kanojo wa* omoikitte *señsee ni hoñtoo no koto o hanashita.* (彼女は思い切って先生にほんとうのことを話した) She *dared* to tell the truth to her teacher.
omoikitte ... suru (〜...する) make up one's mind to do.

o'**moiko**̧l**m·u** おもいこむ (思い込む) *vi.* (-kom·i-; -kom·a-; -koñ-de ⓒ)
1 believe; be under the impression. (⇨ shiñjiru)
2 take...for granted: *Miñna kare ga yuushoo suru mono to* omoikoñde *ita.* (みんな彼が優勝するものと思い込んでいた) Everyone *took it for granted* that he would win the championship.

o'**moi-no-hoka** おもいのほか (思いの外) *adv.* unexpectedly; surprisingly. (⇨ añgai)

o'**moitodoma**̧l**r·u** おもいとどまる (思い止まる) *vt.* (-todomar·i-; -todomar·a-; -todomat-te ⓒ) change one's mind; hold oneself back. (⇨ akirameru)

o'**moitsuki** おもいつき (思い付き) *n.* idea; thought: *Sore wa yoi* omoitsuki *desu.* (それは

良い思いつきです) That is a good *idea.* (⇨ omoitsuku)

o'**moitsu**̧l**k·u** おもいつく (思い付く) *vt.* (-tsuk·i-; -tsuk·a-; -tsu·i-te ⓒ) hit on; think of: *umai kañgae o* omoitsuku (うまい考えを思いつく) *hit on* a good idea. (⇨ omoitsuki)

o'**moiyari** おもいやり (思いやり) *n.* consideration; thoughtfulness; sympathy: *Kare wa hoka no hito ni taishite* omoiyari *ga aru.* (彼はほかの人に対して思いやりがある) He *is considerate* to others.

o'**mokurushi**̧l·**i** おもくるしい (重苦しい) *a.* (-ku) heavy; gloomy; oppressive; stifling.

o'**momuki** おもむき (趣) *n.* **1** attractive atmosphere; charm: *Kono niwa wa* omomuki *ga aru.* (この庭は趣がある) This garden has its *charm.*
2 look; appearance: *Kaateñ de heya no* omomuki *ga kawatta.* (カーテンで部屋の趣が変わった) Because of the curtains the *appearance* of the room changed.

o'**mo-na** おもな (主な) *attrib.* chief; principal; main; leading: *Nihoñ no* omo-na *toshi* (日本の主な都市) the *major* cities in Japan.

o'**moni** おもに (重荷) *n.* heavy load; burden: *Ryooshiñ no kitai ga kare no* omoni *datta.* (両親の期待が彼の重荷だった) The expectations of his parents were a *burden* to him.

o'**mo ni** おもに (主に) *adv.* chiefly; mainly; mostly.

o'**moñji**̧l·**ru** おもんじる (重んじる) *vt.* (omoñji-te Ⓥ) respect; make much of; value. (↔ karoñjiru)

o'**mo-omoshi**̧l·**i** おもおもしい (重々しい) *a.* (-ku) (of speech, attitude, etc.) grave; dignified; serious.

o'**mosa** おもさ (重さ) *n.* weight. (⇨ omoi[1]; mekata)

o'**moshiro**̧l·**i** おもしろい (面白い) *a.* (-ku) interesting; amusing;

funny; exciting. (↔ tsumaranai)

o｢**mota·i** おもたい (重たい) *a.* (-ku) heavy. (⇨ omoi¹)

o｢**mote**¹ おもて (表) *n.* **1** front; the right side; surface. (↔ ura)
2 front door:
Omote *kara haitte kudasai.* (表から入ってください) Please come in through the *front door.* (↔ ura)
3 outside; the outdoors:
Omote *ni dare-ka tatte imasu.* (表にだれか立っています) There is someone standing *outside.*
4 (of baseball) the first half.

o｢**motemoñ** おもてもん (表門) *n.* front gate. (⇨ uramoñ)

o｢**mo**¹·**u** おもう (思う) *vt.* (omo·i-; omow·a-; omot-te C)
★ '*Omou*' refers to having thoughts and '*kañgaeru*' implies thinking about, pondering, considering, but there is some overlap in meaning.
1 think; believe:
Sore *wa uso da to* omou. (それはうそだと思う) I *think* that is a lie.
2 consider; regard:
Kare *wa yuushuu na señshu da to* omoimasu. (彼は優秀な選手だと思います) I *consider* him to be an excellent player.
3 expect:
Soko *de kare ni au to wa* omowanakatta. (そこで彼に会うとは思わなかった) I *never expected* I would meet him there.
4 want; wish; hope:
Yoroshikereba, sochira *ni ukagaitai to* omoimasu. (よろしければ、そちらにうかがいたいと思います) Provided it is convenient, I *would like* to pay you a visit. ★ In the pattern '...tai to omou,' '*omou*' is used to soften the force of '*tai*' and as such does not have a very specific meaning.
5 intend; be going to:
Kare *wa isha ni naroo to* omotte iru. (彼は医者になろうと思っている) He *intends* to become a doctor.
6 think of:

Kare *wa itsu-mo byooki no haha no koto o* omotte iru. (彼はいつも病気の母のことを思っている) He always *thinks of* his sick mother. (⇨ kañgaeru)

o｢**mo**¹**u-zoñbuñ** おもうぞんぶん (思う存分) *adv.* (~ ni) to the full; to one's heart's content.

o｢**mowaku** おもわく (思惑) *n.* expectation; calculation:
Watashi *no* omowaku *wa hazureta.* (私の思惑ははずれた) My *calculations* turned out to be wrong.

o｢**mo**¹**wazu** おもわず (思わず) *adv.* involuntarily; unconsciously; instinctively:
Sono shashiñ o mite, omowazu *waratte shimatta.* (その写真を見て、思わず笑ってしまった) I *could not help* laughing when I saw the picture.

o｢**mu**¹**subi** おむすび (お結び) *n.* rice ball. (⇨ onigiri)

o｢**mu**¹**tsu** おむつ *n.* diaper; nappy.

o｢**ñ**¹ おん (恩) *n.* obligation; favor; kindness:
Go-oñ *wa wasuremaseñ.* (ご恩は忘れません) I will never forget your *kindness.*

o｢**ñ**² おん (音) *n.* **1** (phonetics) speech sound.
2 the reading of a Chinese character taken from the original Chinese pronunciation. (⇨ kuñ)

o｢**ñ**- おん (御) *pref.* (used to indicate respect or politeness):
★ More formal than '*o-*,' but limited in use.
Oñ-ree *mooshi agemasu.* (御礼申し上げます) Please accept my *sincere thanks.*

o｢**naji** おなじ (同じ) ★ '*Onaji*' is the form that precedes a noun. It is not followed by '*na*' or '*no.*'
1 same; similar; alike:
Watashi *mo kore to* onaji *jisho o motte imasu.* (私もこれと同じ辞書を持っています) I have the *same* dictionary as this. (⇨ onajiku)
2 equivalent; equal:
Kono *Nihoñgo to mattaku* onaji

Eego wa arimaseñ. (この日本語とまっ
たく同じ英語はありません) There is no
English expression that is exactly
equivalent to this Japanese.
(⇨ dooitsu; dooyoo¹)

o**na**jiku おなじく(同じく) *adv.*
similarly; in like manner:
Kare mo kimi to onajiku *gorufu ga
suki da.* (彼も君と同じくゴルフが好きだ)
He is fond of playing golf *like*
you. (⇨ onaji)

o**naka** おなか(お腹) *n.* bowels;
stomach: ★ More polite than
'*hara.*'
Onaka ga suita. (おなかがすいた) I *am
hungry.*

onaka ga ookii (～が大きい) (*euphemistic*) be pregnant. (⇨ hara¹)

o**ñbiñ** おんびん(音便) *n.* euphonic
change in the pronunciation of a
word. (⇨ APP. 1)

o**ñbu** おんぶ *n.* piggyback; picka-
back. (⇨ obusaru)
oñbu suru (～する) *vt.* 1 carry a
child piggyback.
2 rely on; depend upon.

o**ñchuu** おんちゅう(御中) *n.* (*formal*) Messrs. ★ Used after the
name of a firm or office on an
envelope.

o**ñdañ** おんだん(温暖) *a.n.* (～ na,
ni) (of climate) temperate; mild.

o**ñdo** おんど(温度) *n.* temperature; heat. (⇨ shitsuoñ)

o**ñdokee** おんどけい(温度計) *n.*
thermometer. ★ In Japan, the
temperature is measured in Celsius. (⇨ kañdañkee; sesshi)

o-**ne**esañ おねえさん(お姉さん) *n.*
1 someone else's older sister.
(↔ o-niisañ)
2 (as a term of address) my older
sister. ★ When referring to one's
own older sister, '*ane*' is used.

o-**negai** おねがい(お願い) *n.* favor;
request:
O-negai ga aru ñ desu ga. (お願いが
あるんですが) I have a *favor* to ask of
you.
o-negai suru (～する) *vt.* request;

ask: *Kore kara mo yoroshiku* o-
negai shimasu. (これからもよろしくお願
いします) I*'d appreciate* your support in the future. (⇨ negai)

o**ñgaku** おんがく(音楽) *n.* music;
the musical art.

o**ñgakuka** おんがくか(音楽家) *n.*
musician.

o**ñgaku**kai おんがくかい(音楽会) *n.*
concert.

o**ni**¹ おに(鬼) *n.* 1 demon; fiend;
ogre.
2 (of the game of tag) " it. "

o**ni**giri おにぎり(お握り) *n.* rice
ball. (⇨ omusubi)

o**ni-go**kko おにごっこ(鬼ごっこ) *n.*
the game of tag.

o-**ni**isañ おにいさん(お兄さん) *n.*
1 someone else's older brother.
2 (as a term of address) my older
brother. ★ When referring to
one's own older brother, '*ani*' is
used. (⇨ o-neesañ)

o**ñna** おんな(女) *n.* woman;
female. ★ Often has a derogatory
connotation; '*josee*' is preferable
in many uses. (↔ otoko) (⇨ fujiñ¹;
josee)

o**ñnade** おんなで(女手) *n.* female
breadwinner:
Kanojo wa oñnade *hitotsu de sañ-
niñ no kodomo o sodateta.* (彼女は女
手ひとつで3人の子どもを育てた) She
brought up three children all by
herself.

o**ñna**-no-ko おんなのこ(女の子) *n.*
girl; daughter. (↔ otoko-no-ko)
(⇨ musume)

o**ñnarashi**i おんならしい(女らしい)
a. (-ku) womanly; feminine; lady-
like. (↔ otokorashii) (⇨ josee-
teki)

o**no**-ono おのおの(各々) *n.*
(*slightly formal*) each:
Hito ni wa ono-ono *choosho to tañsho ga arimasu.* (人にはおのおの長所と
短所があります) *Each* person has
merits and shortcomings.
(⇨ kakuji; meemee)

o**ñsee** おんせい(音声) *n.* voice;

vocal sound.

o⌐**ñseñ** おんせん (温泉) *n.* hot spring; spa.

o⌐**ñsetsu** おんせつ (音節) *n.* syllable.

o⌐**ñshiñ-futsuu** おんしんふつう (音信不通) *n.* no news; no correspondence.

o⌐**ñshitsu** おんしつ (温室) *n.* hothouse; greenhouse.

o⌐**ñtai** おんたい (温帯) *n.* temperate zone. ((⇨ kañtai; nettai))

o⌐**o¹** おう (王) *n.* **1** king. ((↔ jo-oo))
2 king; magnate:
hyaku-juu no oo (百獣の王) the *king of beasts* / *sekivu-oo* (石油王) an oil *magnate*.

o⌐**o²** おお *int.* oh; aah; well:
★ Used to express admiration, wonder, sorrow, etc.
Oo, suteki da. (おお、すてきだ) *Oh, how fantastic.* ((⇨ aa²))

oo- おお (大) *pref.* big; many; heavy; special:
oo-doori (大通り) a *main* street / *oo-goe* (大声) a *loud* voice.

-oo *infl. end.* [attached to the stem of a consonant-stem verb] ((⇨ -yoo))
1 intend; want:
Boku wa beñgoshi ni naroo to omotte imasu. (ぼくは弁護士になろうと思っています) I *intend to become* a lawyer.
2 be about to do:
Kare no uchi e ikoo to shitara, kare ga tazunete kita. (彼の家へ行こうとしたら、彼が訪ねてきた) I *was on the point of going* to his house, when he came to see me.
3 let's:
Teñrañ-kai o mi ni ikoo. (展覧会を見に行こう) *Let's go* to see the exhibition.

o⌐**oa**⌐**me** おおあめ (大雨) *n.* heavy rain. ((⇨ kosame))

o⌐**obaa** オーバー *a.n.* (~ na, ni) exaggerated. ((⇨ oogesa))
oobaa suru (~する) *vi.* exceed; go beyond. ((⇨ chooka))

o⌐**obo** おうぼ (応募) *n.* application; entry.
oobo suru (~する) *vi.* apply for; enter for. ((⇨ mooshikomu))

o⌐**odañ¹** おうだん (横断) *n.* crossing; traversing:
oodañ-hodoo (横断歩道) a pedestrian *crossing*.
oodañ suru (~する) *vt.* go across; cross; traverse. ((⇨ wataru))

o⌐**odañ²** おうだん (黄疸) *n.* jaundice.

o⌐**odo**⌐**ori** おおどおり (大通り) *n.* main street; thoroughfare.

o⌐**oeñ** おうえん (応援) *n.* help; support; backing.
ooeñ suru (~する) *vt.* help; support; back up; cheer.

o⌐**oeñ**⌐**dañ** おうえんだん (応援団) *n.* cheering party; rooters.

o⌐**o-e**⌐**ru** オーエル *n.* female office worker. ★ Often written as 'OL,' an abbreviation of 'office lady.'

o⌐**ofuku** おうふく (往復) *n.* coming and going; going and returning. ((↔ katamichi))
oofuku suru (~する) *vi.* go and come back; make a round trip.

o⌐**ofuku-ha**⌐**gaki** おうふくはがき (往復葉書) *n.* reply-paid postcard. ((⇨ hagaki))

o⌐**oga**⌐**kari** おおがかり (大掛かり) *a.n.* (~ na, ni) great; large-scale:
oogakari na kooji (大がかりな工事) *large-scale* construction works. ((⇨ daikibo))

o⌐**ogata** おおがた (大型) *n.* large size:
oogata no taifuu (大型の台風) a *large* typhoon / *oogata no reezooko* (大型の冷蔵庫) a *large* refrigerator. ((⇨ chuugata; kogata))

o⌐**ogesa** おおげさ (大袈裟) *a.n.* (~ na, ni) exaggerated:
Kare no hanashi wa itsu-mo oogesa da. (彼の話はいつも大げさだ) His stories are always *exaggerated*.

o⌐**ogo**⌐**e** おおごえ (大声) *n.* loud voice:
oogoe o dasu (大声を出す) *raise one's voice.* ((↔ kogoe))

oˈoguchi おおぐち (大口) *n.* **1** big [large] mouth:

ooguchi o akete *warau* (大口を開けて笑う) laugh *with one's mouth wide open*. (⇨ kuchi¹)

2 big:

ooguchi *no chuumoñ o morau* (大口の注文をもらう) receive a *big* order.

oˈohaba おおはば (大幅) *a.n.* (~ na, ni) large; big; drastic; substantial:

Jugyoo-ryoo *ga* oohaba *ni agatta*. (授業料が大幅に上がった) Tuition fees have gone up *substantially*.

oˈo·i おおい (多い) *a.* (-ku) many; much; numerous:

Nihoñ *wa jishiñ ga* ooi. (日本は地震が多い) Earthquakes are *common* in Japan. (↔ sukunai)

oˈoi ni おおいに (大いに) *adv.* greatly; very (much):

ooi ni *yorokobu* (大いに喜ぶ) be *highly* pleased.

oˈoiˈsogi おおいそぎ (大急ぎ) *n.* being urgent; being pressed:

ooisogi *de eki e iku* (大急ぎで駅へ行く) *rush* to the station.

oˈoji·ru おうじる (応じる) *vi.* (ooji-te Ⅴ) **1** meet (a demand, order, etc.); accept; satisfy; respond.

2 be appropriate; be suitable (to one's ability); makeshift:

nooryoku *ni* oojita *shoku o sagasu* (能力に応じた職を探す) look for employment that *is appropriate* to one's abilities.

oˈokata¹ おおかた (大方) *adv.* **1** probably; perhaps:

Ookata *soñna koto daroo to omotte imashita*. (おおかたそんなことだろうと思っていました) I thought that was *perhaps* the case.

2 almost; nearly:

Sono atarashii ie wa ookata *deki-agarimashita*. (その新しい家はおおかたでき上がりました) The new house is *almost* finished. (⇨ daitai)

oˈokata² おおかた (大方) *n.* people in general:

Ookata *no yosoo-doori, Seebu ga*

yuushoo *shimashita*. (おおかたの予想通り, 西武が優勝しました) As generally expected, the Seibu Lions won the pennant.

oˈokeˈsutora オーケストラ *n.* (symphony) orchestra; orchestral music.

oˈokiˈ·i おおきい (大きい) *a.* (-ku) **1** big; large:

ookii *tsukue* (大きい机) a *large* desk. (↔ chiisai) (⇨ ooki-na)

2 (of degree) great:

Fugookaku *no shokku wa* ooki-katta. (不合格のショックは大きかった) Failure in the exam came as a *great* shock.

ookiku naru (大きくなる) grow up.

oˈoki-na おおきな (大きな) *attrib.* big; large; great:

Yotee *ni* ooki-na *heñkoo wa nakatta*. (予定に大きな変更はなかった) There was no *great* change in the schedule. (↔ chiisa-na) (⇨ ookii)

oˈokisa おおきさ (大きさ) *n.* size; dimensions; volume:

ookisa *o hakaru* (大きさを測る) measure the *size*. (⇨ daishoo; suñpoo)

oˈoku おおく (多く) *n., adv.* many; much:

Kañkyaku *no* ooku *wa kodomo-tachi datta*. (観客の多くは子どもたちだった) *Most* of the audience were children.

oˈokyuu おうきゅう (応急) *n.* emergency; temporary; makeshift:

★ Usually used in compounds.

ookyuu-teate (応急手当) *first aid*.

oˈomiˈzu おおみず (大水) *n.* flood:

oomizu *ga deru* (大水が出る) *be flooded*.

oˈomuˈgi おおむぎ (大麦) *n.* barley.

oˈomuˈkashi おおむかし (大昔) *n.* ancient times; antiquity.

oˈopuñ¹ オープン *n.* opening.

oopuñ suru (~する) *vi.* open.

oˈopuñ² オープン *a.n.* (~ na, ni) frank; open to the public.

oˈorai オーライ *n.* all right; O.K.:

Hassha oorai. (*said by train conductors, etc.*) (発車オーライ) It is all *right* to depart.

o˥osee おうせい (旺盛) *a.n.* (~ na, ni) full of energy; eager: *Kodomo-tachi wa shokuyoku oosee da.* (子どもたちは食欲おうせいだ) Children have a *good* appetite.

o˥osetsu おうせつ (応接) *n.* reception (of a visitor).
oosetsu suru (~する) *vt.* receive (a guest).

o˥osetsuma おうせつま (応接間) *n.* drawing room.

o˥osetsu˥shitsu おうせつしつ (応接室) *n.* reception room.

o˥otai おうたい (応対) *n.* reception; meeting.
... ni ootai suru (...に~する) *vi.* receive (callers); deal with; wait on (customers).

o˥oteñ おうてん (横転) *n.* turning sideways; overturning.
ooteñ suru (~する) *vi.* turn sideways; overturn.

o˥oto˥bai オートバイ *n.* motorcycle; motorbike.

o˥o˥·u おおう (覆う) *vt.* (oo-i-; oo-w-a-; oot-te C̄) cover; veil; envelop. (⇨ tsutsumu)

o˥oya おおや (大家) *n.* owner of a house for rent; landlord; landlady. (⇨ jinushi)

o˥oyoo おうよう (応用) *n.* application; adaptation; practice.
ooyoo suru (~する) *vt.* apply; adapt; put to use.

o˥oyo˥rokobi おおよろこび (大喜び) *n.* delight; glee; joy:
Kare-ra wa shiai ni katte, ooyorokobi datta. (彼らは試合に勝って、大喜びだった) They *were overjoyed* at winning the match.

o˥oyoso おおよそ (大凡) *n.* outline:
Keekaku no ooyoso o hanashite kudasai. (計画のおおよそを話してください) Please tell us the *general outline* of your plan.
— *adv.* roughly; approximately; about. (⇨ oyoso)

o˥oyuki おおゆき (大雪) *n.* heavy fall of snow; heavy snowfall.

(↔ koyuki) (⇨ yuki[1])

o˥oza˥ppa おおざっぱ (大雑把) *a.n.* (~ na, ni) rough; general:
Oozappa ni mitsumotte, hyakumañ-eñ kakarimasu. (おおざっぱに見積もって、100万円かかります) Estimating *roughly*, it will cost a million yen.

o˥oze˥e おおぜい (大勢) *n.*, *adv.* crowd (of people).

o˥ppai おっぱい *n.* = chichi[2].
★ Infant word for mother's milk or breast.

o˥ppara˥·u おっぱらう (追っ払う) *vt.* (-para-i-; -paraw-a-; -parat-te C̄) = oiharau.

o˥ro おれ (俺) *n.* (rude) I
★ Used by men. The plural form is '*ore-tachi.*' (⇨ omae)

o-˥ree おれい (お礼) *n.* ★ Polite form of '*ree.*' (⇨ ree[2])
1 thanks; gratitude:
Sono uchi o-ree ni ukagaimasu. (そのうちお礼に伺います) I will shortly pay you a visit *to thank you.*
2 reward; fee; remuneration.
o-ree (o) suru (~(を)する) *vt.* give a reward; pay a fee.

or˥eñji-ka˥ado オレンジカード *n.* a magnetic card with which one can buy Japan Railway tickets from vending machines.

o˥re˥·ru おれる (折れる) *vi.* (ore-te V̄) 1 break; give way:
Yuki no omomi de ki no eda ga oreta. (雪の重みで木の枝が折れた) The branches *broke* under the weight of the snow. (⇨ oru[1])
2 give in; yield to.
3 turn:
Sono kuruma wa hidari ni oreta. (その車は左に折れた) The car *turned* left.

o˥ri[1] おり (折) *n.* occasion; time; chance:
Kono tsugi kare ni atta ori, yoroshiku o-tsutae kudasai. (この次彼に会った折、よろしくお伝えください) Please give him my best regards the next *time* you see him.
ori o mite (~をみて) at the first

opportunity.

o⌐**ri**⌐**gami** おりがみ (折り紙) *n.* origami; colored paper for paper folding.

o⌐**rimono** おりもの (織物) *n.* textile; fabric.

o⌐**ri**⌐**ru** おりる (降りる・下りる) *vi.* (ori-te V) **1** get off (a vehicle); step down. 《↔ noru¹》《⇨ gesha; orosu¹》
2 come [go] down; step down: *kaidañ o oriru* (階段を下りる) *go down* stairs.
3 (of frost and dew) fall: *Kesa wa hidoi shimo ga orita.* (今朝はひどい霜が降りた) This morning the frost *was thick.*
4 quit (a position, etc.); resign.

o⌐**ritatam·u** おりたたむ (折り畳む) *vt.* (-tatam·i-; -tatam·a-; -tatañde C) fold; collapse (an umbrella). 《⇨ tatamu》

o⌐**roka** おろか (愚か) *a.n.* (~ na, ni) foolish; silly; stupid.

o⌐**roshi**¹ おろし (卸し) *n.* wholesale. 《⇨ kouri; orosu²; toñya》

o⌐**ro**⌐**soka** おろそか (疎か) *a.n.* (~ na, ni) neglectful; negligent: *beñkyoo o orosoka ni suru* (勉強をおろそかにする) *neglect* one's studies.

o⌐**ro**⌐**s·u**¹ おろす (降ろす・下ろす) *vt.* (orosh·i-; oros·a-; orosh·i-te C)
1 drop; let off:
Tsugi no shiñgoo de oroshite kudasai. (次の信号で降ろしてください) Please *drop* me *off* at the next traffic light. 《↔ noseru¹》《⇨ oriru》
2 unload; discharge; take down.
3 pull down; roll down; lower: *buraiñdo o orosu* (ブラインドを下ろす) *lower* the blinds.
4 withdraw (a deposit).

o⌐**ro**⌐**s·u**² おろす (卸す) *vt.* (orosh·i-; oros·a-; orosh·i-te C) sell; wholesale:
Kono shoohiñ wa hitotsu señ-eñ de oroshite imasu. (この商品は一つ千円で卸しています) We *wholesale* these goods at 1,000 yen apiece.

o⌐**r·u**¹ おる (折る) *vt.* (or·i-; or·a-; ot-te C) **1** break; snap:
Kare wa hidari-ashi no hone o otta. (彼は左足の骨を折った) He *broke* a bone in his left leg.
2 fold:
Kanojo wa origami o otte, tsuru o tsukutta. (彼女は折り紙を折って、つるを作った) She *folded* a piece of paper into a crane.

o⌐**r·u**² おる (織る) *vt.* (or·i-; or·a-; ot-te C) weave.

o⌐**r·u**³ おる (居る) *vi.* (or·i-; or·a-; ot-te C) be; exist:
1 [with an animate subject] (humble equivalent of '*iru*'):
Shujiñ wa ima ie ni orimasu. (主人は今家におります) My husband *is* at home now.
2 [with an inanimate subject] (polite equivalent of '(-*te*) *iru*'):
Kochira wa ima yuki ga futte orimasu. (こちらは今雪が降っております) It *is* now snowing here.

o⌐**rugañ** オルガン *n.* organ:
orugañ o hiku (オルガンをひく) *play the organ.*

o⌐**sae**⌐**ru** おさえる (押さえる) *vt.* (osae-te V) **1** hold (down):
Kono roopu o shikkari osaete kudasai. (このロープをしっかり押さえてください) Please *hold* this rope tightly.
2 catch; arrest:
Doroboo wa geñkoohañ de osaerareta. (泥棒は現行犯で押さえられた) The thief *was caught* red-handed.

o⌐**sama**⌐**r·u**¹ おさまる (収まる) *vi.* (osamar·i-; osamar·a-; osamat-te C) **1** fit; be kept:
Sono tana ni kono hoñ ga zeñbu osamarimasu ka? (その棚にこの本が全部収まりますか) Will these books all *fit* onto that shelf? 《⇨ osameru¹》
2 take office:
Kare wa kaichoo ni osamatta. (彼は会長に収まった) He *took* the post of chairman.

o⌐**sama**⌐**r·u**² おさまる (治まる) *vi.* (osamar·i-; osamar·a-; osamat-te C) **1** (of turmoil) settle (down); be settled. (⇨ **osameru**²)

2 (of the wind) calm down; die down.

o**ˈsamaˈr·uˈ³** おさまる(納まる) *vi.*
(osamar·i-; osamar·a-; osamat-te ⓒ) be paid:
Anata no zeekiñ ga mada osa-matte imaseñ. (あなたの税金がまだ納まっていません) Your taxes *have* not *been paid* yet. (⇨ **osameru**³)

o**ˈsameˈ·ruˈ¹** おさめる(収める) *vt.*
(osame-te Ⅴ) **1** put away (in); store; keep:
Tsukatta doogu wa moto no tokoro ni osamemashita. (使った道具は元の所に収めました) I *put* the tools *away* in their proper place. (⇨ **osamaru**¹)

2 get (a grade, mark); obtain; gain; attain:
Kare wa yuushuu na seeseki o osameta. (彼は優秀な成績を収めた) He *obtained* distinguished grades.

o**ˈsameˈ·ruˈ²** おさめる(治める) *vt.*
(osame-te Ⅴ) **1** rule; govern; reign: *kuni o osameru* (国を治める) *govern* a country.
2 settle; put down:
sawagi o osameru (騒ぎを治める) *settle* a disturbance. (⇨ **osamaru**²)

o**ˈsameˈ·ruˈ³** おさめる(納める) *vt.*
(osame-te Ⅴ) **1** pay (a fee, charge, tax, etc.):
jugyoo-ryoo [zeekiñ] o osameru (授業料[税金]を納める) *pay* one's tuition [tax]. (⇨ **osamaru**³)
2 supply; deliver:
Chuumoñ no shina wa getsumatsu made ni osamemasu. (注文の品は月末までに納めます) We will *deliver* the goods ordered by the end of the month.
3 accept:
Doo-ka kore o o-osame kudasai. (どうかこれをお納めください) Please *accept* this.

o**ˈsanaˈ·i** おさない(幼い) *a.* (-ku)
1 very young.
2 childish; immature:
Ano hito wa toshi no wari ni osa-

nai. (あの人は年の割に幼い) He is very *immature* for his age.

o-**ˈsatsu** おさつ(お札) *n.* paper money; bill; note. (⇨ **satsu**)

o**ˈsechi-ryoˈori** おせちりょうり(お節料理) *n.* special dishes served on the first three days of the New Year.

o-**ˈseebo** おせいぼ(お歳暮) *n.*
= **seebo**.

o**ˈseji** おせじ(お世辞) *n.* compliment; flattery:
hito ni oseji o iu (人にお世辞を言う) *flatter* [*compliment*] a person.

o**ˈshaˈberi** おしゃべり(お喋り) *n.* chat; chatter.
oshaberi (o) suru (～(を)する) *vi.* chat away; chatter.
— *a.n.* (～ na) talkative; gossipy.

o**ˈshaˈre** おしゃれ(お洒落) *n.* dressing up; smart dresser.
oshare (o) suru (～(を)する) *vi.* get dressed up.

o**ˈshie** おしえ(教え) *n.* teaching; instruction. (⇨ **oshieru**)

o**ˈshie-ru** おしえる(教える) *vt.*
(oshie-te Ⅴ) **1** teach (a lesson); instruct. (↔ **osowaru**) (⇨ **oshie**)
2 tell (information); show (the way).

o**ˈshiˈ·i** おしい(惜しい) *a.* (-ku)
1 regrettable; unlucky:
Ii chañsu o nogashite, oshii koto o shita. (いいチャンスを逃して、惜しいことをした) It was too *bad* that I let a great opportunity slip by.
2 precious; dear:
Dare de mo inochi ga oshii. (だれでも命が惜しい) Life is *dear* to everyone. (⇨ **oshimu**)
3 too good:
Kono mañneñhitsu wa suteru no ga oshii. (この万年筆は捨てるのが惜しい) This fountain pen is *too good* to throw away. (⇨ **mottainai**)

o**ˈshiire** おしいれ(押し入れ) *n.* closet; storage cupboard.

o**ˈshiˈkko** おしっこ *n.* pee; piddle; urine. ★ Often used by

young children. (⇨ shooben)

o⌐**shiko**⌐**m·u** おしこむ (押し込む) vi.
(-kom·i-; -kom·a-; -kon-de C)
push; thrust; stuff:
*Kare wa kaban ni hon o oshiko-
nda.* (彼はかばんに本を押し込んだ) He
stuffed the books into his bag.

o⌐**shimai** おしまい (お仕舞い) n.
end; finish:
*Kyoo wa kore de oshimai ni shi-
yoo.* (きょうはこれでおしまいにしよう)
Let's finish off here for today.
(⇨ shimai²)

o⌐**shi**⌐**m·u** おしむ (惜しむ) vt. (o-
shim·i-; oshim·a-; oshin-de C)
1 grudge; spare:
*Kare wa musume no tame ni
hiyoo o oshimanakatta.* (彼は娘のた
めに費用を惜しまなかった) He *spared
no* expense for his daughter.
2 regret:
Minna ga kare no shi o oshinda.
(みんなが彼の死を惜しんだ) Every-
body *regretted* his death.
(⇨ oshii)

o⌐**shiroi** おしろい (白粉) n. face
powder.

o⌐**shitsuke**⌐**·ru** おしつける (押し付
ける) vt. (-tsuke-te V) 1 push
against; press against; thrust.
2 force (an unwelcome job) onto
a person.

o⌐**shiyose**⌐**·ru** おしよせる (押し寄せ
る) vi. (-yose-te V) crowd;
throng; surge:
*Oozee no hito ga shin-kyuujoo ni
oshiyoseta.* (大勢の人が新球場に押し
寄せた) Many people *crowded* into
the new ballpark.

o⌐**shoku** おしょく (汚職) n. corruption; graft; bribery.

o-⌐**shoosui** おしょうすい (お小水) n.
urine. ★ A common euphemism
used in hospitals. (⇨ shooben)

o⌐**so·i** おそい (遅い) a. (-ku) 1 (of
time) late:
Kotoshi wa haru ga osoi. (今年は
春が遅い) Spring is *late* in coming
this year. (↔ hayai¹)
2 (of motion) slow. (↔ hayai²)

o⌐**sonae** おそなえ (お供え) n. 1 offering. (⇨ sonaeru²)
2 rice-cake offering.

o⌐**so**⌐**raku** おそらく (恐らく) adv.
perhaps; probably; possibly;
likely. (⇨ tabun; tashika)

o⌐**sore**¹ おそれ (虞れ) n. 1 fear:
*Kyoo wa ame no osore wa arima-
sen.* (きょうは雨のおそれはありません)
There is no *fear* of rain today.
2 possibility; likelihood:
*Sono jikken wa shippai suru oso-
re ga arimasu.* (その実験は失敗するお
それがあります) The experiment *is
likely* to fail.

o⌐**sore**¹² おそれ (恐れ) n. terror;
horror; dread. (⇨ osoreru)

o⌐**so**⌐**reirimasu** おそれいります (恐
れ入ります) (humble) thank you
very much:
O-kokorozukai osoreirimasu. (お心
づかい恐れ入ります) Your kind con-
sideration *is much appreciated.*
osoreirimasu ga (〜が) excuse
me, but: **Osoreirimasu ga mado
o shimete itadakemasu ka?** (恐れ
入りますが窓を閉めていただけますか)
Excuse me, but would you mind
closing the window?

o⌐**sore**¹**·ru** おそれる (恐れる) vi.
(osore-te V) fear; dread; be
afraid; be frightened.
(⇨ osore²; osoroshii)

o⌐**soroshi**¹**·i** おそろしい (恐ろしい) a.
(-ku) fearful; terrible; horrible.
(⇨ osoreru; kowai)

o⌐**soro**⌐**shiku** おそろしく (恐ろしく)
adv. very; awfully; terribly:
Kyoo wa osoroshiku samui. (きょう
はおそろしく寒い) Today is a *terribly*
cold day.

o⌐**so**¹**·u** おそう (襲う) vt. (oso·i-;
osow·a-; osot-te C) 1 attack;
assault; raid.
2 (of disaster, tragedy, etc.) hit;
strike:
Taifuu ga Kantoo chihoo o osotta.
(台風が関東地方を襲った) A ty-
phoon *struck* the Kanto district.

o⌐**sowar·u** おそわる (教わる) vi.

(osowar·i-; osowar·a-; osowat-
te C) be taught; learn:
*Tanaka señsee kara Nihoñgo o
osowaru* (田中先生から日本語を教わ
る) *learn* Japanese from Miss
Tanaka. ((↔ oshieru))

o⸢ssha⸣r·u おっしゃる (仰る) *vt.*
(ossha·i-; osshar·a-; osshat-te
C) say: ★ Honorific equivalent
of '*iu.*'
Nañ to osshaimashita ka? (何とおっ
しゃいましたか) What was it you
said?

o⸢s·u⸣¹ おす (押す) *vt.* (osh·i-; o-
s·a-; osh·i-te C) 1 push; press;
shove; thrust.
2 stamp; seal:
han o osu (判を押す) *affix* a seal.

o⸢su⸣² おす (雄) *n.* male; he:
osu no saru (雄の猿) a *male* monkey / *osu-neko* (雄猫) a *tomcat.*
((↔ mesu))

o⸢tagaisama おたがいさま (お互い
様) being in the same circumstances:
*Kyuuryoo ga yasui no wa otagai-
sama da.* (給料が安いのはお互いさまだ)
We are in the same boat — having
a low salary.

o-⸢taku⸣ おたく (お宅) *n.* 1 someone else's house: ★ Usually
refers to the house of the listener.
Asu o-taku ni ukagaimasu. (あすお
宅に伺います) I'll visit *your house*
tomorrow.
2 you: ★ Polite equivalent of
'*anata.*'
*Kono kabañ wa o-taku no desu
ka?* (このかばんはお宅のですか) Is this
bag *yours?*

o-⸢tazune⸣¹ おたずね (お尋ね) *n.*
(*polite*) question; inquiry.
o-tazune suru (〜する) *vt.* ask;
inquire; question. ((⇨ tazuneru¹))

o-⸢tazune⸣² おたずね (お訪ね) *n.*
(*polite*) visit.
o-tazune suru (〜する) *vt.* pay a
visit. ((⇨ tazuneru²))

o-⸢tea⸣rai おてあらい (お手洗い) *n.*
(*polite*) toilet; lavatory. ((⇨ te-

o-⸢te⸣tsudai-sañ おてつだいさん
(お手伝いさん) *n.* home help;
housemaid.

o⸢to⸣¹ おと (音) *n.* sound; noise.

o⸢togiba⸣nashi おとぎばなし (お伽
話) *n.* fairy tale; nursery tale.
((⇨ doowa))

o⸢toko⸣ おとこ (男) *n.* man; male.
★ Has no derogatory connotation like '*oñna.*' ((⇨ dañsee))

o⸢toko⸣-no-ko おとこのこ (男の子)
n. boy; son. ((↔ oñna-no-ko))

o⸢tokorashi⸣·i おとこらしい (男らし
い) *a.* (-ku) (*appreciative*) manly;
masculine. ((↔ oñnarashii))
((⇨ dañsee-teki))

o-⸢tokui(-sañ) おとくい(さん)(お得
意(さん)) *n.* good customer.

o⸢tona おとな (大人) *n.* grown-up;
adult. ((↔ kodomo))

o⸢tonashi⸣·i おとなしい (大人しい) *a.*
(-ku) 1 (of a disposition) quiet;
gentle; mild; meek; obedient.
2 (of a color, a pattern) quiet;
soft; sober.

o-⸢to⸣ochañ おとうちゃん (お父ちゃ
ん) *n.* father; dad. ★ Used chiefly by small children. ((↔ o-kaa-
chañ))

o-⸢to⸣osañ おとうさん (お父さん) *n.*
father; dad. ((↔ o-kaasañ)) ((⇨ chichi¹))

o⸢tooto⸣ おとうと (弟) *n.* one's
younger brother. ★ When referring to someone else's, '*otooto-
sañ*' is usually used. ((↔ ani))

ot⸢oroe⸣ おとろえ (衰え) *n.* decline; weakening; failing:
kiokuryoku no otoroe (記憶力の衰
え) the *failing* of one's memory.
((⇨ otoroeru))

o⸢toroe⸣·ru おとろえる (衰える) *vi.*
(otoroe-te V) become weak;
fail; decline:
Taifuu wa otoroete kita. (台風は衰
えてきた) The typhoon *has lost its
force.* ((⇨ otoroe))

o⸢tor·u おとる (劣る) *vi.* (otor·i-;

otor·a-; otot-te Ⓒ be inferior; fall below.

o⌐toshimono おとしもの (落とし物) *n.* lost article [property]; something dropped by mistake. (⇨ otosu)

o⌐to⌐s·u おとす (落とす) *vt.* (otosh·i-; otos·a-; otosh·i-te Ⓒ)
1 drop:
Kare wa fooku o yuka ni otoshita. (彼はフォークを床に落とした) He *dropped* his fork on the floor. (⇨ ochiru)
2 lose:
Saifu o doko de otoshita *no ka wakarimaseñ.* (財布をどこで落としたのかわかりません) I do not know where I *lost* my purse.
3 reduce; lower:
supiido o otosu (スピードを落とす) *reduce* speed / *koe o* otosu (声を落とす) *lower* one's voice. (⇨ ochiru)
4 remove makeup; take out (stains, etc.). (⇨ ochiru)
5 fail (an examinee). (⇨ ochiru)

o⌐to⌐toi おととい (一昨日) *n.* the day before yesterday.

o⌐to⌐toshi おととし (一昨年) *n.* the year before last.

o⌐tozure⌐·ru おとずれる (訪れる) *vi.* (otozure-te Ⓥ) visit; call. (⇨ hoomoñ; tazuneru²)

o⌐tsukaresama おつかれさま (お疲れ様) you must be tired; thank you for your hard work.
★ Used to express thanks to a person for doing something on one's behalf. '*Otsukaresama deshita.*' is used to superiors. (⇨ -sama)

o-⌐tsuri おつり (お釣り) *n.* change: *O-tsuri wa totte oite kudasai.* (お釣りはとっておいてください) Please keep the *change*. (⇨ tsuri²)

o⌐tto おっと (夫) *n.* husband.
★ '*Otto*' refers either to one's own husband, or is used as a generic term for husband. (↔ tsuma) (⇨ shujiñ)

o-⌐u¹ おう (追う) *vt.* (o·i-; ow·a-;

ot-te Ⓒ **1** chase; go after. (⇨ oikakeru)
2 drive away:
Kare wa sono chii o owareta. (彼はその地位を追われた) He *was driven* from his position.

o-⌐u² おう (負う) *vt.* (o·i-; ow·a-; ot-te Ⓒ) **1** carry (a load) on one's back. (⇨ seou)
2 assume (responsibility).
3 get wounded [injured]; suffer (an injury):
juushoo o ou (重傷を負う) *suffer* severe injury / *soñgai o* ou (損害を負う) *suffer* a loss.

o-⌐wabi おわび (お詫び) *n.* (*polite*) apology. (⇨ wabi; wabiru)

o-⌐wañ おわん (お椀) *n.* = wañ¹.

o⌐wari おわり (終わり) *n.* end; close. (↔ hajime) (⇨ owaru)

o⌐war·u おわる (終わる) *vi.* (owar·i-; owar·a-; owat-te Ⓒ) finish; end; be over. (⇨ oeru; owari; shuuryoo)

o⌐ya おや (親) *n.* parent(s). (↔ ko)

o⌐ya⌐¹ おやっ *int.* oh; oh dear; dear me; good heavens:
Oya', are wa nañ no oto da? (おやっ、あれは何の音だ) *Oh!* What's that sound?

o⌐yako おやこ (親子) *n.* parent and child.

o⌐yaoya おやおや *int.* well; oh; oh dear; good heavens. ★ Intensive equivalent of '*oya*.'

o⌐yasumi nasa⌐i おやすみなさい (お休みなさい) good night; sleep well.

o⌐ya⌐tsu おやつ (お八つ) *n.* **1** coffee [tea] break.
2 snack; refreshments.

o⌐yayubi おやゆび (親指) *n.* thumb. ★ In Japanese, the thumb is considered one of the fingers.

o⌐yobi および (及び) *conj.* (*formal*) and; both...and...:
Shimee oyobi *juusho o kinyuu no koto.* (氏名および住所を記入のこと)

Enter *both* name *and* address.
((⇨ soshite; to²))

o「yobos·u およぼす (及ぼす) *vt.*
(oyobosh·i-; oyobos·a-; oyo-
bosh·i-te C) exert (influence);
cause (harm). ((⇨ oyobu))

o「yob·u および (及ぶ) *vi.* (oyob·i-;
oyob·a-; oyoñ-de C) 1 extend;
spread; reach:
Kare no keñkyuu wa hiroi hañi ni
oyobu. (彼の研究は広い範囲に及ぶ)
His researches *extend* over a
wide field. ((⇨ oyobosu))
2 (of time) last:
Kare no shukuji wa sañjup-puñ ni
mo oyoñda. (彼の祝辞は 30 分にも及
んだ) His congratulatory address
lasted all of thirty minutes.
3 match:
Suugaku de wa kare ni oyobu
mono wa imaseñ. (数学では彼に及ぶ

者はいません) There is no one who
can *match* him in math.
4 (in the negative) do not need:
Anata wa kuru ni wa oyobimaseñ.
(あなたは来るには及びません) You *don't*
need to come.

o「yo「g·u およぐ (泳ぐ) *vi.* (oyog·i-;
oyog·a-; oyo·i-de C) swim.

o-「yomesañ およめさん (お嫁さん)
n. bride. ((⇨ yome))

o「yoso およそ (凡そ) *adv.*
1 about; nearly. ((⇨ yaku²))
2 (with a negative) quite; entirely:
Soñna koto o shite mo oyoso imi
ga arimaseñ (そんなことをしてもおよそ
意味がありません) Even if you did
that kind of thing, it would be
quite meaningless.

o-「yu おゆ (お湯) *n.* hot water.
((⇨ yu))

P

-pa ぱ (羽) *suf.* counter for birds
and rabbits. ((⇨ -wa; APP. 4))

pa「ama パーマ *n.* permanent
wave; perm.

pa「ase「ñto パーセント *n.* percent;
per cent. ((⇨ bu²; wari))

pa「atii パーティー *n.* 1 (of an occasion) party:
paatii *o hiraku [okonau]* (パーティー
を開く[行う]) give a *party*.
2 (of a group) party. ((⇨ ikkoo¹))

pa「chiñko パチンコ *n.* pinball
(game); pachinko.

pa「chipachi ぱちぱち *adv.* (~ to)
(the sound or action of crackling,
clapping, etc.):
Kareki ga pachipachi (to) moeta.
(枯れ木がぱちぱち(と)燃えた) The dry
trees burned *with a crackling*
sound.

-pai ぱい (杯) *suf.* counter for
glassfuls or cupfuls. ((⇨ -hai;
APP. 4))

pa「ipu パイプ *n.* pipe; tube;

cigarette holder.

-paku ぱく (泊) *suf.* counter for
overnight stays. ((⇨ APP. 4))

pa「ñ パン *n.* bread; toast; roll;
bun.

pa「ñfure「tto パンフレット *n.* pamphlet; brochure; leaflet.

pa「ñku パンク *n.* flat tire; punc-
ture.
pañku suru (~する) *vi.* have a flat
tire; be punctured.

pa「ñtii-suto「kkiñgu パンティース
トッキング *n.* panty hose.

pa「ñtsu パンツ *n.* underpants;
briefs; shorts. ★ Not usually
used for '*trousers*.'

pa「ñya パンや (パン屋) *n.* bakery;
baker.

pa「pa パパ *n.* dad; daddy; papa;
father. ((⇨ mama²))

pa「rapara¹ ぱらぱら *adv.* (~ to)
(the sound or action of droplets
or small objects falling or pages
being turned):

Ame ga parapara *(to) futte kita.*
(雨がぱらぱら(と)降って来た) The rain
has started to *spatter down*.

pa⌐rapara² ぱらぱら *adv.* (the
state of being sparse):
Dono sharyoo mo jookyaku wa
parapara *datta.* (どの車両も乗客はぱ
らぱらだった) There were *just a few*
passengers on every train.

pa⌐sapasa¹ ぱさぱさ *adv.* (～ to;
～ suru) (the state of being dry
and bland):
Kono pañ wa pasapasa *shite iru.*
(このパンはぱさぱさしている) This
bread *is all dried up*.

pa⌐sapasa² ぱさぱさ *adv.* dry
and brittle:
Kami ga pasapasa *da.* (髪がぱさぱさ
だ) My hair *is dry and brittle*.

pa⌐sokoñ パソコン *n.* personal
computer.

pa⌐supo⌐oto パスポート *n.* passport. (⇨ ryokeñ)

-patsu ぱつ (発) *suf.* counter
used with bullets, shells and
large fireworks. (⇨ APP. 4)

pa⌐tto ぱっと *adv.* suddenly; all
at once; quickly:
Ii kañgae ga patto *ukañda.* (いい考
えがぱっと浮かんだ) A great idea *suddenly* occurred to me.
patto shinai (～しない) unattractive; inconspicuous; dull.

pe⌐chakucha ぺちゃくちゃ *adv.*
(～ to) (used to express the manner of chattering or prattling):
pechakucha *(to) shaberu* (ぺちゃくち
ゃ(と)しゃべる) *chatter away*.

pe⌐epaa-te⌐suto ペーパーテスト *n.*
written test.

pe⌐kopeko¹ ぺこぺこ *a.n.* (～ na,
ni) (the state of being hungry):
Onaka ga pekopeko *da.* (おなかがぺこ
ぺこだ) I am very *hungry*.

pe⌐kopeko² ぺこぺこ *adv.* (～ to;
～ suru) (bow) humbly.

-peñ ぺん (遍) *suf.* counter for
the number of times. (⇨ APP. 4)

pe⌐ñchi ペンチ *n.* cutting pliers.

pe⌐ñki ペンキ *n.* paint:

kabe ni peñki *o nuru* (壁にペンキを塗
る) *paint* a wall. (⇨ toryoo)

pe⌐rapera¹ ぺらぺら *a.n.* (～ na,
ni) fluent; glib; voluble:
Kare wa Nihoñgo ga perapera
desu. (彼は日本語がぺらぺらです) His
Japanese is *fluent*.
— *adv.* (～ to) talkatively; noisily. (⇨ berabera)

pe⌐rapera² ぺらぺら *a.n.* (～ na/
no, ni) (of paper, board, etc.)
thin; flimsy. (⇨ usui)

pi⌐chipichi ぴちぴち *adv.* (～ to;
～ suru) (the state of being
young, fresh and vigorous):
Sono shoojo wa pichipichi *(to)
shite ita.* (その少女はぴちぴち(と)してい
た) The girl was *young and fresh*.

pi⌐imañ ピーマン *n.* green pepper; pimento.

pi⌐ipii ぴいぴい *adv.* (～ to; ～
suru) 1 (the song of birds):
Tori ga piipii *(to) naite iru.* (鳥がぴ
いぴい(と)鳴いている) Birds *are chirp-
ing*.
2 (of a financial condition) badly
off; hard up:
Kare wa ima piipii *shite iru.* (彼は
今ぴいぴいしている) He *is short of
money* right now.

pi⌐kapika¹ ぴかぴか *a.n.* (～ na/no,
ni) shining; glittering.

pi⌐ka⌐pika² ぴかぴか *adv.* (～ to)
(the state of glittering, twinkling,
etc.):
Inazuma ga pikapika *to hikatta.*
(稲妻がピカピカと光った) There was a
flash of lightning.

-piki ぴき (匹) *suf.* counter for
small animals, fish and insects.
(⇨ APP. 4)

pi⌐kunikku ピクニック *n.* picnic.
★ Used for a pleasure trip which
includes a picnic. Not used in
the sense of a meal out of doors.

pi⌐kupiku ぴくぴく *adv.* (～ to;
～ suru) (the state of twitching):
Uki ga pikupiku *shite iru.* (浮きがぴ
くぴくしている) The float *is bobbing
up and down*.

pi˥ñku ピンク *n*. pink. ★ Suggests something risqué, like 'blue' in English. *e.g.* piñku-*eega* (ピンク映画) a *pornographic* movie. (⇨ momoiro)

pi˥ñto ピント *n*. focus: piñto *ga amai* [*zurete iru*] (ピントがあまい[ずれている]) be out of *focus*.
piñto-hazure (〜外れ) be wide of the mark. (⇨ mato)

pi˥ta˥ri ぴたり *adv*. (〜 to)
1 closely; tightly.
2 suddenly; right away: *Sono kusuri o noñdara, itami ga* pitari (to) tomatta. (その薬を飲んだら、痛みがぴたりと止まった) The pain *went right away* after I took the medicine.
3 exactly perfectly: *Yosoo ga* pitari (to) *atatta*. (予想がぴたり(と)当たった) My forecast hit the mark *exactly*.

pi˥tchi ピッチ *n*. pace; speed: *Koosoo-biru ga kyuu*-pitchi *de keñsetsu sarete iru*. (高層ビルが急ピッチで建設されている) High-rise buildings are being built at a fast *pace*.

pi˥tta˥ri ぴったり *adv*. (〜 no, to; 〜 suru) **1** = pitari.
2 right: *Kono fuku wa anata ni* pittari *de-su*. (この服はあなたにぴったりです) These clothes are *just right* for you.

-po ほ (歩) *suf*. counter for steps. (⇨ APP. 4)

po˥kapoka ぽかぽか *adv*. (〜 to; 〜 suru) **1** (the state of being nice and warm): *Yooki ga* pokapoka *shite ite kimochi ga ii*. (陽気がぽかぽかしていて気持ちがいい) The weather is *nice and warm*.
2 (of beating) repeatedly.

po˥kka˥ri ぽっかり *adv*. (〜 to)
1 (the state of floating): *Shiroi kumo ga sora ni* pokkari (to) *ukañde iru*. (白い雲が空にぽっかり(と)浮かんでいる) There *is* a white cloud *suspended* in the sky.
2 (the state of being wide open): *Michi ni ana ga* pokkari aite ita. (道に穴がぽっかり開いていた) There *was* a hole *gaping wide open* in the road.

-poñ ほん (本) *suf*. counter for long cylindrical objects. (⇨ APP. 4)

po˥ñdo ポンド *n*. **1** pound sterling.
2 pound (unit of weight).

-ppo˥˙i っぽい *suf*. (*a*.) (-ku) [attached to a noun, the continuative base of a verb, or the stem of an adjective] **1** something like; resembling; -ish: *Kare ni wa* kodomo-ppoi *tokoro ga aru*. (彼には子どもっぽいところがある) He has some *childish* points.
2 tending; looking: shime-ppoi (湿っぽい) *dampish* / yasu-ppoi *fuku* (安っぽい服) *cheap-looking* clothes.

po˥suto ポスト *n*. mailbox.

po˥tsupotsu ぽつぽつ *adv*. (〜 to) **1** (the state of small drops falling): *Ame ga* potsupostu *futte kita*. (雨がぽつぽつ降ってきた) The rain started *splattering down in drops*.
2 (the state of things occurring sporadically): *Joohoo ga* potsupostu *haitte kita*. (情報がぽつぽつ入ってきた) The reports *trickled in*.

po˥tto ポット *n*. thermos [vacuum] bottle; teapot; coffee pot.

-puñ ふん (分) *suf*. counter for minutes. (⇨ APP. 4)

pu˥ñpuñ ぶんぶん *adv*. (〜 to; 〜 suru) **1** (a strong smell): *Kanojo wa koosui o* puñpuñ (to) *sasete ita*. (彼女は香水をぶんぶん(と)させていた) She *smelt strongly* of perfume.
2 (the state of being angry): *Kare wa okotte* puñpuñ *shite iru*. (彼は怒ってぶんぶんしている) He *is absolutely furious*.

pu˥ragu プラグ *n*. electric plug.

pu˥rasu プラス *n*. **1** plus.
(⇨ tasu)
2 advantage; gain; asset.
(↔ mainasu)
    purasu suru (〜する) *vt*. add.

pu˥rasuchi˥kku プラスチック *n*.
plastic. ★ Refers only to rigid
substances; vinyl is called
'*biniiru*.'

pu˥rattoho˥omu プラットホーム *n*.
railroad station platform.
(⇨ hoomu˥)

pu˥re˥zeňto プレゼント *n*. present; gift.
    purezeňto suru (〜する) *vt*. give
a present. (⇨ miyage; okurimono)

-puri ぶり (振り) *suf*. = -buri.

pu˥riňto プリント *n*. **1** handout;
copy; mimeographed copy.

2 (of a photograph) print.
    puriňto suru (〜する) *vt*. make a
handout [copy].

pu˥ripuri ぷりぷり *adv*. (〜 to;
〜 suru) (the state of being angry): puripuri suru (ぷりぷりする) *be
very angry*.

pu˥ro[1] プロ *n*. professional; pro.
(⇨ seňmoňka)

pu˥ro[2] プロ *n*. theatrical agency.
★ Originally from the shortened
form of English 'production.'

pyu˥upyuu ぴゅうぴゅう *adv*.
(〜 to) (used to express a shrill
sound):
Soto wa tsumetai kaze ga pyuu-
pyuu (to) *fuite ita*. (外は冷たい風がぴ
ゅうぴゅう(と)吹いていた) The cold
wind *was whistling* outside.

R

-ra ら(等) *suf*. **1** (used to form
the plural of a noun referring to
a person): ★ Used with reference to equals or subordinates.
'*-tachi*' is more common.
boku-ra (ぼくら) *we*; *us* / kare-ra
(彼ら) *they*; *them* / kodomo-ra (子
どもら) *children*.
2 (used to form the plural of a
pronoun referring to a thing):
kore-ra (これら) *these* / sore-ra (それ
ら) *those*.

ra˥ameň ラーメン *n*. Chinese
noodles. (⇨ chuuka-soba; iňsuta-
ňto-raameň)

ra˥igetsu らいげつ(来月) *n*. next
month. (⇨ koňgetsu; seňgetsu)

ra˥imu˥gi ライむぎ(ライ麦) *n*. rye.

ra˥ineň らいねん(来年) *n*. next
year. (⇨ kotoshi; kyoneň)

ra˥inichi らいにち(来日) *n*. visit
to Japan.
    rainichi suru (〜する) *vi*. visit
[come to] Japan.

ra˥ishuu らいしゅう(来週) *n*. next

week. (⇨ koňshuu; seňshuu)

ra˥isu ライス *n*. cooked [boiled]
rice. ★ Refers to cooked rice
served on Western plates. When
referring to rice served in Japanese-style bowls, use the word '
gohaň.'

ra˥jio ラジオ *n*. radio:
rajio o tsukeru [*kesu*] (ラジオをつける
[消す]) turn on [off] the *radio*.

ra˥kkyoo らっきょう *n*. baker's
garlic.

ra˥ku[1] らく(楽) *n*. ease; comfort;
relief.
    — *a.n*. (〜 na, ni) **1** comfort-
able; easy:
*Kusuri o noňdara, raku ni narima-
shita*. (薬を飲んだら、楽になりました) I
felt more *comfortable* after taking
the medicine.
2 simple; easy:
Kono nimotsu o hakobu no wa raku *desu*. (この荷物を運ぶのは楽です) It
is quite *easy* to carry this baggage.

ra⌐kudai らくだい (落第) n. failure; flunking.
rakudai suru (〜する) vi. fail; flunk; repeat the same grade in school.

ra⌐kugo らくご (落語) n. comic story. ★ Told by a professional raconteur and with a witty ending.

ra⌐kunoo らくのう (酪農) n. dairy farming.

ra⌐kuseñ らくせん (落選) n. defeat in an election. (↔ tooseñ)
rakuseñ suru (〜する) vt. 1 be defeated in an election.
2 be rejected. *Kanojo no e wa rakuseñ shita.* (彼女の絵は落選した) Her painting *was rejected.*

ra⌐ñ¹ らん (欄) n. column; space.

ra⌐ñ² らん (蘭) n. orchid.

ra⌐ñboo らんぼう (乱暴) n. violence; rudeness. (⇨ booryoku)
rañboo suru (〜する) vi. 1 use violence; behave rudely.
2 violate; rape:
josee ni rañboo suru (女性に乱暴する) *rape* a woman.
— a.n. (〜 na, ni) violent; rude; rough; reckless:
Ano ko wa rañboo da. (あの子は乱暴だ) That child is *rude and rough.*

ra⌐ñpu¹ ランプ n. lamp.

ra⌐ñpu² ランプ n. exit [entrance] ramp of an expressway.

ra⌐ñshi らんし (卵子) n. ovum. (⇨ seeshi³)

-rare·ru られる infl. end. (-rare-te Ⅴ) [attached to the negative base of a vowel-stem verb and 'kuru,' and itself inflected like a vowel-stem verb] (⇨ -reru)
1 (indicates the passive) be...-ed:
Kanojo wa señsee ni homerareta. (彼女は先生にほめられた) She *was praised* by her teacher.
2 (indicates a sense of suffering, loss, etc.): ★ Usually used with reference to unfavorable occurrences.

Kitaku no tochuu de ame ni furareta. (帰宅の途中で雨に降られた) I *was caught* in the rain on my way home.
3 (indicates the potential) can:
Kono mi wa taberaremaseñ. (この実は食べられません) You *cannot eat* this fruit.
4 (indicates the natural potential): ★ Used when something naturally or involuntarily comes to mind.
Chichi no byooki no koto ga añjirareru. (父の病気のことが案じられる) I *cannot help worrying* about my father's illness.
5 (indicates the honorific):
Tanaka sañ no kawari ni Yamada-sañ ga korareru soo desu. (田中さんの代わりに山田さんが来られるそうです) I hear that Mr. Yamada will *come* in place of Mr. Yamada.

ra⌐shi¹·i らしい a. (-ku) [follows a noun, adjective, adjectival noun, the dictionary form or the *ta*-form of a verb or the copula]
1 look like; seem:
Kono ike wa kanari fukai rashii. (この池はかなり深いらしい) This pond *seems* rather deep.
2 they say; I hear:
Kare wa kaisha o yameru rashii. (彼は会社を辞めるらしい) *They say* that he is leaving the company.

-rashi¹·i らしい suf. (a.) (-ku) typical of; just like; befitting:
★ Added to a noun to make an adjective.
Soñna koto o suru nañte kimi-rashiku nai. (そんなことをするなんて君らしくない) It is not *like you* to do such a thing. / otoko-rashii *taido* (男らしい態度) a *manly* attitude.

re⌐e¹ れい (例) n. 1 example; instance: ree o ageru (例をあげる) give an *example*.
2 case:
mare na ree (まれな例) a rare *case*.
3 custom; habit; practice:
Soo suru no ga Nihoñ no ree desu.

(そうするのが日本の例です) It is a Japanese *custom* to do so.

re᛬e² れい (礼) *n.* **1** thanks; gratitude:
ree o noberu (礼を述べる) express one's *thanks*. (⇨ o-ree)
2 reward; fee:
Watashi wa o-ree ni ichimañ-eñ kare ni ageta. (私はお礼に1万円彼にあげた) I gave him 10,000 yen as a *reward*.

re᛬e³ れい (礼) *n.* bow; salute:
Seeto-tachi wa señsee ni ree o shita. (生徒たちは先生に礼をした) The pupils *bowed* to the teacher. (⇨ aisatsu)

re᛬e⁴ れい (零) *n.* zero; naught. (⇨ zero)

re᛬eboo れいぼう (冷房) *n.* air conditioning.
reeboo suru (〜する) *vt.* air-condition. (↔ dañboo)

re᛬ebuñ れいぶん (例文) *n.* example; illustrative sentence.

re᛬egai れいがい (例外) *n.* exception.

re᛬egi れいぎ (礼儀) *n.* manners; courtesy; politeness:
Ano hito wa reegi o shiranai. (あの人は礼儀を知らない) He does not understand the meaning of *manners*.

re᛬eka れいか (零下) *n.* below zero: reeka juugo-do (零下15度) fifteen degrees *below zero*.

re᛬ekiñ れいきん (礼金) *n.* reward; fee; thank-you money. ★ Money given to the landlord when renting an apartment or house. It is not refundable. (⇨ shikikiñ; yachiñ)

re᛬ekoku れいこく (冷酷) *a.n.* (〜 na, ni) cruel; heartless; coldhearted.

re᛬ekyaku れいきゃく (冷却) *n.* cooling; refrigeration.
reekyaku suru (〜する) *vi., vt.* cool; chill; refrigerate. (⇨ hiyasu) (↔ kanetsu)

re᛬esee れいせい (冷静) *a.n.*

(〜 na, ni) calm; cool-headed:
Haha wa itsu-mo reesee desu. (母はいつも冷静です) My mother is always *calm and composed*.

re᛬esu¹ レース *n.* race:
reesu ni katsu [makeru] (レースに勝つ[負ける]) win [lose] a *race*.

re᛬esu² レース *n.* lace:
reesu no kaateñ (レースのカーテン) a *lace* curtain.

re᛬etañ れいたん (冷淡) *a.n.* (〜 na, ni) cold; indifferent; coldhearted.

re᛬etoo れいとう (冷凍) *n.* freezing; refrigeration:
reetoo-niku (冷凍肉) *frozen* meat.
reetoo suru (〜する) *vt.* freeze; refrigerate. (⇨ reezoo)

re᛬eto᛬oko れいとうこ (冷凍庫) *n.* freezer. (⇨ reezooko)

re᛬ezoo れいぞう (冷蔵) *n.* cold storage; refrigeration.
reezoo suru (〜する) *vt.* refrigerate. (⇨ reetoo)

re᛬ezo᛬oko れいぞうこ (冷蔵庫) *n.* refrigerator; icebox. (⇨ reetooko)

-reki れき (歴) *suf.* career; experience; history:
gaku-reki (学歴) one's academic *career* / shoku-reki (職歴) one's working *experience*.

re᛬ekishi れきし (歴史) *n.* history. ★ 'Nihoñ no rekishi' is often shortened to 'Nihoñ-shi.'

re᛬ekishi-teki れきしてき (歴史的) *a.n.* (〜 na, ni) historic:
rekishi-teki ni yuumee na tera (歴史的に有名な寺) a *historically* famous temple. (⇨ rekishi)

re᛬ako᛬odo レコード *n.* record; disk: rekoodo o kakeru (レコードをかける) play a *record*.

re᛬amoñ レモン *n.* lemon. ★ In Japan the word suggests something fresh and pleasant.

re᛬añai れんあい (恋愛) *n.* love:
Futari wa reñai-chuu desu. (二人は恋愛中です) Those two *are in love*.
reñai suru (〜する) *vi.* fall in love.

re￣ñga れんが (煉瓦) n. brick.

re￣ñgoo れんごう (連合) n. coalition; alliance; union: reñgoo-koku (連合国) the *Allied* Powers.
reñgoo suru (〜する) vi., vt. combine; ally; unite.

re￣ñjitsu れんじつ (連日) adv. (〜 no) every day; day after day. (⇨ mainichi)

re￣ñpoo れんぼう (連邦) n. federation; union: reñpoo-seefu (連邦政府) a *federal* government.

re￣ñraku れんらく (連絡) n. connection; contact.
reñraku suru (〜する) vi., vt. connect; contact; get in touch.

re￣ñshuu れんしゅう (練習) n. practice; drill; exercise; training; rehearsal:
reñshuu-*mondai* (練習問題) a *practice* exercise [drill].
reñshuu suru (〜する) vt. practice; drill; train; rehearse.

re￣ñsoo れんそう (連想) n. association of ideas.
reñsoo suru (〜する) vt. remind; bring to mind; associate.

re￣ñtai-hoshooniñ れんたいほしょうにん (連帯保証人) n. surety; person who accepts responsibility for another.

re￣ñtogeñ レントゲン n. X-rays; Roentgen rays.

re￣ñzoku れんぞく (連続) n. continuation; succession; series.
reñzoku suru (〜する) vi. continue; go on; last. (⇨ tsuzuku)

re￣ñzu レンズ n. lens:
totsu [oo] reñzu (凸[凹]レンズ) a convex [concave] *lens*.

re￣po￣oto レポート n. 1 term paper; written report. ★ Students commonly call their term papers '*repooto*.' (⇨ roñbuñ)
2 news report.
repooto suru (〜する) vt. report (for a newspaper); cover.

-re·ru れる infl. end. (-re-te Ⅴ) [attached to the negative base of a consonant-stem verb, and itself inflected like a vowel-stem verb. '*Suru*' becomes '*sareru*.'] (⇨ -rareru; sareru)
1 (indicates the passive) be...-ed: Watashi wa inu ni te o kamareta. (私は犬に手をかまれた) I *was bitten* on the hand by a dog.
2 (indicates a sense of suffering, loss, etc.): ★ Usually used with reference to unfavorable occurrences.
Yuube wa akañboo ni nakarete, yoku nemurenakatta. (夕べは赤ん坊に泣かれて、よく眠れなかった) I could not sleep well last night because the baby was crying.
3 (indicates the potential) can: Kono saki wa ikaremaseñ. (この先は行けません) You *cannot go* any further than this.
4 (indicates the natural potential): ★ Used when something naturally or involuntarily comes to mind.
Koñdo no shiai de wa kare no katsuyaku ga kitai sareru. (今度の試合では彼の活躍が期待される) A remarkable performance *is expected* of him in the coming match.
5 (indicates the honorific): Shachoo wa moo kitaku saremashita. (社長はもう帰宅されました) The president *has* already *left* for home.

re￣ssee れっせい (劣勢) n. inferiority; inferior position.
— a.n. (〜 na, ni) inferior. (↔ yuusee) (⇨ otoru)

re￣ssha れっしゃ (列車) n. railroad [railway] train. ★ Usually refers to a long-distance train. (⇨ deñsha; kisha²)

re￣tsu れつ (列) n. row; line; queue. (⇨ gyooretsu)

-retsu れつ (列) suf. counter for rows or columns:
zeñ-retsu (前列) the front *row* / koo-retsu (後列) the back *row* / Yoko ni ichi-retsu ni narabi nasai. (横に1列に並びなさい) Please get

into one *line* across.

re⌐tteru レッテル *n.* label:
'*gekiyaku*' *no* retteru (「劇薬」のレ
ッテル) a *label* of 'poison' / *Kare
wa kechi da to iu* retteru *o hara-
rete iru.* (彼はけちだというレッテルをはら
れている) He *is labeled* as a stingy
man.

re⌐ttoo¹ れっとう (列島) *n.* chain
of islands; archipelago:
Nihoñ rettoo (日本列島) the Japanese *Archipelago.* (⇨ guñtoo)

re⌐ttoo² れっとう (劣等) *n.* inferiority; low grade:
rettoo-*kañ* (劣等感) an *inferiority*
complex / rettoo-*see* (劣等生) a
poor student.

ri⌐eki りえき (利益) *n.* 1 profit;
gains:
juumañ-eñ no rieki *o eru* (10万円
の利益を得る) make a *profit* of
100,000 yen. (↔ kessoñ)
(⇨ mooke; saisañ)
2 benefit; good:
Kono torihiki ga otagai no rieki *ni
naru koto o nozomimasu.* (この取引
がお互いの利益になることを望みます) I
hope this business will prove of
mutual *benefit.*

ri⌐juñ りじゅん (利潤) *n.* profit:
rijuñ *o tsuikyuu suru* (利潤を追求す
る) pursue *profits.* (⇨ rieki)

ri⌐ka りか (理科) *n.* 1 science;
natural science.
2 the department of science:
Kare wa rika-kee *ni susuñda.* (彼は
理科系に進んだ) He took the *science
course.* (⇨ buñka²)

ri⌐kai りかい (理解) *n.* understanding; appreciation. (↔ murikai)
rikai suru (〜する) *vt.* understand; appreciate. (⇨ wakaru)

ri⌐kishi りきし (力士) *n.* sumo
wrestler. (⇨ sumoo)

ri⌐koñ りこん (離婚) *n.* divorce.
rikoñ suru (〜する) *vi.* get divorced. (⇨ bekkyo)

ri⌐koo りこう (利口) *a.n.* (〜 na,
ni) clever; wise; smart:
Kono inu wa totemo rikoo *desu.*

(この犬はとても利口です) This dog is
very *intelligent.* (⇨ kashikoi)

ri⌐ku りく (陸) *n.* land; shore.
(↔ umi')

ri⌐ku⌐guñ りくぐん (陸軍) *n.* army.
(⇨ Jieetai; kaiguñ; kuuguñ)

ri⌐kujoo りくじょう (陸上) *n.*
1 land; shore:
Rikujoo *o itta hoo ga añzeñ desu.*
(陸上を行ったほうが安全です) It is
safer to go by *land.* (⇨ kaijoo²)
2 = rikujoo-kyoogi.

ri⌐kujoo-kyo⌐ogi りくじょうきょう
ぎ (陸上競技) *n.* track and field;
track-and-field events:
rikujoo-kyoogi-*joo* (陸上競技場) an
athletic field.

ri⌐kutsu りくつ (理屈) *n.* 1 reason; logic:
Kare no iu koto wa rikutsu *ni atte
iru.* (彼の言うことは理屈に合っている)
What he says is in conformity
with *logic.*
2 argument:
Kare wa nañ ni de mo rikutsu *o iu.*
(彼は何にでも理屈を言う) He puts
forth an *argument* about everything.

ri⌐ñgo りんご (林檎) *n.* apple.

ri⌐ñji りんじ (臨時) *n.* 1 special;
extraordinary:
riñji-*ressha* (臨時列車) a *special*
train / riñji-*kyuugyoo* (臨時休業)
an *unscheduled* holiday.
2 temporary; provisional:
riñji *no shigoto* (臨時の仕事) a *temporary* job. (⇨ riñji ni)

ri⌐ñjiñ りんじん (隣人) *n.* one's
neighbor; people in the neighborhood.

ri⌐ñji ni りんじに (臨時に) *adv.* temporarily; specially; provisionally:
Kare o riñji ni *yatotta.* (彼を臨時に
雇った) We employed him *temporarily.* (⇨ riñji)

ri⌐ppa りっぱ (立派) *a.n.* (〜 na,
ni) 1 respectable; worthy;
praiseworthy; honorable.
(⇨ erai')
2 wonderful; magnificent; splen-

did; excellent.

ri￟ppoo¹ りっぽう（立方）*n.* cube: *go*-rippoo-*meetoru* (5 立方メートル) five *cubic* meters. (↔ heehoo)

ri￟ppoo² りっぽう（立法）*n.* law making; legislation: Rippoo-*kikañ wa kokkai desu.* (立法機関は国会です) The *legislative* organ is the Diet. (⇨ sañkeñ-buñritsu)

ri￟reki りれき（履歴）*n.* one's personal history; one's career. (⇨ keereki)

ri￟re￟kisho りれきしょ（履歴書）*n.* personal history; curriculum vitae.

ri￟riku りりく（離陸）*n.* takeoff (of an airplane). ririku suru (～する) *vi.* take off. (↔ chakuriku)

ri￟roñ りろん（理論）*n.* theory: riroñ *o jissai ni ooyoo suru* (理論を実際に応用する) apply *theory* to practice.

ri￟see りせい（理性）*n.* reason: risee *o ushinau* (理性を失う) lose one's *reason*.

ri￟shi りし（利子）*n.* interest: Tooza-yokiñ *ni wa* rishi *ga tsukanai.* (当座預金には利子がつかない) A checking account yields no *interest*. (↔ gañkiñ)

ri￟soku りそく（利息）*n.* = rishi.

ri￟soo りそう（理想）*n.* ideal: takai risoo *o idaku* (高い理想を抱く) have lofty *ideals*.

ri￟soo-teki りそうてき（理想的）*a.n.* (～ na, ni) ideal: Kono basho wa teñtai-kañsoku ni risoo-teki *da.* (この場所は天体観測に理想的だ) This spot is *ideal* for astronomical observations.

ri￟sshiñ-shusse りっしんしゅっせ（立身出世）*n.* success in life. risshiñ-shusse suru (～する) *vi.* succeed in life; get ahead in life. (⇨ shusse)

-ritsu りつ（率）*suf.* rate; percentage; proportion: shitsugyoo-ritsu (失業率) the un-

employment *rate* / toohyoo-ritsu (投票率) the voter *turnout*. (⇨ wariai)

ri￟ttaa リッター *n.* liter. ★ Often used when referring to gasoline. (⇨ rittoru)

ri￟ttai りったい（立体）*n.* three-dimensional object; solid.

ri￟ttai-ko￟osa りったいこうさ（立体交差）*n.* two-level crossing; overpass system.

ri￟ttai-teki りったいてき（立体的）*a.n.* (～ na, ni) solid; three-dimensional.

ri￟ttoru リットル（立）*n.* liter: mizu *ni*-rittoru (水 2 リットル) two *liters* of water. (⇨ rittaa)

ri￟yoo りよう（利用）*n.* use; utilization. riyoo suru (～する) *vt.* use; utilize; make use of; take advantage of. (⇨ tsukau)

ri￟yuu りゆう（理由）*n.* reason; cause; grounds. (⇨ wake)

ro￟kka￟kukee ろっかくけい（六角形）*n.* hexagon.

ro￟kotsu ろこつ（露骨）*a.n.* (～ na, ni) candid; plain; open; outspoken: Kare wa rokotsu *ni fumañ o arawashita.* (彼は露骨に不満を表した) He expressed his dissatisfaction *openly*.

ro￟ku ろく（六）*n.* six. (⇨ muttsu; APP. 3)

ro￟ku-gatsu ろくがつ（六月）*n.* June. (⇨ APP. 5)

ro￟kumaku ろくまく（肋膜）*n.* pleura.

ro￟ku-na ろくな（碌な）*attrib.* (with a negative) (no) good: Kotoshi wa roku-na koto *ga nakatta.* (今年はろくなことがなかった) *Nothing good* has happened to me this year.

ro￟ku ni ろくに（碌に）*adv.* (with a negative) (not) well; (not) properly; hardly: Kyoo wa isogashikute, roku ni sho-kuji *o shite imaseñ.* (きょうは忙しくて、

ろくに食事をしていません) I have been so busy today that I haven't eaten *properly*. (⇨ rokuroku)

ro「kuoñ ろくおん (録音) *n.* recording; transcription.

　rokuoñ suru (〜する) *vt.* record; tape.

ro「kuroku ろくろく *adv.* (with a negative) (not) well; hardly; scarcely:

　Yuube wa rokuroku *nenakatta.* (ゆうべはろくろく寝なかった) I slept *badly* last night. (⇨ roku ni)

-roñ ろん (論) *suf.* theory; essay; comment:

　*kyooiku-*roñ (教育論) educational *theory* / *buñgaku-*roñ (文学論) an *essay* on literature.

ro「ñbuñ ろんぶん (論文) *n.* essay; thesis; paper:

　*hakase-*roñbuñ (博士論文) a doctoral *dissertation*. (⇨ repooto)

ro「ñji-ru ろんじる (論じる) *vt.* (roñji-te Ⅴ) discuss; argue; treat.

ro「ñri ろんり (論理) *n.* logic:

　Kimi no roñri *ni wa tsuite ikemaseñ.* (君の論理にはついていけません) I cannot follow your *logic*.

ro「ñri-teki ろんりてき (論理的) *a.n.* (〜 na, ni) logical:

　Kare wa roñri-teki *na setsumee o shita.* (彼は論理的な説明をした) He gave a *logical* explanation.

ro「o ろう (労) *n.* labor; pains; trouble:

　Kanojo wa kesshite roo *o oshimanai.* (彼女は決して労を惜しまない) She never spares *pains*.

ro「odoo ろうどう (労働) *n.* (manual) labor; work:

　roodoo-*jikañ* [*jookeñ*] (労働時間 [条件]) *working* hours [conditions].

　roodoo suru (〜する) *vi.* labor; work. (⇨ hataraku)

ro「odoo-ku「miai ろうどうくみあい (労働組合) *n.* labor union; trade union. (⇨ kumiai)

ro「odo「osha ろうどうしゃ (労働者) *n.* laborer; worker.

ro「ogo ろうご (老後) *n.* one's old age.

ro「ohi ろうひ (浪費) *n.* waste; extravagance. (⇨ muda)

　roohi suru (〜する) *vt.* waste. (↔ setsuyaku)

ro「ojiñ ろうじん (老人) *n.* old people; aged man [woman]; the aged. (↔ wakamono)

ro「ojiñ-ho「omu ろうじんホーム (老人ホーム) *n.* home for old people; nursing home for the aged.

ro「oka ろうか (廊下) *n.* corridor; passage.

ro「oma「ji ローマじ (羅馬字) *n.* Roman letters; Roman alphabet. (⇨ inside front cover)

ro「oryoku ろうりょく (労力) *n.* labor; effort; service.

ro「oso「ku ろうそく (蠟燭) *n.* candle; taper.

ro「shutsu ろしゅつ (露出) *n.*

　1 outcropping:

　iwa no roshutsu (岩の露出) an *outcropping* of rock.

　2 exposure:

　Kono shashiñ wa roshutsu *ga fusoku shite iru.* (この写真は露出が不足している) This picture is *underexposed*.

　roshutsu suru (〜する) *vt.* expose; bare: *hada o* roshutsu *suru* (肌を露出する) *bare* one's body.

ru「i るい (類) *n.* kind; sort. (⇨ shurui)

ru「iji るいじ (類似) *n.* similarity; likeness; resemblance.

　ruiji suru (〜する) *vi.* be similar [alike]; resemble. (⇨ niru²)

ru「su るす (留守) *n.* absence:

　Chichi wa rusu *desu.* (父は留守です) My father *is not at home* now.

ru「subañ るすばん (留守番) *n.* looking after the house during a person's absence.

rya「ku りゃく (略) *n.* abbreviation; omission. (⇨ shooryaku; tañshuku)

rya「kugo りゃくご (略語) *n.* abbreviated word; abbreviation.

rya`ku¹s·u** りゃくす (略す) vt. (rya-kush·i·; ryakus·a·; ryakush·i·te C) abbreviate. (⇨ shooryaku)

ryo`hi りょひ (旅費) n. traveling expenses.

ryo`kaku りょかく (旅客) n. passenger; traveler. ★ Also pronounced 'ryokyaku.'

ryo`ka¹kuki りょかくき (旅客機) n. passenger plane. ★ Also pronounced 'ryokakki.'

ryo`kañ りょかん (旅館) n. Japanese inn. ★ The rooms have tatami floors, and the rate usually includes breakfast and dinner. (⇨ yado; yadoya)

ryo`keñ りょけん (旅券) n. passport. (⇨ pasupooto)

ryo`koo りょこう (旅行) n. trip; journey; tour; travel. (⇨ tabi¹)
ryokoo suru (～する) vi. travel; make a trip.

-ryoku りょく (力) suf. power: sui-ryoku (水力) hydraulic power / seeji-ryoku (政治力) political power.

ryo`kucha りょくちゃ (緑茶) n. green tea. (⇨ o-cha)

ryo`kyaku りょきゃく (旅客) n. = ryokaku.

ryo¹o¹ りょう (量) n. 1 quantity; amount. (↔ shitsu) (⇨ buñryoo)
2 volume:
Kootsuu no ryoo ga sañ-neñ de ni-bai ni natta. (交通の量が3年で2倍になった) The volume of traffic doubled in three years.

ryo¹o² りょう (寮) n. dormitory.

ryo¹o³ りょう (良) n. (of a grade rating) being good or satisfactory; B or C in schoolwork. (⇨ ka²; yuu²)

ryo¹o⁴ りょう (猟) n. shooting; hunting: ryoo ni dekakeru (猟に出かける) go shooting [hunting].

ryo¹o⁵ りょう (漁) n. 1 fishing; fishery: ryoo ni iku (漁に行く) go fishing.
2 catch:
Kyoo wa ryoo ga sukunakatta. (き

ょうは漁が少なかった) We had a poor catch today.

ryo¹o- りょう (両) pref. both: ryoo-koku (両国) both countries / ryoo-niñ (両人) both people.

-ryoo りょう (料) suf. charge; fee; rate:
deñwa-ryoo (電話料) a telephone charge / jugyoo-ryoo (授業料) a tuition fee. (⇨ -chiñ; -dai²)

ryo`oashi りょうあし (両足) n. both feet [legs]. (⇨ ryoote)

ryo¹odo りょうど (領土) n. territory; possession; domain:
Kono shima wa Nihoñ no ryoodo desu. (この島は日本の領土です) This island is Japanese territory.

ryo`ogae りょうがえ (両替) n. money exchange.
ryoogae suru (～する) vt. exchange (dollars into yen); change.

ryo`ogawa りょうがわ (両側) n. both sides. (⇨ katagawa)

ryo`ohashi りょうはし (両端) n. both ends. (⇨ katahashi)

ryo`oho¹o りょうほう (両方) n. both; both parties [sides]:
Kare wa jookañ gekañ, ryoohoo tomo yoñde shimatta. (彼は上巻下巻, 両方とも読んでしまった) He read both Volume 1 and Volume 2. (⇨ katahoo)

ryo¹oji りょうじ (領事) n. consul.

ryo`oji¹kañ りょうじかん (領事館) n. consulate.

ryo`okai¹ りょうかい (了解) n. understanding; agreement; consent: ryookai o eru [motomeru] (了解を得る[求める]) obtain [ask for] a person's consent.
ryookai suru (～する) vt. understand; consent.

ryo`okai² りょうかい (領海) n. territorial waters.

ryo`okiñ りょうきん (料金) n. rate; charge; fee; fare. (⇨ daikiñ; uñchiñ)

ryo`okoo りょうこう (良好) a.n. (～ na, ni) good; excellent; satisfactory:

Kotoshi no kome no shuukaku wa ryookoo deshita. (今年の米の収穫は良好でした) The rice harvest this year was *excellent*. (⇨ yoi¹)

ryoˈori りょうり (料理) *n.* cooking; cookery; cuisine; dish; food.
　ryoori suru (～する) *vt.* cook; prepare. (⇨ suiji)

ryoˈosañ りょうさん (量産) *n.* mass production.
　ryoosañ suru (～する) *vt.* massproduce.

ryoˈosha りょうしゃ (両者) *n.* both of the two people; each other: *Ryoosha no setsumee ga kuichigatte ita.* (両者の説明が食い違っていた) Their accounts contradicted *each other*.

ryoˈoshi りょうし (漁師) *n.* fisherman.

ryoˈoshiñ¹ りょうしん (両親) *n.* one's parents.

ryoˈoshiñ² りょうしん (良心) *n.* conscience: *Ryooshiñ ni yamashii koto wa arimaseñ.* (良心にやましいことはありません) I have a clear *conscience*.

ryoˈoshu りょうしゅ (領主) *n.* feudal lord.

ryoˈoshuusho りょうしゅうしょ (領収書) *n.* receipt: *Ryooshuusho o moraemasu ka?* (領収書をもらえますか) May I have a *receipt*, please? (⇨ uketori)

ryoˈoshuushoo りょうしゅうしょう (領収証) *n.* voucher; receipt.

ryoˈote りょうて (両手) *n.* both hands; both arms. (⇨ katate; ryooashi)

ryuˈu りゅう (龍) *n.* dragon.

-ryuu りゅう (流) *suf.* **1** style; type; way:
　jiko-ryuu (自己流) one's own *way*

(of doing things).
　2 class; rate; grade: *ichi*-ryuu (一流) first *class* / *ni*-ryuu (二流) second *rate* / *chuu*-ryuu (中流) middle *grade* / *joo*-ryuu (上流) upper *class*.
　3 flow; stream; current: *deñ*-ryuu (電流) electric *current* / *shi*-ryuu (支流) a *tributary*.

ryuˈuchijoo りゅうちじょう (留置場) *n.* detention house; lockup.

ryuˈudoˈoshoku りゅうどうしょく (流動食) *n.* liquid food [diet].

ryuˈugaku りゅうがく (留学) *n.* studying abroad.
　ryuugaku suru (～する) *vi.* study abroad; go abroad for study.

ryuˈugaˈkusee りゅうがくせい (留学生) *n.* student studying abroad; foreign student.

ryuˈuhyoo りゅうひょう (流氷) *n.* drift ice; ice floe.

ryuˈukañ りゅうかん (流感) *n.* influenza; flu: *ryuukañ ni kakaru* (流感にかかる) catch *influenza*.

ryuˈukoo りゅうこう (流行) *n.* fashion; vogue; popularity: *ryuukoo-ka* (流行歌) a *popular* song.
　ryuukoo suru (～する) *vi.* come into fashion; be in fashion; be popular.

ryuˈuneñ りゅうねん (留年) *n.* remaining in the same class.
　ryuuneñ suru (～する) *vi.* repeat the same class for another year. (⇨ rakudai)

ryuˈuniñ りゅうにん (留任) *n.* remaining in office.
　ryuuniñ suru (～する) *vi.* remain in office.

S

sa¹ さ(差) *n.* difference; gap; margin:
sedai no sa (世代の差) a generation *gap*. (⇨ chigai)

sa² さ *p.* 1 (used when casually emphasizing one's thoughts or opinions):
Kyoo dekinakereba, ashita suru sa. (きょうできなければ, あしたするさ) If I can't do it today, *well* then, I'll do it tomorrow.
2 (used to indicate a strong reaction):
Nani o baka na koto o itte iru no sa. (何をばかなことを言っているのさ) What nonsense you are talking!
3 (used after a phrase to hold the attention of the listener):
Kono aida karita hoñ sa, moo yoñjatta. (この間借りた本さ, もう読んじゃった) The book I borrowed from you the other day... *Well*, I've already read it.

-sa さ *suf.* (*n.*) [added to the stem of an adjective or to an adjectival noun to form a noun] atsu-sa (暑さ) *heat* / seekaku-sa (正確さ) *exactness*.

saa さあ *int.* now; here; well; come on:
Saa, hajimeyoo. (さあ, 始めよう) *Okay*, let's start. (⇨ sate)

saabisu サービス *n.* 1 service:
Kono ryokañ wa saabisu ga yoi [warui]. (この旅館はサービスが良い[悪い]) The *service* at this Japanese inn is good [poor].
2 discount; no charge; extra:
Kono eñpitsu o saabisu ni agemasu. (この鉛筆をサービスにあげます) I will throw in this pencil as an *extra*.

saabisu (o) suru (〜を(を)する) *vi., vt.* 1 give a service; attend to.
2 make a discount; give away for nothing.

saabisuryoo サービスりょう(サービス料) *n.* service charge.

saakuru サークル *n.* club:
saakuru-*katsudoo* (サークル活動) *club* activities (at college).

sabaku さばく(砂漠) *n.* desert.

sabi さび(錆び) *n.* rust; tarnish.

sabi·ru さびる(錆びる) *vi.* (sabite Ⓥ) rust; get rusty. (⇨ sabi)

sabishii さびしい(寂しい; 淋しい) *a.* (-ku) lonely; forlorn; deserted. (↔ nigiyaka) (⇨ wabishii)

saboru サボる *vt.* (sabor·i-; sabor·a-; sabot-te Ⓒ) (*colloq.*) play truant [hooky]; loaf on the job; cut classes.

saboteñ サボテン(仙人掌) *n.* cactus. ★ Sometimes pronounced '*shaboteñ*.'

sadamar·u さだまる(定まる) *vi.* (sadamar·i-; sadamar·a-; sadamat-te Ⓒ) be decided; be fixed:
Kono natsu wa teñkoo ga sadamaranai. (この夏は天候が定まらない) This summer the weather *is* quite *changeable*. (⇨ sadameru)

sadame·ru さだめる(定める) *vt.* (sadame-te Ⓥ) 1 provide; stipulate; lay down (a rule).
2 decide (an aim, goal, etc.); fix; set. (⇨ sadamaru)

sadoo さどう(茶道) *n.* tea ceremony. (⇨ cha-no-yu)

sae さえ *p.* (not) even:
★ Used for extreme examples.
Ichi-nichi-juu tabemono wa mochiroñ, mizu sae kuchi ni shinakatta. (一日中食べ物はもちろん, 水さえ口にしなかった) No food of course, but not *even* water, passed my lips all day long.

sae ...-ba [-tara] (〜...ば[たら]) (just) as long as; if only: ★ Used to indicate an emphatic condition. *O-kane sae areba, nañ de mo dekiru.*(お金さえあれば、何でもできる) *Just as long as you have* money, you can do anything.

sa⌈egi⌉r·u さえぎる (遮る) *vt.* (saegir·i-; saegir·a-; saegir·te [C]) interrupt; obstruct; block: *kaateñ de hikari o saegiru*(カーテンで光をさえぎる) *block out* the light with a curtain.

sa⌈ezu⌉r·u さえずる (囀る) *vi.* (saezur·i-; saezur·a-; saezur·te [C]) (of a bird) sing; twitter; chirp; warble. ((⇨ naku²)

sa⌈ga⌉r·u さがる (下がる) *vi.* (sagar·i-; sagar·a-; sagar·te [C]) 1 go down; fall; lower; drop: *Kioñ ga kyuu ni sagatta.*(気温が急に下がった) The temperature *has* suddenly *gone down.* ((↔ agaru) ((⇨ sageru)
2 step back; stand back.

sa⌈gas·u さがす (捜す・探す) *vt.* (sagash·i-; sagas·a-; sagash·i-te [C]) look for; seek; search.

sa⌈ge⌉·ru さげる (下げる) *vt.* (sage·te [V]) 1 lower; pull down: *nedañ o sageru*(値段を下げる) *lower* the price. ((↔ ageru¹) ((⇨ sagaru)
2 hang; wear (a pendant). ((⇨ sagaru)
3 move back; draw back: *teeburu o ushiro e sageru*(テーブルを後ろへ下げる) *move* a table *back.*
4 clear away (dishes); take away.

sa⌈gi⌉¹ さぎ (詐欺) *n.* fraud; swindle; deception: *sagi o hataraku*(詐欺を働く) practice a *deception.* ((⇨ damasu)

sa⌈gi⌉² さぎ (鷺) *n.* heron.

sa⌈gur·u さぐる (探る) *vt.* (sagur·i-; sagur·a-; sagur·te [C]) 1 grope for; fumble for; feel for: *poketto o saguru*(ポケットを探る) *fumble* in one's pocket.
2 sound out (a person's intention); feel out.

sa⌈gyoo さぎょう (作業) *n.* (factory) work; operation.

sagyoo suru (～する) *vi.* work.

sa⌈i⌉ さい (際) *n.* time; occasion: *Hijoo no sai wa kono botañ o oshite kudasai.*(非常の際はこのボタンを押してください) Press this button in *case* of emergency. ((⇨ toki)

sa⌈i-⌉¹ さい (再) *pref.* re-; again: *sai-nyuukoku*(再入国) re-entry into a country / sai-*koñ*(再婚) re-marriage.

sa⌈i-⌉² さい (最) *pref.* (often translated into English as most..., -est): *sai-dai*(最大) the larg*est* / sai-*shoo*(最小) the small*est* / sai-zeñ (最善) the *best* / sai-aku (最悪) the *worst.*

-sai¹ さい (歳) *suf.* age; years old: *Haha wa juuhas-sai de kekkoñ shimashita.*(母は18歳で結婚しました) My mother married at the *age* of eighteen.

-sai² さい (祭) *suf.* festival; anniversary: *gojuu-neñ-sai*(50年祭) the fiftieth *anniversary* / buñka-sai (文化祭) a cultural *festival.*

sa⌈ibai さいばい (栽培) *n.* growing; cultivation. **saibai suru** (～する) *vt.* grow; raise; cultivate: *oñshitsu de bara o saibai suru*(温室でばらを栽培する) *grow* roses in a greenhouse.

sa⌈ibañ さいばん (裁判) *n.* trial; judgment; court. ((⇨ soshoo)

sa⌈iba⌉ñkañ さいばんかん (裁判官) *n.* judge.

sa⌈ibañsho さいばんしょ (裁判所) *n.* courthouse; a court of justice.

sa⌈iboo さいぼう (細胞) *n.* (of biology) cell.

sa⌈ichuu さいちゅう (最中) *n.* (in) the middle (of): *Eñkai no saichuu ni kare wa seki o tatta.*(宴会の最中に彼は席を立った) He left his seat in the *middle* of the party. ((⇨ massaichuu)

sa⌈idaa サイダー *n.* soda pop. ★ From English 'cider,' but not made from apples and non-alcoholic.

sa⌐idai さいだい (最大) *n.* the largest [biggest]; the greatest; maximum. (↔ saishoo¹)

sa⌐ifu さいふ (財布) *n.* wallet; (coin) purse.

sa⌐igai さいがい (災害) *n.* disaster; calamity:
saigai *o* koomuru (災害を被る) suffer from a *disaster* / saigai-chi (災害地) a *disaster* area.

sa⌐igo¹ さいご (最後) *n.* **1** the last; the end:
Kore ga saigo no chañsu desu. (これが最後のチャンスです) This is the *last* chance. (↔ saisho)
2 once: ★ Used like a conjunction.
Kare ni kane o kashitara saigo, kaeshite moraemaseñ. (彼に金を貸したら最後, 返してもらえません) *Once* you lend him money, you can never get it back.

sa⌐igo² さいご (最期) *n.* end of one's life:
hisañ na saigo o togeru (悲惨な最期を遂げる) *die* in misery.

sa⌐ihoo さいほう (裁縫) *n.* sewing; needlework.

sa⌐ijitsu さいじつ (祭日) *n.* national holiday; festival day. (⇨ APP. 6)

sa⌐ijoo さいじょう (最上) *n.* the best: saijoo *no shina* (最上の品) the *highest* quality article. (↔ saitee) (⇨ saikoo)

sa⌐ikai さいかい (再開) *n.* reopening; resumption.
saikai suru (〜する) *vt.* reopen; resume: Kaigi *wa gogo ni-ji ni* saikai saremasu. (会議は午後2時に再開されます) The meeting will *be reconvened* at 2:00 P.M.

sa⌐ikeñ さいけん (再建) *n.* reconstruction; rebuilding.
saikeñ suru (〜する) *vt.* reconstruct; rebuild.

sa⌐ikiñ¹ さいきん (最近) *n.* recent date.
— *adv.* recently; lately:
Saikiñ *yatto Nihoñgo no shiñbuñ*
ga yomeru yoo ni narimashita. (最近やっと日本語の新聞が読めるようになりました) Just *recently*, I have at last become able to read Japanese newspapers. (⇨ kono-goro)

sa⌐ikiñ² さいきん (細菌) *n.* germ; bacteria. (⇨ baikiñ)

sa⌐ikoo さいこう (最高) *n.* **1** the highest:
Kyoo wa kotoshi saikoo no atsusa datta. (きょうは今年最高の暑さだった) Today it was the *highest* temperature of the year. (↔ saitee)
2 best; supreme; maximum: saikoo *sokudo* (最高速度) the *maximum* speed.

Sa⌐iko⌐osai さいこうさい (最高裁) *n.* Supreme Court. ★ Shortened form of 'Saikoo-saibañsho.'

Sa⌐ikoo-saibañsho さいこうさいばんしょ (最高裁判所) *n.* Supreme Court.

sa⌐iku さいく (細工) *n.* **1** work; workmanship:
Kono kagu no saiku wa subarashii. (この家具の細工はすばらしい) The *workmanship* of this furniture is excellent.
2 artifice; tactics:
Ano hito no saiku wa te ga koñde iru. (あの人の細工は手が込んでいる) He uses very skillful *tactics*.

sa⌐iñ サイン *n.* **1** signature; autograph. ★ Comes from English 'sign,' but used as a noun in Japanese. (⇨ shomee)
2 sign; signal:
rañnaa ni toorui no saiñ o dasu (in baseball) (ランナーに盗塁のサインを出す) *signal* a runner to steal.
saiñ suru (〜する) *vi.* sign; autograph.

sa⌐inañ さいなん (災難) *n.* misfortune; disaster; accident:
sainañ ni au (災難にあう) meet with a *misfortune*.

sa⌐inoo さいのう (才能) *n.* ability; talent; gift:
sainoo o hakki suru (才能を発揮する) give full play to one's *ability*.

sa⌐isañ さいさん (採算) n. profit; gain:
saisañ ga toreru [torenai] (採算がとれる[とれない]) be profitable [unprofitable]. (⇨ rieki)

sa⌐iseñ さいせん (賽銭) n. offertory; money offering.

sa⌐ishi さいし (妻子) n. one's wife and children; a man's family.

sa⌐ishite さいして (際して) on the occasion of:
Shuppatsu ni saishite señsee kara chuui ga atta. (出発に際して先生から注意があった) The teacher gave us advice when we were going to depart.

sa⌐isho さいしょ (最初) n. 1 beginning; start:
hoñ o saisho kara saigo made yomu (本を最初から最後まで読む) read a book from beginning to end. (↔ saigo')
2 (the) first:
Saisho ni hatsugeñ shita no wa Yamada-sañ desu. (最初に発言したのは山田さんです) It was Mr. Yamada who spoke first.

sa⌐ishoku さいしょく (菜食) n. vegetable diet.
saishoku suru (〜する) vi. live on vegetables.

sa⌐ishoo[1] さいしょう (最小) n. the smallest; minimum. (↔ saidai)

sa⌐ishoo[2] さいしょう (最少) n. the least; the smallest. (⇨ saitee)

sa⌐ishuu[1] さいしゅう (最終) n. the last; the final:
Kore ga saishuu no kettee desu. (これが最終の決定です) This is our final decision.

sa⌐ishuu[2] さいしゅう (採集) n. collection.
saishuu suru (〜する) vt. collect; gather: koñchuu o saishuu suru (昆虫を採集する) collect insects.

sa⌐isoku さいそく (催促) n. demand; reminder.
saisoku suru (〜する) vt. press; urge; ask: Watashi wa kare ni kashita kane no heñsai o saisoku

shita. (私は彼に貸した金の返済を催促した) I pressed him to repay the money I loaned him.

sa⌐itee さいてい (最低) n. 1 the lowest:
Señgetsu wa uriage ga saitee datta. (先月は売上が最低だった) Last month sales were the lowest.
2 the worst; minimum:
Shikeñ wa saitee no deki datta. (試験は最低の出来だった) I got the worst mark in the examination. (↔ saikoo)

sa⌐iteñ さいてん (採点) n. grading; marking; scoring.
saiteñ suru (〜する) vt. grade; mark; score: tooañ o saiteñ suru (答案を採点する) mark test papers.

sa⌐iwai さいわい (幸い) a.n. (〜 na, ni) happy; lucky; fortunate.
— adv. happily; luckily; fortunately: ★ Often used in the form '〜 ni mo.'
Saiwai (ni mo) o-teñki ni megumaremashita. (幸い(にも)お天気に恵まれました) Fortunately, we were blessed with good weather.
(⇨ shiawase)

sa⌐iyoo さいよう (採用) n. adoption; acceptance; employment.
saiyoo suru (〜する) vt. adopt; accept; employ: Sono kaisha wa joshi o juu-mee saiyoo shita. (その会社は女子を10名採用した) The company took on ten women.

sa⌐ji[1] さじ (匙) n. spoon.

sa⌐ka[1] さか (坂) n. slope; hill:
saka o noboru [oriru] (坂を上る[下りる]) go up [down] a slope.

sa⌐kae[1]・ru さかえる (栄える) vi. (sakae-te Ⅴ) prosper; flourish; thrive.

sa⌐ka[1]i さかい (境) n. border; boundary. (⇨ kyookai[1])

sa⌐kañ さかん (盛ん) a.n. (〜 na, ni) 1 prosperous; flourishing; thriving.
2 energetic; active; vigorous:
Kanojo wa ima sakañ ni e o kaite iru. (彼女は今盛んに絵をかいている)

She now *actively* paints pictures.

3 popular; enthusiastic:
Nihoñ wa yakyuu ga sakañ *desu.*
(日本は野球が盛んです) Baseball is
popular in Japan.

sa⌐kana¹ さかな (魚) *n.* fish.
(⇨ sakanaya; tsuru⌐)

sa⌐kana² さかな (肴) *n.* side dish.
★ Relishes eaten as an accompaniment to drinking.
(⇨ tsumami²)

sa⌐kanaya さかなや (魚屋) *n.*
fish dealer; fishmonger; fish
shop.

sa⌐kanobo⌐r·u さかのぼる (遡る) *vi.*
(-nobor·i-; -nobor·a-; -nobot-te
Ⓒ) **1** go [sail] upstream.
2 (of a practice, convention, custom, etc.) go back; date from.

sa⌐kari さかり (盛り) *n.* **1** the
height:
Sakura no hana wa sakari *o sugimashita.* (桜の花は盛りを過ぎました)
The cherry blossoms are now
past their *best.*
2 prime; bloom; flower:
Kare wa hataraki-zakari *ni
nakunatta.* (彼は働き盛りに亡くなった)
He died in his *prime.* ★ 'Sakari'
usually changes to 'zakari' in
compounds.
3 (of animals) heat; rut.

sa⌐kariba さかりば (盛り場) *n.* the
busiest quarters of a city; amusement quarters.

sa⌐kasa さかさ (逆さ) *n.* inver-
sion; reverse:
sakasa ni suru (逆さにする) *turn
upside down.*

sa⌐kaya さかや (酒屋) *n.* liquor
store; sake shop; sake dealer.

sa⌐kazuki¹ さかずき (杯) *n.* sake
cup. (⇨ tokkuri)

sa⌐ke¹ さけ (酒) *n.* **1** sake; fer-
mented rice beverage.
2 alcoholic drink; liquor:
Kare wa sake *ni tsuyoi [yowai].*
(彼は酒に強い[弱い]) He can [can't]
hold his *drink.*

sa⌐ke² さけ (鮭) *n.* salmon.

★ Sometimes pronounced '*shake.*'

sa⌐kebi(go⌐)e さけび(ごえ) (叫び
(声)) *n.* cry; shout; yell; scream;
shriek. (⇨ sakebu)

sa⌐keb·u さけぶ (叫ぶ) *vi.* (sake-
b·i-; sakeb·a-; sakeñ-de Ⓒ)
shout; cry out; yell; scream.
(⇨ donaru)

sa⌐ke¹·ru¹ さける (避ける) *vi.* (sa-
ke-te Ⓥ) avoid; avert; evade;
shun:
Sono jiko o sakeru *no wa fukanoo
datta.* (その事故を避けるのは不可能だっ
た) It was impossible to *avert* the
accident.

sa⌐ke¹·ru² さける (裂ける) *vi.* (sa-
ke-te Ⓥ) tear; split; rip:
Shatsu ga kugi ni hikkakatte, sa-
kete *shimatta.* (シャツがくぎに引っかか
って、裂けてしまった) My shirt got
caught on a nail and *ripped.*
(⇨ saku⌐)

sa⌐ki さき (先) *n.* **1** point; tip;
end; head:
yubi no saki (指の先) the *tip* of a
finger.
2 future:
Saki *no koto wa wakarimaseñ.* (先
のことはわかりません) I do not know
what will happen in the *future.*
3 (~ *ni*) in advance; beforehand:
Saki *ni daikiñ o haratte kudasai.*
(先に代金を払ってください) Please pay
in advance. (↔ ato⌐)
4 ahead;
Chichi wa saki *ni dekakemashita.*
(父は先に出かけました) My father left
ahead of us.
5 previous; former:
Watashi ga saki *ni nobeta-toori
yatte gorañ nasai.* (私が先に述べた通
りやってごらんなさい) Try to do it just
as I told you *previously.*

sa⌐kihodo さきほど (先程) *n., adv.*
(*formal*) a little while ago; some
time ago. ★ A little more formal
than '*sakki.*'

sa⌐kka さっか (作家) *n.* writer;
author; novelist.

sa⌐kkaa サッカー *n.* soccer; association football.

sa⌐kkaku さっかく（錯覚）*n.* illusion; imagination.
sakkaku suru (～する) *vi.* have an illusion. (⇨ gokai)

sa⌐kki さっき *n., adv.* a little while ago; some time ago. (⇨ sakihodo)

sa⌐kkyoku さっきょく（作曲）*n.* musical composition:
sakkyoku-ka (作曲家) a *composer*.
sakkyoku suru (～する) *vi., vt.* compose; write music.

sa⌐k·u[1] さく（咲く）*vi.* (sak·i-; sa-k·a-; sa·i-te Ⓒ) (of a flower) blossom; come out; bloom. (⇨ hiraku)

sa⌐k·u[2] さく（裂く）*vt.* (sak·i-; sa-k·a-; sa·i-te Ⓒ) 1 tear; split; rip; rend. (⇨ sakeru[2])
2 separate; break up (relation, friendship, etc.).

sa⌐ku[3] さく（柵）*n.* fence; railing.

sa⌐ku[4] さく（策）*n.* plan; scheme; measure; policy:
saku o neru (策を練る) carefully work out a *plan*.

sa⌐k·u[5] さく（割く）*vt.* (sak·i-; sa-k·a-; sa·i-te Ⓒ) spare (time); give:
Isogashikute zeñzeñ jikañ ga sakemaseñ. (忙しくて全然時間が割けません) I am too busy to *spare* any time.

sa⌐ku- さく（昨）*pref.* last:
saku-jitsu (昨日) *yesterday* / saku-neñ (昨年) *last* year. (↔ yoku-)

sa⌐kubañ さくばん（昨晩）*n.* (*formal*) last night; yesterday evening. (⇨ sakuya)

sa⌐kubuñ さくぶん（作文）*n.* essay; composition.

sa⌐kuhiñ さくひん（作品）*n.* work; production; creation.

sa⌐kuiñ さくいん（索引）*n.* index.

sa⌐kujitsu さくじつ（昨日）*n.* (*formal*) yesterday. (⇨ kinoo[1])

sa⌐kumotsu さくもつ（作物）*n.* crops; farm products.

sa⌐kuneñ さくねん（昨年）*n.* (*formal*) last year. (⇨ kyoneñ)

sa⌐kura さくら（桜）*n.* cherry tree; cherry blossoms. ★ The cherry blossom is Japan's national flower.

sa⌐kusee[1] さくせい（作成）*n.* drawing up; making out.
sakusee suru (～する) *vt.* draw up; make out (a contract).

sa⌐kusee[2] さくせい（作製）*n.* = seesaku[1].

sa⌐kuseñ さくせん（作戦）*n.* strategy; tactics; operations.

sa⌐kusha さくしゃ（作者）*n.* author; writer; artist.

sa⌐kushi さくし（作詞）*n.* writing a lyric [song]:
sakushi-ka [-sha] (作詞家[者]) a *songwriter*.

sa⌐ku⌐ya さくや（昨夜）*n.* last night; yesterday evening. (↔ koñya)

-sama さま（様）*suf.* ★ Polite equivalent of '*-sañ*.'
1 Mr.; Mrs.; Miss: ★ Used in formal situations but more of a written than conversational form. *Tanaka*-sama (田中様) *Mr.* [*Mrs.*; *Miss*] Tanaka.
2 (used to express respect): ★ Added to a kinship word or a name signifying a post or position.
oji-sama (おじ様) *uncle* / shichoo-sama (市長様) *mayor*.
3 (used to express appreciation): ★ Added to a word meaning labor or hard work. Not used when speaking to one's superiors, but '*-sama deshita*' is often used to superiors. (⇨ otsukaresama; gokuroosama)

sa⌐ma⌐s·u[1] さます（冷ます）*vt.* (sa-mash·i-; samas·a-; samash·i-te Ⓒ) 1 cool:
o-yu o samasu (お湯を冷ます) *cool* hot water. (⇨ sameru[1])
2 spoil; dampen:
hito no netsu o samasu (人の熱を冷

ます) *dampen* a person's enthusiasm. (⇨ sameru¹)

sa⌐ma¬s·u² さます (覚ます) *vt.* (samash·i-; samas·a-; samash·i-te [C]) **1** wake up; awake. (⇨ okiru; sameru²)
2 awaken; sober up:
Yoi o samashite kara, uñteñ shi nasai. (酔いを覚ましてから、運転しなさい) Please drive your car after you *have sobered up*. (⇨ sameru²)

sa⌐matage¬·ru さまたげる (妨げる) *vt.* (samatage-te [V]) disturb; obstruct; prevent.

sa⌐ma¬zama さまざま (様々) *a.n.* (~ na, ni) various; different; all kinds of. (⇨ iroiro¹)

sa⌐me¬·ru¹ さめる (冷める) *vi.* (same-te [V]) **1** cool; get cold. (⇨ samasu¹)
2 (of a feeling, enthusiasm, etc.) cool down.

sa⌐me¬·ru² さめる (覚める) *vi.* (same-te [V]) **1** wake up; awake.
2 come to one's senses; sober up:
Kare no kotoba de mayoi ga sameta. (彼の言葉で迷いが覚めた) His words *brought* me *to my senses*. (⇨ samasu²)

sa⌐me¬·ru³ さめる (褪める) *vi.* (same-te [V]) (of color) fade; go out: iro ga sameru (色がさめる) *be discolored*.

sa⌐mu¬·i さむい (寒い) *a.* (-ku) cold; chilly; freezing. (↔ atatakai; atsui²) (⇨ samusa; suzushii)

sa⌐muke¬ さむけ (寒気) *n.* chill; cold fit: samuke *ga suru* (寒気がする) have a *chill*.

sa⌐musa さむさ (寒さ) *n.* cold; cold weather. (↔ atsusa¹)

sa⌐ñ¬ さん (三・参) *n.* three; third: *eñpitsu* sañ-*boñ* (鉛筆 3 本) *three* pencils / sañ-*neñ* (3 年) *three* years. (⇨ APP. 3)

sa⌐ñ² さん (酸) *n.* acid. (↔ arukari)

-sañ¹ さん *suf.* **1** (used to express respect and friendliness):

★ Added to a family or given name. (⇨ -kuñ)
*Yamamoto-*sañ (山本さん) *Mr.* [*Mrs.; Miss*] Yamamoto
2 (used after a kinship word): oji-sañ (おじさん) *uncle* / oba-sañ (おばさん) *aunt*.
3 (used to express appreciation in certain set phrases): ★ Not used when speaking to one's superiors.
Otsukare-sañ. (お疲れさん) *You must be tired.* / Go-kuroo-sañ. (ご苦労さん) *Thank you for your help*. (⇨ -sama)

-sañ² さん (山) *suf,* Mount; Mt,:
★ Added to the name of a mountain. *Fuji-*sañ (富士山) *Mt*. Fuji. (⇨ -yama)

sa⌐ñbutsu さんぶつ (産物) *n.* product; produce.

sa⌐ñchi さんち (産地) *n.* producing district; production center.

sa⌐ñfujiñka さんふじんか (産婦人科) *n.* obstetrics and gynecology: sañfujiñka-i (産婦人科医) an *obstetrician and gynecologist*. (⇨ fujiñka)

sa⌐ñ-gatsu さんがつ (三月) *n.* March. (⇨ APP. 5)

Sa⌐ñgi¬iñ さんぎいん (参議院) *n.* the House of Councilors:
Sañgiiñ *giiñ* (参議院議員) a member of *the House of Councilors*. (⇨ Shuugiiñ; kokkai)

sa⌐ñgo さんご (珊瑚) *n.* coral.

sa⌐ñgyoo さんぎょう (産業) *n.* industry.

sa⌐ñka¹ さんか (参加) *n.* participation; joining.
sañka suru (~する) *vi.* participate; take part in; join. (⇨ deru (3))

sa⌐ñka² さんか (酸化) *n.* oxidation.
sañka suru (~する) *vi.* oxidize.

sa⌐ñkaku さんかく (三角) *n.* triangle. (⇨ shikaku²)

sa⌐ñka¬kukee さんかくけい (三角形) *n.* triangle.

sa⌐ñkeñ-buñritsu さんけんぶんり

つ（三権分立） *n.* separation of the three powers of administration, legislation, and judicature. (⇨ shihoo²; gyoosee; rippoo⁷)

sa⌐ñketsu さんけつ（酸欠） *n.* oxygen shortage.

sa⌐ñkoo さんこう（参考） *n.* reference; information; consultation: *Kono hoñ o* sañkoo *ni shi nasai.* （この本を参考にしなさい） You *should refer* to this book.

sa⌐ñkoosho さんこうしょ（参考書） *n.* study-aid book; student handbook; reference book.

sa⌐ñma さんま（秋刀魚） *n.* Pacific saury.

sa⌐ñmyaku さんみゃく（山脈） *n.* mountain range [chain].

sa⌐ñpai さんぱい（参拝） *n.* visit to a shrine or temple for worship.
　sañpai suru （～する） *vi.* go and worship. (⇨ omairi)

sa⌐ñpatsu さんぱつ（散髪） *n.* men's haircut; men's hairdressing. (⇨ tokoya)
　sañpatsu suru （～する） *vi.* have a haircut.

sa⌐ñpo さんぽ（散歩） *n.* walk; stroll:
　sañpo *ni iku* [*deru*]（散歩に行く[出る]) go for a *walk*.
　sañpo suru （～する） *vi.* take a walk.

sa⌐ñryuu さんりゅう（三流） *n.* third-class; third-rate. (⇨ ichiryuu; niryuu)

sa⌐ñsee¹ さんせい（賛成） *n.* agreement; approval; support; favor.
　sañsee suru （～する） *vt.* agree; approve; be in favor. (↔ hañtai)

sa⌐ñsee² さんせい（三世） *n.* Sansei; the third generation of Japanese immigrants; a member of this generation. (⇨ issee²; nisee)

sa⌐ñshoo さんしょう（参照） *n.* reference.
　sañshoo suru （～する） *vt.* see; refer to: *jiteñ o* sañshoo *suru* （辞典を参照する） *consult* a dictionary.

sa⌐ñso さんそ（酸素） *n.* oxygen.

sa⌐ñsu⌐u さんすう（算数） *n.* arithmetic. (⇨ suugaku)

sa⌐ñtoo さんとう（三等） *n.* third class; third prize; third place. (⇨ ittoo; nitoo)

sa⌐ñzañ さんざん（散々） *a.n.* (~ na) severe; terrible:
Tozañ wa ame de sañzañ *datta.* （登山は雨でさんざんだった） Our mountain climbing was *ruined* by the rain.
　— *adv.* severely; terribly:
Sono seeto wa señsee ni sañzañ *shikarareta.* （その生徒は先生にさんざんしかられた） The pupil was *severely* scolded by his teacher.

sa⌐o¹ さお（竿） *n.* pole; rod.

sa⌐ppa⌐ri¹ さっぱり *adv.* (~ suru)
1 feel refreshed:
Furo ni haittara, sappari *shita.* （ふろに入ったら、さっぱりした） I felt *nice and fresh* after taking a bath.
2 (of clothes) neat:
Kanojo wa itsu-mo sappari *shita fukusoo o shite iru.* （彼女はいつもさっぱりした服装をしている） She is always dressed *neatly*.
3 (of personality) frank; openhearted.
4 (of a dish, taste, etc.) simple; plain; light.

sa⌐ppa⌐ri² さっぱり *adv.* **1** no good:
Shikeñ no kekka wa sappari *datta.* （試験の結果はさっぱりだった） The exam result was *no good*.
2 (with a negative) not at all:
Roshiago wa sappari *wakarimaseñ.* （ロシア語はさっぱりわかりません） I do not understand Russian *at all*. (⇨ sukoshi mo)

sa⌐ra さら（皿） *n.* plate; dish; platter; saucer.

sa⌐raineñ さらいねん（再来年） *n.* the year after next. (⇨ kotoshi; raineñ)

sa⌐raishuu さらいしゅう（再来週） *n.* the week after next. (⇨ raishuu)

sa⌐ra ni さらに（更に） *adv.* further; even [still] more:

Yoru ni naru to, ame wa sara ni tsuyoku natta. (夜になると，雨はさらに強くなった) The rain became *even* heavier as night fell.

sa⌐rari¹imañ サラリーマン *n.* office worker; white-collar worker; salaried worker. ★ Refers to male workers. Female workers are often called '*oo-eru*' (OL). (⇒ oo-eru)

sa⌐rasara さらさら *adv.* (~ to) (the sound or state of moving or proceeding smoothly):
Kaze de ki no ha ga sarasara to natte iru. (風で木の葉がさらさらと鳴っている) The leaves are *rustling* in the wind.

sa⌐ra·u¹ さらう (攫う) *vt.* (sara·i-; saraw·a-; sarat-te [C]) 1 sweep away:
Kodomo ga nami ni sarawareta. (子どもが波にさらわれた) A child *was swept away* by the waves.
2 kidnap:
Kare no hitori musume ga sarawareta. (彼の一人娘がさらわれた) His only daughter *was kidnapped*.
3 carry off (a victory); win (popularity, etc.).

sa⌐ra·u² さらう (浚う) *vt.* (sara·i-; saraw·a-; sarat-te [C]) clean; dredge: *ike o sarau* (池をさらう) *dredge* a pond.

sare·ru される *vt.* (sare-te [V]) 1 (honorific equivalent of '*su-ru*'):
Señsee mo shusseki sareru soo desu. (先生も出席されるそうです) I hear that the teacher will also *be present*.
2 be done: ★ The passive of '*suru*.'
Watashi wa kare ni ijiwaru sareta. (私は彼に意地悪された) I *was treated* meanly by him.

sa⌐r·u¹ さる (去る) *vi.* (sar·i-; sar·a-; sat-te [C]) leave; pass; resign:
Taifuu wa sarimashita. (台風は去りました) The typhoon *has passed*.

sa⌐ru² さる (猿) *n.* monkey; ape.

sa⌐ru- さる (去る) *pref.* last:
Sono jikeñ wa saru itsuka ni okotta. (その事件は去る五日に起こった) The incident occurred on the fifth of *this* [*last*] month.

sa⌐sae·ru ささえる (支える) *vt.* (sasae-te [V]) 1 prop up:
Tana o boo de sasaeta. (棚を棒で支えた) I *propped up* the shelf with a stick.
2 support (a family, group, organization, etc.).

sa⌐sa⌐r·u ささる (刺さる) *vi.* (sasar·i-; sasar·a-; sasat-te [C]) stick; prick:
Hari ga yubi ni sasatta. (針が指に刺さった) A needle *pricked* my finger.

sa⌐sa⌐yaka ささやか *a.n.* (~ na, ni) small; humble; modest:
shomiñ no sasayaka na negai (庶民のささやかな願い) a *modest* request from common folk.

sa⌐serare·ru させられる *vt.* (-rare-te [V]) be made to do:
Watashi wa toire no sooji o saserareta. (私はトイレの掃除をさせられた) I *was made* to clean the toilet. (⇒ saseru; -rareru)

sa⌐se·ru させる *vt.* (sase-te [V]) 1 make someone do; cause someone to do:
Koochi wa señshu ni mainichi reñshuu saseta. (コーチは選手に毎日練習させた) The coach *made* the players *practice* every day.
2 let someone do; allow someone do:
Watashi wa kare-ra ni yaritai-yoo ni saseta. (私は彼らにやりたいようにさせた) I *let* them *do* as they wished.

-sase·ru させる *infl. end.* (-sase-te [V]) [attached to the negative base of a vowel-stem verb and '*kuru*,' and itself inflected like a vowel-stem verb]
1 make someone do; cause someone to do:
Kare no kañgae o kaesaseru no

wa muzukashii.(彼の考えを変えさせるのはむずかしい) It is difficult to *make* him *change* his mind. (⇨ -seru)

2 let someone do; allow someone to do:
Sono ko ni suki na dake tabesasete yari nasai.(その子に好きなだけ食べさせてやりなさい) *Let* the child *eat* as much as he likes. (⇨ -seru)

sa⌐shiage·ru さしあげる(差し上げる) *vt.* (-age-te Ⅴ) (*honorific*) give; present. (⇨ ageru)

sa⌐shidas·u さしだす(差し出す) *vt.* (-dash·i-; -das·a-; -dash·i-te Ⅽ)
1 hold out (one's hand); reach out.
2 hand in; present; submit:
hookokusho o sashidasu(報告書を差し出す) *submit* a report. (⇨ teeshutsu)

sa⌐shi⌐hiki さしひき(差し引き) *n.* balance; total. (⇨ gookee)

sa⌐shimi さしみ(刺身) *n.* slices of raw fish for eating.

sa⌐shitsukae さしつかえ(差し支え) *n.* (with a negative) difficulty; obstruction; harm:
Sashitsukae nakereba, ashita kite kudasai.(差しつかえなければ、あした来てください) *If it is not inconvenient,* I would like you to come tomorrow. (⇨ sashitsukaeru)

sa⌐shitsukae·ru さしつかえる(差し支える) *vi.* (-tsukae-te Ⅴ) interfere; affect; have difficulty. (⇨ sashitsukae)

sa⌐shizu さしず(指図) *n.* directions; instructions; orders.
sashizu suru (〜する) *vt.* direct; instruct; order. (⇨ shiji)

sa⌐so·u さそう(誘う) *vt.* (saso·i-; sasow·a-; sasot-te Ⅽ) **1** invite; ask; allure; tempt:
Watashi wa sukii ni ikoo to kanojo o sasotta.(私はスキーに行こうと彼女を誘った) I *asked* her to come skiing.
2 cause (tears, laughter, etc.).

sa⌐ssa to さっさと *adv.* quickly;

promptly: **sassa to** *aruku*(さっさと歩く) walk *quickly*.

sa⌐sshi さっし(察し) *n.* understanding; guess; judgment:
Kare wa sasshi *ga ii* [*warui*].(彼は察しがいい[悪い]) He is quick [slow] to *understand*. (⇨ sassuru)

sa⌐ssoku さっそく(早速) *adv.* immediately; promptly.

sa⌐ssoo to さっそうと *adv.* smartly; dashingly:
Kare wa atarashii fuku de sassoo to arawareta.(彼は新しい服でさっそうと現れた) He showed up *smartly* dressed in a new suit.

sa⌐ss·uru さっする(察する) *vt.* (sassh·i-; sassh·i-; sassh·i-te Ⅰ) **1** guess; presume; suppose. (⇨ suisoku)
2 appreciate; understand:
O-kimochi wa o-sasshi itashimasu.(お気持ちはお察しいたします) I *appreciate* how you feel.

sa⌐s·u¹ さす(指す) *vt.* (sash·i-; sas·a-; sash·i-te Ⅽ) **1** point; show; indicate:
Dore ga hoshii ka, yubi de sashi nasai.(どれが欲しいか、指で指しなさい) *Point* to the one you want.
2 mean; refer to:
Anata no koto o sashite, itta wake de wa arimaseñ.(あなたのことを指して、言った訳ではありません) I do not mean to imply that I *was referring* to you.
3 (in a classroom) call on.

sa⌐s·u² さす(刺す) *vt.* (sash·i-; sas·a-; sash·i-te Ⅽ) **1** stab; pierce; thrust.
2 (of an insect) sting; bite:
Hachi ni te o sasareta.(蜂に手を刺された) I *was stung* on the hand by a bee.
3 (in baseball) throw out.

sa⌐suga さすが(流石) *adv.*
1 (〜 ni) truly; indeed:
Sasuga ni Fuji-sañ wa utsukushii.(さすがに富士山は美しい) Mt. Fuji is *truly* beautiful.
2 (〜 no) even:

Sasuga no *kare mo tsui ni maketa.*
(さすがの彼もついに負けた) *Even he
finally suffered a defeat.*
3 (~ ni/wa) just as one might
expect:
Sasuga wa *taika da. Migoto na e
da.* (さすがは大家だ。みごとな絵だ)
*That's just what one would ex-
pect* of a master. It's a wonderful
painting.

sa⌐tchuuzai さっちゅうざい (殺虫
剤) *n.* insecticide.

sa⌐te さて *int.* now; well:
★ Used at the beginning of a sentence.
Sate, *tsugi no gidai ni utsurimasu.*
(さて、次の議題に移ります) *Now we
are going to move on to the next
topic.* (⇨ saa)

sa⌐toimo さといも (里芋) *n.* taro.

sa⌐too さとう (砂糖) *n.* sugar.

sa⌐tor·u さとる (悟る) *vt.* (sator·i-;
sator·a-; satot·te Ⓒ) **1** realize;
find:
Koto no juudai-sa o satotta. (事の
重大さを悟った) I *realized* the importance of the matter.
2 sense (danger):
Kiken o satotte, *kare wa sugu nigeta.* (危険を悟って、彼はすぐ逃げた)
Sensing danger, he quickly escaped.

sa⌐tsu さつ (札) *n.* paper money;
bill; note. ★ 'O-satsu' is more
common when used indepen-
dently. (⇨ kahee; shihee)

-satsu さつ (冊) *suf.* volume;
copy. ★ Counter for books and
magazines.

sa⌐tsuee さつえい (撮影) *n.* photo-
graphing; shooting.
satsuee suru (~する) *vt.* take a
picture; photograph; shoot.
(⇨ toru)

sa⌐tsujin さつじん (殺人) *n.*
homicide; murder:
satsujin-jiken (殺人事件) a *murder*
case / satsujin-han (殺人犯) a *mur-
derer.*

sa⌐tsumaimo さつまいも *n.*

sweet potato.

sa⌐tsutaba さつたば (札束) *n.* roll
[wad] of bills.

sa⌐tto さっと *adv.* quickly; suddenly:
Doa ga satto *hiraita.* (ドアがさっと開
いた) The door opened *suddenly.*

sa⌐wagashi⌐·i さわがしい (騒がしい)
a. (-ku) noisy; boisterous.
(⇨ sawagi; sawagu; soozooshii)

sa⌐wagi さわぎ (騒ぎ) *n.* noise;
tumult; disturbance:
sawagi o okosu (騒ぎを起こす)
cause a *disturbance.* (⇨ sawagu;
sawagashii)

sa⌐wag·u さわぐ (騒ぐ) *vi.* (sawa-
g·i-; sawag·a-; sawa·i·de Ⓒ)
1 make a noise; clamor.
2 make merry:
Minna de uta o utatte sawaida. (み
んなで歌を歌って騒いだ) We all sang
and *made merry.* (⇨ sawagi)
3 make a fuss:
Ano kashu wa ima masukomi de
sawagarete imasu. (あの歌手は今マ
スコミで騒がれています) *A great fuss is
now made of* that singer by the
media. (⇨ sawagi)

sa⌐war·u[1] さわる (触る) *vi.* (sawa-
r·i-; sawar·a-; sawat·te Ⓒ)
touch; feel:
Tenjihin ni sawaranai de kudasai.
(展示品に触らないでください) *Don't
touch* the exhibits.

sa⌐war·u[2] さわる (障る) *vi.* (sawa-
r·i-; sawar·a-; sawat·te Ⓒ)
1 hurt (a person's feelings); get
on (a person's nerves); offend.
2 affect; be harmful (to health):
Nomi-sugi wa karada ni sawaru.
(飲み過ぎは体にさわる) Drinking to
excess *affects* the health.

sa⌐wa⌐yaka さわやか (爽やか) *a.n.*
(~ na, ni) fresh; refreshing;
crisp; pleasant:
sawayaka na asa no kuuki (さわやか
な朝の空気) the *refreshing* morning air.

sa⌐yona⌐ra さよなら (*informal*)
goodbye. (⇨ sayoonara)

sa⌐yoo さよう（作用）*n.* action;
operation; function:
sayoo to hañ-sayoo（作用と反作用）
action and reaction.

sa⌐yoona⌐ra さようなら（左様なら）
goodbye; so long.

sa⌐yuu さゆう（左右）*n.* right and
left. 《↔ jooge》《⇨ ue-shita》
sayuu suru（～する）decide; influence; control: *Sono moñdai
ga señkyo o ookiku sayuu shita.*
（その問題が選挙を大きく左右した）
That matter greatly *influenced*
the election.

sa⌐zo さぞ *adv.* surely; I am
sure:
*Okaasañ wa sazo yorokoñda de-
shoo.*（お母さんはさぞ喜んだでしょう）*I
am sure* your mother was very
pleased.

sa⌐zuka⌐r·u さずかる（授かる）*vi.*
(sazukar·i-; sazukar·a-; sazukat-
te Ⓒ) be given [awarded]; be
blessed:
kodomo o sazukaru（子どもを授かる）
be blessed with a child. 《⇨ sazu-
keru》

sa⌐zuke⌐·ru さずける（授ける）*vt.*
(sazuke-te Ⓥ) award (a prize);
confer (a title); grant. 《⇨ sazu-
karu》

se せ（背）*n.* **1** back:
uma no se ni noru（馬の背に乗る）
ride on a horse's *back* / se o no-
basu（背を伸ばす）straighten one's
back. 《⇨ senaka》
2 = see[1].

se⌐biro せびろ（背広）*n.* business
suit; lounge suit.

se⌐dai せだい（世代）*n.* generation.

se⌐e[1] せい（背）*n.* height of a person; stature. 《⇨ se》

se⌐e[2] せい（性）*n.* sex. ★ The act
of sex is called 'sekkusu.'

se⌐e[3] せい（姓）*n.* family name;
surname.

se⌐e[4] せい（精）*n.* energy; vigor.
see o dasu（～を出す）work hard.

se⌐e[5] せい（所為）*n.* **1** blame;
fault:

*Sore wa watashi no see de wa ari-
maseñ.*（それは私のせいではありません）
It's not my *fault*.
2 because of; due to: ★ Indicates an unfavorable cause or
reason.
*Deñsha ga okureta no wa yuki no
see desu.*（電車が遅れたのは雪のせいで
す）The train was late *because of*
the snow. 《⇨ okage》

-see せい（製）*suf.* made in [by;
of]; -made:
garasu-see no kabiñ（ガラス製の花
瓶）a vase *made* of glass.

se⌐ebetsu せいべつ（性別）*n.* distinction of sex.

se⌐ebi せいび（整備）*n.* maintenance; repair; improvement.
seebi suru（～する）*vt.* maintain;
service; improve.

se⌐ebo せいぼ（歳暮）*n.* year-end
gift. ★ Usually with 'o-.' Japanese people customarily send
'o-seebo' to those to whom they
feel indebted. 《⇨ chuugeñ》

se⌐ebuñ せいぶん（成分）*n.* ingredient; component.

se⌐ebutsu せいぶつ（生物）*n.*
living thing; creature. 《⇨ iki-
mono》

se⌐ebyoo せいびょう（性病）*n.*
venereal disease.

se⌐echoo せいちょう（成長・生長）*n.*
growth. ★ '成長' is usually
used for animals and '生長' for
plants.
seechoo suru（～する）*vi.* grow:
seechoo shite *otona ni naru*（成長
して大人になる）*grow* into a man
[woman].

se⌐edo せいど（制度）*n.* system;
institution:
atarashii seedo o mookeru（新しい
制度を設ける）establish a new *system.*

se⌐e-eki せいえき（精液）*n.* se-
men; sperm.

se⌐efu せいふ（政府）*n.* government; administration.

se⌐efuku[1] せいふく（制服）*n.* uniform. (⇨ fuku²; yoofuku)

se˨efuku² せいふく (正副) *n.* original and duplicate:
shorui o seefuku ni-tsuu sakusee suru (書類を正副2通作成する) make out documents in *duplicate* / seefuku gichoo (正副議長) the *chairman and vice-chairman*.

se˨egeˈñ せいげん (制限) *n.* restriction; limit: seegeñ o kuwaeru (制限を加える) impose *restrictions*.
seegeñ suru (～する) *vt.* restrict; limit. (⇨ toosee)

se˨egi せいぎ (正義) *n.* justice; right.

se˨ehiñ せいひん (製品) *n.* product; article; goods.

se˨ehoˈokee せいほうけい (正方形) *n.* square.

se˨eiku せいいく (成育・生育) *n.* growth. ★ '成育' is usually used for animals and '生育' for plants.
seeiku suru (～する) *vt., vi.* grow: Ine wa juñchoo ni seeiku shite imasu. (稲は順調に生育しています) The rice plants *are coming along* nicely. (⇨ seechoo)

se˨eji せいじ (政治) *n.* politics; government; administration.

se˨ejika せいじか (政治家) *n.* statesman; politician.

se˨ejiñ せいじん (成人) *n.* adult; grown-up.
seejiñ suru (～する) *vi.* become an adult; come of age. (⇨ seeneñ²)

se˨ejiñbyoo せいじんびょう (成人病) *n.* adult diseases; diseases which are often connected with aging.

se˨ejitsu せいじつ (誠実) *a.n.* (～ na, ni) sincere; honest; faithful:
Kare wa yakusoku o seejitsu ni jikkoo shita. (彼は約束を誠実に実行した) He *faithfully* carried out his promise.

se˨ejoo せいじょう (正常) *a.n.* (～ na, ni) normal; ordinary:
Taioñ wa seejoo desu. (体温は正常

です) My temperature is *normal*. (↔ ijoo³)

se˨ejooka せいじょうか (正常化) *n.* normalization.
seejooka suru (～する) *vt.* normalize: kokkoo o seejooka suru (国交を正常化する) *normalize* diplomatic relations.

se˨ejuku せいじゅく (成熟) *n.* ripeness; maturity.
seejuku suru (～する) *vt.* ripen; mature.

se˨ekai せいかい (正解) *n.* correct answer.

se˨ekaku¹ せいかく (性格) *n.* character; disposition; personality.

se˨ekaku² せいかく (正確) *a.n.* (～ na, ni) correct; accurate; precise; exact. (↔ fuseekaku)

se˨ekatsu せいかつ (生活) *n.* life; living; livelihood:
seekatsu-hi (生活費) *living* expenses. (⇨ seekee¹)
seekatsu (o) suru (～(を)する) *vi.* live; make a living. (⇨ kurasu¹)

se˨ekee¹ せいけい (生計) *n.* one's living; one's livelihood:
seekee o tateru (生計を立てる) earn a *living*.

se˨ekee² せいけい (整形) *n.* orthopedic surgery; plastic surgery.
seekee suru (～する) *vt.* have plastic surgery.

se˨ekee-geˈka せいけいげか (整形外科) *n.* orthopedics.

se˨ekeñ せいけん (政権) *n.* political power:
Hoshutoo ga geñzai seekeñ o nigitte iru. (保守党が現在政権を握っている) The conservative party is now in *power*.

se˨eketsu せいけつ (清潔) *a.n.* (～ na, ni) **1** clean; neat: toire o seeketsu ni shite oku (トイレを清潔にしておく) keep the toilet *clean*. (↔ fuketsu)
2 honest:
seeketsu na seejika (清潔な政治家) an *honest* politician.

se˨eki せいき (世紀) *n.* century.

se｢ekoo¹ せいこう（成功）n. success; prosperity; achievement.
seekoo suru (～する) vi. succeed; be successful. (↔ shippai)

se｢ekoo² せいこう（性交）n. sexual intercourse.
seekoo suru (～する) vi. have sexual intercourse.

se｢eko｢oi せいこうい（性行為）n. sexual act.

se｢ekyuu せいきゅう（請求）n. demand; claim; request:
seekyuu-sho (請求書) a *bill*; a *request for payment*.
seekyuu suru (～する) vt. demand; claim; request; charge.

se｢emee¹ せいめい（生命）n. life. (⇨ inochi)

se｢emee² せいめい（姓名）n. one's full name. (⇨ namae)

se｢emee³ せいめい（声明）n. statement; declaration; announcement: seemee o dasu (声明を出す) make a *statement*.

se｢emitsu せいみつ（精密）a.n. (～ na, ni) precise; detailed; minute:
seemitsu-*keňsa* (精密検査) a *detailed* (health) examination.

se｢emoň せいもん（正門）n. front gate; main entrance.

se｢eneň¹ せいねん（青年）n. youth; young man. (⇨ shooneň)

se｢eneň² せいねん（成年）n. full age; majority:
seeneň ni tassuru (成年に達する) *come of age*. (⇨ seejiň)

se｢eneňga｢ppi せいねんがっぴ（生年月日）n. date of one's birth.

se｢enoo せいのう（性能）n. efficiency; performance; power:
Kono kamera wa seenoo *ga yoi.* (このカメラは性能が良い) This camera *works well*.

se｢eoň せいおん（清音）n. voiceless sound. ★ Japanese syllables with a consonant that is not voiced, *i.e.* か (*ka*), さ (*sa*), ち (*chi*), ほ (*ho*). (⇨ dakuoň; haň-dakuoň; inside front cover)

se｢ereki せいれき（西暦）n. Christian era; A.D.

se｢eri¹ せいり（整理）n. tidying up; putting things in order.
seeri suru (～する) vt. **1** tidy up; put in order; arrange. **2** cut down; reduce:
juugyooiň o seeri suru (従業員を整理する) *reduce* the number of employees.

se｢eri² せいり（生理）n. physiology; menses:
seeri *ni naru* (生理になる) have one's monthly *period*.

se｢eritsu せいりつ（成立）n. coming into existence; formation; conclusion.
seeritsu suru (～する) vi. come into existence; be formed; be concluded: *Atarashii naikaku ga* seeritsu shita. (新しい内閣が成立した) A new cabinet *was formed*.

se｢eryoku せいりょく（勢力）n. influence; power; strength.

se｢e-sa｢betsu せいさべつ（性差別）n. sexism; sex discrimination.

se｢esaku¹ せいさく（製作）n. manufacture; production of machinery.
seesaku suru (～する) vt. manufacture; produce. (⇨ seezoo)

se｢esaku² せいさく（制作）n. production of works of art.
seesaku suru (～する) vt. produce: *atarashii eega o* seesaku suru (新しい映画を制作する) *make* a new movie.

se｢esaku³ せいさく（政策）n. policy:
gaikoo seesaku (外交政策) a foreign *policy*.

se｢esaň せいさん（生産）n. production; manufacture:
seesaň-daka (生産高) *output*.
seesaň suru (～する) vt. produce; manufacture. (↔ shoohi)

se｢esaň｢sha せいさんしゃ（生産者）n. producer; maker; manufacturer. (↔ shoohisha)

se｢eseki せいせき（成績）n.

school record; grade; result.

se⌐eshi[1] せいし (生死) n. life and death:
Kare no seeshi wa fumee desu. (彼の生死は不明です) Nobody knows whether he is *alive or not.*

se⌐eshi[2] せいし (制止) n. holding back; control.
seeshi suru (～する) vt. stop; hold back; restrain. (⇨ tomeru[1])

se⌐eshi[3] せいし (精子) n. sperm. (↔ rañshi)

se⌐eshiki せいしき (正式) a.n. (～ na, ni) formal; official; regular: seeshiki *kaiiñ* (正式会員) a *regular member*

se⌐eshiñ せいしん (精神) n.
1 mind; soul:
seeshiñ-*byoo* (精神病) a *mental* disease / seeshiñ-*ryoku* (精神力) *mental* power.
2 spirit:
keñpoo no seeshiñ (憲法の精神) the *spirit* of the constitution.

se⌐eshiñ-teki せいしんてき (精神的) a.n. (～ na, ni) mental; spiritual:
Chichi-oya no shi wa kare ni totte ooki-na seeshiñ-teki *dageki datta.* (父親の死は彼にとって大きな精神的打撃だった) His father's death was a great *mental* blow to him.

se⌐eshitsu せいしつ (性質) n.
1 nature; disposition; character.
2 property; quality:
abura ga mizu ni uku to iu seeshitsu *o riyoo suru* (油が水に浮くという性質を利用する) make use of oil's *property* of floating on water.

se⌐esho[1] せいしょ (清書) n. fair copy; making a fair copy.
seesho suru (～する) vt. make a fair copy.

se⌐esho[2] せいしょ (聖書) n. the Bible; Testament:
kyuuyaku seesho (旧約聖書) the Old *Testament* / *shiñyaku* seesho (新約聖書) the New *Testament.*

se⌐eshuñ せいしゅん (青春) n. youth; the period of adolescence.

se⌐esoo せいそう (清掃) n. cleaning: seesoo-*sha* (清掃車) a *garbage truck*; a *dustcart.*
seesoo suru (～する) vt. clean: *heya* [*dooro*] *o* seesoo suru (部屋[道路]を清掃する) *clean* a room [street]. (⇨ sooji)

se⌐etaa セーター n. sweater.

se⌐etee せいてい (制定) n. enactment; establishment.
seetee suru (～する) vt. enact; establish: *hooritsu o* seetee suru (法律を制定する) *enact* laws.

se⌐e-teki せいてき (性的) a.n. (～ na, ni) sex; sexual; sexy: see-teki *iyagarase* (性的いやがらせ) *sexual* harassment.

se⌐eteñ せいてん (晴天) n. fair weather. (↔ uteñ)

se⌐etetsu せいてつ (製鉄) n. iron manufacture:
seetetsu-*jo* (製鉄所) an *ironworks.*

se⌐eto せいと (生徒) n. pupil; student. ★ College students are called '*gakusee.*'

se⌐etoñ せいとん (整頓) n. order.
seetoñ suru (～する) vt. put in order; tidy up. (⇨ totonoeru)

se⌐etoo[1] せいとう (正当) a.n. (～ na, ni) just; right; good: fair: *Kare ni wa* seetoo *na riyuu ga arimasu.* (彼には正当な理由があります) He has a *good* reason. (↔ futoo)

se⌐etoo[2] せいとう (政党) n. political party. (⇨ APP. 8)

se⌐eyaku せいやく (制約) n. restriction; restraint; limitation: *yosañ no* seeyaku (予算の制約) budgetary *limitations.*
seeyaku suru (～する) vt. limit; restrict; restrain.

Se⌐eyoo せいよう (西洋) n. the West: seeyoo-*ryoori* (西洋料理) *Western* cooking. (↔ Tooyoo)

Se⌐eyo⌐ojiñ せいようじん (西洋人) n. Westerner; European. (↔ Tooyoojiñ)

se⌐eza せいざ (正座) n. sitting in a formal posture. ★ To sit upright on the floor with one's shins folded under the haunches and the knees facing out.

se͞ezee せいぜい（精々）*adv.*
1 as...as possible:
Seezee o-yasuku shite okimasu. (せいぜいお安くしておきます) We will give you *as* big a discount *as possible*.
2 (of cost, time, quantity, etc.) at (the) best [most]:
Soko made iku no ni kakatte mo, seezee ichi-jikan desu. (そこまで行くのにかかっても、せいぜい1時間です) You can get there in an hour *at the most*.

se͞ezon せいぞん（生存）*n.* existence; survival:
seezon-sha (生存者) a survivor.
seezon suru (～する) *vi.* exist; survive; live.

se͞ezoo せいぞう（製造）*n.* manufacture; production.
seezoo suru (～する) *vt.* manufacture; produce; make. ((⇨ see-saku¹; tsukuru¹)

se͞kai せかい（世界）*n.* **1** the world:
sekai isshuu suru (世界一周する) go around *the world*.
2 circle; sphere; realm:
seeji no sekai (政治の世界) political *circles*.

se͞kaseka せかせか *adv.* (～ to; ～ suru) (the state of being restless or busy):
Kare wa itsu-mo sekaseka shite iru. (彼はいつもせかせかしている) He is always *restless*.

se͞ka·s·u せかす（急かす） *vt.* (sekash·i·; sekas·a·; sekash·i·te C) hurry; rush; press:
Sonna ni sekasanai de kudasai. (そんなにせかさないでください) Please *don't rush* me like that. (⇨ seku)

se͞ken せけん（世間）*n.* the world; the public; society:
seken no chuumoku o atsumeru (世間の注目を集める) attract *public* attention.

se͞ki¹ せき（席）*n.* seat; one's

place: ((⇨ zaseki)
seki ni tsuku (席に着く) take one's seat / seki o tatsu [hanareru] (席を立つ[離れる]) stand up from [leave] one's seat.

se͞ki¹² せき（咳）*n.* cough; coughing: seki o suru (せきをする) *cough*.

-seki （隻） *suf.* counter for large ships: guñkañ is-seki (軍艦一隻) a warship.

se͞kiba͞rai せきばらい（咳払い）*n.* cough.
sekibarai (o) suru (～を）する) *vi.* clear one's throat.

se͞kidoo せきどう（赤道）*n.* equator.

se͞kigaiseñ せきがいせん（赤外線）*n.* infrared rays. ((↔ shigaiseñ)

se͞kiju͞uji せきじゅうじ（赤十字）*n.* the Red Cross:
Nihoñ Sekijuujisha (日本赤十字社) the Japanese *Red Cross Society*.

se͞kiniñ せきにん（責任）*n.* responsibility; duty; obligation; liability:
sekiniñ ga aru (責任がある) be *responsible*.

se͞kita̚ñ せきたん（石炭）*n.* coal:
sekitañ o horu (石炭を掘る) mine *coal*.

se͞kitate·ru せきたてる（急き立てる） *vt.* (-tate-te Ⅴ) urge; hurry; hasten; press:
Hayaku repooto o kaku yoo ni kare o sekitateta. (早くレポートを書くように彼をせきたてた) I *urged* him to write his school report soon. ((⇨ sekasu)

se͞kiyu せきゆ（石油）*n.* petroleum; kerosene: sekiyu-sutoobu (石油ストーブ) a *kerosene* heater.

se͞kkaku せっかく（折角）*adv.*
1 in spite of one's efforts:
Sekkaku kita no ni doobutsu-eñ wa yasumi datta. (せっかく来たのに動物園は休みだった) Although we *took the trouble* to come, the zoo was closed.
2 (～ no) kind:
Sekkaku no o-maneki desu ga so-

no hi wa tsugoo ga tsukimaseñ.
(せっかくのお招きですがその日は都合がつきません) Thank you very much for your *kind* invitation, but I cannot make it on that day.

3 (~ no) precious; rare:
Sekkaku no kikai o nogashita. (せっかくの機会を逃した) I let a *rare* opportunity slip by.

se⌈**kkee** せっけい (設計) *n.* plan; design.
　sekkee suru (~する) *vt.* plan; design (a house, car, etc.).

se⌈**kkeñ** せっけん (石鹸) *n.* soap.

se⌈**kkiñ** せっきん (接近) *n.* approach; access.
　sekkiñ suru (~する) *vi.* approach; come [go] near.

se⌈**kkusu** セックス *n.* sexual intercourse; sex. ★ Japanese '*sekkusu*' is used only in this meaning.

se⌈**kkyoku-teki** せっきょくてき (積極的) *a.n.* (~ na, ni) positive; active; aggressive. 《↔ shookyoku-teki》 (⇨ shookyoku-teki)

se⌈**k·u** せく (急く) *vi.* (sek·i-; se-k·a-; se·i-te Ⓒ) hurry; be impatient. (⇨ isogu)

se⌈**kuhara** セクハラ *n.* sexual harassment. (⇨ iyagarase)

se⌈**ma**⌉**·i** せまい (狭い) *a.* (-ku) small; narrow:
Dooro ga semakute, uñteñ shinikui. (道路が狭くて、運転しにくい) The road is so *narrow* that it is difficult to drive along it. 《↔ hiroi》

se⌈**ma**⌉**r·u** せまる (迫る) *vi.* (semar·i-; semar·a-; semat-te Ⓒ)
1 draw near; approach; be at hand:
Shuppatsu no hi ga sematte kita. (出発の日が迫ってきた) The day of departure *is drawing near.*
2 force; press; urge:
Daijiñ wa sono jikeñ no sekiniñ o toware, jiniñ o semarareta. (大臣はその事件の責任を問われ、辞任を迫られた) The minister *was urged* to take responsibility for the affair

and resign. 《⇨ shiiru》

se⌈**me**⌉**·ru**[1] せめる (攻める) *vt.* (se-me-te Ⓥ) attack; invade. 《↔ mamoru》 (⇨ osou)

se⌈**me**⌉**·ru**[2] せめる (責める) *vt.* (se-me-te Ⓥ) blame; accuse; criticize:
Señsee wa kare no fuchuui o semeta. (先生は彼の不注意を責めた) The teacher *criticized* him for his carelessness.

se⌈**mete** せめて *adv.* at least; just; only:
Semete neñ ni ni-kai wa keñshiñ o uketa hoo ga yoi. (せめて年に2回は検診を受けたほうがよい) You should undergo a medical examination twice a year *at least.*

se⌈**mi** せみ (蟬) *n.* cicada.

se⌈**ñ**[1] せん (線) *n.* line:
señ o hiku (線を引く) draw a *line.*

se⌈**ñ**[2] せん (千) *n.* one thousand. 《⇨ APP. 3》

se⌈**ñ**[3] せん (栓) *n.* stopper; cork:
gasu [suidoo] no señ o hiraku [shimeru] (ガス[水道]の栓を開く[締める]) turn on [off] the *gas [water].*

se⌈**ñ**[4] せん (選) *n.* selection:
señ ni hairu [moreru] (選に入る[漏れる]) be [not] selected.

-señ せん (線) *suf.* transport system; line:
Chuuoo-señ no deñsha (中央線の電車) trains on the Chuo *Line.* 《⇨ -bañseñ》

se⌈**naka** せなか (背中) *n.* one's back.

se⌈**ñbazu**⌉**ru** せんばづる (千羽鶴) *n.* a thousand folded paper cranes on a string. ★ Often used in praying for recovery from illness. 《⇨ tsuru[3]》

se⌈**ñbee** せんべい (煎餅) *n.* Japanese rice cracker.

se⌈**ñcha** せんちゃ (煎茶) *n.* green tea of middle grade. (⇨ o-cha)

se⌈**ñchi** センチ *n.* centimeter. ★ Shortened form of '*señchi-meetoru.*'

se⌈**ñchi-me**⌉**etoru** センチメートル

(糎) *n.* centimeter. ★ The shortened form '*senchi*' is more common. (⇨ senchi)

se¦nchoo せんちょう(船長) *n.* captain (of a ship).

se¦nden せんでん(宣伝) *n.* advertisement; publicity; propaganda.
senden (o) suru (〜(を)する) *vt.* advertise; propagandize. (⇨ kookoku)

se¦nge¦n せんげん(宣言) *n.* declaration; proclamation; announcement.
sengen (o) suru (〜(を)する) *vt.* declare; proclaim; announce: *chuuritsu o sengen suru* (中立を宣言する) *declare* one's neutrality.

se¦ngetsu せんげつ(先月) *n.* last month. (⇨ kongetsu; raigetsu)

se¦ngo せんご(戦後) *n.* the postwar period; after the war. (↔ senzen)

se¦ni せんい(繊維) *n.* fiber: *goosee[kagaku]-seni* (合成[化学]繊維) synthetic [chemical] *fiber*.

se¦njitsu せんじつ(先日) *n.* the other day; a few days ago; some time ago:
Senjitsu *wa doomo.* (先日はどうも) Thank you very much for *the other day.*

se¦nkoo せんこう(専攻) *n.* academic specialty; special field; major.
senkoo suru (〜する) *vt.* major in; specialize in.

se¦nkyo せんきょ(選挙) *n.* election:
senkyo-*ken* (選挙権) the right *to vote* / senkyo-*undoo* (選挙運動) an *election* campaign.
senkyo suru (〜する) *vt.* elect; vote for. (⇨ toohyoo)

se¦nmen せんめん(洗面) *n.* washing one's face:
senmen-*doogu* (洗面道具) one's *washing* things.

se¦nmenjo せんめんじょ(洗面所) *n.*
1 washroom; lavatory.
★ In an ordinary Japanese house,

the bathtub and the toilet are installed in separate rooms.
2 washstand.

se¦nme¦nki せんめんき(洗面器) *n.* washbowl; washbasin.

se¦nmon せんもん(専門) *n.* specialty; special subject.

se¦nmonka せんもんか(専門家) *n.* specialist; expert; professional.

se¦nmu (to¦rishimari¦yaku) せんむ(とりしまりやく)(専務(取締役)) *n.* senior [executive] managing director; senior vice president.

se¦nnuki せんぬき(栓抜き) *n.* corkscrew; bottle opener.

se¦nobi せのび(背伸び) *n.* standing on tiptoe.
senobi (o) suru (〜(を)する) *vi.*
1 stand on tiptoe; stretch oneself.
2 (*fig.*) aim too high.

se¦npai せんぱい(先輩) *n.* one's senior; elder:
Kare wa watashi no san-nen senpai desu. (彼は私の3年先輩です) He is my *senior* by three years. (↔ koohai)

se¦npu¦uki せんぷうき(扇風機) *n.* electric fan.

se¦nro せんろ(線路) *n.* railroad [railway] track; line.

se¦nryoo¹ せんりょう(占領) *n.* occupation; possession; capture.
senryoo suru (〜する) *vt.* occupy; have all to oneself.

se¦nryo¦o² せんりょう(染料) *n.* dye; dyestuffs.

se¦nse¦e せんせい(先生) *n.* teacher; professor; doctor.

se¦nshi せんし(戦死) *n.* death in battle.
senshi suru (〜する) *vi.* be killed in war.

se¦nshu せんしゅ(選手) *n.* player; athlete: *yakyuu no senshu* (野球の選手) a baseball *player*.

se¦nshuu せんしゅう(先週) *n.* last week. (↔ konshuu)

se¦nshu¦uraku せんしゅうらく(千秋楽) *n.* the last day of a Grand

Sumo Tournament; the last day of a public performance.

se￢ꞌnsoo せんそう (戦争) *n.* war; battle; fight. (↔ heewa)
señsoo (o) suru (〜(を)する) *vi.* make war; go to war.

se￢ꞌnsu せんす (扇子) *n.* folding fan. (⇒ uchiwa²)

se￢ꞌntaku¹ せんたく (洗濯) *n.* wash; washing; laundry.
señtaku suru (〜する) *vt.* wash; do the laundry. (⇒ hoshimono; señtakumono)

se￢ꞌntaku² せんたく (選択) *n.* choice; selection; option:
señtaku *o* ayamaru (選択を誤る) make the wrong *choice*.
señtaku suru (〜する) *vt.* choose; select. (⇒ erabu)

se￢ꞌntakuki せんたくき (洗濯機) *n.* washing machine; washer.

se￢ꞌntakumono せんたくもの (洗濯物) *n.* laundry; washing:
señtakumono *o* hosu (洗濯物を干す) hang the *washing* out to dry. (⇒ señtaku¹)

se￢ꞌnteñ-teki せんてんてき (先天的) *a.n.* (〜 na, ni) native; innate; inborn:
señteñ-teki *na* sainoo (先天的な才能) *innate* talent. (↔ kooteñ-teki)

se￢ꞌntoo¹ せんとう (先頭) *n.* the head; the lead:
ikkoo no señtoo *ni* tatte aruku (一行の先頭に立って歩く) walk at the *head* of the group.

se￢ꞌntoo² せんとう (戦闘) *n.* battle; combat; fight; action.

se￢ꞌntoo³ せんとう (銭湯) *n.* public bath. (⇒ furo; furoya)

se￢ꞌnzai せんざい (洗剤) *n.* detergent: chuusee-señzai (中性洗剤) a neutral *detergent*.

se￢ꞌnzeñ せんぜん (戦前) *n.* the prewar period; before the war. (↔ señgo)

se￢ꞌnzo せんぞ (先祖) *n.* ancestor; forefathers. (↔ shisoñ)

se￢ꞌoꞏu せおう (背負う) *vt.* (seoꞏi-; seowꞏa-; seot-te Ⓒ) **1** carry (a load) on one's back.
2 shoulder (responsibility). (⇒ ou²)

se￢ꞌrifu せりふ (台詞) *n.* words; one's lines: serifu *o* wasureru (せりふを忘れる) forget one's *lines*.

se￢ꞌroñ せろん (世論) *n.* public opinion. (⇒ yoroñ)

-se·ru せる *infl. end.* (-se-te Ⓥ) [attached to the negative base of a consonant-stem verb and itself inflected like a vowel-stem verb]
1 make someone do; cause someone to do:
Kare ni sugu heñji *o* kakasemasu. (彼にすぐ返事を書かせます) I'll *make* him *write* his answer immediately. (⇒ -saseru)
2 let someone do; allow someone to do:
Watashi ni mo kono hoñ *o* yomasete kudasai. (私にもこの本を読ませてください) Please *allow me* as well to *read* this book.

se￢ꞌsse to せっせと *adv.* hard; busily:
Kanojo wa itsu-mo sesse to hataraite iru. (彼女はいつもせっせと働いている) She always works *diligently*.

se￢ꞌsshi せっし (摂氏) *n.* Celsius; centigrade. ★ The Fahrenheit scale is not used in Japan.

se￢ꞌsshoku せっしょく (接触) *n.*
1 contact; touch; connection:
Kono puragu wa sesshoku ga warui. (このプラグは接触が悪い) This plug gives a bad *connection*.
2 contact with a person.
sesshoku suru (〜する) *vi.*
1 contact; touch: Kare no jiteñsha ga kuruma to sesshoku shite, kare wa taoreta. (彼の自転車が車と接触して、彼は倒れた) His bicycle *bumped* into a car and he fell over.
2 get in touch. (⇒ sessuru)

se￢ꞌssui せっすい (節水) *n.* water saving.
sessui suru (〜する) *vi.* save water; use water sparingly.

se⌈ss·uru せっする（接する）vi.
(sessh·i-; sessh·i-; sessh·i-te
①) **1** touch:
Deñseñ ga noki ni sesshite iru.（電
線が軒に接している）The electric
wire *touches* the eaves.
2 come into contact with (a person); see.
3 attend to (a guest, customer,
etc.); deal with.
4 border; abut:
Nihoñ wa dono gaikoku to mo sesshite imaseñ.（日本はどの外国とも接
していません）Japan does not *border*
any foreign countries.

se⌈tchi せっち（設置）n. formation; establishment; installation.
setchi suru (～する) vt. form; establish; install.

se⌈tomono せともの（瀬戸物）n.
china; porcelain; earthenware.

se⌈tsu[1] せつ（説）n. **1** theory:
atarashii setsu o tateru（新しい説を
立てる）put forward a new *theory*.
2 opinion; view:
Kare wa jibuñ no setsu o magenakatta.（彼は自分の説を曲げなかった）
He didn't change his own *views*.

se⌈tsu[2] せつ（節）n. **1** occasion;
time; when:
*Kochira e o-ide no setsu wa zehi
o-tachiyori kudasai.*（こちらへお出で
の節はぜひお立ち寄りください）By all
means, please drop in *when* you
happen to be in the neighborhood. (⇨ toki)
2 (of grammar) clause.
3 section; paragraph; phrase.

se⌈tsubi せつび（設備）n. equipment; facilities; accommodations.
setsubi suru (～する) vt. equip;
accommodate. (⇨ setchi)

se⌈tsubuñ せつぶん（節分）n. the
day before the start of spring.
★ Usually falls on February 2 or
3. On the evening of this day,
Japanese conduct the 'Bean-Throwing' ceremony and scatter
roasted soybeans to drive away

evil spirits.

se⌈tsudañ せつだん（切断）n. cutting; severance; amputation.
setsudañ suru (～する) vt. cut
off; sever; amputate. (⇨ kiru[1])

se⌈tsudeñ せつでん（節電）n.
power saving.
setsudeñ suru (～する) vi. save
electricity.

se⌈tsujoku せつじょく（雪辱）n.
vindication of one's honor; revenge.

se⌈tsumee せつめい（説明）n. explanation; illustration:
setsumee-*sho*（説明書）an *explanatory* leaflet; written *instructions*.
setsumee (o) suru (～(を)する) vt.
explain; illustrate; demonstrate.

se⌈tsuritsu せつりつ（設立）n. establishment; foundation.
setsuritsu suru (～する) vt. set
up; establish; found.

se⌈tsuyaku せつやく（節約）n.
economy; saving; thrift.
setsuyaku suru (～する) vt. economize; save; cut down. (↔ roohi) (⇨ keñyaku)

se⌈tsuzoku せつぞく（接続）n. connection; joining; link.
setsuzoku suru (～する) vi., vt.
join; connect.

se⌈tsuzoku[1]**shi** せつぞくし（接続
詞）n. (of grammar) conjunction.

se⌈wa[1] せわ（世話）n. **1** care:
Oosaka ni itta toki, obasañ no sewa ni narimashita.（大阪に行ったと
きおばさんの世話になりました）When I
went to Osaka, I *was looked after*
by my aunt.
2 trouble:
hito ni sewa o kakeru（人に世話を
かける）cause *trouble* to others.
3 help; kindness:
Anata no o-toosañ ni wa taiheñ o-sewa ni natte imasu.（あなたのお父さ
んには大変お世話になっています）I do
appreciate the *help* I always receive from your father.
4 recommendation; introduction.

sewa (o) suru (〜を する) *vt.*
1 take care of; look after; attend.
2 recommend; introduce: *Ueki-ya-san ga ii daiku-san o sewa shi-te kureta.* (植木屋さんがいい大工さんを世話してくれた) Our gardener was kind enough to *recommend* a good carpenter.

-sha しゃ (車) *suf.* car; vehicle: *jidoo-sha* (自動車) a motor *vehicle* / *res-sha* (列車) a long-distance *train.*

sha「be「r・u しゃべる (喋る) *vi.* (shaber-i-; shaber-a-; shabet-te C̄) chat; chatter; talk. (⇨ hanasu¹; kataru)

sha「bushabu しゃぶしゃぶ *n.* thin slices of beef and vegetables cooked portion by portion in boiling water on the table.

sha「choo しゃちょう (社長) *n.* president of a company; managing director.

sha「dan しゃだん (遮断) *n.* cutting off; interruption: *shadan-ki* (遮断機) a railroad *crossing gate.*
shadan suru (〜する) *vt.* cut off; interrupt; hold up. (⇨ tomeru¹)

sha「doo しゃどう (車道) *n.* roadway; carriageway. (↔ hodoo)

sha「gai しゃがい (車外) *n.* outside a vehicle [train]: *shagai no fuukee* (車外の風景) the view *from a train.* (↔ shanai)

sha「gam・u しゃがむ *vi.* (shagam-i-; shagam-a-; shagan-de C̄) crouch; squat.

sha「in しゃいん (社員) *n.* company employee. (⇨ juugyooin; shokuin)

sha「kai しゃかい (社会) *n.* society; the world: *shakai ni deru* (社会に出る) go out into the *world* / *shakai-hoshoo* (社会保障) *social* welfare guarantee / *shakai-kyooiku* (社会教育) *adult* education / *shakai-shugi* (社会主義) *socialism.*

sha「kkin しゃっきん (借金) *n.* debt; loan: *Watashi wa yaku hyakuman-en*

shakkin ga aru. (私は約100万円借金がある) I am in *debt* for about a million yen.
shakkin (o) suru (〜を する) *vi.* borrow money.

sha「kkuri しゃっくり *n.* hiccup: *shakkuri ga deru* (しゃっくりが出る) have the *hiccups.*

sha「ko しゃこ (車庫) *n.* garage; carbarn. (⇨ gareeji)

sha「men しゃめん (斜面) *n.* slope; slant: *yama no shamen o noboru* (山の斜面を登る) go up the *slope* of a mountain.

sha「nai しゃない (車内) *n.* inside a vehicle [train]: *Shanai wa kinen desu.* (車内は禁煙です) Smoking is prohibited *in the train* [bus]. (↔ shagai)

sha「re しゃれ (洒落) *n.* joke; witty remark; pun: *share o iu* [tobasu] (しゃれを言う[とばす]) crack a *joke.*

sha「rin しゃりん (車輪) *n.* wheel: *jitensha no sharin* (自転車の車輪) the *wheels* of a bicycle.

sha「ryoo しゃりょう (車両) *n.* vehicle; railway car.

sha「see しゃせい (写生) *n.* sketch; sketching.
shasee suru (〜する) *vt.* make a sketch.

sha「setsu しゃせつ (社説) *n.* editorial; leading article.

sha「shin しゃしん (写真) *n.* photograph; picture: *shashin o toru* (写真を撮る) take a *photograph.*

sha「shi「nki しゃしんき (写真機) *n.* camera.

sha「shoo しゃしょう (車掌) *n.* train [bus] conductor; guard.

sha「tai しゃたい (車体) *n.* body of a car; frame.

sha「tsu シャツ *n.* shirt; undershirt; underwear. ★ The type of shirt with which one wears a necktie is called '*waishatsu.*'

shi¹ し *p.* 1 and (also): ★ Used for emphatic listing.
Ano mise wa ryoori ga oishii shi,

fuñiki mo ii. (あの店は料理がおいしいし、雰囲気もいい) The food in that restaurant is good, *and also* there is a pleasant atmosphere. (⇨ to²; to ka)

2 (used at the end of an incomplete sentence in order to leave the rest to the imagination of the listener):
Asobi ni ikitai shi, o-kane wa nai shi ... (遊びに行きたいし、お金はないし…) I want to go off and enjoy myself, but I have no money, *and...*

shi¹² し(市) *n.* city.

shi³ し(詩) *n.* poem; poetry; verse.

shi¹⁴ し(四) *n.* four. ★ '四' is usually pronounced 'yoñ,' as the pronunciation 'shi' suggests 'death.' (⇨ APP. 3)

shi¹⁵ し(氏) *n.* **1** Mr:
Suzuki-shi ga gichoo ni erabareta. (鈴木氏が議長に選ばれた) *Mr.* Suzuki was elected chairman.
2 family:
Tokugawa-shi (徳川氏) the Tokugawa *family*.

shi¹⁶ し(氏) *n.* he; him:
Shi no keñkoo o shukushite, kañpai shiyoo. (氏の健康を祝して、乾杯しよう) Let's toast *his* health.

shi¹⁷ し(死) *n.* death.

shi「age しあげ(仕上げ) *n.* finish:
Kono teeburu wa shiage ga suteki da. (このテーブルは仕上げがすてきだ) This table has a nice *finish*. (⇨ shiageru)

shi「age」・ru しあげる(仕上げる) *vt.* (shiage-te Ⅴ) finish; complete. (⇨ shiage)

shi「ai しあい(試合) *n.* match; game; bout; competition.
shiai (o) suru (~(を)する) *vi.* play a game; have a match; compete.

shi「asa」tte しあさって *n.* three days from today. (⇨ asatte)

shi「awase しあわせ(幸せ) *n.* happiness; blessing; fortune. (⇨ saiwai)
— *a.n.* (~ na, ni) happy; fortu-

nate; lucky. (↔ fukoo; fushiawase) (⇨ koofuku)

shi「ba しば(芝) *n.* turf; grass.

shi「bafu しばふ(芝生) *n.* lawn; grass.

shi「bai しばい(芝居) *n.* **1** play; drama; performance:
shibai o mi ni iku (芝居を見に行く) go to see a *play*.
2 put-on; acting: (⇨ kyoogeñ)
Ani ga okotta no wa shibai desu. (兄が怒ったのは芝居です) My brother's anger is just a *put-on*.

shi「ba」raku しばらく(暫く) *adv.*
1 for a while [minute]:
Shibaraku, o-machi kudasai. (しばらく、お待ちください) Please wait *a little while*.
2 for the time being:
Shibaraku kono hoteru ni taizai shimasu. (しばらくこのホテルに滞在します) I will be staying in this hotel *for the time being*.
Shibaraku (buri) desu ne. (~(ぶり)ですね) I haven't seen you for a long time.

shi「ba」r・u しばる(縛る) *vt.* (shibar・i-; shibar・a-; shibat-te ⓒ)
1 tie; bind:
Kanojo wa kizuguchi o hootai de shibatta. (彼女は傷口を包帯でしばった) She *bound up* the wound with a bandage.
2 (of time) restrict; bind:
jikañ ni shibarareru (時間に縛られる) *be restricted* by time.

shi「bashiba しばしば(屡々) *adv.* many times; often; frequently. (⇨ tabitabi)

shi「basu しバス(市バス) *n.* city bus. ★ This is a bus operated by a city. (⇨ shideñ)

shi「bire」・ru しびれる(痺れる) *vi.* (shibire-te Ⅴ) be numbed; be paralyzed:
Ashi ga shibirete tatenai. (足がしびれて立てない) I cannot stand up because my feet *are asleep*.

shi「boo¹ しぼう(志望) *n.* wish; desire; plan:

shiboo-sha (志望者) an *applicant*.
shiˈboo suru (～する) *vt.* want;
desire; plan. (⇨ nozomu')

shiˈboo² しぼう (死亡) *n.* death:
shiboo-jiko (死亡事故) a *fatal* accident.
shiboo suru (～する) *vi.* die; be
killed. (⇨ shinu)

shiˈboo³ しぼう (脂肪) *n.* fat;
grease:
Kono niku wa shiboo ga ooi. (この
肉は脂肪が多い) This meat is *fatty*.
(⇨ abura²)

shiˈboˈr·u しぼる (絞る) *vt.* (shibor·i-; shibor·a-; shibot-te ⓒ)
1 squeeze; press: remoñ o shi-
boru (レモンを絞る) *squeeze* a lemon.
2 wring:
Nureta taoru o shibotte, hoshita.
(濡れたタオルを絞って、干した) I *wrung*
the wet towel and put it out to
dry.

shiˈibuˈl·i しぶい (渋い) *a.* (-ku)
1 (of taste) bitter; sharp and
astringent.
2 (of color) sober; quiet; refined:
Kare wa itsu-mo shibui fukusoo o
shite iru. (彼はいつも渋い服装をしてい
る) He is always dressed in *quiet
good taste*.
3 (of countenance) sullen:
shibui kao o suru (渋い顔をする)
make a *sour* face.
4 tight-fisted:
Ano hito wa kane ni shibui. (あの人
は金に渋い) He is *stingy*.

shiˈbuˈr·u しぶる (渋る) *vi.* (shi-
bur·i-; shibur·a-; shibut-te ⓒ)
hesitate; be reluctant:
Kare wa kanojo ni au no o shi-
butta. (彼は彼女に会うのを渋った) He
was reluctant to meet her.

shiˈchiˈl しち (七) *n.* seven.
(⇨ nana; nanatsu; APP. 3)

shiˈchi-gatsuˈl しちがつ (七月) *n.*
July. (⇨ APP. 5)

shiˈchoˈloˈl しちょう (市長) *n.*
mayor.

shiˈchoˈloˈ² しちょう (支庁) *n.* the

regional branch of a government
agency.

shiˈchoˈloˈ³ しちょう (市庁) *n.* = shiyakusho.

shiˈdai しだい (次第) *n.* 1 the instant; the moment: ★ Follows
the continuative base of a verb.
Kekka ga wakari shidai o-shirase
shimasu. (結果がわかり次第お知らせし
ます) We will inform you *as soon
as* we know the results.
2 being dependent:
Seekoo suru ka shinai ka wa
anata no doryoku shidai desu. (成
功するかしないかはあなたの努力次第です)
Whether you succeed or not *depends* on your own efforts.
(⇨ yoru')
3 circumstances:
Koo-iu shidai de asu no kaigi ni
wa shusseki dekimaseñ. (こういう次
第であすの会議には出席できません) Un-
der these *circumstances*, I cannot
attend tomorrow's meeting.
(⇨ wake)
4 order; program:
shiki-shidai (式次第) the *program*
of a ceremony.

shiˈdai ni しだいに (次第に) *adv.*
gradually; by degrees; little by
little.

shiˈdareyaˈnagi しだれやなぎ (垂
れ柳) *n.* weeping willow.

shiˈdeñ してん (市電) *n.* streetcar; tram. ★ This is a streetcar
operated by a city. (⇨ shibasu)

shiˈdooˈl しどう (指導) *n.* guidance; direction; leadership; instruction: shidoo-sha (指導者) a
leader; a *guide*.
shidoo suru (～する) *vt.* guide;
direct; coach; instruct; teach.
(⇨ oshieru)

shiˈdooˈ² しどう (私道) *n.* private
road [path].

shiˈgaiˈl しがい (市街) *n.* the
streets; city; town. (⇨ machi)

shiˈlgaiˈ² しがい (市外) *n.* suburbs;
outskirts:
shigai-deñwa (市外電話) an *out-*

of-town telephone call.
(↔ shinai) (⇨ koogai¹)

shiˈgalseñ しがいせん (紫外線) *n.*
ultraviolet rays. (↔ sekigaiseñ)

shiˈgamitsuˈk·u しがみつく *vi.*
(-tsuk·i-; -tsuk·a-; -tsu·i·te ○)
cling to; hang [hold] on to.

shi-ˈgatsu¹ しがつ (四月) *n.* April.
(⇨ APP. 5)

shiˈgeki しげき (刺激) *n.* stimulation; stimulus; incentive.
shigeki suru (〜する) *vt.* stimu-
late; excite; provoke.

shiˈgeñ しげん (資源) *n.* resources: *teññeñ-shigeñ o kaihatsu
suru* (天然資源を開発する) develop
natural *resources.*

shiˈgeˈr·u しげる (茂る) *vi.* (shiger·
i·; shiger·a·; shiget·te ○)
(of plants) grow thickly; (of
weeds) be overgrown.

shiˈgoto しごと (仕事) *n.*
1 work; job; business.
2 position; work; job; employment:
*Kare wa ima shigoto o sagashite
iru tokoro desu.* (彼は今仕事を探して
いるところです) He is now seeking
employment.

shiˈhai しはい (支配) *n.* rule; government; control:
shihai-sha (支配者) a *ruler.*
shihai suru (〜する) *vt.* rule;
govern; control; dominate.

shiˈhaˈiniñ しはいにん (支配人) *n.*
manager (of a store, restaurant,
etc.).

shiˈharai しはらい (支払い) *n.* payment:
*Shiharai wa getsumatsu ni nari-
masu.* (支払いは月末になります) *Payment* will be made at the end of
the month. (⇨ shiharau)

shiˈharaˈ·u しはらう (支払う) *vt.*
(-hara·i·; -haraw·a·; -harat·te
○) pay; defray:
*Koñgetsu wa gasu-dai ni ichimañ-
eñ shiharatta.* (今月はガス代に1万円
支払った) This month I *paid*
10,000 yen for gas. (⇨ harau)

shiˈhatsu しはつ (始発) *n.* 1 the
first train; the first run.
(↔ shuudeñ(sha); shuusha)
2 starting:
*Sono ressha wa Shiñjuku shihatsu
desu.* (その列車は新宿始発です) That
train *starts* from Shinjuku.

shiˈhee しへい (紙幣) *n.* paper
money. (⇨ satsu; kooka³)

shiˈhoñ しほん (資本) *n.* capital;
fund:
shihoñ-ka (資本家) a *capitalist* /
shihoñ-shugi (資本主義) *capitalism.*

shiˈhoˈlo¹ しほう (四方) *n.* all
sides; all around:
*Sono mura wa shihoo o yama ni
kakomarete iru.* (その村は四方を山に
囲まれている) The village is surrounded *on all sides* by mountains.

shiˈhoo² しほう (司法) *n.* juris-
diction:
shihoo-keñ (司法権) *judicial
power* / shihoo-shikeñ (司法試験)
a *bar* examination. (⇨ sañkeñ-
buñritsu)

shiˈiñ しいん (子音) *n.* consonant.
(⇨ boiñ; APP. 1)

shiˈire しいれ (仕入れ) *n.* stock-
ing; buying in:
shiire *kakaku* (仕入れ価格) the
buying price (⇨ shiireru)

shiˈireˈ·ru しいれる (仕入れる) *vt.*
(shiire·te Ⅴ) 1 stock (goods);
lay in stock. (⇨ shiire)
2 get (information).

shiˈiˈ·ru しいる (強いる) *vt.* (shii·te
Ⅴ) force; compel; press:
Kare wa jishoku o shiirareta. (彼は
辞職を強いられた) He *was forced* to
resign.

shiˈitsu シーツ *n.* bed sheet.

shiˈizuñ-oˈfu シーズンオフ *n.* off-
season.

shiˈji¹ しじ (指示) *n.* directions;
instructions.
shiji suru (〜する) *vt.* direct; instruct; indicate.

shiˈji² しじ (支持) *n.* support;
backing.

shiji suru (～する) *vt.* support; back up. (⇨ kooeñ⁴)

shi「jiñ しじん (詩人) *n.* poet.

shi「joo しじょう (市場) *n.* market: shijoo-*choosa* (市場調査) a *market* survey.

shi「juu しじゅう (始終) *adv.* always; all the time; very often. (⇨ itsu-mo)

shi「ka¹ しか (鹿) *n.* deer; stag; hind.

shi「ka² しか (歯科) *n.* dentistry: shika-i (歯科医) a *dentist*. (⇨ haisha¹)

shika³ しか *p.* 1 only; except for; ★ Used after a noun or counter in negative sentences. *Kanojo wa kodomo ga hitori* shika *inakatta.* (彼女は子どもが一人しかいなかった) She had *only* one child. (⇨ dake; nomi²; bakari)
2 no other way: ★ Used after a verb in the dictionary form. *Koo nattara moo yaru* shika *arimaseñ.* (こうなったらもうやるしかありません) If such is the case, there is *nothing* for us *but* to go ahead and do it.

shi「kaeshi しかえし (仕返し) *n.* revenge; retaliation.

shi「kai しかい (司会) *n.* master of ceremonies; chairperson.

shi「kake しかけ (仕掛け) *n.* device; mechanism; gadget.

shi「kake¹・ru しかける (仕掛ける) (-kake-te Ⓥ) 1 start (a quarrel): *Kare wa watashi ni keñka o* shikakete kita. (彼は私にけんかをしかけてきた) He *picked* a quarrel with me.
2 set (a trap); plant (a bomb).

shi「kaku¹ しかく (資格) *n.* 1 qualification; capacity: shikaku no aru *kyooshi* (資格のある教師) a *qualified* teacher.
2 license; certificate: isha no shikaku o toru (医者の資格を取る) get a doctor's *license.*

shi「kaku¹² しかく (四角) *a.n.* (～ na, ni) square. (⇨ shikakui)

shi「kaku³ しかく (死角) *n.* dead angle; blind spot.

shi「kaku¹・i しかくい (四角い) *a.* (-ku) square: shikakui *teeburu* (四角いテーブル) a *square* table (⇨ shikaku²; marui)

shi「ka¹kukee しかくけい (四角形) *n.* quadrangle; tetragon.

shi「kame-ru しかめる *vt.* (shikame-te Ⓥ) frown; grimace: *Kanojo wa sono shirase o kiite, kao o* shikameta. (彼女はその知らせを聞いて，顔をしかめた) She *frowned* on hearing the news.

shi「ka¹mo しかも (然も) *conj.*
1 moreover; besides: *Kanojo wa shigoto ga hayai.* Shikamo *shiñchoo da.* (彼女は仕事が速い。しかも慎重だ) She does her work very quickly; *moreover,* she is careful.
2 yet; still; nevertheless: *Kare wa kikeñ ni chokumeñ shi,* shikamo *heezeñ to shite ita.* (彼は危険に直面し，しかも平然としていた) He faced dangers, *and yet* he still remained calm.

shi「kar・u しかる (叱る) *vt.* (shikar・i-; shikar・a-; shikat-te Ⓒ) scold; reprove. (⇨ okoru²)

shi「ka¹shi しかし (然し) *conj.* but; however. (⇨ da ga; keredo (mo); tokoro ga)

shi「kashi-na¹gara しかしながら (然し乍ら) *conj.* however; but. ★ More formal than 'shikashi.'

shi「kata しかた (仕方) *n.* way; method: tadashii *beñkyoo no* shikata (正しい勉強のしかた) the right *way* of studying.

shi「katana¹・i しかたない (仕方ない) *a.* (-ku) ★ Polite forms are 'shikatanai desu' and 'shikata arimaseñ.' 'Shikata ga nai' is also used in the same meaning.
1 (*pred.*) cannot help doing; be no use doing: *Suñda koto wa* shikatanai. (済んだことは仕方ない) What is done, *is done.* (⇨ shiyoo ga nai)

2 (-ku) unwillingly; against one's will:
Watashi wa shikatanaku *sansee shita.* (私は仕方なく賛成した) I approved it *reluctantly*.
-te shikatanai (て〜): *Ikitakute shikatanai.* (行きたくて仕方ない) I'm *dying to go* there.

shi「ke¬e しけい (死刑) *n.* death penalty.

shi「ke¬ñ しけん (試験) *n.* examination; test: shikeñ *o ukeru* (試験を受ける) take an *examination*.
shikeñ (o) suru (〜(を)する) *vt.* test; experiment. (⇨ tesuto)

shi「keñkañ しけんかん (試験管) *n.* test tube. (⇨ kañ²)

shi「ki¬¹ しき (四季) *n.* the four seasons.

shi「ki¬² しき (指揮) *n.* **1** command; direction: shiki *o toru* (指揮をとる) assume *command*.
2 conducting (an orchestra).
shiki suru (〜する) *vt.* command (a ship); direct (a business); conduct (an orchestra).

shi「ki¬³ しき (式) *n.* **1** ceremony: shiki *o okonau* (式を行う) hold a *ceremony*. (⇨ -shiki)
2 expression; formula: shiki *de arawasu* (式で表す) express something in a *formula*.

-shiki しき (式) *suf.* **1** ceremony: *sotsugyoo-shiki* (卒業式) a graduation *ceremony* / *kekkoñ-shiki* (結婚式) a wedding *ceremony*.
2 way; style; fashion: *Nihoñ-shiki no toire* (日本式のトイレ) a Japanese-*style* toilet.

shi「kibu¬toñ しきぶとん (敷き布団) *n.* mattress; sleeping pad.

shi「kichi しきち (敷地) *n.* site; lot; ground.

shi「ki¬kiñ しききん (敷金) *n.* deposit. ★ Money paid to a landlord as a pledge for the rental contract. It is returnable. (⇨ keñrikiñ; reekiñ; yachiñ)

shi「ki¬ñ しきん (資金) *n.* fund; capital: shikiñ *o tsukuru* (資金を

つくる) raise *funds*. (⇨ motode)

shi「kiri しきり (仕切り) *n.* **1** partition; compartment:
heya no shikiri *o toru* (部屋の仕切りを取る) remove the *partitions* of a room. (⇨ shikiru)
2 (of sumo wrestling) the warm-up process before a bout:
shikiri-*naoshi o suru* (仕切り直しをする) toe the mark again.

shi「kiri ni しきりに (頻りに) *adv.* very often; continually; eagerly.

shi「ki¬r·u しきる (仕切る) *vt.* (shikir·i-; shikir·a-; shikit-te Ⓒ) divide; partition:
kaateñ de heya o futatsu ni shikiru (カーテンで部屋を2つに仕切る) *divide* the room into two with curtains. (⇨ shikiri)

shi「kisai しきさい (色彩) *n.* color; coloration; coloring.

shi「kka¬ri しっかり *adv.* (〜 to; 〜 suru) **1** firmly; tightly:
Kono tsuna ni shikkari *(to) tsukamari nasai.* (この綱にしっかり(と)つかまりなさい) Please take hold of this rope *firmly*.
2 hard; steadily; bravely:
Shikkari *(to) beñkyoo shi nasai.* (しっかり(と)勉強しなさい) Study *hard.* / Shikkari shi nasai. (しっかりしなさい) *Pull yourself together*.
shikkari shite iru [shita] (〜している[した]) *firm*; reliable:
Kono tatemono wa kiso ga shikkari shite iru. (この建物は基礎がしっかりしている) The foundations of this building *are firm*.

shi「kke しっけ (湿気) *n.* moisture; humidity; damp.

shi「kki¬¹ しっき (漆器) *n.* lacquerware. (⇨ urushi)

shi「kki¬² しっき (湿気) *n.* = shikke.

shi「k·u しく (敷く) *vt.* (shik·i-; shik·a-; shi·i-te Ⓒ) lay; spread; cover; stretch:
Doozo zabutoñ o shiite *kudasai.* (どうぞ座布団を敷いてください) Please *take* a cushion and sit down.

shi「kuji¬r·u しくじる *vt.* (-jir·i-;

-jir·a-; -jit·te C| fail; blunder; make a mistake. (⇨ shippai)

shiˈkumi しくみ (仕組み) *n.* structure; mechanism; setup: *koñpyuutaa no shikumi* (コンピュータ ーのしくみ) the *working* of a computer.

shiˈkuˈshiku しくしく *adv.* **shikushiku (to) itamu** (〜（と）痛 む) have a dull pain. **shikushiku (to) naku** (〜（と）泣く) sob; weep.

shiˈkyuu[1] しきゅう (至急) *n., adv.* urgently; immediately: *Shikyuu go-heñji o kudasai.* (至急 ご返事を下さい) Please let us have your reply *promptly*.

shiˈkyuu[2] しきゅう (子宮) *n.* womb; uterus.

shiˈma[1] しま (島) *n.* island.

shiˈma[2] しま (縞) *n.* stripe: *aoi shima no nekutai* (青い縞のネク タイ) a tie with blue *stripes*.

shiˈmai[1] しまい (姉妹) *n.* sisters. (⇨ kyoodai)

shiˈmai[2] しまい (仕舞い) *n.* end: *Hajime kara shimai made kare wa damatte ita.* (始めからしまいまで彼は黙 っていた) He kept silent from beginning to *end*. (⇨ oshimai)

shiˈmaˈr·u[1] しまる (閉まる) *vi.* (shimar·i-; shimar·a-; shimat·te C|) **1** close; be closed: *Kono doa wa jidoo-teki ni shimari-masu.* (このドアは自動的に閉まります) This door *closes* automatically. (⇨ shimeru[1])
2 (of a shop) shut: *Sono mise wa hachi-ji ni shimari-masu.* (その店は8時に閉まります) That shop *shuts* at eight. (⇨ shimeru[1])

shiˈmaˈr·u[2] しまる (締まる) *vi.* (shimar·i-; shimar·a-; shimat·te C|) **1** be tightened; become firm: *Neji wa shikkari shimatte imasu.* (ねじはしっかり締まっています) The screws *are* good and *tight*. (⇨ shimeru[2])
2 become tense:

Kyoo no kare wa shimatte iru. (き ょうの彼は締まっている) He *is tense* today.
3 be frugal: *Kanojo wa nakanaka shimatte iru.* (彼女はなかなか締まっている) She *is* very *frugal* with money.

shiˈmaˈsu します do: ★ Polite *masu*-form of '*suru.*' *Daigaku o detara nani o shimasu ka?* (大学を出たら何をしますか) What will you *do* after college? (⇨ suru[1])

shiˈmatsu しまつ (始末) *n.* disposal; management; settlement: *Kono ko wa shimatsu ni oenai.* (こ の子は始末に負えない) This child is *unmanageable*.
shimatsu ga warui (〜が悪い) be impossible to handle.
shimatsu (o) suru (〜（を）する) *vt.* dispose of; tidy up; put in order.

shiˈmatsusho しまつしょ (始末書) *n.* written apology. ★ Submitted to superiors by those who have caused an accident or made a blunder.

shiˈmaˈtta しまった *int.* gosh!; oh no!: *Shimatta! Teeki o wasureta.* (しまっ た. 定期を忘れた) *Gosh!* I have forgotten my commuter pass.

shiˈma·u[1] しまう (仕舞う) *vi.* (shima·i-; shimaw·a-; shimat·te C|) stop (work); leave off: *Kyoo wa itsu-mo yori hayaku shigoto o shimatta.* (きょうはいつもより早 く仕事をしまった) Today I *left off* working earlier than usual.

shima·u[2] しまう (仕舞う) (shima·i-; shimaw·a-; shimat·te C|) ★ Follows the *te*-form of a verb. In conversation '*-te＋shimau*' becomes '*-chau*,' and '*-de＋shi-mau*' becomes '*-jau*.'
1 have done; (have) finished doing: ★ Used to emphasize the recent completion or occurrence of an action. *Shukudai wa moo yatte shimai-*

mashita [yatchaimashita]. (宿題は
もうやってしまいました[やっちゃいました])
I *have* already *finished* my homework.
2 end up doing; go and do:
★ Used in reference to unfavorable consequences.
Kotori ga shiñde shimatta [shiñ-
jatta]. (小鳥が死んでしまった[死んじゃっ
た]) The bird *went and died*.

shiˈmaˑu³　しまう (仕舞う) *vi.* (shi-
maˑi-; shimawˑaˑ-; shimat-te Ⓒ)
put away; put back; keep.
《⇨ katazukeru》

shiˈmauma　しまうま (縞馬) *n.*
zebra.

shiˈmee¹　しめい (氏名) *n.* full
name. ★ Literally 'family name'
(氏) and 'personal name' (名).
《⇨ namae》

shiˈmee²　しめい (使命) *n.* mission: shimee *o hatasu* (使命を果た
す) carry out one's *mission*.

shiˈmee³　しめい (指名) *n.* nomi-
nation; designation; appointment:
shimee-*tehai* (指名手配) institu-
ting a search for an *identified
criminal*.
shimee suru (～する) *vt.* nomi-
nate; designate; name.

shiˈmekiri　しめきり (締め切り) *n.*
deadline. 《⇨ shimekiru²》

shiˈmekirˑu¹　しめきる (閉め切る) *vt.*
(-kirˑi-; -kirˑaˑ-; -kit-te Ⓒ) close
[shut] up:
Ame ga hidoi no de amado o shi-
mekitte *oita*. (雨がひどいので雨戸をし
めきっておいた) The rain was so
heavy that I *kept* the shutters
closed.

shiˈmekirˑu²　しめきる (締め切る) *vt.*
(-kirˑi-; -kirˑaˑ-; -kit-te Ⓒ) close:
Boshuu wa koñgetsu ippai de shi-
mekirimasu. (募集は今月いっぱいで締
め切ります) Applications will *be
closed* at the end of this month.
《⇨ shimekiri》

shiˈmenawa　しめなわ (注連縄) *n.*
sacred straw festoon. ★ A twist-

ed rice-straw rope hung with
strips of white paper.

shiˈmeppoˌˑi　しめっぽい (湿っぽい)
a. (-ku) **1** wet; damp; humid;
moist:
Kono taoru wa shimeppoi. (このタオ
ルはしめっぽい) This towel is *damp*.
2 gloomy:
Kyoo wa shimeppoi *hanashi wa
yameyoo*. (きょうはしめっぽい話はやめよ
う) Let's put *gloomy* topics aside
today.

shiˈmeˌˑru¹　しめる (閉める) *vt.*
(shime-te Ⓥ) close; shut:
Mado o shimete *kudasai*. (窓を閉め
てください) Please *shut* the window.
《↔ akeru¹》《⇨ shimaru¹》

shiˈmeˌˑru²　しめる (締める) *vt.*
(shime-te Ⓥ) **1** fasten:
shiito-beruto o shimeru (シートベルト
を締める) *fasten* one's seatbelt.
2 put on (neckties, belts, etc.):
★ '*shimete iru*' = wear.
3 lock:
doa no kagi o shimeru (ドアの鍵を締
める) *lock* a door. 《⇨ shimaru²》
4 add up; total:
Shimete *ichimañ goseñ-eñ ni narimasu*. (締めて1万5千円になります)
Adding it up, it comes to 15,000
yen.

shiˈmerˑu³　しめる (湿る) *vi.* (shi-
merˑi-; shimerˑaˑ-; shimet-te Ⓒ)
get damp; get moist.

shiˈmeˌˑru⁴　しめる (占める) *vt.*
(shime-te Ⓥ) occupy; hold:
*Kare wa kaisha de juuyoo na
chii o* shimete *iru*. (彼は会社で重要
な地位を占めている) He *occupies* an
important position in the company. 《⇨ toru¹》

shiˈmeˌsˑu　しめす (示す) *vt.* (shi-
meshˑi-; shimesˑaˑ-; shimesh-i-te
Ⓒ) show; point out; indicate.

shiˈmi　しみ (染み) *n.* stain; spot;
blot.

shiˈmijiˌˑmi　しみじみ *adv.* (～ to)
deeply; really; keenly; quietly:
Byooki o shite, shimijimi *(to) keñkoo no taisetsu na koto ga wakat-

ta.(病気をして, しみじみ(と)健康の大切なことがわかった) I *keenly* realized the importance of good health when I became ill.

shi¹miñ しみん(市民) *n.* citizen: shimiñ-keñ (市民権) *citizenship.*

shi¹mi·ru しみる(染みる) *vi.* (shimi-te Ⅴ) **1** smart; sting; (of medicine) irritate:
Kono kusuri wa sukoshi shimimasu.(この薬は少ししみます) This medicine *stings* a little.
2 (of kindness, gentleness) touch:
Kare no shiñsetsu ga mi ni shimita.(彼の親切が身にしみた) His kindness *deeply touched* me.
3 (of cold) pierce:
Samusa ga mi ni shimita.(寒さが身にしみた) The cold *chilled* me to the bone.

shi¹mo しも(霜) *n.* frost.

shimo² しも *p.* (used with a negative) (not) always; (not) necessarily: ★ Used mainly with '*kanarazu.*'
Doryoku shite mo, kanarazu shimo *seekoo suru to wa kagiranai.*(努力しても, 必ずしも成功するとは限らない) Even if you make every effort, it *doesn't always follow* that you will succeed.

shi¹mo- しも(下) *pref.*
1 lower:
shimo-*te* (下手) the *lower* part; the left of the stage / shimo-*za* (下座) a *lower* seat. ((↔ kami-)
2 the second:
shimo-*hañki* (下半期) the *second* half of the year. ((↔ kami-)
3 last:
shimo-*futa-keta* (下2桁) the *last* two figures.

shi¹moñ しもん(指紋) *n.* fingerprints.

shi¹ñ¹ しん(芯) *n.* core; lead; wick:
eñpitsu no shiñ (鉛筆のしん) the *lead* of a pencil / *roosoku no* shiñ (ろうそくのしん) the *wick* in a candle.

shi¹ñ² しん(心) *n.* heart; spirit:
Kare wa shiñ *wa yasashii hito da.*(彼は心はやさしい人だ) He is kind at *heart.* ((⇨ kokoro)

shi¹ñ- しん(新) *pref.* new:
shiñ-*kiroku* (新記録) a *new* record / shiñ-*seehiñ* (新製品) a *new* product.

shi¹na しな(品) *n.* **1** article; goods. ((⇨ shinamono)
2 quality; brand:
Kono kabañ wa shina *ga yoi [warui].*(このかばんは品が良い[悪い]) This bag is of good [bad] *quality.*

shi¹nabi·ru しなびる(萎びる) *vi.* (shinabi-te Ⅴ) wither; shrivel. ((↔ kareru)

shi¹nai しない(市内) *n.* city; within the city. ★ This only applies to a city which is designated as '*shi.*' ((↔ shigai²) ((⇨ tonai)

shi¹namono しなもの(品物) *n.* article; goods. ((⇨ shina)

shi¹na¹yaka しなやか *a.n.* (~ na, ni) soft and tender; flexible; supple: shinayaka *na eda* (しなやかな枝) a *supple* branch.

shi¹ñ-Bee しんべい(親米) *n.* pro-American. ((↔ hañ-Bee)

shi¹ñboo しんぼう(辛抱) *n.* patience; endurance; perseverance.
shiñboo suru (~する) *vi., vt.* be patient; endure; persevere. ((⇨ gamañ)

shi¹ñboozuyo¹·i しんぼうづよい(辛抱強い) *a.* (-ku) patient; persevering; tenacious.

shi¹ñbuñ しんぶん(新聞) *n.* newspaper; paper. ((⇨ furushiñbuñ)

shi¹ñchiku しんちく(新築) *n.* new building; new construction.
shiñchiku suru (~する) *vt.* build; construct. ((⇨ tateru²)

shi¹ñchoo¹ しんちょう(身長) *n.* stature; height.

shi¹ñchoo² しんちょう(慎重) *a.n.* (~ na, ni) careful; cautious; prudent. ((↔ keesotsu)

shi¹ñchuu しんちゅう(真鍮) *n.* brass.

shiˈñdai しんだい（寝台）n. bed; berth: shiñdai-*sha*（寝台車）a *sleeping* car.

shiˈñdañ しんだん（診断）n. diagnosis: shiñdañ-*sho*（診断書）a *medical* certificate.
shiñdañ suru（～する）vt. diagnose.

shiˈñdo¹ しんど（震度）n. seismic intensity; intensity of a quake on the Japanese scale of eight.

shiˈñdo² しんど（進度）n. progress:
shiñdo *ga hayai* [*osoi*]（進度が速い[遅い]）make fast [slow] *progress*.

shiˈñdoo¹ しんどう（振動）n. vibration; swing; oscillation.
shiñdoo suru（～する）vt. vibrate; swing; oscillate.

shiˈñdoo² しんどう（震動）n. quake; tremor.
shiñdoo suru（～する）vi. shake; quake; tremble.

shiˈñfuˈzeñ しんふぜん（心不全）n. heart failure.

shiˈñgaˈkki しんがっき（新学期）n. new school term.（⇨ gakki¹）

shiˈñgaku しんがく（進学）n. going on to a school of the next higher level.
shiñgaku suru（～する）vi. enter a school of a higher grade.

shiˈñgoo しんごう（信号）n. signal; traffic light:
shiñgoo *o mamoru* [*mushi suru*]（信号を守る[無視する]）observe [ignore] a *traffic signal*.

shiˈnimonoguˈrui しにものぐるい（死に物狂い）n. desperation:
shinimonogurui *ni* [*de*] *nigeru*（死に物狂いに[で]逃げる）run away for *dear life*.

shiˈñjiñ しんじん（新人）n. new star; new employee; rookie.

shiˈñjiˈ-ru しんじる（信じる）vt. (shiñji-te Ⅴ) **1** believe:
Anata no iu koto o shiñjimasu.（あなたの言うことを信じます）I *believe* what you say.
2 trust:

Watashi wa kare o shiñjite imasu.（私は彼を信じています）I *trust* him.
3 be sure; be confident:
Kanojo wa kitto seekoo suru to shiñjimasu.（彼女はきっと成功すると信じます）I *am confident* that she will succeed.
4 believe in (religions).
（⇨ shiñkoo²）

shiˈñjitsu しんじつ（真実）n. truth; reality; fact.（⇨ shiñsoo）

shiˈñju しんじゅ（真珠）n. pearl.

shiˈñjuu しんじゅう（心中）n. double suicide; taking someone into death with one.
shiñjuu suru（～する）vi. commit a double suicide.（⇨ muri-shiñjuu）

shiˈñkee しんけい（神経）n.
1 nerve:
Kare wa me no shiñkee o yararete imasu.（彼は目の神経をやられています）His visual *nerves* are damaged.
2 sensitivity:
shiñkee ga surudoi [nibui]（神経が鋭い[鈍い]）be sensitive [insensitive].

shiˈñkeeka しんけいか（神経科）n. neurology: shinkeeka-i（神経科医）a *neurologist*.

shiˈñkeˈeshitsu しんけいしつ（神経質）a.n.（～ na, ni）nervous:
shiñkeeshitsu na hito（神経質な人）a *nervous* person.

shiˈñkeñ しんけん（真剣）a.n.（～ na, ni）serious; earnest:
Watashi wa shiñkeñ desu.（私は真剣です）I am *serious*.（⇨ majime）

shiˈñkiñ-koˈosoku しんきんこうそく（心筋梗塞）n. myocardial infarction.

shiˈñkoku しんこく（深刻）a.n.（～ na, ni）serious; grave:
Jitai wa shiñkoku desu.（事態は深刻です）The situation is *grave*.（⇨ kibishii）

shiˈñkoñ しんこん（新婚）n. newly-married:
Ano futari wa shiñkoñ hoyahoya desu.（あの二人は新婚ほやほやです）They are *recently married*.

shi⸢ñkoo[1] しんこう (進行) *n.*
progress; advance.
shiñkoo suru (～する) *vi.* move;
progress; advance. (⇨ susumu)

shi⸢ñkoo[2] しんこう (信仰) *n.* faith;
belief.
shiñkoo suru (～する) *vt.* believe
in (Buddhism). (⇨ shiñjiru)

shi⸢ñkuu しんくう (真空) *n.* vacuum.

shi⸢ñkuukañ しんくうかん (真空管)
n. vacuum tube; valve. (⇨ kañ[2])

shi⸢ñneñ[1] しんねん (新年) *n.* new
year; the New Year. (⇨ shoogatsu)

shi⸢ñneñ[2] しんねん (信念) *n.* belief; faith; conviction:
shiñneñ *o tsuranuku* [*magenai*] (信
念を貫く [曲げない]) stick to [do not
deviate from] one's *faith*.

shi⸢ñnyuu しんにゅう (侵入) *n.* invasion; intrusion; raid.
shiñnyuu suru (～する) *vi.* invade; intrude; break into.

shi⸢-noo-koo-shoo しのうこうし
ょう (士農工商) *n.* the four classes
in Japanese feudal society, from
the highest to the lowest; war-
riors, farmers, artisans, and mer-
chants.

shi⸢ñpai しんぱい (心配) *n.* **1** anxiety; worry; concern; fear.
2 care; help:
Ojisañ ga shuushoku no shiñpai o
shite kureta. (おじさんが就職の心配を
してくれた) My uncle *helped* me
find employment.
shiñpai suru (～する) *vt.* worry;
fear; care; be troubled.
— *a.n.* (～ na) worried; anxious; uneasy. (⇨ kigakari; fuañ)

shi⸢ñpañ しんぱん (審判) *n.*
1 (of sports) umpire; referee.
2 judgment:
kainañ ni tsuite shiñpañ *o kudasu*
(海難について審判を下す) pass *judg-
ment* on a marine accident.

shi⸢ñpi しんぴ (神秘) *n.* mystery.

shi⸢ñpi-teki しんぴてき (神秘的)
a.n. (～ na, ni) mysterious.

shi⸢ñpo しんぽ (進歩) *n.* progress;
advance; improvement.
shiñpo suru (～する) *vi.* progress;
advance; improve.

shi⸢ñpo-teki しんぽてき (進歩的)
a.n. (～ na, ni) progressive;
advanced:
Kare no kañgae wa shiñpo-teki *da.*
(彼の考えは進歩的だ) His thinking
is *forward-looking.* (↔ hoshu-
teki)

shi⸢ñpu[1] しんぷ (神父) *n.* father.
★ A priest or clergyman in the
Roman Catholic church.
(⇨ bokushi)

shi⸢ñpu[2] しんぷ (新婦) *n.* bride.
★ Used only at a wedding ceremony or reception. (⇨ shiñroo)

shi⸢ñrai しんらい (信頼) *n.* trust;
confidence.
shiñrai suru (～する) *vt.* trust;
rely on.

shi⸢ñri[1] しんり (心理) *n.* state of
mind; psychology:
shiñri-gaku (心理学) *psychology.*

shi⸢ñri[2] しんり (真理) *n.* truth:
Kimi no iu koto ni wa ichimeñ no
shiñri ga aru. (君の言うことには一面の
真理がある) There is some *truth* in
what you say.

shi⸢ñriñ しんりん (森林) *n.* forest;
woods. (⇨ mori; hayashi)

shi⸢ñroo しんろう (新郎) *n.* bridegroom; groom. ★ Used only at
a wedding ceremony or reception. (⇨ shiñpu[2])

shi⸢ñrui しんるい (親類) *n.* relative; relation. (⇨ shiñseki)

shi⸢ñryaku しんりゃく (侵略) *n.*
invasion; aggression.
shiñryaku suru (～する) *vt.* invade.

shi⸢ñryoo しんりょう (診療) *n.*
medical treatment:
shiñryoo-jo (診療所) a *clinic*; a *dis-
pensary.*
shiñryoo suru (～する) *vt.* treat (a
patient). (⇨ chiryoo)

shi⸢ñsatsu しんさつ (診察) *n.*
medical examination.

shiňsatsu suru (～する) *vt.* examine; see: *isha ni* shiňsatsu shite morau (医者に診察してもらう) *see* a doctor.

shi「ňsee[1] しんせい (申請) *n.* application; request: shiňsee-*sho* (申請書) an *application* form; a written *application*. **shiňsee (o) suru** (～(を)する) *vt.* apply for. (⇨ mooshikomu)

shi「ňsee[2] しんせい (神聖) *a.n.* (～ na) sacred; holy; divine: shiňsee *na basho* (神聖な場所) a *holy* place.

shi「ňseki しんせき (親戚) *n.* relative; relation. (⇨ shiňrui)

shi「ňseň しんせん (新鮮) *a.n.* (～ na, ni) fresh; new; green: shiňseň *na yasai* (新鮮な野菜) *fresh* vegetables.

shi「ňsetsu しんせつ (親切) *n.* kindness; kindliness; tenderness. — *a.n.* (～ na, ni) kind; kindly; friendly; hospitable: *Nihoň de wa miňna ga* shiňsetsu *ni shite kuremashita.* (日本ではみんなが親切にしてくれました) Everyone was *kind* to me in Japan. (↔ fushiňsetsu)

shi「ňshi しんし (紳士) *n.* gentleman.

shi「ňshiki しんしき (神式) *n.* Shinto rites: shiňshiki no *kekkoň* (神式の結婚) a *Shinto* wedding. (⇨ busshiki)

shi「ňshiň しんしん (深々) *adv.* (～ to) (the state of increasing darkness or cold, or snow falling): *Yoru ga* shiňshiň to fukete iku. (夜がしんしんと更けていく) The night *is getting far advanced*.

shi「ňshitsu しんしつ (寝室) *n.* bedroom.

shi「ňshoku しんしょく (浸食) *n.* erosion. **shiňshoku suru** (～する) *vt.* erode; eat away.

shi「ňsho「osha しんしょうしゃ (身障者) *n.* abbreviation for '*shiňtai-shoogaisha*.' (⇨ shiňtai-shoogaisha)

shi「ňshutsu しんしゅつ (進出) *n.* advance. **shiňshutsu suru** (～する) *vt.* advance; make one's way: *kesshoo-seň ni* shiňshutsu suru (決勝戦に進出する) *advance* to the finals.

shi「ňsoo しんそう (真相) *n.* the truth; fact: *Sono* shiňsoo *wa dare mo shirimaseň.* (その真相はだれも知りません) Nobody knows the *true facts*.

shi「ňtai しんたい (身体) *n.* body; constitution: shiňtai-*keňsa* (身体検査) a *physical* examination. (⇨ karada)

shi「ňtai-shooga「isha しんたいしょうがいしゃ (身体障害者) *n.* physically handicapped person; disabled person.

Shi「ňtoo しんとう (神道) *n.* Shintoism; Shinto.

shi「ň・u しぬ (死ぬ) *vi.* (shin・i-; shin・a-; shiň-de Ⓒ) die; be killed: ★ A rather blunt expression. '*Nakunaru*' is more polite. *Chichi wa gaň de* shinimashita. (父はがんで死にました) My father *died* of cancer. (↔ ikiru) (⇨ shiboo[2])

shi「ňya-ho「osoo しんやほうそう (深夜放送) *n.* late-night broadcasting.

shi「ňyoo しんよう (信用) *n.* confidence; trust; faith; reliance. **shiňyoo suru** (～する) *vt.* trust; put confidence in; rely on.

shi「ňyoo-ku「miai しんようくみあい (信用組合) *n.* credit union (association). ★ Operates as a bank for medium and small-sized enterprises.

shi「ňyuu しんゆう (親友) *n.* close friend; one's best friend.

shi「ňzeň しんぜん (親善) *n.* friendship; goodwill: shiňzeň *o hakaru* (親善を図る) promote *friendly relations*.

shi⌐ɴzeɴ-ke⌐kkoɴ しんぜんけっこん（神前結婚）*n.* wedding according to Shinto rites.

shi⌐ɴzoo しんぞう（心臓）*n.* heart. **shiɴzoo ga tsuyoi [yowai]** (〜が強い[弱い]) be bold [timid]: *Kare wa shiɴzoo ga tsuyoi.* (彼は心臓が強い) He is *stout-hearted*.

shi⌐ɴz·u·ru しんずる（信ずる）*vt.* (shiɴj·i·-; shiɴj·i·-; shiɴj·i·-te □) = shiɴjiru.

shi⌐o¹¹ しお（塩）*n.* salt.

shi⌐o¹² しお（潮）*n.* tide. shio *no michi-hi* (潮の満ち干) the ebb and flow of the *tide*.

shi⌐okara⌐ i しおからい（塩辛い）*a.* (-ku) salty. (⇒ karai)

shi⌐oɴ しおん（子音）*n.* = shiiɴ.

shi⌐ore·ru しおれる（萎れる）*vi.* (shiore-te □) 1 (of a plant) wither; wilt; fade. (⇒ kareru) 2 (of a person) be dejected.

shi⌐ppai しっぱい（失敗）*n.* failure; mistake. **shippai suru** (〜する) *vi.* fail. (↔ seekoo¹) (⇒ shikujiru)

shi⌐ppitsu しっぴつ（執筆）*n.* writing: shippitsu-sha (執筆者) a *writer*; an *author*. **shippitsu suru** (〜する) *vt.* write: hoɴ [roɴbuɴ] o shippitsu suru (本[論文]を執筆する) *write* a book [an essay].

shi⌐ppo¹ しっぽ（尻尾）*n.* tail. (⇒ o¹)

shi⌐rabe¹¹ しらべ（調べ）*n.* examination; investigation; questioning: shirabe o ukeru (調べを受ける) be *examined*. (⇒ torishirabe)

shi⌐rabe¹² しらべ（調べ）*n.* melody; tune.

shi⌐rabemono しらべもの（調べ物）*n.* something to check up on.

shi⌐rabe·ru しらべる（調べる）*vt.* (shirabe-te □) 1 examine; inspect; investigate: kaji no geɴiɴ o shiraberu (火事の原因を調べる) *investigate* the cause of a fire. (⇒ soosa²)

2 consult (a reference book); look up: *Sono go no imi o jisho de shirabeta.* (その語の意味を辞書で調べた) I *consulted* the dictionary for the meaning of the word.

shi⌐rase しらせ（知らせ）*n.* news; information; report: *Kare kara nani-ka shirase ga arimashita ka?* (彼から何か知らせがありましたか) Has there been any *news* from him? (⇒ shiraseru)

shi⌐rase·ru しらせる（知らせる）*vt.* (shirase-te □) let know; inform; tell; report. (⇒ shirase)

shi⌐razu-shi⌐razu しらずしらず（知らず知らず）*adv.* (〜 ni) without knowing it; unconsciously: *Kodomo wa shirazu-shirazu (ni) kotoba o oboeru.* (子どもは知らず知らず(に)言葉を覚える) Children learn language *unconsciously*.

shi⌐ri¹ しり（尻）*n.* buttocks; bottom. ★ Often with 'o-.'

shi⌐riai しりあい（知り合い）*n.* acquaintance: *Ano hito wa taɴ-naru shiriai desu.* (あの人は単なる知り合いです) He is just an *acquaintance*.

shi⌐riizu シリーズ *n.* series; serial.

shi⌐ritsu¹ しりつ（私立）*n.* private: ★ Sometimes '*watakushiritsu*' to distinguish it from '*shiritsu*²'(市立). shiritsu-*daigaku* (私立大学) a *private* university [college]. (↔ kooritsu¹)

shi⌐ritsu² しりつ（市立）*n.* municipal: ★ Sometimes '*ichiritsu*' to distinguish it from '*shiritsu*¹'(私立). shiritsu *no toshokaɴ* (市立の図書館) a *municipal* library.

shi⌐ro¹ しろ（白）*n.* 1 white. (⇒ shiroi)

2 innocence: *Kare wa zettai ni shiro da to omou.* (彼は絶対に白だと思う) I am quite sure that he is *innocent*. (↔ kuro)

shi⌐ro² しろ（城）n. castle.

shi⌐ro⌐·i しろい（白い）a. (-ku) white; (of skin) fair; (of hair) gray.

shi⌐ro-kuro しろくろ（白黒）n. black and white:
shiro-kuro no fuirumu（白黒のフイルム）black-and-white film.

shi⌐rooto しろうと（素人）n. amateur; layman. (↔ kurooto)

shi⌐r·u¹ しる（知る）vt. (shir·i-; shir·a-; shit-te ⓒ) **1** know; have knowledge of; be acquainted with; ★ The form 'shitte iru' is used rather than 'shiru.'
Kanojo no deñwa-bañgoo o shitte imasu ka?（彼女の電話番号を知っていますか）Do you know her phone number?
2 realize; notice; be aware:
Koñna ni osoi to wa shiranakatta.（こんなに遅いとは知らなかった）I did not realize it was this late.
3 discover; find:
Kare wa jibuñ ga machigatte iru koto o shitta.（彼は自分が間違っていることを知った）He found that he was wrong.

shi⌐ru² しる（汁）n. juice; soup.

shi⌐rubaa-shi⌐ito シルバーシート n. seat reserved for the elderly or handicapped on trains or buses. ★ Literally 'silver seat.'

shi⌐ruko¹ しるこ（汁粉）n. sweet thick soup made from red beans with pieces of rice cake. ★ Often with 'o-.'

shi⌐rushi しるし（印）n. **1** mark; check; sign:
kami ni shirushi o tsukeru（紙に印をつける）put a mark on paper.
2 token:
o-ree no shirushi to shite（お礼の印として）in token of one's gratitude.

shi⌐rus·u しるす（記す）vt. (shirush·i-; shirus·a-; shirush·i-te ⓒ) (formal) write down. (⇨ kaku¹)

shi⌐ryoo しりょう（資料）n. material; data:

roñbuñ no tame no shiryoo o atsumeru（論文のための資料を集める）collect material for an essay.

shi⌐satsu しさつ（視察）n. inspection; observation.
shisatsu suru（～する）vt. inspect; observe.

shi⌐see しせい（姿勢）n. posture; carriage; position:
Kare wa shisee ga ii [warui].（彼は姿勢がいい[悪い]）He has a fine [poor] posture.

shi⌐señ しせん（支線）n. branch line (of a railroad).

shi⌐setsu しせつ（施設）n. **1** facilities.
2 (euphemistically) institution; home; mental hospital.

shi⌐sha¹ ししゃ（死者）n. dead person; the dead.

shi⌐sha² ししゃ（支社）n. branch office. (⇨ shiteñ)

shi⌐sha-gonyuu ししゃごにゅう（四捨五入）n. rounding off.
★ To round up to the nearest whole number when the figure is 5 and above, and round down when the figure is 4 and below. (⇨ kiriageru; kirisuteru)

shi⌐sho⌐osha ししょうしゃ（死傷者）n. casualties:
Sono jiko de tasuu no shishoosha ga deta.（その事故で多数の死傷者が出た）There were many dead and injured in the accident.

shi⌐shutsu ししゅつ（支出）n. expenditure; outgoings; expense. (↔ shuunyuu) (⇨ shuushi¹)
shishutsu suru（～する）vt. pay; expend. (⇨ shiharau)

shi⌐shuu ししゅう（刺繍）n. embroidery.
shishuu (o) suru（～(を)する）vt. embroider.

shi⌐soku しそく（四則）n. the four basic operations of arithmetic. (⇨ keesañ)

shi⌐soñ しそん（子孫）n. descendant; offspring. (↔ señzo; soseñ)

shi⌐soo しそう（思想）n. thought;

shi「sso しっそ (質素) *a.n.* (~ *na*, *ni*) simple; plain; homely:
Kare no seekatsu wa shisso desu.
(彼の生活は質素です) His way of living is *plain and simple*.

shi「su「u しすう (指数) *n.* index number: *bukka-shisuu* (物価指数) a price *index*.

shi「ta¹ した (下) *n.* 1 under; below:
Ki no shita de inu ga nete iru. (木の下で犬が寝ている) There is a dog asleep *under* the tree. (↔ ue¹)

2 down; downward:
Kono erebeetaa wa shita e ikimasu. (このエレベーターは下へ行きます) This elevator is going *down*. (↔ ue¹)

3 bottom. (↔ ue¹)

4 junior; younger:
Kanai wa mittsu shita desu. (家内は 3 つ下です) My wife is three years *younger* than me. (↔ ue¹)

shi「ta¹² した (舌) *n.* tongue.

shi「tagae¹·ru したがえる (従える) *vt.* (shitagae-te Ⅴ) make (a person) follow; be accompanied by:
buka o shitagaeru (部下を従える) *be attended* by one's subordinates. (⇒ shitagau)

shi「tagaki したがき (下書き) *n.* draft:
supiichi no shitagaki o suru (スピーチの下書きをする) *make a draft* of one's speech.

shi「tagatte¹ したがって (従って)
★ Used in the pattern '... *ni shitagatte*.' **1** in accordance with:
Subete, kare no sashizu ni shitagatte okonatta. (すべて、彼の指図に従って行った) We have done everything *in accordance with* his instructions. (⇒ shitagau)

2 as:
Taifuu no sekkiñ ni shitagatte, fuu-u ga tsuyoku natta. (台風の接近に従って、風雨が強くなった) *As the* typhoon drew nearer, the wind

got stronger and the rain heavier. (⇒ tsurete)

shi「tagatte² したがって (従って) *conj.* (*formal*) therefore; consequently; accordingly. ★ Used at the beginning of a sentence.

shi「taga·u したがう (従う) *vi.* (shitaga-i-; shitagaw-a-; shitagat-te Ⓒ) obey; follow; observe:
iiñkai no kettee ni shitagaimasu. (委員会の決定に従います) We will *abide by* the decision of the committee. (⇒ shitagaeru)

shi「tagi したぎ (下着) *n.* underwear; underclothes.

shi「tai したい (死体) *n.* dead body; corpse.

shi「taku したく (支度) *n.* preparation; arrangements.
shitaku (o) suru (~(を)する) *vi.* prepare; get ready. (⇒ yooi¹)

shi「tamachi したまち (下町) *n.*
1 the lower section of a city.
2 the old part of Tokyo.
★ Such as Asakusa and Kanda where family industries and commerce used to thrive. (↔ yamanote)

shi「tashi¹·i したしい (親しい) *a.* (-ku) friendly; familiar; intimate; close:
shitashii tomodachi (親しい友だち) a *good* friend / *shitashii kañkee* (親しい関係) *close* relations.

shi「tashimi¹ したしみ (親しみ) *n.* friendly feeling; affection:
Watashi wa kanojo no hitogara ni shitashimi o kañjita. (私は彼女の人柄に親しみを感じた) I *felt myself drawn* to her because of her personality.

shi「tashi¹m·u したしむ (親しむ) *vi.* (-shim·i-; -shim·a-; -shiñ-de Ⓒ)
1 be familiar [intimate]:
Sono otogibanashi wa kodomo-tachi ni shitashimarete imasu. (そのおとぎ話は子どもたちに親しまれています) That fairy tale *is familiar* to children.
2 enjoy; take an interest:

dokusho ni shitashimu (読書に親しむ) *enjoy* reading. (⇨ shitashimi)

shiˈtateˈ·ru したてる(仕立てる) *vt.* (shitate-te Ⅴ) **1** tailor; make: *Kare wa atarashii suutsu o it-chaku* shitateta.(彼は新しいスーツを一着仕立てた) He *had* a suit *made*. **2** raise; educate; train (a person).

shiˈtauke したうけ(下請け) *n.* subcontract; subcontractor: *Kare wa sono shigoto o* shitauke *ni dashita.*(彼はその仕事を下請けに出した) He gave the work to a *subcontractor*.

shiˈtee してい(指定) *n.* appointment; designation: shitee-*seki* [-*keñ*] (指定席[券]) a *reserved* seat [seat ticket]. **shitee suru** (〜する) *vt.* appoint; designate; specify.

shiˈteki してき(指摘) *n.* indication. **shiteki suru** (〜する) *vt.* point out; indicate.

shiˈteñ してん(支店) *n.* branch office [store; shop]. (⇨ shisha¹)

shiˈtetsu してつ(私鉄) *n.* private railroad [railway].

shiˈtoˈshito しとしと *adv.* (〜 to) (the state of fine rain falling): *Ame ga* shitoshito *(to) futte iru.* (雨がしとしと(と)降っている) The rain is falling *softly*.

shiˈtoˈyaka しとやか(淑やか) *a.n.* (〜 na, ni) graceful; gentle: shitoyaka *na josee* (しとやかな女性) a *graceful and modest* woman. (⇨ joohiñ)

shiˈtsu しつ(質) *n.* quality: *Ryoo yori mo* shitsu *ga taisetsu desu.* (量よりも質が大切です) *Quality* matters more than quantity. (↔ ryoo¹)

-shitsu しつ(室) *suf.* room: kyoo-shitsu (教室) a class*room* / yoku-shitsu (浴室) a bath*room*.

shiˈtsuboo しつぼう(失望) *n.* disappointment; discouragement. **shitsuboo suru** (〜する) *vi.* be disappointed. (⇨ gakkari)

shiˈtsuˈdo しつど(湿度) *n.* humidity: *Kyoo wa* shitsudo *ga takai* [*hikui*]. (きょうは湿度が高い[低い]) The *humidity* is high [low] today.

shiˈtsuˈgai しつがい(室外) *n.* outside a room; outdoors. (↔ shitsunai)

shiˈtsugyoo しつぎょう(失業) *n.* unemployment. **shitsugyoo suru** (〜する) *vt.* lose one's job; be out of work.

shiˈtsuke しつけ(躾) *n.* training; discipline; manners: *Chichi wa* shitsuke *ga kibishi-katta.* (父はしつけが厳しかった) My father was very particular about our *upbringing*.

shiˈtsukoˈ·i しつこい *a.* (-ku) **1** persistent; stubborn; importunate: *Onaji koto o* shitsukoku *iwanai de kudasai.*(同じことをしつこく言わないでください) Please stop going *on and on* about the same thing. **2** (of food) heavy; cloying; greasy.

shiˈtsumoñ しつもん(質問) *n.* question; inquiry. **shitsumoñ suru** (〜する) *vt., vi.* ask a question.

shiˈtsuˈnai しつない(室内) *n.* inside a room: shitsunai-*sooshoku* (室内装飾) interior decoration. (↔ shitsugai)

shiˈtsuoñ しつおん(室温) *n.* room temperature. (⇨ oñdo)

shiˈtsuˈree しつれい(失礼) *n.* impoliteness. **shitsuree suru**(〜する) *vi.* **1** I'm sorry; Excuse me: *Kinoo wa rusu o shite,* shitsuree shimashita. (きのうは留守をして, 失礼しました) *I am sorry* that I was not at home yesterday. **2** I must be going: *O-saki ni* shitsuree shimasu.(お先に失礼します) Now *I must be going.* — *a.n.* (〜 na) impolite; discourteous; rude. (⇨ busahoo)

shiˈtto しっと (嫉妬) *n.* jealousy; envy.

shitto suru (〜する) *vt.* be jealous of; envy. (⇨ yakimochi)

shiˈwa しわ (皺) *n.* **1** wrinkle: *Kare wa hitai ni shiwa o yoseta.* (彼は額にしわを寄せた) He *wrinkled* his forehead.
2 crease: *airoñ de zuboñ no shiwa o nobasu* (アイロンでズボンのしわを伸ばす) iron out the *creases* in the trousers.

shiˈwaza しわざ (仕業) *n.* one's doing; work: *Kore wa dare no shiwaza desu ka?* (これはだれのしわざですか) Whose *doing* is this?

shiˈyaˈkusho しゃくしょ (市役所) *n.* municipal [city] office; city hall. (⇨ kuyakusho)

shiˈyoo[1] しよう (使用) *n.* use; employment.
shiyoo suru (〜する) *vt.* use; employ. (⇨ tsukau)

shiˈyoo[2] しよう (私用) *n.* private use; private business: *shiyoo no deñwa* (私用の電話) a *private* telephone call.

shiˈyoo ga naˈ·i しようがない (仕様がない) *a.* (-ku) ★ Also pronounced 'shoo ga nai.' Polite forms are 'shiyoo ga nai desu' and 'shiyoo ga arimaseñ.'
1 (*pred.*) be helpless; have no choice: *Dame nara, shiyoo ga nai. Hoka no hito ni tanomimasu.* (だめなら、しようがない。ほかの人に頼みます) If your answer is 'No,' *there is no more to be said.* I will ask someone else. (⇨ shikatanai)
2 (*attrib.*) good-for-nothing: *Aitsu wa shiyoo ga nai yatsu da.* (あいつはしようがないやつだ) He is a *good-for-nothing.*

shiˈyuu しゆう (私有) *n.* private possession: *shiyuu-zaisañ* (私有財産) *private* property / *shiyuu-chi* (私有地) *private* land.

shiˈzai しざい (資材) *n.* material; raw material.

shiˈzeñ しぜん (自然) *n.* nature: *Hokkaidoo ni wa mada shizeñ ga nokotte iru.* (北海道にはまだ自然が残っている) The *natural environment* still survives in Hokkaido.
— *a.n.* (〜 na, ni) natural: *shizeñ ni furumau* (自然に振る舞う) behave *naturally.* (↔ fushizeñ)
— *adv.* naturally; automatically.

shiˈzeñ ni しぜんに (自然に) *adv.* of oneself; automatically; spontaneously: (⇨ hitoride ni) *Kaze wa shizeñ ni naotta.* (かぜは自然に治った) My cold cured *itself.*

shiˈzuka しずか (静か) *a.n.* (〜 na, ni) **1** quiet; still: *shizuka na ashioto* (静かな足音) *quiet* footsteps / *shizuka ni aruku* (静かに歩く) walk *quietly.* (↔ urusai)
2 calm; soft: *Kyoo no umi wa shizuka da.* (きょうの海は静かだ) The sea is *calm* today. (⇨ arai[1])

shiˈzuku[1] しずく (滴) *n.* drop: *Jaguchi kara mizu no shizuku ga ochite iru.* (蛇口から水のしずくが落ちている) *Water is dripping* from the tap.

shiˈzumaˈr·u しずまる (静まる) *vi.* (shizumar·i-; shizumar·a-; shizumat-te Ⓒ) calm [quiet] down; subside: *Kaze ga shizumatta.* (風が静まった) The wind *has died down.* (⇨ shizumeru[2])

shiˈzume·ru[1] しずめる (沈める) *vt.* (shizume-te Ⓥ) sink; submerge; put under water. (⇨ shizumu)

shiˈzumeˈ·ru[2] しずめる (静める) *vt.* (shizume-te Ⓥ) calm; quiet; soothe; appease: *Kare wa koofuñ shita kañkyaku o shizumeta.* (彼は興奮した観客を静めた) He *calmed* the excited spectators. (⇨ shizumaru)

shiˈzum·u しずむ (沈む) *vi.* (shizum·i-; shizum·a-; shizuñ-de Ⓒ) **1** sink; go down:

Sono fune wa akkenaku shizuňde *shimatta.*(その船はあっけなく沈んでしまった) The ship *sank* quickly. (⇨ chiňbotsu; shizumeru¹)

2 be depressed:
Kare wa naze-ka shizuňde ita.(彼はなぜか沈んでいた) He *was depressed* for some reason or other.

sho- しょ(諸) *pref.* various:
sho-*koku*(諸国) *various* countries / sho-*seňsee*(諸先生) *teachers*. (⇨ kaku-)

-sho¹ しょ(所) *suf.* place; office; institute:
juu-sho(住所) an *address* / jimu-sho(事務所) an *office*. (⇨ -jo)

-sho² しょ(書) *suf.* writing; letter; book: buň-sho(文書) a *document* / doku-sho(読書) *reading*.

sho¹batsu しょばつ(処罰) *n.* punishment; penalty:
shobatsu *o ukeru*(処罰を受ける) receive *punishment*.
shobatsu suru(〜する) *vt.* punish.

sho¹buň しょぶん(処分) *n.* **1** disposal:
Gomi no shobuň *ni komatte imasu.*(ごみの処分に困っています) I do not know what to do about *getting rid of* the rubbish.
2 punishment:
Kare wa uňteňmeňkyo-teeshi no shobuň o uketa.(彼は運転免許停止の処分を受けた) He *was punished* by having his driving license suspended.
shobuň suru(〜する) *vt.* **1** dispose of; do away with; get rid of: *ie o* shobuň *suru*(家を処分する) *sell off* one's house.
2 punish; discipline.

sho¹chi しょち(処置) *n.* measure; treatment; disposal.
shochi suru(〜する) *vt.* deal with; treat; dispose of: *moňdai o umaku* shochi suru(問題をうまく処置する) *deal with* a problem skillfully.

sho¹chuu-mi¹mai しょちゅうみま

い(暑中見舞い) *n.* summer greeting card. ★ A postcard sent to inquire after a person's health in the hot season.

sho¹ho しょほ(初歩) *n.* the first step; rudiments.

sho¹kki しょっき(食器) *n.* tableware; the dishes.

sho¹koku しょこく(諸国) *n.* various countries.

sho¹kuba しょくば(職場) *n.* one's place of work; office; one's job.

sho¹ku¹butsu しょくぶつ(植物) *n.* plant; vegetation.

sho¹kubutsu¹eň しょくぶつえん(植物園) *n.* botanical garden. (⇨ doobutsueň)

sho¹kudoo¹ しょくどう(食堂) *n.* dining room; cafeteria; eating place; restaurant.

sho¹kudoo² しょくどう(食道) *n.* gullet; esophagus.

sho¹kudo¹osha しょくどうしゃ(食堂車) *n.* dining car.

sho¹ku¹gyoo しょくぎょう(職業) *n.* occupation; profession; job; business.

sho¹kuhi しょくひ(食費) *n.* food expenses; board.

sho¹kuhiň しょくひん(食品) *n.* food; foodstuffs: shokuhiň-teňkabutsu(食品添加物) a *food* additive.

sho¹ku¹iň しょくいん(職員) *n.* staff; staff member; personnel. (⇨ juugyooiň; shaiň)

sho¹kuji しょくじ(食事) *n.* meal; diet.
shokuji (o) suru(〜(を)する) *vi.* have a meal.

sho¹ku¹motsu しょくもつ(食物) *n.* food. (⇨ shokuryoo¹)

sho¹kuniň しょくにん(職人) *n.* artisan; craftsman.

sho¹ku¹ryoo¹ しょくりょう(食料) *n.* foodstuffs. ★ Often refers to food other than staples. (⇨ shokuryoo²)

sho¹ku¹ryoo² しょくりょう(食糧) *n.* food; provisions. ★ Often refers to staple food. (⇨ shokuryoo¹)

sho⸢kutaku⸣¹ しょくたく（食卓）*n.* dining table.

sho⸢kutaku⸣² しょくたく（嘱託）*n.* part-time employee; nonregular employee.

sho⸢kuyoku⸣ しょくよく（食欲）*n.* appetite:
shokuyoku *ga aru* [*nai*]（食欲がある［ない］）have a good [poor] *appetite*.

sho⸢kyuu⸣ しょきゅう（初級）*n.* beginner's class:
shokyuu *Nihoñgo*（初級日本語）Japanese for *beginners*. (⇨ chuu-kyuu; jookyuu)

sho⸢mee⸣ しょめい（署名）*n.* signature; autograph.
shomee suru (〜する) *vi.* sign; autograph: *keeyakusho ni* shomee suru（契約書に署名する）*sign* a contract. (⇨ saiñ)

sho⸢miñ⸣ しょみん（庶民）*n.* ordinary citizen; common people; average person.

sho⸢motsu⸣ しょもつ（書物）*n.* (*formal*) book. (⇨ hoñ)

sho⸢mu⸣ しょむ（庶務）*n.* general affairs:
shomu-*ka*（庶務課）the *general affairs* section (of a company).

sho⸢o⸣¹ しょう（省）*n.* ministry: *Gaimu-*shoo（外務省）the *Ministry* of Foreign Affairs. (⇨ APP. 7)

sho⸢o⸣² しょう（性）*n.* nature; disposition; temperament.
shoo ni au (〜に合う) be congenial to one: *Ima no shigoto wa kare no* shoo ni atte iru *yoo da.*（今の仕事は彼の性に合っているようだ）The present work seems to *be suited* to him.

sho⸢o⸣³ しょう（賞）*n.* prize; reward; award:
shoo *o toru* [*morau*]（賞を取る［もらう］）win a *prize*.

sho⸢o⸣⁴ しょう（章）*n.* **1** chapter: *dai is-*shoo（第１章）*Chapter* 1.
2 badge; emblem: *kaiiñ-*shoo（会員章）a membership *badge*.

sho⸢o⸣⁵ しょう（小）*n.* smallness:

Saizu wa dai to shoo *ga arimasu.*（サイズは大と小があります）There are two sizes: large and *small*. (⇨ dai¹)

sho⸢o-⸣ しょう（小）*pref.* small; minor: shoo-*gekijoo*（小劇場）a *small* theater / shoo-*kibo*（小規模）*small* scale. (↔ dai-¹)

sho⸢obai⸣ しょうばい（商売）*n.* business; trade; occupation.
shoobai (o) suru (〜（を）する) *vi.* do business; engage in trade; deal in.

sho⸢obeñ⸣ しょうべん（小便）*n.* piss; urine. ★ Often pronounced 'shoñbeñ.' ★ Considered vulgar and advisable not to use in public.
shoobeñ (o) suru (〜（を）する) *vi.* urinate: *tachi-*shoobeñ *o suru*（立ち小便をする）*urinate* in the street. (↔ daibeñ; fuñ²; kuso)

sho⸢oboo⸣ しょうぼう（消防）*n.* fire fighting: shooboo-*sho*（消防署）a *fire* station / shooboo-*sha*（消防車）a *fire* engine.

sho⸢obu⸣ しょうぶ（勝負）*n.* game: shoobu *ni katsu* [*makeru*]（勝負に勝つ［負ける］）win [lose] a *game*.
shoobu suru (〜する) *vi.* have a game; fight. (⇨ tatakau)

sho⸢ochi⸣ しょうち（承知）*n.* knowing; being aware (of); consent: *Go-*shoochi *no yoo ni, kare wa señgetsu taishoku shimashita.*（ご承知のように、彼は先月退職しました）*As you know*, he retired last month.
shoochi suru (〜する) *vi.*
1 know; be aware (of); understand: *Sono koto wa yoku* shoochi *shite imasu.*（そのことはよく承知しています）I *am well aware* of that.
2 consent; agree; permit: *Chichi wa yatto watashi-no keekaku o* shoochi *shite kureta.*（父はやっと私の計画を承知してくれた）My father finally *agreed* to my plan.

sho⸢o-chiku⸣-bai しょうちくばい（松竹梅）*n.* pine, bamboo and

Japanese apricot. ★ These three plants are used together in making symbolic decorations on happy occasions. (⇨ matsu²; take¹; ume)

sho⌐ochoo¹ しょうちょう(象徴) *n.* symbol.
　shoochoo suru (～する) *vt.* symbolize.

sho⌐ochoo² しょうちょう(小腸) *n.* the small intestine.

sho⌐odaku しょうだく(承諾) *n.* consent; agreement; permission; acceptance.
　shoodaku suru (～する) *vt.* consent; agree; permit; accept.

sho⌐odoku しょうどく(消毒) *n.* disinfection; sterilization.
　shoodoku suru (～する) *vt.* disinfect; sterilize: *kizuguchi o shoodoku suru* (傷口を消毒する) *disinfect* a wound.

sho⌐o-ene しょうエネ(省エネ) *n.* energy-saving.

sho⌐ogai¹ しょうがい(障害) *n.*
　1 obstacle; obstruction; barrier: *shoogai ni butsukaru* (障害にぶつかる) encounter an *obstacle*.
　2 defect; impediment: *Kare wa geñgo-shoogai ga aru.* (彼は言語障害がある) He has a speech *defect*.

sho⌐ogai² しょうがい(生涯) *n.* one's whole life: *shiawase na shoogai o okuru* (幸せな生涯を送る) lead a happy *life*.

sho⌐oga⌐kkoo しょうがっこう(小学校) *n.* elementary school. (⇨ gakkoo)

sho⌐ogakukiñ しょうがくきん(奨学金) *n.* scholarship.

sho⌐oga⌐kusee しょうがくせい(小学生) *n.* elementary school pupil; schoolchild. (⇨ seeto)

sho⌐o ga na⌐i しょうがない *a.* (-ku) = shiyoo ga nai.

sho⌐ogatsu しょうがつ(正月) *n.* the New Year; January.

sho⌐ogi しょうぎ(将棋) *n.* Japanese chess.

sho⌐ogo しょうご(正午) *n.* noon; midday. (⇨ o-hiru)

sho⌐oguñ しょうぐん(将軍) *n.* general; shogun.

sho⌐ogyoo しょうぎょう(商業) *n.* commerce; business: *shoogyoo-kookoo* (商業高校) a *commercial* high school.

sho⌐ohai しょうはい(勝敗) *n.* result of a game [battle]; victory or defeat.

sho⌐ohi しょうひ(消費) *n.* consumption; expenditure: *shoohi-zee* (消費税) a *consumption* tax.
　shoohi suru (～する) *vt.* consume; expend (time, energy, etc.). (↔ seesañ)

sho⌐ohiñ¹ しょうひん(商品) *n.* commodity; goods; merchandise. (⇨ shinamono)

sho⌐ohiñ² しょうひん(賞品) *n.* prize; trophy.

sho⌐ohi⌐sha しょうひしゃ(消費者) *n.* consumer. (↔ seesañsha)

sho⌐oji しょうじ(障子) *n.* paper sliding door; shoji screen.

sho⌐oji⌐ki しょうじき(正直) *n.* honesty; uprightness.
　— *a.n.* (～ na, ni) honest; frank; straightforward: *Hoñtoo no koto o shoojiki ni hanashite kudasai.* (本当のことを正直に話してください) Please speak the truth *frankly*.

sho⌐oji·ru しょうじる(生じる) *vi.* (shooji-te Ⅴ) arise; happen; come about; result: *Gakusee no aida de fumañ ga shoojita.* (学生の間で不満が生じた) Discontent *arose* among the students.

sho⌐ojo しょうじょ(少女) *n.* young [little] girl. (↔ shooneñ)

sho⌐ojoo¹ しょうじょう(賞状) *n.* certificate of merit [commendation].

sho⌐ojo⌐o² しょうじょう(症状) *n.* (disease) symptom; condition.

sho⌐oka¹ しょうか(消化) *n.* digestion.

shooka suru (〜する) *vi.*, *vt.* digest; assimilate.

sho￢oka² しょうか (消火) *n.* fire extinguishing [fighting]:
shooka-ki (消火器) a *fire extinguisher* / shooka-señ (消火栓) a *fire hydrant*.
shooka suru (〜する) *vt.* extinguish a fire; fight a fire.

sho￢okai¹ しょうかい (紹介) *n.* introduction; presentation.
shookai suru (〜する) *vt.* introduce; present.

sho￢okai² しょうかい (商会) *n.* firm; company: *Sakamoto* shookai (坂本商会) Sakamoto & *Co.*

sho￢oko しょうこ (証拠) *n.* proof; evidence:
shooko *o dasu* (証拠を出す) produce *evidence*.

sho￢okyoku-teki しょうきょくてき (消極的) *a.n.* (〜 na, ni) negative; passive. (↔ sekkyoku-teki)

sho￢omee¹ しょうめい (証明) *n.* proof; evidence; testimony:
shoomee-sho (証明書) a *certificate*.
shoomee suru (〜する) *vt.* prove; testify; certify.

sho￢omee² しょうめい (照明) *n.* lighting; illumination:
teñjihiñ ni shoomee *o ateru* (展示品に照明を当てる) direct a *light* onto an exhibit.
shoomee suru (〜する) *vt.* light; illuminate.

sho￢omeñ しょうめん (正面) *n.* the front; facade; the area in front. (⇒ mae)

sho￢omoo しょうもう (消耗) *n.* exhaustion; consumption.
shoomoo suru (〜する) *vi.*, *vt.* exhaust; consume.

sho￢oneñ しょうねん (少年) *n.* (little) boy; lad. (↔ shoojo)

sho￢onika しょうにか (小児科) *n.* pediatrics:
shoonika-i (小児科医) a *pediatrician*.

sho￢oniñ¹ しょうにん (承認) *n.* approval; recognition; permission:

shooniñ *o eru* [*morau*] (承認を得る [もらう]) get *permission*.
shooniñ suru (〜する) *vt.* approve; recognize; permit.
((⇒ kyoka))

sho￢oniñ² しょうにん (商人) *n.* merchant; tradesman; dealer; storekeeper; shopkeeper.

sho￢oniñ³ しょうにん (証人) *n.* witness.

sho￢oniñ⁴ しょうにん (昇任) *n.* promotion. (⇒ shooshiñ)

sho￢orai しょうらい (将来) *n.* future; the time [days] to come. (⇒ mirai)

sho￢oree しょうれい (奨励) *n.* encouragement.
shooree suru (〜する) *vt.* encourage; recommend: *supootsu o* shooree suru (スポーツを奨励する) *encourages* sports.

sho￢ori しょうり (勝利) *n.* victory: *attoo-teki na* shoori *o osameru* (圧倒的な勝利をおさめる) gain an overwhelming *victory*. (↔ haiboku)

sho￢oryaku しょうりゃく (省略) *n.* omission; abridgment; abbreviation. (⇒ ryaku; ryakusu; tañshuku)
shooryaku suru (〜する) *vt.* omit; abridge; abbreviate.

sho￢oryo￢o しょうりょう (少量) *n.* a small quantity [amount]. (↔ tairyoo; taryoo)

sho￢osai しょうさい (詳細) *n.* details; particulars:
Shoosai *wa ato de o-shirase shimasu*. (詳細は後でお知らせします) We will inform you of the *particulars* later on. (↔ gaiyoo)
— *a.n.* (〜 na, ni) detailed; particular; minute; full. (⇒ kuwashii)

sho￢osetsu しょうせつ (小説) *n.* novel; story; fiction:
shoosetsu-ka (小説家) a novelist.

sho￢osha¹ しょうしゃ (商社) *n.* trading company; business firm.

sho￢osha² しょうしゃ (勝者) *n.* winner; victor. (↔ haisha²)

sho⌐oshiñ しょうしん（昇進）*n.*
promotion.
  shooshiñ suru (〜する) *vi.* be
promoted.

sho⌐oshoo しょうしょう（少々）*adv.*
a little [few]; a moment [min-
ute]:
  Shooshoo o-machi kudasai. (少々
お待ちください) Please wait *a moment.* (⇨ sukoshi)

sho⌐osu⌐u[1] しょうすう（少数）*n.* a
small number; minority. (↔ tasuu)

sho⌐osu⌐u[2] しょうすう（小数）*n.*
decimal: shoosuu-*teñ* (小数点) a
decimal point.

sho⌐otai[1] しょうたい（招待）*n.* invitation:
  shootai *o ukeru* [*kotowaru*] (招待
を受ける[断わる]) accept [decline] an
invitation.
  shootai suru (〜する) *vt.* invite.

sho⌐otai[2] しょうたい（正体）*n.* a
person's true colors [character];
true nature.

sho⌐oteñ[1] しょうてん（商店）*n.*
store; shop. (⇨ mise)

sho⌐oteñ[2] しょうてん（焦点）*n.*
focus:
  shooteñ *ga atte iru* [*inai*] (焦点が合
っている[いない]) be in [out of] *focus.*

sho⌐otoo しょうとう（消灯）*n.*
turning off the lights.
  shootoo suru (〜する) *vi.* turn off
[put out] the lights.

sho⌐ototsu しょうとつ（衝突）*n.*
  1 collision; crash:
  deñsha no shoototsu-*jiko* (電車の衝
突事故) a *collision* between trains.
  2 clash; conflict:
  rigai no shoototsu (利害の衝突) a
clash of interests.
  shoototsu suru (〜する) *vi.*
  1 collide; run into; crash.
  2 clash; conflict: *Guñshuu wa
keekañ-tai to shoototsu shita.* (群衆
は警官隊と衝突した) The crowd
clashed with the police. (⇨ butsukaru)

sho⌐oyu しょうゆ（醤油）*n.* soy

sauce. (⇨ miso)

sho⌐ri しょり（処理）*n.* management; disposal; treatment.
  shori suru (〜する) *vt.* handle;
deal with; manage.

sho⌐rui しょるい（書類）*n.* document; papers.

sho⌐sai しょさい（書斎）*n.* room for
study.

sho⌐tchuu しょっちゅう *adv.* (*informal*) always; very often.
  (⇨ itsu-mo)

sho⌐toku しょとく（所得）*n.* income; earnings:
  shotoku-*zee* (所得税) an *income* tax.

sho⌐oyo しょうよ（賞与）*n.*
  = boonasu.

sho⌐yuu しょゆう（所有）*n.* possession; ownership:
  shoyuu-*butsu* (所有物) one's *possessions* / shoyuu-*sha* (所有者) an
owner.
  shoyuu suru (〜する) *vt.* possess;
own. (⇨ motsu)

sho⌐zoku しょぞく（所属）*n.* one's
position [post; place].
  ... ni shozoku suru (...に〜する) *vi.*
belong to; be attached to.

shu[1] しゅ（種）*n.* kind; sort; class;
type:
  *Kono shu no hoñ ga yoku urete
imasu.* (この種の本がよく売れています)
Books of this *kind* are selling well.
  (⇨ shurui)

shu[2] しゅ（主）*n.* the chief [princi-
pal] thing:
  *Kono jigyoo wa kanemooke ga shu
de wa nai.* (この事業は金もうけが主では
ない) It is not the *main purpose* of
this enterprise to make money.
  (⇨ shu to shite)

shu[3] しゅ（主）*n.* the Lord:
  shu *Iesu Kirisuto* (主イエスキリスト)
Jesus Christ, *Our Lord.*

-shu しゅ（酒）*suf.* alcoholic drink:
  Nihoñ-shu (日本酒) Japanese *sake* /
budoo-shu (ぶどう酒) *wine.*

shu⌐bi しゅび（守備）*n.* defense;
guard; fielding:
  Ano señshu wa shubi ga umai. (あの

選手は守備がうまい) That player is good at *fielding*.

shubi suru (〜する) *vi.* defend; guard. ((↔ koogeki)) ((⇒ mamoru))

shuˈchoo しゅちょう (主張) *n.* insistence; claim; assertion; opinion.
shuchoo suru (〜する) *vt.* insist; maintain; claim: *jibuñ no keñri o* shuchoo suru (自分の権利を主張する) *assert* one's rights.

shuˈdai しゅだい (主題) *n.* subject; theme:
shudai-ka (主題歌) a *theme* song.

shuˈdañ しゅだん (手段) *n.* means; measures; step:
shudañ o toru (手段をとる) take a *step* [*measures*]. ((⇒ hoosakuˈ))

shuˈee しゅえい (守衛) *n.* guard; doorkeeper.

shuˈeñ しゅえん (主演) *n.* having a leading role; the leading actor [actress].
shueñ suru (〜する) *vi.* play the leading role; star.

shuˈfu[1] しゅふ (主婦) *n.* housewife.

shuˈfu[2] しゅふ (首府) *n.* capital; metropolis. ((⇒ shuto))

shuˈgi しゅぎ (主義) *n.* principle; doctrine:
Kare wa jibuñ no shugi o magenakatta. (彼は自分の主義を曲げなかった) He did not deviate from his *principles*.

shuˈgo しゅご (主語) *n.* (of grammar) subject of a sentence.

shuˈjiñ しゅじん (主人) *n.* **1** storekeeper; employer; owner.
2 husband. ★ *shujiñ*=one's own husband; *go-shujiñ*=someone else's husband. ((⇒ otto))

shuˈju しゅじゅ (種々) *n.* many kinds; various. ((⇒ iroiroˈ))

shuˈjutsu しゅじゅつ (手術) *n.* operation. ★ Often pronounced '*shijitsu*.'
shujutsu (o) suru (〜(を)する) *vt.* operate; be operated on.

shuˈkañ しゅかん (主観) *n.* subjectivity.

shuˈkañ-teki しゅかんてき (主観的) *a.n.* (〜 na, ni) subjective:
Kare wa shukañ-teki na ikeñ o nobeta. (彼は主観的な意見を述べた) He gave his *subjective* opinion. ((↔ kyakkañ-teki))

shuˈkketsu しゅっけつ (出血) *n.* bleeding; hemorrhage:
shukketsu o tomeru (出血を止める) stop the *bleeding*.
shukketsu suru (〜する) *vt.* bleed.

shuˈkkiñ しゅっきん (出勤) *n.* going to work; attendance.
shukkiñ suru (〜する) *vt.* go to work; go [come] to the office.

shuˈkkoku しゅっこく (出国) *n.* departure from a country:
shukkoku-tetsuzuki (出国手続き) *departure* formalities.
shukkoku suru (〜する) *vt.* leave a country; get out of a country. ((↔ nyuukoku))

shuˈkudai しゅくだい (宿題) *n.*
1 homework; assignment.
2 open [pending] question:
Kono moñdai wa tsugi no kai made shukudai ni shite okimashoo. (この問題は次の会まで宿題にしておきましょう) *Let's leave* this matter *as it is* until the next meeting.

shuˈkujitsu しゅくじつ (祝日) *n.* national [legal; public] holiday. ((⇒ APP. 6))

shuˈkusaiˈjitsu しゅくさいじつ (祝祭日) *n.* national [public] holiday; red-letter day; festival.
★ Combination of '*shukujitsu*' (祝日) and '*saijitsu*' (祭日).

shuˈkushoo しゅくしょう (縮小) *n.* reduction; curtailment.
shukushoo suru (〜する) *vt.* reduce; curtail: guñbi o shukushoo suru (軍備を縮小する) *reduce* armaments. ((↔ kakudai))

shuˈkuˈs·u しゅくす (祝す) *n.* (shukush·i-; shukus·a-; shukush·i-te C) (*formal*) congratulate; celebrate. ((⇒ iwau))

shuˈmi しゅみ (趣味) *n.* **1** hobby; pastime; interest.
2 taste:

Kanojo wa kiru mono no shumi *ga ii [warui].* (彼女は着る物の趣味がいい[悪い]) She has fine [poor] *taste* in clothes.

shu˥niñ しゅにん (主任) *n.* head; chief; boss: *kaikee-*shuniñ (会計主任) the *chief* accountant.

shu˥ñkañ しゅんかん (瞬間) *n.* moment; instant: *Sore wa* shuñkañ *no dekigoto datta.* (それは瞬間の出来事だった) It was something that happened in an *instant*.

...(shita) shuñkañ (...(した)~) the moment (one has done...): *Hako no futa o aketa* shuñkañ *bakuhatsu shita.* (箱のふたを開けた瞬間爆発した) *The moment* I took off the lid, the box exploded.

shu˥ñki しゅんき (春季) *n.* spring; springtime. (⇒ kaki³; shuuki²; tooki⁴)

shu˩ppañ¹ しゅっぱん (出版) *n.* publication; publishing: shuppañ-*sha* (出版社) a *publishing* company; a *publisher*.

shuppañ suru (~する) *vt.* publish; issue. (⇒ dasu (3); deru (11))

shu˩ppañ² しゅっぱん (出帆) *n.* sailing; departure.

shuppañ suru (~する) *vi.* set sail; leave; depart.

shu˩ppatsu しゅっぱつ (出発) *n.* departure; start.

shuppatsu suru (~する) *vi.* leave; start; depart; set out. (↔ toochaku) (⇒ deru (1))

shu˩ppiñ しゅっぴん (出品) *n.* exhibition; display.

shuppiñ suru (~する) *vt.* exhibit; display.

shu˩rui しゅるい (種類) *n.* kind; sort; variety: (⇒ rui; shu¹) *Kore wa nañ to iu* shurui *no inu desu ka?* (これは何という種類の犬ですか) What *kind* of dog is this?

shu˩sai しゅさい (主催) *n.* sponsorship; promotion: shusai-*sha* (主催者) a *sponsor*; a *promoter*.

shusai suru (~する) *vt.* organize; sponsor; host.

shu˥shi しゅし (趣旨) *n.* aim; object; point: *O-hanashi no* shushi *wa yoku wakarimashita.* (お話しの趣旨はよくわかりました) I've understood the *point* of what you are saying.

shu˩shoku しゅしょく (主食) *n.* staple food.

shu˩shoo しゅしょう (首相) *n.* prime minister; premier. (⇒ Soori-daijiñ)

shu˩ssañ しゅっさん (出産) *n.* birth; childbirth; delivery.

shussañ suru (~する) *vi., vt.* give birth. (⇒ umu²)

shu˩sse しゅっせ (出世) *n.* success in life; promotion.

shusse suru (~する) *vi.* succeed in life; be promoted. (⇒ risshiñ-shusse)

shu˩ssee しゅっせい (出生) *n.* birth: ★ Also pronounced '*shus-shoo.*' shussee-*chi* (出生地) a *birthplace*.

shu˩sseki しゅっせき (出席) *n.* presence; attendance.

shusseki suru (~する) *vt.* attend; be present. (↔ kesseki) (⇒ deru (3))

shu˩sshiñ しゅっしん (出身) *n.* 1 the place where one was born: *Kare wa Kyooto no* shusshiñ *desu.* (彼は京都の出身です) He *comes from* Kyoto.

2 graduate: *Watashi wa kono daigaku no* shusshiñ *desu.* (私はこの大学の出身です) I am a *graduate* of this university.

shu˩sshoo しゅっしょう (出生) *n.* birth. (⇒ shussee)

shu˩tai しゅたい (主体) *n.* main constituent; core: *Sono chiimu wa wakai hito ga* shutai *ni natte imasu.* (そのチームは若い人が主体になっています) The team *is made up mainly* of young players.

shu˩tchoo しゅっちょう (出張) *n.* business [official] trip.

shutchoo suru (〜する) *vi.* make a business [an official] trip.

shu「to しゅと(首都) *n.* capital; metropolis:
shuto-*keñ* (首都圏) *Tokyo* and the surrounding region / shuto-*koo-soku-dooro* (首都高速道路) the *Metropolitan* Expressway.

shu「toku しゅとく(取得) *n.* (*formal*) acquisition.
shutoku suru (〜する) *vt.* acquire; obtain; get possession of. (⇨ toru')

shu」to shite しゅとして(主として) *adv.* mainly; chiefly; mostly:
Kaiiñ wa shu to shite shufu desu. (会員は主として主婦です) The members are *mostly* housewives.

shu「tsueñ しゅつえん(出演) *n.* appearance (on TV, the stage, etc.).
shutsueñ suru (〜する) *vi.* appear; perform.

shu「tsujoo しゅつじょう(出場) *n.* participation; entry:
shutsujoo-sha (出場者) a *participant*; a *contestant*.
shutsujoo suru (〜する) *vi.* take part in; participate in.

shu「u¹ しゅう(週) *n.* week.

shu「u² しゅう(州) *n.* state (of the U.S., Australia, etc.); county.

shu「uchaku しゅうちゃく(執着) *n.* attachment; adherance.
... ni shuuchaku suru (...に〜する) *vi.* adhere to; be attached to:
jibuñ no añ ni saigo made shuu-chaku suru (自分の案に最後まで執着する) *adhere* to one's own plan till the last.

shu「uchaku¹-eki しゅうちゃくえき (終着駅) *n.* terminal station.

shu「uchuu しゅうちゅう(集中) *n.* concentration:
shuuchuu-*goou* (集中豪雨) a *localized* torrential downpour.
shuuchuu suru (〜する) *vi., vt.* concentrate; focus; center. (↔ buñsañ)

shu「udañ しゅうだん(集団) *n.* group; mass:

shuudañ *o tsukuru* (集団を作る) form a *group*.

shu「udeˉñ(sha) しゅうでん(しゃ) (終電(車)) *n.* the last train of the day. (↔ shihatsu)

shu「ugeki しゅうげき(襲撃) *n.* attack; assault; raid.
shuugeki suru (〜する) *vt.* raid; attack.

Shu「ugiˉiñ しゅうぎいん(衆議院) *n.* the House of Representatives:
Shuugiiñ *giiñ* (衆議院議員) a member of the *House of Representatives*. (⇨ Sañgiiñ; kokkai)

shu「ugoo しゅうごう(集合) *n.*
1 gathering; meeting; assembly:
shuugoo-*jikañ* [-*basho*] (集合時間 [場所]) the *meeting* time [place].
2 (of mathematics) set:
shuugoo-*roñ* (集合論) *set* theory.
shuugoo suru (〜する) *vi.* gather; meet; assemble. (⇨ atsumaru)

shu「uheñ しゅうへん(周辺) *n.* vicinity; neighborhood; outskirts. (⇨ mawari)

shu「ui しゅうい(周囲) *n.* **1** circumference. (⇨ mawari)
2 surroundings; circumstances:
Shuui *ga urusakute, beñkyoo ga dekinakatta.* (周囲がうるさくて, 勉強ができなかった) I couldn't devote myself to my study because of the noisy *surroundings*.

shu「ukai しゅうかい(集会) *n.* meeting; assembly; gathering.

shu「ukaku しゅうかく(収穫) *n.* crop; harvest.
shuukaku suru (〜する) *vt.* harvest; crop.

shu「ukañ¹ しゅうかん(習慣) *n.* habit; custom; practice:
Hayaku okiru no wa yoi shuukañ *desu.* (早く起きるのは良い習慣です) It is a good *habit* to get up early.

shu「ukañ² しゅうかん(週間) *n.* week:
Kootsuu Añzeñ Shuukañ (交通安全 週間) Traffic Safety *Week*.

shu「ukaˉñshi しゅうかんし(週刊誌) *n.* weekly magazine.

shuˈuki[1] しゅうき（周期）*n*. cycle; period:
keeki no shuuki（景気の周期）a business [trade] *cycle*.

shuˈuki[2] しゅうき（秋季）*n*. fall; autumn.《⇨ kaki³; shuñki; tooki⁴》

-shuˈuki しゅうき（周忌）*suf*. anniversary of a person's death:
*Kyoo wa haha no sañ-*shuuki *desu.*（きょうは母の 3 周忌です）Today is the third *anniversary* of our mother's death.

shuˈukiñ しゅうきん（集金）*n*. collection of money.
shuukiñ suru（〜する）*vt*. collect money.

shuˈuki-teki しゅうきてき（周期的）*a.n.*（〜 na, ni）periodical:
Kono kazañ wa shuuki-teki *ni baku-hatsu shimasu.*（この火山は周期的に爆発します）This volcano erupts *periodically*.

shuˈukyoo しゅうきょう（宗教）*n*. religion: shuukyoo *o shiñjiru*（宗教を信じる）believe in *religion*.

shuˈumatsu しゅうまつ（週末）*n*. weekend.《⇨ heejitsu》

-shuˈuneñ しゅうねん（周年）*suf*. anniversary: ★ Used for a happy event.
*is-*shuuneñ *kineñbi*（一周年記念日）the first *anniversary*.

shuˈuniñ しゅうにん（就任）*n*. assumption of office; inauguration.
shuuniñ suru（〜する）*vi*. take office; assume.

shuˈunyuu しゅうにゅう（収入）*n*. income; earnings; revenue.（↔ shishutsu）《⇨ kasegi》

shuˈunyuu-iˈñshi しゅうにゅういんし（収入印紙）*n*. revenue stamp. ★ Often called '*iñshi*,' and put on a bond, deed, etc.

shuˈuri しゅうり（修理）*n*. repair; mending.
shuuri suru（〜する）*vt*. repair; mend; fix: *ie o* shuuri suru（家を修理する）*repair* a house.

shuˈuryoo しゅうりょう（終了）*n*. end; close.

shuuryoo suru（〜する）*vi., vt*. end; close.（↔ kaishi）《⇨ owaru》

shuˈusee[1] しゅうせい（修正）*n*. amendment; revision; modification.
shuusee suru（〜する）*vt*. amend; revise; modify; correct.

shuˈusee[2] しゅうせい（習性）*n*. habit; behavior:
saru no shuusee *o keñkyuu suru*（猿の習性を研究する）study the *behavior* of monkeys.

shuˈusha しゅうしゃ（終車）*n*. the last train [bus].（↔ shihatsu）

shuˈushi[1] しゅうし（収支）*n*. incomings and outgoings; revenue and expenditure.（⇨ shuunyuu; shishutsu）

shuˈushi[2] しゅうし（終始）*adv*. from beginning to end; throughout.
shuushi suru（〜する）*vi*. remain the same from beginning to end.

shuˈushoku しゅうしょく（就職）*n*. finding employment.
... ni shuushoku suru（...に〜する）*vi*. find work at; get a position at.

shuˈushokugo しゅうしょくご（修飾語）*n*.（of grammar）modifier; qualifier.

shuˈushuu しゅうしゅう（収集）*n*. collection.
shuushuu suru（〜する）*vt*. collect: *kitte o* shuushuu suru（切手を収集する）*collect* stamps.（⇨ atsumeru）

shuˈuteñ しゅうてん（終点）*n*. terminal station; terminus.（↔ kiteñ）

shuˈutokuˈbutsu しゅうとくぶつ（拾得物）*n*. article found; find.（⇨ hirou）

shuˈuyoo しゅうよう（収容）*n*. accommodation; seating.
shuuyoo suru（〜する）*vt*. accommodate; admit.

shuˈuzeñ しゅうぜん（修繕）*n*. = shuuri.

shuˈyaku しゅやく（主役）*n*. the leading part [role]; lead.

shuᵊyoo しゅよう（主要）*a.n.*
(~ na) important; chief; principal; main:
shuyoo-*sañgyoo* （主要産業）*major* industries / shuyoo-*toshi* （主要都市）*chief* cities.

soᵊba¹ そば（側）*n.* 1 side:
Sono ko wa haha-oya no soba kara hanareyoo to shinakatta. （その子は母親のそばから離れようとしなかった）The child wouldn't leave his mother's *side.*
2 (~ ni) next to; near; beside:
Chuushajoo wa eki no soba ni arimasu. （駐車場は駅のそばにあります）The parking lot is *next to* the station.

soᵊba² そば（蕎麦）*n.* buckwheat (noodles).

soᵊbieᵊru そびえる（聳える）*vi.* (sobie-te Ⅴ) rise; tower:
Me no mae ni sobiete iru no ga Komagatake desu. （目の前にそびえているのが駒ヶ岳です）That mountain *rising high* before us is Mt. Komagatake.

soᵊbo そば（祖母）*n.* one's grandmother. （↔ sofu）（⇒ o-baasañ）

soᵊboku そぼく（素朴）*a.n.* (~ na, ni) simple; unsophisticated:
soboku *na hitogara* （素朴な人柄）an *unsophisticated* personality.

soᵊchira そちら*n.* ★ More polite than 'sotchi.'
1 there; over there: ★ Refers to a direction or a place close to the listener.
Sochira ga deguchi desu. （そちらが出口です）*That way* is the exit.
2 that one; the other one: ★ Refers to something closer to the listener than the speaker.
Sochira no o misete itadakemasu ka? （そちらのを見せていただけますか）May I take a look at *that* one?
3 you; your side:
Sochira no tsugoo no yoi toki ni itsu de mo oide kudasai. （そちらの都合の良いときにいつでもおいでください）Please come any time when it is

convenient to *you.* （⇒ achira; kochira）

soᵊdachi¹ そだち（育ち）*n.*
1 growth:
Kotoshi wa ine no sodachi ga yoku nai. （ことしは稲の育ちが良くない）This year the *growth* of rice is not good. （⇒ sodatsu）
2 upbringing; breeding:
Watashi wa Tookyoo sodachi desu. （私は東京育ちです）I *grew up* in Tokyo. （⇒ sodatsu）

soᵊdateᵊru そだてる（育てる）*vt.* (sodate-te Ⅴ) bring up; raise; cultivate; train:
Kare wa ooku no yuushuu no señshu o sodateta. （彼は多くの優秀な選手を育てた）He *has trained* many excellent players. （⇒ sodatsu）

soᵊdatsᵊu そだつ（育つ）*vi.* (sodach-i-; sodat-a-; sodat-te C) grow (up):
Riñgo wa koko de wa sodachimaseñ. （りんごはここでは育ちません）Apples *do not grow* here. （⇒ sodateru; sodachi）

soᵊde そで（袖）*n.* sleeve.

soᵊeᵊru そえる（添える）*vt.* (soe-te Ⅴ) attach; add; garnish:
Okurimono ni tegami o soeta. （贈り物に手紙を添えた）I *attached* a letter to the gift.

soᵊfu そふ（祖父）*n.* one's grandfather.

soᵊfuto-kuriᵊimu ソフトクリーム*n.* soft ice-cream (in a cone).

soᵊkkuᵊri そっくり*a.n.* (~ na/no, ni) similar; like:
Kanojo wa haha-oya ni sokkuri desu. （彼女は母親にそっくりです）She is *exactly like* her mother.
— *adv.* all; wholly; entirely:
Mochimono o sokkuri nusumareta. （持ち物をそっくり盗まれた）I had *all* my things stolen.

soᵊko¹ そこ*n.* 1 that place; there: ★ Refers to a place near the listener and slightly distant from the speaker.
Suutsukeesu wa soko ni oite kuda-

sai. (スーツケースはそこに置いてください) Leave the suitcase *there*, please. 《⇨ asoko; doko; koko¹》

2 there: ★ Refers to a place previously mentioned.
Saisho wa Oosaka e iki, soko kara Okayama e ikimasu. (最初は大阪へ行き、そこから岡山へ行きます) First I go to Osaka, and from *there* to Okayama.

3 that: ★ Refers to a subject mentioned by the listener.
Soko no tokoro o moo ichido itte kudasai. (そこの所をもう一度言ってください) Will you please repeat *what* you have just said?

4 then; when: ★ Refers to a particular time.
Dekakeyoo to shitara, soko e deñwa ga kakatte kita. (出かけようとしたら、そこへ電話がかかってきた) I was just going out, *when* the telephone rang.

so「ko² そこ (底) *n*. **1** bottom:
baketsu no soko (バケツの底) the *bottom* of a bucket.

2 sole:
Kutsu ni atarashii soko o tsukete moratta. (靴に新しい底をつけてもらった) I had new *soles* put on my shoes.

so「ko de そこで *conj.* so; therefore. ★ Used at the beginning of a sentence.

so「kona¹·u そこなう (損なう) *vt.* (sokona·i-; sokonaw·a-; sokonat-te Ⓒ) spoil; ruin; injure:
keñkoo o sokonau (健康を損なう) *ruin* one's health.

-sokona¹·u そこなう (損なう) (-sokona·i-; -sokonaw·a-; -sokonat-te Ⓒ) miss; fail to (do): ★ Occurs as the second element of compound verbs. Added to the continuative base of a verb.
deñsha ni nori-sokonau (電車に乗りそこなう) *miss* a train.

so「ko¹ra そこら *n.* **1** around there:
Megane nara, sokora ni aru hazu desu. (眼鏡なら、そこらにあるはずです)

As for your glasses, they should be somewhere *around there*.

2 all over the place:
Karada ga sokora-juu itai. (体がそこらじゅう痛い) I have aches and pains *all over* my body.

3 approximately; or so:
Sono kamera nara, sañmañ-eñ ka sokora de te ni hairimasu. (そのカメラなら、3万円かそこらで手に入ります) That camera is available at 30,000 yen *or so*.

-soku そく (足) *suf.* counter for footgear. 《⇨ APP. 4》

so「kubaku そくばく (束縛) *n.* restraint; restriction.
sokubaku suru (〜する) *vt.* restrain; restrict: *geñroñ no jiyuu o sokubaku suru* (言論の自由を束縛する) *restrict* freedom of speech.

so「kumeñ そくめん (側面) *n.* side; flank: *sokumeñ kara kare o eñjo suru* (側面から彼を援助する) help him *indirectly*.

so「kuoñ そくおん (促音) *n.* doubled consonant. ★ Represented in writing by a small '*tsu*' (っ). *e.g.* itta (行った). 《⇨ APP. 1》

so「ku¹ryoku そくりょく (速力) *n.* speed:
zeñ-sokuryoku de hashiru (全速力で走る) run at full *speed*. 《⇨ sokudo; supiido》

so「kuryoo そくりょう (測量) *n.* survey; measurement.
sokuryoo suru (〜する) *vt.* make a survey; measure.

so「kushiñ そくしん (促進) *n.* promotion; furtherance.
sokushiñ suru (〜する) *vt.* promote; further; hasten: *booeki o sokushiñ suru* (貿易を促進する) *encourage* foreign trade.

so「kutatsu そくたつ (速達) *n.* special [express] delivery.

so「kutee そくてい (測定) *n.* measurement.
sokutee suru (〜する) *vt.* mea-

sure; check: *kuruma no hayasa o
sokutee suru* (車の速さを測定する)
measure the speed of a car.

so「mar·u そまる(染まる) *vi.* (so-
mar·i-; somar·a-; somat-te ⓒ)
1 dye; be tinged:
Kono kiji wa yoku somaru. (この生
地はよく染まる) This cloth *takes dye*
well. (⇨ someru)
2 be adversely influenced (by
one's surroundings).

so「matsu そまつ(粗末) *a.n.*
(~ na, ni) **1** poor; plain; humble:
somatsu *na shokuji o suru* (粗末な
食事をする) have a *frugal* meal.
2 careless; rough; rude:
hoñ o somatsu *ni atsukau* (本を粗末
に扱う) handle books *roughly*.

so「me·ru そめる(染める) *vt.* (some-
te ⓥ) dye; tinge:
Kanojo wa kami o chairo ni someta.
(彼女は髪を茶色に染めた) She *dyed*
her hair brown. (⇨ somaru)

so「mu「k·u そむく(背く) *vi.* (so-
muk·i-; somuk·a-; somu·i-te ⓒ)
disobey; disregard; violate:
Kare wa ryooshiñ no kitai ni somu-
ite, *shikeñ ni shippai shita.* (彼は両
親の期待に背いて、試験に失敗した)
Contrary to his parents' hopes, he
failed the exam.

so「ñ そん(損) *n.* loss.
soñ (o) suru (~(を)する) *vt.* lose;
suffer a loss.
— *a.n.* (~ na, ni) disadvantageous. (↔ toku²) (⇨ soñshitsu)

so「nae」 そなえ(備え) *n.* preparations; provision; defense.
(⇨ sonaeru¹)

so「nae」·ru¹ そなえる(備える) *vt.*
(sonae-te ⓥ) **1** prepare; provide:
Roogo ni sonaete *chokiñ shite
imasu.* (老後に備えて貯金しています) I
am saving up *for* my old age.
(⇨ sonae)
2 equip; furnish:
*Kono kyooshitsu ni wa koñpyuutaa
ga* sonaete *arimasu.* (この教室にはコン
ピューターが備えてあります) Computers

are installed in this classroom.

so「nae」·ru² そなえる(供える) *vt.*
(sonae-te ⓥ) offer:
Watashi wa kare no haka ni hana o
sonaeta. (私は彼の墓に花を供えた) I
offered flowers at his grave.

so「naetsuke そなえつけ(備え付け)
n. equipment; fittings:
Doozo sonaetsuke *no shokki o o-
tsukai kudasai.* (どうぞ備え付けの食器
をお使いください) Please feel free to
use the tableware *kept here*.
(⇨ sonaetsukeru)

so「naetsuke」·ru そなえつける(備え
付ける) *vt.* (-tsuke-te ⓥ) provide;
furnish; equip; install:
*Kono heya ni wa hitsuyoo na kagu
ga subete* sonaetsukete *aru.* (この部
屋には必要な家具がすべて備え付けてある)
This room *is fully equipped* with
all the necessary furniture.
(⇨ sonaetsuke)

so「ñchoo¹ そんちょう(尊重) *n.* respect; high regard; esteem.
★ The grammatical object is
usually inanimate.
soñchoo suru (~する) *vt.* respect;
make much of. (⇨ soñkee)

so「ñchoo² そんちょう(村長) *n.* village chief; the head of a village.

so「ñdai そんだい(尊大) *a.n.* (~ na,
ni) arrogant; haughty; self-im-
portant:
Kare no soñdai *na taido ni hara ga
tatta.* (彼の尊大な態度に腹が立った) I
got angry at his *arrogant* attitude.

so「ñgai そんがい(損害) *n.* damage;
loss:
Taifuu wa sono machi ni ooki-na
soñgai *o ataeta.* (台風はその町に大きな
損害を与えた) The typhoon caused
great *damage* to the town.

so「ñkee そんけい(尊敬) *n.* respect;
esteem; reverence. ★ The grammatical object is usually a person
or the actions of a person.
soñkee suru (~する) *vt.* respect;
esteem. (⇨ soñchoo¹)

so「ñna そんな *attrib.* **1** such; like
that: ★ Refers to something men-

tioned or done by the listener.
Soñna *kanashi-soo na kao o shinai
de kudasai.*(そんな悲しそうな顔をしない
でください) Please don't put on *such*
a sad look.
2 that; such: ★ Refers to something mentioned by the listener.
"Kare wa shutchoo-chuu desu."
"Soñna hazu wa arimaseñ."(「彼は
出張中です」「そんなはずはありません」)
"He is on a business trip." "*That*
cannot be true." (⇒ **añna**; **doñna**;
koñna)

so「ñna ni そんなに *adv.* that; like
that; such; so:
Soñna ni *isogu hitsuyoo wa arimaseñ.*(そんなに急ぐ必要はありません) You
needn't be in *such* a hurry.
(⇒ **añna ni**; **doñna ni**; **koñna ni**)

so「no その *attrib.* **1** the; that:
★ Refers to something which is
located away from the speaker
and close to the listener.
Sono *shio o totte kudasai.*(その塩を
とってください) Could you pass me
the salt, please.
2 the; that; it: ★ Refers to a person or thing just mentioned.
"Uchi wa eki no sugu soba desu."
"Sono eki wa kyuukoo mo tomarimasu ka?"(「家は駅のすぐそばです」「そ
の駅は急行も止まりますか」)"My
house is near the station." "Do
the expresses also stop at *that*
station?" (⇒ **ano**; **dono**; **kono**)

so「no-aida そのあいだ (その間) *adv.*
during the time; in the meantime; all the while. (⇒ **aida**)

so「no¹-hoka そのほか (その他) *n.*
the rest; the others:
Sono-hoka *no koto wa watashi ga
yarimasu* (そのほかのことは私がやります)
I will do *the rest*.
 — *adv.* (~ ni) else; besides:
Sono-hoka *(ni) nani-ka shitsumoñ
wa arimasu ka?* (そのほか(に)何か質問
はありますか) Are there *any other*
questions? (⇒ **hoka**)

so「no-mama そのまま (その儘) *n.*
1 the present state [situation]; as

it is [stands]:
Kañja *wa* sono-mama *nekasete oite
kudasai.*(患者はそのまま寝かせておいてく
ださい) Please leave the patient
sleeping *as he is.* (⇒ **mama¹**)
2 immediately:
Kodomo *wa gakkoo kara kaeru to*
sono-mama *asobi ni dekaketa.* (子
どもは学校から帰るとそのまま遊びに出かけ
た) The child came home from
school and *immediately* went out
to play. (⇒ **mama¹**)

so「no-uchi そのうち (その内) *adv.*
(~ ni) soon; before long; someday; sometime:
Sono-uchi *ame mo agaru deshoo.*
(そのうち雨も上がるでしょう) The rain
should let up *soon.*

so「no ue そのうえ (その上) *conj.*
besides; moreover:
Kare *wa yokubari de,* sono ue
kechi datta.(彼は欲張りで, その上けち
だった) He was greedy, and *besides*
he was stingy.

so「ñshitsu そんしつ (損失) *n.*
loss: soñshitsu *o ataeru
[koomuru]* (損失を与える[被る]) cause
[suffer] a *loss.* (⇒ **soñ**)

so「ñzai そんざい (存在) *n.* existence; presence; being.
soñzai suru (~する) *vi.* exist.

so「o¹ そう *adv.* **1** yes; no:
★ Used to express agreement
with a question, regardless of
whether it is affirmative or negative.
*"Anata wa Doitsu no kata desu
ka?" "Soo desu."* (「あなたはドイツの方
ですか」「そうです」) "Are you German?" "*That's right.*" / *"Anata
wa o-sake o nomimaseñ ne?" "Soo
desu. Zeñzeñ nomimaseñ."* (「あなた
はお酒を飲みませんね」「そうです. 全然飲
みません」) "You don't drink, do
you?" "*That's right.* I don't drink
at all."
2 so; like that; in that way:
Watashi *wa* soo *omoimasu.* (私はそ
う思います) I think *so.* (⇒ **aa¹**; **doo**;
koo)

so「oдeñ そうでん (送電) *n.* (kooš-

so᷄o² そう *n.* they say; I hear; I understand: ★ Preceded by a non-polite style predicate in either the present or past tense.
Yamada-saṅ wa teṅkiṅ ni naru soo desu. (山田さんは転勤になるそうです) *I hear* that Mr. Yamada is to be transferred. (⇨ mitai; rashi; yoo²)

so᷄o³ そう *int.* really; good:
"*Kuji ni atatta yo.*" "*Soo, yokatta ne.*" (「くじに当たったよ」「そう、よかったね」) "I won in the lottery."
"*Really?* That's great!"

so᷄o⁴ そう (層) *n.* **1** layer; stratum: *gaṅseki no soo* (岩石の層) a rock *stratum*
2 class; bracket:
chishiki-soo (知識層) the *intelligentsia* / *kooshotokusha-soo* (高所得者層) the high income *bracket*.

so᷄o- そう (総) *pref.* all; general; total: *soo-seṅkyo* (総選挙) a *general* election / *soo-jiṅkoo* (総人口) the *total* population.

-soo そう *suf. (a.n.)* look; seem; appear: ★ Attached to the continuative base of a verb, or the stem of an adjective, or to an adjectival noun. The adjectives '*yoi*' and '*nai*' take the form '*yosa-soo*' and '*nasa-soo*.'
Ame ga furi-soo da. (雨が降りそうだ) *It looks like rain.*

so᷄oba そうば (相場) *n.* **1** market price; rate.
2 speculation:
Sooba de soṅ o shita. (相場で損をした) I have lost money in *speculation*.

so᷄ochi そうち (装置) *n.* device; equipment; apparatus:
Sono heya ni wa daṅboo-soochi ga nakatta. (その部屋には暖房装置がなかった) There was no *kind of heating* in the room.

so᷄odaṅ そうだん (相談) *n.* talks; consultation; conference.
soodaṅ suru (～する) *vi., vt.* talk; consult; confer. (⇨ kyoogi²)

so᷄odeṅ そうでん (送電) *n.* transmission of electricity; power supply.
soodeṅ suru (～する) *vt.* transmit [supply] electricity.

so᷄odoo そうどう (騒動) *n.* disturbance; trouble; riot:
soodoo o okosu (騒動を起こす) make a *disturbance*.

so᷄ogeṅ そうげん (草原) *n.* grasslands; plain.

so᷄ogo そうご (相互) *n.* mutual; reciprocal:
soogo no rikai o fukameru (相互の理解を深める) promote *mutual* understanding. (⇨ tagai)

so᷄ogo no᷄ ri᷄ire そうごのりいれ (相互乗り入れ) *n.* mutual use of each other's railroad tracks; mutual trackage agreement.

so᷄ogoo そうごう (総合) *n.* synthesis; generalization.
soogoo suru (～する) *vt.* put together; synthesize.

so᷄oi¹ そうい (相違) *n.* difference; divergence:
ikeṅ no sooi (意見の相違) a *difference* of opinion.
sooi suru (～する) *vi.* differ; diverge. (⇨ chigau; kotonaru)

so᷄oi² そうい (総意) *n.* the general opinion [will]; the consensus.

so᷄o-iu そういう *attrib.* **1** such; like that; that kind of: ★ Refers to something mentioned by the listener.
"*Kinoo Maruyama-saṅ to iu kata ga tazunete kimashita.*" "*Soo-iu hito wa shirimaseṅ.*" (「きのう丸山さんという方が訪ねて来ました」「そういう人は知りません」) "A Mrs. Maruyama came to see you yesterday." "I don't know *such* a person."
2 that: ★ Refers to what the speaker previously mentioned.
Soo-iu wake de kyoo no kaigi ni wa shusseki dekimaseṅ. (そういう訳できょうの会議には出席できません) *That's* why I am unable to attend today's meeting. (⇨ aa-iu; doo-iu; koo-iu)

so⌐oji そうじ (掃除) *n.* cleaning.
  sooji (o) suru (～(を)する) *vt.* clean;
  sweep; dust. (⇨ seesoo)
so⌐oji⌐ki そうじき (掃除機) *n.* (vacuum) cleaner.
so⌐ojuu そうじゅう (操縦) *n.* operation; maneuvering.
  soojuu suru (～する) *vt.* operate;
  pilot; fly; steer: *hikooki* [*fune*] *o*
  soojuu suru (飛行機[船]を操縦する)
  pilot a plane [ship].
so⌐okai そうかい (総会) *n.* general
  meeting:
  kabunushi-sookai o hiraku (株主総
  会を開く) hold a *general meeting* of
  stockholders.
so⌐okiñ そうきん (送金) *n.* remit-
  tance of money.
  sookiñ suru (～する) *vi.* send
  money; remit.
so⌐oko そうこ (倉庫) *n.* ware-
  house; storehouse.
so⌐o-oñ そうおん (騒音) *n.* noise;
  din.
so⌐ori そうり (総理) *n.* abbreviation for ‘*Soori-daijiñ*.’
  Soori-*fu* (総理府) the *Prime Minister*’s Office.
So⌐ori-da⌐ijiñ そうりだいじん (総理
  大臣) *n.* Prime Minister; Premier.
so⌐oritsu そうりつ (創立) *n.* establishment; foundation.
  sooritsu suru (～する) *vt.* establish; found.
so⌐oryo⌐oji そうりょうじ (総領事) *n.*
  consul general.
so⌐oryooji⌐kañ そうりょうじかん (総
  領事館) *n.* consulate general:
  Nihoñ sooryoojikañ (日本総領事館)
  the Japanese *Consulate General*.
so⌐osa¹ そうさ (捜査) *n.* criminal
  investigation; search; manhunt.
  soosa suru (～する) *vt.* investigate.
  (⇨ shiraberu)
so⌐osa² そうさ (操作) *n.* operation;
  handling; manipulation.
  soosa suru (～する) *vt.* operate (a
  machine); handle; manipulate.
so⌐osaku¹ そうさく (創作) *n.* cre-

soosaku suru (～する) *vt.* create;
  originate; write.
so⌐osaku² そうさく (捜索) *n.*
  search; manhunt.
  soosaku suru (～する) *vt.* make a
  search.
so⌐oshiki そうしき (葬式) *n.* funeral (service): ★ Often ‘*o-soo-
  shiki*.’
  sooshiki *o suru* [*itonamu*] (葬式をす
  る[営む]) perform a *funeral service*.
so⌐o shita⌐ra そうしたら *conj.*
  1 after that; after all: ★ Used at
  the beginning of a sentence.
  *Ichi-jikañ mo matta. Soo shitara
  yatto kare ga arawareta.* (1時間も待
  った。そうしたらやっと彼が現れた) I waited a full hour. *After that* he at
  last showed up.
  2 then; if so; in that case:
  *Motto majime ni beñkyoo shi nasai.
  Soo shitara baiku o katte agemasu.*
  (もっとまじめに勉強しなさい。そうしたらバイ
  クを買ってあげます) Try to study
  more seriously. *If you do*, I will
  buy you a motorcycle. (⇨ soo
  sureba)
so⌐o-shite そうして *conj.* and
  then:
  Soo shite *kare wa shushoo ni niñ-
  mee sareta.* (そうして彼は首相に任命さ
  れた) *And then* he was appointed
  prime minister. (⇨ soshite)
  — *adv.* that way; like that:
  Soo shite *yaru no ga ichibañ da.* (そ
  うしてやるのが一番だ) The best way to
  do it is *like that*.
so⌐oshoku そうしょく (装飾) *n.*
  decoration; ornament.
  sooshoku suru (～する) *vt.* decorate (an interior); ornament.
so⌐osoo¹ そうそう *int.* yes; oh;
  come to think of it; I remember:
  *Soosoo, ano hito wa Yamada-sañ
  desu.* (そうそう、あの人は山田さんです)
  Come to think of it, he is Mr.
  Yamada.
so⌐osoo² そうそう (草々) *n.* Sincerely yours. ★ Polite way of
  ending a formal letter which

begins with 'zeñryaku.'
(⇨ tegami)

so｢osu ソース n. sauce. ★ In Japan it often refers to a thick brown sauce.

so｢o sure｣ba そうすれば conj. then; if so; in that case: ★ Used at the beginning of a sentence.
Kono kusuri o nomi nasai. Soo sureba, sugu yoku narimasu. (この薬を飲みなさい. そうすれば, すぐよくなります) Take this medicine. If you do so, you will soon get better.

so｢otoo¹ そうとう (相当) n. worth:
Kare ni goseñ-eñ sootoo no shina o okutta. (彼に 5,000 円相当の品を贈った) I presented him with an article worth five thousand yen.
... ni sootoo suru (...に～する) vi. be equivalent to; correspond to.

so｢otoo² そうとう (相当) a.n.
(～ na/no, ni) considerable; quite; decent:
Kare no sukii no udemae wa sootoo na mono desu. (彼のスキーの腕前は相当なものです) His skill at skiing is quite something.
— adv. pretty; a lot:
Kyoo wa sootoo atsuku nari-soo da. (きょうは相当暑くなりそうだ) I think it is going to be quite hot today.

so｢ozoo¹ そうぞう (想像) n. imagination; fancy; supposition:
soozoo ga tsukanai (想像がつかない) have no idea.
soozoo suru (～する) vt. imagine; fancy; guess.

so｢ozoo² そうぞう (創造) n. creation.
soozoo suru (～する) vt. create.

so｢ozooshi｣-i そうぞうしい (騒々しい) a. (-ku) noisy; boisterous.
(⇨ sawagashii)

so｢ra¹ そら (空) n. the sky; the air.

so｢ra² そら int. look; there: ★ Not used to superiors.
Sora, watashi no itta toori da. (そら, 私の言ったとおりだ) There, I told you so. (⇨ sore²)

so｢re¹ それ n. **1** that; it: ★ Refers to something which is located away from the speaker and close to the listener.
Sore wa dare no hoñ desu ka? (それはだれの本ですか) Whose book is that?
2 that; it: ★ Refers to something mentioned by the listener.
"Jiko no koto shitte imasu ka?" "Sore wa itsu no koto desu ka?" (「事故のこと知っていますか」「それはいつのことですか」) "Do you know about the accident?" "When did it take place?"
3 it: ★ Refers to something previously mentioned.
Kinoo kasa o kaimashita ga, sore o doko-ka e okiwasurete shimaimashita. (きのう傘を買いましたが, それをどこかへ置き忘れてしまいました) I bought an umbrella yesterday, but I have left it somewhere. (⇨ are¹; dore¹; kore)

so｢re² それ int. there; now; look:
Sore, isoge. (それ, 急げ) Look, hurry up! (⇨ sora²)

so｢re da｣ kara それだから conj. so; that is why: ★ Used at the beginning of a sentence.
Kanojo wa seekaku ga yoi. Sore da kara tomodachi ga takusañ iru. (彼女は性格が良い. それだから友だちがたくさんいる) She has a nice personality. That is why she has got a lot of friends.

so｢re de それで conj. **1** and; then:
Sore de anata wa doo omoimasu ka? (それであなたはどう思いますか) And what is your opinion?
2 therefore:
Netsu ga ari, sore de gakkoo o yasumimashita. (熱があり, それで学校を休みました) I had a fever, therefore I was absent from school.
— adv. now:
Sore de jijoo ga wakarimashita. (それで事情がわかりました) Now I have understood the circumstances.

s｢ore de｣ mo それでも conj. but;

still; nevertheless; however:
★ Used at the beginning of a sentence.
Muzukashii ka mo shirenai. Sore de mo yaru shika nai. (難しいかもしれない。それでもやるしかない) It may be difficult. *Nevertheless*, there is nothing for it but to have a go.

so「re de」wa それでは *conj.* 1 if that is the case; if so; in that case:
★ Used at the beginning of a sentence.
"Watashi mo sono eega o mitai to omotte imasu." "Sore de wa, issho ni ikimaseñ ka?" (「私もその映画を見たいと思っています」「それでは、一緒に行きませんか」) "I want to see that movie as well." *"In that case*, shall we go together?"
2 well; then: ★ Used at the beginning of a sentence.
Sore de wa, kyoo wa kore de owarimasu. (それでは、きょうはこれで終わります) *Well then*, we will finish here for today.

so「re do」koro ka それどころか on the contrary: ★ Used at the beginning of a sentence.
"Ima hima desu ka?" "Sore dokoro ka, isogashii saichuu desu." (「今暇ですか」「それどころか、忙しい最中です」) "Are you free now?" *"Quite the opposite.* I am very busy right now."

so「re ja」(a) それじゃ(あ) *int.* well (then): 《⇨ de wa²》
Sore jaa, mata ashita. (それじゃあ、またあした) *Well*, see you tomorrow.

so「re kara それから *conj.* and then; after that; afterward.

so「re-(k)kiri それ(っ)きり *adv.*
1 (with a negative) since:
Sore-(k)kiri kanojo kara tayori wa arimaseñ. (それ(っ)きり彼女から便りはありません) I haven't heard from her *since then.* 《⇨ are-(k)kiri》
2 all; no more than that:
Anata no chokiñ wa sore-(k)kiri shika nai no desu ka? (あなたの貯金はそれっきりしかないのですか) Are your

savings *no more than* that?
《⇨ kore-(k)kiri》

so「re ma」de それまで(それ迄) up to that time; till then:
Kare no shoobai wa sore made umaku itte ita. (彼の商売はそれまでうまくいっていた) His business was successful *up to that time.*

so「re na」ra それなら *conj.* if so; in that case: ★ Used at the beginning of a sentence.
"Ogotte ageru yo." "Sore nara issho ni itte mo ii." (「おごってあげるよ」「それならいっしょに行ってもいい」) "I'll be glad to treat you." *"If so*, I'll come along with you."

so「re ni それに *conj.* and; besides; moreover: ★ Often used at the beginning of a sentence.
Koko wa yachiñ ga yasui shi, sore ni eki ni mo chikai. (ここは家賃が安いし、それに駅にも近い) The rent for this house is low, *and moreover* it is near the station.

so「re to」mo それとも *conj.* or:
Ocha ni shimasu ka, sore tomo koohii ni shimasu ka? (お茶にしますか、それともコーヒーにしますか) Do you wish green tea, *or* would you like coffee?

so「re wa so」o to それはそうと incidentally; by the way:
★ Used at the beginning of a sentence when changing the subject.
Sore wa soo to, otoosañ no guai wa doo desu ka? (それはそうと、お父さんの具合はどうですか) *By the way*, how is your father's health?
《⇨ tokoro de》

so「re」zore それぞれ *n., adv.* each; respectively:
Shussekisha wa sorezore ikeñ o nobemashita. (出席者はそれぞれ意見を述べました) The participants expressed their *respective* views.

so「robañ そろばん(算盤) *n.* abacus.

so「roe」・ru そろえる(揃える) *vt.* (soroe-te Ⅴ) 1 arrange properly; put in order:
kaado o arufabetto juñ ni soroeru

（カードをアルファベット順にそろえる）*ar-range* cards *in* alphabetical *order*. (⇨ sorou)

2 get ready; collect: *Hitsuyoo na shorui wa zeñbu so-roemashita.* (必要な書類は全部そろえました) I *got* all the necessary documents *ready.* (⇨ sorou)

3 make even: *ki o onaji takasa ni soroeru* (木を同じ高さにそろえる) *make* the trees the same height. (⇨ sorou)

so╹rosoro そろそろ *adv.* **1** (of time) soon; before long; almost: *Sorosoro shitsuree shimasu.* (そろそろ失礼します) *Now* I must be getting along. (⇨ ma-mo-naku)

2 (~ to) (of movement) slowly; little by little.

so╹ro╹・u そろう (揃う) *vi.* (soro-i-; sorow・a-; sorot-te C)

1 gather; meet; assemble: *Zeñiñ jikañ-doori ni sorotta.* (全員時間通りにそろった) Everyone *assembled* at the appointed time.

2 be equal; be even; be uniform: *Kare-ra wa miñna fukusoo ga sorotte ita.* (彼らはみんな服装がそろっていた) Their clothes *were* all *the same.* (⇨ soroeru)

3 be [become] complete: *Koko ni wa Sheekusupia zeñshuu ga sorotte imasu.* (ここにはシェークスピア全集がそろっています) We *have* a complete set of Shakespeare's works here. (⇨ soroeru)

so╹r・u[1] そる (剃る) *vi.* (sor・i-; sor・a-; sot-te C) shave: *kao o soru* (顔をそる) *shave* one's face.

so╹r・u[2] そる (反る) *vi.* (sor・i-; sor・a-; sot-te C) warp; curve; bend.

so╹señ そせん (祖先) *n.* ancestor; forefathers. (↔ shisoñ) (⇨ señzo)

so╹shiki そしき (組織) *n.* **1** organization; formation; system.

2 tissue.

soshiki suru (~する) *vt.* organize; form; compose: *roodoo-kumiai o soshiki suru* (労働組合を組織する)

organize a labor union.

so╹shite そして *conj.* and; and then: ★ A very common word for connecting words and clauses. *Furo ni hairi, soshite sugu ni nemashita.* (風呂に入り、そしてすぐに寝ました) I took a bath, *and then* went to bed right away. (⇨ soo-shite)

so╹shitsu そしつ (素質) *n.* the makings; quality; aptitude: *Kare ni wa seerusumañ no soshitsu wa nai.* (彼にはセールスマンの素質はない) He does not have the *makings* of a salesman.

so╹shoo そしょう (訴訟) *n.* suit; lawsuit: *soshoo o okosu* (訴訟を起こす) file a *suit.* (⇨ saibañ)

so╹sog・u そそぐ (注ぐ) *vt., vi.* (sosog・i-; sosog・a-; soso・i-de C)

1 pour; water: *potto ni o-yu o sosogu* (ポットにお湯を注ぐ) *pour* hot water into a thermos flask.

2 concentrate; devote oneself to; focus: *Kare wa jibuñ no keñkyuu ni zeñryoku o sosoida.* (彼は自分の研究に全力を注いだ) He *put* everything into his studies.

3 flow: *Kono kawa wa Taiheeyoo ni sosogu.* (この川は太平洋に注ぐ) This river *flows* into the Pacific Ocean.

so╹sokkashi╹・i そそっかしい *a.* (-ku) hasty; careless; thoughtless.

so╹tchi[1] そっち *n.* (*colloq.*) = sochira. **1** that; over there: *Sotchi no o misete kudasai.* (そっちのを見せてください) Please show me *that* one.

2 (*colloq.*) you: *Kono moñdai ni tsuite sotchi no kañgae wa doo desu ka?* (この問題についてそっちの考えはどうですか) What are *your* thoughts on this matter? (⇨ atchi; dotchi; kotchi)

so╹tchoku そっちょく (率直) *a.n.* (~ na, ni) frank; straightforward; candid. (⇨ zakkubarañ)

so╹to そと (外) *n.* outside; outdoors. (↔ uchi²; naka¹)

so⌈togawa そとがわ (外側) *n.* the outside; exterior:
Kono doa wa sotogawa *ni hiraki-masu.* (このドアは外側に開きます) This door opens *outward*. (↔ uchigawa)

so⌈tsugyoo そつぎょう (卒業) *n.* graduation.
sotsugyoo suru (~する) *vt.* graduate; finish. (↔ nyuugaku) (⇨ deru (5))

so⌈tto そっと *adv.* quietly; softly; lightly; gently:
Kare wa heya kara sotto *dete itta.* (彼は部屋からそっと出て行った) He went out of the room *quietly*.

so・⌈u¹ そう (沿う) *vi.* (so・i-; so-w・a-; sot-te C) 1 go [run] along; (⇨ -zoi)
Watashi-tachi wa kawa ni sotte *aruita.* (私たちは川に沿って歩いた) We walked *along* the riverbank.
2 be done according to:
Shigoto wa saisho no keekaku ni sotte *susumerareta.* (仕事は最初の計画に沿って進められた) The work was continued *according to* the original plan.

so・⌈u² そう (添う) *vt.* (so・i-; so-w・a-; sot-te C) meet (expectations); answer; come up to:
Go-kitai ni sou *yoo, doryoku itashi-masu.* (ご期待に添うよう、努力いたします) I will make every effort to *meet* your expectations.

su¹ す (巣) *n.* nest; web; comb.

su⌉² す (酢) *n.* vinegar.

su⌈barashi⌉・i すばらしい (素晴らしい) *a.* (-ku) wonderful; splendid; excellent:
subarashii *keshiki* (すばらしい景色) a *splendid* view. (⇨ migoto)

su⌈bashiko⌉・i すばしこい *a.* (-ku) nimble; quick:
subashikoi *kodomo* (すばしこい子ども) a *nimble* child. (⇨ subayai)

su⌈baya⌉・i すばやい (素早い) *a.* (-ku) quick; nimble:
Seefu wa sono jitai ni subayaku

taioo shita. (政府はその事態にすばやく対応した) The government *promptly* dealt with the situation. (⇨ subashikoi)

su⌈be⌉r・u すべる (滑る) *vi.* (sube-r・i-; suber・a-; subet-te C)
1 slip; slide; glide: subette *korobu* (滑って転ぶ) *slip* and fall down.
2 fail (an examination).

su⌈bete すべて (全て) *n., adv.* all; everything:
Subete *watashi no sekiniñ desu.* (すべて私の責任です) I am responsible for *everything*.

su⌈dare すだれ (簾) *n.* bamboo blind; reed screen.

su⌈de⌉ すで (素手) *n.* empty hand; bare hand:
Watashi wa sono sakana o sude de *tsukamaeta.* (私はその魚を素手で捕まえた) I caught that fish with my *bare hands*.

su⌉de ni すでに (既に) *adv.* already; previously; before; long ago:
Deñwa o shitara, kare wa sude ni *dekakete ita.* (電話をしたら、彼はすでに出かけていた) When I telephoned, he had *already* left.

su⌈e すえ (末) *n.* 1 end:
Koñgetsu sue *ni kare wa Burajiru e ikimasu.* (今月末に彼はブラジルへ行きます) He is leaving for Brazil at the *end* of this month. (⇨ -matsu)
2 after: ★ Follows the past of a verb.
Yoku kañgaeta sue *o-kotae itashi-masu.* (よく考えた末お答えいたします) I will give a reply *after* thinking it over carefully.
3 youngest child: sue *no musu-ko* (末の息子) the *youngest* son.

su⌈ekko すえっこ (末っ子) *n.* the youngest child.

su⌈e・ru すえる (据える) *vt.* (sue-te V) 1 set; place; fix:
hoñbako o heya no sumi ni sueru (本箱を部屋の隅に据える) *place* a bookcase in a corner of the room.

2 appoint:

Shachoo wa jibuñ no musuko o kookeesha ni sueta. (社長は自分の息子を後継者に据えた) The president *appointed* his son as his successor.

su⌐gasugashi˥·i すがすがしい (清々しい) *a.* (-ku) fresh; refreshing; bracing:

Yoku nemureta no de kesa wa sugasugashii. (よく眠れたのできさはすがすがしい) I slept well, so I feel *refreshed* this morning.

su˥gata すがた (姿) *n.* figure; shape:

Sono otoko no sugata ni mioboe ga atta. (その男の姿に見覚えがあった) I recognized the *figure* of that man.

sugata o arawasu (〜を現す) appear; come into view.

sugata o kesu (〜を消す) disappear.

su˥gi すぎ (杉) *n.* Japanese cedar.

-sugi すぎ (過ぎ) *suf.* **1** (of times and dates) past; after:

Ima hachi-ji go-fuñ-sugi desu. (今8時5分過ぎです) It is now five *past* eight. (↔ -mae˥)

2 (of age) over; past:

Chichi wa nanajuu-sugi desu. (父は70過ぎです) My father is *over* seventy. (↔ -mae˥)

3 too much: ★ Added to the continuative base of a verb.

Tabe-sugi wa keñkoo ni yoku arimaseñ. (食べ過ぎは健康に良くありません) Eating *too much* is not good for the health. (⇨ -sugiru)

su⌐gi˥·ru すぎる (過ぎる) *vi.* (sugi-te Ⅴ) **1** (of time) pass; be over:

Are kara ni-neñ (ga) sugimashita. (あれから2年(が)過ぎました) Since then two years *have* passed.

2 pass through:

Ressha wa moo Hiroshima o sugimashita. (列車はもう広島を過ぎました) The train *has* already *passed through* Hiroshima.

3 be past:

Kare wa go-juu o sugite iru to omoimasu. (彼は50を過ぎていると思います) I

think he *is past* fifty.

-sugi·ru すぎる (過ぎる) (-sugi-te Ⅴ) over-; too much: ★ Occurs as the second element of compound verbs. Added to the continuative base of a verb or the stem of an adjective.

hataraki-sugiru (働きすぎる) *over*work / *omo-sugiru* (重すぎる) be *too* heavy.

su⌐go˥·i すごい (凄い) *a.* (-ku)

1 (*informal*) great; superb; fantastic:

Shiñjuku wa sugoi hito datta. (新宿はすごい人だった) There was a *large* crowd in Shinjuku.

2 drastic; dreadful; horrible:

sugoi jishiñ (すごい地震) a *frightful* earthquake.

3 (-ku) awfully; terribly; extremely:

Kono hoñ wa sugoku omoshiroi. (この本はすごくおもしろい) This book is *terribly* interesting.

su⌐go˥s·u すごす (過ごす) *vt.* (sugosh·i-; sugos·a-; sugosh·i-te Ⓒ) pass; spend; idle away:

Watashi-tachi wa teñto de ichi-ya o sugoshita. (私たちはテントで一夜を過ごした) We *spent* the night in a tent.

su⌐gosugo すごすご *adv.* (〜 to) dejectedly; with a heavy heart:

Shakkiñ o kotowarareta kare wa sugosugo (to) hikisagatta. (借金を断られて彼はすごすご(と)引き下がった) Having been refused a loan, he *dejectedly* withdrew.

su˥gu すぐ (直ぐ) *adv.* **1** (of time) at once; right away; soon.

2 (of distance) just; right:

Eki wa sugu soko desu. (駅はすぐそこです) The station is *just* over there.

3 easily; readily:

Kare wa sugu okoru. (彼はすぐ怒る) He gets angry *easily*.

su⌐gure˥·ru すぐれる (優れる) *vi.* (sugure-te Ⅴ) excel; surpass.

su⌐ibokuga すいぼくが (水墨画) *n.* a drawing in Indian ink.
《⇨ sumie》

su⌐ibuñ すいぶん (水分) *n.* water; moisture; juice:
suibuñ no ooi *kudamono* (水分の多い果物) *juicy* fruit.

su⌐ichoku すいちょく (垂直) *a.n.* (~ nà, ni) perpendicular; vertical. (↔ suihee)

su⌐ichuu すいちゅう (水中) *n.* underwater; in the water:
suichuu *ni tobikomu* (水中に飛び込む) jump *into the water.*

su⌐ideñ すいでん (水田) *n.* paddy; paddy field. (⇨ ta¹; tañbo)

su⌐idoo すいどう (水道) *n.* 1 water supply [service]:
Kono suidoo no mizu *wa nomemasu ka?* (この水道の水は飲めますか?). Is this *tap water* good to drink?.
2 channel: *Buñgo*-suidoo (豊後水道) the Bungo *Channel.*

su⌐idookañ すいどうかん (水道管) *n.* water pipe; water main. (⇨ kañ²)

su⌐iee すいえい (水泳) *n.* swimming; bathing. (⇨ oyogu)

su⌐igara すいがら (吸い殻) *n.* cigarette butt [end]:
suigara-ire (吸い殻入れ) an *ashtray.*

su⌐igiñ すいぎん (水銀) *n.* mercury.

su⌐ihee すいへい (水平) *a.n.* (~ na, ni) horizontal; level. (↔ suichoku)

su⌐iheeseñ すいへいせん (水平線) *n.* horizon. ★ The line where the sky and the sea meet. (⇨ chiheeseñ)

su⌐iji すいじ (炊事) *n.* cooking; kitchen work. (⇨ ryoori)
suiji (o) *suru* (~する) *vi.* cook.

su⌐ijuñ すいじゅん (水準) *n.* level; standard: *seekatsu*-suijuñ (生活水準) the *standard* of living.

su⌐ika すいか (西瓜) *n.* watermelon.

su⌐imaseñ すいません (*colloq.*) = sumimaseñ.

su⌐imeñ すいめん (水面) *n.* the water surface.

su⌐imiñ すいみん (睡眠) *n.* sleep:
suimiñ *o toru* (睡眠をとる) have a *sleep.*

su⌐ioñ すいおん (水温) *n.* water temperature.

su⌐iri すいり (推理) *n.* reasoning; inference; guess.
suiri *suru* (~する) *vt.* reason; infer; deduce.

su⌐iryoku すいりょく (水力) *n.* waterpower:
suiryoku *hatsudeñsho* (水力発電所) a *hydroelectric power* plant. (↔ karyoku)

su⌐iryoo すいりょう (推量) *n.* guess; surmise; inference.
suiryoo *suru* (~する) *vt.* guess; surmise; conjecture. (⇨ suisoku)

su⌐isañbutsu すいさんぶつ (水産物) *n.* marine products.

su⌐iseñ¹ すいせん (推薦) *n.* recommendation.
suiseñ *suru* (~する) *vt.* recommend. (⇨ susumeru²)

su⌐iseñ² すいせん (水仙) *n.* narcissus; daffodil.

su⌐iseñ-beñjo すいせんべんじょ (水洗便所) *n.* flush toilet. (⇨ beñjo)

su⌐ishiñ すいしん (推進) *n.* propulsion; drive.
suishiñ *suru* (~する) *vt.* propel; push on with. (⇨ susumeru¹)

su⌐ishitsu すいしつ (水質) *n.* quality of water.

su⌐ishoo すいしょう (水晶) *n.* crystal.

su⌐iso すいそ (水素) *n.* hydrogen.

su⌐isoku すいそく (推測) *n.* guess; conjecture.
suisoku *suru* (~する) *vt.* guess; conjecture; speculate.

su⌐isui すいすい *adv.* (~ to) lightly; easily:
Ike no koi ga suisui (to) *oyoide iru.* (池でこいがすいすい(と)泳いでいる) The carp *are gliding* through the pond.

su⌐itchi スイッチ *n.* switch:
hiitaa no suitch o ireru [kiru] (ヒーターのスイッチを入れる[切る]) *switch on* [*off*] a heater.

su⌐itoˈr・u すいとる (吸い取る) *vt.* (-tor・i-; -tor・a-; -tot-te Ⓒ) suck up; soak up; absorb (water).

su⌐iyoˈo(bi) すいよう(び) (水曜(日)) *n.* Wednesday. (⇨ APP. 5)

su⌐izoo すいぞう (膵臓) *n.* pancreas.

su⌐ji すじ (筋) *n.* **1** line; stripe:
akai suji *no haitta tii-shatsu* (赤い筋
の入った T シャツ) a T-shirt with red
stripes.

2 muscle; tendon; sinew:
ashi no suji *o itameru* (足の筋を痛め
る) hurt a *tendon* in one's leg.

3 string:
mame no suji *o toru* (豆の筋を取る)
remove the *strings* from beans.

4 story; plot:
Hanashi no suji *wa heeboñ datta.*
(話の筋は平凡だった) The *story* was
commonplace.

5 sense; logic:
Kimi no iu koto wa suji *ga tooranai.*
(君の言うことは筋が通らない) There is
no *sense* in what you say.

su⌐ke⌐eru スケール *n.* scale; caliber:
sukeeru *no ooki-na jigyoo* (スケールの
大きな事業) a large *scale* enterprise.

su⌐keeto スケート *n.* ice skating.

su⌐ke⌐juuru スケジュール *n.*
schedule; program:
sukejuuru *o tateru* (スケジュールを立て
る) make out a *schedule*.

su⌐ki¹¹ すき (好き) *a.n.* (~ na, ni)
like; be fond of; love:
Tanaka-sañ wa e o kaku no ga suki
desu. (田中さんは絵をかくのが好きです)
Ms. Tanaka *likes* to paint pictures.
(↔ kirai) (⇒ daisuki)

suki na yoo ni (~ようなに) as one
likes [wishes].

su⌐ki² すき (隙) *n.* **1** unguarded
moment; chance:
Dare mo inai suki *ni tsumamigui o
shita.* (だれもいないすきにつまみ食いをした)
I took some snacks *while no one
was around*.

2 fault; flaw:
Kare no toobeñ ni wa suki *ga
nakatta.* (彼の答弁にはすきがなかった)
There were no *flaws* in his answer.

3 space; room:
*Suutsukeesu wa ippai de sono hoñ
o ireru* suki *wa arimaseñ.* (スーツケー
スはいっぱいでその本を入れるすきはありませ

ん) The suitcase is full and there is
no *room* for the book.

su⌐ki³ すき (鋤) *n.* plow; spade.

su⌐ki⌐i スキー *n.* ski; skiing:
sukii *ni iku* (スキーに行く) go *skiing*.

su⌐kima すきま (隙間) *n.* **1** opening; gap; space:
kabe no sukima (壁のすき間) an
opening in the wall.

2 chink; crack:
mado-garasu no sukima (窓ガラスのす
き間) a *crack* between window-
panes.

su⌐kito⌐or·u すきとおる (透き通る) *vi.*
(-toor·i-; -toor·a-; -toot-te C) be
transparent; be seen through:
sukitootta *garasu* (透き通ったガラス)
transparent glass. (⇒ toomee)

su⌐kiyaki すきやき (すき焼き) *n.*
sukiyaki. ★ A dish of sliced beef
and vegetables cooked in a shallow iron pan.

su⌐ki⌐zuki すきずき (好き好き) *n.*
a matter of taste:
Hito ni wa sorezore sukizuki *ga arimasu.* (人にはそれぞれ好き好きがあります)
People have their *different tastes*.
(⇒ konomi)

su⌐kka⌐ri すっかり *adv.* completely; perfectly:
Sono koto o sukkari *wasurete ita.*
(そのことをすっかり忘れていた) I had *completely* forgotten about it.

su⌐kki⌐ri すっきり *adv.* ~ to;
~ suru) (the state of being refreshed, neat, clear-cut or simple):
Furo ni haittara, kibuñ ga sukkiri
shita. (ふろに入ったら、気分がすっきりし
た) I felt *refreshed* after taking a
bath.

su⌐ko⌐shi すこし (少し) *n., adv.*
1 a few [little]; some:
O-cha o moo sukoshi *kudasai.* (お茶
をもう少し下さい) Please give me a *little* more tea. (↔ takusañ) (⇒ shooshoo)

2 a bit; somewhat:
Kono michi o sukoshi *iku to hashi
ni demasu.* (この道を少し行くと橋に出
ます) Go along this road *a bit* and

you will come to a bridge.
3 a short time:
Kono heñ de sukoshi *yasumima-shoo.* (この辺で少し休みましょう) Let's take *a short* rest somewhere around here.

su'ko'shi mo すこしも (少しも) *adv.* (with a negative) (not) at all; (not) in the least:
Sono eega wa sukoshi mo *omoshiroku nakatta.* (その映画は少しもおもしろくなかった) The film was *not in the least* interesting. (⇨ chitto-mo)

su'koshi-zu'tsu すこしずつ (少しずつ) *adv.* little by little; gradually.

su'ku' すく (空く) *vi.* (suk·a-; su-k·i-; su·i-te C) **1** become less crowded:
Deñsha wa suite ita. (電車はすいていた) The train *was* rather *empty.*
2 (of a stomach) become empty:
Onaka ga sukimashita. (おなかがすきました) I feel *hungry.*

su'k·u' すく (好く) *vt.* (suk·i-; su-k·a-; su·i-te C) like; love:
Kare wa miñna ni sukarete iru. (彼はみんなに好かれている) He *is liked* by everybody.

su'kui すくい (救い) *n.* **1** help; rescue:
sukui *o motomete sakebu* (救いを求めて叫ぶ) cry out for *help.*
(⇨ sukuu')
2 relief; saving grace:
Sono jiko de shisha ga denakatta no ga sukui *datta.* (その事故で死者がでなかったのが救いだった) It was a great *relief* that there were no fatalities in the accident.

su'kuna'·i すくない (少ない) *a.* (-ku) few; little; small; scarce; short:
Koñgetsu wa ame ga sukunakatta. (今月は雨が少なかった) We have had *little* rain this month. (↔ ooi)

su'ku'naku-tomo すくなくとも (少なくとも) *adv.* at least; not less than:
Kono kimono wa sukunaku-tomo *sañjuumañ-eñ wa shimasu.* (この着

物は少なくとも 30 万円はします) This kimono costs *at least* 300,000 yen.

su'ku·u' すくう (救う) *vt.* (suku·i-; sukuw·a-; sukut-te C) save; rescue; help:
Isha wa watashi no inochi o sukutte kureta. (医者は私の命を救ってくれた) The doctor *saved* my life. (⇨ sukui)

su'ku·u'² すくう (掬う) *vt.* (suku·i-; sukuw·a-; sukut-te C) scoop (up); dip (up); ladle.

su'ma'ato スマート *a.n.* (~ na, ni) nice-looking; stylish; slender:
Kanojo wa itsu-mo fukusoo ga sumaato *da.* (彼女はいつも服装がスマートだ) Her clothes are always *chic.* (⇨ iki²)

su'mai すまい (住まい) *n.* **1** address:
O-sumai wa dochira desu ka? (お住まいはどちらですか) May I ask *where you live?*
2 home; house; residence:
Koko wa kari no sumai *desu.* (ここは仮の住まいです) This is my temporary *residence.* (⇨ juukyo)

su'ma'na·i すまない (済まない) *a.* (-ku) sorry; inexcusable:
Kimi ni wa hoñtoo ni sumanai *koto o shimashita.* (君には本当にすまないことをしました) I really did something *unpardonable* to you. (⇨ kokoro-gurushii; sumimaseñ)

su'mase'·ru すませる (済ませる) *vt.* (sumase-te V) finish; get through:
Moo chuushoku wa sumasemashita *ka?* (もう昼食は済ませましたか) *Have* you *finished* lunch yet? (⇨ sumasu')

su'ma's·u' すます (済ます) *vt.* (su-mash·i-; sumas·a-; sumash·i-te C) **1** finish; settle:
Kare wa shiharai o sumasanai *de dete ikoo to shita.* (彼は支払いを済まさないで出て行こうとした) He tried to leave *without paying* the bill. (⇨ sumaseru)
2 manage (with); make do;

Nihoñgo no beñkyoo ni jisho nashi de sumasu koto wa dekimaseñ. (日本語の勉強に辞書なして済ますことはできません) In studying Japanese, one cannot *do* without a dictionary.

su｜ma｜s･u² すます(澄ます) *vi.* (sumash･i-; sumas･a-; sumash･i-te C|) put on airs:
Kanojo wa sumashite ita. (彼女は澄ましていた) She *was* prim and proper.

su｜mi¹ すみ(隅) *n.* corner.

su｜mi¹² すみ(炭) *n.* charcoal.

su｜mi¹³ すみ(墨) *n.* India [Chinese] ink; ink stick.

su｜mi｜e すみえ(墨絵) *n.* India-ink painting. (⇨ suibokuga)

su｜mimase｜ñ すみません **1** excuse [pardon] me; I'm sorry:
Go-meewaku o o-kakeshite, sumimaseñ. (ご迷惑をおかけして、すみません) I am sorry for causing you a lot of trouble.
2 thank you:
Tetsudatte itadaite, sumimaseñ. (手伝っていただいて、すみません) Thank you very much for helping me. (⇨ arigatoo)

su｜mire すみれ(菫) *n.* violet (flower).

su｜moo すもう(相撲) *n.* sumo wrestling. (⇨ rikishi)

su｜m･u¹ すむ(住む) *vi.* (sum･i-; sum･a-; suñ-de C|) live; reside:
★ Used in the '-te iru' form when referring to where a person currently lives.
Watashi wa apaato ni suñde imasu. (私はアパートに住んでいます) I *am living* in an apartment.

su｜m･u² すむ(済む) *vi.* (sum･i-; sum･a-; suñ-de C|) be finished; come to an end; get through:
Yatto shigoto ga suñda. (やっと仕事が済んだ) At last work *is finished*.

su｜m･u³ すむ(澄む) *vi.* (sum･i-; sum･a-; suñ-de C|) become clear:
Koñya wa sora ga suñde iru. (今夜は空が澄んでいる) Tonight the sky *is clear*.

su｜na すな(砂) *n.* sand; grain of sand.

su｜nao すなお(素直) *a.n.* (~ na, ni) gentle; mild; obedient:
Sono ko wa watashi no iu koto o sunao ni kiita. (その子は私の言うことを素直に聞いた) The child listened *obediently* to what I said.

su｜na｜wachi すなわち(即ち) *conj.* (*formal*) that is (to say); namely.

su｜ne¹ すね(脛) *n.* shank; shin.

su｜ñpoo すんぽう(寸法) *n.* measure; measurements; size:
suñpoo o toru [hakaru] (寸法をとる [測る]) measure the *size*. (⇨ ookisa)

su｜ñzeñ すんぜん(寸前) *n.* just [right] before:
Sono kaisha wa toosañ sunzeñ datta. (その会社は倒産寸前だった) The company was *on the verge* of bankruptcy.

su｜pa｜supa すばすば *adv.* (~ to) (with) quick puffs: ★ Used to express the action of smoking heavily.
tabako o supasupa (to) suu (たばこをすばすば(と)吸う) *puff away* at a cigarette.

su｜piido スピード *n.* speed:
supiido-ihañ (スピード違反) a *speeding* violation. (⇨ hayasa; sokudo)

su｜po｜otsu スポーツ *n.* sport(s):
supootsu o suru (スポーツをする) go in for a *sport*.

su｜ppa｜･i すっぱい(酸っぱい) *a.* (-ku) acid; sour; vinegary.

su｜ra すら *p.* even; if only:
★ Used for extreme examples.
Kodomo ni sura dekiru no da kara anata ni dekinai wake ga nai. (子どもにすらできるのだからあなたにできない訳がない) *Even* a child can do it, so there is no reason you can't. (⇨ sae)

su｜rasura すらすら *adv.* (~ to) smoothly; easily; fluently; readily.

su｜rechiga･u すれちがう(すれ違う) *vi.* (-chiga･i-; -chigaw･a-; -chigat-te C|) pass by:

Michi de señsee to surechigatta. (道で先生とすれ違った) I *passed* my teacher on the road.

su｢ri すり (掏摸) *n.* pickpocket. 《⇨ suru⁴》

su｢ri｣ppa スリッパ *n.* scuffs; mules. ★ From English 'slippers.'

s･u｢ru｣¹ する *vt.* (sh･i-; sh･i-; sh･i-te ①) **1** do (something): *kaimono o suru* (買い物をする) *do* the shopping / *señtaku o suru* (洗濯をする) *do* the washing.

2 have (a wash, walk, etc.): *shokuji o suru* (食事をする) *have* a meal / *oshaberi o suru* (おしゃべりをする) *have* a chat / *keñka o suru* (けんかをする) *have* a fight.

3 take (a bath, break, etc.): *nyuuyoku o suru* (入浴する) *take* a bath / *hirune o suru* (昼寝をする) *take* a nap.

4 make (a decision, discovery, etc.): *yakusoku o suru* (約束をする) *make* a promise / *iiwake o suru* (言い訳をする) *make* excuses.

5 play (baseball, chess, etc.): *yakyuu o suru* (野球をする) *play* baseball / *torañpu o suru* (トランプをする) *play* cards.

6 (of an article, goods, etc.) cost: *Kono yubiwa wa sañmañ-eñ shimashita.* (この指輪は 3 万円しました) This ring *cost* me 30,000 yen.

7 put on (a scarf, gloves, etc.): *tebukuro o suru* (手袋をする) *put on* gloves / *Kanojo wa kiiroi mafuraa o shite ita.* (彼女は黄色いマフラーをしていた) She *was wearing* a yellow muffler.

... ga suru (...が～) there is...: *Yoi kaori ga suru.* (良い香りがする) *There is* a nice smell.

... koto ni suru (...ことに～) decide: *Atarashii terebi o kau koto ni shimashita.* (新しいテレビを買うことにしました) I *have decided* to buy a new television.

... ni suru (...に～) **1** make into: *Tanaka-sañ o gichoo ni shimashoo.* (田中さんを議長にしましょう) *Let's*

make Mr. Tanaka the chairman.

2 choose; decide: *"Kimi wa nani ni suru?" "Boku wa toñkatsu ni suru."* (「君は何にする」「ぼくはとんかつにする」) "What *would* you *like* to eat?" "I'll *have* a pork cutlet."

... o shite iru (...をしている) **1** be doing: *Haha wa señtaku o shite imasu.* (母は洗濯をしています) My mother *is doing* the washing.

2 work as; be engaged: *Ani wa isha o shite imasu.* (兄は医者をしています) My older brother *is* a doctor.

3 have (a shape, color, etc.): *Kanojo wa ooki-na me o shite iru.* (彼女は大きな目をしている) She *has* large eyes.

... to shitara (...としたら) as; when: *Dekakeyoo to shitara, deñwa ga kakatte kita.* (出かけようとしたら、電話がかかってきた) *As* I was about to go out, there was a phone call.

su｢r･u｣² する (刷る) *vt.* (sur･i-; sur･a-; sut-te ©) print: *Kono meeshi wa doko de surimashita ka?* (この名刺はどこで刷りましたか) Where *did* you *get* this name card *printed*?

su｢r･u｣³ する (擦る) *vt.* (sur･i-; sur･a-; sut-te ©) **1** strike (a match); rub.

2 lose (at gambling).

su｢r･u｣⁴ する (掏る) *vt.* (sur･i-; sur･a-; sut-te ©) pick; lift: *Watashi wa deñsha no naka de saifu o surareta.* (私は電車の中で財布をすられた) I *had* my wallet *lifted* in the train. 《⇨ suri》

su｢rudo｣･i するどい (鋭い) *a.* (-ku) **1** (of a blade, a claw, etc.) sharp; pointed.

2 (of a look, pain, etc.) sharp; acute: *senaka no surudoi itami* (背中の鋭い痛み) an *acute* pain in one's back.

3 (of a person etc.) sharp; keen: *kañsatsu ga surudoi* (観察が鋭い) have a *keen* eye.

su｢rume するめ (鯣) *n.* dried squid. 《⇨ ika²》

su｢rusuru するする *adv.* (~ to) easily; smoothly:
Saru wa surusuru (to) ki ni nobotta. (猿はするする(と)木に登った) The monkey climbed up the tree *with perfect ease.*

su｢ru to すると *conj.* 1 and; then:
Kare wa neyoo to shite ita. Suru to deñwa ga natta. (彼は寝ようとしていた。すると電話が鳴った) He was going to sleep. *Just then* the telephone rang.
2 in that case:
"*Ashita no yohoo wa ame desu.*" "*Suru to uñdookai wa chuushi desu ne.*" (「あしたの予報は雨です」「すると運動会は中止ですね」) "Tomorrow the forecast is for rain." "*In that case,* we will have to cancel the athletic meet, won't we?"

su｢shi¹ すし (寿司・鮨) *n.* sushi. ★ Vinegared rice balls topped with slices of raw fish or egg.

su｢so すそ (裾) *n.* 1 hem; bottom:
kimono no suso (着物のすそ) the *hem* of a kimono.
2 foot: *yama no suso* (山のすそ) the *foot* of a mountain.

su｢su すす (煤) *n.* soot.

su｢sume･ru¹ すすめる (進める) *vt.* (susume-te Ⅴ) 1 proceed with (a procedure, project, etc.); carry forward: *kooshoo o susumeru* (交渉を進める) *proceed with* the negotiations. (⇨ susumu)
2 promote; further:
sekai heewa o susumeru (世界平和を進める) *promote* world peace.
3 put forward (the hand of a clock [watch]). (↔ okuraseru) (⇨ susumu)

su｢sume･ru² すすめる (勧める) *vt.* (susume-te Ⅴ) 1 advise; suggest; persuade:
Watashi wa kare ni tabako o yameru yoo susumeta. (私は彼にたばこをやめるよう勧めた) I *advised* him to give up smoking.
2 recommend:
Señsee wa sono jisho o seeto ni

susumeta. (先生はその辞書を生徒に勧めた) The teacher *recommended* that dictionary to the pupils.
3 offer (a dish, drink, etc.).
4 tell; ask; invite:
Kare wa watashi ni kutsurogu yoo susumeta. (彼は私にくつろぐよう勧めた) He *told* me to make myself comfortable.

su｢sum･u すすむ (進む) *vi.* (susum-i-; susum･a-; susuñ-de Ⓒ)
1 proceed; travel:
Watashi-tachi wa kita ni mukatte susuñda. (私たちは北に向かって進んだ) We *proceeded* northward.
2 (of a clock [watch]) gain; be fast. (↔ okureru) (⇨ susumeru¹)
3 (of a procedure, project, etc.) make progress; advance.
4 (of diseases) get worse.
5 (of appetite) be good:
Kyoo wa shoku ga susumanai. (きょうは食が進まない) I *do not have a good appetite* today.

su｢sur･u すする (啜る) *vt.* (susur-i-; susur･a-; susut-te ⒸC) sip; slurp; suck:
o-cha o susuru (お茶をすする) *sip* tea / *hana o susuru* (鼻をすする) *sniffle.*

su｢ta｢a スター *n.* actor [actress, singer, player, etc.]; star.

su｢ta｢ato スタート *n.* start; getaway.
sutaato suru (~する) *vi.* start; begin. (⇨ hajimaru)

su｢tairi｢suto スタイリスト *n.*
1 fashion-conscious person.
2 adviser on the hairstyle and clothes of models and actors.

su｢ta｢iru スタイル *n.* 1 figure:
Kanojo wa sutairu ga ii. (彼女はスタイルがいい) She has a good *figure.*
2 style:
Seekatsu no sutairu ga kawatta. (生活のスタイルが変わった) Life-*styles* have changed.

su｢ta｢jiamu スタジアム *n.* stadium.

su｢ta｢suta すたすた *adv.* (~ to) briskly; hurriedly: ★ Used to express a way of walking.

Kare wa sutasuta *to toori no hoo e aruite itta.*(彼はすたすたと通りの方へ歩いて行った) He walked *briskly* toward the street.

su˦te˥eki ステーキ *n.* steak; beefsteak.

su˦teki すてき (素敵) *a.n.* (~ na) nice; splendid; marvelous; great: *Kimi no aidea wa* suteki *da.*(君のアイデアはすてきだ) That idea of yours is *brilliant.*

su˦te·ru すてる (捨てる) *vt.* (sute-te Ⓥ) **1** throw away; cast off; dump. **2** abandon; give up; forsake: *inochi o* suteru (命を捨てる) *throw away* one's life.

su˦to˥ スト *n.* strike. (⇨ sutoraiki)

su˦to˥obu ストーブ *n.* heater. ★ Comes from English 'stove' but never refers to an apparatus for cooking food.

su˦to˥ppu ストップ *n.* stop; halt. **sutoppu suru** (~する) *vi.* stop. (⇨ tomaru)

su˦tora˥iki ストライキ *n.* strike: *Sutoraiki wa ma-mo-naku chuushi sareta.*(ストライキは間もなく中止された) The *strike* was soon called off. (⇨ suto)

su˦tto すっと *adv.* (~ suru) (feel) refreshed [relieved]: *Nayami o uchiakete kimochi ga* sutto shita.*(悩みを打ち明けて気持ちがすっとした) *A burden was removed from my mind* after I disclosed my worries.

su·˦u˥ すう (吸う) *vt.* (su·i-; su-w·a-; sut-te Ⓒ) **1** breathe (in): *asa no shiñseñ na kuuki o* suu (朝の新鮮な空気を吸う) *breathe* the fresh morning air.

2 sip; sup; suck; absorb: *Akañboo ga haha-oya no chichi o* sutte iru.(赤ん坊が母親の乳を吸っている) A baby *is sucking* at her mother's breast.

3 smoke: *Tabako o* sutte *mo ii desu ka?* (たばこを吸ってもいいですか) May I *smoke?*

su˦u˥² すう (数) *n.* number. (⇨ APP. 3)

su˦ugaku すうがく (数学) *n.* mathematics. (⇨ sañsuu)

su˦uhai すうはい (崇拝) *n.* worship; admiration; cult. **suuhai suru** (~する) *vt.* worship; admire; adore.

su˦uji すうじ (数字) *n.* numeral; figure.

su˦upaa(-ma˥aketto) スーパー (マーケット) *n.* supermarket.

su˦upu スープ *n.* soup; broth.

su˦ushi すうし (数詞) *n.* (of grammar) numeral.

su˦war·u すわる (座る) *vi.* (suwar·i-; suwar·a-; suwat-te Ⓒ) sit (down); take a seat. (⇨ kakeru¹)

su˦yasuya すやすや *adv.* (~ to) calmly; quietly; peacefully: ★ Used to express the state of sleeping: *Akañboo wa* suyasuya *(to) nemutte imasu.*(赤ん坊はすやすや(と)眠っています) The baby is sleeping *peacefully.*

su˦zu¹ すず (鈴) *n.* bell.

su˦zu² すず (錫) *n.* tin.

su˦zume すずめ (雀) *n.* sparrow.

su˦zuri˥ すずり (硯) *n.* inkstone.

su˦zushi˥·i すずしい (涼しい) *a.* (-ku) cool; refreshing. (↔ atatakai) (⇨ samui)

T

ta˥¹ た (田) *n.* (rice) paddy. (⇨ tañbo)

ta˥² た (他) *n.* the rest; the other; the others. (⇨ hoka)

-ta た *infl. end.* [attached to verbs, adjectives, and the copula] ★ The *ta*-form of a verb is made by dropping the final '*-te*' of the

te-form of a verb and adding '-*ta*.' When the *te*-form is '-*de*,' add '-*da*.' The *ta*-form of an adjective is made by dropping the final '-*i*,' and adding '-*katta*.' The *ta*-form of the copula is '*datta*.'
(⇨ APP. 2)

1 (indicates an action or a situation in the past):
Kesa wa go-ji ni okita. (今朝は 5 時に起きた) I *got up* at five this morning.

2 (indicates an action or a situation which is just finished or completed):
Kare wa ima dekaketa tokoro desu. (彼は今出かけたところです) He *has* just *gone out*. (⇨ -tara)

3 (used to ask for confirmation or agreement):
Go-chuumoñ no shina wa kore deshita ne. (ご注文の品はこれでしたね) This *is* the article you ordered, isn't it?

4 (used to make a clause which modifies a noun):
Ano shiroi fuku o kita hito wa dare desu ka? (あの白い服を着た人はだれですか) Who is that person *wearing white*?

ta⌐ba たば (束) *n.* bundle; bunch:
tegami no taba (手紙の束) a *bundle* of letters.

ta⌐bako たばこ (煙草) *n.* cigarette; cigar; tobacco:
tabako o suu [nomu] (たばこを吸う[のむ]) smoke a *cigarette*.

ta⌐bane¬ru たばねる (束ねる) *vt.* (tabane-te Ⓥ) bundle; tie up in a bundle.

ta⌐bemo¬no たべもの (食べ物) *n.* food; diet.

ta⌐be¬ru たべる (食べる) *vt.* (tabe-te Ⓥ) **1** eat (food); have; take. (⇨ kuu; meshiagaru)
2 live on:
Hito-tsuki gomañ-eñ de wa tabete ikemaseñ. (ひと月 5 万円では食べていけません) One *cannot live* on fifty thousand yen a month.

ta⌐bi¬¹ たび (旅) *n.* trip; journey; tour; travel. (⇨ ryokoo)

ta⌐bi¬² たび (足袋) *n.* Japanese socks. ★ The front part is separated into two, the big toe and the other four toes.

ta⌐bi¬³ たび (度) *n.* **1** every time:
Kono shashiñ o miru tabi ni nakunatta chichi o omoidasu. (この写真を見るたびに亡くなった父を思い出す) *Every time* I look at this photo I recall my dead father.
2 occasion:
Kono tabi wa go-kekkoñ omedetoo gozaimasu. (この度はご結婚おめでとうございます) *Congratulations* on this, the *occasion* of your wedding.

ta⌐bitabi たびたび (度々) *adv.* often; many times; repeatedly. (⇨ shibashiba)

ta⌐boo たぼう (多忙) *a.n.* (~ na/no) busy. (⇨ isogashii)

ta⌐buñ たぶん (多分) *adv.* probably; perhaps; maybe:
Tabuñ kanojo wa konai deshoo. (たぶん彼女は来ないでしょう) *Maybe* she won't come. (⇨ osoraku; tashika)

-tachi たち (達) *suf.* [attached to nouns indicating people and animals] (indicates the plural).
★ Note there are two uses: *señsee-tachi* =the teachers / the teacher(s) and others.

ta⌐chiagar·u たちあがる (立ち上がる) *vi.* (-agar·i-; -agar·a-; -agatte Ⓒ) stand up; rise up:
Kokumiñ wa dokusai-seeji ni taishite tachiagatta. (国民は独裁政治に対して立ち上がった) The people *rose up* against the dictatorship.

ta⌐chiba たちば (立場) *n.* **1** position; situation:
Kochira no tachiba mo rikai shite kudasai. (こちらの立場も理解してください) I hope you will understand our *position*.
2 standpoint:
Chigatta tachiba kara arayuru kanoosee o kañgaemashita. (違った

立場からあらゆる可能性を考えました）
We considered all possibilities from a different *standpoint*.

ta⌐chidomar·u たちどまる（立ち止まる）*vi.* (-domar·i-; -domar·a-; -domat-te C) stop; pause; stand still. (⇨ tomaru')

ta⌐chiiri たちいり（立ち入り）*n.* entrance; entry:
Koko wa tachiiri kiñshi *desu.* (ここは立ち入り禁止です) This area is *off-limits*. (⇨ tachiiru)

ta⌐chii⌐r·u たちいる（立ち入る）*vi.* (-ir·i-; -ir·a-; -it-te C) 1 trespass; enter:
taniñ no tochi ni tachiiru (他人の土地に立ち入る) *trespass* on other people's land. (⇨ tachiiri)
2 meddle; pry into:
Kono moñdai ni wa tachiiritaku *arimaseñ.* (この問題には立ち入りたくありません) I don't wish to *meddle* in this problem.

ta⌐chimachi たちまち（忽ち）*adv.* in a moment; in no time:
Kineñ-kitte wa tachimachi *uri-kireta.* (記念切手はたちまち売り切れた) The commemorative stamps were sold out *in no time*.

ta⌐chisar·u たちさる（立ち去る）*vi.* (-sar·i-; -sar·a-; -sat-te C) leave; go away.

ta⌐chisuku⌐m·u たちすくむ（立ち竦む）*vi.* (-sukum·i-; -sukum·a-; -sukuñ-de C) be [stand] petrified:
Osoroshii kookee o mite, watashi wa sono ba ni tachisukuñde *shimatta.* (恐ろしい光景を見て、私はその場に立ちすくんでしまった) I *stood rooted* to the spot at the horrible sight.

ta⌐chiyor·u たちよる（立ち寄る）*vi.* (-yor·i-; -yor·a-; -yot-te C) drop in; stop by.

ta⌐da¹ ただ（唯）*adv.* only; simply; just:
Ima wa tada *kekka o matsu bakari desu.* (今はただ結果を待つばかりです) There is nothing to be done now but *simply* wait for the re-

sults. (⇨ tañ ni)

ta⌐da² ただ（只）*n.* no charge; free:
Kono katarogu wa tada *desu.* (このカタログはただです) There is *no charge* for this catalog.

ta⌐dachi ni ただちに（直ちに）*adv.* at once; immediately; directly:
Ikkoo wa tadachi ni *shuppatsu shita.* (一行はただちに出発した) The party *immediately* set out. (⇨ sugu)

ta⌐daima¹ ただいま（唯今）*n., adv.* now; (at) present; soon:
Tadaima *no jikoku wa ku-ji juu-go-fuñ desu.* (ただいまの時刻は9時15分です) The time *now* is fifteen minutes past nine.

ta⌐daima² ただいま I'm home; I've just gotten back. ★ A greeting used by a person who has just come home. (⇨ okaeri nasai)

ta⌐dashi ただし（但し）*conj.* (*formal*) but; however; provided. (⇨ shikashi)

ta⌐dashi⌐·i ただしい（正しい）*a.* (-ku) correct; right; proper:
Kimi no hañdañ wa tadashikatta. (きみの判断は正しかった) Your decision was *correct*.

ta⌐da⌐s·u ただす（正す）*vt.* (tadash·i-; tadas·a-; tadash·i-te C)
1 correct; rectify:
ayamari o tadasu (誤りを正す) *correct* the errors.
2 reform; straighten:
shisee o tadasu (姿勢を正す) *straighten* one's posture.

ta⌐dayo⌐·u ただよう（漂う）*vi.* (tadayo·i-; tadayow·a-; tadayot-te C) 1 drift; float:
Shiroi booto ga kaijoo o tadayotte *iru.* (白いボートが海上を漂っている) There *is* a white boat *afloat* on the sea.
2 be filled with:
Kaijoo ni wa nekki ga tadayotte *ita.* (会場には熱気が漂っていた) The hall *was alive* with excitement.

ta⌐do⌐oshi たどうし（他動詞）*n.*

ta⌐doritsu⌐k·u たどりつく (辿り着く) *vi.* (-tsuk·i-; -tsuk·a-; -tsu·i-te C̄) manage to arrive; work one's way.

ta⌐e⌐ru[1] たえる (耐える) *vi.* (tae-te V̄) bear; stand; endure: *kurushii seekatsu ni taeru* (苦しい生活に耐える) *endure* a hard life.

ta⌐e⌐ru[2] たえる (絶える) *vi.* (tae-te V̄) 1 become extinct; die out. 2 (of contact, relations, etc.) be cut off; come to an end: *Deñwa no koshoo de kare to no reñraku ga taeta.* (電話の故障で彼との連絡が絶えた) With the phone out of order, communication with him *was broken*.

ta⌐ezu たえず (絶えず) *adv.* always; continually; constantly.

ta⌐gai たがい (互い) *n.* each other; one another: ★ Often with 'o-.' *Kare-ra wa o-tagai ni tasukeatta.* (彼らはお互いに助け合った) They helped *each other*. (⇨ soogo)

-taga⌐r·u たがる *suf.* (*vi.*) (-tagar·i-; -tagar·a-; -tagat-te C̄) [attached to the continuative base of a verb] want (to do); be eager (to do): ★ Indicates the wishes and hopes of a person other than the speaker. (⇨ -tai) *Kare wa nañ de mo shiritagaru.* (彼は何でも知りたがる) He *is eager to know* everything.

ta⌐gaya⌐s·u たがやす (耕す) *vt.* (tagayash·i-; tagayas·a-; tagayash·i-te C̄) cultivate (land); till; plow. (⇨ koosaku[1])

ta⌐gu⌐r·u たぐる (手繰る) *vt.* (tagur·i-; tagur·a-; tagut-te C̄) haul in [up]; draw in: *tsuna o taguru* (綱をたぐる) *haul up* a rope.

ta⌐i[1] たい (対) *n.* versus; between: *sañ tai ni de katsu* (3 対 2 で勝つ) win by a score of three *to* one.

ta⌐i[2] たい (鯛) *n.* sea bream.

ta⌐i[3] たい (隊) *n.* party; company; band.

-ta·i たい *infl. end.* (*a.*) (-ku) [attached to the continuative base of a verb] want (to do); would like (to do): ★ Indicates the speaker's wishes or a desire to do something. (⇨ -tagaru) *Watashi wa nani-ka uñdoo ga* [o] *shitai.* (私は何か運動が[を]したい) I *want to do* some exercise. (⇨ ga[1])

ta⌐idañ たいだん (対談) *n.* talk between two people; interview. **taidañ suru** (～する) *vi.* have a talk.

ta⌐ido たいど (態度) *n.* attitude; manner; behavior.

ta⌐ifu⌐u たいふう (台風) *n.* typhoon.

ta⌐igai たいがい (大概) *n.* (～ no) most; nearly all: *taigai no hito* (たいがいの人) *most* people. — *adv.* usually; generally: *Nichiyoobi wa taigai ie ni imasu.* (日曜日はたいがい家にいます) On Sundays I am *generally* at home. (⇨ taitee)

ta⌐igaku たいがく (退学) *n.* withdrawal from school; expulsion from school. (⇨ teegaku[1]) **taigaku suru** (～する) *vi.* leave school.

ta⌐iguu たいぐう (待遇) *n.* 1 treatment; terms; pay: *Ano kaisha wa taiguu ga yoi* [warui]. (あの会社は待遇が良い[悪い]) That company *pays* its employees *well* [*badly*]. 2 service: *Kono ryokañ wa taiguu ga yoi.* (この旅館は待遇が良い) The *service* at this inn is good. **taiguu suru** (～する) *vt.* treat; pay.

Ta⌐ihe⌐eyoo たいへいよう (太平洋) *n.* Pacific Ocean. (⇨ Taiseeyoo)

ta⌐iheñ たいへん (大変) *a.n.* (～ na) 1 very; awful; terrible: *Ryokoo de wa taiheñ na keekeñ o shimashita.* (旅行ではたいへんな経験をしました) I had an *awful* experience during the trip.

2 (of quantity) a lot of:
Sono shoobai ni wa taiheñ na shi-kiñ ga iru. (その商売にはたいへんな資金がいる) You need *a lot of* funds for that business.
3 hard; difficult:
Kare o settoku suru no wa taiheñ desu. (彼を説得するのはたいへんです) It is *hard* to persuade him.
4 serious; grave:
Taiheñ na machigai o shite shimatta. (たいへんな間違いをしてしまった) I have made a *serious* mistake.
— *adv.* (~ ni) very much; greatly; extremely.

ta⌐iho たいほ (逮捕) *n.* arrest.
  taiho suru (~する) *vt.* arrest.

ta⌐ihoo たいほう (大砲) *n.* heavy gun; cannon.

ta⌐iiku たいいく (体育) *n.* physical education.

ta⌐iiñ たいいん (退院) *n.* leaving the hospital.
  taiiñ suru (~する) *vi.* leave the hospital; be discharged from the hospital. (↔ nyuuiñ) (⇨ byooin)

ta⌐iji たいじ (退治) *n.* getting rid of; extermination.
  taiji suru (~する) *vt.* get rid of; exterminate: *gokiburi o taiji suru* (ごきぶりを退治する) *get rid of* cockroaches.

ta⌐ijoo たいじょう (退場) *n.* leaving; exit.
  taijoo suru (~する) *vi.* leave; exit: *butai kara taijoo suru* (舞台から退場する) *leave* the stage. (↔ nyuujoo; toojoo)

ta⌐ijuu たいじゅう (体重) *n.* one's body weight.

ta⌐ika たいか (大家) *n.* authority; expert; great master.

ta⌐ikai たいかい (大会) *n.* **1** convention; mass [general] meeting. **2** tournament; contest: *tenisu-taikai* (テニス大会) a tennis *tournament*.

ta⌐ikaku たいかく (体格) *n.* physique; constitution; build.

ta⌐ikee たいけい (体系) *n.* system; organization.

ta⌐ikee-teki たいけいてき (体系的) *a.n.* (~ na, ni) systematic.

ta⌐ikeñ たいけん (体験) *n.* personal experience.
  taikeñ suru (~する) *vt.* experience; undergo. (⇨ keekeñ)

ta⌐ikiñ たいきん (大金) *n.* large sum of money.

ta⌐iko たいこ (太鼓) *n.* drum: *taiko o tataku* (太鼓をたたく) beat a *drum*.

ta⌐ikoo たいこう (対抗) *n.* competition; rivalry.
  taikoo suru (~する) *vi.* match; equal; compete. (⇨ kyoosoo)

ta⌐ikutsu たいくつ (退屈) *a.n.* (~ na) tedious; boring; dull.
  taikutsu suru (~する) *vi.* be bored; be weary. (⇨ akiru)

ta⌐ioñ たいおん (体温) *n.* body temperature:
  taioñ o hakaru (体温を測る) take a person's *temperature*.

ta⌐ioñkee たいおんけい (体温計) *n.* clinical thermometer.

ta⌐ipu¹ タイプ *n.* type; kind.

ta⌐ipu² タイプ *n.* typewriter; typing.
  taipu suru (~する) *vt.* type.

ta⌐ira たいら (平ら) *a.n.* (~ na, ni) flat; even; level:
  taira na yane (平な屋根) a *flat* roof.

ta⌐iriku たいりく (大陸) *n.* continent.

ta⌐iritsu たいりつ (対立) *n.* opposition; antagonism; confrontation.
  tairitsu suru (~する) *vi.* be opposed; confront: *rigai ga tairitsu suru* (利害が対立する) interests *are in conflict*.

ta⌐iryoku たいりょく (体力) *n.* physical strength; powers.

ta⌐iryoo たいりょう (大量) *n.* a large quantity. (↔ shooryoo)

ta⌐isaku たいさく (対策) *n.* measure; countermeasure:
  taisaku o neru (対策を練る) work out *countermeasures*.

ta⌐isee たいせい (体制) *n.* system;

structure; establishment.
((↔ han-taisee))

Ta「ise「eyoo たいせいよう（大西洋）
n. Atlantic Ocean. ((⇨ Taihee-yoo))

ta「iseki たいせき（体積）*n.* volume; capacity. ((⇨ menseki))

ta「isen たいせん（大戦）*n.* great war:
dai ni-ji sekai taisen（第二次世界大戦）the Second World *War*.

ta「isetsu たいせつ（大切）*a.n.*
(~ na, ni) important; valuable; precious. ((⇨ kanjin; daiji))

ta「isha たいしゃ（退社）*n.* leaving one's office; resignation; retirement. ((↔ nyuusha)) ((⇨ taishoku))
taisha suru（~する）*vi.* leave one's office; resign; retire.

ta「ishi たいし（大使）*n.* ambassador.

ta「ishi「kan たいしかん（大使館）*n.* embassy.

ta「ishita たいした（大した）*attrib.*
1 a lot of; great:
Kare no shageki no udemae wa taishita *mono da.*（彼の射撃の腕前はたいしたものだ）His skill in shooting is *quite* something.
2 (with a negative) not very; not much of:
Kare no kega wa taishita *koto wa nakatta.*（彼のけがはたいしたことはなかった）His injury was *nothing* serious.

ta「ishite¹ たいして（大して）*adv.*
(with a negative) very (much):
Taishite *o-yaku ni tatezu, mooshi-wake arimasen.*（たいしてお役に立てず、申し訳ありません）I am sorry that I could not be of *much* assistance.

ta「ishite² たいして（対して）
★ Used in the pattern '… *ni tai-shite.*'
1 to; against; regarding:
Go-shitsumon ni taishite *o-kotae shimasu.*（ご質問に対してお答えします）I will reply *to* your question.
((⇨ taisuru))
2 in contrast to [with]:
Sono keekaku ni nenchoosha ga

sansee shita no ni taishite, *wakai hito-tachi wa hantai shita.*（その計画に年長者が賛成したのに対して、若い人たちは反対した）*In contrast to* the elderly people's support of the plan, the young were against it.

ta「ishoku たいしょく（退職）*n.* retirement; resignation.
taishoku suru（~する）*vi.* retire; resign; leave one's company. ((⇨ taisha))

ta「ishoo¹ たいしょう（対象）*n.* object; subject:
Kono shina wa kazee no taishoo *ni narimasu.*（この品は課税の対象になります）These goods are *subject to* taxation.

ta「ishoo² たいしょう（対照）*n.* contrast; comparison.
taishoo suru（~する）*vt.* contrast; compare. ((⇨ kuraberu))

ta「ishoo³ たいしょう（対称）*n.* symmetry.

ta「ishoo⁴ たいしょう（大将）*n.* general; admiral.

ta「ishuu たいしゅう（大衆）*n.* the general public; the people; the masses.

ta「isoo¹ たいそう（体操）*n.* gymnastics; physical exercise; calisthenics. ((⇨ undoo))

ta「isoo² たいそう（大層）*adv.* very (much); greatly:
Kanojo wa sono e ga taisoo *ki ni itte iru yoo datta.*（彼女はその絵がたいそう気に入っているようだった）She seemed to like the picture *very much*. ((⇨ hijoo))

ta「is・u・ru たいする（対する）*vi.* (ta-ish・i-; tais・a-; taish・i-te ⓒ)
… *ni taisuru* (…に~) to; against:
Sono mondai ni taisuru *taisaku o tatenakereba naranai.*（その問題に対する対策を立てなければならない）We have to work out countermeasures *against* the problem.
((⇨ taishite²))

ta「itee たいてい（大抵）*n.* (~ no) most; just about:
Taitee *no kodomo wa chokoreeto*

ga suki desu.(たいていの子どもはチョコレートが好きです) *Most* children like chocolate.
— *adv.* usually; generally. (⇨ taigai)

ta￢itoo たいとう(対等) *a.n.*
(～ na/no, ni) equal; even:
otagai ni taitoo *no tachiba de hanashiau* (お互いに対等の立場で話し合う) talk with each other on an *equal* footing. (⇨ byoodoo)

ta￢iyaku たいやく(大役) *n.* important task [duty]:
taiyaku *o hatasu* (大役を果たす) carry out an *important duty*.

ta￢iyoo¹ たいよう(太陽) *n.* the sun.

ta￢iyoo² たいよう(大洋) *n.* ocean:
taiyoo*-kooroseñ* (大洋航路船) an *ocean* liner.

ta￢iyoo-ne￢ñsuu たいようねんすう (耐用年数) *n.* period of durability; life.

ta￢izai たいざい(滞在) *n.* stay (at a place); visit.
taizai *suru* (～する) *vi.* make a stay. (⇨ tomaru²)

ta￢ka たか(鷹) *n.* hawk; falcon.

ta￢ka･i たかい(高い) *a.* (-ku)
1 high; tall; lofty. (↔ hikui) (⇨ takasa)
2 expensive; high; dear:
Tookyoo wa bukka ga takai. (東京は物価が高い) The price of goods in Tokyo is *high*. (↔ yasui)
3 (of status, position, degree, etc.) high:
Kachoo wa Suzuki-sañ o takaku *hyooka shite iru.* (課長は鈴木さんを高く評価している) The manager thinks *highly* of Mr. Suzuki. (↔ hikui)
4 (of sound, voice) loud; high-pitched. (↔ hikui)

ta￢kama￢r･u たかまる(高まる) *vi.* (takamar･i-; takamar･a-; taka-mat-te Ⓒ) rise; increase:
hyooban ga takamaru (評判が高まる) *rise* in popularity. (⇨ taka-meru)

ta￢kame￢･ru たかめる(高める) *vt.*

(takame-te Ⓥ) raise; increase; improve:
kokumiñ no seekatsu-suijuñ o takameru (国民の生活水準を高める) *increase* the people's standard of living. (⇨ takamaru)

ta￢kara￢ たから(宝) *n.* treasure. (⇨ takaramono)

ta￢kara￢kuji たからくじ(宝くじ) *n.* public lottery (ticket). (⇨ kuji)

ta￢karamono￢ たからもの(宝物) *n.* treasure; heirloom. (⇨ takara)

ta￢kasa たかさ(高さ) *n.* 1 height; altitude: *biru no* takasa (ビルの高さ) the *height* of a building. (⇨ haba; takai)
2 pitch; loudness:
oto no takasa *o choosetsu suru* (音の高さを調節する) control the *pitch* [*loudness*] of a sound.

ta￢ke¹ たけ(竹) *n.* bamboo. (⇨ shoo-chiku-bai)

ta￢ke¹² たけ(丈) *n.* 1 length:
sukaato no take o mijikaku suru (スカートの丈を短くする) *shorten* a skirt.
2 height: take *ga nobiru* (丈がのびる) *grow tall*.

ta￢ki たき(滝) *n.* waterfall.

ta￢kibi たきび(焚火) *n.* open-air fire; bonfire.

ta￢kkyuu たっきゅう(卓球) *n.* table tennis; ping-pong.

ta￢kkyuubiñ たっきゅうびん(宅急便) *n.* (*trade name*) express home delivery.

ta￢ko¹ たこ(蛸) *n.* octopus.

ta￢ko² たこ(凧) *n.* kite.

ta￢ko³ たこ(胼胝) *n.* callus; corn.

ta￢k･u¹ たく(炊く) *vt.* (tak･i-; ta-k･a-; ta･i-te Ⓒ) cook (rice); boil. (⇨ niru¹)

ta￢k･u² たく(焚く) *vt.* (tak･i-; ta-k･a-; ta･i-te Ⓒ) burn (fuel):
sekitañ [*maki*] *o* taku (石炭[まき]を たく) *burn* coal [firewood]. (⇨ moyasu)

ta￢ku³ たく(宅) *n.* ⇨ o-taku.

ta￢kumashi￢･i たくましい(逞しい) *a.* (-ku) 1 strong; robust:
takumashii *karada* (たくましい体) a

robust physique.
2 powerful:
takumashii *soozooryoku* (たくましい 想像力) a *powerful* imagination.

ta⌈kumi たくみ (巧み) *a.n.* (~ na, ni) skillful; clever:
hoochoo o takumi *ni tsukau* (包丁 を巧みに使う) wield a kitchen knife with *skill*.

ta⌈kusa⌉ñ たくさん (沢山) *n., adv.*
1 many; much; a lot of:
Kare wa hoñ o takusañ *motte imasu.* (彼は本をたくさん持っています) He has *a lot of* books. (↔ suko-shi; shooshoo) (⇔ ikutsu mo)
2 enough; sufficiently:
Kare no jimañ-banashi wa moo takusañ *da.* (彼の自慢話はもうたくさん だ) I have had *enough* of his boasting.

ta⌈kushii タクシー *n.* taxi:
takushii *o hirou* (タクシーを拾う) pick up a *taxi* / takushii-*noriba* (タクシー 乗り場) a *taxi* stand. (⇔ haiyaa)

ta⌈kuwae⌉·ru たくわえる (蓄える) *vt.* (takuwae-te Ⓥ) save; put away; store:
roogo no seekatsu-shikiñ o taku-waeru (老後の生活資金を蓄える) *save* money to provide for one's old age.

ta⌈ma⌉ たま (球) *n.* **1** (of base-ball, billiards, etc.) ball.
2 light bulb. (⇔ deñkyuu)

ta⌈ma⌉ たま (玉) *n.* ball; bead.

ta⌈ma⌉ たま (弾) *n.* bullet.

ta⌈ma⌉go たまご (卵) *n.* egg:
tamago-*yaki* (卵焼き) an *omelet*. (⇔ hañjuku; yude-tamago)

ta⌈mane⌉gi たまねぎ (玉葱) *n.* onion. (⇔ negi)

ta⌈ma ni たまに *adv.* (~ wa) once in a while; occasionally; rarely:
Kare to wa tama ni *shika aimaseñ.* (彼とはたまにしか会いません) I meet him only *rarely*.

ta⌈marana⌉i たまらない (堪らない) *a.* (-ku) ★ Polite forms are '*tama-ranai desu*' and '*tamarimaseñ.*'

unbearable; intolerable.
-te tamaranai (て~) **1** so...that one cannot stand...: Sabishikute tamaranai. (寂しくてたまらない) I *am so lonely that* I *cannot stand* it.
2 be eager; be dying: *Jibuñ no kuruma ga* hoshikute tamaranai. (自分の車が欲しくてたまらない) I *can-not wait to have* my own car.

ta⌈mar·u⌉ たまる (溜まる) *vi.* (ta-mar·i-; tamar·a-; tamat-te Ⓒ) collect; pile up; accumulate; gather:
Tana no ue ni hokori ga tamatta. (棚の上にほこりがたまった) Dust *has collected* on the shelf. (⇔ tameru¹)

ta⌈mar·u⌉ たまる (貯まる) *vi.* (ta-mar·i-; tamar·a-; tamat-te Ⓒ) be saved:
Kare wa daibu o-kane ga tamatta *yoo da.* (彼はだいぶお金がたまったようだ) He seems to *have saved up* quite a bit of money. (⇔ tameru²)

ta⌈mashii たましい (魂) *n.* soul; spirit.

ta⌈matama たまたま (偶々) *adv.* by chance. (⇔ guuzeñ)

ta⌈me⌉ ため (為) *n.* **1** for the sake of; for the benefit of:
Watashi wa kimi no tame *ni, soo shita no desu.* (私は君のために、そうし たのです) I did so *for* your own sake.
2 for the purpose of; in order to:
Kanojo wa ryokoo e iku tame *ni, o-kane o tamete iru.* (彼女は旅行へ 行くために、お金をためている) She is saving money *for the purpose of* going on a trip.
3 because of; owing to; as a result of:
Byooki no tame *ni, paatii ni dera-renakatta.* (病気のために、パーティーに 出られなかった) I could not attend the party *because of* my illness.

ta⌈mei⌉ki ためいき (溜息) *n.* sigh:
ooki-na tameiki *o tsuku* (大きなため 息をつく) give a deep *sigh*.

ta｢mera˥・u ためらう（躊躇う）vi.
(tamera・i-; tameraw・a-; tame-
rat-te ⓒ) hesitate; waver; hang
back. (⇨ chuucho)

ta｢me・ru¹ ためる（溜める）vt. (ta-
me-te Ⓥ) store; cumulate:
amamizu o tameru（雨水をためる）
collect and store rainwater.
(⇨ tamaru¹)

ta｢me・ru² ためる（貯める）vt. (ta-
me-te Ⓥ) save (money); amass.
(⇨ tamaru²)

ta｢meshi˥ ni ためしに（試しに）adv.
tentatively; on trial.

ta｢me˥s・u ためす（試す）vt. (tame-
sh・i-; tames・a-; tamesh・i-te ⓒ)
try; test:
*Kore wa kare no nooryoku o ta-
mesu ii chañsu da.*（これは彼の能力を
試すいいチャンスだ）This is a good
chance to *test* his ability.

ta｢mo˥ts・u たもつ（保つ）vi. (ta-
moch・i-; tamot・a-; tamot-te ⓒ)
keep; hold; maintain; preserve;
retain:
keñkoo [wakasa] o tamotsu（健康
[若さ]を保つ）*stay* healthy [young].

ta｢na たな（棚）n. shelf; rack.

ta｢nabata たなばた（七夕）n. the
Star Festival celebrated on July
7.

ta｢ñbo たんぼ（田圃）n. rice paddy.
(⇨ suideñ; ta¹)

ta｢ñchoo たんちょう（単調）a.n.
(～ na, ni) monotonous; dull:
*Tañchoo na seekatsu ni wa akima-
shita.*（単調な生活には飽きました）I
am tired of my *dull* life.

ta｢ne たね（種）n. 1 seed: *tane o
maku*（種をまく）sow [plant] *seeds.*
2 cause; source:
*Musume no koto ga itsu-mo shiñ-
pai no tane desu.*（娘のことがいつも心
配の種です）Our daughter is always
a *cause* of anxiety.

ta｢ñgo たんご（単語）n. word; vocabulary.

ta｢ni たに（谷）n. valley; gorge.

ta｢ñi たんい（単位）n. unit; (of a
school) credit.

ta｢niñ たにん（他人）n. others;
unrelated person.

ta｢ñjoo たんじょう（誕生）n. birth.
tañjoo suru（～する）vi. be born.
(⇨ umareru)

ta｢ñjo˥obi たんじょうび（誕生日）n.
birthday.

ta｢ñjuñ たんじゅん（単純）a.n.
(～ na, ni) 1 simple:
tañjuñ na shigoto（単純な仕事）a
simple task.
2 (of people, ways of thinking,
etc.) simple-minded.

ta｢ñka¹ たんか（単価）n. unit price.

ta｢ñka² たんか（担架）n. stretcher:
tañka de hito o hakobu（担架で人を
運ぶ）carry a person on *stretcher.*

ta｢ñka³ たんか（短歌）n. Japanese
poem consisting of 31 syllables.
★ The syllables are arranged in
five lines of 5, 7, 5, 7 and 7.

ta｢ñkeñ たんけん（探検）n. exploration; expedition.
tañkeñ suru（～する）vt. explore.

ta｢ñki¹ たんき（短期）n. a short
(period of) time. (↔ chooki)

ta｢ñki² たんき（短気）n., a.n.
(～ na) short temper; short-
tempered.

ta｢ñkoo たんこう（炭鉱）n. coal
mine.

ta｢ñ-naru たんなる（単なる）attrib.
mere; simple; only:
Sore wa tañ-naru uwasa desu.（そ
れは単なるうわさです）That is a *mere*
rumor.

ta｢ñ ni たんに（単に）adv. only;
merely; simply:
*Watashi wa tañ ni shitte iru koto
o hanashita dake desu.*（私は単に知
っていることを話しただけです）I have
just told them *only* what I know.
(⇨ tada¹)

ta｢ no たの（他の）attrib. other;
another:
ta no hito [moñdai]（他の人[問題]）
another person [problem].
(⇨ hoka)

ta｢nomi たのみ（頼み）n. request;
favor:

Anata ni tanomi *ga aru no desu ga.* (あなたに頼みがあるのですが) I have a *favor* to ask of you. (⇨ tano-mu)

ta⌐nomoshi⌐⸱i たのもしい (頼もしい) *a.* (-ku) reliable; promising; trustworthy.

ta⌐no⌐m⸱u たのむ (頼む) *vt.* (ta-nom⸱i⸱-; tanom⸱a⸱-; tanon⸱-de Ⓒ)
1 ask (a favor); beg:
Watashi wa kare ni tasuke o tanonda. (私は彼に助けを頼んだ) I *asked* him for assistance. (⇨ tanomi)
2 order (goods); call (in); hire:
Honya ni hon o tanonda ga shina-gire datta. (本屋に本を頼んだが品切れだった) I *ordered* a book at the bookshop, but it was out of stock.

ta⌐noshi⌐⸱i たのしい (楽しい) *a.* (-ku) enjoyable; cheerful; happy. (⇨ tanoshimi; tanoshimu)

ta⌐noshi⌐mi たのしみ (楽しみ) *n.*
1 pleasure; enjoyment; amusement; diversion. (⇨ tanoshii; tanoshimu)
2 hope; expectation:
O-ai dekiru no o tanoshimi ni shite imasu. (お会いできるのを楽しみにしています) I *am looking forward to* seeing you.

ta⌐noshi⌐m⸱u たのしむ (楽しむ) *vt., vi.* (-shim⸱i⸱-; -shim⸱a⸱-; -shin⸱-de Ⓒ) enjoy; have a good time. (⇨ tanoshii; tanoshimi)

ta⌐npaku⌐shitsu たんぱくしつ (蛋白質) *n.* protein.

ta⌐nseñ たんせん (単線) *n.* single track (railroad). (↔ fukuseñ)

ta⌐nshiñ-fu⌐niñ たんしんふにん (単身赴任) *n.* taking up a new post and leaving one's family behind: tañshin-funinsha (単身赴任者) a *business bachelor.*

ta⌐nsho たんしょ (短所) *n.* short-comings; weak point; fault. (↔ choosho)

ta⌐nshuku たんしゅく (短縮) *n.* shortening; curtailment; reduction.

tañshuku suru (～する) *vt.* shorten; reduce: *eegyoo-jikañ o* tañshuku suru (営業時間を短縮する) *shorten* business hours. (↔ eñ-choo)

ta⌐ñso たんそ (炭素) *n.* carbon.

ta⌐ñsu たんす (簞笥) *n.* chest of drawers; wardrobe.

ta⌐ñtoo たんとう (担当) *n.* charge: tañtoo-sha (担当者) the person *in charge.*

tañtoo suru (～する) *vt.* be in charge (of); take charge (of):
Kanojo wa kaikee o tañtoo shite imasu. (彼女は会計を担当しています) She *is in charge of* accounting. (⇨ ukemotsu)

ta⌐nuki たぬき (狸) *n.* raccoon dog.

ta⌐ore⸱ru たおれる (倒れる) *vi.* (ta-ore-te Ⓥ)
1 fall; topple:
Taifuu de taiboku ga taoreta. (台風で大木が倒れた) A big tree *fell down* in the typhoon. (⇨ taosu)
2 become sick; (of a person) die; be killed:
karoo de taoreru (過労で倒れる) *collapse* from overwork.

ta⌐oru タオル *n.* towel.

ta⌐o⌐s⸱u たおす (倒す) *vt.* (taosh⸱i⸱-; taos⸱a⸱-; taosh⸱i⸱-te Ⓒ)
1 throw [push] down; knock down; tip. (⇨ taoreru)
2 beat; defeat; overthrow:
Kare wa yokozuna o taoshita. (彼は横綱を倒した) He *beat* the sumo grand champion. (⇨ taoreru)

ta⌐ppu⌐ri たっぷり *adv.* (～ to) fully; enough; in plenty:
Yosañ wa tappuri (to) arimasu. (予算はたっぷり(と)あります) We have *ample* funds.

-tara たら *infl. end.* [attached to verbs, adjectives, and the copula]
★ The *tara*-form is made by adding '-ra' to the *ta*-form. (⇨ APP. 2)
1 if:
a (used in a conditional sentence):

Kirai dattara, *tabenakute mo ii desu yo.* (嫌いだったら、食べなくてもいいですよ) *If you do not like it, you don't have to eat it.* (⇨ ttara)

b (used in unreal or imaginary conditionals):
Byooki de nakattara, ryokoo e ikeru ñ da ga. (病気でなかったら、旅行へ行けるんだが) *If I were not ill, I would be able to go on a trip.* (⇨ -ba¹)

c (used in fixed, introductory expressions):
Yoroshikattara, kono heya o o-tsukai kudasai. (よろしかったら、この部屋をお使いください) *If it is convenient for you,* please use this room.

2 when:
a (used to indicate a cause or reason): ★The second clause is often in the past.
Kanojo ni okurimono o shitara, totemo yorokoñde kureta. (彼女に贈物をしたら、とても喜んでくれた) *When* I gave her a present, she was very pleased.

b (used when an action occurs immediately after the *tara*-clause):
Kuukoo ni tsuitara, o-deñwa shimasu. (空港に着いたら、お電話します) I will phone you *on arriving* at the airport.

c (used when the action in the *tara*-clause leads to an unexpected occurrence): ★The second clause is in the past.
Yamada no uchi e ittara, rusu datta. (山田の家へ行ったら、留守だった) I went to Yamada's, but he was not at home.

-tara (doo desu ka) (～(どうですか)) what about; why don't you:
Koko de mattara, doo desu ka? (ここで待ったら、どうですか) *What about if* we wait here?

ta˥ra˥s·u たらす（垂らす）*vt.* (tara-sh·i-; taras·a-; tarash·i-te [C])
1 drop (liquid); drip:

Kare wa hitai kara ase o tarashite ita. (彼は額から汗を垂らしていた) He had sweat *dripping* from his brow. (⇨ tareru)

2 hang down:
okujoo kara tsuna o tarasu (屋上から綱を垂らす) *hang down* a rope from the roof. (⇨ tareru)

-ta˥razu たらず（足らず）*suf.* less than; not more than:
hyaku-peeji-tarazu no hoñ (100 ページ足らずの本) a book of *less than* 100 pages.

ta˥remaku たれまく（垂れ幕）*n.* banner hanging vertically; drop curtain.

ta˥re˥·ru たれる（垂れる）*vi.* (tare-te [V]) **1** drip; (of liquid) dróp:
Jaguchi kara mizu ga tarete *imasu.* (蛇口から水が垂れています) Water *is dripping* from the faucet. (⇨ tarasu)

2 hang; dangle:
Kanojo no kami wa kata made tarete ita. (彼女の髪は肩まで垂れていた) Her hair *hung down* to her shoulders. (⇨ tarasu)

-tari たり *infl. end.* [attached to verbs, adjectives, and the copula] ★The *tari*-form is made by adding '-ri' to the *ta*-form. (⇨ APP. 2)

1 (indicates state(s) or action(s) occurring simultaneously or in succession): ★Used usually in pairs, '...-tari ...-tari.'
Sono heya ni wa hito ga detari haittari shite ita. (その部屋には人が出たり入ったりしていた) Some people *were going into* the room, and others *were coming out*.

2 (indicates an example): ★Often followed by 'nado'.
Watashi wa donattari nado shimaseñ. (私はどなったりなどしません) I will not do such a thing as *shouting*.

ta˥ri·ru たりる（足りる）*vi.* (tari-te [V]) be enough; be sufficient. (⇨ juubuñ)

ta˥ryoo たりょう（多量）*a.n.*

(~ na/no, ni) a large quantity
[amount] (of):
*Remoñ wa bitamiñ o taryoo ni
fukuñde iru.*(レモンはビタミンを多量に
含んでいる) Lemons *are* rich in vitamins. (↔ shooryoo) (⇨ tairyoo)

ta`shika` たしか (確か) *a.n.* (~ na,
ni) sure; certain; positive:
Kare ga kuru no wa tashika desu.
(彼が来るのは確かです) It is *certain*
that he will come. (↔ futashika)
—— *adv.* probably; perhaps; possibly:
*Ano hito wa tashika watashi yori
wakai hazu desu.*(あの人は確か私よ
り若いはずです) He is *younger than
me, if I'm not mistaken.* (⇨ chigainai; osoraku; tabuñ)

ta`shikame`·ru たしかめる (確かめ
る) *vt.* (tashikame-te [V]) make
sure; confirm; check.

ta`shi`zañ たしざん (足し算) *n.*
(of arithmetic) addition.
(↔ hikizañ)

ta`shoo` たしょう (多少) *n.* (a large
or small) number; (a large or
small) quantity.
—— *adv.* some; a little; a few:
*Nihoñ ni wa tashoo shiriai ga
imasu.*(日本には多少知り合いがいます)
I have *a few* acquaintances in
Japan.

ta`ssha` たっしゃ (達者) *a.n.*
(~ na, ni) 1 healthy; in good
health. (⇨ geñki)
2 proficient; expert; well:
Kanojo wa suiee ga tassha desu.
(彼女は水泳が達者です) She is an
expert swimmer.

ta`ss·uru` たっする (達する) *vi., vt.*
(tassh·i-; tassh·i-; tassh·i-te [I])
1 reach; arrive. (⇨ tsuku)
2 amount; reach:
*Higai wa hyakumañ-eñ ni tasshi-
ta.*(被害は 100 万円に達した) The
damage *amounted* to one million
yen.
3 attain; achieve:
*Wareware wa mokuteki o tasshi-
ta.*(われわれは目的を達した) We at-

tained our purpose.

ta`s·u` たす (足す) *vt.* (tash·i-; ta-
s·a-; tash·i-te [C]) add; plus.
(↔ hiku; herasu)

ta`suka`r·u たすかる (助かる) *vi.*
(tasukar·i-; tasukar·a-; tasukat-
te [C]) 1 be saved; be rescued;
survive. (⇨ tasukeru)
2 (of aid, help, cooperation, etc.)
be helpful:
*Anata no go-kyooryoku ga areba,
hijoo ni tasukarimasu.*(あなたのご協
力があれば, 非常に助かります) If we
have your cooperation it will *be a
great help.* (⇨ tasukeru)

ta`suke`r·u たすける (助ける) *vt.*
(tasuke-te [V]) 1 help; assist; support:
*Kanojo ga nimotsu o hakobu no o
tasukete yatta.*(彼女が荷物を運ぶの
を助けてやった) I *helped* her carry
the baggage. (⇨ tasukaru)
2 save; rescue:
*Kare wa oboreyoo to shite iru ko-
domo o tasuketa.*(彼はおぼれようとし
ている子どもを助けた) He *saved* the
child who was about to drown.
(⇨ tasukaru)

ta`su`u たすう (多数) *n.* a large
[great] number; majority.
(↔ shoosuu)

ta`takai` たたかい (戦い) *n.* 1 war;
battle. (⇨ tatakau)
2 struggle:
hiñkoñ to no tatakai (貧困との戦い)
the *struggle* against poverty.
(⇨ tatakau)

ta`taka·u` たたかう (戦う) *vi.* (tata-
ka·i-; tatakaw·a-; tatakat-te [C])
1 fight; struggle:
dokuritsu no tame ni tatakau (独
立のために戦う) *fight* for independence. (⇨ tatakai)
2 (of a game, match) play.

ta`ta`k·u たたく (叩く) *vt.* (tatak-
·i-; tatak·a-; tata·i-te [C])
1 beat; hit; knock; slap:
doa o tataku (ドアをたたく) *knock* on
the door.
2 attack; criticize:

Yatoo wa seefu no seesaku o ta-taita.(野党は政府の政策をたたいた) The opposition *attacked* the government's policy.

ta⌐tami たたみ(畳) *n.* tatami (mat). 《⇨ -joo⁵》

ta⌐tam·u たたむ(畳む) *vt.* (tatam·i-; tatam·a-; tatañ-de C) **1** fold; double: *futoñ o tatamu* (ふとんをたたむ) *fold up* the bedding. **2** collapse (a desk, umbrella, etc.). **3** close down (a shop).

ta⌐te たて(縦) *n.* **1** length: ★ The vertical distance from end to end. *tate no señ o hiku* (縦の線を引く) draw a *vertical* line. 《↔ yoko》 **2** (～ni) lengthwise; vertically.

ta⌐tegaki たてがき(縦書き) *n.* vertical writing. 《↔ yokogaki》

ta⌐tekae·ru たてかえる(立て替える) *vt.* (-kae-te V) pay (for someone else); lend.

ta⌐temae たてまえ(建て前) *n.* principle; theory; opinion; official stance: *tatemae to hoñne* (建て前と本音) the *principle* and the practice. 《↔ hoñne》

ta⌐te⌐mono たてもの(建物) *n.* building. 《⇨ keñchiku》

ta⌐te⌐ru¹ たてる(立てる) *vt.* (tate-te V) **1** set up; put up; stand: *tatefuda o tateru* (立て札を立てる) *put up* a notice board. 《⇨ tatsu¹》 **2** raise (dust); make (a noise). 《⇨ tatsu²》

ta⌐te⌐ru² たてる(建てる) *vt.* (tate-te V) build; erect: *tera o tateru* (寺を建てる) *build* a temple. 《⇨ tatsu²》

ta⌐teuri-ju⌐utaku たてうりじゅうたく(建て売り住宅) *n.* ready-built house. ★ Often called '*tateuri*.'

ta⌐tole¹ たとえ(譬え・例え) *n.* simile; metaphor; example.

ta⌐toe² たとえ(仮令) *adv.* even if; no matter what...: *Tatoe anata ga hañtai shite mo watashi wa ikimasu.*(たとえあなたが

反対しても私は行きます) *Even if* you are against it, I'm going.

ta⌐to⌐eba たとえば(例えば) *adv.* for example [instance]; such as.

ta⌐toe⌐ru たとえる(譬える・例える) *vt.* (tatoe-te V) compare to; use a simile [metaphor].

ta⌐ts·u¹ たつ(立つ) *vi.* (tach·i-; tat·a-; tat-te C) **1** (of a person or an animal) stand; stand up: *seki o tatsu* (席を立つ) *get up* from a seat. **2** (of a thing) stand. **3** (in an election) run; stand: *Koñdo no señkyo ni wa dare ga tachimasu ka?* (今度の選挙にはだれが立ちますか) Who *is running* in the coming election? **4** (of steam, smoke, dust, etc.) rise. 《⇨ tateru¹》

ta⌐ts·u² たつ(建つ) *vi.* (tach·i-; tat·a-; tat-te C) be built; be erected; be set up: *Kiñjo ni mañshoñ ga tatta.* (近所にマンションが建った) A condominium *was built* in my neighborhood. 《⇨ tateru²》

ta⌐ts·u³ たつ(絶つ) *vt.* (tach·i-; tat·a-; tat-te C) break off; sever; cut off: *gaikoo kañkee o tatsu* (外交関係を絶つ) *break off* diplomatic relations.

ta⌐ts·u⁴ たつ(経つ) *vi.* (tach·i-; tat·a-; tat-te C) (of time) pass by; go by: *Chichi-oya ga nakunatte kara sañ-neñ tatta.* (父親が亡くなってから３年たった) Three years *have passed* since my father died. 《⇨ keeka》

ta⌐ts·u⁵ たつ(発つ) *vt.* (tach·i-; tat·a-; tat-te C) start; leave; depart. 《⇨ shuppatsu》

ta⌐ts·u⁶ たつ(断つ) *vt.* (tach·i-; tat·a-; tat-te C) quit; give up (smoking, alcohol, etc.).

ta⌐tta たった *adv.* only; just; no more than: *Eki made koko kara tatta go-fuñ* *desu.* (駅までここからたった 5 分です) It takes *no more than* five minutes from here to the station.

ta⌈ue⌉ たうえ (田植え) *n.* rice-planting; transplantation of rice seedlings.

ta⌈wara⌉ たわら (俵) *n.* straw bag.

ta⌈yasu⌉¹·i たやすい *a.* (-ku) easy; simple:
Koñna moñdai wa tayasuku *tokemasu.* (こんな問題はたやすく解けます) I can *easily* solve a problem like this. (⇨ yasashii¹)

ta⌈yori⌉¹ たより (便り) *n.* letter; news. (⇨ tegami)

ta⌈yori⌉² たより (頼り) *n.* reliance; dependence; trust. (⇨ tayoru)
tayori ni naru [naranai] (〜になる [ならない]) reliable [unreliable].

ta⌈yo⌉r·u たよる (頼る) *vt.* (tayo-r·i-; tayor·a-; tayot-te C) rely [count] on; depend on:
Kare wa mada oya ni tayotte iru. (彼はまだ親に頼っている) He still *depends* on his parents.

ta⌈zune⌉·ru¹ たずねる (尋ねる) *vt.* (tazune-te V) 1 ask; inquire; question. (⇨ kiku¹)
2 look for; search for (a person): *nikushiñ o* tazuneru (肉親を尋ねる) *look for* one's relatives.

ta⌈zune⌉·ru² たずねる (訪ねる) *vt.* (tazune-te V) visit; call on [at]; come [go round] to see.

te¹ て (手) *n.* 1 hand.
2 means; way:
Keesatsu wa arayuru te *o tsuku-shite, sono ko o sagashita.* (警察はあらゆる手を尽くして、その子を捜した) The police tried every possible *means* to find the child.
3 kind; brand:
Kono te *no mono ga yoku ure-masu.* (この手のものがよく売れます) Articles of this *kind* sell very well.
te ga denai (〜が出ない) cannot possibly buy.
te ni ireru (〜に入れる) get; obtain.

te o dasu (〜を出す) start; dabble: *kabu ni* te o dasu (株に手を出す) *dabble* in stocks.
te o nuku (〜を抜く) cut corners.
te o tsukeru (〜をつける) start; set about.

-te て *infl. end.* [attached to the *ku*-form of an adjective. For the *te*-form of verbs, see APP. 2]
★ The *te*-form of the copula is '*de.*'
1 and: ★ Used to link similar items in a parallel relationship.
Terebi no nyuusu wa hayakute seekaku da. (テレビのニュースは速くて正確だ) The news on TV is *quick and* correct.
2 since; after: ★ Used to indicate a temporal sequence.
Kanojo wa daigaku o dete, *sugu kekkoñ shita.* (彼女は大学を出て、すぐ結婚した) She got married soon *after* graduating from college.
3 with: ★ Used when two actions occur almost simultaneously.
Kare wa udegumi o shite, *nani-ka kañgaete ita.* (彼は腕組みをして、何か考えていた) He was thinking about something *with* his arms folded.
4 because; since: ★ Used to indicate a cause or reason.
Kinoo no bañ wa atsukute, *nemu-renakatta.* (きのうの晩は暑くて、眠れなかった) I could not sleep last night *for* the heat. (⇨ kara⁴; no de)
5 by; on: ★ Used to indicate a means or method.
Kanojo wa jiteñsha ni notte, *kai-mono ni ikimashita.* (彼女は自転車に乗って、買い物に行きました) She went shopping *by* bicycle.
6 but: ★ Used to indicate a contrast or opposition.
Koñna ni doryoku shite, *mada de-kinai.* (こんなに努力して、まだできない) I have tried so hard, *but* I still cannot do it.
7 (used with other verbs such as '*iru,*' '*miru,*' '*oku,*' '*morau,*' '*age-*

ru,' 'kureru,' etc.):
Ima Nihoñgo o naratte imasu. (今日本語を習っています) I am now *studying* Japanese.

te⌈a⌉rai てあらい (手洗い) *n.* toilet; restroom; lavatory. ⟪⇨ beñjo⟫

te⌉-ashi てあし (手足) *n.* hand and foot; arms and legs; limbs.

te⌉ate てあて (手当て) *n.* **1** medical treatment [care]:
ookyuu-teate *o ukeru* (応急手当てを受ける) receive first *aid.*
2 allowance; bonus:
juutaku[*tsuukiñ*]-teate (住宅[通勤]手当て) a housing [commuting] *allowance.* ⟪⇨ boonasu; shooyo⟫
teate (o) suru (〜(を)する) *vt.* treat (an illness).

te⌈bana⌉s·u てばなす (手放す) *vt.* (-banash·i-; -banas·a-; -banash·i-te Ⓒ) part with; sell; give up. ⟪⇨ uru[1]⟫

te⌈baya⌉·i てばやい (手早い) *a.* (-ku) quick:
Kare wa tebayaku *heya o katazuketa.* (彼は手早く部屋を片づけた) He *quickly* straightened up his room.

te⌉biki てびき (手引き) *n.* guide; guidebook; handbook.
tebiki (o) suru (〜(を)する) *vt.* guide; lead; help.

te⌈bu⌉kuro てぶくろ (手袋) *n.* glove. ⟪⇨ kutsushita⟫

te⌉buri てぶり (手振り) *n.* gesture; signs. ⟪⇨ miburi⟫

te⌈chi⌉gai てちがい (手違い) *n.* mistake; fault; accident.

te⌈choo てちょう (手帳) *n.* small notebook; pocket diary.

te⌈da⌉suke てだすけ (手助け) *n.* help; assistance:
tedasuke ni naru (手助けになる) *be helpful.*
tedasuke (o) suru (〜(を)する) *vt.* help; assist. ⟪⇨ tetsudau⟫

te⌈eañ ていあん (提案) *n.* proposal; suggestion; motion.
teeañ (o) suru (〜(を)する) *vt.* propose (a plan); suggest; move.

te⌈eboo ていぼう (堤防) *n.* riverbank; embankment; levee. ⟪⇨ dote⟫

te⌈echi ていち (低地) *n.* lowlands; low ground. ⟪↔ koochi[3]⟫

te⌈edeñ ていでん (停電) *n.* blackout; power failure; power cut.
teedeñ suru (〜する) *vi.* (of electric power) fail; be cut off.

te⌉edo ていど (程度) *n.* degree; extent; standard; level:
Sono uwasa wa aru teedo *made hoñtoo desu.* (そのうわさはある程度まで本当です) The rumor is true to some *extent.*

te⌈egaku[1] ていがく (停学) *n.* suspension from school (as punishment). ⟪⇨ taigaku⟫

te⌈egaku[2] ていがく (低額) *n.* small sum of money. ⟪⇨ koogaku⟫

te⌈eiñ ていいん (定員) *n.* (seating) capacity; the fixed number.

te⌈eka[1] ていか (低下) *n.* fall off; decline; deterioration.
teeka suru (〜する) *vi.* fall; drop; lower. ⟪↔ jooshoo⟫ ⟪⇨ sagaru⟫

te⌈eka[2] ていか (定価) *n.* fixed [list] price.

te⌉eki ていき (定期) *n.* **1** fixed period:
kaigoo o teeki *ni hiraku* (会合を定期に開く) hold meetings at *regular intervals.*
2 commutation [season] ticket. ⟪⇨ teekikeñ⟫

te⌈eki⌉keñ ていきけん (定期券) *n.* commutation [season] ticket. ⟪⇨ kaisuukeñ⟫

te⌈ekoku ていこく (定刻) *n.* the scheduled [appointed] time.

te⌈ekoo ていこう (抵抗) *n.* **1** resistance; opposition.
2 reluctance:
Kare ni au no wa nañto-naku teekoo o kañjimasu. (彼に会うのは何となく抵抗を感じます) I *am* rather *reluctant* to meet him.
teekoo suru (〜する) *vi.* resist; oppose.

te⌈ekyoo ていきょう (提供) *n.* offer; sponsorship.

teekyoo suru (〜する) vt. offer; provide; donate. (⇨ ataeru)

te⌐ekyu'ubi ていきゅうび (定休日) n. regular holiday.

te⌐ema テーマ n. theme; subject; topic.

te⌐enee ていねい (丁寧) a.n.
(〜 na, ni) **1** polite; courteous; kind: teenee ni ojigi suru (丁寧におじぎする) bow politely.
2 careful; close; thorough: kanji o teenee ni kaku (漢字を丁寧に書く) write Chinese characters carefully.

te⌐eneego ていねいご (丁寧語) n. polite word [expression].

te⌐enen ていねん (定年) n. retirement age; age limit.

te⌐eon ていおん (低温) n. low temperature. (↔ koo-on)

te⌐epu テープ n. (of a cassette, video, etc.) tape; ticker tape; ribbon; adhesive tape.

te⌐eryuujo ていりゅうじょ (停留所) n. bus [streetcar] stop. ★ A train station is 'eki.' (⇨ basutee)

te⌐esai ていさい (体裁) n. appearance; show; style. (⇨ kakkoo')
teesai ga warui (〜が悪い) feel awkward.

te⌐esee ていせい (訂正) n. correction; revision.
teesee suru (〜する) vt. correct: ayamari o teesee suru (誤りを訂正する) correct a mistake. (⇨ naosu')

te⌐esha ていしゃ (停車) n. (of a train, bus, etc.) stop. (↔ hassha)
teesha suru (〜する) vi. stop.

te⌐eshi ていし (停止) n. **1** stop; halt. (↔ zenshin')
2 suspension; cessation: kaku-jikken no teeshi (核実験の停止) the suspension of nuclear tests.
teeshi suru (〜する) vi., vt.
1 come to a stop; halt. (⇨ tomaru')
2 suspend (business, payment).

te⌐eshi'see ていしせい (低姿勢) n. modest attitude; low profile. (↔ kooshisee)

te⌐eshoku ていしょく (定食) n. fixed meal; table d'hôte.

te⌐eshutsu ていしゅつ (提出) n. submission; presentation.
teeshutsu suru (〜する) vt. submit; turn [send] in; present. (⇨ dasu; sashidasu)

te⌐ga'kari てがかり (手掛かり) n. clue; key; track:
Hannin wa nani mo tegakari o nokosanakatta. (犯人は何も手がかりを残さなかった) The culprit left no traces behind.

te⌐gami てがみ (手紙) n. letter: tegami o dasu [uketoru] (手紙を出す[受け取る]) send off [receive] a letter. (⇨ buntsuu; tayori')

te⌐gara' てがら (手柄) n. credit; meritorious deed:
Kono seekoo wa kimi no tegara da. (この成功は君の手柄だ) Credit for this success goes to you.

te⌐garu てがる (手軽) a.n. (〜 na, ni) handy; easy; light: tegaru na jisho (手軽な辞書) a handy dictionary.

te⌐giwa' てぎわ (手際) n. skill; craftsmanship; efficiency:
Kare wa tegiwa yoku sono kooshoo o matometa. (彼は手ぎわよくその交渉をまとめた) He concluded the negotiations with skill.

te⌐hai てはい (手配) n. arrangements; preparations.
tehai (o) suru (〜を(を)する) vt.
1 arrange; prepare; get ready.
2 search: Sono jiken no yoogisha wa zenkoku ni tehai sarete imasu. (その事件の容疑者は全国に手配されています) The suspect in that case is being searched for nationwide.

te⌐hazu てはず (手筈) n. arrangements; plan; program: tehazu o totonoeru (手はずを整える) make arrangements.

te⌐ho'n てほん (手本) n. model; example; pattern.

te⌐ire' ていれ (手入れ) n. **1** care: Kono niwa wa teire ga yukitodo-

ite iru.(この庭は手入れが行き届いている) This garden *is well cared for*.
2 raid; crackdown:
keesatsu no teire (警察の手入れ) a police *raid*.

teire (o) suru (〜(を)する) *vt.*
1 take care of; care for; repair.
2 raid; crack down on.

te￢jina てじな(手品) *n.* magic; conjuring trick.

te￢juñ てじゅん(手順) *n.* plan; order; process; arrangement:
Subete wa tejuñ-*doori umaku itta.* (すべては手順どおりうまくいった) Everything went well according to *plan*.

te￢ka￢geñ てかげん(手加減) *n.* allowance; discretion; consideration.
tekageñ (o) suru (〜(を)する) *vt.* make allowances; use discretion; take into consideration.

te￢kazu てかず(手数) *n.* trouble. (⇨ tesuu)

te￢ki てき(敵) *n.* enemy; opponent; rival. (↔ mikata²)

-teki てき(的) *suf. (a.n.)* (〜 na, ni) concerning; having a certain character; resembling: ★ Added to a noun, usually of Chinese origin. '-*teki na [ni]*' is often equivalent to English '-al [-ally].'
roñri-*teki ni setsumee suru* (論理的に説明する) explain *logically* / ippañ-*teki na kañgae* (一般的な考え) a *common* notion.

te￢kigi てきぎ(適宜) *a.n.* (〜 na, ni), *adv.* appropriate; proper; suitable. (⇨ tekitoo)

te￢kii てきい(敵意) *n.* hostility; enmity. (↔ kooi²)

te￢kikaku てきかく(的確) *a.n.* (〜 na, ni) accurate; exact; precise.

te￢kisee てきせい(適性) *n.* aptitude: tekisee-*keñsa* (適性検査) an *aptitude* test.

te￢kisetsu てきせつ(適切) *a.n.* (〜 na, ni) suitable; appropriate; proper. (⇨ fusawashii)

te￢kis·u￢ru てきする(適する) *vi.* (tekish·i-; tekis·a-; tekish·i-te C) be suitable; be good:
Kono shokubutsu wa shokuyoo ni tekishite imasu.(この植物は食用に適しています) This plant *is good* for food.

te￢kisuto テキスト *n.* textbook. ★ Shortened form of '*tekisuto bukku*' (textbook). (⇨ kyooka-sho)

te￢kitoo てきとう(適当) *a.n.* (〜 na, ni) **1** suitable; good: tekitoo *na kikai ni* (適当な機会に) on a *suitable* occasion. (↔ fute-kitoo) (⇨ tekisetsu)
2 (of work, method, etc.) irresponsible; taking things easy:
Muri shinai de, tekitoo ni yaroo. (無理しないで、適当にやろう) *Let's take it easy* and not push ourselves too hard.

te￢kiyoo てきよう(適用) *n.* application.
tekiyoo suru (〜する) *vt.* apply (a rule).

te￢kkiñ てっきん(鉄筋) *n.* steel rod [bar]: tekkiñ-*koñkuriito* (鉄筋コンクリート) *ferroconcrete*.

te￢kkyoo てっきょう(鉄橋) *n.* iron bridge; railroad bridge.

te￢ko てこ(梃子) *n.* lever.

te￢kubi てくび(手首) *n.* wrist.

te￢ma￢ てま(手間) *n.* time; labor; trouble: tema *o habuku* (手間を省く) save *labor*.

te￢mae てまえ(手前) *n.* **1** (〜 ni, de) this side; before:
Koosateñ no temae de *tomatte kudasai.*(交差点の手前で止まってください) Please stop the car *before* you come to the intersection.
2 presence:
Ryooshiñ no temae *sono ko wa otonashiku shite ita.*(両親の手前その子はおとなしくしていた) The child remained quiet in the *presence* of her parents.

te￢mane￢ki てまねき(手招き) *n.* beckoning.

temaneki suru (〜する) *vt.* beckon. (⇨ maneku)

-te mo ても [*te*-form of a verb or adjective plus the particle '*mo*']
1 (even) if; though:
Ame ga futte mo *shiai wa arimasu.* (雨が降っても試合はあります) *Even if* it rains, we will have the game. (⇨ tatoe[2])
2 however; whatever:
Doñna ni sono shigoto ga tsurakute mo *watashi wa yarimasu.* (どんなにその仕事がつらくても私はやります) I will carry out the task *however painful it is.*

te˥moto てもと (手元) *n.* hand:
jisho o temoto *ni oku* (辞書を手元に置く) keep a dictionary at *hand.*

te˥ñ[1] てん (点) *n.* **1** dot; spot.
2 score; grade; mark. (⇨ teñsuu)
3 point; respect:
Sono teñ *ni moñdai ga aru.* (その点に問題がある) There is a problem on that *point.*

te˥ñ[2] てん (天) *n.* **1** the sky.
2 Heaven; Providence.

-teñ[1] てん (店) *suf.* store; shop; office:
sho-teñ (書店) a bookstore / *kissa*-teñ (喫茶店) a coffee *shop* / *shi*-teñ (支店) a branch *office.*

-teñ[2] てん (展) *suf.* exhibition:
ko-teñ (個展) a one-man *show.*

te˥na˥oshi てなおし (手直し) *n.* readjustment; rectification; alteration; improvement.
tenaoshi suru (〜する) *vt.* readjust; rectify; alter; improve. (⇨ naosu[1])

te˥ñchi てんち (天地) *n.* **1** heaven and earth; universe.
2 land; world: *jiyuu no* teñchi (自由の天地) a free *land.*
3 top and bottom:
Kono shashiñ wa teñchi *ga gyaku da.* (この写真は天地が逆だ) This photo is *upside down.*

te˥ñdoñ てんどん (天丼) *n.* a bowl of rice topped with deep-fried shrimp and vegetables.

te˥ñgoku てんごく (天国) *n.* heaven; Heaven; paradise. (↔ jigoku)

te˥ni˥motsu てにもつ (手荷物) *n.* carry-on baggage; hand luggage: tenimotsu-*azukarijo* (手荷物預かり所) a *checkroom*; a *left-luggage office.*

te˥ñiñ てんいん (店員) *n.* sales-clerk; salesman; saleswoman.

te˥ñjoo てんじょう (天井) *n.* ceiling; roof.

te˥ñkai てんかい (展開) *n.* development.
teñkai suru (〜する) *vi., vt.* develop; unfold; spread out (⇨ hirogaru)

te˥ñkee てんけい (典型) *n.* type; model; specimen.

te˥ñkee-teki てんけいてき (典型的) *a.n.* (〜 na, ni) typical; model.

te˥ñkeñ てんけん (点検) *n.* examination; check; inspection.
teñkeñ suru (〜する) *vt.* examine; check; inspect: *Gasoriñ-sutañdo de kuruma o* teñkeñ *shite moratta.* (ガソリンスタンドで車を点検してもらった) I *had* my car *checked* at a gas station. (⇨ shiraberu)

te˥ñki てんき (天気) *n.* weather; fine weather:
Kyoo wa teñki *da.* (きょうは天気だ) It's *fine* today. (⇨ kaisee[2]; teñkoo)

te˥ñkiñ てんきん (転勤) *n.* transfer.
teñkiñ suru (〜する) *vi.* be transferred.

te˥ñki-yo˥hoo てんきよほう (天気予報) *n.* weather forecast [report].

te˥ñkoo てんこう (天候) *n.* weather conditions. (⇨ teñki)

te˥ñmo˥ñgaku てんもんがく (天文学) *n.* astronomy.

te˥ñneñ てんねん (天然) *n.* nature: teñneñ-*gasu* (天然ガス) *natural* gas / teñneñ-*kineñbutsu* (天然記念物) a *Natural* Monument.

te˥ñno˥o てんのう (天皇) *n.* emperor: ★ This only refers to the

Emperor of Japan.
Teñnoo-heeka (天皇陛下) *His Majesty the Emperor*. (⇨ Koogoo)

te-「no」-hira てのひら (手の平) *n.* the flat of the hand; palm.

te「ñpo テンポ *n.* tempo; pace; speed.

te「ñpura てんぷら (天ぷら) *n.* tempura. ★ A dish of seafood and vegetables, which are dipped in batter and deep-fried.

te「ñra」ñkai てんらんかい (展覧会) *n.* exhibition; show.

te「ñsai[1] てんさい (天災) *n.* natural disaster [calamity].

te「ñsai[2] てんさい (天才) *n.* genius.

te「ñshi てんし (天使) *n.* angel.

te「ñshoku てんしょく (転職) *n.* change of one's job.
teñshoku suru (～する) *vi.* change one's occupation.

te「ñsu」u てんすう (点数) *n.* mark; point; score:
shikeñ de ii teñsuu *o toru* (試験でいい点数を取る) get a good *mark* on the test. (⇨ teñ[1])

te「ñteki てんてき (点滴) *n.* intravenous drip infusion.

te「ñtoo てんとう (点灯) *n.* lighting.
teñtoo suru (～する) *vt., vi.* turn [switch] on a light; be turned on.

te「nugui てぬぐい (手拭) *n.* hand towel. ★ It is made of rough cotton cloth.

te「o」kure ておくれ (手遅れ) *n.* being too late; being beyond cure:
Ima to natte wa teokure *da.* (今となっては手遅れだ) It is *too late* now.

te「ppañ てっぱん (鉄板) *n.* iron [steel] plate:
teppañ-*yaki* (鉄板焼き) meat and vegetables cooked on an *iron plate*.

te「ppoo てっぽう (鉄砲) *n.* gun:
teppoo *o utsu* (鉄砲を撃つ) fire a *gun*.

te「ra」 てら (寺) *n.* (Buddhist) temple. ★ Also '*o-tera*.' (⇨ jiñja)

te「rashiawase」-ru てらしあわせる (照らし合わせる) *vt.* (-awase-te [V])

compare with; check; test by comparison. (⇨ kuraberu)

te「ra」s・u てらす (照らす) *vt.* (terash-i-; teras-a-; terash-i-te [C]) light; shine; illuminate. (⇨ teru)

te「rebi テレビ *n.* television (set); television (program); TV.

te「rehoñ-ka」ado テレホンカード *n.* telephone card. ★ A prepaid plastic card against which charges are debited when using a public phone.

te「r・u てる (照る) *vi.* (ter-i-; ter-a-; tet-te [C]) shine; blaze:
Taiyoo ga kañkañ to tette iru. (太陽がかんかんと照っている) The sun *is shining* brightly. (⇨ terasu)

te「ruteru-bo」ozu てるてるぼうず (照る照る坊主) *n.* a simple, small doll, which children hang outside in the hope of it bringing good weather.

te「saki」 てさき (手先) *n.* 1 finger; hand:
Kare wa tesaki *ga kiyoo [bukiyoo] da.* (彼は手先が器用[不器用]だ) He is good [clumsy] with his *hands*.
2 tool; agent:
booryokudañ no tesaki (暴力団の手先) the *tool* of a criminal gang.

te「suri てすり (手摺り) *n.* rail; handrail.

te「suto テスト *n.* test; quiz. (⇨ shikeñ)
tesuto (o) suru (～(を)する) *vt.* give a test: *kikai no seenoo o* tesuto suru (機械の性能をテストする) *test* the performance of a machine.

te「su」u てすう (手数) *n.* trouble:
Kare no okage de daibu tesuu *ga habuketa.* (彼のおかげでだいぶ手数が省けた) Thanks to him, we were able to save much *trouble*.

te「su」uryoo てすうりょう (手数料) *n.* commission; service charge.

te「tsu てつ (鉄) *n.* iron.

te「tsubiñ てつびん (鉄瓶) *n.* iron

kettle. (⇨ yakañ²)

te「tsuboo」 てつぼう (鉄棒) n.
horizontal bar; iron bar.

te「tsuda」i てつだい (手伝い) n.
1 help; assistance. (⇨ tetsudau)
2 help(er); assistant:
Dare-ka tetsudai o yokoshite kuda-sai. (だれか手伝いをよこしてください)
Please send *someone to help.*

te「tsuda」.u てつだう (手伝う) vt.
(tetsuda-i-; tetsudaw-a-; tetsu-dat-te Ⓒ) help; assist:
Watashi wa kanojo no shigoto o tetsudatta. (私は彼女の仕事を手伝った) I *helped* her with her work.
(⇨ tetsudai)

te「tsudoo」 てつどう (鉄道) n. rail-road; railway.

te「tsu」gaku てつがく (哲学) n.
philosophy.

te「tsuya」 てつや (徹夜) n. staying up all night.
tetsuya suru (〜する) vi. stay up all night.

te「tsu」zuki てつづき (手続き) n.
procedure; formalities.

te「ttee」 てってい (徹底) n. thor-oughness; completeness.
tettee suru (〜する) vi. be thor-ough; be complete.

te「ttee-teki」 てっていてき (徹底的) a.n. (〜 na, ni) thorough; ex-haustive:
tettee-teki ni choosa suru (徹底的に調査する) make a *thorough* inves-tigation.

-te wa ては [*te*-form of a verb or adjective plus the particle '*wa*']
1 (the '*-te wa*' clause indicates a condition and the following clause the natural or obvious re-sult or conclusion):
Soñna ni tsukarete ite wa, shigoto ni naranai. (そんなに疲れていては、仕事にならない) If you are so tired, you will not be able to do your job properly.
2 (used to indicate an objection or prohibition):
Abunai tokoro e itte wa ikemaseñ.
(危ない所へ行ってはいけません) You *must not go* to dangerous places.
★ Note: '-te wa' becomes '-cha' in informal speech, and '*de wa*' becomes '*ja*.' e.g. *Soko e itcha ikenai yo.* (そこへ行っちゃいけないよ) Don't *go* there. (⇨ de wa²)

-nakute wa naranai [dame da]
(なくてはならない[だめだ]) must; should: ★ The form '*-nakereba*' is used similarly. (⇨ -ba³)
Kodomo wa hayaku nenakute wa dame desu. (子どもは早く寝なくてはめです) Children *should go to bed* early.

te「wake」 てわけ (手分け) n. divi-sion of labor.
tewake suru (〜する) vi. divide; separate; share.

te「za」wari てざわり (手触り) n.
feel; touch:
tezawari *ga yawarakai* (手触りが柔らかい) be soft to the *touch.*

ti「sshu-pe」epaa ティッシュペーパー n. tissue; Kleenex (*trade name*). ★ Also called simply '*tis-shu*.' (⇨ chirigami)

to¹ と p. 1 with; from: ★ Used after a noun.
Watashi wa kare to *yoku tenisu o shimasu.* (私は彼とよくテニスをします) I often play tennis *with* him.
2 to; into: ★ Used to indicate a resulting change.
Kaji de subete ga hai ni natta. (火事ですべてが灰となった) Everything was reduced *to* ashes in the fire.
3 from; as; to: ★ Used in ex-pressing difference, similarity, or comparison.
Kore to *onaji mono o kudasai.* (これと同じ物を下さい) Please give me the same one *as* this.
4 that: ★ Used as a quotative particle.
Ashita wa hareru to *omoimasu.* (あしたは晴れると思います) I think it will be fine tomorrow.
5 (used after adverbs, especially those signifying state, condition

or manner and after onomato-
poeias):

Dokaṇ to ooki-na oto ga shita. (ドカ
ンと大きな音がした) There was a
loud *bang*.

to² と *p.* and: ★ Used to enu-
merate or list two or more nouns.
naifu to fooku (ナイフとフォーク) a
knife *and* fork.

to³ と (戸) *n.* door.

to⁴ と (都) *n.* metropolis. ★ An
administrative division of Japan,
but only used with reference to
Tokyo.

to｢bas·u¹ とばす (飛ばす) *vt.* (toba-
sh·i-; tobas·a-; tobash·i-te [C])
1 fly; let [make] fly:
mokee hikooki o tobasu (模型飛行
機を飛ばす) *fly* a model airplane.
2 blow off:
*Kaze de seṇtakumono ga toba-
sareta.* (風で洗濯物が飛ばされた) The
washing *was blown down* by the
wind.
3 drive fast:
*Kare wa moo-supiido de baiku o
tobashita.* (彼は猛スピードでバイクを飛
ばした) He *drove* his motorbike at
a furious speed.
4 skip; omit:
*Watashi wa sono shoosetsu o to-
basanai de yoṇda.* (私はその小説を
飛ばさないで読んだ) I read the novel
without skipping.
5 make (a joke); spread:
joodaṇ o tobasu (冗談を飛ばす)
crack a joke / *dema o tobasu* (デマ
を飛ばす) *spread* a false rumor.
6 sputter; splash:
doromizu o tobasu (泥水を飛ばす)
splash muddy water.

to｢basu² とバス (都バス) *n.* a bus
or the bus transportation system
operated by the Tokyo Metropolitan Government. (⇨ basu)

to｢biaga｢r·u とびあがる (飛び上がる)
vi. (-agar·i-; -agar·a-; -agat-te
[C]) **1** jump; leap; spring to
one's feet.
2 fly up:

Hibari ga mugibatake kara tobia-
gatta. (ひばりが麦畑から飛び上がった)
A skylark *flew up* from the
wheat field.

to｢bida｢s·u とびだす (飛び出す) *vi.*
(-dash·i-; -das·a-; -dash·i-te [C])
jump out; run out; rush out.

to｢biko｢m·u とびこむ (飛び込む) *vi.*
(-kom·i-; -kom·a-; -koṇ-de [C])
jump [plunge] into; dive into:
puuru ni tobikomu (プールに飛び込
む) *jump into* a pool.

to｢bimawa｢r·u とびまわる (飛び回
る) *vt.* (-mawar·i-; -mawar·a-;
-mawat-te [C]) fly about; bustle
about; romp about.

to｢bino｢k·u とびのく (飛び退く) *vi.*
(-nok·i-; -nok·a-; -no·i-te [C])
jump back [aside].

to｢bino｢r·u とびのる (飛び乗る) *vi.*
(-nor·i-; -nor·a-; -not-te [C])
jump on [into] (a vehicle).
(↔ tobioriru)

to｢biori｢·ru とびおりる (飛び下りる)
vi. (-ori-te [V]) jump down; leap
down. (↔ tobinoru)

to｢bira とびら (扉) *n.* **1** door.
2 (of a book) title page.

to｢bita｢ts·u とびたつ (飛び立つ) *vi.*
(-tach·i-; -tat·a-; -tat-te [C]) fly
away; (of an airplane) take off.

to｢bitsu｢k·u とびつく (飛び付く) *vi.*
(-tsuk·i-; -tsuk·a-; -tsu·i-te [C])
jump at; leap at.

to｢boshi｢·i とぼしい (乏しい) *a.*
(-ku) scanty; scarce; poor:
*Kimi wa mada keekeṇ ga tobo-
shii.* (きみはまだ経験が乏しい) You
are still *lacking* in experience.

to｢botobo とぼとぼ *adv.* (~ to)
(a weary or weak way of walking): tobotobo (to) aruku (とぼとぼ
(と)歩く) *plod along*.

to｢b·u¹ とぶ (飛ぶ) *vi.* (tob·i-; to-
b·a-; toṇ-de [C]) **1** (of a bird, aircraft) fly.
2 (of a person) fly; travel by
plane:
*Kare wa Sapporo made hikooki
de* toṇda. (彼は札幌まで飛行機で飛ん

だ) He *flew* to Sapporo by plane.
3 rush; fly:
Kare wa jiko no geñba e toñda.
(彼は事故の現場へ飛んだ) He *rushed*
to the scene of the accident.
(⇨ isogu))

to「bu² とぶ (跳ぶ) *vi.* (tob·i-; to-
b·a-; toñ-de [C]) jump; leap; hop.
(⇨ haneru))

to「chi とち (土地) *n.* **1** land; lot;
soil: tochi o tagayasu (土地を耕す)
cultivate the *soil.* (⇨ akichi))
2 place:
*Kono tochi ni kita no wa hajimete
desu.* (この土地に来たのは初めてです)
This is the **first time** that I've
visited this *place.*

to「chuu とちゅう (途中) *n.* on the
way; halfway:
*Yuubiñkyoku wa eki e iku tochuu
ni arimasu.* (郵便局は駅へ行く途中に
あります) The post office is *on the
way* to the station.

to「chuu-ge¹sha とちゅうげしゃ (途
中下車) *n.* (train) stopover.
tochuu-gesha suru (～する) *vi.*
stop over. (⇨ gesha; oriru))

to「dana とだな (戸棚) *n.* cupboard; closet.

to「den とでん (都電) *n.* a streetcar
or the streetcar system operated
by the Tokyo Metropolitan
Government. (⇨ tobasu²))

to「doke¹·ru とどける (届ける) *vt.*
(todoke-te [V]) **1** send; deliver;
take; bring:
*Kono kagu o jitaku made todo-
kete kudasai.* (この家具を自宅まで届
けてください) Please *deliver* this furniture to my house. (⇨ todoku))
2 report; notify:
Toonañ o keesatsu ni todoketa.
(盗難を警察に届けた) I *reported* the
theft to the police.

to「do¹k·u とどく (届く) *vi.* (todo-
k·i-; todok·a-; todo·i-te [C])
1 arrive; get to:
Sokutatsu ga todokimashita. (速達
が届きました) A special delivery *has
arrived.* (⇨ todokeru))

2 reach:
*Tana no ano hoñ ni te ga todoki-
masu ka?* (棚のあの本に手が届きます
か) Can you *reach* that book on
the shelf?

to-「doo-fu-ke¹ñ とどうふけん (都
道府県) *n.* all the major administrative divisions within Japan.
(⇨ map (inside back cover)))

to「ga¹r·u とがる (尖る) *vi.* (togar-
r·i-; togar·a-; togat-te [C]) taper
off to a point; be sharp.
★ Often pronounced '*toñgaru.*'

to「ge¹ とげ (刺) *n.* prick; splinter:
Toge ga yubi ni sasatta. (とげが指に
刺さった) I got a *splinter* in my
finger.

to「ge¹·ru とげる (遂げる) *vt.* (toge-
te [V]) accomplish; achieve;
attain; realize:
mokuteki o togeru (目的を遂げる)
accomplish one's purpose.

to「gire¹·ru とぎれる (途切れる) *vi.*
(togire-te [V]) break; be interrupted:
*Deñwa ga natte, kaiwa ga togire-
ta.* (電話が鳴って、会話が途切れた)
The phone rang and our conversation *was interrupted.*

to¹g·u とぐ (研ぐ) *vt.* (tog·i-; to-
g·a-; to·i-de [C]) **1** sharpen (a
knife); whet; grind.
2 wash (rice).

to¹ho とほ (徒歩) *n.* walking:
Eki made toho de jup-puñ desu.
(駅まで徒歩で10分です) It takes ten
minutes to *walk* to the station.
(⇨ aruku))

to「i とい (問い) *n.* question.
(↔ kotae) (⇨ shitsumoñ))

to「iawase といあわせ (問い合わせ)
n. inquiry. (⇨ toiawaseru))

to「iawase¹·ru といあわせる (問い合
わせる) *vt.* (-awase-te [V]) inquire; make inquiries:
*Sono hoñ ga aru ka shoteñ ni toi-
awaseta.* (その本があるか書店に問い合
わせた) I *inquired* at a bookstore
whether the book was there.
(↪ toiawase))

to「ika」es・u といかえす (問い返す) *vi.*
(-kaesh・i・; -kaes・a・; -kaesh・i・te
C) ask again; ask back; repeat
one's question. (⇨ kiku')

to「ire トイレ *n.* toilet; lavatory.
(⇨ beñjyo)

to「ishi といし (砥石) *n.* whetstone.

to「itada」s・u といただす (問い質す)
vt. (-tadash・i・; -tadas・a・; -ta-
dash・i・te C) question closely;
inquire. (⇨ kiku')

to「jikome」・ru とじこめる (閉じ込め
る) *vt.* (-kome-te V) shut up;
lock up; confine.

to「jikomi とじこみ (綴じ込み) *n.*
file: *shiñbuñ no tojikomi* (新聞の
とじ込み) a newspaper *file*. (⇨ toji-
komu')

to「jiko」m・u とじこむ (綴じ込む) *vt.*
(-kom・i・; -kom・a・; -koñ-de C)
file (papers); keep on file. (⇨ tojikomi; tojiru')

to「ji」mari とじまり (戸締まり) *n.*
locking of doors.
   tojimari (o) suru (〜(を)する) *vi.*
lock up.

to「ji」・ru' とじる (閉じる) *vt.* (toji-te
V) close; shut:
me o tojiru (目を閉じる) *close* one's
eyes / *hoñ o tojiru* (本を閉じる) *shut*
a book / *mise o tojiru* (店を閉じる)
close a store.

to「ji」・ru² とじる (綴じる) *vt.* (toji-te
V) bind; keep on file:
pañfuretto o hotchikisu de tojiru
(パンフレットをホッチキスで綴じる) *staple*
a pamphlet together.

to「ka とか (都下) *n.* 1 Tokyo
Metropolitan area.
   2 the cities, towns and villages
of Metropolitan Tokyo, but ex-
cluding the 23 wards. (⇨ toshiñ)

to ka とか *p.* 1 and; or: ★ Used
to link representative examples
of a class.
Yasumi ni wa tenisu to ka *gorufu
o shimasu.* (休みにはテニスとかゴルフを
します) I go in for sports *like* tennis *and* golf on holidays. (⇨ ya')
   2 or someone [something]:

★ Used when unable to recall
something accurately.
Tanaka-sañ to ka *iu hito kara deñwa ga arimashita.* (田中さんとかいう
人から電話がありました) There was a
phone call from a Mr. Tanaka *or
someone.*

to「kai とかい (都会) *n.* city; town.

to「kaku とかく (兎角) *adv.* having
a tendency; being likely:
*Wareware wa tokaku jikañ o mu-
da ni shi-gachi desu.* (われわれはとか
く時間をむだにしがちです) We *are apt*
to waste time.

to「ka」s・u とかす (溶かす) *vt.* (toka-
sh・i・; tokas・a・; tokash・i・te C)
melt; dissolve; liquefy; fuse;
thaw: *shio o mizu ni tokasu* (塩
を水に溶かす) *dissolve* salt in water.
(⇨ tokeru')

to「kee とけい (時計) *n.* clock;
watch. ★ '*Tokee*' is a general
word for watches and clocks.

to「kekom・u とけこむ (溶け込む) *vi.*
(-kom・i・; -kom・a・; -koñ-de C)
1 melt; dissolve:
shio ga tokekoñda mizu (塩が溶け
込んだ水) water in which salt *is dis-
solved.*
   2 adapt oneself (to the environment).

to「ke」・ru' とける (溶ける) *vi.* (toke-
te V) melt; dissolve. (⇨ tokasu)

to「ke」r・u² とける (解ける) *vi.* (toke-
te V) 1 (of a problem) be
solved:
*Kono moñdai wa nakanaka toke-
nai.* (この問題はなかなか解けない) This
problem *is not* easily *solved.*
(⇨ toku')
   2 (of a knot) come loose; come
untied. (⇨ toku')
   3 (of suspicion) be cleared; disappear. (⇨ toku')

to「ki」 とき (時) *n.* 1 time; hour:
Sono moñdai wa toki *ga kaiketsu
shite kureru deshoo.* (その問題は時
が解決してくれるでしょう) *Time* will
take care of the problem.
   2 when; while:

Shitsumoñ ga aru toki wa te o age nasai. (質問があるときは手を上げなさい) *When* you have a question, please raise your hand.

3 occasion; case:

Hijoo no toki wa kono doa o akete kudasai. (非常のときはこのドアを開けてください) Please open this door *in the event of* an emergency.

to「kidoki ときどき (時々) *adv.* from time to time; once in a while. (⇨ shibashiba)

to「ki¹ ni wa ときには (時には) *adv.* sometimes; at times; once in a while:

Toki ni wa dare datte machigai o shimasu. (時にはだれだって間違いをします) Everyone makes mistakes *at times.*

to「kkeñ とっけん (特権) *n.* privilege: *tokkeñ-kaikyuu* (特権階級) the *privileged* classes.

to「kku ni とくに (疾っくに) *adv.* long ago; a long time ago: *Kare wa tokku ni dekakemashita.* (彼はとっくに出かけました) He left *long ago.*

to「kkuri とっくり (徳利) *n.* sake flask. (⇨ sakazuki)

to「kkyo とっきょ (特許) *n.* patent: *tokkyo o toru* (特許を取る) take out a *patent.*

to「kkyuu とっきゅう (特急) *n.* limited [special] express. (⇨ kyuukoo¹)

to「ko とこ (床) *n.* bed. (⇨ futoñ) *toko ni tsuku* (〜につく) go to bed; (be sick) in bed.

to「konoma とこのま (床の間) *n.* tokonoma; alcove in a Japanese house.

to「koro¹ de ところで *p.* [follows the past tense of a verb, adjective, or the copula] even if: ★ The first clause introduces a condition and the second clause specifies a disagreeable or unfavorable consequence.

Kore kara isshoo-keñmee yatta

tokoro de, moo maniawanai daroo. (これから一生懸命やったところで、もう間に合わないだろう) *Even if* you were to do your best from now on, it would be too late.

-ta [-da] tokoro de wa (た[だ]〜は) as far as; according to:

★ The first clause puts a limit on the personal opinion or prediction in the second clause.

Watashi no kiita tokoro de wa, mata kabu ga sagaru rashii. (私の聞いたところでは、また株が下がるらしい) *As far as I have heard*, stocks will apparently continue to fall in value.

— *conj.* **1** well; now: ★ Used at the beginning of a sentence. *Tokoro de koñdo wa nani o shimasu ka?* (ところで今度は何をしますか) *Well*, what shall we do this time?

2 by the way: ★ Used at the beginning of a sentence. *Tokoro de okaasañ wa o-geñki desu ka?* (ところでお母さんはお元気ですか) *By the way*, is your mother in good health? (⇨ sore wa soo to)

to「korodo¹koro ところどころ (所々) *n., adv.* here and there; several places.

to「koro¹ ga ところが *p.* when: ★ Follows the past tense of a verb, adjective or the copula. The second clause strongly suggests a realization or discovery occasioned by the action or state in the first clause. Similar to '-tara.' (⇨ -tara)

Kare no uchi ni itta tokoro ga, kare wa dekaketa ato datta. (彼の家に行ったところが、彼は出かけたあとだった) *When* I got to his house, he had already left.

— *conj.* but; while: ★ Used at the beginning of a sentence. *Chichi wa otooto ni wa yasashii. Tokoro ga boku ni wa kibishii.* (父は弟には優しい。ところがぼくには厳しい) My father is very gentle with my

to￢koya とこや (床屋) n. barber-shop; barber. (⇨ sañpatsu)

to￢k･u¹ とく (解く) vt. (tok･i-; to-k･a-; to･i-te Ⓒ) 1 untie; undo; unpack; loosen:
himo no musubime o toku (ひもの結び目を解く) untie the knot in a piece of string. (⇨ tokeru²)
2 solve (a problem). (⇨ kaitoo²)
3 dismiss; discharge; relieve:
Kare wa ma-mo-naku geñzai no niñmu o tokareru deshoo. (彼は間もなく現在の任務を解かれるでしょう) He will be relieved of his current duties very soon.

to￢ku² とく (得) n. profit; benefit.
— a.n. (~ na, ni) profitable; advantageous; economical.
(↔ soñ) (⇨ yuuri)

to￢k･u³ とく (説く) vt. (tok･i-; to-k･a-; to･i-te Ⓒ) persuade; talk into; preach:
hotoke no michi o toku (仏の道を説く) preach the way of Buddha.

to￢kubai とくばい (特売) n. sale; bargain sale.
tokubai (o) suru (~(を)する) vt. sell at a special price.

to￢kubetsu とくべつ (特別) a.n. (~ na/no, ni), adv. special; extra; particular; exceptional:
tokubetsu ni chuui o harau (特別に注意を払う) take special care.
(⇨ toku ni)

to￢kuchoo とくちょう (特徴) n. characteristic; feature. (⇨ tokushoku)

to￢ku￢i とくい (得意) a.n. (~ na/no, ni) 1 good; favorite:
Kanojo wa ryoori ga tokui desu. (彼女は料理が得意です) She is good at cooking. (↔ nigate)
2 proud; triumphant:
Kare wa jibuñ no keekeñ o tokui ni natte hanashita. (彼は自分の経験を得意になって話した) He talked about his experiences in a proud manner.

to￢kuisaki とくいさき (得意先) n. custom; customer:
tokuisaki o mawaru (得意先を回る) make the rounds of the customers.

to￢ku ni とくに (特に) adv. specially; especially; particularly:
Kotoshi no natsu wa toku ni atsukatta. (今年の夏は特に暑かった) This summer was especially hot.
(⇨ kotoni; tokubetsu)

to￢kushoku とくしょく (特色) n. characteristic; feature.
(⇨ tokuchoo)

to￢kushu とくしゅ (特殊) a.n. (~ na, ni) special; particular; unique; unusual:
tokushu na jijoo (特殊な事情) special circumstances.

to￢kutee とくてい (特定) n. specification.
tokutee suru (~する) vt. specify:
Sono kaisha wa meekaa o tokutee shite kita. (その会社はメーカーを特定してきた) The company specified the manufacturer.

to￢kuyuu とくゆう (特有) a.n. (~ na/no, ni) peculiar; characteristic; proper:
Kono o-matsuri wa Nihoñ tokuyuu no mono desu. (このお祭りは日本特有のものです) This festival is peculiar to Japan. (⇨ dokutoku)

to￢mar･u¹ とまる (止まる) vi. (to-mar･i-; tomar･a-; tomat-te Ⓒ) 1 (of a moving thing) stop; pull up:
Kono deñsha wa kaku eki ni tomarimasu. (この電車は各駅に止まります) This train stops at every station. (⇨ teeshi; tomeru¹)
2 cease; stop:
Suidoo no mizumore ga tomatta. (水道の水漏れが止まった) The leak in the water pipe has stopped.
(⇨ tomeru¹)
3 (of electricity [water, gas, etc.] supply) fail; be cut off:
Jiko de deñki ga tomatta. (事故で電気が止まった) The electricity failed because of an accident.

4 (of a bird) perch; alight; settle.

to¯mar·u² とまる (泊まる) *vi.* (to-mar·i·; tomar·a·; tomat·te [C])
1 (of a person) stay; lodge: *inaka no ryokañ ni* tomaru (田舎の旅館に泊まる) *stay* at a country inn. (⇨ -haku; taizai; tomeru²)
2 (of a ship) lie at anchor.

to¯me·ru¹ とめる (止める) *vt.* (to-me·te [V]) **1** stop; bring to a halt; park:
Hoteru no mae de kuruma o to-meta. (ホテルの前で車を止めた) I *stopped* the car in front of the hotel. (⇨ tomaru¹)
2 stop; forbid; prohibit: *Futari no keñka o tometa.* (二人のけんかを止めた) I *stopped* their quarrel.

to¯me·ru² とめる (泊める) *vt.* (to-me·te [V]) lodge; put up; accommodate:
Kare o sono bañ uchi ni tomete yatta. (彼をその晩家に泊めてやった) I *put* him *up* for the night. (⇨ tomaru²)

to¯me·ru³ とめる (留める) *vt.* (to-me·te [V]) pin; tape; fasten: *posutaa o kabe ni byoo de* tomeru (ポスターを壁にびょうで留める) *fix* a poster to a wall with tacks.

to¯mi とみ (富) *n.* wealth; riches; fortune.

tomo¹ とも *p.* **1** all; both: *Watashi no kyoodai wa sañ-niñ* tomo *isha desu.* (私の兄弟は3人とも医者です) *All* three of my brothers are doctors.
2 at the ...-est: ★ Indicates an approximate limit.
Sukunaku tomo ichi-nichi ichi-jikañ wa uñdoo o shita hoo ga yoi. (少なくとも1日1時間は運動をしたほうが良い) You should do *at least* one hour's exercise every day.

tomo² とも *p.* certainly; sure; of course: ★ Used when confidently expressing one's opinions or thoughts. Used mainly by men.

"Tetsudatte kurenai ka?" "Ii tomo." (「手伝ってくれないか」「いいとも」) "Won't you give me a hand?" "*Only* too pleased to."

tomo³ とも (友) *n.* friend. (⇨ tomodachi; yuujiñ)

-tomo とも (共) *suf.* **1** both; all; (with a negative) neither; none: *Watashi no kodomo wa sañ-niñ-tomo shoogakusee desu.* (私の子どもは3人とも小学生です) *All* three of my children are elementary school pupils.
2 including:
Kono yadoya no ryookiñ wa sho-kuhi-tomo ip-paku ichimañ-eñ desu. (この宿屋の料金は食費とも一泊1万円です) The charge for one night at this inn is 10,000 yen, *including* the cost of meals. (⇨ fukumeru)

to¯moba¯taraki ともはたらき (共働き) *n.* husband and wife both working.

to¯modachi ともだち (友達) *n.* friend; companion. (⇨ tomo³; yuujiñ)

to¯mokaku ともかく *adv.*
1 = tonikaku.
2 regardless of; apart from: *Hoka no hito wa* tomokaku, *watashi wa hañtai desu.* (ほかの人はともかく，私は反対です) *Regardless of* the others, I am against it.

to¯moka¯segi ともかせぎ (共稼ぎ) *n.* = tomobataraki.

to¯mona¯·u ともなう (伴う) *vi.* (-na·i·; -naw·a·; -nat·te [C])
1 take; bring; be accompanied: *Kare wa kazoku o* tomonatte do-raibu ni dekaketa. (彼は家族を伴ってドライブに出かけた) He went for a drive *with* his family.
2 bring about (danger); go together; involve:
Kono shigoto wa kikeñ o tomonai-masu. (この仕事は危険を伴います) This work *involves* danger.

to¯mo ni ともに (共に) *adv.* **1** together; with:

Señsee wa seeto to tomo ni kyoo-shitsu no sooji o shita.(先生は生徒とともに教室の掃除をした) The teacher cleaned the classroom *together* with the students.

2 both; as well as:
Watashi-tachi futari wa tomo ni shiken ni ukarimashita.(私たち二人はともに試験に受かりました) We *both* passed the examination. (⇨ ryoohoo)

3 as:
Toshi o toru to tomo ni kioku-ryoku wa otoroemasu.(年をとるとともに記憶力は衰えます) *As* one grows older, one's memory becomes poor.

to┌mor·u ともる（点る） vt. (tomor·i·; tomor·a·; tomot-te Ⓒ) be lit; burn:
Sono koya ni wa ranpu ga tomotte ita.(その小屋にはランプがともっていた) A lamp *was burning* in the cabin. (⇨ tsuku')

to┐m·u とむ（富む） vi. (tom·i·; tom·a·; ton-de Ⓒ) abound (in); be rich (in):
Kare no supiichi wa yuumoa ni tonde ita.(彼のスピーチはユーモアに富んでいた) His speech *was full* of humor.

to┌nae┐·ru となえる（唱える） vt. (tonae-te Ⓥ) **1** recite; chant; utter:
nenbutsu o tonaeru（念仏を唱える） *chant* (Buddhist) prayers / banzai o tonaeru（万歳を唱える） *cry* 'ban-zai.'

2 advocate; advance:
Watashi no iken ni igi o tonaeru hito wa inakatta.(私の意見に異議を唱える人はいなかった) There was nobody who *raised* objections to my opinion.

to┐nai とない（都内） n. (within) the Tokyo Metropolitan area. (⇨ shinai)

to┌nari となり（隣） n. **1** next-door neighbor; the house next door.
2 next:

Tonari no seki wa aite imasu ka?（隣の席は空いていますか） Is that seat *next* to you free?

to┌naria┐wase となりあわせ（隣り合わせ） n. being side by side.

to┌nbo とんぼ n. dragonfly.

to┌nbo-ga┐eri とんぼ返り n.
1 somersault.
2 quick round trip:
Tonbo-gaeri de Nagano e itte kita.(とんぼ返りで長野へ行ってきた) I made a *quick visit* to Nagano.

to┌nda とんだ attrib. terrible; unexpected; serious:
Sore wa tonda sainan deshita ne.(それはとんだ災難でしたね) It was *quite* an unfortunate occurrence, wasn't it? (⇨ tonde mo nai)

to┌nde mo na┐·i とんでもない
1 absurd; outrageous; terrible; unexpected.
2 (used to express strong negation):
"Watanabe-san wa rikon shita soo desu ne." "Tonde mo nai."（「渡辺さんは離婚したそうですね」「とんでもない」）"I hear Mrs. Watanabe got divorced." "*Goodness, no!*"

to┌nga┐r·u とんがる vi. = togaru.

to┐nikaku とにかく（兎に角） adv. anyway; in any case; at any rate. (⇨ izure)

to┌nkatsu とんカツ（豚カツ） n. deep-fried breaded pork cutlet.

tono ko┌to┐ da [desu] とのことだ[です] I hear that...; they say that...:
Jee-aaru no unchin henkoo wa sugu ni jisshi sareru to no koto desu.(JRの運賃変更はすぐに実施されるとのことです) *They say that* the changes in JR fares will soon be put into effect.

to┌nton¹ とんとん adv. (~ to) (the sound of a quick light strike):
tonton to doa o nokku suru oto (とんとんとドアをノックする音) a *knock* on the door.

to┌nton² とんとん a.n. (~ na, ni)

toojoo

(*informal*) even; equal; the same:
Keehi o sashihiku to soñ-eki wa toñtoñ desu.(経費を差し引くと損益はとんとんです) If we deduct the expenses, gains and losses are *equal.*

to「ñya とんや(問屋) *n.* wholesale store; wholesaler. (⇨ oroshi)

to「o「¹ とう(十) *n.* ten. ★ Used when counting. (⇨ juu'; APP. 3)

to「o「² とう(党) *n.* (political) party. (⇨ APP. 8)

to「o「³ とう(塔) *n.* tower; pagoda; steeple.

too- とう(当) *suf.* this; current:
too-chi (当地) *this* city [town; country] / too-teñ (当店) *this* store.

-too¹ とう(等) *suf.* **1** class; grade: it-too (1 等) first *class* / ni-too (2 等) second *class.*
2 prize:
Kyoosoo de it-too ni natta.(競争で1 等になった) I won first *prize* in the race.

-too² とう(頭) *suf.* counter for large animals:
uma it-too (馬 1 頭) *one* horse / ushi go-too (牛 5 頭) five *head* of cattle. (⇨ -hiki)

to「oañ とうあん(答案) *n.* examination answer sheet. (↔ moñdai) (⇨ kotae)

to「obañ とうばん(当番) *n.* turn; duty:
Is-shuukañ ni ichi-do sooji toobañ ni atarimasu.(一週間に一度掃除当番にあたります) I take my *turn* to clean the room once a week.

to「obuñ とうぶん(当分) *adv.* for the time being; for some time.

to「ochaku とうちゃく(到着) *n.* arrival: toochaku-jikoku (到着時刻) the *arrival* time.
toochaku suru (～する) *vi.* arrive (at one's destination). (↔ shuppatsu) (⇨ tsuku')

to「odai とうだい(灯台) *n.* lighthouse.

to「ofu とうふ(豆腐) *n.* soybean curd; tofu.

to「oga「rashi とうがらし(唐辛子) *n.* red pepper.

to「oge「 とうげ(峠) *n.* **1** the top of a mountain pass.
2 peak; height:
Atsusa wa ima ga tooge da.(暑さは今が峠だ) Now is *the hottest time* of the year.
tooge o kosu [koeru] (～を越す [越える]) **1** cross over a peak.
2 get over the hump; overcome a difficulty.

to「ohyoo とうひょう(投票) *n.* vote; poll; ballot.
toohyoo (o) suru (～(を)する) *vt.* vote; cast a vote. (⇨ señkyo)

to「o・i とおい(遠い) *a.* (-ku) **1** far; distant; a long way. (↔ chikai')
2 (of time, relation, etc.) remote; distant:
Damu no kañsee wa mada tooi hanashi da.(ダムの完成はまだ遠い話だ) The completion of the dam is *a long way off.*

to「oitsu とういつ(統一) *n.* unity; unification; standardization.
tooitsu suru (～する) *vt.* unify; standardize: kakaku o tooitsu suru (価格を統一する) *standardize* prices.

to「oji「¹ とうじ(当時) *n.* at that time; then:
Tooji wa shokuryoo ga fusoku shite ita.(当時は食料が不足していた) *At that time* there was a shortage of food.

to「oji「² とうじ(冬至) *n.* the winter solstice (about December 22). (⇨ geshi)

to「ojitsu とうじつ(当日) *n.* that day; the very day:
Kare wa toojitsu ni natte, kesseki no reñraku o shite kita.(彼は当日になって、欠席の連絡をしてきた) When *the day* came he reported that he would be absent.

to「ojoo とうじょう(登場) *n.* appearance; entrance. (↔ taijoo)

toojoo suru (～する) *vi.* appear (on stage); enter.

to˥oka とおか (十日) *n.* ten days; the tenth day of the month. (⇨ APP. 5)

to˥okee とうけい (統計) *n.* statistics: tookee *o toru* (統計をとる) collect *statistics*.

to˥oki[1] とうき (陶器) *n.* earthenware; pottery; ceramics. (⇨ jiki[3])

to˥oki[2] とうき (登記) *n.* registration (of a house or land).
　tooki suru (～する) *vt.* register.

to˥oki[3] とうき (投機) *n.* speculation (in stocks); venture.

to˥oki[4] とうき (冬季) *n.* winter; wintertime. (⇨ kaki[3]; shuñki; shuuki[2])

to˥okoo とうこう (登校) *n.* school attendance: tookoo-*kyohi* (登校拒否) refusal to *attend school*.
　tookoo suru (～する) *vi.* go to [attend] school. (↔ gekoo)

to˥oku とおく (遠く) *n.* a long way (off):
　Amari tooku *made asobi ni itte wa ikemaseñ.* (あまり遠くまで遊びに行ってはいけません) You must not go and play too *far off*. (↔ chikaku)

to˥okyoku とうきょく (当局) *n.* the authorities:
　*shi-*tookyoku *kara kyoka o morau* (市当局から許可をもらう) get permission from the ciy *authorities*.

to˥oma˥wari とおまわり (遠回り) *n.* roundabout way; detour:
　Kono michi o iku to toomawari *ni narimasu.* (この道を行くと遠回りになります) If we go this way it will be *farther*.
　toomawari (o) suru (～(を)する) *vi.* make a detour. (↔ chikamichi)

to˥omee とうめい (透明) *a.n.* (～ na, ni) transparent; clear: toomee *na garasu* (透明なガラス) *transparent* glass. (⇨ sukitooru)

to˥oniñ とうにん (当人) *n.* **1** the person concerned.
　2 oneself:

Sono uwasa ni tooniñ *wa heeki datta.* (そのうわさに当人は平気だった) He *himself* was indifferent to the rumor. (⇨ hoññiñ)

to˥ori[1] とおり (通り) *n.* street; road.

to˥ori[2] とおり (通り) *n.* as; like:
　Kare wa itsu-mo no toori *ku-ji ni shussha shita.* (彼はいつものとおり 9 時に出社した) He came to the office at nine *as* usual.

-toori/doori とおり/どおり *suf.*
　1 kind; sort:
　*Jikkeñ wa iku-*toori *mo yatte mimashita.* (実験はいくとおりもやってました) We carried out the experiment in many different *ways*.
　2 about; approximately:
　*Shigoto wa hachi-bu-*doori *owarimashita.* (仕事は 8 分どおり終わりました) *About* eighty percent of the work has been finished.

to˥orikakar·u とおりかかる (通り掛かる) *vi.* (-kakar·i-; -kakar·a-; -kakat-te C) pass by casually; come along.

to˥orinuke とおりぬけ (通り抜け) *n.* passing through; through passage:
　Toorinuke *kiñshi.* (*sign*) (通り抜け禁止) No *Thoroughfare*. (⇨ toorinukeru)

to˥orinuke[1]**·ru** とおりぬける (通り抜ける) *vi.* (-nuke-te V) go [pass] through:
　toññeru o toorinukeru (トンネルを通り抜ける) *pass through* a tunnel.

to˥orisugi·ru とおりすぎる (通り過ぎる) *vi.* (-sugi-te V) pass; go by; go past. (⇨ tooru)

to˥oroku とうろく (登録) *n.* registration; entry.
　tooroku suru (～する) *vt.* register; enter: *shoohyoo o* tooroku suru (商標を登録する) *register* a trademark.

to˥oroñ とうろん (討論) *n.* discussion; debate; argument: tooroñ-*kai* (討論会) a *debate*; a *panel discussion*.
　tooroñ suru (～する) *vi.* discuss;

debate; argue.

to⌐or·u とおる (通る) *vi.* (toor·i-; toor·a-; toot-te C) 1 (of a vehicle, person, etc.) go; pass:
Kono dooro wa jidoosha ga yoku toorimasu. (この道路は自動車がよく通ります) Many cars *pass* along this road.
2 (of a bill, proposal, etc.) pass; be approved:
Kaisee-ań wa kinoo iińkai o tootta. (改正案はきのう委員会を通った) The amended bill *passed* the committee yesterday. (⇨ toosu)
3 (of a public vehicle) run:
Deńsha wa nijup-puń goto ni tootte imasu. (電車は20分毎に通っています) The trains *come by* every twenty minutes.
4 (of a word, sentence, passage, etc.) make sense:
Kono buńshoo wa imi ga tooranai. (この文章は意味が通らない) This sentence *does not convey* any meaning.
5 (of a voice) carry.

to⌐osań とうさん (父さん) *n.* (*informal*) father; dad; daddy. (↔ kaasań) (⇨ chichi¹; o-toosań)

to⌐osee とうせい (統制) *n.* control; regulation.
toosee suru (～する) *vt.* control; regulate. (⇨ seegeń)

to⌐oseń とうせん (当選) *n.* 1 election; win in an election. (↔ rakuseń)
2 winning a prize:
tooseń-sha (当選者) the *winner of a prize.*
tooseń suru (～する) *vi.* be elected; win a prize. (⇨ ataru)

to⌐oshi とうし (投資) *n.* investment.
tooshi suru (～する) *vi.* invest; put money in.

to⌐osho とうしょ (投書) *n.* letter; complaint [suggestion] by letter.
toosho suru (～する) *vi., vt.* write in (to a newspaper).

to⌐os·u とおす (通す) *vt.* (toosh·i-;

toos·a-; toosh·i-te C) 1 let (a person) pass:
Sumimaseń ga chotto tooshite kudasai. (すみませんがちょっと通してください) Excuse me, but would you *let* me *pass*, please? (⇨ tooru)
2 let in; admit:
Biniiru wa hikari wa toosu ga mizu mo kuuki mo toosanai. (ビニールは光は通すが水も空気も通さない) Plastic sheets *let in* light, but *let through* neither water nor air. (⇨ tooru)
3 show in (a guest, etc.); usher in:
O-kyaku-sań o heya ni tooshi nasai. (お客さんを部屋に通しなさい) Please *show* the guest into the room.
4 thread; pierce:
hari ni ito o toosu (針に糸を通す) *thread* a needle. (⇨ tooru)
5 approve; pass (a bill). (⇨ tooru)
6 stick to (one's opinion); persist:
Kare wa akumade jibuń no shuchoo o toosoo to shita. (彼はあくまで自分の主張を通そうとした) He persistently *stuck* to his assertion.
7 continue; remain (in a certain state):
Kare wa isshoo dokushiń de tooshita. (彼は一生独身で通した) He *remained* single all his life.

to⌐otatsu とうたつ (到達) *n.* arrival; attainment.
tootatsu suru (～する) *vi.* reach; attain. (⇨ tassuru)

to⌐otee とうてい (到底) *adv.* (with a negative) not possibly; by any means:
Sońna koto wa tootee fukanoo desu. (そんなことはとうてい不可能です) That kind of thing is *quite* impossible. (⇨ totemo)

to⌐oteń とうてん (読点) *n.* Japanese-language comma (、). ★ An English-language comma (,) is called '*końma.*' (⇨ kuteń) to⌐oto⌐b·u とうとぶ (尊ぶ) vt. (-to-b·i-; -tob·a-; -toñ-de C) value; respect: inochi o tootobu (命を尊ぶ) value life.

to⌐oto⌐·i とうとい (尊い・貴い) a. (-ku) precious; valuable; noble: tootoi kyookuñ (貴い教訓) an invaluable lesson / tootoi gisee (尊い犠牲) a high sacrifice.

to⌐otoo とうとう (到頭) adv. ★ More informal than 'tsui ni'
1 at last; finally:
Kare wa tootoo sono añ o akirameta. (彼はとうとうその案をあきらめた) At last he gave up the plan.
2 after all:
Kanojo wa tootoo sugata o misenakatta. (彼女はとうとう姿を見せなかった) She did not show up after all.

To⌐oyoo とうよう (東洋) n. the Orient; the East:
Tooyoo shokoku (東洋諸国) Oriental [Eastern] countries. (↔ Seeyoo)

To⌐oyo⌐ojiñ とうようじん (東洋人) n. an Oriental. (↔ Seeyoojiñ)

to⌐ozai とうざい (東西) n. east and west. (↔ nañboku)

to⌐ozaka⌐r·u とおざかる (遠ざかる) vi. (-zakar·i-; -zakar·a-; -zakat-te C) 1 go away; fade away.
2 keep away:
Saikiñ gorufu kara toozakatte imasu. (最近ゴルフから遠ざかっています) I haven't played golf recently. (⇒ toozakeru)

to⌐ozake⌐·ru とおざける (遠ざける) vt. (-zake-te V) keep away; avoid; ward off:
Kare wa yuujiñ o toozakete iru. (彼は友人を遠ざけている) He keeps his friends at a distance. (⇒ toozakaru)

to⌐ozeñ とうぜん (当然) a.n. (~ na/no, ni) reasonable; natural; expected. (⇒ atarimae)
— adv. naturally; of course:
Toozeñ, kimi mo iku beki da. (当然、きみも行くべきだ) Of course, you should go, too.

to⌐ppa とっぱ (突破) n. breakthrough; overcoming.
toppa suru (~する) vt. break through; overcome: nañkañ o toppa suru (難関を突破する) overcome a difficulty.

to⌐ra とら (虎) n. tiger.

to⌐rae⌐·ru とらえる (捕らえる) vt. (torae-te V) 1 catch; arrest:
Keesatsu wa sono doroboo o toraeta. (警察はその泥棒を捕らえた) The police caught the thief. (⇒ tsukamaeru)
2 capture:
Kanojo no eñgi wa kañshuu no kokoro o toraeta. (彼女の演技は観衆の心を捕らえた) Her performance captured the hearts of the audience.

to⌐ra⌐kku トラック n. truck; lorry.

to⌐ra⌐ñpu トランプ n. playing cards. ★ Not used in the sense of 'trump(s),' as in bridge or whist.

to⌐re⌐·ru¹ とれる (取れる) vi. (tore-te V) 1 come off; be removed:
Shatsu no botañ ga toreta. (シャツのボタンがとれた) A button has come off my shirt. (⇒ toru¹)
2 (of pains) go away:
Kizu no itami ga toreta. (傷の痛みがとれた) The pain from the cut has gone away. (⇒ toru¹)
3 (of a word, sentence, passage, etc.) can be interpreted:
Kono buñ wa futatsu no imi ni toreru. (この文は二つの意味にとれる) This sentence can be interpreted in two ways. (⇒ toru¹)

to⌐re⌐·ru² とれる (捕れる) vi. (tore-te V) (of an animal) be caught. (⇒ toru²)

to⌐re⌐·ru³ とれる (採れる) vi. (tore-te V) (of a plant) be produced; be grown. (⇒ toru³)

to⌐ri とり (鳥) n. 1 bird; fowl; poultry.
2 chicken. (⇒ toriniku)

to⌐ria⌐ezu とりあえず (取り敢えず) adv. first of all; for the present:

Toriaezu *biiru o sañ-boñ kudasai*. (とりあえずビールを3本下さい) *To start with*, please give us three bottles of beer.

to⌐riage-ru とりあげる (取り上げる) *vt*. (-age-te Ⓥ) **1** pick up: *juwaki o toriageru* (受話器を取り上げる) *pick up* the telephone receiver.
2 adopt (a proposal); accept (an opinion).
3 take up for discussion: *Sono moñdai wa tsugi ni* toriage-masu. (その問題は次に取り上げます) We will *take up* that problem next.
4 deprive (someone of a qualification, license, etc.); cancel.

to⌐riatsukai とりあつかい (取り扱い) *n.* treatment; handling. (⇨ to riatsukau)

to⌐riatsuka-u とりあつかう (取り扱う) *vt*. (-atsuka·i-; -atsukaw·a-; -atsukat-te Ⓒ) treat; handle; deal in [with]:
Kono shinamono wa chuui shite toriatsukatte *kudasai.* (この品物は注意して取り扱ってください) Please *handle* these goods with care. (⇨ toriatsukai)

to⌐ridas·u とりだす (取り出す) *vt*. (-dash·i-; -das·a-; -dash·i-te Ⓒ) take out; pick out; produce:
Kanojo wa baggu kara techoo o toridashita. (彼女はバッグから手帳を取り出した) She *took out* a small notebook from her bag.

to⌐rihazus·u とりはずす (取り外す) *vt*. (-hazush·i-; -hazus·a-; -hazush·i-te Ⓒ) take away; remove.

to⌐ri⌐hiki とりひき (取り引き) *n.* business; dealings; transaction.
torihiki (o) suru (~(を)する) *vi., vt.* do business; make a deal.

to⌐rii とりい (鳥居) *n.* torii.
★ The gateway at the entrance of a Shinto shrine.

to⌐riire⌐·ru とりいれる (取り入れる) *vt*. (-ire-te Ⓥ) **1** take in:
señtakumono o toriireru (洗濯物を

取り入れる) *take in* the washing.
2 gather in (a crop); harvest.
3 adopt (an idea, opinion, etc.); introduce.

to⌐rikae とりかえ (取り替え) *n.* exchange; replacement. (⇨ koo-kañ; torikaeru)

to⌐rikae·ru とりかえる (取り替える) *vt*. (-kae-te Ⓥ) change; exchange; replace; renew:
Kanojo wa teeburu-kurosu o atarashii no to torikaeta. (彼女はテーブルクロスを新しいのと取り替えた) She *changed* the tablecloth for a new one. (⇨ torikae)

to⌐rikaes·u とりかえす (取り返す) *vt*. (-kaesh·i-; -kaes·a-; -kae-sh·i-te Ⓒ) get back; recover; regain.

to⌐rikakar·u とりかかる (取り掛かる) *vi*. (-kakar·i; -kakar·a-; -kakat-te Ⓒ) begin; start; set about:
shigoto ni torikakaru (仕事に取りかかる) *set to* work.

to⌐rikakom·u とりかこむ (取り囲む) *vt*. (-kakom·i-; -kakom·a-; -ka-koñ-de Ⓒ) surround; gather around. (⇨ torimaku)

to⌐rikeshi とりけし (取り消し) *n.* cancellation; withdrawal. (⇨ torikesu)

to⌐rikes·u とりけす (取り消す) *vt*. (-kesh·i-; -kes·a-; -kesh·i-te Ⓒ) cancel; take back; withdraw:
yoyaku o torikesu (予約を取り消す) *cancel* one's reservation. (⇨ tori-keshi)

to⌐rikumi とりくみ (取り組み) *n.* (of sumo wrestling) match; bout. (⇨ torikumu)

to⌐rikum·u とりくむ (取り組む) *vi*. (-kum·i-; -kum·a-; -kuñ-de Ⓒ) wrestle with; tackle; be engaged in:
Kare wa ima sono moñdai ni tori-kuñde imasu. (彼は今その問題に取り組んでいます) He *is* now *tackling* the problem. (⇨ torikumi)

to⌐rimak·u とりまく (取り巻く) *vt*. (-mak·i-; -mak·a-; -ma·i-te Ⓒ)

surround:

Señsee wa seeto-tachi ni torima-kareta.(先生は生徒たちに取り巻かれた) The teacher *was surrounded* by her pupils.

to｢rimodo｣s·u とりもどす(取り戻す) *vt.* (-modosh·i-; -modos·a-; -modosh·i-te C) get back; recover; regain:

keñkoo o torimodosu(健康を取り戻す) *regain* one's health.

to｢rinigas·u とりにがす(取り逃がす) *vt.* (-nigash·i-; -nigas·a-; -nigash·i-te C) fail to catch; miss. (⇨ nigasu)

to｢riniku とりにく(鶏肉) *n.* chicken meat; poultry.

to｢rinozo｣k·u とりのぞく(取り除く) *vt.* (-nozok·i-; -nozok·a-; -nozoi-te C) take away; remove. (⇨ nozoku｣)

to｢rishimari とりしまり(取り締まり) *n.* control; regulation; crackdown. (⇨ torishimaru)

to｢rishimari｣yaku とりしまりやく (取締役) *n.* director (of a company).

to｢rishima｣r·u とりしまる(取り締まる) *vt.* (-shimar·i-; -shimar·a-; -shimat-te C) control; crack down:

Ima yopparai-uñteñ o torishimatte imasu.(今酔っ払い運転を取り締まっています) They *are* now *cracking down* on drunken driving. (⇨ torishimari)

to｢rishirabe とりしらべ(取り調べ) *n.* questioning; investigation; examination. (⇨ torishiraberu)

to｢rishirabe｣·ru とりしらべる(取り調べる) *vt.* (-shirabe-te V) examine (a suspect, etc.); investigate; inquire into:

Keesatsu wa yoogisha o torishirabete iru.(警察は容疑者を取り調べている) The police *are examining* the suspect. (⇨ torishirabe)

to｢ritsugi とりつぎ(取り次ぎ) *n.* agency; agent; wholesaler.

to｢ritsu｣g·u とりつぐ(取り次ぐ) *vt.*

(-tsug·i-; -tsug·a-; -tsu·i-de C)

1 act as an agent:

Go-chuumoñ wa watashi-domo ga toritsuide orimasu.(ご注文は私どもが取り次いでおります) We will *act as agent* for what you order. (⇨ toritsugi)

2 convey (a message, telephone, etc.); answer.

to｢ritsuke·ru とりつける(取り付ける) *vt.* (-tsuke-te V) 1 install; furnish; equip; fit.

2 obtain (consent, permission, etc.):

Sono koto ni kañshite chichi no dooi o toritsuketa.(そのことに関して父の同意を取り付けた) I *obtained* my father's consent regarding that matter.

to｢robi とろび(とろ火) *n.* very slow heat; low fire.

to｢r·u¹ とる(取る) *vt.* (tor·i-; tor·a-; tot-te C) 1 take; take hold of; seize:

Kare wa hoñdana kara jisho o totta.(彼は本棚から辞書を取った) He *took* a dictionary from the bookshelf.

2 get; take; receive; obtain; win:

Kyoo wa yasumi o torimashita.(きょうは休みをとりました) I *took* a day off today.

3 take off; remove:

Kare wa booshi o totte, aisatsu shita.(彼は帽子をとって、挨拶した) He *took off* his hat and greeted me.

4 steal; rob:

Watashi wa jiteñsha o dare-ka ni torareta.(私は自転車をだれかにとられた) I *had* my bicycle *stolen* by someone. (⇨ nusumu)

5 subscribe to (a newspaper, magazine); buy:

Watashi mo onaji shiñbuñ o totte imasu.(私も同じ新聞をとっています) I also *take* the same newspaper.

6 eat; have:

Moo chuushoku wa torimashita

ka? (もう昼食はとりましたか) *Have you already had lunch?*

7 take; make out; interpret; understand:
Watashi ga itta koto o waruku toranai de kudasai. (私が言ったことを悪くとらないでください) *Do not take my words amiss.*

8 take up; occupy (a place):
Kono tsukue wa basho o tori-sugiru. (この机は場所をとり過ぎる) This desk *takes up* too much space. ((⇒ shimeru⁴)

9 record; write down:
bañgumi o bideo ni toru (番組をビデオにとる) *record* a program on video / *kiroku o toru* (記録をとる) *keep* records.

10 charge (a fare, fee, etc.); demand:
Ano ryokañ wa ip-paku nimañ-eñ mo torimasu. (あの旅館は一泊 2 万円もとります) That inn *charges* all of 20,000 yen for one night.

to｢r·u² とる (捕る) *vt.* (tor·i-; to-r·a-; tot-te Ⓒ) catch (an animal, fish, etc.); get.

to｢r·u³ とる (採る) *vt.* (tor·i-; to-r·a-; tot-te Ⓒ) **1** gather; pick (a plant).
2 adopt (a proposal, suggestion, etc.); choose; employ; engage.

to｢r·u⁴ とる (撮る) *vt.* (tor·i-; to-r·a-; tot-te Ⓒ) take (a picture). ((⇒ satsuee)

to｢ryoo とりょう (塗料) *n.* paint. ((⇒ peñki)

to｢shi¹ とし (年) *n.* year; age.

to｢shi² とし (都市) *n.* city; towns and cities.

to｢shigoro としごろ (年頃) *n.*
1 marriageable age:
toshigoro no musume (年ごろの娘) a daughter of *marriageable age.*
2 about the same age:
Watashi ni mo añta to onaji toshigoro no musuko ga imasu. (私にもあんたと同じ年ごろの息子がいます) I also have a son *of your age.*

to｢shiñ としん (都心) *n.* the heart

[center] of Tokyo. ((⇒ toka)

to｢shi-shita としした (年下) *n.* junior in age. ((↔ toshi-ue)

to shite として **1** as; for: ★ Indicates a role, position or qualification.
Yamamoto-shi wa taishi to shite Chuugoku ni hakeñ sareta. (山本氏は大使として中国に派遣された) Mr. Yamamoto was sent to China *as* ambassador.
2 not even a...: ★ Used after words such as '*hitori*,' '*ichi-nichi*,' '*ichi-do*,' etc., with a negative.
Dare hitori to shite kare o tasukeyoo to shinakatta. (だれ一人として彼を助けようとしなかった) *Not a single* person tried to help him.

to｢shito｣tta としとった (年とった) old; aged.

to｢shi｣tsuki としつき (年月) *n.* years. ((⇒ neñgetsu)

to｢shi-ue としうえ (年上) *n.* senior in age. ((↔ toshi-shita)

to｢shiyori¹ としより (年寄り) *n.* old person [people]. ((↔ wakamono)

to｢sho としょ (図書) *n.* books. ((⇒ hoñ)

to｢shokañ としょかん (図書館) *n.* (public) library. ((⇒ toshoshitsu)

to｢sho｣keñ としょけん (図書券) *n.* book token. ★ Often given as a gift.

to｢sho｣shitsu としょしつ (図書室) *n.* library; reading room. ★ Usually refers to a library in a school or an office. ((⇒ toshokañ)

to｢ssa とっさ (咄嗟) *n.* (~ no) sudden; instant:
tossa no dekigoto (とっさの出来事) an *unexpected* occurrence.

to｢ssa ni とっさに (咄嗟に) *adv.* immediately; instinctively.

to su｢reba とすれば if; supposing; on the assumption that...: ★ The particle '*to*' plus the provisional of '*suru*.' The second clause indicates a judgment or inference based on the supposi-

tion in the first clause.
*Kimi ga dekinai to sureba, tabuň
dare ni mo dekinai deshoo.* (君がで
きないとすれば、たぶんだれにもできないでし
ょう) *If* you are unable to do this,
I doubt that anyone can.
(⇨ -tara; to¹)

to「taň¹ とたん (途端) *n.* the moment; just as...:
*Furo ni hairoo to shita totaň (ni)
deňwa ga naridashita.* (ふろに入ろう
としたとたん(に)電話が鳴りだした) *Just
as* I was about to get into the
bath, the phone started ringing.
(⇨ shuňkaň)

to「taň² トタン *n.* galvanized iron.

tote とて *p.* even if: ★ Used
when a fact is presented or an
assumption made but the subse-
quent result or inference is contrary to expectation.
Shippai shita tote gakkari suru na.
(失敗したとてがっかりするな) *Even if*
you've failed, do not be discouraged.

to「temo とても *adv.* ★ Also 'tot-
temo.' **1** very; really; awfully;
extremely:
Kono hoň wa totemo omoshiroi.
(この本はとてもおもしろい) This book
is *very* interesting.
2 (with a negative) not possibly;
by any means:
*Koňna muzukashii moňdai wa
totemo tokemaseň.* (こんな難しい問
題はとても解けません) I cannot *possibly* solve this sort of difficult
problem. (⇨ tootee)

to「tonoe「・ru ととのえる (整える・調
える) *vt.* (-noe-te V) **1** prepare;
get ready:
yuushoku o totonoeru (夕食を整え
る) *get* dinner *ready*. (⇨ totonou)
2 make tidy; dress:
kami o totonoeru (髪を整える) *fix*
one's hair.
3 settle; arrange (a marriage).
(⇨ totonou)

to「tono「・u ととのう (整う・調う) *vi.*
(-no・i-; -now・a-; -not-te C)

1 be ready; be prepared; be completed:
Juňbi ga sukkari totonotta. (準備
がすっかり整った) The arrangements
are fully *completed*. (⇨ totonoeru)
2 be settled; (of a marrige) be
arranged. (⇨ totonoeru)

to「tsuzeň とつぜん (突然) *a.n.*
(~ na/no, ni) sudden; abrupt;
unexpected.
— *adv.* suddenly; abruptly;
unexpectedly: *Totsuzeň deňwa
ga natta.* (突然電話が鳴った) *Suddenly* the phone rang.

to「tte¹ とって to; for: ★ Used in
making judgments or evalua-
tions. Used in the pattern '... *ni
totte.*'
*Kaigai-ryokoo wa watashi ni totte
wasurerarenai omoide desu.* (海外
旅行は私にとって忘れられない思い出で
す) The overseas trip is an unfor-
gettable memory *to* me.

to「tte² とって (取っ手) *n.* handle;
knob; pull; grip:
nabe no totte (なべの取っ手) the
handle of a pan / *doa no totte* (ド
アの取っ手) a doorknob.

to「ttemo とっても *adv.* = totemo.

to「・u とう (問う) *vt.* (to・i-; tow・a-;
to・u-te C) **1** ask; inquire:
hito no aňpi o tou (人の安否を問う)
ask about a person's safety.
(⇨ tazuneru')
2 (in the negative) care; mind:
Nedaň wa toimaseň. (値段は問いま
せん) I *don't care* about the price.

to wa ka「gira「nai とはかぎらない
(とは限らない) not necessarily; not
always: ★ This phrase is often
preceded by '*kanarazu shimo.*'
The polite equivalent is '*to wa
kagirimaseň.*'
Takai mono ga ii to wa kagiranai.
(高いものがいいとは限らない) Expen-
sive things are *not necessarily*
good. (⇨ kagiru)

to「zaň とざん (登山) *n.* mountain
climbing; going up a mountain.

tozañ (o) suru (～(を)する) *vi.* climb a mountain.

tsu⌉ba つば(唾) *n.* spit; saliva: *michi ni* tsuba o haku (道につばを吐く) spit *on the road.*

tsu⌈baki⌉[1] つばき(唾) *n.* = tsuba.

tsu⌉baki[2] つばき(椿) *n.* camellia.

tsu⌈bame つばめ(燕) *n.* swallow (bird).

tsu⌈basa つばさ(翼) *n.* wing.

tsu⌈bo[1] つぼ(壺) *n.* pot; jar; vase.

tsu⌈bo[2] つぼ(坪) *n.* tsubo.
★ Unit of area. 1 tsubo = 3.3 square meters.

tsu⌈bomi⌉ つぼみ(蕾) *n.* flower bud.

tsu⌉bu つぶ(粒) *n.* grain; drop: *kome*-tsubu (米粒) *grains* of rice / *oo*-tsubu *no ame* (大粒の雨) large *drops* of rain.

-tsu⌉bu つぶ(粒) *suf.* counter for grain and small round objects: *kome hito*-tsubu (米1粒) *a grain* of rice / *mame* go-tsubu (豆5粒) *five* beans.

tsu⌈bure·ru つぶれる(潰れる) *vi.* (tsubure-te [V]) **1** be crushed; be smashed; collapse. ⟪⇨ tsubusu⟫
2 (of a company) go bankrupt.

tsu⌈bur·u つぶる(瞑る) *vt.* (tsubur·i-; tsubur·a-; tsubut-te [C]) close [shut] (one's eyes).

tsu⌈bus·u つぶす(潰す) *vt.* (tsubush·i-; tsubus·a-; tsubush·i-te [C]) **1** crush; smash: *Kare wa hako o fuñzukete* tsubushita. (彼は箱を踏んづけてつぶした) He stepped on the box and *crushed* it. ⟪⇨ tsubureru⟫
2 thwart (a plan, project, etc.); ruin.
3 kill [pass] (time).

tsu⌈buyaki つぶやき(呟き) *n.* mutter; murmur; grumble. ⟪⇨ tsubuyaku⟫

tsu⌈buya⌉k·u つぶやく(呟く) *vi.* (tsubuyak·i-; tsubuyak·a-; tsubuya·i-te [C]) murmur; mutter; grumble. ⟪⇨ tsubuyaki⟫

tsu⌈chi⌉ つち(土) *n.* **1** earth; soil; mud.
2 the ground: *bokoku no* tsuchi *o fumu* (母国の土を踏む) stand on the *ground* of one's homeland.

tsu⌉e つえ(杖) *n.* stick; cane.

tsu⌈geguchi つげぐち(告げ口) *n.* tattle; talebearing.
tsugeguchi (o) suru (～(を)する) *vt.* tell on; let on.

tsu⌈ge·ru つげる(告げる) *vt.* (tsuge-te [V]) (*formal*) tell; inform; report.

tsu⌈gi⌉ つぎ(次) *n.* next: Tsugi (*no eki*) *wa Ueno desu.* (次(の駅)は上野です) The *next* station is Ueno. ⟪⇨ kondo; tsugitsugi⟫

tsu⌈giko⌉m·u つぎこむ(注ぎ込む) *vt.* (-kom·i-; -kom·a-; -koñ-de [C]) put into; invest: *Kare wa chokiñ o kabu ni* tsugikoñda. (彼は貯金を株につぎ込んだ) She *invested* her savings in stocks.

tsu⌈gime つぎめ(継ぎ目) *n.* joint; seam: *Isu no* tsugime *ga yuruñde iru.* (いすの継ぎ目がゆるんでいる) The *joints* of the chair are loose.

tsu⌈gi⌉tsugi つぎつぎ(次々) *adv.* (～ ni, to) one after another; in succession.

tsu⌈goo つごう(都合) *n.* convenience; opportunity; circumstances.
tsugoo ga tsuku (～がつく) suit one's convenience.
tsugoo o tsukeru (～をつける) manage to do.

tsu⌈g·u[1] つぐ(注ぐ) *vt.* (tsug·i-; tsug·a-; tsu·i-de [C]) pour; fill: *Kanojo wa o-cha o* tsuide kureta. (彼女はお茶をついでくれた) She *poured* me some tea.

tsu⌈g·u[2] つぐ(次ぐ) *vi.* (tsug·i-; tsug·a-; tsu·i-de [C]) be [come] next to: ★ Used in the patterns '*... ni tsugu*' and '*... ni tsuide.*' *Oosaka wa Tookyoo ni* tsugu *daitokai desu.* (大阪は東京に次ぐ大都会

です) *Next* to Tokyo, Osaka is the biggest city.

tsu「g·u³ つぐ (継ぐ) *vt.* (tsug·i-; tsug·a-; tsu·i-de [C]) succeed; inherit; take over.

tsu「i¹ つい (対) *n.* pair: *Kono yunomi-jawañ wa tsui ni natte imasu.* (この湯飲み茶わんは対になっています) These teacups make a *pair*.

tsu「i² つい *adv.* 1 (of time and distance) just; only: *Tsui sakihodo koko ni tsuita tokoro desu.* (つい先ほどここに着いたところです) I got here *just* a little while ago.
2 carelessly; by mistake.

-tsui つい (対) *suf.* counter for a pair: *it*-tsui *no yunomi-jawañ* (一対の湯飲み茶碗) a *pair* of teacups.

tsu「ide¹ ついで (序で) *n.* chance; opportunity; convenience: *Sono hoñ o o-kaeshi itadaku no wa* tsuide *no toki de kekkoo desu.* (その本をお返しいただくのはついでのときで結構です) It will be perfectly all right if you return the book at your *convenience*.

tsu「ide² ついで (次いで) *adv.* next to; after: *Daitooryoo ni* tsuide *shushoo ga eñzetsu shita.* (大統領に次いで首相が演説した) The prime minister gave his speech *after* that of the president.

tsu「ide ni ついでに (序でに) *adv.* while; on the way: *Hoñya e iku* tsuide ni *kitte mo katte kimasu.* (本屋へ行くついでに切手も買って来ます) I will buy some stamps *on my way* to the bookstore.

tsu「ihoo ついほう (追放) *n.* exile; expulsion; purge. **tsuihoo suru** (〜する) *vt.* exile; banish; deport; oust.

tsu「ika ついか (追加) *n.* addition; supplement. **tsuika suru** (〜する) *vt.* add; sup-

plement: *Biiru o ato ni-hoñ* tsuika *shite kudasai.* (ビールをあと2本追加してください) Please *bring us two more bottles* of beer.

tsu「i ni ついに (遂に) *adv.* 1 at last; finally. (⇒ tootoo)
2 (with a negative) after all: *Kanojo ni nañ-do mo tegami o dashita ga,* tsui ni *heñji ga konakatta.* (彼女に何度も手紙を出したが、ついに返事がこなかった) I wrote her many times, but *ended up* getting no answer.

tsu「iraku ついらく (墜落) *n.* (of an airplane) fall; crash. **tsuiraku suru** (〜する) *vi.* fall; crash. (⇒ ochiru)

tsu「itachi¹ ついたち (一日) *n.* the first day of the month. (⇒ APP. 5)

tsu「ite ついて (就いて) ★ Used in the pattern '... *ni tsuite.*'
1 about; on; concerning: ★ Indicates the topic under discussion. *Atarashii seefu ni* tsuite *doo omoimasu ka?* (新しい政府についてどう思いますか) What do you think *about* the new government?
2 per; for: ★ Indicates proportions or ratios. Also in the pattern '... *ni tsuki.*' *Chuusha-ryookiñ wa ichi-jikañ ni* tsuki *sañbyaku-eñ desu.* (駐車料金は1時間につき300円です) The parking fee is 300 yen *per* hour.

tsu「iya「s·u ついやす (費やす) *vt.* (tsuiyash·i-; tsuiyash·a-; tsuiyash·i-te [C]) spend (time, money); waste; consume.

tsu「kae·ru¹ つかえる (支える) *vi.* (tsukae-te [V]) 1 be choked; be stopped; be blocked: *Gesuikañ ni nani-ka ga* tsukaete *iru.* (下水管に何かがつかえている) There is something *blocking* the drain.
2 be too big to go into: *Piano wa doa ni* tsukaete *naka ni hairanakatta.* (ピアノはドアにつかえて中

に入らなかった) The piano *was too
big* for the door and could not go
into the room.

tsuˈkae·ru² つかえる（仕える）*vi.*
(tsukae-te [V]) serve; wait on.

tsuˈkai つかい（使い）*n.* **1** errand:
kodomo o tsukai ni yaru（子どもを
使いにやる）send a child on an
errand.
2 messenger; bearer.

tsuˈkaihataˈs·u つかいはたす（使い
果たす）*vt.* (-hatash·i-; -hatas·a-;
-hatash·i-te [C]) use up; exhaust:
kozukai o tsukaihatasu（小遣いを使
い果たす）*use up* all one's pocket
money.

tsuˈkaikomi つかいこみ（使い込み）
n. embezzlement; misappropria-
tion. (⇨ tsukaikomu)

tsuˈkaikoˈm·u つかいこむ（使い込
む）*vt.* (-kom·i-; -kom·a-; -koñ-
de [C]) embezzle (company
money). (⇨ tsukaikomi)

tsuˈkaikonaˈs·u つかいこなす（使い
こなす）*vt.* (-konash·i-; -konas·a-;
-konash·i-te [C]) make good use
of; have a good command of.

tsuˈkainareˈ·ru つかいなれる（使い
慣れる）*vi.* (-nare-te [V]) be accustomed to using:
Kono waapuro wa tsukainarete
imasu.（このワープロは使い慣れています）
I *am accustomed to using* this
word processor.

tsuˈkaisute つかいすて（使い捨て）
n. throwaway; disposable:
tsukaisute *kamera*（使い捨てカメラ）a
throwaway camera / tsukaisute
raitaa（使い捨てライター）a *disposable*
lighter.

tsuˈkamae·ru つかまえる（捕まえる）
vt. (tsukamae-te [V]) catch; arrest (a thief). (⇨ taiho)

tsuˈkamar·u つかまる（捕まる）*vi.*
(tsukamar·i-; tsukamar·a-; tsuka-
mat-te [C]) be caught; be ar-
rested:
*Sono seeto wa kañniñgu o shite
iru tokoro o* tsukamatta.（その生徒
はカンニングをしているところを捕まった）

The pupil *was caught* in the act
of cheating. (⇨ tsukamaeru)

tsuˈkaˈm·u つかむ（摑む）*vt.* (tsu-
kam·i-; tsukam·a-; tsukañ-de [C])
1 catch; hold:
Kare wa ikinari watashi no ude o
tsukañda.（彼はいきなり私の腕をつかん
だ）He suddenly *caught* me by
the arm.
2 get (money); grasp (a meaning,
intention, etc.); seize (an opportunity).

tsuˈkareˈ つかれ（疲れ）*n.* fatigue;
tiredness; exhaustion. (⇨ tsukareru)

tsuˈkareˈ·ru つかれる（疲れる）*vi.*
(tsukare-te [V]) get tired; be
tired out; be exhausted:
Kyoo wa zañgyoo de tsukaremashita.（きょうは残業で疲れました）
Today I *am tired* from overtime
work. (⇨ tsukare)

tsuˈka·u つかう（使う）*vt.* (tsuka-
i-; tsukaw·a-; tsukat-te [C])
1 use; handle; operate:
kikai o tsukau（機械を使う）*handle*
a machine. (⇨ shiyoo').
2 spend (money, time); use.
3 employ; handle; manage:
arubaito o tsukau（アルバイトを使う）
employ a part-timer.
4 speak (a language); write:
Eego o tsukatte *mo ii desu ka?*（英
語を使ってもいいですか）Is it all right
if I *speak* English?
5 use (a nonmaterial thing):
atama o tsukau（頭を使う）*use* one's
head / *ki o* tsukau（気を使う）*worry*
/ *shiñkee o* tsukau（神経を使う）*pay*
careful attention to.

tsuˈkekuwaeˈ·ru つけくわえる（付
け加える）*vt.* (-kuwae-te [V]) add;
append. (⇨ kuwaeru)

tsuˈkemono つけもの（漬け物）*n.*
pickles. ★ Vegetables pickled in
salt and rice bran. (⇨ tsukeru')

tsuˈkeˈ·ruˈ つける（付ける）*vt.*
(tsuke-te [V]) **1** attach (medicine); apply; spread (butter,
jam):

suutsukeesu ni nafuda o tsukeru
(スーツケースに名札をつける) *attach* a
name tag to one's suitcase.
2 fix (equipment); install:
Kuruma ni eakoñ o tsukete moratta. (車にエアコンをつけてもらっ
た) I *had* an air conditioner *installed*
in my car.
3 write (a memo, diary, etc.):
nikki o tsukeru (日記をつける) *write*
a diary.
4 give (a mark); grade:
*Señsee wa kare no tooañ ni ii teñ
o* tsuketa. (先生は彼の答案にいい点を
つけた) The teacher *gave* his answer a high mark.
5 tail; follow:
Kanojo wa dare-ka ni tsukerarete
ita. (彼女はだれかにつけられていた) She
was being followed by someone.

tsu「ke」・ru² つける (着ける) *vt.*
(tsuke-te Ⅴ) **1** put on (a dress,
ring, etc.): ★ '*tsukete iru*'=wear.
atarashii doresu o mi ni tsukeru
(新しいドレスを身に着ける) *put on* a
new dress.
2 drive (a car) up to; draw (a
ship) alongside:
geñkañ ni kuruma o tsukeru (玄関
に車を着ける) *drive* a car up to the
entrance.

tsu「ke・ru」³ つける (点ける) *vt.*
(tsuke-te Ⅴ) switch on: light;
set fire:
deñki o tsukeru (電気をつける)
switch on the electricity / *tabako
ni hi o* tsukeru (たばこに火をつける)
light a cigarette. (⇨ tsuku⁴)

tsu「ke・ru」⁴ つける (漬ける) *vt.* (tsuke-te Ⅴ) pickle; preserve:
Niku o shio ni tsukete *hozoñ shita.*
(肉を塩に漬けて保存した) I *salted* the
meat to preserve it. (⇨ tsuke-
mono)

tsu「ki」¹ つき (月) *n.* month.
(⇨ APP. 5)
tsu「ki」¹² つき (月) *n.* the moon.
tsu「ki」¹³ つき (付き) *n.* **1** adher-
ence; stickiness:
Kono nori wa tsuki *ga yoi* [*warui*].

(この糊は付きが良い[悪い]) This glue
sticks well [*badly*].
2 combustion:
Kono raitaa wa tsuki *ga warui.* (こ
のライターは付きが悪い) This lighter
does not light easily.

-tsuki つき (付き) *suf.* with:
*Kono rajio wa ichi-neñ-kañ no
hoshoo-*tsuki *desu.* (このラジオは1年
間の保証付きです) This radio comes
with a one-year guarantee.

tsu「kiai」 つきあい (付き合い) *n.* association; friendship; acquaintance:
Kare to wa nagai tsukiai *desu.* (彼
とは長いつきあいです) I *have known
him* for a long time. (⇨ tsukiau)

tsu「kiatari」 つきあたり (突き当たり)
n. the end of a street.

tsu「kiata」r・u つきあたる (突き当た
る) *vi.* -atar・i・; -atar・a・; -atat-te
Ⅽ) **1** run into; collide; run
against:
Torakku ga deñchuu ni tsuki-
atatta. (トラックが電柱に突き当たった)
The truck *ran into* a utility pole.
2 face (a problem, difficulties,
etc.):
muzukashii moñdai ni tsukiataru
(むずかしい問題に突き当たる) *come up
against* a tough problem.

tsu「kia」・u つきあう (付き合う) *vi.*
(-a・i・; -aw・a・; -at-te Ⅽ) associate with; keep company with.
(⇨ tsukiai)

tsu「kigime」 つきぎめ (月極め) *n.*
(of payment) monthly:
Watashi wa chuushajoo o tsuki-
gime *de karite iru.* (私は駐車場を月
ぎめでかりている) I rent a parking
space *by the month.*

tsu「ki」hi つきひ (月日) *n.* time;
years. (⇨ neñgetsu)

tsu「kioto」s・u つきおとす (突き落と
す) *vt.* (-otosh・i・; -otos・a・; -oto-
sh・i-te Ⅽ) push over; thrust
down:
gake kara hito o tsukiotosu (がけか
ら人を突き落とす) *push* a person *off*
a cliff.

tsu⌈ki¹⌉·ru つきる(尽きる) vi. (tsu-ki-te Ⓥ) run out; be exhausted.

tsu⌈kisa⌉s·u つきさす(突き刺す) vt. (-sash·i-; -sas·a-; -sash·i-te Ⓒ) stick; pierce; stab. (⇨ sasu²)

tsu⌈kisoi つきそい(付き添い) n. attendance; attendant; escort. (⇨ tsukisou)

tsu⌈kiso·u つきそう(付き添う) vt. (-so·i-; -sow·a-; -sot-te Ⓒ) accompany; attend; escort:
Haha-oya wa byooki no kodomo ni tsukisotta. (母親は病気の子どもに付き添った) The mother *attended* her sick child. (⇨ tsukisoi)

tsu⌈kitoba⌉s·u つきとばす(突き飛ばす) vt. (-tobash·i-; -tobas·a-; -tobash·i-te Ⓒ) thrust away; send flying:
Kare wa watashi o tsukitobashita. (彼は私を突き飛ばした) He *pushed* me *away*.

tsu⌈kitome¹⌉·ru つきとめる(突き止める) vt. (-tome-te Ⓥ) trace; locate; ascertain:
uwasa no dedokoro o tsukitomeru (うわさの出所を突き止める) *trace* the source of the rumor.

tsu⌈kitsuke¹⌉·ru つきつける(突き付ける) vt. (-tsuke-te Ⓥ) point (a weapon); confront with (evidence).

tsu⌈kko¹⌉m·u つっこむ(突っ込む) vi. (-kom·i-; -kom·a-; -koñ-de Ⓒ) thrust into; dip into; run into:
poketto ni te o tsukkomu (ポケットに手を突っ込む) *dip* one's hand into one's pocket.

tsu⌈k·u¹ つく(着く) vi. (tsuk·i-; tsuk·a-; tsu·i-te Ⓒ) 1 arrive (at); get (to); reach:
Ikkoo wa buji, sañchoo ni tsuita. (一行は無事, 山頂に着いた) The party safely *arrived* at the summit. (⇨ toochaku)
2 touch; reach:
Teñjoo ga hikui no de atama ga tsuki-soo da. (天井が低いので頭がつきそうだ) The ceiling is so low that my head almost *touches* it.

3 sit down; take a seat:
seki ni tsuku (席に着く) *take* a seat / *shokutaku ni* tsuku (食卓に着く) *sit down* to a meal.

tsu⌈k·u² つく(付く) vi. (tsuk·i-; tsuk·a-; tsu·i-te Ⓒ) 1 stick; adhere:
Kore wa nori de wa tsukimaseñ. (これは糊では付きません) We *cannot stick* these with paste.
2 be stained:
Te ni iñku ga tsuite imasu yo. (手にインクが付いていますよ) Your hands *are stained* with ink.
3 have; carry; include:
Kono zasshi ni wa furoku ga tsuite imasu. (この雑誌には付録が付いています) This magazine *has* a supplement.
4 take the side of; side with.
5 (of seed, fruit, etc.) bear; yield; take root; bear (interest).

tsu⌈k·u³ つく(就く) vi. (tsuk·i-; tsuk·a-; tsu·i-te Ⓒ) 1 take; hold; be engaged:
too no iiñchoo no chii ni tsuku (党の委員長の地位に就く) *take* the post of party chairperson.
2 take lessons from; study under (a person).

tsu⌈k·u⁴ つく(点く) vi. (tsuk·i-; tsuk·a-; tsu·i-te Ⓒ) catch fire; be lighted. (⇨ tsukeru³)

tsu⌈k·u⁵ つく(突く) vi. (tsuk·i-; tsuk·a-; tsu·i-te Ⓒ) 1 poke; stab; prick; spear:
Kare wa watashi no wakibara o hiji de tsuita. (彼は私の脇腹をひじで突いた) He *poked* me in the ribs with his elbow.
2 toll (a bell); strike; bounce (a ball).

tsu⌈k·u⁶ つく(吐く) vt. (tsuk·i-; tsuk·a-; tsu·i-te Ⓒ) tell; sigh:
uso o tsuku (うそをつく) *tell* a lie / *tameiki o tsuku* (ため息をつく) *give* a sigh.

tsu⌈kue つくえ(机) n. desk.

tsu⌈kuri¹ つくり(旁) n. the right-hand element of a Chinese char-

acter. ★ Often the phonetic element of the character. ((⇨ bushu;
heñ³))

tsuˈkuˈr·u¹ つくる (作る) vt. (tsu-
kur·i-; tsukur·a-; tsukut-te Ⓒ)
1 make; form; shape; manufacture: ((⇨ tsukuru²))
ki de inugoya o tsukuru (木で犬小
屋を作る) *make* a kennel of wood.
2 write; compose; make:
shi o tsukuru (詩を作る) *write* a
poem / *keeyakusho o tsukuru* (契
約書を作る) *draw up* a contract.
3 grow; raise:
kome [*yasai*] *o tsukuru* (米[野菜]を
作る) *grow* rice [vegetables]. Ⓒ
4 form; organize:
retsu o tsukuru (列を作る) *form* a
line / *roodoo-kumiai o tsukuru* (労
働組合を作る) *organize* a labor
union.
5 cook; make:
yuushoku o tsukuru (夕食を作る)
cook dinner.

tsuˈkuˈr·u² つくる (造る) vt. (tsu-
kur·i-; tsukur·a-; tsukut-te Ⓒ)
1 build; construct:
ie o tsukuru (家を造る) *build* a
house / *hashi o tsukuru* (橋を造る)
construct a bridge. ((⇨ tsukuru¹))
2 mint; coin:
kooka o tsukuru (硬貨を造る) *mint*
coins / *shihee o tsukuru* (紙幣を造
る) *print* paper money.
3 create:
atarashii toshi o tsukuru (新しい都
市を造る) *create* a new city / *tee-eñ
o tsukuru* (庭園を造る) *create* a garden.
4 brew: *biiru o tsukuru* (ビールを
造る) *brew* beer.

tsuˈkuˈs·u つくす (尽くす) vt. (tsu-
kush·i-; tsukus·a-; tsukush·i-te
Ⓒ) **1** exhaust (energy); use up;
consume:
Kare wa zeñryoku o tsukushita.
(彼は全力を尽くした) He *has done*
his best.
2 devote oneself; serve:
Kanojo wa byooki no otto no tame

ni tsukushita. (彼女は病気の夫のため
に尽くした) She *did all she could*
for her sick husband.

tsuˈkuzuˈku つくづく adv. (~ to)
1 (of dislike) utterly; really:
*Kono wabishii seekatsu ga tsuku-
zuku iya ni natta.* (このわびしい生活が
つくづくいやになった) I am *utterly* disgusted at this lonely life.
2 carefully; intently:
*Watashi wa kore made no jiñsee
o tsukuzuku (to) furikaette mita.*
(私はこれまでの人生をつくづく(と)振り返
ってみた) I *carefully* looked back
on my life so far.

tsuˈma つま (妻) n. wife.
★ '*I suma*' refers to one's own
wife, or is used as a generic term
for wife. '*Kanai*' is used only in
the first sense. (↔ otto)

tsuˈmami¹ つまみ (摘まみ) n.
1 knob: *tsumami o mawasu* (つ
まみを回す) turn a *knob*.
2 pinch:
hito-tsumami no shio (一つまみの塩)
a *pinch* of salt. ((⇨ tsumamu)

tsuˈmami² つまみ n. light snacks;
hors d'oeuvre.

tsuˈmamigui つまみくい (つまみ食
い) n. eating with the fingers;
sneaking a bite of food.
tsumamigui suru (~する) vt. eat
secretly.

tsuˈmam·u つまむ (摘まむ) vt. (tsu-
mam·i-; tsumam·a-; tsumañ-de
Ⓒ) pick up; pinch:
*Kamikuzu o tsumañde kuzukago
ni ireta.* (紙くずをつまんでくずかごに入れ
た) I *picked up* the scraps of paper
and put them into the litter bin.

tsuˈmaraˈna·i つまらない (詰まらな
い) a. (-ku) **1** uninteresting;
boring:
Sono shiai wa tsumaranakatta. (そ
の試合はつまらなかった) The match
was *not exciting*. (↔ omoshiroi)
2 trifling; foolish; worthless:
Tsumaranai mono desu ga doozo.
(つまらないものですがどうぞ) This is
nothing special, but I hope you

will accept it. (⇒ kudaranai)

tsu⌐mari つまり (詰まり) *conj.* that is; in short; in a word; after all: Tsumari *sore ga kimi no iitai koto desu ne.* (つまりそれが君の言いたいことですね) *In short,* that is what you want to say, isn't it? (⇒ kekkyoku; yoo-suru ni)

tsu⌐ma¬r·u つまる (詰まる) *vi.* (tsumar·i-; tsumar·a-; tsumat-te C) **1** be stopped; be choked up; clog: *Kaze o hiite, hana ga tsumatta.* (かぜをひいて、鼻が詰まった) I have a cold so my nose *is stuffed up.* **2** be full; be filled up; be packed: *Kaban no naka wa shorui ga ippai tsumatte ita.* (かばんの中は書類がいっぱい詰まっていた) The briefcase *was packed* full of papers. (⇒ tsumeru)

tsu⌐masaki つまさき (爪先) *n.* tiptoe; tip.

tsu⌐mazuk·u つまずく (躓く) *vi.* (-zuk·i-; -zuk·a-; -zu·i-te C) **1** stumble; trip. **2** (of a project, plan, etc.) fail; go wrong: *Watashi-tachi no keekaku wa saisho kara tsumazuita.* (私たちの計画は最初からつまずいた) Our plan *went wrong* from the beginning.

tsu⌐me つめ (爪) *n.* nail; claw.

tsu⌐mekake·ru つめかける (詰めかける) *vt.* (-kake-te V) besiege; throng; crowd. (⇒ atsumaru)

tsu⌐me¬·ru つめる (詰める) *vt.* (tsume-te V) **1** pack; stuff; fill; plug; stop: *Danbooru-bako ni hon o tsumeta.* (段ボール箱に本を詰めた) I *packed* the books in the cardboard boxes. (⇒ tsumaru) **2** move over; stand [sit] closer: *Moo sukoshi oku e tsumete kudasai.* (もう少し奥へ詰めてください) Will you *move back* a little more, please? **3** shorten (time); cut (hair).

tsu⌐meta·i つめたい (冷たい) *a.* (-ku) **1** (of temperature) cold; cool; chilly: tsumetai *nomimono* (冷たい飲み物) a *cold* drink / tsumetai *kaze* (冷たい風) a *chill* wind. (↔ atsui) **2** (of a person's attitude) cold; cool: tsumetai *kotoba* (冷たい言葉) *cold* words / tsumetai *hito* (冷たい人) a *coldhearted* person. (↔ atatakai)

tsu⌐mi つみ (罪) *n.* sin; crime; offense: tsumi *o okasu* (罪を犯す) commit a *sin* [*crime*].

tsu⌐mori つもり (積もり) *n.* **1** intention; purpose; idea: *Sono koto wa kare ni iwanai* tsumori *desu.* (そのことは彼に言わないつもりです) I do not *plan* to tell him about that. **2** thought; expectation; conviction: *Kare ni kite moraeru* tsumori *de ita.* (彼に来てもらえるつもりでいた) I *expected* that he would come. **3** attitude; frame of mind: *Kondo shippai shitara, kubi da kara sono* tsumori *de.* (今度失敗したら、首だからそのつもりで) If you fail again, you will be fired, so *be prepared* for that.

tsu⌐mor·u つもる (積もる) *vi.* (tsumor·i-; tsumor·a-; tsumot-te C) accumulate; be piled up: *Yuki ga takusan tsumotta.* (雪がたくさん積もった) The snow *lies* very deep.

tsu⌐m·u¹ つむ (積む) *vt.* (tsum·i-; tsum·a-; tsun-de C) **1** pile (up); heap (up); stack. (⇒ kasaneru) **2** load: *torakku ni zaimoku o tsumu* (トラックに材木を積む) *load* a truck with lumber. **3** accumulate (experience, exercise, etc.).

tsu⌐m·u² つむ (摘む) *vt.* (tsum·i-; tsum·a-; tsun-de C) pick; gather; pluck; nip: *nohara de hana o tsumu* (野原で花

をつむ) *gather* flowers in the field.

tsu⌐na¹ つな (綱) *n.* rope; cord.

tsu⌐nagari つながり (繋り) *n.* connection; relation. (⇨ tsunagaru)

tsu⌐nagar·u つながる (繋がる) *vi.* (tsunagar·i-; tsunagar·a-; tsunagat-te Ⓒ) **1** connect; link: *Atarashii hashi de Hoñshuu to Shikoku ga tsunagatta.* (新しい橋で本州と四国がつながった) Honshu and Shikoku *were linked* by new bridges. (⇨ tsunagu)
2 be related; be linked: *Watashi wa kare to chi ga tsunagatte imasu.* (私は彼と血がつながっています) I *am related* to him by blood. (⇨ tsunagari)

tsu⌐nage·ru つなげる (繋げる) *vt.* (tsunage-te Ⓥ) = tsunagu.

tsu⌐nag·u つなぐ (繋ぐ) *vt.* (tsunag·i-; tsunag·a-; tsuna·i-de Ⓒ) **1** tie; fasten; chain: *inu o ki ni tsunagu* (犬を木につなぐ) *tie* a dog to a tree. (⇨ tsunagaru)
2 connect; join: *hoosu o shookaseñ ni tsunagu* (ホースを消火栓につなぐ) *connect* a hose to a fire hydrant.

tsu⌐nami つなみ (津波) *n.* tidal wave; tsunami.

tsu⌐ne ni つねに (常に) *adv.* (*slightly formal*) always; habitually. (⇨ itsu-mo)

tsu⌐ne⌐r·u つねる (抓る) *vt.* (tsuner·i-; tsuner·a-; tsunet-te Ⓒ) pinch; nip: *Kanojo wa watashi no ude o tsunetta.* (彼女は私の腕をつねった) She *pinched* me on the arm.

tsu⌐no¹ つの (角) *n.* horn; antler.

tsu⌐ra·i つらい (辛い) *a.* (-ku) hard; tough; painful; bitter: *tsurai shigoto* (つらい仕事) *hard* work / *tsurai omoi o suru* (つらい思いをする) have a *bitter* experience.

tsu⌐ranu⌐k·u つらぬく (貫く) *vt.* (-nuk·i-; -nuk·a-; -nu·i-te Ⓒ) **1** pierce; run through; penetrate: *Tama wa kabe o tsuranuita.* (弾は

壁を貫いた) The bullet *went through* the wall.
2 carry through; accomplish: *Kare wa jibuñ no shiñneñ o tsuranuita.* (彼は自分の信念を貫いた) He *maintained* his convictions *to the end*.

tsu⌐re つれ (連れ) *n.* companion.

tsu⌐re·ru つれる (連れる) *vt.* (tsure-te Ⓥ) take (a person); bring (a person); be accompanied: *Watashi wa kodomo o doobutsueñ e tsurete itta.* (私は子どもを動物園へ連れて行った) I *took* the children to the zoo.

tsu⌐rete つれて *conj.* accordingly; consequently.
... *ni tsurete* (…に〜) as...: *Toshi o toru ni tsurete tairyoku ga yowaru.* (年を取るにつれて体力が弱る) *As* one grows older, one's strength decreases. (⇨ shitagatte)

tsu⌐ri¹ つり (釣り) *n.* fishing; angling. (⇨ tsuru)

tsu⌐ri² つり (釣り) *n.* change. ★ Often with '*o-*'. (⇨ o-tsuri; tsuriseñ)

tsu⌐riai つりあい (釣り合い) *n.* balance; proportion; harmony. (⇨ tsuriau)

tsu⌐ria⌐u つりあう (釣り合う) *vi.* (-a·i-; -aw·a-; -at-te Ⓒ) balance; be in proportion; be in harmony; match. (⇨ tsuriai)

tsu⌐ribashi つりばし (吊り橋) *n.* rope bridge; suspension bridge.

tsu⌐riseñ つりせん (釣り銭) *n.* small change: *Tsuriseñ no nai yoo ni o-negai shimasu.* (つり銭のないようにお願いします) Please have the *exact amount* ready. (⇨ o-tsuri)

tsu⌐r·u¹ つる (釣る) *vt.* (tsur·i-; tsur·a-; tsut-te Ⓒ) fish; angle; catch. (⇨ tsuri)

tsu⌐r·u² つる (吊る) *vt.* (tsur·i-; tsur·a-; tsut-te Ⓒ) hang; suspend: *kaateñ o tsuru* (カーテンをつる) *hang*

curtains / *kubi o* tsuru (首をつる)
hang oneself. (⇨ tsurusu)

tsu┌ru³ つる (鶴) *n.* crane.
(⇨ kame; señbazuru)

tsu┌rus·u つるす (吊す) *vt.* (tsu-
rush·i·; tsurus·a·; tsurush·i·te
Ⓒ) hang; suspend:
señtakumono o tsurusu (洗濯物をつ
るす) *hang out* the washing.
(⇨ tsuru¹)

tsu┌tae·ru つたえる (伝える) *vt.*
(tsutae·te Ⓥ) 1 tell; inform;
notify; communicate.
2 hand down (a tale, custom, religion, etc.); introduce. (⇨ tsuta-
waru)

tsu┌ta·u つたう (伝う) *vt.* (tsuta·i·;
tsutaw·a·; tsutat·te Ⓒ) go
along:
yane o tsutatte *nigeru* (屋根を伝っ
て逃げる) flee from roof *to* roof.

tsu┌tawar·u つたわる (伝わる) *vi.*
(tsutawar·i·; tsutawar·a·; tsuta-
wat·te Ⓒ) 1 (of information,
rumor, etc.) spread; travel; circulate. (⇨ tsutaeru)
2 (of a tale, tradition, etc.) come
down; be handed down. (⇨ tsutaeru)
3 be transmitted; be introduced:
Bukkyoo ga Nihoñ ni tsutawatta
no wa roku-seeki nakaba desu. (仏
教が日本に伝わったのは6世紀半ばです)
It is in the mid-sixth century
that Buddhism *was introduced*
into Japan. (⇨ tsutaeru)

tsu┌toma┌r·u つとまる (勤まる) *vi.*
(-mar·i·; -mar·a·; -mat·te Ⓒ) be
fit; be equal:
Sono shigoto ga watashi ni tsu-
tomaru *ka doo ka shiñpai desu.* (そ
の仕事が私に勤まるかどうか心配です) I
am worried whether I *am equal*
to the job.

tsu┌tome┐¹ つとめ (勤め) *n.* work;
job. (⇨ tsutomeru¹)

tsu┌tome┐¹² つとめ (務め) *n.* duty;
task:
Kare wa tsutome *o rippa ni hata-*

shita. (彼は務めを立派に果たした) He
discharged his *duties* splendidly.
(⇨ tsutomeru²)

tsu┌tome┐·ru¹ つとめる (勤める) *vt.*
(-me·te Ⓥ) work for; serve:
Kanojo wa shoojigaisha ni tsu-
tomete *imasu.* (彼女は商事会社に勤
めています) She *works for* a trading
company. (⇨ kiñmu; tsutome¹)

tsu┌tome┐·ru² つとめる (務める) *vt.*
(-me·te Ⓥ) act as:
Kare wa kaigi de gichoo o tsu-
tometa. (彼は会議で議長を務めた)
He *acted* as chairman at the conference. (⇨ tsutome²)

tsu┌tome┐·ru³ つとめる (努める) *vt.*
(-me·te Ⓥ) try; make efforts;
endeavor. (⇨ doryoku)

tsu┌tomesaki つとめさき (勤め先)
n. one's place of employment.
(⇨ kaisha)

tsu┌tsu つつ (筒) *n.* pipe; tube;
cylinder.

tsu┌tsu┌k·u つつく (突つく) *vt.* (tsu-
tsuk·i·; tsutsuk·a·; tsutsu·i·te Ⓒ)
poke; peck; nudge.

tsu┌tsu┌m·u つつむ (包む) *vt.* (tsu-
tsum·i·; tsutsum·a·; tsutsuñ·de
Ⓒ) 1 wrap; pack:
mono o kami ni tsutsumu (物を紙に
包む) *wrap* a thing *up* in paper.
2 cover; veil:
Yama zeñtai ga moya ni tsutsu-
marete ita. (山全体がもやに包まれてい
た) The whole mountain *was
covered* in mist.

tsu┌tsushimi┐ つつしみ (慎み) *n.*
modesty; prudence; discretion;
self-control. (⇨ tsutsushimu)

tsu┌tsushi┐m·u つつしむ (慎む) *vt.*
(-shim·i·; -shim·a·; -shiñ·de Ⓒ)
1 be careful; be discreet; be prudent; be cautious:
koodoo o tsutsushimu (行動を慎む)
be prudent in one's conduct.
2 refrain from; be moderate:
sake o tsutsushimu (酒を慎しむ) *cut
down on* one's drinking.

tsu┌u つう (通) *n.* authority;
expert:

Ano hito wa kabuki no tsuu *desu.* (あの人は歌舞伎の通です) He is an *authority* on kabuki.

tsu⌐uchi つうち (通知) *n.* notice; notification; information.
tsuuchi suru (〜する) *vt.* notify; inform.

tsu⌐ugaku つうがく (通学) *n.* traveling to school; attending school. (⇨ zaigaku)
tsuugaku suru (〜する) *vi.* go to school. (⇨ tsuukiñ)

tsu⌐uji つうじ (通じ) *n.* bowel movement; evacuation; stool.

tsu⌐uji·ru つうじる (通じる) *vi.* (tsuuji-te Ⅴ) **1** lead; run:
Kono michi wa eki e tsuujite imasu.* (この道は駅へ通じています) This road *leads* to the station.
2 (of a telephone) get through:
Kanojo no uchi ni deñwa o shita ga tsuujinakatta.* (彼女の家に電話をしたが通じなかった) I telephoned her house but I *could not get through.*
3 be understood; make oneself understood:
Watashi no iu koto ga aite ni tsuujinakatta.* (私の言うことが相手に通じなかった) I *could not make myself understood* to the other party.
4 be well-informed; be familiar:
Kare wa sono kaisha no naibu-jijoo ni tsuujite iru.* (彼はその会社の内部事情に通じている) He *is well-informed* on the internal affairs of the company.

tsu⌐ujoo つうじょう (通常) *n., adv.* usually; generally:
Neñmatsu mo tsuujoo-doori ee-gyoo itashimasu.* (年末も通常どおり営業いたします) We will be conducting business *as usual* at the end of the year. (⇨ futsuu⌐)

tsu⌐uka つうか (通過) *n.* passage.
tsuuka suru (〜する) *vi.* pass:
Kyuukoo wa kono eki o tsuuka shimasu.* (急行はこの駅を通過します) The express *does not stop* at this station.

tsu⌐uki つうき (通気) *n.* ventila-

tion; air permeabilty.

tsu⌐ukiñ つうきん (通勤) *n.* commutation; going to work.
tsuukiñ suru (〜する) *vi.* commute; go to work.

tsu⌐ukoo つうこう (通行) *n.* passing; passage; traffic:
*ippoo-*tsuukoo (一方通行) a *one-way* street.
tsuukoo suru (〜する) *vi.* pass; go along. (⇨ tooru)

tsu⌐u-pi⌐isu ツーピース *n.* two-piece woman's suit.

tsu⌐uro つうろ (通路) *n.* passage; way; aisle.

tsu⌐ushiñ つうしん (通信) *n.* correspondence; communication.
tsuushiñ suru (〜する) *vi.* correspond; communicate.

tsu⌐uyaku つうやく (通訳) *n.* interpretation; interpreter:
tsuuyaku *o tooshite hanasu* (通訳を通して話す) speak through an *interpreter.*
tsuuyaku suru (〜する) *vt.* interpret. (⇨ dooji-tsuuyaku)

tsu⌐uyoo つうよう (通用) *n.* popular use; circulation; currency.
tsuuyoo suru (〜する) *vi.* be used; be accepted; be valid.

tsu⌐uya つや (艶) *n.* gloss; luster; polish.

tsu⌐uyo⌐·i つよい (強い) *a.* (-ku) **1** strong; powerful; intense. (↔ yowai) (⇨ tsuyosa)
2 (... ni) be good at:
Kare wa suuji ni tsuyoi.* (彼は数字に強い) He *is good* at figures. (↔ yowai)
3 (... ni) be able to resist; withstand:
Watashi wa samusa ni tsuyoi.* (私は寒さに強い) I *can easily stand* the cold. (↔ yowai) (⇨ tsuyosa)

tsu⌐uyoki つよき (強気) *a.n.* (〜 na, ni) bold; aggressive; optimistic:
Kare wa itsu-mo tsuyoki da.* (彼はいつも強気だ) He is always *firm and resolute.* (↔ yowaki)

tsu⸢yoma⸣r・u つよまる（強まる）*vi.*
(-mar・i・; -mar・a・; -mat-te 🄲)
become strong; increase in power [strength]. (⇨ tsuyomeru)

tsu⸢yome⸣・ru つよめる（強める）*vt.*
(-me-te 🅅) strengthen; inten-
sify; emphasize:
ryookoku no musubitsuki o tsu-
yomeru（両国の結びつきを強める）
strengthen the ties between two
countries. (↔ yowameru)(⇨ tsu-
yomaru)

tsu⸢yosa つよさ（強さ）*n.*
strength; power, force:
kaze no tsuyosa *o hakaru*（風の強さ
を測る）measure the *force* of the
wind. (⇨ tsuyoi)

tsu⸢yu¹ つゆ（露）*n.* dew; dew-
drop.

tsu⸢yu² つゆ（梅雨）*n.* the rainy
season. ★ The period from June
to July, when there are many
rainy days. (⇨ baiu; uki¹)

tsu⸢yu³ つゆ（汁）*n.* soup; sauce;
juice. ★ Often called 'o-tsuyu.'
(⇨ shiru²)

tsu⸢zuke・ru つづける（続ける）*vt.*
(tsuzuke-te 🅅) continue; go on;
keep up:
Doozo hanashi o tsuzukete *kudasai.*（どうぞ話を続けてください）*Go on*
with your story, please. (⇨ tsuzuku)

tsu⸢zuki つづき（続き）*n.* contin-
uance; continuation; sequel:
Sono hanashi no tsuzuki *ga kikitai.*
（その話の続きが聞きたい）I want to
hear the *rest* of the story. (⇨ tsuzuku)

tsu⸢zuk・u つづく（続く）*vi.* (tsu-
zuk・i・; tsuzuk・a・; tsuzu・i-te 🄲)
1 continue; go on; last:
Seeteñ ga is-shuukañ tsuzuita.（晴
天が一週間続いた）The fine weath-
er *continued* for a week. (⇨ tsuzukeru; tsuzuki)

2 follow:
Watashi-tachi wa kare ni tsuzuite
sono heya ni haitta.（私たちは彼に続
いてその部屋に入った）We went into
the room, *following* him.
(⇨ shitagatte¹)

3 lead; extend:
*Kono namikimichi wa ichi-kiro
hodo* tsuzukimasu.（この並木道は１
キロほど続きます）This avenue of
trees *extends* for about one kilometer.

tsu⸢zumi¹ つづみ（鼓）*n.* Japanese
hand drum. ★ Beaten with the
fingertips.

tta⸢ra¹ ったら *p.* (used to mark
the topic of a sentence): ★ Follows a noun or the dictionary
form of a verb. An informal
form mainly used by women.
Uchi no ko ttara, *asoñde bakari
ite, sukoshi mo beñkyoo shinai.*（う
ちの子ったら、遊んでばかりいて、少しも勉
強しない）*That child of ours!* He
plays around all the time, and
does not study one bit.

... ttara nai (...～ない) (used for
emphasis or exaggeration):
Kono tokoro mainichi isogashii
ttara nai.（このところ毎日忙しいったら
ない）These days I *am rushed off
my feet* every day.

(t)tara² (っ)たら *p.* = (t)teba.

(t)teba (っ)てば *p.* (used when
emphasizing one's thoughts or
opinions to someone who appears not to understand):
★ Sometimes used as a retort or
contradiction. Use 'teba' after 'ñ,'
otherwise 'tteba.'
"Hayaku ikoo yo." "Wakatte iru
tteba.*（「早く行こうよ」「わかっているっ
てば」）"Let's hurry up and get
along." "Okay, okay, *I understand.*"

U

-u う *infl. end.* = -oo.

uꜜba¹·u うばう(奪う) *vt.* (ubai·i-; ubaw·a-; ubat·te C) take by force; snatch; rob; deprive.

uꜝchi¹ うち(家) *n.* **1** house; home; family. (⇒ ie¹)
2 (~ no) my; our:
uchi no *chichi* (うちの父) *my* father / uchi no *gakkoo* [*kaisha*] (うちの学校[会社]) *our* school [company].

uꜝchi² うち(内) *n.* **1** inside:
Kono doa wa uchi *kara hiraku.* (このドアは内から開く) This door opens from the *inside.* (↔ soto)
(⇒ naka¹)
2 (~ ni) in; within; before:
Kuraku naranai uchi *ni kaerima-shoo.* (暗くならないうちに帰りましょう) Let's go back *before* it gets dark.
3 (~ kara) of; out of:
Kono itsutsu no uchi *kara hitotsu tori nasai.* (この五つのうちから一つ取りなさい) Take one *out of* these five.

uꜝchiake·ru うちあける(打ち明ける) *vt.* (-ake-te Ⅴ) confide; confess; unburden.

uꜝchiawase うちあわせ(打ち合わせ) *n.* previous arrangement.
(⇒ uchiawaseru)

uꜝchiawase·ru うちあわせる(打ち合わせる) *vt.* (-awase-te Ⅴ) arrange; make arrangements beforehand. (⇒ uchiawase)

uꜝchigawa うちがわ(内側) *n.* the inside; interior:
hako no uchigawa (箱の内側) the *inside* of a box. (↔ sotogawa)

uꜝchikeshi うちけし(打ち消し) *n.* denial; negation. (⇒ uchikesu)

uꜝchikes·u うちけす(打ち消す) *vt.* (-kesh·i-; -kes·a-; -kesh·i-te C) deny (the rumor); negate.
(⇒ uchikeshi)

uꜝchikir·u うちきる(打ち切る) *vt.* (-kir·i-; -kir·a-; -kit·te C) dis-

continue; break off (negotiations).

uꜝchikom·u うちこむ(打ち込む) *vt.* (-kom·i-; -kom·a-; -koñ-de C) **1** drive; shoot; smash:
jimeñ ni kui o uchikomu (地面にくいを打ち込む) *drive* a stake into the ground.
2 devote oneself to.

uꜝchiwa¹ うちわ(内輪) *n.* **1** private; family:
uchiwa *dake no atsumari* (内輪だけの集まり) a *private* meeting / uchi-wa *no kekkoñ-shiki* (内輪の結婚式) a *family* wedding.
2 conservative; moderate:
Hiyoo wa uchiwa *ni mitsumotte, gojuumañ-eñ kakarimasu.* (費用は内輪に見積もって、50万円かかります) *Conservatively* estimated, the cost is half a million yen.

uꜝchi¹wa² うちわ(団扇) *n.* round fan made of paper and bamboo.

uꜝchiwake うちわけ(内訳) *n.* breakdown (of expenditures); item; detail.

uꜝchuu うちゅう(宇宙) *n.* the universe; the cosmos; space.

uꜝde うで(腕) *n.* **1** arm; forearm.
2 ability; skill:
Kare wa saikiñ gorufu no ude ga agatta. (彼は最近ゴルフの腕が上がった) He has recently improved his *skill* in golf. (⇒ udemae)

uꜝdedo¹kee うでどけい(腕時計) *n.* wristwatch. (⇒ tokee)

uꜝdegumi¹ うでぐみ(腕組み) *n.* folding one's arms:
udegumi *o shite kañgaeru* (腕組みをして考える) think with one's *arms folded.*

uꜝdemae うでまえ(腕前) *n.* skill; ability. (⇒ ude)

uꜝdoñ うどん *n.* noodles.

uꜝe¹ うえ(上) *n.* **1** on:

Kanojo wa yuka no ue ni juutañ o shiita. (彼女は床の上にじゅうたんを敷いた) She laid a carpet *on* the floor. 《↔ shita¹》

2 over; above:
Hikooki wa yama no ue o toñde ita. (飛行機は山の上を飛んでいた) The plane was flying *over* the mountain. 《↔ shita¹》

3 up; upstairs:
Kanojo wa esukareetaa de ue ni ikimashita. (彼女はエスカレーターで上に行きました) She went *up* in the escalator. 《↔ shita¹》

4 top:
Sono hoñ wa ichibañ ue no tana ni arimasu. (その本はいちばん上の棚にあります) The book is on the *top* shelf. 《↔ shita¹》

5 senior; older:
Shujiñ wa watashi yori go-sai ue desu. (主人は私より5歳上です) My husband is five years *older* than me. 《↔ shita¹》

6 superior:
Kono koocha no hoo ga sore yori shitsu ga ue desu. (この紅茶の方がそれより質が上です) This tea is *superior* in quality to that one. 《⇨ otoru》

7 after:
Sono koto wa ryooshiñ to soodañ no ue kimemasu. (そのことは両親と相談の上決めます) I will decide that matter *after* discussing it with my parents.

u「e」¹²　うえ (飢え) *n.* hunger; starvation. 《⇨ ueru》

u「eki　うえき (植木) *n.* garden tree [plant]; potted plant.

u「e・ru　うえる (植える) *vt.* (ue-te Ⓥ) plant (a tree); sow; grow.

u「e」・ru²　うえる (飢える) *vi.* (ue-te Ⓥ) be [go] hungry; starve. 《⇨ ue²》

u「e」-shita　うえした (上下) *n.* up and down. 《↔ sayuu》《⇨ jooge》

u「gai　うがい (含嗽) *n.* gargling.
ugai suru (～する) gargle.

u「goka」s・u　うごかす (動かす) *vt.* (ugokash・i-; ugokas・a-; ugokash・i-te Ⓒ) **1** move (a table).
2 operate (a machine, vehicle, etc.); run; start. 《⇨ ugoku》
3 (of feelings, emotions) touch; move; influence:
Sono tegami wa kanojo no kokoro o ugokashita. (その手紙は彼女の心を動かした) That letter *touched* her heart. 《⇨ ugoku》

u「goki」　うごき (動き) *n.* **1** movement; motion. 《⇨ ugoku》
2 activity; action.
booryokudañ no ugoki o shiraberu (暴力団の動きを調べる) investigate the *activities* of criminal gangs.
3 trend; development:
yo no naka no ugoki (世の中の動き) social *trends*. 《⇨ ugoku》

u「go」k・u　うごく (動く) *vi.* (ugok・i-; ugok・a-; ugo・ite Ⓒ) **1** move; budge; stir:
Kare wa kega o shite, ugokemaseñ. (彼はけがをして、動けません) He has hurt himself and *cannot move*. 《⇨ ugokasu; ugoki》
2 (of a machine, vehicle, etc.) work; run:
Kono kuruma wa deñki de ugoku. (この車は電気で動く) This car *runs* on electricity. 《⇨ ugokasu》
3 act; get about:
Ima ugoku no wa keñmee de wa arimaseñ. (今動くのは賢明ではありません) It is not wise to *act* now.
4 (of feelings, emotions) be influenced; be moved; be touched.

u「kabe・ru　うかべる (浮かべる) *vt.* (ukabe-te Ⓥ) **1** float; set afloat. 《⇨ ukabu》
2 show (one's feeling); express:
namida o ukaberu (涙を浮かべる) *have* tears in one's eyes. 《⇨ ukabu》

u「kab・u　うかぶ (浮かぶ) *vt.* (ukab・i-; ukab・a-; ukañ-de Ⓒ)
1 float (on the water). 《⇨ ukaberu》
2 (of an idea) come into; occur.
3 (of tears, countenance) appear:

Kanojo no me ni namida ga ukañda. (彼女の目に涙が浮かんだ) Tears *appeared* in her eyes. (⇨ ukaberu)

uˈkaga·u うかがう (伺う) *vt.* (ukaga·i-; ukagaw·a-; ukagat-te Ⓒ)
1 (*humble*) visit; call on [at]:
Asu o-taku ni ukagatte *mo yoroshii desu ka?* (あすお宅にうかがってもよろしいですか) Is it all right if I *call on* you at home tomorrow?
2 (*humble*) ask:
Ukagaitai *koto ga aru ñ desu ga.* (うかがいたいことがあるんですが) There are some questions I'd like to ask you.
3 (*humble*) hear; be told:
Anata wa teñkiñ sareta to ukagatte *orimasu ga.* (あなたが転勤されたとうかがっておりますが) I *hear* that you have been transferred.

uˈkeire·ru うけいれる (受け入れる) *vt.* (-ire-te Ⓥ) accept (a demand, request, proposal, etc.); grant.

uˈkemi[1] うけみ (受け身) *n.* passive; passive sentence. (⇨ -rareru; -reru)

uˈkemochi うけもち (受け持ち) *n.* charge; responsibility. (⇨ ukemotsu)

uˈkemots·u うけもつ (受け持つ) *vt.* (-moch·i-; -mot·a-; -mot-te Ⓒ) take charge of; be in charge of:
Dare ga kono kurasu o ukemotte *imasu ka?* (だれがこのクラスを受け持っていますか) Who *is in charge of* this class? (⇨ ukemochi)

uˈke[1]**·ru** うける (受ける) *vt.* (uke-te Ⓥ) 1 catch (a ball).
2 receive (an invitation); get; obtain (permission).
3 suffer:
ooki-na higai o ukeru (大きな被害を受ける) *suffer* heavy damage.
4 take (an examination); sit for.
5 *vi.* be popular:
Sono sakka no shoosetsu wa josee no aida de ukete iru. (その作家の小説は女性の間で受けている) That author's novels *are popular* among

women. (⇨ niñki)

uˈketome·ru うけとめる (受け止める) *vt.* (-tome-te Ⓥ) 1 catch (a ball); stop; take.
2 take (a situation); deal with:
jitai o reesee ni uketomeru (事態を冷静に受け止める) *take* the situation calmly.

uˈketori うけとり (受取) *n.* accepting; receipt. (⇨ ryooshusho; uketoru)

uˈketor·u うけとる (受け取る) *vt.* (-tor·i-; -tor·a-; -tot-te Ⓒ) 1 receive; get; take; accept:
tegami o uketoru (手紙を受け取る) *receive* a letter. (⇨ uketori)
2 interpret; take:
Ima no wa joodañ to shite uketotte *kudasai.* (今のは冗談として受け取ってください) Please *take* what I have just said as a joke.

uˈketsug·u うけつぐ (受け継ぐ) *vt.* (-tsug·i-; -tsug·a-; -tsu·i-de Ⓒ) succeed to; inherit:
Otto ga shiñda ato, tsuma ga jigyoo o uketsuida. (夫が死んだ後, 妻が事業を受け継いだ) The wife *succeeded* to the business after her husband's death.

uˈketsuke うけつけ (受付) *n.*
1 receptionist; reception desk.
2 acceptance. (⇨ uketsukeru; ukeireru)

uˈketsuke·ru うけつける (受け付ける) *vt.* (-tsuke-te Ⓥ) accept; receive:
Gañsho wa koñgetsu-matsu made uketsukemasu. (願書は今月末まで受け付けます) We *accept* applications until the end of this month. (⇨ uketsuke)

uˈki[1] うき (雨季) *n.* the rainy season. (↔ kañki[2]) (⇨ baiu; tsuyu[1])

uˈki[2] うき (浮き) *n.* float (on a fishing line).

uˈkka[1]**ri** うっかり *adv.* (~ to; ~ suru) carelessly; inadvertently.

uˈk·u うく (浮く) *vi.* (uk·i-; uk·a-; u·i-te Ⓒ) 1 float; rise to the surface. (⇨ ukabu)

2 (of cost, expense) be saved:
Kare no kuruma ni nosete moratta no de takushii-dai ga uita.(彼の車に乗せてもらったのでタクシー代が浮いた) I got a lift in his car, so the taxi fare *was saved*.

u˥ma˩ うま(馬) *n.* horse.

u˥ma˩·i うまい(旨い) *a.* (-ku)
1 skillful; good:
Kare wa unten ga umai.(彼は運転がうまい) He is *good* at driving. (⇨ joozu))
2 (of an idea, a project, etc.) great; good: umai *kangae* (うまい考え) a *great* idea.
3 (of food) delicious; good.
★ Used mainly by men. (⇨ oishii))
4 successful; profitable; lucky:
Subete umaku *ikimashita.* (すべてうまくいきました) Everything worked out *well*.

u˥mare うまれ(生まれ) *n.* birth; descent:
Watashi wa umare *mo sodachi mo Tookyoo desu.* (私は生まれも育ちも東京です) I *was born* and brought up in Tokyo. (⇨ umareru))

u˥mare·ru うまれる(生まれる) *vi.* (umare-te ꓦ) be born; come into existence. (⇨ tanjoo; umare; umu˥))

u˥maretsuki うまれつき(生まれ付き) *n., adv.* by nature:
Kanojo no koe ga ii no wa umaretsuki *desu.*(彼女の声がいいのは生まれつきです) Her fine voice is something she *was born with*.

u˥mar·u うまる(埋まる) *vt.* (umar-i-; umar-a-; umat-te ꒞) be buried; be filled up:
Kaijoo wa hito de umatta.(会場は人で埋まった) The hall *was filled* with people. (⇨ umeru))

u˥me うめ(梅) *n.* ume; Japanese apricot; *Prunus mume.*

u˥meboshi うめぼし(梅干し) *n.* pickled Japanese apricot.

u˥mekigo˩e うめきごえ(呻き声) *n.* groan; moan.

u˥me˩k·u うめく(呻く) *vi.* (umek-i-; umek-a-; ume·ite ꒞) groan; moan.

u˥me·ru うめる(埋める) *vt.* (ume-te ꓦ) **1** bury; fill in:
Kanojo wa gomi o atsumete, niwa ni umeta.(彼女はごみを集めて、庭に埋めた) She gathered up the trash and *buried* it in the garden. (⇨ uzumeru))
2 make up for (a loss, deficit). (⇨ umaru))

u˥metate うめたて(埋め立て) *n.* land reclamation. (⇨ umetateru))

u˥metate˩·ru うめたてる(埋め立てる) *vt.* (-tate-te ꓦ) reclaim; fill up; recover. (⇨ umetate))

u˥mi¹ うみ(海) *n.* sea; ocean. (↔ riku))

u˥mi² うみ(膿) *n.* pus; discharge. (⇨ umu²))

u˥m·u¹ うむ(生む) *vt.* (um·i-; m·a-; un-de ꒞) **1** give birth to; breed; lay (an egg). (⇨ umareru))
2 produce; give rise to; yield.

u˥m·u² うむ(膿む) *vi.* (um·i-; um·a-; un-de ꒞) suppurate; fester; form pus. (⇨ umi²))

u˥mu³ うむ(有無) *n.* existence; presence:
Keeken no umu *wa toimasen.*(経験の有無は問いません) We do not mind *whether* you have experience *or not*.

umu o iwasezu (～を言わせず) willy-nilly; forcibly.

u˥n¹ うん(運) *n.* luck; fortune; chance:
Kare wa un *ga ii* [warui].(彼は運がいい[悪い]) He is *lucky* [*unlucky*]. (⇨ unmee))

u˥n² うん *int.* (*informal*) all right:
"*Kore tetsudatte kureru kai.*" "Un, *ii yo.*"(「これ手伝ってくれるかい」「うん、いいよ」) "Can you help me with this?" "*Okay*, fine."

un to iu (～と言う) say yes.

u˥nagi うなぎ(鰻) *n.* eel:
unagi *no kabayaki* (うなぎのかば焼き) broiled *eel*. (⇨ kabayaki))

u⌐na⌐r·u うなる (唸る) *vi.* (unar·i-; unar·a-; unat-te Ⓒ) **1** groan; moan; growl.
2 (of a motor, engine, etc.) howl; roar.

u⌐nazuk·u うなずく (頷く) *vi.* (unazuk·i-; unazuk·a-; unazu·i-te Ⓒ) nod (in agreement); approve.

u⌐ñchiñ うんちん (運賃) *n.* fare; charge; freight. (⇨ ryookiñ)

u⌐ñdoo うんどう (運動) *n.* **1** exercise; sport.
2 movement; campaign: *koogai hañtai no uñdoo* (公害反対の運動) anti-pollution *campaigns*.
uñdoo (o) suru (〜を(を)する) *vi.* take exercise; campaign (for a cause).

u⌐ñdoojoo うんどうじょう (運動場) *n.* playground; playing field.

u⌐ñdo⌐okai うんどうかい (運動会) *n.* sports day; athletic meet.

u⌐ñee うんえい (運営) *n.* management; operation; administration.
uñee (o) suru (〜を(を)する) *vt.* manage; operate; administer: *jigyoo o uñee suru* (事業を運営する) *manage* a business.

u⌐ñga うんが (運河) *n.* canal.

u⌐ñmee うんめい (運命) *n.* fate; destiny. (⇨ uñ')

u⌐ñpañ うんぱん (運搬) *n.* carriage; conveyance; transport.
uñpañ suru (〜する) *vt.* carry; convey; transport.

u⌐ñteñ うんてん (運転) *n.* driving; operation.
uñteñ (o) suru (〜を(を)する) *vi., vt.* drive; run; operate.

u⌐ñte⌐ñshu うんてんしゅ (運転手) *n.* driver; chauffeur; motorman.

u⌐ñto うんと *adv.* (*informal*) hard; severely; much: *uñto beñkyoo suru* (うんと勉強する) study *hard*.

u⌐nubore うぬぼれ (自惚れ) *n.* conceit; self-conceit; vanity. (⇨ unuboreru)

u⌐nubore·ru うぬぼれる (自惚れる) *vi.* (unubore-te Ⓥ) flatter oneself; be conceited. (⇨ unubore)

u⌐ñyu うんゆ (運輸) *n.* transport: *uñyu-gaisha* (運輸会社) a *transport* company.

u⌐o うお (魚) *n.* fish. (⇨ sakana')

u⌐oi⌐chiba うおいちば (魚市場) *n.* fish market.

u⌐ra うら (裏) *n.* **1** the back; the wrong side; the reverse. (↔ omote)
2 back door: *ura e mawaru* (裏へ回る) go round to the *back door*. (↔ omote)
3 back; rear: *ie no ura no niwa* (家の裏の庭) the garden in the *rear* of the house. (↔ mae)
4 (of baseball) the second half. (↔ omote)
5 hidden part; shady side: *ura no imi* (裏の意味) a *hidden* meaning.

u⌐raga⌐eshi うらがえし (裏返し) *n.* inside out; turning over. (⇨ uragaesu)

u⌐raga⌐es·u うらがえす (裏返す) *vt.* (-gaesh·i-; -gaes·a-; -gaesh·i-te Ⓒ) turn over; turn inside out: *suteeki o uragaesu* (ステーキを裏返す) *turn* a steak *over*. (⇨ uragaeshi)

u⌐ragi⌐r·u うらぎる (裏切る) *vt.* (-gir·i-; -gir·a-; -git-te Ⓒ) betray; disappoint (someone's hopes).

u⌐raguchi うらぐち (裏口) *n.* back door [entrance].

ur⌐aguchi-nyu⌐ugaku うらぐちにゅうがく (裏口入学) *n.* backdoor admission to a university.

u⌐rami⌐ うらみ (恨み) *n.* grudge; spite; ill-feeling. (⇨ uramu)

u⌐ramoñ うらもん (裏門) *n.* back [rear] gate. (↔ omotemoñ)

u⌐ra⌐m·u うらむ (恨む) *vt.* (uram·i-; uram·a-; urañ-de Ⓒ) bear a grudge; think ill of. (⇨ urami)

u⌐ra-omote うらおもて (裏表) *n.* the top side and the bottom side; both sides.

ura-omote ga aru (〜がある) two-faced.

u⌐rayamashi⌐.i うらやましい (羨ましい) a. (-ku) envious; jealous. (⇨ urayamu)

u⌐raya⌐m.u うらやむ (羨む) vt. (urayam·i-; urayam·a-; urayañ·de C) envy; be envious. (⇨ urayamashii)

u⌐re·ru¹ うれる (売れる) vi. (ure-te V) 1 sell; be sold. (⇨ deru (16)) 2 (of an entertainer, etc.) be popular; be famous:
Sono kashu no na wa sekeñ ni yoku urete imasu. (その歌手の名は世間によく売れています) The name of the singer is well known to everybody.

u⌐re⌐·ru² うれる (熟れる) vi. (ure-te V) ripen:
Kono suika wa mada urete inai. (このすいかはまだ熟れていない) This watermelon is not ripe yet.

u⌐reshi⌐.i うれしい (嬉しい) a. (-ku) glad; happy; pleased. (⇨ yorokobu) (↔ kanashii)

u⌐ri うり (瓜) n. type of melon; vegetable such as a gourd, squash, cucumber, etc.
uri-futatsu (うり二つ) double(s); look-alike(s).

u⌐riage うりあげ (売り上げ) n. sales; proceeds; turnover:
uriage o nobasu (売り上げを伸ばす) increase the sales.

u⌐riba うりば (売り場) n. counter; department; office:
omocha uriba (おもちゃ売り場) the toy department.

u⌐ridashi うりだし (売り出し) n. opening sale; bargain [special] sale. (⇨ uridasu)
uridashi-chuu no (〜中の) up-and-coming: uridashi-chuu no kashu (売り出し中の歌手) a singer coming into popularity. (⇨ niñki)

u⌐rida⌐s·u うりだす (売り出す) vt. (-dash·i-; -das·a-; -dash·i-te C) 1 put on sale; offer for sale.

(⇨ uridashi; uru¹)
2 win a reputation; become popular. (⇨ uridashi)

u⌐rikire うりきれ (売り切れ) n. sell-out; being out of stock. (⇨ urikireru)

u⌐rikire⌐·ru うりきれる (売り切れる) vi. (-kire-te V) be sold out; be out of stock. (⇨ urikire)

u⌐rimono うりもの (売り物) n. article for sale; selling point.

u⌐roko うろこ (鱗) n. (of fish) scale.

u⌐rouro うろうろ adv. (〜 to; 〜 suru) (an aimless or uneasy way of walking):
Hen na otoko ga urouro (to) arukimawatte iru. (変な男がうろうろ(と)歩き回っている) There is a strange fellow hanging around.

u⌐r·u¹ うる (売る) vt. (ur·i-; ur·a-; ut-te C) 1 sell. (↔ kau¹) 2 betray (one's country, organization, friend, etc.); sell out.

u⌐·ru² うる (得る) vt. (e-te V) (literary) gain. (⇨ eru)

u⌐rusa⌐.i うるさい (煩い) a. (-ku) 1 noisy. (⇨ yakamashii) 2 (of a demand, request, etc.) annoying; nagging:
Kodomo ga omocha o katte kure to urusai. (子どもがおもちゃを買ってくれとうるさい) My child is pestering me to buy him a toy.
3 strict:
Watashi-tachi no señsee wa urusai. (私たちの先生はうるさい) Our teacher is strict.
4 particular:
Chichi wa koohii no aji ni urusai. (父はコーヒーの味にうるさい) My father is particular about the taste of his coffee.

u⌐rushi うるし (漆) n. Japanese lacquer; japan. (⇨ shikki¹)

u⌐ryoo うりょう (雨量) n. rainfall; precipitation.

u⌐sagi うさぎ (兎) n. rabbit; hare.

u⌐shi うし (牛) n. cattle; bull; cow; ox.

u⌐**shina·u** うしなう (失う) *vt.* (ushi-
na·i-; ushinaw·a-; ushinat-te C)
1 lose; be deprived of:
shoku o ushinau (職を失う) *lose*
one's job.
2 miss (an opportunity).

u⌐**shiro** うしろ (後ろ) *n.* **1** back;
rear: *kuruma no ushiro no seki*
(車の後ろの席) the *back* seat of a
car. (↔ mae)
2 behind:
Ushiro *kara osanai de kudasai.* (後
ろから押さないでください) Stop push-
ing from *behind.* (↔ mae)

u⌐**shiro**⌐**ashi** うしろあし (後ろ足) *n.*
hind leg. (⇨ maeashi)

u⌐**so** うそ (嘘) *n.* **1** lie; fib:
Kare wa heeki de uso o tsuku. (彼
は平気でうそをつく) He makes no
bones about telling *lies.*
2 falseness:
Sono uwasa wa uso da to wakatta.
(そのうわさはうそだとわかった) I found
out that the rumor was *false.*

u⌐**sugi** うすぎ (薄着) *n.* being
lightly dressed. (↔ atsugi)
usugi (o) suru (〜を) する) *vi.* be
lightly dressed; wear light
clothes.

u⌐**sugura·i** うすぐらい (薄暗い) *a.*
(-ku) dim; dusky. (⇨ kurai¹)

u⌐**su·i** うすい (薄い) *a.* (-ku)
1 thin:
usui *kami* [*hon*] (薄い紙 [本]) a *thin*
sheet of paper [book]. (↔ atsui³)
2 (of taste) weak; thin; lightly-
seasoned. (↔ koi¹)
3 (of color) light. (↔ koi¹)
4 (of hair) thin; sparse:
kami ga usuku *naru* (髪が薄くなる)
lose one's hair.
5 (of possibility) few; little.

u⌐**sume·ru** うすめる (薄める) *vt.*
(usume-te V) dilute; water
down.

u⌐**ta**⌐ うた (歌) *n.* **1** song.
(⇨ utau)
2 'tanka' poem:
uta *o yomu* (歌を詠む) compose a
'*tanka*' poem. (⇨ tañka³; waka)

u⌐**tagai** うたがい (疑い) *n.*
1 doubt. (⇨ gimoñ; utagau)
2 suspicion:
utagai *o idaku* (疑いを抱く) have a
suspicion. (⇨ utagau)

u⌐**taga·u** うたがう (疑う) *vt.* (uta-
ga·i-; utagaw·a-; utagat-te C)
doubt; suspect. (⇨ utagai)

u⌐**tago**⌐**e** うたごえ (歌声) *n.* singing voice.

u⌐**ta·u** うたう (歌う) *vt.* (uta·i-;
utaw·a-; utat-te C) sing (a
song). (⇨ uta)

u⌐**teñ** うてん (雨天) *n.* rainy weather; rain. (↔ seeteñ)

u⌐**ts·u**¹ うつ (打つ) *vt.* (uch·i-;
ut·a-; ut-te C) **1** hit; strike;
knock:
kanazuchi de kugi o utsu (金づちで
くぎを打つ) *strike* a nail with a hammer. (⇨ tataku)
2 (of a clock) strike.

u⌐**ts·u**² うつ (撃つ) *vt.* (uch·i-;
ut·a-; ut-te C) shoot (a rifle);
fire.

u⌐**tsukushi**¹⌐**i** うつくしい (美しい) *a.*
(-ku) (*slightly literary*) beautiful;
pretty; handsome:
utsukushii *josee* (美しい女性) a
beautiful woman / utsukushii *koe*
(美しい声) a *sweet* voice. (⇨ kiree)

u⌐**tsumuk·u** うつむく (俯く) *vi.*
(-muk·i-; -muk·a-; -mu·i-te C)
look down; hang one's head.

u⌐**tsurikawari** うつりかわり (移り
変わり) *n.* change; transition:
kisetsu no utsurikawari (季節の移り
変わり) the *changes* of the seasons.

u⌐**tsu**⌐**r·u**¹ うつる (移る) *vi.* (utsu-
r·i-; utsur·a-; utsut-te C)
1 move (to a plae); shift.
(⇨ utsusu¹)
2 move on to (a new topic, subject, etc.). (⇨ utsusu¹)
3 be infected; catch:
Kaze wa utsuri-*yasui.* (かぜはうつりや
すい) Colds *are catching.*
(⇨ utsusu¹)

u⌐**tsu**⌐**r·u**² うつる (写る) *vi.* (utsur-
r·i-; utsur·a-; utsut-te C) (of a

photograph) be taken; come out.
(⇨ utsusu²)

u῾tsu῾r·u³ うつる (映る) vi. (utsur·i-; utsur·a-; utsut-te Ⓒ) be reflected; be mirrored. (⇨ utsusu³)

u῾tsu῾s·u¹ うつす (移す) vt. (utsush·i-; utsus·a-; utsush·i-te Ⓒ)
1 move; remove; transfer.
(⇨ utsuru¹)
2 give; infect:
Watashi wa anata ni kaze o utsusareta. (私はあなたにかぜをうつされた) I got a cold from you. (⇨ utsuru¹)

u῾tsu῾s·u² うつす (写す) vt. (utsush·i-; utsus·a-; utsush·i-te Ⓒ)
1 take (a photo). (⇨ utsuru²)
2 copy; trace:
kokuban ni kaite aru koto o nooto ni utsusu (黒板に書いてあることをノートに写す) copy what is written on the blackboard into one's notebook.

u῾tsu῾s·u³ うつす (映す) vt. (utsush·i-; utsus·a-; utsush·i-te Ⓒ)
reflect; mirror; project:
suraido o sukuriiñ ni utsusu (スライドをスクリーンに映す) project slides onto the screen. (⇨ utsuru³)

u῾tsuwa うつわ (器) n. 1 container; vessel.
2 ability; caliber:
utsuwa no ookii [chiisai] hito (器の大きい[小さい]人) a man of high [poor] caliber.

u῾ttae うったえ (訴え) n. 1 lawsuit; legal action.
2 appeal; complaint.
(⇨ uttaeru)

u῾ttae῾·ru うったえる (訴える) vt. (uttae-te Ⓥ) 1 bring an action; file a suit. (⇨ uttae)

2 complain (illness, etc.):
zutsuu o uttaeru (頭痛を訴える) complain of headaches.
3 appeal; protest (one's innocence).
4 resort (to violence).

u῾ttooshi῾·i うっとうしい (鬱陶しい) a. (-ku) gloomy; depressing; annoying.

u῾wagi うわぎ (上着) n. coat; jacket.

u῾waki うわき (浮気) n. being fickle; being unfaithful.
uwaki (o) suru (～(を)する) vi. have an affair; be unfaithful.
— a.n. (～ na) fickle; unfaithful: uwaki na hito (浮気な人) a person of easy virtue.

u῾wasa うわさ (噂) n. rumor; gossip; hearsay.
uwasa (o) suru (～(を)する) vi. talk about; gossip about.

u῾yama῾·u うやまう (敬う) vt. (-ma·i-; -maw·a-; -mat-te Ⓒ) respect; worship:
ryooshiñ o uyamau (両親を敬う) respect one's parents.

u῾zu῾maki うずまき (渦巻) n. whirlpool; eddy.

u῾zumar·u うずまる (埋まる) vi. (-mar·i-; -mar·a-; -mat-te Ⓒ)
1 be buried. (⇨ uzumeru)
2 be filled; overflow:
Hiroba wa oozee no guñshuu de uzumatta. (広場は大勢の群衆でうずまった) The plaza was overflowing with people. (⇨ umeru; uzumeru)

u῾zume·ru うずめる (埋める) vt. (-me-te Ⓥ) bury. (⇨ umeru; uzumaru)

W

wa¹¹ わ (輪) n. circle; ring; loop.
wa¹² わ (和) n. 1 unity; harmony: hito no wa (人の和) good teamwork.

2 sum; total: wa o motomeru (和を求める) work out the sum.

wa³ は p. 1 (used to mark the topic of a sentence): ★ Used

when the speaker wants to add something new about the topic.
Kore wa *watashi no jisho desu.* (これは私の辞書です) *This* is my dictionary. (⇨ ga¹)

2 (used in making contrasts and comparisons):
Ame wa *futte imasu ga* kaze wa *arimaseñ.* (雨は降っていますが風はありません) *Raining it is,* but there is no *wind.*

3 (used with a negative in a contrastive sense):
Watasha wa tabako wa suimaseñ. (私はたばこは吸いません) I *don't smoke* (but I do drink).

4 (used to indicate a limit):
Koko kara eki made jup-puñ wa *kakarimaseñ.* (ここから駅まで10分はかかりません) It does not take *as much as* ten minutes from here to the station. (⇨ mo²)

wa⁴ わ *p.* **1** (used to indicate emotions, such as admiration):
★ Used mainly by women.
Watashi mo gaikoku e ikitai wa. (私も外国へ行きたいわ) I too *want to* go abroad.

2 (used for slight emphasis):
★ Used mainly by women.
Watashi ga iku wa. (私が行くわ) I *am going.*

3 (used to emphasize emotions or feelings of surprise):
Deñsha de ashi o fumareru wa, *saifu o* nusumareru wa, *kyoo wa hidoi hi datta.* (電車で足を踏まれるわ、財布を盗まれるわ、きょうはひどい日だった) My foot *got stepped on* in the train and my purse *was stolen.* What an awful day it has been today!

-wa わ (羽) *suf.* counter for birds and rabbits. (⇨ APP. 4)

wa˺a わあ *int.* hurray; hurrah; gee; wow.

wa˺apuro ワープロ *n.* word processor.

wa˺bi わび (詫び) *n.* apology.
★ Often '*o-wabi.*' (⇨ wabiru)

wa˺bi·ru わびる (詫びる) *vt.* (wabi-te Ⅴ) apologize; make an apology. (⇨ wabi)

wa˺bishi˥·i わびしい (侘びしい) *a.* (-ku) lonely; miserable; dreary. (⇨ mijime; sabishii)

wa˺buñ わぶん (和文) *n.* Japanese; Japanese writing.

wa˺dai わだい (話題) *n.* topic; subject of conversation.

wa˺dakamari わだかまり (蟠り) *n.* bad feeling; grudge.

wa˺ee-ji˺teñ わえいじてん (和英辞典) *n.* Japanese-English dictionary for Japanese people.
(⇨ eenichi-jiteñ; eewa-jiteñ; nichiee-jiteñ)

wa˺fuku わふく (和服) *n.* kimono; traditional Japanese costume.
★ More formal than 'kimono.'
(↔ yoofuku) (⇨ kimono)

wa˺fuu わふう (和風) *n.* Japanese style: wafuu *no ie* (和風の家) a *Japanese-style* house. (↔ yoofuu)

wa˺ga わが (我が) *attrib.* my; our: waga-*sha* (わが社) *our* company / waga-*ya* (わが家) *our* house.

wa˺gamama˥ わがまま (我儘) *n.* selfishness; willfulness: wagamama *o toosu* (わがままを通す) *get one's way.* (⇨ katte²)
— *a.n.* (~ na, ni) selfish; willful; egoistic.

wa˺ga˺shi わがし (和菓子) *n.* Japanese confectionery. (↔ yoogashi)

wa˺gomu わゴム (輪ゴム) *n.* rubber band.

wa˺ishatsu ワイシャツ *n.* shirt; dress shirt. ★ Refers to a shirt with which a tie can be worn.

wa˺iwai わいわい *adv.* (~ to) noisily; boisterously: waiwai (*to*) *sawagu* (わいわい(と)騒ぐ) make *a lot of noise.*

wa˺ka わか (和歌) *n.* = tañka³.

wa˺ka˥·i わかい (若い) *a.* (-ku)
1 young; youthful.
2 immature; inexperienced; green:

Soñna koto o iu nañte kimi mo mada wakai. (そんなことを言うなんてきみもまだ若い) You are still *green* to say that sort of thing.

3 (of numbers) low.

wa⌐ka⌐me わかめ (若布) *n.* wakame seaweed. ★ Often served in miso soup.

wa⌐kamono わかもの (若者) *n.* young people; youth. (↔ roojiñ; toshiyori)

wa⌐kare⌐ わかれ (別れ) *n.* parting; separation; farewell:

Moo o-wakare shinakereba narimaseñ. (もうお別れしなければなりません) Now, I *have* to say good-bye. (⇨ wakareru²)

wa⌐kare⌐·ru¹ わかれる (分かれる) *vi.* (wakare-te Ⓥ) branch off; divide; fork; split. (⇨ wakeru)

wa⌐kare⌐·ru² わかれる (別れる) *vi.* (wakare-te Ⓥ) part; say good-bye; separate; divorce. (⇨ wakare)

wa⌐ka⌐r·u わかる (分かる・判る・解る) *vi.* (wakar·i-; wakar·a-; wakat-te Ⓒ) **1** understand:

Watashi no itte iru koto ga wakarimasu ka? (私の言っていることがわかりますか) *Do* you *understand* what I am saying? (⇨ rikai)

2 know:

Ashita no koto wa wakarimaseñ. (あしたのことはわかりません) *Nobody knows* what will happen tomorrow.

3 turn out; prove:

Kekkyoku kare wa mujitsu to wakatta. (結局彼は無実とわかった) He *turned out* to be innocent after all.

wa⌐kas·u わかす (沸かす) *vt.* (wakash·i-; wakas·a-; wakash·i-te Ⓒ) **1** boil; heat:

furo o wakasu (ふろを沸かす) *get* a bath *ready*. (⇨ waku²)

2 excite:

Kare no subarashii puree wa kañshuu o wakashita. (彼のすばらしいプレーは観衆を沸かした) His fine play

excited the spectators. (⇨ waku²)

wa⌐ke わけ (訳) *n.* **1** reason; cause; grounds:

Futari no rikoñ no wake o shiritai. (二人の離婚の訳を知りたい) I'd like to know the *reason* for their divorce.

2 case; circumstances:

Soo-iu wake nara, dekiru dake no koto wa shimasu. (そういう訳なら、できるだけのことはします) If that is the *case*, I will do what I can. (⇨ jijoo)

3 meaning:

Kono buñ wa nani o itte iru no ka wake ga wakaranai. (この文は何を言っているのか訳がわからない) I cannot make out the *meaning* of this sentence.

4 sense:

Shachoo wa wake no wakaru hito desu. (社長は訳のわかる人です) Our president is a *sensible* man.

wa⌐ke⌐·ru わける (分ける) *vt.* (wake-te Ⓥ) **1** divide; distribute; share:

rieki o miñna de wakeru (利益をみんなで分ける) *divide* the profits among everyone. (⇨ wakareru¹)

2 classify:

Zoosho o bumoñ-betsu ni waketa. (蔵書を部門別に分けた) I *classified* the book collection according to the different categories. (⇨ buñrui)

wa⌐ke wa nai わけはない (訳はない) (*polite*＝wake wa arimaseñ) **1** there is no reason for…; it cannot be…:

Kare ga soñna ni isogashii wake wa nai. (彼がそんなに忙しいわけはない) It *cannot be* that he is so busy.

2 easy; simple:

Jiteñsha ni noru no nañ ka wake wa nai. (自転車に乗るのなんかわけはない) It is *quite easy* to ride a bicycle.

wa⌐ki⌐ わき (脇) *n.* **1** under one's arm:

Kanojo wa waki *ni hoñ o kakaete*

ita.(彼女はわきに本を抱えていた) She was carrying some books *under her arm.*

2 side:

Chuushajoo wa sono mise no waki *ni arimasu.*(駐車場はその店のわきにあります) The parking lot is at the *side* of the shop.

wa'kibara わきばら (わき腹) *n.* one's side:

Kare wa watashi no wakibara *o tsutsuite chuui shita.*(彼は私のわき腹をついて注意した) He cautioned me by poking me in *the ribs.*

wa'kimi[1] わきみ (脇見) *n.* looking away; glancing aside:

wakimi-*uñteñ*(わき見運転) driving a car *without keeping one's eyes on the road.*

wakimi (o) **suru** (～(を)する) *vi.* look away.

wa'ki-no'l-shita わきのした (脇の下) *n.* armpit.

wa'ku[1] わく (枠) *n.* **1** frame:

mado no waku (窓の枠) a window *frame.*

2 limit:

waku *o koeru* (枠を越える) go beyond the *limit.*

wa'k·u[2] わく (沸く) *vi.* (wak·i-; wak·a-; wa·i-te C) **1** (of water) boil; be heated. (⇨ wakasu)

2 be excited. (⇨ wakasu)

wa'kuwaku わくわく *adv.*

wakuwaku suru (～する) get nervous; be exited; be thrilled.

wa'ñ[1] わん (椀) *n.* bowl. ★ Often 'o-wañ.' (⇨ moribachi)

wa'ñ[2] わん (湾) *n.* bay; gulf:

Tookyoo wañ (東京湾) Tokyo *Bay.*

wa'na わな (罠) *n.* trap; snare:

wana *ni kakaru* (わなにかかる) be caught in a *trap.*

wa'ni わに (鰐) *n.* crocodile; alligator.

wa'ñpi'isu ワンピース *n.* dress; female one-piece garment.

wa'ñwañ わんわん **1** bow-wow. **2** (young children's word) doggie.

wa'ra わら (藁) *n.* straw.

wa'rai わらい (笑い) *n.* laugh; laughter:

warai *o koraeru* (笑いをこらえる) suppress one's *laughter.* (⇨ warau)

wa'raigo'le わらいごえ (笑い声) *n.* laughing voice; laughter. (↔ nakigoe')

wa'ra·u わらう (笑う) *vi.* (wara·i-; waraw·a-; warat-te C) **1** laugh; grin; smile. (⇨ warai) **2** laugh at; ridicule; make fun of.

wa're-na'gara われながら (我ながら) *adv.* if I do say so myself:

Ware-nagara *yoku yatta to omoimasu.*(われながらよくやったと思います) I think I did rather well, *if I may say.*

wa're-ru われる (割れる) *vi.* (ware-te V) **1** break; smash:

Sara o otoshita ga warenakatta. (皿を落としたが割れなかった) I dropped the plate, but it *didn't break.* (⇨ kowareru; waru)

2 (of opinions, organization, group, etc.) be divided; split. (⇨ wakareru)

wa'reware われわれ (我々) *n.* (*formal*) = watashi-tachi. we. ★ 'wareware no'=our; 'wareware o'=us. Used mainly by men.

wa'ri わり (割) *n.* **1** rate; ratio:

sañsee to hañtai no wari (賛成と反対の割) the *ratio* of supporters and opponents. (⇨ wariai)

2 (unit of ratio) ten percent. (⇨ bu')

wari ni awanai (～に合わない) do not pay; be unprofitable. (⇨ au')

wa'riai わりあい (割合) *n.* rate; ratio; percentage. (⇨ wari)

— *adv.* (～ ni) comparatively; relatively:

Kyoo wa wariai (ni) *suzushii.*(きょうは割合(に)涼しい) It is *fairly* cool today.

wa'riate わりあて (割り当て) *n.* assignment; allotment; quota. (⇨ wariateru)

wa͞riate¹·ru わりあてる (割り当てる) *vt.* (-ate-te V̄) assign (a task); allot; allocate. (⇨ wariate)

wa͞riba¹shi わりばし (割り箸) *n.* disposable wooden chopsticks. (⇨ hashi²)

wa͞ribiki わりびき (割引) *n.* discount; reduction. (⇨ waribiku)

wa͞ribi¹k·u わりびく (割り引く) *vt.* (-bik·i·; bik·a·-; -bi·i·te C̄) discount; reduce. (⇨ waribiki) *Geñkiñ nara* waribikimasu. (現金なら割り引きます) We will *make a discount* if you pay in cash.
waribiite kiku (割り引いて聞く) don't take a person's story at face value.

wa͞rikañ わりかん (割り勘) *n.* each paying his [her] own way: *Kañjoo wa* warikañ *ni shimashoo.* (勘定は割り勘にしましょう) *Let's split* the bill.

wa͞riko¹m·u わりこむ (割り込む) *vi.* (-kom·i·; -kom·a·-; -koñ-de C̄) 1 squeeze oneself: *mañiñ deñsha ni* warikomu (満員電車に割り込む) *squeeze oneself into* a crowded train.
2 jump a line; cut in.
3 break into (a conversation).

wa͞ri ni わりに (割に) *adv.* 1 comparatively; rather; fairly: *Kare wa* wari ni *kimuzukashii.* (彼は割に気むずかしい) He is *rather* hard to please.
2 in proportion to; for: *Kare wa toshi no* wari ni *fukete mieru.* (彼は年の割に老けて見える) He looks old *for* his age.

wa͞ri¹zañ わりざん (割り算) *n.* (of arithmetic) division. (↔ kakezañ)

wa͞r·u わる (割る) *vt.* (war·i-; war·a·-; wat-te C̄) 1 break; smash: *tamago o* waru (卵を割る) *break* an egg. (⇨ wareru)
2 split; chop: *maki o* waru (まきを割る) *chop* logs.
3 divide: *Juu-ni* waru yoñ wa sañ desu. (12

割る 4 は 3 です) Twelve *divided by* four is three. (⇨ warizañ)
4 dilute: *uisukii o mizu de* waru (ウイスキーを水で割る) *dilute* the whisky with water. (⇨ mizuwari)

wa͞rugi¹ わるぎ (悪気) *n.* evil intention; ill will; malice. (⇨ akui)

wa͞ru¹·i わるい (悪い) *a.* (-ku) 1 bad; evil; wrong: *Uso o tsuku no wa* warui *koto desu.* (うそをつくのは悪いことです) It is *wrong* to tell a lie. (↔ yoi¹)
2 (of quality, weather, harvest) bad; poor; inferior. (↔ yoi¹)
3 (of a situation, state, etc.) bad; sick; ill-timed: *Kyoo wa buchoo no kigeñ ga* warui. (きょうは部長の機嫌が悪い) The general manager is in a *bad* mood today. (↔ yoi¹)
4 (of luck) bad; unlucky: *Kare wa uñ ga* warukatta *dake da.* (彼は運が悪かっただけだ) He was just *unlucky.* (↔ yoi¹)
5 troublesome; harmful: *Tabako wa keñkoo ni* warui. (たばこは健康に悪い) Cigarettes are bad for the health.

wa͞ru¹kuchi わるくち (悪口) *n.* slander; (verbal) abuse: *hito no* warukuchi *o iu* (人の悪口を言う) *speak ill of* others.

wa͞¹sai わさい (和裁) *n.* Japanese dressmaking; kimono making. (↔ yoosai)

wa͞¹shitsu わしつ (和室) *n.* Japanese-style room. (↔ yooshitsu)

wa͞¹sho わしょ (和書) *n.* book published in the Japanese language; Japanese book. (↔ yoosho)

wa͞¹shoku わしょく (和食) *n.* Japanese food. (↔ yooshoku²)

wa͞¹suremono わすれもの (忘れ物) *n.* something left behind: wasuremono-*toriatsukaijo* (忘れ物取り扱い所) a *lost-and-found* office. (⇨ okiwasureru; wasureru)

wa「sure・ru わすれる（忘れる）*vt.*
(wasure-te ⓥ) **1** forget:
*Yuube wa akari o kesu no o wa-
surete shimatta.* （ゆうべは明りを消す
のを忘れてしまった）I *forgot* to turn
out the lights last night.
2 leave behind:
*Deñsha no naka ni kasa o wasu-
rete shimatta.* （電車の中に傘を忘れて
しまった）I *have left* my umbrella
on the train. (⇨ wasuremono)

wa「ta」 わた（綿）*n.* cotton.

wa「takushi わたくし（私）*n.*
= watashi.

wa「takushi-do」mo わたくしども
（私共）*n.* (*humble*) we; our company [office; store]. ★ Used by
service personnel.

wa「takushi」ritsu わたくしりつ
（私立）*n.* = shiritsu¹.

wa「tar・u わたる（渡る）*vi.* (wata-
r・i-; watar・a-; watat-te ⓒ)
1 cross; go across; go over:
Kare wa dooro o hashitte watatta.
（彼は道路を走って渡った）He ran
across the street.
2 (of a bird) migrate; (of religion, custom, etc.) be introduced.

wa「tashi わたし（私）*n.* (*polite*=
watakushi) I: ★ 'watashi no' =
my; 'watashi o' = me. Words
indicating personal reference are
less commonly used in Japanese
than in English.
(*Watashi wa*) *kinoo Yamada-sañ
ni aimashita.* （（私は）きのう山田さん
に会いました）I met Mr. Yamada
yesterday.
The following are situations in
which the use of '*watashi*' is
natural:
1 (when contrasting oneself with
someone else):
Watashi ni mo misete kudasai.
（私にも見せてください）Please let *me*
have a look at it, too.
2 (when mentioning oneself for

the first time): ★ When the
topic is already about oneself,
'*watashi*' is normally not used.
Watashi wa Suzuki to iimasu. （私
は鈴木と言います。）*My name* is
Suzuki.

wa「tashibu」ne わたしぶね（渡し
船）*n.* ferry. ★ A small boat
used to carry passengers across a
river. (⇨ fune)

wa「tashi」-tachi わたしたち（私達）
n. we. ★ 'watashi-tachi no'=
our; 'watashi-tachi o' = us.
(⇨ wareware)

wa「tas・u わたす（渡す）*vt.* (wata-
sh・i-; watas・a-; watash・i-te ⓒ)
1 give; hand over:
*Kono tegami o kanojo ni wata-
shite kudasai.* （この手紙を彼女に渡し
てください）Please *give* her this letter.
2 lay (a board); stretch (a rope,
bridge, etc., between).

wa「za-to わざと（態と）*adv.* on
purpose; intentionally; deliber-
ately. (⇨ koi³)

waza-to-rashii （〜らしい）put-on;
unnatural.

wa「zawaza わざわざ（態々）*adv.*
specially; expressly:
*O-isogashii tokoro o wazawaza
oide itadaki, arigatoo gozaimasu.*
（お忙しいところをわざわざお出でいただき、
ありがとうございます）Thank you very
much for *taking the trouble* to
come here when you are so busy.

wa「zuka わずか（僅か）*a.n.* (〜 na,
ni) few; little; slight:
*Hoñno wazuka na hito ga sono kai
ni shusseki shita.* （ほんのわずかな人が
その会に出席した）Only *a few* people attended the party.
— *adv.* only:
*Kyooto ni wa wazuka mikka ita
dake deshita.* （京都にはわずか三日い
ただけでした）I was in Kyoto for
only three days. (⇨ hoñno)

Y

ya¹ や *p.* and: ★ Used to link nouns which are representative of their class.
Sono o-kane de hoñ ya jisho o kaimashita. (そのお金で本や辞書を買いました) I bought books, dictionaries, *and the like*, with that money. (⇨ dano; to²; to ka; yara)

ya² や *p.* as soon as: ★ Follows the dictionary form of a verb. Also '*ya ina ya.*' (⤷ Ina)
Kare wa uchi ni kaeru ya (ina ya) kabañ o oite, mata tobidashite itta. (彼は家に帰るや(いなや)かばんを置いて, また飛び出して行った) *No sooner* had he come home *than* he put down his bag and rushed out again. (⇨ sugu)

ya¹³ や (矢) *n.* arrow: *ya o iru* (矢を射る) shoot an *arrow.* (↔ yumi)

ya' やっ *int.* 1 aha: ★ An exclamation of satisfaction or surprise.
Ya', mitsuketa. (やっ, 見つけた) *Aha!* I have found it.
2 hi; ya:
Ya', hisashiburi da ne. (やっ, 久しぶりだね) *Hi!* It has been a long time, hasn't it?

-ya や (屋) *suf.* store; shop; person: *yao-ya* (八百屋) a *greengrocery* / *sakana-ya* (魚屋) a fish *shop*.

ya¹**a** やあ *int.* (*informal*) hi; hello.

ya「bañ やばん (野蛮) *a.n.* (~ na, ni) savage; barbarous:
yabañ na kooi (野蛮な行為) a *barbarous* act.

ya「bure¹**-ru**¹ やぶれる (破れる) *vi.* (yabure-te ⓥ) 1 tear; be torn; rip; be ripped:
Kono kami wa sugu yabureru. (この紙はすぐ破れる) This paper *tears* easily. (⇨ yaburu¹)
2 (of relationship, balance, etc.) break down; come to nothing:

Kanojo no kekkoñ seekatsu wa sañ-neñ de yabureta. (彼女の結婚生活は3年で破れた) Her married life *came to an end* after three years. (⇨ yaburu¹)

ya「bure¹**-ru**² やぶれる (敗れる・破れる) *vi.* (yabure-te ⓥ) (of a competitor) lose; be beaten. (⇨ yaburu²)

ya「bu「r・u¹ やぶる (破る) *vt.* (yabur・i-; yabur・a-; yabut-te ⓒ) 1 tear; rip; break:
Kare wa sono tegami o yabutte suteta. (彼はその手紙を破って捨てた) He *ripped up* the letter and threw it away. (⇨ yabureru¹)
2 break (a promise, agreement, record, etc.).

ya「bu「r・u² やぶる (敗る・破る) *vt.* (yabur・i-; yabur・a-; yabut-te ⓒ) beat; defeat. (⇨ yabureru²)

ya「chiñ やちん (家賃) *n.* (of an apartment, house, etc.) rent.

ya「do やど (宿) *n.* 1 inn; hotel. (⇨ ryokañ; yadoya)
2 lodging:
Watashi wa kare ni hito-bañ yado o kashite yatta. (私は彼に一晩宿を貸してやった) I gave him a night's *lodging*.

ya「doya やどや (宿屋) *n.* Japanese-style hotel; Japanese inn. (⇨ ryokañ; yado)

ya「gate やがて *adv.* by and by; before long; in the course of time.

ya「gu やぐ (夜具) *n.* bedding; bedclothes.

ya「ha「ri やはり *adv.* (*intensive* = yappari) 1 as expected:
Yahari anata ga yosoo shita toori ni narimashita. (やはりあなたが予想したとおりになりました) Things turned out *just as you had expected*.
2 still; nonetheless; after all:
Kare wa Ima mo yahari Kama-

kura ni suñde imasu. (彼は今もやはり鎌倉に住んでいます) He *still* lives in Kamakura.

3 too; also: ★ In the pattern '... *mo yahari.*'

Kare no musuko mo yahari *señsee desu.* (彼の息子もやはり先生です) His son is *also* a teacher.

ya￹i やい *int.* (*rude*) hey.

ya￹ji やじ (野次) *n.* jeering; hoot. (⇨ yajiru)

ya￹ji・r・u やじる (野次る) *vt.* (yajir-i-; yajir-a-; yajit-te Ⓒ) jeer; hoot; jeer; hoot; boo. (⇨ yaji)

ya￹ji￹rushi やじるし (矢印) *n.* arrow sign.

ya￹jiuma やじうま (野次馬) *n.* curious onlooker; rubberneck: yajiuma-koñjoo (やじ馬根性) *curiosity.* (⇨ kookishiñ)

ya￹kamashi￹・i やかましい (喧しい) *a.* (-ku) 1 noisy; loud. (↔ shizuka) (⇨ urusai)

2 (of a rule, regulation, etc.) strict.

3 (of a person) particular: *tabemono ni* yakamashii (食べ物にやかましい) be *particular* about food. (⇨ urusai)

ya￹kañ¹ やかん (夜間) *n.* night; nighttime. (↔ hiruma; nitchuu)

ya￹kañ² やかん (薬缶) *n.* teakettle; kettle.

ya￹kedo やけど (火傷) *n.* burn; scald.

yakedo suru (〜する) *vi.* get burned; get scalded.

ya￹ke・ru やける (焼ける) *vi.* (yakete Ⓥ) 1 burn; be burned: *Sono mise wa sakuya no kaji de yaketa.* (その店は昨夜の火事で焼けた) That shop *burned down* in last night's fire. (⇨ yaku¹)

2 be broiled; be grilled; be roasted; be baked; be toasted. (⇨ yaku¹)

3 be tanned; get sunburned. (⇨ yaku¹)

4 be discolored: *Kono kiji wa iro ga* yake-yasui. (こ

の生地は色が焼けやすい) This cloth *quickly becomes discolored.*

ya￹kimashi やきまし (焼き増し) *n.* additional print of a photo.

yakimashi suru (〜する) *vt.* make an additional print [copy].

ya￹kimo￹chi やきもち (焼き餅) *n.* toasted rice cake. (⇨ mochi)

yakimochi o yaku (〜を焼く) get jealous. (⇨ shitto)

ya￹kitori やきとり (焼き鳥) *n.* chunks of chicken barbecued on a bamboo skewer: yakitori-ya (焼き鳥屋) a *yakitori restaurant.*

ya￹kkai やっかい (厄介) *n.* burden; trouble: *hoka no hito ni* yakkai *o kakeru* (ほかの人にやっかいをかける) cause other people a lot of *trouble.*

— *a.n.* (〜 na, ni) troublesome; burdensome.

yakkai ni naru (やっかいになる) depend on; stay.

ya￹kki やっき (躍起) *a.n.* (〜 ni) eager; excited; heated; vehement: *Kare wa* yakki ni natte, *sono uwasa o hitee shita.* (彼は躍起になって、そのうわさを否定した) He *vehemently* denied the rumor.

ya￹kkyoku やっきょく (薬局) *n.* pharmacy; drugstore.

ya￹ku・u¹ やく (焼く) *vt.* (yak-i-; yak-a-; ya-i-te Ⓒ) 1 burn: *kimitsu-shorui o* yaku (機密書類を焼く) *burn* classified documents.

2 tan; get a tan. (⇨ yakeru)

3 broil; grill; roast; bake; toast; barbecue. (⇨ yakeru)

ya￹ku￹¹² やく (役) *n.* 1 role; part. (⇨ yakuwari)

2 position; post: *buchoo no* yaku (部長の役) the *post* of manager.

yaku ni tatsu (〜に立つ) be useful; be helpful. (⇨ yakudatsu)

ya￹ku³ やく (約) *adv.* about; some; nearly. (⇨ oyoso)

ya￹ku￹⁴ やく (訳) *n.* translation. (⇨ hoñyaku; tsuuyaku; yakusu)

-yaku やく (薬) *suf.* medicine;
drug; pill:
suimiñ-yaku (睡眠薬) a sleeping
pill / *doku-yaku* (毒薬) *poison.*

ya「kuda1ts・u やくだつ (役立つ) *vi.*
(-dach・i-; -dat・a-; -dat・te C) be
of use; be useful; be helpful.

ya「kugo やくご (訳語) *n.* word;
term; equivalent translation.

ya「kuhiñ やくひん (薬品) *n.* medicine; drug; chemical. (⇨ kusuri)

ya「kume1 やくめ (役目) *n.* duty;
role. (⇨ yaku²; yakuwari)

ya「kuniñ やくにん (役人) *n.* government official; public servant.

ya「kusha やくしゃ (役者) *n.* actor;
nctress. (⇨ haiyuu)

ya「kusho1 やくしょ (役所) *n.* government office:
shi-yakusho (市役所) a city *hall* /
ku-yakusho (区役所) a ward *office.*

ya「kusoku やくそく (約束) *n.*
promise; engagement; appointment.
yakusoku ga chigau (〜が違う)
differ from what was promised.
yakusoku suru (〜する) *vt.* promise; make an appointment.

ya「ku1s・u やくす (訳す) *vt.* (yakus-
sh・i-; yakus・a-; yakush・i-te C)
translate; put...into.... (⇨ yaku⁴)

ya「kuwari1 やくわり (役割) *n.*
part; role: *juuyoo na yakuwari o
hatasu* (重要な役割を果たす) play an
important *role.* (⇨ yaku²)

ya「kyuu やきゅう (野球) *n.* baseball.

ya「ma1 やま (山) *n.* **1** mountain;
hill. ★ A hill with a gentle slope
and lower than '*yama*' is called
'*oka.*' (⇨ oka)
2 heap; pile:
gomi no yama (ごみの山) a trash
heap / *hoñ no yama* (本の山) a *pile*
of books.
3 climax; juncture:
Sono jikeñ wa yama o mukaeta.
(その事件は山を迎えた) The affair
has reached a critical *juncture.*
4 guess:

Yama ga atatta [hazureta]. (やまが
当たった[はずれた]) My *guess* hit
[missed] the mark.

-yama やま (山) *suf.* Mount; Mt.:
Mihara-yama (三原山) *Mount*
Mihara. (⇨ -sañ²)

ya「maimo やまいも (山芋) *n.* yam.

ya「maku1zure やまくずれ (山崩れ)
n. landslide.

ya「manote やまのて (山の手)
1 the hilly section of a city.
2 the residential section of a
city; uptown. (↔ shitamachi)

ya「mawake1 やまわけ (山分け) *n.*
equal division; going halves.
(⇨ buñpai)
yamawake (ni) suru (〜(に)する)
vt. divide equally; go shares.

ya「me・ru1 やめる (止める) *vt.* (ya-
me-te V) **1** stop; discontinue.
(⇨ yamu¹; yosu)
2 give up; abandon:
tabako o yameru (たばこをやめる)
give up smoking. (⇨ akirameru)

ya「me・ru2 やめる (辞める) *vt.* (ya-
me-te V) resign (one's post);
quit.

ya「mi1 やみ (闇) *n.* **1** darkness.
2 black-marketing; illegal trade.

ya「m・u1 やむ (止む) *vi.* (yam・i-;
yam・a-; yañ-de C) (of rain)
stop; (of wind) die down.
(⇨ yameru)

ya「m・u2 やむ (病む) *vt., vi.* (ya-
m・i-; yam・a-; yañ-de C) be
taken sick; suffer from:
zeñsoku o yamu (ぜんそくを病む) *suffer from* asthma. (⇨ byooki)

ya「mu1naku やむなく *adv.* =
yamu o ezu.

ya「mu o e1nai やむをえない (やむを
得ない) unavoidable; inevitable.

ya「mu o e1zu やむをえず (やむを得
ず) *adv.* reluctantly; unwillingly.

ya「ne やね (屋根) *n.* roof.

ya「nushi やぬし (家主) *n.* landlord; landlady.

ya「oya やおや (八百屋) *n.* vegetable store; greengrocery; green-
grocer.

ya⌐ppa⌐ri やっぱり *adv.* (*intensive*) = yahari.

yara やら *p.* what with...:
★ Used in the pattern '... yara ... yara' to link nouns or verbs.
Beñkyoo yara, arubaito yara de, isogashii. (勉強やら、アルバイトやらで、忙しい) *What with* my studies *and* my part-time job, I am busy. (⇨ ya¹)

ya⌐reyare やれやれ *int.* well:
★ Used to express a sigh of relief.
Yareyare, yatto shigoto ga owatta. (やれやれ、やっと仕事が終わった) *Well, well*, the job is at last finished. (⇨ hotto)

ya⌐rikata やりかた (やり方) *n.* way; method:
Sono yarikata o oshiete kudasai. (そのやり方を教えてください) Please show me *how to do it.* (⇨ hoo¹; hoohoo)

ya⌐rikome·ru やりこめる (遣り込める) *vt.* (-kome-te C) argue a person down; talk down.

ya⌐rinaoshi やりなおし (やり直し) *n.* redoing; doing over again. (⇨ yarinaosu)

ya⌐rinao⌐s·u やりなおす (やり直す) *vt.* (-naosh·i-; -naos·a-; -naosh·i-te C) do over again; make a fresh start. (⇨ yarinaoshi)

ya⌐ri⌐tori やりとり (やり取り) *n.* exchange; giving and taking:
okurimono no yaritori (贈り物のやり取り) an *exchange* of presents.

ya⌐r·u¹ やる (遣る) *vt.* (yar·i-; yar·a-; yat-te C) 1 do; play:
★ More informal than 'suru.'
tenisu o yaru (テニスをやる) *play* tennis.
2 keep; run:
Chichi wa hoñya o yatte imasu. (父は本屋をやっています) My father *runs* a bookstore.
3 eat; drink; have; smoke:
Kare wa tabako wa yaranai ga, sake wa yaru. (彼はたばこはやらないが、酒はやる) He *does not* smoke, but *drinks.*

ya⌐r·u² やる (遣る) *vt.* (yar·i-; yar·a-; yat-te C) 1 give: ★ Never used toward one's superiors.
kodomo ni o-kashi o yaru (子どもにお菓子をやる) *give* candy to a child / hana ni mizu o yaru (花に水をやる) *water* the flowers. (⇨ ageru¹)
2 send (a letter).

ya⌐sai やさい (野菜) *n.* vegetable; greens.

ya⌐sashi·i¹ やさしい (易しい) *a.* (-ku) easy; simple; plain.

ya⌐sashi·i² やさしい (優しい) *a.* (-ku) gentle; tender; kind:
kimochi no yasashii hito (気持ちの優しい人) a *kindhearted* person.

ya⌐se·ru やせる (痩せる) *vi.* (yase-te V) lose weight; become thin.

ya⌐shiki やしき (屋敷) *n.* mansion; residence; premises.

ya⌐shiñ やしん (野心) *n.* ambition: yashiñ-ka (野心家) an *ambitious* person.

ya⌐shina·u やしなう (養う) *vt.* (yashina·i-; yashinaw·a-; yashinat-te C) 1 support; sustain; feed:
ikka o yashinau (一家を養う) *support* one's family.
2 cultivate; develop; build up:
jitsuryoku o yashinau (実力を養う) *cultivate* one's proficiency.

ya⌐su⌐·i やすい (安い) *a.* (-ku) cheap; low; inexpensive; reasonable. (↔ kooka²; takai)

-yasu⌐·i やすい (易い) *suf.* (a.) (-ku) easy; apt: ★ Added to the continuative base of a verb.
Kare no buñshoo wa yomi-yasui. (彼の文章は読みやすい) His prose is *easy* to read. (↔ -gatai; -nikui; -zurai)

ya⌐sume⌐·ru やすめる (休める) *vt.* (yasume-te V) rest; relax:
karada o yasumeru (体を休める) *rest* one's body. (⇨ yasumu)

ya⌐sumi やすみ (休み) *n.* 1 rest; break; respite:
hito-yasumi suru (ひと休みする) take a *rest.* (⇨ yasumu)

2 absence:
Kare wa kyoo wa yasumi *desu.*
(彼はきょうは休みです) He *is off* today.
(⇨ yasumu)

3 being closed:
Kono depaato wa suiyoobi ga yasumi *desu.* (このデパートは水曜日が休
みです) This department store *is
closed* on Wednesdays. (⇨ yasumu)

4 holiday; vacation. (⇨ kyuuka)

ya⌐sumono やすもの (安物) *n.*
cheap article.

ya⌐su⌐m·u やすむ (休む) *vi.* (ya-
sum·i-; yasum·a-; yasuñ-de C)
1 take a rest; relax. (⇨ yasumeru; yasumi)
2 be absent; stay away; take a
holiday. (⇨ yasumi)
3 go to bed; sleep. (⇨ neru¹; oya-
sumi nasai)

ya⌐suppo¹·i やすっぽい (安っぽい) *a.*
(-ku) cheap; tawdry:
yasuppoi *kabañ* (安っぽいかばん) a
cheap-looking bag.

ya⌐tara ni やたらに (矢鱈に) *adv.*
freely; haphazardly; thought-
lessly; at random.

ya⌐too やとう (野党) *n.* the opposition party; the opposition.
(↔ yotoo)

ya⌐to¹·u やとう (雇う) *vt.* (yato·i-;
yatow·a-; yatot-te C) employ
(a person); hire.

ya⌐tsu やつ (奴) *n.* (sometimes
derog.) fellow; guy; chap.

ya⌐tte k·u¹ru やってくる (やって来る)
vi. (k·i-; k·o-; k·i-te ⫢) **1** come
along; appear; turn up. (⇨ kuru)
2 continue to do:
Moo juu-neñ kono shigoto o yatte
kimashita. (もう10年この仕事をやって
来ました) I *have* already *been doing*
this job for ten years.

ya⌐tto やっと *adv.* **1** at last; at
length; finally.
2 just; barely:
yatto *maniau* (やっと間に合う) be
barely in time. (⇨ yooyaku)

ya⌐ttsu¹ やっつ (八つ) *n.* eight.

★ Used when counting.
(⇨ hachi¹; APP. 3)

ya⌐ttsuke¹·ru やっつける *vt.* (yat-
tsuke-te Ⅴ) beat; criticize.

ya⌐wara¹ka やわらか (柔らか) *a.n.*
(~ na, ni) **1** soft; tender:
yawaraka *na kusshoñ* (柔らかなクッ
ション) a *soft* cushion. (↔ katai)
2 gentle; mild:
yawaraka *na hizashi* (柔らかな日ざ
し) *mild* sunshine.
3 flexible; supple:
yawaraka *na karada* (柔らかな体) a
supple body. (⇨ yawarakai)

ya⌐waraka¹·i やわらかい (柔かい・軟
かい) *a.* (-ku) **1** soft; tender:
yawarakai *niku* (柔らかい肉) *tender*
meat. (↔ katai)
2 gentle; mild: yawarakai *koe*
(柔らかい声) a *gentle* voice.
3 (of a way of thinking, etc.)
flexible; supple. (↔ katai)
(⇨ yawaraka)

ya⌐ya やや (稍) *adv.* a little;
somewhat:
Keeki wa yaya *yoku natte imasu.*
(景気はややよくなっています) Business
conditions are improving *slightly*.
(⇨ sukoshi)

ya⌐yakoshi¹·i ややこしい *a.* (-ku)
(*colloq.*) complicated; intricate;
complex.

yo¹¹ よ (世) *n.* **1** world:
kono [*ano*] yo (この[あの]世) this
[the other] *world.*
2 times; age.
yo ni deru (~に出る) make one's
debut.
yo o saru (~を去る) pass away.
(⇨ shinu)

yo¹² よ (夜) *n.* night. (⇨ yoru¹)

yo³ よ *p.* **1** (used when emphasizing one's thoughts, feeling or
opinions, or when reminding
someone of something):
Hayaku shinai to okuremasu yo.
(早くしないと遅れますよ) *Look*, you
will be late unless you hurry up.
2 (used to indicate an invitation
or order):

Issho ni ikimashoo yo.（いっしょに行きましょうよ）*Come on, let's go together.*

3 (used to indicate disapproval of someone's thoughts or actions):
Soko de nani o shite iru ñ da yo. (*by men*)（そこで何をしているんだよ）What are you up to there?

4 (*formal*) (used as a form of address):
Waga ko yo.（我が子よ）Oh, my child! / *Kami* yo.（神よ）Oh, God!

-yo よ（余）*suf.* over; more than:
nijuu-yo-neñ（20余年）*more than twenty years.*

yo˺ake˺ よあけ（夜明け）*n.* dawn; daybreak.

yo˺bi よび（予備）*n.* spare; extra:
yobi *no taiya* [*kagi*]（予備のタイヤ[鍵]）a spare tire [key]. (⇨ yooi˺)

yo˺bidashi よびだし（呼び出し）*n.*
1 summons:
yobidashi *o ukeru*（呼び出しを受ける）get a *summons.* (⇨ yobidasu)
2 paging. ★ Usually '*o-yobidashi.*' (⇨ yobidasu)
3 (of sumo wrestling) match announcer.

yo˺bida˺s·u よびだす（呼び出す）*vt.* (-dash·i-; -das·a-; -dash·i-te Ⓒ)
1 call; page. (⇨ yobidashi)
2 call [ring] up:
Taroo o deñwa-guchi ni yobidashite *kudasai.*（太郎を電話口に呼び出してください）Please *call* Taro to the phone. (⇨ yobidashi)
3 summon:
Kare wa saibañsho ni yobidasareta.（彼は裁判所に呼び出された）He *was summoned* to court. (⇨ yobidashi)

yo˺bikake よびかけ（呼び掛け）*n.* appeal; plea:
kaku-jikkeñ hañtai no yobikake（核実験反対の呼びかけ）an *appeal* against a nuclear test. (⇨ yobikakeru)

yo˺bikake˺·ru よびかける（呼び掛ける）*vt.* (-kake-te Ⓥ) **1** call (out);

address (a person).
2 appeal to (the public). (⇨ yobikake)

yo˺bikoo よびこう（予備校）*n.* cramming school. ★ A school for students who need extra help to pass the university entrance exam.

yo˺bisute よびすて（呼び捨て）*n.* calling a person's name without any title of courtesy.

yo˺boo よぼう（予防）*n.* prevention; precaution; protection.
yoboo *suru*（〜する）*vt.* prevent; protect: *mushiba o* yoboo suru（虫歯を予防する）*prevent* tooth decay.

yo˺boo-chu˺usha よぼうちゅうしゃ（予防注射）*n.* preventive shot [injection].

yo˺b·u よぶ（呼ぶ）*vt.* (yob·i-; yob·a-; yoñ-de Ⓒ) **1** call; call [cry] out: *takushii o* yobu（タクシーを呼ぶ）*call* a taxi.
2 invite:
Paatii ni wa kare o yobitai.（パーティーには彼を呼びたい）I *would like to invite* him to the party.
3 give a name; call.

yo˺buñ よぶん（余分）*a.n.* (〜 na, ni) extra; spare; additional. (⇨ yokee)

yo˺chi よち（余地）*n.* room (for improvement); space.

yo˺fu˺kashi よふかし（夜更かし）*n.* staying up late at night.
yofukashi *suru*（〜する）*vi.* stay up late at night; keep late hours. (↔ asa-neboo)

yo˺fuke˺ よふけ（夜更け）*n.* late hours of the night; midnight. (⇨ yonaka)

yo˺gore よごれ（汚れ）*n.* dirt; stain; soil. (⇨ yogoreru; yogosu)

yo˺gore·ru よごれる（汚れる）*vi.* (yogore-te Ⓥ) become dirty; be soiled; be stained; be polluted. (⇨ yogosu; yogore)

yo˺gos·u よごす（汚す）*vt.* (yogosh·i-; yogos·a-; yogosh·i-te Ⓒ)

make dirty; soil; stain; pollute. (⇨ yogoreru)

yo｢hodo よほど（余程）*adv.*
1 very; much; greatly:
Kare wa yohodo *noñda rashii.*（彼はよほど飲んだらしい）He seemed to have drunk *a lot*.
2 nearly; almost:
Yohodo *tsutome o yameyoo ka to omoimashita.*（よほど勤めを辞めようかと思いました）I *almost* decided to quit my job.

yo｢hoo よほう（予報）*n.* forecast:
teñki yohoo（天気予報）a weather *forecast*.
yohoo suru（～する）*vt.* forecast

yo｣i¹ よい（良い・善い）*a.* (-ku)
good; fine; excellent:
★ More formal than '*ii*.'
yoi *kañgae*（良い考え）a *good* idea / yoi *shirase*（良い知らせ）*good* news / yoi *teñki*（良い天気）*fine* weather. (↔ warui) (⇨ ryookoo)
... hoo ga yoi（...ほうが～）= hoo ga ii.
-te mo yoi（ても～）can; may:
Kono arubamu o mite mo yoi desu ka?（このアルバムを見てもよいですか）*Can* I *have a look* at this photo album?

yo｣i² よい（酔い）*n.* drunkenness; intoxication: yoi ga sameru（酔いがさめる）*sober up*. (⇨ you)

yo｣isho よいしょ *int.* heave ho; here we go.

yo｣jinobor･u よじのぼる（よじ登る）*vi.* (-nobor･i-; -nobor･a-; -nobot-te C) climb (up); clamber (up). (⇨ noboru')

yo｣ka よか（余暇）*n.* leisure; free [spare] time. (⇨ hima)

yo｣kee よけい（余計）*a.n.* (～ na) unnecessary; needless:
Yokee *na o-sewa desu.*（よけいなお世話です）It's *none* of your business.
— *adv.* (～ ni) (the) more; extra; too many [much]. (⇨ yobuñ)

yo｣ke｣･ru よける（避ける）*vt.* (yo-ke-te V) avoid; dodge:
kaze o yokeru（風をよける）*avoid*

the wind / *ame o* yokeru（雨をよける）*seek shelter* from the rain.

yo｣ki よき（予期）*n.* anticipation; expectation. (⇨ yosoo)
yoki suru（～する）*vt.* expect; anticipate.

yo｣kiñ よきん（預金）*n.* deposit; money on deposit; savings.
★ A deposit in a bank is generally called '*yokiñ*,' and savings put in the post office are called '*chokiñ*.'
yokiñ suru（～する）*vi., vt.* make a deposit.

yo｣kka よっか（四日）*n.* four days; the fourth day of the month. (⇨ APP. 5)

yo｣ko よこ（横）*n.* **1** width.
★ The horizontal distance from side to side. (↔ tate) (⇨ haba)
2 side:
Kanojo wa watashi no yoko *ni suwatta.*（彼女は私の横に座った）She sat at my *side*.
3 (～ ni) sideways; crossways:
Kani wa yoko *ni aruku.*（かには横に歩く）Crabs walk *sideways*.

yo｣kogaki よこがき（横書き）*n.* horizontal writing. (↔ tategaki)

yo｣kogao よこがお（横顔）*n.* (of a face) profile.

yo｣kogi｣r･u よぎる（横切る）*vt.* (-gir･i-; -gir･a-; -git-te C) cross; go across: *dooro o* yokogiru（道路を横切る）*cross* a road.

yo｣ko｣s･u よこす（寄越す）*vt.* (yo-kosh･i-; yokos･a-; yokosh･i-te C) **1** send; hand over: ★ The recipient is the speaker.
Musuko wa metta ni tegami o yokosanai.*（息子はめったに手紙をよこさない）My son *rarely sends* me letters.
2 make a person come to the speaker or writer:
O-ko-sañ o itsu de mo uchi e asobi ni yokoshite *kudasai.*（お子さんをいつでもうちへ遊びによこしてください）Please *send* your child to play at our house anytime.

yo⌐ku[1] よく (欲) *n.* greed; ava-
rice; desire:
Kare wa yoku *ga fukai.*(彼は欲が深
い) He *is greedy.*

yo⌐ku[2] よく (良く) *adv.* **1** well;
fully; thoroughly:
Ossharu koto wa yoku *wakarimashita.*(おっしゃることはよくわかりました)
I understand *perfectly* what you
say.
2 kindly; favorably:
Kare wa itsu-mo watashi ni yoku
shite kuremasu.(彼はいつも私によくし
てくれます) He always treats me
kindly.
3 (used to express wonder, or
disapproval):
Yoku *kega o shimaseñ deshita ne.*
(よくけがをしませんでしたね) It's *a miracle* that you were not injured, isn't
it?

yo⌐ku[3] よく *adv.* frequently; often: *Kare wa* yoku *kaze o hiku.*
(彼はよくかぜをひく) He *often* catches
colds.

yo⌐ku- よく (翌) *pref.* next; following:
yoku-*go-gatsu tooka* (翌 5 月 10 日)
the *following* day, that is, May 10.

-yoku よく (欲) *suf.* desire; lust:
*chishiki-*yoku (知識欲) *thirst for
knowledge* / *kiñseñ-*yoku (金銭欲)
desire for money.

yo⌐kuasa よくあさ (翌朝) *n.* the
next [following] morning.
(↔ kesa) (⇒ yokuchoo)

yo⌐kubari[1] よくばり (欲張り) *a.n.*
(~ na, ni) greedy; avaricious:
yokubari *na hito* (欲張りな人) an
avaricious person. (↔ muyoku)
(⇒ yokubaru)

yo⌐kuba⌐r·u よくばる (欲張る) *vi.*
(-bar·i-; -bar·a-; -bat-te ⓒ) be
greedy; be avaricious. (⇒ yokubari)

yo⌐kuboo よくぼう (欲望) *n.* desire; appetite; craving:
yokuboo *o mitasu [osaeru]* (欲望を
満たす[抑える]) satisfy [overcome]
one's *cravings.*

yo⌐kuchoo よくちょう (翌朝) *n.*
(*formal*) the next [following]
morning. (⇒ yokuasa)

yo⌐kugetsu よくげつ (翌月) *n.*
the next [following] month.
(↔ koñgetsu; raigetsu; señgetsu)

yo⌐kujitsu よくじつ (翌日) *n.* the
next [following] day. (↔ zeñjitsu)

yo⌐kuneñ よくねん (翌年) *n.* the
next [following] year. (↔ kotoshi; kyoneñ)

yo⌐kushitsu よくしつ (浴室) *n.*
bathroom; bath. ★ In Japanese
houses, the bath and toilet are in
separate rooms.

yo⌐kushuu よくしゅう (翌週) *n.*
the next [following] week.
(⇒ raishuu)

yo⌐me よめ (嫁) *n.* **1** bride:
yome *ni iku* (嫁に行く) *marry into
a family.* (↔ muko) (⇒ o-yome-
sañ)
2 daughter-in-law. (↔ muko)

yo⌐mi[1] よみ (読み) *n.* **1** reading.
(⇒ yomu)
2 judgment; calculation; insight:
Kare wa yomi *ga fukai [asai].*(彼
は読みが深い[浅い]) He is a man of
deep [shallow] *insight.* (⇒ yomu)

yo⌐miga⌐er·u よみがえる (蘇る) *vi.*
(-gaer·i-; -gaer·a-; -gaet-te ⓒ)
come back to life; come to oneself; (of memory, impression, etc.)
revive; be refreshed.

yo⌐mi-kaki よみかき (読み書き) *n.*
reading and writing.

yo⌐mikata よみかた (読み方) *n.*
reading; pronunciation; interpretation.

yo⌐m·u よむ (読む) *vt.* (yom·i-;
yom·a-; yoñ-de ⓒ) **1** read:
hoñ o yomu (本を読む) *read a book*
/ *koe o dashite* yomu (声を出して読
む) *read aloud.*
2 read (a person's intention,
mind, etc.); fathom. (⇒ yomi)

yo⌐ñ よん (四) *n.* four. (⇒ shi[4]; yottsu; APP. 3)

yo⌐naka[1] よなか (夜中) *n.* midnight; the middle of the night.

yo-「no」-naka よのなか（世の中）*n.* the world; times; society: *Kare wa yo-no-naka no koto o yoku shitte iru.* (彼は世の中のことをよく知っている) He has seen much of *the world.* (⇨ yo')

yo「o」¹ よう（用）*n.* something to do; business: *Konban wa yoo ga arimasu.* (今晩は用があります) I have *something to do* this evening. (⇨ yooji')

yoo ga nai (～がない) be no longer useful.

yoo o tasu (～を足す) do one's business; *(euphemism)* go to the toilet.

yoo² よう（様）*a.n.* (～ na, ni)
1 seem; look: ★ Used to indicate a judgment based on sight, sound, or smell. *Kare wa sono koto o zeñzeñ oboete inai yoo da.* (彼はそのことを全然覚えていないようだ) He *does not seem* to remember that at all.
2 like; similar to; of the kind: *Watashi mo kare no yoo na kashu ni naritai.* (私も彼のような歌手になりたい) I wish to be a singer *like* him.
3 to the effect that: *Yamada-sañ ga kaisha o yameru yoo na hanashi o kikimashita.* (山田さんが会社を辞めるような話を聞きました) I heard something *to the effect* that Miss Yamada was leaving the company.
4 such; sort: ★ Usually in a negative expression, often with '*kesshite.*' *Watashi wa kesshite uso o tsuku yoo na niñgeñ de wa arimaseñ.* (私は決してうそをつくような人間ではありません) I am certainly not the *sort* of person who tells lies.

yoo ni (～に) 1 as; like: *Watashi wa itsu-mo no yoo ni roku-ji ni okita.* (私はいつものように6時に起きた) I got up at six *as* usual.
2 so that; so as to: *Miñna ni kikoeru yoo ni ooki-na koe de hana-*

shite kudasai. (みんなに聞こえるように大きな声で話してください) Please speak in a loud voice *so that* everyone can hear you.

yoo ni iu [tanomu] (～に言う[頼む]) tell [ask]: *Kodomo ni rusubañ suru yoo ni itta.* (子どもに留守番するように言った) I *told* the child to look after the house during my absence.

yoo ni naru (～になる) reach the point where: *Nihoñgo ga hanaseru yoo ni narimashita.* (日本語が話せるようになりました) I *have reached the stage* at which I can speak Japanese.

yoo ni shite iru (～にしている) make it a rule to: *Shokuji no ato wa ha o migaku yoo ni shite imasu.* (食事の後は歯を磨くようにしています) I *make it a rule* to brush my teeth after meals.

-yoo よう *infl. end.* [attached to the continuative base of a vowel-stem verb. Irregular verbs are '*shiyoo*' (*suru*) and '*koyoo*' (*kuru*)] (⇨ -oo)
1 intend; want: *Ashita wa hayaku okiyoo.* (あしたは早く起きよう) I *will get up* early tomorrow.
2 let's: *Issho-ni terebi o miyoo.* (一緒にテレビを見よう) *Let's watch* TV together.

-(y)oo to suru ((よう)～とする) be about to; try: *Uchi o deyoo to shita toki, deñwa ga natta.* (家を出ようとしたとき、電話が鳴った) When I *was about to* leave home, the telephone rang.

yo「obi」 ようび（曜日）*n.* day of the week. (⇨ APP. 5)

yo「oboo」 ようぼう（要望）*n.* request; requirement: *yooboo ni oojiru [kotaeru]* (要望に応じる[応える]) meet a person's *requirements*

yooboo suru (～する) *vt.* ask for; request.

yo⌐**obuñ** ようぶん (養分) *n.* nourishment; nutriment.

yo⌐**ochi** ようち (幼稚) *a.n.* (~ na, ni) childish; immature:
yoochi *na kañgae* (幼稚な考え) a *childish* way of thinking.

yo⌐**ochi**⌐**eñ** ようちえん (幼稚園) *n.* kindergarten. (⇨ gakkoo)

yo⌐**oda**⌐**i** ようだい (容体) *n.* condition of a patient.

yo⌐**odate**⌐**ru** ようだてる (用立てる) *n.* (-date-te Ⅴ) lend (money).

yo⌐**ofuku** ようふく (洋服) *n.* Western clothes; suit; dress. (⇨ fuku²) (↔ kimono; wafuku)

yo⌐**ofuu** ようふう (洋風) *n.* Western style:
yoofuu *no ie* (洋風の家) a *Western-style* house. (↔ wafuu)

yo⌐**oga** ようが (洋画) *n.* Western [European] painting; oil painting; foreign film.

yo⌐**oga**⌐**shi** ようがし (洋菓子) *n.* cake; Western-style confectionery. (↔ wagashi)

yo⌐**ogi** ようぎ (容疑) *n.* suspicion:
yoogi *o ukeru* (容疑を受ける) *be suspected* / yoogi *o harasu* (容疑を晴らす) *dispel suspicion*.

yo⌐**ogo**¹ ようご (用語) *n.* term; word; terminology.

yo⌐**ogo**² ようご (擁護) *n.* support; protection.
yoogo suru (~する) *vt.* support; protect: *keñpoo o yoogo suru* (憲法を擁護する) *support* the constitution.

yo⌐**ogu** ようぐ (用具) *n.* tool; instrument.

yo⌐**oi**¹ ようい (用意) *n.* preparation; arrangement; readiness.
yooi (o) suru (~(を)する) *vt.* prepare; arrange; get ready. (⇨ juñbi; shitaku)

yo⌐**oi**² ようい (容易) *a.n.* (~ na, ni) easy; simple:
Kono kawa o oyoide wataru no wa yooi *de nai.* (この川を泳いで渡るのは容易でない) It is not *easy* to swim across this river. (⇨ kañtañ)

yo⌐**oji**¹ ようじ (用事) *n.* business; things to do; engagement:
yooji *o sumasu* (用事を済ます) finish one's *job*. (⇨ yoo¹)

yo⌐**oji**² ようじ (幼児) *n.* infant; very young child.

yo⌐**ojiñ** ようじん (用心) *n.* care; caution; precaution: yoojiñ-boo (用心棒) a *bodyguard*; a *bouncer*.
yoojiñ suru (~する) *vi.* take care; be careful. (↔ buyoojiñ)

yo⌐**ojiñbuka**⌐**i** ようじんぶかい (用心深い) *a.* (-ku) cautious; watchful; careful. (↔ keesotsu) (⇨ chuuibukai; shiñchoo²)

yo⌐**oka** ようか (八日) *n.* eight days; the eighth day of the month. (⇨ APP. 5)

yo⌐**oke**⌐**ñ** ようけん (用件) *n.* business. (⇨ yooji¹)

yo⌐**oki**¹ ようき (容器) *n.* container.

yo⌐**oki**² ようき (陽気) *a.n.* (~ na, ni) cheerful; lively; merry.

yo⌐**oki**³ ようき (陽気) *n.* weather:
Ii yooki *desu ne.* (いい陽気ですね) Pleasant *weather*, isn't it?

yo⌐**okyuu** ようきゅう (要求) *n.* demand; requirement; claim.
yookyuu suru (~する) *vt.* demand; require; claim. (⇨ motomeru)

yo⌐**omoo** ようもう (羊毛) *n.* wool.

yo⌐**o-oñ** ようおん (拗音) *n.* palatalized consonant. ★ The palatalized sound is represented by a smaller や, ゆ and よ (ャ, ュ, ョ) after the *i*-row *kana* letter of the appropriate consonant: *kya* (きゃ), *kyu* (きゅ), *kyo* (きょ). (⇨ inside front cover; APP. 1)

yo⌐**oryo**⌐**o**¹ ようりょう (要領) *n.*
1 point; essentials:
Kare no setsumee wa yooryoo *o ete iru.* (彼の説明は要領を得ている) His explanation is to the *point*.
2 knack:
Yatto kuruma no uñteñ no yooryoo *ga wakatta.* (やっと車の運転の要領がわかった) At last I got the *knack* of driving a car.

yooryoo ga ii [warui] (～がいい [悪い]) clever [clumsy]: *Kare wa yooryoo ga ii [warui].* (彼は要領がいい[悪い]) He is *quick and smart [slow and dull]*.

yo͞oryoo² ようりょう (容量) *n.* capacity; volume; bulk. (⇨ taiseki)

yo͞osai ようさい (洋裁) *n.* dressmaking. (↔ wasai)

yo͞osee ようせい (養成) *n.* training; education.
　yoosee suru (～する) *vt.* train; educate; foster.

yo͞oshi¹ ようし (要旨) *n.* outline; summary; the gist.

yo͞oshi² ようし (養子) *n.* adopted [foster] child.

yo͞oshitsu ようしつ (洋室) *n.* Western-style room. (↔ washitsu)

yo͞osho ようしょ (洋書) *n.* book published in a European language. (↔ washo)

yo͞oshoku¹ ようしょく (養殖) *n.* culture; farming: *yooshoku-shiñju* (養殖真珠) a *cultured* pearl.
　yooshoku suru (～する) *vt.* raise; farm: *masu o yooshoku suru* (ますを養殖する) *raise* trout.

yo͞oshoku² ようしょく (洋食) *n.* Western food; Western dishes. (↔ washoku)

yo͞oso ようそ (要素) *n.* element; factor; constituent.

yo͞osu ようす (様子) *n.* **1** condition; the state of affairs: *yoosu o ukagau* (様子をうかがう) see *how things stand*.
　2 appearance; looks: *machi no yoosu* (町の様子) the *look* of the town. (⇨ moyoo)

yo͞o-su͞ru ni ようするに (要するに) *adv.* in short; in a word; after all.

yo͞oteñ ようてん (要点) *n.* point; essence; the gist:
O-hanashi no yooteñ wa tsukamemashita. (お話の要点はつかめました) I

got the *point* of your talk.

yo͞oto ようと (用途) *n.* use: *Purasuchikku wa yooto ga hiroi.* (プラスチックは用途が広い) Plastics have many *uses*.

yo͞oyaku ようやく (漸く) *adv.*
　1 at last; finally. (⇨ tsui ni)
　2 barely; with difficulty: *Saishuu doñsha ni yooyaku ma niaimashita.* (最終電車にようやく間に合いました) I was *barely* in time for the last train. (⇨ yatto)

yo͞pparai よっぱらい (酔っぱらい) *n.* drunken person; drunk: *yopparai-uñteñ* (酔っぱらい運転) *drunken* driving.

yo͞reba よれば (依れば) according to: ★ Indicates the source or authority of information received. *Teñki-yohoo ni yoreba, ashita wa ame ni naru rashii.* (天気予報によれば、あしたは雨になるらしい) *According to* the weather forecast, it will evidently rain.

yo͞ri より *p.* **1** ...than: ★ Used to make comparisons. *Watashi wa koohii yori koocha no hoo ga suki desu.* (私はコーヒーよりも紅茶のほうが好きです) I like tea rather *than* coffee.
　2 (*formal*) at; from; than: ★ Indicates a point of origin in time or space. (⇨ kara³)
Kyoo no kaigi wa sañ-ji yori hajimemasu. (きょうの会議は3時より始めます) We will start today's meeting *at* three.

yo͞rikaka͞r·u よりかかる (寄り掛かる) *vi.* (-kakar·i-; -kakar·a-; -ka-kat-te Ⓒ) **1** lean on; recline against: *kabe ni yorikakaru* (壁に寄り掛かる) *lean against* a wall.
　2 rely on: *Kare wa mada oya ni yorikakatte iru.* (彼はまだ親に寄り掛かっている) He still *relies on* his parents.

yo͞rimichi よりみち (寄り道) *n.* dropping in; stopover: *yorimichi o suru* (寄り道をする) *stop on the way*.

yo⌐riwake⌐·ru よりわける (選り分ける) *vt.* (-wake-te Ⅴ) sort out; classify.

yo⌐roi よろい (鎧) *n.* armor.

yo⌐roke⌐·ru よろける *vi.* (-ke-te Ⅴ) stagger; totter; stumble.

yo⌐rokobi よろこび (喜び) *n.* joy; pleasure; delight; rapture. (↔ kanashimi) (⇨ yorokobu)

yo⌐roko⌐b·u よろこぶ (喜ぶ) *vi.* (-kob·i-; -kob·a-; -koñ-de Ⓒ) be glad; be pleased; be delighted. (↔ kanashimu) (⇨ yorokobi)

yorokoñde ... suru (喜んで...する) be glad to do: Yorokoñde *o-tetsudai shimasu.* (喜んでお手伝いします) I will *be glad to* help you.

yo⌐roñ よろん (世論) *n.* public opinion: yoroñ-*choosa* (世論調査) a *public opinion* poll. (⇨ seroñ)

yo⌐roshi·i よろしい (宜しい) *a.* (-ku) ★ Formal alternative of '*ii.*'
1 all right; fine; good: Juñbi wa yoroshii deshoo ka? (準備はよろしいでしょうか) You are *ready*, I assume?
2 had better; should: Kare no iu toori ni shita hoo ga yoroshii desu yo. (彼の言うとおりにしたほうがよろしいですよ) You *had better* do as he tells you.
3 can; may: Kono deñwa o tsukatte mo yoroshii desu ka? (この電話を使ってもよろしいですか) *May* I use this telephone? (⇨ yoi')

yo⌐roshiku よろしく (宜しく) *adv.*
1 (used to express one's hopes for friendship or favor): Hajimemashite. Doozo yoroshiku o-negai shimasu. (始めまして。どうぞよろしくお願いします) How do you do? *It is a pleasure to meet you.* ★ Greeting used when first meeting someone. / Kono shigoto o yoroshiku tanomimasu. (この仕事をよろしく頼みます) *I would be grateful for your help* with this job.
2 (used to express one's regards or best wishes): O-toosañ ni yoroshiku o-tsutae kudasai. (お父さんによろしくお伝えください) Please give my *regards* to your father.

yo⌐royoro よろよろ *adv.* (~ to; ~ suru) staggeringly; totteringly; falteringly. (⇨ hyorohyoro')

yo⌐ru' よる (夜) *n.* night. (↔ asa') (⇨ bañ'; yo²)

yo⌐r·u² よる (寄る) *vi.* (yor·i-; yor·a-; yot-te Ⓒ) 1 draw near; come [go] close.
2 drop in (at a person's house).

yo⌐r·u³ よる (因る・依る) *vi.* (yor·i-; yor·a-; yot-te Ⓒ) 1 depend: Shuukaku wa teñkoo ni yorimasu. (収穫は天候によります) The crop *depends* on the weather. (⇨ shidai)
2 be based; according to: Kono monogatari wa jijitsu ni yotte kakaremashita. (この物語は事実によって書かれました) This story was written, *based* on fact.
3 be caused; owing to: Kaji wa tabako no fushimatsu ni yoru mono datta. (火事はたばこの不始末によるものだった) The fire was one *caused by* not extinguishing a cigarette. (⇨ yotte)

yo⌐sañ よさん (予算) *n.* budget: yosañ o tateru (予算を立てる) make a *budget.*

yo⌐seatsume よせあつめ (寄せ集め) *n.* medley; odds and ends: yoseatsume no chiimu (寄せ集めのチーム) a *scratch* team. (⇨ yoseatsumeru)

yo⌐seatsume⌐·ru よせあつめる (寄せ集める) *vt.* (-atsume-te Ⅴ) collect; gather up; bring together. (⇨ yoseatsume)

yo⌐se·ru よせる (寄せる) *vt.* (yose-te Ⅴ) 1 bring [draw] up: Akari o motto hoñ no soba e yose nasai. (あかりをもっと本のそばへ寄せなさい) *Bring* the light *closer* to the book.
2 put [push] aside:

Tsukue o mado no waki ni yoseta.
(机を窓のわきに寄せた) I *put* the desk
next to the window.

yo⌐shi よし (良し・好し) *int.* well;
good; all right; OK:
Yoshi, *soo shiyoo.* (よし、そうしよう)
Well, let's do so.

yo⌐shi⌐ashi よしあし (善し悪し) *n.*
good or bad; right or wrong.
yoshiashi da (〜だ) have good
and bad points: *Hima ga aru no
mo* yoshiashi da. (暇があるのもよしあ
しだ) *It is not always good* to have
ample leisure time.

yo⌐shiyoshi よしよし *int.* (used
when consoling someone):
Yoshiyoshi. *Moo nakanai de.* (よし
よし。もう泣かないで) *Come come.*
You must stop crying now.

yo⌐shuu よしゅう (予習) *n.* preparation (of one's lessons).
(↔ fukushuu)

yo⌐so⌐ よそ (他所) *n.* **1** (〜 no)
another (place); some other
(place). (⇨ hoka)
2 another person:
kodomo o yoso ni azukeru (子ども
をよそに預ける) leave one's child in
the care of *another*.

yo⌐soo よそう (予想) *n.* expectation; anticipation; guess:
Yosoo ga atarimashita [hazurema-
shita]. (予想が当たりました[外れました])
My *guess* proved right [wrong].
yosoo suru (〜する) *vt.* expect;
anticipate; guess; predict.

yo⌐s·u よす (止す) *vt.* (yosh·i-;
yos·a-; yosh·i-te Ⓒ) stop; give
up; quit:
tabako o yosu (たばこをよす) *give up*
smoking / *gakkoo o* yosu (学校をよ
す) *quit* school. (⇨ yameru¹)

yo⌐tee よてい (予定) *n.* plan;
schedule; program:
yotee o tateru (予定を立てる) make
a *plan* / yotee o henkoo suru (予定
を変更する) change a *schedule*.
yotee suru (〜する) *vt.* plan;
schedule; expect.

yo⌐too よとう (与党) *n.* the ruling

[government] party. (↔ yatoo)

yo⌐tsukado よつかど (四つ角) *n.*
crossroads; intersection.

yo⌐tte よって (依って) ★ Used in
the pattern '... ni yotte.'
1 by: ★ Used with a passive
verb and indicates the agent of a
passive sentence.
*Kono zoo wa yuumee na chooko-
kuka ni* yotte *tsukurareta mono
desu.* (この像は有名な彫刻家によって
作られたものです) This statue is one
that was made *by* a famous sculp-
tor. (⇨ yoru³)
2 because of; due to: ★ Indicates cause or reason.
Señsoo ni yotte *ooku no hito ga
nikushiñ o ushinaimashita.* (戦争に
よって多くの人が肉親を失いました)
Many people lost their families
because of the war. (⇨ de¹)
3 with; by; through; of: ★ Indicates means, method or material.
Miñna no kyooryoku ni yotte *sono
shigoto wa hayaku owatta.* (みんな
の協力によってその仕事は早く終わった)
The work was finished early
with the cooperation of everyone.
4 (differ) from...to...: ★ Used in
expressions indicating variety or
disparity.
Fuuzoku shuukañ wa kuni ni yotte *chigaimasu.* (風俗習慣は国によっ
て違います) Manners and customs
vary *from* country *to* country.

yo⌐ttsu よっつ (四つ) *n.* four.
★ Used when counting.
(⇨ shi⁴; yoñ; APP. 3)

yo⌐·u よう (酔う) *vi.* (yo·i-; yo-
w·a-; yot-te Ⓒ) **1** get tipsy;
become drunk. (⇨ yoi²; yowa-
seru)
2 get sick:
fune [kuruma] ni you (船[車]に酔う)
get seasick [carsick].
3 be intoxicated; be elated:
Señshu-tachi wa shoori ni yotte
ita. (選手たちは勝利に酔っていた) The
players *were elated* at the victory.

yo「wa」・i よわい (弱い) *a.* (-ku)

1 weak:

Haha wa karada ga yowai. (母は体が弱い) My mother is physically *weak*. (↔ tsuyoi)

2 dim; low:

yowai hikari (弱い光) a *dim* light / *Gasu no hi o yowaku shi nasai.* (ガスの火を弱くしなさい) *Turn down* the gas. (↔ tsuyoi)

3 (... ni) (of knowledge, etc.) be poor at; weak:

Watashi wa kañji ni yowai. (私は漢字に弱い) I *am poor* at Chinese characters.

4 (... ni) be affected easily:

Chichi wa sake ni yowai. (父は酒に弱い) My father *cannot hold* his liquor very well. (↔ tsuyoi)

yo「waki よわき (弱気) *a.n.*

(~ na, ni) weak-minded; timid; pessimistic. (↔ tsuyoki)

yo「wame」・ru よわめる (弱める) *vt.* (yowame-te Ⅴ) weaken; turn down (the gas). (↔ tsuyomeru) (⇨ yowamaru)

yo「wa」r・u よわる (弱る) *vi.* (yowar-i-; yowar-a-; yowat-te Ⓒ)

1 become weak; weaken. (⇨ yowameru)

2 be perplexed; be in a fix:

Kodomo ni nakarete, yowatta. (子どもに泣かれて、弱った) I *was at a loss* when the child was crying.

yo「wase」・ru よわせる (酔わせる) *vt.* (yowase-te Ⅴ) **1** make a person drunk. (⇨ you)

2 charm; enchant:

Kare no eñsoo wa choochuu o yowaseta. (彼の演奏は聴衆を酔わせた) His performance *enchanted* the audience. (⇨ you)

yo「yaku よやく (予約) *n.* **1** reservation; booking:

yoyaku o toru [torikesu] (予約をとる [取り消す]) make [cancel] a *reservation*.

2 subscription (to a magazine).

3 appointment (with a dentist).

yoyaku suru (~する) *vt.* reserve; book; subscribe; make an appointment.

yo「yuu よゆう (余裕) *n.* margin; room; leeway.

yu」 ゆ (湯) *n.* **1** hot water. ★ Often 'o-yu.'

2 (hot) bath.

-yu ゆ (油) *suf.* oil:

seki-yu (石油) *petroleum* / *too-yu* (灯油) *kerosene*.

yu「bi」 ゆび (指) *n.* finger; thumb; toe.

yu「bisa」s・u ゆびさす (指さす) *vt.* (-sash-i-; -sas-a-; -sash-i-te Ⓒ) point to [at]:

kabe no e o yubisasu (壁の絵を指す) *point to* a picture on the wall.

yu「biwa ゆびわ (指輪) *n.* ring:

yubiwa o hameru (指輪をはめる) put on a *ring*.

yu「dañ ゆだん (油断) *n.* carelessness; inattention; negligence.

yudañ suru (~する) *vi.* be careless; be inattentive; be negligent. (⇨ yoojiñ)

yu「de」・ru ゆでる (茹でる) *vt.* (yude-te Ⅴ) boil: *tamago o yuderu* (卵をゆでる) *boil* an egg.

yu「de-ta」mago ゆでたまご (茹で卵) *n.* boiled egg. (⇨ hañjuku; tamago)

yu「e ni ゆえに (故に) *conj.* (*formal*) therefore; consequently; hence.

yu「game・ru ゆがめる (歪める) *vt.* (yugame-te Ⅴ) distort; twist: *kao o yugameru* (顔をゆがめる) *screw up* one's face. (⇨ yugamu)

yu「gam・u ゆがむ (歪む) *vi.* (yugam-i-; yugam-a-; yugañ-de Ⓒ) be twisted; be distorted; be warped; lean. (⇨ yugameru)

yu「ge ゆげ (湯気) *n.* steam.

yu「i-itsu ゆいいつ (唯一) *n.* one and only:

Kare no yui-itsu no tanoshimi wa tsuri desu. (彼の唯一の楽しみは釣りです) His *only* pastime is fishing.

yu「ka ゆか (床) *n.* floor: *itabari no yuka* (板張りの床) a boarded *floor*.

yu「kai ゆかい (愉快) *a.n.* (~ na,
ni) pleasant; enjoyable; jolly;
amusing. (↔ fuyukai)

yu「kata ゆかた (浴衣) *n.* informal
summer kimono.

yu「ketsu ゆけつ (輸血) *n.* blood
transfusion.
yuketsu suru (~する) *vi.* trans-
fuse: *kañja ni* yuketsu suru (患者
に輸血する) *give* a patient a *blood
transfusion*.

yu「ki¹ ゆき (雪) *n.* snow:
Yuki ga futte kita. (雪が降ってきた)
It *has begun to snow*.

yu「ki² ゆき (行き) *n.* (=iki²) going
(to a destination):
Deñsha wa yuki wa koñde ita ga,
kaeri wa suite ita. (電車は行きはこん
でいたが、帰りはすいていた) The train
was crowded *on the way there*,
but not crowded on the way
back. (↔ kaeri) (⇒ iku; yuku)

-yuki ゆき (行き) *suf.* bound for:
Oosaka-yuki no ressha (大阪行きの
列車) a train *bound for* Osaka.

yu「kichigai ゆきちがい (行き違い) *n.*
1 crossing each other:
Tegami ga yukichigai ni natte shimatta. (手紙が行き違いになってしまっ
た) Our letters *have crossed each
other*.
2 misunderstanding.

yu「kidomari ゆきどまり (行き止ま
り) *n.* dead end. (⇒ ikidomari)

yu「kisaki ゆきさき (行き先) *n.*
= yukusaki.

yu「kku¹ri ゆっくり *adv.* (~ to)
1 slowly; without hurry; leisurely.
2 good; plenty of:
Deñsha ni wa yukkuri maniaimasu.
(電車にはゆっくり間に合います) We are
in *plenty* of time for the train.
yukkuri suru (~する) *vi.* take
one's time; stay long.

yu「k·u ゆく (行く) *vi.* (yuk·i-; yu-
k·a-; it-te C) = iku.

yu「kue ゆくえ (行方) *n.* whereabouts.

yu「kue-fu¹mee ゆくえふめい (行方

不明) *n.* missing:
Yama de go-niñ ga yukue-fumee
ni natta. (山で5人が行方不明になっ
た) Five people *have gone missing*
in the mountains.

yu「kusaki ゆくさき (行く先) *n.*
destination; whereabouts.
(⇒ ikusaki; yukue)

yu「kusue ゆくすえ (行く末) *n.*
future. (⇒ shoorai)

yu「me¹ ゆめ (夢) *n.* dream; ambition:
Isha ni naru no ga kare no yume
desu. (医者になるのが彼の夢です) It is
his *dream* to become a doctor.

yu「mi¹ ゆみ (弓) *n.* bow:
yumi o iru (弓を射る) *shoot an
arrow*. (↔ ya²)

yu「nomi¹ ゆのみ (湯呑) *n.* cup;
teacup. (⇒ chawañ)

yu「nyuu ゆにゅう (輸入) *n.*
import; importation.
yunyuu suru (~する) *vt.* import.
(↔ yushutsu)

yu「re-ru ゆれる (揺れる) *vi.* (yurete Ⓥ) **1** shake; tremble; sway.
2 waver:
Sono moñdai de kanojo no kokoro
wa yurete iru. (その問題で彼女の心は
揺れている) Her heart *is wavering*
over that problem.

yu「ru¹·i ゆるい (緩い) *a.* (-ku)
1 loose; lax:
Kono kutsu wa sukoshi yurui. (この
靴は少しゆるい) These shoes are a
little *too big* for me. (↔ kitsui)
(⇒ yurumeru; yurumu)
2 (of a curve, slope, etc.) gentle.
(↔ kyuu¹) (⇒ yuruyaka)
3 slow:
yurui tama o nageru (ゆるい球を投げ
る) pitch a *slow* ball. (↔ hayai²)

yu「rume¹·ru ゆるめる (緩める) *vt.*
(yurume-te Ⓥ) **1** loosen; unfasten; relax:
beruto o yurumeru (ベルトをゆるめる)
loosen one's belt. (⇒ yurumu;
yurui)
2 make less strict; relax:
Tookyoku wa kooki o yurumeta.

（当局は警戒をゆるめた）The authorities *relaxed* their vigilance. (⇨ yurumu)

3 slow down:
Kuruma wa sakamichi de supiido o yurumeta. (車は坂道でスピードをゆるめた) The car *slowed down* on the slope.

yuˈruˈmˈu ゆるむ (緩む) *vi.* (yurum·i-; yurum·a-; yuruñ-de Ⓥ)
1 become loose; loosen. (⇨ yurui; yurumeru)
2 soften; abate:
Samusa ga yuruñde kita. (寒さがゆるんできた) It *has become less* cold.

yuˈrushi ゆるし (許し) *n.* permission; pardon. (⇨ kyoka; yurusu)

yuˈruˈsˈu ゆるす (許す) *vt.* (yurush·i-; yurus·a-; yurush·i-te Ⓒ)
permit; allow; forgive:
Go-busata o o-yurushi kudasai. (ごぶさたをお許しください) *Forgive* me for not contacting you for so long. (⇨ kañbeñ; kyoka; yurushi)

yuˈruˈyaka ゆるやか (緩やか) *a.n.* (~ na, ni) gentle; slow:
yuruyaka na saka (ゆるやかな坂) a *gentle* slope. (↔ kitsui)

yuˈshutsu ゆしゅつ (輸出) *n.* export; exportation.
yushutsu suru (~する) *vt.* export. (↔ yunyuu)

yuˈsoo ゆそう (輸送) *n.* transport; transportation.
yusoo suru (~する) *vt.* transport; carry.

yuˈsugˈu ゆすぐ (濯ぐ) *vt.* (yusug·i-; yusug·a-; yusu·i-de Ⓒ)
rinse out; wash out:
señtakumono o yusugu (洗濯物をゆすぐ) *rinse* one's laundry.

yuˈsurˈuˈ¹ ゆする (揺する) *vt.* (yusur·i-; yusur·a-; yusut-te Ⓒ)
shake; rock; swing; roll.

yuˈsurˈuˈ² ゆする (強請る) *vt.* (yusur·i-; yusur·a-; yusut-te Ⓒ)
extort; blackmail.

yuˈtaka ゆたか (豊か) *a.n.* (~ na, ni) abundant; ample; rich; affluent:

yutaka na shigeñ (豊かな資源) *abundant* resources. (↔ mazushii; toboshii)

yuˈttaˈri ゆったり *adv.* (~ to; ~ suru) at ease; comfortably; loosely:
guriiñsha no zaseki ni yuttari to suwaru (グリーン車の座席にゆったりと座る) sit *comfortably* in a first class train seat.

yuˈruˈ¹ ゆう (言う) *vi.* (i·i-; yuw·a-; yut-te Ⓒ) = iu.

yuˈuˈ² ゆう (優) *n.* (of a grade, rating) being excellent; A (in schoolwork). (⇨ fuka; ka²; ryoo³)

yuˈube¹ ゆうべ (夕べ) *n.* yesterday evening; last night. (⇨ sakuya)

yuˈube² ゆうべ (夕べ) *n.* (*literary*) evening: *oñgaku no yuube* (音楽の夕べ) a musical *evening*.

yuˈubiñ ゆうびん (郵便) *n.* **1** mail [postal] service; mail: *yuubiñ-bañgoo* (郵便番号) *zip* [*postal*] code / *yuubiñ-chokiñ* (郵便貯金) *postal* savings.
2 postal matter; mail.

yuˈubiˈñbutsu ゆうびんぶつ (郵便物) *n.* = yuubiñ (2).

yuˈubiˈñkyoku ゆうびんきょく (郵便局) *n.* post office. ★ 〒 is the emblem of '*yuubiñkyoku.*'

yuˈuboku ゆうぼく (遊牧) *n.* nomadism: *yuuboku-miñzoku* (遊牧民族) a *nomadic* tribe.

yuˈuboo ゆうぼう (有望) *a.n.* (~ na, ni) promising; hopeful.

yuˈudachi ゆうだち (夕立) *n.* sudden, heavy shower on a summer afternoon.

yuˈudoku ゆうどく (有毒) *a.n.* (~ na, ni) poisonous.

yuˈueki ゆうえき (有益) *a.n.* (~ na, ni) useful; helpful; instructive. (↔ mueki)

yuˈugai ゆうがい (有害) *a.n.* (~ na, ni) harmful; injurious; bad. (↔ mugai)

yuˈugata ゆうがた (夕方) *n.* evening. (⇨ asa¹; bañ¹; yuube¹)

yuˈugure ゆうぐれ (夕暮れ) *n.*

evening. (⇨ yuugata; ban¹)

yu⌐uhañ ゆうはん (夕飯) *n.* supper; dinner. (⇨ yuushoku)

yu⌐uhi ゆうひ (夕日) *n.* the evening [setting] sun. (↔ asahi)

yu⌐ujiñ ゆうじん (友人) *n.* friend. (⇨ tomo³; tomodachi)

yu⌐ujoo ゆうじょう (友情) *n.* friendship.

yu⌐ukai ゆうかい (誘拐) *n.* kidnapping; abduction.
yuukai suru (〜する) *vt.* kidnap; abduct.

yu⌐ukañ¹ ゆうかん (勇敢) *a.n.* (〜 na, ni) brave; courageous:
yuukañ *ni tatakau* (勇敢に闘う) fight *courageously*.

yu⌐ukan² ゆうかん (夕刊) *n.* evening paper; the evening edition of a newspaper. (↔ chookañ¹) (⇨ shiñbuñ)

yu⌐uki ゆうき (勇気) *n.* courage; bravery.

yu⌐ukoo¹ ゆうこう (友好) *n.* friendly relationship; friendship:
yuukoo *o fukameru* (友好を深める) promote *friendship*.

yu⌐ukoo² ゆうこう (有効) *a.n.* (〜 na, ni) effective; valid. (↔ mukoo²)

yu⌐umee ゆうめい (有名) *a.n.* (〜 na, ni) famous; well-known; notorious. (↔ mumee)

yu⌐umeshi ゆうめし (夕飯) *n.* (*informal*) supper; dinner. (⇨ yuushoku)

yu⌐umoa ユーモア *n.* humor; joke.

yu⌐unoo ゆうのう (有能) *a.n.* (〜 na) able; capable; competent. (↔ munoo)

yu⌐uri ゆうり (有利) *a.n.* (〜 na, ni) advantageous; favorable. (↔ furi¹)

yu⌐uryoku ゆうりょく (有力) *a.n.* (〜 na, ni) influential; strong; leading. (↔ muryoku)

yu⌐uryoo ゆうりょう (有料) *n.* charge:
Kono tenrankai wa yuuryoo desu.

(この展覧会は有料です) There is a *charge* for this exhibition. (↔ muryoo)

yu⌐usee ゆうせい (優勢) *n.* superiority; lead:
yuusee *o tamotsu* (優勢を保つ) retain one's *superiority*.
— *a.n.* (〜 na, ni) superior; leading. (↔ ressee)

yu⌐useñ ゆうせん (優先) *n.* priority; precedence; preference:
yuuseñ-*juñi* (優先順位) the order of *priority*.
yuuseñ suru (〜する) *vi.* have priority; take precedence.

yu⌐useñ-ho⌐osoo ゆうせんほうそう (有線放送) *n.* closed-circuit [cable] broadcasting.

yu⌐ushoku ゆうしょく (夕食) *n.* supper; dinner. (⇨ yuuhañ; bañsañ)

yu⌐ushoo ゆうしょう (優勝) *n.* victory; championship.
yuushoo suru (〜する) *vi.* win the victory [championship].

yu⌐ushuu ゆうしゅう (優秀) *a.n.* (〜 na) excellent; superior; outstanding.

yu⌐usoo ゆうそう (郵送) *n.* sending by mail; post:
yuusoo-ryoo (郵送料) *postage*.
yuusoo suru (〜する) *vt.* mail; post; send by mail [post].

yu⌐utoo ゆうとう (優等) *n.* academic honors:
yuutoo *de daigaku o sotsugyoo suru* (優等で大学を卒業する) graduate from college with *honors*.

yu⌐u-utsu ゆううつ (憂鬱) *a.n.* (〜 na, ni) depressing; gloomy; melancholy.

yu⌐uwaku ゆうわく (誘惑) *n.* temptation; lure; seduction.
yuuwaku suru (〜する) *vt.* tempt; lure; seduce (a woman).

yu⌐uyake ゆうやけ (夕焼け) *n.* glow of the sunset. (↔ asayake)

yu⌐uyu⌐u ゆうゆう (悠々) *adv.* (〜 to) **1** easily; without difficulty:

yuuyuu to katsu (ゆうゆうと勝つ) win an *easy* victory.

2 calmly; sedately; leisurely: *Kare wa sono ba kara* yuuyuu *to tachisatta*. (彼はその場からゆうゆうと立ち去った) He *calmly* went away from the spot.

yuˈuzuu ゆうずう (融通) *n.*

1 adaptability; flexibility: *Ano hito wa* yuuzuu *ga kiku* [kika-nai]. (あの人は融通がきく[きかない]) He *is flexible and versatile* [*rigid and literal-minded*].

2 loan (of money); financing.

yuuzuu suru (～する) *vt.* accommodate; lend.

yuˈzur·u ゆずる (譲る) *vt.* (yuzur·i-; yuzur·a-; yuzut-te Ⓒ)

1 hand over; transfer: *kooshiñ ni michi o yuzuru* (後進に道を譲る) *make way* for the younger generation.

2 give; offer; sell: *Shooneñ wa basu de roojiñ ni seki o yuzutta*. (少年はバスで老人に席を譲った) The boy *gave up* his seat to an elderly person on the bus.

3 concede; make a concession.

Z

zaˈazaa ざあざあ *adv.* (～ to) hard: ★ The sound of heavy rainfall.
Ame ga zaazaa *(to) futte kita*. (雨がざあざあ(と)降ってきた) The rain *began to pour down*.

zaˈbuñ ざぶん *adv.* (～ to) with a splash: ★ The sound of a heavy object falling into water.
Kare wa zabuñ *to kawa ni ochita*. (彼はざぶんと川に落ちた) He fell into the river *with a splash*.

zaˈbuˈtoñ ざぶとん (座布団) *n.* cushion for sitting on.

zaˈdaˈñkai ざだんかい (座談会) *n.* discussion meeting; round-table talk.

-zai ざい (剤) *suf.* medicine; drug; dose: yaku-zai (薬剤) a *medicine* / ge-zai (下剤) a *laxative*.

zaˈigaku ざいがく (在学) *n.* being in school [college].
zaigaku suru (～する) *vi.* attend a school; be in school.
(⇨ tsuugaku)

zaˈiko ざいこ (在庫) *n.* stock: *Sono hoñ wa* zaiko *ga kirete imasu*. (その本は在庫が切れています) The book is out of *stock*.

zaˈimoku ざいもく (材木) *n.* wood; lumber; timber.

zaˈiryoˈo ざいりょう (材料) *n.* material; stuff; ingredient.

zaˈisañ ざいさん (財産) *n.* property; fortune.

zaˈisee ざいせい (財政) *n.* finance: zaisee *ga kurushii* (財政が苦しい) be in *financial* difficulties.

zaˈiseki[1] ざいせき (在籍) *n.* registration; enrollment: zaiseki-*sha* (在籍者) a *registered* person.
zaiseki suru (～する) *vi.* be registered; be enrolled.

zaˈiseki[2] ざいせき (在席) *n.* being at one's own seat [desk].
zaiseki suru (～する) *vi.* be at one's desk.

zaˈitaku ざいたく (在宅) *n.* being at home: ★ Often with 'go-.' *Yukari-sañ wa go-zaitaku desu ka?* (ゆかりさんはご在宅ですか) Is Yukari *at home*?
zaitaku suru (～する) *vi.* be at home.

zaˈkka ざっか (雑貨) *n.* sundries; miscellaneous goods.

zaˈkkubarañ ざっくばらん *a.n.* (～ na, ni) (*informal*) frank; candid; outspoken. (⇨ sotchoku)

zaˈñdaka ざんだか (残高) *n.* balance; the remainder (in an account, etc.).

zaⁿgyoo ざんぎょう (残業) *n.*
overtime (work): zaⁿgyoo-*teate*
(残業手当) *overtime* pay.
zaⁿgyoo (o) suru (〜(を)する) *vi.*
work overtime.

zaⁿkoku ざんこく (残酷) *a.n.*
(〜 na, ni) cruel; atrocious;
brutal.

zaⁿneⁿ ざんねん (残念) *a.n.*
(〜 na, ni) sorry; regrettable;
repentant:
*Anata ga paatii ni derarenai no
wa* zaⁿneⁿ *desu.* (あなたがパーティーに
出られないのは残念です) I am *sorry*
that you cannot come to the
party.
zaⁿneⁿ-nagara (〜ながら) re-
grettably; unfortunately.

zaⁿpi ざっぴ (雑費) *n.* miscellaneous [sundry] expenses; inci-
dental expenses.

zaⁿseki ざせき (座席) *n.* seat:
zaseki *o yoyaku suru* (座席を予約す
る) reserve a *seat.* (⇨ seki¹)

zaⁿsetsu ざせつ (挫折) *n.* set-
back; collapse.
zasetsu suru (〜する) *vi.* miscar-
ry; collapse; be discouraged.

zaⁿshiki¹ ざしき (座敷) *n.* tatami-
matted reception room with a
'tokonoma.'

zaⁿshoo ざしょう (座礁) *n.*
stranding; going aground.
zashoo suru (〜する) *vi.* go [run]
aground.

zaⁿsshi ざっし (雑誌) *n.* magazine;
periodical. (⇨ hoⁿ)

zaⁿssoo ざっそう (雑草) *n.* weed:
niwa no zassoo o toru (庭の雑草をと
る) *weed* the garden. (⇨ kusa)

zaⁿtaku ざたく (座卓) *n.* a low
table placed in a Japanese-style
room.

zaⁿtsu ざつ (雑) *a.n.* (〜 na, ni)
careless; sloppy; slipshod; rough:
Kare wa shigoto ga zatsu *da.* (彼は
仕事が雑だ) He is *careless* in his
work.

zaⁿtsudaⁿ ざつだん (雑談) *n.* chat;
light conversation.

zaⁿtsuoⁿ ざつおん (雑音) *n.* noise;
static.

zaⁿtto ざっと *adv.* **1** briefly;
roughly:
shorui ni zatto *me o toosu* (書類に
ざっと目を通す) *briefly* look through
the papers. (⇨ hitotoori)
2 about; approximately.

zaⁿttoo ざっとう (雑踏) *n.* crowd;
throng; congestion.
zattoo suru (〜する) *vi.* be crowded; be thronged.

zaⁿwazawa ざわざわ *adv.*
(〜 to) **1** (the murmur heard
when many people are together):
Kaijoo-nai wa zawazawa (*to*) *shite
ita.* (会場内はざわざわ(と)していた)
There was a *stirring* in the hall.
(⇨ gayagaya)
2 (the sound of leaves rustling in
the wind):
Tsuyoi kaze ni ki no ha ga zawazawa (*to*) *yurete iru.* (強い風に木の葉
がざわざわ(と)揺れている) The leaves
are rustling in the strong wind.

zaⁿyaku ざやく (座薬) *n.* supposi-
tory.

ze ぜ *p.* (*colloq.*) (used to emphasize one's opinions or wishes):
★ Used by men.
Sorosoro dekakeyoo ze. (そろそろ出か
けようぜ) *Well,* let's be going now.

zeⁿe ぜい (税) *n.* tax; taxation.
(⇨ zeekiⁿ)

zeⁿekaⁿ ぜいかん (税関) *n.* customs; customhouse:
zeekaⁿ-*shiⁿkokusho* (税関申告書) a
customs declaration.

zeⁿekiⁿ ぜいきん (税金) *n.* tax;
duty: zeekiⁿ *o osameru* (税金を納
める) pay a *tax.*

zeⁿemuⁿsho ぜいむしょ (税務署) *n.*
tax office.

zeⁿetaku¹ ぜいたく (贅沢) *n.* lux-
ury; extravagance.
— *a.n.* (〜 na, ni) luxurious;
extravagant; lavish.

zeⁿhi¹ ぜひ (是非) *adv.* surely; by
all means; at any cost:
Kai ni wa zehi *shusseki shite ku-*

dasai. (会にはぜひ出席してください) *Be sure* to attend the party. ((⇨ ⁼zehi-tomo))

zeʼhi² ぜひ (是非) *n.* right and/or wrong.

zeʼhi-tomo ぜひとも (是非共) *adv.* an emphatic form of '*zehi¹*.'

zeʼkkoo¹ ぜっこう (絶好) *n.* (~ no) ideal; perfect:
zekkoo *no kikai o nogasu* (絶好の機会を逃す) let a *golden* opportunity slip by.

zeʼkkoo² ぜっこう (絶交) *n.* breach; breaking off relations.
zekkoo suru (~する) *vi.* break off one's friendship.

zeʼkkyoo ぜっきょう (絶叫) *n.* shout; scream; exclamation.

zeʼñ¹ ぜん (善) *n.* good; right:
zeñ *to aku* (善と悪) *right* and wrong. ((↔ aku³)) ((⇨ zeñaku))

zeʼñ² ぜん (禅) *n.* Zen.

zeʼñ-¹ ぜん (全) *pref.* all; whole:
zeñ-*sekai* (全世界) the *whole* world / zeñ-*zaisañ* (全財産) one's *whole* fortune.

zeʼñ-² ぜん (前) *pref.* the former; ex-:
zeñ-*Soori-daijiñ* (前総理大臣) the *former* prime minister. ★ 'Moto (no) Soori-daijiñ' is a *previous* prime minister. ((⇨ moto²))

-zeñ ぜん (前) *suf.* before:
señ-zeñ (戦前) *before* the war / shoku-zeñ (食前) *before* a meal.

zeʼñaku ぜんあく (善悪) *n.* right and wrong; good and evil. ((⇨ zeñ¹; aku³))

zeʼñbu ぜんぶ (全部) *n.* all; everything; total.

zeʼñgo ぜんご (前後) *n.* before and after; in front and in the rear; back and forth.
zeñgo *o wasureru* (~を忘れる) forget oneself.
zeñgo suru (~する) *vi.* be reversed.

-zeʼñgo ぜんご (前後) *suf.* about; around: yoñjus-sai-zeñgo (40 歳前後) *about* forty years old.

zeʼñhañ ぜんはん (前半) *n.* the first half: nijus-seeki zeñhañ (20 世紀前半) *the first half* of the twentieth century. ((↔ koohañ))

zeʼñiñ ぜんいん (全員) *n.* all the members.

zeʼñjitsu ぜんじつ (前日) *n.* the day before; the previous day. ((⇨ yokujitsu))

zeʼñkai ぜんかい (全快) *n.* complete recovery.
zeñkai suru (~する) *vi.* recover completely.

zeʼñki ぜんき (前期) *n.* the first half year; the first term [semester]. ((↔ kooki))

zeʼñkoku ぜんこく (全国) *n.* the whole country; all parts of the country.

zeʼñkoku-teki ぜんこくてき (全国的) *a.n.* (~ na, ni) nationwide; all over the country.

zeʼñmetsu ぜんめつ (全滅) *n.* annihilation; total destruction.
zeñmetsu suru (~する) *vi.* be annihilated; be totally destroyed.

zeʼñpañ ぜんぱん (全般) *n.* the whole:
Nihoñ buñka zeñpañ no chishiki (日本文化全般の知識) a *general* knowledge of Japanese culture.

zeʼñpañ-teki ぜんぱんてき (全般的) *a.n.* (~ na, ni) on the whole; all in all.

zeʼñryaku ぜんりゃく (前略) *n.* Dear Mr. [Mrs., Miss, Ms.]...; Dear Sir [Sirs, Madam]. ★ Used in the salutation of an informal letter. The corresponding complimentary close is 'soosoo.' ((⇨ haikee¹; soosoo))

zeʼñryoku ぜんりょく (全力) *n.* all one's strength:
zeñryoku *o tsukusu* (全力を尽くす) *do one's best.*

zeʼñsha ぜんしゃ (前者) *n.* the former. ((↔ koosha²))

zeʼñshiñ¹ ぜんしん (前進) *n.* advance; progress.
zeñshiñ suru (~する) *vi.* go

ahead; advance; progress.

ze⌐ñshiñ² ぜんしん (全身) *n.* the whole body:
Sono ko wa zeñshiñ *doro-darake datta.* (その子は全身泥だらけだった) The child was covered with mud *all over*.

ze⌐ñsoku ぜんそく (喘息) *n.* asthma.

ze⌐ñsoku⌐ryoku ぜんそくりょく (全速力) *n.* full speed.

ze⌐ñtai ぜんたい (全体) *n.* the whole; all: *machi* zeñtai (町全体) *the whole* town.

ze⌐ñtee ぜんてい (前提) *n.* premise; assumption.

ze⌐ñto ぜんと (前途) *n.* future; one's way:
zeñto *yuuboo na wakamono* (前途有望な若者) a *promising* young man.

ze⌐ñzeñ ぜんぜん (全然) *adv.*
1 (with a negative) not at all; never:
Kare ni tsuite wa zeñzeñ *shirimaseñ.* (彼については全然知りません) I know nothing *at all* about him.
2 completely; entirely; altogether. (⇒ mattaku)

ze⌐ro ゼロ (零) *n.* zero; nothing. (⇒ ree²)
zero kara yarinaosu (〜からやり直す) start from scratch once more.

ze⌐tsuboo ぜつぼう (絶望) *n.* despair; hopelessness.
zetsuboo suru (〜する) *vi.* despair; give up hope.

ze⌐tsuboo-teki ぜつぼうてき (絶望的) *a.n.* (〜 na, ni) desperate; hopeless.

ze⌐tsueñ ぜつえん (絶縁) *n.*
1 breaking off relations.
2 insulation: zetsueñ-*teepu* (絶縁テープ) *insulating* tape.
zetsueñ suru (〜する) *vi.* sever relations.

ze⌐ttai ぜったい (絶対) *n., adv.* absoluteness; absolutely:
Koko de wa kañtoku no meeree wa zettai *desu.* (ここでは監督の命令は絶対です) Around here the team man-

ager's orders are *final*.

ze⌐ttai ni ぜったいに (絶対に) *adv.*
1 absolutely; surely:
Koko nara zettai ni *añzeñ desu.* (ここなら絶対に安全です) Provided you are here, you will be *absolutely* safe.
2 (with a negative) never; by no means:
Kono himitsu wa zettai ni *hito ni iimaseñ.* (この秘密は絶対に人に言いません) *Under no circumstances*, will I tell this secret to anybody.

zo ぞ *p.* (colloq.) **1** (used rhetorically to oneself in confirming an opinion): ★ Used by men.
Nañ da ka heñ da zo. (何だか変だぞ) *I am sure* something or other is wrong.
2 (used to emphasize one's opinions or wishes): ★ A potentially rude form. Used to close friends and those of lower status. (⇒ ze)
Sorosoro dekakeru zo. (そろそろ出かけるぞ) *Well*, let's be off now.

-zoi ぞい (沿い) *suf.* along:
*yama-*zoi *no michi* (山沿いの道) a road *along* the foot of a mountain. (⇒ sou¹)

zo⌐kugo ぞくご (俗語) *n.* slang; slang word.

zo⌐ku·s·u ぞくす (属す) *vi.* (-sh·i-; -s·a-; -sh·i-te C) belong to; come under.

zo⌐kuzoku¹ ぞくぞく (続々) *adv.* (〜 to) in succession; one after another.

zo⌐kuzoku² ぞくぞく *adv.* (〜 suru) (the state of feeling chilliness or being excited):
Netsu ga aru no ka, karada ga zokuzoku *suru.* (熱があるのか, 体がぞくぞくする) I must have a fever because I *have the shivers*.

zo⌐ñji·ru ぞんじる (存じる) *vi.* (zoñji-te V) ★ Used in the forms '*zoñjimasu*' and '*zoñjite*.' The plain form '*zonjiru*' is never used. The honorific equivalent is '*gozoñji desu*.' (⇒ gozoñji)

1 (*humble*) know:
Yamada-sañ no koto wa yoku zoñ-jite orimasu. (山田さんのことはよく存じております) I *know* Mr. Yamada very well. (⇨ **shiru**)
2 (*humble*) hope; feel; think:
Kooee ni zoñjimasu. (光栄に存じます) I *feel* honored.

zo'ñza'i そんざい *a.n.* (~ na, ni) rude; rough; careless; impolite.

zo'o ぞう (象) *n.* elephant.

zo'odai そうだい (増大) *n.* increase; enlargement.
zoodai suru (~する) *vi., vt.* increase. (↔ **geñshoo**) (⇨ **zooka**)

zo'ogeñ そうげん (増減) *n.* increase and/or decrease.; fluctuation; variation.
zoogeñ suru (~する) *vi., vt.* increase and/or decrease; fluctuate; vary.

zo'oka ぞうか (増加) *n.* increase:
jiñkoo no zooka (人口の増加) an *increase* in population.
zooka suru (~する) *vi., vt.* increase. (↔ **geñshoo**) (⇨ **zoodai**)

zo'okiñ そうきん (雑巾) *n.* duster; dust cloth; floor cloth.

zo'okyoo そうきょう (増強) *n.* reinforcement; increase; buildup.
zookyoo suru (~する) *vt.* reinforce; strengthen: *yusooryoku o zookyoo suru* (輸送力を増強する) *augment* the transport capacity.

zo'oni ぞうに (雑煮) *n.* soup with rice cakes, chicken and vegetables, served during New Year celebrations. (⇨ **shoogatsu**)

zo'ori ぞうり (草履) *n.* zori; Japanese flat sandals.

zo'oseñ そうせん (造船) *n.* shipbuilding:
zooseñ-jo (造船所) a *shipyard*.

zo'osho ぞうしょ (蔵書) *n.* a collection of books; one's personal library.

zo'oshuu そうしゅう (増収) *n.* increase of income [revenue]. (↔ **geñshuu**)

zo'rozoro ぞろぞろ *adv.* (~ to)

in a stream; one after another.

zu ず (図) *n.* drawing; figure; diagram; illustration.

zu'bo'ñ ズボン *n.* trousers; slacks; pants.

zu'ibuñ ずいぶん (随分) *adv.* very (much); really; a lot; quite:
Kono heñ wa mukashi to zuibuñ kawarimashita. (この辺は昔とずいぶん変わりました) This area has changed *a lot* from the old days.

zu'ihitsu ずいひつ (随筆) *n.* essay:
zuihitsu o kaku (随筆を書く) write an *essay*.

-zu ni ずに = -nai'+-de.

zu'ñzuñ ずんずん *adv.* (~ to) quickly; rapidly; on and on.

-zura'i づらい (辛い) *suf.* (*a.*) (-ku) hard; difficult: ★ Added to the continuative base of a verb.
Kono hoñ wa ji ga chiisakute yomi-zurai. (この本は字が小さくて読みづらい) This book has small print and is thus *difficult* to read. (↔ -yasui) (⇨ -gatai; -nikui)

zu'ra'ri ずらり *adv.* (~ to) in a line [row]:
Butai ni odoriko ga zurari to naranda. (舞台に踊り子がずらりと並んだ) The dancers formed a *straight line* on the stage.

zu'ra'su ずらす *vt.* (zurash·i-; zuras·a-; zurash·i-te Ⓒ) **1** shift; move a little. (⇨ **zureru**)
2 put off; postpone:
nittee o zurasu (日程をずらす) *move back* the schedule. (⇨ **zureru**)

zu'ire ずれ *n.* difference; gap:
kañgaekata no zure (考え方のずれ) a *difference* of views. (⇨ **zureru**)

zu'ire'·ru ずれる *vi.* (zure-te Ⓥ)
1 be shifted; be not in the right place. (⇨ **zurasu**)
2 be put off:
Shigoto ga haitte, yotee ga isshuukañ zuremashita. (仕事が入って、予定が1週間ずれました) Because some work has come in, my schedule *is* a week *off*. (⇨ **zurasu**)
3 deviate:

Kare no ikeñ wa teema to sukoshi zurete iru. (彼の意見はテーマと少しずれ ている) His opinion *is* a bit *off* the topic. ((⇨ zure)

zuˈruˈ·i ずるい *a.* (-ku) cunning; tricky; unfair.

zuˈruzuru ずるずる *adv.* (～ to) trailingly; draggingly:
Kare wa zuruzuru (*to*) *heñji o noba-shita.* (彼はずるずる(と)返事を延ばした) He *kept on* putting off his reply.

zuˈsañ ずさん (杜撰) *a.n.* (～ na) careless; slipshod; faulty.

-zuˈtai づたい (伝い) *suf.* along:
señro-zutai no michi (線路づたいの道) a road *running beside* the railway lines.

zuˈtazuta ni ずたずたに *adv.* to pieces; to shreds.

-zuˈtsu ずつ (宛) *suf.* 1 of each; for each; to each: ★ Indicates distribution.
Kono kami o hitori-zutsu ichi-mai tori nasai. (この紙を一人ずつ1枚取りな さい) *Each of you* take a sheet of this paper.
2 at a time: ★ Indicates repetition.
Sukoshi-zutsu arukeru yoo ni nari-mashita. (少しずつ歩けるようになりまし た) *Little by little* I have reached the stage where I am able to walk.

zuˈtsuu ずつう (頭痛) *n.* headache.
zutsuu no tane (～の種) a source of worry.

zuˈtto ずっと *adv.* 1 (with a comparative) much; far:
Kare wa watashi yori zutto *wakai.* (彼は私よりずっと若い) He is *much* younger than I. ((⇨ haruka ni)
2 (of time) long:
Zutto ato ni natte, sono koto ni ki ga tsukimashita. (ずっと後になって、そ のことに気がつきました) I noticed that a *long* time afterward.
3 all the time; all the way.

zuˈuzuushiˈ·i ずうずうしい (図々しい) *a.* (-ku) impudent; pushy; shameless. ((⇨ atsukamashii)

APPENDIX 1

Guide to Japanese Pronunciation

1. Standard pronunciation of the Japanese language

The variety of Japanese of greatest practical importance for foreign learners is that called **Standard Japanese**. This is understood throughout Japan. The pronunciation of Standard Japanese is based on that of educated people who were born and brought up in Tokyo, or its vicinity.

2. Vowels
2.1 Short and Long Vowels

The vowel system of Japanese (hereafter abbreviated to J) is much simpler than that of English (abbreviated to E). It consists of five short vowels **i, e, a, o, u**, and the corresponding long vowels. Long vowels may also be interpreted as double vowels, and in this dictionary they are written **ii, ee, aa, oo, uu**. It should be noted that the distinction between short and long vowels is significant in Japanese in that it affects the meanings of words. For example, *i* (stomach) vs. *ii* (good), *tesee* (handmade) vs. *teesee* (correction), *kado* (corner) vs. *kaado* (card), *toru* (take) vs. *tooru* (pass), *kuki* (stem) vs. *kuuki* (air).

In pronouncing a long vowel, foreign learners should nearly double the length of the corresponding short vowel. E speakers are especially advised not to lengthen J short vowels, but to cut them short.

2.2 i and ii (い, イ and いー, イー)

J **i** is phonetically [i] and [iː]. It is close to the French vowel in *qui*, *ici*, etc. E short *i*-vowel in words like *sit*, *miss* is halfway between J **i** and **e**, and, if used, sometimes sounds like **e** to Japanese listeners. It would be better for E-speaking learners to make their *i*-vowel more like long *e*, though they must cut it short. On the other hand, E long *e*-vowel in *be*, *seat*, etc. can safely be used for J **ii**.

2.3 e and ee (え, エ and えー, エー)

J **e** is phonetically halfway between [e] and [ɛ], and is close to the short *e*-vowel in *get*, *less*, etc. The *a*-vowel in *day*, *late*, etc. can safely be used for J **ee**, though the latter is less diphthongal than the former.

2.4   a and aa (あ, ア and あー, アー)

Phonetically between [a] and [ɑ], J **a** has rather a wide range. The nearest vowel to this is British (abbreviated to B hereafter) E short *u*-vowel in *cut*, *fun*, etc. J **a** is halfway between American (abbreviated to A) E short *u*-vowel (*hut*, *luck*, etc.) and short *o*-vowel (*not*, *lock*, etc.) The initial part of the long *i*-vowel in *ice*, *fine*, etc. will also do for J **a**.

Learners are warned against using E short *a*-vowel in *back*, *man*, etc., since this sometimes sounds a little like **e** to Japanese listeners. E *a*-vowel in words like *father*, *Chicago* can be used for J **aa**.

2.5   o and oo (お, オ and おー, オー)

J **o** is phonetically halfway between [o] and [ɔ]. The nearest approach to this vowel is the initial part of A E long *o*-vowel in *go*, *most*, etc., or the B E *au*-vowel in *cause*, *law*, etc., but these should be cut short. B E short *o*-vowel in *hot*, *lock*, etc. is too open for J **o**, and A E short *o*-vowel in *hot*, *lock*, etc. is more like J **a** than J **o**. The nearest vowel to J **oo** is B E *au*-vowel, A E *au*-vowel being too open. It is also like A E long *o*-vowel in *go*, *road*, etc., though less diphthongal. British learners (especially those from southern England) should never use their long *o*-vowel in *go*, *road*, etc., because it sometimes sounds like **au** to Japanese listeners.

2.6   u and uu (う, ウ and うー, ウー)

J **u** is phonetically [ɯ], that is, it lacks the lip-rounding which accompanies the *u*-vowel of most European languages. Therefore learners are advised not to round the corners of their mouths, but to draw them back when making this vowel. This also holds true in the pronunciation of long **uu**.

2.7   Devoicing of vowels

J vowels, especially **i** and **u** are often devoiced (i.e. become voiceless) when they do not carry the accent nucleus (see 5.) and occur between voiceless consonants, or occur at the end of a word or an utterance, preceded by a voiceless consonant. The devoicing is represented by a small circle under the phonetic symbols thus [i̥] and [ɯ̥]. For example, *chikara* [tʃi̥kara] (strength), *pittari* [pi̥ttari] (closely), *ashi* [aʃi̥] (reed); *suppai* [sɯ̥ppai] (sour), *futoi* [ɸɯ̥toi] (thick), *karasu* [karasɯ̥], etc. In the final **su** in ...*masu*. or ...*desu*., **u** is very often devoiced or dropped completely, and the preceding **s** is compensatorily lengthened. However, failure to devoice these **i**'s and **u**'s does not impair intelligibility.

3. Consonants

3.1 k (ka か, カ, ki き, キ, ku く, ク, ke け, ケ, ko こ, コ; kya きゃ, キャ, kyu きゅ, キュ, kyo きょ, キョ)

Phoetically [k]. It is like E *k* in *keep, cold,* etc., but the aspiration, or *h*-like sound, after J **k** is weaker than in E.

3.2 g (ga が, ガ, gi ぎ, ギ, gu ぐ, グ, ge げ, ゲ, go ご, ゴ; gya ぎゃ, ギャ, gyu ぎゅ, ギュ, gyo ぎょ, ギョ)

Phonetically [g]. It is like E *g* in *get, good,* etc. In the middle of words like *kago* (basket), *agaru* (rise) and in the particle *ga* (が), **g** is often pronounced [ŋ] (as in E *sing*) in traditional standard J, but [ŋ] is currently being replaced by [g]. Foreign learners can safely use ⌈g⌉ in these positions.

3.3 s (sa さ, サ, su す, ス, se せ, セ, so そ, ソ)

Phonetically [s], the sound in E *set, soon,* etc.

3.4 sh (shi し, シ, sha しゃ, シャ, shu しゅ, シュ, sho しょ, ショ)

Phonetically [ʃ]. It is like E *sh* in *shine, short,* etc., but lacks the lip-protrusion which often accompanies E *sh*.

3.5 z (za ざ, ザ, zu ず, ズ, ze ぜ, ゼ, zo ぞ, ゾ)

At the beginning of words, J **z** is phonetically [dz], like E *ds* in *cards, leads,* etc. In the middle of words it is usually [z], like E *z* in *zone, lazy,* etc. However, *z* is always intelligible in all positions.

3.6 j (ji じ, ジ; ja じゃ, ジャ, ju じゅ, ジュ, jo じょ, ジョ)

Phonetically [dʒ], the sound in E *judge, George,* etc.

3.7 t (ta た, タ, te て, テ, to と, ト)

Phonetically dental [t] with the tip of the tongue against the front upper teeth, rather than against the teethridge as in the E *t* in *time, talk,* etc., which, however, can safely be used. The aspiration after J **t** is weaker than in E. American learners are warned against using their *t* before a weak vowel as in words like *city, matter,* because it sometimes sounds like **r** to Japanese listeners.

3.8 d (da だ, ダ, de で, デ, do ど, ド)

Phonetically [d] pronounced in the same way as J **t** but with voice. However, the E *d* as in in *dark, date,* etc., can safely be used for J **d**. Again, Americans should avoid using their *d* before a weak vowel as in *ladder, pudding,* etc., since it sometimes sounds like **r** to Japanese listeners.

3.9 ch (chi ち, チ; cha ちゃ, チャ, chu ちゅ, チュ, cho ちょ, チョ)

Phonetically [tʃ], the sound in E *church, nature,* etc.

3.10 ts (tsu つ, ツ)

Phonetically [ts], the sound in E *cats, roots,* etc. English speakers often find it difficult to say [ts] initially as in *tsuzuku* (continue), *tsuru* (crane). You can practice this sound by saying it in words like *cat's-eye* and then omitting the first part of that word (*ca*).

3.11 n (na な, ナ, ni に, ニ, nu ぬ, ヌ, ne ね, ネ, no の, ノ; nya にゃ, ニャ, nyu にゅ, ニュ, nyo にょ, ニョ)

Phonetically dental [n], not alveolar as the E *n* in *night, none,* etc., but this causes no practical problems. It is more important that foreign learners should distinguish this sound from ñ treated in 3.20.

3.12 h (ha は, ハ, hi ひ, ヒ, he へ, ヘ, ho ほ, ホ; hya ひゃ, ヒャ, hyu ひゅ, ヒュ, hyo ひょ, ヒョ)

Phonetically [h], the sound in E *house, hold,* etc. To be more exact, the **h** before **i** and **y** is phonetically [ç], the sound heard in German *ich.* [ç] is accompanied by more friction in the mouth than E *h*.

3.13 f (fu ふ, フ)

Phonetically [ɸ]. Though spelled with **f**, it is slightly different from the *f* in European languages. While European *f* is formed with the lower lip against the upper teeth, the J **f** is produced with the upper and the lower lips close together. The friction sound of J **f** is weaker than European *f*.

3.14 b (ba ば, バ, bi び, ビ, bu ぶ, ブ, be べ, ベ, bo ぼ, ボ; bya びゃ, ビャ, byu びゅ, ビュ, byo びょ, ビョ)

Phonetically [b]. Like E *b* in *be, ball,* etc.

3.15 p (pa ぱ, パ, pi ぴ, ピ, pu ぷ, プ, pe ぺ, ペ, po ぽ, ポ; pya ぴゃ, ピャ, pyu ぴゅ, ピュ, pyo ぴょ, ピョ)

Phonetically [p]. It is like E *p* in *pay, post,* etc., but the aspiration after J **p** is weaker than in E.

3.16 m (ma ま, マ, mi み, ミ, mu む, ム, me め, メ, mo も, モ; mya みゃ, ミャ, myu みゅ, ミュ, myo みょ, ミョ)

Phonetically [m], the sound in E *meet, most,* etc.

3.17 y (ya や, ヤ, yu ゆ, ユ, yo よ, ヨ)

Phonetically [j], the semivowel corresponding to the vowel **i** [i]. It is like the sound in E *yes, you,* etc. **ya, yu, yo** can follow consonants such as **p, b, k, g, h, m, n** and form one syllable. In that case the resulting combinations are called **yoo-on**.

3.18 r (ra ら, ラ, ri り, リ, ru る, ル, re れ, レ, ro ろ, ロ; rya りゃ, リャ, ryu りゅ, リュ, ryo りょ, リョ)

Phonetically, J **r** is often a retroflex stop [d] initially and flap [ɾ] between vowels. Unlike E and other European *r*, it is made with a single tap of the tip of the tongue against the front upper teeth. It sometimes sounds like *d* to a European ear.

3. 19 w (wa わ, ワ)

Phonetically [ɥ], the semivowel corresponding to the vowel **u** [ɯ]. Like J **u**, it lacks lip-rounding which usually accompanies European *w*-sound.

3. 20 ñ (ん, ン)

ñ is peculiar to J. Learners should never confuse this sound with **n** treated in 3.11. Though usually spelled with the same letter **n** in the Roman alphabet, **n** and ñ are quite different in J. While **n** is a pure consonant and is always followed by a vowel or **y**, ñ appears word-finally, before a consonant, a vowel, and **y**, but never at the beginning of a word. ñ is called hatsuoñ. It is always long enough to make a syllable by itself (see 4). Besides, ñ has the following varieties according to the position in which it appears. The phonetic property common to all the following variants is that they are syllabic nasals. Thus,

(1) in word-final position: Phonetically syllabic [N], a rather difficult sound for foreign learners. It is made further back than E *ng* [ŋ] (between the backmost part of the tongue and uvula). Examples *eñ* (yen), *hoñ* (book).

(2) before z, j, t, d, ch, ts, n, and r: Phonetically syllabic [n], nearly the same as E *n*, but longer. Examples *bañzai* (hurrah), *heñji* (answer), *kañtoku* (manager), *koñdo* (this time), *deñchi* (cell), *kañtsuu* (penetration), *oñna* (woman), *señro* (rail).

(3) before f, b, p, and m: Phonetically syllabic [m], the same as E *m*, but longer. Examples *iñfure* (inflation), *biñboo* (poverty), *kiñpatsu* (blonde), *koñmori* (thickly).

(4) before k and g: Phonetically syllabic [ŋ], the same as E *ng*, but longer. Examples *keñka* (quarrel), *sañgo* (coral).

(5) before s and sh: To be phonetically exact, a nasalized vowel [ĩ], but learners may use [N] in this position. Examples *keñsa* (inspection), *deñsha* (electric train). English-speaking people are advised not to use their *n* here, because they often insert a *t*-sound between *n* and the following *s* or *sh*. The result is *nts* or *nch*, which may sometimes be unintelligible to a Japanese listener.

(6) before h, y, w, and a vowel: Phonetically nasalized vowels like [ĩ], [ẽ], [ũ], etc. Learners, however, may use [N] in these positions. Examples *hañhañ* (fifty-fifty), *pañya* (bakery), *deñwa* (telephone), *heñi* (variation), *dañatsu* (oppression). They should

never use *n* in these positions, since the resulting pronunciation would often be unintelligible. Note the following distinctions: *hiñi* (dignity) vs. *hi ni* (by a day), *kiñeñ* (no smoking) vs. *kineñ* (commemoration), *fuñeñ* (smoke of a volcano) vs. *funeñ* (non-flammable).

3. 21   Double consonants (っ, ッ)

In J, double consonants appear in the combination of **kk**, **ss**, **ssh** (**s**+**sh**), **tt**, **tch** (**t**+**ch**), **tts** (**t**+**ts**), and **pp** as in *sekkeñ* (soap), *bessoo* (villa), *issho* (together), *kitto* (certainly), *itchi* (agreement), *mittsu* (three), *suppai* (sour). English-speaking learners are warned against regarding them as single consonants as in *lesson*, *butter*, *catcher*, etc. They should pronounce them twice as the *c*'s in *thick cloud*, *sh*'s in *reddish shoes*, *t*'s in *hot tea*, *tch* in *hit children*, *p*'s in *hope peace*, etc. To Japanese ears, the first part of a double consonant is considered an independent sound and is counted as consituting another syllable (see 4.). For example, while the second **t** in *kitto* (certainly) is the "normal" **t**, the first **t** is regarded as an independent sound referred to as **sokuoñ** and is written with a smaller *kana* letter っ, ッ (the Roman letter **q** is used by some linguists to represent it, as in *kiqto*), and the word is counted as making three syllables (not two). Likewise, *sekkeñ* (i.e. *seqkeñ*) constitutes three syllables. Note the following distinctions between single and double consonants: *sekeñ* (world) vs. *sekkeñ* (soap), *sasoo to* (in order to stab) vs. *sassoo to* (smartly), *hato* (pigeon) vs. *hatto* (surprisedly), *ichi* (location) vs. *itchi* (agreement), *mitsu* (honey) vs. *mittsu* (three), *supai* (spy) vs. *suppai* (sour).

4.   Syllables

J syllables (to be more exact, beats, or technically, morae) are normally composed of a consonant and a vowel in that order, the exceptions being **ñ** ん, ン (see 3.20) and **q** っ, ッ (see 3.21). See the table of the J syllabary on the front endpaper. J syllables tend to be of nearly equal length, though **ñ** and **q** are usually pronounced slightly shorter. Thus, *teashi* (limbs) (three syllables) is said nearly three times longer than *te* (hand) (one syllable).

5.   Accent

J does not have an accent system of strong and weak stress like E, and each syllable is said with nearly equal strength. Instead, J has a pitch accent system. The degrees of the pitch of voice depend on the rate of vibration of the vocal cords. When the vibration is fast the pitch is high, and when the rate is slow the pitch is low. The accent patterns of standard J are most clearly explained in terms of two significant levels of pitch: **high** and **low**, and the **accent nucleus**. Words are divided into two classes: words with and without an accent nucleus. In all words which have an accent nucleus, the syllable where the nucleus falls and the preceding syllables (except the first one which is automatically low) are pronounced high, and every syllable that follows the nucleus is said low. In this dictionary accent nucleus is marked with ˺, and the automatic rise on the second syllable is marked with ˹. Thus,

(1) Words with an accent nucleus on the first syllable are: *hi*˺ (fire), *ne*˺*ko* (cat), *i*˺*nochi* (life), *so*˺*rososo* (slowly).

(2) Words with a nucleus on the second syllable are: *i*˹*nu*˺ (dog), *ko*˹*ko*˺*ro* (mind), *i*˹*ke*˺*bana* (flower arrangement).

(3) Words with a nucleus on the third syllable are: *o*˹*toko*˺ (man), *a*˹*maga*˺*sa* (umbrella), *ka*˹*rai*˺*bari* (bravado).

(4) Words with a nucleus on the fourth syllable are: *o*˹*tooto*˺ (younger brother), *wa*˹*tashibu*˺*ne* (ferry boat), *shi*˹*dareya*˺*nagi* (weeping willow).

(5) Words without an accent nucleus are automatically pronounced with the first syllable low and all the succeeding syllables are kept high (though actually with a slight gradual descent). They are: *hi* (day), *u*˹*shi* (cattle), *ka*˹*tachi* (shape), *to*˹*modachi* (friend). Compare the following pair of phrases: *hi*˺ *ga* (the fire is…) and *hi*˹*ga* (the day is…), the former *hi* having a nucleus on it, the latter *hi* without a nucleus.

A word may lose its original accent pattern when it becomes a part of a compound word which then has its own accent pattern as a single word. Thus, *ga*˹*ikoku* (foreign country) and *yu*˹*ubiñ* (mail) but *ga*˹*ikoku-yu*˺*ubiñ* (foreign mail), *o*˺*ñgaku* (music) and *ga*˹*kkoo* (school), but *o*˺*ñgaku-ga*˺*kkoo* (music school), and so on. In this dictionary, only those compounds given as main entries are marked with accent.

APPENDIX 2

Outline of Japanese Grammar

1 Noun

Japanese nouns have no gender or case. There is no distinction between singular and plural: *hoñ* (本) means 'a book' or 'books.' But some suffixes are used to indicate the plural: *kare-ra* (they), *kodomo-tachi* (children). Some nouns are capable of forming plurals by reduplication, sometimes with sound changes: *yama-yama* (mountains), and *hito-bito* (people).

1. 1 There is a large class of nouns whose function is chiefly grammatical. They are used in making phrases in which these nouns are preceded by a modifier. For example, *kita toki* (when I came), *mita koto* (what I saw), *nani-ka taberu mono* (something to eat), etc. Other examples of such nouns are *aida, tame, tokoro, wake,* etc.

2 Verb

Verbs are classified into the following three groups: consonant-stem verbs, vowel-stem verbs and irregular verbs.

2. 1 Consonant-stem verb (*u*-verbs)

The verbs in this group have a consonant preceding final '*u*' in the dictionary form. Note that all verbs ending in vowel plus '*u*' in their dictionary form are also consonant stem verbs; the original '*w*' in these verbs has simply been lost in the modern language: *kawu > kau, hirowu > hirou,* etc.

Consonant-stem verbs are marked Ⓒ in this dictionary.

2. 2 Vowel-stem verb (*ru*-verbs)

The verbs in this group end with a final '*-ru*' preceded by '*i*' or '*e*' in the dictionary form. However, not all verbs that end thus are vowel-stem verbs, since there are some consonant-stem verbs which end with '*-iru*' or '*-eru.*'

> *hairu* (enter), *hashiru* (run), *iru* (need), *kiru* (cut), *shiru* (know), *kaeru* (return).

Vowel-stem verbs are marked Ⓥ in this dictionary.

2. 3 Irregular verb

There are only two irregular verbs, *suru* (do) (and those verbs formed with *suru*: *mensuru*, *tassuru*, etc.) and *kuru* (come), which are irregular only in their stems.

Irregular verbs are marked ☐ in this dictionary.

3   Conjugations of Verbs

Basic Verb Forms

	Ending	Consonant-stem verbs		Vowel-stem verb	Irregular verb	Irregular verb
Dictionary form	-u	kak·u (write)	yob·u (call)	tabe·ru (eat)	s·uru (do)	k·uru (come)
masu-form	-masu	kaki-masu	yobi-masu	tabe-masu	shi-masu	ki-masu
Negative	-nai	kaka-nai	yoba-nai	tabe-nai	shi-nai	ko-nai
te-form	-t[d]e	kai-te	yoñ-de	tabe-te	shi-te	ki-te
ta-form	-t[d]a	kai-ta	yoñ-da	tabe-ta	shi-ta	ki-ta
tara-form	-t[d]ara	kai-tara	yoñ-dara	tabe-tara	shi-tara	ki-tara
tari-form	-t[d]ari	kai-tari	yoñ-dari	tabe-tari	shi-tari	ki-tari
Desiderative	-tai	kaki-tai	yobi-tai	tabe-tai	shi-tai	ki-tai
Provisional	-ba	kake-ba	yobe-ba	tabere-ba	sure-ba	kure-ba
Tentative	-oo -yoo	kak-oo	yob-oo	tabe-yoo	shi-yoo	ko-yoo
Imperative	-e -ro	kak-e	yob-e	tabe-ro	shi-ro	ko-i
Potential	-eru -rareru	kak-eru	yob-eru	tabe-rareru	(dekiru)	ko-rareru
Passive	-reru -rareru	kaka-reru	yoba-reru	tabe-rareru	sa-reru	ko-rareru
Causative	-seru -saseru	kaka-seru	yoba-seru	tabe-saseru	sa-seru	ko-saseru
Causative-passive	-serareru -saserareru	kaka-serareru	yoba-serareru	tabe-saserareru	saserareru	ko-saserareru

3.1   Dictionary form

This is the form by which verbs are listed in the dictionary. The dictionary form of all Japanese verbs ends in '*u*.' This form is in fact the non-past tense of a verb.

Watashi wa Iku. (I go/will go.)

3.2 Continuative form (*masu*-form)

The continuative base of a consonant-stem verb is made by replacing the final '*u*' with '*i*': *kaku* (write) > *kaki-masu*. In the case of a vowel-stem verb, it is made by dropping the final '*ru*': *taberu* (eat) > *tabe-masu*. Irregular verbs are: *suru* (do) > *shi-masu*, *kuru* (come) > *ki-masu*. The following five formal, polite verbs are slightly irregular in dropping '*r*' in their continuative forms.

gozaru (be)	*gozari-masu* > *gozai-masu*
irassharu (go, come)	*irasshari-masu* > *irasshai-masu*
kudasaru (give)	*kudasari-masu* > *kudasai-masu*
nasaru (do)	*nasari-masu* > *nasai-masu*
ossharu (say)	*osshari-masu* > *osshai-masu*

'*-masu*' is used to make the tone of speech polite, and has no concrete meaning in itself.

The conjugation of '*-masu*'

Negative	-maseñ
te-form	-mashi-te
ta-form	-mashi-ta
ba-form	-masure-ba
Tentative	-mashoo

3.3 Negative form (*nai*-form)

The negative base of a consonant-stem verb is made by replacing the final '*u*' with '*a*': *kaku* (write) > *kaka-nai*. In modern Japanese '*w*' is retained only before '*a*,' so those verbs which end in vowel plus '*u*' in the dictionary form in the modern language, but which had an original '*w*' (see 2.1), retain this in the negative form: *ka(w)u* > *kawa-nai*, *hiro(w)u* > *hirowa-nai*. In the case of a vowel-stem verb, the negative base is made by dropping the final '*ru*': *taberu* (eat) > *tabe-nai*. Irregular verbs are: *suru* (do) > *shi-nai*, *kuru* (come) > *ko-nai*.

The conjugation of '*nai*'

te-form	-naku-te
ta-form	-nakat-ta
ba-form	-nakere-ba

3.4 Gerund (*te*-form)

In the case of a vowel-stem verb, the gerund is made by adding '*te*' to the stem.

In the consonant-stem conjugation, however, the verbs undergo sound changes according to the final consonant of the stem.

ka-	ku	ka-	i	-te	write
oyo-	gu	oyo-	i	-de	swim
to-	bu	to-	ñ	-de	jump
no-	mu	no-	ñ	-de	drink
shi-	nu	shi-	ñ	-de	die
hana-	su	hana-	shi	-te	speak
ka-	u	ka-	t	-te	buy
no-	ru	no-	t	-te	ride
ma-	tsu	ma-	t	-te	wait

For the uses of the *te*-form, see under the main entry for '*-te*.' The past tense (*ta*-form) is simply made be replacing the '*-te*' with '*-ta*.'

3.5 Provisional form (*ba*-form)

The provisional form of a verb is made by replacing the final '*-u*' with '*e*' and adding '*-ba*.' This is equivalent to stating that the *ba*-form of a verb is made by dropping the final '*-u*' and adding '*-eba*': *kaku* (write) > *kake-ba*, *taberu* (eat) > *tabere-ba*. Irregular verbs are *suru* (do) > *sure-ba* and *kuru* (come) > *kure-ba*.

This form is also called the conditional form. It indicates the circumstances under which the situation or action in the main clause will be possible.

3.6 Tentative form

The tentative form of a consonant-stem verb is made by changing the final '*u*' to '*oo*': *kaku* (write) > *kak-oo*. In the case of a vowel-stem verb, it is made by changing the final '*-ru*' to '*-yoo*': *taberu* (eat) > *tabe-yoo*. Irregular verbs are *suru* (do) > *shi-yoo*, *kuru* (come) > *ko-yoo*. This form conveys the probable mood and indicates possibility, probability, belief, doubt, etc.

3.7 Imperative form
The imperative form of a consonant-stem verb is made by replacing the final '*u*' with '*e*': *kaku* (write) > *kak-e*. In the case of a vowel-stem verb, it is made by replacing the final '*ru*' with '*ro*': *taberu* (eat) > *tabe-ro*. The irregular verbs are *suru* (do) > *shi-ro* and *kuru* (come) > *ko-i*. This form constitutes a brusque imperative.

The imperative forms of the formal, polite verbs are as follows:

> *gozaru* (be)   no form
> *irassharu* (go, come) > *irasshai*
> *kudasaru* (give)   > *kudasai*
> *nasaru* (do)   > *nasai*
> *ossharu* (say)   > *osshai*

3.8 Other verb forms
Forms not dealt with in this 'Outline' can be referred to under the relevant 'ending' in the body of the dictionary.

4 Intransitive and transitive verbs

4.1 Intransitive verb (*vi.*)
An intransitive verb is a verb which is used without a direct object: *aku* (open), *tomaru* (stop), *iku* (go), *kuru* (come), etc.

4.2 Transitive verb (*vt.*)
A transitive verb is a verb which is used with a direct object. The object is usually followed by the particle '*o.*' However, it does not necessarily follow that every noun followed by '*o*' is a direct object, since '*o*' can also denote a location: *kado o magaru* (turn a corner).

Many transitive verbs have intransitive verb partners: *okosu* (wake) / *okiru* (get up), *miru* (look at) / *mieru* (be visible).

Pairs of transitive and intransitive verbs

vt.	*vi.*	Examples
-eru	-aru	*ageru* (raise) / *agaru* (rise)
-eru	-u	*tsukeru* (attach) / *tsuku* (stick)
-u	-eru	*toru* (take) / *toreru* (be taken)
-asu	-u	*chirasu* (scatter) / *chiru* (be scattered)
-su	-ru	*kaesu* (return) / *kaeru* (come back)

In the case of a small number of verbs, the transitive and intransitive forms are the same: *owaru* (end), *hiraku* (open), etc.

Among the large class of verbs formed by noun plus *suru*, some are transitive, some are intransitive, and some are both transitive and intransitive.

sakusee suru (*vt.*) (I) make (something).

shippai suru (*vi.*) (I) fail.

teñkai suru (*vt.*) (I) develop (something).

(*vi.*) (Something) develops.

5 Copula

The informal form is *da* and the polite form is *desu*.

The conjugation of the copula

	informal	polite
Sentence final form	da	desu
Negative	de nai (ja nai)	de wa arimaseñ (ja arimaseñ)
te-form	de	deshite
ta-form	datta	deshita
ba-form	nara (ba)	deshitara (ba)

6 Adjective

The dictionary form of adjectives ends with '*i.*' Adjectives occur in attributive position: *Kore wa furui kuruma desu.* (This is an old car.), or in predicative position: *Kono kuruma wa furui.* (This car is old.) An adjective can stand by itself as a complete sentence. For example, *Furui* means '(Something) is old.'

Basic adjective forms

Dict. form	samu·i (cold)
ku-form	samu-ku
Negative	samu-kunai
te-form	samu-kute
ta-form	samu-katta
ba-form	samu-kereba

7 Adjectival noun

Adjectival nouns have some functions that ordinary nouns have, and other functions which are similar to adjectives. This class of words is sometimes simply called '*na* word,' since the word '*na*' is used to link an adjectival noun to the following noun or adjectival noun which it modifies. An adjectival noun followed by '*ni*' is an adverb. In this dictionary, '*na*' is treated as a variant of the copula and '*ni*' is a particle indicating manner, and they are written separately: *shizuka na umi* (calm sea), *shizuka ni aruku* (walk quietly).

8 Adverb

Adverbs modify verbs, adjectives and other adverbs. There are true adverbs and derived adverbs. True adverbs include *sugu* (immediately), *mattaku* (very much), *hakkiri* (clearly), etc.
Derived adverbs:

1 Adjectival nouns with the particle '*ni*.'
   shizuka ni (quietly)
2 The *ku*-form of adjectives.
   hayaku (early), *osoku* (slowly), etc.
3 The *te*-form of verbs.
   aratamete (again), *kononde* (willingly), etc.

9 Interrogative words

When interrogative words are followed by the particles '*ka*' or '*mo*,' or the gerund of the copula plus '*mo*' (i.e. *de mo*), the resulting combinations take on a variety of meanings.

	with 'ka'	with 'mo'		with 'de mo'
		(affirm. verb)	(neg. verb)	
dare (who)	someone	everyone	no one	anyone
dore (which of three or more)	some (one)	every one	none	any one
dochira (which of two)	either	both	neither	either
doo (how)	somehow	every way	no way	any way
doko (where)	somewhere	everywhere	nowhere	anywhere
itsu (when)	sometime	always	never	any time
nani (what)	something	(not used)	nothing	anything

10 Attributive

Attributive refers to a class of words which do not change their form. Some of these correspond to English pronominal adjectives: *kono* (this), *sono* (that), *ano* (that over there), *dono* (which), *koñna* (this kind of), *soñna* (that kind of), *añna* (that kind of), *doñna* (what kind of). *Ooki-na* (large), *chiisa-na* (small), *okashi-na* (funny), etc. are also considered attributives. They cannot be classified as adjectival nouns, even though they are followed by '*na*,' because *ooki*, *chiisa* and *okashi* without '*na*' can neither be used as nouns nor be followed by the copula *da* (*desu*).

ko- here (near the speaker)	so- there (far from the speaker and near the listener)	a- over there (far from both speaker and listener)	do- question
kore this (one)	sore that (one)	are that (one)	dore? which (one)?
kono this	sono that	ano that (over there)	dono? which?
koko here	soko there	asoko over there	doko? where?
kochira this side	sochira that side	achira that side	dochira? which side?
koñna this kind of	soñna that kind of	añna that kind of	doñna? what kind of?
koo like this	soo like that	aa like that	doo? how?

11 Conjunction

A conjunction is a word or phrase which is used to link words, phrases, clauses, or sentences. Many Japanese conjunctions are a combination of two or more words: *sore de* (therefore), *soo suru to* (then).

12 Inflected ending

Inflected endings are attached to a base of a verb, the stem of a verb or adjective, or the copula in order to give a wide range of additional meanings to that verb, adjective or copula: '*-ba*' in *ikeba*, '*-nai*' in *oishikunai*, '*-ta*' in *deshita*, etc.

13 Particle

Particles (*wa*, *ga*, *mo*, *o*, etc.) are unchanging in form and used to indicate the topic, subject, object, etc. of a Japanese sentence as well as functioning in a way similar to prepositions in English: *kara* (away from), *ni* (toward), etc. They are placed after a noun, clause, or sentence, and are sometimes called 'postpositions.'

14 Interjection

An interjection is a word which expresses a strong feeling such as surprise, pain, horror and so on.

aa (oh), *iya* (no), *hora* (look), etc.

15 Prefix

A prefix is a meaning element or a group of meaning elements added to the beginning of a word to form a new word. The new word is written as one word, or sometimes a hyphen is used.

dai- (big), *doo-* (the same), *sai-* (again), etc.

16 Suffix

A suffix is a meaning element or a group of meaning elements added to the end of another word to form a new word; suf. (*a.*) and suf (*a.n.*) indicate that the derived forms are an adjective or adjectival noun respectively.

-dañ (group), *-juu* (through), *-ryuu* (style), etc.

APPENDIX 3

Numbers

Native Japanese counting system

1	hi˹to˺tsu	6	mu˹ttsu˺
2	fu˹tatsu˺	7	na˹na˺tsu
3	mi˹ttsu˺	8	ya˹ttsu˺
4	yo˹ttsu˹	9	ko˹ko˹notsu
5	i˹tsu˺tsu	10	to˹o
		?	i˹kutsu

Chinese-derived system

1	i˹chi˹ (一)	100	hya˹ku˹ (百)
2	ni˹ (二)	200	ni-˹hyaku
3	sa˹ñ (三)	300	sañ˹-byaku
4	shi˹, yo˹ñ (四)	400	yoñ˹-hyaku
5	go˹ (五)	500	go-˹hyaku
6	ro˹ku˹ (六)	600	rop-˹pyaku
7	na˹na, shi˹chi˹ (七)	700	na˹na˹-hyaku
8	ha˹chi˹ (八)	800	hap-˹pyaku
9	ku˹, kyu˹u (九)	900	kyu˹u-hyaku
10	ju˹u (十)	1,000	se˹ñ (千)
11	ju˹u-ichi˹	2,000	ni-˹se˹ñ
12	ju˹u-ni˹	3,000	sa˹ñ-ze˹ñ
13	ju˹u-sañ	4,000	yo˹ñ-se˹ñ
14	ju˹u-shi˹, ju˹u-yoñ˹	5,000	go-˹se˹ñ
15	ju˹u-go	6,000	ro˹ku-se˹ñ
16	ju˹u-roku˹	7,000	na˹na-se˹ñ
17	ju˹u-shichi˹, ju˹u-na˹na	8,000	ha˹s-se˹ñ
18	ju˹u-hachi˹	9,000	kyu˹u-se˹ñ
19	ju˹u-ku, ju˹u-kyu˹u	10,000	i˹chi-ma˹ñ (1 万)
20	ni˹-juu	100,000	ju˹u-ma˹ñ
30	sa˹ñ-juu	1,000,000	hya˹ku-ma˹ñ
40	yo˹ñ-juu	10,000,000	se˹ñ-ma˹ñ
50	go-˹ju˹u	100,000,000	i˹chi˹-oku (1 億)
60	ro˹ku-ju˹u	1,000,000,000	ju˹u-oku
70	shi˹chi-ju˹u, na˹na˹-juu	10,000,000,000	hya˹ku˹-oku
80	ha˹chi-ju˹u	100,000,000,000	se˹ñ-oku
90	kyu˹u-juu	1,000,000,000,000	i˹t-choo (1 兆)

APPENDIX 4 Counters

	-fuń (分) minutes	-hai (杯) cups	-haku (泊) stays	-hatsu (発) shots	-heń (週) times	-hiki (匹) fish	-ho (歩) steps	-hoń (本) bottles	-kai (階) floors	-keń (軒) houses	-soku (足) shoes	-wa (羽) birds
1	i'p-puń	i'p-pai	i'p-paku	i'p-patsu'	i'p-peń	i'p-piki'	i'p-po	i'p-poń	i'k-kai	i'k-keń	i's-soku'	i'chi'-wa
2	ni'-fuń	ni'-hai	ni'-haku	ni'-hatsu	ni'-heń	ni'-hiki	ni'-ho	ni'-hoń	ni'-kai	ni'-keń	ni'-soku	ni'-wa
3	sa'ń-puń	sa'ń-bai	sa'ń-paku	sa'ń-patsu	sa'ń-beń	sa'ń-biki	sa'ń-po	sa'ń-boń	sa'ń-gai	sa'ń-geń	sa'ń-zoku	sa'ń-ba
4	yo'ń-puń	yo'ń-hai	yo'ń-haku	yo'ń-hatsu	yo'ń-heń	yo'ń-hiki	yo'ń-ho	yo'ń-hoń	yo'ń-kai	yo'ń-keń	yo'ń-soku	yo'ń-wa
5	go'-fuń	go'-hai	go'-haku	go'-hatsu	go'-heń	go'-hiki	go'-ho	go-'hoń	go-'kai	go'-keń	go'-soku	go'-wa
6	ro'p-puń	ro'p-pai	ro'p-paku	ro'p-patsu'	ro'p-peń	ro'p-piki'	ro'p-po	ro'p-poń	ro'k-kai	ro'k-keń	ro'k-soku'	ro'ku'-wa
7	na'na'-fuń	na'na'-hai	na'na'-haku	na'na'-hatsu	na'na'-heń	na'na'-hiki	na'na'-ho	na'na'-hoń	na'na'-kai	na'na'-keń	na'na'-soku	na'na'-wa
8	ha'p-puń	ha'p-pai	ha'p-paku	ha'p-patsu'	ha'p-peń	ha'p-piki'	ha'p-po	ha'p-poń	ha'k-kai	ha'k-keń	ha's-soku'	ha'chi'-wa
9	kyu'u-fuń	kyu'u-hai	hyu'u-haku	kyu'u-hatsu	kyu'u-heń	kyu'u-hiki	kyu'u-ho	kyu'u-hoń	kyu'u-kai	kyu'u-keń	kyu'u-soku	kyu'u-wa
10	ji'p-puń ju'p-puń	ji'p-pai ju'p-pai	ji'p-paku ju'p-paku	ji'p-patsu' ju'p-patsu'	ji'p-peń ju'p-peń	ji'p-piki' ju'p-piki'	ji'p-po ju'p-po	ji'p-poń ju'p-poń	ji'k-kai ju'k-kai	ji'k-keń ju'k-keń	ji's-soku' ju's-soku'	ji'p-pa ju'p-pa
How many	na'ń-puń	na'ń-bai	na'ń-paku	na'ń-patsu	na'ń-beń	na'ń-biki	na'ń-po	na'ń-boń	na'ń-gai	na'ń-geń	na'ń-zoku	na'ń-ba

APPENDIX 5

Days, Weeks and Months

1st	tsuˈitachi¹	11th	juˈu-ichi-nichi¹	21st	niˈjuu-ichi-nichi
2nd	fuˈtsuka	12th	juˈu-ni-nichi¹	22nd	niˈjuu-ni-nichi
3rd	miˈkka	13th	juˈu-saˈñ-nichi	23rd	niˈjuu-sañ-nichi
4th	yoˈkka	14th	juˈu-yokka	24th	niˈjuu-yokka
5th	iˈtsuka	15th	juˈu-go-nichi	25th	niˈjuu-go-nichi
6th	muˈika	16th	juˈu-roku-nichi¹	26th	niˈjuu-roku-nichi
7th	naˈnu[o]ka	17th	juˈu-shichi-nichi¹	27th	niˈjuu-shichi-nichi
8th	yoˈoka	18th	juˈu-hachi-nichi¹	28th	niˈjuu-hachi-nichi
9th	koˈkonoka¹	19th	juˈu-ku-nichi	29th	niˈjuu-ku-nichi
10th	toˈoka	20th	haˈtsuka	30th	saˈñjuˈu-nichi
				31st	saˈñjuu-ichi-nichi

niˈchiyoˈoˈ(bi)	日曜(日)	Sunday	
geˈtsuyoˈoˈ(bi)	月曜(日)	Monday	
kaˈyoˈoˈ(bi)	火曜(日)	Tuesday	
suˈiyoˈoˈ(bi)	水曜(日)	Wednesday	
moˈkuyoˈoˈ(bi)	木曜(日)	Thursday	
kiˈñyoˈoˈ(bi)	金曜(日)	Friday	
doˈyoˈoˈ(bi)	土曜(日)	Saturday	

January	iˈchi-gatsu¹
February	ni-ˈgatsu¹
March	saˈñ-gatsu
April	shi-ˈgatsu¹
May	goˈ-gatsu
June	roˈku-gatsu¹
July	shiˈchi-gatsu¹
August	haˈchi-gatsu¹
September	kuˈ-gatsu
October	juˈu-gatsu¹
November	juˈu-ichi-gatsu¹
December	juˈu-ni-gatsu¹

APPENDIX 6

National Holidays

January	1	Gañjitsu	New Year's Day
January	15	Seejiñ-no-hi	Coming-of-Age Day
February	11	Keñkoku-kineñ-no-hi	National Foundation Day
ca. March	21	Shuñbuñ-no-hi	Vernal Equinox Day
April	29	Midori-no-hi	Greenery Day
May	3	Keñpoo-kineñbi	Constitution Day
May	5	Kodomo-no-hi	Children's Day
September	15	Keeroo-no-hi	Respect-for-the-Aged Day
ca. Sept.	23	Shuubuñ-no-hi	Autumnal Equinox Day
October	10	Taiiku-no-hi	Health-Sports Day
November	3	Buñka-no-hi	Culture Day
November	23	Kiñroo-kañsha-no-hi	Labor Thanksgiving Day
December	23	Teñnoo-tañjoobi	The Emperor's Birthday

APPENDIX 7

Japanese Government Ministries and Agencies

Gaimu-shoo （外務省）	Ministry of Foreign Affairs
Hoomu-shoo （法務省）	Ministry of Justice
Jichi-shoo （自治省）	Ministry of Home Affairs
Keñsetsu-shoo （建設省）	Ministry of Construction
Koosee-shoo （厚生省）	Ministry of Health and Welfare
Moñbu-shoo （文部省）	Ministry of Education
Nooriñ-suisañ-shoo （農林水産省）	Ministry of Agriculture, Forestry and Fisheries
Ookura-shoo （大蔵省）	Ministry of Finance
Roodoo-shoo （労働省）	Ministry of Labor
Tsuusañ-shoo （通産省）	Ministry of International Trade and Industry
Uñyu-shoo （運輸省）	Ministry of Transport
Yuusee-shoo （郵政省）	Ministry of Posts and Telecommunications

Booee-choo (防衛庁) Defense Agency
Booeeshisetsu-choo (防衛施設庁) Defense Facilities Administration Agency
Buñka-choo (文化庁) Agency for Cultural Affairs
Chuushoo-kigyoo-choo (中小企業庁) Small and Medium Enterprise Agency
Hokkaidoo kaihatsu-choo (北海道開発庁) Hokkaido Development Agency
Kagaku-gijutsu-choo (科学技術庁) Science and Technology Agency
Kaijoohoañ-choo (海上保安庁) Maritime Safety Agency
Kainañshiñpañ-choo (海難審判庁) Marine Accidents Inquiry Agency
Kañkyoo-choo (環境庁) Environment Agency
Keesatsu-choo (警察庁) National Police Agency
Keñsatsu-choo (検察庁) Public Prosecutor's Office
Keezaikikaku-choo (経済企画庁) Economic Planning Agency
Kishoo-choo (気象庁) Meteorological Agency
Kokudo-choo (国土庁) National Land Agency
Kokuzee-choo (国税庁) National Tax Administration Agency
Kooañchoosa-choo (公安調査庁) Public Security Investigation Agency
Kunai-choo (宮内庁) Imperial Household Agency
Okinawa kaihatsu-choo (沖縄開発庁) Okinawa Development Agency
Riñya-choo (林野庁) Forestry Agency
Shakaihokeñ-choo (社会保険庁) Social Insurance Agency
Shigeñ-enerugii-choo (資源エネルギー庁) Agency of Natural Resources and Energy
Shokuryoo-choo (食糧庁) Food Agency
Shooboo-choo (消防庁) Fire Defense Agency
Soomu-choo (総務庁) Management and Coordination Agency
Suisañ-choo (水産庁) Fisheries Agency
Tokkyo-choo (特許庁) Patent Office

APPENDIX 8

Japanese Political Parties

Jiyuu Miñshutoo (自由民主党)	Liberal Democratic Party
Nihoñ Shakaitoo (日本社会党)	Social Democratic Party of Japan
Koomeetoo (公明党)	Komeito Party
Miñshatoo (民社党)	Japan Democratic Socialist Party
Nihoñ Kyoosañtoo (日本共産党)	Japanese Communist Party
Shakai Miñshu Reñgoo (社会民主連合)	United Social Democratic Party

APPENDIX 9

Japanese Historical Periods and Eras

Joomoñ-jidai	縄 文 時 代	8,000 – 300 B.C.
Yayoi-jidai	弥 生 時 代	300 B.C. – A.D. 300
Kofuñ-jidai	古 墳 時 代	A.D. 300 – 710
Nara-jidai	奈 良 時 代	710 – 794
Heeañ-jidai	平 安 時 代	794 – 1192
Kamakura-jidai	鎌 倉 時 代	1129 – 1333
Muromachi-jidai	室 町 時 代	1336 – 1573
Señgoku-jidai	戦 国 時 代	ca. 1480 – ca. 1570
Azuchi-Momoyama-jidai	安土・桃山時代	1573 – 1603
Edo-jidai	江 戸 時 代	1603 – 1867
Meeji-jidai	明 治 時 代	1868 – 1912
Taishoo-jidai	大 正 時 代	1912 – 1926
Shoowa-jidai	昭 和 時 代	1926 – 1989
Heesee-jidai	平 成 時 代	1989 –

After 1868, 'jidai' refers to emperors' names.

APPENDIX 10

Chronological Table of Eras

1868	Meeji	1	1911		44	1954		29
1869	明治	2	1912	Meeji	45	1955		30
1870		3	1913	Taishoo	2	1956		31
1871		4	1914	大正	3	1957		32
1872		5	1915		4	1958		33
1873		6	1916		5	1959		34
1874		7	1917		6	1960		35
1875		8	1918		7	1961		36
1876		9	1919		8	1962		37
1877		10	1920		9	1963		38
1878		11	1921		10	1964		39
1879		12	1922		11	1965		40
1880		13	1923		12	1966		41
1881		14	1924		13	1967		42
1882		15	1925		14	1968		43
1883		16	1926	Taishoo	15	1969		44
1884		17	1927	Shoowa	2	1970		45
1885		18	1928	昭和	3	1971		46
1886		19	1929		4	1972		47
1887		20	1930		5	1973		48
1888		21	1931		6	1974		49
1889		22	1932		7	1975		50
1890		23	1933		8	1976		51
1891		24	1934		9	1977		52
1892		25	1935		10	1978		53
1893		26	1936		11	1979		54
1894		27	1937		12	1980		55
1895		28	1938		13	1981		56
1896		29	1939		14	1982		57
1897		30	1940		15	1983		58
1898		31	1941		16	1984		59
1899		32	1942		17	1985		60
1900		33	1943		18	1986		61
1901		34	1944		19	1987		62
1902		35	1945		20	1988		63
1903		36	1946		21	1989	Shoowa	64
1904		37	1947		22	1990	Heesee	2
1905		38	1948		23	1991	平成	3
1906		39	1949		24	1992		4
1907		40	1950		25	1993		5
1908		41	1951		26	1994		6
1909		42	1952		27	1995		7
1910		43	1953		28	1996		8

APPENDIX 11

Essential English–Japanese Vocabulary List

Use this list to determine the basic translation of English words that you do not know in Japanese. Additional information, usage notes, and references to synonyms may be found under the entry in the main dictionary.

A

abandon hooki suru
ability nooryoku
able dekiru
about yaku
above ue
absolutely zettai
absorb kyuushuu suru
accent akuseñto
accept ukeireru
accident jiko
accomplish togeru
according yoru
account kañjoo
accurate seekaku
accurately seekaku
achievement gyooseki
acid sañ
across wataru
act eñjiru
action koodoo
active sekkyoku-teki; kappatsu
activity katsudoo
ad kookoku
adapt ooyoo suru
add kuwaeru; tasu
addition tsuika
additional tsuika; yobuñ
address juusho
admit mitomeru
adopt saiyoo suru
adult otona
advance shiñpo; susumu
advantage yuuri
adventure bookeñ
adverb fukushi
affair jikeñ; koto
affect eekyoo suru

afraid osoreru
after ato; nochi
afternoon gogo
again futatabi
against hañtai
age neñree; toshi
ago mae
agree itchi suru; dooi suru
agreement itchi; keeyaku
agriculture noogyoo
ahead saki
aid eñjo
aim nerau; mezasu
air kuuki
airplane hikooki
airport kuukoo
alcohol arukooru
alive ikiru
all subete; zeñbu
allow yurusu
almost hotoñdo
alone hitori
along sou; -zoi
already sude ni
also mata
although keredo
altitude koodo
altogether zeñzeñ
aluminum arumi
always itsu-mo
amaze bikkuri
America Beekoku
American Beekoku
among aida
amount gaku
ancestor señzo
ancient mukashku
and soshite; to
anger ikari
angle kakudo
angrily okoru

angry okoru
animal doobutsu
announce happyoo suru
announcement happyoo
another hoka
answer kotaeru; heñji
answers kotaeru; heñji
ant ari
anxious shiñpai
any dore
anyone dare-ka
anything nani-ka
anyway tonikaku
anywhere doko de mo
apartment apaato
appeal uttae
appear arawareru
appearance gaikañ; shutsueñ
apple riñgo
apply mooshikomu
appointment yakusoku; yoyaku
approach chikazuku
appropriate tekisetsu
approximately ooyoso
April shi-gatsu
area chiiki; meñseki
argument giroñ
arithmetic sansuu
arm ude
arms buki
army rikuguñ
around mawari
arrange totonoeru

arrangement uchiawase
arrive tsuku
arrow ya
art bijutsu
article kiji
artificial jiñkoo-teki
artist geejutsuka
as to shite
ash hai
ask kiku; tazuneru
asleep nemuru
assembly shuukai
association koosai
assume katee suru
astronomy teñmoñgaku
at de; ni
Atlantic Taiseeyoo
atmosphere fuñiki
atom geñshi
atomic geñshi
attach tsukeru
attack osou
attempt kokoromiru
attend shusseki suru
attention chuui
attitude taido
attract hikitsukeru
attraction miryoku
audience chooshuu
August hachi-gatsu
aunt oba
author sakka
authority keñi
automatic jidoo
automobile jidoosha
autumn aki
average heekin
avoid sakeru
awake okosu
aware kizuku

B
baby akañboo
back ushiro
background haikei
bacteria saikiñ
bad warui
bag fukuro; kabañ
baggage nimotsu
bake yaku
balance barañsu

ball tama
balloon fuuseñ
band bañdo
bank giñkoo
bar boo
barely karoojite
bark hoeru
base kiso; kichi
baseball yakyuu
basis kiso
basket kago
basketball basuketto-booru
bath furo
bathroom furoba; yokushitsu
battery deñchi
battle tatakai
bay wañ
be da
beach kaigañ
bean mame
bear kuma
beard hige
beast kemono
beat tataku
beautiful utsukushii
because da kara
become naru
bed beddo
bedroom shiñshitsu
bee hachi
beef gyuuniku
before mae
beg tanomu
begin hajimeru
beginning hajime
behave furumau
behavior koodoo
behind ushiro
being soñzai
believe shiñjiru
bell kane
belong zokusu
below shita
belt obi
bend mageru; magaru
benefit rieki
beside soba
besides sono ue
best saikoo
bet kakeru

better hoo ga ii
between aida
beyond koeru
Bible seesho
bicycle jiteñsha
big ookii
bill kañjoo
bird tori
birth tañjoo
birthday tañjoobi
bit sukoshi
bite kamu
bitter nigai
black kuro
blade ha
blanket moofu
blend mazeru
block fusagu
blood chi
blossom hana
blow fuku
blue aoi
board ita
boat booto
body jiñtai; karada
boil wakasu
bold daitañ
bone hone
book hoñ
boot nagagutsu
border kyookai
born umareru
borrow kariru
boss jooshi
both ryoohoo
bother meewaku
bottle biñ
bottom soko
bound hazumu
bow ojigi
bowl wañ
box hako
boy otoko-no-ko
brain atama
branch eda
brass shiñchuu
brave yuukan
bread pañ
break kowareru
breakfast chooshoku
breast mune
breath iki
breathe kokyuu suru

breathing kokyuu
breeze kaze
brick reñga
bride hanayome
bridge hashi
brief mijikai
bright akarui
brilliant
  hanabanashii
bring motte kuru
Britain Eekoku
broad hiroi
broom hooki
brother kyoodai
brown chairo
brush burashi
bubble awa
bucket baketsu
build tateru
building tatemono
bull ushi
bunch fusa
bundle taba
burn moyasu
burst bakuhatsu
bury hoomuru
bus basu
business shoobai
busy isogashii
but shikashi
butcher nikuya
butterfly choo
button botañ
buy kau
buying koonyuu
by de; ni; yoru

C
cabbage kyabetsu
cactus saboteñ
cage kago
cake keeki
call yobu
calm shizuka
camera shashiñki
campaign undoo
can dekiru; kañ
canal uñga
cancel torikesu
candle roosoku
candy ame
cannon taihoo
cap booshi

capable yuunoo
cape misaki
capital shuto
captain señchoo
capture toraeru
car kuruma
carbon tañso
cardboard atsugami
care shiñpai
career keereki
careful chuuibukai
cargo kamotsu
carrot niñjiñ
carry hakobu
carve kizamu
case haai; hako
cash geñkiñ
castle shiro
cat neko
catch tsukamu
cattle ushi
cause geñin
cave hora-ana
ceiling teñjoo
cell saiboo
center chuushiñ
century seeki
certain tashika
certificate shoomee-
  sho
chain kusari
chair isu
challenge chooseñ
chamber heya
championship
  yuushoo
chance kikai
change kaeru
chapter shoo
character moji
characteristic
  tokuchoo
charge ryookiñ
chase ou
cheap yasui
check teñkeñ
cheek hoo
cheer hagemasu
cheerful tanoshii
chemistry kagaku
cherry sakura
chest mune
chew kamu

chicken niwatori
chief -choo
chiefly shu to shite
child kodomo
chimney eñtotsu
chin ago
choice señtaku
choose erabu;
  señtaku suru
chopsticks hashi
Christian Kirisuto-
  kyooto
Christianity Kirisuto-
  kyoo
Christmas
  Kurisumasu
church kyookai
cigarette tabako
circle eñ
circumstances jijoo
cities shi
citizen shimiñ
city shi
civilization buñmee
claim shuchoo
class kurasu
classification buñrui
classify buñrui suru
classroom kyooshitsu
clay neñdo
clean seeketsu
cleaning sooji
clear hareru
clearly hakkiri
clerk jimuiñ
clever kashikoi
cliff gake
climate kikoo
climb noboru
clock tokee
close chikai;
  shimaru; missetsu
cloth nuno
clothes kimono
clothing kimono
cloud kumo
club bu
clue tegakari
coach koochi
coal sekitañ
coast kaigañ
coat uwagi
code añgoo

coffee koohii
coin kooka
cold kaze; samui
collar eri
collect atsumeru
collection shuushuu
college daigaku
color iro
column rañ
combination
  kumiawase
combine
  kumiawaseru
come kuru
comfort nagusameru
comfortable kiraku
command shiki
commerce shoogyoo
committee iiñkai
common futsuu
commonly futsuu
communicate
  tsuushiñ suru
communication
  tsuushiñ
companion aite
company kaisha
compare hikaku suru
comparison hikaku
complete kañzen
completeness kañzen
complex fukuzatsu
complicated
  fukuzstsu
compose koosee
  suru; tsukuru
composition koosee
concept gaineñ
concern shiñpai;
  kañkee
conclusion ketsuron
concrete gutai-teki
condition jootai;
  jookeñ
conditions jijoo
conduct kooi; shiki
confidence shiñrai
conflict shoototsu
confusion koñrañ
congress gikai
connect setsuzoku
  suru
connection setsuzoku

consider kañgaeru
considerable sootoo
consist naru
consonant shiiñ
constantly taezu
constitution taikaku
construct keñsetsu
  suru
construction
  keñsetsu
consul ryooji
consulate ryoojikañ
contact sesshoku
contain fukumu
container yooki
contents naiyoo
contest kyoogi
continent tairiku
continue tsuzukeru;
  tsuzuku
contract keeyaku
contrast taishoo
contribute kifu suru
contribution kifu
control kañri; toosee
convenient beñri
conversation kaiwa
cook ryoori
cool suzushii
copper doo
copy utsusu
coral sañgo
cord nawa
corner kado; sumi
correct tadashii;
  teesee suru
correspond tsuushiñ
  suru
correspondence
  tsuushiñ
cost hiyoo
costume ishoo
cottage bessoo
cotton meñ
cough seki
council kaigi
count kazoeru
country inaka; kuni
countryside inaka
county guñ
couple futari
courage yuuki
course koosu

court saibañ
cousin itoko
cover oou
cow ushi
crack hibi
crash tsuiraku
crawl hau
create soozoo suru
creation soozoo
creature seebutsu
creep hau
crime hañzai
crop shuukaku
cross yokogiru
crowd komu
crown kañmuri
cruel zañkoku
crush tsubusu
cry naku
crystal suishoo
culture buñka
curiosity kookishiñ
current nagare
curtain maku
curve magaru
custom shuukañ
customer kyaku
customs kañzee
cut kiru
cutting setsudañ
cycle shuuki

D

dad o-toosañ
dairy rakunoo
damage soñgai
damp shikke
dance odori
danger kikeñ
dangerous kikeñ;
  abunai
dark kurai
data shiryoo
date hinichi
daughter musume
dawn yoake
day hi; hiru
daytime hiruma
deal torihiki
dear kawaii
death shi
December juuni-
  gatsu

decide kettee suru
decision kettee
declare señgeñ(o) suru
deep fukai
deer shika
defeat haiboku
defense boogyo
definite meekaku
degree teedo
delay okure
delicious oishii
delight yorokobi
deliver watasu
demand yookyuu
density mitsudo
dentist haisha
deny hitee suru
department bu
department store depaato
depend tayoru
deposit azukeru
depth fukasa
describe byoosha suru
description byoosha
desert sabaku
design sekkee
desire yokuboo
desk tsukue
despite kakawarazu
destroy kowasu
detail shoosai
determination kesshiñ
determine kesshiñ suru
develop hattatsu suru
development hattatsu
device soochi; kufuu
diagram zu
diameter chokkee
diamond daiya
dictionary jisho
die shinu
diet shokuji
differ chigau
difference chigai
difficult muzukashii
difficulty koñnañ

dig horu
dim kasuka
dining room shokudoo
dinner yuushoku
direct chokusetsu-teki
direction hookoo
directions sashizu
directly chokusetsu
dirt chiri
dirty kitanai
disappear kieru
disappointment shitsuboo
discount waribiki
discover mitsukeru
discovery hakkeñ
discuss hanashiau
discussion giroñ
disease byooki
dish sara; ryoori
display chiñretsu
distance kyori
distant tooi
distinction kubetsu
distinguish kubetsu suru
distribution buñpai
district chiku
dive moguru
divide wakeru
division buñpai
do suru
doctor isha
dog inu
doll niñgyoo
dollar doru
do not nai
door to
doorway iriguchi
dot teñ
double bai
doubt utagau
down shita
dozen daasu
drag hikizuru
dragon ryuu
drama geki
draw hiku
drawing e
dream yume
dress ishoo

drift hyooryuu
drill kuñreñ
drink nomu
drive uñteñ
driver uñteñshu
driving uñteñ
drop otosu; shizuku
drug kusuri
drugstore yakkyoku
drum taiko
dry kawaku
duck kamo
dull nibui
during aida
dust hokori
duty gimu

E

each kaku
eager nesshiñ
eagerly shikiri ni
ear mimi
early hayai
earn kasegu
earth chikyuu
earthquake jishiñ
ease raku
easily kañtañ; surasura
east higashi
easy kañtañ
eat taberu
echo hañkyoo
economic keezai-teki
economy keezai
edge hashi
educate kyooiku suru
education kyooiku
effect kooka
effective kooka-teki
efficient nooritsu-teki
effort doryoku
egg tamago
eight hachi; yattsu
either dochira mo; mo
elect señkyo suru
election señkyo
electric deñki
electricity deñki
element yooso
elephant zoo
else hoka

embassy taishikañ
emergency kiñkyuu
emotional kañjoo-
teki
employ yatou
empty kara
encourage hagemasu
end owari
enemy teki
energy geñki
engagement
yakusoku
engine -kikañ
engineer gishi
England Eekoku
English Eego
enjoy tanoshimu
enormous bakudai
enough juubuñ
enter hairu
entirely zeñzeñ
entrance iriguchi;
nyuujoo
envelope fuutoo
environment
kañkyoo
equal hitoshii
equator sekidoo
equipment setsubi
equivalent sootoo
error ayamari
escape nigeru
especially toku ni
essential hoñshitsu-
teki
establish setsuritsu
suru
estimate mitsumori
even taira; sae
evening bañ
event dekigoto
ever katsute
every mai-
everybody miñna
every day mainichi
everyone miñna
everything subete
everywhere doko mo
evidence shooko
exact seekaku
exactly choodo
examination shikeñ
examine shiraberu

example ree
excellent subarashii
except jogai suru
exception jogai
exchange kookañ
excitement koofuñ
excuse iiwake
exercise uñdoo
exhibition teñrañkai
exist soñzai suru
existence soñzai
expand hirogaru
expect kitai suru
expedition tañkeñ
expense hiyoo
expensive takai
experience keekeñ
experiment jikkeñ
expert señmoñka
explain setsumee
suru
explanation
setsumee
exploration tañkeñ
explore tañkeñ suru
explosion bakuhatsu
export yushutsu
expose bakuro suru
express hyoogeñ suru
expression hyoogeñ
extend hirogaru
extent hirosa
extra yobuñ
extreme kyokutañ
extremely kiwamete
eye me

F

face mukau; kao
fact jijitsu
factor yooso
factory koojoo
fail shippai suru
failure shippai
faint kasuka
fair koohee
fairly kanari
fall ochiru; aki
false uso
familiar shitashii
family kazoku
famous yuumee
fan señpuuki

fancy kuusoo
far tooi
fare ryookiñ
farm noojoo
farmer nooka
fascination miryoku
fashion ryuukoo
fast hayai
fasten shimeru
fat shiboo
father chichi
fault machigai
favor kooi
favorite daisuki
fear osore
fearful osoroshii
feast gochisoo
feather hane
feature tokuchoo
February ni-gatsu
federal reñpoo
feed esa
feel kañjiru
feeling kañjoo
fellow yatsu
female josee; oñna
fence saku
fertile koeru
fever netsu
few sukunai
field nohara
fierce mooretsu
fight tatakau
figure keesañ; suuji
file tojikomi
fill mitasu
film eega; maku
final saishuu
finally tsui ni
find mitsukeru
fine ii; geñki
finger yubi
finish owaru
fire hi; kaji
firm katai; kaisha
firmly shikkari
first saisho
fish sakana
fisherman ryooshi
fishing tsuri
fit au
five go; itsutsu
fix shuuri

flag hata
flame honoo
flat taira
flee nigeru
flesh niku
flight biñ
float uku
flood koozui
floor kai; yuka
flour kona
flow nagareru
flower hana
fly tobu
fog kiri
fold tatamu
follow shitagau
fond suki
food tabemono
fool baka
foolish baka
foot ashi
for tame
force chikara
forehead hitai
foreign gaikoku
foreigner gaikokujiñ
forest mori
forever itsu made
    mo
forget wasureru
forgot wasureru
form katachi
formal keeshiki-teki
former saki
formula kooshiki
fortunate saiwai
fortune uñ
fossil kaseki
found setsurItsu suru
four yoñ; yottsu
fox kitsune
fraction buñsuu
frame waku
free jiyuu; tada
freedom jiyuu
freeze kooru
freight kamotsu
frequency kaisuu
frequently
    shibashiba
fresh shiñseñ
Friday kiñyoo
friend tomodachi

friendly shiñsetsu
frightened kowagaru
frog kaeru
from kara
front mae
frontier kokkyoo
frost shimo
fruit kudamono
fuel neñryoo
full ippai
fully kanzeñ
fun omoshiroi
function kinoo
funny okashii
fur ke
furniture kagu
furthermore nao
future mirai

G

gain eru
game shiai
garage gareeji
garden niwa
gas gasu
gasoline gasoriñ
gate moñ
gather atsumeru
gathering atsumari
gear haguruma
generally ippañ ni
generation sedai
gentle yasashii
gentleman shiñshi
gently sotto
geography chiri
get morau
get off oriru
get on noru
get up okiru
ghost bakemono
gift okurimono
girl oñna-no-ko
give ataeru
glad yorokobu
glance hitome
glass garasu; koppu
glasses megane
globe chikyuu
glove tebukuro
glue nori
gnaw kajiru
go iku

goal mokuhyoo
god kami
gold kiñ
good yoi
good–bye sayoonara
goods shoohiñ
grade kyuu
gradually shidai ni
grand idai
grandfather sofu
grandmother sobo
grape budoo
grasp haaku
grass kusa
grave haka
gravitation iñryoku
gray hai-iro
grease abura
great ookii
greatly ooi ni
greedy yokubari
green midori
greet aisatsu suru
grill yaku
grin warau
ground jimeñ; tsuchi
group dañtai
grow seechoo suru;
    sodatsu
growth seechoo
guard mihari
guess suisoku
guest kyaku
guide añnai
gulf wañ
gun juu

H

habit shuukañ
hair ke
half hañbuñ
halfway tochuu
hall hooru
hammer kanazuchi
hand te
handle totte
handsome utsukushii
hang tsurusu
happen okoru
happening dekigoto
happy koofuku;
    shiawase
harbor minato

hard katai; tsurai
hardly hotoñdo
harm gai
harmful yuugai
harmony choowa
harvest shuukaku
hat booshi
hatch kaeru
hate nikumu
have motsu
haze kasumi
he kare
head atama
headache zutsuu
health keñkoo
hear kiku
heart shiñzoo
heat netsu
heaven teñgoku
heavy omoi
heel kakato
height takasa
hello moshimoshi
help tasukeru
helpful yakudatsu
hen niwatori
her kanojo no
here koko
hero eeyuu
hey oi
hide kakureru;
  kakusu
high takai
highly ooi ni
hill oka
hire yatou
his kare no
history rekishi
hit utsu
hobby shumi
hold motsu
hole ana
holiday kyuujitsu
home ie; katee
honest shoojiki
honey mitsu
honor meeyo
hope kiboo
horizon suiheeseñ
horizontal suihee
horn tsuno
horse uma
hospital byooiñ

hot atsui
hotel yado
hour jikañ
house ie; uchi
household katee
how doñna ni
however keredo
huge kyodai
human niñgeñ
humor yuumoa
hundred hyaku
hunger ue
hungry ueru
hunting ryoo
hurry isogu
hurt kizu
husband otto
hut koya
hydrogen suiso

I
I watashi
ice koori
idea kañgae
if moshi
ill byooki
illustration setsumee
image imeeji
imagination soozoo
imagine soozoo suru
immediately tadachi
  ni
import yunyuu
important juuyoo
impossible fukanoo
impression iñshoo
improvement kairyoo
in naka; ni
include fukumu
income shuunyuu
increase fueru
increasingly
  masumasu
indeed naruhodo
independence
  dokuritsu
index sakuiñ
indication shiteki
individual kojiñ
industry sañgyoo
influence eekyoo
information joohoo
inhabitant juumiñ

inn ryokañ
insect mushi
inside naka
insistence shuchoo
instance ree
instant shuñkañ
instead kawari
instruction oshie;
  sashizu
instrument doogu
intelligent chiteki
intention tsumori
interest kyoomi
interesting omoshiroi
interior naibu
international
  kokusai-teki
interpreter tsuuyaku
interrupt chuudañ
  suru
interview meñkai
into naka
introduce shookai
  suru
introduction shookai
invent hatsumee
  suru
invention hatsumee
investigation choosa
invite shootai suru
involve makikomu
iron tetsu
island shima
issue hakkoo
it sore
item koomoku
it sore
itself jishiñ

J
jacket uwagi
January ichi-gatsu
Japan Nihoñ
Japanese Nihoñjiñ
jar biñ
jaw ago
jet jettoki
jewelry hooseki
job shigoto
join kuwawaru
joint kyoodoo
joke joodañ
journey ryokoo

joy yorokobi
judgment hañdañ
juice juusu
July shichi-gatsu
jump tobu
June roku-gatsu
just choodo
justice seegi

K

keep tamotsu
kettle yakañ
key kagi
kick keru
kill korosu
kind shiñsetsu;
  shurui
kindly shiñsetsu
king oo
kitchen daidokoro
kite tako
knee hiza
knife naifu
knock tataku
know shiru
knowledge chishiki

L

label retteru
labor roodoo
laboratory
  jikkeñshitsu
lack fusoku
lad shooneñ
ladder hashigo
lady fujiñ
lake mizuumi
lamp rañpu
land tochi
landscape keshiki
language kotoba
lap hiza
large ookii
largest saidai
last saigo
late osoi
later ato
latter koosha
laugh warau
laughter warai
lavatory beñjo
law hooritsu
lawn shibafu

lawyer beñgoshi
lay shiku
layer soo
lead michibiku
leader shidoo-sha
leaf ha
league doomee
lean motareru
leap tobu
learn manabu
learning gakumoñ
least saishoo
leather kawa
leave saru
left hidari
leg ashi
legend deñsetsu
length nagasa
lens reñzu
less sukunai
lesson jugyoo
let saseru
letter moji; tegami
level suihee
liberty jiyuu
library toshokañ
license meñkyo
lid futa
lie uso; neru
life inochi; seekatsu
lifetime isshoo
lift mochiageru
light karui; akari;
  deñki; tsukeru
lightbulb tama
lightly sotto
lightning inazuma
like suki
limit seegeñ
line señ
lip kuchibiru
lipstick kuchibeni
liquid ekitai
list hyoo
listen kiku
literature buñgaku
little chiisai; sukunai
live sumu
lively nigiyaka
living seekatsu
load ni
lobster ebi
location ichi

lock kagi
lonely sabishii
long nagai
look miru
loop wa
loose yurui
lose nakusu
loss fuñshitsu
lot kuji
love ai
lovely kawaii
low hikui
lowest saitee
luck uñ
lucky uñ
luggage nimotsu
lumber zaimoku
lump katamari
lunch chuushoku
lung hai

M

machine kikai
magazine zasshi
magic mahoo
magnificent rippa
mail yuubiñ
main omo-na
mainly omo ni
maintain iji suru
major señkoo
majority tasuu
make tsukuru
male dañsee; otoko
man hito; dañsee
manage shori suru
manner taido
manufacture seezoo
many ool
map chizu
March sañ-gatsu
march kooshiñ
mark shirushi
market ichiba
marriage kekkoñ
marry kekkoñ suru
mass katamari;
  shuudañ
master masutaa suru
match shiai
mate aite
material zairyoo
mathematics suugaku

matter koto
May go-gatsu
may ka mo shirenai
maybe tabuñ
mayor shichoo
me watashi o
meal shokuji
meaning imi
means shudañ
measure hakaru
measurement
  sokutee
meat niku
medicine kusuri;
  igaku
medium chuu
meet au
meeting kaigi
melody merodii
melt tokeru
member kaiiñ
memory kioku
mental seeshiñ-teki
mention iu
merchant shooniñ
merely hoñno
merry yooki
metal kiñzoku
meter meetoru
method hoohoo
middle mañnaka
midnight mayonaka
might chikara
mild odayaka
milk gyuunyuu
million hyaku-mañ
mind kokoro
mineral koobutsu
mining koogyoo
minister daijiñ
minority shoosuu
minute fuñ
mirror kagami
Miss misu; sañ
miss nogasu
missing yukue-fumee
mistake machigai
mix mazeru
mixture koñgoo
model mokee
modern geñdai-teki
moist shimeru
moisture shikke

mold kata
molecule buñshi
mom o-kaasañ
moment shuñkañ
Monday getsuyoo
money o-kane
monkey saru
monster bakemono
month tsuki
mood kibuñ
moon tsuki
more motto
moreover sono ue
morning asa
mosquito ka
moss koke
most mottomo
mostly shu to shite
mother haha
motion ugoki
mountain yama
mouse nezumi
mouth kuchi
move ugoku; ugokasu
movement ugoki
movie eega
Mr. sañ
Mrs. sañ
much ooi; ooku
mud nukarumi
multiplication
  kakezañ
multiply kakeru
muscle kiñniku
museum
  hakubutsukañ
music oñgaku
must chigainai
my watashi no
mysterious shiñpi-
  teki
mystery shiñpi

N

nail tsume
name namae
narrow semai
nation kokka
national kokuritsu
natural shizeñ
nature shizeñ
navy kaiguñ
near chikai; soba

nearly chikaku;
  hotoñdo
neat kiree
neatly kichiñto
necessary hitsuyoo
neck kubi
need hitsuyoo
needle hari
negative shookyoku-
  teki
neighbor riñjiñ
neighborhood kiñjo
neither mo
nerve shiñkee
nervous
  shiñkeeshitsu
nest su
net ami
never kesshite
nevertheless sore de
  mo
new atarashii
news nyuusu
newspaper shiñbuñ
next tsugi
nice suteki
night yoru
nine ku; kokonotsu
nitrogen chisso
no iie; nai
noise soo-oñ
noisy urusai
noon hiru
normal seejoo;
  futsuu
north kita
nose hana
not nai
note memo
notebook nooto
nothing nani mo
notice kizuku
noun meeshi
November juuichi-
  gatsu
now ima
nowhere doko mo
nucleus geñshikaku;
  kaku
number kazu; suu
numeral suuji
numerous ooi

nurse kañgo fu
nut mi

O

object taishoo
observe kañsatsu suru
obtain eru
obvious akiraka
occasion kikai; baal
occasionally tama ni
occupation shokugyoo
occupy señryoo suru
occur okoru
ocean umi
o'clock ji
October juu-gatsu
odd heñ
odor nioi
of no
offer teekyoo
office jimusho; kaisha
official kooshiki
often shibashiba
oh oo
oil abura
old furui
on ue; ni
once ichido
one ichi; hitotsu
only dake; tada
onto ni
open akeru; hiraku
opening kaishi
operate soosa suru
opinion ikeñ
opportunity kikai
opposite hañtai
or mata-wa
orchestra ookesutora
order chuumoñ; juñ
ordinary futsuu
organ orugañ
organize soshiki suru
origin kigeñ
original moto
originally hoñrai
other hoka; ta
ought beki
our watashi-tachi no
outdoors soto

outline gaiyoo
outside soto
over ue; koeru
overcome katsu
own motsu
owner mochinushi
oxygen sañso

P

pace ashinami
Pacific Ocean Taiheeyoo
pack tsumeru
package kozutsumi
pail baketsu
pain itami; kutsuu
paint kaku
painting e
pair kumi
pale aojiroi
palm te-no-hira
pan nabe
papa papa
paper kami
parade kooshiñ
paragraph setsu
parallel heekoo
parent oya
parentheses kakko
park kooeñ
part bubuñ
particle joshi
particular tokubetsu
particularly toku ni
partly bubuñ-teki
partner aite
party paatii; kai
pass tooru
passage tsuukoo
passenger jookyaku
passport pasupooto
past kako
paste nori
pasture bokujoo
path michi
patient kañja
pattern kata
pay harau
peace heewa
peach momo
peak choojoo
pearl shiñju
peculiar dokutoku

pencil eñpitsu
people hito
per tsuite
percent paaseñto
perfect kañzeñ
perform eñjiru
performance eñgi
perhaps osoraku; tabuñ
period kikañ
permanence eekyuu
permit kyoka suru
person hito
personal kojiñ-teki
personality kosee
phone deñwa
photograph shashiñ
phrase setsu
physical shiñtai
pick hirou; tsumu
picnic pikunikku
picture e
piece -mai
pig buta
pigeon hato
pile tsumu
pillow makura
pilot soojuu suru
pin tomeru
pine matsu
pink piñku
pipe paipu
pitch nageru
pitcher mizusashi
place basho; oku
plain meehaku; shisso
plan keekaku
plane hikooki
plant shokubutsu
plastic purasuchikku
plate sara
plateau koogeñ
platform hoomu
play asobu
player señshu
playground uñdoojoo
pleasant yukai
please doozo
pleasure tanoshimi
plenty tappuri
plot iñboo
plow suki

plus tasu
poem shi
poet shijiñ
point sasu; saki
pointed surudoi
poison doku
pole boo
police keesatsu
policeman keekañ; juñsa
policy seesaku
polish migaku
polite teenee
politics seeji
pond ike
poor mazushii
popular ryuukoo
population jiñkoo
porch geñkañ
port minato
portion bubuñ
position ichi; chii
positive sekkyoku-teki
possess shoyuu suru
possession shoyuu
possible kanoo
possibly osoraku
post yuusoo
postage stamp kitte
postcard hagaki
pot tsubo
potato jagaimo
pound poñdo
pour sosogu; tsugu
powder kona
power chikara
powerful chikarazuyoi
practical jitsuyoo-teki
practice reñshuu
pray inoru
precious kichoo
prefer konomu
prepare juñbi suru
presence shusseki
present shusseki suru; geñzai
president daitooryoo; shachoo
press osu
pressure atsuryoku
pretend furi o suru

pretty kiree
prevent fusegu
previous saki
price nedañ
pride hokori
principal omo-na
principle geñri
print iñsatsu suru
private kojiñ-teki
prize shoo
probably osoraku; tabuñ
problem moñdai
procedure tetsuzuki
proceed susumu
process katee
produce seesañ suru
product seehiñ
profession shokugyoo
professional señmoñka
professor kyooju
profit rieki
program bañgumi
progress shiñpo
project keekaku
promise yakusoku
pronoun daimeeshi
pronounce hatsuoñ suru
proof shoomee
proper tekisetsu
property zaisañ
proportion tsuriai
propose teeañ suru
protect hogo suru
proud hokoru
prove shoomee suru
provide kyookyuu suru
public kookyoo
publicity señdeñ
publish shuppañ suru
pull hiku
punctuation kutooteñ
pupil seeto
purchase kau
pure juñsui
purple murasaki
purpose mokuteki
push osu

put oku
puzzle nazo

Q
quality shitsu
quantity ryoo
queen jo-oo
queer heñ
question shitsumoñ
quick hayai
quiet shizuka
quietly shizuka; sotto
quite sootoo

R
rabbit usagi
race reesu
radio rajio
raft ikada
rail tesuri
railroad tetsudoo
rain ame
rainbow niji
raise ageru
range hañi
rank kaikyuu
rapid hayai
rare mare
rarely metta ni
rat nezumi
rate ritsu; wariai
rather mushiro
raw nama
ray kooseñ
razor kamisori
reach tsuku; todoku
reaction hañnoo
read yomu
reader dokusha
ready yooi
real hoñtoo
realize jitsugeñ suru
really jissai wa
rear ushiro
reason riyuu
recall omoidasu
receipt ryooshuusho
receive uketoru
recent saikiñ
recognize mitomeru
recommend suiseñ suru
record kiroku

red aka
reduce herasu
refer sañshoo suru
reflect hañsha suru
refrigerator reezooko
refuse kotowaru
regard minasu
region chihoo; chiiki
regular kisoku-teki
relation kañkee
relative shiñseki
relatively hikaku-teki
release kaihoo
relief añshiñ
religion shuukyoo
remain nokoru
remarkable
    mezamashii
remember oboeru
remind omoidasu
remove toru
rent kariru
repair shuuri
repeat kurikaesu
replace kawaru
reply heñji; kotaeru
report hookoku
represent hyoogeñ
    suru
require yookyuu suru
rescue sukuu
research choosa
resource shigeñ
respect soñkee
response hañnoo
responsibility
    sekiniñ
rest yasumi
restaurant shokudoo
result kekka
return kaeru; kaesu
reveal abaku
review fukushuu
revolution kakumee
rewrite kakinaosu
rib hone
rice kome; gohañ
rich hoofu
rid nozoku
ride noru
rifle juu
right migi; tadashii
rim fuchi

ring naru
ripe jukusu
rise agaru
river kawa
road dooro
roar hoeru
rock iwa
rod sao
role yaku
roll korogaru
roof yane
room heya
root ne
rope nawa
rose bara
rough arai
round marui
route michijuñ
row retsu
rub kosuru
rubber gomu
rug juutañ
rule kisoku
ruler monosashi
run hashiru
rush sekasu

S
sad kanashii
safe añzeñ
safety añzeñ
sail ho
salary kyuuryoo
sale hañbai
salmon sake
salt shio
same onaji
sample mihoñ
sand suna
satellite eesee
satisfy mañzoku suru
Saturday doyoo
save tameru;
    tasukeru
saw nokogiri
say iu
scale memori
scatter chirabaru
scene keshiki; bameñ
school gakkoo
science kagaku
scientific kagaku-teki
scientist kagakusha

scissors hasami
score teñsuu
scratch kaku
scream sakebu
sea umi
seal fuu
search sagasu
season kisetsu
seat seki
second byoo
secret himitsu
section setsu
secure añzeñ
see miru
seed tane
seek sagasu
seem mieru
seize tsukamu
seldom metta ni
select erabu
selection señtaku
sell uru
send okuru
sense kañkaku
sensitive biñkañ
sentence buñ
separate wakareru
September ku-gatsu
series reñzoku
serious juudai;
    majime
serve tsukaeru; dasu
service saabisu
set sueru
settle kaiketsu suru;
    kimaru
settlement kaiketsu
seven shichi; nanatsu
several ikutsu ka
severe kibishii
sew nuu
sex see
shadow kage
shake furu
shallow asai
shape katachi
share wakeru
sharp surudoi
she kanojo
shed koya
sheep hitsuji
sheet -mai; shiitsu
shelf tana

shell kai
shelter hinañ
shine kagayaku
ship fune
shirt shatsu
shock odoroki
shoe kutsu
shoot utsu
shop mise
shopping kaimono
shore kishi
short mijikai
shortly ma-mo-naku
should beki
shoulder kata
shout sakebu
show miseru
shrine jiñja
shut shimeru; tojiru
sick byooki
side gawa
sidewalk hodoo
sigh tameiki
sight kookee
sightseeing kañkoo
sign aizu; saiñ
signal shiñgoo
silence chiñmoku
silk kinu
silly oroka
silver giñ
similar niru
simple kañtañ;
    tañjuñ
since -irai
sing utau
single hitotsu
sink shizumu
sister shimai
sit suwaru
site shikichi
situation jookyoo
six roku; muttsu
size ookisa
sketch shasee
skill gijutsu
skillful takumi
skin hada; kawa
sky sora
sleep nemuru
sleepy nemui
slender hosonagai
slice -kire

slide suberu
slight wazuka
slope saka
slow osoi
slowly yukkuri
small chiisai
smart rikoo
smell nioi
smile hohoemu
smoke kemuri
smooth nameraka
snake hebi
snore ibiki
snow yuki
so soo
soap sekkeñ
society shakai
soft yawarakai
softly sotto
soil tsuchi
soldier guñjiñ
solid kotai
solve kaiketsu suru
some ikutsu ka;
    sukoshi
somebody dare-ka
someday itsu-ka
somehow nañ to ka
someone dare-ka
something nani-ka
sometime itsu-ka
sometimes toki ni wa
somewhat yaya
somewhere doko-ka
son musuko
song uta
soon sugu
sorry sumanai
sort shurui
soul seeshiñ;
    tamashii
sound oto; naru
soup suupu
south minami
space sukima; uchuu
spare yobi
spark hibana
speak hanasu
speaker hanashite
special tokubetsu
specify tokutee suru
speech hanashi
speed sokudo

spend tsuiyasu;
    tsukau
sphere kyuu
spider kumo
spin kaiteñ
spirit seeshiñ
spite kakawarazu;
    akui
splash haneru
splendid rippa;
    subarashii
split saku
sport uñdoo
spot basho; shimi
spread hirogeru
spring haru
square shikaku;
    hiroba
stability añtee
staff shokuiñ
stage butai
stair dañ
stamp kitte
stand tatsu
standard hyoojuñ
star hoshi
stare mitsumeru;
    niramu
start hajimeru;
    shuppatsu
state jootai
statement seemee
station eki
stay tomaru
steadily chakuchaku
steady chakujitsu
steal nusumu
steam jooki
steep kewashii
stem kuki
step kaidañ
stick boo; sasaru
sticky nebaru
stiff katai
still mada; shizuka
stir kakimawasu
stock chozoo; kabu
stomach i
stone ishi
stop tomaru; yameru
store mise
storm arashi
story hanashi

stove sutoobu
straight massugu
strange heñ
straw wara
stream nagare
street toori
strength chikara
stress atsuryoku
stretch haru
strike utsu
string himo
stripe shima
stroke naderu
strong tsuyoi
structure koozoo
struggle mogaku
student gakusee
study beñkyoo suru
stuff zairyoo; tsumeru
style kata; sutairu
subject shudai
substance busshitsu
substitute kawaru
subtract hiku
subway chikatetsu
succeed seekoo suru
success seekoo
successful seekoo
such soñna
sudden totsuzeñ
suffer ukeru;
　koomuru
sufficient juubuñ
sugar satoo
suggest teeañ suru
suit au; niau
suitable tekitoo
sum gookee
summer natsu
sun taiyoo
Sunday nichiyoo
sunlight nikkoo
sunrise hinode
sunset hinoiri
supper yuushoku
supply kyookyuu
support sasaeru
suppose katee suru
sure tashika
surely kitto
surface hyoomeñ
surprise odorokasu
surround kakomu

surroundings shuui;
　kañkyoo
survive ikinokoru
swallow nomikomu
sweat ase
sweep haku; sooji
　suru
sweet amai
swim oyogu
swimming suiee
swing shiñdoo
switch tsukeru;
　suitchi
sword katana
syllable oñsetsu
symbol shoochoo
system seeshiki

T

table hyoo;
　shokutaku
tail o
take toru; motsu
tale monogatari
talk hanasu
tall takai
tap jaguchi
tape teepu
target mato
task tsutome
taste aji
tasty oishii
tax zee
taxi takushii
tea o-cha
teach oshieru
teacher señsee
team kumi
tear namlda; saku
technique gijutsu
telegram deñpoo
telephone deñwa
telescope booeñkyoo
television terebi
tell hanasu
temperature oñdo
temple tera
ten juu; too
tend -gachi
tendency keekoo
tender yawarakai
tension kiñchoo
term yoogo; kikañ

terms jookeñ
terrible osoroshii
territory ryoodo
terror kyoofu
test shikeñ
than yori
thank kañsha suru
thanks arigatoo;
　kañsha
that sore; are
the sono; ano
theater gekijoo
theme teema
then sore kara
theory riroñ
there soko; asoko
therefore shitagatte
thermometer
　oñdokee
they kare-ra
thick atsui
thief doroboo
thin usui
thing koto; mono
think kañgaeru;
　omou
third sañ
this kore
thorough tettee-teki
thought kañgae
thousand señ
thread ito
threaten odosu
three sañ; mittsu
throat nodo
through -juu
throw nageru
thrust tsukkomu
thumb oyayubi
thunder kaminari
Thursday mokuyoo
ticket kippu
tide shio
tie shibaru
tiger tora
tight kitsui
tightly shikkari
till made
timber zaimoku
time jikañ; toki
tin suzu
tip saki
tired tsukareru

tissue soshiki
title daimee
to e; ni
tobacco tabako
today kyoo
toe yubi
together issho ni
toilet toire
tomorrow ashita
tone chooshi
tongue shita
tonight koñya
too mo
tool doogu
tooth ha
top ue; choojoo
topic wadai
toss hooru
total gookee
touch sawaru
tough tsurai
tour ryokoo
toward ni
towel taoru
tower too
town machi
toy omocha
trace ato
trade booeki; shoobai
tradition deñtoo
traffic kootsuu
trail hikizuru
train ressha
translate yakusu
transportation
   kootsuu
trap wana
travel ryokoo
treasure takara
treat toriatsukau
treatment taiguu
tree ki
trial kokoromi
triangle sañkaku
trick damasu
trip ryokoo
troops guñ; guñtai
tropic nettai
trouble meewaku;
   moñdai
truck torakku
true hoñtoo
trunk miki

trust shiñyoo
truth shiñjitsu
try tamesu
tube kuda
Tuesday kayoo
tune chooshi
turn mawaru;
   mawasu
turtle kame
twist nejiru
two ni; futatsu
type kata; teñkee

U

ugly minikui
umbrella kasa
uncle oji
under shita
underground chika
understand wakaru
understanding rikai
underwater suichuu
underwear shitagi
unexpected igai
unhappy fukoo
uniform seefuku
union reñgoo
unique dokutoku
unit tañi
unite reñgoo suru
United States
   Beekoku
universe uchuu
university daigaku
unknown michi
until made
unusual ijoo;
   mezurashii
up ue
upper jooryuu
upright massugu
upset hikkurikaeru
upstairs ue; nikai
use tsukau
useful beñri; yuueki
useless mueki
usual futsuu
usually futsuu;
   itsu-mo

V

vacation kyuuka
vacuum shiñkuu

valley tani
valuable kichoo
value kachi
vapor jooki
variation heñka
various iroiro
vary heñka suru
vast koodai
vegetable yasai
verb dooshi
vertical suichoku
very hijoo; totemo
vessel fune
vibration shiñdoo
victory shoori
view nagame
village mura
vinegar su
violent rañboo
visible mieru
visit hoomoñ
visitor kyaku
vocabulary goi
voice koe
volcano kazañ
volume taiseki
vote toohyoo
vow chikai
vowel boiñ
voyage kookai

W

wages chiñgiñ
waist koshi
wait matsu
wake okiru
walk aruku
wall kabe
want hoshii; -tai
war señsoo
warm atatakai
warn keekoku suru
wash arau
waste muda
watch miru; tokee
water mizu
wave nami
way hoohoo; michi
we watashi-tachi
weak yowai
wealth tomi
weapon buki
wear kiru

weary taikutsu
weather teñki
weave oru
web su
wedding kekkoñshiki
Wednesday suiyoo
weed zassoo
week shuu
weigh hakaru
weight omosa
welcome kañgee
well joozu
well-known yuumee
west nishi
wet nureru
what nani
wheat komugi
wheel shariñ
when itsu; toki
where doko
whether doo ka
which dochira;
   dotchi
while aida
whip muchi
whistle fue
white shiro
who dare
whole zeñtai
why naze

wide hiroi
width hirosa
wife tsuma
will ishi
win katsu
wind kaze
window mado
wine budooshu
wing hane
winter fuyu
wipe fuku
wire harigane
wisdom chie
wise kashikoi
wish negau; nozomu
with to
within -nai; uchi
without nai
woman joosee
wonder fushigi
wonderful subarashii
wood ki
woods mori
wool ke
word kotoba
work shigoto;
   hataraku
worker roodoosha
world sekai
worm mushi

worry shiñpai
worse warui
worst saitee
worth kachi
wound kizu
wrap tsutsumu
write kaku
writer sakka
wrong warui

X
X-ray reñtogeñ

Y
yard niwa
year toshi; neñ
yell sakebu
yellow kiiro
yes hai
yesterday kinoo
yet mada
you anata; kimi
young wakai
youth seeneñ;
   seeshuñ

Z
zero ree
zone chiiki
zoo doobutsueñ